ND
SWEDEN
FINLAND
NORWAY
RUSSIA
GREAT BRITAIN
DENMARK
ESTONIA
LATVIA
LITHUANIA
BELARUS
LAND
NETH.
POLAND
GERMANY
BELGUM
LUX.
CZECH
UKRAINE
SLOVAKIA
LIECH.
AUST
HUNGARY
MOLD.
FRANCE
SW.
SLO.
CRO.
BO.
HER.
YUGO.
ITALY
BULGARIA
ALB.
MACE.
GEORGIA
ARM.
AZER.
SPAIN
UGAL
GREECE
TURKEY
KAZAKHSTAN
MONGOLIA
UZBEKISTAN
KYRGYZSTAN
TURKMENISTAN
TAJIKISTAN
N. KOREA
S. KOREA
JAPAN
CHINA
MALTA
TUNISIA
SYRIA
CYPRUS
LEB.
ISRAEL
IRAQ
IRAN
AFGHAN-ISTAN
JORDAN
MOROCCO
KUWAIT
ALGERIA
LIBYA
EGYPT
SAUDI ARABIA
BAHRAIN
UNITED ARAB EMIR.
NEPAL
BHUTAN
BANGLADESH
INDIA
MYANMAR (BURMA)
TAIWAN
VIETNAM
LAOS
PACIFIC OCEAN
OMAN
RITANIA
MALI
NIGER
CHAD
SUDAN
YEMEN
THAILAND
CAMBODIA
PHILIPPINES
ERITREA
DJIBOUTI
BURKINA FASO
GUINEA
BENIN
NIGERIA
ETHIOPIA
SRI LANKA
NE
IVORY COAST
BERIA
CENTRAL AFRICAN REP.
GHANA
TOGO
CAMEROON
SOMALIA
BRUNEI
MALAYSIA
UGANDA
KENYA
EQUATORIAL GUINEA
GABON
RWANDA
DEM. REP. OF THE CONGO
REP. OF THE CONGO
INDIAN OCEAN
SEYCHELLES
INDONESIA
BURUNDI
TANZANIA
PAPUA NEW GUINEA
CABINDA (ANGOLA)
TIC
EAN
COMOROS
ANGOLA
ZAMBIA
MALAWI
MOZAMBIQUE
MADAGASCAR
MAURITIUS
NAMIBIA
ZIMBABWE
BOTSWANA
REUNION (FRANCE)
AUSTRALIA
SWAZILAND
SOUTH AFRICA
LESOTHO
TARCTICA

COMPREHENSIVE VOLUME

Fourth Edition

WORLD HISTORY

Jiu-Hwa L. Upshur
Eastern Michigan University

Janice J. Terry
Eastern Michigan University

James P. Holoka
Eastern Michigan University

Richard D. Goff
Eastern Michigan University

George H. Cassar
Eastern Michigan University

WADSWORTH

THOMSON LEARNING™

Australia • Canada • Mexico • Singapore • Spain
United Kingdom • United States

WADSWORTH
THOMSON LEARNING

Editorial Director: Clark G. Baxter
Senior Development Editor: Sharon Adams Poore
Assistant Editor: Jennifer Ellis
Editorial Assistant: Jonathan Katz
Executive Marketing Manager: Diane McOscar
Marketing Assistant: Kasia Zagorski
Project Manager: Dianne Jensis Toop
Senior Manufacturing Supervisor: Barbara Britton
Permissions Editor: Joohee Lee
Production Service: Hal Lockwood, Penmarin Books
Text Designer: Janet Bollow
Photo Researcher: Connie Hathaway
Copy Editor: Kevin Gleason
Cover Designer: Janet Bollow
Cover Photo Researcher: Lisa Jeanne Graf
Cover Images: Art Today, Corel Corporation, Instructional Resources Corporation
Cover Printer: Phoenix Color
Compositor: Thompson Type
Printer: Quebecor/World

Printed in the United States of America
1 2 3 4 5 6 7 05 04 03 02 01

ISBN: 0-534-58725-9

Wadsworth/Thomson Learning
10 Davis Drive
Belmont, CA 94002-3098
USA

For more information about our products, contact us:
Thomson Learning Academic Resource Center
1-800-423-0563
http://www.wadsworth.com

International Headquarters
Thomson Learning
International Division
290 Harbor Drive, 2nd Floor
Stamford, CT 06902-7477
USA

UK/Europe/Middle East/South Africa
Thomson Learning
Berkshire House
168-173 High Holborn
London WC1V 7AA
United Kingdom

Asia
Thomson Learning
60 Albert Street, #15-01
Albert Complex
Singapore 189969

Canada
Nelson Thomson Learning
1120 Birchmount Road
Toronto, Ontario M1K 5G4
Canada

About the Authors

JIU-HWA L. UPSHUR received her B.A. at the University of Sydney in Australia and Ph.D. in history at the University of Michigan. She is the author of two catalogs on Chinese art and many articles on Chinese history and has lived and traveled extensively in China, Taiwan, and other parts of Asia. She is co-author of *The Twentieth Century: A Brief Global History* (6th edition, 2001) and co-editor of *Lives and Times: Readings in World History* (1994). She served on the world history committee of the College Board between 1993 and 1999. She is currently a member of the review board of Teaching World History for the Twentieth Century, funded by the National Endowment for the Humanities and the National Advisory Committee for Social Studies of the Educational Testing Service.

JANICE J. TERRY is a graduate of the School of Oriental and African Studies, University of London. She is author of *The Wafd, 1919–1952: Cornerstone of Egyptian Political Power, Mistaken Identity: Arab Stereotypes in Popular Writing,* and numerous articles on contemporary events in western Asia. Dr. Terry has lived and traveled extensively throughout western Asia and Africa. She is co-author of *The Twentieth Century: A Brief Global History* (6th edition, 2001). In 1990, she received an award for excellence in teaching from the state of Michigan.

JAMES P. HOLOKA received his B.A. from the University of Rochester, his M.A. from SUNY, Binghamton, and his Ph.D. from the University of Michigan, where he was a Rackham Prize Fellow. He has taught Greek and Latin, classical humanities, and ancient history since 1974; he received a teaching excellence award in 1980 and a scholarly recognition award in 1991. He is a published translator and the author of three textbooks and over eighty scholarly articles and reviews in such journals as *American Historical Review; Classical World; Greek, Roman, and Byzantine Studies;* and *Transactions of the American Philological Association.*

RICHARD D. GOFF received his B.A. and Ph.D. from Duke University and his M.A. from Cornell University. He has taught courses in Western civilization and specializes in teaching twentieth-century world history. He is the author of *Confederate Supply* and encyclopedia articles on southern U.S. history and culture. In 1983 he received a distinguished faculty service award. He is co-author of *The Twentieth Century: A Brief Global History* (6th edition, 2001), and lead author of R. Goff et al., *A Survey of Western Civilization* (2nd edition, 1997).

GEORGE H. CASSAR received his B.A and M.A. from the University of New Brunswick and his Ph.D. from McGill University. He is currently Professor of History at Eastern Michigan University, where he has taught European and military history since 1968. His output is extensive and includes half a dozen books on various aspects of the First World War as well as co-authorship of *A Survey of Western Civilization* (2nd edition, 1997). In 1985 he received the prestigious Faculty Award for Research and Publication from Eastern Michigan University. He is currently working on a book about Kitchener and British strategy during the Great War.

Brief Contents

Contents

Maps

Preface

Modern communications and transportation have linked the world's continents closer together and made them more integrated politically, economically, and culturally than ever before. Our technological society is predicated on a world economy and depends on a precarious ecological balance that makes events in the forests of Brazil or the deserts of Africa and Asia vitally important to people all around the globe.

Many institutions of higher learning have come to realize that students need insights into the historical backgrounds of other cultures in order to respond effectively to the currents that make us all citizens of a global village. As a result, many are now emphasizing world history as an essential part of the basic undergraduate curriculum, rather than traditional courses in Western civilization.

The five authors set out to produce a truly global and well-balanced world history text. We have expertise in different regions, periods, and topics of history, including the classics and Greco-Roman history, modern Europe, military history, the Western Hemisphere, the Islamic world, American history, and South and East Asia. We are conversant in more than a half-dozen ancient and modern languages. Each has more than thirty years' experience teaching college survey courses of Western and world history and advanced courses in special subjects. All have extensive experience in writing successful textbooks and editing primary source materials in world history and Western civilization. The result is a smooth integration of diverse materials.

Our first edition, widely adopted across the United States and Canada, was a success. Our second and third editions were even more successful. Thus encouraged, we have now made additional improvements to further enhance this fourth edition.

While other world history textbooks have stressed specific themes, human civilizations, in our view, have produced too rich a tapestry of experience to limit our examination of them to any single theme. Our consistent goal has been not only to show students the diversity and distinctive qualities of the various civilizations, but to trace their social, cultural, and economic influences and interactions. Furthermore, we point out the many dimensions of the lives of individual men and women across cultures, religions, social classes, and times.

Several distinctive features of our book bear enumeration.

First, we have divided world history into seventeen chapters, each highlighting a major trend (emergence of civilization, early empires, invasion and disruption, and so on) during a distinct chronological era. The subsections of each chapter are devoted to the areas of the world affected by this trend. This effective organization has been continued from previous editions, with revisions based on the latest discoveries and advances in scholarship. Chapter 17 has been carefully reworked and updated to incorporate recent events.

Second, we have placed twelve comparative essays at strategic points in the book. These lay the groundwork for the historical concepts examined in detail in subsequent chapter sections. For example, the essay "The Defining Characteristics of Great Empires," which discusses the dynamics of large states, precedes Chapter 4, which covers the roughly contemporary Hellenistic, Roman, Mauryan, and Han Empires. For this edition, we have added quotations from original sources at the opening of each essay to demonstrate the pertinence of such material and to heighten the essays' interest and relevance.

Third, we have included many charts and maps; each chapter features helpful maps to accentuate the geographical contexts of historical events. In each chapter the "Summary and Comparisons" section is accompanied by a timeline of important events that occurred during the period covered by that chapter, an important learning aid for students.

Fourth, we have chosen many new, attractive illustrations, all in full color, to bring to life events, individuals, and locations of historical interest. As the old adage says, a picture is worth a thousand words. This book abounds with good pictures, some never before published. About a quarter of the illustrations in this edition are new, and many are unique.

Fifth, we have added new boxes to each chapter; most of these consist of quotations from primary sources. Students, reviewers, and professors have praised this engaging and useful enhancement of the text.

Sixth, expanding on a successful feature, we have added more short essays entitled "Lives and Times Across Cultures." These informative, often offbeat, and entertaining pieces present facts and details of life not found in traditional textbooks.

Seventh, Pat Manning at the World History Center, Northeastern University, has created one "Connections Box" per chapter that integrates one of four themes (migrations, technology, family, and culture) with three technologies (the *Migration CD-ROM,* the World Wide Web, and *InfoTrac College Edition*). Students will receive a copy of the *Migrations CD-ROM* and free access to *InfoTrac College Edition* with the purchase of their new textbook. See the *Instructor's Manual* for more details.

Eighth, the chapter summaries, titled "Summary and Comparisons," stress the comparative aspect of historical study. Since each chapter contains much information about diverse regions of the world, this emphasis on comparison ensures a better integration of the various materials of a given chapter and a clearer overall view of world events.

Ninth, at the end of each chapter we have compiled an updated list of sources to guide interested students to well-written monographs, fiction, dramas, films, and television programs that provide historical perspective. We have also added selections of appropriate, exciting, and carefully screened Internet resources.

Tenth, the publisher has put together an invaluable package of ancillary materials. These include aids for instructors:

- **Instructor's Manual and Testbank.** Includes a multimedia guide, chapter outlines, recommended readings, paper topics, identification questions, multiple-choice questions, short-essay questions, and new to this edition, Internet resources. One comprehensive volume.
- **ExamView for Windows and Macintosh.** Create, deliver, and customize tests and study guides (both print and online) in minutes with this easy-to-use assessment and tutorial system. ExamView offers both a Quick Test Wizard and an Online Test Wizard that guide you step by step through the process of creating tests, while its unique "WYSIWYG" capability allows you to see the test you are creating on the screen exactly as it will print or display online. You can build tests of up to 250 questions using up to 12 question types. Using ExamView's complete word-processing capabilities, you can enter an unlimited number of new questions or edit existing questions.
- ***Map Acetates and Commentary for World History, 2002 Edition.*** Contains maps from the text and from other sources as well as commentary on each map. The commentary, by James Harrison of Siena College, includes not only the text caption but also additional points of interest about the map, such as what it shows and its relevance to the study of world history. Possible discussion questions for student involvement are included.
- **HistoryLink 2002.** This is an advanced PowerPoint presentation tool containing text-specific lecture outlines, figures, and images that allows you to quickly deliver dynamic lectures. In addition, it provides the flexibility to customize each presentation by editing what we have provided or by adding your own collection of slides, videos, and animations. All of the map acetates and selected photos have also been incorporated into each of the lectures. In addition, the extensive Map Commentaries for each map slide are available through the Comments feature of PowerPoint.
- **Wadsworth Video Library: History.** Recommended Films for the Humanities & Sciences videos are available free upon adoption, subject to terms of the Wadsworth video policy.
- **CNN Today Video: *World History, Volumes I and II.*** Launch lectures with riveting footage from CNN, the world's leading twenty-four-hour global news television network. CNN Today: *World History, Volumes I and II,* allows you to integrate the news-gathering and programming power of CNN into the classroom to show students the relevance of course topics to their everyday lives. Organized by topics covered in a typical course, these videos are divided into short segments—perfect for introducing key concepts. A Wadsworth/Thomson Learning exclusive.
- **Slide Set.** A set of 150 slides of photos taken throughout the world.
- **Sights and Sounds of History Videodisk/Video.** Short, focused video clips, photos, artwork, animations, music, and dramatic readings are used to bring life to historical topics and events that are most difficult for students to appreciate from a textbook alone. For example, students will experience the grandeur of Versailles and the defeat felt by a German soldier at Stalingrad. The video segments (average length, four minutes) are available on VHS and make excellent lecture launchers.

The following ancillaries are also available for students:

- ***Study Guide for World History, Volumes I and II.*** The study guide contains identifications, true-or-false questions, essay study questions, for further reading, and map exercises.
- ***InfoTrac College Edition.*** This online library allows students to study and learn about history at any time of the day or night. The online database gives students access to full-length articles from more than 900 scholarly and popular periodicals, updated daily, and dating back as far as four years. Periodicals include *Historian, Smithsonian,* and *Harper's* magazines. Free with every new copy of the text.
- ***Migrations in History CD-ROM.*** Free with every new copy of the text. An interactive multimedia curriculum on CD-ROM by Patrick Manning and the World History Center. Includes over 400 primary source documents; analytical questions to help the student develop his/her own interpretations of history; timelines; and additional suggested resources, including books, films, and websites.
- ***Map Exercise Workbook, Volumes I and II.*** Prepared by Cynthia Kosso of Northern Arizona University, this workbook features approximately thirty exercises. Designed to help students feel comfortable with maps by having them work with different kinds of maps and identify places in order to improve their geographic understanding of world history.
- ***Document Exercise Workbook, Volumes I and II.*** Prepared by Donna Van Raaphorst of Cuyahoga Community College, this workbook provides a collection of exercises based on primary sources in history.
- ***Journey of Civilization CD-ROM.*** This CD-ROM takes the student on eighteen interactive journeys through history. Enhanced with QuickTime movies, animations, sound clips, maps, and more, the journeys allow students to engage in history as active participants rather than as readers of past events.
- ***Internet Guide for History*** by John Soares. Section One introduces students to the Internet and includes tips for searching on the web. Section Two introduces students to methods of doing history research and lists URL sites by topic.
- ***Magellan World History Atlas.***
- ***Lives and Times: A World History Reader.*** Assembled by two of the text authors, James Holoka and Jiu-Hwa Upshur, the reader includes 150 short and lively selections, most of them biographical.
- **Web Tutor on WebCT or Blackboard.** This web-based teaching and learning tool is rich with study and mastery tools, communication tools, and course content. Use Web Tutor to provide virtual office hours, post syllabi, set up threaded discussions, track student progress with the quizzing material, and more. For students, Web Tutor offers real-time access to a full array of study tools, including flashcards (with audio), practice quizzes, online tutorials, and web links. Professors can customize the content by uploading images and other resources, adding web links, or creating their own practice materials. Web Tutor also provides rich communication tools, including a course calendar, asynchronous discussion, "real time" chat, and an integrated e-mail system.
- **Web page.** Both instructors and students will enjoy our web page. Visit Historic Times, the Wadsworth History Resource Center at http://history.wadsworth.com. From this full-service site, instructors and students can access many selections, such as a career center, lessons on surfing the web, and links to great history-related websites. Students can also take advantage of the online Student Guide to *InfoTrac College Edition,* featuring lists of article titles with discussion and critical-thinking questions linked to the articles to invite deeper examination of the material. Instructors can visit book-specific sites to learn more about our texts and supplements, and students can access chapter-by-chapter resources for the book, interactive quizzes, and a lively "Join the Forum" online bulletin board.

In sum, we have striven to make this book not only accurate and informative but also exciting for students and other readers. Our textbook combines key characteristics to work effectively in various learning situations. It offers a clear narrative focusing on major historical forces and concepts, uncluttered by minute detail. This edition gives greater attention to social, economic, cultural, and gender history in order to provide a more balanced and comprehensive account of human experience.

We have nevertheless kept our book relatively short—short enough to be suitable for courses at most colleges, so that instructors may assign supplementary readings without overwhelming their students.

To provide a true world perspective, we have adopted several special conventions. First, because the text will be used mostly in North American colleges, we have based our general chronology on the traditional Christian/Western calendar; however, we have designated year dates as B.C.E. (Before the Common Era) instead of B.C. (Before Christ) and C.E. (Common Era) instead of A.D. (Anno Domini). Next, wherever possible we have eliminated Eurocentric geographical terms such as *Far East, Levant, New World,* and the like. Finally, we have generally transliterated (rather than Latinized or Anglicized) names and terms from their original language; thus, *Qur'an* instead of *Koran, Tanakh* instead of *Old Testament,* and (post-1949) *Mao Zedong* instead of *Mao Tsetung* and *Beijing* instead of *Peking* (see also "Romanizing Chinese Words" at the end of this volume). However, we have made exceptions of such familiar Westernized spellings as *Confucius, Averroës, Christopher Columbus,* and *Aztec.*

An enterprise of this magnitude and complexity succeeds only through the dedicated efforts of many people. Wadsworth Publishing secured the services of reviewers whose insights and information materially strengthened this and the previous three editions. The list follows this preface.

We wish to thank our colleagues at Eastern Michigan University—in particular, Ronald Delph and Joseph Engwenyu for their assistance at several stages in the writing—and Gersham Nelson, head of the History Department, for his constant support and encouragement. Nancy Snyder and her assistants were stalwart helpers in handling innumerable practical and technological chores. Raymond Craib at Yale University supplied information and text on women's history and Mexican history. From the outset of this project, Sally Marks, in Providence, Rhode Island, has been exceptionally helpful in suggesting improvements. We also wish to thank Margot Duley of Eastern Michigan University and Richard Edwards of the University of Michigan for making available to us photographs of historical interest from their personal collections. We are grateful to John Nystuen of the University of Michigan for photographing some of the artifacts illustrated in this edition. The authors' spouses furnished copious practical and moral support and showed a high tolerance for hectic writing and production schedules. Thanks also go to Pat Manning at the World History Center at Northeastern University and his graduate assistants, Stacy Tweedy, Tiffany Olson, and Bin Yang. A final word of thanks goes to Clark Baxter, Sharon Adams Poore, Nancy Crochiere, and other members of the Wadsworth Publishing team for their patient attention to all manner of details. Their collective skills have once again transformed our project into a most attractive textbook.

THE AUTHORS

Reviewers

Charles F. Ames, Jr.
Salem State College

Jay Pascal Anglin
University of Southern Mississippi

Gary Dean Best
University of Hawaii at Hilo

Charmarie Blaisdell
Northeastern University

Edward L. Bond
Alabama Agricultural and Mechanical University

Patricia Bradley
Auburn University at Montgomery

Cynthia Brokaw
University of Oregon

Antoinette Burton
Indiana State University

Antonio Calabria
University of Texas

Daniel P. Connerton
North Adams State College

Lane Earns
University of Wisconsin at Oshkosh

John Anthony Eisterhold
University of Tennessee

Angela Hudson Elms
University of Louisiana

Edward L. Farmer
University of Minnesota

William Wayne Farris
University of Tennessee

Gary R. Freeze
Erskine College

Ronald Fritze
Lamar University

Ray C. Gerhardt
Texas Lutheran College

Marc Jason Gilbert
North Georgia College

Steven A. Glazer
Graceland College

Joseph M. Gowaskie
Rider College

Zoltan Kramar
Central Washington University

Susie Ling
Pasadena City College

Lawrence S. Little
Villanova University

Craig A. Lockard
University of Wisconsin at Green Bay

Raymond M. Lorantas
Drexel University

Delores Nason McBroome
Humboldt State University

Susan Maneck
Murray State University

C. P. Mao
Texas Lutheran University

Robroy Meyers
El Camino College

Timothy E. Morgan
Christopher Newport University

Terry Morris
Shorter College

Henry Myers
James Madison University

Cecil C. Orchard
Eastern Kentucky University

James L. Owens
Lynchburg College

Oliver B. Pollak
University of Nebraska at Omaha

Dennis Reinhartz
University of Texas at Arlington

Cynthia Schwenk
Georgia State University

Wendy Singer
Kenyon College

Paul D. Steeves
Stetson University

Cheryl Thurber
Shippensburg University

Hubert van Tuyll
Augusta State University

Pingchao Zhu
University of Idaho

Introduction: Paleolithic and Neolithic Cultures Around the World

HUMAN DEVELOPMENT IN THE OLD STONE AGE

THE NEOLITHIC FOOD-PRODUCING REVOLUTION IN WEST ASIA

NEOLITHIC TIMES IN EUROPE

NEOLITHIC TIMES IN AFRICA

NEOLITHIC TIMES IN ASIA

NEOLITHIC TIMES IN THE WESTERN HEMISPHERE

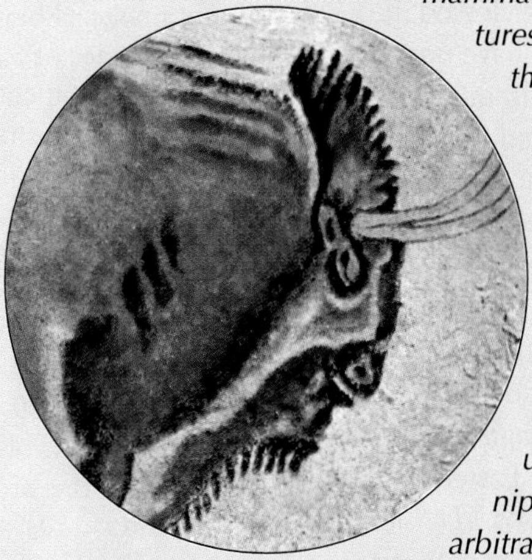

What are we? To the biologist we are . . . Homo sapiens sapiens. *. . . But what is particularly interesting about our species? For a start, we walk upright on our hind legs at all times, which is an extremely unusual way of getting around for a mammal. There are also several unusual features about our head, not least of which is the very large brain it contains. . . . Unlike the apes, we are not covered by a coat of thick hair. . . . Very probably this has something to do with [the fact that] the skin is richly covered with millions of microscopic sweat glands. . . . Our forelimbs, being freed from helping us to get about, possess a very high degree of manipulative skill. . . . No other animal manipulates the world in the extensive and arbitrary way that humans do. . . . Unlike any other animal, we have a spoken language which is characterized by a huge vocabulary and a complex grammatical structure. . . .*

*All [these] . . . are characteristics of a very intelligent creature, but humans are more than just intelligent. Our sense of justice, our need for aesthetic pleasure, our imaginative flights and our penetrating self-awareness, all combine to create an indefinable spirit which I believe is the "soul."**

*Richard E. Leakey, *The Making of Mankind* (New York: Dutton, 1981), pp. 18, 20.

This passage by anthropologist Richard Leakey states the dual nature of human beings—physical and spiritual. Students of history are particularly concerned to identify how these various distinguishing traits have found expression in the accomplishments of mankind. Such historical study records advances in production of food, in technology, in the building of social groups and their habitations, and in general in the more efficient control of the environment. It also seeks to define what it is to be human. This means that historians also study the ways human beings have viewed the world around them, that is, how people have understood its working through science, answered unfathomable questions through religion, and expressed their thoughts in art, literature, and philosophy.

Through such investigation, students of history have ascertained that, to begin with, humans survived precariously through hunting and gathering. Eventually, after hundreds of thousands of years, humans living in several continents created first the agricultural and then the urban revolutions noted in the passage above, thus bringing about civilized life in both the Eastern and Western Hemispheres. This section of *World History* surveys these initial advances of humankind. It first discusses what modern researchers have reconstructed about the emergence of the human species and about life in the hunter-gatherer era around the world. It then takes up the dramatic material changes brought by the invention of agriculture.

Human Development in the Old Stone Age

The story of humanity's achievement began with the Paleolithic or Old Stone Age sometime around 2,000,000 B.C.E., probably in East Africa, as the famous finds in the Olduvai Gorge show. (The labeling of Ages as "Stone," "Bronze," and "Iron" refers to the materials used in the making of tools at a given stage in history.) After 1,000,000 B.C.E., hominids of the *Homo erectus* type moved out of East Africa into West Asia, Europe, East Asia, and Indonesia. This whole vast stretch of time cannot be described with great confidence or detail because there are no written records to illumine it. Instead, we have had to rely on the conclusions and conjectures which modern scientists have drawn from materials obtained from archaeological excavations.

In response to changes in the natural environment, Old Stone Age people made physical and cultural adaptations fundamental for subsequent human development. Crucial physiological refinements included the ability to stand and walk easily in an upright position, changes in the position and size of teeth (especially the canines) in response to changing diet, the evolution and increasing dexterity of an opposable thumb, and changes in the size and configuration of the skull.

Particularly dramatic was the doubling of their brain size. This gave men and women mental superiority over other species, demonstrated in creating artifacts, particularly tools. They could both expand and perfect their cultural equipment and transmit knowledge of how to use that equipment through language, the most flexible and finely calibrated tool of all.

A series of four major ice ages, marked by the movement of ice sheets hundreds of feet thick over vast areas of the earth, stimulated human development. The glaciations changed land formations, sea levels, and plant and animal life and habitats. People had to be innovative and able to modify their patterns of living to survive. Many animals, solely dependent on physical equipment for their survival, were often unable to adjust to changing environmental conditions and became extinct.

By 100,000 B.C.E., modern humans (*Homo sapiens sapiens*) had evolved in Africa. By 40,000 B.C.E. they had occupied the areas originally settled by *Homo erectus,* and afterwards spread into northern Eurasia and into Australia. The South Pacific was settled much later, between 1100 B.C.E. and 1300 C.E.

Modern *Homo sapiens* also migrated through Siberia, across to Alaska, and then east and south throughout North America. Most scholars think that, as in Australia, the greater number of movements occurred during the last ice ages, when glaciers locked up some of the world's water, thus lowering sea levels and exposing land bridges.

As elsewhere in the world at this time, these *Homo sapiens* migrants were still hunters and gatherers, fire-users with chipped stone tools, whose relics in the Western Hemisphere date from about 40,000 B.C.E. By 20,000 B.C.E. humans had arrived in Middle America (the southern two-thirds of Mexico and parts of current Central America south to Panama). It appears that they soon spread thereafter throughout South America, although isolated archaeological finds hinting at settlements even as early as 30,000 B.C.E. may require a revision of our chronology.

The Arctic zone of North America, though it was on the migration route from Asia, was in fact the last part of the continent to be settled. The earliest Paleolithic culture of the Eskimos dates to about 7000 B.C.E. in the region of the Bering Strait. Succeeding cultures known as Pre-Dorset and Dorset combined influences from East Asia and from regions to the south in North America. They were characterized by hunting of caribou, rabbits, and birds, with a gradual shift to fishing and the hunting of polar bears and marine creatures such as walrus and seals. By the first millennium B.C.E., these Eskimo cultures were prevalent in the Arctic from

The Ascent of Mankind

*Fossil skulls have been found in Southern Africa . . . which establish the characteristic structure of the head when it began to be man-like. . . . A historic skull, found [in 1924] . . . at a place called Taung, by . . . Raymond Dart . . . is [that of] a baby, five to six years old. . . . Dart called this creature Australopithecus [Southern Ape]. . . . For me the little Australopithecus baby has a personal history. In 1950, . . . I was asked to do a piece of mathematics. Could I combine a measure of the size of the Taung child's teeth with their shape, so as to discriminate them from the teeth of apes? I had never held a fossil skull in my hands, and I was by no means an expert on teeth. But it worked pretty well; and it transmitted to me a sense of excitement which I remember at this instant. I, at over forty, having spent a lifetime in doing abstract mathematics about the shape of things, suddenly saw my knowledge reach back two million years and shine a searchlight into the history of man. . . . I do not know how the Taung baby began life, but to me it still remains the primordial infant from which the whole adventure of man began.**

*Jacob Bronowski, The Ascent of Man (Boston: Little Brown, 1973), pp. 28–30.

Thus Jacob Bronowski described the excitement he felt as he looked at a bit of evidence of ancient human life on our planet. The title of his book, *The Ascent of Man,* is an allusion to Charles Darwin's famous book *The Descent of Man,* published a century earlier, which advanced evidence for the hypothesis that human beings had evolved from more primitive life forms. Darwin's claim released a torrent of controversy by its challenge to the traditional belief in the biblical story of Creation, but it also stimulated the sciences of physical anthropology and archaeology. Researchers have made stunning discoveries about the ancestry of our species through excavations at sites such as the Olduvai Gorge in East Africa and Hsihoutu in Shansi province in China. Their work has yielded insights into the earliest achievements that brought humanity from primitive origins to the creation of civilized life, from crude stone implements to spacecraft, from the rudiments of spoken language to the art of poetry, from nomadic hunting and gathering to the complex socioeconomic and political structures of city life.

Alaska in the west through northern Canada to Greenland in the east.

By the late Paleolithic era, human beings around the world had (1) manufactured a range of stone or bone implements (knives, scrapers, borers) and weapons (blades, bows and arrows, spears and spear throwers), (2) controlled fire for cooking and for giving heat and light, (3) developed spoken language in addition to the nonverbal gestures used by all primates, (4) formulated an artistic tradition, seen for example in the famous cave paintings at Lascaux in France and Altamira in Spain, (5) created ritual practices connected chiefly with fertility and with burial of the dead, and (6) organized themselves into social groups for more efficient collection and sharing of food.

Also by late Paleolithic times, human beings had probably acquired the superficial physical traits conventionally known as racial. Differences in skin, hair, and eye color, in size and shape of the nostrils, and perhaps in stature and cranial shape likely resulted from adaptation to environmental conditions in various parts of the world.

The Neolithic Food-Producing Revolution in West Asia

Because Paleolithic humans lived by hunting animals and by gathering wild fruits, nuts, and grains, they needed a relatively large space to support even a single family. This severely restricted the size of human communities and made settled life in one area impossible, since the group had to follow its food supply and move in conjunction with animal migrations and vegetation cycles. Only when people shifted from the random collection of food to its regular cultivation did they overcome such limitations. In the Neolithic or New Stone Age, humans assured themselves of a regular food supply by developing agricultural techniques and domesticating food-producing animals. Stable food supplies in turn produced a rapid increase in population and the founding of permanent settlements, which later became the

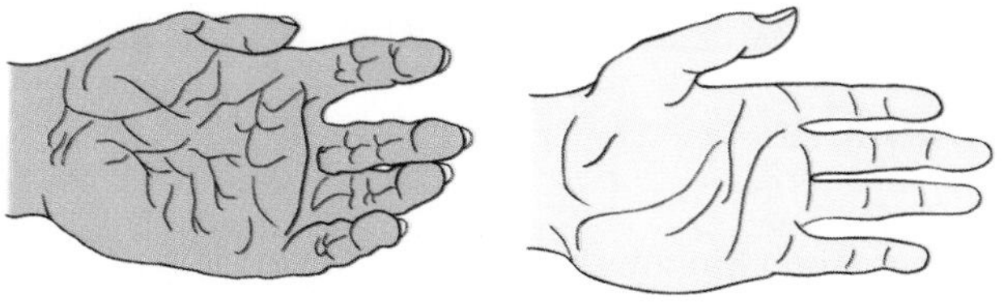

Simian and human hands are roughly similar, but the longer, highly mobile thumb is especially useful to human beings.

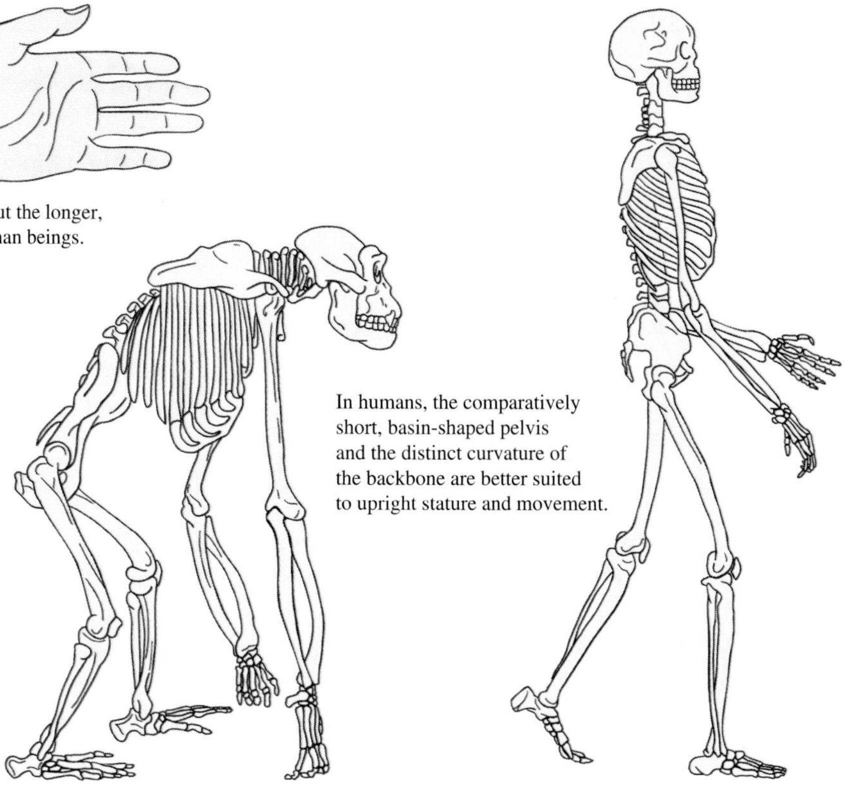

Although humans and gorillas have the same number of teeth and bones, evolution has given them quite distinct forms: apes possess large, strong canines set in massive jaws, while humans have smaller canines set in a more curved row, permitting side-to-side mastication.

In humans, the comparatively short, basin-shaped pelvis and the distinct curvature of the backbone are better suited to upright stature and movement.

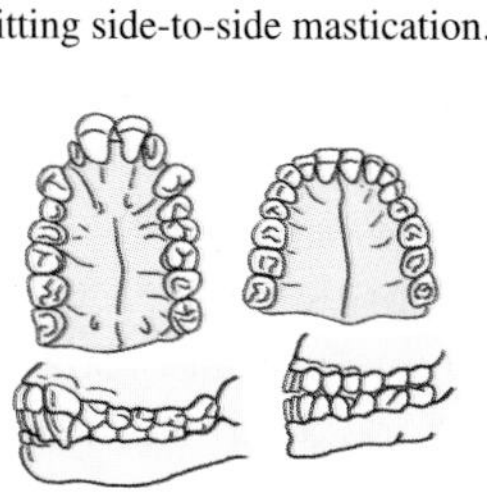

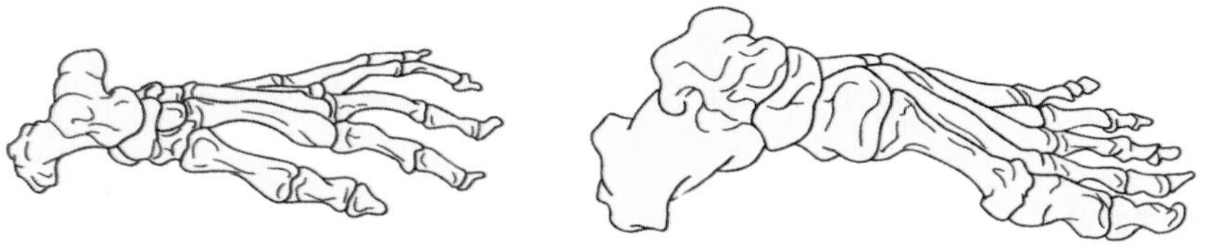

Comparisons of the Skeletal Structures of Humans and Apes.

The gorilla's foot differs from the human foot in the length of its toes, the more lateral location of the big toe, and the absence of an arch, which imparts a spring to the human gait.

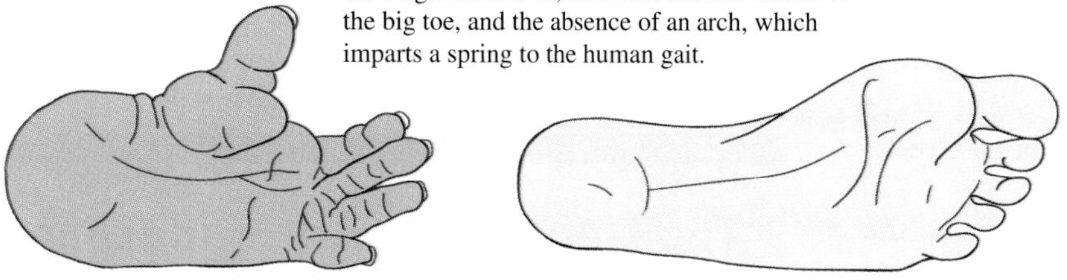

basis for the more complex social structures and more dynamic technologies of urban civilization. These characteristics of the Neolithic revolution varied from region to region and emerged much earlier in some parts of the world than in others. Indeed, to speak of a "revolution" is somewhat misleading, since the transformation in most areas was very gradual. Still, in terms of the vast time frame of human evolution, the change was comparatively quick. In 10,000 B.C.E., 100 percent of the world's population of ca. 10 million were hunters and gatherers; by 1500 C.E., only 1 percent of the world's roughly 350 million people were hunters and gatherers; today, less than 0.001 percent of the world's population—for example, Eskimos, African !Kung San people, and the aborigines of Australia—still live in pre-Neolithic conditions.

With the retreat of the last ice age, beginning around 10,000 B.C.E., climatic conditions in that part of West Asia called the Fertile Crescent became well suited to raising grain and domesticating animals. The valleys and foothills of this region were home to the wild ancestors of domesticable plants (barley, wheat, millet, and so on) and animals (goats, donkeys, and the like). During a transitional period, the Mesolithic or Middle Stone Age (10,000 to 7000 B.C.E..), at places like Mount Carmel in Palestine, humans made tentative efforts to move from hunting-gathering subsistence methods to the systematic harvesting of grain.

By 7000 B.C.E. the residents of West Asia had developed the true farming villages that typify the Neolithic era. These centers consisted of at most a few thousand inhabitants engaged in the cultivation of wheat, barley, peas, beans, and lentils and in the raising of goats, sheep, pigs, and cattle. These early farmers continued to supplement their diet with wild fruits, nuts, and grains. They lived in caves or pit houses or huts made of mud, reeds, logs, or stones, grouped in small open communities or in larger fortified towns like Jericho, in the Jordan Valley near the Dead Sea, or Çatal Hüyük in the Anatolian Peninsula (modern Turkey). The point of such communities was to concentrate labor both for agricultural work—plowing, sowing, harvesting, and the like—and for the protection of the farmland on which the community's survival now depended.

Early farmers also devised techniques for making porridge, bread, and beer, and developed ovens for cooking and, later, for firing pottery. (Pottery in particular is a joy for archaeologists because it is almost imperishable and once a culture starts to make pottery, it leaves behind a trail of broken shards, often distinctively decorated and therefore datable.) They wove baskets and textiles from wool and flax, and began to work metals like gold, silver, and copper. Finally, they discovered the wheel and made wagons and pottery wheels, and they invented the plow, which superseded digging sticks and hoes. Food surpluses freed some members of the community, generally males, to become at least part-time specialists: smiths, potters, weavers, artists, and perhaps priests.

Gender roles in Neolithic communities were affected by the production of food surpluses. Plow agriculture required the physical strength of males, rather than of females, whose energies were taken up by pregnancy and the nursing and rearing of children. Animal husbandry, too, was likely a male occupation. The males' control of surpluses of livestock, meat, pelts, and grain gave them an economic advantage that translated into the leisure to develop and engage in the specializations mentioned above. In short, males managed production, while to women fell the lifetime-consuming and labor-intensive tasks of reproduction.

Once the agricultural revolution had occurred in the Fertile Crescent, it quickly spread to other regions in Asia, North Africa, and Europe. By contrast, farming emerged independently in North and South America (see Map I.1). In all these areas, the revolution in food production enabled humans to take the next major step toward civilization, from village to city. Before turning to that major change, we will consider Neolithic culture elsewhere in the world.

Neolithic Times in Europe

The earliest agricultural villages in Europe appeared about 6500 B.C.E. in Greece, probably as a result of colonization by Anatolians across the Aegean. The farmers lived in square mudbrick buildings, sometimes with one larger building as a meeting place. Their economy centered on the raising of sheep and the cultivation of wheat and legumes. By 4000 B.C.E., Neolithic settlements had spread throughout Europe along two major routes: the Vardar-Danube-Rhine corridor, and the coastal areas of the Mediterranean Sea. Wooden longhouses were . . . more common than mud brick huts outside the Balkans. Initially, the pattern of farming settlements was dictated by the location of fertile soil that had resulted from the weathering of loess (layers of wind-blown dust that had formed like silt along the rims of glaciers in earlier times). Eventually, however, as incoming farmers carved land from the European forests, the hunters who had lived there since the early postglacial period (ca. 10,000 B.C.E.) left their former mode of life to swell the ranks of the agriculturalists.

The earliest progress toward civilization on the European continent took place along the Mediterranean coasts, especially in the Balkan and Italian peninsulas. Northern and western Europe was another matter; this area made few contributions (mainly in the form of natural resources) to the general advance of civilization before 500 B.C.E. It was largely unreceptive to external cultural influences (metalworking was an exception). Literacy, for example, came very late, imposed by conquerors. However, one ancient European art form does remain noteworthy: the megalithic (literally "large stone") constructions scattered from Scandinavia in the north to Corsica, Sardinia, and Malta in the south. Some of these are older than the great pyramids of Giza in Egypt, though they are by comparison very crude both in form and arrangement. Many of them are tombs; others are laid out in symmetrical patterns selected for religious or astronomical reasons. The most famous of these megaliths is Stonehenge in southern England. Here, in late Neolithic and early Bronze Age times (c. 2800–1800 B.C.E.), the prehistoric builders collected about 136 massive stones, some as large as thirty feet long and weighing fifty tons. The megaliths, transported over some eighteen miles, were assembled in a hundred-foot-diameter circle with an inner horseshoe consisting of five massive post and lintel gateways. The structure as a whole is aligned to the movements of sun, moon, and stars at specific points in the year, thus constituting a kind of gigantic observatory. All this argues a remarkably precise awareness of astronomical movements, unassisted by the mathematical theorems later developed by Babylonians and Egyptians. Stonehenge also bespeaks both an elaborate cooperation of labor activity and a careful organization of religious and social observances.

Neolithic Times in Africa

The Neolithic Revolution spread to the Nile Valley between 5000 and 4000 B.C.E. Wheat and barley, and

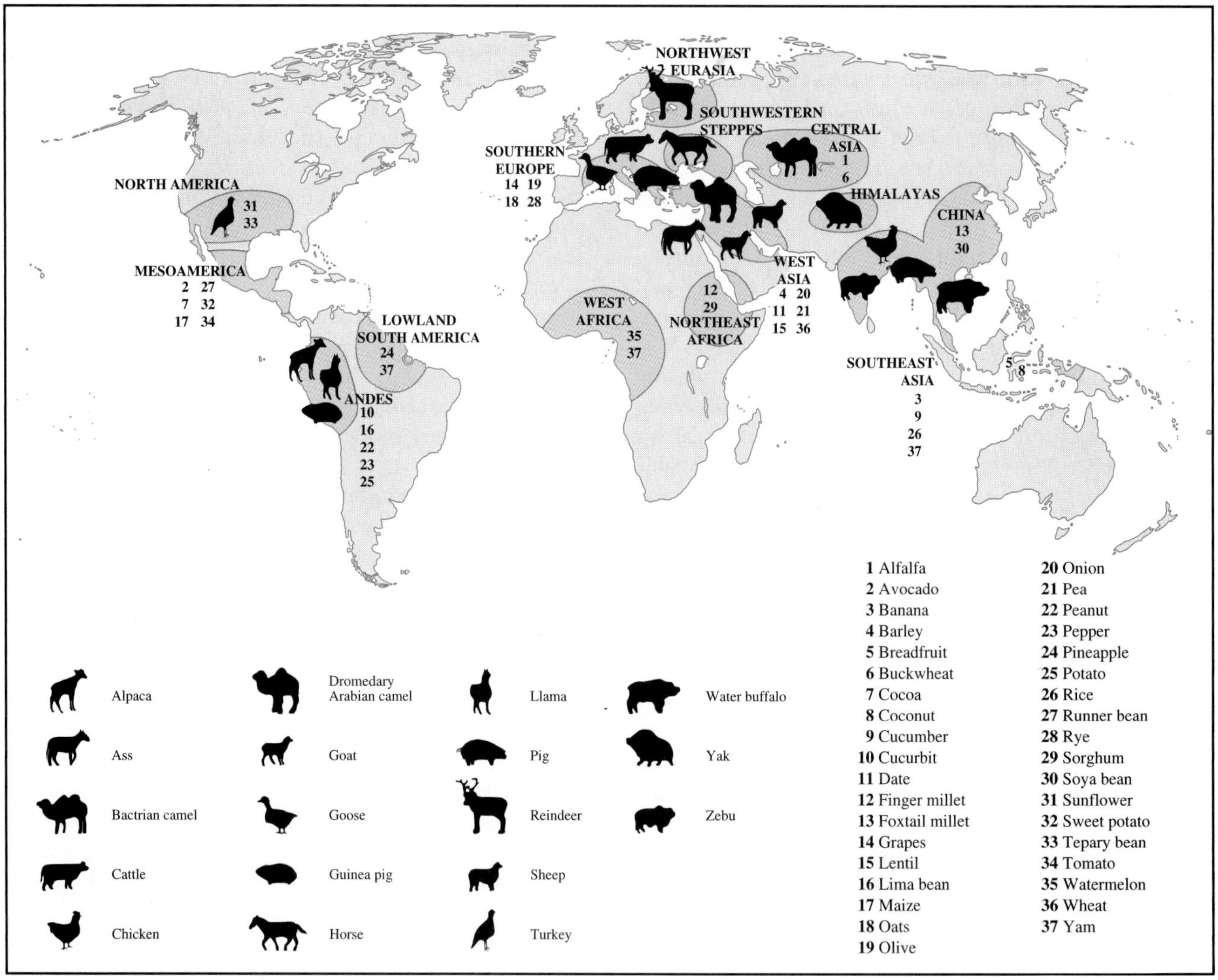

Map I.1 The Origins of Agricultural Crops and of Domestic Animals. This map shows the areas where particular plant and animal species were first cultivated or domesticated. Some species (for example, the pig) seem to have developed independently in different areas. In most cases, however, contact between neighboring cultures facilitated the rapid spread of plant and animal cultivation around the globe.

goats, sheep, and pigs were introduced very likely from the Fertile Crescent, especially Palestine and Mesopotamia. Irrigation by control of the Nile flood started at this time. Such developments laid the agricultural foundations for the first historical dynasties of ancient Egypt, beginning about 3000 B.C.E., discussed later in this chapter. Elsewhere, African peoples in the Saharan region, which did not become uninhabitably arid till after 3000 B.C.E., adopted the domestication of animals and, more slowly, the practice of agriculture from the neighboring Nile Valley. With the desiccation of the Sahara, these peoples carried their Neolithic skills with them in migrations to central and western Africa, though hunting-gathering cultures persisted in many areas. The barrier that the Sahara desert imposed by 2500 B.C.E. prevented the spread of the urban civilization that flowered with such magnificence in Old Kingdom Egypt. It was not until the first millennium B.C.E. that settled agricultural life and the practice of metallurgy became more widespread in sub-Saharan Africa. In all cases, however, the scarcity of water has meant that African peoples engaged in long-term agriculture have lived within the limits of a precariously balanced ecological system.

A very few African peoples remained at the hunter-gatherer stage till quite recently. Thus anthropologists could observe directly the cultural implications of changeover to an agricultural mode of life, for example, among the !Kung San people (formerly called "bushmen") of southern Africa (the ! symbolizes an explosive sound or "click" common to the language). Here the transition to settled farming meant a shift from the mentality of sharing to that of saving. Among hunter-gather-

Corbis-Bettmann

Altamira Wall Painting. A section of the famous paleolithic wall paintings in the caves of Altamira, Spain. Similar paintings and carvings, found in caves throughout Europe from southern Spain and France in the west to the Ural Mountains in the east, testify to the wide dispersion of Paleolithic culture.

ers, survival of the group depends on the sharing of food collected into a common supply by all members, and all who contribute in any way to the general store of food are valued equally, regardless of sex. Among farmers, by contrast, a desire to conserve for oneself what one has produced is predominant. There is also an intensified possessiveness of and willingness even to fight for land that one has labored long and hard to make productive. Socially, hunter-gatherer !Kung exhibited little differentiation in status or rigidity in the definition of sex roles. Among agriculturalist !Kung, however, women are confined to work in the fields, while men tend to animals. Because there is often a surplus of animals and not of crops, the men gain power by controlling cattle as a medium of exchange for other goods or for money; thus the work of the women is undervalued. The division of gender roles begins even in childhood: in hunter-gatherer societies, children play together in the same manner. By contrast, the children of !Kung farmers split by sex: girls' play is modeled on the behavior of women, boys' on that of men.

Neolithic Times in Asia

The Neolithic age in India dates from about 5000 B.C.E. It was centered in modern day Baluchistan and Sind in northwest India, then well watered and wooded, today almost a waterless desert. Several distinct cultures evolved, distinguished from each other by different types of painted pottery and burial practices. Pottery figurines made by these Neolithic peoples show that they practiced fertility rites (Mother Goddess, phallic symbols) and that the bull was important to them. The Neolithic Age came to an end around 2500 B.C.E. with the beginning of the Indus civilization. This also is the subject for the next chapter.

The Neolithic Age began in China about 6000 B.C.E. with three separate Neolithic cultures. The first was in North China, called the Yangshao culture, whose people lived in semisubterranean round and rectangular houses and cultivated millet. Another was located in the Hwai (a river in east-central China) and lower Yangtze valleys, where rice was grown. A third, which extended along the South China coast and possibly included coastal Southeast Asia and Taiwan, cultivated edible tubers (taro and yam) and fruit. Each culture had its distinct and characteristic pottery ware. In time each outgrew its immediate surroundings and interactions resulted. Around 3000 B.C.E., silkworms were domesticated and weaving of silk cloth began. At about the same time, technology for working neghrite jade, an extremely hard stone, was developed. The Chinese have been making jade tools, ornaments, and ritual items ever since.

Around 2500 B.C.E., an advanced late Neolithic culture, the Lungshan, developed in northeastern China. Its people made a thin, high-fired, almost porcelain-quality pottery on the wheel, began to work metals, had specialized crafts, and began to live in small urban settlements. Differentiated graves indicate the development of a ranked society. According to traditional accounts, great rulers of this period created the first dynasty, called the Hsia. To date, we have no documentary evidence of the Hsia dynasty. Undoubtedly, however, the Lungshan culture provided a basis for later development of the first documented dynasty, the Shang, which began around 1700 B.C.E. The Shang dynasty and its immediate successors will be examined in Chapter 2.

Although the earliest Japanese written records date from about 500 C.E., archaeology and Chinese records enable us to reconstruct information for earlier periods. The archaeological record shows that the first Japanese culture, called the Jomon (rope pattern), appeared during the third millennium B.C.E. It is named after pots made and decorated by coiling clay. These people did not practice agriculture, but were hunters and gatherers. To judge from the huge shell mounds they left behind, shellfish was important to their diet.

About the third century B.C.E., in western Japan, there emerged a Neolithic culture that made pottery on wheels, knew both bronze and iron, and used irrigation to grow rice. It is called the Yayoi culture after one of its sites. Strong Chinese influence is suggested in the introduction of irrigation and in the Han bronze mirrors, weapons, and coins found at Yayoi sites. Technology

CONNECTIONS IN MIGRATION

Migration in World History

The "Connections" box found in each chapter of this volume focuses on various linkages, or common themes, in world history. These essays locate connections in the past, encourage you to explore how your own interests are tied to issues in history, and link this textbook to the Migration CD-ROM, the Internet, and InfoTrac. If you practice finding connections in world history, you will see the patterns underlying all the complexity of our past, have a much better understanding of the present, and be better able to predict the future.

Humans are a migratory species. Our ancestors settled the planet in a series of early wanderings from Africa to all of the earth's other landmasses. In every era, beginning with the Paleolithic and Neolithic eras, people have moved to new environments, developing new ways of life and new communities. In moving, they have not only changed their lives, but also modified their surroundings. World history, in one sense, is a repetition and elaboration of this basic pattern in individual lives.

Consider the migrations discussed in this introductory chapter. They include the movement of people from Africa to every other continent, and the later movements of food crops and domestic animals beginning more than 5,000 years ago. Because migration is always about at least two places, it helps us think about connections across the world.

Now consider the issues of greatest importance to you personally. These issues may deal with family, career, education, beliefs, lifestyle, or other questions. How many of these issues present you with a choice between moving and staying put? How many persons or material goods of importance to you are affected by issues of migration?

With the above points in mind, open and explore Unit 1 of your Migration CD-ROM. There you will find thirty documents about migration in the present and in the past 500 years. Read through the documents and look for patterns or concepts that underlie each. Now open the "Notebook" in the Migration CD-ROM, and write your thoughts on the question, "What can we learn about world history and ourselves by studying migration?" The point of this essay is for you to formulate issues—that is, to write out your own statement of what you hope to learn in world history, and how the concept of migration, both in the past and in your own life, might connect to issues of importance to you.

transfer is evident in the local imitation of metal prototypes introduced from China.

The earliest Chinese historic records containing definite information on Japan were compiled in the third century B.C.E.. They provide interesting information about the political and social organization of the island people whom the Chinese called Wa. According to the records, the Wa were divided into many tribes, ruled over by hereditary kings and queens. The most powerful tribe, called the Yamatai (possibly a rendition of Yamato, the old capital district of the later Japanese imperial line), was ruled by a queen who was also a high priestess. The Chinese also commented on the marked social differences between members of society.

Neolithic Times in the Western Hemisphere

In the Western Hemisphere, undisputed evidence of Mesolithic farming exists in the semiarid Mexican highlands, but the climate, at least in the areas where the first civilizations rose, is less favorable to preserving the evidence archaeologists need than are the deserts of Mesopotamia or Egypt. Nevertheless, the early Middle Americans had domesticated gourds by 6500 B.C.E., and they selectively bred maize (commonly called "corn") into a cultivated staple between 7000 and 3500 B.C.E. In comparison, the first cereals were grown in the area of present-day Europe about 3000 B.C.E.

Maize would be the agricultural basis for the development of later civilization in Middle America, filling the role that rice did in Asia and cereals did in the Middle East. Weighed against those staples, maize produces more nourishment with less effort than rice or wheat and can grow in drier conditions. The Middle American peoples recognized their debt to the crop: maize gods figure in every Middle American culture as equals, at least, of rain and other environmental deities.

From 3500 to 2500 B.C.E., roughly contemporaneously with the civilization of Sumer and the founding of Egypt's dynasties, permanent Neolithic settlements appeared in Middle America. The oldest pottery found

2,500,000 B.C.E.	Earliest evidence of stone tools
2,000,000	Earliest examples of the genus *Homo*
1,000,000	Premodern humans spread out of Africa
100,000	Appearance of *Homo sapiens sapiens* in East Africa
40,000	*Homo sapiens* in the Western Hemisphere
15,000	Cave paintings at Altamira and Lascaux
10,000	Retreat of the last ice age Transition from Paleolithic to Mesolithic era Beginnings of agriculture
7000	The Neolithic Revolution in West Asia Cultivation of maize in Mesoamerica
6500	Earliest agricultural villages in Europe
6000	Neolithic period begins in China
5000	Agriculture in the Nile Valley Neolithic settlements in Mesoamerica
3000	Neolithic period in India Cultivation of silkworms Megalithic construction begins at Stonehenge Desiccation of the Sahara
2500	Neolithic settlements begin in Peru

dates to about 2500 B.C.E. By 1500 B.C.E., full-time agriculturists had appeared in the central highlands and the Gulf Coast regions of Middle America. The earliest known civilization in the Western Hemisphere, the Olmec, appeared here south of Vera Cruz; it will be taken up in Chapter 1.

Turning to South America, in Peru some farming of both gourds and cotton took place before 2500 B.C.E. In this early phase, many cultural centers existed in different river valleys, but intervening highlands limited contact between them. We know from the archaeological record that sedentary cultures evolved between 2500 and 1800 B.C.E. in most of the river valleys, with the people there, as well as some of the highland groups, building temples and altars. On the seacoast, the basis of the economy was not agriculture, although farming was done in the fertile soil that seasonal flooding left on the rivers' banks. The main source of food was the sea, which provided not only fish, shellfish, and birds but also seaweed. By the end of this period, some highlanders grew maize, the cultivation of which had spread from Middle America, although most still depended largely on hunting and gathering. Unlike the Middle Americans, the Peruvians domesticated animals, and they had the dog, guinea pigs, and fowl for food; and the American cousins of the camel family—the llama, alpaca, guanaco, and vicuña—for carrying burdens and also for wool. Along the central coast, pottery appeared about 1800 B.C.E. and may represent a diffusion of the technology from Colombia, where it was being made by about 3100 B.C.E. Cultivation of the potato, whose later export to Europe profoundly affected the Old World, was general in suitable climates. During the period when pottery was just beginning, some of the Peruvian coastal cities also began to raise peanuts and manioc. Because those plants originated east of the Andes, their presence on the Peruvian coast argues long-range trade.

Selected Sources

Annaud, Jean-Jacques, director. *Quest for Fire.* 1982. This film depicts a variety of Stone Age discoveries, including fire starting and spoken language.

Barber, Elizabeth W. *Women's Work: The First 20,000 Years: Women, Cloth, and Society in Early Times.* 1994. An informative book that draws on archaeological and other evidence for the development of weaving and many other aspects of women's lives; covers the era from later Paleolithic through classical Greece.

*Bronowski, Jacob. *The Ascent of Man.* 1973. Chapters 1 and 2 of this best-seller, based on the BBC television series, offer a lively account of Stone Age developments.

*Available in paperback.

*Chang Kwang-chih. *The Archaeology of Ancient China*. 3d ed. 1977. The most authoritative book on the subject. Many illustrations, maps, and charts make it interesting and informative.

*Ehrenberg, Margaret. *Women in Prehistory*. 1989. An interesting study of deductions that can be made about the important role of women in Stone Age cultures.

Fagan, Brian M. *The Journey from Eden: The Peopling of Our World*. 1990. A useful treatment of human evolution and migration patterns in Paleolithic times.

Fiedel, Stuart J. *Prehistory of the Americas*. 1988. A recent and splendid attempt to integrate the new knowledge about pre-Colombian America that has appeared in many fields.

Gimbutas, Marija A. *The Civilization of the Goddess: The World of Old Europe*. 1991. A good examination of the question of prehistoric religions and the place of mother goddesses in early human culture.

*Hawkes, Jacquetta. *The Atlas of Early Man: The Rise of Man across the Globe from 35,000 B.C. to A.D. 500*. 1976; rev. ed. 1993. An extremely well-written book, enhanced by more than 1,000 superb illustrations and maps.

*Leakey, Richard E., and Roger Lewin. *Origins Reconsidered: In Search of What Makes Us Human*. 1992. A readable and well-illustrated update of the popular first edition of Leakey's discussion of human origins.

Lloyd, Seton. *The Archaeology of Mesopotamia: From the Old Stone Age to the Persian Conquest*. Rev. ed. 1984. An excellent survey of the origins and early course of civilization in Mesopotamia.

Mohen, J. P. *The World of Megaliths*. 1990. A current discussion of the megalithic monuments and their builders in the Neolithic era.

Piggott, S. *Prehistoric India*. 1950. Still the classic work on this subject.

Wilson, Peter J. *The Domestication of the Human Species*. 1988. Particularly strong on prehistoric social evolution, land settlement patterns, and dwellings.

Internet Links

The Cave of Lascaux

http://www.culture.gouv.fr/culture/arcnat/lascaux/en

This well-designed website, maintained by the French Ministry of Culture, offers accurate information about the discovery and significance of the famous caves and their spectacular paintings.

Human Prehistory: An Exhibition

http://users.hol.gr/~dilos/prehis.htm

A series of "Exhibition Rooms" featuring helpful graphics and text discussing advances in our understanding of human prehistory.

Ice Ages

http://www.museum.state.il.us/exhibits/ice_ages

This site is based on a special exhibition at the Illinois State Museum; it focuses on life 16,000 years ago in the region of present-day midwestern United States. The user may "visit" paleontologists at work in various cave excavations.

Paleolithic Art

http://www.mc.maricopa.edu/anthro/exploratorium/art/paleoart.html

An excellent selection of Paleolithic rock art, such as the Lascaux paintings, with helpful text, including a *Time* magazine article, "Behold the Stone Age," by Robert Hughes.

Stone Age Habitats

http://www.personal.psu.edu/users/w/x/wxk116/habitat

This very well-illustrated source features reconstructions of Paleolithic dwellings excavated at European and Asian sites; includes a link to "Stone Age Handaxes."

COMPARATIVE ESSAY 1

The Defining Characteristics of Civilization

Appetite for food and sex is nature.

Kao Tzu, fourth-century B.C.E. philosopher.

The range of variations is infinitely wider in food than in sex. . . . People who have the same culture share the same food habits, that is, they share the same assemblage of food variables. People of different cultures share different assemblages of food variables. We might say that different cultures have different food choices.

K. C. Chang, *Food in Chinese Culture: Anthropological and Historical Perspectives* (New Haven: Yale University Press, 1977), p. 3.

The first cities appeared in the Fertile Crescent and Egypt about 3000 B.C.E. as a result of the Agricultural Revolution, which began in those regions after about 10,000 B.C.E. This momentous achievement enabled humans to acquire food with much greater efficiency and regularity and in greater quantities than had been possible during the earlier hunting-gathering stage. Thus larger groups of people could live from the produce of less land. As food production increased, so did population and consequently population density. More efficient food production led to a surplus that allowed some people to engage in specialized occupations. Trade developed as a result. These advances changed the human condition so significantly that they are collectively termed the Agricultural Revolution.

Some historians speculate that agriculture spread from the Fertile Crescent and Egypt to other parts of the globe. This thesis is difficult to prove, however, and it is possible that agriculture was independently invented in several areas of the world and under different geographic conditions. For example, most early centers of the Agricultural Revolution in Asia and North Africa were located in the temperate zones, and most early civilizations began in large river valleys: the Tigris-Euphrates in Mesopotamia, the Nile in Egypt, the Indus in India, and the Huang Ho in China. However, the Amerindians of Mesoamerica and South America developed advanced civilizations in tropical jungles, in hot arid highlands and coasts, and in cool plateaus and uplands, but not along major river valleys. These cultures differed in their food assemblages (for example, cereal grains in West Asia, rice in East Asia, maize in Mesoamerica), and in the evolution of city-based societies. Thus no set rules regarding the preconditions for civilization are universally applicable.

Many people use the word *civilized* to mean "urbane" or "sophisticated." The term is often applied to one's own group; other groups are deemed to be less civilized or uncivilized "barbarians." For example, the Greeks considered the Persians "barbarians" because they did not speak Greek and embrace Greek cultural values; in the same way, the Persians called the Arabs barbarians, and the Chinese referred to most of their neighbors by the same epithet. In North America, the Inuit and Sioux spoke of themselves as "human beings" or "the people," as if those outside their group were somehow less than human. The origin myths of many peoples support such claims.

Professionals who deal with the past use the word *civilized* in a neutral, descriptive way. Increasingly, historians tend to define civilization in terms of urbanization. Whatever the particular circumstances of their origin, early civilizations manifested similar urban characteristics: new and specialized vocations, advances in the arts and technology, and complex political and cultural institutions. Physically, a city is functionally distinct from the surrounding countryside, often with defensive walls demarcating the entire city or at least its religious and administrative center. It also includes palaces, temples, private residences, and markets. Socially, most early cities included people of distinct social classes and occupational groups, ranging from the ruling elite and religious leaders to artisans, merchants, and slaves.

The city-centered government also ruled surrounding territories, often by military force. It also organized labor for public works. Depending on the resources at their disposal, governments devoted great technological and artistic skills to building canals and dikes, roads, palaces, rulers' tombs, and monuments.

Another approach to defining civilization is to link it with writing. In the opinion of some, no matter how urbanized and how technologically, culturally, and artistically advanced a culture is, it must also have a system of writing to be termed civilized. Applying this criterion to Amerindian cultures, the Maya and the Aztecs were civilized but the Olmec and Inka were not.

Another issue related to the concept of civilization is the meaning of the term *prehistoric*. Most of us use the term to mean "primitive," as in the sense of Neolithic "cave dwellers." Some professionals, however, use *prehistoric* in a special technical sense to denote a culture that had no writing or whose writing has not been deciphered. According to this point of view, an era is designated *historic* if written materials provide us with a deeper understanding of its culture than can be gained from archaeological artifacts alone. Thus, although the people of the Indus civilization used writing, their civilization is prehistoric, because the few surviving samples of their writing remain undeciphered.

This essay has defined civilization and its preconditions largely in material terms. In closing our discussion, we must also remember that every civilization represents a triumph of the human spirit. In the words of Arnold J. Toynbee, a renowned historian of world civilizations:

How are we to describe . . . any . . . of the ten or twenty civilizations which we can count up on our fingers? In human terms . . . , each of these civilizations is . . . a distinctive attempt at a single great common human enterprise . . . , an effort to perform an act of creation. (Civilization on Trial *[New York: Oxford University Press, 1948], p. 55)*

The next two chapters will focus on the distinguishing features and achievements of the world's oldest known civilizations in West Asia and Africa, along the Mediterranean, in Central and South America, and in South and East Asia.

Early Civilization in West Asia, Africa, the Aegean, and the Western Hemisphere

1

On [the shield, Hephaestus] wrought in all their beauty two cities of mortal men. And there were marriages in one, and festivals. They were leading the brides along the city from their maiden chambers under the flaring of torches, and the loud bride song was arising. The young men followed the circles of the dance, and among them the flutes and lyres kept up their clamor as in the meantime the women standing each at the door of her court admired them. The people were assembled in the marketplace, where a quarrel had arisen, and two men were disputing over the blood price for a man who had been killed. One man promised full restitution in a public statement, but the other refused and would accept nothing. Both then made for an arbitrator, to have a decision; and people were speaking up on either side, to help both men. But the heralds kept the people in hand, as meanwhile the elders were in session on benches of polished stone in the sacred circle and held in their hands the staves of the heralds who lift their voices. The two men rushed before these, and took turns speaking their cases, and between them lay on the ground two talents of gold, to be given to that judge who in this case spoke the straightest opinion.

But around the other city were lying two forces of armed men shining in their war gear. For one side counsel was divided whether to storm and sack, or share between both sides the property and all the possessions the lovely citadel held within it. But the city's people were not giving way, and armed for an ambush. Their beloved wives and their little children stood on the rampart to hold it, and with them the men with age upon them, but meanwhile the others went out. . . .

But the other army . . . went after, and soon overtook them. These stood their ground and fought a battle by the banks of the river, and they were making casts at each other with their spears bronze-headed; and Hate was there with Confusion among them, and Death the destructive.

The Iliad of Homer, trans. Richmond Lattimore (Chicago: University of Chicago Press, 1951), pp. 388–389.

In this passage from Homer's epic story of the Trojan War, we read the description of a shield adorned with an elaborate relief sculpture that the smith-god Hephaestus has crafted for the greatest of the Greek heroes, Achilles. The subject matter of the god's art is a tale of two cities, of peace and of war, of the good things and the bad of civilized life. The Shield of Achilles depicts the human potential for both creativity and destruction. This chapter surveys the results of that potential in several of the earliest civilizations around the world.

The study of ancient societies is rewarding for many reasons. There is the allure of origins, of people in remote times and distant places who were first in so many crucial endeavors. The early inhabitants of West Asia, Egypt, the Aegean area, and, in the Western Hemisphere, of Mesoamerica and the Andean region confronted the problems of survival and developed the earliest examples of civilized life. The cities of Mesopotamia, Babylon, and Ur of the Chaldees, the ever-fascinating great pyramids at Giza, the massive sculpted heads at the Olmec city of La Venta, the Lion Gate in the imposing walls at Mycenae, and the spectacular royal palace at Persepolis in Iran—all are the visible signs of energetic people who had marvelous creative talents and ambition to match. Because of their remoteness in time, these civilizations have an air of the exotic and mysterious. We cannot help but be curious about the conditions of life and the personal motivations of the people who fashioned these ancient worlds: in short, what made them tick? To pursue this question is to explore the early, prototypical accomplishments of the human race. Such study is its own reward.

For the student of history, there are additional reasons for studying ancient civilizations. This chapter and the next examine the cultural traits of a number of peoples who built some of the earliest societies based on an urban mode of existence. The preconditions for those societies and their political, social, economic, and cultural common denominators are sketched in the preceding comparative essay. Though the early civilizations examined in this chapter died out in the course of history, they demand attention because of their lasting contributions to subsequent societies: the development of writing, city living, metal working, hydraulic engineering, complex governments, rational codes of law, and quasi-monotheistic religions.

For students living in Western societies, the study of ancient civilizations, as indeed of world history itself, is a good antidote to Eurocentrism (overemphasis on European historical achievements). For West Asia and Africa were the cradles of the very earliest civilizations, and it is increasingly clear that the first European civilization, ancient Greece, owed a large debt to its non-European predecessors. Furthermore, great civilizations were emerging in the rain forests and highlands of Mesoamerica and on the Peruvian coast and the adjacent slopes of the Andes long before the heyday of the classical Greeks.

Mesopotamian Civilization

The fenlands are in bloom, the fields are green,
The uplands are drenched, the dykes are watered;
Ravine and slope carry down the mountain-torrents
That rush into the dykes, watering the fields.
The soil . . . becomes a plantation,
The grass grows in wood and in meadow,
The bountiful womb of the earth is opened,
Giving plenteous food for cattle and abundance for the homes of men.
An ox and a horse struck up a friendship.
The rich pasture had sated their bellies,
And glad of heart they lay resting.
The ox opened his mouth to speak, and said to the horse, glorious in battle:
"I seem to have been born under a lucky star:
From beginning to end of the year I find food;
I have fodder in abundance and spring water in profusion. . . .
Change thy way of life and come away with me!"
[Said the horse:] "Strong brass to cover my body
Have they put upon me, and I wear it as a garment.
Without me, the fiery steed,
Nor king nor prince nor lord nor noble fares upon his way . . . .
The horse is like a god, stately of step,
*Whilst thou and the calves wear the cap of servitude."**

*Sabatino Moscati, *The Face of the Ancient Orient* (Garden City, NY: Doubleday, 1962), pp. 85–86.

This Assyrian beast fable offers a parable of the contrasting aspects of civilized life. The ox praises the settled and orderly life of peace, an idyllic life in a land

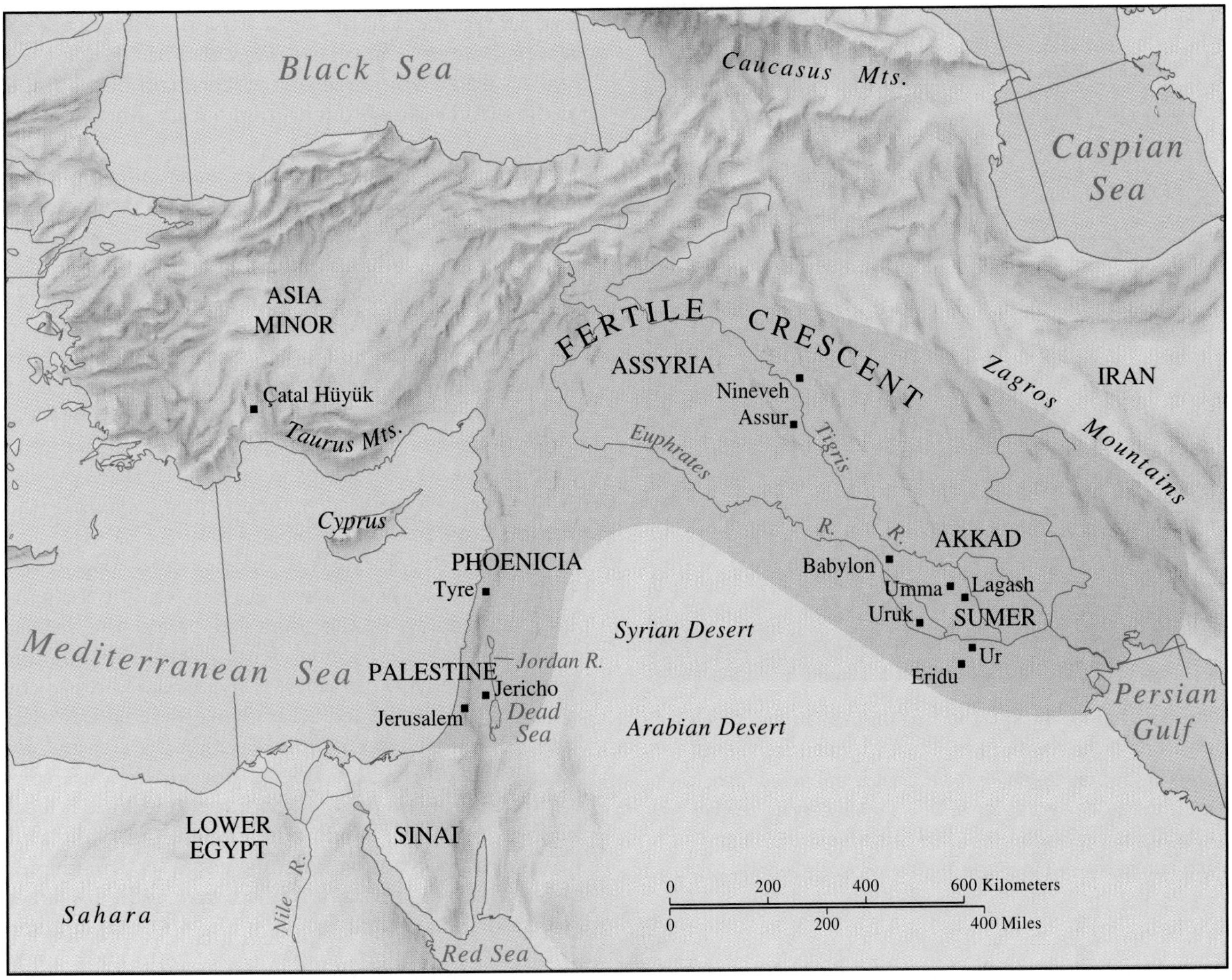

Map 1.1 Ancient Mesopotamia. The two great rivers of Mesopotamia flow out of Anatolia (present-day Turkey): in Mesopotamia the Euphrates runs some 800 miles and the Tigris about 440, from northwest to southeast, before they join as the present-day Shatt al-Arab, whose 100-mile course ends in the Persian Gulf.

made lush and fertile by the efforts of men and women who build dikes, divert water, sow seeds, reap the harvest, and raise the animals. The horse, by contrast, praises war, scorning the slavish life of its bovine friend and glorying in the armor and magnificence of the great warriors, lords, and kings who depend on it for success in battle. The following section examines both peace and war in several ancient Mesopotamian civilizations.

The Sumerian Exemplar of Civilized Life

The constituents of civilization appeared first in Mesopotamia (Greek for "the land between the rivers"), in the Tigris and Euphrates river valleys of West Asia. Climatically, Mesopotamia, a region larger than Texas, was sometimes a hot, arid dust bowl, but at other times suffered from unpredictable floods and unhealthful swamps. To surmount these problems, a succession of peoples over the centuries—Sumerians, Babylonians, Assyrians, and Chaldeans—mobilized large, well-organized labor forces that gained control over the water supply by constructing and maintaining a system of canals, dikes, drainage ditches, and reservoirs. Properly irrigated and cultivated, Mesopotamian crops yielded as much as a hundredfold return on seed planted and thus supported a much larger population than regions outside Mesopotamia still practicing Neolithic agriculture.

Soon after 3500 B.C.E. the Sumerians began to exploit the potential of the lower Tigris-Euphrates Valley. They built several city-states of ten to fifty thousand inhabitants, notably Ur, Uruk, and Lagash, and sustained themselves both by the agricultural produce of the land they controlled and by trade, which provided various imported goods and materials in exchange for surplus crops

University of Pennsylvania, Museum of Archaeology and Anthropology (U. 12357)

Ram Caught in a Thicket. This mid-third-millennium sculpture is one of the most beautiful objects found in the royal tombs at the Sumerian city of Ur. Standing seventeen inches high and made of gold, silver, lapis lazuli, copper, and other materials, it foreshadows the ram caught in a thicket that Abraham sacrificed in place of his son Isaac (Genesis 22:13).

of cereals and vegetables. On this agricultural base the Sumerians erected in the next 1,500 years a civilization of great sophistication and durability essentially based on a cluster of independent city-states that occasionally made war on each other. Because the Sumerians established enduring patterns for Mesopotamian civilization, they receive the greatest attention here.

The Sumerian city-states showed a striking advance in agriculture, architecture, engineering, and technology over the farming villages of the Neolithic era. The Sumerians parceled out the land in tracts of almost geometrical regularity, and efficiently watered them through an elaborate irrigation system of dams and canals, with smaller channels supplying individual plots. They built a network of roads and waterways and used pack asses, wagons, boats, and barges to carry goods to the urban center.

Sumerian social, economic, and political life was as elaborately organized and controlled as were its natural surroundings. Around 85 percent of the inhabitants of a city were little more than human farm machines. Most were slaves or tenant farmers who went out from the city to their plots or to the water control works and, by ceaseless toil, produced the abundant crops that sustained their society. They exchanged part of their produce for the wares of the city's artisans—metal workers, weavers, potters, and others. They also bartered for the foods available from fisherfolk, bakers, and brewers and for the merchandise brought from outside Mesopotamia by a host of traders.

This intense economic activity made Sumerian cities very impressive indeed. Fortifications were common. The city wall at Uruk, for example, nearly six miles in circuit, enclosed about 1,000 acres and contained some 900 defense towers. Within the walls were thousands of humble farmers' hovels and the more elaborate homes of civic and priestly officials and other members of the upper class. Though one could find some broad and straight avenues, the city as a whole gave the impression of a densely packed hive. Most conspicuous were the temples, set apart in walled-off enclosures and often raised on distinctive, stepped artificial mounds called *ziggurats* (the probable inspiration of the biblical tower of Babel).

Much of the peasants' produce went to support the many religious and civic activities controlled by the temples. Increasingly, in the Sumerian period the secular leaders of the state became identical with the religious hierarchy. The *ensi* (city ruler) was considered the agent of the city god and acted on his behalf. He coordinated the various temple communities within the city and assigned work on public buildings and on the water-control installations. He imposed taxes and made legal decisions of various kinds. The city ruler also dictated the foreign policy of the state, including its defense policy and trade relations. The soldiers were under his direct command. Recognized by his subjects as the supreme earthly authority, the *ensi* was given gifts and shown other signs of deference.

Writing is one of the most notable achievements of the Sumerians. Archaeologists have found thousands of clay tablets inscribed in cuneiform ("wedge-shaped"; see the illustration) dating from nearly all periods of Mesopotamian civilization. These tablets mainly record business transactions, inventories of supplies, production and taxation figures, and wage payments. They show, too, that the Mesopotamians employed such mathematical functions as multiplication and division and had devised both a base 12 system of numerical computation and a calendar correlated to the phases of the moon.

Cuneiform records give invaluable insights into the Sumerians' view of the world. Anthropomorphic (having human forms and/or personalities) deities, all-powerful and often fickle, populated their religion. The gods were chiefly personifications of natural forces: Inanna, goddess of fertility; Enlil, storm god of earth, wind, and air; Ereshkigal, queen of the underworld; Dumuzi, cyclically dying god of vegetation. Humans were subject to these and a whole host of lesser but still awe-inspiring divine forces.

Sumerian religion offered no comforting theology of love and salvation and no clearly defined ethical code by which men and women might order their individual lives.

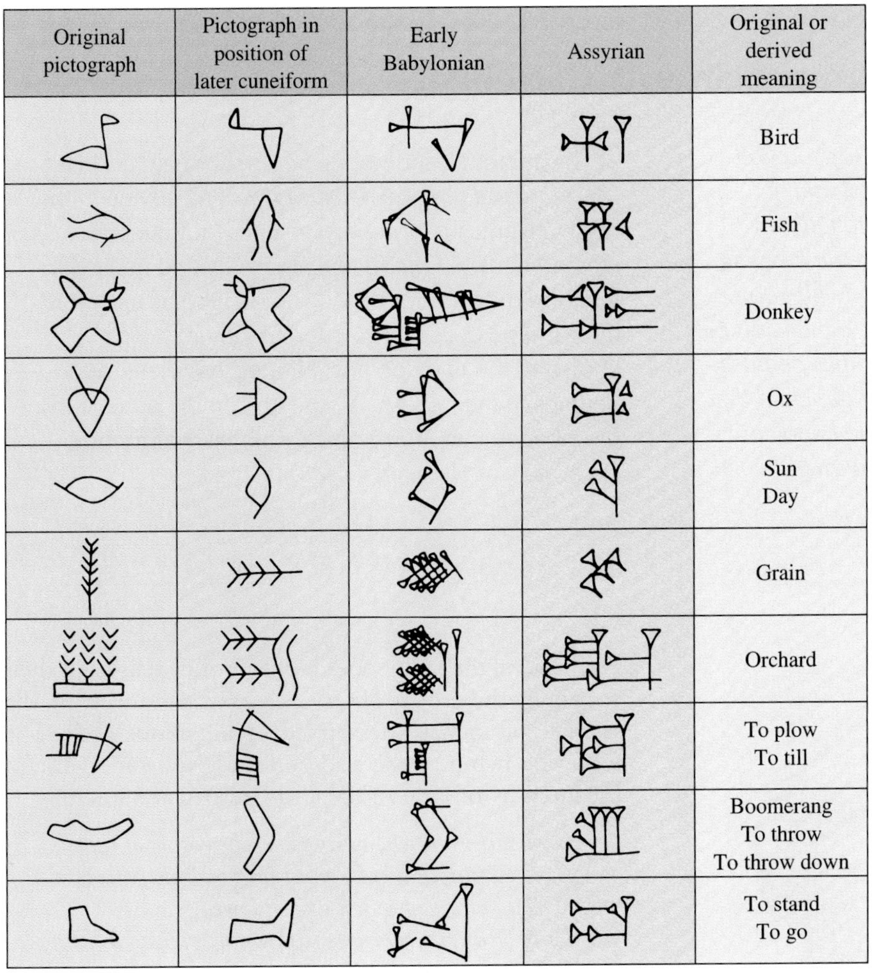
Original pictograph
Pictograph in position of later cuneiform
Early Babylonian
Assyrian
Original or derived meaning
Bird
Fish
Donkey
Ox
Sun
Day
Grain
Orchard
To plow
To till
Boomerang
To throw
To throw down
To stand
To go

Evolution of Sumerian Writing. After earlier experimentation with pictographic writing, the Sumerians devised a script called cuneiform (wedge-shaped). Since this system of signs transcribed sounds rather than pictures or ideas, it was adaptable to other languages as well; thus cuneiform writing was used by the Babylonians and Assyrians.

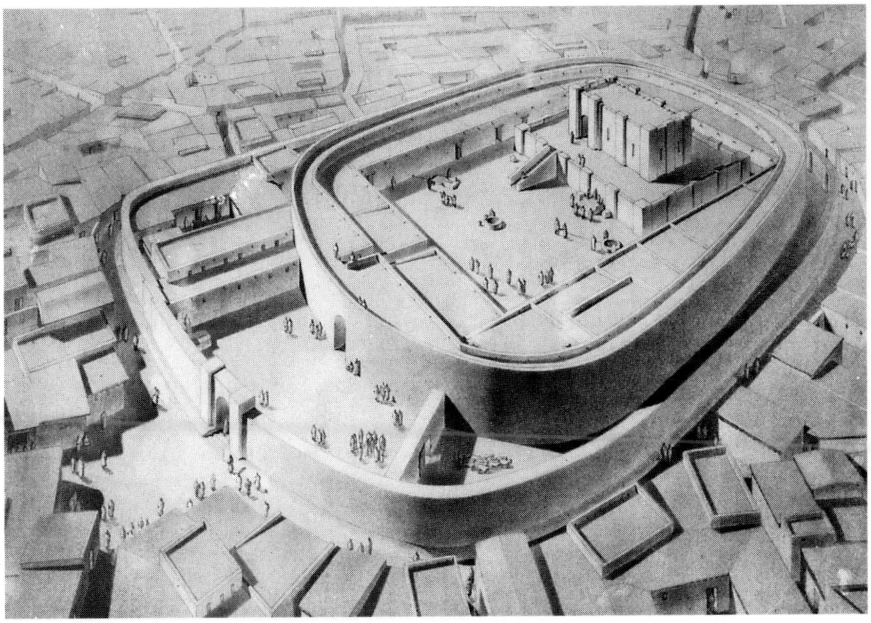

Courtesy of the Oriental Institute/University of Chicago

Sumerian Temple. A reconstruction of an early temple at Khafajah in present-day Iraq. Such elevated buildings dominated the vista of the city as the gods dominated the Sumerian worldview. Because the Sumerians worked chiefly with mudbricks, the resulting architecture was and is less impressive than that of the Egyptians and Greeks, who used limestone, granite, and marble in more elaborate and durable structures.

"Fill Your Belly with Good Things"

*Gilgamesh, where are you hurrying to? You will never find that life for which you are looking. When the gods created man they allotted him death, but life they retained in their own keeping. As for you, Gilgamesh, fill your belly with good things; day and night, night and day, dance and be merry, feast and rejoice. Let your clothes be fresh, bathe yourself in water, cherish the little child that holds your hand, and make your wife happy in your embrace; for this too is the lot of man.**

The attractive and nubile Siduri, barmaid and vintner to the gods, gives this consoling advice to the hero Gilgamesh during his unsuccessful quest for eternal life. The *Epic of Gilgamesh* was composed in the third millennium B.C.E., some 1,500 years before the earliest European literature (Homer). It was known to the Babylonians, Hittites, Assyrians, and perhaps to the Greeks. A seventh-century B.C.E. copy inscribed in cuneiform on clay tablets was found by excavators at Nineveh in 1853.

**N. K. Sandars, trans.,* The Epic of Gilgamesh, *rev. ed. (Baltimore: Penguin, 1972), p. 102.*

Iraq Museum, Baghdad. Photograph: AKG London

King Sargon I. Sargon I, ruler of Akkad, founded a dynasty that dominated the cities of Sumer for two centuries. This imposing sculptural head was found at Nineveh and dates to around 2350 B.C.E.

Humans might only hope to ensure the security of their society by the proper observance of rituals, involving the sacrifice of animals, demanded by imperious gods. The following hymn to the god Ninurta gives some sense of the intensity of "fear of the lord" in ancient Sumer:

> *Lord Ninurta who vanquishes the houses of the*
> *rebellious lands, great lord of Enlil,*
> *You, with power you are endowed. . . .*
> *Lord Ninurta, when your heart was seized by anger,*
> *You spat venom like a snake. . . .*
> *Lord Ninurta, of the house of the contentious and*
> *disobedient, you are its adversary,*
> *Of their city, you are its enemy.* (Trans. S. N. Kramer)

Further, after death one could expect to experience only a shadowy, limbolike existence in the underworld. The outlook here is in striking contrast to the more optimistic expectations of Egyptian religion. Still, there was a time for laughter and dancing as well as for weeping and mourning, as may be seen in such literary remains as the great *Epic of Gilgamesh*.

Political and Cultural Developments of the Babylonians, Assyrians, and Chaldeans

After 2400 B.C.E. the land of Mesopotamia witnessed political upheavals and shifts in centers of power. New peoples rose to prominence by gradual infiltration or by conquest. The rulers of Akkad (2350–2150), known as Sargonids after King Sargon I, subjugated the city-states of Sumer and forced them into a federation under Akkadian direction. However, this early instance of empire building was terminated by the violent incursion of outside groups. A later reassertion of Sumerian control (2150–1950) was cut short by an invasion of the Amor-

"I Cut Their Throats Like Lambs"—Memoirs of an Assyrian Warrior-King

*With the weapons of [the god] Assur, my lord, and the terrible onset of my attack, I stopped their advance, I succeeded in surrounding them [or turning them back], I decimated the enemy host with arrow and spear. All of their bodies I bored through like a sieve. . . . Speedily I cut them down and established their defeat. I cut their throats like lambs. I cut off their precious lives [as one cuts] a string. Like the many waters of a storm, I made [the contents of] their gullets and entrails run down upon the wide earth. My prancing steeds, harnessed for my riding, plunged into the streams of their blood as [into] a river. The wheels of my war chariot, which brings low the wicked and the evil, were bespattered with blood and filth. With the bodies of their warriors I filled the plain, like grass. [Their] testicles I cut off, and tore out their privates like the seeds of cucumbers. . . . Their hands I cut off. The heavy rings of brightest gold [and] silver which [they had] on their wrists I took away. With sharp swords I pierced their belts and seized the girdle daggers of gold and silver which [they carried] on their persons. . . . The chariots and their horses, whose riders had been slain at the beginning of the terrible onslaught, and who had been left to themselves, kept running back and forth. . . . I put an end to their [the riders'] fighting. [The enemy] abandoned their tents and to save their lives they trampled the bodies of their [fallen] soldiers, they fled like young pigeons that are pursued. They were beside themselves . . . they held back their urine, but let their dung go in their chariots. In pursuit of them I dispatched my chariots and horses after them. Those among them who had escaped, who had fled for their lives, wherever they [my charioteers] met them, they cut them down with the sword.**

The ruler who records one of his military successes with such relish in the inscription quoted above was Sennacherib (704–681 B.C.E.). This typically brutal Assyrian warrior-king established an imperial capital at Nineveh on the Tigris River, using thousands of slave laborers to construct the royal palaces and monuments of the new city.

**Daniel D. Luckenbill,* Ancient Records of Assyria and Babylonia, *vol. 2 (Chicago: University of Chicago Press, 1927), pp. 126–128.*

ites, who organized the city-states of Sumer and Akkad into an empire centered at Babylon.

This Old Babylonian Empire lasted four centuries. The Babylonians assimilated and refined many of the elements of Sumerian civilization, just as Rome later built on Greek cultural foundations. To cite one example, the law code of Hammurabi (1792–1750 B.C.E.), Babylon's most famous dynast, set out in an orderly way, in some 280 articles, the body of law as it had evolved over 1,500 years of Mesopotamian history. Designed to replace capricious blood feuds as the basis for justice, Hammurabi's laws dealt in a ponderous, rational manner with a wide variety of actionable offenses. Most of the code was primarily concerned with indebtedness and breach of business contracts (reflecting a commercial orientation among the Mesopotamians), but it also applied to marriage, adultery, and divorce, legitimacy and inheritance, incest, treatment of slaves, personal injury and property damage, and even medical malpractice. Clearly evident in the code is a stratification of society into upper, lower, and slave classes. The penal aspects are dominated by the law of retaliation, "an eye for an eye." As with many early codifications of law, Hammurabi's code imposed harsh penalties—including capital punishment for many crimes—usually according to the status of the aggrieved party. For example, it stipulated, "If a physician performed a major operation on a free man with a bronze lancet and has caused the free man's death, or he opened up the eye-socket of a free man and has destroyed his eye, they shall cut off his hand" (trans. Theophile J. Meek), while the same offense against a slave entailed only replacement of the damaged "property." The general severity of the law code was necessitated in part by the absence of a highly developed ethical doctrine in Mesopotamian religion.

The Babylonians also improved on Sumerian innovations in mathematics and science, especially astronomy. In religion, their deity Marduk presided over a pantheon of Sumerian gods with Babylonian names: for example, Babylonian Ishtar was equivalent to Sumerian Inanna. These deities would survive in various guises down through the periods of Assyrian and Chaldean predominance.

The sudden arrival around 1550 B.C.E. of the Kassites from the neighboring Iranian highlands to the east brought another transition in the sequence of Mesopotamian civilizations. The Kassites in their turn melded

Assyrian Relief Sculpture. This sculpture, done in low relief, shows the Assyrian king Assurbanipal (reigned 668–630 B.C.E.) participating in a hunt. The elaborate dress of both rider and horse signifies the high status of the king.

with existing Babylonian civilization and remained dominant in Sumer and Akkad for some 400 years.

During the Kassite period, the focus of Mesopotamian development shifted northward. Between about 1300 and 900 B.C.E. the Assyrians rose to prominence in northern Mesopotamia. Although the Kassites for a time prevented consolidation of the entire Tigris-Euphrates Valley, ruthless Assyrian militarism won out after 900 and reached its peak in the careers of a succession of victorious warrior-kings. By the seventh century nearly all of Asia Minor (present-day Turkey), Mesopotamia, Syria, Palestine, and Egypt were at one time or another under Assyrian domination

In 612, however, another Iranian people, the Medes, allied with resurgent Babylon, succeeded in destroying Assyrian power at its center, the capital of Nineveh. The Neo-Babylonian or Chaldean era that followed was a time of conquests of foreign lands, though not on the Assyrian scale. The most famous Neo-Babylonian king, Nebuchadnezzar (reigned 605–562), beautified Babylon with such adornments as the Hanging Gardens (an elaborate terraced garden area) and the magnificently decorated Ishtar Gate; he also sought to revive Babylonian religious devotion.

Religion in the Chaldean period of Mesopotamia was marked by equating the gods with planets: for example, Ishtar (later, Venus), Marduk (later, Jupiter), and so on. The Chaldeans were the best astronomers of the ancient world; they developed a detailed method of time reckoning, employing a seven-day week and a day of twelve 120-minute hours. Astronomy had also a religious or astrological function. Chaldeans believed that charting the positions and movements of the planets and the stars provided a key that would reveal the intentions of the gods, thus enabling mankind to foresee future events.

The long story of Mesopotamian civilization closed in 539 B.C.E., when the Persian ruler Cyrus conquered Babylon and incorporated Mesopotamia into his huge empire.

African Civilization

*One generation of men passes to another, and God, who knows characters, has hidden Himself,. . . so worship God upon his way. . . . The soul goes to the place it knows. . . . Beautify your mansion in the West, embellish your place in the necropolis with straightforwardness and just dealing; . . . more acceptable is the character of the straightforward man than the ox of the wrongdoer. Serve God, that He may do the like for you, with offerings for replenishing the altars and with carving; . . . God is aware of whoever serves Him. Provide for men, the cattle of God, for He made heaven and earth at their desire. He suppressed the greed of the waters, he gave the breath of life to their noses, for they are likenesses of Him which issued from His flesh. He shines in the sky for the benefit of their hearts; He has made herbs, cattle, and fish to nourish them. He has killed His enemies and destroyed His own children, because they had planned to make rebellion; He makes daylight for the benefit of their hearts, and He sails around in order to see them,. . . and when they weep, He hears.**

*Leonard H. Lesko, trans., "Egyptian Religion: An Overview," in *The Encyclopedia of Religion,* vol. 5, ed. M. Eliade (New York: Macmillan, 1987), p. 41.

The passage quoted above comes from an ancient Egyptian "coffin text" (so called because it was painted inside a coffin) of about 2040 B.C.E. It provides a concise summary of the theology and philosophy of the religion of Re, the sun god, whose cult was preeminent through most of Egyptian history. Re is a hidden, all-knowing, and just god. His gifts of life and of the good things of the world must be matched by humankind's worship of his godhead and fair treatment of fellow human beings. The pyramids of Giza are the most lasting testimony of the Egyptians' faithfulness to these central beliefs in the power and justice of their gods and of the kings thought to be descended from them. They also bespeak a thriving society of teeming thousands whose labor—skilled and unskilled—was mustered and directed by a highly sophisticated organization. Ancient Egyptian civilization, the earliest to develop on the continent of Africa, has fascinated later ages both because of its great antiquity and because of the marvelous works of art and architecture that have outlived it.

The Land of the Nile and the Emergence of Egyptian Civilization

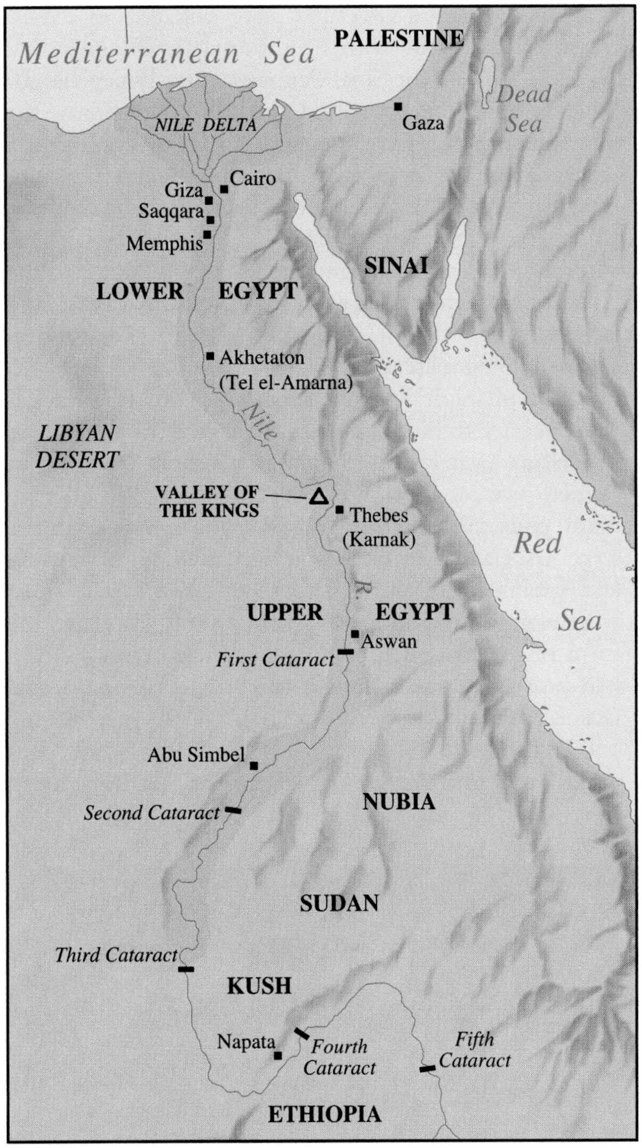

Map 1.2 Ancient Egypt. The Nile—the longest river in the world—literally defines the country of Egypt. Its sources are in the lakes of Ethiopia and Uganda, which give rise to the Blue and White Niles. These two join at Khartoum in Sudan. The river is about one-half mile wide, and its valley is about five miles wide down to a point just west of present-day Cairo, where the river divides to form the great Nile delta on the Mediterranean. Throughout Egyptian history, 95 percent of the population has lived in the Nile valley and delta.

Because of the topographical uniformity of its location, Egyptian civilization (see Map 1.2) was more homogeneous, both geographically and politically, than was the case in Mesopotamia, with its numerous, densely populated city-states. Compared with Mesopotamia, Egypt had few cities; administrative activity was highly centralized and concentrated in a few major capitals, such as Memphis and Thebes. The mass of people in Egypt lived in thousands of villages more or less evenly distributed in the twelve thousand square miles of arable land in the valley and delta of the mighty Nile, where the dependable pulse of the river's yearly cycle of flood and subsidence regulated Egyptian life. The arid land was fertile only where its waters reached or could be made to reach.

Besides bringing water during its annual flood stage, June to October, the Nile brought deposits of some 200 million tons of rich, fertile soil and minerals per year. The diversion of floodwaters and draining of swamplands in the Nile Valley made Egypt the most productive agricultural land of the ancient world. The reliable rhythm of the Nile also affected the people of Egypt in subtler ways: in particular, it fostered a more optimistic outlook on life, a confidence in the natural order of things that is not evident in, for example, Mesopotamia.

Menes, the first king of Egypt's First Dynasty (royal family line), is credited with unifying Upper and Lower Egypt around 3000 B.C.E. The next 2,000 years of Egyptian history are customarily divided into three periods of strong political unity, the Old, Middle, and New Kingdoms, separated by periods of weak central government, social unrest, and foreign invasions.

The preeminent central authority in the Old Kingdom was the pharaoh, a god-king, seen variously as the son or the manifestation of certain deities. He exercised his supreme will through a simple but rigid hierarchy ranging from royal agents and elite nobles to local officials who ruled some forty administrative districts. This political superstructure and the many building projects and other activities it supervised were supported by the tremendous agricultural surplus produced by the mass of peasants. The god-governed state engaged in exploration of and trade with neighboring lands, including Nubia, Ethiopia, the Sinai Peninsula, and Phoenicia. To build monuments or flood-control installations, the pharaohs dictated the enlistment and provisioning of a large, skilled labor force: masons and stonecutters, sculptors, carpenters, and painters, as well as construction managers, surveyors, draftsmen, scribes, and others. These worked chiefly during the inundation phase of the Nile's cycle, when transport by water was easiest and farm workers were free to quarry, haul, and position stone building materials.

The pharaoh wielded such extensive powers because service to him on any state project was a religious as well as a civic duty. Egyptian religion, like that of Sumer, was a thoroughgoing polytheism (belief in many gods), in which most major and minor divinities were associated with the agrarian rhythms of fertility and germination, death and regeneration. The gods were mainly anthropomorphic, but could also have the form of a beast, such as a beetle, bull, or snake, or a half-beast, such as a human torso with the head of a jackal, crocodile, or cow.

Perhaps the most universal Egyptian myths concerned the god Osiris, slain by the evil Set but reborn through the efforts of his sister/wife Isis. Osiris was the father of Horus, who, in most periods of Egyptian history, was embodied in the person of the king. After death, the pharaoh became one with Osiris, the king of the dead who influenced the life cycles governing the natural world. In a continuing cycle, the new pharaoh, his son, was the dutiful Horus, who led the state in the worship of his father Osiris. Thus the security not only of the state but also of the whole universe was directly linked to the well-being of the king, both during and after his life on earth. He had to be accorded all due honors and signs of deference in this life as well as in the next. This accounts for the practice of mummification, which was an attempt to ensure the continued comfort and goodwill of the deceased king in the afterworld. Hence, too, the fantastic expenditure of time and resources on funeral monuments, temples, and tombs, of which the pyramids are the most notable.

Early in their history, the ancient Egyptians evolved and perfected the pyramid, the architectural form that has ever after been the distinguishing mark of their civilization. Of the Great Pyramids built at Giza, the largest is that of Khufu (or Cheops), which dates from about 2600 B.C.E. It was 460 feet high and 755 feet on each side, and was made from some 2.3 million stone blocks

LIVES AND TIMES ACROSS CULTURES

Diverse Burial Customs

Death, birth, and marriage are the cardinal events in all societies throughout history. Humans have evolved a wide range of rituals of celebration and mourning. Burial practices vary depending on the climate and topography in which various societies have emerged. In tropical, hot regions where bodies decompose quickly, or in densely populated areas like India, corpses are often cremated and the ashes returned to the land, air, or sea. In hot desert regions like the Middle East, simple burials are held usually within twenty-four hours of death.

As civilizations became more complex, so too did burial practices. Powerful and wealthy rulers and elites were often buried in huge, ornate tombs and adorned with costly jewels and clothing. In Han China, rulers were buried with full regalia and replicas of their armies, horses, and trappings of power. Similarly, in the Western Hemisphere, Chaco and Aztec warriors were buried with their armor, gold jewelry, and armaments.

The burial customs of the ancient Egyptians were among the most complex in human history. The pyramids in Giza and tombs in the Valleys of the Kings and Queens are 3,000-year-old monuments to the Egyptian preoccupation with death and the afterlife. The burial chamber of the pharaoh Tutankhamon, uncovered by Howard Carter in 1922, contained a veritable treasure trove of artifacts. Upon seeing the chamber for the first time, Carter exclaimed that he saw "wonderful things, strange animals, statues and gold, everywhere the glint of gold." One elaborately painted chest took Carter three weeks to unpack. The items found in "King Tut's" tomb—including gold jewelry, alabaster vases, and a jewel-inlaid, golden funerary mask—amaze and delight even present-day viewers.

Career Counseling in Ancient Egypt

The washerman's day is going up, going down. All his limbs are weak, [from] whitening his neighbor's clothes every day, from washing linen.

The maker of pots is smeared with soil, like one whose relations have died. His hands, his feet are all full of clay; he is like one who lives in the bog.

The cobbler mingles with vats. His odor is penetrating. His hands are red with madder [dye], like one who is smeared with blood. He looks behind him for the kite, like one whose flesh is exposed.

The watchman prepares garlands and polishes vase-stands. He spends a night of toil just as one on whom the sun shines.

The merchants travel downstream and upstream. They are as busy as can be, carrying goods from one town to another. . . . But the tax collectors carry off the gold, that most precious of metals.

The ships' crews from every house [of commerce], they receive their loads. They depart from Egypt for Syria, and each man's god is with him. [But] not one of them says: "We shall see Egypt again!"

The carpenter who is in the shipyard carries the timber and stacks it. If he gives today the output of yesterday, woe to his limbs! The shipwright stands behind him to tell him evil things. . . .

*The scribe, he alone, records the output of all of them. Take note of it!. . . Set your sight on being a scribe. . . . You will not be like a hired ox.**

The preceding passage is from an ancient Egyptian document (the *Papyrus Lansing* in the British Museum) dating to about 1150 B.C.E. It is part of a letter of advice written to a young man about to decide on a profession. The document provides some interesting reflections on the conditions of work in a variety of jobs.

**Miriam Lichtheim, comp.* Ancient Egyptian Literature: A Book of Readings, *vol. 2,* The New Kingdom *(Berkeley: University of California Press, 1976), pp. 168–173.*

averaging 2.5 tons each. The whole was sheathed with limestone casing blocks (stripped in later centuries to supply building stone for new cities like Cairo) that gave the pyramid the appearance of one massive unit. The complex at Giza—the three Great Pyramids and the famous Sphinx—was only one of many Old Kingdom burial places in the region of Memphis; some eighty tombs are marked by pyramids.

The Pyramids at Giza are among the best examples of Egyptian architecture, not only in scale but also in the precision of their construction. This is particularly remarkable considering the lack of sophisticated hoisting equipment. It is likely that earthen ramps were used to haul the stones up and into position. Moreover, the tombs and temples, here and elsewhere in Egypt, were adorned with magnificent sculptures (full-figure and relief), paintings, and hieroglyphic inscriptions. The last were perhaps inspired by a knowledge of cuneiform, but they differ from that script by combining pictographs with syllable signs and letter signs. Thus the Egyptians did not develop true alphabetic writing.

Although the pyramids were the eternal homes of royalty, the possibility of life after death was open to others besides the pharaoh, as the evidence of nobles' tombs indicates. Moreover, Egyptian religion had a slight ethical emphasis, a concern for justice that we do not see in Mesopotamia. The gods ruled a cosmos based on the Egyptian notion of moral right. The pharaoh was expected to treat his subjects equitably, and those subjects were required to be fair in their dealings with one another. Those with the means to do so were to assist the less well off, such as widows and orphans.

Discontinuities and the Rise and Decline of an Imperial Culture

Just as Sumerian archetypes gave an enduring pattern to Mesopotamian civilization, the Old Kingdom originated many aspects of the political, religious, and artistic worldview of the Egyptians. In Mesopotamia, change often came as a result of intrusions from the Iranian uplands to the east and north or from Arabia to the west and south. Egypt, by contrast, was better protected from invasion by vast tracts of uninhabitable desert wasteland. Internal social and political upheavals, however, occasionally led to weakness and disunity.

During the first intermediate period (2150–2050 B.C.E.), the central administration was replaced by a fragmented system of hereditary local leadership. The

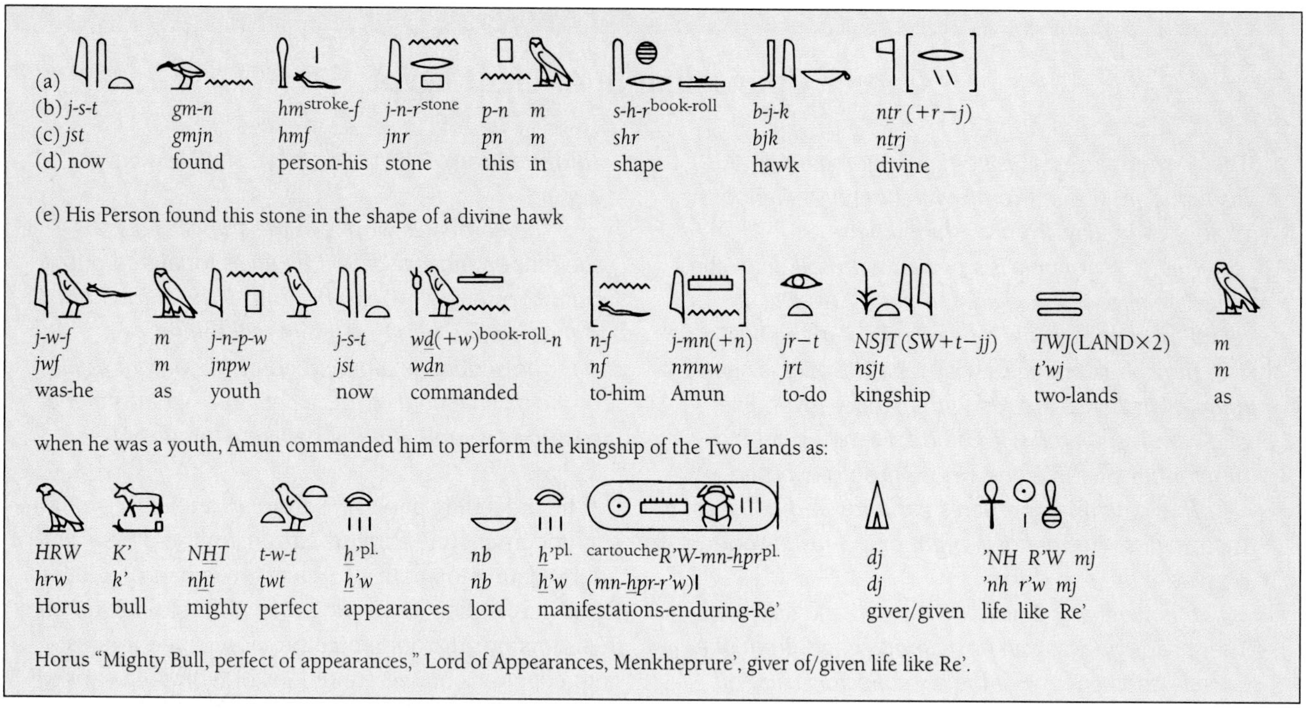
(a)
(b) j-s-t gm-n hmstroke-f j-n-rstone p-n m s-h-rbook-roll b-j-k ntr (+r−j)
(c) jst gmjn hmf jnr pn m shr bjk ntrj
(d) now found person-his stone this in shape hawk divine
(e) His Person found this stone in the shape of a divine hawk
j-w-f m j-n-p-w j-s-t wd(+w)book-roll-n n-f j-mn(+n) jr−t NSJT(SW+t−jj) TWJ(LAND×2) m
jwf m jnpw jst wdn nf nmnw jrt nsjt t'wj m
was-he as youth now commanded to-him Amun to-do kingship two-lands as
when he was a youth, Amun commanded him to perform the kingship of the Two Lands as:
HRW K' NHT t-w-t h'pl. nb h'pl. cartoucheR'W-mn-hprpl. dj 'NH R'W mj
hrw k' nht twt h'w nb h'w (mn-hpr-r'w)I dj 'nh r'w mj
Horus bull mighty perfect appearances lord manifestations-enduring-Re' giver/given life like Re'
Horus "Mighty Bull, perfect of appearances," Lord of Appearances, Menkheprure', giver of/given life like Re'.

Egyptian hieroglyphic writing. This example of Egyptian hieroglyphic writing is from a temple of Thutmose IV (reigned 1406–1398 B.C.E.). Line (a) shows original hieroglyphics, (b) and (c) show two kinds of transcription, (d) gives a word-by-word translation, and (e) gives a smooth English version. Hieroglyphic writing passed out of use around 400 C.E. It remained undeciphered until the discovery of the Rosetta stone (now in the British Museum) by the French during their occupation of Egypt in 1799. The stone bears an inscription from the reign of Ptolemy V (196 B.C.E.) in three versions: hieroglyphic Egyptian, demotic Egyptian, and Greek. Using this as a key, the French scholar Jean François Champollion was able to decipher hieroglyphic writing in 1822.

succeeding Middle Kingdom (2050–1750) had its capital at Thebes, some 400 miles up the Nile from Memphis; Upper and Lower Egypt were reunited. About 1750, however, either a succession of weak kings or stiffer competition from local nobility with royal aspirations apparently once again eroded central authority. Vulnerable because of its domestic disarray, Egypt suffered the "Great Humiliation," a successful invasion, probably from Palestine, by a people whom the Egyptians called the Hyksos. Unlike the Amorites or the Kassites, who were ultimately absorbed by the civilizations they attacked in Mesopotamia, the Hyksos remained an alien force. They maintained themselves in lower Egypt by superior military ability and technology: the horse-drawn chariot and improved weapons. After about 200 years they were ejected by Theban rulers, who were in turn followed by the ambitious and imperialistic kings of the New Kingdom era.

The Egyptian Empire, as the New Kingdom (1550–1150 B.C.E.) is sometimes labeled, restored much of the prestige lost during the Hyksos occupation. Egyptian control again reached across the Sinai into Palestine and Syria and to the Euphrates. At home, foreign conquest meant peace and prosperity; tribute and valuable materials poured into Egypt. Strong trade contacts were developed, for example, with the land of "Punt," in the region of modern Somalia, and with Arabia; these contacts brought incense, ivory, myrrh, and slaves to Egypt in exchange for jewelry, weapons, and tools. The pride taken in these achievements can be seen in the art and architecture sponsored by the conquering pharaohs of the New Kingdom, who launched massive building programs to honor the gods and to publicize and magnify their own accomplishments. The colossal temple complex of Amon at Karnak near Thebes is an especially noteworthy example, as are the huge, lavishly furnished temples and tombs built in the Valley of the Kings across the Nile from Thebes and at Abu Simbel above Aswan. The tomb of an unimportant king, Tutankhamon (reigned 1352–1344), which escaped grave robbers, gives us a tantalizing glimpse of the wealth of these kings and nobles of imperial Egypt. The discovery of the tomb of Tutankhamon (or "King Tut") by the British archaeologist Howard Carter in 1922 caused a worldwide sensation and a frenzy of interest in ancient Egypt, seen in new styles of architecture and interior decoration, as well

VCG/FPG

G. Clyde/FPG

Temple at Abu Simbel. Pictured is the façade of the great temple at Abu Simbel with its colossal figures of Ramses II (reigned 1290–1224 B.C.E.), more than sixty feet in height. At a cost of $40 million, a UNESCO team of German, Italian, French, and Swedish engineers dismantled and moved the temple to higher ground to prevent its submersion by the rising waters of Lake Nasser after the completion of the Aswan High Dam; the move took four years (1964–1968).

as in such popular entertainments as the horror film *The Mummy*. As Carter himself said in recalling the discovery:

> A feeling of intrusion had descended heavily upon us with the opening of the doors, heightened, probably, by the almost painful impressiveness of a linen pall, decorated with golden rosettes, which dropped above the inner shrine. We felt that we were in the presence of the dead King and must do him reverence, and in imagination could see the doors of the successive shrines open one after the other till the innermost disclosed the King himself.

Amenhotep IV (reigned 1369–1353 B.C.E.), unlike most of the militaristic pharaohs who preceded him, was most notable for his innovations in religion. A rebel in his attitudes toward art and theology, he recognized as gods only himself and the solar disk, Aton. He changed his name to Akhenaton ("it pleases Aton") and founded a new capital called Akhetaton ("place of the Glory of Aton") at present-day Tel el-Amarna (see Map 1.2). Compared with the polytheism prevalent in the ancient world, his religion closely approached monotheism. Akhenaton and his queen, Nefertiti, are familiar from artistic depictions. The pharaoh's reform efforts, however, were short-lived. His successor, Tutankhamon, reinstated the previous polytheism with Amon as chief deity, pleasing the numerous priests who derived wealth and prestige at the restored capital of Thebes and elsewhere. Indeed, the ever-rising power of the various priesthoods, which Akhenaton had tried to curb, was a principal symptom of yet another decline of the central authority.

Egypt after 1100 B.C.E. was only intermittently a unified state. Despite sporadic reassertions of independence, Egypt proper never regained the political autonomy and confident imperialism of its glorious past. Ancient Egyptian history became an adjunct of Kushitic, Assyrian, Persian, Macedonian, and Roman history.

The Kushite Kingdom in Upper Egypt and the Sudan

Once an extension of the ancient Egyptian empire, the Kushite kingdom emerged as an independent power by 700 B.C.E. Located around the border of present-day

© Bolton Picture Library

Coffin Mask of Tutankhamon. This impressive mask, which adorned the coffin of King Tutankhamon, is made of gold and lapis lazuli. It depicts the deceased king as the sun god Aton, thus assuring him, by the magical law of similarity, an eternal existence in his afterlife.

Egypt and Sudan, with their capital at Napata, the Kushites had long served as intermediaries for the transport of goods traded between the Egyptian kingdom and eastern Africa. In the course of their contacts with, and eventual subjugation by, Egypt, the Kushites assimilated many of the cultural, religious, and social values of ancient Egypt.

As Egypt declined in military strength and cultural dynamism, the Kushite kingdom evolved into a distinctive Sudanic empire. By 750 B.C.E., Kushite kings began attacking the weakened Egyptian forces and, under King Shabako (reigned 707–696 B.C.E.), conquered Egypt. After almost 100 years of rule over Egypt, the Kushite empire was attacked by the stronger military might of the Assyrians. Following the Assyrian conquest of Egypt, the Kushites hastily withdrew to the Sudan. By 591 the Egyptians renewed their attacks on the Kushites, who then moved their capital further south to Meroë. Meroë, approximately 100 miles north of contemporary Khartoum, had substantial deposits of iron ore and wood, good grazing land for cattle, and a navigable harbor; it also had control of the rich gold mines in the Sudan (known in Rome as Nubia).

In Meroë, the Kushites prospered from trade with Egypt and East Africa. Documents and relics indicate that the Kushites also had indirect contacts with China, India, and Arabia. Following the Macedonian conquest of Egypt in 332 B.C.E., they also established close relations with the Greeks. Much of Meroë's prosperity was based on the production of high-grade iron used to manufacture weapons. Meroë was known throughout the Hellenistic world as an iron-producing center, and remnants of slag heaps from smelting factories are still visible around the ancient monuments of the city. As Meroë declined in wealth and power, some Kushites may have migrated to West Africa, where they transmitted their skills in iron production and knowledge of the lost-wax process for bronze casting. At present it is not known whether these skills were transmitted from East Africa or whether West African societies developed the techniques independently.

Once literate in the Egyptian language, the Kushites gradually developed a written language of their own; based on hieroglyphics, the signs have yet to be interpreted. As a result, much of what is known about

Tomb of an Egyptian Queen. Shown here is a painting of Nefertari, the favorite wife of Ramses II. This scene from the Queen's tomb, which is among the most beautifully decorated Egyptian tombs, shows Nefertari accompanied by the goddess Isis.

Giraudon/Art Resource

Kushite society has been transmitted in accounts by foreign travelers, traders, or historians who had contact with the Kushite Empire.

It is known that the Kushites were literate and had an extremely hierarchical society similar to that of ancient Egypt. The ruling families lived lavishly, owned slaves, and were probably revered as divine. Most Kushites earned their livelihoods from herds of cattle, sheep, and goats. The many depictions of royal women in sculptures and reliefs on temples may indicate that the society was matrilineal. Documentary evidence shows that the Kushite kingdom was ruled by a queen in 45 B.C.E. The extensive ruins of temples, palaces, and pyramids around Meroë attest to the wealth, building skills, and complexity of the society. Pottery, sculpture, and other objects show influences of pharaonic, Hellenistic, and sub-Saharan African societies. As in Egypt, Kushite royalty and nobility, along with their personal possessions, were buried in lavish tombs. Some of these tombs have provided archaeologists with a rich source of information about the Kushites; however, many of these tombs and other Kushite monuments have not yet been excavated, and much remains to be learned.

Early Aegean Civilization

At a depth of twenty-five feet from the surface of the [Mycenaean] Acropolis, [Heinrich] Schliemann cried out, "Sophia! Sophia!"

When she joined him . . . she exclaimed, "My God!"

He had found three bodies "smothered"—Schliemann's word—in gold. Each body was draped with five gold diadems; two of the bodies were each adorned with gold laurel leaves. The sepulcher, cut out of rock, also contained "many curious objects," including cow-shaped idols, fragments of colored glass, small knives of obsidian, the fragments of a gold-plated silver vase, a

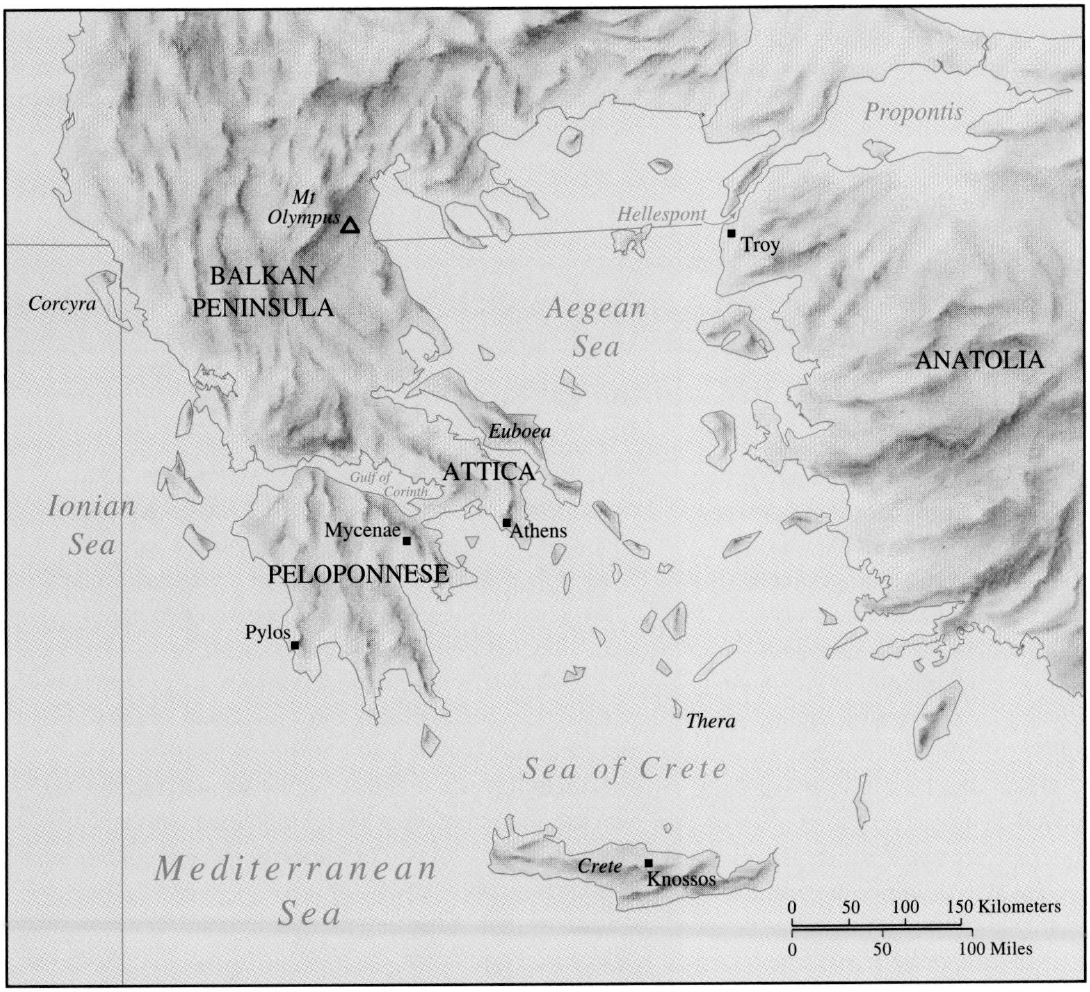

Map 1.3 Greece and the Aegean Basin. Shown in this map are the mainland regions and islands that were the home of Aegean civilization. Some of the more important Bronze Age sites are indicated.

bronze knife. The bones and skulls had been preserved but they had suffered so much from moisture that when he reached out and touched them, they dissolved as if in a dream. . . .

*Returning to the surface in a frenzy, he ordered the work gangs to dig up the whole area beneath the other grave markers. Schliemann behaved like a man possessed.**

*Arnold C. Brackman, *The Dream of Troy* (New York: Mason & Lipscomb, 1974), pp. 180–81.

This passage captures the thrill of discovery that makes archaeology so appealing. Of course, when Schliemann was excavating at Mycenae in 1876, the science was in its infancy and many mistakes were made; as one scholar put it, Schliemann excavated as if he were digging for potatoes, and the atmosphere was more that of a treasure hunt than of a scientific investigation. Schliemann has even been accused of "salting" his dig sites with modern forgeries. Today, as a mature field of study, archaeology involves careful examination of sites and painstaking methods of handling, labeling, and recording materials brought to light. There still remains, however, the romantic allure of revealing the lives of men and women who lived thousands of years ago. This was particularly the case for Schliemann, who later claimed to be seeking to verify the Homeric poems, with their glorious and bloodthirsty kings and warriors, magnificent palaces, and heroic quests and warfare. However rudimentary his efforts at Troy and "golden Mycenae," he proved that Homer's world of heroes was not merely a figment of poetic imagination. This section focuses on the earliest civilizations of the Aegean region.

The Flowering of Minoan Civilization

The Aegean world encompassed the southern end of the Balkan Peninsula (see Map 1.3), the west coast of Asia Minor, the islands that dot the Aegean and Ionian Seas, and the large islands of Crete and Cyprus. This region (in land area about the size of Alabama) was not so blessed as Mesopotamia or Egypt with fertile soil or other natural resources. Its physical geography consisted of many mountains, small and scattered coastal plains and river valleys, and the ever-present sea.

Such topographical features contributed to the political fragmentation of the Aegean world and the scarcity of arable land; less than 20 percent of the land was fit for cultivation, and even in antiquity the land suffered from deforestation and generally poor soil management. The area was hot and arid in summer, in winter cool and moderately watered by rainfall. The grapevine

LIVES AND TIMES ACROSS CULTURES

Risking Death to Gain the Favor of the Gods

Many early cultures around the world have sought to pay homage to supernatural powers by means of perilous athletic contests. Among the Olmec, for example, such competitions centered on ball games in which the losing participants often lost their lives. Spectators at these events no doubt also felt the presence of supernatural forces. The general intent was probably to placate the gods and to ensure their good will toward the community.

Similarly, the Minoan people of Bronze Age Crete appear to have enjoyed life-threatening feats of acrobatic skill. A number of famous wall-paintings and sculptures depict young athletes performing death-defying vaults over charging bulls. Since archaeological evidence from Crete features bulls in contexts of religious sacrifice, it seems likely that the bull-jumping events were designed, like the Mesoamerican athletic competitions, to honor or influence the gods. So, too, in classical Greece and Rome, the athletic games at Olympia, Delphi, and hundreds of other sites, while not generally life-endangering, were held to honor gods such as Zeus and Apollo.

The Roman gladiatorial contests are perhaps the best-known examples of the association of physical competition with the awe-inspiring force of death. Though they became thoroughly secularized, the bloody Roman games likely originated with an earlier, Etruscan practice of a specialized type of human sacrifice, in which pairs of warriors fought to the death as part of the funeral rites in honor of deceased noblemen.

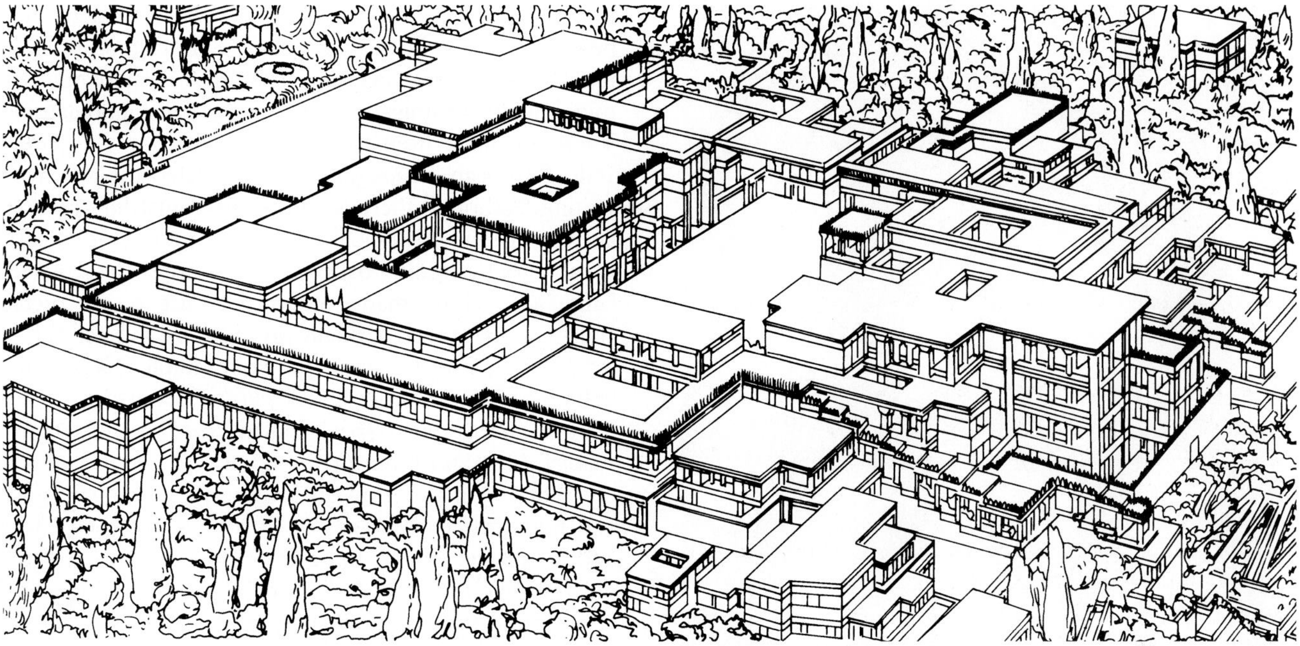

Knossos. An artist's rendering of the great Minoan palace complex discovered by Sir Arthur Evans at Knossos, on Crete. The palace's mazelike complexity may have inspired the myth of the labyrinth, in which the Greek hero Theseus slew the Minotaur.

and the olive tree were best suited to the soil and weather of the region, though wheat and barley were grown on virtually every acre of suitable land. There was sufficient grazing land for sheep and goats, but not usually for cattle and horses. It was and is a beautiful region, one of stunning contrasts, of crystalline skies and "wine-dark" seas, of brilliant, sun-drenched vistas of steep river valleys and mountain peaks.

Human beings had lived in the Aegean area in the Neolithic era (7000–3000 B.C.E.) and, in a few places, even earlier. Around 3000, a change occurred, marked by new types of pottery and the introduction of metallurgy (specifically in bronze, hence the term Bronze Age). This transition from Stone to Bronze Age likely reflects the arrival of a new people. In the next 1,500 years the most rapid cultural advances in the region took place on the large island of Crete, on the southern edge of the Aegean Sea, where the Minoan civilization flourished.

The culture of the Minoans was unknown until modern times, when Sir Arthur Evans excavated Knossos (see Map 1.3), beginning in 1899. He uncovered a vast, multistory palace complex and eventually found that the astonishingly rich and distinctive Minoan civilization had pervaded the whole island, some 150 miles long by 35 miles wide. The palace walls and floors were brightly decorated with fresco paintings showing plants and animals and aquatic and marine life. People were pictured in a wide variety of activities, including ritual sports such as the famous bull-jumping events. The style of this art was vivid and distinctively impressionistic.

Less is known about the people who built and adorned the palaces. The architectural grandeur implies a strongly centralized administration, as does the evidence of two nonalphabetic forms of writing, called Linear A (used to transcribe the language of Crete) and Linear B (used to transcribe Greek). Inscribed clay tablets contain inventories of raw materials and manufactured goods, of agricultural production and stored goods, suggesting that Crete was heavily populated and that the various palace centers controlled surrounding farmsteads, pastures, and villages.

A king called "Minos," perhaps an honorific title, controlled the palace complex, and was assisted by a corps of specially trained bureaucrats and scribes who supervised and recorded the activities of farmers, artisans, and slaves. Priests may have been in charge of religious observances, in which the bull figured prominently; whether the animal was a sacrificial offering or a god image is unclear, but it may have provided the kernel of the myth of the Minotaur, a monster usually depicted as a man with the head of a bull, who was slain by the Athenian hero Theseus. Snake-handling mother goddesses, sacred trees, and caves also figured in Minoan religion. As in Egypt and Mesopotamia, fertility, death, and regeneration were major concerns of this religion.

The people of Crete had learned from Egypt how to construct ships that could sail the Mediterranean.

Boxing Children. This charming fresco painting comes from the island of Thera (present-day Santorini) and dates to the time of the volcanic eruption around 1625 B.C.E. The fresco is in the typical style of the Minoan civilization of Crete and surrounding islands.

Though we have stories of Cretan naval vessels dominating neighboring islands and even mainland sites, the influence of the Minoans appears to have been commercial and cultural rather than imperialistic. Unlike the Mycenaeans later, they neither protected their palaces by fortifications nor included military scenes and weapons in their art.

The Minoan civilization was dealt crippling blows by a devastating earthquake around 1700 B.C.E. and a huge volcanic eruption on the neighboring island of Thera around 1625. The Minoans seem not to have recovered fully from these disasters when, sometime after 1380, their palaces were again destroyed, this time by Indo-European invaders, the Mycenaeans. Minoan traditions, however, continued to live in the culture of the conquerors.

The Advent of the Indo-Europeans

Beginning in the third millennium B.C.E. and continuing into the first millennium C.E., a new linguistic class of people, the Indo-Europeans, radiated out from the steppe region north of the Black Sea into Greece, Anatolia (Asia Minor), Iran, and India. Written records for the earliest periods of Indo-European migration are very scarce and appear only after the migrating peoples settled in their new homes. The languages recorded are distinct (including Greek, Hittite, Persian, and Sanskrit) and reflect a mingling of immigrant and indigenous populations. There are no written specimens whatever of the parent Indo-European language, which antedated the advent of writing. Although there is controversy regarding particular word roots, it is possible to recreate some of its basic vocabulary by arguing backward from later, "descendant" languages. Thus, many dictionaries list reconstructed Indo-European roots (usually preceded by an asterisk [*]) for words in modern languages. For example, **bhrater* lies behind Sanskrit *bhratar,* Greek *phrater,* Latin *frater,* German *Bruder,* French *frère,* Italian *fratello,* and English *brother, friar,* and *fraternal.*

Since so many modern tongues, including English and most other languages of Europe as well as of Iran and, to a lesser extent, India are Indo-European (see the illustration), linguists and historians have given special attention to the history of its speakers. By recreating the vocabulary of this protolanguage, specialists may reconstruct details of the lives of its speakers and their community. Deductions from vocabulary provide a different perspective on a society than does archaeology. The lack of a general word for sea argues that the original Indo-Europeans were an inland people, unfamiliar with seafaring. Indo-Europeans had words for time and the seasons that reflect life in an agricultural society. Words for plowing, sowing, plucking, and grinding, as well as for furrow, wheat, rye, and so forth point to the cultivation of grains. The vocabulary also attests to the domestication of animals (cows, sheep, pigs, horses) and, in the technical sphere, to weaving, pottery manufacture, metal working (copper and possibly bronze), and the use of carts with solid (not spoked) wheels. That the Indo-Europeans also had a word for apple trees, but not for citrus fruits, indicates a northern rather than Mediterranean locale. Words for fish were rare and there were none for camel, lion, or tiger.

As regards socioeconomic matters, the Indo-Europeans had many terms for familial relations within a strongly patriarchal (father-ruled) society and for the household or tribal groups of households as basic units. There were also words for fortified high places. Kingship or warlordship and priesthood appear to have been complementary aspects of political sovereignty. The principles of gift exchange and mutual obligation binding hosts and guests, familiar from later Greek customs, existed in Indo-European society. The invaders infused various indigenous Neolithic peoples with an active, mobile, patriarchal, and aggressive culture. When they conquered and joined or merged with civilized societies, they often adopted or assimilated many elements of those cultures.

The impact of an early Indo-European culture may be gauged from the accomplishments of the Hittites in

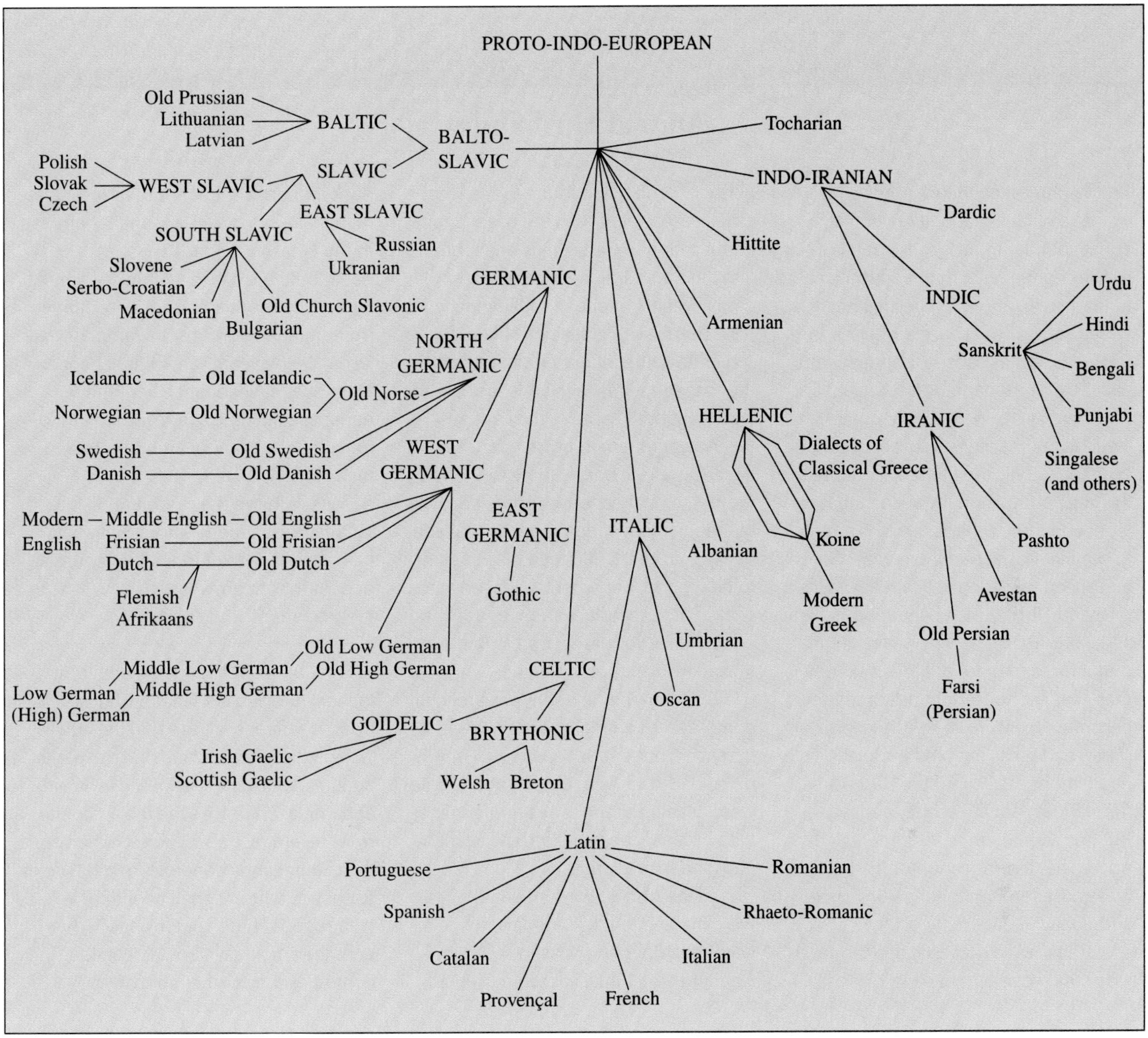

The Indo-European Family of Languages. This chart shows the principal languages of the family in an arrangement indicating genetic relationships and geographic distribution.

the second millennium B.C.E. Although Mesopotamia and Egypt enjoyed for two millennia the best natural resources and strongest political organizations in West Asia, archaeologists have shown that another very significant power was located in Asia Minor. The Hittites came to this region sometime before 2000, as part of the general movement of Indo-European peoples mentioned above. Between 1600 and 1200, the Hittites played a major role in the power politics of West Asia. This was in part due to a technology they monopolized for a time: iron working. The use of iron weapons, together with another innovation, the chariot, gave the Hittites a decided advantage in warfare. Iron was also used in the manufacture of improved farming implements. The Hittites successfully invaded Babylonia and fought a great battle against New Kingdom Egypt at Kadesh in Syria. The Egyptian pharaoh, Ramses II, later decorated many temple walls with carved depictions of his exploits at this battle, though in fact the battle was a draw. The Hittites themselves then fell to a new wave of Indo-European invaders after 1200.

In western Asia Minor, the chief successor state of the Hittites was the kingdom of Lydia, which rose to prominence beginning in the eighth century. The Lydians enjoyed the economic advantages of excellent farmland and rich natural resources. The Greek cities that

CONNECTIONS IN TECHNOLOGY

Animal Husbandry

The domestication of animals has taken place gradually over the course of human history, but it has been of vital significance to the advance of human civilization. Domestic animals were used as both sources of labor in the fields and as beasts of burden, and also as an important food source.

Chickens and pigs were domesticated in Southeast Asia several thousand years ago. Their use helped account for the large population increase in that region, and they facilitated the migration of populations within the region. Goats and sheep were domesticated in western Asia and North Africa beginning as early as 15,000 years ago. They were an important source of food, hides, and other materials for household use, and they became a measure of wealth. Herds of sheep and goats enabled populations to move more easily, and their use spread throughout Africa, Europe, and Asia. But not without an environmental price: The desertification of the Sahara was caused in part by browsing sheep and goats.

Cattle were domesticated as much as 10,000 years ago in western Asia, northern Africa, and India. Cattle were closely associated with the rise of grain farming: they were used as draft animals and their manure provided fertilizer for crops. The technique of milking may have begun with goats and sheep, but its spread to cattle increased dramatically the amount of milk available for human consumption. People of the central Asian steppes tamed horses somewhat later. The use of horses increased once they were hitched to two-wheeled chariots—initially by Indo-European-speaking peoples around 2000 B.C.E.—and later to plows and four-wheeled wagons. In central Asia, people learned to train and equip horses for riding, and a new stage in warfare and sport emerged.

The camel, one of the most recently domesticated animals, was first used by humans around 4,000 years ago in Arabia and central Asia. Once good saddles were developed in the first millennium B.C.E., camels became widely used for transport in arid areas.

In the Andes, llamas and alpacas were made into pack animals, while water buffaloes and yaks in southern Asia and the Himalayas were used as pack and draft animals and as a source of milk. Reindeer served similar purposes in the Eurasian Arctic.

While we naturally think of animal taming and domestication as resulting from human decisions, the animals may also have played a role in the change. Dogs may have joined Paleolithic human settlements while seeking food, initiating the domestication process themselves.

As with the development of agriculture, the domestication of animals has been important in enabling human populations to grow and to develop their economy and society.

---

1. Enter the search term "Neolithic" in the InfoTrac Subject Guide. Choose "Periodical references" and find the article "Eneolithic (Copper Age) horse exploitation in the Eurasian steppes: diet, ritual and riding." What are the main conclusions regarding horse domestication and the cultural and economic importance of the horse in the steppe Eneolithic? What data support these conclusions? What does the article say about Eneolithic domestication of other animals?

had sprung up in western Asia Minor became tribute-paying subject states of Lydia. In Greek accounts of his life, the last and most famous of Lydian kings, Croesus, became an archetype of the fabulously wealthy eastern potentate. It is thus fitting that the Lydians' principal gift to posterity should have been the invention of coined money.

The Rise and Fall of Mycenaean Warrior-Kings

The Greeks, another Indo-European people active at the same time as the Hittites, played a more influential role in world history. Around 2000, the first Greek speakers arrived on the tip of the Balkan Peninsula and founded powerful states centering on citadels at Athens, Pylos, Mycenae (from which the culture gets its name), and other sites. These were the heroes that the Greek poets spoke of, people called Achaeans in Homer's epic poems. The uncovering of Troy and Mycenae by Heinrich Schliemann in the 1870s sent shock waves through the scholarly world.

Each Mycenaean site was a heavily fortified center from which a king governed surrounding territory. Administrative organization was quite intricate and, as on Crete, was overseen by a corps of bureaucrats and scribes who classified, counted, and recorded millions of bits of information in Linear B.

This civilization was wealthy and, at least in its art, cosmopolitan. It imported amber from the Baltic Sea

The Creation of Homer's Epic Poems

The Homeric poems belong to the period of transition from an oral to a literary technique. . . . Homer . . . was an oral poet living in an age of writing. Oral songs can be collected either by phonograph apparatus, which is obviously out of the question here; or by dictation to a scribe; or by a literate oral poet who has been asked to write down his song for someone else who, for some reason, wants it in writing. The last of these possibilities is highly unlikely, because the oral poet, if he is at all literate, can have only a smattering of writing, if he is to remain an oral poet. Had he enough facility in writing to record 27,000 lines of text [of the Iliad *and the* Odyssey*], his style could not be that of an oral technique, which Homer's demonstrably is. In my own mind there remains no doubt that Homer dictated the* Iliad *to someone else who wrote it down, because the Homeric poems have all the earmarks of dictated texts of oral epic songs.**

Albert Lord reached these conclusions about the origins of our texts of the Homeric poems on the basis of knowledge gained while he did field research with his teacher and mentor, Milman Parry. This research was conducted among illiterate singer-poets in Yugoslavia during the 1930s. Lord's theory of the oral dictated text has won wide acceptance among students of Homer and other early oral traditions of epic poetry.

**Albert B. Lord, "Homer's Originality: Oral Dictated Texts,"* Transactions of the American Philological Association, *84 (1953) 131.*

coast, ivory from Syria, alabaster from Crete, lapis lazuli from Mesopotamia, and even ostrich eggs from Nubia in Africa. At Mycenae, excavation revealed royal graves exceedingly rich in gifts, including crowns, sword scabbards, pommels of ivory and gold, bronze daggers inlaid with scenes of lion hunts, vases of gold, silver, bronze, and alabaster, numerous articles of jewelry, arrowheads, boars' tusks like those of a helmet in Homer's *Iliad,* axes, tridents, and many other valuables. The workmanship is very fine and points to influence from Asia Minor, Egypt, and especially Crete. Schliemann thought one of the gold masks he found was the death mask of Homer's King Agamemnon, and indeed the stern and angular features do give an impression of majesty and a will to power.

How did Mycenaean royalty acquire such wealth and power? A far-flung network of trade contacts and a firm agricultural base offer part of the answer, but warfare played an important role too. The weapons buried with

René Burri/Magnum

Mycenaean Gold Death Mask. This is the most imposing and best-known of a number of gold masks found in the shaft graves in the citadel of Mycenae. Heinrich Schliemann erred by three centuries when he identified the portrait as that of Agamemnon. The mask was actually made around 1525 B.C.E. by the repoussé process, in which a thin plate of metal is hammered into a mold from the back.

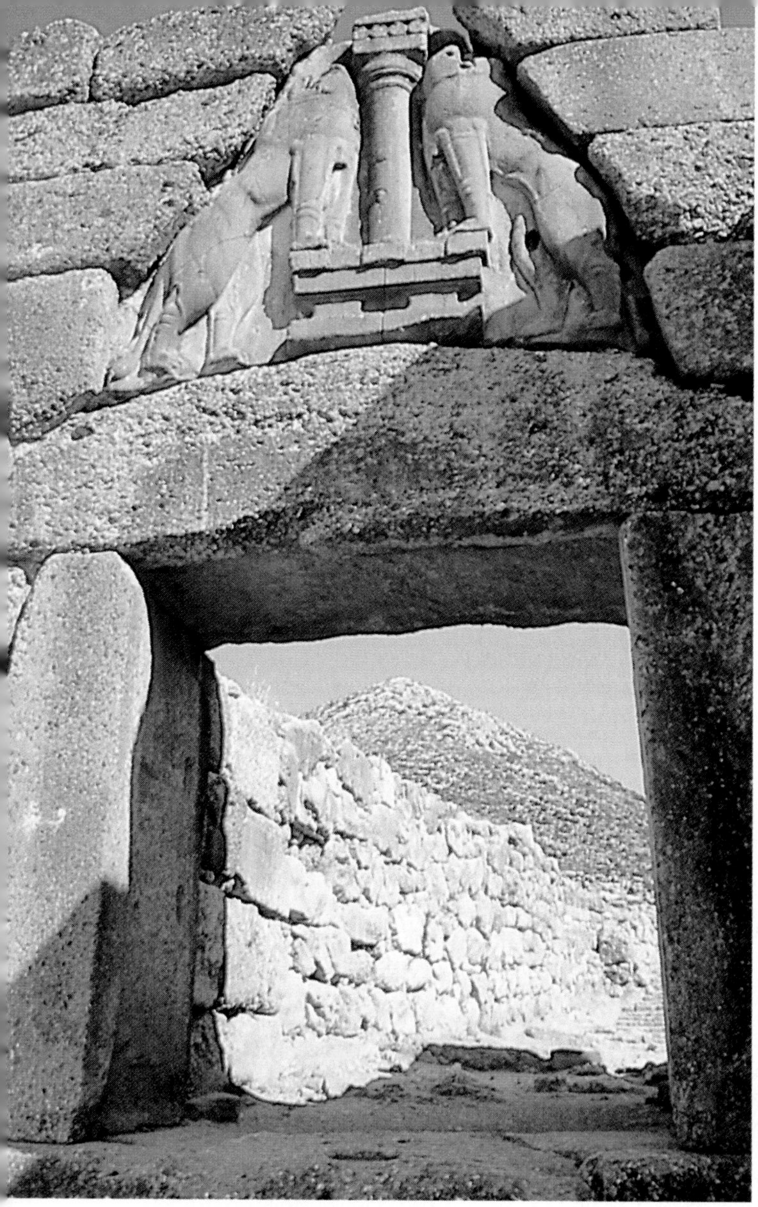

Walter S. Clark/Photo Researchers, Inc

The Lion Gate at Mycenae. The massive structure of the main entrance to the citadel at Mycenae. The lions stand symmetrically in a heraldic pose on either side of a central, Minoan-style column resting on two altars. This earliest piece of monumental sculpture in Europe (c. 1250 B.C.E.) symbolizes the religious and political power of the Mycenaean king.

Bronze Age Bureaucrats

*Astonishing and significant is the omniscience, the insatiable thirst for intimate detail [of Mycenaean officials]. Sheep may be counted up to a glittering total of twenty-five thousand: but there is still a purpose to be served by recording the fact that one animal was contributed by Komawens and another by Etewano. Restless officialdom notes the presence in Pesero's house of one woman and two children; the employment of two nurses, one girl, and one boy, in a Cretan village; the fattening of an insignificant number of hogs. . . ; the existence somewhere of a single pair of brassbound chariot wheels labelled "useless,"—these things and hundreds more of the same type were duly recorded in the palaces of Pylos and Knossos.**

The records described in this passage come from thousands of clay tablets inscribed with the nonalphabetic script called Linear B. For a half century after their first discovery by archaeologists in 1900, it was thought that the language of the tablets was not Greek. Then, in 1952, a young British architect named Michael Ventris deciphered Linear B and showed it to be a primitive form of Greek. This amazing discovery forced researchers to rewrite the history of Greek civilization.

**Denys L. Page,* History and the Homeric Iliad *(Berkeley: University of California Press, 1959), p. 181.*

the warrior-kings show this, and so do the massive fortification walls later built to protect Mycenaean fortresses. The walls at Mycenae were adorned by the Lion Gate, the first large-scale sculpture in Europe. Indeed, the Mycenaeans engaged in one of the most famous military conflicts in ancient history. Around 1200 B.C.E. they attacked and destroyed Troy, located at the northwest corner of Asia Minor near the Dardanelles. The Trojan War was celebrated in heroic song orally transmitted by epic poets down to the eighth century, when the *Iliad* and the *Odyssey* of Homer were recorded in a written form made possible by the adaptation of the Phoenician alphabet to the transcription of the Greek language (see Chapter 3).

Homer's great poems are the earliest landmarks of European literature. Greek myth told of the abduction of Helen, the most beautiful woman on earth, from her husband Menelaus by the Trojan prince Paris. The Greek expedition to Troy, which in legend lasted ten years, was mounted to recover Helen. In fact, the real goal of the mission was the wealth of Troy, which was a great center of textile manufacturing and likely also extracted toll payments from ships passing through the nearby Dardanelles Straits. Whatever the actual goal and the true scale of the Trojan War of legend, it was for the Greeks the earliest major event in their history.

Around 1200 B.C.E., most Mycenaean centers were devastated by roving warriors during the movement of the "Sea Peoples" in the eastern Mediterranean region. There followed a large-scale influx from the north of Dorians, a culturally backward Greek subgroup. Internal strife may also have hastened the Mycenaean world's demise. By 1050 a whole civilization had disappeared, with its royal ruling elite, administrative apparatus, writing system, monumental art and architecture, transport and trade networks, armed forces, fortifications and citadels, and elaborate burial practices. In the period that followed, the Greek dark age, down to 800, the population of Greater Greece fell by about 80 percent. Many people had died in the times of trouble just before and during the Dorian invasion; others fled to new settlements on the west coast of Asia Minor. Although Lefkandi on the island of Euboea and a very few other sites remained active in trading with cities in the eastern Mediterranean, commercial contacts with lands outside the Aegean basin virtually ceased, and in most cases loosely organized tribal groups replaced the former strongly centralized governments.

The Dorians completed the ethnic picture of the Greek people and created a great divide in Greek history. For Greece in the dark age witnessed a transition to another, quite distinct civilization, which will be discussed in Chapter 3.

Ancient Persian Civilization

When I entered Babylon as a friend and . . . established the seat of the government in the palace of the ruler under jubilation and rejoicing, Marduk, the great lord, induced the magnanimous inhabitants of Babylon to love me, and I was daily endeavoring to worship him. My numerous troops walked around in Babylon in peace; I did not allow anyone to terrorize any place of the country of Sumer and Akkad. . . . As to the inhabitants . . . , I abolished the yoke which was against their standing. I brought relief to their dilapidated housing, putting an end to their main complaints. Marduk, the great lord, was well pleased with my deeds and sent friendly blessings to myself, Cyrus, the king who worships him, to Cambyses, my son . . . as well as to all my troops, and we all praised his godhead joyously, standing before him in peace.

*All the kings of the entire world from the Upper to the Lower Sea, those who are seated in throne rooms . . . , as well as all the kings of the West lands living in tents, brought their tributes and kissed my feet in Babylon.**

*James B. Pritchard, ed., *The Ancient Near East: An Anthology of Texts and Pictures* (Princeton: Princeton University Press, 1958), pp. 207–208.

Leaders of new regimes often sing their own praises while damning their predecessors. In the passage above, Cyrus the Great, founder of the mighty Persian Empire, describes the allegedly happy acceptance of his rule by the conquered people and gods of Babylon. While civil discord during the reign of the last Chaldean king, Nabonidus, had in fact made life miserable for many, we may doubt whether Cyrus's contemporaries fully realized the significance of the changes the "king of kings" had made in the political map of ancient West Asia.

The Rise of the Persian Empire

The Persians lived in a number of tribes dispersed throughout southwestern Iran. They were ethnically related to their overlords, the Medes, a warrior people who temporarily controlled Upper Mesopotamia, Syria, and Iran. During the reign of Cyrus (559–530 B.C.E.), the Indo-European-speaking Persians achieved a spectacularly swift rise to power that radically changed the political map of West Asia. In 550 they not only freed themselves from Median authority but conquered their former masters and annexed their territory. The Lydian king, Croesus, now made the mistake of attacking the Persians; in 547 he lost both his life and his kingdom. The realm of the Chaldeans, which was suffering from political disorder internally, fell to Persian arms in 539.

Cyrus next turned his attention to the northeastern quadrant of his far-flung dominions. In 530 he died in Bactria (modern Turkestan) defending the Persian Empire's frontier on the Jaxartes River against nomadic invaders. Cyrus's son and successor, Cambyses (reigned 530–522), added Egypt to the empire. Faced with a major revolt within his empire and perhaps afflicted with mental illness, Cambyses committed suicide in 522. After a period of bloody civil strife, a rather distant relative of the royal Achaemenid family, Darius I (reigned 522–486), became king.

During his long reign, Darius proved as energetic and effective as his forerunners. He eventually enlarged the empire to the Indus River in the east, the Caucasus Mountains in the north, and Upper Egypt in the south, while in the west he seized a foothold in Europe.

Darius made his most significant contribution in creating one model for the organization and administration of large empires composed of ethnically, religiously, and linguistically diverse groups. Royal inscriptions, for example, were written in three official languages: Persian, Elamitic, and Babylonian. In the ancient world, only the Roman Empire would surpass the Persian in the degree of unity achieved despite cultural differences among subject peoples. Imperial China attained a similar degree of administrative unity, but among a population that was much more culturally and ethnically homogeneous. The empire Darius and his predecessors had fashioned embraced various tributary kingdoms and twenty provinces. Although strategically stationed garrisons ensured military control, the Persians allowed considerable

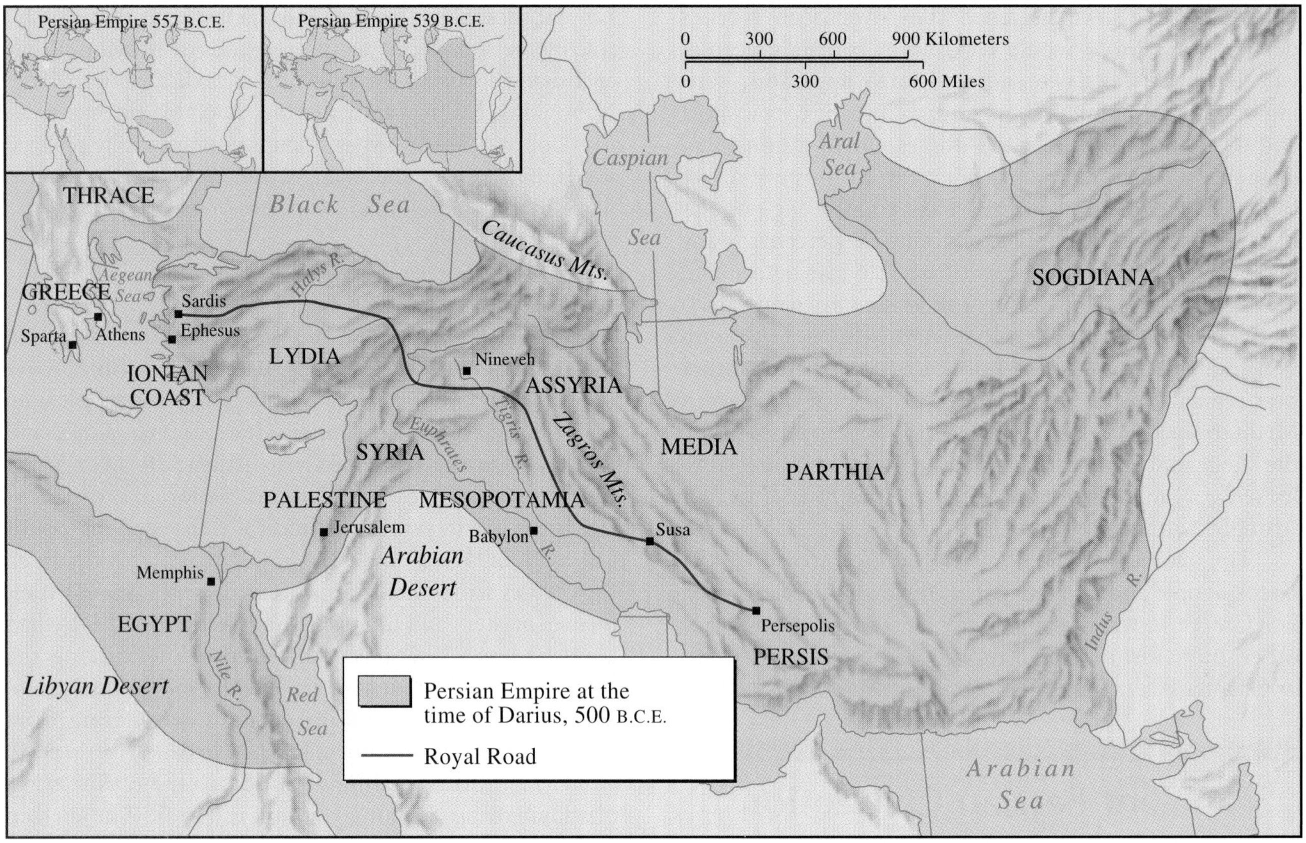

Map 1.4 Persian Empire. The Persian Empire at its greatest extent was by far the largest of the ancient West Asian imperial domains.

Archers of the Persian Royal Guard. This relief sculpture, done in colored brick, depicts two members of the imperial guard. It adorned the palace of King Darius I at Susa.

Musée du Louvre, © Photo R.M.N.

autonomy in local governments and respected religious preferences. The relative leniency of Persian rule as compared with the earlier Assyrian hegemony enabled Darius to recruit willing mercenary forces both for maintaining internal security and for defending borders.

Military and civil officials were drawn primarily from the elite of the Iranian nobility. Darius appointed provincial governors called satraps, who enjoyed considerable individual autonomy, to collect tribute, taxes, soldiers, and military provisions for delivery to the king, whose personal supervisors, called "Eyes and Ears," made regular rounds of the provinces. The revenue generated by this method not only paid administrative expenses but also ensured brimming royal treasuries. Although internal uprisings did occur, especially at times of transition in leadership, the administrative apparatus Darius set in place endured until Alexander's conquest in 330 B.C.E.

To ease the task of governing their huge empire, the Persian monarchs created the most elaborate public works system yet seen in West Asia. Communication (including a postal system) and transport were facilitated by an extensive network of good roads, including the Royal Road from Ephesus on the Aegean to Susa, some 1,600

The Great King Darius Crushes a Rebellion

I am Darius, the great king, the king of kings, the king of Persia, the king of the provinces, the son of Hystaspes, the grandson of Arsames, the Achaemenian. . . .

Says Darius the king—There are eight of my race who have been kings before me; I am the ninth; nine of us have been kings in succession. . . .

Says Darius the king—Then I went to Babylon against that Nidintabelus, who was called Nabochodrossor. The people of Nidintabelus held the Tigris; there they were posted, and they had boats. There I approached with a detachment in rafts. I brought the enemy into difficulty. I carried the enemy's position. Ahura Mazda brought help to me. By the grace of Ahura Mazda I crossed the Tigris. There I slew many of the troops of Nidintabelus. On the 26th day of the month Atriyata, then it was we so fought.

Says Darius the king—Then I went to Babylon. When I arrived near Babylon, at the city named Zazana, on the Euphrates, there that Nidintabelus, who was called Nabochodrossor, came with his forces against me, to do battle. Then we fought a battle. Ahura Mazda brought help to me. By the grace of Ahura Mazda I slew many of the troops of that Nidintabelus—the enemy was driven into the water—the water destroyed them. On the 2nd day of the month Anamaka, then it was we so fought.

Says Darius the king—Then Nidintabelus with the horsemen that were faithful to him fled to Babylon. Then I went to Babylon. By the grace of Ahura Mazda I both took Babylon, and seized that Nidintabelus. Then I slew that Nidintabelus at Babylon.

Says Darius the king—While I was at Babylon, these are the countries which revolted against me: Persia, Susiana, Media, Assyria, Armenia, Parthia, Margiana, Sattagydia, Sacia. . . .

*Says Darius the king—[After his lieutenants had quelled many of the revolts] then I went out from Babylon. I proceeded to Media. When I reached . . . a city . . . named Kudrusia, there that Phraortes, who was called king of Media, came with an army against me, to do battle. Then we fought a battle. Ahura Mazda brought help to me; by the grace of Ahura Mazda, I entirely defeated the army of Phraortes. On the 26th day of the month Adukanish, then it was we thus fought the battle.**

This passage is from an inscription carved around 520 B.C.E. on a cliff face near the site of one of Darius's famous battles. The Persian king records a successful mission to quell a rebellion mounted against him after the death of his predecessor, Cambyses.

*Henry Rawlinson, trans., "The Behistun Inscription of Darius" [1847], in The Greek Historians, vol. 2, ed. Francis R. B. Godolphin (New York: Random House, 1942), pp. 623–628.

miles away in Iran. These were to be traveled by armies, ambassadors, distinguished visitors, prisoners of war, caravans, and merchants. Only Han China and the Roman Empire equaled or surpassed the Persian Empire in their elaborate public works systems. Darius also provided for a uniform standard of weights and measures and, borrowing an idea from Lydia, introduced gold and silver coinage.

Master of all this was the supreme autocrat, Darius, the earthly viceroy of Ahura Mazda, the Zoroastrian god of light. To quote one inscription, he was "the great king, king of Kings, king of the countries possessing many kinds of people, king of this great earth far and wide." In the Greek world, the earlier Mycenaean kings had been mere local warlords by comparison; the powers of the Persian kings were to be rivaled by a Greek only briefly in the reign of Alexander the Great, who saw himself as their supplanter and successor. Roman emperors provide the closest analogy to the Persian model of absolute monarchy, although the earlier (and wiser) emperors tried to avoid the appearance of such unlimited monopoly of power.

Persian Culture and Religion

Persia's artistic and intellectual accomplishments did not match its military and governmental performance. Little literature was produced, except for the Avesta, the collected sacred scriptures of Zoroastrianism. Science and mathematics did not advance beyond the substantial

The Genius of Zoroaster

*With a history of some three thousand years, Zoroastrianism is one of the most ancient living religions. It is the most important and best-known religion of ancient, or pre-Islamic, Iran. . . . It was . . . the religion of Iran under the rule of the Iranian-speaking Aryan populations, members of the Aryan or Indo-Iranian group of the more extended Indo-European family. Another name for Zoroastrianism, Mazdaism, is derived from the name of the religion's supreme god, Mazda ("wise"), or Ahura Mazda ("wise lord"). . . . The primary innovation of Zoroastrianism, which sets it apart from the religions of other Indo-European peoples, . . . is its emphasis on monotheism. . . . The concept of Ahura Mazda as the creator of heaven and earth, day and night, and light and darkness, . . . as well as the ethical context in which Zarathustra conceived his answer to the problem of evil, demonstrates that the prophet was an original thinker, a powerful religious figure who introduced radical changes to the spiritual and cultural world in which he was reared.**

It is important in assessing the achievement of the Persians to avoid the bias of ancient Greek historians like Herodotus. In writing of political and military affairs, they often labeled the Persians "barbarians" and saw their civilization as culturally decadent and, because monarchical, politically despotic. The truth is that Persian religious beliefs at any rate were in crucial ways very much in advance of contemporary Greek polytheism.

**Gherardo Gnoli, "Zoroastrianism," in* Religions of Antiquity, *ed. R. M. Seltzer (New York: Macmillan, 1989), pp. 128, 131.*

inheritance from Babylonia and Egypt. In art and architecture, Assyria, Babylonia, Greece, and Egypt often provided the models and sometimes the expertise: Greek stonecutters and sculptors, for example, worked on the mammoth palace complexes at Susa and Persepolis. In at least one respect, the Persian structures were novel, for they were erected to celebrate not the gods but an earthly ruler of a mighty empire, the all-powerful "king of kings."

The Persians did show great originality in religion. The traditional Iranian religion was a typical Indo-European polytheism, whose chief officials were magi (priest-astrologers). In the early sixth century, however, a reformer named Zoroaster (Zarathustra in Persian), removed the magical elements from the religion. According to the new faith, Zoroastrianism, the world was ruled not by a horde of supernatural beings but by one only. Representing goodness, light, and truth, Ahura Mazda was the supreme being, but he was opposed by another supernatural power, Ahriman, who represented darkness and evil. The two were locked in a universal struggle, which Ahura Mazda was destined to win. On a future judgment day, all human beings, living and dead, would be consigned to heaven or hell. This notion of last judgment later figured significantly in Christianity and Islam. Zoroastrianism was a strongly ethical religion; it taught that men and women possessed free will and were expected to avoid sin and abide by divine laws. Each person's choices mattered in the struggle. The king of kings himself was a devotee and example to his people. Later, Mithras, Ahura Mazda's lieutenant, played a prominent part in the religious ferment of the Roman Empire. Zoroastrianism, though modified by resurgence of old Iranian ritual and magic and by contact with other religious traditions, survived the fall of the Persian Empire to Macedon and the subsequent period of Hellenistic overlordship. After the Arab conquest, it was handed on from generation to generation during Mongol hegemony and the reign of Muslim rulers in Persia. Today there are small Zoroastrian communities in Iran and more influential ones among the Parsee of India (for example, in Bombay) and Pakistan.

In warfare, politics, religion, and material culture, the Persian Empire equaled or surpassed its West Asian predecessors. It brought lasting stability to a vast region of diverse peoples and cultures. In the ancient world, only the Roman Empire and Han China would match that achievement.

Amerindian Civilization

I [came] face to face with Colossal Head Number 1, buried up to its eyes near the base of the great mound at La Venta. Now, retrieved and revered anew, it stares sightlessly with a certain air that seems to me to verge *on smugness, perhaps because it has survived a span of time that began long before the Parthenon rose on the heights above Athens.**

*George E. Stuart, "New Light on the Olmec," *National Geographic* 184 (November 1993): 104.

Standing up to eleven feet tall, these intimidating sculptures portray the rulers of the city-states of the early Olmec culture of Mesoamerica. They are among the most impressive archaeological finds from the early Amerindian civilizations that arose in the Western Hemisphere beginning in 1800 B.C.E., some 1,200 years after humans had established civilizations in Mesopotamia and Egypt. One cultural center, Andean civilization, originated on the Pacific coast of present-day Peru and quickly extended into the Andean highlands from Ecuador to Chile. The other center of civilization arose in Mesoamerica (present-day eastern Mexico, Guatemala, Belize, El Salvador, and western Honduras) about 400 years later.

The University Art Museum, University of Pennsylvania, neg. #T4-132c3

A Chavin Jaguar. This stone mortar was carved in the shape of a puma, or jaguar. Stone carving was a specialty of the Chavin, and the jaguar was an important figure in Peruvian and Andean culture as well as in Mesoamerica.

Map 1.5 Early Peruvian-Andean Civilization. The Chavin culture (900–300 B.C.E.) was the first stage of a series of increasingly sophisticated Amerindian cultures that first flourished on the coast of present-day Peru and spread up into the high plateaus of the Andes. The Chavin built monumental religious structures and were experts in making fine pottery and exquisite gold jewelry.

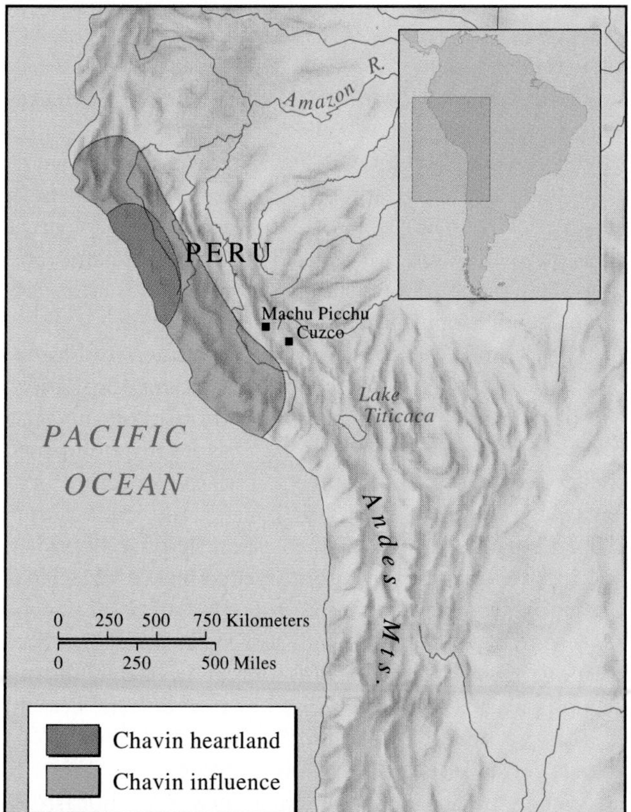

Archaeologists are currently undertaking extensive projects in both Mesoamerica and the Andes, and their investigations are quickly enlarging our understanding of the antiquity, complexity, and geographic extent of these Amerindian civilizations. In this section of the text we focus on the two earliest Amerindian cultures, Chavin society along the arid coast of Peru and Olmec society in the humid rain forests along the Gulf of Mexico southeast of Vera Cruz.

The Opening of Andean Civilization: The Chavin Culture

The Andean cultural area, a region of great environmental diversity where the distance from the ocean shore to high mountain valleys averages seventy miles, is best conceived of on a vertical rather than a horizontal scale. Off the coast, a cold current supports a rich marine life that usually provides a major element of the diet of the dwellers on the narrow, arid coastal plain. On occasion, however, the waters run warm, producing the effect called El Niño, destroying marine life and disrupting the interior climates. The narrow coastal plain is cut by some forty rivers that bring the fertile soil down from the adjacent highlands. Amerindian farmers grew maize, vegetables, avocados, potatoes, and peanuts on the soil deposits in these short, narrow valleys. As one moves into the Andean foothills and mountains that rise next to the arid plains, rainfall increases, and the puna, a high plateau of varying elevations interspersed among the Andean mountain ranges, is well watered. The Amerindians living in these uplands grew maize at the lower levels and potatoes farther up and herded llamas and alpacas on the high grasslands. Some Andean villagers attended to all three areas by walking a few miles up or down the slopes. The warm eastern face of the Andes drops down into the Amazon basin; here the inhabitants grew cotton and coca and gathered tropical fruit.

The civilizations in the Andean region existed in relative isolation from those of Mesoamerica. All that exists of Peru's history before the Spanish Conquest is the archaeological record of nonliterate peoples, which can reveal much about the way that people lived, but less about why they did so. By 3000 B.C.E. the Amerindians had established permanent agricultural settlements on the coast and shortly thereafter in the Andean highlands, and by 2700 the inhabitants were making pottery. By 1800 B.C.E. Amerindians were building religious centers marked by large stone buildings throughout Ecuador and Peru, both on the coast and in the highlands.

The first known widespread civilization in Peru was the Chavin culture, which flourished from 900 to 200 B.C.E. Archaeologists have uncovered some aspects of this culture, and it is known that the Chavin religion promoted two deities that archaeologists call the Smiling God and the Staff God. The Chavin religion was so powerful that in less than a century its missionaries won converts throughout the vast area of Peru; yet scholars to date have little knowledge of its ideas or rituals. Chavin artwork was as influential as its religion. Its artisans worked in ceramics, textiles, and jade; jaguars were a key motif. In these years, metals were smelted for the first time, almost solely for decoration. Chavin artisans first worked with gold and copper and later with silver, platinum, and tin. They also began to cast bronze, also usually for decoration, not for tools or weapons.

About 350 B.C.E. major changes occurred. Coastal populations began to build major irrigation works, a hint that population growth may have been pressing on natural resources. Many Peruvian cities began to build strong fortifications, and their art began to feature warriors, an indication that cities were warring with each other over control of neighboring farmlands. Urban centers constructed fortifications, undertook prolonged wars, built irrigation systems, and allocated water, suggesting that strong central authority and stratified social systems had developed by this stage. By 200 B.C.E. the Chavin culture had faded away in a welter of urban ministates.

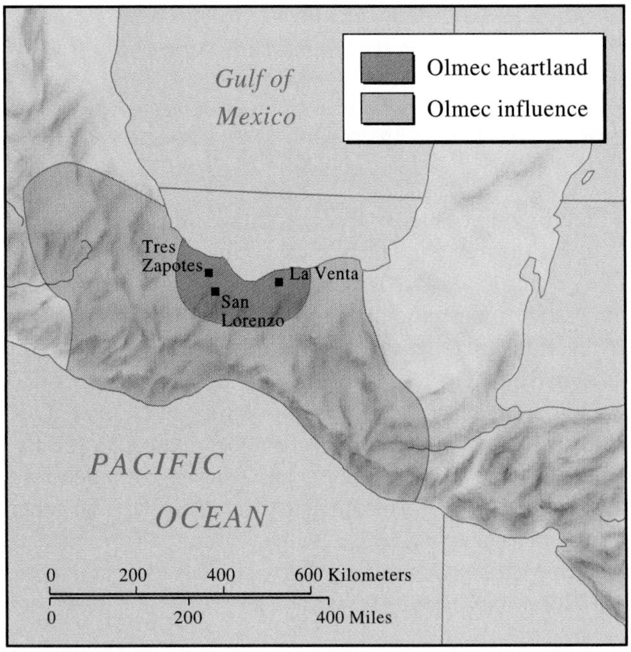

Map 1.6 Early Mesoamerican Civilization. The Olmec culture (1200–500 B.C.E.) was the first stage of a series of increasingly sophisticated Amerindian cultures centered in Mesoamerica (present-day eastern Mexico, Guatemala, Belize, and western Honduras) for almost 3,000 years. The Olmec built large earthen temple mounds, imported huge boulders that they carved into likenesses of their rulers, and set up an extensive trading network throughout the area.

The Advent of Mesoamerican Civilization: The Olmec

Mesoamerica is a geographic area of great variety in altitude and rainfall, and the Amerindian cultures there developed in many different environments. The great mountain spine that runs from Alaska to the tip of South America dominates the physical terrain of Mesoamerica, running close to the Pacific coast. There are, however, extensive lowlands, including the Yucatán Peninsula, along the Gulf of Mexico and the Caribbean Sea. Rainfall varies over different lowland and highland areas.

Olmec society appeared about 1400 B.C.E. Most archaeological excavations have centered on the area southeast of Vera Cruz, but work at new sites in the highlands south of Mexico City and in southern Guatemala has revealed additional centers of Olmec culture.

As early as 2200 B.C.E., the Olmec were living in agricultural villages, cultivating large maize crops in the lush, steamy environment along the gulf coast, supplementing their diet with abundant seafood and shellfish, game, and dogs. The plentiful food supply supported an increasingly populous and sophisticated village and town life.

The Olmec were traders as well as farmers and fisherfolk. They prospered by selling and trading throughout Mesoamerica. They trafficked in tar, rubber, salt, fine clay for pottery, metal ores for coloring, basalt for monuments, shells, skins, exotic bird feathers, cacao, jade, incense, medicines, textiles, obsidian (volcanic glass), and jadite (a special variety of jade). The Olmec especially prized obsidian and jadeite. In cultures without smelted metals, obsidian is particularly valuable because, properly worked, it can be made into razor-sharp, though somewhat brittle, tools or weapons. Access to obsidian sources in the highlands around present-day Mexico City was an important element in the rise and fall of Mesoamerican civilizations. The Olmec craved jadeite for religious purposes.

Where traders went, cultural influence was not far behind. Artifacts found over a wide area of Mesoamerica indicate that the Olmec traders also spread their culture to less advanced maize-growing villages in the central highlands of Mexico and founded a major city, Copan, in southern Guatemala 400 miles from the Olmec heartland.

The culture of the Olmec dominated Mesoamerican civilization from 1400 to 500 B.C.E. Recent studies now indicate that both writing and the famous Mesoamerican calendar (described in the Maya section in Chapter 7), first known to be employed at Monte Alban in the highlands about 450 B.C.E., may have originated in Olmec civilization.

Like the Chavin before them and the Maya after them, the Olmec lived in a world of ministates. In the Olmec heartland three major centers based on temple complexes—San Lorenzo (1400–900 B.C.E.), Tres Zapotes (900–350 B.C.E.), La Venta (900–350 B.C.E.)—arose. San Lorenzo was the first religious center in the Western Hemisphere, and the sacred ball game (described below) may have originated there. As with the Chavin culture, what we know about the Olmec comes from archaeological assessments. At the San Lorenzo stage in Olmec culture, there is no sign of writing.

La Venta, the largest Olmec city, best illustrates aspects of Olmec culture. It was situated on an island whose population numbered about 18,000; another 350,000 people lived in adjacent areas. La Venta was symmetrically laid out on an axis eight degrees west of true north and was dominated by a pyramid of packed earth more than one hundred feet high, probably flattened on top to serve as the center of religious ceremonies. A number of lower mounds were probably the sites of other public buildings or homes for the nobility. In the hot climate, both private homes and public buildings were apparently made with thatched roofs and open walls to catch any cooling drafts. The city was guarded by huge, stern-visaged heads that proclaimed to all outsiders, human and nonhuman, the temporal and spiritual power of La Venta's rulers.

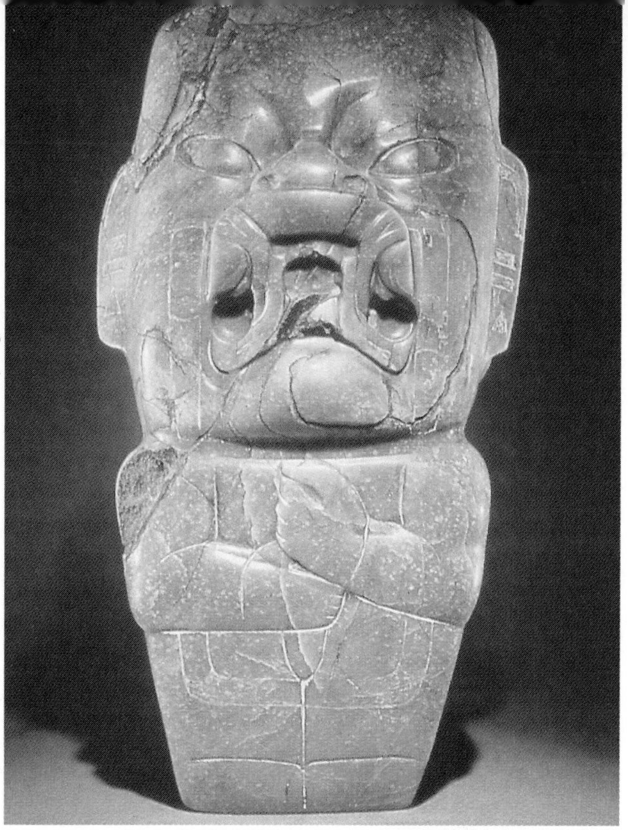

Courtesy of Library Services, American Museum of Natural History, neg. 1298

A Were-Jaguar. The jaguar, depicted here on a ceremonial axe carved before 600 B.C.E., was an important motif in Olmec-influenced areas of Mesoamerica. The ferocious eyes and extended fangs show how the Olmec had created a fearsome supernatural world.

The Head of an Olmec Ruler. The most striking artistic expressions of the Olmec culture are the heads carved from basalt boulders, apparently advertising the authority of specific rulers. This particular six-foot representation was carved about 700 B.C.E.

Foto Film/Art Resource

The Olmec, and the Amerindian cultures that succeeded them in Mesoamerica, constructed their temples and other major buildings without the wheel, metal tools, or draft animals. Olmec farmers, probably working in the dry season as forced labor, hauled burdens such as the ten-ton monumental heads; they used rafts on waterways where possible and sleds and rolling poles on land where necessary. Historians of ecology see the lack of draft animals as the greatest handicap for the Olmec, because these animals not only perform labor but also provide a ready source of high-protein food.

La Venta was a center for artisans, traders, and farmers who lived in a highly stratified society dominated by a class of nobles and absolute rulers. Unlike the Chavin, Olmec artisans did little metalworking, but rather concentrated their efforts on sculpting, whether huge stone heads or tiny jadite jewelry. Overall, the artistic and spiritual power of the Olmec artisans was immense. Most of the numerous Mesoamerican cultures that followed the Olmec—including the Maya and the Aztec—show distinct Olmec influence.

La Venta was above all a religious complex. What precisely the Olmec asked of their gods is not clear, because

3000 B.C.E.	King Menes unifies Egypt
	Bronze metallurgy in West Asia
	Great Pyramids at Giza
	Olmec agricultural villages in Mesoamerica
2000	Indo-Europeans arrive in Balkan Peninsula
	Hammurabi's Code
	Hyksos domination in Egypt
	Height of Minoan civilization on Crete
	Eruption of Thera
	Akhenaton and Nefertiti rule in Egypt
	Rise of Olmec civilization in Mesoamerica
	Introduction of chariot warfare by the Hittites
	The Trojan War
	Collapse of Mycenaean civilization
1000	Spread of iron metallurgy
	Kushite kingdom in Africa
	Amerindian Chavin culture begins to flourish in Peru
	Greeks adopt Phoenician alphabet
	Homer composes *Iliad* and *Odyssey*
	Zoroaster in Persia
	Nebuchadnezzar builds the Hanging Gardens in Babylon
	Persian royal road network
	Conquests of King Cyrus
500	

they had plenty of rain, an unfailing agriculture, and no strong enemies. Perhaps, as in many religions, they sought the continuation of the natural order, praying that their state would not fall to social anarchy or natural catastrophes.

The Olmec and later Mesoamericans depicted most of their gods as part human and part animal, a practice also common in ancient Egyptian and Indian religions. At different times, the eagle, the serpent, the alligator, and the jaguar rose to special distinction. The jaguar, a fearsome predator in nature, was even more terrible and powerful when deified; jadeite was the medium chosen to represent the jaguar god.

Like all humans, the Olmec had death rituals. They evidently believed in an underworld. The seated figures they commonly carved may have been their rulers sitting in the passageway to that underworld. The rulers, in animal-shaman form, could perhaps pass in and out of the underworld as mediators, and determine who went there and under what conditions.

The Olmec developed the "divine" or "sacred" ball game that later spread into almost every Mesoamerican culture, although they did not construct the walled enclosures for it that became typical later. The ball game was an athletic contest in which the object was to put a heavy rubber ball through a tight-fitting ring set vertically in a wall at both ends of the court. The players could not use their hands, but powered the ball by bouncing it off heavy plates on their forearms, chests, and hips. There may have been professional teams that played for money and glory; apparently there was considerable betting. Certainly in later Mesoamerican civilizations and probably in the Olmec, the players often fought for high stakes—their lives. In these instances, the ball game served as a ritual for the perpetuation of the state. A captured ruler and his men, suitably weakened, were forced to play in a hopeless contest against the local ruler and his rested men. The captives eventually lost the game and were sacrificed to the gods. The ball game in later times also played a role in predicting the future and had other religious overtones.

Summary and Comparisons

The story of civilization begins in Mesopotamia, a fertile land claimed from swamp and desert by dint of hard work that became the locus for the development of cities. Around 3500 B.C.E. the Sumerians, who lived in the region, began an urban mode of life with a diversified social structure and labor force. The development of writing both facilitated public and private business transactions and made possible the creation of a rich literary tradition. The Babylonians added further refinements in mathematics, astronomy and the calendar, and law; the Assyrians' achievements were in imperialism and military conquest. Finally, in the Chaldean or Neo-Babylonian phase, Mesopotamian civilization was revitalized under Nebuchadnezzar.

In Egypt, too, regular crop production supported a vibrant and long-lived civilization. In the Old Kingdom, the god-king pharaoh presided over a strongly centralized government, and massive labor forces built irrigation systems and the Great Pyramids. Priests supervised the rituals of an elaborate polytheism. Later, New Kingdom pharaohs built an Egyptian Empire that extended into West Asia. They, too, engaged in extensive building programs at Karnak, Abu Simbel, the Valley of the Kings, and elsewhere. The New Kingdom also experimented briefly with a form of monotheism.

In the Aegean region, Crete and the southern Balkan Peninsula saw the flourishing of Minoan-Mycenaean civilization. Mycenaean culture emerged from the mixture of indigenous elements and borrowings from Crete by a Greek-speaking Indo-European people around 2000 B.C.E. The Minoan-Mycenaean culture excelled in painting, sculpture, jewelry, and architecture. The surviving written materials show a degree of literacy in both Crete and Greece. A combination of disruptive forces, including foreign invasion, brought an end to the Mycenaean world.

The Persians, also an Indo-European people, reshaped West Asia when Cyrus fashioned a larger and better-organized empire than any up to Roman times. Racially, linguistically, and religiously diverse populations were governed through a carefully devised network of semiautonomous local officials. The public works infrastructure included an unprecedented imperial road network. Culturally, Zoroastrianism brought an advance in beliefs about the nature of the divine and superseded the older, more traditional Iranian polytheism.

In the Western Hemisphere, civilization appeared in the Mesoamerican rain forests and highlands and also in the coastal and Andean region centered in present-day Peru, again because of a thriving agriculture. Amerindian cultures built cities around religious complexes. There was extensive internal trade within the cultures, but apparently little or none between them. The Chavin culture in Peru, like that of the Mesopotamians, demonstrated advanced engineering skills in constructing an extensive irrigation system.

Amerindian religious practices flourished and spread widely; typical were painstakingly constructed temples and arenas for sacred ball games. Artwork was impressive, including the monumental sculpted heads of the Olmec and the advanced metalwork of the Chavin culture. In these matters the Western Hemisphere civilizations were as advanced as those elsewhere in the world.

The magnitude of the material and intellectual developments of early civilizations described in this chapter is impossible to overestimate. Certainly the differences stand out. Geographically, some cultures, like Egypt and Mesopotamia, developed in great river valleys, others on the edge of the sea or in steaming jungles. Urbanization for some of these cultures, as in Mesopotamia, meant large cities that reorganized a prosperous agricultural society for commerce. For other societies, like Egypt and the Olmec, it meant having a religious center for the most effective communication with the powers of the next world. Some, such as Persia, were conquering civilizations that could sustain military operations in far away lands; some, like the Chavin, stayed home. Some civilizations, like Mesopotamia, Persia, and the Olmec, added to the sum of human knowledge in mathematics, astronomy, highway engineering, hydraulics, and the calendar; others specialized in body adornments. Though some of these early cultures remained completely illiterate, in others literacy could mean prayers for priests only, commercial and stockyard receipts, or even transcriptions of poetry.

If one were to seek a common denominator, perhaps the most pervasive underlying factor in the human experience was the striving for order. The impulse to exploit the order of nature had earlier led to agriculture. The need to impose order on the relationships of men and women to the environment and to one another now led to civilized communities. The attempt to detect order in the dispositions of the invisible powers also stimulated more complex intellectual speculation. Egyptians; Mesopotamians; Indo-European peoples like the Hittites, Persians, and Greeks; and Amerindians all attempted to grasp and somehow control the workings of their world and have influence on the other world. They did this by developing mathematics and astronomy, some by creating writing systems, and all by applying their religious insights. In all these arenas, later participants in the various civilizations of the world were heavily indebted to their ancient forebears. Chapter 2 will round out the picture of early civilizations by examining those of South and East Asia.

Selected Sources

Archaeology. This reasonably priced magazine (six issues annually) provides information on recent discoveries and interpretations of archaeological sites around the world. Excellent photographs.

Brosius, Maria. *Women in Ancient Persia (559–331 B.C.).* 1996. An excellent, very current examination of a neglected subject.

Burger, Richard. *Chavin and the Origins of Andean Civilization.* 1992. A good, well-illustrated overview of Chavin culture as it has been revealed by archaeological excavation.

*Burstein, Stanley, ed. and trans. *Ancient African Civilizations: Kush and Axum.* 1997. Based on Greek and Roman sources, the collection describes the cultures and governments of two major African kingdoms.

*Castleden, Rodney. *Minoans: Life in Bronze Age Crete.* 1990. A very attractive presentation of the evidence about Minoan Crete.

*Available in paperback.

*Chadwick, John. *The Mycenaean World.* 1976. A well-written general account with helpful illustrations.

*Crawford, Harriet. *Sumer and the Sumerians.* 1991. A good, concise treatment of the Sumerian people and their achievements.

*Ferry, David, trans. *Gilgamesh: A New Rendering in English Verse.* 1992. A recent, lively translation of the world's first heroic epic.

Ghirshman, Roman. *Persia: From the Origins to Alexander the Great.* Trans. S. Gilbert and J. Emmons. 1964. An excellent, highly readable survey.

*Gurney, O. R. *The Hittites.* Rev. ed. 1990. A good, concise work on the subject.

*Harris, James E., and Kent R. Weeks. *X-Raying the Pharaohs.* 1973. This description of a radiological examination of mummies in the Egyptian Museum in Cairo includes an astounding "Portfolio of Pictures."

Hawkes, Jacquetta. *King of the Two Lands.* 1966. A historical novel set in the time of Akhenaton and Nefertiti, by an eminent British archaeologist.

*Hobson, Christine. *The World of the Pharaohs: A Complete Guide to Ancient Egypt.* 1987; reprinted 1993. A clearly organized treatment with marvelous color illustrations.

*Knapp, A. Bernard. *The History and Culture of Ancient West Asia and Egypt.* 1988. A succinct, current survey.

*Latacz, Joachim. *Homer: His Art and His World.* Trans. James P. Holoka. 1996. This recent study places the great Greek epic poet in his historical and literary contexts. Contains helpful discussions of the *Iliad* and the *Odyssey.*

*Mallory, J. P. *In Search of the Indo-Europeans: Language, Archaeology, and Myth.* 1989. A recent work with many illustrations; includes a judicious assessment of rival theories.

Markman, Roberta H., and Peter T. *The Flayed God: The Mythology of Mesoamerica.* 1992. A combination of original text and contemporary commentary that leads the reader into the mythology of the Mesoamerican cultures.

*Phillipson, David W. *African Archaeology.* 2d ed. 1993. A revised version of the author's broad survey of the archaeology of Africa, beginning with the origins of humankind. Well illustrated.

*Pritchard, James B. *The Ancient Near East: An Anthology of Texts and Pictures.* 1958. A convenient, widely available collection of interesting and important materials.

*Romer, John. *Ancient Lives: Daily Life in the Egypt of the Pharaohs.* 1984. A fascinating study of daily lives of the people—on all social strata—in a village near ancient Thebes.

Soustelle, Jacques. *The Olmecs: The Oldest Civilization in Mexico.* Trans. Helen R. Lane. 1985. The distinguished French anthropologist shows his affection for the Olmec in this work.

Stuart, George E. "New Light on the Olmec." *National Geographic* 184, no. 5 (1993) 88.

Welsby, Derek A. *The Kingdom of Kush: The Napatan and Meroitic Empires.* 1996; reprinted 1998. This up-to-date examination of these very ancient civilizations is enhanced by more than 200 illustrations.

Wilber, Donald N. *Persepolis: The Archaeology of Parsa, Seat of the Persian Kings.* 1969. A well-written and illustrated presentation of the ancient Persian capital.

*Wood, Michael. *In Search of the Trojan War.* 1985. A well-illustrated and clearly written account of the archaeological adventures of the search for ancient Troy; a companion to the six-part BBC television series.

Internet Links

Ancient Persia
http://home.wxs.nl/~lende045/ANET.htm
Included here are several ancient documents, among them the famous Behistun inscription, in which Darius I commemorates his military victories. Nicely illustrated.

Chavin Culture
http://www.anthro.mankato.msus.edu/prehistory/latinamerica/south/cultures/chavin.html
This site provides a brief description of Chavin culture and links to discussions and illustrations of a number of topics centering on Latin American prehistory.

Greek Art and Architecture: Mycenaean Civilization
http://harpy.uccs.edu/greek/mycenae.html
A collection of excellent photographs of Mycenae, its environs, and its major architectural remains.

History of Ancient Egypt
http://www.library.nwu.edu/class/history/B94/
This website, developed as part of a course on the History of Ancient Egypt at Northwestern University, contains extensive text, visual aids (maps, photos, diagrams), bibliography, and Internet links to other resources pertinent to both Egypt and Nubia.

Minoan Civilization
http://dilos.com/region/crete/evans.html
This site, drawing in part on the holdings of the Iraklion Museum on Crete, offers succinct text material and a superb Image Gallery relevant to most of the major sites of Minoan civilization.

Mycenae
http://www.tulane.edu/lester/text/Ancient.World/Mycenae/Mycenae.html
A useful collection of images of Mycenaean sites and art objects.

Oriental Institute Virtual Museum
http://www-oi.uchicago.edu/OI/MUS/QTVR96/QTVR96.html
Maintained by the University of Chicago's Oriental Institute, this is an excellent source of information about the ancient Near East, based on the holdings of the institute.

Photo Gallery of Ancient Mesopotamia
http://www.stolaf.edu/people/kchanson/photogal.html
Besides the high-quality images presented here, there is also a lengthy selection from the Code of Hammurabi.

Sumerian Mythology
http://pubpages.unh.edu/~cbsiren/sumer-faq.html#A1.3.1
This website provides very accurate, quite extensive information about many aspects of Sumerian religious beliefs, including major deities, notions of the underworld, and biblical parallels.

The Early Civilizations of South and East Asia

2

*Hitherto it has commonly been supposed that the pre-Aryan peoples of India were on an altogether lower plane of civilization than their Aryan [Caucasian, Indo-European] conquerors; that to the latter they were much what the Helots were to the Spartans, . . .—a race so servile and degraded, that they were commonly known as Dasas or slaves. . . . Never for a moment was it imagined that five thousand years ago, before ever the Aryans were heard of, the Punjab and Sind, if not other parts of India as well, were enjoying an advanced and singularly uniform civilization of their own, closely akin but in some respects even superior to that of contemporary Mesopotamia and Egypt. . . . They exhibit the Indus people of the fourth and third millennia B.C., in possession of a highly developed culture.**

*In [1899], Liu Tieh-yun. . .was visiting the capital [Peking] as a house guest of Wang I-yung. The host of Liu Tieh-yun was attacked by malarial fever. The doctor's prescriptions included an ingredient of decayed tortoise shell purchased at the drug store. On the tortoise shells Liu Tieh-yun saw seal characters, which he picked out and showed to his host; both of them were somewhat astonished at this discovery. Wang, a student of bronze inscriptions, immediately realized that these tortoise shells must be ancient. He went to the drugstore, to inquire about the source of supply of these ingredients. The manager told him that they came from T'ang-yin and Anyang of Honan province. They were sold at a very low price. Liu Tieh-yun went to the drugstore in the city and purchased them all.***

*John Marshall, ed., *Mohenjo-Daro and the Indus Civilization* (Delhi: Indological Book House, 1973), pp. v, vii.
**Li Chi, *Anyang* (Seattle: University of Washington Press, 1997), p. 8.

The author of the first passage quoted above, Sir John Marshall, headed the first systematic excavation of Indus sites in the 1920s. Workers digging foundations for a railway line in the Indus River valley uncovered remains of brick walls and streets that, as archaeologists confirmed, belonged to the earliest civilization on the Indian subcontinent, a discovery as exciting and important as those of Heinrich Schliemann at Troy in Asia Minor and Mycenae in Greece.

In the second passage, from the journal of a specialist in ancient Chinese writing, the writer tells of the accidental discovery of the earliest specimens of writing, incised on tortoise shells and scapula bones of cattle, and the tracing of those items to the last capital of the Shang dynasty at Anyang. Scientific excavations began at Anyang in the late 1920s just when Marshall was working along the Indus River.

These passages illustrate how archaeological work has enormously increased our knowledge of the past and unlocked its secrets throughout the world. This chapter looks at South Asia (the Indian subcontinent) and East Asia, which is dominated by China. South Asia is bounded by the Hindu Kush range in the northwest and the Himalayas in the northeast, the Arabian Sea in the southwest, and the Bay of Bengal in the southeast. It comprises five nations: India, Pakistan, Bangladesh, Nepal, and Sri Lanka. East Asia is situated between the Pacific Ocean to the east, the Gobi Desert to the north, and the Tien Shan and Himalaya mountains on the west. China, Korea, and Japan occupy eastern Asia.

As happened slightly earlier in Mesopotamia and Egypt, civilizations in South and East Asia first emerged in the Indus River valley in India and the Yellow River valley in China, because the rivers made transportation easy and brought silt that renewed the soil's fertility. China was isolated from other ancient civilizations by the nearly impassable Gobi Desert and the high Himalayas and Tien Shan; the Hindu Kush posed a somewhat lesser barrier between India and western Asia. Current archaeological evidence points to independent indigenous developments of higher civilization in these two regions from Neolithic times.

Both regions underwent periodic invasions that brought new settlers. The Aryan invaders who superseded the first Indus civilization infused large numbers of settlers of a different racial makeup and linguistic heritage. In China, by contrast, the earliest historic dynasty was overtaken by people of the same racial and cultural background, so that its early development suffered no discontinuity. As a result, the people of historic northern India spoke Indo-European languages introduced by the Aryans, while southern Indians spoke languages of the indigenous Dravidian group. No such divide affected the Chinese, whose current writing system evolved in form directly from the first extant script.

The Indus Civilization

The most striking feature of the Indus Civilization is its homogeneity. Within the farthest limits of the Indus Empire its uniform products are easily distinguishable from those of the Mesopotamian and Egyptian civilizations. This remarkable uniformity in the form and content of its products should be attributed to the early realization of the advantages of standardization on the part of the Harappans. Wherever they settled down they introduced a uniform system of civic administrations, built towns and cities on identical gridiron plans with neatly laid-out streets and lanes, maintained a high standard of public sanitation, used similar earthen and metalwares, produced the same types of tools and weapons, and organized trade of a uniform pattern. Even the sizes of houses and bricks, tools and ornaments were standardized. . . .

*Another remarkable feature of the Indus Civilization is its individuality, which was zealously guarded against any serious inroads by alien cultures. In spite of extensive trade contacts with the Mesopotamians and Egyptians, Harappans did not adopt the western system of writing. The rectangular steatite seals and cubical stone weights of the Indus people differed as much from the duck- and barrel-shaped weights and cylinder seals of the Mesopotamians as did their pictographic script from the cuneiform writing of the latter.**

*S. R. Rao, *Lothal and the Indus Civilization* (New York: Asia Publishing House, 1973), p. 5.

S. R. Rao is an eminent Indian archaeologist of the Indus civilization and author of the above passage. Since the 1920s, the excavation of dozens of sites along the Indus River and in other parts of northwestern India and Pakistan has led him and other archaeologists to conclude that this highly developed civilization was homogeneous. They also agree that the Indus civilization remained unique in important ways despite extensive trade with Mesopotamia and other regions to the west.

The Land of India

The Indian subcontinent, also called South Asia, is a little less than half the size of the United States. It is bor-

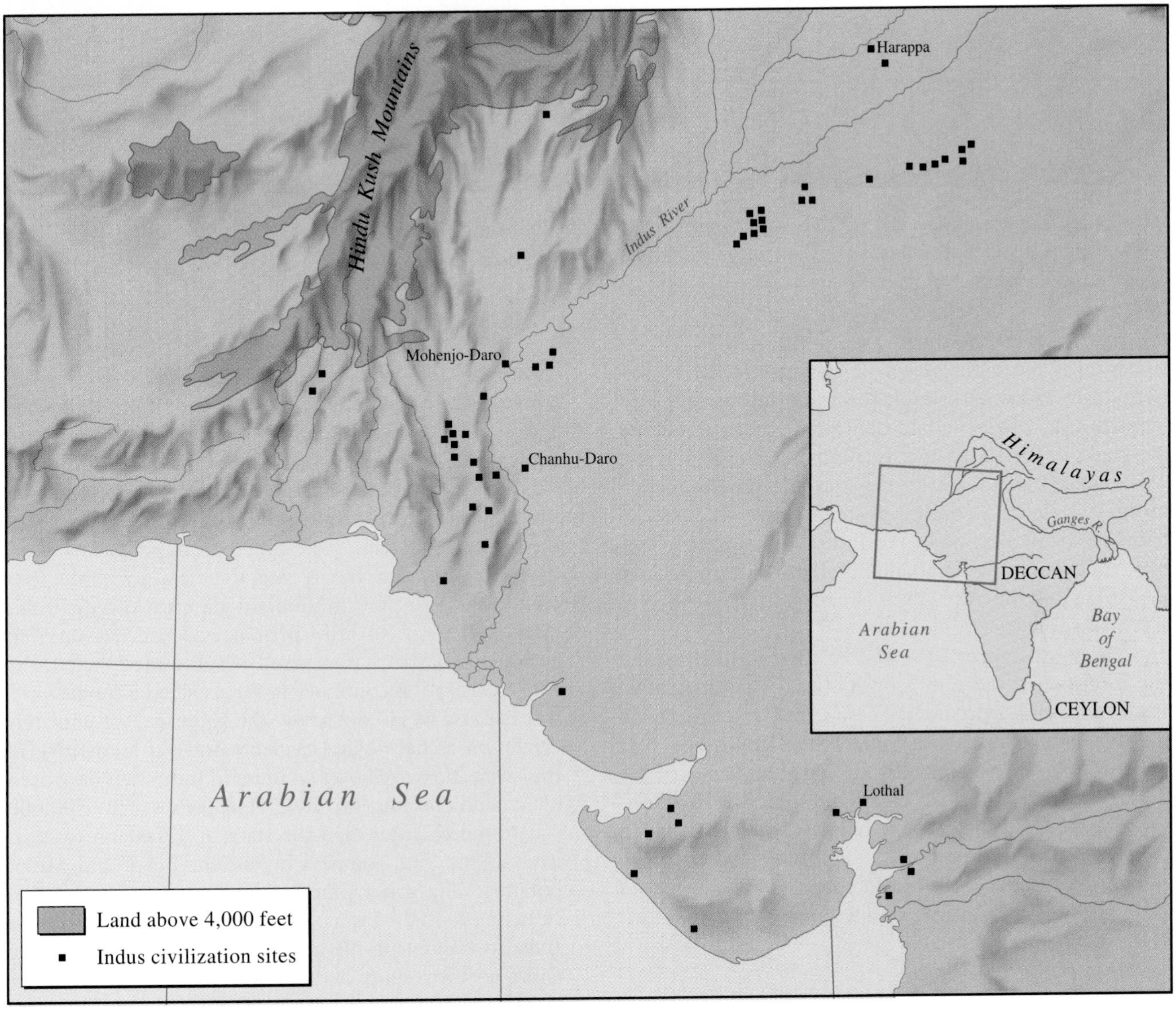

Map 2.1 Indus Valley Civilization. The earliest civilization on the Indian subcontinent flourished between 2500 and 1500 B.C.E. in an 800-mile stretch extending along the banks of the Indus River and its tributaries to the coast of the Arabian Sea. Indus cities were planned and prosperous, and the peoples traded with other parts of India and Mesopotamia.

dered on the north by the Hindu Kush and Himalayas, the latter the world's tallest mountain range; with their extensions to the east and west, these separate India from the rest of Asia and make it a distinct subcontinent. Formidable though the mountains are, they did not prevent the movement of settlers, traders, and warriors to and from India. The mountains are also the source of two great river systems. To the west is the Indus, which gave its name to India and which empties into the Arabian Sea. To the east the Ganges joins the Brahmaputra to form the largest delta in the world, as the two mighty rivers empty into the Bay of Bengal. The Thar, or Desert of Rajastan, divides the Indus from the Ganges River. In more recent times the Gangetic Plain, together with that of the Brahmaputra, has been the heartland of India.

South of the great river plains is peninsular India, whose core is the Deccan Plateau, bordered by the Eastern and Western Ghats, or hills, and beyond them, the coastal plains. The Tamil Plain at the southeastern tip of the peninsula is home to a distinct ethnic and cultural group. Geographically the island of Sri Lanka (formerly Ceylon) is a continuation of south India. From north to south the subcontinent spans approximately 2,000 miles.

India has a wide variety of climates, from cold winters in the Himalayan foothills to searing summers in the northern plains, to year-round high temperatures in the south. Climate and natural conditions have changed

Indus Seals. Many seals of engraved stone have been found throughout the Indus Valley and in Mesopotamia. A variety of animals and humanlike figures are found on the seals, as well as characters of an undeciphered pictographic writing that is unrelated to any other known writing system.

significantly since the dawn of civilization. From Neolithic times down through the third and second millennia B.C.E. when the first civilization developed along the banks of the Indus and its tributaries, the region was well watered and featured marshes and jungles. Later, more arid climatic conditions in the lower Indus contributed to the decline of the Indus civilization. By the time Alexander the Great and his army reached this area in 326 B.C.E., much of it was already a barren desert, as it remains today.

The most important feature in the Indian climate is the monsoon ("the rain"), which comes pelting down from June until September. These rains bring relief from the suffocating heat, turn the parched land green, and make agriculture possible. To this day, the quality of the harvest depends on the intensity and timing of the monsoon season. Not surprisingly, Indians look on rain-laden dark clouds and thunder and lightning as beneficent signs from heaven. Between October and May hardly a drop of rain falls in most of India, making irrigation indispensable for farming.

The Beginning of the Indus Civilization

By around 3000 B.C.E., Neolithic peoples who lived in the Indus valley evolved the first civilizations in India, just as civilizations were emerging in the Nile and Tigris-Euphrates valleys. Sites and artifacts of the earliest stages of the Indus civilization are found sixty-eight feet below ground level along the banks of the Indus, much below the water table, making archaeological work extremely difficult. Successively higher levels show continuous development from Neolithic beginnings. Unlike Egypt and Mesopotamia, however, where much of our knowledge comes from written records, the Indus civilization must be reconstructed from other evidence. Although a system of writing developed in the Indus valley, the longest surviving inscription is only twenty-five words; most specimens of Indus writing are short pictographic inscriptions averaging five words, carved on little seals about one inch square or in diameter. The carvings likely were used as stamps to mark ownership of merchandise; they probably represent personal or company names, or short prayers. Most seals also have carved animals or deitylike figures. Thousands of seals have been found throughout the Indus valley and also in Mesopotamia, but no Indian equivalent of a Rosetta Stone has been discovered that unlocks the secrets of the language. Pottery shards predating the Harappan era of the culture bear cruder versions of the pictographic seals, indicating that the script was an indigenous invention. In any case, the messages on the seals are too short to allow meaningful glimpses into the Indus culture. Because so little written evidence has survived and because what has survived is still undeciphered, the Indus civilization continues to be classified as prehistoric.

Because we do not know the language, we must rely chiefly on archaeological evidence for our knowledge of this civilization. Well over a thousand Indus sites have been identified, covering an area of approximately 300,000 square miles, larger than the state of Texas and twice as large as the area occupied by ancient Egypt and Mesopotamia. The geographic boundaries of the civilization stretch beyond the Indus valley to include all northwestern India to Kashmir in the north, Delhi in the east, and the entire northern shore of the Arabian Sea. The three largest cities excavated bear the modern names Harappa, in Punjab; Mohenjo-Daro, in Sind, 400 miles to the southwest beside the Indus in present-day Pakistan; and Lothal, on the coast in present-day India. Many features, such as the size of bricks and the urban plans, including an elevated mound in each city center, were uniform throughout the area. Hence, archaeologists refer to the civilization as the Harappan culture or the Indus Empire.

An Urban Culture: Mohenjo-Daro

Since Mohenjo-Daro is the best preserved and one of the most systematically excavated cities of the Indus culture, it stands as the prototype for other cities in the region. Mohenjo-Daro was centered around an artificial mound, about fifty feet high, which was fortified by a brick wall with towers. Stores of ammunition stones indicate that this was a citadel. The citadel also has a great bath or tank, thirty-nine feet by twenty-three feet, flanked by a large pillared hall and small cell-like rooms. Archaeologists guess that the pool and hall served a religious or ritual purpose. Since no palace that might have housed royal rulers has been found, archaeologists further deduce that a high priest or a college of priests may have ruled the city. Scholars also surmise that the ritual tanks found alongside Hindu temples in later India may have had their origin in the great bath of the Indus cities. A magnificent granary of brick and timber, with loading platform and ventilation holes, completes the structures on the citadel.

Below the citadel spreads a well-laid-out city, perhaps the earliest example of urban planning. The main broad avenues were oriented north-south; they were intersected by lesser east-west lanes in a grid system. Certain parts of the town were designated for shops; other areas were used by other occupational groups. All buildings were made of baked bricks of uniform size, suggesting a powerful centralized authority.

Merchants' houses in the prosperous residential districts were substantial; the ground floor was about thirty feet square on average, and many had second and third stories. No windows faced the street; instead the rooms opened on a central courtyard. This style of house is found in India today and throughout tropical and temperate areas from China to North Africa. On both the ground and second floors were bathrooms with drains flowing to underground sewers that ended in soak pits (like our septic tanks). Some houses had private wells, but public wells at street intersections provided water for those without them. These features, the state granary, and the sentry boxes found scattered throughout the city could only have been maintained by a highly sophisticated government.

The workers' living quarters also indicate a prosperous economy. They lived comfortably by the standards of the era (and even by present-day living standards of Indian workers) in two-room cottages, with bathrooms with bathing platforms and toilets lined with brick supports for seating, each unit being about twelve feet by twenty feet in Mohenjo-Daro and even bigger in Harappa.

Society and Economy

Anthropologists who have studied the skeletal remains of the Indus people conclude that several racial groups were represented among them. Adults ranged between five feet five inches and five feet nine inches in height. The average life span was around thirty years (the norm for Indians until the early twentieth century). Then as now, most of the noncity dwellers farmed. The main food crops were wheat, barley, peas, sesame, melon, and dates. We cannot be certain whether they irrigated their crops, but we do know they were the first people in the world to grow and weave cotton. Their domestic animals included humped cattle, horses, goats, sheep, pigs, and fowl. Elephants figure in the seals, but we do not know whether they had been tamed; in any case, their ivory was widely used.

Trade flourished. Boats carried goods along the Indus River and the seacoast to West Asia. Lothal, a major seaport, had the world's oldest scientifically designed docks in an artificial basin that took into consideration the water level of high and low tides. Land routes connected the Indus valley with other parts of India. A bead factory found at Lothal has ten rooms and measures 5,380 square feet. Indus artists made jewelry from lapis lazuli (a semiprecious stone possibly from Afghanistan), gold, turquoise from Iran, conch shells

Randy Olson/NGS Image Collection

An Archaeological Dig in Progress. The Indus people built with bricks. Workers here have uncovered an ancient drainage channel that once carried waste water out of the city.

Artist's Drawing Recreating an Indus-Era Market. Lothal and other cities specialized in beadmaking for local purchase and for export. Here a merchant is weighing semiprecious stones such as turquoise and lapis lazuli used for making beads.

from the Arabian Sea, and locally mined carnelian. Perishable items such as textiles and woods may also have been exchanged. Numerous Indus seals and pottery items found in Mesopotamia testify to trade between the two civilizations. Sumerian and Akkadian cuneiform documents from about 2400–2000 B.C.E. mention a land called Dilmun or Telmun in the east with which there was organized trade; these documents may have referred to the Indus civilization.

Indus artisans displayed talent in a large number of basic crafts. They used the wheel to make pottery vessels of many shapes and sizes for food, drink, cooking, and storage. They also created utensils of stone, ivory, copper, bronze, and silver. They used the lost-wax method, as did the ancient Greeks, to cast metal ornaments and tools, in contrast to the piece mold method of the ancient Chinese. Some ivory combs, copper mirrors, beads made from a variety of materials, and gold and silver jewelry show very fine workmanship and artistry. The many toys and games, such as miniature terra cotta animals, whistles, rattles, and bird cages, show the loving care that adults must have lavished on their children. From excavations in other parts of northern India, it is clear that the Indus culture had a wide influence beyond its immediate region.

Indus Religion

In the absence of written documents, it is difficult to write definitively about the religion of the Indus people. As we observed, archaeologists speculate that they used the Great Bath and the adjoining Assembly Hall in Mohenjo-Daro for religious and ritual purposes, and that a college of priests lived in the rows of small rooms nearby. Excavations have revealed neither temples nor monumental sculptures nor large religious statues such as those in Egypt. However, "fire altars" were found, suggesting the practice of fire worship, perhaps similar to that practiced by later, Vedic peoples. Many terra cotta figurines have been discovered, like those found in sites from Egypt to Iran. The pregnant-looking female figurines, often molded together with children, may represent the Great Mother or nature goddesses. Analogous female nature deities were widespread in the Eastern Mediterranean. There are also nude male figurines; the best example is a three-faced horned figure, nude except for his jewelry, seated with crossed legs in the yoga position and surrounded by four animals—an elephant, a tiger, a rhinoceros, and a buffalo. This image has been called a prototype of Shiva, the later three-faced Hindu god of death, destruction, and fertility, and the lord of beasts.

Indus people may also have worshiped trees and animals, including the bull, which is very common on the seals and in later Hinduism is strongly associated with Shiva. The cow, however, though a nearly universal symbol of later Hinduism, is absent from Indus imagery. The dead were carefully buried in cemeteries, laid out with their heads to the north. Grave goods, though not elaborate, include painted pottery jars, occasionally weapons, and sometimes a sacrificed sheep or goat. We do not know the significance of the burial practices.

The End of Indus Civilization

Civilizations rise and fall for complex reasons. No single cause can account for the decline of the widely distributed Indus civilization, nor can a definite date be assigned to its end. One apparent cause was extensive flooding, likely a result of deforestation and overgrazing. But even more important were major geological changes in the beginning of the second millennium B.C.E. These included coastal uplifts in the northern shores of the Arabian Sea that moved several Indus-era ports as much as thirty-five miles inland. Such dramatic changes ruined the lives and economies of the people in the lower Indus region but left unscathed the life of Harappa farther upriver. We may deduce the interruption of long-distance trade from the almost complete disappearance of seals in the late levels of Mohenjo-Daro and Lothal. The uplift prevented the river's water from reaching the sea and created huge shallow lakes upstream—a condition that probably persisted for decades. Flooding would explain the layers of silt as much as seventy feet deep around Mohenjo-Daro, and the huge embankments, some twenty-five feet high, and other community projects built to keep out the floodwaters. Since such flood-control mechanisms are major undertakings, smaller towns and settlements were no doubt simply abandoned to the floodwaters. In time the floodwaters spilled over the natural barriers and the river resumed its course to the sea. The people of Mohenjo-Daro were then left with the massive task of reinforcing or replacing flood-damaged structures.

This process was repeated at least five times at Mohenjo-Daro. The people, worn out and impoverished by the repeated efforts to fight the floods, endured declining living standards, evidenced in the shoddier construction of later houses, built on the ruins of their predecessors or on artificial platforms raised to avoid flood crests. Economic decline and population pressures are visible everywhere as shanty towns superseded spacious residences and rabbit warrens overspread once neatly laid out streets. Around 1900 B.C.E. the Indus River changed course and a parallel river, the Saravasti, dried up, further contributing to the economic ruin.

Then invading barbarian settlers from the west, descending on the Indus plains through the passes of the Hindu Kush, brought additional pressures to bear. Defensive measures are evident in the last centuries of the Indus cities. Mohenjo-Daro's great citadel was fortified by a brick wall with towers, and Harappa's massive turreted walls were forty feet wide at the base and thirty-five feet tall; its western gate was wholly blocked up to repel invaders from the west. In the centuries after 2000 B.C.E., newcomers settled in villages in outlying areas. Their crude pottery was coarser than the vessels made by the Indus peoples. Fleeing refugees must have streamed into the walled cities for protection, causing further economic and social strains. A potter's kiln built in the middle of a street indicates collapsing municipal standards. Caches of hoarded jewelry speak eloquently of the breakdown of law and order.

Before the end came, most of the inhabitants of Mohenjo-Daro had fled. Several groups of skeletons have been found in dead-end streets, strewn helter-skelter with axe and knife wounds in the skulls, or huddled by wells, then covered by debris. These remains vividly suggest how the last stragglers met their doom. Fires probably destroyed the sacked city. The bodies must have been burnt or buried to prevent contamination.

Harappa and other nearby settlements, which had not suffered previous decline, were abruptly and permanently abandoned. The inhabitants either fled at the threat of invasion or were expelled. At Chanhu-Daro, farther downriver, Indus inhabitants were replaced by squatters, whose huts had fireplaces, a feature unknown to Indus architecture, suggesting that the owners had come from colder climates. Among the scattered remains of the newcomers are copper axes and swords with reinforcing midribs superior to anything the Indus people possessed.

By about 1500 B.C.E., the Indus civilization had perished. While scholars still debate the precise individual causes, it clearly succumbed to a combination of factors. Deforestation and degradation of the environment and natural catastrophes first weakened both the morale and the economy of the Indus peoples. Then, from the north

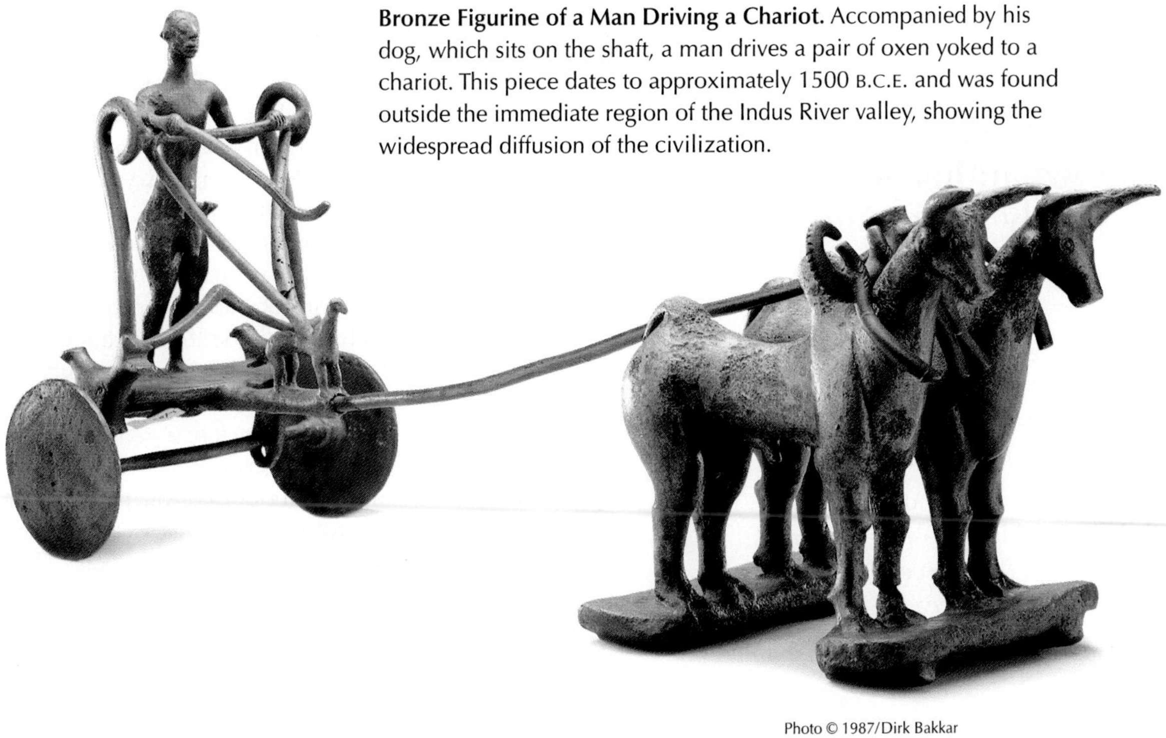

Bronze Figurine of a Man Driving a Chariot. Accompanied by his dog, which sits on the shaft, a man drives a pair of oxen yoked to a chariot. This piece dates to approximately 1500 B.C.E. and was found outside the immediate region of the Indus River valley, showing the widespread diffusion of the civilization.

Government of Pakistan, Department of Archeology and Museums

Bearded Man Found at Mohenjo-Daro. Very little statuary from the Indus civilization has been discovered. We do not know whether this figure was a deity or a man.

and west, came waves of dynamic and warlike invaders and settlers called Aryans, wielding superior weapons and riding swift and terrifying horse-drawn chariots.

The Aryan Invasion and Early Vedic Age

To Indra

I will declare the manly deeds of Indra, the first that he
achieved, the thunder-wielder.
He slew the dragon, then disclosed the waters, and cleft
the channels of the mountain torrents.

He slew the dragon lying on the mountain; his
heavenly bolt of thunder Tvashtar fashioned.
Like lowing kine in rapid flow descending the waters
glided downward to the ocean.

Impetuous as a bull, he chose the Soma, and in three
beakers drank the juices.
The Bounteous One grasped the thunder for his
weapon, and smote to death this first born
of the dragons.

When Indra, thou hadst slain the dragon's first born,
and overcome the charms of the enchanters,
Then, giving life to sun and dawn and heaven, thou
foundest not one foe to stand against thee.

Indra with his own great and deadly thunder smote into
pieces Vritra, worst of Vritras,
As trunk of trees, what time the axe hath felled them,
low on the earth so lies the prostrate dragon.

He, like a mad weak warrior, challenged Indra, the
great impetuous many-slaying hero.
He, brooking not the clashing of the weapons, crushed—
*Indra's foe—the shattered forts in falling.**

*Robert O. Ballou, ed., *The Bible of the World* (New York: Viking, 1939), pp. 5–6.

These six verses of a hymn to Indra are from the Rig-Veda, the holiest book of the Aryans who settled in India and also of Hinduism, a religion that developed out of the beliefs of the Aryans and the indigenous Indian peoples. For generations the Aryan priests memorized the songs of praise in a language that was Indo-European and closely related to Greek and Latin. About 1000 B.C.E., these songs were written down in Sanskrit, an alphabetical script of the Indo-European family. Indra was an important god in the *Rig-Veda*. This hymn portrays him as a hard-drinking warrior who killed dragons and demolished forts. He was also the god of thunder and the bringer of rain.

The word *Aryan* is the Anglicized form for *Aryas* in Sanskrit. It means "noble of birth and race," as the fair-complexioned invaders described themselves, in contrast to the natives whom they called *dasas*, meaning dark skinned, or of "dasa color." *Dasa* in Sanskrit came to mean "slave." Sometime after 2000 B.C.E. the Aryans pushed through the mountain passes that separate Afghanistan from northwestern India. The movement spanned several centuries and included many tribes that sometimes fought each other. Tools and weapons of bronze and copper discovered in northwestern India in association with the early Aryans are very similar in type and date to those found in south Russia, the Caucasus, and Iran. They suggest that the Aryan invaders of India were closely related to the Indo-Europeans who spilled over Europe and Iran in equally dynamic migrations in about the same period.

In material development, the Aryans were less advanced than the people of the Indus civilization. They were not city dwellers, and after conquering the Indus cities, they abandoned them to ruin. There were no significant cities in India for the next 1,000 years, and the remains of the villages with houses of wood and other perishable materials have long since vanished. Thus India from 1500 to 500 B.C.E. is almost an archaeological blank; knowledge about it comes mainly from literary sources.

Early Vedic Society and Economy

The earliest literary sources for the history of India are the hymns and prayers of the Rig-Veda, the literature of the Aryan invaders. These hymns are primarily addressed to male deities. They were memorized by the priests for recital at religious ceremonies, as they are to the present day. After about 1000 B.C.E. and the appearance of writing, the hymns were compiled and written down. Although primarily religious and metaphysical in character, the Vedas and other early writings do contain some historical reference points that supply information about the life of the community during the 1,000-year period of the Vedic Age.

The Aryans were organized according to tribes, each ruled by a hereditary chief, called a *raja* (related to the Latin word *rex*, or "king"). The main function of the raja was to lead his people in war. He was not absolute and had to consult a tribal assembly before making decisions. He had no religious function, except to order sacrifices and provide support for the priests, who were important because they composed, memorized, and passed down to succeeding generations of priests the hymns of the Rig-Veda and other sacred works. They also presided at ceremonies and conducted sacrifices to maintain cosmic order and ensure tribal prosperity in peace and victory in war.

Aryan society was already divided into social classes before the invasion. As the Aryans settled in India among dark-skinned indigenous people, they put more stress on purity of bloodline and class divisions. By the end of the early Vedic period, society had been divided into four great classes; children were born into their father's class and could not change it. This division was given religious sanction. The groupings were based on function and on skin color, called *varna* in Sanskrit. Thus the old tribal class structure was expanded to include people of different skin complexion. In English the word "caste" or "class" is commonly used to refer to these groups. They were, in descending order, the priests (*brahmans*), the warriors (*kshatriyas*), the landholders and artisans (*vaisyas*), and the serfs and servants (*sudras*). The first three castes included the fair-skinned Aryans, while the fourth consisted of the dark-skinned natives. In later centuries the originally intended racial distinctions became blurred as the religion of the Aryans outpaced their physical penetration of India. Thus in South India where there were few Aryans, members of all castes tended to be non-Aryans. These basic divisions, with many subdivisions, survive to the present.

The Aryan social unit was the patrilineal and patriarchal family. Marriages were usually monogamous and apparently indissoluble. Although the wife and mother enjoyed respect, a woman was definitely subordinate to her husband. Daughters were less desired than sons. The Rig-Veda describes unmarried young men and women mixing freely and does not indicate that married women were secluded, as became normal in later times.

Hymn of the Primeval Man

From that all-embracing sacrifice
were born the hymns and chants,
from that the metres were born,
from that the sacrificial spells were born.

Thence were born horses,
and all beings with two rows of teeth.
Thence were born cattle,
and thence goats and sheep

When they divided the Man,
into how many parts did they divide him?
What was his mouth, what were his arms,
what were his thighs and his feet called?

The Brahman was his mouth,
of his arms was made the warrior,
his thighs became the vaisya,
of his feet the sudra was born.

The moon arose from his mind,
from his eyes was born the sun,
from his mouth Indra and Agni,
from his breath the wind was born.

From his navel came the air,
from his head there came the sky,
from his feet the earth, the four quarters from his ear,
*thus they fashioned the worlds.**

The preceding verses from a hymn in the Rig-Veda describe how the universe and all within it were created and justify a social order in which humans were divided into four major categories, each with its function. These four divisions are called "castes" in English (*varna*, meaning "color" in Sanskrit). Each caste is subdivided into occupational or geographic groups called *jati*, which remain the foundation of Hindu society.

*A. L. Basham, *The Wonder That Was India* (New York: Grove Press, 1954), pp. 240–241.

© Charles & Josette Lenars/Corbis

Indra. An important Vedic god, Indra is here depicted as the king of heaven, trailing clouds and accompanied by celestial nymphs. This figure is part of a Buddhist cave wall painting dating to between the fifth and seventh centuries C.E. By then Indra had been supplanted in worship by other deities, but he remained a celestial god to both Hindus and Buddhists.

The Aryans practiced a mixed pastoral and farming economy. They prized cattle for status and wealth; they valued horses as well, though mainly for military reasons. Domestic animals included sheep (for wool), goats, and dogs. Cows did not have the sacred status of later times, nor were there strictures against eating meat. Most people were farmers and lived in villages. Arable land appears to have been privately owned, but grazing land was probably held in common and manuring and irrigation were practiced. Artisans such as carpenters, metalworkers and tanners formed subcastes, plied their specialties, and lived in both towns and villages. Most trade was by barter, but cattle were also used as currency in important exchanges. There is no information about international trade in the Vedic Age as there was in the Indus era, and no Vedic Age artifacts have been discovered outside India.

Religion

Our knowledge of early Aryan religion comes from the Rig-Veda. By the time its hymns were written down hundreds of years after they had been composed, many of the words used in them had become archaic and their meanings unclear. The hymns therefore represent an amalgamation of the beliefs of several different Aryan tribes and are not systematic. Nevertheless, hymns from the Rig-Veda are still recited at weddings and funerals and in the daily devotions of brahmans, and they remain part of the living Hindu tradition.

The objects of Aryan worship were the devas, a Sanskrit word related to *deus*, which means "god" in Latin. Foremost among the gods was Indra, who in some respects resembled the Greek god Zeus, a successful warrior who killed the dasas and demolished their forts. Agni was the fire god (compare Latin *ignis* which means fire), also god of the hearth and home. He accepted the sacrifices offered by humans and carried them to the other gods, and as such was an intermediary between gods and humans. Soma was both a god and a hallucinogenic drink made from a hemp-type plant and drunk at religious ceremonies. Yama was the lord of the dead. Rudra was the archer god, who was feared and avoided because his arrows brought disease; but he was also the healer god and gave good health to those he liked. Varuna was the ethical god and guardian of the moral order who abhorred sin and punished sinners by inflicting them with disease, especially dropsy, and by condemning them to a gloomy House of Clay after death. Aryans who had performed the proper rites, however, were believed to feast forever in happiness after they died. The Vedas tell of many other gods, demigods, divine musicians, gnomes, goddesses, and *apsarases*, who were similar to the nymphs of the Greeks. Unfortunately, ancient India never did have the equivalent of a Homer or Hesiod of ancient Greece, so we do not have a clear genealogy of the deities of the Aryans, and their relationships are often unclear.

Aryan religion centered on many kinds of sacrifices, ranging from the daily domestic hearth sacrifices performed by the head of the family to the great sacrifices ordered by rulers and chiefs, presided over by many brahmans, and requiring the slaughter of many animals. The goal in each case was to gain the favor of gods, who were believed to descend to earth, partake of the offerings, and then bless the participants by granting their requests for success in war, health, long life, children, good crops, and so forth. The participants drank soma, felt bigger than life, and were rewarded with a sense of well-being.

Aryan religious ceremonies became more complex with the passage of time. Their correct performance came to be regarded as essential not only to individual and community well-being but also to the maintenance of the cosmic order.

The Appearance of Writing

Sanskrit and all other Indo-European languages are related because they all trace back to the spoken tongue of common ancestors who lived in the steppes of the Eurasian plains around 4,000 years ago. Many key Sanskrit, Greek, and Latin words obviously share the same origin, and many grammatical rules of the three ancient languages are similar. The Rig-Veda, which is written in the earliest surviving form of Sanskrit, bears the same relationship to later classical Sanskrit as Homeric Greek to classical Greek.

By the time the Rig-Veda was written, its language was already archaic. Classical Sanskrit, which developed in the first centuries of the first millennium B.C.E., had a less complex grammar and included new words, many borrowed from non-Aryan languages. Even then it was probably never used by ordinary Aryan peoples, who spoke dialects with simpler grammar. The spoken or vernacular tongues were called Prakrits, which literally means "unrefined" or popular languages, as opposed to the "perfected" or "refined" or "Sanskrit" of the scholars. Because Sanskrit was used by the priests (and probably by other members of the upper class) and by government officials, it became a universal language for the subcontinent. Even now brahman scholars from different parts of India can communicate with one another through Sanskrit.

Although writing began around 1000 B.C.E., no document from earlier than the third century B.C.E. has survived. By the time the Vedas were written down, classical Sanskrit had evolved so much from Vedic Sanskrit that scholars and priests concerned with preserving the purity of the religious texts developed the sciences of linguistics and grammar. The oldest extant Indian linguistic text dates to the fifth century B.C.E. and explains obsolete Vedic words. Toward the end of the fourth century B.C.E. a great grammar book, entitled *Eight Chapters*, was written. Sanskrit became standardized, and also perhaps fossilized after the completion of the *Eight Chapters*. It ceased to develop, whereas the Prakrits evolved into modern vernaculars.

The languages of south India belong to the Dravidian group. They are unrelated to Indo-European languages although in time many Sanskrit words were incorporated into their vocabularies. The oldest Dravidian written language is Tamil. The earliest literature in the Tamil language dates to the beginning of the common era.

The Late Vedic Age

Satyakama son of Jabala said to his mother: "Mother, I want to be a student. What is my family?"

"I don't know your family, my dear," she said. "I had you in my youth, when I travelled about a lot as a servant—and I just don't know! My name is Jabala, and yours is Satyakama Jabala."

He went to Gautama Haridrumata, and said: "I want to be your student, sir. May I come?"

"What is your family, my friend?" he asked.

"I don't know my family, sir," he answered. "I asked my mother, and she said that she had me in her youth, when she used to travel about a lot as a servant. . . . She said that as she was Jabala and I was Satyakama. I was to give my name as Satyakama Jabala."

*"Nobody but a true brahman would be so honest!" he said. . . . "Go and fetch me fuel, my friend, and I will initiate you, for you have not swerved from the truth."**

*Robert O. Ballou, ed., *The Bible of the World* (New York: Viking, 1939), p. 254.

This passage from an Upanishad extols the virtue of honesty. Ethical behavior was one of the qualities given high emphasis in the quest for truth and salvation that characterized the late Vedic age (about 1000–500 B.C.E.), the five centuries between the composition of the Rig-Veda and the age of the Buddha. Old rituals and sacrifices to the Aryan tribal gods had lost their appeal, and the goal of thinking people was to seek truth and understand the nature of the brahman, or the essential divine reality of the universe. In so doing, scholars brought about new philosophical developments within the existing religious pattern and founded new, breakaway religions.

Our sources of the period are still predominantly sacred literature and the Upanishads, essays that deal with religious and philosophical questions. In addition, there are epic tales about the period, though they were written later. The greatest of those epics is the *Mahabharata*, which survives in two versions; both tell the story of a gigantic war that began in a dispute over the dynastic succession in the Kuru tribe and eventually involved all of India. Corroborative evidence shows that between the tenth and ninth centuries a great war did take place, probably centered in modern-day Delhi. The names of many of the heroes in the epic may indeed be those of contemporary chieftains. However, it is not possible to reconstruct an accurate political history from the epic. Since archaeological work on this era of Indian history is far less comprehensive than that done in Greece, the *Mahabharata* is of even less use to the historian of India than the *Iliad* is to historians of ancient Greece. Both epics served the purpose of providing models of heroic behavior to their societies.

Despite the scarcity of sources, it is known that during the Late Vedic period Aryan society expanded across northern India along the Himalayan foothills and the Jumna and Ganges Plains to the Bay of Bengal. The center of culture and political power in India shifted from the Indus to the Ganges Valley. The earlier conquered land of Sind and the Punjab (which means "five rivers" because of its location on the upper Indus, where five tributaries converge on the main river) were almost forgotten and, when mentioned, were described as inhabited by the impure, that is non-Aryan, people. Tribal groups had formed into territorial states with permanent capital cities and rudimentary administrative systems. The kings, almost exclusively kshatriyas, now wielded judicial as well as military power. The formerly powerful tribal assemblies were discarded, replaced by courtiers who served the kings.

Late Vedic Society and Economy

The Late Vedic Age was more advanced economically and materially than the previous era. As the tribes settled down and cleared forests, agriculture became more important than animal herding. Most people lived in villages, but the texts mention cities; Ujjian, for example, retains its seventh-century name unchanged. Situated in the present state of Vindhya Pradesh, it was then the capital city of a kingdom and a holy city; it is still sacred to Hinduism.

The texts also note many subcastes of craftsmen and new grain crops. While many continued to eat meat, others began to regard meat eating with disfavor, because new ideals of respect for animal life were developing. There is some, but not conclusive, evidence that India once more traded with Mesopotamia in this period. Caste distinctions became more pronounced and rigid; the members of all four castes found their lives more strictly regulated. Brahmans and kshatriyas, however, increasingly enjoyed privileges denied to vaisyas and sudras, and the gap between the top and bottom of society grew wider. At the top, brahmans enjoyed immense power and prestige, for they were indispensable to the conduct of sacrifices and the maintenance of a correct relationship between this world and the cosmic order. At the lower end, the sudras were regarded as impure. The size of the sudra caste grew constantly, as conquered or assimilated tribal people were added to Aryan-dominated society.

Unlike some other ancient civilizations, Vedic society did not have large numbers of slaves, and no caste of slaves as such existed. Slavery existed, however. War captives became slaves to the victors until ransomed. Undesirable work that some societies relegated to slaves was given to people later known as outcastes or untouchables, a group lower than sudras. Outcastes were considered ritually impure; they were assigned menial and unpleasant tasks, served the rest of society, and were excluded from the Aryan social order. Some outcastes were descended from conquered aborigines. Others were descended from men and women who had been "outcasted" because of severe infractions of caste rules. Still others might have been members of professions that came to be considered impure in the new moral scheme.

Indirect evidence warrants the conclusion that in this period the position of women declined from its earlier relatively high level. Child marriages, in which young girls were sent to live under the authority of their husbands' parents, were common, and had the effect of keeping young women subordinated. Another new practice allowed upper-caste men to take concubines or secondary wives from the sudra caste.

Religion

During the Late Vedic period two religious trends emerged. First, brahman religious leaders challenged the kings' pretensions to political absolutism. Second, men not traditionally associated with religious leadership, as well as some brahmans who were dissatisfied with traditional ways, began to offer new religious ideas that challenged the established religious rituals and prescribed sacrifices. One of these ideas was the doctrine of ***karma*** (literally "deed"), which held that one's position in this life is the result of deeds and actions in past lives, and that one's present deeds will affect future lives as the soul passes from life to life into infinity. This doctrine of the transmigration of souls—that the soul moves from one

Lessons from the Upanishads

"Fetch me a fruit of the banyan tree."

"Here is one, sir."

"Break it."

"I have broken it sir."

"What do you see?

"Very tiny seeds, sir."

"Break one."

"I have broken it, sir."

"Now what do you see?"

"Nothing, sir."

"My son," the father said, "what you do not perceive is the essence, and in that essence the mighty banyan tree exists. Believe me, my son, in that essence is the Self of all that is. That is the True, that is the Self. And you are that Self, Svetaketu!"

"Put this salt in water, and come to me in the morning."

The son did as he was told. The father said: "Fetch the salt." The son looked for it, but could not find it, because it had dissolved.

"Taste the water from the top," said the father. "How does it taste?"

"Of salt," the son replied.

"Taste from the bottom. How does it taste?"

"Of salt," the son replied.

*Then the father said, "You don't perceive that the one Reality exists in your own body, my son, but it is truly there. Everything which is has its being in that subtle essence. That is Reality! That is the Soul! And you are that, Svetaketu!"**

The dominant theme of the Upanishads was a search for knowledge or understanding of the mystery of this unintelligible world and one's place in it. These two passages from an Upanishad assert that salvation is found through knowledge of or realization of the individual self (the *atman*) and the absolute self (*brahman*). The wise person realizes that the two are the same, and his highest quest is then to seek a synthesis of the two. When one achieves that, one is freed from transmigration.

*Robert O. Ballou, ed., *The Bible of the World* (New York: Viking, 1939), pp. 250–251.

body to another from life to life—gave an ethical content to one's actions, and it explained and justified the inequalities in Aryan society. It also linked all forms of life into one comprehensive system that included humans, animals, insects, and, according to some, even inanimate matter. The belief in karma, that one's conduct determined one's status in future existences, became fundamental to all religions originating in India.

The political changes discussed earlier and the development of new ethical and religious ideals combined to cause a pessimistic outlook on the world that is characteristic of the Late Vedic period. This mood caused several developments; one was the trend toward asceticism. Ascetics were men, and occasionally women, of any caste, whose quest for wisdom had led them to abandon the material world in favor of a life of wandering and meditation. They also performed mystical exercises requiring great discipline of both mind and body, with the goal of developing their psychic faculties and insights beyond ordinary understanding. Similarly, in classical Greece, Socrates, in the *Phaedo*, said that the true philosopher is in training for death (that is, the final separation of the soul from the body and its distractions). The ascetic way of life had ancient roots in India. Some hymns of the Rig-Veda even mention a class of holy men who, as a result of meditation and the practice of austerities, acquired great wisdom and powers of perception beyond ordinary people's understanding.

By about 600 B.C.E., toward the end of the Vedic Age, asceticism had become very widespread, and it was through the ascetics rather than the orthodox brahman priests that new religious teachings developed. Some ascetics, in groups or alone, wandered the country, teaching and debating with one another. Others lived rather permanently on the outskirts of towns and villages. Some groups were led by a senior teacher. The movement toward asceticism was certainly in part a protest against the pretensions of the brahmans and their sacrificial cult, though some brahmans who felt the traditional cult to be inadequate also became ascetics.

The Upanishads

The greatest creation of the Late Vedic Era was the Upanishads, a collection of 108 essays dealing with ethical questions, written between 800 and 300 B.C.E. Literally, *upanishad* means "sitting near," and refers to students sitting near a teacher to learn esoteric doctrines from him. Not all those essays are important, nor do they teach a consistent point of view. We know the names of some of the authors, but most of the essays were anonymous group efforts. Just as the Greek philosopher Plato and Chinese philosopher Confucius explained their ideas in dialogue form, so many of the Upanishads contain dialogues, questions and answers between students and teachers.

The general tendency of the Upanishads was toward monism, a metaphysical system in which reality is conceived as a unified whole. Ritual and magic were discouraged as futile when applied without enlightenment, and faith and good works were considered inadequate. The goal of the Upanishads was to seek the knowledge and wisdom that the Vedas did not give. Eventually, the ideas explored in the Upanishads found their way into the new orthodoxy of the Hindu religion that emerged from the synthesis of old and new ideas. In this way, the Upanishads became accepted as an orthodox part of the Vedic literature that for more than 2,000 years has formed the basis of Hinduism, the religion that emerged from early Aryan religion and later additions. The strength of the teaching of the Upanishads is its all-embracing approach, which overrides all barriers of caste and every external and internal difference between believers.

The ideas expressed in the Upanishads, however, were so esoteric and complex that they influenced only the small number of people capable of understanding them. They were entirely too difficult for the vast masses of the people and hence did not permeate downward. The most immediate result of the movement was to widen the gap between the intellectuals and ordinary people.

Meanwhile, the common people began to put their faith in hitherto unimportant deities who now seemed to answer their needs. Most important among them were Shiva and Vishnu, who replaced Indra and Varuna, who had been important earlier. Also known as Rudra, Shiva may have become popular because of his identification with a deity often depicted on Indus seals. Shiva was associated with death and destruction, but also with fertility, something everyone desired. Worshippers appealed to Vishnu for deliverance from distress; he was also identified with Krishna, who taught morality and virtue. These two gods continued from late Vedic to modern times as the most popular deities in Hinduism.

Another result of the religious mood of the late Vedic period is the development of two new religions that sought to change and reform some of the prevailing religious ideas and practices. They are Buddhism and Jainism, and will be discussed in Chapter 4.

China from the Neolithic Age to the Shang Dynasty

Examining into antiquity we find that the Emperor Yao was called Fang-hsun. He was reverent, intelligent, accomplished, sincere and mild. He was sincerely respectful and capable of modesty. His light covered the four extremities of the empire and extended to Heaven above and the earth below. He was able to make bright his great virtue, and bring affection to the nine branches of the family. When the nine branches of the family had become harmonious, he distinguished and honored the hundred clans. When the hundred clans had become illustrious, he harmonized the myriad states. The numerous people were amply nourished and prosperous and became harmonious. . . .
[As he grew older Yao searched for a successor from among all his subjects, and found Shun the best qualified.]

*The emperor said: "Come you, Shun, in the affairs on which you have been consulted, I have examined your words; your words have been accomplished and capable of yielding fine results for three years; do you ascend to the imperial throne." Shun considered himself inferior in virtue and was not pleased. But in the first month, the first day, he accepted the abdication of Yao in the Temple of the Accomplished Ancestor.**

*William T. de Bary, ed., *Sources of Chinese Tradition*, vol. 1 (New York: Columbia University Press, 1960), pp. 8–9. Reprinted with permission.

Until the twentieth century, Chinese were taught that Kings Yao and Shun were historic figures who reigned around 2200 B.C.E. They were revered for their sincerity, reverence, and unselfishness, and for the golden age that their reigns brought. Later rulers were exhorted to emulate them. Since there is no proof that they existed, we can only regard them as culture heroes. In this section we will find out how civilization began in China, how traditional Chinese looked at their past, and how modern archaeology has added to our knowledge of ancient China.

The Land of China

China, a country of continental dimensions, today extends some 2,500 miles from the Pamir Mountains in the west to the Pacific Ocean in the east and over 2,000 miles from the Amur River in the north to the Indochinese border in the south. At 3.7 million square miles, it is slightly larger than the 3.6 million square miles of the United States. This area varies greatly in topography, climate, and vegetation, ranging from subarctic taiga (evergreen forests) in the northeast to tropical jungles in the southwest, from the steppes and deserts of Chinese Turkestan in the northwest to the high plateau of Tibet in the west and the temperate river valleys of the east. Although it is possible to cross the broad deserts and scale the high mountains that separate China from the other civilizations of Asia, the length of the journey and the difficulties and dangers associated with such travel have tended to isolate China from other lands. Conversely, the great river valleys and coastal plains make internal communications relatively easy and thus have helped unify the Chinese.

China can be divided into two broad parts, north and south. The Yellow River dominates North China. It brings the water and deposits the layers of silt on which agriculture depends; it has also since the earliest times brought cruel floods that have given it the name "China's sorrow." Hot in summer and cold in winter, the North China plains receive little rainfall. Here barley and millet are the main crops, and the donkey and oxen are the chief draft animals.

The Tsingling Mountains separate the drainage basins of the Yellow and the Yangtze Rivers. The Yangtze valley and the Hsi (West, also called Pearl) River valley farther south constitute South China. A coastal plain of varying width extends along the entire coastline. Southern China receives abundant rainfall and has mild winters and hot summers. It is the land of double and triple crops each year, paddy rice and water buffalo, and canals and lakes. Contrasts abound between the harsh north and the verdant south (see Map 2.2).

The Study of Ancient China

The Chinese have a tradition and history that has continued unbroken to the present. Unlike the earliest Indian oral traditions and written documents, which dealt with religion and philosophy, ancient Chinese writings were from the beginning concerned with historiography, or the recording of historic events, with an emphasis on socially applicable morals and virtues.

Early records told of ancient culture heroes who ruled in succession starting from 2850 B.C.E. The greatest was Huang-ti (Yellow Emperor), considered the founding father of the Chinese state because he defeated the neighboring barbarians and united the Chinese

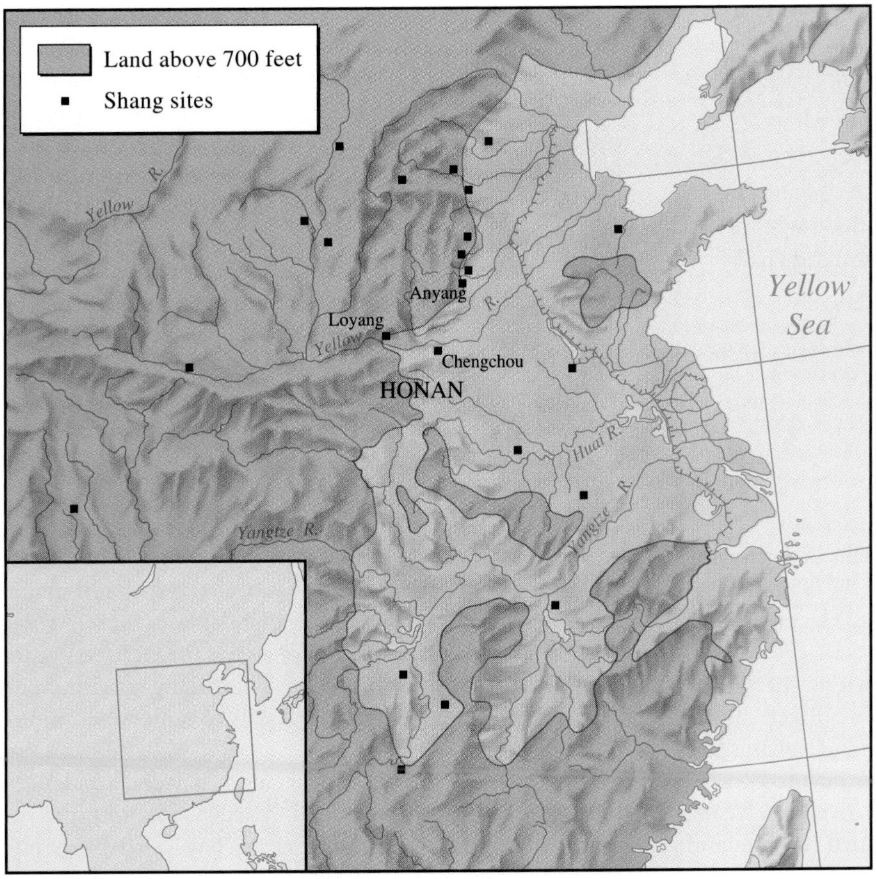

Map 2.2 Shang China. Most archaeological sites of the Shang dynasty are found along the lower reaches of the Yellow River, the heartland of early Chinese civilization, although some are located along the Yangtze and its tributaries. The last Shang capital, Anyang, is located in modern Honan province.

An Idealized View of Antiquity

*At the time when men still followed the Great Way, all under Heaven was owned in common. Men were chosen for their ability and talent. Their teaching was reliable and they cultivated harmony. People of ancient times treated not only their nearest relatives as relatives and not only their own children as children. . . . There was employment for the strong and the young were given the opportunity to grow up. Widows, orphans, those left on their own, and invalids were all provided for. Men had their work and women their shelter. They accumulated provisions because they did not wish anything to be thrown away, but they were not supposed to amass goods for themselves. They toiled because they did not wish goods to be anything but the result of their own efforts. But they were not supposed to do this for the sake of personal advantage. Therefore selfish schemes did not arise and robbers, thieves, and rebels were not in evidence. They went out without shutting the door. This was called the Great Harmony.**

Centuries later, Confucius and Confucians viewed the earliest antiquity as a golden age when virtue reigned and selfishness did not exist. They were undoubtedly exhorting the people of their times to live up to high ideals and to encourage them that such ideals were realizable, because they had once been reality.

*Attributed to Confucius, from the *Li Chi,* vol. 1, trans. James Legge (1885; reprint, New Hyde Park, NY: University Books, 1967), pp. 364–366.

people throughout the Yellow River plain. To this day Chinese call themselves descendants of the Yellow Emperor. He was followed by others such as Yao and Shun, whom posterity regarded as sage kings.

Another culture hero was Yu, known as the Great, because he dredged channels of the Yellow River, allowing the floodwaters to flow to the sea and solving the problem of recurring floods. He was so devoted to his work that he never returned home in over ten years, even when he passed by his gate and heard his wife and children weeping in loneliness. Yu was made ruler because of his successful flood control work, and was so loved that when he died the people set aside the man he had chosen to succeed him and put his son on the throne. Thus began the first dynasty, the Hsia (c. 2205–1766 B.C.E.). Little is known about the Hsia kings until the last, who was a tyrant. He was overthrown by a subordinate named Tang the Successful, who founded the Shang dynasty (c.1766–1122 B.C.E.). The last Shang king was a debauched tyrant who in turn was deposed by his subordinate, who founded the Chou dynasty (1122–256 B.C.E.). This, in very brief outline, is how early history was taught to Chinese children until the beginning of the twentieth century.

The Rise of the Shang Dynasty, 1766–1122 B.C.E.

The Agricultural Revolution, evident in the domestication of plants and animals and the appearance of pottery, began in China around 7000 B.C.E. Communities existed in isolation until about 4000 B.C.E., when they began to interact with one another, though remaining independent from other emerging civilizations. Although archaeologists have found many remains that corroborate traditional accounts of the Hsia, no written documents of that era have survived. Thus the Hsia dynasty remains prehistoric.

The Shang dynasty was centered in modern-day Honan province (an area south of the Yellow River in northeastern China). We are not sure of the extent of its political power and its relationship with the peoples of other parts of China. Since the systematic excavation of its last capital began at Anyang in 1928, scores of other Shang sites have been found and investigated. Some major sites might have been earlier capitals of the dynasty. For example, Chengchow in north Honan was probably the second Shang capital, called Ao in ancient records. Excavations have been in progress in Chengchow since the 1950s, and study of the findings reveals that the area was continuously occupied since Neolithic times. The city was rectangular in shape, surrounded by a wall of rammed earth estimated to have been over thirty feet in height, over sixty feet thick at the base, and totaling almost two and half miles in circumference. As with the construction of the Great Pyramids in Egypt, a huge labor force was mobilized to build major Chinese public works. Experts calculate that it took 10,000 men working 330 days a year for eighteen years to build the wall around Ao. The Shang government clearly had the organizational skill to supervise monumental projects.

Within the city walls were large palaces, residences for aristocrats, and ceremonial quarters. Pits with the remains of human sacrificial victims have also been unearthed. Artisans and workers lived close to their work in tamped-earth houses. Remains of these houses are found near kiln sites, bronze foundries, and workshop areas, located outside the walls. Scattered farmhouses dot the countryside. Artifacts made of bronze, jade, and other materials abound throughout, but no writing has been found, either here or at the other presumed pre-Anyang capitals. We can therefore only deduce from nonwritten information that Chengchow (Ao) was an important political and ceremonial center. Pottery and other artifacts of the last Shang phase at Chengchow are of poorer quality, which suggests that by then the center of power had moved elsewhere.

The last twelve kings of Shang ruled from Yin, near present-day Anyang, for 273 years until the dynasty fell; hence the last phase of the Shang is also called the Yin dynasty. When the curious purchasers of the inscribed tortoise shells began to inquire as to their place of origin, the trail led to Anyang, where a major archaeological dig began in 1928.

Anyang was an impressive capital. Eleven large tombs that belonged to the kings have been found. Twelve kings had ruled from Anyang, but the twelfth and last king died in his burning palace as his capital fell and was not given a kingly burial. Smaller tombs in the royal cemetery apparently belonged to other members of the royal family. Unlike the Egyptians, whose rulers were buried in pyramids and tombs carved into cliffs, the Shang kings were buried in underground chambers not unlike those found in the royal cemetery at Mycenae. Each tomb was about thirty feet deep, oblong in shape, with a central burial chamber containing a coffin surrounded by objects of jade, bronze, shell, pottery, and other materials. Remains of human sacrificial victims were found interred in the main chamber and scattered in other parts of the grave, as were dogs, and horses harnessed to chariots. Chariot drivers were buried beside their vehicles. Similarities between Shang chariots and those discovered in burial mounds in the Caucasus region in western Asia led to speculation that Shang China might have had contact with cultures to the west.

All the royal graves excavated up to 1975 had been robbed in ages past, but in 1975 a hitherto undisturbed grave was found. This lavish grave belonged to Lady Hao, the powerful wife of a mighty Shang king who reputedly had sixty-four wives. Her name frequently appeared in oracle bone inscriptions. She led troops in war, owned her own estates, and was the mother of some of the king's children. Thus she had merited an elaborate send-off to the next life. Her grave contains the remains of sixteen sacrificed humans and six dogs. It also held more than 1,600 objects, including many bronzes, jades, ivories, pottery, stone carvings, and 7,000 cowrie shells (used as currency). Originally a building had stood over the grave; it was used for ceremonies and sacrifices conducted in her honor.

Collection of Jiu-Hwa L. Upshur, photograph by John Nystuen

Neolithic Pots. Both pieces, a large earthenware jar and a bowl, were made by Neolithic farmers in northwestern China between 4000 and 3000 B.C.E. Found in graves, they originally contained food and were buried in the belief that people in the afterlife needed the same things they had in this life. These vessels were handmade by the coiling method and painted with abstract designs in red, black, and white.

The key "documents" that give us an understanding of the Shang dynasty are 20,000 inscribed oracle bones buried in Shang government archives. Questions to the gods were written on these bones, and answers from the gods were recorded there as well. Modern Chinese writing evolved from the script incised into the scapula bones of oxen and inner shells of tortoises. Most of the words have been deciphered. We know that Shang scribes kept government records that they wrote down with brush and ink on slips of bamboo or wood that were bound together and rolled up in the fashion of modern slat screens, but these have long since perished. Some Shang bronze ritual vessels also had inscriptions cast into their lids or bases, but they, like the Indus seals, contained only a few characters identifying the vessel and the clan names of the owners. Major excavations in other parts of China that are contemporary with those of the Shang dynasty show cultures that are at the same time similar and different from that at Anyang, but without artifacts bearing explanatory inscriptions.

Shang Government

The Shang oracle bones were used for divination, the art of telling future events through consulting the supernatural, a practice found worldwide that was also used by the Neolithic peoples of China. Not until the Anyang period of the Shang dynasty did the bones contain writing. The Shang king's diviner would inscribe a question on the prepared bone or shell, dig a small pit part way through the piece, and then apply a heated metal rod to the pit, which would cause the shell or bone to crack. The nature of the crack indicated the answer. A typical bone or shell contains a date, followed by "The diviner X asks on behalf of the king . . ."; then comes the question, for example, "Is the drought caused by ancestor X?" or "If we raise an army of 3,000 men to drive X away from Y, will we succeed?" The diviner then recorded the answer. A final statement sometimes gave the outcome, which occasionally differed from the first answer. Other oracles were in the nature of reports to ancestors. Since

Shang Oracle Bones. Thousands of inscribed tortoise shells and scapula bones have been unearthed in Anyang. Used for divination, they are the earliest surviving examples of Chinese writing and a rich storehouse of information on the Shang dynasty.

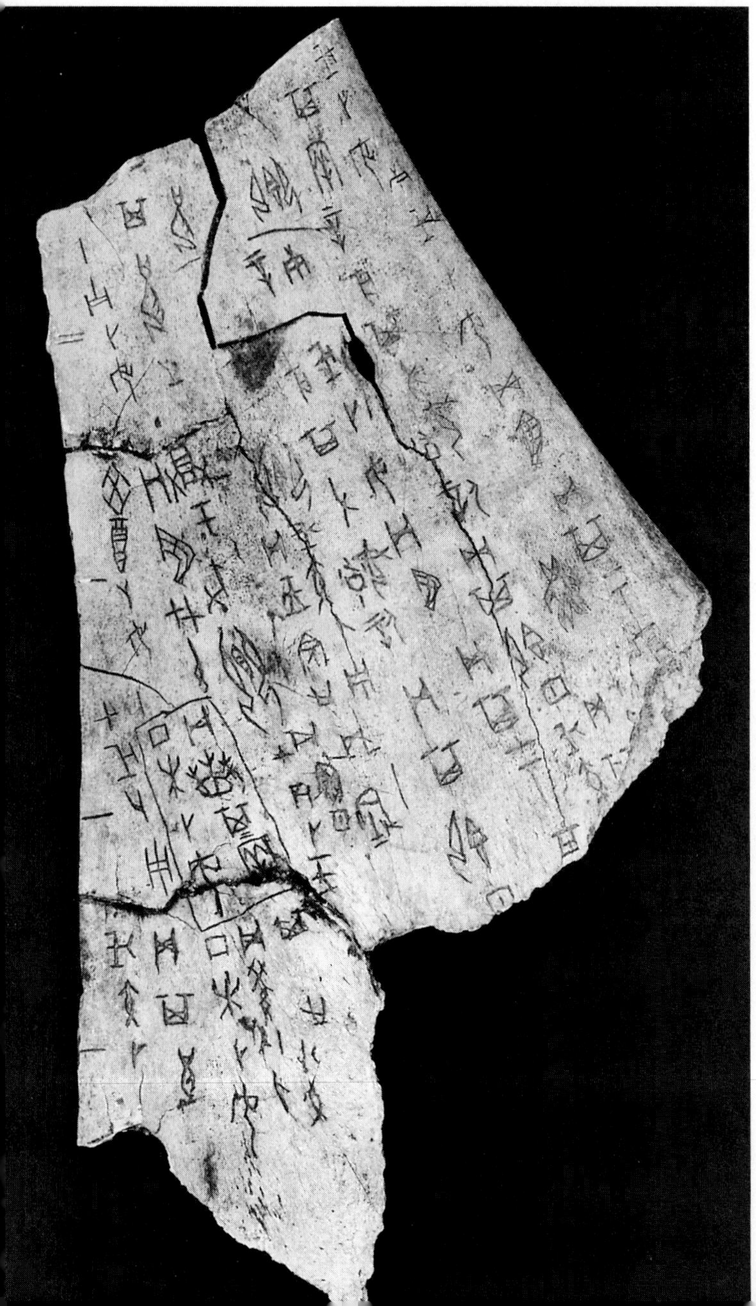

Courtesy of the C. V. Starr East Asian Library, Columbia University

it was believed that the spirits of royal ancestors could influence events, Shang monarchs regularly offered elaborate sacrifices to propitiate those spirits.

The Shang is a historic dynasty because in addition to archaeological evidence, we now possess copious contemporary documentation about it deciphered from the oracle bone inscriptions. The king's relationship to the ancestor who was the object of a sacrifice was important and was always clearly stated, allowing reconstruction of clear genealogies of the royal family. Oracle bone inscriptions also contained information about Shang government, state, society, and economy, as well as insights into the kings' private lives and relationships with their ancestors. The inscriptions have also corroborated much of the information about the Shang recorded in the later historic texts.

The king was the central focus of the Shang dynasty and the succeeding Chou dynasty. A poem written during the early Chou proclaimed:

Everywhere under Heaven
Is no land that is not the king's.
To the borders of all those lands
None is but the king's slave.

Historians are not sure whether the Shang state and society were based on tribal alliances or a form of feudalism, in which the king delegated power to noblemen who owed him allegiance and responsibilities such as taxes and contribution of troops in war. We do know that from his capital city, the king ruled through a complex and highly stratified governmental network. Numerous offices and titles are mentioned in the oracle bone inscriptions, but we are not sure of the functions of many of them. Only the king could consult and offer sacrifices to his ancestors and other spirits. Although this was an important source of the king's power and its results affected the whole nation, the king himself, unlike the Egyptian pharaoh, was not considered divine. Ancestors and their living descendants had reciprocal obligations; therefore, for the health and safety of the state, the king had to offer the correct sacrifices to the particular ancestor at the appropriate times. A proper offering should secure the desired response from the ancestral spirit. The king should then make another offering to the ancestor in thanksgiving. This concept of reciprocal responsibility is the essence of ancestor worship practiced by the Chinese.

The king was responsible for correct relations with the wider spirit world as well. The most important spirit was the impersonal high god called Ti, who appointed kings to rule on his behalf and demanded moral uprightness and integrity from all kings, a concept called the mandate of heaven. Heaven appointed a worthy man to rule and allowed him to pass the kingship to his descendants so long as they ruled with justice and compassion and carried out their religious duties. If they failed to do

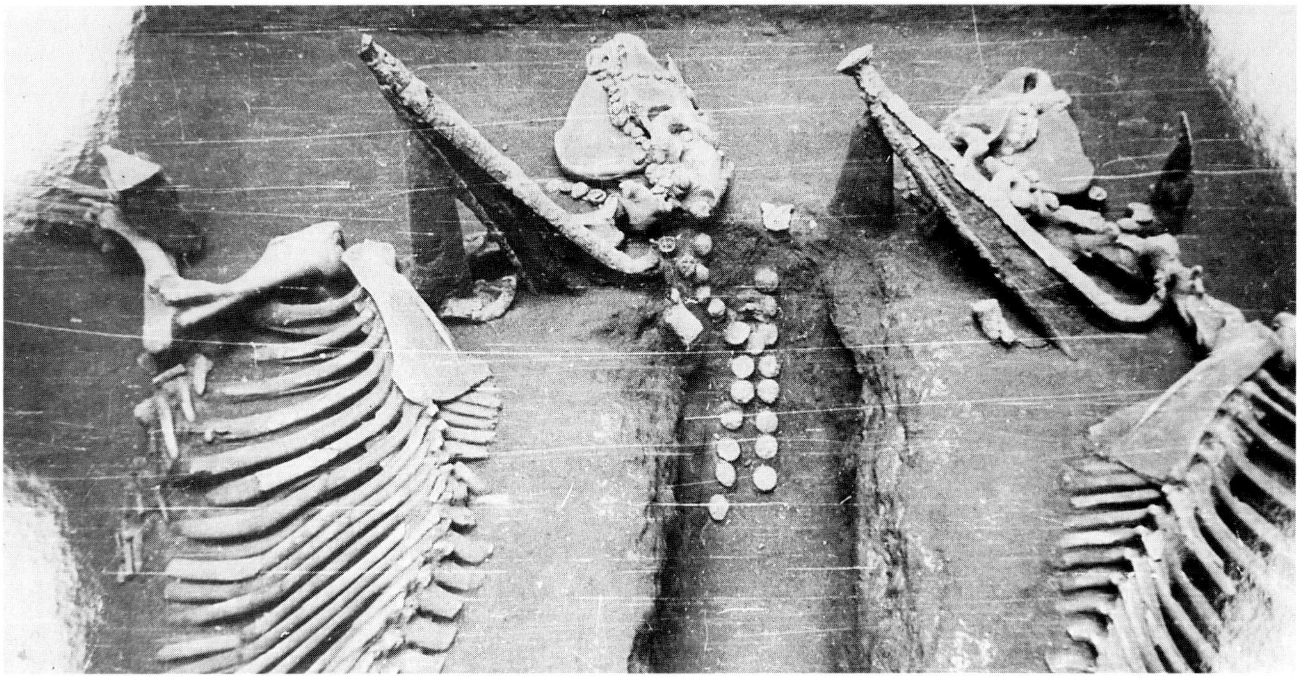
Robert Harding Picture Library

Royal Tombs at Anyang. Eleven kings were buried in huge underground tombs at the royal cemetery at Anyang, the last Shang capital. They were interred with thousands of precious items such as bronze ritual vessels and weapons, jades, and ivory ornaments. Dogs, horses, and slaves were sacrificed and buried in the tombs to serve their masters in the next world. This picture shows the remains of two horses lying in front of the chariot they once pulled.

so, heaven would cut its mandate and appoint another ruler.

Shang kings also led their troops in war. Sometimes calling up 5,000 or more men at a time, they conducted campaigns against neighboring groups; those with non-Chinese cultures were referred to as "barbarians." At first the Shang kings made war mostly in North China, but later they expanded southward along the coast and probably into the Yangtze region. The king and the nobles rode to battle in horse-drawn chariots. They and the soldiers used a variety of bronze weapons, including axes, spears, daggers, and metal-tipped arrows. Prisoners of war became slaves and victims in sacrificial burials, and were also buried in building foundations. When not warring, the kings and their nobles held large hunts for sport and for food.

Society and Economy during the Shang Era

A great gap existed between the rulers and the ruled in Shang society. At the top of society were the royal and aristocratic families, who were organized according to patrilineal clans and kept careful genealogies. Since the royalty and nobility practiced polygyny (one man with more than one wife), and since the economy could not have supported an ever-increasing leisure class, it is reasonable to assume that some offspring of the nobility must have been regularly demoted to commoner status. Nobles were rewarded with strings of cowrie shells acquired from South China and Southeast Asia, which were probably used for major transactions. There was also an artisan class such as jade carvers and bronzesmiths, who lived in or around the towns. We do not know of their social status, but since they performed services that needed skills, it is reasonable to assume that they were well treated. Most of the trade must have been in barter form, since there was no coinage beside the cowrie shells.

At the bottom of society were the slaves. Some slaves were acquired deliberately in wars against the Shang's non-Chinese neighbors, while others were convicted criminals who were enslaved as punishment. Slaves were often sacrificed in royal burials and other rituals. The vast majority of the people, however, were not slaves. They were farmers, who probably had the status of serfs, meaning that they were tied to the land and had to give part of their crops to the lord.

By Shang times the hunting-herding-farming economy of the Neolithic Age had given way to a predominantly farming one. Where there was arable land, the landscape was dotted with villages of semisubterranean houses of adobe and thatch. Fieldwork was primarily for men; the common word meaning "male" is a pictograph that combines a symbol representing a field and another

LIVES AND TIMES ACROSS CULTURES

Royal Tombs in Bronze Age Greece and China

Many ancient cultures buried artifacts with the dead for use in the next world. Such burials prove belief in a next world and also help posterity reconstruct life in ancient times. Excavated tombs of Bronze Age rulers of Mycenaean Greece corroborate descriptions of *The Iliad,* just as the royal graves of Shang dynasty rulers at Anyang authenticate passages of the *Books of History and Poetry.*

The following passage describes burial objects found by Heinrich Schliemann during his excavation of one of six shaft graves inside the city wall at Mycenae in Greece.

*The five bodies in Grave IV had been literally smothered in costly burial offerings. . . . Among the finds were . . . a silver vase in the form of a bull's head . . . with golden horns . . . ; three remarkable and awe-inspiring gold face masks . . . , apparently modeled on the actual features of the deceased; two large gold signet rings showing chariot scenes of battle and hunting; a massive gold bracelet; gold breastplates, diadems and a "shoulder-belt"; nine golden goblets and vases, including the famous "cup of Nestor"; . . . more than 400 beads of amber; . . . thirty-two copper cauldrons; . . . various adornments for armor and weapons; obsidian arrowheads; perforated boar's tusks; forty-six bronze swords and daggers; four lances; three knives; numerous terra-cotta vases.**

The next passage is from an archaeological report listing items found in a Chinese queen's tomb from the Shang dynasty in the fourteenth century B.C.E.

*At least sixteen human [sacrificial victims] were buried in the tomb. . . . There were also six dogs . . . more than 1,600 objects in addition to almost 7,000 pieces of cowrie shells [used as large-denomination money]. Of the 1,600 plus buried objects, there were more than 440 bronze pieces, over 590 jade items, over 560 bone objects; in addition there were over 70 stone objects, several ivory carvings, pottery objects, two made from sea shells and one from a large sea shell. After preliminary study of the burial items, and the deciphering of the inscriptions on the bronze vessels, it would seem that most of them had been the accumulated possessions of the owner of the grave; and that a minority of the pieces had been made expressly as sacrificial items of the person buried.***

*William A. McDonald, *Progress into the Past: The Rediscovery of Mycenaean Civilization* (Bloomington: Indiana University Press, 1967), pp. 61–62.

**Kaogu Xuebao, 1977, no. 2, Peking Institute of Archaeology, Chinese Academy of Social Sciences, pp. 59–60, trans. Jiu-Hwa L. Upshur.

meaning work. Since bronze was a luxury metal, farming implements were made of wood, bone, or stone. The major crops were millet, barley, wheat, and vegetables. Women did domestic chores. The pictograph for "woman" or "wife" combined a symbol for female and a symbol of a broom. Women also tended silkworms, spun, and wove. Domesticated animals include horses (used for chariot-pulling only, not for riding or field work), oxen, pigs, sheep, dogs, and fowls. Pork was the staple meat. Animal bones and tusks were used for arrow heads, small tools, and ornaments. Animals were sacrificed in ancestral and other rites; their meat was probably later eaten. Animals were also buried with their owners.

There is no indication in Shang times or in later ages that the Chinese used milk or milk products from any of their milk-producing animals. Yet they were in constant contact with nomadic herders living on the northern rim of their world who relied on milk products. In fact, one can observe a contrast in dietary patterns among the peoples of Europe and Asia based on their use or avoidance of dairy products. In East Asia the people of China, Korea, Japan, Indochina, and Malaya do not use milk products, while all Indo-Europeans (including the Aryans of India), the Semites, Scythians, Turks, and Mongols have used them since early times. The reason for this difference is not clear.

Science, Arts, and Crafts

Chinese tradition says that the Yellow Emperor first established the sixty-year cycle as the basis of calculating time and that the Hsia dynasty fixed the lunar calendar of 366 days a year. To the present day the Chinese call the

LIVES AND TIMES ACROSS CULTURES

Feasting in Bronze Age Greece and China

We have considerable evidence of foods consumed by Bronze Age people. Although little documentary evidence about the diet of ordinary people is available, great literary writings from ancient Europe and Asia depict the feasts of rulers, nobles, and heroes.

The following excerpt is from Homer's *Odyssey*. The hero Odysseus has been washed ashore in the land of the peace-loving and somewhat decadent Phaiakians, who show him much hospitality and assist him on his journey home. In the passage quoted here, the Phaiakian king, Alkinoös, has ordered a great feast for his distinguished visitor, complete with musical entertainment by the blind minstrel, Demodokos, who may be a self-portrait by Homer.

> *[They] made their way to the great house of Alkinoös, and the porticoes and enclosures and rooms were filled with people assembling, there were many men there, both old and young ones, and for them Alkinoös made a sacrifice, twelve sheep, eight pigs with shining tusks, and two drag-footed oxen. These they skinned and prepared and made the lovely feast ready. The herald came near bringing with him the excellent singer. . . . Pontonoös set a silver-studded chair out for him in the middle of the feasters . . . and set beside him a table and a fine basket, and beside him a cup to drink whenever his spirit desired it.**

The second quotation, from the Chou dynasty, vividly describes the delicacies and delicious dishes that family members have prepared in hopes of enticing the soul of a departed loved one to share the meal. The Chinese have always prepared elaborate dishes to commemorate special occasions involving beloved deceased family members. After ceremonially entreating the souls to enjoy their offerings, family members sit down to the lavish meal.

The Summons of the Soul

Oh soul, come back! Why should you go far away?
All your household have come to do you honour; all kinds of good food are ready;
Rice, broom-corn, early wheat, mixed all with yellow millet;
Bitter, salt, sour, hot and sweet; there are dishes of all flavours.
Ribs of fatted ox cooked tender and succulent;
Sour and bitter blended in the soup of Wu;
Stewed turtle and roast kid, served up on yam sauce;
Geese cooked in sour sauce, cassaroled duck, fried flesh of the great crane;
Braised chicken, seethed tortoise, high-seasoned, but not to spoil the taste;
Fried honey-cakes of rice flour and malt-sugar sweetmeats;
Jadelike wine, honey-flavoured, fills the winged cups;
Ice-cooled liquor, strained of impurities, clear wine, cool and refreshing;
*Here are laid out the patterned ladles, and here is sparkling wine.***

*Richmond Lattimore, trans., *The Odyssey of Homer* (New York: Harper, 1965), pp. 122–123.

**K. C. Chang, ed., *Food in Chinese Culture: Anthropological and Historical Perspectives* (New Haven: Yale University Press, 1977), p. 32.

lunar calendar on which their traditional festivals are based the Hsia calendar. Many oracle bones of the Shang recorded solar and lunar eclipses and noted predictions of their occurrences. From this it would seem that the men who cast oracles were also astronomers and mathematicians. Records show that the decimal system originated during the Shang and was in use at least by the fourteenth century B.C.E. The ability to chart the movement of heavenly bodies, predict eclipses, regulate the calendar, and define the agricultural season became recognized as the prerequisite for rulership. The Shang oracle specialists were probably the predecessors of the Board of Astronomers of the Chinese government of later eras.

The most remarkable products of the Shang dynasty are bronze ritual vessels that art historians consider unequalled in technical excellence and beauty. The art of

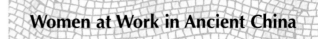

The Nelson-Atkins Museum of Art, Kansas City, MO (Purchase: Nelson Trust) 41–43

Shang Bronzes. Bronze ritual vessels made by Shang craftsmen are unsurpassed in artistry and technical virtuosity. Most are richly ornamented with stylized animals whose meanings are lost. Many vessels have survived because they were buried with the dead.

Women at Work in Ancient China

With the spring days the warmth begins,
And the oriole utters its songs.
The young women take their deep baskets,
And go along the small paths,
Looking for the tender [leaves of the] mulberry tree . . .
In the silkworm month they strip the mulberry branch of their leaves,
And take their axes and hatchets,
To lop off those that are distant and high;
Only stripping the young trees of their leaves.
In the seventh month the shrike is heard;
In the eighth month, they begin their spinning,
They make dark fabrics and yellow,
Our red manufacture is very brilliant,
*It is for the lower robes of our young princes.**

Ancient records tell mostly about the doings of kings and the mighty. However, the *Book of Poetry,* an ancient collection of anonymously written songs and poems, is a good source about the lives of the common people. Besides housework, women also tended the silk worms and spun and wove cloth. Common people wore linen cloth woven from hemp, while the rich wore garments of silk.

**The Chinese Classics,* vol. 4: *Book of Poetry,* trans. James Legge (London, 1871), pp. 228–229.

bronze casting developed around 2000 B.C.E., in the late Neolithic Age. In early west Asia, India, and Europe, bronze was made by the lost-wax method, whereby a wax model of the object is encased in a clay mold; as molten metal is poured in, the wax melts (is lost) and is replaced by the metal. By contrast, the Chinese cast their vessels in ceramic piece molds. This way very large vessels could be made with complex decorations (the largest Shang vessels found weigh about 1,500 pounds). This method of bronze casting came naturally to the Chinese, who were already skilled in pottery making. Indeed, the Shang potter made a high-fired, glazed pottery close to stoneware. Shang pottery and bronze pieces often shared the same shapes and forms of decoration. Pottery making was widespread, but bronze foundries were found only at major urban centers close to ore sites, where they constituted large-scale operations with divisions of labor. Bronzesmiths must have been respected artisans.

Art historians have classified over two dozen distinct forms of bronze ritual vessels, which fall into three categories according to use: for storage, food, and liquids, mainly alcoholic beverages. Most pieces were decorated, some elaborately, with stylized images of real or mythological birds and animals, arranged symmetrically. Styles of decoration varied with time and region from abstract to realistic. Many pieces survived because they were buried with the dead, as the practice of ancestor worship dictated. For over 1,000 years, Chinese connoisseurs have collected Shang ritual bronze pieces; early collectors had attributed magical qualities to these unearthed treasures. Such practices and superstitious beliefs led to the looting of early tombs. Shang bronzesmiths also made weapons, chariot fittings, horse harnesses, and mirrors.

Shang artisans also worked extensively in jade and other materials. Like bronze, jade was a luxury item used in rituals and buried with the dead. The Shang jade carvers improved upon the skills of their Neolithic forebears. Their raw material, nephrite jade, came from present-day northwestern China, a considerable distance from the Shang urban centers. The abundance in Shang culture of jade and cowrie shells, both of which came from lands outside of Shang political control, indicates international

Asian Art Museum of San Francisco, The Avery Brundage Collection, Chong-Moon Lee Center for Asian Art and Culture B60 J908

Jade Disk. From time immemorial, a circular disk with a perforated center was used in rituals to symbolize heaven. This jade disk dates to the period between the Late Neolithic Age and the Shang dynasty in the second millennium B.C.E. Nephrite jades come from central Asia, and its presence in China is evidence of long-distance trade.

trade. Shang artisans also fashioned utilitarian and decorative objects from stone, ivory, and bone. They invented lacquer by extracting sap from a lacquer tree and applying the liquid to a surface such as wood to form a glossy, waterproof coating. They also worked gold and silver. However, gold was not abundant in ancient China, and gold objects did not have the significance there that they did in most other early cultures.

A Pictographic Script

Although signs and symbols are found on pottery as early as 5000 B.C.E., they are isolated and cannot be considered written language. The earliest extant written records date to the fourteenth century B.C.E., by which time the script exhibited a maturity of stylization that presupposes a centuries-long evolution.

Chinese writing is unrelated to other writings. It is a nonalphabetic script, consisting of symbols or graphs. A good modern dictionary will list over 40,000 graphs, most of which have evolved since Shang times. There are three basic kinds of graphs: (1) Pictographs are conventionalized picture symbols of an object such as the sun and moon. (2) Ideographs frequently are formed by combining two or more pictographs, for example, pictographs of the sun and moon placed side by side mean "bright" or "brilliant." (3) Logographs are formed by combining either a pictograph or an ideograph to indicate meaning and a symbol to give a key to pronunciation. For example, the pictograph of a horse is pronounced "ma," but when it is combined with a pictograph for woman the new word is still pronounced "ma" but means mother. The great majority of words in the Chinese vocabulary are logographs. All three kinds of graphs were evident in late Shang writing.

The Chou Dynasty

*Now that the king has received the mandate, unbounded is the grace, but also unbounded is the solicitude. Oh, how can he be but careful! Heaven has removed and made an end to the great state Yin's mandate. There are many former wise kings of Yin in Heaven, and the later kings and people here managed their mandate. But in the end [under the last king] wise and good men lived in misery so that, leading their wives and carrying their children, wailing and calling to Heaven, they went to where no one could come and seize them. Oh, Heaven had pity on the people of the four quarters, and looking with affection and giving its mandate, it employed the zealous ones [the leaders of the Chou]. May the king now urgently pay careful attention to his virtue . . . may he not neglect the aged elders. Then he will comprehend our ancient men's virtue, nay, still more it will occur that he is able to comprehend and endeavor to follow Heaven.**

*William T. de Bary, ed., *Sources of Chinese Tradition*, vol. 1 (New York: Columbia University Press, 1960), p. 11. Reprinted with permission.

Thus the people of China heard their new Chou rulers justify their conquest of the Shang (Yin) dynasty as the will or mandate of heaven. Around 1120 B.C.E. the leaders of the Chou from northwest China overthrew the Shang dynasty and set up their own rule. They then issued a series of proclamations to explain to the people why they had overthrown the Shang and why the people should submit to their rule. Appealing to the mandate of heaven, they told their new subjects that the last Shang king had forfeited his right to rule by his personal immorality and tyrannical government. Ti had then cut off the Shang's mandate to rule and transferred it to the deserving house of Chou. The concept of the mandate of heaven has remained the cornerstone of Chinese political thinking down to the twentieth century.

After the overthrow of the Shang in 1122 B.C.E., the Chou established the longest-lasting dynasty in Chinese history, ending in 256 B.C.E. This long period is

A Lesson in Politics: The Victor's Point of View

*Heaven then greatly ordered Wen Wang [King Wen] to destroy the great Yin [Shang] and greatly received its mandate; its state and people as a result became orderly." In contrast: "He [King Shou, last ruler of the Shang] was greatly excessive in wine. He did not think of ceasing his licentiousness. His heart was malign and he was unable to fear death. Crimes existed in the city of Shang and in the state of Yin, but for the extinction he had no anxiety. . . . Therefore heaven sent down destruction on Yin and had no mercy for Yin, it was due to his excesses. Heaven is not tyrannical, people themselves draw guilt upon themselves.**

Early Chou rulers used this theme frequently when they lectured their newly conquered subject peoples. They insisted that it was heaven's will that the people obey their new masters. In applying a moral dimension to rulership, however, the early Chou kings were also introducing a weapon with a double edge. In other words, heaven could just as easily turn against them if they failed to live up to high standards.

*James Legge, trans., *The Chinese Classics: A Translation*, vol. 3.2: *The Book of History* (London: Trubner, 1865), pp. 284–288.

subdivided into the Western Chou (1122–771 B.C.E.) and the Eastern Chou (770–256 B.C.E.). During the Chou dynasty, Chinese civilization underwent fundamental changes that brought the end of the formative era and the beginning of the imperial era, whose political and philosophical systems lasted for the next 2,000 years.

The Chou Conquest

Toughened by years of fighting non-Chinese tribes, the Chou people emerged out of the plain of Chou, situated on the northwestern frontier of the agricultural basin of North China. Shang oracle bone inscriptions described them at different times as both enemies and as allies. Although in the twelfth century B.C.E. the Shang looked on the Chou as semibarbarous country cousins, a Shang king had made an alliance with the house of Chou by giving a kinswoman to the Chou leader in marriage and then conferring on him the title Chief of the West (see Map 2.3).

Parts of the earliest texts that have survived, the *Shu Ching* (Book of History) and *Shih Ching* (Book of Poetry) were written during the early Chou and described and justified their destruction of the Shang. The first undoubtedly historic leader of the Chou was King Wen (the Cultivated or Accomplished), who laid plans to take on the Shang. The *Shu Ching* justified his actions as in obedience to heaven's wishes.

King Wen's son, King Wu (the Martial) defeated and destroyed the Shang. In accounts that clearly show a Chou bias, King Shou, the last Shang ruler, is described as deserving death in his burning palace at Yin as the dynasty fell to Chou troops. Wu died soon after his victory and left the throne to his young son. As the new king was only a boy, his uncle, the Duke of Chou, became regent. The duke completed the conquest of Shang lands and laid down the institutional basis for what became a long-lived dynasty. He lectured his nephew about the duties of the ruler, and the people about bowing to the will of heaven. When his nephew came of age, the duke handed him the reins of government and retired. Chinese have ever since celebrated King Wen, King Wu, and the Duke of Chou as three of their greatest rulers, and the early Chou as a Golden Age.

Several documentary sources contribute to our knowledge of the early Chou. Although Chou rulers also used divination to find out the will of heaven and of their ancestors, their oracle bones did not contain lengthy inscriptions. Instead, they cast long inscriptions on the surfaces of their bronze ceremonial vessels to document and report major events such as victories and the granting of fiefdoms to royal relatives or allies.

In addition to the information provided by the inscribed vessels, some documents in the *Shu Ching*, and some of the poems in the *Shih Ching*, we have also the *Li Chi*, or Book of Rituals, which describes the organization of the Chou government and the rituals, ceremonies, and etiquette of the Chou court. Tradition says that the *Li Chi* was written by the Duke of Chou. Since the duke, his brother, and his father were considered exemplary rulers by later generations, the government structure, rites, and ceremonies of the *Li Chi* are accepted as evidence of a golden age worthy or study and emulation.

Ruling a land approximately the size of modern France, Chou kings were unable to govern the entire kingdom effectively. They therefore devised a political and economic system called feudalism, which worked in the following way. The king ruled a royal domain directly; he also supervised a central government assisted by six ministers, each responsible for an aspect of administration. The king assigned the remaining land as fiefdoms to his relatives and created marriage ties with meritorious nonrelatives to whom he also awarded fiefdoms. These lords administered the king's laws in their domains, assisted by royal inspectors; they were expected to visit the royal court

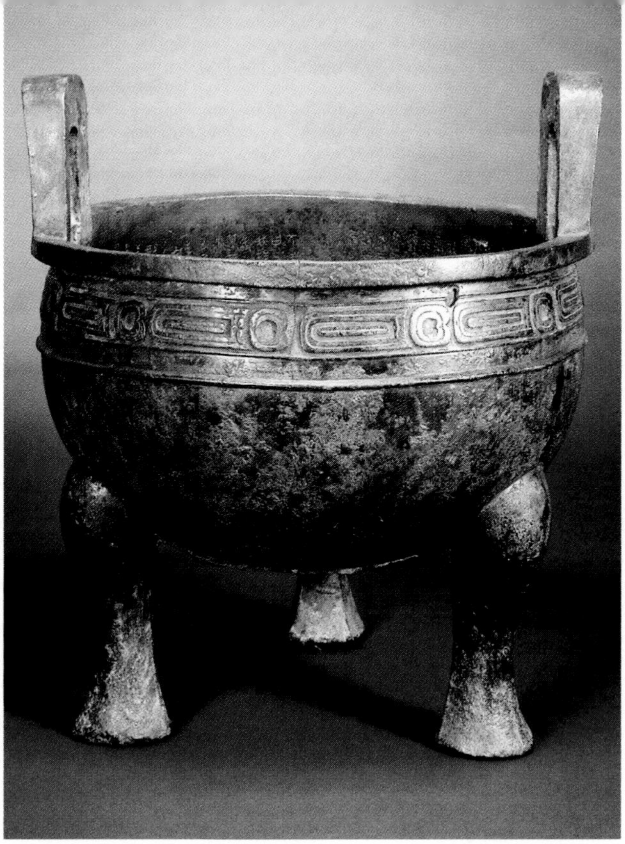

National Palace Museum, Taipei, Taiwan, Republic of China

Inscribed Bronze Cauldron. Much of our knowledge of the early Chou dynasty comes from long inscriptions on bronze vessels that were cast to commemorate important events. This monumental three-legged cauldron, commissioned by the Duke of Mao, has a 500-word inscription cast into the interior (a rubbing of the inscription is shown below).

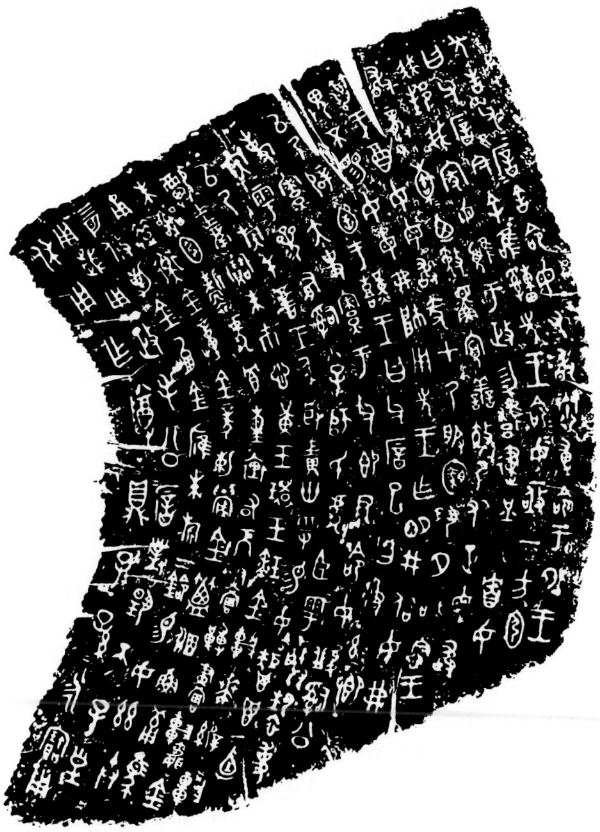

at prescribed intervals as demonstrations of their loyalty, to contribute substantive revenues to the king's treasury as well as symbolic tribute, and provide military contingents when needed. The lords received their titles at investiture ceremonies at the Chou ancestral temple, and their heirs had to be confirmed by the king. Each fiefdom was called a *kuo*, represented by a pictogram of a walled and guarded territory. The Chou royal domain, the heartland of the nation, was called *chung-kuo*, meaning central state. Later *chung-kuo* came to mean the Middle Kingdom or China.

Western Chou Society and Economy

The early Chou kings were city builders. Likewise the nobles built smaller towns from which they ruled their domains. The proliferation of archaeological sites throughout this long dynasty shows population growth and a trend toward urbanization. This trend was especially pronounced during the Eastern Chou; records show that at least seventy-eight cities were built between 722 and 480 B.C.E.

Hao, capital of Western Chou (situated in the Chou homeland), and Loyang, built by the Duke of Chou as a second capital to administer the eastern conquests (and later the capital of the Eastern Chou), would under various names be the sites of China's capital for the next 2,000 years. So many Chou sites have been identified and excavated that a picture of urban life of that time can be reconstructed. Most early Chou towns were administrative and ceremonial centers and were walled and fortified.

As under the Shang, rank and position were inherited, classifying people according to hereditary social classes. Atop the social ladder were the aristocrats, who ranged from members of the royal family downward through a graded nobility to the knights. The aristocrats were polygynous, organized into patrilineal clans, and kept careful genealogies of their families. Farmers were serfs, bound to the land they tilled, and transferred with the land at each investment of land to a new lord.

Late Chou writers recreated an idealized land tenure system that they attributed to the Duke of Chou and called the well-field system. The name comes from the pictograph for a well (for drawing water), which resembles a tick-tack-toe design, with nine components. Supposedly the early Chou villages were divided into units of eight families, each farming a plot. Villagers lived in a central plot, the ninth one, where presumably the well was located, and farmed it in common for the lord. Such a detailed land distribution was probably impossible for an ancient government. Yet the concept is so simple and just that it has inspired every reformer in China down to the twentieth century. It is another reason that later Chinese recall the early Chou as a golden age.

Unlike India, China had no priestly class after the Shang, because the kings and nobles officiated at their own ancestral sacrifices and ceremonies and appealed

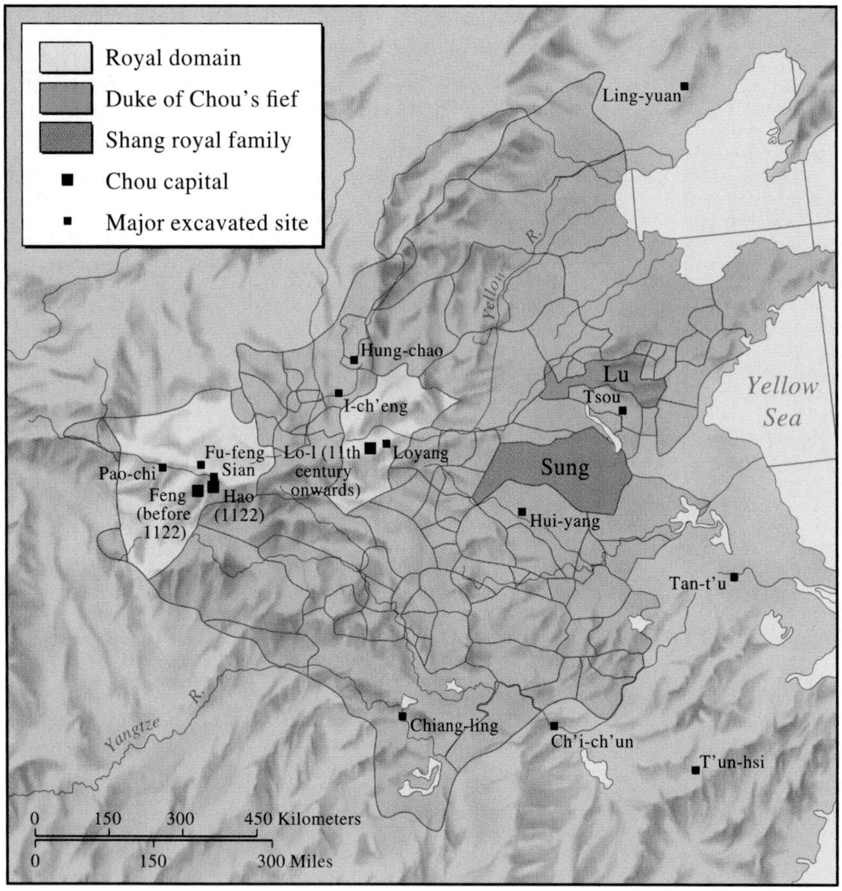

Map 2.3 Western Chou China, Eleventh to Ninth Centuries B.C.E. The victorious house of Chou divided its territories into fiefs and granted them to relatives, allies, and even surviving relatives of the previous Shang dynasty, while retaining only a core territory that it ruled directly as *chungkuo* or royal (central) domain. During its initial centuries, the Chou royal house was powerful and exercised control over the feudal vassals.

directly to their ancestors' spirits. Artisans congregated in towns to serve the needs of the governing nobles and lived in their separate quarters. They probably enjoyed a higher status than the serfs. As the population grew, so did trade and a merchant class. Merchants and artisans in Chou China, as in medieval Europe, had no defined place in the feudal hierarchy, as they had in the Indian caste system. Slavery declined and slaves did not play an important role economically. Few excavated Chou tombs contained remains of human sacrificial victims.

As in Shang times, the cowrie shell, strung in decimal units, was the big-denomination currency. Records tell of kings awarding lords ten to twenty strings of cowrie shells for meritorious service, and the notable event would be inscribed in a specially cast bronze vessel. Standard lengths of silk rolled in bolts, jade, pearls, dogs, horses, and measures of grain were other items mentioned as media of exchange. Metal coins did not come into use until the fifth century B.C.E.

By the sixth century B.C.E., a number of major improvements in agriculture had taken place and become widespread: irrigation, animal-drawn plows, crop rotation, and fertilization. During the fifth century, iron farming implements were introduced. These improvements revolutionized agriculture, increased food production, and led to rapid population growth. Chinese began to move into lands hitherto occupied by aboriginal tribes. Scarcity of land also brought about intensive use of what was available, and hunting and herding as a way of life were gradually abandoned in favor of agriculture.

Chou Religion

Religious practices of the Shang continued and evolved during the Chou period. Kings and commoners alike worshiped the spirits of their ancestors. All believed that in the life following death one needed essentially the same things one had needed on earth. Thus people buried food, drink, and other material goods, according to what they could afford, with the dead. Most of the commemorative bronze vessels cast and inscribed by Chou lords contained the following sentence: "May my sons and grandsons forever treasure and use this vessel."

The specialists or priests who had cast and inscribed oracle bones for Shang kings seem to have disappeared, and owing to the dominance of ancestor worship in religious life, they were not replaced by other priests or magicians. From king to commoner, each invoked his own ancestors for blessing and assistance, and every family's life centered on its ancestral temple or shrine. The practice of human and animal sacrifices to serve the powerful in death declined and died out and came to be denounced in later Chou writings.

Ti, the high god of the Shang, in time came to be identified with Tien or heaven, the chief Chou deity. Tien might have begun as the "great man," as its pictograph, clearly that of a man, would suggest. In time, Tien became a "Great Spirit," a vast, impersonal, supreme deity. The Chou ruler bore the title of *wang,* or king, as had the Shang sovereign. However, in accordance with the doctrine that the Chou rulers had inherited the mandate of heaven, the Chou monarch was also called Son of Heaven. This mandate theoretically could only be maintained by the king's descendants if they, too, carried out heaven's wishes. Otherwise, as had happened to the Shang, the mandate could be revoked and transferred to a more worthy recipient.

The king's ancestral temple was the center of affairs for the kingdom. All important state affairs took place there, and all events of consequence were reported to the king's ancestral spirits. Separate altars were constructed, each for a specific purpose; for example, one for worshiping heaven, another for worshiping earth and the soil, and still others in honor of various spirits. It was the king's responsibility to officiate at ceremonies in honor of heaven, the soil, and the various spirits at appropriate times.

The Eastern Chou

During the dynasty's first three centuries, the Chou rulers expanded their realm and united all of North China under their rule. However, with the passing of time, early kinship ties loosened, the kings' authority declined, and the feudal lords began to identify more with their hereditary territories than with the royal court. By the ninth century B.C.E. kings were experiencing difficulties in dealing with warlike barbarians in both the north and south, and regional lords were beginning to ignore the king's orders and to fight among themselves. In 771 B.C.E. the king was killed in a campaign against a northern tribe, and the western capital, Hao, was overrun. The remnant government fled eastward to Loyang, which had been made the second capital of the dynasty by the Duke of Chou.

This flight marked the end of the exercise of real power by the Chou kings, who reigned but no longer ruled; in time they were consulted only on such issues as genealogy and ritual. The period between 770 and 256 B.C.E. is called the Eastern Chou. The royal domain of the house of Chou was now tiny compared with the extent of the larger feudal states.

The Eastern Chou was an unstable and violent age, marked by many wars. Diplomacy was important, as evidenced by the many interstate alliances, often cemented by marriages. After 680 B.C.E. one ruler, but never the Chou king, was always recognized as the hegemon (*pa*), or predominant lord, who maintained some order. So many wars characterized the last 150 years of the Chou dynasty that it was called the Era of Warring States; during the period 132 states were finally reduced to one.

Since chariot warfare was unsuitable in the hilly northwest or in the wet Yangtze Valley, chariots were replaced by massed infantry and cavalry formations. If contemporary records can be believed, some states fielded infantry numbering in the hundreds of thousands. Military leaders who needed to counter the northern horse-riding nomads created cavalry units, which became the standard auxiliary of Chinese armies. By the fifth century more lethal iron weapons had replaced bronze ones. The crossbow, a Chinese invention that had a more powerful and longer draw than the composite bow and was worked by a precisely cast metal trigger mechanism, came into widespread use. Warfare became more destructive as a result.

Bronze Bell. Most early Chou bronzes continued the Shang tradition, but new shapes were also introduced. This bell was part of a set; different-sized bells produced different notes when struck. Bells provided music during religious and court rituals.

National Palace Museum, Taipei, Taiwan, Republic of China

CONNECTIONS IN TECHNOLOGY

Rice Cultivation in East Asia

The cultivation of Asian rice developed gradually over thousands of years in several stages. The first stage was systematic collection of wild rice in all the areas of southern and eastern Asia where it grew. The second stage was domestication—the regular cultivation of "dry" or "upland" rice, watered by rain. It is likely that this breakthrough occurred some 8,000 years ago in South China, when that region was inhabited not by Chinese speakers but by speakers of languages related to the Thai, Vietnamese, and Austronesian languages of today. Different types of wild rice were domesticated in West Africa, and wild rice was harvested systematically in the Great Lakes regions of North America.

A third stage was the development of wet rice, in which the plants grow under water. Its place of origin is not known with certainty, but by 3000 B.C.E. this wet rice, which gave higher yields and required less land but more labor than dry rice, was established in India and in much of Southeast Asia and South China. Farming implements changed only gradually in this time: farmers continued to use the same stone, bone, shell, and wooden farming implements until about 600 to 500 B.C.E., when cast iron came into use. There is little evidence that metal tools, irrigation networks, or draft animals were in use before that time.

Only with time did Chinese empires and Chinese-speaking peoples become leaders in rice production. In China, the early societies of the north depended largely on millet and wheat. As the Ch'in and Han dynasties spread their power to the south, and as Chinese-speaking settlers moved south of the Yangtze Valley, rice became more important in the Chinese diet.

A fourth stage in rice cultivation came at this point, in the third century B.C.E., as the Ch'in dynasty began to expand irrigation techniques. Before irrigation, farmers had to work near fairly large streams and carry water from wells or reservoirs to terraced fields. The Han dynasty (c. 200 B.C.E.–200 C.E.) implemented a policy of intensive land clearing and promoted more sophisticated agricultural techniques. Paddy fields, filled with water and separated by earthen banks, were linked with bamboo conduits bringing in water from high ground springs, while sluices let water flow from one paddy to the next to circulate oxygen to the plants' roots.

Japan, in the later times of the Tokugawa era (1600–1868), experienced a technological boom in rice agriculture. Prior to this time, rice had been used much like currency, and the value of rice affected the cost of everything else. Improvements in seeds, irrigation networks, drainage systems, and farming implements provided the food that contributed to an explosion in Japan's population, which rose to 30 million.

---

1. Enter the search term "rice" in the Infotrac Subject Guide. Choose "Periodical references" and find the four articles on rice domestication in the December 1998 issue of *Antiquity*. Read "The origins and dispersal of rice cultivation." What are the main conclusions of the article? What evidence is used to draw those conclusions? Pick one of the three remaining articles and answer the same two questions.

2. Go to http://www.riceweb.org/. What important aspects of the history of rice cultivation supplements the information you learned from the essay above and from the InfoTrac articles? Then, visit http://www.asiarice.org/sections/riceheritage/riceheritage.html. In what ways has rice cultivation shaped the culture of Asia?

In 256 B.C.E. King Cheng of the northwestern state of Ch'in eliminated the house of Chou; by 221 he had crushed the other warring states. In unifying all the land that had once been in the Chou domain, he renamed the national dynasty Ch'in, which became China. That story will be covered in the next chapter.

Eastern Chou Society and Economy

The system of family government that had characterized the early Chou no longer sufficed for an increasingly complex society. Hereditary posts declined, replaced by a system in which promotions were determined by merit. For the first time in Chinese history, men of commoner status rose to important political positions. Most of the new bureaucrats, however, were not commoners, but belonged to the lower aristocracy of knights, called *shih*. Others of the shih class who were disappointed in their quest for public office or who felt disaffected by the chaotic conditions became teachers and developed philosophies to correct the evils and problems of the age. Their ideas, too, will be explored in the next chapter.

Whereas early Chou cities were mostly administrative and religious centers created and inhabited by the feudal lords, their retainers, and the artisans who served their needs, many new cities built during the Eastern Chou were industrial and commercial centers.

The large number of cities built during the last centuries of the Chou underscores a growing population and the rise of the merchant class. Whereas the old cities had a wall that enclosed the lords' residences and government buildings, now a second enclosed area sometimes appeared for ordinary residential and commercial quarters. We have one population estimate for a city of the Warring States period: Lin-tzu, capital city of the state of Ch'i, in northeast China, had 70,000 households, or roughly a third of a million people. There are also accounts of Lin-tzu's bustling traffic, amusement quarters, street markets, and wholesale brokers' businesses.

Rulers eager to increase their revenues encouraged commerce. From the fifth century on, metal coinage became widespread. Inscriptions identified the states that issued them, and different sizes and weights distinguished the denominations. Early coins were shaped like miniature spades and knives. A round coin with a square hole in the center suitable for stringing was first issued by the state of Ch'in. After 221 B.C.E. the format became standard throughout China. Such coins strung in units of 1,000 remained the basic Chinese currency until the early twentieth century.

Three significant improvements in agriculture were made during the Eastern Chou. First was water control, vital for bringing land in the upper Yellow River valley under cultivation, controlling floods, and allowing irrigated rice cultivation in the upper Yangtze plains. Engineers improved diking techniques, and systematic irrigation became widespread. Second was the introduction of fertilization and crop rotation. Third, and perhaps most important, was the introduction of iron farming implements, sharply increasing the amount of land an individual farmer could cultivate. Iron tools also facilitated the clearing of virgin lands. As the Chinese people expanded the area of land under cultivation and more intensely colonized the land they already occupied, the population reached sixty million by the end of the era. As the population grew, the feudal land tenure system of the early Chou was gradually replaced by that of freehold farmers. Rulers discovered that free farmers worked harder and produced more than land-bound serfs and also fought better to protect their interests. The northwest frontier state of Ch'in took the lead in ending the feudal land tenure and in building irrigation works. Both policies were key to the Ch'in's ultimate success in unifying China. By the end of the Chou dynasty, all the essential technological characteristics of traditional Chinese farming had been introduced.

2500 B.C.E.	Urban civilization in the Indus Valley Era of Chinese culture heroes
	Mythical Hsia dynasty in China
2000	
	Tang the Successful establishes the Shang dynasty
1500	Aryans and other factors destroy Indus civilization Early Vedic Age Earliest extant Chinese writing
	Anyang capital of Shang China Kings Wen and Wu establish Chou dynasty Duke of Chou
1000	Books of Poetry, History, Rites, Change Rig-Veda Late Vedic Age Eastern Chou
	Spring and Autumn era Upanishads written in India
500	Iron weapons, crossbow, metal tools, and coins
	Warring States era *Eight Chapters*
200	

Summary and Comparisons

This chapter has examined the early developments of two great Asian civilizations. Higher civilization in both India and China rose from indigenous Neolithic cultures in large river valleys. Major archaeological work, begun in both countries in the 1920s, has not only verified information from certain ancient texts but also added enormous quantities of new knowledge.

The Indus, or Harappan, civilization began in northwestern India before 2500 B.C.E. and flourished for more than a thousand years. Although a very advanced urban and trading culture, this civilization is classified as prehistoric because its pictographic script remains undeciphered. After a gradual decline caused by extensive flooding and deforestation, the weakened Indus civilization fell around 1500 B.C.E. to Indo-European nomads called Aryans, who came from the steppes of Eurasia. Not being city-dwellers, the Aryans abandoned the Indus cities, settled in the Indus valley, and gradually migrated eastward to the Gangetic plain. They subjugated the darker-skinned indigenous people and developed a hierarchy of conquering and conquered peoples, which we call the caste system. The Rig-Veda, the most sacred text of the Aryans and of later Hinduism, contains hymns alluding to the Aryan conquest. It and other Vedas were written down in an Indo-European language called Sanskrit between 1000 and 500 B.C.E.

The millennium between approximately 1500 and 500 B.C.E. is divided into the Early and Late Vedic Ages because of marked cultural differences between the two periods. Notably, Aryan society became predominantly agricultural during the late Vedic Age, and the economy became specialized and commercial. Religious changes included the emergence of new deities and the ideas of karma and reincarnation. The search for new answers to life's questions led to the writing of the Upanishads, essays on the nature of human destiny. In time the new deities and the Upanishads were incorporated into Hinduism.

China's first dynasty, the Shang (1766–1122 B.C.E.), was centered in the Yellow River valley. Shang civilization is classified as historic because of writing found incised on tortoise shells and scapula bones of large animals used for divination by Shang kings. These written remains tell us much about Shang government, society, and beliefs. The modern Chinese language is directly descended from the Shang script.

The most beautiful objects from the Shang are bronze vessels, used in rites of ancestor worship and buried in royal and aristocratic tombs. They were made by the piece mold method, unique to China. Bronzesmiths and other craftsmen evidently enjoyed higher status than serfs, who farmed the land.

In 1122 B.C.E., the Shang dynasty ended, overthrown by the Chou, who continued beliefs and institutions as they found them, leaving Chinese civilization essentially unchanged. The Chou conquest expanded the Chinese heartland geographically to include all of the Yellow River valley and parts of the Yangtze River valley. The gradual decline of the house of Chou after 771 B.C.E. resulted in political turmoil as powerful feudal lords competed for supremacy and the right to impose a national dynasty on a reunified land.

There are striking similarities between the first great civilizations of India and China. Both were rooted in indigenous Neolithic cultures; both were riverine, urban, literate, and metal working; and both invented pictographic written scripts. However, because the extensive written remains of the Shang have been deciphered, we know much more about this civilization than that of the Indus Valley, where the scanty extant engravings on seals are not yet understood. Our ability to decode Shang documents makes it a historic civilization, while the Indus remains prehistoric. Shang written materials give us key information about Shang kings and their relations to one another, their gods, and their worship. In contrast, we know nothing for certain about the Indus government or religion.

Both the Indus people and the Shang were excellent builders. Because the Indus buildings were constructed with bricks, there are extensive physical remains of Indus cities, while little survives of the wood and tamped-earth structures of the Shang. The Indus people buried their dead carefully in cemeteries, but without elaborate grave goods. The Aryans cremated their dead, a practice that continued in India, leaving archaeologists with few material remains. On the other hand, the Shang and Chou peoples have left tombs that are treasure troves because of the Chinese custom of burying the dead sumptuously with everything they might need in the next world.

Similarly, both peoples traded far afield, the Indus people with the older Mesopotamian civilization, where documents mention people we infer to be from the Indus region. There is no evidence yet that the Vedic peoples carried on international trade. Both the Shang and Chou traded with Southeast and Central Asia, but their preliterate trading partners left no written records.

Social organization differed sharply in India and China. We cannot reconstruct social patterns in the Indus culture without written evidence, but we know that social distinctions in India became sharper as the Vedic Age progressed, apparently owing to racial distinctions between the conquering Aryans and the indigenous dasas. The Chinese, on the other hand, were racially homogeneous, which meant a gradual erasing of hereditary distinctions by the late Chou dynasty.

Both the Indus Empire and the Shang dynasty came to violent ends. While the Indo-Aryan conquerors had a different culture from the conquered Indus people, on whom they imposed a new language, religion, and social organization, the Chou who overthrew the Shang shared the same traditions, beliefs, and written language, which continued to evolve uninterrupted by political change. Chou bronze wares followed the shapes and decorations of pieces made under the Shang, showing shared artistic traditions and rituals. Thus the transition from one dynasty to another was much less disruptive in China than in India.

By the end of the Vedic Age in India and the Chou dynasty in China, each civilization had achieved a degree of homogeneity. Among Indians, homogeneity was based on shared religious beliefs, social organization, and (among north Indians) languages derived from Sanskrit. Among Chinese, a common historical and political tradition, writing, and ancestor worship created cohesiveness. Although India had no tradition of political unity, in China such unity was indelibly rooted in the earliest folk memory.

Selected Sources

*Basham, A. L. *The Wonder That Was India.* 1954. Many maps and photos and a well-organized text make this book a pleasure to read.

———, ed. *Cultural History of India.* 1969. Numerous experts contributed to this informative book.

*Chang Kwang-chih. *The Archaeology of Ancient China.* 4th ed. 1986. The most authoritative book on the subject. Many photos, illustrations, maps, and charts make it interesting and informative.

———. *Shang Civilization.* 1980. Professor Chang has pieced together a fascinating jigsaw puzzle from archaeological and textual evidence of China's first historic dynasty.

*———, ed. *Food in Chinese Culture: Anthropological and Historical Perspectives.* 1977. A storehouse of interesting information.

Cheng Te-k'un. *Archaeology in China.* Vol. I: *Prehistoric China.* 1986. A concise and clear account, with photos, charts, and maps.

———. *Archaeology in China.* Vol. II: *Shang China.* 1960. Profusely illustrated with drawings and photos, this comprehensive book examines what archaeologists have learned about the Shang.

———. *Archaeology in China.* Vol. III: *Chou China.* 1963. This book is as authoritative as Professor Cheng's other books in the series.

*de Bary, William T., ed. *Sources of Chinese Tradition.* Vol. I. 1960. A source book of readings.

*———, ed. *Sources of Indian Tradition.* Vol. I. 1958. A source book of readings with helpful introductions.

Fairservice, Walter A., Jr. *The Roots of Ancient India.* 1971. A comprehensive survey of India from the earliest humans to the Aryan invasion.

Feuerstein, Georg, Subash Kak, and David Frawley. *In Search of the Cradle of Civilization.* 1995. Provocative new studies and interpretations regarding ancient India.

Gupta, S. P., ed. *The "Lost" Sarasvati and Indus Civilizations.* 1995. Includes very recent scholarship by many experts.

*Hsu Cho-yun. *Ancient China in Transition, An Analysis of Social Mobility, 722–222 B.C.* 1965. A brief, interesting account.

Ke Yuan. *Dragons and Dynasties: An Introduction to Chinese Mythology.* 1993. Good stories, well explained.

Li, Chi. *Anyang.* 1977. Li supervised the first excavation of Anyang, the last Shang capital, during the 1920s and 1930s.

Majumdar, R. C. *Ancient India,* 1968. A clearly written history of India up to about 1200 C.E.

———. *Concise History of Ancient India.* 3 vols. 1977. An authoritative work.

Rawson, Jessica, ed. *Mysteries of Ancient China: New Discoveries of the Early Dynasties.* 1996. The first account in English of over 200 new archaeological discoveries in China. Richly illustrated.

Smith, Brian K. *Classifying the Universe: The Ancient Indian Varna System and the Origins of Caste.* 1994. A scholarly book on the role of caste in ancient Indian religion and culture.

Spear, Percival, ed. *The Oxford History of India.* 4th ed. 1981. An authoritative book written by many experts and updated with new information.

*Temple, Robert. *The Genius of China: 3,000 Years of Science, Discovery and Invention.* 1986. Concise, well-written, and beautifully illustrated, this book summarizes China's scientific contributions.

*Thapar, Romila. *A History of India.* Vol 1. 1968. A good, concise history from the beginning of Indian civilization to the sixteenth century.

Internet Links

Wagner, Donald B. *Iron and Steel in Ancient China.* 1993. Recent archaeological finds have been incorporated into this study of the development of an important technology.

Watson, William. *Early Civilization in China.* 1966. Lavishly illustrated and clearly written, this book traces the evolution of humans in China from Paleolithic times to the end of the Chou.

Wheeler, Mortimer. *The Indus Civilization: Supplementary Volume to the Cambridge History of India.* 3d ed. 1968. Written by the man who supervised the excavation of Harappa and other sites, with many photos and illustrations.

Chinese Bronzes of the Shang Dynasty

http://www.smcm.edu/academics/aldiv/art/webcourses/arth100/monumentality/shang/shhome.html

This site contains helpful text and illustrations on many aspects of the art of bronze working during the Shang period.

Warring States Project

http://www.umass.edu/wsp/

This very elaborate resource, a project of the University of Massachusetts at Amherst, is devoted to the study of early Chinese texts, including the "Original Analects."

*Available in paperback.

Chronology: Ancient India
http://www.itihaas.com/ancient/index.html
A helpful chronological outline with links to informative texts on the various eras and events of Indian history.

Harappa
http://www.harappa.com/welcome.html
This very extensive site features detailed information about Indus Valley civilization; plentiful graphics with photographs, site plans, and maps; and a "walkabout" of the archaeological venue at Harappa.

Indus Valley Civilization Daily Life: 3000–1500 B.C.
http://members.aol.com/Donnclass/Indialife.html#INDUS
This site provides information about daily life in ancient India, including food, clothing, housing, entertainment, transportation, and art. Links to other sites relevant to ancient Indian life and religion.

COMPARATIVE ESSAY 2

Great Faiths and Philosophies

And the angel of the Lord called unto Abraham . . . and said, "By myself have I sworn, says the Lord, for because you have done this thing, and have not withheld your son, your only son [Isaac]: That in blessing I will bless you, and in multiplying I will multiply your seed as the stars of the heaven, and as the sand which is upon the sea shore; and your seed shall possess the gate of his enemies; And in your seed shall all the nations of the earth be blessed; because you have obeyed my voice."

King James Version of the Holy Bible, Genesis, Chapter 22, with slight changes.

* * * * *

Homer and Hesiod have ascribed to the gods everything shameful and reprehensible among mankind: theft, adultery, and mutual deception. . . .

Xenophanes

* * * * *

Regarding the gods, I can't tell if they exist or not, nor what they look like, for many things preclude such knowledge: the obscurity of the subject, and the brevity of our lives.

Protagoras

* * * * *

We don't know yet how to serve men, how can we know about serving spirits? . . .

Devote yourself to the proper demands of the people, respect the ghosts and spirits but keep them at a distance—this may be called wisdom.

Confucius

Although all peoples across the globe have believed in some supernatural power over the universe, their conceptions of that power have varied. The passages quoted above show some of these differing attitudes. Thus, in Judaism an all-powerful, monotheistic deity makes a promise to Abraham as the representative of the Hebrew people. In Greek religion, by contrast, polytheistic deities were often depicted as exhibiting the same vices and virtues as mere humans. This led certain Greek philosophers to skepticism about the existence, or at any rate our conception, of such humanlike gods. On the other hand, though the Chinese philosopher Confucius did not question the existence of the gods, he did recommend keeping a safe distance from them.

By the fifth century B.C.E., and even earlier in Palestine, a number of great religious and philosophical systems had evolved. Jews, Greeks, Indians, and Chinese learned from such remarkable thinkers as the Hebrew prophets, Socrates, Gautama Buddha, and Confucius.

What made these beliefs so appealing and durable? The primary function of religions and philosophies is to explain the meaning of human life and death and to find order in the universe. Religion and philosophy follow different paths and answer somewhat different human needs. Religions demand faith and offer supernatural explanations for the human condition in this life and beyond. Philosophies, on the other hand, are concerned with existing life and society and seek explanations through rational inquiry. In some of the cultures discussed in Chapter 3, many religions and philosophies competed for allegiance, and in the crucible of time only the most useful and appealing survived. For example, in China the era between 600 and 300 B.C.E. is called "The Hundred Schools"; out of this competition Confucianism eventually emerged triumphant.

Most early humans were awed by inexplicable occurrences in life and nature. They could not account for such rhythms of nature as the rising and setting of the sun, the cycle of the seasons, meteorological events, the mystery of birth, aging, and death. Unable to explain these events, people attributed them to supernatural powers.

The belief that there was a power or powers beyond human control caused fear and anxiety, and the desire to ensure right relations with that power. The belief systems described here tried to assuage or lessen the anxieties that earlier faiths had failed to dispel. The great religions provided a sense of harmony and spiritual well-being by spelling out the terms for a right relationship with the divine. They taught their adherents to visualize the divine power as a person—for example, Buddha, Vishnu, and Yahweh—amenable to the supplications of human beings. The faithful believed they could communicate with the deity by prayer and ritual to ensure harmony and good fortune. The Jews, for example, codified their relationship with Yahweh through a covenant or pact. In return for obedience to Him, Yahweh promised His worshipers prosperity and protection.

Greek philosophy and Confucian teaching, on the other hand, stressed universal patterns that could be grasped by human reason and understanding. Early Greek philosopher-scientists sought to explain the mystery of the universe and its workings by observation and rational analysis rather than through supernatural explanations. A knowledge of these patterns would allow people to order their lives in accord with them.

The major religions and philosophies survived because they offered codes of conduct and provided workable ethical bases for society. Their teachings were eventually codified in authoritative scriptures or canons. The Hebrew scriptures, the Buddhist canons, the Confucian Classics, the Taoist *Tao-te Ching,* and the Hindu Upanishads are among such guidebooks for right living. Although no Greek philosophical text attained the status of a sacred book, Greek philosophers were also concerned with questions of ethical conduct, in part because they found that traditional Greek religion lacked moral consistency. The lasting Greek contribution was thus not a code of religious beliefs, but rather a conviction that human reason, exercised in careful observation and logical argumentation, might discover the laws that both govern the order of nature (physics) and provide the key for right living (ethics).

In summary, these religious and philosophical systems gave a strong sense of security and purpose to the men and women who embraced them, and they provided effective guidance for a meaningful existence. Further, each one contained a distinctive mixture of precepts and ethical principles that exerted an especially powerful psychological attraction for its adherents.

We may ask why so many great belief systems arose across two continents in the same general time span. There is no definitive answer to this question. However, during this period, India, China, Greece, and Palestine all experienced profound social, economic, and political changes. These changes and the insecurities they generated stimulated philosophers and religious leaders to revise old, no-longer-sufficient philosophical and religious systems or to develop new ones. The resulting combinations of beliefs, practices, and perspectives obviously met very basic psychological and spiritual needs. Along with two later religions, Christianity and Islam, which shared many of the same characteristics as those discussed here, the belief systems discussed in Chapter 3 continue to be profoundly influential up to the present day.

The Flowering of Great Faiths and Philosophies

3

Strange, indeed, would be my conduct, O men of Athens, if I who, when I was ordered by the generals whom you chose to command me at [the battles of] Potidaea and Amphipolis and Delium, remained where they placed me, like any other man, facing death—if now, when . . . God orders me to fulfill the philosopher's mission of searching into myself and other men, I were to desert my post through fear of death, or any other fear. . . .

I might justly be arraigned in court for denying the existence of the gods, if I disobeyed the oracle [of Apollo] because I was afraid of death, fancying that I was wise when I was not wise. . . . No one knows whether death, which men in their fear apprehend to be the greatest evil, may not be the greatest good. . . . But I do know that injustice and disobedience to a better, whether God or man, is evil and dishonourable. . . . Therefore if you [were to] let me go now, and . . . if you [were to] say to me,

"Socrates, this time we will not mind [your accusers] and you shall be let off, but upon one condition, that you are not to enquire and speculate in this way any more, and that if you are caught doing so again you shall die," . . . I would reply:

"Men of Athens, I honour and love you; but I shall obey God rather than you, and while I have life and strength I shall never cease from the practice and teaching of philosophy, exhorting any one whom I meet and saying . . .

'You, my friend,—a citizen of the great and mighty and wise city of Athens,—are you not ashamed of heaping up the greatest amount of money and honour and reputation, and caring so little about wisdom and truth and the greatest improvement of the soul, which you never regard or heed at all?'" . . .

And I shall repeat the same words to every one whom I meet. . . . For know that this is the command of

*God; and I believe that no greater good has ever happened in the state than my service to the God. For I do nothing but go about persuading you all, old and young alike, not to take thought for your persons or your properties, but first and chiefly to care about the greatest improvement of the soul.**

*Plato, *Apology* (trans. Benjamin Jowett).

In 399 B.C.E., the philosopher Socrates was tried on charges of atheism and of corrupting the youth of Athens. In his speech defending himself against these charges, Socrates offered the justification above for living a life of intellectual inquiry and urging others to do the same.

Elsewhere in this defense speech, Socrates says, "the unexamined life is not worth living." Indeed, Socrates lived his life, and ultimately died, in an unwavering commitment to the principles expressed in his speech. In this chapter, we will consider several cultures across the Eurasian continent during the first millennium B.C.E. that first and chiefly cared about the soul. The Hebrews of Palestine, the Greeks of many city-states, the Indians of the Late Vedic Age, and the Chinese of the Eastern Chou dynasty developed religions and philosophies that influenced future generations both within and well beyond their original homelands.

As stated in the essay "Great Faiths and Philosophies," religions and philosophies based on the archaic past already permeated and gave structure to ancient civilizations. However, during the middle of the first millennium B.C.E., religious and philosophical innovators challenged, and sometimes discarded, old values and beliefs at critical junctures when they proved inadequate or outdated. In the process new religions, philosophies, and systems of government emerged.

This chapter begins with a study of the evolution of the world's first great monotheistic faith: Judaism. The Hebrews' ethical religion was based on a covenant or pact with God that would sustain them through great adversities. Judaism, because of its influence on Christianity and Islam, also represents how a people small in numbers can have more long-term influence in history than many huge empires.

Greek culture flourished with astonishing inventiveness in philosophy, government, the sciences, and the arts among the city-states of mainland and island Greece. In politics, the world is indebted to Greece, above all, for participatory government. Like the Hebrews, the Greeks were not numerous and established no great empires. Again like the Hebrews, their contribution to the human spirit far outpaced their political sway and would guide and inspire much of humanity to the present.

In India, the mid-period of the first millennium B.C.E. not only produced new philosophies that altered the direction of the Vedic religion (discussed in the previous chapter), but also developed two new religions: Buddhism and Jainism. Buddhism became a universal religion and gave ethical meaning and guidance to countless millions across South, East, and Southeast Asia. It challenged Vedism/Hinduism in India, brought higher civilization to Southeast Asia, and was so influential even in a highly civilized land such as China that Chinese civilization can be divided by this encounter into the pre- and post-Buddhist eras.

The centuries that produced Buddhism and Jainism in India produced new philosophies in China. Of the many, or Hundred Schools of philosophies, that developed in China during this era, two have dominated Chinese thought to the present: Confucianism and Taoism. Confucianism sought to instill in people the values of virtue, love, humanity, and duty to bring about a golden age. Taoism taught escape from a chaotic and immoral world. These two philosophies complemented each other. During the closing centuries of the first millennium, it was the amoral philosophy called Legalism that provided the discipline and force that restored unity to divided China.

Civilization in Palestine and Phoenicia

The Lord said to Abram, "Go forth from your native land and from your father's house to the land that I will show you.

I will make of you a great nation,
And I will bless you;
I will make your name great,
And you shall be a blessing.
I will bless those who bless you
And curse him that curses you;
And all the families of the earth
Shall bless themselves by you."

*Abram went forth as the Lord had commanded him.**

*Genesis 12:1–4, from *Tanakh: A New Translation of the Holy Scriptures according to the Traditional Hebrew Text* (Philadelphia: Jewish Publication Society, 1985), p. 18.

Belief in a covenant, or special arrangement with God, pervades Hebrew scriptures and marks a crucial ethical departure from the polytheistic systems of Mesopotamia, Egypt, and Greece. In the developed Hebrew view, one and only one God existed; and this God looked with special love upon the men and women who worshiped him and duly obeyed his laws. Monotheism (belief in only one God) made possible a self-consistent code of ethics. The Hebrew people made their chief contribution to civilization in religion, not in politics or military conquest.

The part of West Asia known as Syria-Palestine and as Canaan was not the center of any major kingdom or empire; it was, however, the midpoint on the route of conquerors from the powerful states of Egypt or Mesopotamia marching to attack each other. Its land was less productive agriculturally than the fertile river valleys that were home to powerful nations elsewhere in West Asia. Nonetheless, two very important cultural groups, the Israelites and the Phoenicians, appeared in this region. The Israelites conceived a religious faith that has exercised a lasting influence on humankind. The Phoenicians created the alphabet and spread it with their trade throughout the Mediterranean world and beyond.

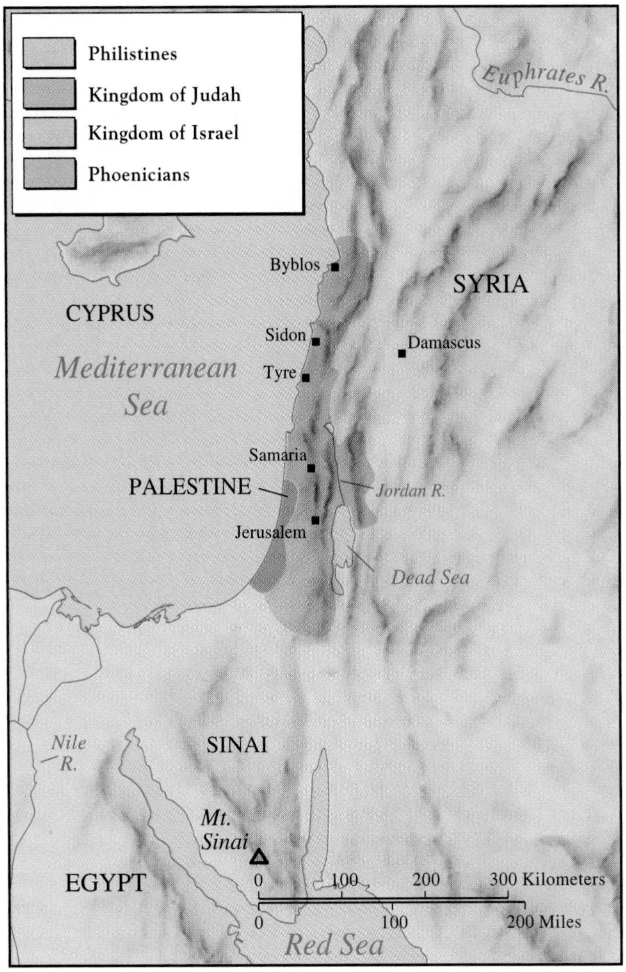

Map 3.1 Ancient Palestine. This map shows the northern and southern kingdoms of the ancient Hebrews and the adjacent areas inhabited by the Phoenicians and Philistines.

Israelite Political History

In the historical big picture, the Hebrews were neither numerous nor politically dominant. In fact, they were often victimized by powerful neighbors. Their monotheism and their recurrent covenants with God, however, made them uniquely important in the history of civilization.

From about 2000 B.C.E. onward, the Semitic-speaking Hebrews moved from the surrounding deserts of Syria and Arabia, where they had subsisted as nomads, into less desolate regions of West Asia. According to their records, one contingent, led by Abraham, migrated from Ur in Babylonia to Canaan (Palestine). Later, sometime before 1600, certain Israelites (so called from Israel, another name for Jacob, Abraham's grandson) went to Egypt to avoid famine in Palestine; there they suffered oppression and fled in a mass exodus around 1300, under the leadership of Moses, who united his followers in the worship of God. Once again in Palestine, the Israelites exchanged a nomadic for an agricultural mode of existence, engaging in military actions to acquire and defend territory. In time, they intermingled with the original population and adopted various aspects of Canaanite culture, including the institution of private ownership of property. The Israelites succeeded in gaining a hold on territory in Palestine, an area not then controlled by any powerful state. After about 1200, however, another invading people, the Philistines, also entered the region, at first along the coast, but then, by force of arms, farther inland as well. The Philistines were militarily more advanced than their new Canaanite and Israelite neighbors, with better organization and superior (iron) weaponry.

As often happens in history, the Israelites responded to the threat of a strong external opponent by moving toward greater internal unity. During the period 1025–928 B.C.E., the twelve tribes of Israel were joined in a united monarchy under three successive king-generals. The first king of Israel, Saul (reigned 1025–1004), did not attain the needed full cooperation of the various tribes and achieved little before meeting his death in battle at Gilboa against the Philistines. His successor, David (reigned 1004–965), gained both victory on the battlefield and political harmony within the united kingdom. He ended the threat posed by the Philistines, ultimately restricting them to the area of five towns in the coastal region near Gaza. David then annexed the remaining Canaanite areas and established a royal capital at Jerusalem, making that city the political, military,

The British Museum

Relief Sculpture from the Palace of Sennacherib. This sculpture from the royal palace at Nineveh shows captive Israelites being presented to the Assyrian king, Sennacherib (seated on throne), in 701 B.C.E.

and religious center of his realm. He forged strong ties with Phoenicia, thereby giving Israel access to the important ports of Tyre and Sidon, through which Israelite olive oil and grain could be traded for cedar, copper, and various luxury materials such as ivory and gold. The economic and political prosperity continued in the reign of David's son, Solomon (reigned 965–928 B.C.E.), who spent lavishly on public construction projects. He built a magnificent temple and royal palace complex at Jerusalem and enlarged the fortifications begun by David. Such projects necessitated unpopular measures, specifically, heavy taxation and forced labor (already begun in the reign of David). After Solomon's death, the Israelites could no longer endure a West Asian–style royal autocracy, and the kingdom (an area about the size of New Jersey) soon split into two parts: Israel in the north and Judah in the south. Because of the resulting division of resources and manpower, the Israelites eventually lost territories outside Palestine and became increasingly vulnerable to attacks by external foes.

In 722 B.C.E., the expanding Assyrian Empire absorbed Israel, whose people were scattered, being remembered in history as the "ten lost tribes." The Chaldean king Nebuchadnezzar conquered Judah in 597 B.C.E. In 586 Jerusalem was destroyed, and many of its leading citizens were deported to Babylon, marking the end of the period of the First Temple. Although the Persian ruler Cyrus allowed the Jews (another name for Hebrews, derived from the name Judah) to return to Jerusalem after his conquest in 539, many chose to stay in Babylonia. The returnees completed a new temple—with Persian approval—in 516. This was the beginning of the period of the Second Temple. Palestine remained under Persian control till the conquest of Alexander the Great in 332. It was thereafter absorbed by various Hellenistic kingdoms. Finally, after a last period of independence, it succumbed to the Roman Empire in 63 B.C.E.

Judaism

The religious history of ancient Israel is important out of all proportion to its political history. The various conquerors of Israel and Judah inflicted massacres, destroyed cities and sanctuaries, and imposed the misery of exile. Whatever their condition, however, the Jews gradually managed to formulate and cling to a monotheistic religious tradition that differed notably from the polytheisms of Mesopotamia, Egypt, India, or China.

For this monotheism we have the evidence of a truly remarkable body of literature, the *Tanakh* (the Holy Scriptures, the first five books of which are called the *Torah*), known to Christians as the Old Testament. These writings comprise two-thirds of "the Book" or Bible (Greek *biblos*) that has codified Judaeo-Christian tradition throughout Western civilization. Tanakh is both a religious text and a rich work of literature. It is unique among West Asian documents in giving such a thorough description of its composers' early history and in relating that history to a particular system of religious beliefs.

The most distinctive aspect of those beliefs is monotheism. Hebrew monotheism was characterized by an elaborate code of moral behavior. Unlike the gods of the West Asian and later Greco-Roman polytheisms, the Hebrew God presented men and women with a consistent code of morality and dictated a covenant under which humans would be rewarded for abiding by that code. The Ten Commandments of the Book of Exodus (20:1–17) are only its essence: Orthodox Judaism contains 613 commandments in the Law.

By contrast, the gods of Egypt and Mesopotamia set out no coherently formulated standards of behavior. Whatever ethical imperatives these deities stood for were vague and subject to suspension or cancellation. Thus mortals, even a hero like Gilgamesh, suffered from a deep-seated insecurity, often finding themselves in the double bind of being punished by one god for obeying another. Sometimes, like the polytheistic deities, the Lord God could be vengeful and jealous as well as paternally nurturing. His ways could be hard to fathom, as in the story of the wealthy and virtuous hero of Tanakh's Book of Job, who is overwhelmed by terrible misfortunes that he seems not to deserve. Nonetheless, Judaism normally furnished its followers with a comprehensive code of ethics by which to live their lives. It offered the assurance that the supreme creator looked on human beings as intrinsically valuable, not as mere playthings of the deities. Neither the Greeks nor the Romans, despite their emphasis on the potentials and achievements of humankind, were to formulate a theology that so emphasized the worth of every individual in the eyes of God.

Despite their code, the Jews, both individually and as a nation, broke the Law and disobeyed their God over and over in scriptural accounts. Moreover, in evolving their monotheistic religion, the Israelites were not insulated from the religious influences of their West Asian neighbors. Elijah, for example, had to prove to his people the superiority of their God to the Canaanite god Baal. Other prophets, like Amos, chastised the Jews for their shortcomings and, like Jeremiah, foresaw the coming of divine punishment in the guise of Babylonian conquest. During the exile in Babylon (586–539 B.C.E.), the "second Isaiah" and Ezekiel sang the praises of the one God and of his chosen people, urging repentance and holding out hope for a return to the promised land and a restoration of the temple at Jerusalem.

Judaic scriptures reflect the attitudes of a rigidly patriarchal society. Women's roles were restricted and their moral worth was often suspect. In part, this stemmed from the struggle of monotheistic Judaism against the polytheistic worship of Canaanite deities, especially the popular fertility-goddess Asherah. Judaism mandated the exclusive worship of a male Father-God, a worship eventually organized and administered by a strictly male priestly caste. Women could, of course, pray and study the scriptures, but one of the principal religious responsibilities of parents was to teach the Torah only to sons.

The Return from Babylon: Free at Last

The Israelites . . . celebrated the dedication of the House of God with joy. And they sacrificed for the dedication of this House of God one hundred bulls, two hundred rams, four hundred lambs, and twelve goats as a purification offering for all of Israel. . . . They appointed the priests in their courses and the Levites in their divisions for the service of God in Jerusalem, according to the prescription in the Book of Moses.

*The returned exiles celebrated the Passover on the fourteenth day of the first month, for the priests and Levites had purified themselves to a man; they were all pure. They slaughtered the Passover offering for all the returned exiles, and for their brother priests and for themselves. The children of Israel who had returned from exile, together with all who had joined them . . . to worship the Lord God of Israel, ate of it. They joyfully celebrated the Feast of Unleavened Bread for seven days, for the Lord had given them cause for joy by inclining the heart of the Assyrian king [Darius] toward them so as to give them support in the work of the House of God, the God of Israel.**

This passage from the Book of Ezra recounts the joy of those former inhabitants of Judah who had returned from the Babylonian Captivity and restored the destroyed temple at Jerusalem. The theme of exile and return is one of special pathos and power in the history and religion of the Jews. The Passover feast (celebrating the "passing over" of the homes of the Israelites when the firstborn of the Egyptians were slain) was itself a commemoration of another time of exodus or release from foreign captivity (in Egypt). Other exiles, however, like the ten lost tribes, were not so fortunate. And there would be further occasions of dispersal from the promised land, in particular, the great Diaspora ("scattering") after the Roman destruction of Jerusalem in 70 C.E. Still, somehow the God of the Israelites seemed to restore his chosen ones, particularly if they had obeyed his prophets (the word means chiefly "teacher") by repenting their transgressions of his laws. In the passage quoted here, the Lord is credited with controlling the mind of king Darius.

*Ezra 6: 16–22, from *Tanakh: A New Translation of the Holy Scriptures according to the Traditional Hebrew Text* (Philadelphia: Jewish Publication Society, 1985), pp. 1500–1501.

When formal education was instituted in ancient Israel, it was limited to males.

The Book of Genesis describes the first woman, Eve, as created from the rib of the first man, Adam. She is thus a secondary creation, somehow inferior to the original male. So, too, Eve's role as the first to sin by eating of the forbidden fruit has often been interpreted as owing to the inherent weakness of the female sex. Though the scriptures do contain stories of virtuous and heroic women, such as Deborah, the prophetess and judge who helped deliver Israel from Canaanite oppression in the Book of Judges, the overall tone of Hebrew tradition and scripture is patriarchal.

The canonical (official) books of Tanakh were assembled between 400 and about 150 B.C.E. and constitute one of the most influential legacies of ancient West Asia. In religious thought, the Hebrews far outstripped their materially more fortunate neighbors. Judaism was to survive as a tremendously influential world religion, both in and of itself and as a major element in the evolution of Christianity and Islam.

The Phoenicians: Catalysts of Culture

By the early first millennium, the Phoenicians had emerged in a coastal strip about the size of Connecticut west of the Lebanon mountains and north of Palestine (see Map 3.1). Neither innovators nor originators of culture, the Phoenicians did facilitate its spread, especially between about 1000 and 700 B.C.E. They were the best mariners and traders of the ancient world, with major home ports at Tyre, Sidon, Berytus (modern Beirut), and Byblos. From these, Phoenician sailors and merchants fanned out to all the centers of commerce in the eastern Mediterranean and eventually even as far away as modern Spain and Great Britain (called the Tin Islands after the rich sources of that rare metal mined in Cornwall). This enabled them to maintain their civilized way of life despite the scarcity of fertile soil in their sector of West Asia. Imports included foodstuffs and raw materials such as grain and metals (for example, copper from Cyprus); exported were timber (cedar in particular) and various manufactured goods, including textiles, bronze and ivory artifacts, and a famous purple dye extracted from the shellfish of the region. On the north coast of Africa, in modern Tunisia, they founded Carthage, a prosperous city that later challenged Rome for control of the western Mediterranean.

The most enduring Phoenician gift to civilization, however, was the alphabet. This script, consisting of a small number of easily learned consonant signs, enormously facilitated the spread of literacy and cultural development. The actual characters seem to have descended from a script used at the town of Byblos. They were simpler to learn and to use than, for example, the more cumbersome and difficult Egyptian hieroglyphics. After 1500 B.C.E. the Phoenicians spread alphabetic writing principally through trade contacts. By the eighth century the Greeks had borrowed it, adding signs to represent vowels. They in turn passed it on to the Romans via the Etruscans. The Greek and Roman alphabets were subsequently adopted by virtually all modern European languages.

Classical Greek Civilization

*I declare that our city is an education to Greece, and I declare that in my opinion each single one of our citizens, in all the manifold aspects of life, is able to show himself the rightful lord and owner of his own person, and do this, moreover, with exceptional grace and exceptional versatility. . . . Athens, alone of the states we know, comes to her testing time in a greatness that surpasses what was imagined of her. . . . Mighty indeed are the marks and monuments of our empire which we have left. Future ages will wonder at us, as the present age wonders at us now. . . . For our adventurous spirit has forced an entry into every sea and into every land; and everywhere we have left behind us everlasting memorials of good done to our friends or suffering inflicted on our enemies.**

*Thucydides, *History of the Peloponnesian War,* trans. R. Warner (Harmondsworth: Penguin, 1954; rev. 1972), pp. 147–148.

In this speech in honor of war dead in 430 B.C.E., the great Athenian statesman and general Pericles patriotically celebrated the civil and military accomplishments of his beloved Athens, assessing with prophetic insight their impression on posterity. The stage for these accomplishments was set earlier, in the Archaic Age, when the Greeks enjoyed freedom from outside interference. Beginning about 500 B.C.E., however, the Greek city-states faced a dire threat from the Persian Empire, which forced the Greek states for once to stand united. Greek victory in that conflict inaugurated a period of brilliant cultural and political achievement, particularly at Athens. Politically, the Persian wars also resulted in the rise and triumph of the Athenian Empire in the era of Periclean Athens. The fifth century closed with the long, debilitating struggle known as the Peloponnesian War, which ended with the triumph of Athens' major rival, Sparta.

The Archaic Revival: New Patterns of Government

In the archaic period (c. 800–c. 500 B.C.E.), renewed contact with West Asia revived Greek architecture, metallurgy, pottery and textile production, and trade. Sea routes linked Greece with many points on the Mediterranean and Black Seas. The Phoenician alphabet was adapted for use in transcribing Greek, and the practice of coining money was adopted from Lydia (a kingdom in Asia Minor); both greatly expedited commercial activities.

In the Greek homelands, however, increasing population and relatively unproductive soil led to starvation, foreclosure, and enslavement for debt. One remedy was to acquire new land. Between 750 and 550 B.C.E., thousands of Greek colonists emigrated to Sicily, southern Italy, southern France, and North Africa, bringing Greek culture to the western Mediterranean. Other Greeks emigrated northward to Thrace, Macedon, and the coasts of the Black Sea. The new settlements were independent states, not units within a unified empire such as the Romans later fashioned.

The Greek city-state, or *polis* (compare English "political"), a city and its immediate rural environs, usually no more than a few hundred square miles, was the setting for momentous experiments in government. Citizen input into domestic and foreign policy set the *polis* off sharply from its West Asian predecessors, where strong monarchies ceded few rights to the common individual. In the early archaic period, most Greek city-states were governed by an aristocratic oligarchy (small ruling elite). After 675 B.C.E., however, changes in military affairs brought changes in government. Greek soldiers now used new advanced, standardized equipment and were carefully drilled and deployed in a phalanx or mass formation of *hoplites* (heavy-armed foot soldiers). The success of this efficient new infantry made all city-states quickly realize that a force of hoplites—the larger the better—was indispensable for "national security." Ordinary citizens, mainly farmers, serving in the hoplite army, displaced aristocratic cavalry as the backbone of the military.

Social and political changes rapidly ensued, as the hoplites sought economic advantages and a voice in

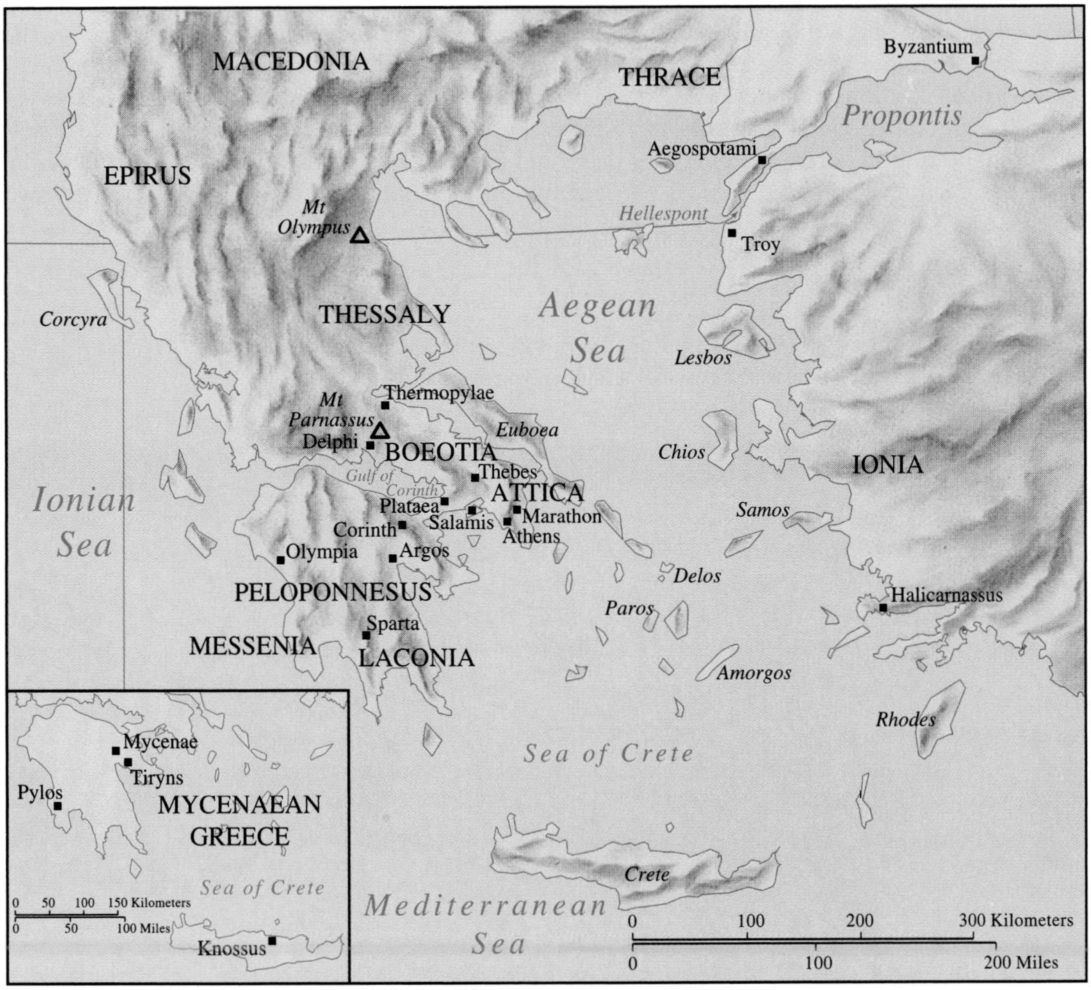

Map 3.2 The Greek Homeland. This map shows major fifth-century Greek city-states, battle sites, and cultural centers in the Balkan Peninsula and on the islands and shores of the Aegean Sea.

government befitting their military importance. They often acquired these by backing a tyrant, that is, a usurper-reformer, generally a disgruntled noble. Typically, the tyrant overpowered his aristocratic opponents with a privately conscripted army of hoplite commoners. He rewarded the commoners by canceling debts and redistributing land. Paradoxically, at Athens tyranny led to democracy, when the tyrant abused his powers, became "tyrannical" in the familiar sense, and was overthrown and replaced by an elected leadership.

Full citizenship in Greece was normally confined to adult male landowners. Women could not vote or hold office, nor could they be recognized in law courts without representation by some male, usually a father, husband, uncle, or brother. Women were, however, highly valued as a means of producing citizen children. In most city-states respectable women were carefully supervised and customarily confined to special quarters within the home, to insure that they had no contact with strange males and thus that the children they bore were legitimate. Women were given in marriage by their fathers or other male relatives who verified their citizenship. A substantial dowry accompanied the new wife; although it reverted with her to her family of origin in the event of divorce, while she was married, the dowry money was managed by her husband. Respectable women all followed the same profession: bearing children, keeping house, and making clothing for family members.

Women who were not tied to a single male through a legal marriage were not considered respectable; such women, generally noncitizens or freedwomen, enjoyed greater freedom of movement outside the home and more diversity in occupations, including small-scale selling of clothing, perfumes, and foodstuffs, wet-nursing, and flute playing. Many, however, turned to prostitution, as *hetairai,* sophisticated call girls or "escorts" for males attending drinking parties, or as *pallakai* (concubines), who, though they lived with one male for a length of time, lacked citizenship status and could not bear legitimate children. Pericles himself fell afoul of this legal restriction when he had a child by his long-time companion, the captivating ex-*hetaira* (and noncitizen) Aspasia. He had to secure a special exemption to have his son, also called Pericles, recognized as a citizen.

Much of the labor force in Greek city-states consisted of slaves, acquired through warfare or trade, who had no legal standing even as human beings. The Greeks and the Romans, though more liberal than, for example, U.S. slave owners in freeing individual slaves, never abolished slavery; slaves could no more be given up than tools. Finally, there were intermediate statuses, like that of the *perioikoi* (non-full-blooded) in Sparta and the *metoikoi* or metics (resident non-Athenians, but normally Greeks) in Athens. Both groups had legal protections, served as soldiers, and played a key role economically, but lacked the right to vote or hold office or sometimes even to own

The Chigi Vase. This archaic-era Corinthian vase (c. 650 B.C.E.) bears a very early representation of hoplite warriors. The phalanx is marching into battle in time to the playing of a piper. The standard hoplite weapons and armor are clearly depicted.

Scala/Art Resource, NY

Faking Citizenship: The Case Against Neara

Stephanus gave [Phano, the daughter of Neaera] in marriage, as being his own daughter, to an Athenian citizen, Phrastor, together with a dowry of 30 minas [the equivalent of about ten years' wages]. When she went to live with Phrastor . . . she was unable to accommodate herself to his ways, but hankered after her mother's habits and the dissolute ways of that household. . . . Phrastor observed that she was not well-behaved nor willing to be guided by him, and . . . he found out for certain that she was not the daughter of Stephanus, but only of Neaera [allegedly a concubine]. . . . Phrastor was most indignant at all this, and . . . turned the young woman out of his house after having lived with her for a year and when she was pregnant; and he refused to return the dowry.

*Stephanus began a suit against him for alimony . . . according to the law enacting that if a man divorce his wife, he shall pay back the dowry. . . . Phrastor also brought an indictment against Stephanus . . . that Stephanus had betrothed to him, an Athenian citizen, the daughter of an alien woman, pretending that the girl was his own daughter, contrary to the following law . . . : "If any person give in marriage an alien woman to an Athenian citizen, pretending that she is related to him, he shall be deprived of his citizen status, and his property shall be confiscated."**

This passage is from a speech delivered in a court case at Athens around 340 B.C.E. At issue is whether Stephanus has given in marriage the daughter of the defendant, a woman named Neaera, whom the prosecution has described as a prostitute/slave, formerly owned by various individuals in Elis, Corinth, and Athens, and now living as the mistress of Stephanus. To recognize the offspring of such a disreputable woman as citizens would threaten the structure of Athenian society and civil law. The harshness of the penalties imposed on offenders shows that this threat was taken very seriously.

*Kathleen Freeman, *The Murder of Herodes and Other Trials from the Athenian Law Courts* (New York: Norton, 1963), p. 205.

land. Political participation in ancient Greece was thus not so inclusive as in modern times.

Athenian and Spartan Social and Political Patterns

Throughout most of Greek history, the most important states were Athens and Sparta. Athens controlled the 1,000-square-mile peninsula of Attica (about the size of Rhode Island) and had the largest population of any Greek city-state (in the mid-fifth century B.C.E., around 300,000, at least one-third of whom were slaves or noncitizens). The lower classes profited when Draco supervised the first written codification of law at Athens (c. 621 B.C.E.). Like Hammurabi's code in Babylonian times, Draco's laws laid down harsh penalties; they were said to have been written in blood (thus the meaning of ***draconian***). Still, they did at least distinguish murder from manslaughter and in general shield the lower classes from arbitrary judgments by aristocratic magistrates. At this time, the indispensable hoplite infantry had little control over their personal destinies. Because their land was not very productive, many were deep in debt to aristocratic creditors. They often forfeited their farms or, worse yet, were sold into slavery. The situation grew potentially explosive.

To forestall violent revolution, aristocrats and commoners granted special powers to the chief ***archon*** (nine archons served as the chief executive officers) in 594. This archon, Solon (c. 640–c. 560), spared the wealthy the radical measure of land redistribution, but canceled debts, forbade debt bondage, and recalled citizens sold into slavery outside Attica. By redefining social status and eligibility for office by wealth rather than birth, and by widening the jurisdiction and composition of juries of citizens, Solon broke the aristocratic monopoly of governmental authority. He also promoted economic development by extending citizenship to immigrant craftsmen, merchants, and traders.

In 508 B.C.E. another reformer, Cleisthenes, ensured more equitable representation of citizens by creating ten large political divisions (tribes) each composed of wards, with residence the chief requirement for citizenship. Each tribe annually elected one archon and chose fifty councilors by lot to serve in a Council of Five Hundred, which managed state finances and foreign policy and determined the agenda for the full assembly of citizens. The latter made the final decisions regarding all weighty matters of domestic and foreign policy and has remained the model of early democratic self-determination. There was also a panel of ten annually elected generals; because, unlike archons, they could be elected repeatedly, the generals came to possess exceptional authority in the Athenian state. Through another innovation, ostracism, the citizenry could vote, using pottery fragments called *ostraca,* to send a dangerously powerful person into a ten-year exile.

Sparta (see Map 3.2) had a government differing in many respects from that of Athens. For example, it retained the archaic institution of kingship; in fact, there were two kings and two royal families. Though these kings were supreme military commanders, civil authority came to be vested in five elected *ephors,* similar to Athenian archons in responsibilities. There was, in addition, a council of thirty elders. An assembly restricted to full-blooded Spartans possessed powers of ratification.

Even more than Athens, Sparta contained a strong class structure. Members of the Spartan ruling elite were called *homoioi* ("equals"). The non-Spartan inhabitants or *perioikoi* ("dwellers around") were free citizens of their own communities but were obliged to serve in Sparta's army and to abide by its foreign policy. The largest population group was the helots or state-owned slaves. The Spartans defeated neighboring Messenia in the seventh century B.C.E. and enslaved its population, forcing them to work on Spartan-controlled land. Freed thus from farm work, full-blooded Spartans made a life-long, absolute commitment to the most rigorous discipline in education and military training (hence the term *spartan* for living under austere conditions), partly to maintain internal security in the face of a vastly larger subject population. The relationship between Spartans and helots was similar in some respects to that between Aryans and dasas in India. Sparta was the greatest military power in Greece until the fourth century B.C.E., but it paid a high price for this supremacy. The Spartans aborted promising earlier developments in art and poetry to devote their energies exclusively to the code of the soldier. History shows a similar stunting of cultural growth among other excessively militaristic societies (for example, the Assyrians or, in modern times, fascist states).

The Persian and Peloponnesian Wars

In 499 B.C.E., some Ionian Greek cities revolted (unsuccessfully) against Persia. Because Athens had assisted the rebels, the Persians sent a punitive expedition against it in 490. At the plain of Marathon, 10,000 hoplites soundly defeated a Persian force over twice as large. Although King Darius's death in 486 postponed a new assault, his son, Xerxes (reigned 486–465 B.C.E.), planned a much larger invasion with both land and sea forces. He ordered a mile-long bridge to be constructed out of ships cabled together across the Hellespont, which divided Europe from Asia, and a canal built through the Mount Athos peninsula to avoid the risk of storms off its cape.

Fortunately for Greece, the Athenian statesman Themistocles (c. 528–462 B.C.E.) realized that sea power was critical. In 483, when a large new vein of silver was discovered in the state-owned mines at Laurium, Themistocles persuaded the assembly of Athenian citizens to use the bonanza to increase their fleet to 200 triremes and to improve the harbor installations. This democratically adopted decision determined the outcome of the Persian wars.

In 481 Athens, Sparta, and some thirty other states formed a league to defend themselves against the Persians. In 480 Xerxes led about 150,000 troops on the 500-mile march to central Greece. The Persians annihilated King Leonidas' Spartan force at the mountain pass of Thermopylae and pushed on to seize Athens, burning the temples on the Acropolis.

Although the Greeks still possessed powerful forces, victory required coordination of the military and naval strengths of Sparta and Athens, respectively. Themistocles engaged the Persian fleet in the narrow strait between the island of Salamis and Attica. There the Greeks used boarding parties of marines, superior oarsmanship, and effective ramming tactics to win a decisive battle. Xerxes withdrew to Asia Minor, leaving behind a large force, which Greek forces crushed at Plataea in 479 B.C.E. The victory ensured the independent development of the Greek city-states for another century and a half.

In 478, some 150 Greek cities of Asia Minor and neighboring islands turned to the strongest naval power, Athens, to form and lead a league called The Athenians and Their Allies (known in modern times as the Delian League because its treasury was on Apollo's sacred island of Delos). The league was created to defend the Aegean region and harass the Persians wherever possible. Members contributed either men and ships or money to maintain an allied fleet under Athenian direction. Sparta, which refused an earlier offer to head the league, did not join, but remained the *hegemon* (leader) of the land-based Peloponnesian League. These alliances of Greek city-states resembled those of Chinese states during the late Chou, though on a smaller scale. In both cases, a common culture superficially united member states. Like Athens and Sparta, the hegemonic states of the Eastern Chou (described later in the chapter) tried to control their allies.

At first, the Delian League benefited Greece by rooting out remaining Persian bases in the Aegean and Asia Minor, suppressing piracy, and fostering seaborne mercantile activity, but Athens transformed the Delian League into an Athenian Empire. The treasury at Delos was removed to Athens, which squelched attempts to leave the alliance and interfered high-handedly in the internal affairs

The Spartans' Last Stand at Thermopylae

*Many of the invaders fell; behind them the company commanders plied their whips, driving the men remorselessly on. Many fell into the sea and were drowned, and still more were trampled to death by their friends. No one could count the number of the dead. The Greeks . . . fought with reckless desperation. . . . They resisted to the last, with their swords if they still had them, and, if not, with their hands and teeth, until the Persians, coming on from the front over the ruins of the wall and closing in from behind, finally overwhelmed them [with arrows and spears].**

For two days, 300 Spartans held the pass at Thermopylae against much larger Persian forces. On the third day, however, the Persians, assisted by a Greek collaborator, brought some of their troops around through the mountains and down to the coast behind Thermopylae. Leonidas and his men, specially chosen from those who had living sons, were thus caught in a slaughterous pincer movement.

*Herodotus, *The Histories,* trans. A. de Sélincourt (Harmondsworth: Penguin, 1954), pp. 492–493.

of member states. Under Pericles' guidance, Athens became the richest and most powerful Greek city-state and the capital of intellectual and artistic activity. Pericles' mistress, the former Milesian prostitute Aspasia, made his home a social gathering place for the intellectual lights of the era. Pericles' imperialistic foreign policy went hand in hand with the increased prosperity of the lower socioeconomic classes at home. In particular, reliance on the fleet gave a new prominence to the thousands of rowers who were paid for manning the ships. This enabled Pericles to win election to the *strategia* (generalship) so routinely that the historian Thucydides wrote of Athens that "though the system was democratic in name, power was actually vested in the leading citizen."

Sparta and many other Greek states feared the growing power of Athens. When Athens attempted to control supplies of grain, timber, and precious metals at their source, the Spartans declared war and prepared to march on Attica. The Peloponnesian War began in 431 B.C.E. and lasted twenty-seven years. Although the Spartans used severely repressive tactics in maintaining the enslavement of helots in their own country, they painted themselves as champions of Greek liberty in the struggle against Athenian imperialism. Pericles' chief task was maintaining good morale, as may be seen from his speech delivered at the funeral for war dead in 430. A far greater crisis, however, arose when Athens lost perhaps one-fourth of its population, including Pericles, to a virulent plague. Peace was negotiated in 421.

In 415 B.C.E. the volatile, high-living Alcibiades (c. 450–404) persuaded the Athenians to send the finest Greek naval force ever assembled to attack the powerful city of Syracuse in Sicily and add the island, with its rich grain production, to the empire—just the sort of endeavor Pericles had advised against. In 413 the campaign ended in complete victory for Syracuse. Although Athens recovered partially from the Sicilian debacle, Sparta built a formidable fleet of its own, thanks in large measure to Persian subsidies, and shifted the theater of the war to Attica and the Aegean. In 405 a Peloponnesian naval victory severed Athens' grain supply route from the Black Sea. The starving Athenians surrendered unconditionally in 404. Their fortifications were dismantled, and they relinquished the empire and their navy.

Greek Intellectual History: From Myth to Philosophy

Despite political fragmentation, all Greeks shared a religious heritage with roots in the Bronze Age. The images of the Olympian gods, named for their home on Mount Olympus, were already fully formed at the very beginning of the archaic period: Zeus, the supreme deity, sky god, wielder of the thunderbolt; Athena, the warrior-goddess and patroness of intellectual endeavor; Aphrodite, the goddess of erotic love; Apollo, the god of music, prophecy, and medicine; and so on. The gods figured in the tales of poet-singers and in the art of vase painters, sculptors, coin designers, and the like. The mythic stories often answered questions as yet unanswerable by science: What caused thunder? Where did a particularly strange black rock come from? They could convey a moral—treat a guest as you would like to be treated—or simply entertain, as good stories have always done.

Certain religious centers gained exceptional prestige among all Greeks. As was the case among the Chaldeans in West Asia and the Shang dynasty in China, the practice of divination was very prominent in Greece, for example, at Delphi, where the city-states vied with one another in erecting sacred monuments at Apollo's oracular shrine. The Greeks also held athletic contests to honor the gods at various sites, especially Olympia in the western Peloponnese.

The principal occasions for the private citizen to worship in Greece (and indeed throughout the ancient

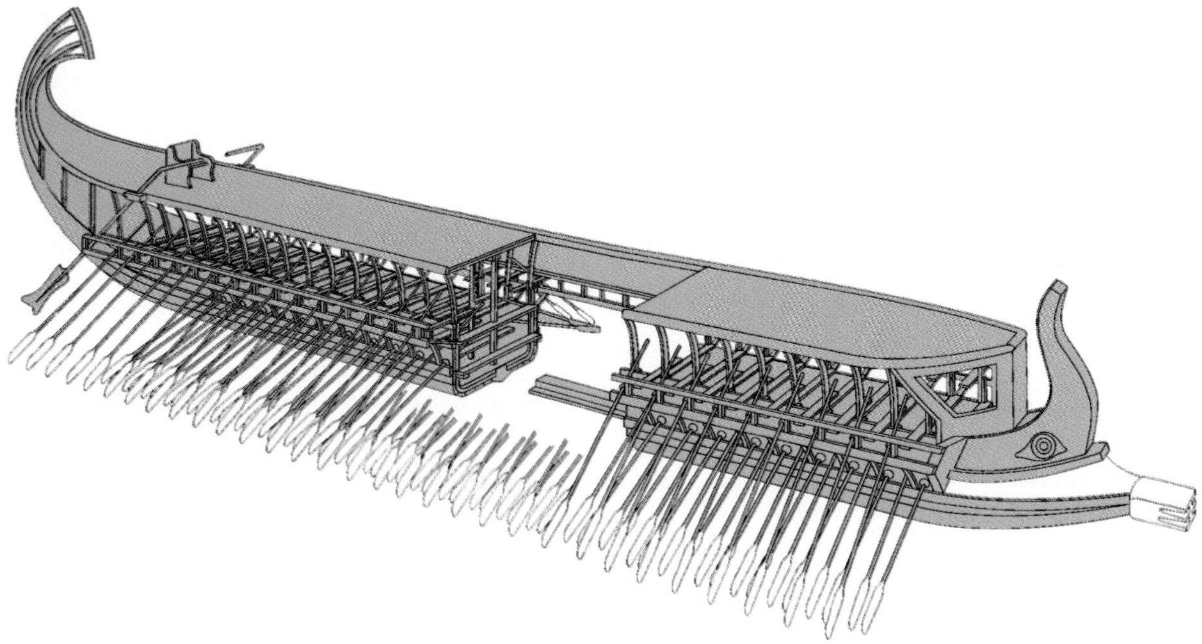

Courtesy of American School of Athens

The Greek Trireme.

Above: A cutaway view of a trireme, the standard Greek warship of the classical period. These vessels were about 120 feet long by 12 feet wide, with crews of about 170 rowers seated on benches in three tiers. The ram at the bow was the ship's main offensive weapon; note also the special steering oars at the stern. *Below:* In 1987 Greek shipbuilders, working from plans made by a British classical scholar and former chief naval architect of the British Ministry of Defense, completed "the first trireme to be launched in 1,500 years." The *Olympias* was the result of two years' work and the expenditure of $700,000 by the Greek government. With a crew of 130 men and 40 women, mostly college-age Britons, the modern replica achieved a speed of 21.7 knots at thirty oar strokes per minute.

CONNECTIONS IN CULTURE

Creation Myths and the Construction of Gender and Social Orders

Like other myths, creation stories often explain or justify "the way things are" by investing the current state of affairs with an aura of venerability and divine causation. The creation stories of the ancient Greeks, for example, are best known from the works of the poet Hesiod, a younger contemporary of Homer. Hesiod's very early version of creation foreshadows the patriarchal social system of the Greeks. According to the myth, man was created first and woman only later, as a punishment inflicted by vengeful gods for the titan Prometheus's theft of fire for men.

> *The father of men and gods [Zeus] . . . bade famous Hephaestus make haste and mix earth with water and to put in it the voice and strength of human kind, and fashion a sweet, lovely maiden-shape, like to the immortal goddesses in face. . . . [And] the Guide, Slayer of Argus [Hermes] contrived within her lies and crafty words and a deceitful nature at the will of loud-thundering Zeus, and the Herald of the gods put speech in her. And he called this woman Pandora, because all they who dwelt on Olympus gave each a gift, a plague to men who eat bread.**

In Plato's *Symposium* the comic poet Aristophanes tells a myth to explain the origins of human sexual preference. In his witty tale, humans were in the beginning double beings, with two heads, four arms and four legs, two sets of genitalia, and dual sets of all other organs. There were three sexes, male-male, male-female, and female-female. They were much stronger than later humans; they could, for instance, run much faster by cartwheeling along on their eight limbs. Soon they challenged the very gods for supremacy in the universe. Zeus in anger cut them into halves. Thus they (like us, their descendants) spent their lives seeking to find their true partners and undo the division imposed by Zeus.

The early Aryan texts in India do not present a clearly defined creator god. This hymn from the Rig-Veda describes the sacrifice of the primeval man by the gods and tells how his body produced the universe and all within. Members of the four Hindu castes were created from different parts of his body, which sanctified the social order of Hinduism.

When the gods made a sacrifice
with the Man as their victim,
Spring was the melted butter,
Summer the fuel,
and Autumn the oblation.

* * *

Then were born horses,
and all beings with two rows
of teeth.
Thence were born cattle,
and thence goats and sheep. . . .
When they divided the Man,
into how many parts did they
divide him?
What were his mouth, what were his
arms,
what were his thighs and his feet
called? . . .
The brahman was his mouth,
of his arms was made the warrior,
his thighs became the vaisya,
of his feet the sudra was born.

* * *

With Sacrifice the gods sacrificed
to Sacrifice—
these were the first of the sacred
laws.
These mighty beings reached the sky,
where are the eternal spirits, the
*gods.***

---

1. Visit http://www.mythinglinks.org/ct~creation.html, a site that provides annotated links to many other sites that detail creation myths from around the world. Pick sites from three different regions and answer the following: What are the similarities and differences in these myths? How do they portray the roles and importance of men and women? How might they affect social relations in their respective societies?

2. Enter "creation" into the Subject Guide and find the article "Share in the light: Native American stories of creation." How do these creation myths differ from the Greek and Hindu myths presented in the connection box? What roles do animals play in the myths? How do the myths portray women?

*Hugh G. Evelyn-White, trans., *Hesiod, the Homeric Hymns, and Homerica*, rev. ed. (Cambridge: Harvard University Press, 1936), pp. 7, 9.

**A. L. Basham, *The Wonder That Was India* (New York: Grove Press, 1959), pp. 240–241.

world) were at the numerous festivals throughout the religious calendar. Unlike most modern religious "services," the festivals of the Greek city-states were public, often state-sponsored, events embracing a broad range of activities and spectacles. The farmer and his family left their homestead and spent part or all of a day traveling, generally on foot, to the city, where for a day or perhaps a few days they attended religious events. During the festivals, they watched an impressive, Fourth of July-like parade of religious officials and worshipers wending its way to the shrine of a particular god or goddess. They might also attend athletic competitions, choral performances,

Erich Lessing/Art Resource

Bronze Statue of a Greek God. This magnificent bronze statue was found in the sea off the island of Euboea. If the lost weapon was a trident, this is Poseidon, if a thunderbolt, Zeus. The statue was made around 460 B.C.E. by the lost-wax method of casting. Slightly over life-size, it is one of the finest surviving Greek bronze sculptures.

poetic recitations, or tragedies and comedies staged to honor the deity. The farmers' visits to the city to pay homage to their gods were thus also civic activities and occasions for popular entertainment. Athenians enjoyed the annual Panathenaic (All-Athenian) festival in honor of the birth of the goddess Athena, with games, musical performances, and recitations of Homeric poetry from "authorized" versions.

As in most ancient religions, including early Judaism, the sacrificial festivals provided the chance for fellow citizens to socialize and, since the core of the actual rites in honor of the many Greek gods was the offering of sacrificial animals and participation in special meals, to consume foods, especially meats, not normally available to them.

The central ceremony took place in the open air; the notion of a church where one sat in quiet, pious, personal devotion to the god was quite alien to the ancient Greeks. The priests and other officials, wearing ornaments and wreaths, led a procession with the sacrificial animal, often a bull, which was also decorated with ribbons or gilded horns, to an altar near a temple or shrine of the god or goddess. A fire blazed on top of the altar; incense often wafted through the air, and typically there was musical accompaniment. The priests or priestesses ritually washed their hands and sprinkled water on the victim. Grains of unground barley (the most ancient agricultural product) were scattered on the ground, the altar, and the victim as prayers were uttered. The officiating priest took a knife and trimmed a few hairs from the animal's head and tossed them in the fire. The victim's throat was then cut, to the accompanying ritual screams of women; care was taken so that the blood fell on the altar, with a bowl sometimes being used to catch and pour the blood.

The sacrificial victim was next disemboweled and carved up. The bones and much of the fat were burned, the savory smoke ascending to the god while the meat itself provided the sacrificial meal for those attending the rite. This was the typical blood sacrifice of the ancient religions. Also, it was the most common form of religious practice in ancient times and is still practiced in some religions today. Thus for the average man or woman, religion meant participating in or witnessing various ritual actions. Unlike the Jews, the Greeks had no sophisticated theology or body of dogma and no sacred book to give moral guidance; they had only "the customs of our ancestors."

Despite frequent, elaborate public rituals, the Olympian gods failed to provide answers to moral and ethical questions or to explain how the physical world worked. Early Greek philosopher-scientists, dissatisfied with simple mythic resolutions of scientific problems, sought to explain the universe by rational inquiry. Some believed that a controlling law (in Greek, a *logos*) underlay the arrangement of basic elements—earth, air, water, and fire; others argued about being and becoming, and the precise nature of appearances and motion. Pythagoras and his followers explored mathematical patterns in the structure of the cosmos and dabbled in theories of the transmigration and reincarnation of souls. In the atomic theory of Democritus, indivisible bits of matter were the basis of all reality. As we will see, in India at approximately the same period, similar questions were being asked by philosophers who wrote their reflections in the Upanishads.

By about 450 B.C.E., however, the inconclusiveness of the natural philosophers brought about the Sophists (wise ones), traveling professors who provided instruction, for a fee, in everything from arts and crafts to medicine, philosophy, and oratory. The chief traits of the Sophists were skepticism and relativism. In their opinion, humans would never ascertain absolute right and wrong or good and evil. What was "good" for one might be bad for another. For the Sophists, the only subjects worth pursuing were held to be those that gave individuals the means to achieve their own ends. In Athens, this meant rhetoric—the theory and practice of persuasive oratory. Skill in speaking could even make the worse case appear to be the better; indeed, *worse* and *better* became meaningless terms. As the Sophist Gorgias put it, "The power of speech over the . . . soul can be compared with the

LIVES AND TIMES ACROSS CULTURES

Big-Time Sports in Ancient Greece

As a people, the ancient Greeks were extremely competitive. This is apparent in the nearly constant warfare between city-states, in the court cases that occupied as many as 6,000 jurors a day at Athens, and even in the dramatic festivals at which prizes were given to the best actor, best playwright, best producer.

Perhaps the most prevalent and beneficial outlet for the Greek competitive spirit, however, was provided by public sporting events. Already in the earliest piece of European literature—Homer's *Iliad* (c. 725 B.C.E.)—the heroes compete with each other in athletic contests held to honor the memory of a fallen comrade. But even earlier, in 776, the Greeks had begun to hold great pan-Hellenic games every fourth year at Olympia to honor their supreme deity, Zeus.

The Olympics and three other especially prestigious festivals held at the Isthmus of Corinth and at Delphi were known as "crown" games, because the only prizes awarded were wreaths of olive, laurel, celery, and pine. So too, in the modern Olympics, instituted in 1896, the winners are awarded only medals of nominal intrinsic value. But, in fact, victorious Olympians, then and now, often enjoyed large financial gains: today by product endorsements, personal appearance fees, and professional contracts; in antiquity by such perks as free lunch every day in the dining commons of the town councilmen and automatic qualification at many other meets that did award substantial monetary and material prizes. (By 500 B.C.E., some fifty sets of prize-awarding games were held at regular intervals; by the first century C.E., the number had risen to over 300.)

In reality, Greek athletes—men only, in the ancient world—were professionals who garnered the same sort of spectacular material gains that the Michael Jordans and Wayne Gretzkys of our time have enjoyed. For example, the victor at the one-stade (c. 200-meter) race at the Panathenaic Games held at Athens each year was awarded 100 jars (c. 900 gallons) of olive oil, which could be sold for 1,200 drachmas, the equivalent of four years' wages for the typical skilled laborer. This for less than thirty seconds of "work."

The slate of events at the Olympics and other meets modeled on them comprised five categories of competition:

- Running: Interest was focused especially on sprints of one or two stades. The longest race was twenty-four stades or about three miles (the twenty-six-mile marathon run is a twentieth-century innovation).
- Combat: Wrestlers were required to win the best of five pins. Boxers fought without regard to weight classification and without any division into rounds with rest periods between; bouts continued till one man was unable to continue or "cried uncle." A third combat event, not included in the modern games, was the pankration or "all force" fight, an almost no-holds-barred struggle in which contestants might punch, kick, choke, or strangle their opponents.
- Throwing: Only the discus and javelin were included; there was no shot put or hammer throw.
- Jumping: Only the long jump was included; this was actually some sort of multiple jump, rather like the modern triple jump. An interesting sidelight was the use of "jumping weights" of two to ten pounds that contestants held in their hands and thrust forward as they leapt, evidently to increase momentum (see illustration).

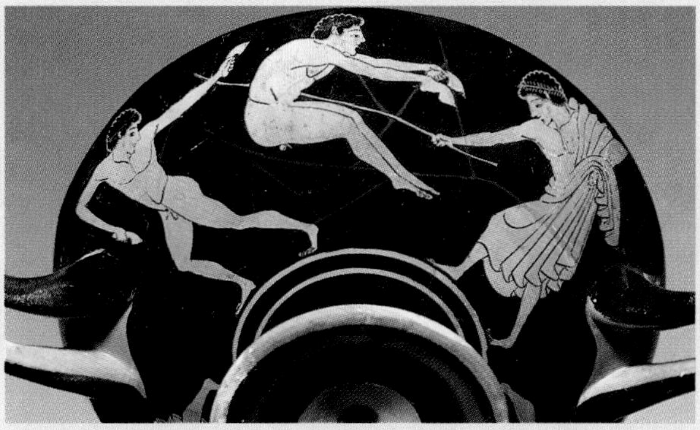

Museum of Fine Arts, Boston (H. L. Pierce Fund, 01.8020).

Athlete Performing Long Jump. This red-figure vase shows an athlete in the middle of a long jump. He is using jumping weights in each hand as he tries to perform his jump to the directions of his trainer (on the right).

- Horse racing: This included bareback riding and chariot driving with horses, colts, and mules.

The throwing and jumping events were held only as part of the "all-round" competition, that is, the pentathlon or five-event contest (the decathlon is a modern innovation). This comprised the one-stade sprint, long jump, discus, javelin, and wrestling.

effect of drugs on the bodily state: just as drugs by driving out different humors from the body . . . different words can induce grief, pleasure or fear; or again, by means of a harmful kind of persuasion, words can drug and bewitch the soul" (trans. K. Freeman). For the Sophists, it was all a matter of using the appropriate words in the proper situation; ethical questions of absolute right and wrong were both unanswerable and irrelevant.

Socrates (469–399 B.C.E.) extended this questioning of old values. As a young man, he dabbled in natural philosophy, but later shifted his focus to the right conduct of life: What is justice and can it be taught? What is love? Is the soul immortal? Unlike the Sophists, Socrates believed that absolute values did in fact exist and that one could strive to know them through dialectic. He solicited definitions from others and tested them by cross-questioning, a procedure known as the Socratic method of inquiry. Since the definitions nearly always crumbled, he sometimes made enemies, but he never lapsed into the relativistic skepticism of the Sophists.

In 399 Socrates was tried on capital charges of atheism and corruption of the young (he made questioners of them). In defending himself against these charges, as recorded in Plato's *Apology* (defense), he portrayed himself as a victim of old prejudices, wrongly lumped together with the amoral Sophists. He stoutly refused to stop his irksome inquiries, maintaining that the unexamined life was not worth living. Found guilty and sentenced to death, Socrates accepted the decision and, as required, drank a poison called hemlock to show his respect for the laws of Athens, by which he had always abided. He argued on his last day that death—the separation of body and soul—was something not to be feared but desired by the true philosopher, since philosophy was a "training for death." The wise man practices an ascetic way of life, as Socrates had famously done throughout his own life, to reduce the bodily distractions that prevent one's intellectual endeavors from reaching their goal. Death eliminates such distractions altogether. Socrates lived and died by these principles, and bequeathed to humanity a method of inquiry and a style of living and seeking the truth, rather than a body of hard and fast doctrine.

View of Delphi. This shows the Temple of Apollo at the great pan-Hellenic oracular shrine at Delphi. The elaborate complex of religious buildings centered on the temple is spectacularly situated on the steep slopes of Mt. Parnassus in central Greece.

Among the pupils of Socrates was Plato (c. 429–347 B.C.E.), whose philosophy profoundly shaped Western intellectual history. Plato's dialogues present brilliantly dramatic conversations between Socrates and his pupil-friends. Plato sharply distinguishes the reality of the five senses from the world of ideas, which is true and unchanging always and everywhere and thus the only proper source of knowledge. The philosopher (lover of wisdom) must cultivate the soul, the seat of reason, and suppress the body's misleading sensory experiences. Plato applied this theory of knowledge to such concepts as beauty, virtue, and justice. In his *Republic,* for example, the participants seek to define the "just man" by constructing a detailed model of a perfectly just state, governed by philosopher-kings, whose education is described in detail. The result is an extraordinary mix of philosophy, political science, educational theory, sociology, psychology, and literary criticism. Some modern critics have called the political theory of the *Republic* oppressive and totalitarian, but it must be remembered that Plato aimed to define the just man and not to draw plans for an actual state.

Plato founded a school called the Academy. His best pupil was Aristotle (384–322 B.C.E.), known to his fellow students as "the brain." For a time the tutor of Alexander the Great, Aristotle later founded his own school, the Lyceum. He rejected Plato's emphasis on a separately existing, unchanging reality and based his own general concepts on logical argumentation and observation of natural phenomena. He systematized logic, ethics, political science, metaphysics, the natural sciences, and literary theory. In the Middle Ages, the Scholastics, including Thomas Aquinas, revered Aristotle, and his biological works remained definitive until the eighteenth century. Dante rightly called him "the master of those who know."

In their long tradition of philosophical inquiry, the Greeks succeeded in two major accomplishments. First, they provided an option to "blind faith." Although the old religious views persisted, thinking persons increasingly turned to a more rational, even scientific, way of explaining the world and seeking guidance to right living. While it brought no final answers to the mysteries of life, philosophy did give to human beings a confidence about their capacity to fathom issues of cause and effect, of moral right and wrong, of the origins of things. Second, Greek rationalism established a very durable mindset, or habit of thinking, for subsequent civilizations.

Vatican Museum

Black-Figure Vase. This splendid black-figure amphora was painted by Exekias c. 530 B.C.E. It shows the epic heroes Achilles (left) and Ajax (right) enjoying "R-and-R" between battles by playing dice: Achilles calls "four" and Ajax "three."

The Greek Origins of European Literature

The impact of the Greeks on literature was as profound as their contributions to philosophical and scientific thought. The Greeks enriched older literary forms such as the epic and lyric, and the Athenians developed drama and history. Written Greek literature began with Homer's *Iliad* and *Odyssey* in the eighth century. Behind them lay a long oral tradition of epic poetry dating back to Mycenaean times and furnishing a common Greek heritage of heroic myth. Children learned their alphabet with the Homeric epics before their eyes and in their ears. Homer's answers to the great questions of human potential faced by Achilles on the battlefield at Troy and by Odysseus during his journey home influenced the mental outlook of every educated Greek. The aristocratic ideal of *arete* (moral and physical excellence) set a standard of heroic behavior for the whole society.

The Indians and Chinese also had venerable oral traditions and heroic tales that served an educational purpose of transmitting ethical values as did the Greek heroic poems. The oral poetry of the early Aryans in India culminated in the composition of the *Mahabharata* and the *Ramayana,* which celebrated the deeds of gods and heroes. Homer's poetry was the closest thing to a Holy Book that the Greeks possessed. Though they were not taken as dogma or as a formal creed, his epics, together with the poet Hesiod's *Theogony,* which recounts the origins and genealogy of the gods, provided an authoritative, early record of the Greek polytheistic system of belief. By contrast, as we have seen, the Rig Veda of ancient India did not present any such clear genealogy of relationships among the gods.

A more down-to-earth, practical strain of Greek literature also emerged in the archaic period. The *Fables* of Aesop normally relate anecdotes from the life of simple folk or animals that carry some moral, often illustrating shrewdness (or lack of it). The fable "Vengeance at Any Price" is typical: "A wasp settled on a snake's head and tormented it by continually stinging. The snake, maddened with the pain and not knowing how else to be revenged on its tormentor, put its head under the wheel of a wagon, so that they both perished together." The moral is that "some men elect to die with their enemies rather than let them live" (trans. S. A. Handford).

The archaic Greeks also developed the lyric, a short poem sung usually to the music of a lyre. The most distinctive aspect of Greek poetry, as compared with that of ancient West Asia, was the prominence of the self-aware individual. The inner life of the poet was appropriate subject matter for serious and not-so-serious writing. Lyric poems were personal, immediate, and flexible in form and content, suitable for recording nearly any experience. The poetess Sappho described the emotional and physiological responses ignited by love:

> *. . . my lips are stricken to silence, under-*
> *neath my skin the tenuous flame suffuses;*
> *nothing shows in front of my eyes, my ears are*
> *muted in thunder.*
> *And the sweat breaks running upon me, fever*
> *shakes my body . . .* (trans. R. Lattimore)

The invention of drama in late sixth-century Athens was one of the most important Greek contributions to civilization. Tragedy evolved from choral lyrics sung at Athenian religious festivals, as singers impersonated gods or heroes and interacted with the chorus in dramatic dialogue. In the fifth century, at the Athenian City Dionysia (festival in honor of Dionysus), three poets each presented three tragedies in competition for prizes. The actors and the chorus of twelve or fifteen singers wore costumes and masks, but there were otherwise few props and little scenery. The theater itself was at first a hillside (the south slope of the Acropolis) with a stage and a circular orchestra in which the chorus danced and sang. Attendance was perhaps as large as 20,000. Admission was inexpensive, and in the time of Pericles the treasury paid for the seats of citizens. Large stone theaters came later, in Hellenistic and Roman times.

For their subjects, playwrights selected and freely modified mythic tales of murder, incest, cannibalism, rape, insanity, parricide, fratricide, infanticide, and suicide. In his *Poetics,* Aristotle said that the crisis of the best plots involved a spectacular coincidence of fall from grace and shocking recognition for the central character, arousing fear and pity in the audience.

Aeschylus (525–456 B.C.E.) wrote plays concerned with major moral and theological issues. In the Oresteian trilogy (*Agamemnon, Libation Bearers,* and *Eumenides*), he wrestled with a thorny question of crime and punishment. Clytemnestra murders her husband Agamemnon, who had sacrificed their daughter Iphigenia to secure safe passage for the Greek expedition to Troy. (Similarly, in Hebrew scriptures, Abraham was willing to sacrifice his son Isaac at the command of God.) Clytemnestra's son Orestes then retaliates by killing her, thereby escaping the Furies (avenging spirits who attack those who kill their kin) of his father but attracting the wrath of his mother's Furies. Orestes escapes the appalling cycle of vengeance only after Athena authorizes a law court to hand down a binding decision. Orestes goes free and vendetta is eliminated, just as it had been historically under such lawgivers as Hammurabi and Draco. Though the human predicament is often painful in the works of Aeschylus, wisdom resulting from suffering ennobles the individual. The Olympian gods ensure ultimate triumph over the forces of darkness and madness.

In the tragedies of Sophocles (c. 496–406 B.C.E.), action arises from personalities subjected to wrenching changes in outlook and fortune. Characters learn not to exceed their limitations or to challenge the gods. Inborn character traits, whether despicable or admirable, may lead to disastrous decisions. In *Oedipus the King,* a man has unwittingly killed his father and married his mother. Oedipus is a conscientious ruler, eager to rid Thebes of a terrible plague by apprehending the murderer of the previous king. Even after he suspects he is the guilty party, Oedipus doggedly pursues the truth. His discovery of that truth destroys his wife/mother and drives him to blind himself. Ironically, the man who at first saw with his eyes but not with his mind later gains inner sight but loses his eyes.

Euripides (c. 485–c. 406 B.C.E.) was attuned to the teachings of the Sophists. His plays are often psychological "thrillers" that question traditional morality. His most powerful works, however, deal with psychological abnormality, with the explosive emotions of men and especially women under stress. The traditional anthropomorphic gods symbolize psychic compulsions. Thus, in the *Hippolytus,* Aphrodite and Artemis represent extremes of sexuality and chastity in Phaedra and her stepson Hippolytus, respectively. Phaedra's supercharged sexual appetite draws her to Hippolytus, who adheres to a cult of virginity, redirecting sexual urges into sadistically obsessive hunting of wild animals. When Hippolytus learns of Phaedra's illicit infatuation and denounces all women with maniacal bitterness, she hangs herself but leaves a note for her husband, Theseus, claiming Hippolytus has raped her. Theseus curses his son, who is trampled to death by his own horses before his father learns the truth.

The Athenians also invented comedy, which, in the Classical period, was strongly satirical. The eleven surviving comedies of Aristophanes (c. 450–c. 385 B.C.E.) are a fantastic mix of serious exposé and uproarious farce, often based on bodily function humor. In *The Clouds,* for example, Aristophanes parodied the Sophists and natural scientists by an outrageous caricature of Socrates, whose eccentric looks and behavior invited such attacks. In *The Knights,* he portrayed the politician and general Cleon, then at the height of his success, as a contemptible dem-

The Code of the Hero in Homer

And now [Sarpedon] spoke in address to Glaukos,
son of Hippolochos:
"Glaukos, why is it you and I are honored before
others with pride of place, the choice meats
and the filled wine cups
in Lykia, and all men look on us as if we were
immortals, and we are appointed a great piece
of land by the banks of Xanthos,
good land, orchard and vineyard, and ploughland
for the planting of wheat?
Therefore it is our duty in the forefront of the
Lykians to take our stand, and bear our part
of the blazing of battle. . . .
Seeing that the spirits of death stand close about
us in their thousands, no man can turn aside
nor escape them, let us go on and win glory for
*ourselves, or yield it to others."**

Sarpedon, a son of Zeus and ally of the Trojans during their war against the Greeks, here summarizes the heroic code. The price of nobility and the material advantages it confers is to risk one's life on the battlefield. Humans are inescapably mortal. Death comes for us all, sooner or later. In Homer, the hero seeks to cheat death by winning glory, which will ensure both prestige in this life and continued life in the memories of men and women.

*Richmond Lattimore, trans., *The Iliad of Homer* (Chicago: University of Chicago Press, 1951), pp. 266–267.

AKG London

Parthenon. The Parthenon was built by the architects Ictinus and Callicrates between 447 and 432 B.C.E. to replace the incomplete temple destroyed by the Persians in 480 and to symbolize Athenian imperial might and cultural superiority. The temple was nearly leveled in 1687 C.E. when a Venetian bombardment set off gunpowder stored in it by the Turks. Though it was restored in the late nineteenth and early twentieth centuries, deterioration caused by atmospheric pollutants and rusting iron clamps has necessitated a complete dismantling and re-restoration, currently in progress.

agogue and a blustering, vulgar, stupid upstart. Aristophanes' antiwar sentiments were given free rein in *Lysistrata;* in that play, Athenian women attempt to end the war by a sex strike against their soldier-husbands, who appear in humorously obvious states of agonizing sexual arousal. That Aristophanes could heap blistering abuse on prominent persons and attack their policies without reprisals attests to the remarkable freedom of speech in classical Athens.

Another major innovation of Greek writing was thoughtful narrative and analytical history, as compared to the rote chronicles of ancient West Asia. Herodotus (c. 484–c. 425 B.C.E.), called the Father of History, was born in Asia Minor but lived at Athens and later at an Athenian colony in Italy. His *History* (from Greek *historia,* "inquiry"), though concentrating on the Persian Wars, also compares the cultures of Persia and Egypt with that of Greece; enlivening the narrative are the author's accounts of his own eyewitness experiences and of oral reports collected on his wide travels. The *History* is full of believe-it-or-not tales of amazing happenings, told in a leisurely and enjoyable style. It is also our best source of information about the Persian wars. Herodotus combined the roles of cultural anthropologist, geographer, and naturalist with that of the historian. Yet for all its advance in trustworthiness over Greek mythology, Herodotus's *History* is still often unreliable. He naively accepted stories of oracular pronouncements, inspired dreams, and other divine interferences in human affairs. His chronology and statistics also are often faulty; for example, his number for the army of Xerxes—5,283,220—is ludicrous.

Thucydides (c. 460–c. 400 B.C.E.) came closer to the critical standards of modern historiography. An Athenian by birth, he began his *History of the Peloponnesian War* just after its outbreak, "expecting it to be a great war and more worthy of recording than previous ones." He served as a general, but in 424 was stripped of his command for failing to relieve the besieged city of Amphipolis. His exile for the remainder of the war freed him to work exclusively on his *History.* Thucydides differed from Herodotus by concentrating on political and military events and more carefully evaluating historical evidence. He believed history should chiefly provide an accurate record and analysis of past events as a basis for intelligent decisions in later times. He adopted a sophistic skepticism by giving no place to the supernatural in human affairs. He believed individuals and states acted out of self-interest, not decency or morality; using a tactic sometimes criticized by modern historians, he composed set speeches to crystallize such motivations. He admired Pericles and the Athenian Empire, but realized that growth in the power of any one state inevitably upset the balance between states. Further, he believed that because states with power either used it or ceased to be powerful, war with its unforeseeable turns and brutalizing effects on people was inevitable.

Greek Art and Architecture

Greek achievements in literature, philosophy, and science were matched by progress in architecture and sculpture. A marvelous sensitivity to balance and beauty

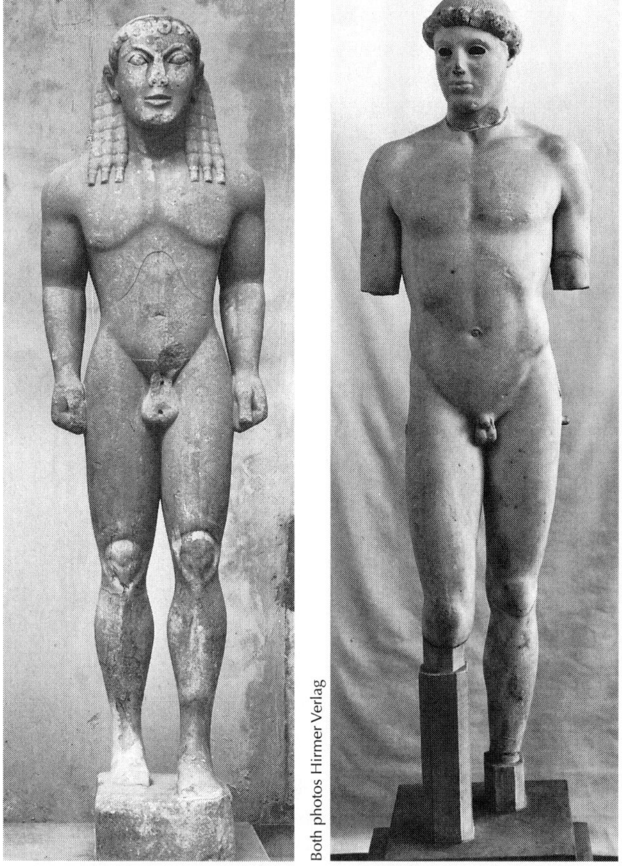

Left: **Archaic Youth Statue.** Note the stiffly impassive frontal pose, left foot forward, arms at sides, hands clenched. These features, together with the broad shoulders, narrow waist, and small flanks, point to Egyptian or Mesopotamian inspiration; c. 600 B.C.E.
Right: **The Kritios Boy.** This statue, done around 480 B.C.E., embodies the Greek ideal of physical perfection. The art historian Kenneth Clark called it "the first beautiful nude in art." The imbalance between the tensed, weight-bearing left leg and the free right leg and the sensual elasticity of the sculptor's rendering of flesh and skin mark a complete break from the four-square rigidity of the archaic youth figures.

in form marked the Greek visual arts as "classic" in their perfection.

The worship of the Olympian gods led to the Greek temple, with its encircling colonnade and carefully worked out proportions, probably inspired by Egyptian models. The Parthenon, built in the heyday of Pericles' Athens, was among the finest architectural expressions of the love of symmetrical proportion and an impressive monument to imperial strength and religious devotion. Unlike Roman temples or Gothic cathedrals, designed to be approached from one direction, Greek temples dominated their surroundings in all directions. The material was fine marble, hauled, at state expense, from quarries a few miles from the city. Forty-six columns surrounded a two-room inner chamber; the smaller room housed the treasury of the Delian League, the larger a magnificent ivory and gold statue of Athena. On the exterior were sculptures of the goddess's birth and of scenes of warfare. The unique continuous frieze running along the top of the chamber illustrated a Panathenaic procession. A remarkable natural serenity pervades the building.

In free-standing, life-size sculpture the Greeks' restrained realism produces a beautiful nobility in diverse renderings of the human figure. Clear influences from Egypt are visible in the archaic-period *kouroi* of "youth" figures. These present a somewhat stiff, four-square stance, with stylized limbs and details of face and hair. By the fifth century, however, the Greeks were producing sculpture in both stone and bronze, such as the Artemisium Zeus and the Kritios Boy, which exhibit a stunning sense of natural proportion and dynamism. The continuous frieze designed by Pheidias to adorn the Parthenon and illustrating a Panathenaic procession is a triumph of the noble, idealizing, "classical" style.

On a much smaller scale, Greek vase painting attained equally high levels of artistry. The black-figure style, which involved the incising of lines to render details and was predominant in the archaic era, gave way in the classical era to the red-figure style, in which details could be rendered more delicately and precisely by strokes of the painter's brush. The vases, which served utilitarian purposes of storage, mixing, and dispensing of water and wine, often depict scenes and characters from myth and saga: for example, Trojan War heroes and gods or scenes from the *Odyssey* or the careers of Herakles or the Athenian hero-king Theseus. But there are also many scenes of daily life: men reclining at symposia or engaged in drunken revels at after-dinner parties, women bathing or drawing water at the well-head, artisans in their workshops, boys at their lessons in the schoolroom.

Unlike bronze sculptures, which were often lost of melted down in later eras, or architectural monuments ruined by the ravages of time and the elements, the ceramic material of vases—or of their fragments—survives remarkably well. Thus, in many museums around the world, vases provide the readiest access to the art of the ancient Greeks.

The Rise of Buddhism and Jainism in India

The monk Gautama has given up injury to life, he has lost all inclination to it; he has laid aside the cudgel and the sword, and he lives modestly, full of mercy, desiring in compassion the welfare of all things living.

He has given up taking what is not given. . . . He accepts what is given to him and waits for it to be given; and he lives in honesty and purity of heart. . . .

He has given up unchastity. . . . He is celibate and aloof. . . .

He has given up false speech. . . . He speaks the truth, he keeps faith, he is faithful and trustworthy, he does not break his word to the world. . . .

He has given up slander. . . . He unites those who are divided by strife, and encourages those who are friends. . . .

He has given up harsh speech. . . .

He has given up frivolous talk. . . .

*He does no harm to seeds or plants. He takes only one meal a day. . . . He will not watch shows, or attend fairs with song, dance, and music. He will not wear ornaments. . . . He will not use a high or large bed. He will not accept gold or silver, raw grain or raw meat. He will not accept women or girls . . . fields or houses. . . . He will not buy or sell, . . . will never bribe, cheat, or defraud. He will not injure, kill or put in bonds, or steal, or do acts of violence.**

*W. T. de Bary, ed., *Sources of Indian Tradition,* vol. 1 (New York: Columbia University Press, 1958), pp. 114–115. Reprinted with permission.

This passage is part of a long essay praising Gautama Buddha's moral virtues. These attributes, codified as the ten precepts or commandments, became the guiding principles for monks, and, in modified form, for lay persons, too. Gautama founded a world religion called Buddhism. Although it later died out in its original land, India, it remains powerful in East and Southeast Asia.

There was much intellectual ferment in India in the middle of the first millennium B.C.E. It was a transitional period from Aryan tribal states to settled territorial kingdoms, from simple village culture to flourishing towns where artisans and merchants plied their trades and prospered, from old rituals and sacrifices to Vedic gods to new religious ideas and ideals. The previous chapter discussed how asceticism grew and intellectual speculations preoccupied the learned in India during the Late Vedic Age. This section will cover the development of the two new religions that contested the domination of the brahmans—Buddhism and Jainism.

The Life of Buddha

Judged by his posthumous effects on the world, Gautama Buddha, founder of Buddhism, was certainly the greatest man ever born on the Indian subcontinent. Like many great men of ancient times, he was the subject of legends and stories that have become intertwined with the facts of his life. Nevertheless, scholars are reasonably sure about some events. He was born around 566 B.C.E., the son of the chief of the Sakyas, a small tribal kingdom at the foothills of the Himalayas near present-day Nepal, and his consort Maya, who died giving birth. His name was Siddhartha and his clan name was Gautama; in Buddhist literature he is called either Gautama or Sakyamuni, which means "sage of the Sakyas." He was brought up amidst luxury by his father and his aunt (who was also his stepmother), was married at sixteen to his beautiful cousin, whom he won in manly contests (as in Greek mythology, several noblemen competed in archery or other contests for the hand of a noble woman in marriage), and by whom he had a son. Visions of old age, sickness, and death troubled him deeply, however, and made him aware of the hollowness of human pleasures. Then one day he saw a holy man in a yellow robe, was attracted by his serenity, and decided to follow his path.

Now thirty years of age, one night Gautama left his father's household, and in an act called the Great Renunciation, stripped off his fine clothes and jewels, cut off his hair, and donned a yellow robe. For six years he wandered and meditated with five other ascetics, torturing himself to find enlightenment, but in vain. Then he decided to follow the middle path or the way of moderation. Accusing him of backsliding, his companions left him in disgust. One day he seated himself beneath a pipal or bo tree and vowed that he would not leave until he had found the solution to suffering.

For forty-nine days and nights he remained beneath the tree meditating, while demons tempted him with pleasure and power and tormented him with pain, but he was unmoved. On the forty-ninth day he knew the truth, the secret of sorrows and what he must do to overcome them. With this knowledge he was fully enlightened and became a Buddha, the Enlightened or Awakened One. He stayed by the tree, now called the *bodhi* tree (tree of wisdom, the holy tree to Buddhists) for another seven weeks, meditating. Then he journeyed to the Deer Park near Banares (or Varanasi, at a place called Sarnath where later a great monument to Buddhism was erected), and preached his first sermon to his five former companions, thus "setting in motion the Wheel of the Law." They became his disciples.

Buddha spent the remainder of his life teaching. He and his disciples spent approximately eight months each year traveling throughout the Ganges Valley, preaching and organizing Buddhist communities. According to one story, a distraught woman clutching her dead infant approached the Buddha and asked if he could restore its life. Buddha told her to go to the nearest town to obtain a handful of mustard seeds (a common spice), but stipulated that the seeds must come from a family that had not suffered death. She returned at the end of the day empty-handed, but though disappointed, she had learned that all suffer the pain of death. She too became a disciple. During the four monsoon months when travel was impossible,

Buddha and his disciples rested and studied in places donated by the pious. As his fame grew, his converts came to include his father and other family members, kings, and humble people. At his stepmother's request, he allowed her to form a community of nuns. Unlike some other holy persons who also appeared to challenge established tradition, he suffered no persecution.

Before his death Buddha admonished his disciples in these words:

> You must be your own lamps, be your own refuge. Take refuge in nothing outside yourselves. . . . A monk becomes his own lamp and refuge by continually looking on his body, feelings, perception, moods, and ideas in such a manner that he conquers the cravings and depressions of ordinary men and is always strenuous, self-possessed, and collected in mind. Whoever among my monks does this, either now or when I am dead, if he is anxious to learn, will reach the summit.

His sorrowing disciples gathered to cremate his remains and then divided his ashes among the various Buddhist communities. In accordance with local custom, stupas (mounds) were built over places where the ashes were deposited and bo trees were planted around them. They became pilgrimage sites because they commemorated his death and enlightenment, respectively.

Soon after his death Buddha's disciples gathered together in council to compile his teachings. A second great council held during the fourth century and a third council called by emperor Asoka around 240 B.C.E. further defined and completed the Buddhist scriptures or canons, called the *Tripitaka* (the Three Baskets, because the palm leaves on which they were written were rolled up and deposited in three basket containers according to classification), after the three sections into which they were divided. These sections were: (1) Conduct—rules of behavior for the *sangha*, or orders of monks and nuns; (2) Discourses—a collection of sermons on doctrine and ethics, later enlarged by the birth stories (*Jataka*) that dealt with the previous incarnations of the Buddha; and (3) Supplementary Doctrine—metaphysical elucidations of ideas presented in the Discourses. The canons were written in Pali, a vernacular language of northern India. The canons and commentaries were completed in the second century C.E. Later additions by Buddhist scholars were not considered canonical works.

All Buddhists derive their views from the words of Gautama Buddha. In time, however, different schools of thought arose, based on different interpretations of the canons. Centuries after the master's death it was impossible to be certain what he had meant by certain words, and people interpreted them according to their own emotional needs and the needs of the time. Eventually each branch, and each of the different sects within each branch, developed its own version of the canons.

The Orthodox: Theravada Buddhism

By the time of the Second Council, different interpretations of the canons had led to a schism within Buddhism over monastic discipline. Those who claimed that they correctly followed the original teachings called their way the *Theravada*, or Teaching of the Elders, as opposed to the followers of the minority dissident camp, who called their way the *Mahayana*, which means the Great Vehicle. At the

V. Panijab/Superstock

The Buddha in a Previous Life. Jataka stories tell about the Buddha's previous incarnations or about moral acts by humans and animals. They were popular among Buddhists as tools for teaching religious ideals. This fourth-century fresco from the Ajanta cave in India tells about the virtuous life of the Buddha in a former incarnation.

Third Council the Theravada school was proclaimed orthodox and members of the Mahayana were expelled.

Gautama did not question the fundamental premises of Indian thought. He believed that *samsara*, or the transmigration of souls, and *karma*, which determine what we are and what we will be, were basic laws that governed the universe. All Indian philosophies agreed that there were endless rounds of rebirths. However, they differed on what *dharma*, or doctrine, to follow in order to escape *samsara*.

In simple terms Buddha explained that life is transient and painful and that the pain is caused by desires, especially by selfish and sexual desires, for they lead to reproduction, which stretches out the chain of life into new suffering. However, the pain can be ended by cultivating detachment from material things; indifference to material things can be achieved by following the Eightfold Path. The goal was *nirvana*, an indescribable state, which Gautama and Theravada Buddhists equated with "the blowing out" or extinction of craving and consequently of suffering; it was a tranquil state realized by those who are freed from desires. In an ever-changing universe, nirvana is the only constant, for it is not part of the universe. A living person can attain nirvana, and once he does, he will never lose it. When he dies he passes into this state forever in the "final blowing out" that releases him from the cycle of reincarnation.

Gautama did not deny that there is happiness in life; but he argued that on balance sorrows always outweigh joy: "As the ocean has one flavor, the flavor of salt," he reputedly said in explanation. Although he did not deny the existence of gods, he insisted that they too are part of the universe, and cannot help us. Gautama also taught that the universe is soulless and that the world soul or *brahman* of the Upanishads is an illusion. As he explained, nothing passes from one life to another in transmigration. Only a new life arises from a chain of events which includes the old. Thus, the original Theravada Buddhism is a religion without gods, without souls.

The leaders of Buddhism were members of the order of monks and nuns called the sangha. Membership was by avocation, and it was not restricted by caste. Gautama did not attack the caste system directly, but he did not recognize it in his own order. Buddhism and Jainism (which we discuss below) were in part a kshatriya protest against the pretensions and domination of the brahman caste and a rejection of caste restrictions. Undoubtedly Gautama's attitudes and activities weakened the caste system, and when Buddhism declined in India, the caste system reasserted its rigid order.

A person could join the sangha as a novice from age eighteen on, but could not gain full admission as a member until at least age twenty and after a period of satisfactory study. A novice underwent a simple ceremony that involved head shaving, donning a yellow robe, and pronouncing the Three Jewels: "I go for refuge to the Buddha; I go for refuge to the Doctrine (dharma); I go for refuge to the Order (sangha)." The novice also promised to obey the Ten Precepts or commandments. Some of the commandments had their equivalents in the later Christian monk's vows of chastity and poverty, but the Buddhist monk, unlike his Christian counterpart, swore no vow of obedience, for the sangha was essentially a community of free men and women with no central authority or chain of command. The monastic vow was not a lifelong bond (even now all young men in such Theravada Buddhist countries as Thailand and Burma are expected to take vows for a specified short period and then return to lay life). A monk might leave or even reenter the order freely, although backsliding is frowned upon.

Monks spent their time chiefly in study and religious exercises; of the latter, the most important were called the Four Sublime Moods, which required one to sit cross-legged and to fill one's mind with the four cardinal virtues—love, pity, joy, and serenity—and to think of all living things in the light of these virtues. Monks who have reached higher levels meditated on more advanced themes, with the ultimate goal of realizing nirvana. To remind them of their vow of poverty, monks went from door to door every morning to beg for food, which they shared with members of the community. As monasteries became wealthy (poverty is enjoined on the individual, not the community), the requirement to beg was either reduced to a formality or dropped entirely.

In a sermon titled "Address to Sigala," Gautama instructed a young man on familial and other relationships, duties, and responsibilities. It said in part:

> Husbands should respect their wives, and comply as far as possible with their requests. They should not commit adultery. They should give their wives full charge of the house, and supply them with fine clothes and jewelry as far as their means permit. Wives should be thorough in their duties, gentle and kind to the whole household, chaste, and careful in housekeeping, and should carry out their work with skill and enthusiasm.
>
> A man should be generous to his friends, speak kindly of them, act in their interest in every way possible, treat them as his equals, and keep his word to them. . . .
>
> Employers should treat their servants and workpeople decently. They should not be given tasks beyond their strength. They should receive adequate food and wages, be cared for in time of sickness and infirmity, and be given regular holidays and bonuses in times of prosperity. They (servants) should rise early and go to bed late in the service of their masters, be content with their just wages, work thoroughly, and maintain their master's reputation.

Unlike the sermon to Sigala, some other sermons and philosophical discourses were difficult for ordinary people to understand, but Jataka stories were not. They therefore became important vehicles for teaching. Like Aesop's *Fables* of ancient Greece, they taught the values

The Sermon that Set the Wheel of Law Turning

1. Now this, O monks, is the noble truth of pain: birth is painful, old age is painful, sickness is painful, death is painful, sorrow, lamentation, dejection, and despair are painful. . . .

2. Now this, O monks, is the noble truth of the cause of pain: that craving, which leads to rebirth, combined with pleasure and lust, finding pleasure here and there, namely the craving for passion, the craving for existence, the craving for non-existence.

3. Now this, O monks, is the noble truth of the cessation of pain: the cessation without a reminder of that craving, abandonment, forsaking, release, non-attachment.

*4. Now this, O monks, is the noble truth of the way that leads to the cessation of pain: this is the noble Eightfold Path, namely, right views, right intention, right speech, right action, right livelihood, right effort, right mindfulness, right concentration. . . .**

The quote contains the crux of Gautama's first sermon at the Deer Park. It is the essence of his enlightenment and the central theme of Buddhist teachings. When he preached that sermon, Gautama set in motion the wheel of the law.

Edward J. Thomas, *The Life of Buddha as Legend and History,* 2nd ed. (New York: Knopf, 1931), p. 87.

of caution and shrewdness in daily life, as well as generosity and self-sacrifice. In the Sibi Jataka, for example, the king of the Sibis (a previous incarnation of Gautama) ransomed a pigeon from a hungry hawk with flesh cut from his own body. Everyone could grasp the moral taught in these stories, which became popular favorites. Through sermons, stories, and examples, Theravada Buddhism taught that all could accumulate merit through individual effort and that all can attain nirvana.

Evolution of the Great Vehicle: Mahayana Buddhism

According to the Pali scriptures, Gautama was not a deity; he had gained his enlightenment by his own efforts after many births, and when he finally entered nirvana, he ceased to affect the universe in any way. The scriptures also taught that there had been other buddhas before Gautama and that there would be others in the future; furthermore, buddhahood was something that everyone could attain just as the holy monks who practiced Gautama's teachings had done. In so doing, a holy monk becomes *arahant* (worthy) and an exemplar for others.

Though inspirational, these teachings also made most people feel inadequate before the challenge of achieving buddhahood. A new interpretation, called *Mahayana* (the Great Vehicle), developed to meet the needs of these believers. In this reinterpreted Buddhism, a great vehicle was found whereby more believers could be carried to nirvana with the help of compassionate beings, called *bodhisattvas.* Mahayana Buddhists called the orthodox school *Hinayana* (Lesser Vehicle), because the self-reliance it demanded of its followers allowed a lesser number to attain nirvana. The nature of nirvana also changed from extinction of the individual soul to a paradise of the blessed. Soon after Gautama's death his followers began to proclaim the phrase: "I go for refuge in the Buddha," as one of the Three Jewels of Buddhism (the other two being dharma and sangha). Mahayana Buddhists interpreted this statement to mean that the master, as distinct from his teaching, was still in some way present and able to help his followers. This point of view led to the deification of Gautama Buddha.

Early Buddhists worshipped outdoors and without statues or images. By the first century B.C.E., however, surviving Buddhist monuments show adoring worshipers honoring symbols of the Buddha, such as his footprint. A little later actual images of the Buddha began to appear as the focus of worship. Although Mahayana Buddhists led the way in this trend, eventually Theravadins followed suit, and Gautama came to be honored in all Buddhist shrines with statues, flowers, incense, and lamps. Bodhisattvas were a hallmark of Mahayana Buddhism. Gautama is portrayed as a bodhisattva in previous incarnations in some Jataka stories. Animals are the heroes of others. One heroic monkey saved his friends from death by making himself a living bridge over the Ganges River so they could escape from hunters by walking over him. Other stories told of wonderfully appealing and compassionate figures who had voluntarily postponed their own buddhahood in order to help other living things achieve the same goal.

Some bodhisattvas had specialized functions, but all answered prayers. Just calling the name of a bodhisattva in sincerity would give merit to the supplicant. Bodhisattvas also became spirits of suffering, taking on the

Collection of the Newark Museum

Photo © RMN—Arnaudet

The Nativity of Gautama. Just as Christians celebrate the nativity of Jesus, Buddhists the world over celebrate Gautama's birth. On the left is a ninth-century southern Indian stone sculpture of Queen Maya, flanked by the god Indra, presenting the infant Gautama to the world, while a goddess stands on her left. The picture on the right is a nineteenth-century Nepalese gilt bronze sculpture of Queen Maya resting under a tree while she was en route to her parents for the birth of her child.

pain and suffering of the world, so that in comparison, the arahants or holy monks admired by Theravada Buddhists seem cold and selfish. By the first century C.E., the idea of a suffering savior, who resembled the Christian idea of a God who gave his life to redeem humanity, became important in Mahayana belief. Scholars agree that the Zoroastrian idea of a savior who will lead the forces of good against those of evil and darkness at the end of the world did influence the Mahayana Buddhist cult of *Maitreya,* or Buddha of the Future, a gentle figure who is worshipped as a bodhisattva.

Mahayana Buddhism also developed the notion that Gautama had been not a mere man, but rather the earthly expression of a great spiritual being. This being had three bodies, and of these only one, the Created Body, had been on earth. Another, the Body of Essence, eternally permeated the universe; the third, the Body of Bliss (called *Amitabha,* or Immeasurable Light), is the presiding deity of the Happy Land, the most important heaven where the blessed are reborn on lotus buds and live in bliss. Though presiding in heaven, Amitabha continues to take a compassionate interest in the world. Some Mahayana sects believe that calling his name in faith will ensure the faithful's rebirth in this Happy Land.

Thus the Great Vehicle not only created a pantheon of noble and compassionate bodhisattvas but transformed nirvana to a land of joy for the blessed. The faithful no longer sought extinction but participation in a land of bliss. Many Mahayana believers preferred the idea of a suffering savior and compassionate saints who answer prayers to the Theravada notion that all humans must find their own way to salvation. Therefore, while both schools agreed that the world is full of suffering, Mahayana is more socially oriented and optimistic. In both forms, Buddhist teachings were less abstract than the nonviolence and abstinence of the Upanishads and more attainable than the severe self-mortification demanded by Jainism. For these reasons Buddhism is called the religion of the middle way.

Jainism

Mahavira means "great hero." It is the title given to Vardhamana, founder of Jainism, the "religion of the conquerors," which also took shape during the Late Vedic Age. It too challenged Vedism and competed with Buddhism. Much of Mahavira's early life resembled that of Gautama Buddha. Like Gautama, Mahavira belonged to the kshatriya caste. Born about 540 B.C.E., he was the second son

Los Angeles County Museum of Art, Nasli and Alice Heeramaneck Collection

Adoration of a Jina. This page from a seventeenth-century illustrated manuscript shows various beings adoring a Jina, one who has conquered desire.

of a minor ruler of northern India, he married and had a daughter, but felt spiritually unfulfilled. After his parents' death, he left home at the age of thirty, with his elder brother's permission, to pursue a life of asceticism. When Mahavira started his wandering life, he wore a suit of clothes, but soon he discarded it as an encumbrance, and for the rest of his life, he went in complete nudity. For twelve years he meditated and subjected his body to the severest punishments. In the thirteenth year, Mahavira found full enlightenment and became a *jina,* or conqueror.

Like Gautama, Mahavira spent the remaining thirty years of his life traveling the Ganges Valley with a band of disciples, teaching his new religion. His followers were called Jains, a derivative of the word *jina*. When he died in 468 B.C.E., at the age of seventy-two, reputedly of self-inflicted starvation, he left a disciplined band of naked monks and many lay followers to continue his work. Jain religious canons were codified about 200 years after Mahavira's death, but they did not take final form until the fifth century C.E.

According to Mahavira, the universe is eternal, divided into an infinite number of cycles, each with an up and a down phase. There have already been twenty-three cycles, the era that spanned his life being the twenty-fourth. Universal emperors and other great men lived during each cycle. When the cycle is at its apex, giant people get all they want from wishing trees and have no need for laws and property. During Mahavira's lifetime the world was in decline and would so continue until the cycle reached its nadir, when the tide would turn and things would improve again.

Jainism holds that there are an infinite number of souls in the universe, all fundamentally equal, but differing in the extent to which the accretion of karmic matter from life to life had dulled the originally bright soul. Salvation is to be found by freeing the soul from matter so that it can regain its original pristine purity. Only then can it enjoy eternal bliss in nirvana, atop the universe, above the highest heaven.

Mahavira taught that life pervades the whole world and that all living things belong to one of five classes of life, locked in the process of birth and rebirth. The highest class includes gods, humans, and certain intelligent animals, down through the lower animals, insects, and plants to inanimate objects such as rocks, fire, and water. Only monks (and nuns, according to one Jain sect) have a chance of escaping the process of reincarnation because of their renunciation of the material life and their strict vows and practice of self-denial. Although lay people cannot obtain release from rebirth in this life, they are nevertheless encouraged to lead strictly moral lives, to undertake frequent retreats into monasteries, and to fast often.

Because the five classes are locked together in the eternal cycle of reincarnation, any action that harms life brings adverse consequences. The following verses from the Jain *Book of Sermons* explains this belief:

Earth and water, fire and wind,
Grass, trees, and plants, and all creatures that move,
Born of egg, born of the womb,
Born of dung, born of liquids—

These are the classes of living beings.
Know that they all seek happiness.
In hurting them men hurt themselves,
And will be born again among them. . . .

The man who lights a fire kills living things
While he who puts it out kills the fire;
Thus a wise man who understands the Law
Should never light a fire.

There are lives in earth and lives in water,
Hopping insects leap into the fire,
And worms dwell in rotten wood.
All are burned when a fire is lighted.

Even plants are beings, capable of growth,
Their bodies need food, they are individuals.
The reckless cut them for their own pleasure
And slay many living things in doing so.

Hence, Jains are sternly enjoined to practice *ahimsa,* which means behaving in a nonviolent or noninjurious way toward living things. Jains are strict vegetarians and are not allowed to wear silk clothing (because silkworm larvae must be killed before the thread can be unwound) or engage in professions that entail killing living things. This includes farming, which involves accidental killing of living organisms and intentional killing of plant life. Hence, monks must eat only food obtained from begging, because they are forbidden to participate in the killing of life that food preparation entails or to light fires. Since Jains could not follow professions that harmed life, they became merchants, bankers, lawyers, and doctors. They are known for their honesty, hard work, and frugality and are a successful people. Splendid Jain temples, built more than a thousand years ago and still well maintained, attest to the wealth and piety of the community. Down to the present the Jain community maintains many charitable institutions for humans and animals. Their contributions to Indian society are much more important than their present population of 7 million people would lead one to expect.

For two centuries after Mahavira's death the Jains were a small community of monks and lay followers, and they were not persecuted. A schism or split occurred at the beginning of the Mauryan dynasty (third century B.C.E.) over the severity of monastic discipline. Two sects of Jain monks, the Space Clad or Sky Clad (naked) and the White Clad (robed in white cloth), emerged, and the schism has never healed.

Although Jains deny the authority of the Vedas and have their own canons, in time they accepted many Hindu gods, though in subordinate positions to the Jain universal emperors. Their domestic rites at birth, marriage, and death do not differ much from those of Hindus, and brahmans are often called in to officiate on those occasions in Jain households. Hence, some Hindus consider Jainism a sect of Hinduism, and Jains a separate group within the four great orders or castes in Hindu society. Such an attitude is typical of the tolerance Indians have traditionally felt toward people of different religious beliefs and practices. In this way a Jain layman could call on a Hindu priest to perform a ceremony at his house, and also donate to a Jain temple and go there for periodic retreats.

Indian culture owes a debt to Jainism. Many Jain monks were scholars of both religious and secular learning; some were noted mathematicians and astronomers. Great libraries associated with Jain temples have preserved many ancient manuscripts. Their fervent support of nonviolence has undoubtedly helped to spread the ideal among non-Jains as well. In modern times, Jainism had a significant influence on Mahatma Gandhi, who was born and raised in a part of India where Jainism was widespread. Gandhi has written about the deep impression the saintly Jain ascetics made on him in his youth.

China: Confucianism, Taoism, and Legalism

*Confucius said: "If a ruler himself is upright, all will go well without orders. But if he himself is not upright, even though he gives orders they will not be obeyed. . . . Lead the people by laws and regulate them by penalties, and the people will try to keep out of jail, but will have no sense of shame. Lead the people by virtue and restrain them by the rules of decorum, and the people will have a sense of shame, and moreover will become good."**

Mencius had an interview with King Hui of Liang. The king said:

"Venerable sir, since you have considered it worth while to journey so far to come here, I assume that you must have brought with you counsels to profit my kingdom—is it not so?"

*Mencius replied, "Why must your majesty speak of profit? I have nothing to offer but benevolence and righteousness. If your majesty asks, 'What will profit my kingdom?' then the great officers will ask, 'What will profit our families?' and the lower officers and people will ask, 'What will profit our persons?' Superiors and inferiors will contend with one another for profit and the state will be endangered. But there has never been a benevolent man who neglected his parents, nor a righteous man who regarded his ruler lightly. Let your majesty then speak only of benevolence and righteousness."***

*William. T. de Bary, ed., *Sources of Chinese Tradition,* vol. 1 (New York: Columbia University Press, 1960), p. 32. Reprinted with permission.
**From *The Mencius* I (1), in H. G. Creel, *Chinese Thought from Confucius to Mao Tse-tung* (New York: Mentor Books, 1953) p. 75.

After their deaths, Confucius and Mencius were honored as China's first and second sages. They were concerned with morals and good government and thought that rulers and educated men had an obligation to set good examples and rule by persuasion rather than threats of punishment. Like the Greek philosopher Plato, they had no success in finding a philosopher-king who would be amenable to their advice. Confucius devoted his later years to teaching, and went on to found a philosophy that would be called Confucianism; Mencius, who lived two centuries later, became the greatest Confucian after the master. Around 100 B.C.E. Confucianism became China's state doctrine.

Philosophy flourished in China between approximately 600–300 B.C.E.; indeed, all the classic philosophies that molded Chinese civilization to the present were rooted in this period. The chaotic conditions of the Eastern Chou dynasty (771–221 B.C.E.) inspired many philosophers to offer their ideas, each claiming that he had the solution to reunite the Chinese world. The philosophies ranged from the very abstract to the very concrete, from idealistic to hedonistic. The great variety of views prompted later Chinese to dub this era that of a Hundred Schools, which happened at about the same time that Hebrew prophets were interpreting God's will in Israel, Greek scientists and philosophers were speculating on moral and cosmic issues, and great religious thinkers were teaching in India.

Some of the teachers were not philosophers in the strict sense. For example, Sun Wu, author of *The Art of War*, was a tactician who analyzed the factors involved in total war, including psychological warfare, intelligence gathering, strategy and mobilization; the work remains useful and even now is often studied in military academies. The three schools that had most influence on China, however, were Confucianism, Taoism, and Legalism.

The Idealist: Confucius and His Teachings

Confucius is the best-known son of China. Few men have so profoundly influenced human lives and history. Confucius (551–479 B.C.E.) was a member of the *shih* (knight) class, the lowest among aristocrats. His family name was K'ung and his given name was Ch'iu, but the Chinese call him K'ung Fu-tzu or Master K'ung, which was Latinized to Confucius by Jesuit missionaries in the seventeenth century. His father died when Confucius was three years old, and he was brought up by a devoted mother in rather humble circumstances. Still, his hobbies were archery and music, which indicate an aristocratic heritage, just as horse riding, music, and the sports of the gymnasium were part of the Greek aristocrat's daily life.

Confucius was ambitious. Because he did not inherit a government position, he had to earn one by his own efforts. Yet he was temperamentally unsuited for a successful career as a politician. His failure to attain responsible public office left him time to study and contemplate, and he finally resigned himself to teaching. He was probably the most learned man of his age. He had a dynamic and revolutionary view of education, which he saw as a means to make government serve the people. Unsurpassed as a teacher, he reputedly imparted his views on life and government to 3,000 students. Soon after his death, about 70 among them, who counted themselves his disciples, compiled his sayings into a book called the *Lun-yu* or *Analects*.

From the *Analects* we know much not only about his views but also about the man, for example:

> In his leisure hours, Confucius was easy in his manner and cheerful in his expression. . . . Confucius fished but not with a net; he shot but not at a roosting bird. . . . When Confucius was pleased with the singing of someone he was with, he would always ask to have the song repeated and would join in himself.

He expressed his love of learning thus:

> At fifteen, I set my heart on learning. At thirty, I was firmly established. At forty, I had no more doubts. At fifty, I knew the will of Heaven. At sixty, I was ready to listen to it. At seventy, I could follow my heart's desire without transgressing what was right.

Confucius believed that human nature was innately good and that it was a moral education that made some people superior, as is reflected in the following sayings by him: "By nature men are pretty much alike; it is learning and practice that set them apart," and, "In education there are no class distinctions."

Confucius wrote a book called the *Chun Chiu (Spring and Autumn)*, a chronicle of his native state Lu from 722 to 479 B.C.E. The *Chun Chiu*, the *Shu Ching* (Book of History), *Shih Ching* (Book of Poetry), *Li Chi* (Book of Rites), and *I Ching* (Book of Change), which dealt with divination and metaphysical concepts, are called the Five Classics. They are the most important canons of Confucianism and are accepted by all Chinese as the distillation of their heritage from ancient times. Some scholars credit Confucius and his disciples with compiling and editing the earlier classics. In any case, they were conservators who prided themselves on preserving and handing down the heritage of the past.

Confucius taught that people must return to virtue and live the ideal of *jen*, which means "humanity, benevolence, and love." When jen is practiced together with *li* (moral and social propriety), society will return to a state of *tao*, or the moral way ordained by heaven and carried out by past sage rulers during the golden age of mythology and the early Chou dynasty.

All individuals exist within society. Moral worth, not birth, makes a person superior. Superior men should devote themselves to public service to bring about general betterment. Leaders should be virtuous and rule by example rather than through fear. When a ruler asked Confucius about government he replied, "If a ruler himself is upright, all will go well without orders. But if he himself is not upright, even though he gives orders they will not be obeyed." To this he added, "Let the prince be prince, the minister be minister, the father father and the son son." He called this concept the rectification of names, meaning that every name carries certain implications. Thus, when a man is called ruler, he should know what is expected of a moral ruler. If he acts according to those ideals, then he is truly a ruler in name as well as in fact. The same holds true for every name in social relationships.

Confucius taught that there are five basic relationships: ruler and minister, father and son, husband and wife, elder and younger sibling, and friend and friend. Each relationship is reciprocal; each person has obligations toward the other. For example, younger siblings should love and respect their older brothers and sisters, who should love and guide the younger ones. The importance of the family is shown by the fact that three of the five relationships are between its members. According to Confucius, the family is the state in microcosm. Older family members give the young ones their first lessons in morality. If the father is kind and just and sets a good example, the family will live in harmony. Likewise if the ruler treats his subjects as a good father does his children, the state will be in good order. Confucius constantly urged filial piety or love and reverence of the young towards the old. What if there is conflict between a son's duty to his father and a higher social duty? Confucius said: "In serving his parents a son may gently remonstrate with them. If he sees that they are not inclined to follow his suggestion, he should resume his reverential attitude but not abandon his purpose. If he is belabored, he will not complain."

Confucius founded a school of moral philosophy, not a religion. He believed in ancestor worship, as did all Chinese, but he shied from speculating about the next world. When asked by a student about the worship of ghosts and spirits, he replied: "We don't know yet how to serve men, how can we know about serving the spirits?" In this he shows a kinship of spirit with Socrates, who similarly was skeptical about conventional notions about life after death.

The Reformer: Mencius and the Confucian Consensus

Confucius had many disciples, who continued his teachings, but the most famous early Confucian was Meng K'o (c. 372–c. 289 B.C.E.), whose Latinized name was Mencius, for Meng Tzu, or Master Meng. Like Confucius, he was born into a *shih* family and lost his father when he was very young. Mencius was raised by his mother, who struggled to give him a good education, moving several times until she found a place near a school. Regretting that he was born too late to know the master, Mencius studied under Confucius's grandson. For a while he traveled from state to state, vainly trying to convice rulers to adopt his ideas, but eventually he settled down to teach. His ideas are set out in a book called *The Mencius,* which became a major Confucian classic.

A brilliant debater, Mencius took on advocates of other schools of philosophy. He also expanded on some ideas not fully developed by Confucius and brought them to their logical conclusion. For example, Confucius said that men should practice jen in dealing with others, but did not fully explain why. Mencius explained that they should do so because human nature is originally good, so every man has the potential for sagehood, but goodness needs to be cultivated and cannot be achieved through a flash of enlightenment.

Mencius was even more insistent than Confucius that the state should be a moral institution and that the head of state should be a moral leader. He declared that such an ideal state had existed when sage men ruled in the golden age. What if the ruler failed to live up to the ideals? Developing Confucius's theory of the rectification of names to its logical conclusion, Mencius said that such a ruler is no king but a "mere fellow" and that the people have the moral right of revolution. He added that rulers should trust the administration to qualified officials and not interfere with their duties, for to do so would be as foolish as trying to tell a skilled jade carver how to carve jade. It is not enough, he continued, for a ruler merely to set good examples. He should also create an environment that will encourage the people to cultivate high standards of morality. He could do this by providing for the economic well-being of his subjects. This had been done, said Mencius, by the Duke of Chou when he created the well-field system. This land distribution system, so simple in concept, has fascinated reformers from Mencius's time to the present; many see it as the ultimate foundation of social justice in an agrarian society.

Mencius's idealism had a practical base. He argued that it is in the enlightened interest of a ruler to treat his people well, for he cannot expect his subjects to practice morality on empty stomachs. Conversely, Mencius warned that if a ruler abuses his people, they have the right to rise up and overthrow him. These teachings earned Mencius the title of the Second Sage (after Confucius), inspired the love of the people, and established his reputation as a scourge of tyrants.

Confucianism was a practical philosophy that emphasized proper conduct, virtuous life, and humanity, which can be learned through the study of history and the classics. It is also an optimistic philosophy that teaches that human nature is good, that both the individual and society are perfectible, and that life can be harmonious and fulfilling for all. Confucianism faced competition, however, from other schools of thought.

The Mystic: Lao Tzu and Taoism

The word *tao* means "the way." If most philosophers agreed upon one thing, it was that the turmoil of the era was the result of the loss of *tao,* however interpreted. While Confucians, the earnest "do-gooders" who attempted to restore the perceived *tao* of the sage kings of antiquity by moral reforms, others reacted to chaotic times by seeking to rise above the mundane because they regarded the world as beyond saving. The philosophy that these recluses developed to justify and give meaning to their nonaction is called Taoism. Next to Confucianism, Taoism is the most important traditional philosophy in Chinese history. In many ways it is precisely the opposite of Confucianism; paradoxically, though, the two doctrines have acted as necessary counterparts of each other, appealing to different sides of the Chinese character.

Tradition credits Lao Tzu (Old Master) with founding Taoism, but there is no proof that such a man existed. After Taoism had established a following, some Taoists claimed that the Old Master had been a senior contemporary of Confucius from the southern state of Ch'u and had worked as an archivist in the royal Chou court. According

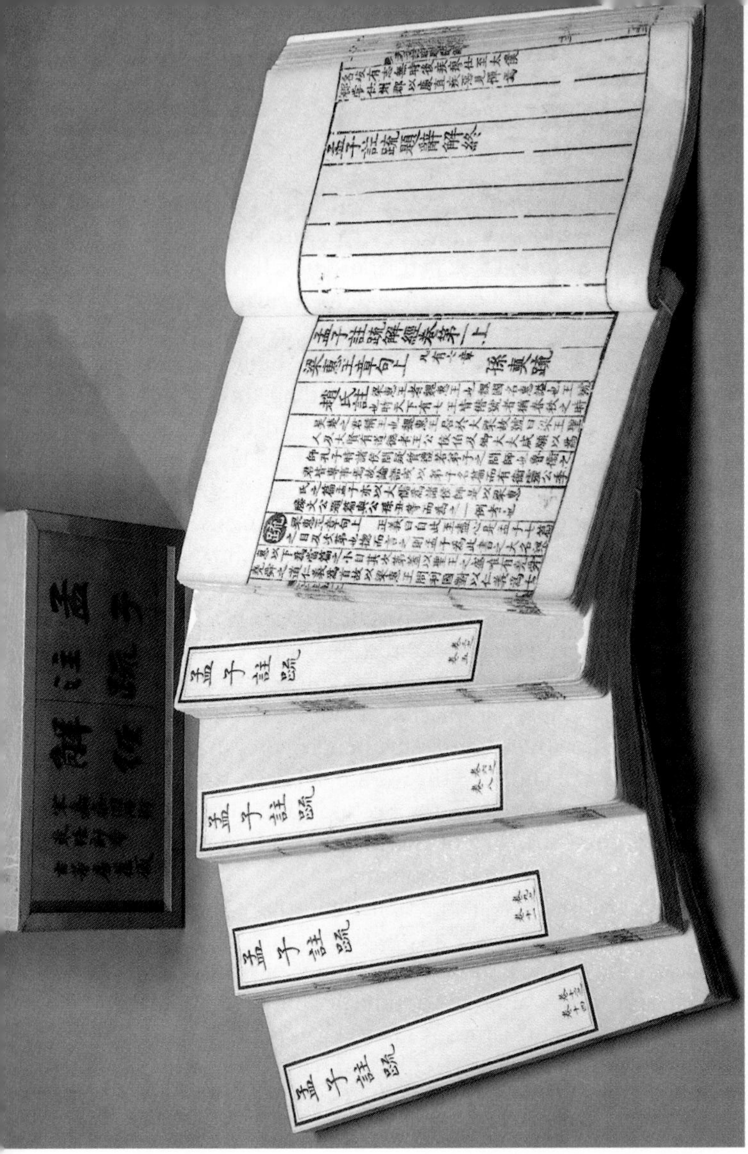

National Palace Museum, Taipei, Taiwan, Republic of China

The Continuity of Tradition. These rare volumes are from a twelfth-century edition of the *Book of Mencius,* with annotations and commentary by a famous scholar of the first century C.E. The Chinese invented paper and printing, which made possible the wide dissemination of important books.

to the same tradition, as an old man Lao Tzu had decided to leave China and head west but had been stopped by border guards who asked him to write down his teachings. After doing so, some stories say, he went to India, where he converted the Buddha to Taoism.

The *Lao Tzu* or *Tao Te Ching* (The Canon of the Way and Virtue) is a work attributed to Lao Tzu. Considered the most important canon of Taoism, the *Lao Tzu* is mostly in poetic form and only 5,000 words long. It is a difficult book—terse, deliberately obscure, and thus open to many interpretations. These characteristics have contributed to its appeal through the generations. It begins thus:

The Tao (way) that can be told of
Is not the eternal Tao;
The name that can be named
Is not the eternal name.
Nameless, it is the origin of Heaven and earth,
Nameable, it is the mother of all things.

In another passage the *Lao Tzu* says: "Those who understand don't talk, and those who talk don't understand." Confucians have delighted in throwing this epigram back at the Taoists, saying that in writing this book, Lao Tzu may have proved that point conclusively!

While many passages of the *Lao Tzu* are puzzling, some are not, for example:

Therefore a sage rules his people thus:
He empties their minds,
And fills their bellies;
He weakens their ambition,
And strengthens their bones.
He strives always to keep the people innocent of knowledge and desires, and to keep the knowing ones from meddling. By doing nothing that interferes with anything, nothing is left unregulated.

This passage sums up the Taoist theory of government. Both Confucians and Taoists agree that a sage should rule, but whereas the Confucian sage-ruler should do many things for the people, the Taoist sage-ruler should do nothing at all. Taoists say the troubles of the world are not caused by governments failing to do enough, but by governments doing too much. They claim that before civilization corrupted people, there had been a golden age:

It was when the Great Tao declined,
That there appeared humanity and righteousness.
It was when knowledge and intelligence arose,
That there appeared hypocrisy.
It was when the six relations lost their harmony,
That there was talk of filial piety and paternal affection.
It was when the country fell into chaos and confusion
That there was talk of loyalty and trustworthiness.
Banish sageliness, discard wisdom,
And the people will be benefitted a hundredfold.
Banish humanity, discard righteousness,
And the people will return to filial piety and parental affection.
Banish skill, discard profit,
And thieves and robbers will disappear.

By virtue (*te* in the canon *Tao-te Ching*), Taoists do not mean the virtues achieved through a moral education, but rather the natural, instinctive qualities of virtue, similar to Plato's ideas of the primitive man in the *Laws.* Taoists therefore strive to return to primitive simplicity, to a time before people were corrupted by the follies of civilization. The *Lao Tzu* thus represents an alternative solution to the political chaos and intellectual turmoil of the late Chou. Like Confucianism, Taoism proposes a way of life and philosophy of government for the elite, the only people who could read and who had the leisure to withdraw to contemplate nature.

Chuang Tzu (Master Chuang, c. 369–286 B.C.E.) was the second great figure, and a historical one, of the Taoist school. He reputedly served as a minor official in one of the states; little is known about him, however, for he seems to have spent much time as a hermit. A book of essays called the *Chuang Tzu* is attributed to him. Like the *Lao Tzu,* it does not depend on methodical argument to convince. It is full of whimsy; animals and insects converse philosophically while men speak nonsense. Moralists, especially Confucians, are lampooned with cutting wit. The Chuang Tzu is sprinkled throughout with anecdotes, of which the following is an example:

> Once Chuang Tzu was fishing in the P'u River when the king of Ch'u sent two of his ministers to announce that he wished to entrust to Chuang Tzu the care of his entire domains.
>
> Chuang Tzu held his fishing pole and, without turning his head, said: "I have heard that Ch'u possesses a sacred tortoise which has been dead for three thousand years and which the king keeps wrapped up in a box and stored in his ancestral temple. Is this tortoise better off dead and with its bones venerated, or would it be better off alive with its tail dragging in the mud?"
>
> "It would be better off alive and dragging its tail in the mud," the two ministers replied.
>
> "Then go away!" said Chuang Tzu, "and I will drag my tail in the mud!"

Chuang Tzu agreed with the *Lao Tzu*'s thesis that the Tao is the underlying principle governing all existence. He denied the Confucian concept that man is the measure of all things. To Chuang Tzu, the human mind was clouded by partial understanding; only the Tao was enduring and eternal. He believed that people must free themselves from their own prejudices and their tendency to judge others in terms of themselves. A person who understood and lived in unity with the Tao would be happy and beyond change and death. Chuang Tzu regarded death as a natural step that followed life in an eternal process of cosmic change; therefore it was not to be feared.

Such was the vision of the early Taoist sages. They extolled nature and urged people to attune themselves to it in order to be happy. They offered no governmental programs except that less is better, until people could return to the state of the childlike innocence of ancient times. A true Taoist should not even urge others to follow the Tao because in so doing he was imposing his own value judgment. However, being human, Taoists joined in competition against other schools of philosophy for acceptance.

The Totalitarians: Legalism

Legalism, the other main challenge to Confucianism, was chronologically the last philosophy to emerge from the Hundred Schools period. It had the greatest impact on the political life of the time. Unlike exponents of the other schools who did not hold important public office, Legalist leaders were high government officials with great power; therefore their primary concern was to find solutions to immediate problems and not to devise theoretical approaches. Like busy politicians, they were impatient with the debates of philosophers, which they condemned as "vain talk." Legalism here does not mean jurisprudence; it refers to the theory and method of political organization and leadership. It developed because the state needed a rational social and political organization to enable it to prosper and to unite China by defeating its rivals in war.

The first book expounding Legalist ideas was *The Lord Shang,* written by Shang Yang (d. 338 B.C.E.). Shang Yang (later rewarded with the title of Lord) was chief minister of the northwestern state of Ch'in and was responsible for organizing a system of government that enabled Ch'in to become powerful, overcome its rivals, and unify China a century later. In his book Lord Shang described the policies that he had successfully implemented, such as the abolition of serfdom and the institution of a centralized, bureaucratic administration. He organized all families into mutual surveillance units, imposed harsh punishments, and rewarded informers. Lord Shang also emphasized the importance of rule by law from which the school derived its name.

Han Fei (d. 233 B.C.E.) was another minister of Ch'in. He too left a book named after himself that added to Lord Shang's theories on Legalism. Han Fei later lost a power struggle, was disgraced, and died in prison at the hands of his fellow Legalist and rival, Li Ssu. Li served as chief minister of Ch'in both during its final drive for unification and afterward. Li, who would also be murdered in prison, synthesized the teachings of Lord Shang and Han Fei and brought them to their highest development. Li and Han's deaths reflect the ruthless and violent power struggles typical of the Legalists.

Legalists had no patience with the Confucians and Taoists, who looked back in time for a golden age. The Legalists maintained that people in the present were neither better nor worse than people in the past; only the conditions were different. Rather than long for a restoration of the past, people should solve new problems with new measures. Han Fei's book cited a story to prove this point:

> There was a plow man of Sung in whose field was a tree stump. When a rabbit scampered headlong into the stump, broke its neck, and died, he abandoned his plow and kept watch over the stump, hoping it would get him more rabbits. But he got no more rabbits and became the laughing stock of the whole state of Sung. Now wanting to apply policies of the former kings in governing people in these times belongs in the very same category as watching over the stump!

The Three Faiths. This sixteenth-century painting shows Confucius in the dominant central position between Gautama Buddha (left), withdrawn in meditation, and Lao Tzu, founder of Taoism (right), looking contented. Legalism was rejected by the Chinese after the brief Ch'in dynasty and does not figure here.

The idea that the human condition was a changing process was revolutionary at that time.

While Confucians and Taoists were concerned to improve the plight of the people, Legalists believed that human nature was evil, that people were naturally selfish, lazy, disobedient, and reluctant to engage in war. Accordingly, the Legalists sought to defend the state's absolute authority against the demands of the people through stringent enforcement of strict laws. Those who contribute to the state should be rewarded lavishly, while wrongdoers should be punished with exemplary harshness. For example, when the crown prince criticized some laws as too harsh, Lord Shang held the prince's teacher responsible and had him branded. When some people then praised the laws, he ordered them banished for daring to voice their opinions. All learned to keep quiet and obey. Officials should receive job assignments on the basis of talent and not birth, and they should be held strictly responsible for their deeds. No one is above the law, and when the laws are complete, the system is foolproof. The ruler need only retain the authority to reward and to punish, and all else will run automatically.

The ultimate Legalist goal was to establish and perpetuate an all-powerful state, protected by all-embracing laws, impersonally administered. Legalists maintained that there were only two types of useful citizens: farmers and soldiers. The farmers' work created wealth, and good soldiers won wars that made the state powerful. Furthermore, the state should be able to mobilize its able-bodied farmers and use them as soldiers when needed. How does the state convince its citizens that they must fight? Lord Shang answered: "If there is no hope of fame except through service in warfare, the people will be ready to lay down their lives. . . . I would have the people told . . . if they fear harm, it will be only by fighting that they can escape it." He concluded: "A country that directed itself to these two ends [agriculture and war] would not have to wait long before it established hegemony or even complete mastery over all other states." He also observed that "a ruler who can make the people delight in war will become king of kings."

Legalists disdained the classics and moral values such as filial piety, sincerity, and humanity. They feared that these books and values would dissuade the people from the single-minded pursuit of agriculture and warfare. They also wished to eliminate many classes of people: aristocrats because they were born to their privileges; artisans because they produced luxury items that catered to the aristocrats; innkeepers because they served travelers, who were apt to be troublesome and to plot against the state; merchants because of their avarice; moralists (Confucians) because they preached filial piety and loyalty to friends, which might create conflict of interest and militate against total loyalty and obedience to the state; philanthropists because they helped the poor, whose condition was due to their own laziness and extravagance; recluses (Taoists) because they were unproductive and also might teach the people falsehoods; sorcerers (diviners) because they taught the people to rely on divine guidance; and last, swashbucklers because they roamed in bands and used their "private swords" to carry out justice on behalf of the oppressed little folks. Legalists opposed formal education, except in practical fields such as medicine and agriculture. They regarded history and philosophy books as especially dangerous because they taught people to think and question, activities that made people discontented.

Some modern scholars call this school Realism instead of Legalism. They argue that its adherents, who rejected tradition, supernatural guidance, and morality and insisted that government be based on the actual facts of

LIVES AND TIMES ACROSS CULTURES

Military Innovations

Late Chou China shared with classical Greece a high frequency of wars (468 wars were fought in China between 463 and 222 B.C.E.). The continual struggles for survival eliminated the lesser states until one, a frontier state called Ch'in, triumphed and unified China. The constant warfare produced armies of up to a million soldiers, new military tactics, and increased social mobility as success was rewarded by upward mobility and failure punished by a drastic drop in status, even to enslavement.

Wars were at first chivalrous affairs between aristocrats fighting from four-horse chariots in individual combat; witness the question by one ruler to another in 632 before the opening of combat: "Will Your Excellency permit our knights and yours to play a game?" Later, large infantry forces using stronger iron rather than bronze weapons and supported by cavalry had mostly replaced the war chariots. The change was dictated by the expense of maintaining the less maneuverable chariots and the expansion of contested areas to regions unsuitable for chariots. Chinese states near nomadic lands had adopted cavalry when fighting the horse-riding nomads; once in use, cavalry forces became common in all wars. Innovative military tactics also became important, leading to the rise of career tacticians. The most famous was Sun Tzu (also known as Sun the Cripple), whose work *The Art of War* is still studied in military academies throughout the world.

In ancient Greece, too, the style of warfare changed dramatically in the archaic era (c. 800–500 B.C.E.). At the beginning of the period, cavalry was the backbone of the military. Since only very wealthy, aristocratic families could afford to allocate precious land for the raising of horses, the nobility was as predominant in the military as it was in civic affairs. In Homer's epic poems, too, we see great kings and heroes conveyed into battle by chariots; they then fought mostly champion against champion in single combat, like Achilles and Hector at the climax of the *Iliad.*

Then, in the seventh century B.C.E., there was a shift toward reliance on infantry. State security came to rest on the special training of large numbers of citizen foot soldiers (much more numerous than aristocrats), uniformly equipped with bronze and iron defensive armor and weaponry. Small-farmer militiamen and later professional infantrymen were the decisive factor in all the major land battles fought during the remainder of ancient Greek and Roman history. Commanders like the Spartan Pausanias, the Athenian Pericles, the Macedonian Alexander the Great, and the Roman Julius Caesar were gifted strategists with the remarkable ability to solve the logistical and tactical problems of mobilizing, moving, and deploying the tens of thousands of men in large infantry forces. Not surprisingly, Caesar's *Commentaries* on his wars in Gaul were the favorite reading of a later military genius—Napoleon Bonaparte.

the world as they existed, were realists. Moreover, they maintain, only such unsentimental and hardnosed policies could have succeeded in ending the chaos of the Era of the Warring States and in unifying China.

The Three Ideologies Compared

Although many schools of philosophy competed for acceptance during the late Chou, we can now say, with the benefit of hindsight, that Confucianism, Taoism, and Legalism were the most important.

Confucians were the idealists. They taught that the goal of life should be the pursuit of goodness and that people should be governed by morality and example, not by harsh laws and punishment. Although they looked back in history for the golden age, they did not extol the past for its own sake, rather they praised certain periods and persons in the past for their virtues and accomplishments. In the process, they also reinterpreted old ideas. For example, the ancient texts talked about *li* as rituals and rites of the aristocratic class. Confucius and Mencius gave li a moral dimension and insisted that it be applied to all people. They also insisted that the aristocracy should be based on merit and not on the accidents of birth. Many centuries later, two of the founding fathers of the United States, John Adams and Thomas Jefferson,

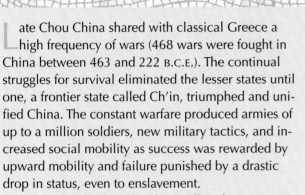

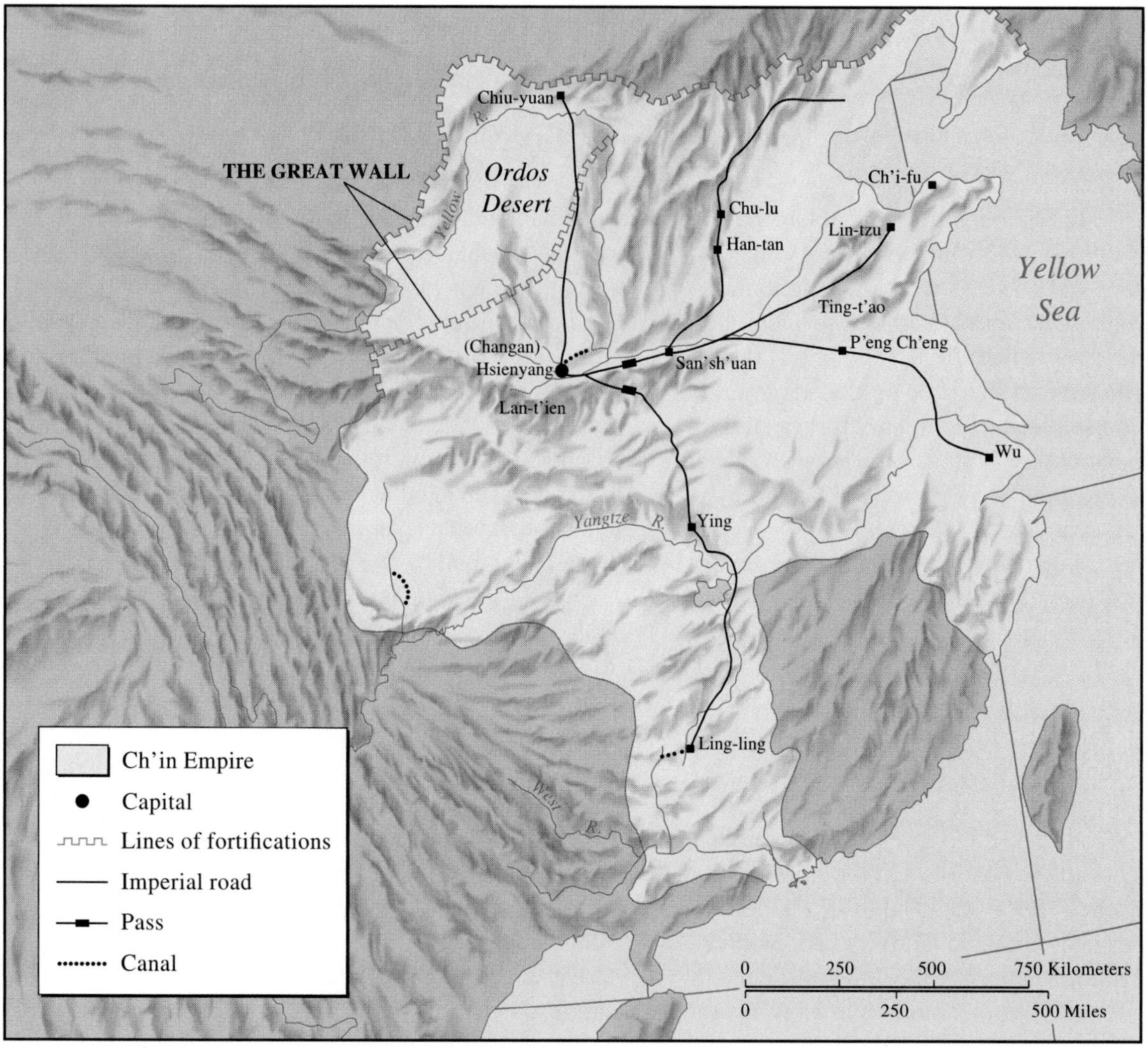

Map 3.3 The Ch'in Empire, 221–206 B.C.E. China was unified in 221 B.C.E., when the Ch'in crushed its rival states. An ambitious program of roads and canals linked the outlying provinces to the capital, Hsienyang, while the Great Wall protected the northern frontiers against nomadic tribes.

advocated a similar concept of the "natural" aristocracy of talent. These reinterpretations of traditional values made Confucians revolutionaries.

Taoists taught that humans were originally innocent but were corrupted by civilization. They believed in a return to nature and innocence, and that less is better, especially in government. They valued passivity and individual freedom and shunned worldly power and position. Although Taoism resembles a recent idea of government called laissez-faire, no government has tried to put Taoism into action as a philosophy.

Legalists were cynical realists. To them the individual had worth only if he could serve the state, whose primary functions were war and expansion. Morality was irrelevant. Like Confucians, they believed there should be no privilege by birth; but instead of raising the common people to a higher standard of conduct by teaching them moral values, Legalists demoted the aristocrats to ordinary people, discarded li and subjected all to harsh impersonal laws. They were amoral technocrats and efficiency experts.

The Brief Rise and Fall of the Ch'in

Although the Era of Warring States produced great philosophies, it was a difficult period for most Chinese. Many yearned for the reestablishment of a strong dynasty that would once again bring peace and order. In the rise of Ch'in, their hopes were both realized and turned into a nightmare. As a national dynasty, Ch'in was short lived, but its importance cannot be measured by its duration, for it left its imprint on the next 2,000 years of Chinese history.

Ch'in was located in northwest China, in what had been the Chou homeland. Its rise in some ways was a re-

LIVES AND TIMES ACROSS CULTURES

Slavery and Volatile Social Status

During the late Chou (772–222 B.C.E.), the breakdown of the feudal order led to social mobility. For example, out of 713 persons mentioned in important historical works describing this period, over one-third or 34% rose from obscure social origins, proving that there were many opportunities for upward mobility. Others lost status. Prisoners of war, especially captured "barbarians," often became slaves and were presented as rewards to victorious generals. For example, in 594, as a reward for adding territory to the state, a Ch'in general was awarded the families of 1,000 defeated barbarians. Nobles and officials from defeated states could also be enslaved: a former official of a state named Kuo was sold as a slave for five pieces of sheepskin, and another source dated to 655 noted that a defeated ruler and his minister were enslaved and given as part of the dowry of a princess of the victor state. An inscription cites the use of horses, silk, and slaves in lieu of money in commercial transactions. Other sources mention the freeing of slaves who had fought well in battles. Men convicted of certain crimes and their family members were enslaved; people could also be enslaved for indebtedness. All these examples indicate the volatility of social status in the wars that culminated in the Ch'in unification of China.

In both Greece and Rome, slavery was an enduring institution throughout antiquity. In Greece, warfare was the most common source of slaves. Defeated enemies, if not put to the sword or ransomed, were enslaved. This is well-attested in the Bronze Age Linear B tablets and in the epic poems of Homer (c. 725 B.C.E.). Later, the Spartans were able to concentrate on being soldiers because they conquered a neighboring territory—Messenia—and made its inhabitants into state-owned serfs. In ancient Greece, citizens could be stripped of their rights and sold into slavery for nonpayment of debts. The Athenian statesman Solon (594) enacted legislation to prevent the enslavement of Athenian citizens for debt, but he did not abolish the institution of slavery itself. Thus, after taking the island of Melos by siege during the Peloponnesian War, the Athenians put all the males to death and sold all the women and children into slavery. Indeed, slavery was so commonplace that the philosopher Aristotle speaks as if a natural law consigned some people to the status of slaves and others to freedom.

The Romans, too, capitalized on the manpower made available by slavery. Success in warfare resulted in the development of a flourishing trade in slaves and bustling slave markets throughout the empire. So many slaves were employed in farm work by the second century B.C.E. that Rome suffered a series of "servile" revolts in which huge armies of runaway slaves defeated Roman legions in battle.

In the following letter, the Stoic philosopher Seneca (c. 4 B.C.E.–65 C.E.) reflects on the vicissitudes of fortune that made one person a master and another a slave.

> *"These people are slaves." No: they are human beings.*
>
> *"These people are slaves." No: they are those with whom you share your roof.*
>
> *"These people are slaves." No: when you consider how much power Chance can exert over you both, they are fellow slaves.*
>
> *That's why I find it ludicrous that there should be people who think it shameful to have dinner with their slave. . . .*
>
> *Each time you remember how much you are entitled to do to your slave, you must remember also just how much your own master is entitled to do to you. "But I don't have any master," you object. The world is still young: perhaps there will come a time when you do have one.**

*Trans. R. Campbell, in Thomas Wiedemann, *Greek and Roman Slavery* (Baltimore: Johns Hopkins Univ. Press, 1981), pp. 233–235.

Robert Harding Picture Library

A Terra Cotta Army. Ranks of life-size infantrymen, horses, and chariots made of pottery are drawn up in battle formation in underground pits that flank the tomb of the First Emperor of the Ch'in. They were intended to protect him in death as his flesh-and-blood forces had in life.

peat of the rise of the Chou almost 1,000 years earlier. Because they were tough frontier people, the Ch'in were looked upon by the more advanced Chinese of the heartland as semibarbarous country cousins. Though their location had exempted the Ch'in from most of the wars with other Chinese states, they were nevertheless experienced in war through frequent fighting with nomadic tribesmen from the steppes.

To its original homeland in modern Shensi, Ch'in had early added Szechuan in the southwest along the upper Yangtze Valley. Both lands were rich in agricultural potential if irrigated. Ch'in engineers produced large-scale irrigation and flood-control works (the systems they created in Szechuan are still in use). Despite harsh laws, Ch'in's abolition of serfdom attracted immigrants to settle and farm. Its location on the edge of the Chinese world also saved it from the ravages of the almost continuous warfare that disrupted the economies of the more centrally located states. As a result of economic prosperity, Ch'in built up huge grain reserves, which allowed it to divert manpower from farming into the army in its final push for unification. Its strategic location made Ch'in territories easy to defend from invaders from the east (where most of the Warring States were), while the same mountain passes that protected it were easy staging points to invade the eastern states. Quick to adopt new advances in knowledge and technology, Ch'in soldiers even anticipated the mustard gas used in the trenches in World War I. They used bellows to pump toxic gas generated from burning mustard seeds and other material into the tunnels of their enemies who were besieging Ch'in cities. Ch'in mapmakers drew relief maps that showed the contours of the land and were therefore useful in warfare. A relief map of his entire realm was reported to have been buried in the tomb of the first Ch'in emperor who later unified China.

Ch'in rulers welcomed talented men from other states. In 356 B.C.E., Lord Shang entered into the service of Ch'in from another state and held the office of chief minister until his death in 338. His Legalist policies made Ch'in the most efficiently run state in its time. Officials were chosen on merit and promoted or demoted on their performance, and free men and women worked as tax-paying and land-owning peasants; men also fought as conscript soldiers. Lord Shang was followed by other technocrats; like him, many were born in other states but had been attracted to Ch'in because of the opportunities it offered.

In 247 B.C.E., King Ch'eng, a vigorous and ambitious young man, succeeded to the Ch'in throne, with Li Ssu his chief minister. They completed the conquest and unification of China in 221. Ch'eng decided that he needed a title greater than "king" to match his prestige. With supreme confidence, he called himself *Shih Huang-ti; shih* means "first" and *huang-ti* means "emperor," a title until then used only for high gods. He further decreed that since his house would rule China for all time, his successors would be designated only by numerals, as second, third emperor, and so on. Although his family did not rule beyond the second emperor, the title *huang-ti* was retained by rulers down to the end of the imperial age, in 1911.

Shih Huang-ti and chief minister Li Ssu formally abolished feudalism in the whole empire and instituted a centralized government. The country was divided into commanderies (provinces), which were subdivided into counties. All offices were nonhereditary, and officials were ultimately responsible to the emperor. Uniform laws, weights, measures, coinage, and written script applied to the whole land. The First Emperor ordered roads built to link parts of the country and to facilitate administration and military movements, in much the same way that the Persian emperors Darius and Xerxes had done and that the Roman government would do later. Carts using the roads were required to have axles of standard length, so that the ruts they made would be uniform. His engineers dug a canal linking a tributary of the Yangtze River with the Pearl River in the extreme south to make it easier to supply an army campaigning in the area. The army conquered and annexed lands that today make up southern China and northern Vietnam. In the north, existing walls built by the feudal states against the nomads (and sometimes against one another) were linked together to form a single defense system called the Great Wall. This monumental engineering project was built with conscript and convict labor; although its construction caused enormous hardships, it provided security along a long and vulnerable frontier.

Shih Huang-ti also built a magnificent capital near the first Chou capital, Hao. Because of good surrounding agricultural lands and strategic location, this general vicinity would continue to be China's capital for the next thousand years. Very little remains of the Ch'in capital, but the huge mound, more than 150 feet high, enclosing the tomb that Shih Huang-ti started to build for himself soon after he unified the country is still a major landmark. Records state that tens of thousands of men spent years building the tomb and that it was furnished with fabulous treasures. Nearby, archaeologists have recently excavated three huge underground pits containing over 7,000 life-size terra cotta horses and men, an army to guard him in death.

Despite his real achievements, the First Emperor has been universally reviled in Chinese memory. Popular folk tales denounce his cruelty and tyranny. Millions were conscripted and many died building his walls, canals, palaces, and tomb. Many more paid crushing taxes to support the projects. Scholars abhorred his attempts at thought control. With the Ch'in unification, the Hundred Schools came to an end. Legalism prevailed; all other schools were outlawed. The government prohibited all intellectual discussions; to question the government's policies became treason. In 213 B.C.E., a law ordered all books other than the history of the House of Ch'in and works on agriculture, medicine, and divination confiscated and burned; the penalty for disobeying was death. Scholars were appalled, many, especially the Confucians, spoke out in protest. The emperor had 460 of them arrested and executed. Even the crown prince was not exempt; when he protested the harshness of the punishment, he was banished to duties along the Great Wall. The book burning destroyed forever many ancient texts, creating gaps in our knowledge of the pre-Ch'in eras. Such techniques of totalitarianism and thought control have been used by other tyrants in other eras throughout the world, attesting to the power of the written word. After the fall of the dynasty, when it was again legal to engage in intellectual activities and to write books, accounts were written of the Ch'in dynasty; most of them had little good to say about the First Emperor and his policies.

Since all decisions came from the all-powerful emperor, he toiled long hours to do his work. In 210 B.C.E., while on an inspection tour that had as its second goal a search for the elixirs of long life, the First Emperor suddenly died at age fifty, probably from overwork and other excesses. A power struggle followed. Li Ssu and the chief eunuch (eunuchs were castrated males who served in the households of monarchs) destroyed the emperor's will and forged an order commanding the crown prince to commit suicide, which he did. Li and the eunuch put a weakling younger son of the emperor on the throne as Second Emperor so they could rule in his name. Soon these two men fell out and Li was murdered. The eunuch then murdered the Second Emperor and put a son of the late crown prince on the throne. The new ruler had the eunuch executed. By then revolts had broken out everywhere. Loyal generals rushed hither and yon trying to put them down, and many defected when they could not, for failure was a crime punishable by death. In 206 B.C.E., the third Ch'in ruler surrendered to the rebels, thus ending the dynasty.

Summary and Comparisons

This chapter examined the story of several major cultures that flowered in the first millennium B.C.E. and shared a concern with religion and morals. Soon, new developments in religion and philosophy led to the abandonment or modification of previous traditions in favor of new systems of belief.

In Greece, India, and China, intellectual speculation did not evolve in the direction of monotheism. The Hebrews, therefore, were the originators of the first true monotheistic faith, one of the most durable and influential in history. Although the political and military triumphs of the ancient Hebrew state were short-lived and had little impact outside Palestine, the Hebrew people nevertheless made a momentous contribution to the future of the human spirit through their religion. Judaism furnished its followers with an elaborately formulated and self-consistent ethical code.

The achievements of the Phoenicians were pragmatic. Their sophisticated ports and expert sailors linked West Asia with distant parts of the Mediterranean. Their sailors and merchants also carried an innovation on which no price could be put—a writing system based on an alphabet.

In the archaic period, the Greek world rebounded materially and culturally from the Dark Age. Male citizens increasingly participated in the affairs of their city states. Pericles broadened the basis of democracy and made Athens a focus of economic and artistic activity. The growth of Athenian power, however, led to the Peloponnesian War and ultimately to the dismantling of the Athenian Empire and the hegemony of Sparta and its allies.

Greece was the center of philosophical investigation into the nature of the universe. Greek commitment to the highest intellectual ideals laid the groundwork for philosophical inquiry and the writing of the first factual histories.

Greek literature and art explored the physical and intellectual potentials of human beings. Within a century of their invention, both tragedy and comedy reached the highest levels of artistry, thanks to the city-states' commitment of time, energy, and money to cultural activities. In architecture and the figural arts, also, the Greeks delighted in balance and symmetry of structure and put human beings and society at the center of focus.

In India during the Late Vedic Age (c. 1000–500 B.C.E.), Aryan culture spread eastward to the Ganges Valley and southward to the Deccan Plateau and peninsular India, adapting to contacts with native peoples and

1300 B.C.E.	
	Moses
1000	
	King David
	First Temple at Jerusalem
	Separate kingdoms of Israel and Judah
650	
	Solon's reforms at Athens
	The Babylonian captivity
	The *Lao Tzu*
	Gautama Buddha, Mahavira
500	
	Hundred Schools of philosophy in China
	Confucius, *Spring and Summer* and *Analects*
	Theravada Buddhism
	Greek-Persian Wars
	The Parthenon
	Pericles
	Sophocles, *Oedipus the King*
	The Peloponnesian War
	First five books of Tanakh codified
	Jain canon
400	
	Trial and death of Socrates
	Plato, *The Republic*
	Mahayana Buddhism
	Mencius, *The Mencius*
	Tripitaka
	Shang Yang, *Lord Shang*
	Aristotle
	Chuang Tzu, *The Chuang Tzu*
300	
	Chou dynasty ends
	Ch'in, Shih Huang-ti, Li-Ssu
	The Great Wall of China
200

experiencing economic transformations. In this era the Upanishads explained the human experience and the relationship with the ultimate. Buddhism and Jainism emerged to play an important part in the future of India and many other parts of Asia.

Despite some differences, the basic views of Jainism, Buddhism, and orthodox Vedism (and Hinduism, a later outgrowth of Vedism) do not disagree: life was governed by universal law or *dharma,* and *karma* or deed determined reincarnation with its painful results; all had as the final goal release, resulting in *nirvana*. However, both of the new faiths deny the validity of the Vedas, the authority of the Brahmans, and the caste system. Similarly, in Greece, Pythagorean teaching about transmigration of souls abandoned traditional religious thinking and offered new, alternative beliefs about the next life.

Gautama Buddha taught the middle way in his Four Noble Truths and Eightfold Path. The greater gains of Buddhism compared with Jainism were due to Buddhism's moderation and more attainable lifestyles, and especially to the popular doctrine of Mahayana Buddhism.

Mahavira, founder of the extremely demanding Jainism, taught a rigorous ethical system that gave special emphasis to the ascetic way of life and to self-denial. So too, in classical Greece, Socrates had sought true knowledge in part by reducing or overriding the physical demands of his body.

Just as political and social ferment in India and Greece around 500 B.C.E. had led to important intellectual and religious developments, similarly, in China, the increasing political chaos of the Eastern Chou (771–256) brought in a period of intellectual turmoil known as the Hundred Schools of Philosophy. Most Chinese philosophers dealt with human relationships in this world, as had the Greek Sophists. The only exception was the school known as Taoism, which advocated passivism, renunciation of civilization, and return to an innocent primitive past. In its advocacy of simplicity and asceticism, Taoism may be likened to Buddhism.

Like the itinerant Greek Sophists, who sought pupils in different city-states, many Chinese philosophers traveled from state to state and attempted to persuade rulers to accept their point of view. Confucius and his disciples were foremost among such dedicated men; they believed that the practice of morality, family responsibility, and virtuous government would bring about a return to the golden age. Confucians were ridiculed by Taoists, who maintained that activism was counterproductive and that the way to achieve peace with oneself was to rise above worldly concerns.

Although Confucianism and Taoism later became the twin mainstreams of Chinese thought, Legalism had an immediate impact on the time. Legalists were cynics about human nature and the nature of power, and were interested only in efficiency and results. Their final goal was an all powerful state ruled by harsh and impersonal laws. So too, the perfectly just state in Plato's *Republic* was marked by an authoritarianism that rigidly determined all the social, political, military, and educational aspects of life. With Legalism as its guiding ideology, the Ch'in triumphed over the other Warring States and unified China in 221 B.C.E. Between 221–206, the Ch'in ruled China ruthlessly and by terror, obliterating many old institutions. As a system of ruling, however, Legalism was intolerable, as the speedy collapse of the Ch'in empire proved.

All of the major Eurasian civilizations examined in this chapter took great strides in developing important new religious and philosophical systems. All fostered remarkable innovations in religious and ethical thought that had a profound influence on many aspects of life both at the time and through later centuries.

Selected Sources

*Baldry, H. C. *The Greek Tragic Theater.* 1971. Especially valuable on the social context of the dramatic festivals and on the mechanics of mounting productions.

*Basham, A. L. *The Wonder That Was India.* 1954. A long chapter deals with religions and includes quotations.

Ben-Sasson, H. H., ed. *A History of the Jewish People.* 1969; trans. 1976. A very thorough account from earliest times down to the mid-twentieth century, by several eminent historians.

*Boardman, John. *Greek Art.* 4th ed. 1996. A good basic introduction to ancient Greek art and architecture from the archaic period to the Hellenistic. Many fine illustrations.

Cook, J. M. *The Persian Empire.* 1983. A good, readable, up-to-date introduction to the political and cultural history of ancient Persia. Nicely illustrated.

Cotterell, Arthur. *The First Emperor of China.* 1981. Makes full use of recent excavations of the terra cotta army to bring to life the life and times of the First Emperor.

Creel, H. G. *Confucius the Man and the Myth.* 1949. Creel first gives a biographical account, then explains the development of the myth, the triumph of Confucianism and its worldwide relevance.

———. *Chinese Thought from Confucius to Mao Tse-Tung.* 1953. Concise, well written, and easy to read.

*de Bary, W. T., ed. *Sources of Indian Tradition.* Vol 1. 1958. Good, short introductory passages explain readings in Buddhist and Jain canons.

*Doody, Margaret. *Aristotle Detective.* 1978. A highly entertaining detective story in which the great philosopher solves the mystery of the violent murder of a prominent Athenian citizen. Realistic background detail.

Edward, J. Thomas. *The Life of Buddha as Legend and History.* 1931. An account of the man and his teachings, the growth of Buddhism, and the myths that surround it.

---

*Available in paperback.

*Fantham, Elaine, et al. *Women in the Classical World: Image and Text.* 1994. This very current collection of essays by a number of experts includes material on the representation of women in literature, the arts, science, and philosophy throughout Greek and Roman history.

*Hesse, Hermann. *Siddhartha.* 1922; Eng. trans. 1951. A novel about one man and his search for enlightenment.

Hirakawa, Akira. *A History of Indian Buddhism: From Sakyamuni to Early Mahayana.* Ed. and trans. Paul Groner. 1990. Good, comprehensive book.

Hornblower, Simon, and Antony Spawforth, eds. *The Oxford Classical Dictionary.* 3rd ed. 1996. The most comprehensive, one-volume resource for all aspects of the world of ancient Greece and Rome. Includes contributions from hundreds of leading specialists.

Jaini, P. S. *The Jain Path of Purification.* 1979. Good summary of Jain teachings.

Lange, Nicholas de. *Judaism.* 1986. A recent account of the characteristics and importance of this world religion.

Levi, Jean. *The Chinese Emperor.* 1987. A novel on the life and times of the First Emperor; describes the murderous intrigues and horror of life in a Legalist state.

*Mazar, Amihai. *Archaeology of the Land of the Bible: 10,000–586 B.C.E.* 1990; rev 1992. Simply the best available work on the topic; thorough and attractively presented.

Moscati, Sabatino. *The World of the Phoenicians.* 1968. A good, readable history by the Director of Semitic Studies at the University of Rome.

*Pomeroy, Sarah, et al. *Ancient Greece: A Political, Social, and Cultural History.* 1999. An extremely well-written narrative history, enriched with illustrations and frequent excerpts from primary sources.

Potok, Chaim. *Wanderings: Chaim Potok's History of the Jews.* 1978. A riveting account of 4,000 years of history by the noted American Jewish novelist, scholar, and rabbi.

*Powell, Barry B. *Classical Myth.* 2nd ed. 1998. A wonderfully thorough treatment, founded on ample selections from ancient sources.

*Renault, Mary. *The Last of the Wine.* 1956; reprinted 1975. One of the best of Renault's excellent historical novels; set in the time of the Peloponnesian War.

Robinson, Richard H., and William L. Johnson. *The Buddhist Religion: A Historical Introduction.* 1982. Covers the development of Buddhism in India and elsewhere.

Schwartz, Benjamin. *The World of Thought in Ancient China.* 1985. A comprehensive exposition of Chinese classical philosophies.

*Starr, Chester G. *Individual and Community: The Rise of the Polis, 800–500 B.C.* 1986. A good, recent presentation of the cultural, economic, and political achievements of the citizens of the Greek polis.

Twitchett, Dennis, and Michael Loewe, eds. *The Cambridge History of China.* Vol. 1: *The Ch'in and Han Empires, 221 B.C.–A.D. 220.* 1986. Definitive treatment by many experts; Chapter 1 deals with the Ch'in Empire.

Vaux, R. de. *The Bible and the Ancient Near East.* 1972. A useful assessment of biblical narratives within the context of the history of the Near East.

*Waley, Arthur. *Three Ways of Thought in Ancient China.* 1939. A short, lucid study of Confucianism, Taoism, and Legalism, with many quotes from original writings of the three schools.

Internet Links

The Ancient Greek World
http://www.museum.upenn.edu/Greek_World/Index.html
This site, based on the collections of the University of Pennsylvania Museum, offers informative descriptions and high-quality graphics in such categories as "Land and Archaeological Time," "Daily Life," "Economy," "Religion and Death."

The Ancient Olympic Games Virtual Museum
http://devlab.dartmouth.edu/olympic/
This attractive website, maintained at Dartmouth University, offers "a plethora of information about these contests that are the forefathers of our modern Olympic Games."

Barrington Atlas of the Greek and Roman World
http://www.unc.edu/depts/cl_atlas/
This site features nearly 100 detailed topographical maps.

Diotima: Materials for the Study of Women and Gender in the Ancient World
http://www.uky.edu/ArtsSciences/Classics/gender.html
A good source of guidance for the study of women's lives in ancient Greece, Rome, Egypt, and West Asia, including extensive course materials, bibliography, links to databases of images and texts in translation.

Introduction to Biblical Judaism
http://www.acs.ucalgary.ca/~elsegal/J_Transp/J01_JudaismIntro.html
Offers a very clear chronological outline of ancient Judaism and the early history of the Jews. Several illustrations and maps.

Mahavira and Jainism
http://www.san.beck.org/EC8-Mahavira.html
This site provides a helpful outline of Jainism, with biographical information, lucid explanations of terms and concepts, and well-chosen quotations from ancient documents.

Perseus Project
http://www.perseus.tufts.edu/
This "evolving digital library" provides access to virtually all classical Greek texts (in translation as well as in the original) commonly read in colleges. Maps, archaeological site plans, and a large collection of photographs and other illustrations make this an invaluable research tool. Includes search facilities.

Resources for the Study of East Asian Language and Thought
http://www.human.toyogakuen-u.ac.jp/~acmuller/index.html
This site offers links to several "virtual libraries" relevant to Buddhism, Confucianism, and Taoism, among other subjects, as well as helpful glossaries of technical terminology.

Su Tzu's Chinese Philosophy Page
http://mars.superlink.net/user/fsu/philo.html
"This page has been designed for the purpose of organizing the resources on Chinese philosophy that can be found in 'cyberspace.'" Contains links to bibliography, large text repositories, and other relevant websites.

COMPARATIVE ESSAY 3

The Defining Characteristics of Great Empires

Most noteworthy by far and most marvelous of all is the grandeur of your concept of citizenship. There is nothing on earth like it. For you have divided all the people of the Empire . . . into two classes: the more cultured, better born, and more influential everywhere you have declared Roman citizens . . . the rest vassals and subjects. . . . Everything lies open to everybody; and no one fit for office or a position of trust is an alien. There exists a universal democracy under one man, the best princeps *[emperor] and administrator.*

Aelius Aristides, in N. Lewis and M. Reinhold, eds., *Roman Civilization, Sourcebook II: Roman Empire* (New York: Harper, 1966), pp. 135–136.

Several great empires—the Hellenistic kingdoms, the Roman Empire, and the Mauryan and Han Empires—flourished between about 300 B.C.E. and 200 C.E. Each unified under one government diverse and often previously antagonistic peoples and states. Each was maintained by huge resources of manpower and materials. The quotation above praises the Roman imperial achievement and the many benefits the empire brought to its citizens.

Empires were secured by powerful military forces, effective bureaucracies, and diplomatic alliances that often included the exchange of hostages and arranged marriages between ruling families. A poem by a homesick Han princess attests to the high individual human cost of dynastic marital affiliations:

My family sent me off to be married
on the other side of heaven;
They sent me a long way to a strange
land, to the king of Wu-sun.
A domed lodging is my dwelling
place, with walls made of felt;
Meat is my food, with fermented
milk as the sauce.
I live with constant thoughts of my
home, my heart is full of sorrow;
I wish I were a golden swan, return-
ing to my home country.

Princess Hsi-chun, in James P. Holoka and Jiu-Hwa L. Upshur, eds., *Lives and Times: A World History Reader,* vol. 1 (Minneapolis/St. Paul: West Publishing, 1995), p. 173.

Although they varied considerably in size and longevity, each empire controlled much more territory and larger populations than a single city or group of settlements. Each of the empires discussed in Chapter 4 controlled lands at least the size of the United States east of the Mississippi. Each had populations numbering in the tens of millions and endured for at least two centuries. Other empires had appeared earlier in history (for example, the Egyptian, Assyrian, and Persian), while others would form later (for example, Aztec, Inka, Ottoman, and Mongol). Although each was distinct, most great empires shared numerous common characteristics.

Successful empires were stable and durable for the following reasons: each had centralized leadership and an efficiently run government. Empires were often headed by a more or less stable hereditary dynasty, bolstered by a social and political elite like the Roman patricians or the great families in Han China. Most successful imperial administrations also recruited at least some officials on the basis of merit and not birth. This was true of the Hellenistic states, Rome under the emperors, and Han China. In fact, many empires relied on their schools to fill administrative positions; the successful ones also gave efficiency ratings and on-the-job training to promising officials, and based promotions on performance. In Han China, administrators were chosen from a pool of formally educated men through recommendation, examination, and efficiency ratings. An imperial university for training bureaucrats had over 30,000 students at its peak. In the Hellenistic states, literacy in Greek was essential for successful advancement in both public and private sectors.

Great empires had uniform currencies and standards of weights and measures that simplified tax collection, government finance, and trade. Rulers issued coins that publicized themselves and their political programs. Reasonable fiscal and tax systems generated sufficient revenues to run the government without overburdening the population. When greed or overwhelming needs caused extortionate taxation, disaffection or rebellion often resulted, presaging eventual decline and fall. The maintenance of an adequate military force always took up the largest share of tax revenues and much manpower.

All empires also required service from their citizens, either as soldiers or as laborers. For example, in Rome all male citizens were obligated to serve in the army, initially without pay. Likewise, the Han government demanded military and corvée service (compulsory, unpaid labor) from its adult males. In time, in both China and Rome, long-term, professional forces superseded inadequate part-time citizen soldiers.

Successful empires possessed weapons and military technology superior to those of their enemies; they also supplemented this technological superiority with defensive installations such as the Great Wall in China and Hadrian's Wall in Roman Britain. Vital empires were almost invariably aggressive, often attacking and absorbing their weak or hostile neighbors. Military strength and wealth from booty brought safety and provided the preconditions for further economic expansion and technological innovation. The resulting prosperity contributed to social harmony and political stability. However, the great expense of garrisoning vast territories with professional soldiers also imposed huge financial burdens that drained treasuries.

Empires had uniform legal codes, which the governments enforced. Examples were Rome's Twelve Tables (and the later Justinian Code) and the Mauryan code engraved on stone pillars. The Roman legal system became the foundation for many later European codes. Similarly, later Chinese and other East Asian legal systems were based on the Han legal code. Muslim empires often based their legal systems on the Qur'an.

All great empires built elaborate public works. Although often constructed by forced labor, the roads, aqueducts, granaries, and irrigation works generally had long-term benefits for all inhabitants, often outlasting the states that built them. The Persians, Romans, and Inkas were especially good civil engineers. Their roadways expedited troop movements, domestic commerce, and international trade. Even today, many Roman highways are still in use. An international overland route, called the Silk Road, linked the Roman and Han Empires. Safe trade and travel along this 6,000-mile route was possible because of the Pax Romana and Pax Sinica. Such domestic and international peace maintained over long periods promoted well-being for millions of people. The mapping and policing of sea lanes and the building of harbors and lighthouses also promoted both domestic and international trade. All empires built lavish public monuments, especially in capital cities. Temples, tombs, and palaces, which had no tangible benefits for ordinary people, nevertheless provided spiritual consolation and inspired pride. Even in ruin, the Roman Colosseum, Asoka's pillars, and the monuments at places like Copán in Central America still inspire awe and admiration.

Great imperial governments also patronized learning, expressed in literature, art, and philosophy. In Han China, the government-sponsored writing of history set the example for succeeding generations. In Ptolemaic Egypt, the government supported research in the sciences and a great library in Alexandria. The emperor Augustus's encouragement of writers resulted in masterpieces of Latin literature such as Vergil's *Aeneid.* The political integration of vast imperial territories also brought about linguistic integration. Latin became the universal language of western Europe, Greek of the eastern Mediterranean, and Chinese of East Asia.

Successful empires instilled a sense of strong allegiance and a spirit of public service in their people. Even after such empires fell, the memories of their grandeur continued to capture the imaginations of later generations. For centuries, western Europeans longed to resurrect the glories of the Roman Empire. The very name of Rome, the eternal city, led Constantinople to be called the "Second Rome," and after Constantinople's fall to the Muslim Ottoman Empire, Russian rulers designated Moscow as the "Third Rome." So too, the Chinese have continued to call themselves the Han people. Asoka's lion serves as the national symbol for modern India.

In Chapter 4 we shall examine several of the world's earliest great empires: the Hellenistic, Roman, Indian, and Chinese. Each had many of the characteristics outlined in this essay.

The Age of Great Empires

4

*When Pausanias [a former favorite and now aggrieved bodyguard of King Philip of Macedon] asked [his teacher] how he could become most renowned, the sophist answered: "by slaying the man whose achievements were the greatest, for the assassin's fame would endure as long as the great man's." Pausanias took this opinion as applicable to his own situation. He immediately resolved to revenge himself during the distractions of the wedding festival [of Philip's daughter]. Having readied horses at the city gates, he went to the entrance of the theater carrying a concealed Celtic dagger. Philip on his arrival bid his companions to enter ahead of him, and with his bodyguard ordered to keep their distance, was by himself. Pausanias darted forward and stabbed the king through his ribs, killing him instantly. Then he made a dash for the gates and his getaway horses . . . . Pausanias nearly made it to the waiting horses, but his shoe caught in a vine and he fell. As he was getting up, Perdiccas and the others overtook him and slew him with their javelins.**

Hsiang Yu invited Liu Pang to stay for a banquet [at the former's military camp]. . . . [During the banquet] several times Fan Tseng [Hsiang Yu's supporter] shot Hsiang Yu meaningful glances, but Hsiang Yu did not respond. Finally Fan Tseng rose and went out. Summoning Hsiang Chuang [another supporter of Hsiang Yu], he said:

"Our lord is too kindhearted. Go in, drink a toast, and offer to perform a sword dance. Then strike the lord of Pei [Liu Pang] down where he sits. If you don't do this, we will all end up his captives."

Hsiang Chuang went in to offer a toast, after which he said, "Our prince is drinking with the lord of Pei, but we have no entertainers in the army. May I perform a sword dance?"

"Very well," said Hsiang Yu.

*Hsiang Chuang drew his sword and began the dance. . . [but] Hsiang Po [a supporter of Liu Pang] followed suit, shielding Liu Pang with his body so that Hsiang Chuang could not strike him.***

*Plutarch, *Life of Alexander*, trans. James P. Holoka, in James P. Holoka and Jiu-Hwa L. Upshur, *Lives and Times: A World History Reader*, vol. 1 (Minneapolis/St. Paul: West Publishing, 1995), p. 143.

**Ssu-ma Ch'ien's *Shih chi* [Records of the Grand Historian], in K. C. Chang, ed., *Food in Chinese Culture: Anthropological and Historical Perspectives* (New Haven: Yale University Press, 1977), p. 64.

Both successful and failed assassinations have had a great impact on history. The first excerpt above describes how a disgruntled bodyguard and lover of King Philip of Macedon picked an opportune moment to kill his master and was himself killed almost immediately afterward. Circumstantial evidence indicates that Philip's son and successor Alexander was implicated in the plot. Alexander had quarreled with his father and was afraid of being disinherited in favor of Philip's son by a new wife. Since Pausanias was killed immediately, we cannot know for certain that Alexander was guilty of patricide.

The second passage recounts a banquet in 206 B.C.E. hosted by Hsiang Yu, the leading candidate to succeed the recently toppled Ch'in dynasty. Liu Pang, his lieutenant and the chief guest at the banquet, was also his main rival. Here the quick reaction by one of Liu Pang's aides foiled an assassination attempt by Hsiang Yu's supporters. Liu Pang went on to destroy Hsiang Yu and founded the successful Han dynasty.

This chapter highlights the principal achievements of four of the greatest empires of the ancient world. Three—the Macedonian/Hellenistic, Mauryan, and Han—were founded by ambitious and opportunistic men who seized the advantages offered by wars, invasions, and assassinations. By contrast, the Roman Empire, though it too saw its share of assassinations, grew by the efforts of many great men building on the achievements of their predecessors.

The Hellenistic kingdoms, unlike the classical Greek city-states, brought Greek culture to large, politically unified territories. The Roman Empire unified the entire Mediterranean basin and spread Greco-Roman culture throughout Europe and much of West Asia. The India of the Mauryan Empire, particularly under emperor Asoka, witnessed unprecedented political and religious unification. In Han dynasty China, a remarkable flowering of culture accompanied military and governmental successes.

A Greek citizen of the Roman Empire, Aelius Aristides, once praised Rome in the following terms:

> You have surveyed the whole world, built bridges of all sorts across rivers, cut down mountains to make paths for chariots, filled the deserts with hostels, and civilized it all with system and order. . . . Before your rule, things were all mixed up topsy-turvy, drifting at random. But with you in charge, turmoil and strife ceased, universal order and the bright light of life and government came in, laws were proclaimed, and the gods' altars acquired sanctity.

Though there is some exaggeration in this adulatory account, it is nevertheless essentially true, and similar words could rightly be addressed not only to Rome but to any of the empires examined in this chapter.

Macedonian Conquest and Hellenistic Empires

*You [Philip] are called to action . . . by your ancestors, by Persian effeminacy, by the famous men, true heroes, who fought against Persia, and most of all by the fitting hour which finds you in possession of greater strength than any previous European, and your adversary in deeper hatred and wider contempt than any monarch in history. . . . What will be the praises sung of you, when it is realized that in the political field you have been the benefactor of all Greek states, and in the military the conqueror of Persia? No achievement can ever be greater than to bring us all out of such warfare to unity of spirit.**

*Isocrates, "Philip," in *Greek Political Oratory*, trans. A. N. W. Saunders (Harmondsworth: Penguin, 1970), pp. 164–165.

The Greek city-states of the fifth century B.C.E. had achieved remarkable triumphs in their economic, cultural, and intellectual life, but they failed to overcome interstate rivalries and to unite their world in a lasting political organization. In the wake of the debilitating Peloponnesian War, no Greek state was powerful enough to control or rally the rest for any length of time. This situation changed forever with the careers of Philip II (reigned 359–336 B.C.E.) and Alexander the Great (reigned 336–323 B.C.E.). The two Macedonian leaders enlarged the Greek world and dramatically changed it both politically and culturally.

In the quotation above from an open letter to Philip II, the Athenian orator Isocrates urges the Macedonian king to lead Greece in a crusade against the Persians. He appeals to long-standing Greek prejudices: freedom-loving, rational, masculine Greeks are contrasted with enslaved, barbarian, effeminate Persians. As usual, however, the Greek states were fatally incapable of united action, and Philip was more interested in gaining supremacy for Macedon than in saving Greece from its chronic internal strife.

By 338 B.C.E. Philip had taken advantage of weaknesses of the old city-state system to establish Macedon as the dominant political and military force in the Greek world. After Philip's death, his son Alexander capitalized on this military superiority to conquer vast territories in Asia and Africa. On his death they were divided into several very large kingdoms, which we designate Hellenistic (the word indicates postclassical Greek civilization from the death of Alexander in 323 into the first century B.C.E.).

The Father: Philip

After the Peloponnesian War, the Spartans for a time maintained a shaky predominance among Greek city-states but lacked the diplomatic and financial savvy of the Athenians; by the mid-fourth century B.C.E., Greece was still a disunified collection of independent city-states. The common folk, disenchanted with endless warfare, lost their patriotic enthusiasm for the polis. Greek soldiers often served as mercenaries for the highest bidder, whether Greek or not.

Before the reign of King Philip II, Macedon was an underdeveloped region in northernmost Greece. Many Greeks thought of Macedonians as hard drinking, backward, and uncivilized. In fact, Macedon was a sleeping giant, with valuable natural resources and huge manpower reserves. Similarly, in China during the Warring States era, the frontiersmen Ch'in people were thought to be uncouth country cousins by the more advanced Chinese of the heartland. Nonetheless, they were able forcibly to unify China as Philip and Alexander subjugated Greece.

Philip first reformed the army, making it fully professional, with the highest standards of discipline and elite units called companions. He increased its size to more than 25,000 men diversified among infantry, light-armed skirmishers, archers, slingers, and cavalry. He also introduced a new, thirteen-foot thrusting spear, better siege machinery, and more effective infantry tactics. Philip funded this crack army by seizing the Mount Pangaeus gold and silver mines. He then defeated the Balkan neighbors who had long plagued Macedon. Philip next unified and modernized his country by redistributing the population into new urban centers and by making better use of arable land. He ushered Macedon into mainstream Greek culture by promoting education and encouraging artists and intellectuals to come to the new royal capital at Pella, where Alexander was born. Philip also dared to aim at political domination of Greece.

The Greek city-states feared this growth of Macedonian power and influence. In a series of speeches known as *Philippics,* the Athenian statesman Demosthenes portrayed Philip as addicted to power. Deciding the time had come for a showdown, the Athenians and Thebans confronted the Macedonians at the battle of Chaeronea in 338 B.C.E., and were crushed by Philip and eighteen-year-old Alexander. Chaeronea ended the tempestuous history of the city-state as the primary Greek political unit. From now on, large empires absorbed the Greek states into new political structures. Greece was only the first of many territories that fell to the expanding power of Macedon.

After Chaeronea, Philip announced his intention to avenge Persian offenses, especially Xerxes' burning of Greek temples 150 years earlier, and envisaged a campaign of glorious conquest in Persia. In 336, however, with preparations for this expedition well under way, he was murdered by a disgruntled member of the royal bodyguard. After the assassination of Philip, the troops proclaimed Alexander king; the chance for glory in the Persian campaign went to the son, not the father.

The Mother: Olympias

Philip's principal instrument of foreign policy was warfare or the threat of it. However, as a means of securing good relations with neighboring states and tribes, he also entered into dynastic marriages—some half dozen altogether. This was his motive in marrying a member of the royal family of Epirus. But his connection with Myrtale, or Olympias as she came to be known, was to be especially important, for she bore him the son—Alexander—who was to succeed him.

Our primary ancient historical sources were composed, virtually without exception, by men. Given the rigidly male-dominated and patriarchal ancient Greek society, it is no surprise that Greek historians often vilified strong-willed women who dared to affect the course of political events or to influence men in positions of power. Olympias is no exception.

The first strike against Olympias was her semibarbaric status: as an Epirote rather than a Macedonian, she was at two removes from the Greek ethnocentric definition of "civilized." She was said to be an enthusiastic devotee of that most foreign-seeming of Greek gods, Dionysus, whose rites involved wild dancing on the mountainsides and the dismemberment and eating raw of sacrificial animals.

The second strike against her was psychological: she was overly sensitive to any slight to her honor and fiercely determined to avenge any such slight. Her relationship to the equally strong-minded Philip was evidently troubled from the outset. And when Philip took a full-blooded Macedonian wife in order to ensure a legitimate heir to his throne, he alienated Olympias irretrievably.

Olympias enjoyed much closer ties to her son than did Philip, who was constantly away campaigning or busy

The Boy Alexander and the Black Stallion

*Philonicus the Thessalian brought the horse Bucephalas to Philip, offering to sell him for thirteen talents; but when they went into the field to try him, they found him so very vicious and unmanageable that he reared up when they endeavored to mount him, and would not so much as endure the voice of any of Philip's attendants. Upon which, as they were leading him away as wholly useless and intractable, Alexander [about ten years old at the time], who stood by, said, "What an excellent horse they are losing for lack of courage and know-how!" Philip . . . said, "Do you reproach your elders, as if you knew more and could better control him yourself?" "I could manage this horse," replied Alexander, "better than others do." "And if you do not," said Philip, "what will you forfeit for your rashness?" "I will pay," answered Alexander, "the whole price of the horse." Everyone laughed at this; and as soon as the wager was settled between them, Alexander immediately ran to the horse, and taking hold of the bridle, turned him directly toward the sun, having noticed that he was disturbed by the movement of his own shadow. Then letting him go forward a little, still keeping the reins in his hands and stroking him gently, when he began to grow eager and fiery, he shed his upper garment and with one bound mounted him firmly. When he was astride him, he gradually drew in the bridle and controlled him without blows or spurs. Then, when he was quite relaxed and ready to run, he let him go full speed, urging him with his voice and his heels. Philip and the others gazed in silence and some anxiety, but seeing him return rejoicing in what he had done, they burst into applause. Philip shed tears of joy and kissed the boy as he dismounted, saying "O my son, look for a kingdom worthy of you, for Macedon is too little for you."**

Philip's words were, of course, prophetic. Alexander kept the mighty Thessalian stallion and rode him in most of the major battles of his career. When the great warhorse died, some twenty years later, in the Indus region after the battle of the Hydaspes River, Alexander named a settlement there Bucephala in his honor.

*John Dryden, trans., "Life of Alexander," sect. 6, in vol. 2 of *Plutarch's Lives*, ed. A. H. Clough (New York: Dutton, 1910), p. 467 (with slight modifications).

governing Macedon. She and her kinfolk were Alexander's first teachers. In the final rift between Olympias and Philip, Alexander sided with his mother. Moreoever, Alexander's future conception of himself as a latter-day Greek mythological hero was nourished from boyhood by his mother's insistence that his true father was Zeus, not Philip at all.

When Philip was assassinated, Olympias understandably shed no tears for the man who had spurned and humiliated her. Some contemporaries even suggested she had engineered the murder. In fact, it is far more likely that Alexander was behind the murder conspiracy, though this cannot be proven. There can be little doubt, however, that Alexander's extremely forceful and compelling personality owed as much to Olympias as to Philip.

The Son: Alexander

The nineteen-year-old Alexander possessed tremendous determination and an unquenchable thirst for power. As a youth, he underwent thorough training in athletics and weapons use; he was a fast runner and rode a horse almost before he walked. Nor was his intellectual development neglected: Philip hired the philosopher Aristotle to be Alexander's tutor. His education gave him a scientific curiosity about the natural world and a deep love for literature, especially the epics of Homer and the odes of the great Boeotian lyric poet, Pindar. Alexander's military training culminated in his command of the attacking wing of the Macedonian forces at Chaeronea. By the time his father was assassinated, he was a great favorite among the troops.

In 336 B.C.E., as Alexander was putting down invasions by Macedon's semibarbaric neighbors, the Greek city-states saw a chance to regain their freedom. When Thebes revolted (with Athenian encouragement), Alexander marched swiftly into Greece and destroyed the city (except for the house Pindar had lived in) as a horrifying example to other would-be rebels. He treated

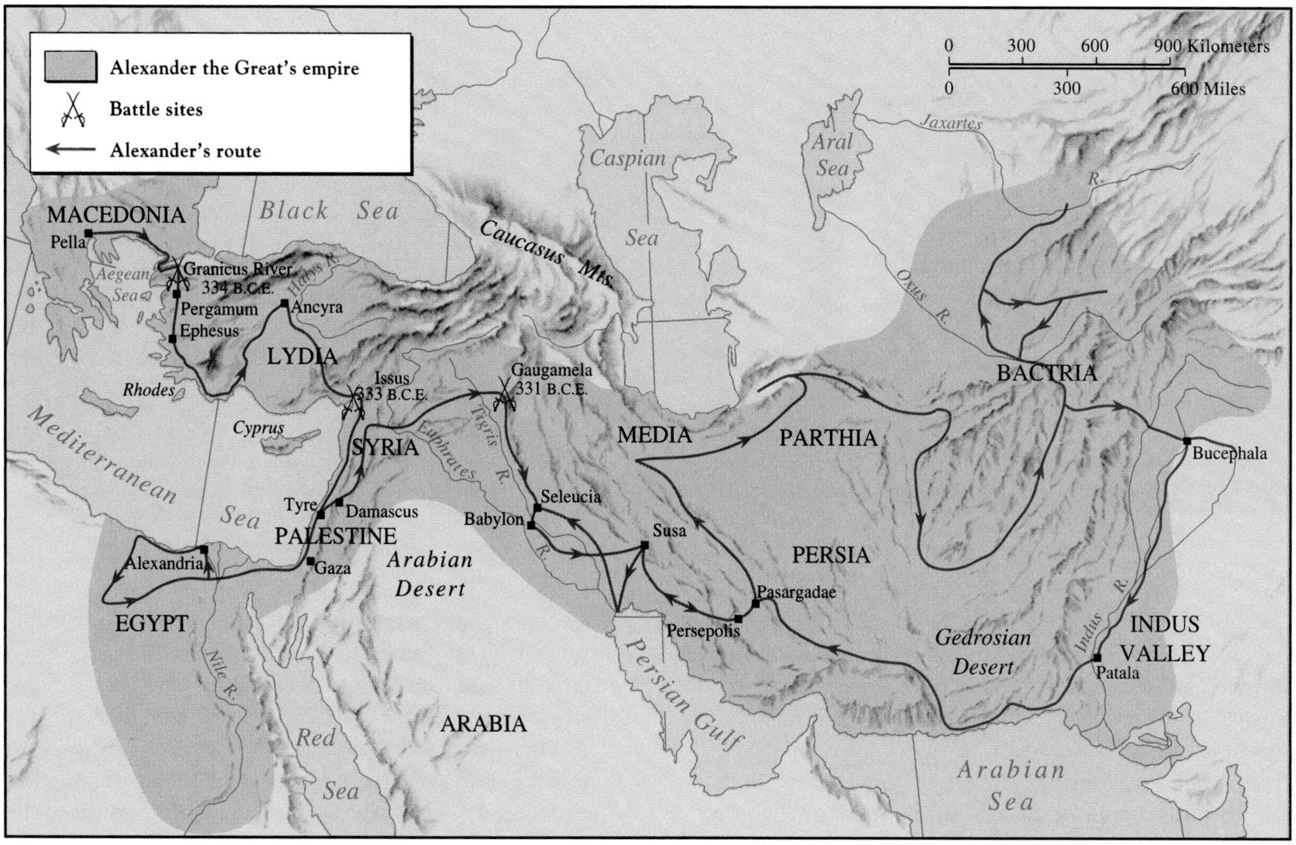

Map 4.1 Conquests of Alexander the Great and the Hellenistic Kingdoms. After the death of Alexander, his far-flung empire, which had never really been stabilized administratively, was carved up during a long series of struggles among his successors. Three major kingdoms emerged by the third century B.C.E.—the Macedonian, the Seleucid, and the Ptolemaic.

Athens much more leniently, out of respect for its cultural history and especially its naval power. Alexander now began his campaign against Persia, crossing the Hellespont in 334 B.C.E. precisely where Xerxes had crossed to attack Greece in 480—the symbolism was obvious. Besides his army of 65,000, Alexander brought with him technicians, road builders, surveyors, administrators, financial officers, and secretary-journalists. In addition, geographers, botanists, zoologists, astronomers, and mathematicians collected information that formed the basis of European knowledge of West Asia and India for many centuries afterward.

In the next decade, Alexander conquered the whole Persian Empire (see Map 4.1). While he was in Asia Minor and Syria-Palestine, Alexander ran the risk that the Persian navy might attack Greece or cut his supply lines at the Hellespont, forcing him to withdraw from Asia. The Persians, however, unwisely decided to give battle on land, first at the Granicus River in 334 B.C.E. and then, under King Darius III himself, at Issus in 333. Alexander won both battles and added the Mediterranean portion of the Persian Empire to his conquests. He marched into Syria and Palestine, where he took Tyre, a key Persian naval base. In Egypt, where he was proclaimed pharaoh, Alexander founded the city of Alexandria in 331. This later became the principal center of Hellenistic cultural development, the most important port in the eastern Mediterranean, and the second most populous city (after Rome) in the history of the ancient world. Alexander also underwent a decisively important religious experience when he consulted at the oasis of Siwah the oracle of Ammon, whom the Greeks equated with Zeus, the god he may have believed was his true father. Though we do not know the content of the oracle's message, since Alexander refused to disclose it till he had spoken with his mother (he died before seeing her), he henceforth believed himself marked out by the gods for even greater achievements than merely punishing the Persians.

Alexander next set out to conquer the heartland of the Persian Empire—modern Iraq and Iran. He beat Darius decisively at Gaugamela near the Tigris in 331. The beaten king escaped and was shortly thereafter assassinated by dissatisfied allies. Alexander then marched

The Granger Collection

Silver Tetradrachm. This four-drachma piece shows a divinized Alexander wearing the royal diadem and the ram's horns symbolic of Zeus Ammon, whose oracle he consulted at the oasis of Siwah. For the first time in Western civilization, coins bore the image of human rulers, as well as of gods. The coin, minted after Alexander's death, demonstrates the artistry of Greek coin designers and die cutters.

triumphantly into Babylon, Susa, and Persepolis, seizing massive booty in gold and silver. At Persepolis, he burned the great royal palaces and temples, avenging the Persian destruction of Greek temples. Turning his war machine eastward to the Indus Valley, Alexander and his troops ran into winter weather in mountainous terrain and torrential monsoon rains. In the main pitched battle of this part of the expedition, Alexander defeated the Indian potentate Porus at the Hydaspes River in 326. Reluctantly yielding to the wishes of his weary troops, Alexander abandoned his plan to march even farther east. The journey back to Persia proved perilous, as the army encountered heavy fighting and suffered tremendous loss of life during a disastrous trek through the Gedrosian desert region.

During his long campaign of conquest, Alexander assumed many of the trappings of Persian royalty, since he saw himself as the successor of the Great King and had come to admire Persian customs. He married the Sogdian princess, Roxane, and encouraged his officers to marry into Iranian nobility. He also promoted a plan of race fusion of his Macedonians and Persians, without much success. He treated Persians and other Iranians as his subjects rather than enemies and recruited a special corps of Iranian troops into the Macedonian army. He even demanded typically Persian signs of obeisance, specifically, prostration before the king. Since, for Greeks, such actions were associated only with the worship of the gods, many of Alexander's veterans resented the apparent arrogance and inaccessibility of their leader.

Alexander was not one to rest on his laurels or devote his life to the administrative tasks of achieving political and social stability in conquered lands. Instead he planned new expeditions to the Arabian Peninsula, Africa, and perhaps the western Mediterranean. In 323, however, he died at Babylon of a fever of unknown origin, possibly malaria. The long journey, wounds suffered in battle, and probably advanced alcoholism had finally exhausted Alexander's marvelous stamina. Although Roxane bore a son, Alexander IV, after Alexander's death, both were murdered.

When Alexander was asked on his deathbed to whom he wished to leave his empire, he answered, "To the strongest." The result was ultimately a division of the empire into three Hellenistic kingdoms: Macedon and Greece; the Seleucid Empire, extending from Asia Minor to India; and the Ptolemaic kingdom, embracing Egypt and, at times, parts of Palestine. These kingdoms differed markedly from the classical city-states. Much larger in territory and ethnically more diverse, they were administered by an elaborate hierarchy headed by a remote, godlike king of Macedonian descent who made the laws, owned much of the land, and was deified after death. Private citizens counted for much less politically than had their fifth-century ancestors and consequently felt little patriotic fervor.

The Hellenistic kingdoms endured for about two or three centuries. Macedon and Egypt fell entirely under Roman domination. The overextended Seleucid empire lost territory too, as the culturally Hellenized kingdoms of Bactria and Parthia split off in its central and eastern sectors; in the West, it succumbed to Roman armies. Ultimately, the Parthians would rule from the Euphrates to the Indus and, with superb cavalry, pose an insoluble military problem for the Romans; they also exploited their profitable position as brokers in the trade between East and West.

A Sophisticated, Cosmopolitan Society and Economy

Although wars occurred, an unprecedented level of cooperation among cities and among Hellenistic kingdoms

A Prenuptial Agreement from Hellenistic Egypt

Apollonia agrees to live with Philiscus in obedience to him, as is appropriate for a wife to her husband, possessing with him the property that they have in common. Philiscus . . . is to provide her with every necessity and a cloak and other possessions . . . at a level appropriate to their means, and Philiscus [may not] . . . bring into the house another wife in addition to Apollonia or a concubine or a catamite nor is he permitted to beget children with another woman so long as Apollonia is alive, nor to set up another household unless Apollonia is in charge of it, and he promises not to throw her out or insult or mistreat her and not to alienate any of their joint property in a way that would be injurious to Apollonia. If Philiscus is shown to have done any of these things or if he has not provided her with the necessities or the cloak or the other possessions as specified, Philiscus must immediately return the dowry of two talents and four thousand drachmas of copper money.

*Similarly, Apollonia is not to stay away for a night or a day from Philiscus' household without Philiscus' knowledge, nor is she to live with another man or to cause ruin to the common household or to bring disgrace on Philiscus in whatever brings disgrace to a husband. If Apollonia voluntarily wants a separation from Philiscus, Philiscus is to return her dowry intact within ten days.**

The passage quoted here is from a papyrus found at Tebtunis in Ptolemaic Egypt and dates to 92 B.C.E. By ancient standards, this is an equitable marriage agreement. The basic responsibilities of both husband and wife are stipulated and the disposition of the dowry and other communal property is carefully defined. The woman Apollonia has been well served by the male relatives who negotiated this marriage contract on her behalf.

*Mary R. Lefkowitz and Maureen B. Fant, *Women's Life in Greece and Rome: A Source Book in Translation,* 2d ed. (Baltimore: Johns Hopkins University Press, 1992), p. 90.

brought stability and prosperity. Greek educators, artisans, merchants, and soldiers moved into recently conquered regions. Trade relations were more secure and extensive, and Greek language and culture pervaded the newly formed kingdoms, at least among the upper classes.

Although most Hellenistic families were farmers, a remarkable growth in manufacturing and international commerce took place. Each region had special commodities, which were exchanged around the Mediterranean and southwestern Asia: grain from Egypt, the Black Sea, and Sicily; olive oil from Attica; wines from Ionia and Syria; salt fish from Byzantium; cheese from Bithynia; prunes from Damascus; glass from Sidon; parchment from Pergamum (in present-day western Turkey), bitumen (used in Egypt for embalming) from the Dead Sea; marble from Paros and Attica; timber from Macedonia and Lebanon; precious purple dye from Tyre; ivory from India and Egypt; gemstones from India and Arabia; frankincense (used as a burnt offering in many religions) from Arabia; balsam from Jericho; and slaves from Thrace, Syria, and Asia Minor.

Enhancing our knowledge of the Hellenistic world are many finds of papyrus in the arid soil of Egypt. The papyri record all sorts of official administrative dealings, as well as private communications and documents including wills, receipts, accounts, letters, lists, and memoranda. Others record agreements regarding marriage, divorce, adoption, apprenticeship and employment, and loans and sales of property and goods.

Hellenistic governments promoted and safeguarded these trade relations. Existing road networks, including those of the Persians, were maintained and expanded; water supply along caravan routes was ensured; efforts were made to suppress piracy; and standard monetary systems were adopted. Certain cities—Rhodes, Delos, Corinth, and Ephesus, in particular—grew wealthy as transit depots. With the rise of Rome in the third century and after, new Italian markets further stimulated commerce.

An Age of Scientific Advances

The Hellenistic kingdoms allocated financial support for various cultural enterprises. The Ptolemies of Egypt, for example, built and supported two important facilities, the first of their kind in history: the great Library of Alexandria and the affiliated "think tank" known as the Museum. Eminent librarians presided over the collection

The Stoic Mind Is a Citadel

Take me and cast me where you will, for there I shall keep my divine part tranquil . . . if it can feel and act according to its proper constitution. Is this change of place sufficient reason why my soul should be unhappy and worse than it was, depressed, expanded, shrinking, frightened? . . .

If you are pained by any external thing, it is not this thing that disturbs you, but your own judgement about it. And it is in your power to wipe out this judgement now. But if anything in your own disposition gives you pain, who hinders you from correcting your opinion? . . .

*Remember that the ruling faculty is invincible, when self-collected it is satisfied with itself, if it does nothing which it does not choose to do, even if it resist from mere obstinacy. . . . Therefore the mind which is free from passions is a citadel, for humans have nothing more secure to which they can fly for refuge and for the future be inexpugnable.**

In this passage, Marcus Aurelius preaches the Stoic doctrine of self-control. The right-thinking person understood that human suffering was a result of an inner response to an outer occurrence. If the mind was correctly trained and attuned to the true nature of the universe, no accident could harm it. Indeed, "accidents" were entirely neutral—simply things that occurred. The Stoic individual possessed a refuge in reason that offered absolute protection from the seemingly harmful events in the world around us.

*Marcus Aurelius, *Meditations,* Book 8, sects. 45–48, trans. George Long, in *The Stoic and Epicurean Philosophers,* ed. Whitney J. Oates (New York: Random House, 1940), p. 550.

of some half-million volumes (papyrus rolls), and the world's first textual critics carefully edited the great works of Greek literature.

The scientific contributions of Hellenistic scholars were especially significant. By 300 B.C.E. Euclid had clearly explained the principles of geometry in his Elements, the basic textbook for the next 2,000 years. The brilliant inventor and mathematician Archimedes of Syracuse (c. 287–212) worked on the geometry of spheres and cones and established the value of pi. Astronomers made surprisingly accurate calculations: a sun-centered theory of the universe was proposed, but the older, earth-centered theory won out, and its formulation by Claudius Ptolemy was not superseded until the work of Copernicus, Galileo, and Newton in the sixteenth and seventeenth centuries. Eratosthenes accurately calculated the circumference of the Earth by comparing the angles of shadow at noon during the summer solstice at two widely separated locations on the same meridian. In biology and medicine, dissection of cadavers and even of living convicts (supplied by King Ptolemy) advanced understanding of anatomy, including the function of the brain and central nervous system and the distinction between veins and arteries.

Hellenistic thinkers showed little interest in applied science and engineering. Under pressure from their rulers and patrons, however, they did produce some new military hardware; Archimedes was as famous for his machines and weaponry as for his mathematical genius; for example, he invented a giant catapult that could hurl 200-pound missiles up to 200 yards.

Escapism and Individualism in Hellenistic Culture

Religion in Hellenistic times was directed more to the spiritual and escapist needs of the individual than to the promotion of civic responsibility. Since the individual was no longer an integral part of a civic group watched over by guardian deities, the old state religion lost its meaning. Needing more immediate emotional satisfaction and assurance of self-worth, people turned to the impressive secret ceremonies of popular new sects known as mystery religions. Cults like those of Dionysus from Greece, Isis from Egypt, and Mithras from Persia offered an escape to a joyful hallucinatory experience of union with a god or goddess, an experience induced by alcohol or drugs, delirious dancing, and sexual frenzy. The promise of immortality was a further attraction. Mystery religions remained popular in the Roman Empire and helped pave the way for Christianity.

For many educated persons, two new philosophical systems—Stoicism and Epicureanism—filled the vacuum left by the waning of the old religion. Zeno of Citium (335–263 B.C.E.) taught in Athens at the Stoa Poikile (painted hall), and his doctrine is thus called "Stoic." Its principal tenets were as follows: First, goodness is based on knowledge. Only the wise person is really virtuous. Second, the truly wise person lives in harmony with nature by means of one's reason, which is part of the divine, universal reason (= God) governing the natural world. It follows that, third, the only good is harmony with nature. External "accidents" like sickness, pain, and death cannot harm the truly good person. Stoicism's emphasis on outwardly directed concepts like duty and civic responsibility later ensured its prevalence in the Roman Empire. Indeed, the Roman Emperor, Marcus Aurelius, was a practicing Stoic whose book of *Meditations* is a masterpiece of Stoic philosophy.

Epicurus (341–270 B.C.E.), who taught at Athens about the same time as Zeno, preached the following principles: First, nothing exists but atoms and void. The soul, like all else, is material and disintegrates like the body; thus it cannot suffer after death. Second, the only good in this life is pleasure, a perfect equilibrium or inner tranquillity, defined as the absence of pain or stress. Third, all our actions should be directed toward the minimizing of pain, that is, toward pleasure. This was an inwardly directed system, recommending withdrawal from society and public life. Its emphasis on pleasure invited charges of vulgar hedonism: Eat, drink, and make merry, for tomorrow you die and will not be held accountable. These perceptions are reminiscent of the charges that some Chinese leveled against Taoists. Despite such accusations and misconceptions, the Epicureans exerted great influence and found their most eloquent proponent in the Roman poet Lucretius.

Stoicism and Epicureanism both offered ethical systems suited to the conditions of life in the Hellenistic world. Rather than focusing exclusively on the search for knowledge about the nature of the universe, they stressed the ability of properly educated individuals to ensure their own happiness. In different ways, each promised release from the psychological and spiritual pain of life in a cosmopolitan world where traditional values were dying.

After the masterpieces of the classical era, literature in the Hellenistic period is disappointing. Menander (c. 342–c. 290 B.C.E.) perfected the New Comedy, whose emphasis, typical of the era, was on private family squabbles rather than the sharp-witted satirical reference to current events and public policy found in Aristophanic Old Comedy. Recent papyrus finds give a clearer impression of this comedy of manners, featuring young lovers, upstart slaves, crotchety old men, and so on. Mistaken identity, contrived or accidental, often motivated the plot. An immensely popular form, New Comedy's influence extended to the Roman stage, in the work of Plautus and Terence, and later to Shakespeare's comedies. The situation comedies of television are modern analogues.

Terme Museum Rome, Photo (c) Archivi Alinari/Art Resource

Statue of a Boxer. One of the favorite subjects of Hellenistic art was the human figure in the throes of intense physical exertion or pain. In this statue of a boxer, probably resting between bouts (there were no rounds), we see a veteran of many fights, which have left him with battle scars, including a broken nose and a cauliflower ear. The leather straps and pads he wears on his forearms and fists, known as "sharp gloves," were designed as much to inflict damage on an opponent as to protect the wearer.

Hellenistic art, best represented in sculpture, is both more ornate and more individualistic than classical art, particularly in its representation of extreme emotion. Artists could still capture classical Greek nobility of form, as in the superb winged Nike of Samothrace, but the supple sensuality of the Venus de Milo is more typical. Humbler, more naturalistic subjects were chosen too: for instance, a gnarled old boxer waiting his turn to compete, or a little girl holding a pet dove. The famous Laocoön group, showing the Trojan priest Laocoön and his two sons being attacked by two sea serpents, symbolically captures the

www.historypictures.com

The Head of Laocoön. The look of agony on the face of Laocoön, a tragic figure drawn from the tale of the Trojan War, well demonstrates the Hellenistic artist's mastery of emotional expression.

essence of war's hellish human price. Its style differs markedly from the sublimity of most Classical sculpture. The discovery of the Laocoön at Rome during the Renaissance created a sensation and profoundly influenced Michelangelo (who viewed it within hours of its discovery), Titian, and Lessing.

Hellenistic artists practiced their art at the behest of the royal families or for wealthy private citizens. They did not, like their classical predecessors, create adornments for the greater glory of the beloved city-state or the gods who watched over it. In this regard, they followed the same trend toward individualism and escapism that can be seen in Hellenistic philosophy and literature.

The Rise and Decline of Roman Power in the Mediterranean World

*The study of history usefully provides a record of all manner of experiences inscribed as it were on a glorious monument. From that record, the reader may choose examples worthy of imitation by himself and by his nation and examples of behavior that are thoroughly disgraceful and to be avoided. If I am not deceived by my love of the work I have set myself in writing history, no republic was ever greater, more virtuous, or abundant in good examples. Into no state did greed and self-indulgence come so late. In no state was there such respect for so long a time for frugality and an austere way of living.**

*Livy, *Ab Urbe Condita,* Book 1, praefatio (translated by James P. Holoka).

These words of praise come from the historian Livy's preface to his magisterial history of Rome. Writing in the late first century B.C.E., he had witnessed the violent upheavals that attended the political transition from Republic to Empire. It was a time of disillusionment among many Roman intellectuals. But Livy found solace in writing the history of his state from its very beginnings. For he found there the record of great achievements and remarkable moral probity. While we may apply a more critical standard in our assessment of Rome's rise to power, the value of studying its history is assured by the influence Roman examples have exerted in the story of civilizations.

Rome had humble beginnings, however, and Romans were not always masters of the world. To explain Rome's rise, we must consider its origins, the social and political practices that gave it internal strength, and the military exploits by which it overcame external threats and conquered great reaches of land. We will examine the resulting Greco-Roman civilization that so shaped the culture and thought of later ages. Finally, we will consider the factors that led to the collapse of Roman power.

The Early Roman Republic

Centrally located in the Mediterranean, Italy has hot and dry summers and mild winters with moderate rainfall. As

www.historypictures.com

Girl with Dove. This charming sculpture of a joyful little girl holding a pet dove illustrates that Hellenistic artists could also render bliss as skillfully as agony in the human face.

Scala/Art Resource

Bronze She-Wolf. This bronze statue (fifth century B.C.E.) represents the most famous city symbol ever devised. The wolf was a kind of totem animal from earliest times: when Romulus and Remus were exposed on the banks of the Tiber by their evil great-uncle, a she-wolf rescued and suckled them. The statue is a fitting symbol of the Roman virtues of warrior prowess and unflinching dedication to family (the twins are a Renaissance addition).

in Greece, the mountainous land separated the population into numerous city-states in valleys or coastal plains, but, with abundant timberland and more cultivatable land, Italy could support large populations.

The history of Rome begins in the eighth century B.C.E., when three major ethnic groups inhabited the Italian peninsula. Greek colonists of the archaic period built towns throughout southern Italy and in Sicily. The Etruscans, who had immigrated in the same period, possibly from Asia Minor, occupied the territory between the Tiber and the Arno Rivers and exerted a crucial influence in culture and religion. Constituting an older ethnic strain than the Greeks and Etruscans were the Italic peoples—Latins, Sabines, and others—in whom were combined a Mediterranean people, perhaps from North Africa, and Indo-Europeans from across the Alps. They were a hardy stock, primarily farmers and herders.

The archaeological record shows that Rome in the eighth century was inhabited by shepherd folk: Latins and Sabines. Etruscan influence in the next three centuries brought progressive urbanization. The Tarquins of Roman myth likely reflect a historical period of Etruscan political and cultural domination. Rome's expulsion of its overlords marked the start of a period of government by elected officials, under a republic.

In the early republic, the population of Rome was sharply divided into patricians and plebeians. The patricians were a hereditary aristocracy that accepted high civic responsibility not just for the sake of power but also because of the dignity conferred by public recognition of services rendered. The plebeians, who comprised the great mass of the free population, farmers, shepherds, small merchants, and artisans, suffered from poverty and oppression by aristocrats. By going on strike or threatening secession, however, the plebeians eventually secured certain essential individual rights and freedoms for all citizens, not just patricians. These included the right to vote for magistrates, the right to have marriages between citizens legally recognized, the right to secure legally binding commercial contracts, and the right to due process in any criminal proceedings. Although the plebeians respected the political competence of the patricians, they successfully agitated for the right to intermarry with patricians and for a written code of law.

The Twelve Tables (449 B.C.E.) marked the beginning of a distinguished history of Roman law, which extended down to the Justinian code of the sixth century C.E. Though excluded from patrician status, plebeians could rise to the rank of *equites* (knights), if they possessed the financial resources to raise horses and serve as cavalry in the army. They also eventually won the right

The Twelve Tables: The Law in Early Republican Rome

When a debt has been acknowledged . . . thirty days must be the legitimate time of grace. After that, the debtor may be arrested by laying on of hands. . . . The creditor may . . . bind [the defaulter] either in stocks or in fetters . . . with a weight no more than fifteen pounds, or with less if he shall so desire. . . . Unless they make a settlement, debtors shall be held in bonds for sixty days. During that time they shall be brought before the praetor's court in the meeting place on three successive market days, and the amount for which they are judged liable shall be announced; on the third market day they shall suffer capital punishment or be delivered up for sale abroad, across the Tiber.

Quickly kill . . . a dreadfully deformed child.

A child born ten months after the father's death will not be admitted into legal inheritance.

Females shall remain in guardianship even when they have attained their majority . . . except Vestal Virgins.

Persons shall mend roadways. If they do not keep them laid with stone, a person may drive his beasts where he wishes.

It is permitted to gather up fruit falling down on another man's farm.

If any person has sung or composed against another person a song such as was causing slander or insult to another, he shall be clubbed to death.

*If a theft has been done by night, if the owner kill the thief, the thief shall be held lawfully killed.**

The Twelve Tables, Rome's earliest written code of law, represented a victory for the plebeian order. Though the code seems to mete out a rough justice, the very fact that it existed in written form shielded, for example, the poor (plebeian) debtor from completely arbitrary punishment by a patrician magistrate. Also, once the law was written down, it could subsequently be amended and refined to create a more rational and humane system of justice. The Twelve Tables also furnishes invaluable evidence for the human condition in early republican Rome: it was an agrarian world, much concerned with questions of property, debt, law and order, and the various rights of family members.

*Naphtali Lewis and Meyer Reinhold, eds., *Roman Civilization, Sourcebook I: The Republic* (1951; reprint, New York: Harper, 1966), pp. 103–104, 106–107.

to serve in the highest public offices. By the early third century, such guarantees of fair play and opportunities for advancement, won by hard struggle, were the inalienable right of every Roman citizen.

Rome, like Greece, was a slave-owning society. Perhaps one-fourth of the population throughout antiquity consisted of slaves acquired through warfare, piracy, and trade. Slaves provided the bulk of the labor force, performing household tasks and the heavy work of farming and mining. Slavery in ancient Rome was also a mechanism for the assimilation of new peoples. The common practice of freeing slaves as a reward for loyal service gave rise to a class of second-class citizens called freedpersons; such large populations of non-Romans were given their freedom that by the late republic perhaps one-half of the citizenry of Rome had slave ancestry.

Although republican Rome never allowed as much participation of common citizens in key governmental decisions as classical Athens had, it did allow for representation of various elements of its society and adjusted to changing needs. The various magistracies were normally annual in tenure and divided among colleagues. Two consuls, elected annually for a one-year term, were the chief civil authorities within the city and commanders of the armed forces. They were empowered to appoint a dictator for a six-month term in times of dire emergency. Other elected officials had responsibility for administering justice; supervising public works; producing games, races, and contests; maintaining official financial accounts; and conducting the census. In addition to the civic magistracies, the Romans elected for life the *pontifex maximus* (chief priest), who presided over the entire apparatus of the state religion. Finally, the Roman Senate was a key advisory body of ex-magistrates who held membership for life. *Senatus Populusque Romanus* (the Senate and Roman People; abbreviated SPQR) was the logo of Roman jurisdiction.

Roman society was based on "piety," the value system that embraced devotion to the gods and to members of one's family, both living and dead. Romans honored the memory of their forefathers and held to their morality of hard work and self-discipline in service to gods, family, and state. As in the teachings of Confucius, the family was a microcosmic state: the father was effectively king and chief priest of the miniature nation of his family. Roman women were educationally and legally disadvantaged, like their Greek sisters, but they could aspire to be *matronae* (mothers of families). In return for her fidelity, fertility, and domesticity, the Roman woman could expect to be revered within her family and Roman society.

Roman religion, like Greek, was polytheistic and involved civic as well as personal duty. Roman beliefs were shaped by foreign influences. The old Italic agricultural gods were modified to parallel Etruscan and/or Greek gods. Venus was equated with Greek Aphrodite, Jupiter with Etruscan Tinia and Greek Zeus, and so on. The goal of Roman religion was *pax deorum* (peace with the gods). Prayers, vows, sacrifices, acts of purification or atonement were all designed to appease gods who were easily angered and liable to inflict punishment on an entire group, guilty and innocent alike. Divination of various kinds was practiced in an effort to ascertain the will of the gods: soothsayers read the stars and the flight patterns of birds and professional "gut watchers" discerned the future in the entrails of sacrificial animals. In return for observance of religious rituals, Romans hoped for favorable answers to their requests for divine assistance.

The Roman Conquest of Italy and the Mediterranean

After 509 B.C.E. Rome joined, and later dominated, a league of Latin cities that defended its fertile plains against the frequent incursions of neighboring hill peoples like the Sabines. Success against these enemies led ultimately to their political absorption and the replacement of Oscan language dialects by Latin. After the setback in 387 of a shattering defeat at the hands of Gauls, fearsome Celtic invaders from across the Alps, the Romans embarked on campaigns of conquest against Gauls and Etruscans to the north and against Samnites and Latins to the south. By 290, Rome controlled more than half of the Italian Peninsula.

Roman predominance in the Italian Peninsula at the beginning of the third century B.C.E. rested on a shrewdly conceived system of annexations and alliances. Rome also established colonies of citizens or, more often, of allies, thus increasing its territory, available manpower, and military strength. Rome's conquests were achieved by an army of unpaid militia conscripted for each campaigning season. Discipline, obedience to authority, and endurance of adversity combined with first-rate training and drill to make the Roman soldier the best the world had yet seen. The efficiency and preparedness of its military were to stand Rome in good stead during its coming struggles against major powers outside the Italian Peninsula.

In the third century Carthage was the major power in the western Mediterranean. Originally founded as a Phoenician colony (called *Poeni* in Latin, giving the adjective "Punic"), its central position in the Mediterranean, near modern Tunis, and its excellent harbor made it a preeminent trading city. It controlled the exchange of gold, silver, and tin from Spain and Africa for wine, textiles, and manufactured goods of its own or from the Hellenistic East. The rise of Rome to a rival first-class power imperiled that advantage.

When Carthage began to expand in Sicily (see Map 4.2), Rome decided in 264 to send troops to the island, thus starting the first Punic War. After Rome built a fleet to match that of the Carthaginians, final victory came in 241 at the high price of 200,000 men and 500 ships lost. Rome's Italian allies and colonists had supplied the needed reserves of manpower and material. The fruits of the hard-earned triumph were sweet. Carthage paid an indemnity of 3,200 talents (200,000 pounds in weight) of silver over the next ten years and ceded its territory in Sicily and, eventually, in Corsica and Sardinia. Rome had acquired its first overseas possessions, and the long process of adapting their government to the requirements of a far-flung empire began in earnest.

Initial hostilities in the second Punic War were ignited by friction in Spain, where members of the Barca family—Hamilcar and later his son Hannibal (247–183)—had been directing the creation of Carthaginian colonies. In 219 Hannibal took by siege the Spanish town of Saguntum, which had contracted an alliance with Rome. War broke out the following year.

Hannibal surprised the Romans by leading men, horses, and combat elephants across the Alps into the Po Valley. By his tactical brilliance and his superior cavalry, he defeated Roman troops sent to stop him, but could not take Rome itself, for the allied cities of central Italy held firm. Instead, he established himself in southern Italy, devastating the territory of those cities that resisted and accepting the cooperation of others.

The tide turned in Rome's favor with the appointment of a brilliant general, Publius Cornelius Scipio (236–183). He succeeded in taking the New Carthage, the nerve center of Punic power in Spain, in 209. Later, Scipio carried the war to North Africa and, after Hannibal was recalled by Carthage, defeated the great general at Zama in 202. In 201 Carthage capitulated, surrendering Spain and agreeing to pay an indemnity of 10,000 talents. The once mighty city survived, only to be razed in 146, after the third Punic War. Rome, now the foremost power in the western Mediterranean, was ready to turn to the Hellenistic East.

LIVES AND TIMES ACROSS CULTURES

Women's Rights: A Test Case in Republican Rome?

During the early part of the second Punic War (218–201 B.C.E.), after a succession of stunning victories by Hannibal (see below), the Roman government passed a special measure to restrict women's possession or display of such luxury items as gold jewelry and expensive clothing. This law remained in force throughout the war and was still not revoked when prosperity returned after its end. As a result, the women of Rome dared to launch a public campaign for its repeal. The historian Livy reports that "the matrons, whom neither counsel nor shame nor their husbands' orders could keep at home, blockaded every street in the city and every entrance to the Forum. As the men came down to the Forum, the matrons besought them to let them, too, have back the luxuries they had enjoyed before, giving as their reason that the republic was thriving and that everyone's private wealth was increasing with every day. This crowd of women was growing daily, for now they were even gathering from the towns and villages. Before long they dared go up and solicit the consuls, praetors, and other magistrates."

One of the consuls for that year, the crusty Marcus Porcius Cato, an arch-conservative and staunch opponent of repeal, delivered a speech attacking the women for their (in his view) outrageous misbehavior and for fomenting a governmental crisis.

*I blushed when, a short while ago, I walked through the midst of a band of women. . . . Our ancestors did not want women to conduct any—not even private—business without a guardian; they wanted them to be under the authority of parents, brothers, or husbands; we (the gods help us!) even now let them snatch at the government and meddle in the Forum and our assemblies. What are they doing now on the streets and crossroads, if they are not persuading the tribunes to vote for repeal? Give the reins to their unbridled nature and this unmastered creature, and hope that they will put limits on their own freedom; unless you do something yourselves, this is the least of the things imposed upon them either by custom or by law which they endure with hurt feelings. They want freedom, nay licence (if we are to speak the truth), in all things. . . . If they are victorious now, what will they not attempt? . . . As soon as they begin to be your equals, they will have become your superiors . . . .**

Speaking against Cato and in favor of repeal was Lucius Valerius, one of the tribunes:

From the very beginning—the reign of Romulus—when the Capitoline had been taken by the Sabines and there was fighting in the middle of the Forum, was not the battle halted by the women's intervention between the two lines? . . . After the kings had been expelled, when the Volscian legions and their general, Marcius Coriolanus, had

As Cicero later said in his *Republic,* "Our people, by defending allies, have become masters of the entire world." When Rhodes and Pergamum appealed to Rome, its armies defeated the Macedonian king in 197. Rome later went to war with the Seleucid kings, again with Macedonia, and with a confederation of Greek states called the Achaean League. The result in each case was Roman victory and the creation of new provinces or puppet states from formerly independent Greek territories. Attalus III (reigned 138–133), the last king of Pergamum, bequeathed his kingdom to Rome, and Rome possessed its first province in Asia.

Between 264 and 133 Rome had won important victories because of the bravery and discipline of the loyal legionary soldiers, and the competence, and sometimes brilliance, of its generals. Rome's military success cost its opponents dearly, as Roman soldiers hunted down and butchered or enslaved Spaniards, Gauls, and Sardinians. Nor were civilized adversaries spared plunder, enslavement, rape, and extortion. As the historian Tacitus cynically said, "Plunder, murder, theft, these they misname empire; and where they make a desert, they call it peace."

By 133 B.C.E., empire building had become Rome's chief industry, a source of glory for the Roman nobility *pitched camp at the fifth milestone, did not the matrons turn away the forces which would have buried the city? When Rome was in the hands of the Gauls, who ransomed it? Indeed the matrons agreed unanimously to turn their gold over to the public need. Not to go too far back in history, in the most recent war, when we needed funds, did not the widows' money assist the treasury?*

Hannibal was in Italy, victorious at Cannae. Already he held Tarentum, Arpi, and Capua. He seemed on the verge of moving against Rome. Our allies had gone over to him. We had no reserve troops, no allies at sea to protect the fleet, no funds in the treasury. . . . Widows and children were donating their funds to the treasury.

*Shall it be our wives alone to whom the fruits of peace and tranquillity of the state do not come? . . . When you, a man, may use purple on your clothes, will you not allow the mother of your family to have a purple cloak, and will your horse be more beautifully saddled than your wife is garbed? . . . They cannot partake of magistracies, priesthoods, triumphs, badges of office, gifts, or spoils of war; elegance, finery, and beautiful clothes are women's badges, in these they find joy and take pride, this our forebears called the women's world. When they are in mourning, what, other than purple and gold, do they take off? What do they put on again when they have completed the period of mourning? What do they add for public prayer and thanksgiving other than still greater ornament? Of course, if you repeal the . . . law, you will not have the power to prohibit that which the law now forbids; daughters, wives, even some men's sisters will be less under your authority—never, while her men are well, is a woman's slavery cast off; and even they hate the freedom created by widowhood and orphanage. They prefer their adornment to be subject to your judgment, not the law's; and you ought to hold them in marital power and guardianship, not slavery; you should prefer to be called fathers and husbands to masters.**

Although Cato and Lucius Valerius hold opposing views on the repeal of the wartime emergency legislation, both speak from a patriarchal bias. Cato blatantly resists the granting of any rights or freedoms that might incite the "unbridled nature" of women. Lucius Valerius recognizes the sacrifices women have historically made in the state's interest and appears to sympathize with their deprivation of signs of status and position. But, while he recommends a more enlightened and kindly exertion of control, all power will remain firmly in the males' hands. In this particular instance, the women prevailed and the offending legislation was revoked.

*Livy, *History of Rome,* 34.1, trans. Maureen B. Fant, in Mary Lefkowitz and Maureen B. Fant, *Women's Life in Greece and Rome: A Source Book in Translation,* 2nd ed. (Baltimore: Johns Hopkins University Press, 1992), pp. 143–146.

and of profits both for the state and for entrepreneurs, businessmen, publicans (tax collectors), and provisioners of the army. New trade routes and markets proliferated in the Mediterranean region. However, many had little share in these profits of empire. The small farmer who had been the mainstay of the early republican state began to disappear. Devastation by Hannibal's army and long neglect of farms caused by military service in the second century ruined many farmers, forcing them off their land. Wealthy senatorial aristocrats bought up the holdings of failed farmers and combined them into vast estates worked by the plentiful slaves obtained through foreign conquests. Dispossessed free men drifted to Rome in search of work or handouts, swelling the ranks of a restless urban population.

For the citizens of Rome, the downside of the greatly enlarged slave labor force was the threat of revolt. Although many literate and skilled slaves from the Greek east found a comfortable life in the homes of wealthy Romans, the great majority of slaves were consigned to hard labor in the fields and mines. Runaways turned to banditry in the Italian countryside and posed a problem of national security: for example, 100,000 rebellious slaves led by the gladiator Spartacus were crushed in 71 B.C.E.,

Corbis

Hannibal. The Carthaginian general shown in this portrait sculpture drew on his brilliance as a tactician to pose the most serious threat to Roman dominance of the Mediterranean in the republican period.

but only after two years at large, during which they inflicted several defeats on Roman legions.

Provincials, too, often suffered from the predations of Roman governors, who were often less interested in fair administration than in enriching themselves through excessive taxation. Inclusion in the empire was thus a mixed blessing.

The Breakdown of the Republic and the Rise of Augustus

By 133 B.C.E., Rome had long since outgrown the makeshift constitution that had served well in early phases of its history. The vast territorial expansion of the empire and the tremendous powers wielded by generals and politicians finally strained the whole framework to the breaking point. Roman history became a tale of power seizures, assassinations, mob violence, political collusion, and, in general, an utter disregard for republican habits of government.

After 133 the political atmosphere in Rome was charged by tension between *populares,* both patrician and plebeian, whose policies generally favored the common people, and *optimates,* again both patrician and plebeian, whose policies generally favored the entrenched senatorial elite. Gaius Marius (157–86 B.C.E.) solved Rome's recruitment problem and acquired a private army by transforming farmer-militiamen into paid professional soldiers. Land grants to discharged veterans accelerated Romanization of outlying parts of the empire and shifted soldiers' allegiance from the civil authorities to the military commander.

Marius's former subordinate Sulla now set the precedent of using military force to achieve his own political ends. Beginning in 83 B.C.E., he fought a bloody civil war against his *populares* opponents and had himself appointed dictator. Because Sulla needed land and money to reward his troops, he set forth proscriptions, lists of public enemies who could be murdered for a reward, including many whose only offenses were their political opinions or their wealth.

In the next thirty years, three new strongmen accumulated fantastic military and political power. Gnaeus Pompeius (106–48 B.C.E.), called Pompey the Great, Marcus Licinius Crassus (c. 112–53 B.C.E.), and Gaius Julius Caesar (100–44 B.C.E.) cooperated for a time to subvert the republican system in favor of their own personal goals, but the uneasy balance of mighty egos finally collapsed.

Julius Caesar had family connections to important *populares* and had served in various high offices. The phenomenal success of Caesar in the Gallic wars of 58–50 B.C.E. upset the tripartite balance of power. He gained for Rome the territory from the Alps to the Atlantic and the North Sea. He also won tremendous booty, shared liberally with his devoted army, which grew from two to thirteen legions. Meanwhile, Crassus's dream of military glory died with him and most of his seven legions on the plains of Mesopotamia, near Carrhae, in 53 B.C.E. The Parthians proudly displayed the captured legionary eagle standards (and Crassus's head on a pike) as trophies. Events now swiftly brought Caesar to supreme power. When the Senate voted that Caesar should lay down his command before returning to Italy, Caesar chose rebellion. He forced Pompey and an army loyal to the Senate to withdraw to Greece. Caesar defeated him in 48 at Pharsalus. Escaping to Alexandria, Pompey was stabbed to death.

Caesar settled matters from one end of the Mediterranean to the other. He established Cleopatra (69–30 B.C.E.) as queen of Egypt, where he remained almost a year. At Rome, Caesar reduced the number of grain dole recipients, carried out public works programs, and revised the calendar, making it solar rather than lunar. Caesar spared Roman citizens who had fought against him in the civil war and even secured offices for former aristocratic opponents, but continued to monopolize power, becoming in 44 *dictator perpetuus* (dictator for

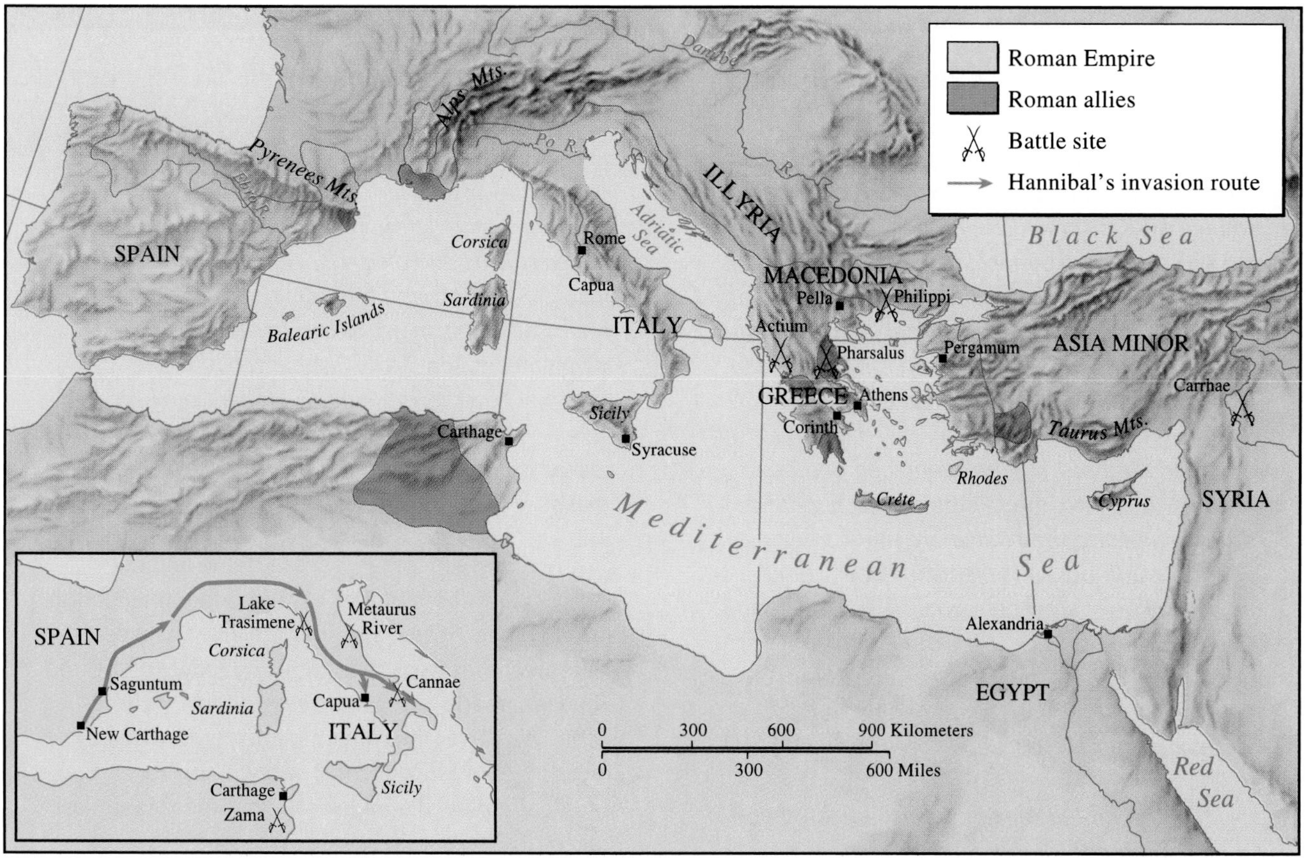

Map 4.2 The Roman World at the Time of the Late Republic. Shown here is the territory under Roman control by about 133 B.C.E. The inset map shows the routes of Hannibal's army and important sites during the second Punic War.

life). This angered jealous aristocrats and alarmed true republicans, including Marcus Junius Brutus (85–42), who murdered Caesar at a meeting of the Senate on the Ides (fifteenth) of March 44 B.C.E.

After Caesar's assassination, no one individual leader was able to consolidate all his powers. Caesar's grandnephew, Gaius Julius Caesar Octavianus—"Octavian" (63 B.C.E.–14 C.E.)—used his vast inherited riches to raise armies and buy influence. After the group responsible for assassinating Caesar was eliminated, Octavian persuaded the western provinces, Italy, and most of the surviving Roman aristocracy that Marc Antony, a colleague of Julius Caesar's who was in control of the eastern provinces of the empire, meant to make Cleopatra joint ruler and shift the center of empire to Alexandria. In 31 Octavian crossed to Greece and defeated Antony and Cleopatra at the naval battle of Actium. At Alexandria the following year, Antony committed suicide to avoid capture, as did Cleopatra, last Hellenistic ruler in the Ptolemaic line from Alexander's day.

Octavian, now left as the single all-powerful ruler, inaugurated the imperial period of Roman history, an epoch that witnessed a fusing of West Asian, Greek, and Roman cultural traditions. He accepted the name Imperator Caesar Augustus (*augustus* means "venerable" or "majestic") and announced his intention to restore republican institutions. However, the next forty-one years brought instead a steady, calculated implementation of a new monarchy, as Augustus's shrewd outward show of respect for republican institutions disguised his monopoly of power. Actually, Augustus genuinely respected most Roman traditions and tried to revive a society demoralized by civil strife.

The emperor's powers were virtually unlimited. He kept exclusive control of the military, which meant ultimate civil authority as well. Augustus's stupendous personal wealth allowed him to win and maintain the people's favor. He built new forum areas, renovated temples, improved roads, and, to keep the urban poor from growing restive, financed public games and kept grain prices artificially low, thereby setting the precedent for later emperors.

Unlike Alexander the Great, Augustus engaged in conquest not for its own sake but to secure borders and to promote the arts of government within them. He

Cleopatra, Last of the Hellenistic Queens

When [Cleopatra] first met Antony she sailed on a golden barge, dressed like Aphrodite. She was not so beautiful as some earlier Macedonian queens, but she possessed a magical charm and a beautiful voice. She was well educated and spoke many languages including Egyptian (unlike many male Ptolemies). . . . Since Antony did not have intellectual aspirations, Cleopatra entertained him as he desired. The two of them enjoyed Oriental luxury, Cleopatra playing the exotic companion to Antony's pleasure, though the debauchery and drunkenness ascribed to her are not in keeping with the traditions of Hellenistic queens, and, as far as we know, she had sexual liaisons with only Caesar and Antony. Legends built up by her enemies are doubtless the source of unflattering accounts, since Cleopatra's competence as a ruler was never questioned, and Egypt remained loyal to her. . . .

She resembled Alexander the Great in her ability and quest for world empire. She posed a major threat to Octavian and Rome. . . . When Octavian finally declared war after Antony had formally divorced Octavia [Octavian's sister], he declared war on Cleopatra alone. . . .

*After being defeated by Octavian, Antony committed suicide and died in Cleopatra's arms. Rather than grace Octavian's triumph, Cleopatra killed herself by allowing an asp to bite her breast. . . . She dominated Antony, and, if she loved him, she certainly never let emotion divert her from her schemes. The Romans feared her as they had feared only Hannibal, and they created a legend that survives to this day.**

More than any other woman of the ancient world, Cleopatra has captured the imagination of biographers, historians, and creative writers. Shakespeare, in particular, in his tragedy *Antony and Cleopatra,* made famous the story of this Hellenistic queen. Whatever the romantic embroidery on her life, as lover of Julius Caesar and wife of Marc Antony, she played a major role in the turbulent last years of the Roman Republic.

*Sarah B. Pomeroy, *Goddesses, Whores, Wives, and Slaves: Women in Classical Antiquity* (New York: Schocken, 1975), pp. 187–188.

succeeded both by his own administrative skills and by those of the men he selected for positions of power. As an economic result of this stability of government, commercial and manufacturing activity flourished during the *Pax Romana* (Roman Peace). Augustus also reopened and made secure trade routes both inside the Mediterranean and outside it, for example, with Arabia, India, and China, via the Red Sea and Indian Ocean.

Roman Cultural Developments

Roman military conquest of the Greek east was paralleled by Greek cultural conquest of Rome in the third and second centuries B.C.E. Greek ways of living and thinking so penetrated Roman society that, as the poet Horace put it "Captive Greece captured its crude conqueror and brought the arts to hayseed Latium."

Their service in campaigns in the Hellenistic kingdoms gave Roman armies a taste for things Greek. They admired magnificent temples and elaborate festivals, enjoyed dramatic performances in splendid theaters and athletic exercises in palestras. They indulged in the creature comforts of public baths, of luxurious mansions adorned with works of art, of sumptuous meals skillfully prepared by master chefs. In imitation of what they had seen in the Hellenistic kingdoms, Roman aristocrats beautified their homes with sculptures and vases and their bodies with jewelry and fabrics from the Greek east. Slaves trained as barbers, doctors, painters, personal secretaries, and tutors brought high prices. Bakeries and taverns began to dot the streets and served imported wines as well as domestic varieties. Dates, peaches, apricots, lemons, plums, cherries, and spices were introduced to Italy from the east.

Also in the second century B.C.E., Epicurean and Stoic philosophers brought their teachings to Rome. Mystery cults, too, like that of Bacchus (in Greek, Dionysus) and of the great mother-goddess Cybele, imported from Asia Minor, first began to make inroads in the traditional beliefs. These alarmed Roman authorities because of their particularly strong appeal to the downtrodden members of society. Bacchus's worshipers were often women seeking to satisfy religious feelings and perhaps to register a disguised protest against male social dominance.

Under the influence of Greek culture, Roman literature made its debut in the late third and early second centuries B.C.E. Plautus (c. 254–184 B.C.E.) and Terence (c. 190–159 B.C.E.) produced the first Latin masterpieces by their adaptations of the Greek comic drama of social mores. The treasure house of Greek literature entered the school curriculum and soon nearly every educated Roman was bilingual and well versed in Greek classics.

Roman literature came of age in the late republic and reached its zenith in the early empire. The first truly great master of Latin language and style was Cicero (106–43 B.C.E.). Among his best-known speeches are the verbal cannon blasts of the *Philippics,* directed against Marc Antony. In a lighter vein are the treatises *On Friendship* and *On Old Age,* delightful reflections on ethical living by a man wise in experience. So great was Cicero's authority as a Latin stylist that, centuries later, one Christian prelate found himself unable to refer to the Holy Spirit in a Latin sermon because there was no word for it in Cicero.

The greatest Roman poet of the republic, Lucretius (c. 94–c. 55 B.C.E.), wrote the *De Rerum Natura (On the Nature of Things),* presenting the central axioms of Epicurean philosophy with consummate artistry and fervent commitment. Lucretius especially admired Epicurus for dispelling the terrors of conventional Greco-Roman religious belief.

Another interesting poet, Catullus (c. 84–c. 54 B.C.E.), was a member of a chic group of avant-garde writers called New Poets. Many of his poems were inspired by his love (and later hatred) for the woman he called Lesbia:

Let's do some living, my Lesbia, and loving,
and not give a damn for the gossip
of all those stern old moralists;
suns can set and then rise up again,
but our brief sunburst goes out just once,
and then it's curtains and the big sleep.
Gimme a thousand kisses, then a hundred,
another thousand, another hundred,
then still another thousand and hundred,
then let's make so many thousands
that we lose track, no counting 'em at all,
so those envious fools can't jinx us
by toting up our kisses.

(Poem 5, translated by Lawrence Smith and James P. Holoka)

According to various sources, this intriguing woman was beautiful, aristocratic, witty, ultrafashionable, nymphomaniacal, adulterous, and perhaps murderous. Other poems relate practical jokes, a visit to the distant grave of a beloved brother, a mock funeral lament for a pet sparrow, and the delight of homecoming after a long absence.

An important aspect of literary production in this period was the influence of the emperor himself. Augustus possessed an exceptional ability to induce the best literary talents to restore the morale of Romans by writing poetry and history that advocated nationalistic ideals of patriotism and morality. Maecenas, the great literary patron of Vergil and Horace, was an indispensable aide to Augustus in this area.

Epicurus and the Human Triumph over Religion

*When human life lay prostrate on the earth oppressed by the heavy burden of religion which seemed to show its head in the heavens, threatening human beings with a terrifying face, it was a Greek who first dared to lift his head and resist its power. He feared neither the tales of gods nor their lightning bolts nor their thunder in the heavens. All these things only spurred his brave spirit to break through the constricting boundaries of nature's gates. The vital force of his intellect carried him past the flaming walls of the universe as he traversed that immense realm in his mind and soul. In triumph he returned to us with knowledge of all that can or cannot come to be, of how each thing has its potentials defined and regulated. In this way, religion was cast down in subjection and we human beings raised to the heavens by his victory.**

Lucretius believed that humankind lived in a benighted and unreasonable state of religious fear before Epicurus developed his philosophy. In particular, men and women lived their lives badly, committing crimes like human sacrifice or unjust war, because they feared reprisals by gods who made contradictory and often irrational demands on them. The typical polytheistic belief in vengeful, fickle, and immoral gods had too long kept people in ethical and intellectual darkness. Epicurus freed humankind from such fears by daring to shed light on the universe with the power of his intellect, which revealed that the gods, if they existed, in fact played no part in our lives and thus posed no threats of punishment.

*Lucretius, *De Rerum Natura,* Book 1, lines 62–79; translated by James P. Holoka.

Rome's Mission

Others will cast more tenderly in bronze
Their breathing figures, I can well believe,
And bring more lifelike portraits out of marble;
Argue more eloquently, use the pointer
To trace the paths of heaven accurately
And accurately foretell the rising stars.
Roman, remember by your strength to rule
Earth's peoples—for your arts are to be these:
To pacify, to impose the rule of law,
*To spare the conquered, battle down the proud.**

In these lines, Vergil identifies the distinctive Roman achievement in history as the art of government: the manifest destiny of the Romans was to unify the earth's peoples into a peaceable order. In Vergil's eyes, this was something to be proud of, surpassing even the artistic and scientific achievements of those "others," the Greeks.

*Virgil, *The Aeneid*, trans. R. Fitzgerald (New York: Random House, 1983), Book 6, lines 847–853.

Between 30 and 19 B.C.E., the greatest Roman poet, Vergil (70–19 B.C.E.), created the *Aeneid*, a masterpiece of world literature. The epic describes the exploits of the hero Aeneas after the fall of Troy. The gods choose Aeneas to lead a band of Trojan refugees on a perilous journey to Italy, where his descendants are to mingle with native Italians and found Rome. Since the gods in the epic gradually disclose the manifest destiny of the Roman Empire, the poem was both foundation myth and mission statement for the Roman people. Without being jingoistic, it gave the Roman world its national epic. The self-effacing Aeneas is unlike Homer's more egocentric heroes. He follows the commands of the gods, even when it means he must leave the homeland he loves or a woman who loves him. The placing of duty above personal interest was precisely the ideal Augustus wished to hold up as a model of patriotic devotion in troubled times.

Another first-magnitude poet of the Augustan period was Horace (65–8 B.C.E.). His *Odes* are compact poems on such universal subjects as love, pleasure, the brevity of life, and art and nature. They are filled with memorable gemlike phrases like *carpe diem* (seize the day) and with patriotic sentiments ("sweet and fitting it is to die for one's country"). Horace also extolled the blessed security and social regeneration of the Augustan age.

Livy (59 B.C.E.–17 C.E.) wrote a massive history of Rome from the founding of the city down to his own day. The *History*, like the *Aeneid*, furnished models of patriotic heroism and morality. Although Livy was less critical in his judgments and handling of sources than, for example, Thucydides, the *History* was both an immediate popular success and influential in later ages.

The greatest Roman historian, however, was Tacitus (c. 56 C.E.–c. 120), whose *Histories* and *Annals* are our best and most extensive narrative of the period from 14 to 96 C.E. Tacitus wrote from the perspective of a man disgusted with both the emperors' abuses of power and the subservience of the aristocratic classes. In his pages, we meet the mistrustful emperor Tiberius listening to the charges of informers and indulging in sexual perversions at his villa on Capri; the genial but naive emperor Claudius, manipulated by scheming wives and freedmen; and, of course, Nero with his uncontrolled passions and delusions of artistic grandeur.

As Tacitus attacked the political impotence of the aristocratic class, the satirist Juvenal (c. 60 C.E.–c. 135) trained the powerful weapon of his biting criticism on its social and moral degeneration. He mercilessly denounced those he felt were corrupting Roman society, especially the immigrant "Greeklings" who excelled in unsavory jobs while seducing the wives and children of native Romans. The satires attack, among others, upper-class married women, Egyptians, homosexuals, soldiers, hypocritical philosophers, and the evil emperor Domitian. Juvenal's transformation of painful moral indignation into literary art has made him the archetypal satirist.

Roman sculpture and painting derived almost entirely from Greek models. Indeed, the thousands of exact Roman reproductions are often our best source for the lost Greek originals. Roman artistic innovation was confined to the ultrarealistic depiction of actual persons, warts and all, particularly in the busts of worthy Romans that adorned homes and tombs. In architecture, however, the Romans did advance beyond Greek models. In particular, they used concrete to alter traditional building types in momentous ways. Roman architects were able to create curvilinear forms—the arch, the vault, the dome—while respecting Greek aesthetic norms of balance and symmetry. These distinctively Roman designs strongly influenced the architecture of later times, particularly the Romanesque.

Huge public baths, sports arenas, and temples were the most typical structures of the new imperial architecture. The amphitheater—essentially a 360-degree version of the Greek theater—first appeared in southern Italy, but the most famous was the Colosseum. It accommodated some 50,000 spectators and was the site of gladiatorial contests, wild animal "hunts," executions of Christians, and even mock sea battles.

The most durable and impressive example of the new imperial architecture was the Pantheon (Temple of

Editorial Photocolor Archives/Art Resource

View of a Roman Town. This photograph shows the forum or "downtown" area of the typical Roman town of Pompeii, which was buried by the volcanic eruption of Mount Vesuvius in 79 C.E. The forum includes a central open space and various surrounding commercial, civic, and religious buildings.

All Gods). Unlike Greek temples, which impress by stunning exterior views, the Pantheon depends on its huge enclosed space for its effect. Its dome was the world's largest till the building of St. Peter's in Vatican City. The Pantheon strongly influenced Renaissance architects and, through them, Thomas Jefferson, in his design for the library rotunda at the University of Virginia.

The Roman spirit emphasized stability, order, and smooth practical function. Although much earlier the Indus people (see Chapter 2) and of course the Greeks (see Chapter 3) had practiced urban planning, Roman civil engineers operated on a much larger scale throughout the vast empire. Every significant town and city in the Roman Empire possessed walls, paved streets, efficient water supply and waste disposal systems, facilities for the preparation, storage, and distribution of food, centers for political, administrative, and judicial functions, temples and associated structures, commercial shops, and recreational and cultural complexes.

Roman engineers built the most durable roads in the world, providing vital transportation and communication arteries throughout the empire. The huge Roman imperial highway system was some 50,000 miles in extent. Construction was done by soldiers or forced labor (slaves and prisoners of war), always with careful attention to good foundation, choice of material, smooth paving, and proper drainage. The Romans were also excellent hydraulic engineers. Large reservoirs situated on high ground fed fountains, baths, and private residences. A constant flow of water through public latrines carried waste out to the sea through the sewer system. When sources were lacking nearby, water was diverted, sometimes over long distances, by aqueducts. At Rome, more than a dozen aqueducts kept 1 million people plentifully supplied, and an extensive underground drainage system emptied into the Tiber.

Politics, Society, and Economics in the Early Empire

Although the immediate successors of Augustus, like him members of the Julio-Claudian family, could not match his managerial skills, they nonetheless maintained stability in domestic and foreign policy. This was despite the eccentricities and even mental aberrations of some of the emperors themselves. Caligula (reigned 37–41) and Nero (reigned 54–68) were psychopaths who committed incest and murdered close family members, Nero even his own mother. Despite such problems at the top, the system Augustus installed was remarkably resilient and durable.

By the second century C.E., succession based on the support of the army and the accident of birth into the imperial family was replaced by one in which each emperor selected and legally adopted his own successor, usually a capable and experienced administrator and/or general.

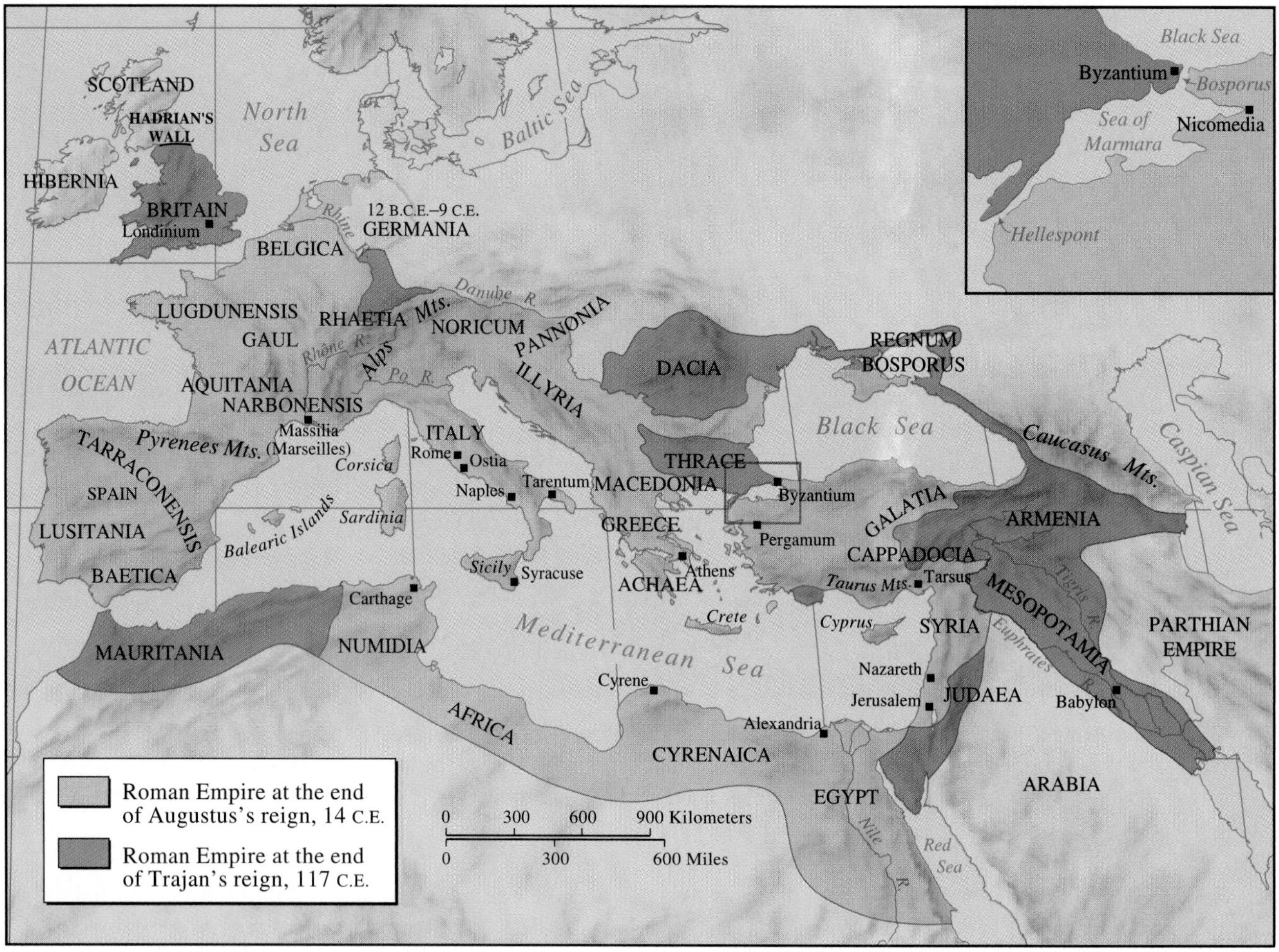

Map 4.3 The Roman Empire from 14 to 117 C.E. Shown here is the Roman Empire in the reign of the emperor Augustus and, a century later, in the reign of the emperor Trajan, when it had reached its greatest extent.

Trajan (reigned 98–117) pleased the masses in Rome by his major building programs and gifts of money. He also enlarged the empire by the addition of Dacia (modern Romania). Hadrian (reigned 117–138) tirelessly traveled throughout the provinces of the empire, personally attending to military security along borders. He everywhere indulged his strong interest in the arts and architecture through the construction and renovation of magnificent temples (including the Pantheon), markets, and other facilities. The general prosperity in the empire continued until 165, when an epidemic (possibly smallpox) caused great loss of life. This severely compromised Rome's military strength, as decreasing Roman manpower and increasing Germanic pressure along the Rhine-Danube frontier overtaxed a defensive system designed to repel one border incursion at a time.

During the early empire, the Roman world was a vast cosmopolitan collection of more than 5,000 towns (see Map 4.3) and their surrounding hinterlands inhabited by a population of 50 to 60 million. Commercial activity flourished because of a uniform currency system, the suppression of piracy, the highway network, and the maintenance of harbors and dockyards. Roman ports saw a constant flow of textiles, grain and other foodstuffs, metals (gold, silver, copper, tin, lead, iron), manufactured goods (glass, pottery, jewelry, paper), and luxury items (silk, ivory, precious gems, spices) from all over the Mediterranean world as well as from Arabia, India, and China.

Besides material advantages, Roman intellectual culture also became widespread in the empire. The Latin language was learned by citizens in the western part of the empire. The modern Romance languages (French, Italian, Spanish, Portuguese, Romanian) are direct descendants of Latin. In the east, Greek persisted in preference to Latin, while in the west educated people were generally bilingual, as the literature and philosophy of both Greece and Rome were transmitted to succeeding generations. Rome showed special originality by creating

LIVES AND TIMES ACROSS CULTURES

"The Going Rate": Wages and Prices in the Roman Empire and China

In 301 C.E., the emperor Diocletian attempted to control the rampant inflation plaguing the late Roman Empire by issuing an "Edict on Maximum Prices," which stipulated limits on wages and prices. Although the edict failed to have the desired effect, it provides modern students with valuable insights into personal income and the cost of goods and services. We can, for example, get an idea of the relative earnings of people in various professions by comparing their wages. Sewer cleaners, camel and mule drivers, shepherds, and farmhands made 25 denarii per day. Scribes made that same amount for 100 lines of fair copy. Wall painters made 75 denarii per day, a sum that arithmetic teachers made per month for each pupil they instructed. Rhetoric or public speaking teachers made 250 denarii per pupil each month. Barbers made 2 denarii per head. Tailors made 60 denarii for a cut-and-finished-hooded cloak of first quality.

While it is impossible to convert ancient Roman monetary units into present-day dollar equivalents, we can get some sense of the real cost of specific items by restating prices in terms of a day's wage. According to Diocletian's Edict, for example, a carpenter or a baker earned up to 50 denarii per day; on that basis, the following prices obtained:

Item	Cost (in days' wages)
20 lbs. wheat	2
20 oz. best-quality wine	.6
20 oz. cheap wine	.2
20 oz. beer	.1
20 lbs. salt	2
20 oz. honey, best quality	.8
1 lb. pork	.25
2 chickens	1.2
1 lb. best-quality fish	.5
100 oysters	2
1 pr. soldier's boots	2
1 pr. women's boots	1.2
1 lb. wool, best quality	3.5
1 lb. wool, 2nd quality	1
1 lb. white silk	240
1 lb. silk, dyed purple	3,000
1 lb. gold	1,000

There were no equivalents of Diocletian's price regulations for China during a similar period. There is nevertheless information on wages and prices for Han China, where a poll tax, which together with the land tax constituted the chief source of revenue, the former at 120 coins per head for adults and 23 for each child between seven and fourteen years old. A Han inscription of 90 C.E. says that a ten-yard roll of undyed silk cloth weighing thirteen ounces had a value of 618 coins. We may compare this with the monthly stipend of between 360 and 3,000 coins paid to officers serving in the northwestern frontier guard. In one case, an officer whose monthly stipend was 900 coins was paid two rolls of silk. Another document from northwestern China during the Han stated that 20,000 coins could purchase two adult female slaves, twenty ox-carts, or ten draft horses.

law schools and recognizing medicine as an important specialization.

Decay and Temporary Recovery in the Later Roman Empire

After 180 a time of troubles set in for the Roman Empire. The era of Roman imperial peace and tranquillity was over. Armed conflict among would-be successors effectively militarized the civil authority of the emperor. Between 235 and 284 more than twenty emperors assumed power, as mutinous legions or imperial guards deposed or murdered the same claimants they had earlier conspired to put on the throne.

Rome also faced increasing defense problems. In the east, the Persians, under the Sassanid dynasty, pushed back Roman legions in the area. The capture of an emperor, Valerian (reigned 253–260), by Persian forces was a

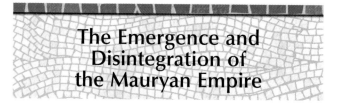

Brian Blake/Photo Researchers

Constantine. This titanic marble head, eight and a half feet in height, remains along with a right hand and sundry other outsized limb fragments of a colossal seated statue of the emperor. The distant gaze of the eyes bespeaks concentration on realms far beyond the ken of puny mortals. The statue (c. 313) graced the basilica of Constantine in Rome.

conspicuous blow to Roman self-esteem. Elsewhere, Germanic tribes made incursions along the Rhine-Danube border and in Britain, and the Dacians frequently broke into the Balkans.

The chaos of the third century was temporarily checked by the reforms of the emperor Diocletian (reigned 284–305). Diocletian staffed the imperial bureaucracy with the best available talent, reorganizing provinces into smaller districts supervised by more officials. In light of the frequency of barbarian invasions, Diocletian believed that the empire had become too large for one man to rule and split it into four administrative sectors. In each, a tetrarch (one-fourth ruler) held supreme authority. Rome was not one of the four imperial capitals and thus faded farther into the background. To meet the defense needs of the empire, Diocletian enlarged the army from 300,000 to 500,000, in part by enlisting barbarians. After Diocletian's resignation in 305, the tetrarchy soon disintegrated in a complicated series of civil wars fueled by personal ambition and the reversion to dynastic inheritance.

By 324 Constantine (reigned 306–337) had emerged as the sole ruler of the Roman Empire. In general, Constantine followed the governmental policies of Diocletian, ruling autocratically and consulting only a few trusted appointees. Constantine prepared the way for the empire's split into eastern and western halves by founding a new imperial capital, Constantinople, on the site of Byzantium. Constantinople (modern Istanbul) commanded a peninsula on the European shore of the Straits of Bosporus, convenient for the direction of military operations along the Danube to the north and against Persia to the east. For over a thousand years, this "second Rome" preserved a residue of Greco-Roman civilization (see Chapter 5) until its fall to the Ottoman Turks in 1453.

The troubles of the third and fourth centuries exerted a powerful disintegrative force on Roman society, economics, and culture. The emperors were forced to siphon wealth from the more prosperous eastern half of the empire to sustain the overburdened west. Increases in spending on defense and the ever-growing imperial bureaucracy led to dire economic difficulties, as imperial tax collectors tightened the screws on a shrinking population of taxpayers. Debasement of coinage caused rampant inflation. Efforts at wage and price controls were no help. Individuals had to be forced to remain in certain essential, but now much less profitable, occupations; these included soldiering, farming, and grain shipping, among others. The nobility retained only honorific titles; true power was in the hands of thousands of petty bureaucrats. Well-to-do landowners, who had in the past voluntarily put their skills and funds at the disposal of government, were now taxed to their limit and laid under legal obligations of public service. The ultimate collapse was near.

The Emergence and Disintegration of the Mauryan Empire

But this last combat with Porus [king of northwest India] took off the edge of the Macedonians' courage, and stayed their further progress into India. For having found it hard enough to defeat an enemy who brought but twenty thousand foot and two thousand horses into the field, [the Greeks] thought they had reason to oppose Alexander's design of leading them on to pass the Ganges too, which they were told was thirty-two furlongs broad and a hundred fathoms deep, and the banks on the further side covered with multitudes of enemies. For they were told the kings of the Gandari-

*tans and Praesians expected them there with eighty thousand horses, two hundred thousand foot, eight thousand armed chariots, and six thousand fighting elephants.**

*Aubrey Stewart and George Long, trans., *Plutarch's Lives,* vol. 3 (London: Bell, 1925), p. 73.

Alexander's incursion into India in 326 B.C.E. was an epoch-making event for both sides. His soldiers were shocked by the formidable heavy cavalry of war elephants the Indians used in battle, the very size of India, which seemed to stretch on endlessly, and the prospect of determined Indian resistance. They refused to march any further and forced their king to turn back. After Alexander's retreat and later death, northwest India was thrown into chaos, but his feats inspired an ambitious young Indian to found the first great Indian empire.

Alexander's invasion had another important and lasting consequence. It opened up direct land and sea communication between India and the Hellenistic kingdoms that Alexander's generals founded in western Asia. Hellenistic artistic traditions influenced Indian art, especially Buddhist art in later centuries. Some scholars believe that contact with Greek gods modified some Indian Buddhist teachings. Indian astronomy was indebted to Hellenistic astronomy and borrowed many terms from Greek.

This section will begin with Alexander's conquest of northwestern India and continue with the Mauryan Empire, the first great Indian empire, and its successor states. It will also explore some of the cultural interactions between India and lands to the west, relying on archaeological remains, coins, inscriptions, and the accounts of foreign (Greek and Chinese) observers. It ends with the successor states that followed the fall of the Mauryan Empire.

Persian and Greek Precursors

Major upheavals culminated in the founding of the Mauryan Empire around 313 B.C.E. As we have seen in Chapter 3, an economic and social revolution had produced Buddhism and Jainism in the sixth century. These religions offered their followers new ethical and social standards that emphasized the individual rather than tribes or castes.

Persian and then Macedonian invasions of northwest India also added to the trauma of the period. In 518 B.C.E., King Darius of Persia had conquered a part of northwest India and made it the twentieth satrapy (province) of the Persian Empire, ruled by Persian appointees. One of the wealthiest in the empire, it paid substantial taxes and supplied numerous soldiers, some of whom participated in the Persian invasion of Greece. Persian power gradually weakened, and the empire fell to Alexander.

In 326 B.C.E., Alexander's conquering army reached northwest India and found many warring states in what had once been the Persian satrapy. Some states submitted to him, others he subdued. He then confronted King Porus (also called Puru), the most powerful ruler in the upper Indus Valley. After a hard-fought battle Porus was brought captive before Alexander, who was so impressed that he confirmed him as a vassal king, restored his lands and even added to them. After Alexander died in 323 B.C.E., his successors, fighting one another to partition his empire, withdrew from newly conquered northwest India. Local revolts broke out, and by 317 the last Greek general had left India.

The Rise of Chandragupta Maurya

Taking advantage of Alexander's death, Chandragupta Maurya, an Indian who may have known the Macedonian conqueror, drove out the remaining Greek forces. He then subdued the tribes in the northwest, marched east, and overthrew a kingdom located along the Ganges. Taking over its capital city, Pataliputra, he proclaimed himself ruler around 313 B.C.E.

Alexander's general Seleucus Nicator succeeded to his empire in Asia. In 305 B.C.E., he set out to reconquer India, failed, then agreed to a treaty in 303 in which Seleucus gave up his claim to India and ceded the Kabul Valley in present-day Afghanistan to Chandragupta in return for 500 elephants. The agreement was cemented by a marriage, perhaps a Seleucid princess was sent to India. Seleucus also sent an ambassador, Megasthenes, to reside at Pataliputra. Chandragupta also exchanged ambassadors with the Ptolemies in Egypt and with other Hellenistic rulers.

Megasthenes wrote a detailed account of India and of life at Chandragupta's court that became the standard source for later classical accounts on India. Although not always accurate, it is nevertheless valuable because it was the first authentic and lengthy account of India by a foreign observer. Another source on this period is the *Arthasastra (Treatise on Polity),* a book reputedly written by Kautilya, a minister to Chandragupta, who some think was the real architect of the Mauryan Empire. The *Arthasastra* is a detailed book that dealt with the theory and practice of government and the laws and administration of the Mauryan Empire.

The *Arthasastra* described a highly organized and thoroughly efficient autocracy. The ruler was assisted by a council of ministers and an elaborate bureaucracy. He was supreme in military and civil affairs and the final arbiter of justice. As in Persia, a network of spies reported to the ruler directly. If accounts can be believed, Chandragupta's army had 600,000 men, 9,000 elephants, chariots, and a naval auxiliary. All were paid directly by the royal treasury.

The capital city Pataliputra (modern Patna), situated at the confluence of the Ganges and Son Rivers, was a grand place. Megasthenes described it as enclosed by a

M. Anand/STSimages.com

Elephants in Combat. Since earliest recorded history, elephants have been used in India for combat and in ceremonial processions. Here, richly caparisoned elephants are shown in battle.

wooden wall approximately nine miles long by two miles wide with 570 towers and sixty-four gates, all protected by a moat. The palaces and other buildings were also made of wood, a good precaution against earthquakes, but highly perishable. Archaeological excavations have confirmed the Greek ambassador's claim that the opulence of the palaces rivaled that of the Seleucid palaces at Susa.

We learn from the *Arthasastra* that a council of thirty men governed the capital city, administering its finances, sanitation, water supply, public buildings, and gardens. The council was divided into six committees, each with a clear-cut function; for example, one supervised industries and another took care of foreigners and pilgrims.

Chandragupta ruled for twenty-four years. Megasthenes wrote admiringly of his energetic administration of justice. Kautilya's account of the Emperor's busy schedule tells us that his days were divided into ninety-minute segments, spent in meditation, meetings with ministers, and receiving reports. His rare public appearances were occasions of pageantry and grandeur as he rode in a golden litter or an elephant-drawn chariot, dressed in embroidered robes of gold and purple, and surrounded by a bodyguard of women. His favorite diversion was the hunt in the royal game preserve, where he shot arrows at game driven before him by beaters. Elaborate precautions were taken to protect him from assassins; he reputedly slept in a different bedroom every night. We know little about his family life or of his end. Jain tradition of doubtful authenticity says he abdicated the throne, became a Jain monk, and fasted to death in the manner of Jain saints.

Bindusara, a son of Chandragupta, succeeded him around 297 B.C.E. and ruled until around 272. He was known as the Slayer of Foes, which suggests that he was a successful warrior. Stories say that he had sixteen wives and 101 sons; the latter may be an exaggeration, since the names of only four sons are known.

Emperor Asoka

Asoka was not Bindusara's eldest son, but while still young, he was given major responsibilities as governor of two strategically located provinces in the northwest, at crossroads of international trade. His first wife was a devout Buddhist; they had a son and a daughter. Buddhist sources tell of a war of succession in which Asoka defeated his inept elder brother, and then had all his other brothers and possible rivals killed. That Asoka was not crowned until four years after his father's death does strongly suggest a disputed succession.

By 269–268 B.C.E., Asoka was firmly in control of the largest empire to that date in Indian history, a realm that included most of modern Afghanistan and all of India except the extreme south. Little is known of the first eight years of his reign. Presumably he spent his time in governing, in family life, and in the accepted pastimes for royalty, including lavish entertaining. As he later said: "Formerly in the kitchen of King [Asoka], many thousands of [animal] lives were daily slaughtered for [making] curries."

Asoka's conquest of Kalinga in southeast India later filled him with such remorse that he changed the direction of his government, and his personal life. He gave up eating meat and commanded his kitchen staff to prepare only vegetarian dishes for everyone. He replaced hunting with pilgrimages to places associated with the life of the Buddha. He also labored hard as king, declaring: "At all times and in all places, whether I am dining or in the ladies' apartments, . . . official reporters should keep me informed of the people's business. . . . At any hour and at any place, work I must for the commonweal." He devoted the rest of his reign to the realizing of Buddhist teachings in laws and deeds. His enthusiastic espousal of Buddhism contributed to its spread in India and beyond. He was to Buddhism what the Roman Emperor Constantine would be to Christianity.

We know much about Asoka's rule because he had his laws and pronouncements carved on stone pillars and on rock surfaces throughout the empire, many of which have survived. He ordered his officials to read these edicts at public gatherings so that ordinary citizens would learn of his commands.

"All men are my children," said Asoka, and although he tolerated all religions, he nevertheless attempted to reform his "children" according to the teachings of Buddha. In application, this meant replacing some traditional practices with the ethics of Buddhism. He relaxed somewhat the stern laws that applied to criminals, although he did not abolish the death penalty. Those condemned to death were given three days' grace to settle their affairs before their sentences were carried out. He prohibited animal slaughter in religious ceremonies, declared many species protected, and encouraged people to become vegetarians, or at least to abstain from eating meat on certain days. Asoka also enjoined his people to cultivate such virtues as obedience to parents, kindness to servants, generosity to friends, and respect to holy men. He told them to be honest and to speak the truth and to give to charity.

Asoka was even ready to hand down disagreeable orders if he believed certain popular pastimes contravened Buddhist ideas. Thus he banned certain festivals where people had a good time eating, dancing, drinking, and watching performances, because he thought they were immoral. He created a new category of officials called morality officers to ensure that his officials conformed to his ideals and lived up to his code of behavior. The morality officers were allowed to pry into people's private lives, even those of the emperor's brothers and sisters. Similarly, Augustus saw moral exhortation and legislation as one of his duties as ruler of Rome.

An Asokan Pillar. Many of the pillars that Asoka ordered erected still stand. The lower part of this pillar is inscribed with the emperor's edict.

Asoka also worked in practical ways to improve the people's daily lives. He set up botanical gardens to cultivate medicinal plants and erected hospitals for both people and animals. He constructed highways and built and maintained rest houses and wells along the routes. He also had fruit and shade trees planted for the benefit of all users.

Many grand religious edifices and new cities were built during Asoka's reign. According to Buddhist literature, he had the Buddha's remains further divided and enshrined in great mounds (*stupas*) throughout his empire to serve as pilgrimage destinations. A Chinese Buddhist pilgrim who visited India in the seventh century C.E. recorded more than eighty *stupas* and other structures associated by tradition with Asoka. That so many had survived or were still remembered a thousand years after his time certainly testifies to his munificent patronage of Buddhism.

Asoka also supported Buddhist missionary activities outside India. Two of his children entered the Buddhist

Asoka Transformed by the Horrors of War

*Eight years after his coronation King Devanampiya Piyadasi [of Gracious Mien, and Beloved of the Gods—a title by which Asoka was addressed] conquered the Kalingas. In that (conquest) one hundred and fifty thousand were deported [as prisoners], 100,000 were killed [or maimed] and many times that number died. Thereafter, with the conquest of Kalinga King D. P. [adopted] the practice of morality, love of morality and inculcation of morality. For there arose in King D. P. remorse for the conquest of Kalinga. For this purpose this rescript on morality has been written that my sons and great grandsons should cease to think of new conquests and in all the victories they may gain they should be content with forbearance and slight punishment. For them the true conquest should be that of morality; all their delight should be delight in morality for benefit in this world and the next.**

Deeply remorseful over the suffering his conquest of Kalinga in southeast India had brought about, Emperor Asoka renounced war as an instrument of policy for himself and his successors. He had this statement carved on a rock pillar as a public confession and manifesto. He also converted to Buddhism and would devote much of his remaining years to the propagation of morality and righteousness according to Buddhist teachings. This fascinating man is revered by Indians as the greatest ruler in their history. Indeed, he ranks as a great ruler in the pageant of humanity.*

*Edict 13, trans. B. G. Gokhale, *Asoka Maurya* (New York: Twayne Publishers, 1966), Appendix.

order and are credited with bringing Buddhism to Ceylon (modern Sri Lanka). They took with them cuttings of the pipal tree under which Gautama had meditated and achieved enlightenment. Some ancient pipal trees on the island reputedly are descended from those cuttings. At a great rock fortress at Sigiriya in Ceylon, surviving frescoes of Buddhist heavenly nymphs from the sixth century C.E. resemble the wall paintings of the Ajanta caves in India (see Chapter 6), an indication of the close cultural (and sometimes political) ties that linked southern India and Ceylon. Recent archaeological studies show that Indians dominated maritime trade in South and Southeast Asia between 200 B.C.E. and 300 C.E.; Buddhist missionaries from India and Ceylon were instrumental in spreading religion as well as Indian commerce and culture throughout the region. They were the forerunners of Indian settlements that would flourish in many parts of Asia in later centuries. Asoka also ordered his ambassadors at the courts of Egypt, Macedonia, the Seleucid Empire, and other states in the west to spread Buddha's message, but with no apparent results.

Around 240 B.C.E., Asoka convened the Third Buddhist Council at Pataliputra. It dealt with differences within the monastic order and completed the compiling of the canons. He then appointed special officers to enforce the monastic discipline and had disobedient monks expelled from their orders. The Roman Emperor Constantine later did much the same thing in dealing with disputes among Christians.

Although an enthusiastic Buddhist, Asoka was tolerant of other faiths. As one of his edicts instructed: "All sects deserve reverence for one reason or another. By thus acting a man exalts his own sect and at the same time does service to the sects of other people." In another edict he advised all to honor brahmans and ascetics. A story about his father Bindusara illustrates the Mauryans' cosmopolitan outlook on religions and philosophies. Bindusara had sent an ambassador to the court of King Antiochus Soter of Syria to request figs, grapes, and a good Greek philosopher, for whom he said he would pay a high price. Antiochus sent him the exotic edibles but said that he could not find a philosopher for sale.

For all his commitment to humanitarian ideals, Asoka was nevertheless the ruler of a mighty empire. Thus, despite renouncing war, he did not disband his army. He warned primitive tribal people on the borders of his empire that if they failed to be persuaded by his *dharma* (moral duty) and infringed on his empire, he had the force to punish them. In other words, like any astute ruler, he continued to maintain a large military for its deterrent effect. His renunciation of war as an instrument of state policy was in itself a great innovation, unique among successful rulers. Some scholars, however, attribute the rapid decline and fall of the Mauryan Empire after Asoka's death in part to his pacifist policy, which they suggest weakened the military.

Although Asoka's edicts are couched in Buddhist terms, they show no interest in theology. Thus, it is possible that Asoka used Buddhism as an instrument to unify his heterogeneous empire. Nevertheless he imbued statecraft with high moral aims. That he was also tolerant of other faiths is proof of his realism as well as of his magnanimity. His reign laid the foundations for one of the greatest conquests in history—Buddhism's peaceful conquest of India, central Asia, Ceylon, Southeast Asia, China, and Japan.

Little is known of Asoka's last years. Some sources say that he became reclusive toward the end and was succeeded by his son, while others say that he was deposed by a grandson. In any event, soon after Asoka's death around 232 B.C.E., his sons and grandsons divided the empire. The last king of the main branch of the line was killed in 185, but several minor families that claimed Mauryan descent ruled parts of India for centuries.

Culture of the Asokan Age

Asoka's long reign, the wide extent of his empire, and contacts with Persia and the Hellenistic world brought about an unprecedented flowering of culture. Buddhist art also began in this period.

The artistic achievements of the Asokan age, however, can only be understood against the background of what had preceded it. The history of art in India between the Indus civilization and the third century B.C.E. is very sketchy. Whereas the Indus people had built with enduring materials, mainly brick, their successors had built with wood, which quickly perished in the humid Indian climate. Likewise sculptures of wood and clay and paintings in perishable media have all vanished. While the Mauryan palaces and even the city wall of Pataliputra continued to be made of wood, India's first stone monumental sculptures date to Asoka's reign.

Thirty spectacular stone pillars, some engraved with inscriptions, were erected at sites throughout the Mauryan Empire under Asoka. Ten have survived in almost perfect condition, others are damaged, still others have disappeared. They are between thirty and forty feet high and each weighs at least forty tons. They are made from hard gray sandstone polished to a lustrous shine. Each pillar is surmounted by a capital and topped by animal sculptures, either singly or in groups, carved in the round. The animals have symbolic importance to Buddhism. They are the lion, whose roar compares with the Buddha's preaching; the horse, which stands for Buddha's renunciation of the world; the elephant, which symbolizes his conception by his mother; the bull, representing strength; and the goose, because a legend says Buddha was the king of geese in an earlier incarnation. The wheel, which represents the sacred law or dharma, is also found on the pillars, placed below the animals. When India gained its independence from Great Britain in 1947, the four-lion Asokan capital was chosen as the nation's emblem and the wheel of law became the centerpiece of the national flag. That leaders of secular and predominantly Hindu modern India would choose these Buddhist emblems as national symbols bespeaks the powerful memory of Asoka and his association with a great past.

©Roger-Viollet

Wall Painting from Ceylon. This fine wall painting of a divine maiden is but one example from a fortress at Sirigaya, in Sri Lanka (formerly Ceylon). The paintings date from the sixth century and are very close stylistically to the wall paintings of Ajanta in India. Since Indian missionaries converted the people of Sri Lanka to Buddhism, that island has remained closely tied culturally to India.

Asoka erected and inscribed his pillars to announce major events in his reign, proclaim laws, and state his Buddhist ideals. He also used them to proclaim the grandeur and extent of his empire. The artistic inspiration for these monumental pieces is difficult to trace. A case can be made for indigenous roots for the bull, lotus, and elephant motif, which were frequently found in the Indus civilization seals. The lion and horse motifs, on the other hand, have a long history in Persian and West Asian art and are probably imported.

The high quality of the sculptures can only have resulted from generations of technical and artistic experience with the medium. We do not know who the stone sculptors were. But since no Indian stone sculptures have been found prior to the Asokan period, and since this art form vanished at the end of his reign, the Asokan monuments were probably made by Hellenistic artists invited by the court of Asoka or by Indians influenced by them.

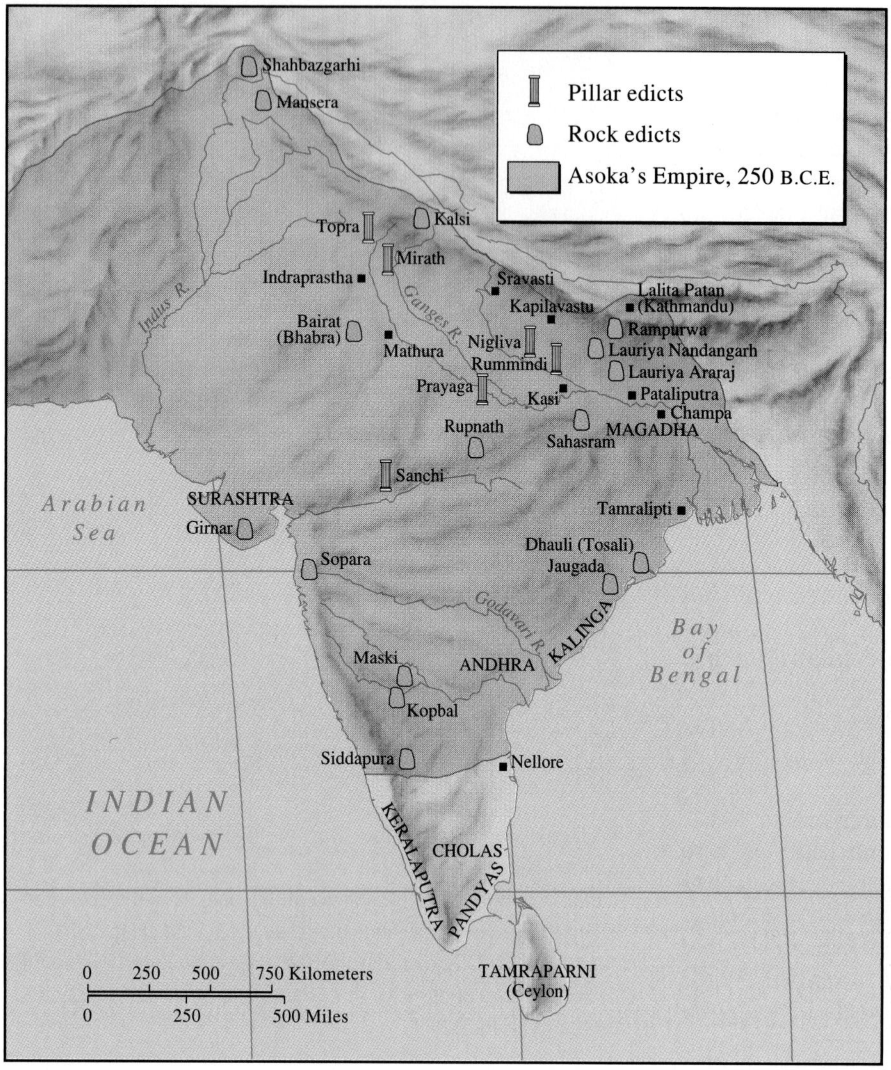

Map 4.4 The Empire of Asoka. Asoka expanded the empire he inherited so that all the Indian subcontinent except the southern tip and part of modern Afghanistan were incorporated into one administration. India was prosperous, and the capital, Pataliputra, was a grand city.

The earliest cave shrines and dwellings also date to Asoka's reign and continued under his successors. For centuries, ascetics had taken shelter in caves during the monsoon season. But the sudden acquisition of skills in stone working, which led to the enlarging of natural caves and to polishing and decorating their surfaces, again suggests Persian and West Asian inspiration, because these techniques already had a long history in Persia and West Asia.

Asoka continued the Vedic and early Buddhist custom of erecting mounds to enshrine the funeral remains of great people. Gautama's disciples had divided his ashes at the first Council and enshrined them under stupas. As Buddhism grew it became a meritorious act for the pious to worship at such sites. Asoka is credited with a further division of the Buddha's remains so that more people could benefit spiritually from visiting them. We know little of the original decoration of Asoka's stupas, since they have been built over in later ages. They were probably hemispheric mounds set on platforms, with flights of steps from four directions that lead to the base. Later on, railings, gateways, and arches were added to enclose and decorate the sites, and these were profusely ornamented with scenes from the Buddha's life and from Jataka stories.

The earliest extant examples of writing since the Indus civilization also date from the reign of Asoka. They survived because they were engraved on stone rather than written on perishable materials. They are his edicts, proclamations, and sermons engraved on rocks, pillars, and cave walls throughout the Mauryan Empire. Persia and Mesopotamia are again the likely sources of inspiration and examples because Indians were first introduced to official proclamations and panegyrics engraved in stone by King Darius I. The language and lettering of the rock edicts varied, indicating that several languages were current in different parts of the Mauryan empire. Most of the inscriptions were written in the Old Brahmi script, from left to right. It is the parent of most of the scripts now current in India. However, those found in the western part of the empire were written in Greek or Aramaic, while those found in the northwest were written in a script then current in Iran. As with ancient Egyptian hieroglyphics, the characters' meanings were lost, and they were not deciphered until 1837, by an Englishman, when modern scholarship on ancient India, called Indology, began.

Extant Buddhist and Jain canons and commentaries were substantially completed during Asoka's time. Nonreligious works, such as the early versions of the epics *Mahabharata* and *Ramayana,* also date from approximately this period, although both were added to and reworked later. In its final form, the *Mahabharata* is seven times as long as the *Iliad* and the *Odyssey* combined. Like the *Iliad,* it is a tale of an epic war fought by gods and men; stories of knightly chivalry, love, piety, duty, and devotion are interwoven with violence and gambling. Written in verse form and narrative style, the following passage tells how princess Damayanti chose as her husband her true love Nala, even though four gods had taken on his appearance in the hope that she would pick one of them by mistake. The theme of competition for a beautiful, royal woman is familiar from the Greek stories of Helen's betrothal and, in the *Odyssey,* the contest for the hand of Penelope.

Robert Harding Picture Library

An Asokan Column Capital. This capital, which adorned one of Asoka's columns, shows powerful, stylized lions standing atop the Buddhist wheel of the sacred law. This capital is the official symbol of the Republic of India.

Then, when the right time had come,
at the auspicious day and hour,
King Bhama invited
the lords of earth to the bride-choice.

When they heard, the lords of earth,
all sick at heart with love,
in haste assembled,
desiring Damayanti.

Like great lions the kings entered
the hall firmly founded,
with its splendid porch
and shining golden columns.

Then on their several thrones
the lords of earth sat down
all decked in fragrant garlands,
with bright gems on their ears.

. . .

Then fair-faced Damayanti
entered the hall,
stealing with her splendor
the eyes and thoughts of the kings.

When the glance of the noble
spectators fell on her limbs
there it was fixed,
and never wavered.

Then, while the names of the kings
were being proclaimed,
the daughter of Bhama saw
five men of the same form.

Whichever of them she looked at
she recognized as Nala.
Wondering in her mind,
the fair one was filled with doubt.

. . .

Thus thinking over and over,
and pondering again and again,
she resolved that the time had come
to take refuge in the gods.
"I heard from the mouth of the swans
that Nala had chosen me as his bride,
and so, if that be true,
may the gods show him to me!

. . .

May the great gods, the world-protectors
take on their own true form,
that I may recognize
the king of men, of good fame!"

When they heard Damayanti,
mournful and piteous
they did as she had asked,
and put on their true forms.

She saw the four gods
sweatless, not blinking their eyelids,
their garlands fresh and free from dust,
not touching the ground with their feet

But the king of Nisadha had a shadow,
his garlands were withered,
his body bore dust and sweat,
and he blinked his eyelids.

The modest long-eyed girl
seized the hem of his garment,
and on his shoulder she placed
the loveliest of garlands.

She chose him for her lord,
she of the fair complexion,
and suddenly all the kings
together shouted and cheered.

And all the gods and sages
thereupon cried bravo.
and shouted at the wonder,
praising Nala the king.

Krishna, an incarnation of Vishnu, and beloved of millions in later Hinduism, is a hero in this great poem. Woven into it is the *Bhagavad-Gita,* a lofty philosophical poem through which Hindus have since learned lessons about morality and religious law. Here Krishna teaches the ideal of duty and action to fulfill one's function in society without personal desire or ambition.

The briefer *Ramayana* resembles the *Odyssey* in that it tells about the hardships and wanderings of the hero, and his faithful wife who waits patiently for his return. The couple's cause triumphed, and they were reunited with the help of the monkey king and his monkey soldiers (hence Hindus revere the monkey and there are temples to Hanuman, the monkey god and Rama's helper). Hindus revere Rama and Sita, the hero and heroine of the *Ramayana,* as the ideal man and woman.

Life under the Mauryans

The Mauryan Empire was richly diverse. In addition to the capital city, Pataliputra, there were several other sizable cities surrounded by strong walls punctuated by lofty watchtowers and pierced by gates. Texts mention city streets lit by torches at night, pleasure parks, assembly halls, and gambling places as well as trading booths and artisans' quarters.

As in the Roman Empire, rulers often sponsored public entertainments for city people. They were usually associated with religious festivals and consisted of singing, dancing, dramatic presentations, chariot races, jousts of arms between men, and animal combats. Asoka was offended by the violence and immorality associated with the festivals and sought to restrict them. Girls and boys from upper classes amused themselves with music, singing, and dancing, and boys and men in addition gambled with dice, and played a game like hockey and a board game that later became chess.

Most people lived in the countryside as farmers, herders, and hunters. Most farmers were sudras and lived in simple mud and thatch houses in villages. Land was owned either by the government or privately. Slavery existed, but the number of slaves was not large. Villages were largely autonomous but paid taxes and dues to the government, customarily one-sixth of the harvest. Agriculture was highly regarded and farmland was supposed to be spared from ravages during wars. Farmers organized themselves for communal projects such as digging irrigation ditches, but were exempted from military and other government services. Then as later, farmers suffered from periodic famines brought on by natural disasters and by locusts. The *Arthasastra* enjoined rulers to store extra food for emergencies and to distribute seeds and food during hard times.

The herdsmen and hunters, also mostly sudras, often lived in tents beyond the pale of the villages. Cattle were always important for their milk, but were rarely butchered for meat. The hunter and trapper were responsible for getting rid of pests and sometimes also for providing food. There was large-scale land clearing for agriculture and the building of irrigation works during the Mauryan dynasty.

Most artisans were vaisyas, an important group living in both cities and villages. Pataliputra's municipal government had a board that supervised artisans in that city. Some villages specialized in one craft, and specialties tended to be passed from father to son. The artisans included ivory and stone workers, painters of frescoes, metal smiths, jewelers, textile weavers, embroiderers, oil-millers (who extracted oils from seeds), bamboo workers, tool makers, and potters, each specialty organized into a guild. Each guild was headed by a foreman or elder who supervised the workers; guilds also performed some of the functions of modern banks. The textile industry employed many women; some worked in shops while others worked at home. New subcastes of artisans were recorded during this time, proof of the proliferation of manufacturing.

Transportation by water was highly developed. Seagoing ships sailed as far away as Burma, the Malay Peninsula, Ceylon, and the Persian Gulf. They navigated by the stars. Most water trade was along north India's well-developed waterways, along the Indus and Ganges

Rivers, and their tributaries. The Mauryan government even established a bureau that built ships and leased them to merchants.

The chief items of trade were silk and cotton textiles, ivory, jewelry, and gold. Some trade was by barter, but it was being replaced by silver and copper coinage. Pataliputra had a special board that supervised trade and commerce. It regulated weights and measures and placed a stamp on items it had inspected. Later, as trade with the Roman Empire flourished, gold and silver coins from Rome became plentiful in India, supplementing locally minted coins. Romans from Pliny the Younger (61–c. 113 C.E.) on regretted their people's appetite for Indian luxuries, especially fine cotton textiles, bought with precious metals. From the west, Indians imported sweet wines, exotic fruits, luxury handicrafts, entertainers, and beautiful girls for the harems of the rich.

Marriages were monogamous for most, polygynous for rulers and aristocrats. There were a few communities that practiced polyandrous marriages (one wife with several concurrent husbands). Most men and women were expected to marry, some of both sexes (fewer women) became ascetics and lived celibate lives and were honored for it. Although some upper class women and female ascetics were well educated, most women were not literate, but neither were most men. *Sati,* or the custom of widow immolation on her late husband's funeral pyre, was practiced by a few. Both men and women wore adornments, upper-class women were especially noted for the richness of their clothing and jewelry.

Successor States to the Mauryan Empire

Jawaharlal Nehru, late prime minister of India, described the confusing state of India after the collapse of the Mauryan Empire in 185 B.C.E. in the following words:

> The Maurya empire faded away and gave place to the Sunga dynasty, which ruled over a much smaller area. . . . In central Asia the Shakas or Scythians had established themselves in the Oxus Valley. The Yueh Chih, coming from farther east, drove them out and pushed them into north India. These Shakas became converts to Buddhism and Hinduism. Among the Yueh Chih, one of the clans, the Kushans, established their supremacy and then extended their sway over northern India. They defeated the Shakas and pushed them still farther south, the Shakas going to Kathiawar and the Deccan. The Kushans thereupon established an extensive and durable empire over the whole of north India and a great part of Central Asia. . . . This borderland state, called the Kushan empire, with its seat near modern Peshawar, and the old university of Taxila near by, became the meeting place of men from many nations. There the Indians met the Scythians, the Yueh Chih, the Iranians, the Bactrian Greeks, the Turks, and the Chinese, and the various cultures reacted on each other.*

*Jawaharlal Nehru, *The Discovery of India,* ed. Robert Crane (New York: Doubleday, 1960), pp. 89–90.

As in Europe after the collapse of Rome, a loose structure of government with less central control emerged. Civil wars became endemic as military adventurers ousted one another in quick succession. In this situation the borderlands became victim to invaders of varying backgrounds and levels of civilization. However, compared to western Europe after the fall of Rome, intellectual and artistic life in India suffered less extensive damage. Some of the invaders who settled in northwestern India were the Bactrian Greeks, Parthians (Iranians or Persians), and Scythians, who introduced Roman, Hellenistic, Persian, and central Asian art, which enriched Indian artistic traditions to form a new synthesis. Mauryan power had never been strong in southern India, and the region remained unaffected by the invasions that disrupted the north during the succeeding centuries.

The Yueh-chih, strongest of all the invading groups, entered India toward the end of the second century B.C.E. They had earlier been driven westward from China's northern border by more powerful nomads, the Hsiung-nu, ancestors of the Huns that later ravaged Europe and invaded the Roman Empire. By 60 C.E. one of the Yueh-chih tribes, the Kushans, had established an empire that stretched from northern India westward to the Caspian Sea. They converted either to Hinduism (mostly to a sect that chiefly worshipped Shiva) or to Buddhism. Kanishka (reigned c. 78–111 C.E.), the greatest Kushan king, was a patron of Buddhist religion and art. After the death of Kanishka, decline set in and the empire broke up during the third century, with remnants surviving until the sixth century.

The reasons for the fall of the Kushan empire remain shrouded in mystery. It may have been due in part to the loss of Afghanistan to Persian control, and with it fresh sources of manpower for the army. Kushan rule, however, left a rich cultural legacy.

Kushan Culture: Buddhism in a Cosmopolitan Setting

The chaos of the post-Mauryan era had no adverse effect on the spread of Buddhism within and beyond India. From northwest India missionaries traveled the Silk Road west to Persia and central Asia and east to China (see the next section). The large number and high quality of Buddhist temple remains in communities in the Kushan realm and along the Silk Road, rich even in ruin, show both the devotion of the believers and the prosperity brought by this international trade in luxuries.

King Kanishka was revered by some Buddhists almost as a second Asoka, and indeed there are many parallels. Like Asoka, he ruled a prosperous and powerful empire and waged victorious wars early in his reign, annexing additional lands. Although a Buddhist, he tolerated other religions, as coins from his reign that include the Hindu god

Shiva, the Roman god Hercules, and Persian deities, show. Like Asoka, he patronized Buddhism by building and repairing shrines and encouraging missionary work. About the year 100 Kanishka called the Fourth Buddhist Council at his capital city, near modern Peshawar on the present-day Pakistan-Afghan border. Five hundred monks attended the council to settle disputes in Buddhism and to collect and compile commentaries on the Tripitaka. He also lavishly patronized Buddhist art.

By the first century, many Buddhists favored community worship of the Buddha as a savior god and some aspired to be saintly bodhisattvas who delayed their own entrance to nirvana to help suffering living beings achieve enlightenment. Many of the devout, however, wished there was an image of Buddha to assist them in their prayers.

The first images of the Buddha date to Kanishka's time, although the origins of the Buddha images are in dispute. Some scholars argue that the likenesses of the Buddha evolved from images of *yakshas,* or earth spirits of Hinduism, and therefore are Indian in origin. Others point out that the Kushans were a non-Indian dynasty and that early Buddhist images show strong Greco-Roman influences. Evidence supports both sides. The two artistic sources express the same subject matter: the image of the Buddha and the stories of his life and previous lives, along with bodhisattvas and other deities associated with Buddhism, including Vedic gods.

Large numbers of the Gandharan, or Greco-Roman-influenced, Buddhist sculptures have been found in the ruins of Taxila, a north Indian center of international commerce and art, and at various sites in Afghanistan and Pakistan. Most are statues that depict the Buddha and bodhisattvas, or are reliefs that describe the Buddha's life or scenes from Buddhist texts. They are characterized by realistic moldings of the human body and accurate delineations of muscles. Many of the stone and stucco (painted plaster) statues and relief carvings of the Buddha and others in Gandhara are so beautifully robed and coifed that they would not have been out of place in imperial Rome. They are distinguishable from their secular counterparts only by their halos (a western import) and their religiously significant hand gestures.

Later Gandharan artists were especially fond of stucco as a medium. This was perhaps due to close sea contacts with Alexandria in Egypt, where at that time the art of working with stucco was well developed. Apparently, a continuing influx of artists and artisans from Roman provinces arrived in India throughout the Kushan period. The imported artists must also have trained local people in their media and styles. It is not surprising then that deities of Greece and Rome are sometimes found in Buddhist scenes.

In the prosperous Bamiyan valley in Afghanistan, at the crossroads of the Silk Road, monks in the fifth century honeycombed a towering cliff wall of the Hindu Kush with grottos and cells, and crowned the complex with three colossal Buddha statues carved from the cliffs. The tallest stands at 175 feet high in its own niche. They were finished with lime plaster and decorated with paintings. The site gave inspiration to pious Chinese pilgrims as they approached India in their long journey and inspired Chinese Buddhists to excavate similar rock grottoes in their homeland. After the eighth century, Bamiyan and other Buddhist sanctuaries in Afghanistan were desecrated by Muslim invaders. They have stood since then amid empty ruins, pockmarked by artillery shells of later Muslim cannons, for which they served as targets. Even in ruin, they stand witness to the energy and creativity that marked the Buddhist centuries in Afghanistan and northwest India.

Mathura was already an art center when the Kushan empire took over. The red sandstone religious statues that its artists produced would adorn Buddhist, Hindu, and Jain holy places for centuries to come. Whereas the Gandharan Buddhas had faces of the Greco-Roman god Apollo and wore togas, those from Mathura are dressed like Indians in thin *dhotis* (loin cloths); *yaksha* spirits became bodhisattvas, surrounded by *nagas* (anthropomorphic serpent figures of ancient Indian lore) and other symbols of Indian mythology. The Mathuran art style survived the fall of the Kushan empire to reach its ultimate development in the following Gupta era. At both centers, Kushan art mirrored social life. Scenes of drunken orgies abound; Gandharan ladies' dresses could have been worn by matrons in any city of the Roman world, while nudity or scanty dress in the Indian fashion is conspicuous in Mathuran figures. Later, when Buddhism spread to China, Korea, and Japan, Greek, Roman, and Persian art forms were introduced to the farthest shores of East Asia.

Coins provide much information and a great deal of the chronology of post-Mauryan dating, since there is very little reliable chronological record otherwise. The Greeks popularized coinage as the medium of exchange, and Indian rulers followed suit. They usually carried images of the issuing ruler on one side and of a deity on the other, along with an inscription. The large quantity of Roman coins found in India supports the contention that India enjoyed a favorable balance of trade against Rome, a circumstance Roman leaders bemoaned. Roman coins were probably circulated as an international currency, which might explain why gold coins issued by Kanishka conformed to the Roman standard. An interesting gold coin bears the image of Buddha on one side, and of Kanishka on the other. Kanishka wears the baggy trousers and tall boots of central Asia, suggesting his nomadic heritage. Although a Buddhist, he is pouring an offering on a fire altar, a Persian religious practice. These coins suggest that initially the conquering rulers worshipped their Hellenistic and Persian deities. But since they were numerically few, they were in time assimilated and became Indianized.

Several centuries of contacts with the West left other legacies. A number of words in Sanskrit and modern Indian languages are borrowed from Greek, especially in the sciences and in astrology, where Indian scholars were very alert to new information. A work titled *Questions of Melinda* (an Indianized name of a minor Hellenistic king, Menander, who converted to Buddhism), though Buddhist in content, shows the stylistic influence of the philosophical dialogues of Plato.

China's First Imperial Age: The Han Dynasty

"Gentlemen, for a long time you have suffered beneath the harsh laws of Ch'in. . . . I hereby promise you a code of laws consisting of three articles only: 1) he who kills anyone shall suffer death; 2) he who wounds another or steals shall be punished according to the gravity of the offense; 3) for the rest I abolish all the laws of Ch'in. Let the officials and people remain undisturbed as before. I have come to save you from injury, not to exploit or oppress you. . . ."

*He sent men to go with the Ch'in officials and publish this proclamation. . . . The people of Ch'in were overjoyed and hastened with cattle, sheep, wine, and food to present to the soldiers, but Liu Chi declined all such gifts, saying: "There is plenty of grain in the granaries. I do not wish to be a burden to the people." With this the people were more joyful than ever and their only fear was that Liu Chi would not become King of Ch'in.**

*William T. de Bary, ed., *Sources of Chinese Tradition,* vol. 1 (New York: Columbia University Press, 1960), pp. 154–155. Reprinted with permission.

In victory Liu Chi (also known as Liu Pang) displayed the essential qualities of compassion and justice that were in sharp contrast to the oppression and tyranny of the government that he had rebelled against. A poor commoner with little education, he was nevertheless a profound psychologist, identifying with the common people and soldiers. These qualities won him the support and respect of the people and explain his success against both the Ch'in and other contenders for power. Liu became the first commoner to found a dynasty. Known as the Han, it was one of the longest lived and most successful in Chinese history. This is the reason why 95 percent of Chinese up to now call themselves the Han

Courtesy of Richard Edwards

Above: **Panoramic View of Rock-Carved Temple at Bamiyan, Afghanistan.** This broad valley was located at the junction of the Silk Road that linked China, India, central Asia, and the Roman Empire. It was a trade center and also became a pilgrimage site after the completion of the rock-carved temple that housed several thousand monks. Two huge Buddha statues dominated; the smaller (120 feet), seated Buddha can be seen here.

Below: **Colossal Buddha.** This enormous Buddha statue stands 175 feet high in a niche shaped as a body halo. Located at a crossroads of international travel, it made an indelible impression on all who passed and was a prototype for similar monuments in China. In 2001 the fanatical Muslim rulers of Afghanistan ordered these two statues and thousands of smaller Buddhist statues and figures in museums in that country destroyed.

Courtesy of Richard Edwards

Bronze Figure of a Kneeling Warrior and Lion Ornament in Gold. Both of these items were excavated in northwestern China and date to circa 500 B.C.E. The warrior (left) is a nomad, probably a Hsiung-nu, with non-Mongolian features, prominent nose, and non-Chinese dress. The gold animal ornament (below) is typical of nomadic art.

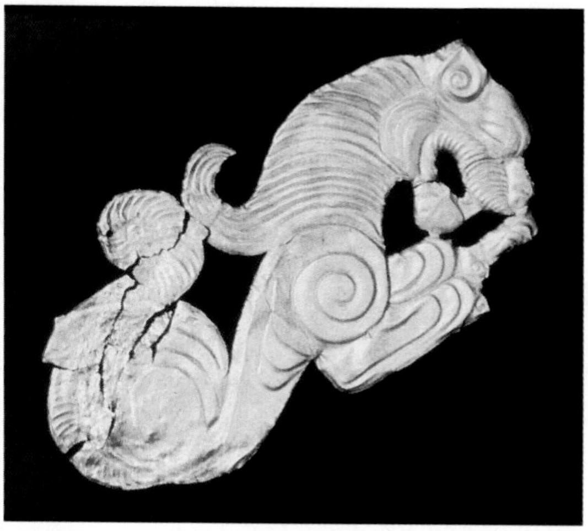

Both photos courtesy of Dolkun Kamberi

people and their language the Han language. Likewise, the Japanese and Koreans call Chinese the Han language. Thus the Han dynasty is to China and East Asia what the Mauryan dynasty is to India and Buddhists throughout Asia. The following pages will explore Han history, achievements, and legacy.

The Han Dynasty, 202 B.C.E.–220 C.E.

Several contenders sought to fill the vacuum created by the fall of the Ch'in dynasty in 206 B.C.E. The winner was Liu Chi, who was proclaimed emperor of the new Han dynasty in 202. History knows him as Han Kao-tsu or High Ancestor of the Han. He was the first commoner to ascend the throne, an event made possible because of the Ch'in abolition of feudalism and the opportunities created by the wars of the preceding centuries. The Han dynasty is divided into two halves, the earlier part was in retrospect called the Western or Former Han, the later part the Eastern or Later Han.

Kao-tsu and his supporters had suffered through the harshness of Ch'in rule and were well aware of the feelings of the people. Establishing his capital at Changan (near the Ch'in capital Hsienyang), Kao-tsu retained the basic structure of the Ch'in government but removed its abuses. For example, he moderated the cruel Ch'in penal code, lifted the ban against intellectual activities, and lightened taxes from two-thirds of the farmer's crop under Ch'in to one-fifteenth. To give the people a chance to rest and recover from years of war, Kao-tsu pursued a foreign policy of conciliation and appeasement toward the powerful northern nomads called Hsiung-nu. In the third century these nomads had formed a powerful confederacy and had menaced China across the entire northern frontier. The Great Wall had not kept out these horse-riding raiders from the steppes. After a disastrous war against the Hsiung-nu, Kao-tsu was forced to bribe them with large annual "gifts" of gold, grain, and silks, and a princess as bride. Kao-tsu died prematurely, in 195 B.C.E. Soon afterward the king of the Hsiung-nu had proposed marriage to his widow, Empress Lu, with the following letter:

> I am a lonely widowed ruler, born amidst the marshes and brought up on the wild steppes in the land of cattle and horses. . . . Your Majesty is also a widowed ruler living in a life of solitude. Both of us are without pleasures and lack any way to amuse ourselves. It is my hope that we can exchange that which we have for that which we are lacking.

Although furious, she was forced to refuse him politely:

> My age is advanced and my vitality is weakening. Both my hair and teeth are falling out, and I cannot even walk steadily. The *shan-yu* [title of Hsiung-nu king] must have heard exaggerated reports. I am not worthy of his lowering himself. But my country has done nothing wrong, and I hope he will spare it.

Empress Lu ruled ably for the next fifteen years and continued Kao-tsu's policies, as did her successors. With peace and frugal government, the economy expanded and production soared, so that despite a further tax cut to one-thirtieth of the crop, the state treasury was full and granaries bulged.

When Emperor Wu (the Martial, reigned 141–87 B.C.E.) ascended the throne, the Chinese people, now fully recovered and confident, were willing to support a new vigorous and aggressive foreign policy. Wu campaigned in the south and regained control of the Pearl River valley and the Red River valley in modern Vietnam, both of which had seceded at the fall of the Ch'in. Another campaign brought southern Manchuria and Korea into the Han Empire. Wu then established a Chinese-style government in the newly annexed regions. He also sponsored Chinese immigration, which gradually resulted in the assimilation or Sinicization (from the Latin *Sinica,* meaning "China") of the local people.

These early wars were preparation for a showdown with the Hsiung-nu; however, Wu needed an ally. Much earlier, the Hsiung-nu had defeated the Yueh-chih, an Indo-European nomadic group north of China. Fleeing westward, the Yueh-chih finally settled in Bactria, in modern Afghanistan and northern Pakistan, converted to Buddhism and founded a state called Kushan.

In 138 B.C.E., Emperor Wu sent a young courtier named Chang Ch'ien to find the Yueh-chih and offer them an alliance against the Hsiung-nu. Chang's journey was one of the most daring travel epics in antiquity. To reach the Yueh-chih, he had to cross Hsiung-nu territory; he was captured, given a Hsiung-nu wife, and made to settle among them and raise a family. Chang escaped after ten years, continued his quest, and finally found the Yueh-chih, but they had no desire to cross swords with the Hsiung-nu again. En route home, Chang was recaptured by the Hsiung-nu, again escaped, finally returning to Changan in 126, with only two of his original staff of a hundred.

Even though he failed in his primary assignment, Chang Ch'ien's account of this trip and his later diplomatic mission to central Asia opened the Chinese to new horizons, peoples, cultures, and products. His information brought about further explorations and trade by land and sea between China, India, Persia, and other lands. His report of "blood sweating" horses (actually, the horses were bleeding, from the bites of tiny mites) later sent Chinese armies campaigning across central Asia to obtain them.

In 133 B.C.E., Wu launched an eighteen-year campaign that evicted the Hsiung-nu from an area bounded by a southward dip of the Yellow River. In 129 they were

Robert Harding Picture Library

The Flying Horse of Kansu. The Han government waged wars, used diplomacy, and traded to obtain these fast horses bred in central Asia. This bronze horse, found in the tomb of a Han general in Kansu in northwestern China, epitomized the qualities of strength and speed the Chinese prized in these "blood-sweating" horses.

The High Cost of Empire

1. Lament of Hsi-chun

My people have married me
In a far corner of Earth;
Sent me away to a strange land,
To the king of the Wu-sun.
A tent is my house,
Of felt are my walls;
Raw flesh my food
With mare's milk to drink.
Always thinking of my own country
My heart is sad within.
Would I were a yellow stork
And could fly to my old home!

2. To His Wife, *by General Su Wu, c. 100 B.C.E.*

Since our hair was plaited and we became man and wife
The love between us was never broken by doubt.
So let us be merry this night together,
Feasting and playing together while the good time lasts
I suddenly remember the distance that I must travel;
I spring from bed and look out to see the time.
The stars and planets are all grown dim in the sky;
Long, long is the road; I cannot stay.
I am going away on service, away to the battle-ground,
And I do not know when I shall come back.
I hold your hand with only a deep sigh;
Afterwards, tears—in the days when we are parted.
With all your might enjoy the spring flowers,
But do not forget the time of our love and pride.
Know that if I live, I will come back again,
And if I die, we will go on thinking of each other.

3. Parting from Su Wu *by Li Ling*

I came ten thousand leagues
Across sandy deserts
In the service of my Prince,
To break the Hun tribes.
My way was blocked and barred,
My arrows and swords broken.
My armies had faded away,
My reputation is gone.
My old mother is long dead.
Although I want to requite my Prince
*How can I return?**

Individual men and women paid a high price for the nation's military and diplomatic successes. Three poems illustrate this point. The first is by princess Hsi-chun. Around 100 B.C.E., she was given in marriage to a client king of Wu-sun, whose land supplied Han with fine horses. Her husband was already an old man and the couple had no common language, so during their occasional meetings they only drank a cup of wine together. The second was by General Su Wu, who wrote it for his wife, before he set out to campaign against the Hsiung-nu. He was captured during the war and held for nineteen years before being released. While Su Wu returned home, a fellow captive chose to stay. In the third poem he explains why.

*Arthur Waley, *Translations from the Chinese* (New York: Knopf, 1941), pp. 18, 52, 53.

cleared from the entire Chinese northern border from Inner Mongolia across Turkestan. Some 700,000 Chinese colonists were sent out to settle the conquered lands, and the Great Wall was extended westward. Beyond it, a string of fortified outposts stretched into Central Asia, which the Chinese called the Western Regions. Chinese protectors-general were appointed to supervise local vassal kings, who were required to pay homage and tribute by coming to Changan and to leave their sons there to be educated and to serve as hostages in a pattern similar to Rome's arrangements with its client states. In return, vassal kings received Chinese titles, lavish gifts, and the right to trade. These conditions were so attractive that rulers in regions like Kashmir in India, which had not been conquered by the Han, voluntarily enrolled themselves as vassals. No more Chinese princesses were sent as brides to Hsiung-nu chieftains. Wu's successors continued his policies against the Hsiung-nu, shattering their power. In 51 the southern branch of the Hsiung-nu submitted to Han rule, while another branch was defeated by the Han in Samarkand and fled westward. The flight of the Hsiung-nu set off a vast westward migration as numerous people were pushed west in a domino effect that continued until the fourth century C.E., when some of them reached the borders of the Roman Empire.

Between 9 and 23 C.E. a usurper attempted and failed to establish his own dynasty. A descendent of the house of Liu reestablished the Han dynasty in 23 C.E. and moved his capital eastward to Loyang, hence the name, Eastern Han, for the era. Loyang is strategically situated at the bank of the River Lo, a tributary of the Yellow River. It had been the capital of the Eastern Chou dynasty.

Restored to power and prosperity, Chinese arms again overawed much of central Asia, and trade and culture flourished. General Pan Ch'ao campaigned all the way to the Caspian Sea, and his vanguard units reconnoitered the shores of either the Persian Gulf or Black Sea. Chinese protectors-general continued to supervise kingdoms across central Asia in the farthest extension of power in its history. Caravans carrying the international luxury trade traveled in safety. The Pax Sinica in the east matched the Pax Romana in the west; together the two empires dominated most of the ancient world.

In the second century, minors on the throne, power struggles between powerful consort families, and economic inequities led to rapid dynastic decline. The upper class became hedonistic, dabbling either in escapist Taoism or the new foreign religion, Buddhism. Ground-down peasants revolted and generals sent to quell them seized power, ending the dynasty in 220. Nevertheless, four centuries of Han rule had firmly established the foundations of traditions and institutions that would continue to the present century and spread the Sinitic civilization across eastern Asia. To later dynasties the Han became the yardstick against which they all measured themselves.

Arthur M. Sackler Museum, Harvard University Art Museums

Model of a Watchtower. This second-century earthenware model of a watchtower standing in a moat has crossbowmen on guard on the parapet of the second-floor balcony. Walls, parapets, and watchtowers guarded China's northern frontier against nomadic raids and invasions.

Han Government

Han emperors presided over a centralized, bureaucratic government headed by a prime minister. Ministries and bureaus had clearly defined functions such as fiscal and judicial affairs, imperial rituals, and the metropolitan police force. The basic local government unit was the county (there were between 1,000 and 1,400 counties); ten to twenty counties formed a commandery (later called a province), headed by a governor. The three-tier government system remains in effect in China to the present and is similar in organization to the three tiers of county, state, and national government of the United States. Governors had to submit detailed annual reports to the central government with statistics on economic conditions, finance, education, justice, and other matters in his commandery. Inspectors sent from the capital regularly investigated local affairs and checked on local officials in a manner similar to the special officials who acted as the "eyes and ears" to the Persian kings.

Kao-tsu had partially restored feudalism by creating a number of principalities and lesser fiefdoms for imperial relatives, in-laws, and meritorious officials. However, the recipients received revenues rather than political power from their fiefs, and their domains were subject to the inspectors and other officials of the central government. Wu's reforms virtually wiped out the princely and noble domains. This separation of government positions from family prerogatives was a great advance in political institutions.

Kao-tsu and his successors failed to control the ambition to power of their wives, mothers, and in-laws. An

LIVES AND TIMES ACROSS CULTURES

Mathematical Problems in the Ancient World

Although the Han school boys' curriculum consisted mainly of the classics and history, they were also given some training in mathematics and exercises related to everyday affairs. Here are examples:

1. A fast horse and a slow horse set out together on the 3000 li [900 kilometers] long journey from Changan to Ch'i. The first day the fast horse travels 193 li, thereafter increasing his speed by 13 li each day. The slow horse covers 97 li on the first day, thereafter reducing his speed by $\frac{1}{2}$ li each day. After reaching Ch'i the fast horse starts his return journey and meets the slow horse. When does the meeting take place and how far has each horse traveled? Answer: After $15\,^{135}/_{191}$ days; the fast horse has traveled $4534\,^{46}/_{191}$ li, and the slow horse $146\,^{145}/_{191}$ li.
2. A man is hired as a salt porter. If he is paid 40 cash for carrying two measures of salt for a distance of 100 li, how much will he be paid for carrying 1.73 measures for a distance of 80 li? Answer: $27\,^{11}/_{15}$ cash.

During his school days in the third century B.C.E., Eratosthenes of Cyrene (in North Africa), was known to his fellow pupils as "Beta" because he excelled in so many subjects as to be nearly (or "second") best in each. In his later life, he was an astronomer, mathematician, poet, and chief librarian at the famous Library of Alexandria in Egypt. The most famous mathematical problem he solved had to do with the circumference of the earth. Eratosthenes had noticed that during the summer solstice, the sun's rays fell vertically at Syene (modern Aswan) some 500 miles up the Nile, but at an angle of 7° at Alexandria to the north, near the mouth of the Nile. Applying basic Euclidean geometrical principles to this observation, Eratosthenes calculated the circumference of the earth. While the precise equivalent in feet or meters of his unit of measure (the stade) is not known, it is nonetheless clear that his computation was amazingly accurate. He also measured the degree of obliquity, or tilt, of the earth's axis.

empress could be powerful because she assisted the emperor in performing rituals and was considered the "mother of the empire," but she was legally subordinate to her husband and could be demoted. Dowager empresses (mothers and grandmothers of reigning emperors) were infinitely more powerful, however, because filial piety required sons to obey their mothers. Empress Lu set the precedent by presiding over the government after Kao-tsu's death, making her son ruler in name only. He could not stop her domineering ways and her extreme cruelty to her husband's concubines and their children, which caused him to suffer a nervous breakdown shortly after ascending the throne. He later abandoned himself to drinking, dying young after a seven-year reign. Dowager Empress Lu then appointed, dismissed, and killed several stepsons in succession; she also appointed members of her family to powerful posts and ruled for fifteen years until her death. Seven other dowager empresses ruled as regents while their sons were minors; some continued to rule even after their sons became adults. As regents they appointed and dismissed emperors and officials, often appointing their relatives and eunuchs to powerful positions, and issued laws. When there was more than one dowager empress (for example, when a mother and grandmother were both alive), feuds between them and their families resulted in coups and battles.

Han government was administered by a professional civil service rather than by hereditary nobles. Men were assigned to positions based on their education, merit, and ability to deal with people effectively. The first requirement for an aspiring official was an education. This requirement favored the rich, because books, which were copied on silk, wood, or bamboo slips, were expensive and rare. Since public service was rewarded with honors and riches, a popular saying held that it was better to bequeath books than gold to one's sons. Local officials were annually required to recommend educated young men of good moral character and send them to the capital city for written and oral exams. Those who passed were then given posts. They served on probation during the first year, and received permanent appointments if they acquitted themselves satisfactorily. Every sixth day was a day of rest, and leaves were granted for illness and for mourning the death of parents. In 124 B.C.E., a national university was established at the capital to prepare young men in the Confucian classics for the civil service. Enrollment was based on a geographic quota so that all areas of the empire were represented; from an original fifty students, their number had grown to 30,000 by the second century. Along with the Ch'in edict that unified the written language, this massive national educational network for training officials proved invaluable in holding together a huge and diverse empire.

Every third year each official received an efficiency rating and report from his superior and was either promoted, demoted, transferred, or dismissed according to his rating and the recommendation of his superior. Aged officials received pensions on retirement. A law of avoidance forbade a man to serve in his home area, to ensure that there would be a national rotation of the civil service and that no one built a power base that might challenge the throne. This rule remained in force until the twentieth century. Subordinate officials in each unit of local government, however, must come from that area to ensure that local voices and interests were heard.

Girls did not attend schools, nor could they take the official exams. However, girls from well-to-do families often received a private education, which included the womanly arts of weaving, embroidery, music, and painting, as well as the classics and poetry. A lady wrote of her education in these lines:

At thirteen I could weave silk,
At fourteen I learnt to cut a garment,
At fifteen I played Kung Hou (a musical instrument),
At sixteen I finished the Book of Odes and other classics,
At seventeen I married thee.

The Han ideal, as in Rome, was the citizen soldier. Adulthood began at twenty, and every male was liable for one year of military service at twenty-three; the three-year delay was intended to allow the citizen time to accumulate savings so that he could serve without pay. Every year after the harvest, until they were fifty-six, men were liable for one month of reserve military duty. Actually, the citizen-soldier concept was impractical for a country the size of China, given the need to defend distant frontiers. Therefore, draft-eligible men who did not wish to serve could pay substitute money that was used for paying draftees and volunteers for longer-term service.

Ruins of hundreds of Han outposts, fortresses, watchtowers, walls, and ramparts across the entire northern frontier testify to the enormous burden of maintaining the Pax Sinica. Frontier garrisons protected the agricultural settlements and horse stud farms for cavalry horses, delivered the mail, and made secure the trade and diplomatic links between China and countries to the west. Because northwestern China had a dry climate, many reports, inventories, regulations, and personal accounts of the Han period have survived. They tell of a rigorous and disciplined life of military duty and farming that kept the empire secure and its prestige high. A fragment of silk from an officer's letter said plaintively: "the distance is long; contacts are rare; my rank is low and my person is humble; exchanges of letters are difficult." Most infantry soldiers carried a 40-inch-long steel sword, twice as long as and much stronger than the bronze sword blade of an earlier time. Iron was also used for javelin tips and arrowheads, knives, and chain-link and fish-scale armor. Throughout world history, camp followers accompanied soldiers on the march and at military encampments. Emperor Wu formally enrolled and supervised prostitutes as a category of camp followers for his far-flung military units.

The cavalry, essential for fighting the Hsiung-nu, supported the infantry in battle; in one campaign 130,000 horses participated—fewer than 30,000 returned. Thus the government gave top priority to obtaining good horses from friendly nomads and to controlling horse-breeding country. The powerful central Asian breeds, unlike the smaller ones native to China, could carry a fully armored soldier into battle. Horses for riding and pulling carriages became a status symbol for the rich. The combination of superior iron weapons, leadership, organization, martial spirit, and cavalry enabled the Han to triumph over the nomads and preserved the peace. Around the end of the Han dynasty, the Chinese first cast stirrups from metal. This important invention gave the rider greater control over his horse, freed his hands, and made mounting and dismounting easier. Nomads spread this Chinese invention westward until it was universally used.

The Land and People

The census of 1 C.E. counted the Han population at 60 million; it was 56.5 million in 157, perhaps more populous than the Roman Empire of the same period. Most Chinese were farmers. Land was privately owned and could be bought and sold. The typical farm family consisted of husband, wife, and three children, working about seventeen acres. In the north, millet, wheat, and barley were the grain crops; in the south, rice. Pigs and fowl were the common meat animal. Fish and tortoise raised in ponds also provided protein.

Wind-powered bellows lowered the cost of making cast-iron tools, now used everywhere; plows were now made entirely of iron. Other technical innovations include a three-legged seeder that could plant three rows of seeds

The British Library

Soldiers' Orders. This wooden slip came from a Han military outpost in northwestern China along the Silk Road. It gives instructions for signaling between posts as follows: "The order will be put up where it can be seen by the soldiers of the section of each post so that all may know it by heart and understand it; a close watch is to be kept and as soon as there is a fire signal the section of the post shall light one in turn. . . ."

simultaneously, an iron harrow, and a leveler. Paired or singly yoked oxen pulled the plow and other farm machinery; by using the nose ring, an innovation, one man could control an oxen team. Archaeologists have found some giant plowshares thought to be ditch diggers. Iron tools enabled the government to build large irrigation projects. Old reservoirs were enlarged and new ones built to hold water for irrigation. Han engineers built the world's first canals that were designed to follow the contour of the land as a way around or over hills. Wells with winches to draw the water and brick-lined spill troughs to funnel water for irrigation became common.

The government encouraged widespread planting of mulberry trees and sericulture (raising silkworms and spinning and weaving silk cloth). Silks were China's most desired export commodity, and bolts of silk were used as currency and given as state gifts. To ensure China's monopoly in silk production, the government prohibited exporting silkworm eggs. Tending silkworms and carding and spinning silk was women's work, and each family in silk-producing areas was required to pay a tax in silk floss and fabric.

Everyone paid a poll tax, and cultivators paid a small land tax. During many years when the state treasury was full, the tax was remitted altogether, once for as long as eleven years. Adult males also spent one month a year in corvée labor, mostly on public works projects after the harvest season.

Despite the general prosperity, the small farmers, as in Rome at this time, found themselves in trouble. Without reserves to tide them over difficulties, farmers often went into debt, and if they could not pay their debt, they lost their land and had to work as sharecroppers, paying 50 percent of their yield to the landowner. Some left the land to become laborers, and the most unfortunate, like poor Athenian farmers before Solon's reforms, had to sell their children or themselves into slavery to pay off their debts. Government attempts at direct relief and schemes to resettle the dispossessed on virgin lands did not solve the fundamental problem of inequity in a free land-tenure system. Those with capital to invest, like wealthy contemporary Romans, accumulated great estates worked by tenants and slaves. The rich estate owner who also enjoyed political connections often could evade taxes. That put a greater strain on the remaining small freeholders. Just as in Rome, the fall of the free peasantry had its corollary in the rise of great families. Individual great families rose and fell, and the government tried to limit the size of estates, but as a class the landowning magnates continued to prosper.

Land ownership thus became an acute social issue. As the dynasty declined, the power of great families increased unrestrained, until some fielded private armies that challenged the government. The worsening economic crisis led to large-scale peasant revolts in the second century, which precipitated the dynasty's downfall.

Cities, Manufacturing, and Commerce

Large urban centers were a characteristic of Han China. Enclosed by a wall sixteen miles in circumference, the capital city Changan was one of the largest in the world, and like Rome, was cosmopolitan and luxurious. It was a planned city of palaces, temples, markets, and private residences; the widest avenues measured 150 feet across. Whereas the Greeks and Romans built in stone, the Chinese (and Indians) used mainly wood, a highly perishable material. Thus not much remains standing from Han times except the tomb mounds for rulers and aristocrats, portions of city walls, and foundations of buildings.

Loyang was smaller, with a maximum total population of half a million. In 131 the state university campus at its outskirts had 240 buildings that housed classrooms and dormitories for 30,000 students. Then as now, citizens complained that many students spent their time boisterously having fun rather than studying. Many towns had specialized functions, such as manufacturing silk or iron, and others were noted for trade, or as garrison and administrative headquarters.

Both manufacturing and commerce flourished, and merchants made fortunes dealing in grain, iron, and salt. The iron industry produced not only weapons and agricultural tools but also common household items such as cooking pots, knives, scissors, and needles. One govern-

Roman Lady in Silk Dress. Everyone of means across Asia and Europe coveted Chinese silk clothes and decorations. This first-century picture shows a wealthy Roman lady fashionably dressed in silk.

ment-owned mine was allotted 100,000 corvée laborers each year to mine iron ore. Blast, reduction, and "steel puddling" furnaces were all in use.

Debates over proper government economic policy raged through much of the period. Confucians agreed with Legalists that merchants were social parasites; both scorned the profit motive as unworthy. Thus they put merchants at the bottom of the social order, below the scholars, farmers, and artisans. Emperor Wu promulgated sumptuary laws that forbade merchants to flaunt their wealth and regulated their other activities. He also nationalized the iron and salt industries and established a liquor licensing system, setting up a pattern that persisted to the twentieth century. He also set up state granaries to stabilize grain prices and to discourage speculation. State-owned factories and workshops were formed in many other fields. Despite these state actions, merchant princes continued to amass fortunes.

Crafts also flourished, as artisans created an extensive array of beautiful objects. Excavated tombs reveal that the metropolitan styles of Changan and Loyang were copied as far afield as Lolang in Korea and central Asia. Gorgeous Han silks were prized throughout the ancient world, and the beautiful articles of lacquer have not been surpassed since. Potters made a wide range of vessels for daily use, some covered with rich green and amber glazes. They also made scaled-down models of houses, animals, and tools that were buried in tombs for "use" by the dead in the spirit world. These grave goods enable us to reconstruct much of Han life.

Bronzesmiths made articles for ritual as well as daily use and decoration that even the middle class could afford. Bronze mirrors were especially prized; thousands have been excavated, even in Korea and Japan, some still with their prices marked on them. Some mirror makers advertised their wares by casting words of praise on them, for example: "The substance of this mirror is pure and bright; the rays it radiates could be compared to those of the sun and moon," and "The mirrors made by the Ye family are handsome and great. They are as bright as the sun and the moon; indeed they are rare to find."

Jade was another ritual as well as luxury item. The securing of the northwest, where nephrite jade was found, made for a steady supply. Because popular superstition had it that jade could preserve the body from decay, royalty had jade burial suits made for themselves. Archaeologists have recovered several jade suits from princely tombs.

The Silk Road: Link between East and West

As the centuries passed, the great civilizations of Eurasia came into increasing contact with one another. Contacts

CONNECTIONS IN MIGRATION

The Silk Road

The term "Silk Road" was coined as recently as the nineteenth century by a European visitor to central Asia, but the network of trade routes bearing that name and linking China and the Black Sea has existed for many centuries. Silk, exported from China, was the most valuable trade good carried along these routes.

Though it is hard to know when the first traders used the Silk Road to cross the Eurasian heartland, the Silk Road grew to prominence in the period from 300 B.C.E. to 300 C.E. The major empires in Asia and the Mediterranean in that period—the Han, Kushan, Mauryan, Hellenistic, and Roman Empires—provided stability and safety for merchants and encouraged long-distance trade.

Many of the merchants came from the so-called oasis states adjoining the central Asian deserts, and trade brought economic advantage to their homelands. The Kushan empire was the most important of those oasis states. From its market towns, trade routes went east to China, south to India, and west to Persia and the Mediterranean.

The cultivation of the silkworm and the weaving of its fiber began in China in the third millennium B.C.E. Chinese silk producers kept their secret until the time of the T'ang Empire in the seventh century C.E., when Chinese monks are said to have smuggled the silkworm cocoons in their canes to Persia and the Byzantine empire.

In exchange for silk fabric, the Chinese desired jade, spices, and horses. For example, when the nomadic Hsiung-nu of central Asia stopped the horse trade to China, an emperor of the Han Empire sent an army to fetch so-called "blood-sweating" horses from the "western region."

The Silk Road encouraged cultural exchange. Dancers, acrobats, and musicians from the west were especially welcome in Chinese courts. Instruments of central Asian origin, such as two- and three-stringed lutes, have become typical Chinese instruments today.

Of even more significance was the spread of religions via the Silk Road. Buddhism, which originated in India, spread to China through the Kushan empire, and from there extended to Korea and Japan. In addition, the Zoroastrian religion of Iran and Nestorian Christianity gained converts all along the Silk Road.

With the decline of the T'ang Empire in the ninth century C.E., the Silk Road diminished in importance. By this time, silk was also produced in Persia, India, and Byzantium, and some silk moved west from China by sea. But commerce along the Eurasian land routes never halted, and today many countries on the Silk Road are trying to improve their communication and cooperation in an effort to increase commerce along this ancient and famous trade route.

---

1. To clarify your picture of the history of the Silk Road, use the index of this text to help you locate the times of major Eurasian empires, such as the Hellenistic, Roman, Kushan, Mauryan, Gupta, Han, and T'ang. Then create a timeline and map to indicate your impression of the rise and fall of commerce along the Silk Road during the timespan of the first empire to the last.

2. Visit these websites on the Silk Road: http://chinapage.com/silkroad.html and http://www.textile-art.com/dun1.html. How did the Silk Road affect religion and culture?

between China and the West resulted from Emperor Wu's victory over the Hsiung-nu, who had blocked access. He then exchanged ambassadors with King Mithridates II of Parthia (modern Iran), giving presents of silk to Mithridates and receiving acrobats and ostrich eggs in return. Trade between China and Parthia followed. Roman descriptions of Crassus' defeat at Carrhae in 53 B.C.E. told of the gleaming silk banners that preceded the Parthian soldiers. Less than ten years later, when Julius Caesar entered Rome in triumph, his procession also had silk banners.

During the early Roman Empire, wealthy women developed an almost insatiable demand for silk fabrics, to the disgust of Roman moralists. The Roman political leader and philosopher Seneca said: "I see garments in which there is nothing to cover either the wearer's body or her shame." Emperor Diocletian's "Edict on Maximum Prices" in 301 rated raw white silk by weight at one quarter the value of gold; if dyed purple, raw silk was rated at triple the value of gold.

The Silk Road that connected the Chinese and Roman Empires and the lands in between began in the Han capital Changan and proceeded westward to Tunhuang, the last Chinese settlement. After crossing mountains and deserts and stopping at oases, it ended at a port of the eastern Mediterranean, where the goods were shipped to Rome. The transshipping made many trading stations en route prosperous. With the Han and Roman Empires in control of most of the route, roads were kept

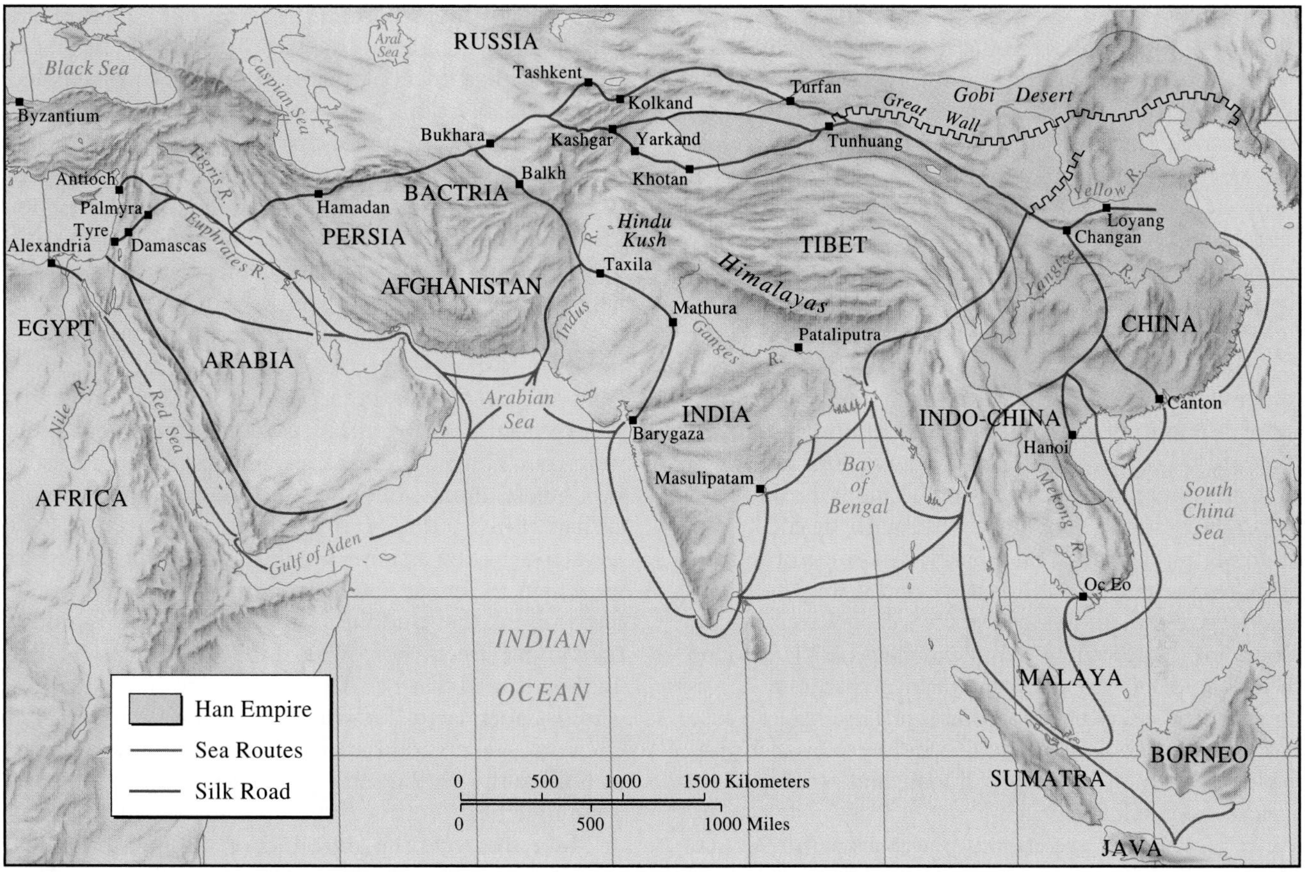

Map 4.5 The Han Empire and the Silk Road. In addition to controlling China, northern Korea, and Vietnam, Han outposts and garrisons dominated central Asia, allowing trade to cross the Silk Road to India, Persia, and the Roman Empire.

open and secure. Silk, both woven and raw, was China's major export; although skins, iron, lacquer, and spices were also exported. From the Roman Empire, China imported wool and linen fabrics, amber, coral, Syrian glass, Egyptian papyrus, wines, and acrobats and entertainers—the latter were status symbols in aristocratic Han households—but above all gold coins and bullion.

In the first century C.E., the Romans developed a sea route to the east, which had a twofold advantage over the land route: ships carried more than draft animals, and they bypassed territory controlled by the difficult and often hostile Parthians. During the reign of Augustus, as many as 120 Roman ships sailed from Red Sea ports for south India every year. Mostly Indian ships carried Roman wares to Southeast Asia and Canton in southern China. They also carried Indian and Southeast Asian products such as ivory, tortoise shell, gems, pearls, precious woods, and spices. Romans were alarmed by their unfavorable balance of trade, which caused a drain on the empire's precious metal reserves. As Emperor Tiberius complained, this outflow paid for "articles that flatter the vanity of women. . . . In exchange for trifles our money is sent to foreign lands and even to our enemies." In the second century, Pliny the Younger claimed that annually this trade drained the Roman treasury by 55 million sesterces paid to India and 45 million to China and Arabia. For comparison, a Roman soldier was paid about four sesterces per day.

The great distance precluded direct communications between the Chinese and Roman governments. Trade dropped off after the third century when political conditions deteriorated first in China and then in the west.

Religious and Intellectual Life

Emperor Kao-tsu and his immediate successors were practical men and had no professed philosophical preferences. Nevertheless, they realized that Legalism had become a liability because of its association with the hated Ch'in dynasty. But they needed dedicated men to help run the government and to dignify it with proper rituals. Enter the Confucians, whose conviction that the place of a scholar was in government and that li or rituals were important in human relations made them natural allies of the imperial system. In 136 B.C.E., Emperor Wu declared Confucianism the official state philosophy and banned students of Legalism from government service. Wu also established a state university with a curriculum based on Confucian works and an embryonic examination system. These measures ensured the dominance of Confucians in the bureaucracy. Without a comparable approach for recruiting officials, the Mauryan dynasty fell quickly. Paradoxically, once in government, the Confucians found that they needed to put into effect certain Legalist techniques and concepts.

Tung Chung-shu (c. 179–c. 104 B.C.E.) was largely responsible for creating an examination system that became the institutional basis of Confucianism as the state ideology. He reinterpreted Confucian teachings and added to them current ideas to make Confucianism the theory of the unified empire. The universe, Tung explained, consisted of heaven, earth, and humans. The emperor was the highest representative of humanity, and it was up to him and the government to interpret the will of heaven and, by moral and beneficent government, help people develop their potential for goodness and maintain harmony. It was the emperor's duty to set a good moral example, to take care of the economic needs of the people, to make it profitable for them to become virtuous, and to help them achieve moral fulfillment.

If he failed to exercise his power properly, the emperor would disrupt cosmic harmony and forfeit the mandate of heaven. To prevent such disasters, Confucians counseled rulers to seek their advice and to take warning from natural portents, which they reported and interpreted. Seasonable weather and abundant harvests meant that heaven was satisfied, while droughts, floods, and strange happenings portended heaven's displeasure. The ruler or son of heaven indeed had heavy responsibilities.

Although a reinterpreted and eclectic Confucianism became the state ideology, other schools were not suppressed. Confucius was exalted as a sage, not a god or king. The spirit of his teachings influenced laws; he was not a lawgiver. Philosophical Taoism had a revival during the Han. Taoist ideas of cultivating self-contentment and seeking harmony with nature provided an outlet from Confucian strictures and allowed a degree of individualism to prevail.

Religious or popular Taoism also enjoyed popularity. Rooted in folk beliefs and superstitions, it was concerned with drugs and potions to prolong life and attain immortality, and with using alchemy to produce gold from base materials. These interests led to experiments and new knowledge in chemistry, pharmacology, and other sciences and to the discovery of the compass, which greatly helped navigation, and of gunpowder later. Many persons may have achieved premature immortality from taking the drugs and potions, but that did not disillusion the true believers, who asserted that the immortals, men and women who had found the secret of everlasting life, had merely pretended to die in order to confound those of little faith. Others participated in group worship and believed in salvation. In late Eastern Han, one religious Taoist group spread so fast that the government, fearing its political implications, acted to suppress it. Thereupon its adherents rebelled, donning a yellow head scarf for identification. The Yellow Turban uprising of 184 C.E., which capitalized on peasant discontent, precipitated the fall of the Han dynasty.

Buddhism had begun to take root by the first century C.E. It spread overland via the Silk Road and by sea from the south. In the second century a number of monks from Persia, central Asian kingdoms, and India were translating Buddhist canons into Chinese, assisted by Chinese monks. Buddhism introduced new concepts such as *karma* and reincarnation, and reinforced existing ideas about compassion. Buddhist meditation and yoga were akin to Taoist practices, leading some Chinese at first to think that Buddhism was a Taoist sect. Buddhist translations freely borrowed Taoist vocabulary. Many Taoists claimed that Lao Tzu had gone to India and converted Gautama to Taoism. Thus second-century Han emperors saw no contradiction when they placed deities of both faiths on the same palace altar and worshipped them together.

In retrospect, the introduction of Buddhism was one of the greatest events in Chinese civilization. After several centuries of assimilation and accommodation, Buddhism would be accepted as one of the three teachings of China, alongside Confucianism and Taoism. As a result, it had a major influence on Chinese thought, art, and literature.

The greatest literary glory of the Han was the writing of history. We have already noted in the previous chapter that the prestige of historical writing is deeply rooted in Chinese civilization. Han historians contributed two great works. The first was the *Shih Chi (Records of the Historian),* a comprehensive history of the world as then known to Chinese, from the era of the culture heroes to the first century B.C.E. It was written by a father and son team, and its format and elegant prose were held up as a model for succeeding historians. It was divided into five sections: basic annals (narrative of important events), chronological tables, monographs (analytical essays on topics of special interest such as music, astronomy, and economic affairs), histories of great families of the past, and biographies (which included lives of statesmen, notable women, thinkers, rogues, and assassins).

This multifaceted approach to history set the standard for later dynastic histories that continued to the present century. Ssu-ma Ch'ien, the son and more famous of the duo, believed that history had two purposes: to give information and to provide moral

550 B.C.E.	
	Beginning of Roman Republic
350	
	Demosthenes Alexander the Great Chandragupta Maurya Kautilya, *Arthasastra* Euclid's *Elements* Stoicism and Epicureanism
	The *Mahabharata* and *Ramayana* Emperor Asoka Third Buddhist Council Scipio defeats Hannibal at Zama
200	Han Kao-tsu founds the Han dynasty Tung Chung-shu
	Emperor Wu Travels of Chang Ch'ien Confucianism becomes the state ideology in China
50	
	Extensive trade along the Silk Road Cicero
	The assassination of Julius Caesar Cleopatra Emperor Augustus Ssu-ma Ch'ien, *Records of the Historian*
1 C.E.	Buddhism spreads in China Eastern Han dynasty
	Pan Ku, Pan Chao, *History of the Former Han Dynasty* King Kanishka Fourth Buddhist Council
100 C.E.	
	Plotinus and Neoplatonism
	Emperor Constantine Compilation of the Talmud
400	

instruction. Like the Athenian historian Thucydides, he invented speeches and dialogues that he felt fitted the historical characters and their situation and brought persons and events to life.

The second great work was titled *The History of the Former [Western] Han Dynasty.* It was begun by Pan Ku (32–92 C.E.), brother and uncle of the great generals, father and son conquerors of central Asia, and finished by his equally famous sister Pan Chao, who also wrote a book of moral instructions for upper-class women. Another famous woman author wrote a multivolume work titled *Lives of Famous Women* that recorded the lives and deeds of over a hundred famous and infamous women up to that time.

Other literary works of the Han dealt with philosophy, poetry, and fiction. In the bibliographical section of the *History of the Former Han Dynasty,* Pan Ku listed 1380 works of fiction, but none has survived.

Summary and Comparisons

This chapter covered the development of several great empires that, after periods of prolonged intellectual ferment and political turmoil, succeeded in imposing unity and order.

The fragmented and weak Greek city states allowed backward and semi-Greek Macedon to rise to ascendancy under Philip and his son, Alexander the Great. Alexander conquered the Persian Empire and controlled territory from Egypt to northwestern India. After his early death, that empire broke up into three Hellenistic states, which were, in their turn, finally absorbed by Rome. Alexander's conquests and the successor Hellenistic states accelerated the spread of Greek culture throughout the eastern Mediterranean and western Asia.

Further west, on the Italian Peninsula, Rome rose to dominance by outstripping neighboring Greek, Etruscan, and Latin cultures. After ousting their Etruscan monarchs and forming a republic, the Romans first dominated the entire peninsula, then, between 264 and 30 B.C.E., wrested control of the Mediterranean from Carthage and the Hellenistic kingdoms. The Roman Empire reached its zenith during the first two centuries C.E., then declined dramatically during the third, when autocratic rulers postponed total collapse by dividing the empire into eastern and western halves.

Alexander's brief incursion into the Indus Valley inspired Chandragupta Maurya to found a dynasty and begin the conquest of an empire that would embrace nearly the entire Indian subcontinent under his successors. The Mauryan Empire reached its zenith under Asoka, who converted to Buddhism, giving it impetus to spread beyond India. Northwest India suffered many invasions by Greeks and Persians after the fall of the Mauryan Empire; the most successful invaders, however, were nomads from China's northwest called Yueh-chih by the Chinese and known as Kushans after they entered India. Kushan power and culture reached its zenith under the great monarch Kanishka around 100 C.E.

Further east, the Han dynasty (202 B.C.E.–220 C.E.), founded by a commoner named Liu Pang, unified the Chinese peoples after a long era of warfare. The Han leaders ended feudalism, adopted Confucianism as a state ideology, and established an educational and examination system that endured in China for two thousand years. Han military success affected Korea in the east, Vietnam in the south, and central Asia in the west.

All four major empires treated in this chapter enjoyed outstanding leadership by great founding leaders and their heirs. Although they did not achieve the same degrees of success or durability, each left a rich legacy to billions of people up to the present day. Alexander the Great, for example, died young, but his powerful generals partitioned his empire and established states that shared many cultural traditions and endowed the eastern Mediterranean world with a degree of cohesion, including a common language for the educated.

Although the Mauryan Empire collapsed soon after the reigns of its three founding rulers, its cultural and religious gains survived and spread far beyond India's frontiers. Despite scholars' knowledge of Sanskrit and Prakrit, languages of Buddhist literature, the Mauryan Empire failed to bequeath a common language to India. This hindered its quest for unity throughout subsequent history.

The Han Empire endured for four centuries, gave its name to most Chinese to the present, left an indelible mark on all east Asian civilizations, and bequeathed a common writing system.

The Roman state lasted longest, in part because it underwent many internal transformations, from monarchy to republic and finally to empire. It, too, left indelible marks on the language, laws, and religion of much of Europe.

Patronage of the arts and other cultural activities under all four empires fostered sacred scriptures, poetry, literature, and philosophy that still exert powerful influences today.

Each of the empires assimilated and civilized disparate peoples and created a common heritage for them. The geographic extent of the Mauryan Empire expanded the notion of India and brought Indian civilization even into southern India and Ceylon (present-day Sri Lanka). Similarly, the Han Empire absorbed many less advanced peoples as heirs of a common Chinese heritage. International trade, travel, and missionary activities made each empire more cosmopolitan, and extended the influences of hitherto insular cultures across continents.

Finally, the political needs of the states and the emotional and spiritual needs of their peoples led to the formation or development of great religions and philosophies. Reinterpreted Confucianism became the moral foundation of the Chinese empire, as Christianity became the official religion of the late Roman Empire (see Chapter 5). New philosophies such as Stoicism and Epicureanism in the Hellenistic states and the further evolution of existing Taoist philosophy in China helped the elite cope with an impersonal world. Higher religions such as Buddhism, Jainism, and Christianity offered moral grounding and spiritual comfort to both the elite and ordinary people, while mystery cults in the Roman Empire and magical Taoist practices in China both consoled and empowered the masses

The great achievements of the Roman, Mauryan, and Han Empires have left a lasting legacy both within and beyond the borders of Europe, India, and China.

Selected Sources

Balsdon, J. P. V. D. *Life and Leisure in Ancient Rome.* 1969. Based on a critical assessment of literary, inscriptional, and archaeological evidence.

Begley, Vimala, and Richard D. De Puma, eds. *Rome and India: The Ancient Sea Trade.* 1991. By many experts on different topics.

*Boardman, John, et al., eds. *The Roman World.* 1988. This volume of the Oxford History of the Classical World contains essays by leading authorities on all aspects of Roman civilization; excellent illustrations.

*Bryher, Winifred. *The Coin of Carthage.* 1963. An entertaining historical novel about the fortunes of two Greek traders trying to make their way in a world convulsed by the second Punic War.

Ch'u, T'ung-tsu. *Han Social Structure.* 1972. Jack L. Dull, ed. Comprehensive in scope and full of human interest and anecdotes.

Erdosy, George. *Urbanism in Early Historic India.* 1988. On the development of cities between 1000 B.C.E. and 300 C.E.

Frye, Richard N. *The Heritage of Central Asia: From Antiquity to the Turkish Expansion.* 1996. This book shows how central Asia connected all the ancient cultures of Europe and Asia.

Gokhale, B. G. *Asoka Maurya.* 1966. A good biography of the man and his age.

Green, Peter. *Alexander the Great.* 1970. This engaging and superbly illustrated biography of Alexander is well-balanced in its assessment of his accomplishments. Covers the career of Philip II also.

Langguth, A. J. *A Noise of War: Caesar, Pompey, Octavian, and the Struggle for Rome.* 1994. A riveting account of a turbulent era by a popular biographer.

*Available in paperback.

*Le Glay, Marcel, et al. *A History of Rome*. Trans. Antonia Nevill. 2d ed. 2000. This comprehensive history of ancient Rome is equipped with excellent graphics: chronologies, illustrations, maps, plans, and a glossary.

Loewe, Michael. *Everyday Life in Early Imperial China*. 1968. Many pictures and drawings help bring back life in China 2,000 years ago.

*Long, A. A. *Hellenistic Philosophy*. 2d ed. 1986. This very helpful study covers Epicureanism, Skepticism, and Stoicism.

*McCullough, Colleen. *The First Man in Rome*. 1990. *The Grass Crown*. 1991. *Fortune's Favorites*. 1993. *Caesar's Women*. 1996. *Caesar*. 1999. These five richly detailed historical novels in the author's "Masters of Rome" series trace, with considerable fictional embroidery, the careers of Marius, Sulla, Pompey the Great, and Julius Caesar, among others.

Pirzzoli-t'Serstevens, Michele. *The Han Dynasty*. 1982. A beautifully illustrated volume with easy-to-read text.

*Plescia, Joseph. *The Bill of Rights and Roman Law: A Comparative Study*. 1995. A fascinating and concise comparison of the development of citizens' rights in ancient Rome and in the U.S. Bill of Rights.

*Pomeroy, Sarah. *Women in Hellenistic Egypt*. 1984. A fascinating account of the lives of women on all social levels during the period.

Power, Martin. *Art and Politics in Early China*. 1992. On interactions between the government and art in Han China.

*Renault, Mary. *Funeral Games*. 1981. A vivid fictionalized treatment of the bloody and chaotic struggle for power by Alexander's successors after 323 B.C.E.

*Scarre, Chris. *The Penguin Historical Atlas of Ancient Rome*. 1995. Contains, in addition to excellent full-color maps and illustrations, a quite detailed, topic-by-topic history of ancient Rome.

Soren, David, et al. *Carthage: Uncovering the Mysteries and Splendors of Ancient Tunisia*. 1990. Much the best general account of ancient Carthage and its civilization from the ninth century B.C.E. to the sixth century C.E.

Soucek, Svat. *A History of Inner Asia*. 2000. A comprehensive look at the peoples of a region important to Indian, Chinese, and other civilizations.

*Southern, Pat. *Augustus*. 1998. The best recent account of the life and times of the first Roman emperor and the system of government he instituted.

*Stoneman, Richard. *Alexander the Great*. 1997. The best brief biography of the Macedonian conqueror.

*Walbank, F. W. *The Hellenistic World*. 1982; rev. ed. 1993. A concise, accurate, up-to-date presentation of political and cultural developments of the era.

Yu Ying-shih. *Trade and Expansion in Han China: A Study in the Structure of Sino-Barbarian Economic Relations*. 1967. Deals with interaction between politics and economics.

Internet Links

The Ancient Greek World
http://www.museum.upenn.edu/Greek_World/Index.html
This site, based on the collections of the University of Pennsylvania Museum, offers informative descriptions and high-quality graphics divided into such categories as Land and Archaeological Time, Daily Life, Economy, and Religion and Death.

China: The Imperial Era
http://www-chaos.umd.edu/history/imperial.html#first
A succinct account of the unification of China in 221 B.C.E., the Han dynasty, the Great Wall, and the Silk Road.

De Imperatoribus Romanis: An Online Encyclopedia of Roman Emperors
http://www.roman-emperors.org/
This scholarly site is an example of the great potential of web-based information sources. It contains detailed biographies of most of the Roman emperors, together with links to images, coins, maps, and the like.

Hellenistic India and the Mauryan Empire
http://members.nbci.com/seleukids/mauryanempire.htm
A brief sketch of the history of the Mauryan Empire is linked to a very extensive webpage presenting translations and comment on the edicts of Asoka.

Images from World History: The Kushan Empire
http://www.hartford-hwp.com/image_archive/
A good selection of graphics depicting art objects and artifacts from the Kushan empire.

In the Footsteps of Alexander the Great
http://www.pbs.org/mpt/alexander/
This site, based in part on Michael Wood's PBS series, offers concise outlines of Alexander's life and career, together with capsule biographies of important figures, a helpful timeline, and hyperlinks to other internet resources.

Pompeii Forum Project
http://jefferson.village.virginia.edu/pompeii/page-1.html
An online examination of the downtown area of a typical Roman town of 20,000. Excellent site plans and text.

The Decline and Fall of Empires

*At Pei-mang how they rise to
Heaven,
Those high mounds, four or five in
the fields!
What men lie buried under these
tombs?
All of them were Lords of the Han
world. . . .
When the dynasty was falling, tumult and disorder rose,
Thieves and robbers roamed like
wild beasts. . . .
They have gone into vaults and
opened the secret doors.
Jewelled scabbards lie twisted and
defaced:
The stones that were set in them,
thieves have carried away,
The ancestral temples are
hummocks in the ground:
The walls that went round them are
all levelled flat.
Over the tombs the ploughshares
will be driven
And peasants will have their fields
and orchards there.
They that were once the lords of a
thousand hosts
Are now become the dust of the
hills and ridges.*

Arthur Waley, *Translations from the Chinese* (New York: Knopf, 1941), pp. 76–77 (poem by Chang Tsai, third century C.E. lamenting the desecration of Han imperial tombs after the fall of the dynasty).

Dynasties [Empires] have a natural life span like individuals . . . as a rule no dynasty lasts beyond the life span of three generations. . . . In a dynasty affected by senility as the result of luxury and rest, it sometimes happens that the ruler chooses helpers and partisans from groups not related to the ruling dynasty but used to toughness. He uses them as an army which will be better able to suffer the hardships of wars, hunger, and privation. This could prove a cure for the senility of the dynasty . . . but only until God permits His command regarding the dynasty to be executed.

Ibn Khaldun, *The Muqaddimah: An Introduction to History,* trans. Franz Rosenthal (Princeton: Princeton University Press, 1967), pp. 135–136.

Why do great empires crumble away or die? Are their deaths inevitable? The Chinese poem above from the third century C.E. describes the robbed and desecrated Han imperial tombs after the fall of that once glorious dynasty. Like empires around the world, the Han Empire had once seemed almost invincible, but it too had fallen into decline and had finally collapsed. Over the centuries, historians have put forth numerous reasons for the demise of empires. For example, Chinese scholars accepted a cyclical theory of history, namely, that growth and prosperity are inevitably followed by decline and fall. Chinese writers also accepted the proposition that periods of unity are followed by disunity and chaos, which in turn give way once more to unity. The great fourteenth-century Arab historian Ibn Khaldun shared these views. Judeo-Christian historians, on the other hand, believed that historic progression served God's purpose, and that history would end when God's kingdom was established on earth. In the nineteenth and twentieth centuries, modern theories range from the Marxist view that all history is the result of class struggle based on economic causes to Arnold Toynbee's hypothesis that empires rise when they meet the physical and spiritual challenges of the people and time and fall when they no longer do so.

The problem with broad theories such as these is that they may lead their exponents to bend, distort, or use facts selectively to prove their case, while ignoring or dismissing important factors that fail to serve their thesis. In fact, the rise and fall of great empires result from many complex reasons, some of which are shared, while in other instances they are specific and unique. Therefore it is difficult and unwise to force the explanation for the fall of empires into a uniform framework. As we shall see in the chapter that follows, empires have characteristically declined and collapsed as a result of a combination of factors.

1. *Dynastic succession.* To paraphrase the great twentieth-century British statesman and historian Winston Churchill, although democratic governments are imperfect, they are nevertheless superior to all other forms of government. In particular, constitutional democracies built on the rule of law have clear rules concerning acquiring, holding, and relinquishing power. No major ancient empire was democratically governed. All were hereditary dynasties, ruled most of the time by men, but sometimes by women. Succession to power was often based on primogeniture or some other form of selection within the ruling family. Inevitably, after some generations, ruling families produced weak heirs due to wine, song, sexual excess, mental deficiency, or other causes, or they left heirs too young to govern capably. Ineffectual leaders and disputed successions generally brought about revolts, usurpations, and

civil wars that toppled the ruling dynasty and contributed to the decline and fall of the empire. For example, the lack of an adult male heir spelled the breakup of Alexander's empire. A disputed succession broke up the Mongol empire two generations after its founding by Genghis Khan. Inferior rulers and minor rulers manipulated by relatives and eunuchs brought about the end of the Mauryan and Han Empires. Disputed succession led to coups that severely undermined the strength of the Roman and Inka Empires, and ended the unity of the Muslim Empire a generation after Muhammad's death.

2. *Bureaucratic corruption.* All effective empires relied on an honest bureaucracy and created checks and balances to ensure it. For example, the Romans emphasized the duty of the upper class to set moral examples and to devote their lives to public service. Han China created state universities and an examination system to educate and select men of integrity and ability for public service. In time, however, all bureaucracies succumbed to corruption, and corrupt governments provoked rebellions; for example, a peasant revolt called the Yellow Turban rebellion contributed to the fall of the Han Empire.
3. *Inequitable economic burdens.* Successful empires depended on sufficient revenues to support the military, bureaucracy, and other arms of government. Sufficient revenues depended on a prosperous population engaged in agriculture, trade, and industries. Those who could evade taxes, however, generally the powerful, often found ways to do so, thereby enhancing their incomes and becoming richer. The resulting shift of the tax burden to the poor and powerless inevitably led to decreased revenue for the government and aroused anger among the taxpayers. A resentful population often revolted, and impoverished governments frequently lacked the resources to put down such revolts, or to secure defenses against outside enemies. A vicious cycle of decline and fall resulted. For example, the rise of large plantations and the concomitant fall of a free farming citizenry contributed to the fall of both Rome and the Han. The inability of the Gupta Empire in India to collect revenues to pay its officials contributed to its collapse, while the system of farming out tax collection to corrupt officials led to the decline of the Ottoman Empire.
4. *Regional, racial, or ethnic tensions.* Great empires were usually composites of numerous racial, ethnic, and religious groups who resisted full integration. The Hellenistic empires never fully integrated the ruling class of Greeks and the subject Egyptians, Persians, and other ethnic groups. In India the reversion to regional states divided by language and ethnicity demonstrates how difficult the Mauryan task of attempting to unite the subcontinent had been. A major weakness of the Aztec Empire was its tenuous control over restless subject peoples, who were often ready to join outsiders against their current masters. Widely disparate regional interests led Emperor Diocletian to divide the Roman Empire into four administrations with four capitals and four leaders. In time the division solidified into two separate empires, each with its official language, traditions, and culture.
5. *Decline of martial spirit.* The existence of a will to fight, or, put another way, the willingness of a populace to sacrifice property or life itself to defend the state, is an intangible but important factor in the rise and fall of many empires. The success of the Roman Empire was in part due to its male citizens' pride in military service. When that spirit declined, Rome was forced to recruit unreliable mercenaries. The need to pay mercenaries drained the treasury. This was also true of the Han and T'ang Empires in China. When the T'ang government needed to recruit barbarian units for the army, the result was a rebellion that almost toppled the dynasty. According to some, the Indian emperor Asoka's emphasis on pacifism and moral persuasion, as state policies sapped the martial spirit of the Indians, contributed to the fall of the Mauryan Empire.
6. *Costly technology.* All successful empires created engineering wonders that helped to sustain them. From China to India, West Asia, the Mediterranean world, and South America, imperial governments built and maintained roads, harbors and waterways, irrigation projects, defensive walls, and other installations.

They maintained granaries to provision troops defending their borders, to relieve famine, and to enhance their economies. The Great Wall of China, the Roman roads and aqueducts, the enormous granary complex of the Inka, and Ptolemaic irrigation works along the Nile River are major examples of the energies expended to maintain safety and enhance the economies of those empires. Whatever their intrinsic merit, however, the expense of initiating and maintaining projects of such magnitude often impoverished the governments that supported them, turning what was originally an advantage into a liability.

7. *Moral decline.* This is an intangible factor. Nevertheless, from Augustus on, Roman leaders decried the decline of their citizens' moral fiber and their increasing self-indulgence and hedonism. Similarly in Han China, the hedonism and extravagance of the upper classes were blamed for the decline of the dynasty. Emperor Asoka of India appointed morality officers to uphold high moral standards, with dubious results.
8. *Escapist or otherworldly religions.* The eighteenth-century historian Edward Gibbon blamed Christianity, which stressed heavenly rather than earthly rewards, for declining civic spirit and other ills of the Roman Empire. He also blamed religious strife among Christians for the increasing chaos of Rome. Likewise many upper-class Han Chinese indulged in otherworldly Buddhism or escapist philosophical Taoism. Emperor Asoka's encouragement of pacific pursuits and the nonviolent teachings of Buddhism and Jainism may also have contributed to weakening the Mauryan Empire.
9. *External enemies.* All successful empires were forged through conquest and maintained through military strength. While defeated enemies schemed for revenge, the wealth generated by powerful empires inspired envy, especially among less affluent neighbors. Thus outsiders awaited opportunities to breach the defenses of the Han and Roman Empires, to loot, settle, and rule the lands they coveted.

Disruption and Renewal in West Asia and Europe

5

I saw how the Northmen had arrived with their wares, and pitched their camp beside the Volga. Never did I see people so gigantic; they are tall as palm trees, and florid and ruddy of complexion. . . . Every one carries an axe, a dagger, and a sword, and without these weapons they are never seen. Their swords are broad, with wavy lines, and of Frankish make. From the tip of the finger-nails to the neck, each man of them is tattooed with pictures of trees, living beings, and other things. The women carry, fastened to their breast, a little case of iron, copper, silver, or gold, according to the wealth and resources of their husbands. Fastened to this case they wear a ring, and upon that a dagger, all attached to their breast. About their necks they wear gold and silver chains. . . . Their most highly prized ornaments consist of small green shells, of one of the varieties which are found in [the bottom of] ships. They make great efforts to obtain these . . . , stringing them as a necklace for their wives.

They are the filthiest race that God ever created. They do not wipe themselves after going to stool, nor wash themselves after a nocturnal pollution, any more than if they were wild asses.

They come from their own country, anchor their ships in the Volga, which is a great river, and build large wooden houses on its banks. In every such house there live ten or twenty, more or fewer. Each man has a couch, where he sits with the beautiful girls he has for sale. Here he is as likely as not to enjoy one of them while a friend looks on. At times several of them will be thus engaged at the same moment, each in full view of the others. Now and again a merchant will resort to a house to purchase a girl, and find her master thus embracing her, and not giving over until he has fully had his will.

Every morning a girl comes and brings a tub of water, and places it before her master. In this he proceeds to wash his face and hands, and then his hair, combing it out over the vessel. Thereupon he blows his nose, and spits into the tub, and, leaving no dirt behind, conveys it all into this water. When he has finished, the girl carries the tub to the man next him, who does the same. Thus she continues carrying the tub from one to another, till each of those who are in the house has blown his nose and spit into the tub, and washed his face and hair. . . .

*If one of their number falls sick, they set up a tent at a distance, in which they place him, leaving bread and water at hand. Thereafter, they never approach nor speak to him, nor visit him the whole time, especially if he is a poor person or a slave. If he recovers and rises from his sick bed, he returns to his own. If he dies, they cremate him; but if he is a slave they leave him as he is, till at length he becomes the food of dogs and birds of prey.**

*Albert Stanburrough Cook, "Ibn Fadlan's Account of Scandinavian Merchants on the Volga in 922," *Journal of English and Germanic Philology* 22 (1923), 56–63.

Civilized life was transformed in the first millennium C.E., a period that spanned the end of the ancient Greco-Roman world and the beginning of the Middle Ages. The civilizations of Europe, West Asia, and North Africa that are examined in this chapter were both the destroyers and the inheritors of Roman culture. In many places, civilization either had never attained or actually receded from the standards of classical Greece and Rome, but in others, equally advanced cultures arose in the aftermath of Rome's fall. In the passage quoted above, Ibn Fadlan, an emissary of the Abbasid caliph Al-Muktadir (reigned 908–932), recounts the strange and revolting habits he observed among the Vikings, a Scandinavian people who had settled along the Volga River (in present-day Russia) in 922 C.E. It vividly portrays the reactions of the sophisticated Arab to the crude and vigorous Vikings, exposing the very different sensibilities of members of two divergent cultures in the Middle Ages.

As noted in the preceding comparative essay, the reasons for the fall of empires are many and varied. Although scholars disagree over the precise reasons for the fall of Rome or Constantinople, there is no doubt that the rising power of the Germanic tribes in Europe and the emergence of a dynamic new Muslim Empire in Arabia first threatened and then overtook the older Roman Empires. After first describing religious and social conditions in first-century Palestine and the spread of Christianity throughout the Roman Empire, this chapter will trace the long decline and destruction of the western, Roman Empire and the gradual disintegration of the eastern, Byzantine Empire.

As we shall see, Germanic peoples and Eurasian nomadic invaders made massive incursions into Europe and western Asia, destroying the western portion of the Roman Empire. This opened the way for a new civilization of the Franks in western Europe during the Carolingian era and the Middle Ages. At the same time, in the eastern portion of the Roman Empire, the Byzantines fashioned a durable imperial government and a distinctive tradition in art and literature. Eventually, however, their empire also manifested the symptoms of internal decay.

Beginning in Arabia in the seventh century, Islam rose to prominence among the major religions of the world. Unlike the Huns and other destructive invaders, the Muslims were agents of constructive change. Like Christianity, Buddhism, and the other great faiths, Islam shaped not only the spiritual but also the temporal lives of its millions of adherents, from India to Spain. In the process Muslims spread their own culture and assimilated elements of Greco-Roman culture, which they later transmitted to western Europe.

Political, Religious, and Social Unrest in Palestine: 63 B.C.E. to 73 C.E.

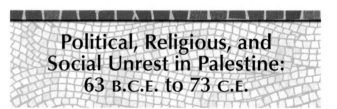

What has become of that great city, the metropolis of the Jewish people, with its protective walls and forts and towers, bursting with war materials and thousands of defenders? The city we thought God had founded? It has been destroyed root and branch, and now the only sign of its existence is the camp of the enemy that destroyed it. A few hapless old men sit and weep by the ashes of the temple precinct; a few women kept alive to sate the lust of the enemy. Who among us in this situation could bear to look on the sun's light any longer, even if he could himself live in safety? Who among us is such an enemy of his fatherland, such a coward, such a lover of life, that he does not regret being alive to see all this? We should all have died rather than see that holy city sacked by enemy hands, that sacred temple so ruined and profaned. We cherished the noble hope of avenging the city. Since that hope has now left us, let us hurry to die honorably. Let us show mercy to ourselves,

*our wives, and our children, while it is still in our power to do so. For we and our children were fated to die; even the fortunate cannot escape death. But nature does not impose on men the necessity of bearing disgrace, slavery, and the sight of our wives and children shamefully treated; such things come to those who refuse to avoid them by seeking death. . . . Let us die unenslaved; as free men with our children and wives, let us depart this life together.**

*B. Niese, ed., *Flavii Iosephi opera*, vol. 6: *De bello Judaico libri vii* (Berlin: Weidmann, 1895; reprinted 1955), trans. James P. Holoka.

This is a passage from a speech given to Jewish rebels by their leader Eleazer in 73 C.E. at the fortress of Masada, where the besieging Roman army is about to break through its defenses. Eleazer encourages his men to cheat the Romans of their victory. Some 960 rebels and their families committed suicide rather than be killed or enslaved by Roman soldiers the following day. This stunning act of defiance marked the last gasp of a revolutionary movement intended to throw off Roman overlordship.

This section will examine the remarkable political, social, and religious conditions of life in Palestine during the century and a half leading up to the failed revolt. This was a crucially important era both for the subsequent history of the Jews and Judaism and for the new world religion—Christianity—which now entered the stage in Palestine.

Masada. This nearly impregnable fortress near the Dead Sea was one of several refuges originally built by Herod the Great in nearly inaccessible places. Held by rebel forces in 73 C.E., it fell to a Roman army after a six-month siege and the mass suicide of its defenders. The Romans finally took the site by constructing a massive earthen ramp.

Palestine under Roman Rule

The direct Roman control of Palestine that Pompey the Great had instituted in 63 B.C.E. was loosened during the reign of King Herod the Great. With Rome's backing, Herod seized power from a rival claimant to the throne and held it throughout a long reign (37–4 B.C.E.), during which Palestine enjoyed peace and prosperity. His new port city of Caesarea Maritima and his lavish project to reconstruct the Temple of Solomon are symbols of the affluence the small Jewish nation enjoyed under Herod. In the latter part of his reign, however, Herod was preoccupied with issues of dynastic succession that led him to monstrous acts such as the execution of members of his own family and the slaughter of the infants after the birth of Jesus (Matthew 2:16–18).

After Herod's death, the Roman authorities divided his kingdom among his sons. This arrangement, however, did not last long, and beginning in 6 C.E. the various parts of the Jewish state again began to come under the direct authority of Rome as the province of Judaea. Roman prefects, including Pontius Pilate (governed 26–36), familiar from the New Testament, and then imperial officials known as procurators ruled the province. These Roman administrators often behaved brutally toward the Jewish population and tolerated massacres of Jews by Greek-speaking inhabitants of the province. These abuses led to uprisings by various militant Jewish groups who used guerrilla tactics in hopes of regaining their freedom.

The subversive and terrorist activities of political resistance groups, especially the Zealots and the Sicarii or "dagger-men," as the Romans called them, eventually caused Rome to take decisive action. The Roman generals (and later emperors) Vespasian and his son Titus led a force of 60,000 troops into the province and crushed the rebellion in a bitterly fought war that resulted in the capture of Jerusalem and the destruction of its great Temple in 70 C.E. Some few pockets of resistance, such as the fortress of Masada near the Dead Sea, were rooted out by 73.

The failure of their revolt and the loss of their temple as a central religious and political focus caused Jews to be scattered around the eastern Mediterranean and even farther afield in a dispersal known as a Diaspora. The character of Jewish life had altered profoundly. In

© Alinari/Art Resource

Detail of the Arch of Titus. This relief sculpture from the triumphal arch erected in the Roman forum shows Roman soldiers carrying off spoils from the sacked city of Jerusalem, including the distinctive menorah or candelabrum.

these new circumstances, Jewish leaders called rabbis began to place greater emphasis on observance of religious and social customs in Jewish communities. Essential to preserving and teaching these customs was the Talmud, a multivolume encyclopedia of Jewish religion. It had been orally accumulated over several centuries in Palestine and Babylonia, receiving final codification early in the sixth century C.E.

Religious Ferment

Reflecting in part these dramatic changes in political life in Palestine under Roman rule, various religious factions within Judaism emerged or became more sharply defined. These groups are familiar from the Christian Gospels and from the writings of the historian Flavius Josephus (born Joseph Ben Matthias), a Jew and Pharisee who became the protégé of the Flavian emperors Vespasian and Titus.

The Pharisees were mainly lay people of various social classes and occupations. They espoused adherence to the Torah (law) in every aspect of life, though they allowed for some flexibility in interpretation of the law. They also stressed prayer, fasting, and the paramount importance of ritual purity. They believed that a savior or Messiah would come to lead their nation against the forces of unbelievers and looked forward to an afterlife with God after the resurrection of the dead.

The Sadducees were a much more socially exclusive party; they belonged to aristocratic families whose members often served as priests. They did not, however, have the same degree of popular approval as the Pharisees, from whom they differed in several key doctrinal matters. For example, the Sadducees did not accept the comparatively new doctrines of resurrection of the dead and an afterlife. Along with the Pharisees, they had a prominent voice in the Sanhedrin (supreme religious and judicial council of the Jews). This theologically conservative party sought accommodation and peaceful coexistence with the Roman political authorities.

The Zealots were a group that advocated revolutionary overthrow of the Roman authorities so that they could establish a free nation based on their religious teachings. Like present-day fundamentalist Muslim revolutionaries, they espoused a very literal reading and strict application of the law. The Zealots and other radical groups, such as the Sicarii, escalated their acts of resistance to the point of open revolt in 66 C.E., with ultimately disastrous results for Judaea, as we have seen.

The preservation and transmission of the Jewish religious doctrines embodied in Mosaic law were the specific responsibility of a class of teachers and legal experts known as scribes. This very honored (though unpaid) occupation drew its practitioners from all social classes and included Pharisees, Sadducees, and Zealots.

A Noble Social Experiment: The Essenes

Amid the factionalism among the Jews under Roman rule, various groups had sought to opt out of the doctrinal strife and bitter political conflicts altogether. These groups withdrew to deserted corners of Judaea to form new communities where they might live according to their own utopian social and religious practices.

One of these separatist groups—the Essenes—is especially well known to us because of a sensational archaeological discovery. In 1947 an Arab shepherd came upon a cave in the hills at Qumran, a mile or so from the northwest coast of the Dead Sea. In it and several others excavated later were hundreds of scrolls written in Hebrew and Aramaic, a related dialect. The Dead Sea Scrolls and extensive archaeological remains at Qumran reveal a monastic community that had its own set of theological tenets and that pursued a simple, self-sufficient existence.

The founder of the community, called the Teacher of Righteousness in the scrolls, probably lived in the mid or late second century B.C.E. Theologically, the Essenes were similar to the Pharisees in their emphasis on the law of Moses, ritual purity, and scrupulous observance of the Sabbath. Unlike the Pharisees, however, they did not believe in the resurrection of the dead. They also considered the Pharisees and other traditional Jewish groups to be corrupt and depraved and saw their own group as the one true Israel, called upon to fight, under the leadership of a Messiah, in an apocalyptic battle of Light against Darkness.

The scrolls indicate that initiation into the community was a three-year process, culminating in an oath that bound members to be just in their dealings with others, to be truthful, to show piety to God, and to discharge the other duties stipulated by the leaders of the sect. Baptism marked the repentance of initiates and entry into the fellowship of "God's Elect."

By the time of Roman rule in the first century C.E., the Qumran community had built an aqueduct and large reservoirs to supply water, a pantry and large kitchen with five fireplaces, a pottery workshop, flour mills and

The Community Rule of Qumran

These are the rules by which they shall judge at a Community Court of Inquiry . . . :

If one of them has lied deliberately in matters of property he shall be excluded from the pure Meal of the Congregation for one year and shall do penance with respect to one quarter of his food. . . .

If any man has uttered the Most Venerable Name even though frivolously, or as a result of shock or for any other reason whatever, while reading the Book or praying, he shall be dismissed and shall return to the Council of the Community no more. . . .

Whoever has deliberately lied shall do penance for six months. . . .

Whoever has borne malice against his companion unjustly shall do penance for . . . one year; and likewise, whoever has taken revenge in any matter whatever.

Whoever has spoken foolishly: three months.

Whoever has interrupted his companion while speaking: ten days.

Whoever has lain down to sleep during an Assembly of the Congregation: thirty days. . . .

Whoever has spat in an Assembly of the Congregation shall do penance for thirty days.

Whoever has been so poorly dressed that when drawing his hand from beneath his garment his nakedness has been seen, he shall do penance for thirty days.

Whoever has guffawed foolishly shall do penance for thirty days. . . .

*Whoever has gone about slandering his companion shall be excluded from the pure Meal of the Congregation for one year and shall do penance. But whoever has slandered the Congregation shall be expelled from among them and shall return no more.**

This passage from the Dead Sea Scrolls illustrates the rigorous rule the Qumran community lived under. Like Calvin's followers in sixteenth-century Geneva (see Chapter 9), members of the sect believed that those chosen to be among the elect by God had to live up to much higher standards than those of other, more conventional factions of believers. The regulations laid down here would have satisfied the strictest monastic orders of medieval Christianity (discussed later in this Chapter).

*Geza Vermes, *The Dead Sea Scrolls in English,* 2d ed. (Harmondsworth: Penguin, 1975), pp. 82–84.

ovens, living quarters, and cemeteries holding the remains of over a thousand people. Another room, where a bench, three tables, and two inkwells were found, appears to have been a writing room—a forerunner of the scriptorium of medieval monasteries. This is likely where the famous scrolls were transcribed.

New Testament scholars have studied the Essene community at Qumran in comparison with elements of Christian doctrine and the communal style of life of early Christian groups. We do not know whether the community had ties to the Zealot groups whose theological outlook was rather like their own. Though they do not seem to have shared the Zealots' enthusiasm for armed insurrection and terrorism, the Essenes suffered the same fate as other Jewish settlements, and the Qumran community was destroyed by Vespasian's legions in 68 C.E.

Palestine in the first century C.E. was a hotbed of religious ideas—reactionary, revolutionary, and conservative. In an atmosphere of political oppression, thinking Jews were wrestling with the question whether their religious convictions could be accommodated to life under Roman rule. Some thought cooperation was the best path, others, like Eleazer's rebel band on Masada, preferred death to despotism. And for many, the best hope for salvation—both political and spiritual—seemed to lie in the coming of a savior or Messiah. Christianity was born in these conditions.

Early Christianity

*Two cities have been formed by two loves: the earthly by the love of self, even to the contempt of God; the heavenly by the love of God, even to the contempt of self. The former, in a word, glories in itself, the latter in the Lord. For the one seeks glory from men; but the greatest glory of the other is God, the witness of conscience. . . . In the one, the princes and the nations it subdues are ruled by the love of ruling; in the other the princes and the subjects serve one another in love. . . . The one delights in its own strength, represented in the persons of its rulers; the other says to its God, "I will love Thee, O Lord, my strength."**

*Augustine, *The City of God,* trans. M. Dods (New York: Random House, 1950), p. 477.

Augustine wrote these words in the final days of the Roman Empire in the West. From the vantage point of an eminent Christian man of learning, he contrasts the earthly city of humanity—most fully realized in Rome itself—with the heavenly city of the Christian God. As the empire of Rome began to show signs of its mortality, many of Augustine's contemporaries also turned their eyes toward visions of more enduring, timeless realms of spiritual truth and divine love. The following section describes the rise and ultimate victory of the Christian religion within the Roman Empire.

The Origins of Christianity

The old Greco-Roman polytheism continued as the official creed of the state during the imperial period. Beginning with the deification of Julius Caesar, the ruler cult expanded the roster of deities, as the Roman Senate voted divine honors for successful and popular emperors after their deaths. In fact, however, a conglomeration of religions had begun to replace the traditional Roman religion during the late republic. As we have seen, mystery religions in honor of Bacchus and Cybele had won enthusiastic followings in Italy by the second century B.C.E. By 100 C.E. the cults of the Persian god Mithras and the Egyptian goddess Isis, among others, had attracted many believers and begun to replace the old religion in the hearts of Roman citizens. Though new to the Roman world, these mystery religions had roots in the distant past of ancient West Asia; their elaborate initiation rituals satisfied deep-seated desires for unity with the deity. The worn-out rituals of Greco-Roman polytheism could not match such powerful inducements to belief.

Amid the Jewish religious fragmentation of the first century C.E., an itinerant Jewish preacher, Jesus of Nazareth (c. 6 B.C.E.–c. 29 C.E.), inaugurated a new religion, Christianity. Many Jews who embraced this faith believed that Jesus was the Messiah (anointed one or savior) whose coming was frequently alluded to in the Old Testament. The Book of Ezekiel, for example, prophesied that a future prince of the house of David would bring salvation to the Jews at the time of the final destruction of the world. Under first Seleucid and then Roman rule, many Jews looked with great expectancy for the coming of an earthly savior who would destroy their oppressors and establish the preeminent power of Israel.

Jesus, however, directed his followers' hopes away from this world toward an otherworldly realm. His teaching emphasized the imminent "coming" of the kingdom of God, a new age of love and justice under God's reign. To prepare for God's kingly rule, men and women were enjoined to love God and their fellow human beings. Like Buddha, Jesus was an "enlightened one." As Buddha had spent forty-nine days and nights in meditation and temptation by demons (see Chapter 3), so Jesus spent forty days and nights in the wilderness, where he fasted and was tempted:

> Jesus was then led by the Spirit into the wilderness, to be tempted by the devil. For forty days and nights he fasted, and at the end of them he was famished. The tempter approached him and said, "If you are the Son of God, tell these stones to become bread." Jesus answered, "Scrip-

Scala/Art Resource

Mosaic from the Tomb of Galla Placidia. This fifth-century mosaic in Ravenna shows (left) bookshelves with texts of the four Gospels. Because Christianity emphasized the good word of Jesus' life and teachings, a new, more easily consulted and durable book form—the codex—replaced the older *volumen* (papyrus roll). The compact codex (about ten by seven inches) usually consisted of vellum (calfskin) or parchment (goatskin) sheets bound together as in a modern book. Constantine had fifty copies of the Christian scriptures written on vellum for the churches of Constantinople.

> ture says, 'Man is not to live on bread alone, but on every word that comes from the mouth of God.'". . .
>
> The devil took him next to a very high mountain, and showed him all the kingdoms of the world in their glory. "All these," he said, "I will give you, if you will only fall down and do me homage." But Jesus said, "Out of my sight, Satan! Scripture says, 'You shall do homage to the Lord your God and worship him alone.'" Then the devil left him; and angels came and attended to his needs. (Matthew 4:1–11, Revised English Bible)

Although Jesus respected the Jewish scriptures, he opposed the Pharisees on matters of Sabbath observance, food laws, and ritual purity. He also believed the priestly Sadducees had corrupted the Jerusalem temple for personal gain. Jesus' popularity with the masses, who "heard him gladly," and his ties with some Zealots made him seem threatening to Roman authority in Judaea, only recently established. When Jesus arrived in Jerusalem, Roman and Jewish officials arrested, tried, convicted, and crucified him as an agitator.

After the death of Jesus, his followers announced he had risen from the dead and was the long-awaited Messiah (in Greek, *Christos,* "anointed one"), adding large numbers to their ranks by their dynamic preaching. Converts underwent ritual baptism; this rite and the common meal of bread and wine (the Eucharist or Lord's Supper) became central ceremonies of Christian observance.

A Jewish convert to Christianity, Paul (c. 3–c. 67 C.E.) of Tarsus carried the new faith to Greek-speaking non-Jews in a series of extensive missionary journeys in Asia Minor, Greece, and Rome. He represented Jesus as a dying and resurrected savior-god who taught that sin so alienated humans from God that only God's grace could save them. According to Paul, God had offered that grace through the life, death, and resurrection of Jesus the Christ.

Paul, who has been aptly called "the apostle to the Gentiles [non-Jews]," was the only first-century partisan of the Christian faith to leave a substantial written legacy. His letters constitute one-fourth of the New Testament, and the Book of Acts is a detailed account of his career. Paul also established numerous Christian churches in Asia Minor and the eastern Mediterranean. He was executed by the authorities in Rome in the time of Nero.

As the new religion attracted large numbers of adherents, Roman authorities abandoned their usual policy of religious toleration. The first recorded persecution of Christians took place after a terribly destructive fire in the city of Rome in 64, when Nero tried to curb rumors blaming him for the disaster by pinning responsibility on the Christians in the city. He imposed horrible penalties, including burning people alive, a common punishment for arson. Before the third century, however, there was no consistent empire-wide policy of persecution. Provincial governors only sporadically enforced the laws against Christianity. For instance, when Pliny the Younger wrote to ask Trajan what should be done about persons accused of being Christians in his province of Bithynia, the emperor answered, "No hard and fast rule may be set down. They are not to be hunted down; if they are brought before you and convicted, they should be punished. Nevertheless, anyone who denies he is Christian and verifies it by supplicating our gods should be pardoned accordingly, however suspicious his past life" (Pliny, *Epistulae,* book 10, no. 97, trans. James P. Holoka). With few exceptions, this rather enlightened policy of Trajan's was adhered to until the mid-third century. Whatever persecutions did occur tended to enhance Christianity's appeal.

Christianity competed effectively with the mystery religions in the Roman Empire in part because of its literature and its organization. Certain lives of Jesus (the Gospels or "good news"), letters by missionaries like Paul, and accounts of Christian teaching were eventually collected in the New Testament, which was joined to the body of Jewish scriptures, termed the Old Testament, to create the Christian Bible. Christian organization early showed a remarkable diversity of specializations, including prophets, teachers, healers, and administrators. Committees composed of elders—members distinguished for their faith and maturity—regulated the activities of each local congregation, whereas its religious services were conducted by a presbyter (priest or minister). Where several congregations existed in the same city, they came to be supervised by a higher official, the bishop.

A Christian Woman Accepts a Martyr's Fate

*After these [executions in the amphitheater], on the final day, they brought in Blandina and a boy named Ponticus about fifteen years old. These two had been made to watch the torments of the other martyrs on previous days. The authorities tried again to constrain them to swear allegiance to their idols, and the mob was enraged by their stubborn refusal to do any such thing. Thus, they ignored the tender years of the boy and did not balk at torturing a woman. They proceeded to put them through the whole course of brutal torments, but could not make them swear allegiance to their gods. Encouraging and assuring Ponticus was his sister, as the pagans [believers in traditional Greek and Roman deities] all witnessed; thus strengthened, he courageously bore the torture and surrendered his spirit in death. Blessed Blandina, kept to the last, counseled her children like a virtuous mother and sent them triumphant to meet the Lord their King. She then eagerly went forth to the same torments her children had suffered, actually glorying in her death as if she were attending a wedding feast and not herself being feasted on by wild animals. She was whipped, torn by beasts, burned by iron, and finally put in a basket and gored by a bull, which savaged her for some time, though she was now unconscious and quite impervious to the pain, thanks to her faith and adherence to her instruction and her communion with Christ. Thus when Blandina was sacrificed, the pagans all granted that no woman had ever endured so many and such awful torments.**

This passage from the Church historian Eusebius describes a particularly savage persecution that took place at Lyons in Gaul in 175–176 C.E. The Roman Empire had been suffering from barbarian invasions and an outbreak of a virulent plague; consequently, a kind of mass hysteria, uncontrolled by an incompetent provincial governor, may explain the brutality of the attacks on Christians. The amazement and sometimes even sympathy of pagans who witnessed the uncanny poise and staunch faith of their Christian victims is a common motif in many biographical accounts of early martyrs. As the Christian writer Tertullian (c. 160–c. 240) put it, "the blood of the martyrs [those killed for their faith] is the seed of the church."

*Eusebius, *Ecclesiastical History,* vol. 1, ed. Kirsopp Lake (Cambridge: Harvard University Press, 1926), book 5, chap. 1, trans. James P. Holoka.

Scala/Art Resource

Christian Communal Meal. This third-century wall painting in the Catacombs of Saint Callixtus depicts the miracle of the loaves and fishes as a prefiguration of the Christian "love feast," or eucharistic meal. This shared Sunday meal commemorated the Last Supper and demonstrated one's membership in the community of the Christian faithful.

The Triumph of Christianity

By the late third century, Christianity had become an increasingly divisive factor in the Roman world. While many were attracted to Christianity for its apparent stability, order, and morality, others blamed it for sapping the empire of its strength by diverting the interest and loyalty of its citizens away from their civic responsibilities. Persecutions became more frequent and widespread. The most notable was begun by Diocletian in 303 and accelerated by his successor, Galerius (reigned 305–311). Churches were destroyed and Christians, especially bishops and other leaders, were hunted down and executed. Sacred scriptures were burned and church holdings seized.

The status of Christianity in the Roman Empire changed with startling suddenness during the fourth century. In 311, on his death bed, Galerius recognized the failure of his religious policy and issued an Edict of Toleration, permitting Christians to practice their faith and rebuild their churches. Constantine, influenced by his mother's devout Christian faith and a prebattle vision of a Christian cross ("In this sign you will conquer"), confirmed this toleration by his Edict of Milan in 313, restoring confiscated Christian properties. He also granted the Christians special favors such as lands and buildings, tax exemptions for their clergy, and permission for their bishops to act as imperial judges. Constantine perhaps envisaged Christianity as a new imperial ideology that could provide unity to a sadly battered empire. Later emperors followed and extended his pro-Christian policies, until by the end of the fourth century Christianity and Judaism were the only legal religions in the empire.

Besides the crucial factors of sincere belief in the Christian God and imperial encouragement of that belief, we may note four reasons for Christianity's final victory over competing faiths and fearsome persecution. First, it was simple in its demand for absolute allegiance, brushing aside the welter of alternative religions and requiring a single, irreversible commitment to one creed. It offered permanent values at a time when political and spiritual absolutes were fast disappearing from the Roman horizon.

Second, it was equalitarian. Like the Hindu Upanishads, which ignored barriers of caste and other differences among believers (see Chapter 3), Christianity stressed the value of every individual soul. It was open to any and all, from the lowest slave (even female slaves) to the emperor. Every soul could be saved, regardless of ethnic origin or social status: "There is no question here of Greek and Jew, circumcised and uncircumcised, barbarian, Scythian, slave and freeman; but Christ is all, and is in all" (Colossians 3:11, Revised English Bible).

Third, Christianity held out the hope of a better life in the world of the heavenly city. This was a compelling enticement when the foundations of the earthly world of the Roman Empire were shaking. Though various mystery cults similarly promised immortality, in the case of Christianity the courage and equanimity of martyrs who endured torturous deaths lent credence to the notion that true believers would gain eternal bliss in the presence of their God. "I am the resurrection and the life. Whoever has faith in me shall live, even though he dies; and no one who lives and has faith in me shall ever die" (John 11:25–26).

Finally, Christianity satisfied the universal need to belong. Founded on the injunction to "Love thy neighbor,"

LIVES AND TIMES ACROSS CULTURES

Women and the Medical Professions in Late Antiquity

As with most other professions in the ancient world, medicine was formally practiced at its highest levels almost exclusively by men. Men performed surgeries, wrote the medical textbooks, instructed students in the medical schools. But on the level of day-to-day attention to patients, women—then as now—were the chief hands-on caregivers, and in much larger numbers than men. One historian has described the circumstances under which women practiced medicine as follows:

> *Medicine was part of the lives of ordinary women. They were agents as well as patients, the first line of defense against illness. Hospitals were available from the late fourth century [C.E.], as one form of Christian charity, but sick people who had homes were usually nursed there: women supervised diet and tried out traditional remedies. Some women were acknowledged experts on illness and medicines generally; others specialized in childbirth and problems associated with reproductive life, including "female complaints" and sexual difficulties. It was easier and cheaper to call on them than to employ a doctor with a professional training. . . .*
>
> *Some women described themselves, or were described by others as* medica *["doctor"]. . . . These women could not attend university lectures or train with doctors, but midwives and nursing attendants could work with doctors, and women caring for the sick could listen as the doctor explained the case to his trainees. According to Soranus [a second-century physician and prolific medical author] . . . , the "complete midwife" understood all the branches of medicine: dietetics, pharmacy, and* cheirourgia*—that is, the "manual work" which includes massage and manipulation as well as the use of instruments.**

The expertise of such women did not go unappreciated, as may be seen from the following epitaph inscribed in the second century C.E.:

> *Farewell, lady Panthia, from your husband. After your departure, I keep up my lasting grief for your cruel death. . . . You guided straight the rudder of life in our home and raised high our common fame in healing—though you were a woman, you were not behind me in skill. In recognition of this your bridegroom Glycon built this tomb for you.***

*Gillian Clark, *Women in Late Antiquity: Pagan and Christian Lifestyles* (Oxford: Clarendon Press, 1993), pp. 63, 67.

**Mary R. Lefkowitz and Maureen B. Fant, *Women's Life in Greece and Rome: A Source Book in Translation,* 2d ed. (Baltimore: Johns Hopkins University Press, 1992), p. 265.

the Christian community shared a value system and manner of living as well as a body of ritual. Persecution only strengthened this bond, as the church assumed the responsibility of caring for its own in a hostile environment, ministering to the indigent and sick, supporting orphans and widows, and supplying a source of self-respect in the lives of thousands of urban poor. Such activities, which were foreign to Greek and Roman religious expression, made the believer's earthly life more tolerable and meaningful, even in the face of adversity, quite apart from the prospect of a life after death.

As the Christians became preeminent in the empire, they devoted increasing attention to defining their beliefs. Ironically, efforts to make simple and clear formulations of the tenets of Christian belief often produced only complexity, confusion, and conflict. Special councils were held to resolve disagreements. From the Council of Nicaea in 325 there emerged the distinctive Christian doctrine of the Trinity and a definitive statement of essential beliefs of Christian faith, the Nicene Creed.

The writings of the church fathers also helped to clarify Christian dogma. Jerome (c. 348–420) mastered Greek and Hebrew and produced a translation into Latin of the whole Bible known as the Vulgate (common or ordinary), because it used an everyday style of language. His translation remained standard for a thousand years.

The greatest church father was Augustine (354–430). As a teacher of rhetoric, he had explored most Roman beliefs and enjoyed many of life's pleasures before embracing Christianity. His *Confessions* recounted the sinfulness—particularly sexual sins—of his earlier life and the importance of God's grace to his rehabilitation. In his *City of God,* written shortly after the Visigothic sack of the city of Rome in 410 (see below), Augustine argues that destruction of the Roman Empire may be part of God's plan and that humans ought to give their permanent allegiance not to the empire but to the city of God.

Some Christians practiced a rigorously disciplined religious life called monasticism and formed communities of monks and nuns, in much the same way as the Buddhist *sangha* was organized, though with greater hierarchic stratification and centralized control than in Buddhist orders. Typically, they vowed themselves to poverty, sexual abstinence, and obedience to superiors. Their day was divided into periods for physical needs such as eating and sleeping, prayer and meditation, study, and, in the Latin West, work. Such communities speeded the Christianization of the countryside, contributed new models for spiritual leadership, and preserved much of classical civilization while transforming it to serve Christian purposes.

The papacy also developed during the period 300–500. Archbishops in the empire's major cities became known as patriarchs. Although there were several patriarchs in the East, in the West there was only one, the patriarch of Rome, also called pope (from Latin *papa* or "father"). The Roman popes asserted that Jesus had granted jurisdiction over the whole church (Matthew 16:16–19) to the apostle Peter, later the first bishop of Rome. The popes claimed that they, as successors of Peter, were the heirs of that authority. This claim caused bitter conflicts in the Roman Empire's Greek-speaking eastern portions. In the Latin-speaking West, however, where no other patriarch existed, papal claims to authority were enforced by a decree that required all bishops in the western Roman Empire to accept them. The following section will describe how, as the Germanic migrations nullified the political power of the Roman emperor in the West, the papacy became a symbol of Christian unity in that area.

Upheaval and Transition in Western Europe

"WAITING FOR THE BARBARIANS"

What are we waiting for, packed in the forum?

The barbarians are due here today.

Why isn't anything going on in the senate?
Why have the senators given up legislating?

Because the barbarians are coming today.
What's the point of senators and their laws now?
When the barbarians get here, they'll do the
legislating.

Why did our emperor set out so early
to sit on his throne at the city's main gate,

Because the barbarians are coming today
and the emperor's waiting to receive their leader. . . .

Why have our two consuls and praetors shown up today
wearing their embroidered, their scarlet togas? . . .

Because the barbarians are coming today
and things like that dazzle barbarians.

And why don't our distinguished orators push
forward as usual
to make their speeches. . . ?

Because the barbarians are coming today
and they're bored by . . . public speaking.

Why this sudden bewilderment . . . ?
(How serious everyone looks.)
Why are the streets . . . rapidly emptying,
everyone going home so lost in thought?

Because . . . the barbarians haven't come.
And some people just in from the border say
there are no barbarians any longer.

Now what's going to happen to us without them?
The barbarians were a kind of solution. *

*C. P. Cavafy, *Selected Poems,* trans. E. Keeley and P. Sherrard (Princeton: Princeton Univ. Press, 1972), pp. 6–7.

In this poem, the Greek author Constantine Cavafy (1863–1933) imagines the state of mind of Romans in the twilight of their empire, as ancient ways of living were giving way before the force of new peoples and new patterns of life. It was, of course, a frightful process, but the Roman Empire had, by the fifth century, lost its strength and its ability to guarantee a secure life for its inhabitants. In this sense, the "barbarians" were, as Cavafy's poem suggests, "a kind of solution" both politically and culturally in the history of western Europe. The present section will describe the fall of Rome and the rise and triumph of the various states that replaced it in western Europe, in particular the Carolingian Empire.

The Fall of the Roman Empire in the West

The Roman Empire after the death of Constantine in 337 struggled unsuccessfully to resist the submersion of its western half under waves of Asiatic and Germanic invaders and immigrants. The Huns, fast-moving horsemen from the steppes of Asia, provided one catalyst of change. Related to the Hsiung-nu who harassed Han China and the Huna or "White Huns" who invaded India, they pushed into central Europe to the north of the Roman Empire, and later, under their king Attila, raided into the empire itself. In the process they displaced many of the German tribes living outside the empire; the Germans in their turn, desiring a more settled existence in the fertile cleared land to the south, poured

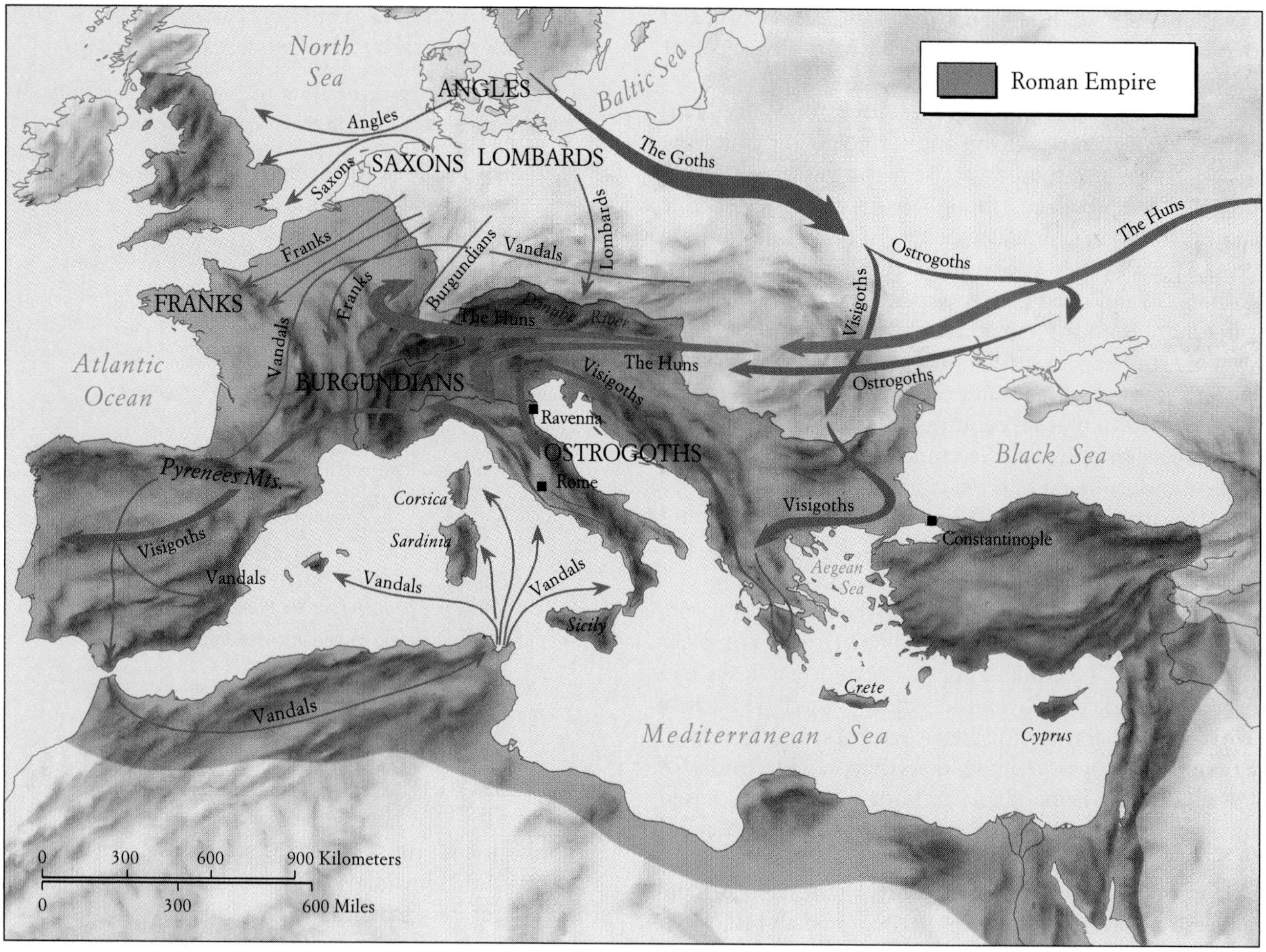

Map 5.1 German Invasion Routes. This map shows the avenues of invasion and immigration followed by the various Germanic tribes that finally overwhelmed the Roman Empire's defenses, beginning in the late fourth and early fifth centuries.

into the Roman Empire. Emperors perished in battle, large tracts of land were successively ceded or stripped away, and finally Rome itself was sacked in 410. In 476, the last Western emperor was deposed by the German leader Odoacer, who became the first barbarian king of Italy (reigned 476–493). The once brilliant light of Roman power in the West flickered out as Visigoths and Ostrogoths, Franks, Burgundians, Vandals, and others divided the territories of the old western empire.

Ancient and present-day scholars have offered various responses to the question of what caused the fall of Rome. Those who emphasize a decay from within point to economic crises caused in part by the bloated imperial bureaucracy and the financial strain it placed on an empire whose inhabitants were unfairly overtaxed and decimated by plagues, poverty, and declining birth rates. Some believe Christianity, with its emphasis on the heavenly Kingdom of God, discouraged the patriotic virtues that had sustained Rome in earlier days; similarly, the later Han Chinese dabbled in escapist Taoism and otherworldly Buddhism. Others cite a loss of traditional Roman moral values as non-Italians and even barbarians gained prominence within the society, the civil administration, and the ranks and officer class of the army. Soil exhaustion, protracted drought, the gradual poisoning of the aristocracy by lead water pipes and lead-containing food storage and cooking vessels, and slavery as an impediment to technological advance are still other causes of decline that scholars have suggested, some more plausibly than others. However, many of these weaknesses also affected the eastern half of the empire, which did not collapse.

The best explanation for the fall of the Roman Empire in the West is the intensified barbarian pressure directed against defense forces spread thin by the great length of the Rhine-Danube frontier. This pressure had been felt since the second century, but as Germanic migration steadily increased in the late fourth and throughout the fifth century, insupportable demands were placed on the military and financial resources of the western half of the empire, where the economic and social structure had long been crumbling.

The Germanic States of Western Europe

In contrast to the Byzantine and Islamic institutions of imperial government and urban life, Germanic society featured family and tribal structures in a rural setting. German families who owned or held land were subject to military service and tax assessment. They sometimes lived in isolated farmsteads, but were more often grouped together in villages. The tribe or people was the aggregate of all persons who lived under the same law, fought in the same army, and recognized a common king. Germanic tribes were patriarchal, and women, on all levels of society, had subordinate roles.

Tribes contained free persons, slaves, and half-free persons later known as serfs. Slaves became less common as settled life replaced migration and reduced slave-raiding activity. Also, many individuals rose out of slavery to become half free, while free persons fell to half-free status under the protection of noble lords. The half-free had to remain on the land they worked, but were not another's personal property. The merchants, clergy, and nobles became the only fully free persons. Nobles maintained their status by intermarrying and collected benefits and privileges from Germanic kings.

Most Germans depended on agriculture for their livelihood. In the great plains of northern Europe, where rainfall was generally plentiful and the seasons moderate, the heavy, wet soil produced two crops per year. However, poor, locally made tools and the lack of fertilizer kept crop yields low, until a heavy plow came into wider use after the sixth century. Because their only method of restoring soil fertility was to let land lie idle, the Germans needed large areas to support relatively few people. They usually settled in small, densely populated communities widely separated from one another, in which all members cooperated in necessary agricultural activities.

The rulers of these scattered peoples retained and modified traditional features of Germanic kingship. Kings moved beyond the status of tribal chiefs by becoming successful war leaders who conquered and ruled territories, not merely people. They gave gifts to loyal followers, as war bands formerly divided booty. The kings maintained the tribal laws and settled disputes between free persons, whereas lords judged disputes among their serfs and slaves. The kings now embodied the tribe's common origin and history, and their succession came to depend on dynastic (family) right rather than individual right.

Germanic rulers also incorporated Christian and Roman elements into their government structure. They used Latin in royal documents and law codes and adopted the biblical practice of anointing the king at accession. Under the church's guidance, kings regarded their subjects as Christians and defense of the faith as one of their royal tasks.

The Roman Tax Collector—"Like a Wild Beast"

What a terrifying individual [the tax-collector] could be is nicely illustrated in . . . the Life of St. John the Almsgiver, *. . . The Saint is represented as thinking about the dreadful monsters he may meet after death, and the only way he can adequately express the appalling ferocity of these wild beasts is to say that they will be "like tax-collectors." Certainly, tax collection from the poor in Roman times was not a matter of polite letters and, as a last resort, a legal action: beating-up defaulters was a matter of routine, if they were humble people. . . . In [Roman-controlled] Egypt . . . local officials would seize taxpayers whom they alleged (rightly or wrongly) to be in default, imprison and ill-treat them, and, with the aid of soldiers and local levies, burn down their houses. . . . According to [the historian] Ammianus [Marcellinus], an Egyptian in the late fourth century would blush for shame if he could not show on his back scars inflicted by the tax-collector's whip.**

One aspect of the economic crisis of an empire that had to support a bloated bureaucracy and a huge military machine was an unfair system of taxation. The rich were often able to evade taxes, while the poor were at the mercy of relentless government officials and tax collectors. In this respect at least, the replacement of Roman authority by Germanic states actually brought relief to many of the empire's inhabitants.

*G. E. M. de Ste. Croix, "The 'Decline and Fall': An Explanation," in Donald Kagan, ed., *The End of the Roman Empire: Decline or Transformation?* 3d ed. (Lexington, MA: Heath, 1992), p. 58.

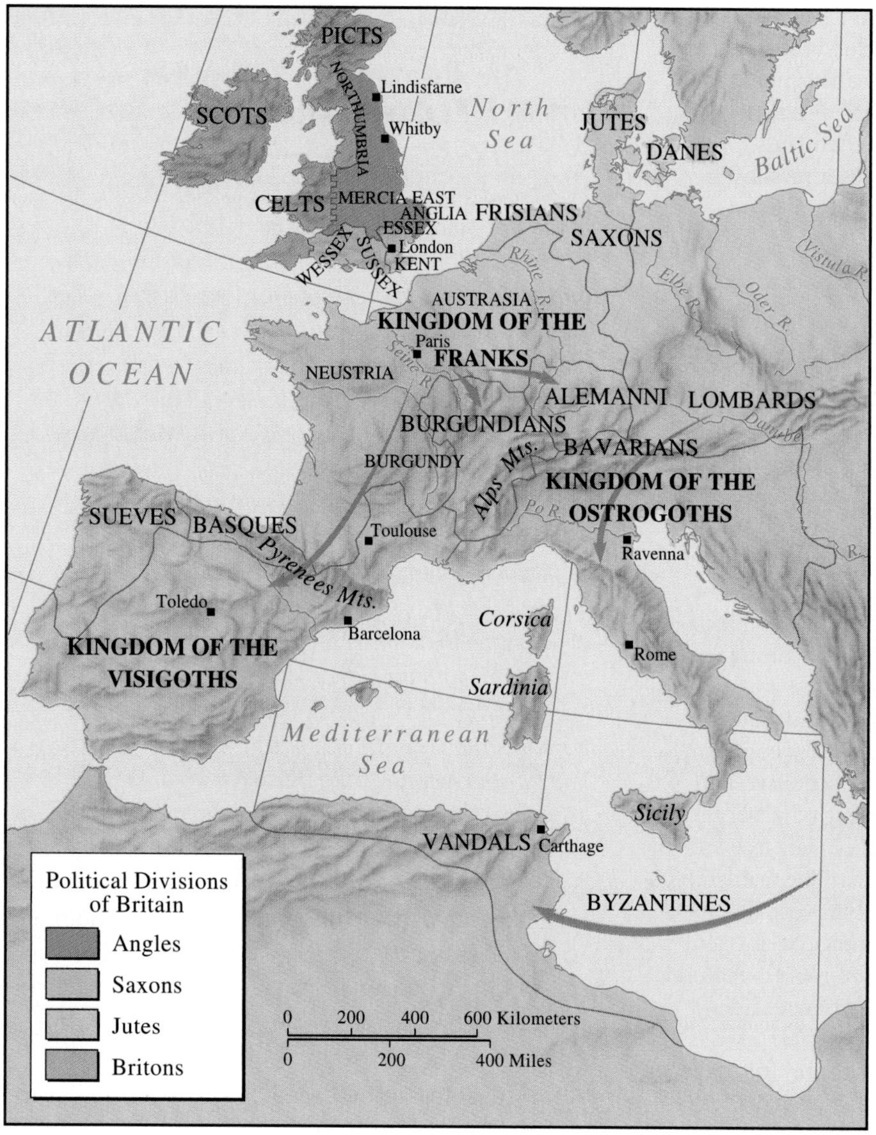

Map 5.2 Germanic States in Europe. Major German states about 500 are shown here; arrows indicate important German advances after that date.

By contrast with the Byzantine and Islamic Empires described later in this chapter, the Germanic peoples of western Europe had difficulty controlling their own territories and were harassed by warlike neighbors. Large landed estates dominated agricultural activity and sought economic self-sufficiency. While trade dwindled and towns decayed, the only significant international institution, the church, became the heir of much of the Roman cultural tradition.

The Triumph and Disintegration of the Carolingian Empire

Out of the preceding patterns of Germanic life, one people, the Franks, rose to prominence under the leadership of a dynamic ruler, King Clovis (reigned 481–511). Instead of separating Romans and Germans, Clovis chose to merge them by requiring both peoples to do military service and permitting intermarriage. Clovis's baptism as a Roman Catholic Christian shortly before 500 separated the Franks from the other Germans, who were Arian Christians. The Franks championed Roman Catholic orthodoxy against the Arians and won the support of the Christianized Roman aristocracy of Gaul. The Roman Catholic clergy supplied Frankish kings with educated advisers and other benefits, such as the flattering legend that the Holy Spirit had descended directly from heaven for Clovis's baptism. The Byzantine emperor later designated Clovis an honorary consul.

The German custom of dividing property among all of a deceased father's sons meant that the sons of Frankish kings often fought among themselves to gain control

Bibliothèque Nationale de France, Paris

Baptism of Clovis. In this artistic recreation of the historic event, bishops on the left and nobles on the right witness the ritual. Above the king, a dove, representing God's Holy Spirit, descends with oil for the ruler's anointing.

of all the territories of their father. Successive generations of the descendants of Clovis followed this process, weakening the monarchy and allowing the Frankish nobles to augment their political power and to assimilate royal lands and wealth.

In the eighth century, the Carolingian family (from the Latin *Carolus,* for "Charles") took control of the Frankish monarchy. Under King Charlemagne the Carolingian Empire was transformed into a restored Roman Empire. On Christmas Day in the year 800, the pope crowned Charlemagne (or Charles the Great; reigned 768–814), deliberately using the Roman titles emperor and Augustus, together with the Byzantine procedures of patriarchal coronation and popular acclamation. Charlemagne, rising from prayer and crowned by God, probably reminded many of Constantine, the first Roman emperor to become a Christian, by whose authority the pope claimed to act. The idea of Rome as the model of a universal state persisted in the notion of a Holy Roman Empire down to 1806.

At its maximum extent under Charlemagne, the Frankish Empire included most of present-day France, Belgium, the Netherlands, and Luxembourg, and portions of Germany, Italy, Switzerland, and Spain. Most of this territory had been wrested from the Frankish Empire's German neighbors and some of it from Muslims in Spain (see the Islamic section of this chapter) and Asiatic tribes from central Eurasia.

At the center of the Carolingian state was a reorganized royal household that included officials supported by the extensive lands held by the royal family. Lacking money, the kings paid those officials with land grants and exemptions from taxation and from visits by royal administrators. Such grants were also made in return for military service, especially by mounted warriors who required land to maintain themselves and their horses. As deteriorating clan and tribal organizations ceased providing customary protection and services, many became personal and economic dependents of noble landowners.

Carolingian dukes had the responsibility for governing large frontier areas known as marches. Counts (controlling territories called counties) became the essential personnel of Carolingian administration; they were required to make frequent public declarations of loyalty and to live in areas where they had no personal connections, administering smaller regions in accordance with local custom. The monarchs sent inspectors to review and when necessary correct the counts' activities. The kings strictly prevented the counts from passing on their offices to their children. Each count served as the king's governor and military commander in one province, assisted by a viscount and one or more judges. Hampering royal control, however, was an insufficiency of counts or supervisors and slow long-distance communications. Strong kings could crush rebellions of counts and dukes, but under weak kings, the nobles sometimes became independent. Nevertheless, Carolingian administration was fairly stable. Although there were differences, the political system established by the Carolingians in many ways resembled the feudal order reputedly established by early Chou kings of China.

In addition to reforming their administration, the Carolingian rulers beginning with Pepin III created the most effective armed forces in western Europe. Usually enjoying a decisive numerical advantage over opponents, their armies consisted primarily of well-armed and highly disciplined infantry, together with smaller groups of cavalry, wearing helmets and mailed coats and armed with swords and spears.

The cooperation of the Carolingian dynasty with the church continued as Charlemagne returned the pope to Rome and restored him to power after his enemies had hounded him from the city. It was mainly in gratitude for this that Pope Leo III crowned Charlemagne Emperor of Rome, thus bestowing prestige beyond that of any other German ruler.

Pepin III and his son Charlemagne owed their success to broad support from church leaders and laity, an effective army, and the weakness of their enemies. However, only a powerful ruler able to enforce loyalty and obedience could manage the weakly unified Carolingian state. Charlemagne's successors lacked that ability, and during the ninth century the Frankish empire disintegrated. Charlemagne's son, Louis, divided his empire and the crown lands among his sons upon his death in 840, thus precipitating a series of civil wars that broke up the Carolingian Empire. Out of the collapse emerged what became a French monarchy and a German monarchy. The nobles, however, increasingly disregarded any central authority and enlarged their own power by in effect dividing the kingdoms into large territorial principalities, further eroding the remnants of Carolingian royal government. Such developments were reminiscent of what had happened in China during the late Chou dynasty.

Map 5.3 The Carolingian Empire. Shown here are the boundaries of the Frankish kingdom before 768 together with surrounding territories acquired during the reign of Charlemagne. The inset shows the division of the Carolingian Empire among Charlemagne's grandsons.

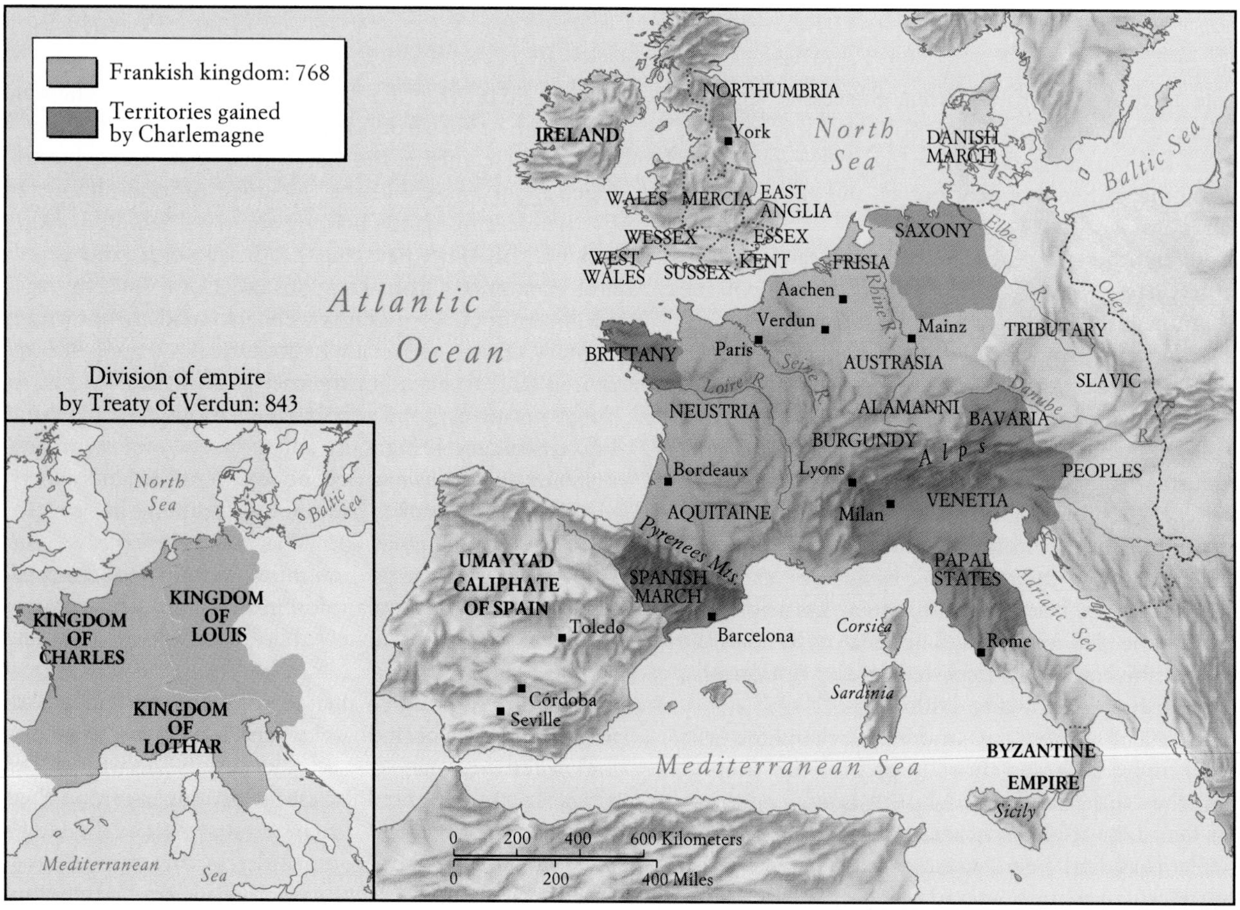

Giraudon/Art Resource

The Coronation of Charlemagne. According to some contemporary writers, the coronation was an unwelcome surprise to Charlemagne, although it clearly required advance preparation and apparently had the monarch's approval.

Religious and Cultural Developments in Early Western Europe

In an increasingly Germanized western Europe, the Christian church faced numerous problems as it assumed the moral, spiritual, and cultural leadership formerly exercised by the Roman Empire. Disappearance of Roman rule in the West deprived the church of imperial support, and the expansion of Islam reduced the territory of Christendom. Furthermore, Greek and Latin churches developed differences in belief, practice, and organization. Superstition, violence, and immorality characterized popular life; most people only vaguely understood or followed Christian teachings. Religious leadership frequently fell to uneducated and morally lax priests, and to bishops better qualified to wield political power than to provide spiritual guidance.

The church responded to these problems on a number of fronts. It infused its ideas of justice and mercy into codes of law, maintaining schools and hospitals, and assisting widows, orphans, and slaves. Monasticism, although introduced to the West before 500, was reformulated by Benedict of Nursia (480–547). He wrote a moderate and humane rule of life for monastic communities based on study, prayer, and physical labor.

To counter the luxury, sexual laxity, and disregard for authority that afflicted some of the clergy, Benedict required vows of poverty, chastity, and obedience, and submission to the absolute authority of an abbot. Pope Gregory I (reigned 590–604) wrote a *Life of Benedict* and promoted the spread of Benedictine monasticism in Europe. Monks and nuns following the Benedictine rule won converts to Christianity and instructed those converts in basic Christian belief and practice.

The other prominent Christian institution, the Roman papacy, gained increasing significance, primarily through the efforts of Gregory I. By adroit land management and shrewd negotiations with Byzantines and Lombards, Gregory made the papacy financially and politically independent. His *Book of Pastoral Care* helped the clergy perform their duties effectively. He also worked to convert German kings from Arianism and sent missionaries to England in

LIVES AND TIMES ACROSS CULTURES

Food for Buddhist and Christian Monks

Buddhist monks and nuns were strictly forbidden to eat meat. In addition, on specified days they had to fast after the noonday meal. On special occasions such as the Buddha's birthday and other days of religious significance or secular celebrations, vegetarian banquets were held at temples for both clerics and laypeople.

Between 838 and 847 a Japanese monk named Ennin traveled and studied in China and kept a detailed diary of his stay. Ennin described a feast for about 750 participants, including monks, nuns, men, women, and children at a famous temple at Mount Wutai. All received equal portions, with seconds given on demand. Although he did not describe the dishes, we gather from other sources that some of them were fashioned to resemble the forbidden meat dishes. Even today Buddhist restaurants among Chinese communities serve "chicken," "meat," and "fish" made from soybeans.

At about the same time, in the Europe of Charlemagne, monasteries complying with the Benedictine rule of life also featured a menu that seems rather ascetic by modern standards. Monks took only one daily meal in winter and two in summer. Although meat (especially pork, beef, mutton, venison, and poultry) was eaten in some monasteries on special feast days, for the most part the menu was vegetarian. The typical meal consisted of three dishes of dairy products, such as cheese, vegetables, and bread or a kind of grain porridge that served as the principal staple of the diet. The members of more austere monasteries restricted themselves to barley bread (often mixed with ashes), gruel, and vegetables, with even poultry and fish forbidden. On Sundays the great treat consisted of a little cheese thinned with water.

597, which in 664 agreed to follow the Roman observance. The Roman hierarchy was aggressive in converting the German and Slavic peoples of central Europe and the Irish, providing western Europe with religious unity.

Ireland became an important center of early medieval cultural and religious activity. Its conversion to Christianity, traditionally attributed to Patrick (389–461), a Roman citizen educated in Gaul, opened the island to continental influences. Irish monasteries became centers of intellectual activity; each had its *scriptorium* (writing room) for the essential work of copying both Christian and classical manuscripts in excellent, clear handwriting and elaborate decorative calligraphy. The Irish copyists also developed the art of illumination (painting brightly colored pictures on manuscripts).

England's conversion to Roman Catholic Christianity stimulated an outburst of literary productivity. The Old English epic of the eighth century, *Beowulf*, recounts the hero's slaying of monsters and a fire-breathing dragon. Although composed in the Germanic heroic tradition, the poem is altruistic in spirit, and it may have been intended as a Christian allegory.

As part of their responsibility for the Christians in their realm, the Carolingian rulers reorganized the administration of the Frankish church, restored old bishoprics and established new ones, and vigorously upheld Latin Christian theology against its challengers. Pepin III and Charlemagne enriched Frankish monasteries and restored them to compliance with the Benedictine rule. The monasteries in turn provided scribes and advisers for royal service. Charlemagne also presented a broadly conceived program for peacefully introducing Christianity among the pagan Saxons and Slavs.

Believing that the quality of the clergy determined the quality of spiritual life, Charlemagne promoted both classical and Christian education, mandating, for example, a teacher of grammar for each cathedral and a teacher of theology for each archbishop's cathedral. Monastic schools concentrated on the liberal arts, and a special palace school was established for educating the sons of Frankish nobles. Scholars whom Charlemagne recruited for this school built a collection of classical writings that preserved and made available earlier knowledge.

Charlemagne stimulated monasteries to become active centers for producing accurate, hand-copied manuscript books, including the Bible, manuals for the conduct of worship services, and the Benedictine rule for monks that was to form the basis of monastic reforms

Magical Practices in the Carolingian Era

Maleficia [sorcery/witchcraft] appeared in many forms. It could impede the growth of another's grain by magic powers . . . or incantations. It rendered a neighbor's cattle sterile or brought harm on others through making knots in a dead person's girdle. Love potions to excite a husband's passion or attract a lover were made from sperm, menstrual blood, and aphrodisiac plants. . . . Bones of the dead, cinders and ashes, hair, pubic hair, different colored strings, various herbs, snails and snakes were used in maleficia, *sterilizing potions, and abortifacients.*

*By far the most popular magical practices were those designed to protect and cure. Prisoners seeking to be free of their bondage, or peasants who feared that their horses would injure themselves, all recited the formulae preserved in Germanic texts. Sick children were carried to the peak of the roof while medicinal herbs were cooked to the recited incantations. Amulets and phylacteries [protective charms] endowed with particular characteristics were sold to anyone who wanted their protection. . . . Models of human limbs were hung from trees or placed at crossroads to procure the healing of an arm or leg. . . . Divination was practiced . . . by . . . paying heed to the direction of smoke, or examining the excrement or liver of animals, climbing to the rooftops, interpreting dreams or opening books at random. . . . Some of the manuscripts which the monks copied carry the magical squares which predicted the course of an illness by combining the letters of the victim's name and the number of the day on which he fell ill.**

The belief in the efficacy of magic or sorcery is both ancient and stubborn. Even in the face of official disapproval (and sometimes active persecution) by civil and religious authorities, many people have always tried to mobilize magical powers to their own benefit or to the detriment of others. The Carolingian Empire, despite its Christian allegiance, was no exception to this sort of activity.

*Pierre Riché, *Daily Life in the World of Charlemagne,* trans. Jo Ann McNamara (Philadelphia: University of Pennsylvania Press, 1978; orig. 1973), pp. 184–185.

during the next several centuries. The monks also produced manuscripts of classical writers as well as of church fathers. More than 8,000 Carolingian manuscripts still exist, and over 90 percent of surviving Roman literature was passed on to later ages in Carolingian manuscript form. This outburst of intellectual and literary activity is sometimes termed the Carolingian Renaissance (rebirth).

Carolingian art, like literature and education, evolved from religious activity and employed late Roman and contemporary Byzantine models and techniques. For example, books priests used to conduct worship services were beautified by illuminations; that is, separate pictures, elaborately decorated book or chapter titles, or large initial letters using traditional Germanic art forms of animals and interlaces. Builders of Carolingian churches usually followed the Roman basilica style, occasionally roofing the atrium to form a porch or adding an enclosed prayer room above the atrium. The architects of Charlemagne's chapel at his capital city of Aachen copied Byzantine imperial models to produce an octagonal building symbolizing the emperor's divinely aided joining together of earth and heaven; Justinian's church of Hagia Sophia at Constantinople served a similar symbolic purpose. Painting on church walls generally made little use of scriptural themes and human forms in order to avoid the appearance of idolatry.

Europe under Siege: A New Wave of Invaders

As the Carolingian Empire disintegrated in the late ninth century, the face of Europe was transformed by new waves of invaders. The Magyars and Vikings produced widespread destruction and disrupted existing institutions and patterns of living. Amid the resulting disorder, successful resisters to those attackers began to establish new social, economic, and political patterns and to form new centers of European development.

Invited from western Asia by the Byzantines to aid in war against the Bulgars, the Magyars, nomadic ancestors of modern Hungarians, occupied the Hungarian basin of the Danube by 900, and soon were raiding Italy, Burgundy, and other Frankish and Germanic territories.

Crucifixion of Christ. Ornate animals and curvilinear decorative designs typified much Germanic art. Here, the Greek letters *alpha* and *omega* hang suspended from the cross's arms to recall Jesus' words: "I am the beginning and the end." A bird representing the Holy Spirit perches atop the cross.

Another group of invaders, Vikings from Scandinavia, raided widely throughout Europe. Their motives included a desire for plunder; dislike of increasing royal authority in Denmark, Norway, and Sweden; overpopulation; climate change; and sheer love of adventure. The Norwegians raided and established settlements in western England and Ireland. Danish Vikings attacked lands on both sides of the English Channel. They conquered the eastern half of England and also seized land at the mouth of the Seine River in Francia, which became the nucleus of the Duchy of Normandy. Well might western Europeans pray, "From the fury of the Northmen, O Lord deliver us." Swedish Vikings crossed the Baltic and worked their way southward across Russia on the extensive north-south river systems, reaching Persia and Constantinople via the Caspian and Black Seas, respectively. They became so numerous that the Latin name *Rus* (for ruddy) that distinguished them from the resident Slavs became applied to the entire land and all its people.

The Vikings also sailed westward across the North Atlantic and in 874 settled in Iceland, establishing the oldest continuously functioning democratic community. Erik the Red, an exile from Iceland, landed on the island of Greenland, and settlements of Europeans soon followed. In 1000, Erik's son Leif sailed farther west and briefly occupied Vinland, probably northern Newfoundland. As royal authority and Christianization increased in Scandinavian lands during the tenth century, the great age of Viking expansion ended.

The absence of effective imperial power in the disintegrating Carolingian Empire left local leaders to develop their own responses to the invaders of the ninth century. In England, Viking raids and English resistance combined to produce a united monarchy. The Danes destroyed all the Anglo-Saxon kingdoms except Wessex, whose king, Alfred the Great (reigned 871–899), effectively opposed them by combating the Vikings at sea and fortifying and garrisoning towns as defensive strongholds. Gradually, Alfred gained authority over Anglo-Saxon lands in the west of England that had escaped Viking rule. By gathering scholars from various lands, he revived literature and learning in England, creating a solid basis for its future development.

In Italy, independent towns, grown prominent as Carolingian authority waned, led the resistance to Magyar and Muslim invaders. Within these towns, bishops became the principal leaders, building town fortifications and collecting tolls and other monies to pay for them. They secured powers and privileges from kings and exercised control of urban defenses, revenues, and courts. Powerful bishops and strong, independent cities continued to play important roles in subsequent centuries of Italian history.

In the eastern regions of the empire, where Carolingian rule was recent, earlier German tribal divisions reemerged in five large duchies, areas dominated by dukes who seized royal lands and powers and controlled the churches in their districts. When the last Carolingian ruler died in 911, the dukes chose one of their number as king to validate their rights and titles to land and to coordinate common defense measures. In the face of persistent Magyar invasions, an able, new dynasty of Saxon rulers (919–1024) emerged to reassert royal authority over the land, which became known as Germany.

In the Carolingian Empire's western areas, the invasions accelerated decentralization of government, as counts and other nobles offered the only meaningful opposition to the invaders, acquired lands and goods, and usurped royal authority. Although Carolingian kings continued to rule until 987, when the last of the line died without heirs, political followed sexual impotence. In the place of the monarchy, aggressive local lords exercised warfare and defense responsibilities and managed royal courts and revenues.

Feudal Relationships

As Carolingian government deteriorated, nobles seeking to provide protection and administer justice combined two well-established Carolingian practices—the personal relationship of vassalage and the landed relationship of benefice or fief—in a set of relationships, new in the west, called feudalism (from Latin *feudum*, "fief"). In vassalage a free man (the vassal) proclaimed his dependence on and faithfulness to another free man (the lord) and promised to serve him, usually militarily. The lord, in return, granted the vassal useful possession, but not ownership, of land called a benefice or fief. Similarly, in China under the Chou dynasty, lords contributed both revenues and homage to the kings and

Culver Pictures

Viking Ship. This ninth-century vessel could carry approximately forty men. Although shallow of draft, these ships were quite seaworthy, carrying Viking invaders across the seas, along the coasts, and up the rivers of Europe.

CONNECTIONS IN MIGRATION

Vikings

Norse mariners navigated great areas of the Northern Hemisphere from the eighth through the thirteenth centuries. With light but effective boats, they traveled from their homeland— present-day Denmark, Sweden, and Norway— in all directions, trading, raiding, conquering, and settling. They set up kingdoms in England, France, Sicily, and Ukraine. They also settled in Iceland, Greenland, and, for a time, in North America.

Norse raiding parties were small but mobile; they relied on the element of surprise to collect booty and captives, then disappear. The location of Paris, far enough up the river Seine to be safe from Norse raids, is one reason that the city served well as the capital of medieval France.

As the Norse (or Northmen or Normans) began their expansion, they celebrated a polytheistic religion. With the passage of time they adopted Christianity and created a runic alphabet. At later stages, these raiders became migrants and conquerors, settling down to become landowners, merchants, diplomats, churchmen, and rulers. In the eleventh century, the Norman duke of northern France became king of England. The Norman King Roger of Sicily was a devout Christian who nonetheless relied heavily on Muslims in his court.

The Norse founders of Novgorod, not far from present-day St. Petersburg, created a trading post that became the kernel of statehood for the eastern Slavs. These Norse were known as "Rus," from which we now have the term "Russian." From Novgorod and Kiev, Norse fleets voyaged southward across the Black Sea in the ninth and tenth centuries for trade and for raids on Constantinople. By way of the Volga River, they crossed the Caspian Sea and raided the inner coast of Persia.

In the Norse homeland, the Danish and Swedish kingdoms came to dominate most of the territories. Their influence declined in the Mongol era, yet each of them became powerful in trade and conquest from time to time thereafter.

---

1. Reread the material on the Norse in the chapter. Did the Norse at home and abroad do more to build organized society or to tear it down? What similarities did the Norse have with the Mongols? Visit http://www.mnh.si.edu/vikings/start.html, the Smithsonian's online exhibition covering the Viking voyages to North America. Where did the Vikings settle? What evidence of their stay has been found? How does the successful completion of the voyage attest to the seaworthiness of Viking ships?

2. Enter the search term "Vikings" in the InfoTrac Subject Guide. Choose "Periodical references" to find articles on the Vikings. Do you find pieces that modify the popular conception of the Vikings as violent marauders? What are some of the important aspects of the Vikings covered in the articles?

received in return confirmation of their social status and of their fiefdoms.

Counts and dukes held their lands as fiefs of the king, lesser nobles held their estates as vassals of counts or dukes, and they in turn granted smaller fiefs to their own vassals. Hence the same person might be the vassal of a greater lord and the lord of lesser vassals. Thorny complications arose when vassals held fiefs from different lords who became enemies. A woman had no property rights and if, as sole survivor, she inherited lands or money from her father, the property became her husband's.

The personal pledges and obligations between lords and vassals theoretically ended when one of them died, but in practice sons normally assumed the loyalties and duties of their fathers. Typically, a vassal owed not only his own personal military service, but often also that of additional knights from his own estates. In addition, he was expected to serve in the lord's court of justice and to feed and house the lord and his traveling companions when required. Vassals also helped to raise a ransom if their lord was captured and gave the lord money on the occasion of the knighting of his eldest son, the marriage of his eldest daughter, and the succession of a son to his father's fief. In return, the lord provided the vassal with military protection and justice through his court.

At first, nobles held large estates whereas lesser vassals, often termed knights, held few if any lands; the nobles led armies into battle whereas knights followed and obeyed. As time passed, knights gradually gained extensive lands, privileges, and jurisdictional rights and married into old noble families, eventually forming a single aristocracy.

Lesser lords and vassals were armed and trained as warriors to preserve the privileges of communities and maintain the safety of the church, but most fought to acquire land and wealth or for the sheer joy of fighting. The armed and mounted knight dominated offensive warfare. Defensive warfare centered on castles, the nobles' fortified homes, which had evolved by the twelfth century into structures built of stone.

Europe in the Middle Ages

Society is divided into three orders. The ecclesiastical order forms one body. The nobles are the warriors and the protectors of churches; they defend all the people, great and small. The unfree is the other class. This unfortunate group possesses nothing without suffering. Supplies and clothing are provided for everyone by the unfree because no free man can live without them.

*Therefore the city of God which is believed to be one is divided into three; some pray, others fight, and the others work. These three groups live together and could not endure separation. The services of one of them allows the work of the other two. Each, by turn, lends its support to all.**

*Adalberon, "Carmen ad Rotbertum regem," in Robert Boutruche, *Seigneurie et féodalité* (Paris: Aubier, 1959), pp. 371–372, trans. in Norton Downs, ed., *The Medieval Pageant* (Princeton: Van Nostrand, 1964), p. 93.

This description, written about 1000, reflects the traditional medieval view of European society as an unchanging interrelationship of three orders or estates. (The terms *medieval* and *Middle Ages* refer to the conventional western division of history into ancient, medieval, and modern.) While this view accurately described many aspects of medieval society, it did not take into account a number of important changes that were underway, changes that would dramatically move Western society away from this three-class division. The present section examines developments in Europe in the period between 900 and 1350.

Economic and Social Changes in the Countryside

From 1000 to 1300, the economy of Europe developed and prospered. Available farmland tripled, and the food supply increased notably, bringing up the population. Europeans resettled lands that had been depopulated by the ninth- and tenth-century invasions and also opened new lands for farming, especially forested and marginal areas, those east of the Elbe River in central Europe, and lands conquered from the Muslims in the Iberian Peninsula. To ensure productivity, medieval farmers adopted the three-field system of cultivation in which only a third (rather than a half) of the land lay fallow (to restore fertility) during the year. Technological improvements like the heavy plow, the shoulder collar for horses, metal horseshoes, and more efficient water and windmills contributed to the jump in food supply. Between 500 and 1300 Europe's population grew from 25 million to more than 70 million.

During the fourteenth century, however, Europe's increasing economic and demographic growth took a sharp reverse. The climate became colder and rainier, causing harvests to shrink and prices to soar. This was a warlike period in which ravaging armies destroyed crops, barns, and mills. Famine became a fact of life. Adding to these troubles, bubonic plague (the "Black Death") ravaged the population. Between 1348 and 1354, perhaps one-third of all Europeans died as the plague spread, in the words of one contemporary, "like fire when it comes in contact with large masses of combustibles." The population did not recover fully till about 1600.

Whether times were easy or hard, peasant farmers and their life pattern constituted the core of medieval society. Most of the farming people of Europe lived in villages ranging from ten to several hundred peasant families, located in manors, units of political governance and economic exploitation controlled by ecclesiastical establishments or by secular nobles. The manors were organized so that they would contain enough villages to produce nearly everything needed by their lords.

The workforce on a manor consisted primarily of families of serfs, semi-free persons linked to the lord and to the land who could not be sold away from their lands. Their village was a cluster of huts surrounded by fields. Each family was assigned several plots or strips, some on the more fertile and some on the less fertile land available to the village. On these plots each family produced food that it used for its own consumption, barter, payment of tithes to the church, and dues to the lord. There was also pasture where plow animals, sheep, and cattle grazed and a wooded area on which the peasants gathered fuel and building materials and where pigs foraged. Usually there was a stream that supplied fish and powered the water mill. Typically there were none of the schools, hospitals, or other amenities sometimes found in medieval towns. The parish church was the center of activity, where villagers celebrated religious holidays, baptisms, and marriages; in the churchyard they found their final resting place. Church bells provided the only timekeeping most people knew, and feast days marked the year's seasons.

Each farm family retained about half its own produce after paying the lord a percentage of the crop for the use of the pasture and woods and fees for the use of the lord's mill and oven. The lord also collected payments when a serf's son inherited his father's holdings or when a serf's daughter married outside the manor. Moreover, the church collected its tithe (10 percent). Serfs also performed labor services for the lord, working his land and repairing roads or carrying firewood.

Art Resource, NY

Medieval Workers. Animals and agricultural workers led a busy existence in medieval times. Oxen fitted with shoulder collars draw a wheeled plow, mainstay of medieval farming. In the left background a planter spreads seeds from the bag slung over his shoulder. On the right, two workers plant a vineyard on a hillside, while the wood gatherers trudge past with their loaded basket. On the far hill a shepherd tends a flock of sheep.

By 1300 some lords, seeking to attract workers to bring new lands under cultivation, offered milder terms of service to peasants and improved the working conditions of their serfs. Some freed them from labor obligations in return for cash payments and allowed them to pay rent in money rather than crops. On occasion, lords granted peasant communities charters that freed them from performing the obligations of serfs and permitted them to pay their dues collectively rather than individually. As wages and prices rose in the West during the fifteenth century, manorial lords sought to increase their cash incomes by raising cattle or sheep or growing commercial agricultural products such as dyestuffs, which required fewer laborers and gave high returns for low costs. Thus by 1500, most western European peasants were no longer serfs owing labor and goods to their lords but renters who had traded the security of serfdom for the freedom to earn or to lose money and livelihood. The gradual waning of feudalism in western Europe resembled what had happened in China during the late Chou dynasty.

While western European peasants were enjoying greater freedom, eastern European peasants were losing what freedom they had. The lords in that area preferred to grow grain for export to western Europe and took advantage of fourteenth- and fifteenth-century wars and other upheavals to acquire large landholdings. They enforced manorial obligations and imposed serfdom even upon formerly free peasants.

In the West, meanwhile, freedom proved to be a mixed blessing, as lords sought to wring maximum rents from their tenants. Moreover, the ravages of war and the taxes of monarchs fell most heavily on peasants, since clergy and nobles were largely exempt from royal taxation. Peasant discontent with the status quo sometimes exploded into rebellions, which were easily defeated by regular armies. Still, the peasants' grievances persisted, and reappeared to trouble later lords and rulers.

The Growth of Trade and the Development of Towns

European commercial activity expanded dramatically from the tenth through the fourteenth century. Whereas early medieval trade had been conducted by local merchants who exchanged perishable items and local commodities for salt, wine, and metals in village markets, by the eleventh century long-distance trade had begun to revive.

Descendants of Viking raiders now traded across the northern seas, bartering furs, timber, fish, and wax for textiles, grain, and wine. To the east, they established commercial relations with the Byzantine and Islamic Empires via the Baltic Sea and the river routes of Russia, trading for Islamic silver or Byzantine gold. By the thirteenth century, Germans had replaced Scandinavians as the primary merchants of northern Europe. The northern trade was primarily in staples: grain, butter, cheese, fish, timber, metals, and salt. German trading towns united in a Hansa (confederation) to preserve their dominant position in commerce.

In the ninth and tenth centuries, Italian port cities, particularly Venice, revived the Mediterranean trade. Byzantine merchant citizens in some Italian port towns traded easily with both the Byzantine Empire and the Muslims; religious differences between eastern and western Christians and between Christians and Muslims posed no obstacles when it came to commercial relations. During the eleventh century, Genoa and Pisa wrested control of the western Mediterranean from the Muslims, but by the late fourteenth century Venice had taken control of the lucrative trade with the East.

The eastern Mediterranean trade was based upon a sophisticated intercontinental commercial network. Venetian merchants exported slaves, timber, iron, and tools to the

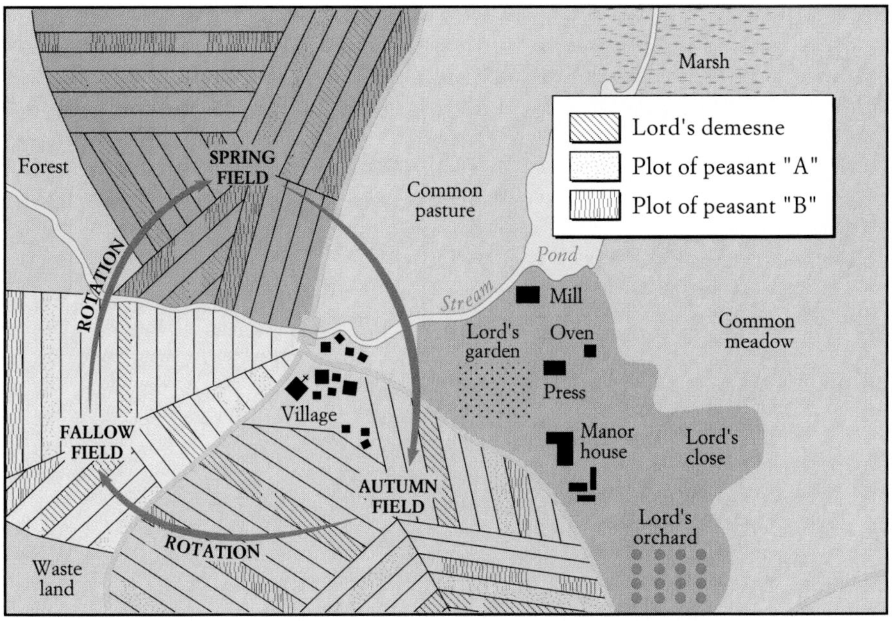

Map 5.4 A Manor. The noble lord dominated the manor; he controlled the best land and the essential services of oven, mill, and press. The operation of the three-field system and the division of land into strips prompted villagers to work together at common tasks.

lands east of the Mediterranean and imported furs, silks, spices, and perfumes from the Byzantines and Muslims, who had brought them from India and China. For a brief time the Mongols permitted Europeans to bypass Islamic middlemen (see Chapter 8) and to trade directly with East Asia. The Venetians sold the Asian luxuries to the upper classes in western Europe, often investing the proceeds in new manufacturing establishments (see below) that were beginning to spring up in Italy.

From the northern and southern seas, trade quickly expanded inland, and by the late twelfth century merchants were moving continuously along Europe's rivers and roads, and commerce was fast displacing agriculture as the most dynamic force in European economic life. During the disastrous fourteenth century, European commercial activity faltered, as population decline diminished markets and wars interfered with commerce.

Manufacturing came later than trade in European economic development. Medieval "manufacturers" were typically craftsmen who produced goods in their own shops and sold them directly to the public. Early manufacturers employed individuals in building construction and textile making, which developed during the medieval period using complex systems of organization. Members of the building trades found employment erecting churches and public buildings in growing towns and cities. As many were wage earners and owned neither the materials nor the tools they used, they resembled factory laborers. Some entrepreneurs used a "domestic" system in which they distributed raw materials to and collected finished products from workers who labored in their homes rather than in a factory.

Enlarged agricultural productivity and increasing commercial activity sparked a growth of town life. Various forms of the German word *Burg* ("fortress")—burg, burgh, bourg, or borough—came to apply to the town, whose inhabitants were called burghers, later known as the bourgeoisie. Compared to the countryside, towns displayed a volatile juxtaposition of individuals and groups in close quarters. Besides merchants and artisans, there were free peasants, runaway serfs, and ambitious younger sons of lesser nobles, as well as masters and students at schools or universities.

Medieval cities and towns were small by present-day European standards. A substantial eleventh-century trading city, such as Bruges, might have only 5,000 inhabitants. Towns grew with commerce, and by 1300 several Italian cities had 100,000 inhabitants each, and Venice held 200,000 persons. Elsewhere, Paris had a population of 80,000, London half that. The Black Death struck cities exceptionally hard, killing up to half their inhabitants.

As the new elements in medieval society, town-dwelling merchants and manufacturers had to struggle to obtain acceptance for their activities, which did not fit the traditional concept of the three estates. To obtain freedom from servile and burdensome tax obligations, they sought charters from the local lord of the land. A lord might grant a charter for a money payment, but sometimes towns had to defeat lords in battle to obtain such documents. A charter usually provided the town's inhabitants freedom from servile obligations, typically permitting them to hold land and buildings for a money rent and forbidding the arbitrary seizure of their property. It also allowed burghers to maintain courts and make laws.

Burghers in northern Italy, whose towns were under the jurisdiction of the Holy Roman Emperor, went still further, seizing control of the cities' defenses, revenues, and

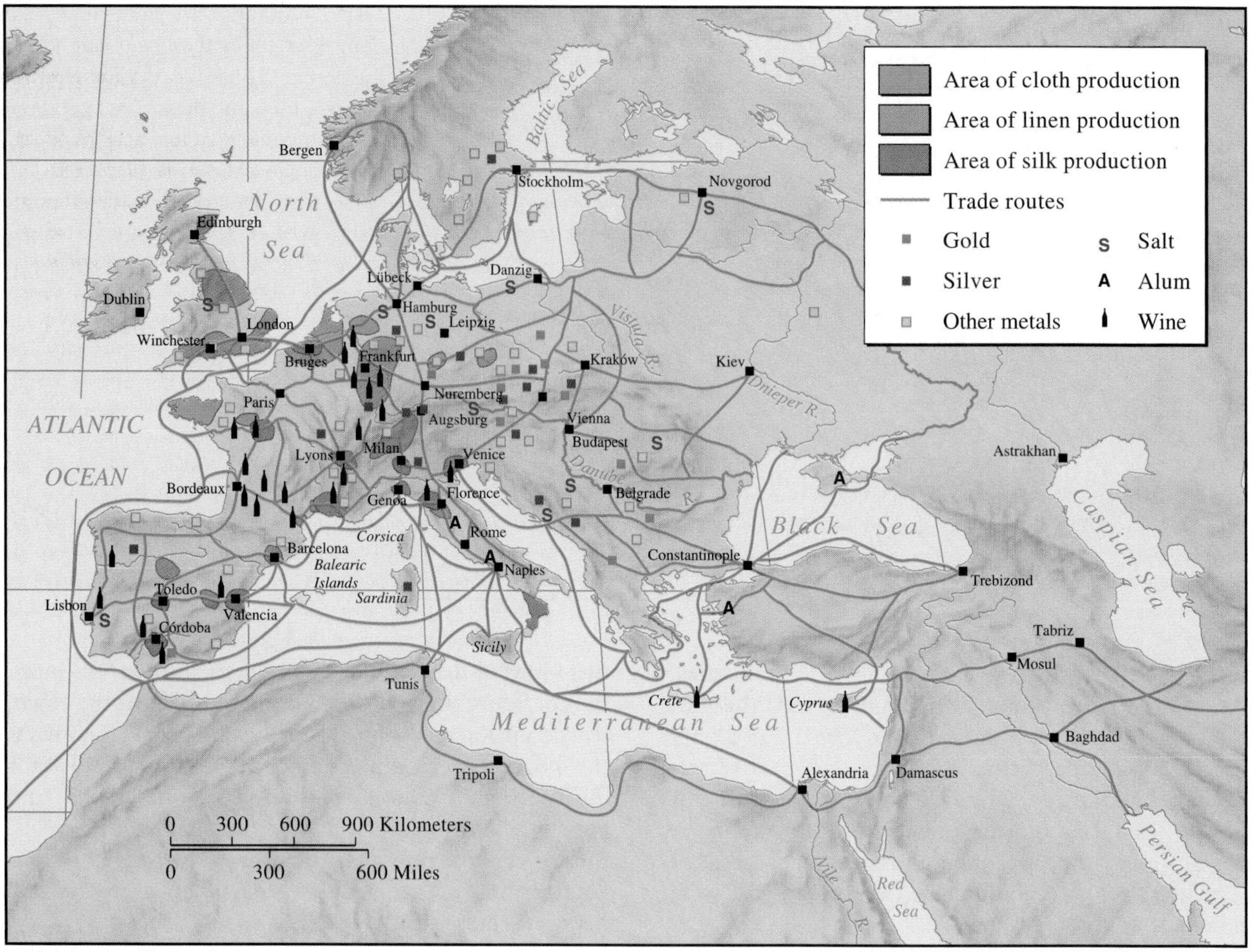

Map 5.5 Medieval Trade Routes. By the end of the thirteenth century, trade routes covered most of western and central Europe. Vikings in early centuries and the German Hansa later controlled commerce in the northern seas. In the south, the Italian cities of Genoa and Venice dominated Mediterranean trade. Overland routes used rivers whenever possible to reduce transportation costs. In eastern Europe, however, trade routes were few, and the economy remained primarily agricultural.

courts, and extending their authority over the surrounding countryside. City leaders began to develop important aspects of a new political order: corporate authority, delegated power, and representative government.

To regulate economic activity, craftsmen and merchants formed "guilds." Merchants' guilds protected their members' interests against outsiders and secured each member a share in the trade available, generally by regulating prices and competition. Similarly, artisans set up craft guilds that supervised wages, prices, labor conditions, quality standards, and methods and amounts of production. Socially, guilds conducted banquets and sponsored religious festivals. They also saw to the proper burial of deceased members and cared for widows and orphans.

Women as well as men found economic opportunities in craft guilds. By 1300, at least 15 of 100 Paris guilds, including garment makers and workers in silk and embroidery, were entirely female. After 1300, however, economic activities for women were increasingly restricted or eliminated. The economic decline of German towns in the period between 1300 and 1500 was due in part to the suppression of flourishing female industries and the replacement of skilled women by unskilled men.

The Theory and Practice of Christianity

Like kings and princes who strove to create stable and effective governments, medieval religious leaders endeavored to centralize the organization and improve the quality of the medieval church. Although by 1000 the rulers of most European peoples had adopted Christianity for themselves and their subjects, the problems of ordering Christian society remained formidable. Viking and Magyar invasions had destroyed not only churches and monasteries but also ecclesiastical institutions, as monarchs converted bishops into vassals with fiefs and diverted the resources of the church to private, family, and "state" purposes.

Significant religious abuses arose from the feudalization of the church and the accompanying lay domination of church offices. Christians frequently decried the ineptitude and immorality of the clergy, who were often ill-educated and appointed for political rather than spiritual reasons. Such appointees sought personal advancement and the control of ecclesiastical property, while showing a shallow, mechanical attitude toward religious life. Many ignored the church's rule of celibacy and either married or had sexual partners, creating further possibilities for the diversion of church lands.

By 1000, efforts to reform the church to eliminate such abuses were underway. As an alternative to local lords controlling the church, eleventh-century reformers created a centralized church bureaucracy under papal control, with its own officers, law, and resources. By the early thirteenth century, the popes directed an extensive bureaucracy through the papal Curia, which was staffed by well-trained clerics in specialized departments handling correspondence and records, finances, judicial cases, and the application of church law. Popes directly asserted their authority over lower levels of church administration either through correspondence or by special emissaries.

A formidable tool for eradicating error in this period was the judicial process known as the Inquisition. Twelfth-century popes ordered bishops to conduct inquests concerning heretics within their dioceses and to punish the guilty by excommunication. Pope Innocent III added confiscation of goods and property to the punishment of heretics. The accused were denied legal counsel, interrogated by torture, and required to prove their repentance by identifying accomplices. Although some found guilty were sentenced to penances or prison terms, the Inquisition was less bloodthirsty than has been presumed; most convicted heretics were in fact put to death by governments, not by the church.

As in earlier centuries, the regimen of the stricter monastic orders, such as the Cluniacs, revitalized monastic discipline. Another monastic group, the Cistercian order, popularized the role of Mary, the mother of Jesus, who became the object of special devotion and veneration as the Blessed Virgin. Important religious feasts were established in her honor and churches and cathedrals were dedicated to her. Jesus Christ's love and compassion could be secured through Mary, who would intercede on behalf of all sinners. The series of prayers known as the rosary deepened popular devotion to Mary.

Pressing religious needs in towns and cities and the threat of heresy prompted the development of mendicant (begging) orders during the early thirteenth century. Mendicant friars rejected life in monasteries and worked in the world while living under a spiritual rule. Relying on donations for the necessities of life, they preached and, by performing charitable deeds, made Christianity relevant to the lives of town dwellers. Dominican friars were broadly educated and specialized in preaching and teaching; they subsequently joined university faculties. Dominicans energetically preached the Gospel to non-Christian Europeans and sought conversions in eastern Mediterranean lands and India.

The Franciscans, founded by Francis of Assisi (1182–1226), espoused a world-embracing joyousness; they spread rapidly throughout Europe, and some became missionaries in Syria and North Africa. They engaged in scholarship and university teaching, forming notable centers of theological study in Paris and Oxford.

Many women, too, found religious withdrawal from the world attractive. Besides professed nuns, lay sisters

The Growth of a Town

*After this, because of the work or needs of those living in the chateau, there began to stream in merchants—that is, dealers in precious goods—who set themselves up in front of the gate, at the chateau's bridge; then there followed tavern-keepers, then inn-keepers to provide the food and lodging for those who came to do business in the presence of the prince, who was often there. Houses began to be built and inns to be made ready, where those were to be lodged who could not be put up inside the chateau. . . . So many dwellings accumulated there that right away it became a large town.**

These words of a contemporary observer describe the beginnings of Bruges (originally Brugge, "the bridge"), one of northern Europe's foremost medieval towns. In central and eastern Europe, outside the territories of the old Roman Empire, new towns were usually founded by colonies of merchants who settled around a fortified stronghold, such as a castle or monastery, strategically located on a major trade route or at the intersection of two or more routes. Such settlers needed services that others came to provide, and settlements quickly grew into towns.

**Documents relatifs à l'histoire de l'industrie et du commerce en France*, ed. Gustave Fagniez, *Collection de textes pour servir à l'étude et l'enseignement de l'histoire*, Vol. I (Paris: Picard, 1898), pp. 54–55, trans. Carolly Erickson, *The Records of Medieval Europe* (Garden City: Doubleday, 1971), pp. 152–153.

from peasant or artisan families performed many menial tasks. Nunneries gave their residents both self-esteem and the respect of society. They also offered women good education and the chance to use organizational and management skills that might otherwise be wasted.

By the thirteenth century, Roman Catholicism was widely prevalent among Europeans, and the beliefs of medieval Christians formed a coherent and integrated system. They believed God was one, almighty, all-knowing, just, and merciful. The universe, created by God, was orderly, and in it human beings had a special place and destiny. By sinning, people had disobeyed God and thus had lost their original righteousness and God's supernatural grace, forfeiting their hope of heaven. Sin rendered men and women incapable of doing good by their own efforts. Therefore, God had sent Jesus Christ to redeem humans and qualify them for heaven. As the custodian of God's grace, the church was an essential intermediary between God and the faithful. By the seven sacraments, the church claimed to bring God's grace to all members at critical junctures of life. Baptism cleansed individuals of original sin and initiated them into the Christian fellowship. At puberty, confirmation reaffirmed a person's membership in the church and gave one additional grace for adult life. Two people might unite their lives in the sacrament of Holy Matrimony, or a person might "marry" the church in holy orders. Extreme unction (anointing with consecrated oil) prepared one for events after death. Christians could receive forgiveness from sin's consequences through the sacrament of penance. They could even receive Jesus Christ's body by partaking of the Eucharist, in which bread and wine

Execution of Heretics. Frequently, as in this thirteenth-century painting, heretics were executed by burning. At left, King Philip II of France sits on his horse. Note the scaffold (upper right) for mass hangings.

were miraculously changed by means of the sacrificial mass into Christ's body and blood.

Saints, too, were believed to intercede with God on behalf of humans. Each town, each trade, even each disease, had its appropriate saint, and prayers and devotion to them were supposed to be especially efficacious. A lively traffic in holy relics (remains of saints) developed. A pilgrim to Venice about 1400 reported seeing there the arm of one saint, the staff of another, the ear of St. Paul, and a tooth of Goliath.

Pilgrimage, journeys to holy sites, although arduous and dangerous, also became increasingly popular acts of devotion and a means to secure grace. Geoffrey Chaucer's *Canterbury Tales*, written in the 1390s, vividly describes the members of such an expedition. A pilgrimage combined religious duty and holiday relaxation; hence pilgrimage routes came to be carefully arranged. Rome and Jerusalem attracted pilgrims from throughout Christendom.

The extent of popular piety, however, should not be exaggerated. The illiterate masses remained uninstructed about basic Christian beliefs and minimally involved in religious observances. Pre-Christian religious practices persisted in many places. Demons and mysterious powers were thought to fill the world and to require appeasement. Persons skilled in "white" magic, knowledgeable in healing by judicious use of herbs and "home remedies," and able to "see" what the future had in store were in great demand.

Jews in Medieval European Life

After Rome had dispersed the Jews in the first and second centuries C.E., they settled throughout West Asia and around the Mediterranean. Life in Christian lands, certainly as compared to Islamic Spain, was difficult and often dangerous for Jews. They were excluded from most occupations, except trading and moneylending; the latter was forbidden to Christians by the church. For self-serving reasons most Christians unreasonably believed that Jews were collectively responsible for Christ's death, that they were active servants of Satan, that they murdered Christian boys and used their blood for secret rituals, and that they poisoned wells and spread disease through the land. Christians executed, lynched, and banished large numbers of Jews. The warriors of the First Crusade massacred Jews in several Rhineland towns. The Third Lateran Council (1179) forbade Christians to live near Jews, thus spurring the growth of the ghetto, a walled section of a city in which Jews were compelled to live. European rulers in need of money exploited popular feeling by expelling Jews and seizing their abandoned property.

Beginning in the ninth and tenth centuries, the ongoing Christian reconquest of Spain forced many Jews to leave Spain in flight from both Muslim and Christian persecution. They joined meager groups of their coreligionists in the north to establish vigorous centers of Jewish life in southern and northeastern France and in the German Rhineland. Other Iberian Jews found refuge in North Africa and Turkey. As persecutions continued in western Europe, many Jews migrated into Poland and Lithuania, forming a major new Jewish population center there.

Feudal Monarchy in Western Europe

During the period from 900 to 1300, kings in some parts of Europe managed to replace the severely decentralized political order of the ninth and tenth centuries with more organized political structures known as feudal monarchies. The office of the king was endorsed by church and scripture, the person of the king was considered sacred, and kings continued to receive honor and prestige. Their primary functions were to provide justice and enforce the king's peace within their realms and to raise and lead national armies to resist external foes.

In addition, as previously discussed, feudal monarchs were overlords of the greater and lesser nobles within the system of feudal relationships, a system they exploited to extend their controls. Feudal kings had the right not only to demand various services and dues in return for their grants but also to recover possession of fiefs forfeited by unfaithful vassals or lost by a vassal's failure to produce heirs.

Despite many rights and responsibilities, feudal monarchs did not have direct authority over the mass of their subjects. Under the feudal structure, monarchs had contact primarily with their chief vassals and the inhabitants of the royal family's own domains. Between the kings and the remainder of their subjects were various levels of lesser vassals, many of whom exercised the rights to wage war, coin money, and dispense justice. Feudal kings thus exercised overlordship while sharing power, rather than wielding unlimited direct authority.

Diffused government was another distinctive aspect of feudal monarchy. In the autocratic and centralized Roman and Byzantine Empires, the ruler used an extensive military and civilian bureaucracy to carry out government services. In contrast, medieval European feudal monarchs, like the Chinese feudal monarchs of the Chou era, governed through a series of relationships in which both they and their vassals personally performed essential public services, administered justice, and waged war.

Feudal monarchies lacked the resources to provide more than limited services. The king derived income primarily from the royal domains and estates he personally owned, feudal payments from vassals, fines, and monies paid by certain churches and monasteries. A council composed of the king's great vassals formally recognized a new king, furnished him with advice and counsel, and judged certain important cases in his name. Between meetings, a smaller body of officials carried on council functions. The great vassals administered local government theoretically in the name of the king but in fact often quite independently.

Feudal monarchy had a varied history. The Holy Roman Empire, inheriting the eastern areas of the former Carolingian Empire, was an example of a feudal monarchy that failed. In the late Middle Ages, the empire was headed by a succession of German kings who engaged in a shifting power struggle with the popes. Although early German rulers succeeded in creating a strong feudal monarchy, their additional imperial responsibilities complicated the task of their successors. Emperors had duties in both Italy and Germany, but usually lacked the resources to make their power truly effective in both places.

The Holy Roman Empire had little significance in European political and religious developments after the death of Frederick II (reigned 1212–1250). Although it eventually expanded to embrace an area as large as that ruled by Charlemagne, the empire itself was merely a loose union of principalities and states. The medieval ideal of an earthly empire peaceably cooperating with the church's dominions remained illusory.

On the other hand, by combining features of Anglo-Saxon and Norman society, England initially became an extremely successful feudal monarchy. During long years of struggle against the Danes, Anglo-Saxon institutions gained strength and maturity, while the descendants of the Danes in Normandy developed efficient feudal governing arrangements there. William of Normandy fused the two sets of institutional relationships by conquering England in 1066. England's small size, its lack of internal divisions, and the swiftness and thoroughness of William I's conquests made its experience unique.

During the twelfth century, England's royal administration became more elaborate and efficient as Henry II (reigned 1154–1189) made England Europe's best-governed state. He closely supervised royal officials and established some government departments at a permanent royal capital at Westminster, near London. Under Henry, royal law replaced a previous patchwork of local laws and customs with a common law governing all English subjects and made justice uniform as well as equitable throughout England.

Throughout most of the thirteenth century, Henry's successors exhibited neither his ability nor his interest in government, and royal authority diminished. The barons forced King John (reigned 1199–1216) to issue in 1215 a Great Charter (*Magna Carta* in Latin). This committed kings to obtain baronial consent before levying new taxes, to administer justice according to established procedures rather than in an arbitrary and capricious manner, and to recognize and permit subjects to enjoy various rights and liberties. Later generations viewed the Magna Carta as a guarantee of fundamental human rights for all.

The reign of Edward I (1272–1307) saw the development of the English Parliament. Edward summoned barons, prelates, royal judges, administrators, shire knights, and members of town governments to parliaments, or formal conferences, to obtain advice on important issues and to support him in times of crisis. The knights and town representatives began to meet separately from the barons, and thereby laid the basis for the division into a House of Commons and a House of Lords. Through the English common law and the operations of Parliament, English kings and their subjects defined their respective rights and responsibilities and forged elements of a national unity.

In France, feudal monarchy developed more slowly than in England, but eventually became a model for other European lands. The reign of Philip IV (1285–1314) brought the development of the medieval French monarchy to its apex. Philip brought additional territories under royal control and consolidated the royal system of justice by making the court of appeals (the Parlement of Paris) its center. The success of his move to tax the French clergy convincingly demonstrated how powerful and secure the French monarchy had become.

To obtain public support for his opposition to the pope, Philip created the Estates General, a parliament-like body composed of members of the three great social classes, or estates: the clergy, nobles, and townspeople. French monarchs used the body as a sounding board for royal policy and a means of stirring up support for royal decisions. However, the Estates General was never permitted to gain the authority that the English Parliament possessed. It had no power base from which to bargain with the king, and never became an integral part of the French government. In France, the crown remained the one great unifying concept, and nobles retained provincial or regional rather than national interests.

The failure of feudal monarchy in the Holy Roman Empire long postponed the development of national unity in Germany and Italy. By contrast, in England and France, the success of feudal monarchy led in varying degrees to strong national states at a comparatively early date.

The Spiritual and Intellectual Life of the Later Middle Ages

During the eleventh and twelfth centuries, expanding royal bureaucracy, an increasingly complex ecclesiastical organization, and reviving commercial activity created a growing demand for educated persons to perform clerical and administrative tasks. Before 1000, most education in Europe had taken place in schools set up in cathedrals or monasteries. In response to the new demand, schools revised their curricula to stress study of the seven liberal arts derived from Greco-Roman civilization: grammar, logic or dialec-

Piety and Pleasure in Latin Poetry

Nigher still, and still more nigh
Draws the day of Prophecy,
Doom'd to melt the earth and sky

Oh, what trembling there shall be,
When the world its Judge shall see,
Coming in dread majesty!

Now the books are open spread;
Now the writing must be read,
Which condemns the quick and dead.

Now, before the Judge severe
Hidden things must all appear;
*Nought can pass unpunish'd here.**

In the third place, I will speak
Of the tavern's pleasure;
Nor shall I find it till I greet
Angels without measure,
Singing requiems for the souls
In eternal leisure
In the public-house to die
Is my resolution;
Let wine to my lips be nigh
At life's dissolution:
That will make the angels cry,
With glad elocution,
"Grant this toper, God on high,
*Grace and absolution!***

Both poems treat the theme of life's end, but in markedly different manners. The first, part of the majestic *Dies Irae (Day of Wrath)* presents the somberness of the Last Judgment in words, meter, and rhyme. The second presents a very different attitude toward life, which the poet's technique helps to emphasize. Both moods were part of medieval life.

*F. J. E. Raby, *A History of Christian-Latin Poetry from the Beginnings to the Close of the Middle Ages*, 2d ed. (Oxford: Clarendon Press, 1953), p. 443.

**John Addington Symonds, ed. and trans., *Wine, Women, and Song: Medieval Latin Students' Songs* (1884; rpt. New York: AMS Press, 1974), pp. 65–66.

tic, rhetoric, arithmetic, geometry, astronomy, and music. By this time, a flood of new knowledge, primarily from the classical Greeks but transmitted and enlarged by Muslim and Jewish scholars, had become available. As artisans and merchants had done previously, scholars organized themselves into guilds known as universities (from Latin *universitas,* meaning "guild" or "society").

The term *university* came to mean a group of scholars working in close proximity and providing a basic program of instruction in the seven liberal arts and in one or more of the higher disciplines of theology, law, or medicine. By completing the six- to eight-year program, a student obtained a master's degree and a license to teach. Bachelor's programs of four to five years' duration developed later, but did not authorize their holders to teach. Universities were highly mobile, and relations between them and their hometowns were frequently strained and occasionally violent. Sometimes students and masters left town and established separate universities elsewhere. Gradually, wealthy patrons endowed colleges and universities with buildings and funds to pay for housing, feeding, and instructing students.

In northern Europe, the focus of study was theology, and scholars labored to improve their understanding of the Christian faith. During the eleventh century, some investigated the value of human reason in comprehending religious truth. Anselm of Bec (1033–1109), who later became archbishop of Canterbury, emphasized the use of logical reasoning in theology, even as a method to prove God's existence. Still, he ultimately subordinated reason to faith: "I do not seek to understand that I may believe, but I believe that I may understand; for this I also believe, that unless I believe I will not understand." By contrast, Peter Abelard (1079–1142), insisted that "by doubting we are led to question, and by questioning we arrive at the truth."

Scholars called "Scholastics" (because they worked in the medieval schools) responded to a challenge posed by the work of Aristotle. The most influential Scholastic thinker was Thomas Aquinas (1225–1274), who, in his massive *Summa Theologica (Summary of Theology),* recognized theology and philosophy as separate realms of knowledge and maintained that properly conducted rational inquiry would support the principles of revelation.

As works of Jewish, Islamic, and Greek philosophy were translated into Latin after their piecemeal recovery from Byzantium and formerly Islamic lands in the twelfth century, studies in logic expanded. Aristotle's *Organon,*

Universitätsbibliothek Heidelberg

Love Scene. Troubadour poets sang of the loves of lords and ladies like the aristocratic couple in this illustration from a fifteenth-century German manuscript. The bird is a falcon, trained by nobles in hunting for sport.

with its emphasis on syllogism and deductive and inductive logic, provided Scholasticism a much needed tool; but Aristotle's rationalism also challenged scholars to harmonize the findings of natural knowledge with the conclusions of religious faith.

Science became another prominent area of medieval intellectual activity, especially with the translation of Greek and Arabic scientific works during the eleventh and twelfth centuries. During the thirteenth century, Roger Bacon (1214–1294), among others, made Oxford a major center of scientific studies. Bacon promoted an inductive investigation method involving observation and experimentation with appropriate instruments and methods. He described the nerve system of the eye, made magnifying glasses, and proposed high-technology warfare employing gigantic mirrors to focus the sun's rays and incinerate opponents.

Medieval Literature, Art, and Architecture

In addition to numerous scholarly writings, medieval writers composed a great quantity and variety of imaginative literature. Several Latin hymns from this period, such as the *Dies Irae (Day of Wrath)* are still sung in churches today. Secular writers also used Latin to produce nonreligious poetry about all aspects of life.

In both quantity and artistic quality, poetry in vernacular languages such as French, German, and English became more important than Latin poetry. During the eleventh century, northern French minstrels began to compose *chansons de geste* (songs of great deeds) and to sing them for audiences of nobles. These action-packed narratives vividly described battles, usually against non-Christian foes, and praised bravery in battle, loyalty to the lord, and generosity to all (including the minstrel!). In French, the *Song of Roland* related with much fictional elaboration a bloody battle between Saracens (Spanish Muslims) and a detachment of Charlemagne's army ambushed in the pass at Roncevaux in the Pyrenees mountains. Its heroic characters became as well-known as those of the *Iliad* and the *Aeneid*. Epics soon appeared in other languages: the Spanish *Song of the Cid*, for example, told of the noble deeds of the eleventh-century heroic "Lord Champion" in the golden age of medieval chivalry. Although these poems and the music of the minstrels often glorified Christian victories against the Muslims, they were often based on forms and images copied from Islamic societies, particularly in Spain.

Meanwhile, minstrels known as troubadours composed lyric poetry in the Provençal dialect of southern France. Troubadour lyrics elaborated an entire art of love that emphasized a lover's good manners and refinement rather than skills in battle and induced nobles to acquire some knowledge of music, poetry, and history. The idea of selecting a marriage partner on the basis of love and serving her faithfully for years made the marriages of some nobles more than business transactions.

A third literary form, the romance, grew from the interaction of troubadour and *chanson de geste* traditions. Romances generally started from a theme or a person of the remote past, but completely disregarded historical accuracy in their treatments. A prominent figure in the romances was Arthur, a semilegendary sixth-century English king who, by the twelfth century, had become a literary archetype of the ideal monarch. Arthur's court at Camelot, full of charming ladies and chivalrous knights, became the imaginary setting for religious sentiment and romantic love.

In addition to epics, lyrics, and romances for noble audiences, medieval writers produced fables, fabliaux, and dramas for town dwellers. Fables were brief moralistic stories featuring animals that symbolized people and their characteristics. Many popular fables came from France and related the exploits of Reynard the Fox, a wily character who consistently outwits his moral but stupid adversaries. *Fabliaux* were satirical poems depicting lives of ordinary people with vigorous and coarse humor while ridiculing conventional morality. In these forerunners of

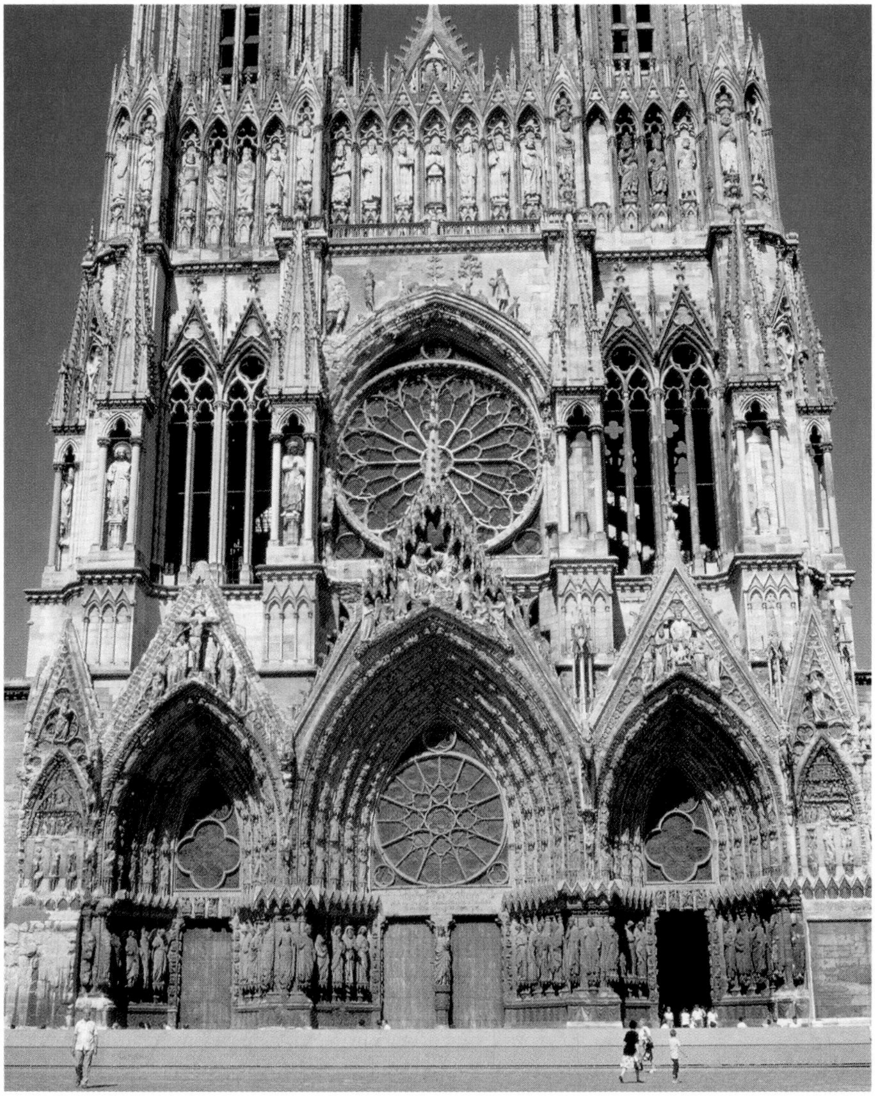

Ulf Sjöstedt/FPC International

Façade of Rheims Cathedral. Elaborate decoration was a typical feature of Gothic architecture and sculpture; note especially the magnificent stained glass window above the central doorway.

the modern short story, all priests and monks are gluttons and lechers, all women are lustful and easily seduced, and praise goes to those who outwit others.

Medieval drama developed from performances in church during religious ceremonies, illustrating in particular events associated with Christmas and Easter. In time, new scenes and incidents were invented, stock characterizations and crude scenery developed, and guilds assumed responsibility for play production. By the thirteenth century, such morality plays emphasized three distinct subjects: saints' lives, biblical stories, and the personification of correct behavior.

Although French and German remained the leading vernacular literatures into the thirteenth century, an Italian, Dante Alighieri (1265–1321), produced the greatest medieval literary masterpiece, *The Divine Comedy.* It describes a journey through hell, purgatory, and paradise, concluding in the awesome presence of God. Dante's guides for that journey were, respectively, Virgil, a spokesman for classical rationalism, Beatrice, an object of romantic and unconsummated but now spiritualized love, and St. Bernard, the epitome of Christian sanctity. The result is a majestic vision of the entire medieval universe.

The artists and artisans of the medieval era created impressive works of architecture, sculpture, and painting that matched the accomplishments of the scholars and writers. So many churches were built (more than 1,500 in France alone during the eleventh century) that a writer shortly after 1000 remarked that the earth was being covered with a white robe of churches.

The architectural style of the eleventh and twelfth centuries is called Romanesque because it used Roman-type building materials and architectural features. Medieval builders employed the Roman basilica plan with certain alterations; it featured a large open rectangular area, called the nave, for accommodating worshipers, and a semicircular apse for the altar and the conduct of religious services. Intersecting aisles were arranged in a cross-shaped floor plan. A continuous barrel-vault roof was supported by massive piers and arches and thick walls with few windows and doors. The atmosphere was one of mysterious darkness but also of castlelike protection.

The twelfth century saw a major innovation in Romanesque architecture, the Gothic style. Influenced by the emphasis of contemporary writers on illumination through prayer and meditation, Gothic architects featured space, light, and height. They unified interior space by replacing the rounded Romanesque arch with the pointed arch, which raised roofs higher above the floor. External buttresses replaced the thick walls of Romanesque churches; this permitted large stained glass windows to flood the building's interior with multicolored light. Sculptors decorated Gothic churches with secular and biblical subjects. The Gothic style remained the dominant European art style into the sixteenth century except in Italy, where interest in classical artistic forms led to the distinctive art style of the Renaissance.

The cathedral became the town's religious center. It was, both physically and spiritually, an ordered unity like that of Thomas Aquinas's *Summa Theologica* or Dante's *Divine Comedy,* combining several distinct but related elements into a structurally coherent whole.

The East Roman or Byzantine Empire

*As the inner part of the temple was seen, and the sun lit its glories, sorrow fled from the hearts of all. . . . And when the first gleam of light, rosy-armed driving away the dark shadows, leaped from arch to arch, then all the princes and peoples with one voice hymned their songs of prayer and praise; and as they came to the sacred courts it seemed to them as if the mighty arches were set in heaven. . . . Whenever anyone enters the church to pray, he realizes at once it is not by any human power or skill, but by the influence of God that it has been built. And so his mind is lifted up to God, and he feels that He cannot be far away, but must love to dwell in this place He has chosen.**

*Procopius, *Buildings,* trans. H. B. Dewing and G. Downey (London: Heinemann, 1940), pp. 11–17, 25–29.

So wrote a Byzantine in contemplation of the magnificent church of Hagia Sophia (Holy Wisdom) in Constantinople. Like the Gothic cathedrals in western Europe, the Hagia Sophia was a symbol of the Byzantine Empire's glorious cultural achievements. As we have seen, Germanic peoples had destroyed the Roman Empire's Mediterranean unity by 500 and ruled large portions of Rome's former domain in the west. However, far from these militarily threatening outside enemies, most of Rome's former eastern territories survived intact as the Byzantine Empire ("Byzantine" referred to an old Greek town Byzantium, incorporated in the imperial capital, Constantinople). Containing the richer and more populated half of the old Roman Empire, the Byzantine state retained Rome's political and social structures and preserved its cultural heritage for a thousand years (476–1453). In the empire, Justinian I (reigned 527–565), perhaps the greatest Byzantine emperor, combined the cultural heritage and political order of classical Greece and Rome with the vitality of the Christian religion. In so doing, he foreshadowed many Byzantine contributions to civilization that rival the work of the architects of Hagia Sophia. This section examines Byzantine accomplishments during the period from 500 to about 1400.

Life in the Byzantine Empire in 500

Freed of heavy expenses for military defense and economic development of the west, the Byzantine Empire prospered economically while remaining socially and ethnically diverse. A top layer of Greek aristocrats ruled over a majority population of Slavs, Arabs, Armenians, Jews, and others. In rural areas, aristocratic nobles held large landed estates, worked by free tenant renters (sharecroppers) called *coloni.* Although the coloni were technically free, they were actually tied to the land by economic necessity.

During the eighth to eleventh centuries, the empire enjoyed relative economic prosperity and agricultural plenty. The government controlled the prices of the staples of the Byzantine diet, bread and olive oil, and manipulated the currency to maintain stability. As in earlier empires from Asia to Europe, the authorities in the Byzantine Empire supervised the upkeep of roads and ports to facilitate trade. Industries, especially the manufacture of brocaded textiles, flourished. In a manner similar to guilds in the west, guilds held monopolies over some manufacturing specialties like textiles, and foreign merchants were encouraged to establish businesses.

The capital, Constantinople, was one of the biggest cities of the age and at its zenith may have had a population of one million. The main street, a sweeping thoroughfare, was lined with shops and a terraced promenade decorated with statues of emperors and popular actresses. An enormous hippodrome or stadium, with seating for 60,000 spectators, was the site of spectacular and exceedingly popular chariot races. Betting on favored teams such as the "blues" or "greens" was a popular pastime and when teams did poorly, it was not uncommon for their supporters to come to blows. These fights sometimes developed into full-scale riots that occasionally threatened the survival of the government.

Erich Lessing/Art Resource

Hagia Sophia. Byzantine rulers were justifiably proud of the Church of Hagia Sophia (Holy Wisdom) with its towering dome. This architectural achievement remains a major monument in present-day Istanbul; the needle-shaped minarets were added by the Ottomans. The Byzantine builders created a huge open space by placing the principal dome atop two half domes. This arrangement so astounded sixth-century contemporaries that they asserted the dome had been let down from heaven.

The wealthy frequently owned slaves to work in their private homes. Large numbers of merchants, artisans, educators, and administrators lived lives of great luxury in large cities or seaside villas located in the European and West Asian sections of the empire. Although members of the ruling elite lived well and reaped the benefits of empire, most people lived on the margin of starvation in one-story city tenements or village huts. As in earlier Greek traditions, men dominated society, and the lives of most women centered on their families and homes; few held any position of political, cultural, or economic importance.

Throughout its long history, the empire steadfastly maintained its identity as the living embodiment of the Roman Empire, but its culture, language, and lifestyle became increasingly Greek. The state paid the instructors at the university of Constantinople, and students often received low or free tuition. Students learned classical Greek writings and followed classical educational traditions taught in classical Greek. However, the coloni and workers spoke a different, common vernacular Greek.

Although Christianity was the official religion, the empire's Christians were divided by theological differences. The church leaders and elite were notoriously disputatious and constantly debated the smallest point of Christian theology, particularly questions involving the nature of Christ and the Trinity. The Orthodox upheld the conclusions of religious councils regarding the Trinity and the nature of Christ, but many non-Orthodox churches, branded as heretical by the Byzantine rulers, differed widely in their beliefs. For example, in eastern Europe (as well as in most of the German states of western Europe) most Christians believed that Jesus was not equal to God. Syria and Egypt, where the populations retained their own rich cultural traditions and local languages and scorned their Greek-speaking rulers, were also strongholds of nontrinitarian Christianity. From Egypt, the

Theodora, Empress of Many Talents

*Theodora, the belly-dancer whom Justinian defied convention to marry . . . was possessed of no ordinary beauty, charm and intelligence. She was a born actress and enjoyed being the centre of attraction as the great lady of the imperial court; and in contrast to her austere husband she revelled in the luxury, pomp and elegance of life in the Great Palace at Constantinople. She shared to the full his conception of the majesty of the Roman Empire. But whereas Justinian belonged to the Latin world and thought like a Roman, Theodora was a Greek or perhaps one may say a Byzantine. But as man and wife they complemented one another. Justinian was devoted to her, and her death in 548 marked a turning-point in his career.**

The wives or mistresses of eminent rulers have often exerted great influence on the course of history. The first Roman emperor, Augustus, found in his wife Livia a source of strength and dependably good advice. By contrast, Agrippina, the wife of the emperor Claudius, ruthlessly manipulated (and finally murdered) her husband in his doddering last years, even inducing him to prefer Nero, her son by a former marriage, to his own direct offspring. Justinian's Theodora, like Pericles' Aspasia, was one of those forceful personalities who overcame a dubious background to capture (and more than repay) the attentions of an important leader.

*Donald M. Nicol, "Justinian I and His Successors, A.D. 527–610," in *Byzantium: An Introduction*, ed. Philip Whitting (New York: Harper, 1973), p. 18.

Coptic Christian church spread into Ethiopia in eastern Africa, where it established a Christian society that survives until the present day (see Chapter 7).

Centered around the eastern Mediterranean, the Nestorians believed that Christ had two separate natures, while the Monophysites argued that Christ's divine nature had absorbed his human nature. Some of these communities still live in present-day Syria, Iraq, and Lebanon. Nestorian missionaries also converted tens of thousands in southern India and China. Some authorities claim that by the ninth century, the Nestorians were the single largest Christian group in the world. Although many of the eastern Christians in western Asia ultimately converted to Islam, theological disputes about the nature of Christ have continued up to the present throughout the Christian world.

Within the Byzantine Empire, the emperor exercised absolute authority over both religious and political matters. He appointed and dismissed officials, issued edicts, sat as the final court of judicial appeal, commanded the military and naval forces, and conducted foreign policy, often seeking to avoid war with rulers and peoples outside the empire. Initially, emperors were chosen from the imperial family by the army and confirmed by the Senate in Constantinople; the mothers and wives of the emperors also often played a key role in the selection of successors. By the fifth century, the patriarch of Constantinople, representing both the people and the church, crowned and consecrated the emperor.

Justinian I

Justinian I, the greatest Byzantine emperor, was an able and active ruler. He was responsible for keeping harmony in what he regarded as a Christian Roman state. He saw his duties as both ecclesiastical, ministering to spiritual needs, and political, attending to earthly affairs. His able and courageous wife, Theodora (c. 500–548), assisted him in those tasks. She restrained his religious zeal and eased tensions between governmental authorities and heretics. Early in his reign, a riot between supporters of rival chariot racing teams spread throughout the city, prompting Justinian and his advisers to consider fleeing the capital, but Theodora urged them instead to stay and fight. When they did, the riot was quelled and the throne secured.

Justinian beautified Constantinople by a large-scale building program, ensuring employment for laborers and also for artists, who added mosaics, sculptures, and icons (pictures of religious figures) to many buildings. Byzantine art became nearly as important as the Greek language in defining Christian faith.

Justinian also systematized Roman law: he directed a committee to compile all Roman legislation and legal commentaries of jurists and to produce a standard textbook for students. The new code, the *Corpus Juris Civilis* (Collection of Civil Law), made Orthodox Christianity the law of the land. Although essentially conservative, it improved the lot of freemen, slaves, and women, and encouraged charitable gifts to the church. The code later become the basis for the civil law of many European and Latin American nations.

In addition, Justinian sought to complete the Christianization of the empire. In 529 he closed the ancient, pre-Christian philosophical schools in Athens. He also restricted the civil rights of so-called heretics; for example, Jews, other non-Christians, and non-Orthodox Christians were prohibited from living within the walls of Constantinople and were barred from many public offices and teaching positions.

Under Justinian, Byzantine literature and learning flourished. Christian teachers stressed the best elements of classical moral training, philosophical thought, and literary craftsmanship. They taught the classical tradition from the Christian viewpoint and wrote on both classical and Christian topics, producing epigrams in the classical Greek manner, poems in elegant Homeric verse, and histories in the style of Herodotus and Thucydides. The subject matter of most literary output, as well as the style, tended to focus on the past; Byzantine writers and artists were not noted for innovation or experimentation.

The Empire's Neighbors

Although he devoted enormous energy to internal matters, Justinian spent most of his reign and much of the empire's wealth on the reconquest of the western Mediterranean, particularly the German-occupied territories in North Africa, the southern coast of Spain, and Italy. Following his death, the Visigoths reconquered southern Spain and a new Germanic group, the Lombards, moved from the Danube Valley to seize much of northern and central Italy. As a result, the Byzantine presence in the west was reduced to North Africa, Sicily, and some regions on the Italian coast, with Ravenna serving as the imperial administrative center.

Justinian's warfare in the west weakened the empire's eastern and northern defenses and created serious problems for his successors. To the north, the Slavs, an Indo-European agricultural people, moved southward through the Danube Valley, now vacated by the Lombards. They entered Macedonia and Greece by 600 and soon thereafter attacked Constantinople. To counter the Lombards and Slavs, seventh-century Byzantine emperors placed civil and military authority in the hands of regional military commanders, and the region's civilian population became the defending army. This ensured the survival of the empire but changed it into a society mobilized for continual warfare. The Byzantines also long enjoyed naval supremacy, thanks in part to "Greek Fire," a petroleum-based incendiary substance that could be discharged from tubes and was not extinguishable by water.

Farther east, Justinian's successors went to war with Persia soon after 600. The Persians, under the Sassanian dynasty that had replaced the Parthians, enjoyed early successes, quickly conquering Syria and Egypt and attacking Constantinople. However, the Byzantines countered by invading Persia and occupying its capital, Ctesiphon (in present-day Iraq). By 628, the Persians were forced to seek peace.

The war with Persia, which brought the Byzantines no long-term territorial gains, exhausted it economically and made it vulnerable to attacks by vigorous new foes.

Scala/Art Resource

Theodora. This spectacular mosaic depicts Theodora arrayed in a jewel-encrusted gown and robe. Dynamic and resourceful, Theodora was a trusted adviser to her husband, the Emperor Justinian I, and became a powerful political figure in her own right.

The Arabs, newly united under Islam, seized Syria and Egypt from the Byzantine Empire and Mesopotamia from the Persians shortly after 630. Two Arab sieges of Constantinople, in 674–678 and 717–718, were unsuccessful; thereafter, the Taurus Mountains dividing Asia Minor from Syria became the Byzantine-Arab frontier. Another Asiatic people, the Bulgars, entered the Balkans from the north late in the seventh century, gaining control of the lower Danube Valley. They integrated the local Slavic peoples into a Bulgar-dominated state. Thus the outer fringes of the empire were lost to increasingly powerful rivals.

Religious Issues

Byzantine wars had religious as well as political dimensions. Justinian fought the Germans as much because they were Arians as because they were occupiers of imperial territory. His successors similarly opposed Slavs and Bulgars as non-Christian pagans. Following Zoroastrianism and

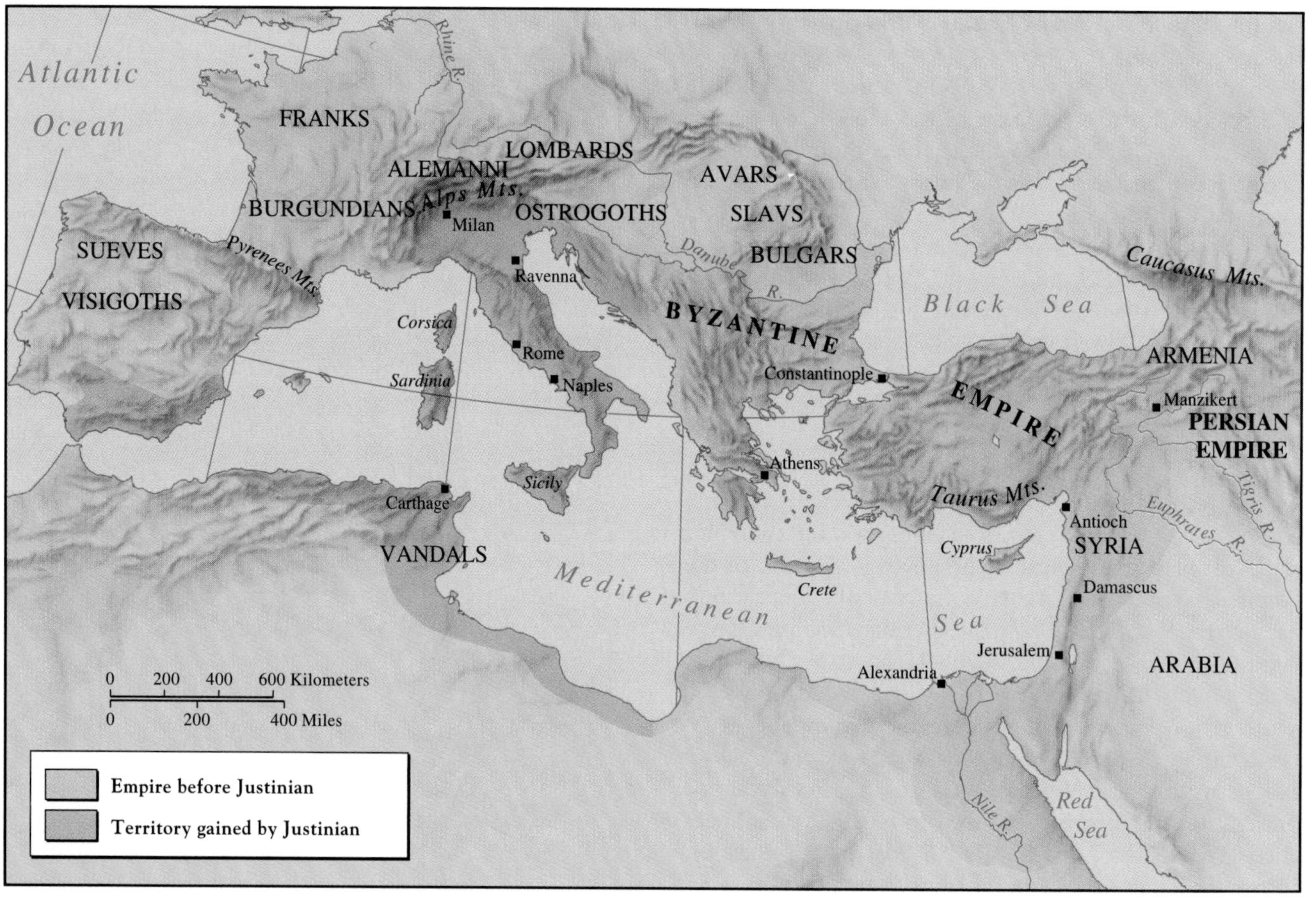

Map 5.6 The Mediterranean in the Time of Justinian. Around 525, after the Germanic migrations into western Europe, the Byzantine Empire occupied only the limited area shown. Justinian I expanded the empire by recovering territories from Goths and Vandals, but some of these gains were lost soon after his death.

Islam, respectively, the Persians and Arabs easily conquered Syria and Egypt in the seventh century, in part because non-Orthodox and Orthodox Christians failed to mount any collective opposition to the invading forces.

Arab and Persian conquests removed Jerusalem, Alexandria, and Antioch from the empire, leaving Constantinople and Rome as the major Christian centers. As time passed, leaders in those two centers often disagreed on religious issues. Believing it was their duty to maintain orthodoxy, Justinian and his successors tried to reestablish doctrinal unity. The bishops of Rome (popes), however, claimed headship of the church and regarded the definition of Christian faith as their responsibility. Doctrines acceptable in the east and proclaimed by bishops in councils under the direction of the patriarch of Constantinople often encountered papal opposition, whereas eastern Catholics often rejected doctrines the west could support. Church councils in the sixth and seventh centuries failed to resolve such conflicts.

In the eighth century, Emperor Leo III (reigned 717–741) created a new rift among Christians. He believed that many of the empire's bright and able men were diverted from state service because they were interested in monastic practices that involved the worship of icons (images of sacred Christian figures). Leo accordingly tried to discredit monasticism by attacking the misuse of icons in eastern churches as idolatrous and by prohibiting their use. This sharply divided the empire's population into iconoclasts (image breakers) and iconodules (image users). Many of latter fled to monasteries or to western imperial territories in south Italy and Sicily. Because the popes opposed the iconoclasts, Leo retaliated by transferring many rich papal lands in Italy to the patriarch of Constantinople. Iconoclasm polarized Latin and Greek Christians and divided the Byzantine Empire even after the ecumenical Council of Nicaea in 787 restored relations between Rome and Constantinople. The dispute over icons was eventually resolved by the Empress Irene (reigned 780–802), who required priests to provide instruction to parishioners on the appropriate use of icons. Irene ruled by brute force and succeeded in imposing her son as successor.

For her service to Christianity, the Church subsequently declared her a saint.

Decline of Empire

During the ninth century, the Byzantine Empire gradually regained some of its former power; emperors reestablished use of icons and restored the empire's financial and military resources. In 867 an ambitious son of Armenian peasants assassinated the reigning emperor and seized the throne as Basil I. Basil established the long-lived Macedonian dynasty (867–1054), which ably led the empire for nearly two centuries.

Byzantine cultural and religious life flourished under the early Macedonians. Literary output grew, while educational activity and interest in classical authors revived. Poems and hymns in praise of saints and prose accounts of their lives were published, while histories and lexicons attested to the Byzantine fascination with the classical past. The emperor Constantine VII (reigned 912–959) patronized scholarly activity and authorized important works describing the administration of the empire and Byzantine court ceremonies. Out of the recurring border wars with Muslims came the *Epic of Digenes Akritas* ("the border warrior born of parents from different ethnic groups"), which resembles western European works such as the *Song of Roland* and the *Song of the Cid*.

In art, the iconoclastic controversy triggered interest in the forms of Greek art popular during Alexander the Great's time, in the historical and secular rather than the ecclesiastical and spiritual, and in Islamic art and its use of ornament. This second golden age of Byzantine art was characterized by the pursuit of dignity, grace, restraint, balance, and refinement.

Under the Macedonian rulers, Byzantine artistic and literary developments continued to copy classical Greek models in which secular taste often contrasted with religious sensitivity. In the decorations of aristocratic homes and in manuscript illuminations, classical themes and mythological or allegorical scenes were popular. The exploitation of their classical inheritance gave the Byzantines superiority over Latin Christianity in literary and artistic achievements in the ninth and tenth centuries.

Byzantine vitality also contributed to cultural and religious expansion. Byzantine emperors considered the late ninth-century conquests and subsequent conversion of Serbians and other Slavs to Orthodox Christianity to be one of their greatest accomplishments. The Bulgars negotiated with both Latin and Byzantine Christians, but the work of Byzantine missionaries and the diplomacy of Byzantine emperors and patriarchs induced the Bulgar ruler to adopt Eastern Orthodox Christianity. By the tenth century, the Bulgar capital of Preslav became a center for training Slavic clergy. They were taught in Old Church Slavonic, a literary language devised by Byzantine missionaries that became a means by which Byzantine culture was infused into eastern and southeastern Europe.

During the tenth century, Kievan Russia began to move into the Byzantine cultural orbit. As trade with the Byzantines grew, Kievan rulers sought closer ties with Constantinople. Prince Vladimir (reigned alone 977–1015), a baptized Christian, married Anna, sister of the Byzantine emperor Basil II (reigned 976–1025). The Bible, saints'

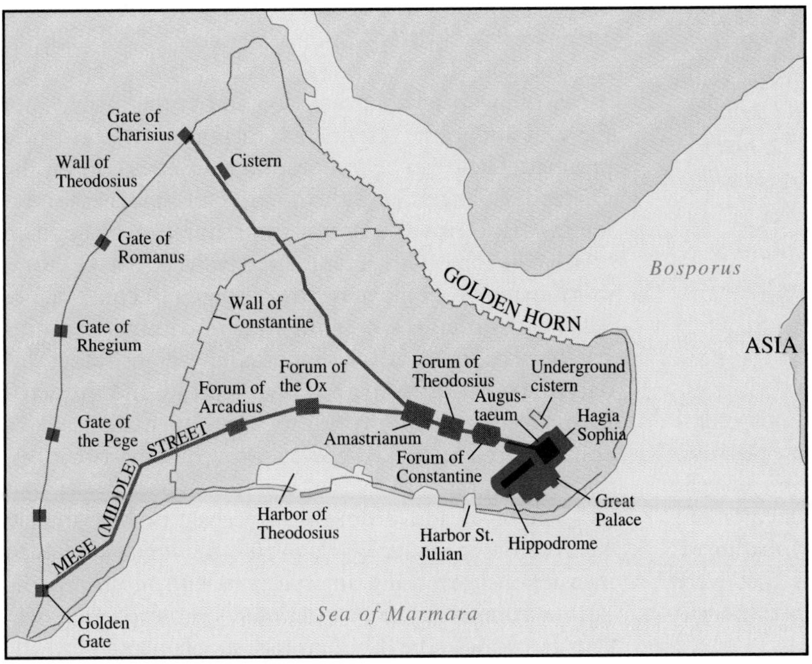

Map 5.7 Constantinople. The capital of the Byzantine Empire, Constantinople was a large city with a lavish complex of imperial buildings and churches. Its location astride the Bosporus provided it with natural defenses that were further strengthened by a series of walls around the city. This map also shows the Hippodrome, where the famous games were held, Hagia Sophia, and the Mese, or middle, street.

lives, and religious service books translated at Preslav from Greek into Old Church Slavonic formed the earliest Russian Christian religious literature.

In southeastern Europe, the Byzantine Empire declined rapidly. Although a series of vigorous emperors from 1081 to 1185 asserted imperial authority, increased commercial connections with Italian cities, and restored Constantinople as a leading cultural center, a subsequent rapid succession of short-lived rulers weakened the empire. By 1200 rebellions in Serbia and Bulgaria led to the establishment of independent states. In 1204 Latin crusaders sacked the capital of Constantinople and made most of the Byzantine Empire a Latin Empire until 1261. Although the Paleologi dynasty (1261–1453) was able to destroy the Latin Empire and recover Constantinople and much of northern Greece, from 1300 onward the Byzantine Empire increasingly became, like central Europe, politically fragmented. Like the Greek and Roman Empires before it, the Byzantine Empire, which had persisted for more than a millennium, disintegrated and finally disappeared. Byzantium was to be replaced during the fifteenth century by a new, non-Christian power, the Ottoman Turks, who, like the Byzantines, had a tradition of absolute rule (see Chapter 8).

Islam and Islamic Empires

The apostle of God became a young man. God protected him from the loose behavior of the pagans. He was the most generous of his people . . . kind to his neighbors, courteous, faithful. . . . He was the bravest of men.

[Muhammad's reactions when he had his first vision as he meditated in a desert cave:] "One came to me with a written scroll, while I was asleep, and said 'Read!' I said 'I cannot read. . . .' He pressed me with it, until I thought death must be nigh. . . . And he said, 'Read in the name of thy Lord who created; He created man from a sensitive drop of blood' [Qur'an 96.1–2]. And he departed. . . .

*And I awoke. . . . And it was as if the scripture were written on my heart."**

*Emel Esin, *Mecca, the Blessed; Madinah, the Radiant* (New York: Crown, 1963), pp. 70, 76.

Thus did the prophet Muhammad's Arabian contemporaries describe the prophet and his first revelation of what was to become one of the world's major religions. Just as Buddha and Jesus had gone to meditate in remote areas, so too, did the prophet Muhammad. There he experienced a series of revelations that were then transmitted first to converts in Arabia and then to growing numbers in Africa and eastern Asia.

Although the peoples in pre-Islamic Arabia were predominantly tribal nomads, Mecca and Medina had been major centers for religious pilgrimages and trade, particularly of frankincense and myrrh from Yemen, for generations. A few Jewish and Christian communities were also scattered about the peninsula; these communities continued to maintain some commercial and cultural ties with the Byzantine Empire, which controlled most of the eastern Mediterranean. Merchants and city dwellers enjoyed a fair degree of prosperity, but most of the population in the Arabian Peninsula lived in either scattered desert oases, where they eked out a subsistence livelihood growing grains, vegetables, and date palms, or as nomads who traveled with herds of camels, goats, and sheep from one life-giving watering hole to the next. The majority of these *bedouin* (tribal people) were animists (believers that inanimate objects like stones, trees, and animals possess spirits or souls), living in what Islamic society would term ignorance.

Muhammad: A Religious and Political Leader

The prophet Muhammad, who came from the Hashim family or branch of the Qurash tribe, was born in Mecca around 570 or 571. He was raised by his grandfather and as an adult married an older widow, Khadijah. Muhammad rapidly gained a reputation as an honest and successful businessman. When he was around forty years old, Muhammad became increasingly religious and began to spend longer periods of time in deep meditation. As early as 610, Muhammad began to have revelations from Allah (God), which were transmitted through the angel Gabriel. Muhammad began to preach the word of Allah and slowly gained adherents to the new religion, Islam (submission to God). The believers in Islam were known as Muslims, or those who submit to the will of God.

Muslims believe in one God and in the prophets of the Old and New Testaments; they include Christ as a prophet. They also believe in progressive revelation, the existence of angels, and the doctrine of the day of judgment. Islam, like Christianity, is a universal religion in which all people who accepted the belief in one God and in Muhammad as his prophet were seen as equal before Allah and within the community. For Muslims, Islam is the perfection of all previous religions, including Judaism and Christianity. As Islam spread and attracted converts around the world, its universal nature and its equal treatment of all believers proved to be two of its major strengths.

The revelations from Allah received by Muhammad were set down in the *Qur'an (Koran),* which contained instructions governing all aspects of human life. As the Islamic community grew in numbers and expanded over vast territories, the Qur'an was supplemented by the

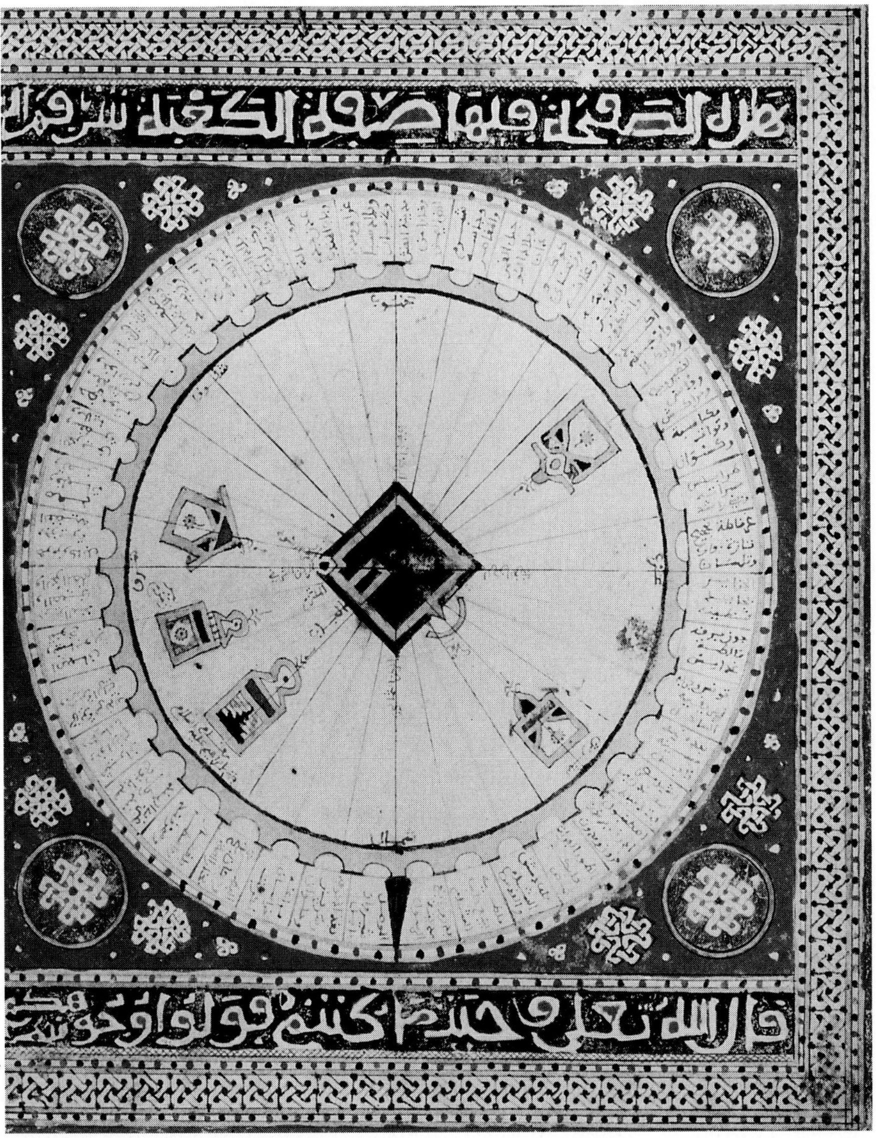

Bibliothèque Nationale de France, Paris

Frontispiece of an Atlas. This Arabic atlas (1551) shows the Ka'bah surrounded by the names of the Islamic nations, connected by lines showing their relative locations. Enclosed by a huge walled courtyard, the Ka'bah remains the holiest site in Islam.

Hadith, which is a collection of the sayings and traditions of the prophet Muhammad. Muslims accept six authoritative collections of the Hadith. In addition, a complex body of law, the *Shari'a,* gradually evolved. The Qur'an, Hadith, and Shari'a provide the guidelines for the conduct of Muslim societies. Over several centuries, differing interpretations of the Qur'an, the Hadith, and the Shari'a led to the formation of several different schools of Islamic law.

A large percentage of Islamic law deals with family matters. In Arabia, where women had previously enjoyed no legal status, Islamic injunctions were a major improvement. As the prophet was known to have said, "Paradise is at the foot of the mother." Under Islamic law, a widow was guaranteed a portion of her husband's estate and could own and dispose of property; women also had the right of divorce in specific instances. These legal rights were granted in Islam centuries before most women in the Christian west obtained such rights. However, in keeping with traditional practice in western Asia, Islamic societies remained patriarchal, the oldest male acting as the leader, provider, and final authority in the family. Muslim law permitted polygamy, which was common in Arabia and much of the rest of the world at the time. A Muslim male could have four wives at any one time if each wife were treated equally. In actual practice only the wealthy could generally afford more than one wife.

In eras when religious tolerance was generally unknown, Islam enjoined believers to grant safe havens to people of the book (Jews and Christians) and usually to Zoroastrians and not to force conversions or to persecute these communities unless they waged war against Muslims. This tolerance, however, was not extended to animists or polytheists such as Hindus.

LIVES AND TIMES ACROSS CULTURES

People of the Book

The three major monotheistic religions—Judaism, Christianity, and Islam—emerged from western Asia and built on many of the same traditions. They are based on belief in one and only one God, creator of the universe and humankind. All three accept Abraham and Moses as important teachers and prophets. Christians believe Jesus was last in a long line of prophets and, in addition, was the son of God. Jews do not accept Jesus as the son of God and continue to await the Messiah's arrival. Although Muslims accept Jesus as a prophet and the virgin birth by Mary, they do not believe in the resurrection. They view Muhammad as the last and greatest of the prophets.

All three stress the written word, each having a sacred text: the Torah for Jews, the Bible for Christians, and the Qur'an for Muslims. These texts provide the basic theology of the religion as well as guidance for daily life, including dietary regulations, religious practices and rites, and a host of instructions for proper behavior. Judaism and Islam also share a common emphasis on law and the duties of believers. The texts provide guidelines for proper daily behavior and the path to salvation after death. They are also rich sources for poetry, stories, and histories of, for example, the creation of the world and early human history.

Although women played important roles in the early history of each religion, such as Sarah in Judaism, the Virgin Mary and Mary Magdalene in Christianity, and Khadijah and Aisha in Islam, all three were organized along patriarchal lines. Men were the religious leaders and interpreters of the sacred texts and law. Rabbis in Judaism, priests and ministers in Christianity, and imams in Islam were traditionally men; indeed, women were frequently barred from holding these positions. Although a few women have become rabbis and ministers in the contemporary era, men continue to dominate the leadership, particularly in conservative branches, of all three religions.

These and other commonalities created a Judeo-Christian-Islamic tradition that had a major impact around the world.

The Qur'an also provides regulations for marriage (including divorce); loaning of money (interest is forbidden); diet; the treatment of women, orphans, and slaves; and the behavior of government. Muslim theologians and legal experts who interpreted and explained Islamic canons were known collectively as the *ulema*. Importantly, Islam, in contrast to early Christianity, did not separate church from state.

Every true Muslim was instructed to follow the five basic pillars: belief in Allah and Muhammad as his prophet, prayer five times a day, the giving of alms, fasting from sunrise to sunset during the month of Ramadan, and the *hajj* or pilgrimage to Mecca once in a lifetime. The observance of these five pillars still serves as the principal means of salvation for Muslims, and nonobservance is believed to lead to eternal suffering in the afterlife.

The hajj commemorates the *hijrah* (flight) in 622 of Muhammad and his followers from the merchants of Mecca, who feared the new religion would threaten both their preeminent political and social status and the wealth they enjoyed from pilgrims coming to worship in the city. The hajj centers on the *Ka'bah*, a cube-shaped shrine in Mecca, which had long been a place of pilgrimage for tribal peoples in the Arabian Peninsula. In addition to its spiritual meaning, the hajj has also enabled diverse and widely scattered Islamic peoples to exchange ideas and goods while maintaining a cohesive structure.

The new Islamic community took refuge in Medina, became the dominant political and social force, and attracted more and more converts. Worried over the growing political and financial power of Muhammad and his followers, the leaders in Mecca launched several armed attacks to destroy the new community. When the Muslims successfully defeated these attacks, they gained more converts. By 629, the Muslims led by Muhammad were strong enough to mount a force of more than 1,000 believers to march on Mecca; by 632 Muhammad had successfully incorporated the city within the new and growing Muslim community. Just a few months after his return to Mecca, however, Muhammad died of a fever. Because Muhammad had left no specific instructions regarding a successor, the community of the faithful immediately gathered together and by consensus selected the first caliph, or leader.

An Inscribed Bowl. Islamic/Arab societies, like the Chinese, held the art of pottery making in extremely high esteem. Ceramic centers flourished in the Islamic world, and pieces were frequently decorated with Arabic inscriptions from the Qur'an or with sayings from the Prophet. The inscription on the bowl shown here reads, "Excellence is a quality of the people of paradise."

The First Four Caliphs and Islamic Conquests

The first caliph, Abu Bakr, had been one of the original converts to Islam. As Muhammad's faithful friend, Abu Bakr was known for his devotion and was widely respected for his wisdom and good humor. Following Muhammad's death, a number of the Arabian tribes had broken with the Islamic community. Abu Bakr immediately appointed loyal chiefs to subdue these revolts. Subsequently, many of the tribal leaders participated in the military conquests of the entire Arabian Peninsula and in expeditions into Syria and Iraq.

After Abu Bakr's death in 634, the Islamic community selected the energetic Umar as the second caliph. Umar's administration was marked by a period of military conquest, as Muslims assimilated widely different areas and peoples into an Islamic Empire. In the east, the Iraqi territories of the old Sassanid Empire were conquered, and in 637 the capital at Ctesiphon fell to Arab/Islamic domination. These military victories brought vast wealth, which was lavishly bestowed upon the soldiers. With promises of military victories and booty, the Islamic armies had little difficulty in attracting recruits.

In following years, Muslim armies met with similar military successes against the Byzantine Empire. Damascus fell to Khalid's forces in 635, and at the decisive battle of Yarmuk in 637, the forces of the Roman emperor were decisively defeated. Jerusalem was incorporated into the Muslim Empire in 638. The Muslims then turned their energies toward Egypt and Africa; in 639 they reached the banks of the Nile, taking Alexandria in 641. Two years later most of Persia had fallen.

Arab women and children accompanied the armies on military campaigns, and women frequently joined the fighting. The Byzantine soldiers, accustomed to women remaining secluded at home, were shocked to see Arab women on the battlefields. At Yarmuk, when the Arab army moved to retreat, women seized swords and tent posts and urged the soldiers to rejoin the battle; some also joined the frontlines on horseback. The result was a complete rout of the Byzantine army.

The Sacred Mosque and Ka'bah at Mecca. This photograph shows the holiest site in the Muslim world during the time of pilgrimage. Although the courtyard can hold a half-million pilgrims, in recent years it has been too small to contain the crowds, which can exceed 4 million worshipers.

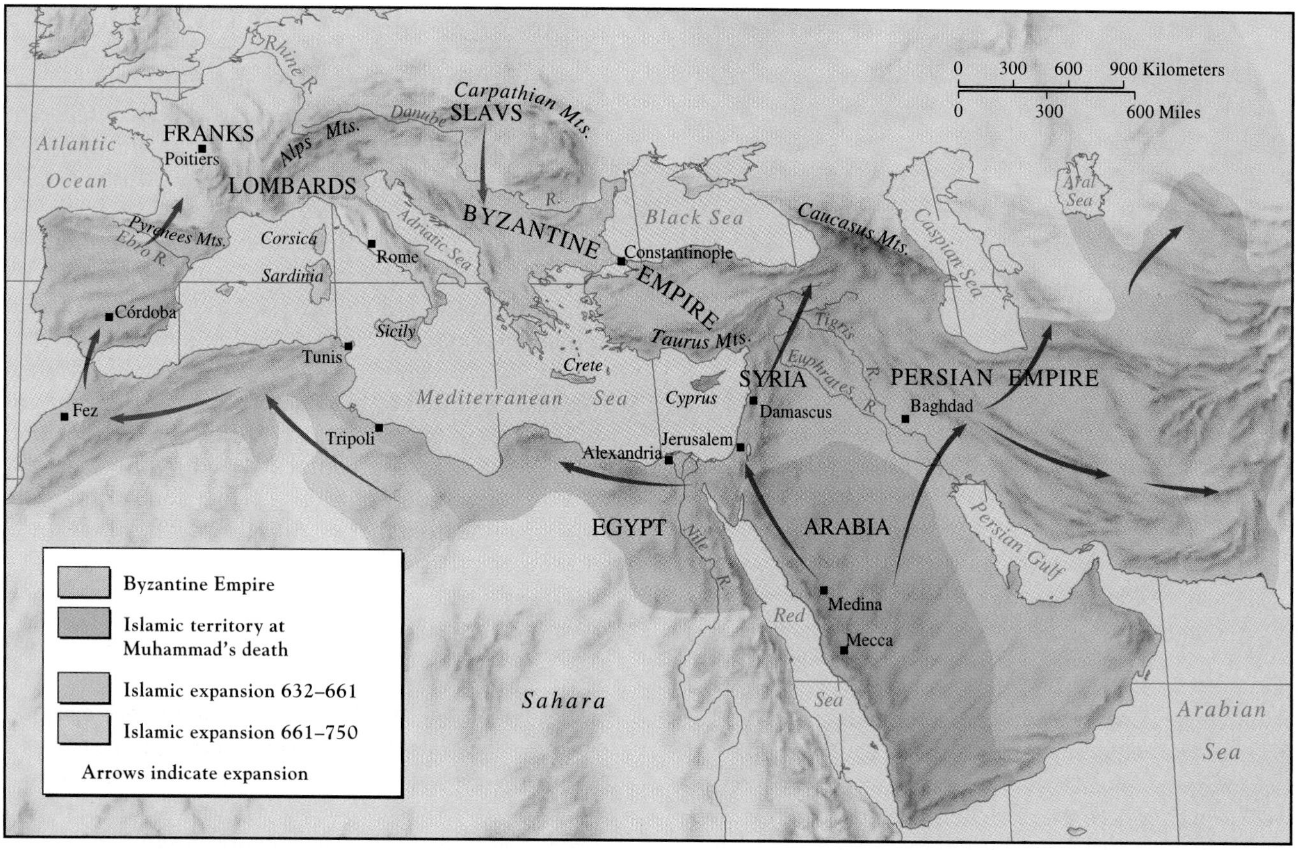

Map 5.8 The Expansion of Islam. Most of Islam's early territorial gains were at the expense of the Persian and Byzantine Empires. The former was entirely absorbed, the latter, already diminished by German gains, lost Syria, Egypt, and all of its North African possessions. Muslims then advanced into the Iberian Peninsula and France in the west and toward the banks of the Indus River in the east.

The extremely rapid expansion of the Muslim/Arab Empire was attributable in part to the weaknesses of the Sassanid and Byzantine Empires. More important to the Muslims' success, however, were their fervent religious belief and the equalitarian nature of the religion, which treated converts as equals within the community. The Muslims' treatment of their new subjects also contributed to their success. In contrast to leaders of earlier empires in Egypt and China, for example, Umar did not attempt to force the conquered peoples to assimilate or to adopt Arabian customs. Umar's decision to interfere as little as possible with the conquered peoples was perhaps his most important contribution to the continued success and endurance of the Islamic Empire. During Umar's caliphate, provincial governors were appointed to administer the new territories; their major job was to collect taxes, which, in many cases, were far lower than those collected by the Byzantine or Sassanid Empires. Hence, many peoples actually welcomed the new rulers and were rapidly absorbed within the Islamic society. Non-Muslims were not forced to convert and were allowed to maintain their own laws, as well as to practice their own religions. They were not permitted to bear arms, however; nor, for example, could their church towers be taller than the highest minaret in a town. In contrast to other societies of the age, which often forced conversions and persecuted or killed people of differing beliefs, the Islamic Empire became known for its relative tolerance of minorities and non-Muslims.

Similarly, Islamic law strictly regulated the treatment of slaves. Muslims could not enslave other Muslims, and the freeing of slaves was encouraged. In contrast to many other societies, particularly in the Western Hemisphere, slaves in the Islamic world were not generally used as agricultural labor on huge plantations, but were kept only as workers and protectors for domestic households or as soldiers in the army.

As the "second founder of Islam," Umar also established a single authoritative version of the Qur'an; all other copies were destroyed, and the Qur'an has remained unchanged since that time. Unfortunately, while praying in Medina, at the very peak of his power, Umar was fatally wounded by a disgruntled slave. On his deathbed Umar appointed a committee of six prominent merchants to select the next caliph.

After some debate the committee chose Uthman, from the powerful Umayyad family, as the third caliph. An elderly man in his seventies, Uthman was not as forceful a leader as his predecessors, and he was widely criticized for favoring members of his own family over the rest of the *umma* (Islamic community). For example, Uthman appointed his cousin Mu'awiyah governor of the flourishing province of Syria. Mu'awiyah proved an able ruler and military strategist, however, ordering the building of the first Islamic fleet, which immediately conquered the islands of Cyprus and Rhodes. With his army and fleet, which made him the dominant military force in the eastern Mediterranean, Mu'awiyah emerged as a powerful leader in his own right.

The Caliph Uthman's leadership was increasingly opposed by faithful Muslims in Medina and in provincial towns on the eastern frontier. An open revolt began in Kufah in Iraq in 655 and soon spread to Medina. In 656 the rebels broke into the caliph's home and assassinated him. Political assassination has often triggered unrest and accelerated changes in the course of history. For example, the assassinations of Uthman and Julius Caesar both sparked struggles for power that ended with the emergence of able administrators and founders of dynastic lines (Mu'awiya and Augustus).

After Uthman's death, once again, the Muslim leaders gathered to select a leader; after a week, the notables agreed to appoint Ali, Muhammad's son-in-law, as the fourth caliph. From the very beginning of his reign, however, Ali met with widespread opposition. So many in Medina were against him, including some who believed he had been implicated in Uthman's death, that Ali fled the city and established his capital in Kufah (in present-day Iraq). Nevertheless, the discontent continued. Aisha, Muhammad's favorite wife, disliked Ali, who had once accused her of infidelity. Astride a camel, Aisha led her supporters into a bloody battle against Ali in 656. Defeated at the so-called Battle of the Camel, in which many of the original followers of the prophet were killed, Aisha was forced to retire to Medina where she died of natural causes several decades later.

Mu'awiyah was to prove a much more dangerous opponent to Ali's supremacy. He refused to resign as virtual ruler of Syria, and he had the support of the powerful Umayyad family. In 657 he challenged Ali's leadership at the battle of Siffin, in northern Syria. Although the battle was essentially a standoff, more and more provinces aligned with Mu'awiyah, who clearly held the preponderance of power. Some of Ali's original followers now turned against him. Known as *Kharijites* (seceders), they were against any sort of compromise and now opposed both Ali and Mu'awiyah. The Kharijites considered themselves to be the only true revolutionaries within the Muslim world. In 661 a Kharijite murdered Ali. His death ended the age of the "rightly guided" caliphs—the first four caliphs, all of whom had either been related to Muhammad or had been his close compatriots.

The Death of a Caliph

*The people rushed upon him, some striking him with their scabbards, others striking him with their fists. A man came at him with a broad iron-tipped arrow and stabbed the front of his throat, and his blood fell on the Koran. Yet even when they were in that state they feared killing him. Uthman was old and he fainted. His wife Na'ila and his daughters wailed loudly. Al-Tujibi came, drawing his sword to thrust it into his belly. When Na'ila protected Uthman, he cut her hand. Then he leaned with his sword upon his chest; and Uthman, Allah bless him, was killed before sundown.**

This emotional description of Caliph Uthman's assassination has all the hallmarks of an eyewitness account. The assassination marked a major turning point in Islamic history after which leadership for the community would be hotly contested.

*From Ibn Jarir al-Tabari (d. 923), "The History of Prophets and Kings," in *The Islamic World*, ed. William H. McNeill and Marilyn Robinson Waldman (New York: Oxford University Press, 1973; reprint, Chicago: University of Chicago Press, 1983), p. 76.

The Umayyad Caliphate

After Ali's death, Mu'awiyah declared himself caliph in Jerusalem in 661 and established Damascus as the new capital of the Islamic Empire. He granted a substantial pension to Hasan, Ali's eldest son and possible rival; Hasan retired from politics and spent the rest of his life in Medina. Mu'awiyah generally appointed able and vigorous governors to oversee the far-flung empire and engaged in lively discussions on governmental policies with the notables in Damascus. Many of the officials were Syrians or had been administrators in the Byzantine Empire. Thus many Byzantine traditions and cultural achievements were assimilated within the Umayyad caliphate. Commanding the strongest army within the empire, Mu'awiyah launched a series of attacks against the remaining territories of the Byzantine Empire in present-day Turkey and, as previously noted, tried but failed to take Constantinople, the Byzantine capital.

The Glorious Umayyads

Our Caliph, successor of God, is the most fortunate; his good omen brings down rain showers from above. He belongs to the most prestigious clan of Quraysh, no other tree can parallel his glorious branch. Following the right and refraining from wrong, his people always endure when tragedy strikes. Their enemy does not dare to fight them, for their resolve is always strong.

They continue to fight till they win;
yet, in peace they are the most magnanimous.
In times of drought they race the winds
to feed and shelter the stricken ones.
Sons of Umayya, your favors are very generous;
*you give without any spite or drudgery.**

These excerpts from a poem in praise of Caliph 'Abd al-Malik by the noted Umayyad poet al-Akhtal (d. 722) reveal the esteem in which many Umayyad Caliphs were held. Writers also sought to win the favor and patronage of the court by penning highly flattering, if not always factually correct, descriptions of the rulers. Writers and poets were similarly supported in the Chinese and other empires.

*Wilson B. Bishai, *Humanities in the Arabic-Islamic World* (Dubuque, Iowa: W. C. Brown, 1973), p. 79.

Simultaneously, Muslim forces in Egypt and northern Africa continued to extend their influence. With Berbers from North Africa and other new African recruits from the sub-Saharan regions, they succeeded in moving across the Strait of Gibraltar in 710 and 711. From there, Tarik, the Berber commander, smashed the Visigoths and incorporated half of Spain under his command. The Muslims called the territory Al-Andalusia, Land of the Vandals, and proceeded to create in Spain a vibrant civilization that was to last for nearly eight centuries. The Muslim forces, known as Moors in western Europe, also made continual forays across the Pyrenees, reaching as far as Tours, only 234 miles south of Paris. Although they remained a military threat for decades, they never succeeded in incorporating France into their empire. As a result, the rest of Europe remained predominantly Christian, while Islamic governments prevailed in the Iberian Peninsula, across North Africa, and in western Asia, excepting for those parts of the Anatolian Peninsula (present-day Turkey) still held by the Byzantine Empire.

During the Umayyad Caliphate, similar expansions occurred in central Asia. Al-Hajjaj, viceroy in the eastern provinces, conquered Samarkand and surrounding territory in central Asia. Simultaneously, Muslim forces marched into northern and western India, conquering the lower Indus Valley (Sind) in 712. The majority of the populations in these territories gradually converted to Islam, and the areas became part of the Islamic world.

The Split between Sunnis and Shi'i

Before his death, Mu'awiyah had his son, Yazid, accepted as his heir and thereby instituted the procedure of hereditary accession to the caliphate. Yazid was a better warrior than administrator, and during his reign a major schism of immense importance to the future Islamic world occurred. After the death of Ali's eldest son Hasan, his younger brother Husayn became the leader of those who had continued to support Ali's cause and to oppose Umayyad rule. Husayn refused to recognize the legitimacy of Yazid. With a small, poorly equipped force, he advanced against Yazid's army. The two rival sides clashed on the field of Kerbala, a city south of contemporary Baghdad on the tenth of Muharram (October 10, 680). Husayn and his badly outnumbered supporters were killed. Husayn's head was cut off and presented in a triumphal display to Yazid.

Husayn's martyrdom became the rallying point for opponents of the Umayyad Caliphate throughout the empire. Their opposition was based on a political division over who should rule, rather than on spiritual differences. The Shi'i or party of Ali maintained that the line of leadership should follow directly through the prophet's family. The Sunni, or Orthodox majority, contended that leadership could be bestowed on any able believer.

Kerbala, where Husayn was buried, became a major point of pilgrimage for the Shi'i, who marked his death in the month of Muharram with passion plays and ceremonies of self-flagellation. Ultimately, the Shi'i would become predominant in present-day Iran, which already differed from the Arabian Peninsula owing to its largely Farsi-speaking population and its unique cultural and historical identity. Shi'i also make up a sizable portion of the populations in present-day Iraq, Lebanon, the eastern Arabian Peninsula, and some other areas of the Islamic world.

The Shi'i ultimately split into a number of different sects, the most important of them being the Twelvers. They recognized the Imams (leaders) through Husayn's children and believed that the twelfth Imam, Muhammad al-Muntazar, disappeared into a cave in 878. According to Twelver Shi'i belief, Muhammad al-Muntazar did not die but went into occultation, a state in which other religious leaders could commune with him while he remained invisible. Twelvers believed that Muhammad al-Muntazar would return as the Mahdi (the rightly guided one) to save the world. As a result, the *mullahs* (clergy) assumed a special role within the Shi'i communities, which continued to look to the clergy for direction and leadership. The Shi'i clergy also established a hierarchy in which particularly knowledgeable and esteemed mullahs became known as *Ayatollahs.* In contrast, the orthodox, or majority, Sunni Muslims had neither an established clergy nor a hierarchy of religious notables.

In addition, a number of other splits developed among the Shi'i. Some argued that the fourth Imam, Zayid, was the last real Imam; they became known as Zayidis and in the contemporary era are found mostly in Yemen. Others held that Isma'il, the seventh in line, should have been recognized as the last infallible Imam. They ultimately established communities in Tunisia and India. From Tunisia their leaders, the Fatimids, established an independent Fatimid Caliphate in Cairo in 969. Cairo subsequently became a rival for power and glory to the eastern capital in Baghdad. (These dynasties are described in Chapter 8.)

The Establishment of the Abbasid Caliphate

The Umayyad Caliphs in Damascus had increasing difficulties keeping the diverse and widely scattered peoples of the empire under their sole control. From the onset, the provinces in North Africa, Spain, and Egypt had been largely self-governing under the local provincial governors.

Meanwhile, the growing wealth and increasingly secular behavior of the Umayyad rulers caused mounting opposition, even in Syria and Arabia. The rulers' lavish lifestyles had also corrupted many within the ruling circles, and it became increasingly difficult to attract recruits to fight for the Umayyads. Rumors that the Umayyad Caliphs drank wine, expressly forbidden to Muslims, and that one caliph even swam in a pool filled with wine, were all used by the Umayyads' opponents to gain adherents from among the devout Muslim/Arab communities.

Rebellions became increasingly frequent. One group, the Abbasids, who were led by the great-grandson of the Prophet Muhammad's uncle, gathered support from the Shi'i and from disgruntled groups in Iraq and Iran. In 747 the Abbasids called for an open revolt against the Umayyad caliphate and within three years had defeated the Umayyads at a decisive battle near the Tigris river. In 750 Damascus fell and the Abbasids promptly attempted to eliminate all members of the Umayyad family. One, Abd al-Rahman I, fled to Spain where he established a new dynasty that lasted for nearly 300 years. The Abbasid leader, Abu al-Abbas, was proclaimed caliph at Kufah in

30 B.C.E.	Crucifixion of Jesus
73	Masada The Gospels
400	Augustine, *City of God* Attila the Hun Last emperor of Rome Justinian I Hagia Sophia
600	Islam: Muhammad The Qur'an Battle of Yarmuk Byzantines use "Greek fire" Split between Shi'i and Sunnis Umayyad Caliphate Abbasid caliphate Islam spreads to East Indies and Iberian Peninsula Umayyad predominance in Spain
800	Charlemagne and the Carolingian Renaissance Olga, princess of Kiev
1000	al-Cid Romanesque architecture Vernacular literatures begin in Europe
1100	Gothic architectural style begins
1200	Francis of Assisi The Magna Carta Beginning of universities in Europe Philip II, "the Fair" Thomas Aquinas, *Summa Theologica*
1300	Dante Alighieri, *The Divine Comedy*

749 and proceeded to establish a new caliphate (see Chapter 8).

Summary and Comparisons

As the Roman Empire declined, the Christian church effectively replaced the collapsing political system as the temporal ruler. In Europe, Christianity swept aside all other competitors and outlived the Roman Empire.

In the fourth and fifth centuries, barbarian invasions finally overwhelmed the defenses of the Western Roman Empire. In contrast to China, where one dynasty led to another with a continuation of most cultural and political institutions, the collapse of Rome led to sharp changes in European institutions and society. Although internal deficiencies of the type discussed in the comparative essay preceding this chapter played a part in its collapse, Rome perished more from assault than from senility. From this point on, the distinctive Greco-Roman civilization was modified at the hands of the Germanic kingdoms of western Europe and the Byzantine Empire to the east, both already on the scene by 500. Another heir, the Islamic Empire, was emerging just over the horizon.

In the Latin west, Germanic peoples practiced subsistence agriculture in tribal societies under weak kings; many African societies were organized along the same lines. In Europe, one people, the Franks, became prominent. By adopting Roman Catholic Christianity and requiring Romans and Germans to work together, King Clovis provided a basis for new political and cultural development. Creative individuals preserved elements of the classical heritage, and innovative religious leaders gave new directions to western European life.

During the period 750–1000, Carolingian rulers unified the Frankish kingdoms and dominated western Europe. They created an adequate, if loosely organized, governmental administration and used an effective army to expand their territories. They also stimulated a modest, mostly religious, literary and artistic activity, sometimes called the Carolingian Renaissance. Charlemagne, the greatest Carolingian ruler, was crowned Holy Roman emperor by the pope in 800. During the ninth century, however, Carolingian rulers engaged in civil wars, and the empire disintegrated into small, weak states, just as similarly organized central powers in western and eastern Asia had disintegrated in earlier centuries.

During the ninth century, Muslim, Magyar, and Viking invaders completed the breakup of the Carolingian Empire and local warlords rose to prominence. Different European regions responded by creating a variety of social and political relationships. Feudalism, a system of mutual obligations between lords and vassals, was the most notable of these new relationships. Kings struggled with popes and the nobility and in many cases increased their political control.

During the medieval period, western and central Europe underwent important economic and cultural changes. The population doubled, agriculture expanded, and town life, trade, and manufacturing grew. Christianity remained vigorous; in particular, monasteries met the religious needs of a generally pious population; however, religious minorities generally were not well treated and Jewish communities, especially in western Europe, suffered increasing discrimination.

A lively cultural life emerged in Europe during this era. The first European universities were founded during the late Middle Ages, encouraging philosophical and theological studies. The rudiments of the modern scientific method and outlook were also established, thanks in part to the translation of Greek and Arabic scientific works. In the late Middle Ages, literature, art, and architecture also reached great heights.

Despite the German conquest of the western portions of the Roman Empire by 500, the eastern Roman or Byzantine Empire continued to prosper. Its rulers retained Rome's political and social structure and fostered both Christianity and secular Greek culture. Justinian I, the greatest Byzantine ruler, codified the law and promoted intellectual and artistic activity.

Just as Rome, weakened by domestic problems, succumbed to outside conquerors, the Byzantine Empire ultimately did, too. By 1200 rebellions in the Balkans had led to the creation of independent states and the growing Arab/Islamic Empire took large pieces of territory in western Asia. In the thirteenth century, Latin crusaders propped up the Byzantine state for a short period of time, but the state never regained its former vitality. This left the way open for its final overthrow by the rising power of the Ottoman Turks.

While the history of the Byzantines was one of gradual decline, that of the Muslims was one of explosive expansion. Islam proved to be not only a dynamic new religion but also a force for political and economic unity. From 622 to 632, under the leadership of the prophet Muhammad, Islam was accepted by most of the tribes in the Arabian Peninsula. The first three caliphs following Muhammad's death initiated a series of military conquests that had established Islamic societies from the Indus River in the east to Spain in the west by 750. Like earlier centrally organized empires in Asia and the Western Hemisphere, the Umayyad caliphs at Damascus fostered a vibrant new culture by encouraging the arts and education. Islamic universities in Cairo and North Africa flourished. Like universities in Christian Europe, Islamic institutions of higher education also emphasized theology and philosophy, albeit from a differing religious and world viewpoint. All in all, Islamic expansion from West Asia to Africa and East Asia was one of the most rapid and far reaching in human history.

Eventually, the Muslim community, like the earlier Byzantine, Mesopotamian, and Egyptian Empires and some Chinese dynasties, also fell prey to open civil strife. This ultimately fragmented the Islamic world into a number of competing political centers. In addition, the community of Muslims split between the Sunnis, who thought the right to rule could be exercised by any believer, and the Shi'i, who maintained that rule should follow through Muhammad, Ali, and their successors. This schism was the major cause for the collapse of the Umayyad Caliphate in Damascus and the emergence of the rival Abbasid Caliphate in Baghdad. Similar divisions in Christianity would later threaten the hegemony of the Catholic church and fragment political leadership in Europe.

Selected Sources

*Abu-Lughod, Janet L. *Before European Hegemony: The World System A.D. 1250–1350.* 1990. An intriguing discussion of the patterns of cultural and commercial interaction across Eurasia in the period covered.

Akkad, Mostapha, dir. *The Message.* A historically correct and spectacular epic film about Muhammad and the early converts to Islam. Also available in videotape.

*Amt, Emilie, ed. *Women's Lives in Medieval Europe: A Sourcebook.* 1993. A valuable collection of primary documents.

*Angold, Michael. *The Byzantine Empire, 1025–1204.* 1997. This political history provides a fine overview of the empire during a key period of change.

Armstrong, Karen. *Islam: A Short History.* 2000. A good, concise overview by a leading theologian.

*Bayard, Tania, ed. and trans. *A Medieval Home Companion: Housekeeping in the Fourteenth Century.* 1991. A handbook of instructions written for his fifteen-year-old bride by an elderly citizen of Paris around 1393.

Benjamin of Tudela. *The Itinerary of Benjamin of Tudela: Travels in the Middle Ages.* Rev. ed. 1987. This twelfth-century travelogue, by a Jewish native of Navarre, contains fascinating descriptions of hundreds of cities: Baghdad, Constantinople, Alexandria, Jerusalem, among others.

*Benko, Stephen. *Pagan Rome and the Early Christians.* 1984. A good account of the collision of paganism and Christianity in the Roman world.

*Brown, Peter. *The World of Late Antiquity: A.D. 150–750.* 1971. Especially valuable for its coverage of religious and cultural developments and of the transition from antiquity to the Middle Ages.

"The Byzantine Empire." Insight Media. Two-part video (thirty minutes each) tracing the empire's glory and long decline.

Chuvin, Pierre. *A Chronicle of the Last Pagans.* Trans. B. A. Archer. 1990. A recent account of the momentous changes in religious life in the Roman Empire as seen from the pagan vantage point.

Clark, Gillian. *Women in Late Antiquity: Pagan and Christian Life-styles.* 1993. An engaging and highly informative treatment of women's lives, based on an intimate familiarity with the primary sources.

*Davis, R. H. C. *A History of Medieval Europe: From Constantine to Saint Louis.* 2d ed. 1988. A thorough, highly readable, and up-to-date history.

*Endress, Gerhard. *An Introduction to Islam.* 1994. A balanced reference work on the basics of Islam and Muslim practices.

"The Five Pillars of Islam." Films for the Humanities. Video on Islamic faith in historical context.

Fleischer, Richard, dir. *The Vikings.* 1958. An adventure story treatment of Viking activities; filmed on location in Norway and Brittany.

*Gardner, John. *Grendel.* 1971. An enthralling short novel that retells the Beowulf story, but from the point of view of the monster!

*Gottfried, Robert S. *The Black Death: Natural and Human Disaster in Medieval Europe.* 1983. An engrossing account of the causes, course, and consequences of the great plague.

*Gregory of Tours. *The History of the Franks.* Trans. Lewis Thorpe. 1976. In this work, a sixth-century bishop describes the history and illuminates the life of his people.

*Hinks, Roger. *Carolingian Art.* 1962. Provides a useful insight into the ideas and values of the period as expressed in painting and sculpture.

*Hourani, Albert. *A History of the Arab Peoples.* 1991. Splendid chapters on social development, demographic movements, and historical issues.

"Islam and Christianity." Films for the Humanities and Sciences. This thirty-minute video explores the long and often hostile relations between two major world religions.

*Kaegi, Walter. *Byzantium and the Early Islamic Conquests.* 1992. A military history of the early clashes between the Byzantine and Muslim Empires.

*Kagan, Donald, ed. *The End of the Roman Empire: Decline or Transformation?* 3d ed. 1992. A good anthology of essays constituting a helpful, brief survey of major theories.

*Kennedy, Hugh. *The Prophet and the Age of the Caliphates.* 1986. An excellent introduction to the rise and growth of Islam to the eleventh century.

*Mattingly, Harold. *Christianity in the Roman Empire.* 1967. An extremely concise and cogent account of the subject; originally a series of lectures.

Medieval Epics. Trans. William Alfred et al. 1963. Includes *Beowulf, The Song of Roland, The Nibelungenlied,* and *The Poem of the Cid.*

Momigliano, Arnaldo. *Essays on Ancient and Modern Judaism.* Ed. S. Berti, trans. M. Masella-Gayley. 1994. The essays on the Jews in ancient Greek and Roman society are especially valuable.

*Moriarty, Catherine. *The Voice of the Middle Ages in Personal Letters, 1100–1500.* 1989. This compendium of

*Available in paperback.

200 letters includes selections from Petrarch, Dèrer, Da Vinci, and Eleanor of Aquitane.

Nicol, Donald MacGillivray. *The Byzantine Lady: Ten Portraits, 1250–1500.* 1994. Fascinating account of women within the empire.

Norwich, John J. *Byzantium: The Decline and Fall.* 1996. A thoughtful analysis, particularly of the schism between the Roman Catholic and the Eastern Orthodox churches.

Reynolds, Susan. *Kingdoms and Communities in Western Europe, 900–1300.* 2d ed. 1997. An excellent, very current study that stresses both social and political history.

*Riché, Pierre. *Daily Life in the World of Charlemagne.* Trans. Jo Ann McNamara. 1978; reprinted 1988. A fascinating survey of the topic; gives an engrossing account of the activities, values, and preoccupations of people on all strata of society.

———. *The Carolingians: A Family Who Forged Europe.* 1983; trans. M. I. Allen. 1993. A thorough investigation of the Carolingian era in medieval history.

Todd, Malcolm. *The Early Germans.* 1992. An account of the changes brought by the migration of Germanic tribes throughout Europe and North Africa between 400 and 600.

*Tuchman, Barbara W. *A Distant Mirror: The Calamitous 14th Century.* 1978. A riveting account, with a focus on the life of a French knight.

Vermes, Geza. *The Complete Dead Sea Scrolls in English.* 1997. This is the best and most complete edition of the scrolls published to date.

Williams, Marty, and Anne Echols. *Between Pit and Pedestal: Women in the Middle Ages.* 1993. Features lively, accurate recreations of the everyday lives of women of many social classes and occupations.

*Wilson, David M. *The Vikings and Their Origins: Scandinavia in the First Millennium.* 1989. An excellent recent treatment of the subject; good illustrations.

*Winston, Richard. *Charlemagne: From the Hammer to the Cross.* 1954. A lively biography of the emperor by a modern popular writer.

Ziegler, Philip. *The Black Death.* 1969. A useful discussion of the social and economic consequences of the plague that swept through Europe in the fourteenth century.

Internet Links

Byzantine Collection: Selected Images
http://www.doaks.org/byzcollimages.html
A beautiful gallery of Byzantine artworks in the Dumbarton Oaks collection.

Interactive Bible/Church History Timeline
http://www.olivetree.com/history/
This helpful site assists in studying significant people and events in biblical history.

Internet Medieval Sourcebook: Selected Sources, Byzantium
http://www.fordham.edu/halsall/sbook1c.html
A huge compendium of primary sources on many aspects of Byzantine history and culture.

Medieval Art
http://www.metmuseum.org/collections/department.asp?dep=17&mark=2#a
This site, part of the Metropolitan Museum of Art's website, features fifty high-quality illustrations with commentary.

Middle Ages: What Was It Really Like to Live in the Middle Ages?
http://www.learner.org/exhibits/middleages/
Produced by the Annenberg/CPB Project Exhibits Collection, this website examines feudal life, religion, homes, clothing, health, arts and entertainment, and town life.

The Rightly-Guided Caliphs
http://www.usc.edu/dept/MSA/politics/firstfourcaliphs.html
A concise account of the first four caliphs and their times, by the National Muslim Student Association of the USA and Canada.

Scrolls from the Dead Sea: The Ancient Library of Qumran and Modern Scholarship
http://sunsite.unc.edu/expo/deadsea.scrolls.exhibit/intro.html
This site provides extensive information about all aspects of the scrolls and the community of people that produced them. Superb text and graphics.

Disruption and Renewal in South and East Asia

6

Then Amaterasu . . . commanded the heir apparent saying:

"Now it is reported that the pacification of the Central Land of the Reed Plains has been finished. Therefore, descend and rule it, as you have been entrusted with it."

Then the heir apparent replied saying:

"As I was preparing to descend, a child was born; his name is Ninigi. . . . This child should descend."

Hereupon, she [Amaterasu] imparted [unto Ninigi] the myriad Maga-Tama beads and the mirror which had been used to lure, as well as the sword . . . and said:

*"This mirror—have [it with you] as my spirit, and worship it just as you would worship in my presence."**

*On September the ninth the decree was given. Henceforth the T'ang Imperial Dynasty was abolished, and the new one was to be called Chou. . . . [Empress Wu] assumed the audacious title "Holy Spirit Emperor." It was an advance from "Holy Mother Divine Sovereign" [a title she had earlier assumed]. At last her ambition was realized. She was a "female emperor," not an empress only. The term "Holy Spirit" constituted also an advance toward divinity.***

**Kojiki*, trans. Donald L. Philippi (Princeton: Princeton University Press; Tokyo: University of Tokyo Press, 1969), pp. 137–140.

**James P. Holoka and Jiu-Hwa L. Upshur, eds., *Lives and Times: A World History Reader* (Minneapolis/St. Paul: West Publishing, 1995), vol. 1, p. 183.

Anthropologists and historians speculate that early human societies were matrilineal. Evidence supports this thesis in Japan, where the Shinto founding myth tells how the Sun Goddess Amaterasu began Japan's imperial line. The items that Amaterasu gave to her grandson became the three imperial treasures that symbolize sovereignty to this day. Early Chinese travelers corroborate the matrilineal thesis with accounts of a Japanese ruler called the sun princess, and a number of empresses in fact ruled during Japan's first historic centuries.

In China, a patrilineal society, with a sharp division between male and female spheres, has prevailed throughout recorded history. Daughters were denied the right of political succession, although mothers and wives often exercised great power in both the government and family. Empress Wu of the T'ang dynasty has the unique distinction of deposing and killing her own sons to succeed her dead husband as female emperor. She gave herself titles that were unprecedented in Chinese history and attempted to establish her own dynasty. Ill health, however, forced her to retire at age eighty and her experiment came to an end.

In both India and China, a period of invasions and upheavals followed the first great imperial age. As in western Europe after the Roman Empire collapsed, when imperial restraints crumbled and new peoples arrived, India experienced an age of innovation and creativity.

The Gupta dynasty reunified northern India in the fourth century C.E.; during its two-century rule, Indian culture reached its golden age. Hinduism began the evolution that has continued to the present day while Buddhism began its irrevocable decline. Islam became a force on the Indian subcontinent from the beginning of the eighth century, and by 1000 C.E. Muslims from central Asia controlled all northern India. Although unable to ward off the invaders, Hinduism and Hindu culture survived. Buddhism, however, vanished from India. The Gupta and post-Gupta period saw the expansion of Indian culture throughout a great part of island and mainland Southeast Asia through a peaceful transmission by Indian traders, missionaries, and immigrants.

China fragmented soon after the collapse of the Han dynasty in 220 C.E.; nomadic invaders ruled the North for three centuries while weak native dynasties ruled the South. Buddhism now became the dominant religion, enriching Chinese civilization with its teachings and the Greco-Roman-Indian artistic traditions. China was reunified in 581 and entered a grand second imperial age under the T'ang dynasty. China was powerful and cosmopolitan under the T'ang, absorbing from other cultures and passing on its great achievements. The following Sung dynasty refined many earlier traditions but failed to continue the diplomatic and military successes of its predecessor. Cultured, urban, and refined, the Sung suffered repeated military reverses before its ultimate conquest by the Mongols in the thirteenth century.

Chinese political power expanded Chinese civilization to Korea and Vietnam starting around 100 B.C.E. Japan voluntarily accepted most aspects of Chinese civilization and sinicized Buddhism. In Southeast Asia, Korea, and Japan, distinctive cultures emerged from the fusing of Indian and Chinese influences with indigenous traditions.

This chapter will explore the forces of disruption and renewal that shaped India and China and their enduring legacies at home and abroad.

India from the Guptas to the Muslim Dynasties

*The people are numerous and happy; they have not to register their households, or attend to any magistrates or their rules; only those who cultivate the royal land have to pay a portion of the gain from it. . . . Throughout the country the people do not kill any living creature, nor eat onion or garlic.**

He caused distress to no man in the city, but he chastised the wicked.

Even in this mean age he did not fail the trust of the people.

He cherished the citizens as his own children and he put down crime.

*He delighted the inhabitants with gifts and honours, and smiling conversation, and he increased their love with informal visits and friendly receptions.***

*H. H. Gowen, *History of Indian Literature* (New York: Appleton, 1931), p. 336.
**A. L. Basham, *The Wonder That Was India* (New York: Grove Press, 1954), p. 104.

The first passage was written by Fa-hsien, a famous Chinese pilgrim who traveled and studied in India during the Gupta period. The second, which was found on a contemporary rock inscription, describes the exemplary provincial administration under an early Gupta king. Both accounts describe a well-governed land under the Gupta dynasty, which had succeeded in uniting northern India. The Guptas and Harsha were the last of the Hindu/Buddhist monarchs to rule over a united and flourishing northern India. Soon after Harsha's death, the region was subjected to centuries of Muslim invasions that permanently changed the religious composition of the subcontinent.

The Gupta Empire, Harsha, and the Rajputs

With the breakup of the Kushan state, northern India was once again fragmented into numerous petty states. Early in the fourth century, a minor prince named Chandra Gupta rose to power in the Delhi region where the Jumna and Ganges Rivers converge. Around 320, after victories in war and marriage to the princess of a powerful tribe, he crowned himself "Great King of Kings," an act that began the Gupta era. By the time he died in 335, the Gupta dynasty ruled the Ganges River valley, the heartland of the earlier Mauryan Empire.

In several respects the early reigns of the Gupta dynasty seemed a reenactment of the Mauryan era. Chandra Gupta I was followed by his son, Samudra Gupta (reigned 335–376). Most of the information about him comes from a eulogy inscribed on an Asokan pillar, praising him as a great warrior who had "violently uprooted" nine kings in northern India, an act that won him the title of "exterminator of all other kings." Samudra Gupta added large parts of northern India to his direct rule and made vassals of the remaining rulers. He was also a cultured man, a capable administrator, tolerant of different religions, and a

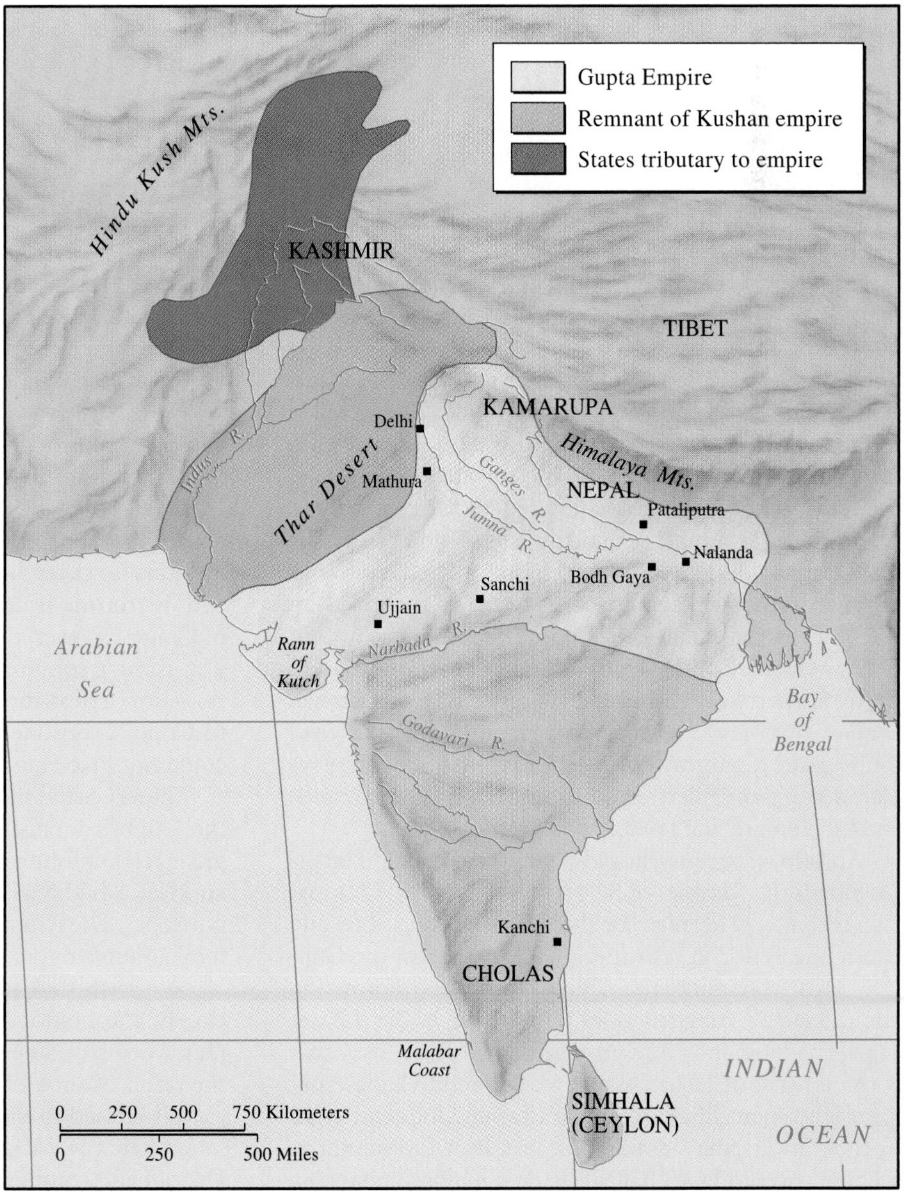

Map 6.1 The Gupta Empire. The great early Gupta rulers conquered most of northern India and gave that area an extended period of peace and prosperity. But even at its height, the Gupta Empire did not control southern India.

patron of the arts. The reign of his son Chandra Gupta II (reigned 376–415) was the high-water mark of the Gupta Empire, to which he added the Deccan region.

The early Gupta dynasty is India's classical age because it established the standards in culture and the arts that later eras looked to for inspiration and example. Just as the Greek ambassador Megasthenes' observations provided insights into the Mauryan Empire, another foreigner, the Chinese Buddhist pilgrim Fa-hsien, supplied information about life in the reign of Chandra Gupta II. Fa-hsien traveled widely in India between 405 and 411 and spoke glowingly of the efficient and benevolent government and a merciful justice system, the rarity of crime, and the generally peaceful state of the land. He marveled that one could travel from one end of India to the other without fear of molestation and without need of passports. On social customs and mores Fa-hsien said: "In this country they do not keep swine or fowls, and do not deal in cattle; they have no shambles [butcher shops] or wine-shops in their market places. In commerce they use cowrie-shells. The Pariahs alone hunt and sell flesh." He also recorded the grandeur of the capital city, Pataliputra, its great religious processions, and the charitable institutions maintained by people of means. Considering the conditions in a divided China and the problems besetting the contemporary late Roman Empire, India under the early Guptas was without doubt the best-governed and most prosperous empire in the world.

The later Guptas, who reigned after 415, were mostly undistinguished rulers, and northern India once again came under attack by invaders. The White Huns, called Huna in India, were nomads from central Asia, who may have been related to the Huns who threatened Europe in the same period. The Huna invaded India repeatedly in the fifth century; much of northwestern India, especially Buddhist establishments in the region, suffered enormous damage from their depredations. Some historians claim that the earlier Chinese defeat of the Hsiung-nu and Gupta resistance of the Huna led other Hunnish tribes to move further west and eventually penetrate the Roman Empire. Resistance to the repeated invasions weakened the Gupta Empire, which disappeared by 550. It was replaced by minor rulers who had once been Gupta vassals and by Hunnish and related tribal states.

In 606 a sixteen-year-old young man named Harsha ascended the throne of a petty state in the Jumna-Ganges valley. He ruled for the next forty-one years and nearly succeeded in restoring the glory days of the Guptas. Two contemporary sources provide information about Harsha (reigned 606–648). One is the *Life of Harsha,* a biography by a protégé named Bana; the other is the journal of Hsuan-tsang, a celebrated Chinese pilgrim who spent fifteen years on the subcontinent, eight of them in Harsha's dominions, and kept a voluminous account. According to Bana, Harsha upon becoming king "went from east to west, subduing all who were not obedient." He was so busy that "the elephants were not unharnessed, nor the soldiers unhelmeted." In six years he had subdued all northern India, but was not able to gain control of the Deccan and the south. He then reigned in peace for thirty-five years.

Harsha was a gifted and energetic ruler. He traveled constantly to render justice and to supervise the government. Although inclined toward Buddhism, he nevertheless patronized all religions. A distinguished scholar and patron of learning, he was also the author of three plays. Harsha was a lavish sponsor of charities and built many hospitals to dispense free medical care to the poor and travelers. According to Hsuan-tsang, on one occasion for seventy-five days Harsha and his retinue distributed the wealth of the treasury and his personal possessions to half a million people, until nothing remained "except for the horses, elephants and military accouterments, which were necessary for maintaining order and protecting the royal estate, nothing remained."

Soon after witnessing Harsha's remarkable largess, Hsuan-tsang, who had been away from home for sixteen years, decided to return to China. He refused all Harsha's gifts except for a fur cloak and money for his traveling expenses. But he was laden with the treasures for which he had come to India. They included 651 manuscripts and numerous relics and images of the Buddha and Buddhist saints. Harsha's escort accompanied the Chinese pilgrim to the frontier of his realm. When Hsuan-tsang arrived at Changan, the Chinese capital, in 646, he was welcomed as a great celebrity by the Chinese emperor, his court, and thousands of ordinary people.

Thanks to the bond established by Hsuan-tsang, Harsha exchanged ambassadors with the Chinese emperor T'ai-tsung. When T'ai-tsung's third envoy arrived in India, however, he found Harsha had been assassinated and his throne usurped. In a remarkable demonstration of Chinese power, the ambassador rushed to Tibet where T'ai-tsung's son-in-law was king, raised an army and returned to defeat the usurper, who was arrested and taken to China as prisoner. Nevertheless, Chinese intervention could not save Harsha's kingdom from disintegration.

Superficially there were many similarities between the Gupta administration and that of the Mauryas. The great accomplishment of the Mauryans had been the creation of a highly centralized empire of continental proportions. The Guptas, however, failed to reduce their local administrators to total obedience. The town and village councils and the professional guilds also remained largely autonomous. Inadequate revenue compelled the Guptas to pay official salaries partly in land grants, with the result of a rise of local power. Thus the king's authority was limited to those areas under his direct control.

When the Mauryan Empire fell, the people of the Deccan and southern India had freed themselves and es-

Life during Harsha's Reign

*With respect to the ordinary people, although they are naturally light-minded, yet they are upright and honourable. In money matters they are without craft, and in administering justice they are considerate. They dread the retribution of another state of existence, and make light of the things of the present world. They are not deceitful in their conduct, and are faithful to their oaths and promises. In the rules of government there is remarkable rectitude, whilst in their behaviour there is much gentleness and sweetness. With respect to criminals and rebels, these are few in number, and only occasionally troublesome. . . . As the administration of the government is founded on benign principles, the executive is simple. The families are not entered on registers, and the people are not subject to forced labour. The private [holdings] of the crown are divided into four principal parts; the first is for carrying out affairs of state and providing sacrificial offerings; the second is for providing subsidies for the ministers and chief officers of state; the third is for rewarding men of distinguished ability; and the fourth is for charity to religious bodies, whereby the field of merit is cultivated. In this way the taxes on the people are light, and the personal service required of them is moderate.**

These comments about India by the Chinese Buddhist pilgrim Hsuan-tsang paint a picture of good government and contented people under Harsha. They agree with observations of other Chinese pilgrims who had visited India somewhat earlier during the Gupta dynasty. In this way Harsha's reign forms the finale of the Gupta era.

**Si-Yu-Ki Buddhist Records of the Western World,* translated from the Chinese of Hiuen Tsiang (A.D. 629) by Samuel Beal (London: Truther, 1884), pp. 83, 87.

tablished independent kingdoms. The inscriptions that have survived, the remains of cave temples, and the records of Chinese pilgrims agree that Buddhism flourished throughout the region in the post-Mauryan centuries. South India was prosperous because it produced spices and precious stones desired by the Romans and other peoples. Since the first century C.E., increased knowledge of the winds and currents brought about a flourishing sea trade between south Indian ports and the Persian Gulf, the Red Sea, Southeast Asia, and China.

Harsha was assassinated in 648. Amidst the political anarchy that followed in northern India, the first of many Muslim armies crossed the mountains in the northwest and appeared at the plains of the Indus in 712. While some Muslims raided and then retreated, others came to stay. In these actions they were no different from earlier invaders, but, whereas the Greeks and central Asian tribal raiders that preceded them had been rapidly assimilated, the Muslims, with their rigidly defined religion, largely retained their separate identities.

Religious Developments: Hinduism and Buddhism

Modern Hinduism gradually emerged during and after the Gupta era. The intellectual basis of Hinduism was revitalized as the brahmans expounded the philosophy of the Upanishads and debated Buddhist theologians. At the same time, in response to the challenge of Buddhist and Jain teachings, ways of life for the ordinary Hindu also began to evolve. They were called the Way of Worship and the Way of Works. All Hindus believed in the law of karma, that deeds had their consequences; they hoped by following dharma or the sacred law, they could finally attain ***moksha*** (release from the round of reincarnations). While some brahmans and ascetics studied the philosophy of the Upanishads and thus followed the Way of Wisdom, most men and women followed the more attainable Way of Worship or the Way of Works.

In the Way of Worship, a devotee chose a personal deity and did his or her bidding, attended temple ceremonies, and took pilgrimages. While the Vedic gods receded in importance, three earlier obscure gods emerged to the forefront. One was Brahma, the creator god and the personified universal spirit of the Upanishads. The primary objects of worship, however, were Vishnu (patron god to many Gupta rulers), the benevolent preserver god, and Shiva, the fearsome god of death and fertility. Myths about the gods were collected in the Puranas, the equivalent of the Bible of popular Hinduism. As the Puranas told believers, Vishnu has been reincarnated nine times, and each time he saved the world from demons and evil forces. His early incarnations, or *avatars*, were in animal form—for example, the Fish, who saved Manu, the father of the human race, from the Cosmic Flood. The seventh incarnation was Rama, the perfect man, the deified hero of the epic *Ramayana*, who is worshipped together with his faithful wife Sita, the ideal woman. The eighth incarnation was Krishna the "dark [skinned]," probably originally a non-Aryan god of the south. Stories about Krishna's pranks as a youth, his popularity with ladies as a young man, and his championship of moral duty as a mature man are known and loved by all Hindus. His ninth incarnation was Gautama Buddha. The admission of Gautama into the Hindu pantheon blurred differences between Hindus and Buddhists and hastened the absorption of Buddhists into the orthodox Hindu fold. After the twelfth century, with the destruction of the remnants of the great Buddhist establishments in northern India by Muslim conquerors, Buddhism finally vanished from the land of its birth. The tenth reincarnation of Vishnu is yet to come. Vishnu was worshipped with his wife Lakshmi, the goddess of good luck; the two are frequently depicted together in affectionate poses.

Shiva. This eighteenth-century painting shows the male and female aspects of the god of destruction with the Bull of Nandi, Shiva's mount and a fertility symbol, below them.

While millions worshipped Vishnu, other millions, mainly in southern India, called themselves devotees of Shiva. In addition to death and fertility, Shiva was identified with the Vedic storm god Rudra and was also patron god of ascetics, lord of the dance, and the embodiment of cosmic energy. Shiva's wife manifested herself in different forms, often as the fertility goddess, perhaps the mother goddess of the Indus civilization. As Durga and Kali, she was bloody and terrible and demanded sacrifices. (Among those who worshipped Kali were members of a small sect called Thuggees, from which the English word "thug" derives. Thuggees specialized in robbing and killing travelers as acts of devotion to Kali.) Their pot-bellied and elephant-headed son Ganesha was the patron god of learning.

The gods and goddesses are represented by statues and pictures and are worshipped at home, in temples, and at special ceremonies with offerings of flowers, food, dance, and incense. Sites associated with them were also the destination of pilgrims. Fertility cults that worshipped the mother goddess and other symbols were popular throughout the land.

While worshipping their personal deities, Hindus were also encouraged to follow the Way of Works. It taught that all persons were born and reared in their respective castes and must follow caste rules. As an inscription of the Gupta dynasty says, good rulers should "keep the castes confined to their respective spheres of duty." In addition, all must repay their debts to parents and ancestors through the proper discharge of duty and responsibility to family, to seers through diligent study and proper respect, to the gods through worship, and to humanity through charity and kindness. In living up to the demands of the Ways of Worship and Works Hindu men and women hoped to acquire good karma and either in this life or future incarnations be able to follow the Way of Wisdom. These essential teachings and practices of Hinduism persist to the present.

The Guptas and Harsha patronized both Hinduism and Buddhism. Leaders of both religions held frequent theological debates. Jewish and Christian communities also appeared in India during this era. Some Jews came to India as refugees after the Great Dispersion of 70 C.E. Their descendents still live in Kerala on the southwestern coast of India, and are divided into two groups: the "white Jews," who claim to have retained their Semitic racial identity, and the "black Jews," who have intermarried with Indians. Most Indian Christians also lived in Kerala. They claimed descent from converts of the apostle Thomas, who had reputedly come to proselytize in India. They professed the Syrian branch of Christianity; many are prominent in modern India.

Art, Architecture, Life, and Culture

Indian art is inextricably linked with religion. Both Buddhist and classical Hindu art reached their peaks during the Gupta era, which saw the synthesis and climax of previous tendencies and produced the classic style that inspired much of the art of the entire Buddhist and Hindu world throughout Asia.

The goal of religious art, in India as elsewhere, was to express devotion and to make religious and philosophical ideals intelligible to all people. The greatest contributions of Gupta artists are their classical representation of the divinities of India. These works combine vigor, refinement, and sublime idealism with a sense of rhythm and movement. In sculptures of the Buddha, the ideal of serenity found its noblest expression and became the standard.

The most impressive surviving Buddhist sites are the cave temples. The grandest is Ajanta, located in the Deccan in an isolated hillside by a river valley. Although the caves were excavated more than a thousand years between the first century B.C.E. and the ninth century C.E., most were built during a great burst of artistic activity in the mid-fifth century. Each of the twenty-nine cave temples is entered through a portal into the main hall where two rows of columns divided the interior into a central nave and side aisles, in much the same way as the interior of Christian basilica churches is divided. At the far end of the hall is either a giant image of the Buddha or a stupa that commemorates his nirvana. A typical hall is sixty-five feet square, with a fourteen-foot-high ceiling. Beyond the halls and cut still deeper into the cliffs are the monks' quarters. Intricately carved columns and capitals, sculptures in the round, and friezes decorate the caves. The Ajanta caves can be compared with the Acropolis, built in Athens a thousand years earlier. Both exemplify the highest artistic accomplishments of their respective culture's classical periods, and both were built to honor the gods and the achievements of the people.

A remarkable number of fresco paintings have survived in Ajanta; they are hailed as among the greatest wall paintings anywhere in the world. Although the subject matter is Buddhist, many scenes are drawn from contemporary life. The depictions of voluptuous ladies and sumptuous scenes illustrate Indian reconciliation of the sensuous and worldly with the spiritual and religious.

Revitalized Hinduism, already strong in the Gupta period, was represented in cave and free-standing temples. In addition to several Ajanta caves that were Hindu, other contemporary cave temples were dedicated exclusively to Hindu deities. Shiva and Vishnu were most often represented in these Hindu shrines. In contrast with the serenity exhibited by Buddha statues, Vishnu and Shiva are often shown in poses full of dynamic energy; they frequently appear in association with their female counterparts. A remarkable eighth-century Hindu temple dedicated to Shiva is located near Ajanta. The immense structure is actually not a building in the conventional sense. It was literally carved out of the rock of a hillside, a rare technical feat.

Metal casting also reached its apogee. The castings range from an eighty-foot-tall copper image of the Buddha at Nalanda to the huge wrought Iron Pillar of Delhi that would have been a feat for even the best foundries of the modern age. The rich variety of gold coins of the Guptas also showed artistic excellence. The highly developed aesthetic sense and excellent mastery of execution of Gupta sculptures made them the ideal and despair of artists of later generations.

Scala/Art Resource

Ajanta Cave Temples. These rock temples were cut into cliffs 250 feet high, standing above a river valley, and date from the first century B.C.E. to the ninth century C.E. This picture shows the façade (or entrance) of a Gupta-era cave temple at Ajanta.

Literature and scholarship in India always depended in part on court patronage. The Guptas patronized many genres of the arts. Literature ranged from refined court poetry to popular fairy tales and fables. "Sinbad the Sailor" and several other stories popularized in *A Thousand and One Nights* originated in India.

Whereas Egyptians wrote on papyrus and the Chinese invented paper, the first surviving Indian books that date to the fifth century were written on birch bark and specially prepared leaves. The resurgence of Hinduism resulted in the revival of Sanskrit, now used in Hindu as well as Buddhist and Jain writings. Other works from this period dealt with law, medicine, and the sciences. Indian scholars devised a sign for zero and worked out a decimal number system, knowledge that was transmitted to the Arabs and later adopted by the rest of the world, which called it the Arabic numeral system. India also led other cultures in knowledge of algebra and is largely credited with founding modern mathematics. Astronomy became a separate discipline. Astronomers found out that the earth was round and rotated on its axis and calculated the length of the year to almost the exact length we know today.

Formal education for men was offered at both brahmanical and Buddhist institutions. The curriculum resembled that in medieval European universities and included theology, grammar, rhetoric, logic, metaphysics, prose and verse composition, and medicine. Interestingly, the first works on veterinary medicine date to Gupta India and dealt mainly with horses and elephants, probably because of their value in the army. The famous university at Nalanda had an international student body that included men from China, Ceylon, and Southeast Asia. Students received free board and tuition from the revenue of lands that had been donated to the monastery. There were no schools for girls, though upper-class girls were taught at home. The only women with a life independent of the family were Buddhist nuns, actresses, courtesans, and prostitutes. The courtesan was a cultured female companion, like the hetaera of ancient Greece and geisha of Japan.

Towns grew, many with specialized functions or crafts for domestic consumption or export. Many towns were planned with streets that were oriented to cardinal points, with drains and wells. The rich lived in brick houses, the poor in houses made with wattled bamboo. Public parks provided places for recreation and musical performances. Popular culture flourished. Frequent religious festivals lent color to daily life. People participated in processions and elaborate religious festivals at richly decorated temples, the dwelling places of gods and goddesses.

The family was patriarchal, land was owned jointly by the extended family, and women were subordinate to men, but children were taught to obey both parents. Marriages were arranged by parents and took place when both parties were very young. Except for those of princes, unions were monogamous. Because of the hot climate, clothing tended to be scanty and loose fitting, except in the cold north, where people wore close-fitting jackets. Men often wore only a loincloth, sometimes with another piece of fabric thrown over the body. Women wore a *sari* or a long piece of cloth wound around the waist in folds, falling to the feet, and draped across the shoulder. Both sexes wore long hair, loose or braided, and both, especially women, adorned themselves with jewelry and flowers.

Hsuan-tsang described Indians as clean and fastidious in manners. He said of their eating habits:

> Before every meal they must have a wash; the fragments and remains are not served up again; the food utensils are not passed on; those which are of pottery or of wood must be thrown away after use, and those which are of

Sensuous Secular Art. These two Indian sculptures, one of a mother and child, the other of a lady striking a sensuous pose, show an appreciation of voluptuous beauty, enhanced by the light clothing and rich jewelry worn by Indians.

Left: Borromeo/Art Resource, NY Right: Nimatallah/Art Resource, NY gold, silver, copper or iron get another polishing. As soon as a meal is over they chew the tooth-stick and make themselves clean. Before they have finished ablutions they do not come in contact with each other.

At death the mighty and humble alike were cremated. The virtuous upper caste widow committed *suttee,* or suicide at the funeral pyre of her husband.

India under the Impact of Islam

In 712, two generations after the death of Harsha, an Arab army conquered Sind, in northwest India, an event heralding the powerful role that Islam would soon play in the history of India. Earlier attackers had been assimilated over time, but these Muslim invaders would not be, because their iconoclastic monotheism was incompatible with Hinduism and Buddhism. Although the zeal of some early Muslim conquerors embittered relations with Hindus, some lower-caste Hindus found dignity in the religious equality that Islam accorded to all believers and converted voluntarily.

The Arab invaders of 712 did not penetrate beyond Sind and generally lived in amity with their neighbors. Meanwhile, the Arabs conquered and converted the Turks of central Asia. Ferocious warriors, now on behalf of Islam, the Turks at first enlisted as bodyguards of their Arab rulers but in time asserted their independence and established their own states. Some Turkic slave bodyguards even established slave dynasties. In 1023 Mahmud of Ghazni, in present-day Afghanistan, rode into India with 30,000 mounted warriors, pillaging and killing as they went. Mahmud called himself the "image-breaker," because he delighted in destroying Hindu and Buddhist places of worship and killing "nonbelievers." His soldiers boasted that they massacred 50,000 Hindus in one Hindu shrine city alone.

Turkish conquerors after Mahmud continued to wreak havoc on Buddhist and Hindu institutions and places of worship. Countless Hindu, Buddhist, and Jain shrines were demolished; some of their stones were recycled to build mosques and monuments to commemorate Muslim power. The Qutb Minar (victory tower) in Delhi was partly built with stones from demolished Hindu and Jain temples. The great Buddhist university at Nalanda, its library filled with priceless manuscripts, was destroyed. Buddhism never recovered from those blows. Hinduism survived in northern India, but without the state patronage that had allowed it to blossom intellectually it turned inward. The caste system became more rigid, and, in compliance with Muslim standards, women became more secluded and wore the veil in public.

Some Indians, most notably the Rajputs of northern India, fought the invaders bravely. *Rajput* means son of a king. Rajputs were kshatriyas (warrior caste), and according to their genealogies they belonged to thirty-two clans that descended from the sun, the moon, and the stars. Modern scholars think that they were descended from the Huna and other previous invaders who had become assimilated and had created fake genealogies to lend themselves greater dignity. Like the knights of medieval Europe and the *samurai* of Japan, they were fiercely proud hereditary warriors. The young Rajputs were brought up on epic stories of old. On reaching puberty, boys went through a ceremony called the binding of the sword, which bound them to a code of honor that included respect for women. The men disdained manual labor; they either fought or hunted and played manly sports. Women enjoyed considerable freedom; they hunted and even went to war with their husbands. On the other hand, when her husband died in battle, a Rajput woman was expected proudly to mount his funeral

Victory Tower. Built around 1200, the Qutb Minar or Victory Tower sits on the site of a demolished Hindu temple. It was built by Muslims to commemorate their conquest of Delhi.

A Rajput Lady's Creed

"Boy, tell me, ere I go, how bore himself my lord?"

"As a reaper of the harvest of battle! I followed his steps as the humble gleaner of his sword. On the bed of honour he spread a carpet of the slain, whereon, a barbarian his pillow, he sleeps ringed by his foes."

"Yet once again, oh boy, tell me how my lord bore himself?"

*"Oh mother, who can tell his deeds. He left no foe to dread or to admire him." She smiled farewell to the boy, and adding, "My lord will chide my delay," sprang into the flame.**

The Rajputs loved epics about heroic deeds in battle and the hunt. The stories, sung by bards, celebrated the heroism of both men and women. In this tale, the widow asked her fallen husband's page about his death at the Muslim siege of Chitor; then she sacrificed her life to honor him. Other tales told of Rajput ladies committing mass suicides at the news of their husbands' deaths in battle, rather than surrender to the Muslims. They built a huge funeral pyre and leapt into the flames.

*H. G. Rawlinson, *India: A Short Cultural History,* p. 202, quoted in James Tod, *Annals and Antiquities of Rajasthan* (London: H. Mitford, 1920), vol. 1, p. 246.

pyre and commit suicide. When not fighting Muslim invaders, Rajputs often fought among themselves. Indian bards composed and recited epic poems that celebrated the brave deeds of Rajput lords and ladies in customs similar to those of the ancient Macedonian chieftains and medieval European knights.

The Rajputs never became a united force and were defeated by the conquering Muslims. Since Hindu society clearly demarcated functions, only the kshatriyas had a duty to fight. On the other hand, when Muslims subjugated ever larger territories, the social cohesiveness of the caste system enabled the Hindus to persevere and thus preserve their way of life.

During these centuries, politically divided southern India escaped Muslim conquest and the ravages suffered by the north. Temple building, culture, and art flourished in the south, and, with northern India under Turkish Muslim rule, it was here that Indian styles and trends in art and architecture persisted. Southern Indian culture also inspired and influenced the Indianized states of Southeast Asia.

Indianized Southeast Asia

The city is twenty li *[three li equals a mile] in circumference and is pierced by five gates, each with two portals. . . . A huge moat protects the wall spanned by massive bridges. Fifty-four stone carved warrior deities stand guard on either side of each bridge, looking huge and fierce. All five gates are similar. . . .*

The city wall is twenty feet tall and made of stone, so well fitted together that grass cannot grow in the crevices. There are no crenellations. . . . On the inside of the wall there is a sloping earthen rampart over a hundred feet wide, pierced by gates that are open during day hours and closed at night, and watched by guards. . . .

In this country most trading is done by women; that is why as soon as a Chinese man arrives in the country he marries a local woman, to help him in business. Every day the market opens at six and continues until noon. Trading is not done in shops, but by displaying the goods on a mat spread on the ground. Each merchant has an allotted space. . . .

*I do not think gold and silver are found in this country, and that is why they desire above all gold and silver from China. Next in demand are lightweight and heavyweight textiles, tin wares, lacquered dishes, celadon glazed ceramics, and mercury, vermilion, paper, sulphur, saltpeter . . . linen, yellow grass cloth, umbrellas, iron pots, copper trays, fresh-water pearls, tung oil, bamboo nets, baskets, wooden combs and needles. . . .**

*James P. Holoka and Jiu-Hwa L. Upshur, eds., *Lives and Times: A World History Reader,* Vol. 1 (Minneapolis/St. Paul: West Publishing, 1995), pp. 278–280.

This description of Angkor Thom, the splendid capital city of the Khmer kingdom, was written by Chou Takuan, a Chinese member of the embassy sent by the Mongol ruler Kubilai Khan to demand Khmer's submission to the Mongol Yuan dynasty in 1296. Chou also described the desirability of many types of Chinese goods and the important role of Khmer women in local commerce, which made them useful wives to Chinese merchants who wished to succeed in business locally.

Indian Economic and Cultural Expansion

Although the nature and extent varied from region to region, Indian influence assumed a major role in the development of Southeast Asia during the first millennium C.E. For this reason Southeast Asia is often referred to as Greater India or Indianized Asia. Similarly, Asia Minor, southern Italy, and Sicily were called Magna Graecia or Greater Greece because the ancient Greeks migrated to those areas where they introduced important elements of Greek culture. Since the beginning of history, Southeast Asia's natural resources had been a magnet for international trade. Indian traders were the first to come; along with brahmans and Buddhist monks, they settled throughout Southeast Asia. Trade and settlement were vehicles for the spread of Indian culture, especially among the elite. Local chiefs modeled themselves on Indian rajas and invited brahmans to perform their court rituals in accordance with the Vedic traditions.

Once the resources of Southeast Asia became known, trade developed on a large scale. Skilled Indian mariners developed seaborne trade routes that carried exotic goods throughout much of Asia and as far as the eastern provinces of the Roman Empire. The early Indian traders ventured to Southeast Asia, where many of the items that the Romans wanted, such as spices, gold, resins, and scented woods, were found. When the Parthians (Iranians) cut off the gold supply from Siberia and declining trade with Rome cut off India from the gold of the Roman Empire, Indians sought an alternative source in Southeast Asia. Some Buddhist *jataka* stories told of princes and nobles sailing abroad to make their fortunes, others mention the Island of Gold to the east of India.

Trade led to settlement that developed into colonies. Local peoples, especially the elite, who admired the sophisticated Indian way of life emulated it. India's cultural influence in Southeast Asia was achieved entirely by peaceful means and continued for over a millennium. No military expeditions were launched from India to maintain Indian power in the lands where its cultural influences held sway. After the fall of the Roman Empire ended the Indian role as middlemen, the increasing demand in India for the products of Southeast Asia supported continued trade. Indian trade served as conduit for religion, as Buddhists and Hindus introduced their faiths throughout the regions, especially in present-day Burma, Thailand, Cambodia, and Java. This direct influence waned after the thirteenth century, however, when Hindu and Buddhist Indian merchants and missionaries were replaced by Indian and Arab merchants of Muslim faith, who also spread Islam.

Except for northern Vietnam, which was a Chinese cultural and political satellite, Chinese contacts with Southeast Asia were mainly mercantile and technical. The Chinese treasured the ivory, pearls, hardwoods, and other products of Southeast Asia, and a small number of

Buddha's Nirvana. This colossal stone image of the reclining Buddha from Polonnaruwa, Sri Lanka (formerly Ceylon), is forty-six feet long. It dates to the twelfth century, when Buddhist missionaries from Ceylon continued to exert great influence in Southeast Asia.

Courtesy of Margot Duley

Chinese merchants settled in the region, as the opening document of this section showed. China also adopted a strain of early-ripening rice from Champa in present-day southern Vietnam. Although most of the merchandise brought by Chinese traders to Southeast Asia has perished, large quantities of Chinese ceramics dating from the Han dynasty and later have survived. Some local peoples called china pots "singing jars" because they made a resonant sound when struck. The ceramics were buried in graves or handed down and preserved as treasured heirlooms. Local potters in Thailand, Vietnam, and other lands learned the technology and art of ceramic making from Chinese potters. Some of their products were modeled after Chinese originals, whereas others reflected local taste. Other Chinese inventions and innovations in agriculture and metallurgy were also passed along to Southeast Asian lands.

Mainland Southeast Asia

Although geographically closest to India, Burma (recently renamed Myanmar) did not come under Indian influence until the Gupta period. Around 500, Theravada Buddhist missionaries arrived from Ceylon and converted the people of Burma to their branch of Buddhism, to which they have remained faithful to the present.

Abundant rice grown with irrigation made Burma prosperous. Pious rulers and people contributed lavishly to build thousands of Buddhist shrines at Pagan on the Irrawady River, the political and cultural center of Burma. Many Burmese monks went to Ceylon for study and ordination. Just as in Ceylon, Pagan shrines were usually stupas, which stood on stepped terraces that symbolized the sacred mountain of the Buddhist cosmos. The Pagan stupa was tall and highly ornate, with a bell-shaped dome.

By the late thirteenth century the dynasty that ruled from Pagan was in decline. In 1271 Kubilai Khan, the Mongol ruler of China (see Chapter 8), sent envoys to Pagan, demanding submission and tribute. The Burmese king refused to receive them. Two years later, when another mission from Kubilai made the same demands, the Burmese king had the envoys executed. This meant war. The victorious Mongols annexed north and central Burma and devastated Pagan. Eventually the Burmese king acknowledged Mongol overlordship, but shortly after these events, Mongol power began to wane and Burma regained its independence. After a period of civil wars, Burma was reunified in the second half of the fourteenth century, but Pagan never regained its ancient glory and never became the capital again.

At the same time that the Buddhist religion and culture flourished in Burma, Indian influences inspired the Khmer people to build magnificent monuments and decorate them with beautiful sculpture and friezes. A Chinese chronicle of the third century described a kingdom called Fu-nan in the Mekong delta in present-day southern Vietnam, which had been founded in the first century by an Indian brahman who married a local princess. Indian culture was thus introduced to southern Indochina. In the seventh century, Fu-nan was conquered by its vassal state, Cambodia, which gave its name to the region.

The full flowering of classic Cambodian (Khmer) civilization between the ninth and the fifteenth centuries was the result of the blending of Indian civilization with Khmer ideas and ideals. At its height, the kingdom of Cambodia ruled present-day Cambodia, Laos, Thailand, parts of Burma, Vietnam, and the Malay Peninsula. Numerous Sanskrit inscriptions engraved in stone give many details of these centuries.

Hinduism and Buddhism came to Cambodia at the same time; Hinduism was preeminent till the twelfth

Map 6.2 Southeast Asia in the Twelfth Century. No one empire dominated either mainland or island Southeast Asia. On the mainland, the Khmer state was at its height; in the islands, various Indianized states warred against each other.

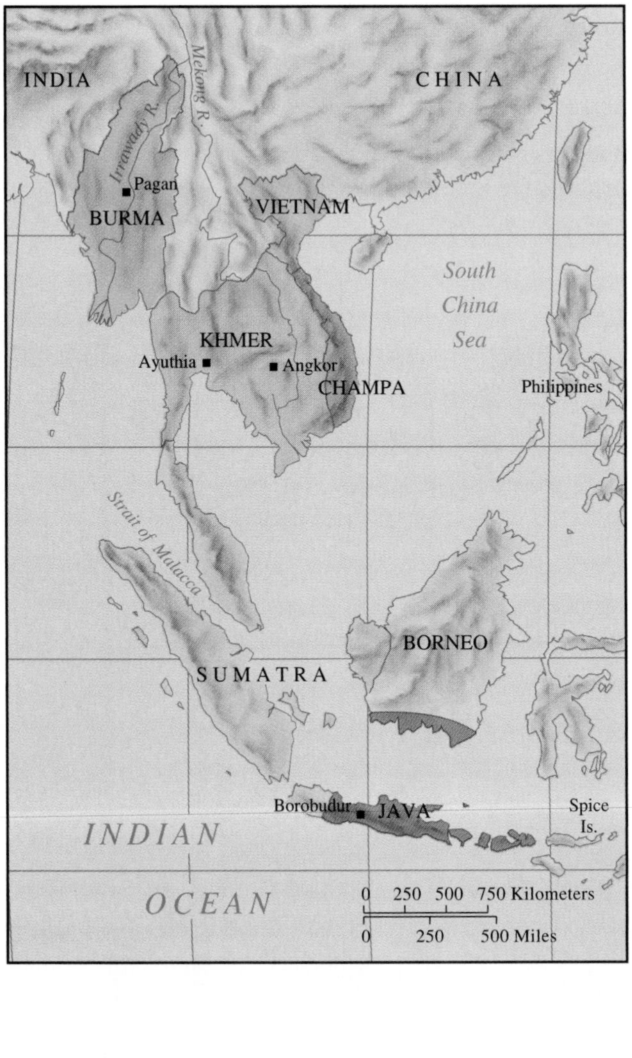

Ray Garner/FPG International

Angkor Wat. Built in the early part of the twelfth century, Angkor Wat was dedicated to the god Vishnu and the king who identified with him. The monument shows the influence of South Indian tradition. Khmer civilization was at its height during this period.

century, Buddhism thereafter, although features of both remain to the present. Both Indian religions merged with local beliefs into a state cult of the god-king. Thus, although temples and statues were dedicated to Vishnu, Shiva, or Buddha, they were really funerary shrines for the divine king who commissioned them and who believed himself to be the earthly incarnation of that god. The art of Cambodia blended and integrated Indian concepts with traditional elements. The facial and physical features depicted in the statues and friezes are Cambodian. Using a folk style that incorporated many elements, Cambodian artists not only integrated Hindu and Buddhist themes but also depicted stories that celebrate Cambodian history and the glory of Khmer rule.

Between the tenth and twelfth centuries, the kings of Cambodia built a capital at Angkor Wat, which even in ruin is one of the architectural wonders of the world. For more than two centuries, each god-king built temples and decorated them with statues and reliefs to outshine those of his predecessors, just as Egyptian pharaohs had done in ancient times.

The most magnificent monument in Angkor Wat was built in the twelfth century as a temple for Vishnu and as a sanctuary of the divine king who identified with him. Here a series of terraced structures culminates in the central shrine 213 feet above the ground. The walls and galleries are decorated with narrative relief carvings of Hindu legends and Khmer history. They depict dancing angels and stories of Vishnu's different incarnation, together with military and other scenes that celebrate the power of the Khmer kings.

In 1177 Angkor Wat was sacked by the forces of Champa, another Indianized state located in present southern Vietnam. After repelling the attackers, the Khmer rulers built a new capital nearby called Angkor Thom, a magnificent square-shaped city surrounded by an eight-mile-long stone wall, and a wide moat (as the Chinese ambassador described in the passage at the beginning of this section) and provided with a remarkably complex drainage and irrigation system. The greatest monument in Angkor Thom is called the Bayan, a Buddhist shrine dedicated to a popular bodhisattva and the king who identified with him. The Bayan is a shrine with a forest of towers; the central one, which dominates the rest, is 150 feet high. All the towers are decorated with giant heads of the bodhisattva-god-king. Miles of friezes portray religious and secular scenes, among them the Khmer army and navy in action against the forces of Champa. The huge expense of building Angkor Wat, Angkor Thom, and other monuments at sites still unexcavated sapped the state's economy and contributed to its eventual decline.

Starting in the fourteenth century, the Khmer kingdom was increasingly threatened by Thai invaders from the west. In 1431 the Thais captured and looted Angkor

Paul Chesley/Tony Stone

The Spice Islands. For two millennia peoples from many cultures have sought the spices produced on these islands of the Indonesian Archipelago. They are sold locally at markets such as this one.

Thom and carried off many prisoners. Without the bureaucracy to supervise and maintain the complex irrigation system, Cambodia's political power, art, and culture went into long decline after this disaster. Those Khmer leaders who survived fled south and established themselves in a new capital called Phnom-Penh, which is still the capital city of Cambodia.

The Thai or "free people" came from the borderlands of Burma, Tibet, and southwestern China. The advancing Chinese, and later the Mongols, had gradually pushed them south. By the twelfth century, the Thais had formed a united government. They were Buddhist converts, having established close ties with Ceylon and Burma and accepted Theravada Buddhism before arriving in Thailand around the twelfth century. Ayuthia, Thailand's first capital, was named after Ayodhia, capital of the legendary kingdom of Rama of the Indian epic *Ramayana*. Although Thais are Buddhist, they were also influenced by Hinduism, as evidenced by their decision to name their capital after a legendary city of Hindu epic. Even today Shiva and other Hindu deities are honored in Thai Buddhist temples and the Thai royal court maintains brahmans to perform religious ceremonies.

Pali, the language of Buddhist scriptures, became Thailand's sacred language, and an alphabet based on Sanskrit became the writing system and remains so today. The Khmer prisoners who settled in Thailand influenced their captors; Thai art and culture showed a heavy debt to Khmer models.

Although the iconography of Thai art, like that of most Southeast Asia, derived from Indian sources, in time it became uniquely Thai and no longer dependent on Gupta or Khmer models.

Island Southeast Asia

In the Gupta and post-Gupta period, Indians brought Mahayana Buddhism to Sumatra, Java, and Malaya. Indian writing systems, art, and architectural styles prevailed throughout the region. When the Chinese Buddhist pilgrim Fa-hsien returned to China from Ceylon by sea in 410 C.E., he sailed on a ship that carried over 200 passengers. Such ships regularly plied the route between Ceylon and the islands in Indonesia where Buddhism had become a thriving religion. In the seventh century, another Chinese pilgrim studied Sanskrit in a monastery with more than 1,000 monks on Sumatra (an island of present-day Indonesia) and wrote that "many kings and chieftains of the Southern Ocean admired and believed in Buddhism."

Java, Sumatra, and other islands attracted traders from China and India, for gold, tin, ivory, camphorwood, and, above all, spices were much in demand in China and India; Indian sailors also carried these items to West Asia for shipping to Europe.

The growing world demand for spices, especially pepper, which was used for preserving meat, had a powerful influence on the history of all Southeast Asia, especially the islands. Two factors outside Southeast Asia played key roles in the economic development of the region: the Crusades and the policy of the Chinese government. The Crusades aroused demand for Asian products in Europe and thus trade between the two continents, much of which either originated in or passed through Southeast Asia. Indian Muslims became middlemen in trade between East Asia, island Southeast Asia, and West Asia, from which the goods were transshipped to the Mediterranean. These merchants were also instrumental in the Islamization of Malaya and the Indonesian islands after the thirteenth century.

The trade policy of Southern Sung China also contributed to the region's economic development. Always in need of revenue to appease or fight its northern nomadic neighbors, the Chinese government encouraged the export of porcelains and other products to Southeast Asia, which stimulated economic development of the region.

The Sung government lacked the power and the desire to dominate Southeast Asia politically, but its successor, the Mongol Yuan dynasty under Kubilai Khan, demanded submission of the petty states on the island of Java. When some Javanese states refused, Kubilai sent a large naval expedition of 1,000 ships and 20,000 men in 1292 to conquer the island. It was a costly failure.

The art of the islands of present-day Indonesia is heavily indebted to India. Some of the greatest examples of Buddhist art are in fact found on Java. Around 800, Mahayana Buddhists at Borobodur on Java built the single largest Buddhist monument. Conceived as a representation of Mount Meru, the World Mountain, it is a succession of terraces. As pious pilgrims climb the terraces, they are symbolically leaving behind the world of desire and moving upward toward spiritual perfection and ultimate union with the cosmic Buddha who dominates the central stupa that crowns the whole edifice. Although the sculpture here follows closely the Gupta style, it also shows characteristics that are uniquely Javanese. The racial type portrayed is Malay rather than Indian, the figural style is softer than that of India, and the scenes depicted are uniquely Javanese. Moreover, the ten miles of relief sculpture of *jataka* stories and of scenes from the life of the Buddha show a narrative tradition that was more developed than in India. Many Hindu temples contemporary with Borododur have also survived on Java. They show the wide range of Indian cultural influences that prevailed on the island.

From the ninth century until the final triumph of Islam after the fourteenth, Hinduism replaced Buddhism as the predominant cultural force on Java and Sumatra. Great shrines were built to worship Shiva, Vishnu, and other deities of the Hindu pantheon. Ganesha, Shiva's son, the elephant-headed and pot-bellied god of learning, was especially popular. He was represented in two aspects, as the benevolent and protective deity and as a fierce god whose throne is ornamented with human skulls.

An extensive literature, written in a Sanskrit-derived alphabet, also date to the Hindu period. The *Ramayana* and *Mahabharata* epics were widely loved throughout the islands. To this day, their stories, modified by Javanese legends, are told in the popular shadow-puppet plays called *wanyang* and in dance and theatrical performances. Thus, although Hinduism survived only on the island of Bali, the influence of Hindu India remains strong in the culture and language of Indonesia to the present day.

Although Chinese ships had traded with the present-day Philippine islands since the beginning of the common era, as Chinese coins and pottery excavated there prove, the islands remained largely isolated and politically fragmented. No stable states emerged, and despite the introduction of Indian writing, few written materials survive. Thus the Philippines did not fully enter the historic era until their conquest by Spain in the sixteenth century. Four centuries of Spanish rule made the Philippines culturally, politically, and socially closer to Latin America than Asia.

Pictures of Life from Stone Reliefs

Two of these [reliefs] show us ploughing. . . . The plough is drawn by a pair of bulls, the yoke resting on the shoulder in front of the hump, with a collar round each beast's neck. The plough itself is the ordinary primitive square shape, by which one side scrapes along the ground and forces the ploughshare into the earth; the other side sticks up with the top bent over to the back and guided by the hand of the ploughman who walks behind and directs it with his left hand, holding a stick in his right. . . .

Another example of work . . . is the potter's. . . . On one side we see the jars already made, on the other side the potter is at work, using a flat stick to get a good shape. Bearers with carrying-poles are bringing large round balls, it may be clay or gourds with water. Women and children are looking on. . . .

*In a goldsmith's [shop] the purchaser, seated opposite to the merchant, is holding a pair of scales, in one scale there is a ring and in the other there seems to be a bag of money.**

Although very little written material has survived describing life in ninth-century Java, the miles of reliefs of Borobodur, some depicting daily life, give vivid pictures of all classes of people in their daily pursuits. They give substance to the saying that a picture is worth a thousand words.

*N. J. Krom, *Barabudur: Archaeological Description,* vol. 2 (The Hague: M. Nijhoff, 1927), pp. 227–229.

China's Second Imperial Age

*At this time in the city of Ch'ang-an there were not more than one hundred families. Weeds and thorns grew thickly as if in a forest. Only four carts could be found in the city. The officials had neither robes of ceremony nor seals. Instead they used tablets of mulberry wood on which their names and rank were inscribed.**

Outside the inner doors, the two court ladies with flowing purple sleeves,
Now turn to the throne to lead the procession from the audience chamber.
The spring wind blows the swirling smoke of incense in the hall,
The sunlight plays across the dazzling robes of the thousand officials.
We hear the striking of the hour from the clepsydra in the high tower,
*As a servitor standing near, I note that the Heavenly Countenance is joyful.***

*Charles P. Fitzgerald, *China: A Short Cultural History* (New York: Praeger, 1961), p. 260.

**Poem by Tu Fu, quoted in *Cities of Destiny,* ed. Arnold Toynbee (New York: McGraw-Hill, 1967), p. 147.

The first excerpt depicts Changan during the fourth century after the once-great capital of the Han Empire had been sacked and plundered by nomadic invaders. The city's desolation symbolizes the ruin of northern China during the age of disunity. The second is a poem by a famous T'ang poet describing a court ceremony of the rebuilt and once-more cosmopolitan Changan during the height of China's second imperial age

As after the end of the Roman and Mauryan Empires, the dissolution of the Han dynasty was followed by three and a half centuries of disruption, wars, and invasions. Just as Christianity and the Latin language eventually built bridges between conquerors and conquered in western Europe and became the basis of a common culture, Buddhism and the Chinese language and culture ultimately united the Chinese and their nomadic rulers. China, however, was more successful in restoring unity and rebuilding an empire than either Rome's successors in western Europe or the Guptas in India.

Political Turmoil and Barbarian Invasions

The age of disunity began in 220 when the ineffectual last emperor of the Han was forced to give two of his daughters to a powerful general in marriage and then to abdicate in favor of his son-in-law. The usurper's heirs soon met the same fate he had meted out to the emperor. The chaos in the Chinese world allowed the regrouped Hsiung-nu to renew their attack. They destroyed Loyang in 311 and burned the imperial library, causing irreparable loss, and in 316 also laid waste to Changan.

North China would be ruled by many groups of nomadic conquerors until the end of the sixth century. The

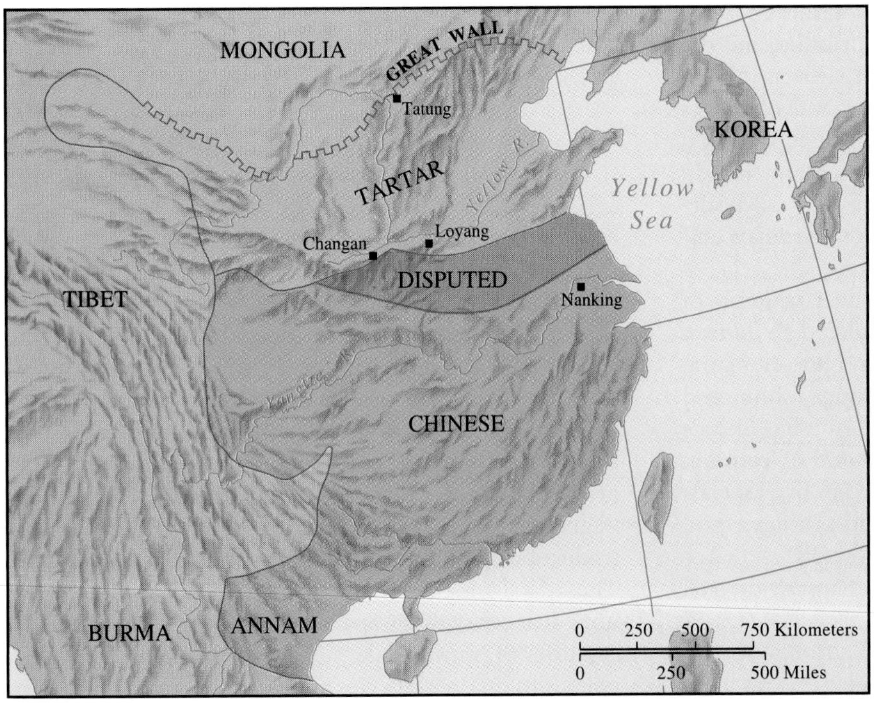

Map 6.3 China in the Age of Disunity. China was partitioned between 317 and 580 C.E. While Hunnish and other nomadic groups called Tartars ruled North China, Chinese dynasties controlled the Yangtze Valley and lands to the south, with a disputed area between. While repeated invasions devastated North China, the south became developed for the first time.

Northern and Southern Chinese Chauvinism

"Though the Wei [T'o-pa] Dynasty [that ruled north China] is indeed prosperous, it is still one of the Five Barbarians. The correct New Year's Day [i.e., the calendar] has been passed down from one generation to the next, and this surely exists only south of the Yangtze. The jade seal of the First Sovereign Ch'in Emperor [seal of legitimate rule] now belongs to the Liang Dynasty [that ruled south China]."

So said the rather drunken guest of honor at a banquet. He was from the southern court sent to the northern capital on a diplomatic mission. To this a northern nobleman replied:

*"You are only using the area of the lower Yangtze as a temporary refuge, and there you live meanly in a corner of the empire. . . . Among your close-cropped gentry, there are none with strong and healthy looks, and your tattooed people [the aborigines] are endowed with bodies that are small and weak. They float about on your three rivers, row about on your five lakes—unaffected by ritual or music, not to be improved by laws and ordinance. Although the prisoners transported to the South under the Ch'in and Han dynasties brought in and intermixed the true Chinese speech [of the north], still the difficult southern languages of Min and Ch'u were not changed for the better. . . . You are steeped in these inherited ways; you have never felt the transforming effects of proper ritual; you are like the people of Yang-t'i [a notorious goiter area] of whom it is said that they don't know that a tumor is a deformity."**

The above exchange is interesting for several reasons. First, it shows that the northern nobleman, a man of nomadic roots, had become entirely Sinicized by the sixth century. By then intermarriage between Chinese and nomads had become so common that few pure bloods could be found any more. Second, it shows that after several centuries of partition, distinct cultures, with different dialects and ways of life, had developed that distinguished northerners from southerners. Third, it reveals the chauvinistic attitude northerners and southerners had toward each other. Each group claimed superiority, regarded itself as the true heirs of the Han, and accused the other of being tainted by lower cultures, whether that of the nomads of the north or that of the aborigines of the south. China would eventually be reunited by a northern nobleman of mixed Chinese and nomadic descent.

*Arthur Wright, *The Sui Dynasty: The Unification of China, A.D. 581–617* (New York: Knopf, 1978), pp. 32–33.

Chinese peasant was reduced to serfdom or to slavery, working for a tiny class of alien rulers. Some of the elite fled to southern China and established a new capital at Nanking on the lower Yangtze. The mountain range that divided the Yellow from the Yangtze drainage basins became the boundary between the northern and southern kingdoms. Short-lived dynasties followed one another in both north and south. By the time China was once more reunified, southern China had built up its population and was fully acculturated. The refugee governments in southern China claimed, with some legitimacy, to be the true successors of the Han and attempted to keep alive ancient traditions. The shift of the center of gravity from northern to southern China would continue after the end of the era of disunity.

Given their small numbers and lack of experience in administering a sedentary people, the conquering rulers of northern China were forced to employ the remaining Confucian officials in their government. The new masters found themselves in a dilemma. To exercise effective control and to enjoy fully their new power, they needed to be located in the Chinese heartland. Thus in 494 the king of the T'o-pa—a Turkic tribe and the most successful and long-lived nomadic dynasty in North China, moved his capital from Tatung, in the frontier between agricultural China and the steppe grasslands, to the former Han capital Loyang. But in moving into China they risked losing their ethnic and cultural identity. In time the T'o-pa rulers became so Sinicized that they banned continued use of T'o-pa tribal names, clothes, and customs. They soon also lost their martial ardor. Since their rule was based on conquest, the softened T'o-pa were soon ousted by other nomads and became merged into the general population. Thus, even in northern China, Chinese culture survived to triumph, assimilating and absorbing the conquerors.

Buddhism in China

Ages of bloodshed are often ages of faith; so it was during the age of division in China. The most important intellectual trend in China during this disruptive period was the growth of Buddhism and its adaptation to Chinese conditions. In the process both Buddhism and China were changed.

Buddhism appealed to members of the upper class in southern China because as exiles from their ancestral homes in the north they needed the consolation of religion. Being literary men, they discussed and studied Buddhist teachings, contacting Buddhist centers in India and Ceylon by sea to obtain original texts. Buddhism reached a high point under Emperor Wu (reigned 502–549) of the southern state of Liang, who compared himself with Asoka by giving up eating meat, forbidding animal sacrifices, convening religious assemblies, and building temples. To honor his father he built a monastic complex of thirty-six buildings that stretched for over two miles and housed a thousand monks. He encouraged people to join the *sangha* (Buddhist religious community) and did so himself several times. Also reminiscent of Asoka, Wu lost control over the government in his later years, and his dynasty quickly declined after his death.

In North China, where chaos frequently prevailed, Buddhist missionaries attached themselves to the ruling princes, who exercised control over the church and sought the monks' advice in return for protecting them. Missionaries from India and central Asia were welcomed in the courts of the nomadic rulers, who found the universalist teachings of Buddhism more congenial than the ideals of Confucianism. Buddhism exerted a civilizing influence on the nomads and also offered consolation to the oppressed peasantry

Until the end of the fourth century, religious movements had gone one way, as missionaries traveled from India and central Asia to China. Fa-hsien was the first recorded Chinese Buddhist monk to travel to Gupta India to study and collect the canons and then return to China. He set off for India by the overland route in 399, studied at all the sites holy to Buddhism, and finally returned to China via Ceylon and the sea route, arriving in 413. He spent his remaining years translating the sutras (scriptural writings) that he had brought back from India into Chinese. Fa-hsien's journals gave valuable information on the history and geography of India and other lands where he had traveled and lived.

Fa-hsien's pathfinding journey started a movement that would continue for three centuries. Pilgrims who traveled to India and the lands in between brought back information and ideas that made Buddhism a vital intellectual force. It was a perilous journey, as a passage from Fa-hsien's journal narrated the real and imagined terrors of crossing the desert indicates:

> In the desert were numerous evil spirits and scorching winds, causing death to anyone who would meet them. Above there were no birds, while on the ground there were no animals. One looked as far as one could in all directions for a path to cross, but there was none to choose. Only the dried bones of the dead served as indication.

Dedicated Buddhist missionaries and translators made their religion dominant throughout China; even sporadic

Courtesy of Dolkun Kamberi

The Caves of the Thousand Buddhas. These cave temples at Bizaklik along the Silk Road in northwestern China were constructed after 300 C.E. The site flourished for centuries as a stop for missionaries, pilgrims, and merchants on an international highway.

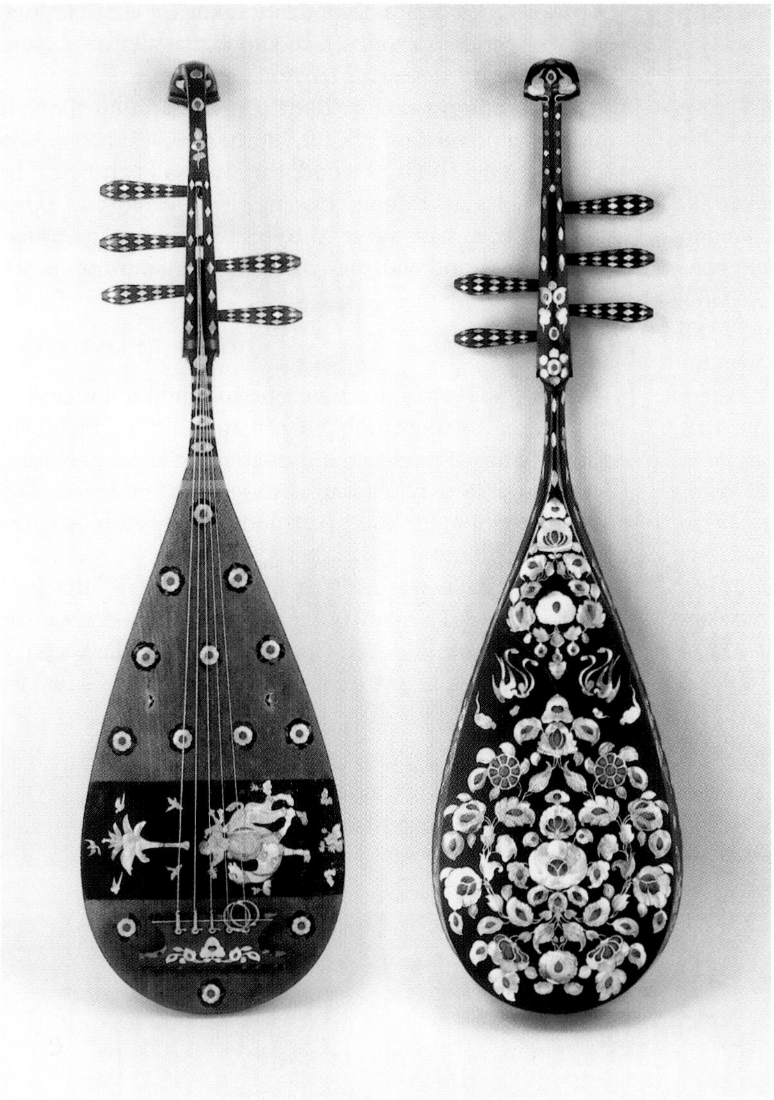

Shoshoin Treasure House, Nara, Japan

Five-String Lute. This Chinese-made musical instrument, shown front and back, probably originated in India, and its mother-of-pearl and tortoise shell decoration shows Persian inspiration. Musicians playing lutes and other instruments participated in T'ang court and religious ceremonies. This lute was taken to Japan, where it had similar functions. From the collection of a seventh-century emperor, it now forms part of Japan's national treasures.

government persecution did little to hinder its growth. Similarly, Christianity had triumphed in the Roman Empire despite periodic persecution. Nevertheless, it would be misleading to equate the triumph of Buddhism in China with that of Christianity in the Roman Empire because, unlike Western monotheistic religions (Judaism, Christianity, and Islam), Buddhism, Taoism, and Confucianism did not demand total loyalty from their followers. Most Chinese found no incompatibility in simultaneously honoring Confucius, worshiping Buddha, and practicing Taoist rites. To express this ideal, the Chinese coined a phrase: "Three ways to one goal," which reflects both Chinese religious tolerance and Buddhism's adaptability.

Classical Greco-Roman-Indian art entered China with Buddhism. Its progress eastward can be easily traced from surviving Buddhist monuments and works of art. The oases of central Asia were the furthest outposts of the classical Greco-Roman world and were also the melting pot where several cultures and peoples met and where merchants, missionaries, pilgrims, and local peoples mingled. Buddhist sculptors were at work at the oasis at Miran on the southern branch of the Silk Road in the third century, and their art, preserved by the dry desert air, shows a definite classical inspiration.

East of Miran, images of Buddha turn up next at Tunhuang, the westernmost Chinese settlement on the Silk Road. Beginning in the fourth century, pious Buddhists excavated cave temples in the cliffs at Tunhuang. Over several hundred years, they honeycombed a whole mountainside with the "Caves of the Thousand Buddhas," decorating them with frescoes that show the gradual fusion of Chinese and imported styles.

Between 460 and 494, an escarpment near the Great Wall outside Tatung (then capital of a northern Chinese dynasty ruled by nomads called T'o-pas), was carved with twenty caves and adorned with Buddhist frescoes and sculptures, the largest image of the Buddha being seventy feet high. The concept of the cave temples was Indian in origin. Stylistically the works were Greco-Roman-Gandharan, reminiscent of the Buddhist cave temple at Bamiyan in Afghanistan, modified to suit Chinese ideals of formalism and stylization.

When the capital of the T'o-pa dynasty was moved east to Loyang, a new series of cave temples was begun outside that city at a site called Lungmen, where work continued with interruptions until the eighth century. According to a recent count, 142,289 Buddhist sculptures still survive at Lungmen. The Lungmen sculptures show a fusion and synthesis of Greco-Roman, Indian, central Asian, and Chinese styles. Many lengthy carved inscriptions that accompany the sculptures also tell of the Sinicization of Buddhism. For example, many of the statues were commissioned by monks and nuns, who dedicated them to benefit the souls of their parents and ancestors. This shows that even in joining the sangha, Chinese monks and nuns retained their family loyalty. People from all social classes participated in commissioning statues and other works of art at Lungmen; they even formed societies that took up donations in order to accumulate funds for that purpose. Many inscriptions expressed the hope that all living things attain salvation, a clearly Mahayana message.

According to one account, Loyang around the year 500 had a population of 500,000 to 600,000 people and 1,367 temples. Built of wood, they have all perished. The cave temples at Tatung, Loyang, Tunhuang, and other sites, however, have survived to testify to the religious fervor of the period and the cosmopolitan nature of its art.

China Reunified: The Sui and T'ang Dynasties

The year 581 was a decisive one in Chinese history: in that year a northern nobleman named Yang Chien proclaimed himself emperor and established the Sui dynasty. Although it lasted only four decades, the Sui dynasty laid the foundation for the great and long-lived T'ang dynasty that followed.

Yang Chien was assisted by his able wife, the Empress Tu-ku. Like many other northern aristocrats at the time, both were of mixed Chinese and nomadic ancestry. Yang wisely used everything at his disposal—military

Map 6.4 T'ang China. The T'ang Empire at its height was more extensive and populous than the Han. The Pax Sinica, maintained by T'ang armies, allowed merchants, missionaries, and pilgrims to travel freely across central Asia to India, Persia, and points west.

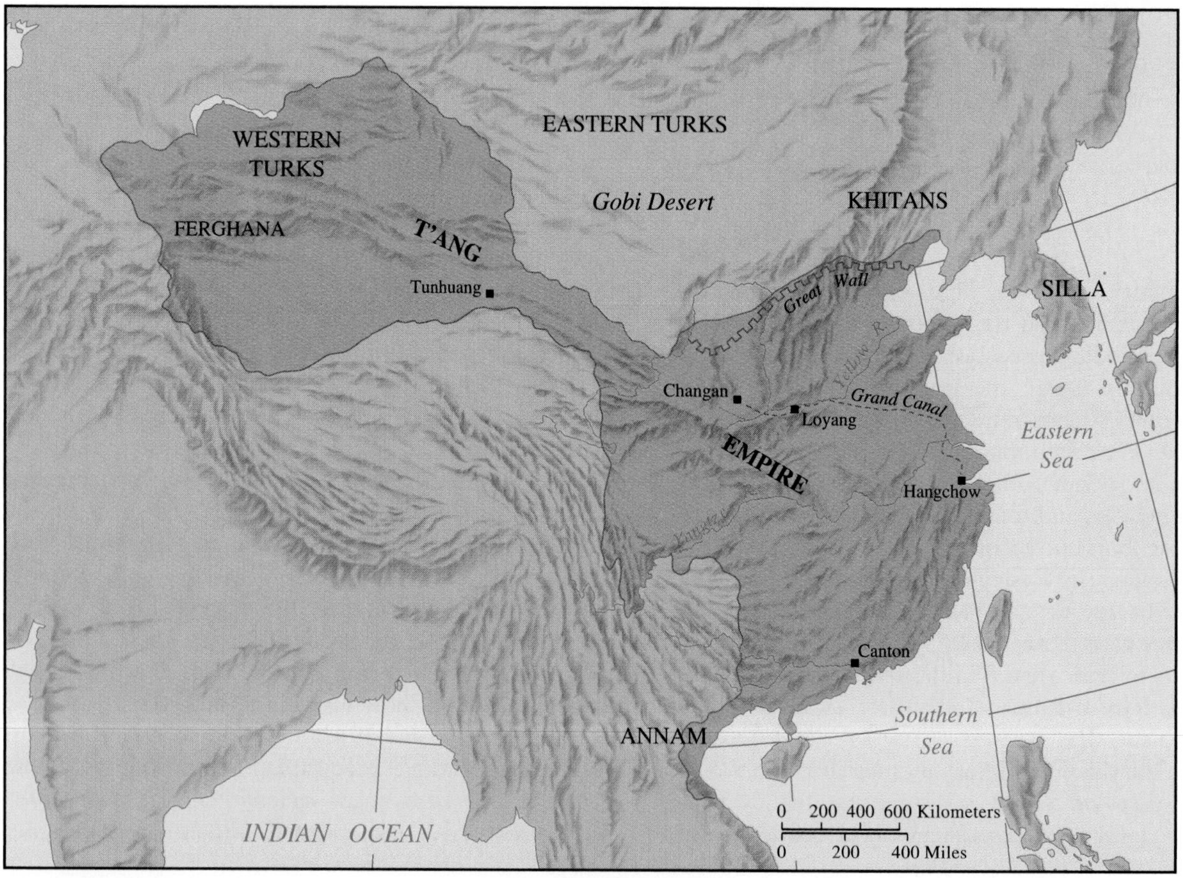

A Famous Battle Charger. The six horses that the T'ang emperor T'ai-tsung rode to his victories are commemorated in relief sculptures. This one and five others guard his tomb outside Changan.

force, diplomacy, religion (Buddhism and Taoism), and philosophy (Confucianism)—to forge an empire of continental proportions. He succeeded more completely than the Guptas in India and Charlemagne in western Europe, because China more than India and western Europe enjoyed the legacy of a unified language, written literary and historical traditions that extolled the ideal of unity, and an experienced bureaucracy that was shaped in Confucian learning and dedicated to public service.

The Sui dynasty did not long survive its frugal and wise founder because Yang Chien's son and heir was an unstable megalomaniac who reputedly murdered his father to gain the throne, as Alexander the Great reputedly had also done. But unlike Alexander's, his foreign military expeditions were costly failures. His overly ambitious public works projects and luxurious court life exhausted the treasury and angered the people. Revolts broke out everywhere, and chaos reminiscent of conditions at the end of the Ch'in again threatened to overtake China.

The chaos was short lived, however, because one rebel named Li Yuan (as the Duke of T'ang, he was a high official in the Sui government) quickly established a new dynasty. The Li family traced its genealogy to a famous Han general, and more fancifully to the mythical Lao Tzu (to whom later Taoist followers had given the surname Li). Most of the credit for Li Yuan's success is due to his second son, Li Shih-min. Then aged seventeen, he persuaded his timid father to revolt, fought to make his cause triumphant, and later succeeded him as emperor T'ai-tsung (the same ruler who sent his ambassador to the court of Harsha). The T'ang dynasty ruled from 618 to 907, an epoch that is remembered as one of the most brilliant in Chinese history. T'ai-tsung is revered as the most heroic ruler of all Chinese history. His generals were deified in popular lore; statues of the six horses he rode in campaigns guard his tomb and were remembered in ballads. Unlike Alexander the Great who named a city after his favorite horse Bucephulus, T'ai-tsung did not name cities after his horses.

T'ai-tsung (reigned 626–649) established Chinese authority across Mongolia, Tibet, Afghanistan, and central Asia. In submitting, the Turks and Mongols acknowledged him their Grand Khan, the first Chinese ruler to be so honored. He was also an able administrator and valued the advice of honest critics. At the death of a minister who was also an outspoken critic, Wei Cheng, he said: "With bronze as a mirror one can correct his improper appearance; with history as a mirror one can understand the rise and fall of nations; with good men as a mirror, one can distinguish right from wrong. I lost one mirror with the passing of Wei Cheng." He tolerated all religions, promoted Confucianism in government and education, patronized Buddhism, and welcomed Nestorian Christians.

T'ai-tsung's son and successor Kao-tsung (reigned 649–683), was best remembered for his infatuation with

LIVES AND TIMES ACROSS CULTURES

Cultural Borrowing and Adaptation—The Chair

Although the chair was a part of life in ancient Egypt, Greece, and Rome, it did not exist in East Asia in antiquity. Until 1,000 years ago, the Chinese sat on mats placed over the floor, as do many Japanese even now. Their nomadic neighbors, and the Persians and Arabs with whom Chinese established contact about 2,000 years ago, also sat on rugs or mats. By the eleventh century, however, the Chinese had changed entirely to sitting on chairs and had altered their domestic architecture, the interior arrangements of rooms, and clothing styles to suit the new furniture.

Historian Charles P. Fitzgerald has studied the introduction of chairs in China and determined that a large folding camp stool, which the Chinese called a *hu-ch'uang* (barbarian bed), was introduced in the second century from the eastern provinces of the Roman Empire. It became popular for informal seating because it elevated the sitter from the sometimes damp and drafty floor, but he still curled his legs on the seat. Fitzgerald further established that by the mid-T'ang dynasty, around 800, the frame chair had been introduced, probably from the Byzantine Empire. The T'ang dynasty was a cosmopolitan period in China when many foreign customs were adopted. The Japanese monk Ennin, who spent many years traveling in China, noted that T'ang officials sat on chairs, but with their legs curled on the seat. Fitzgerald concluded:

> *In the more sophisticated Sung period which soon followed, the break with the old tradition gathered swift momentum. In* A.D. *960 the great officials were furnishing their houses with chairs and tables; in the next century they were even designing their own furniture; by the dawn of the twelfth century the whole nation had given up on the floor and taken to chairs and benches.**

Interestingly, the Koreans and Japanese, who had always modeled their cultures on China, did not follow it in this important transformation.

*Charles P. Fitzgerald, *Barbarian Beds: The Origin of the Chair in China* (Canberra: Australian National University, 1965), pp. 49–50.

Lady Wu, his father's young concubine. At T'ai-tsung's death she was sent to a Buddhist convent. Kao-tsung paid a visit to the convent on the first anniversary of his father's death; when he left, he took Lady Wu with him. She later became her stepson's empress, and then killed and deposed her own sons to become China's only woman "emperor." Empress Wu ruled until she was eighty. She even attempted, but failed, to establish her own dynasty. Old and ill, she was forced to abdicate in favor of one of her surviving sons. Historians criticized the means she used to gain and maintain power (she killed and imprisoned many of her own children, stepchildren, in-laws, and officials who opposed her usurpation) and her scandalous private life—she took numerous young lovers (as did eighteenth-century Russian Empress Catherine the Great). When in her seventies she heard reports that her grandson and granddaughter made fun of her affairs, she ordered them to commit suicide. Nevertheless, she was a capable ruler, who brought Manchuria under Chinese rule and compelled the kings of Korea to acknowledge Chinese overlordship. This relationship between China and Korea continued until the late nineteenth century. She was also a devout Buddhist and endowed many temples.

T'ang prestige and prosperity reached its peak during the reign of Wu's grandson, Ming-huang, or the Brilliant Emperor (reigned 712–756). Ming-huang worked hard for most of his reign and was also a patron of the arts. The most celebrated poets of the age lived in his court and immortalized his reign with their unsurpassed poetry. But Ming-huang lived too long for his own or China's good. At age sixty he fell under the spell of Lady Yang, a young concubine of one of his sons. He took her into his own harem and abandoned himself to the pursuit of pleasure. She was famous for her plumpness and briefly made obesity fashionable; she was also immensely extravagant, which the doting and aged emperor allowed. Ming-huang's neglect of his duties and his elevation of her greedy and incompetent relatives and favorites to power had disastrous results: defeat by an Muslim army, which ended Chinese control of central Asia and destroyed Buddhism in that region, and a major rebellion led by Lady Yang's favorite, a general of Turkic origin and commander of "barbarian" mercenary soldiers. Ming-huang had to sacrifice Lady Yang to appease his angry loyal troops who blamed her for the rebellion and would not fight for him until she had been killed. His sacrificing her and subsequent abdication in humiliation became the subject of a famous romantic poem. Although the rebellion was put down, the central government never fully recovered its authority, nor the dynasty its prestige and vitality. Slow decline set in; the final end came in 907.

An Enlightened Government and a Prosperous Economy

The key to the T'ang dynasty's success was the restoration of a stable central government, aided by the revival of schools and the examination system. The T'ang rulers reinstated and enlarged the Han system of examinations based on Confucian classics as the basis for selecting government officials. The government established a school system from the country up to the imperial university, open to most young men of talent. It administered examinations at regular intervals on several levels, recruited successful candidates into the civil service, and later rated them to determine promotions and dismissals.

Since bright young men were trained in the same curriculum in order to qualify for the examinations and public service, a uniform educational system emerged. Because Confucian ideology was the basis of the examinations, the schools produced a ruling class imbued with the same ethical principles and values. Even Buddhist schools offered a Confucian curriculum that helped poor boys realize their potential. The widespread use of paper, invented in the first century, made books cheaper. However, although printing was invented during the T'ang period, its general use, which would make books still cheaper and more widely available, did not happen until a later era.

The competitive examination system strengthened the T'ang state by turning men of intellectual ability into strong supporters of the government. It created an elite dedicated to government service and to the consensus that the learned and morally worthy should lead and represent public opinion. The perfection of the examination system and the bureaucracy of merit that it produced in T'ang and later eras was one of the greatest achievements of the Chinese civilization and a major reason for its stability and endurance. Their absence was detrimental to the Gupta and Carolingian dynasties' success.

The T'ang era was one of great economic prosperity. International trade flourished, and more caravans plied the Silk Road than during the best Han days. Meanwhile, the Yangtze valley had experienced enormous growth and development and had become the breadbasket (or rice bowl) of China. Realizing this, the Sui rulers built an extensive system of waterways, called the Grand Canal, to link up the Yangtze and lands further south with the Yellow River valley. The enormous drain of manpower and resources required by this project contributed to the popular discontent that ended the Sui dynasty. The Grand Canal allowed the T'ang to tap the abundant resources of the south.

T'ang prosperity was partly based on an ambitious land policy called the "equal field" system. It was an adaptation of the "well-field" system, supposedly instituted by the Duke of Chou, that had helped make the early Chou a golden age. Under the equal field system, all land theoretically belonged to the emperor or the state, which distributed about eighteen acres to every able-bodied man between twenty-one and fifty-nine years of age. Other categories of people—for example, widows who headed families and the elderly—received somewhat smaller allotments. The government then assessed taxes as well as labor on public works projects on the basis of the land allotment. It exempted certain able-bodied males from taxes in return for military service. This complex and largely equitable land and tax policy worked well for over a century. It was made possible by a capable bureaucracy that kept careful census and detailed land survey records.

China and the World Beyond

China was at its most cosmopolitan during the T'ang dynasty. Not until modern times would it again be so open to foreign influences. Two million people lived in Changan and its environs, making it the largest and most populous city in the world (for comparison, Constantinople around 600 had a population of about 1 million). The market places of Changan and other large cities bustled with life; Chinese mingled with people from Japan, Korea, Southeast Asia, India, and the many lands of central and western Asia. Some had come freely to trade, settle, or offer their services; others were brought as slaves. The rich vied with one

Polo Players. A game that originated in Persia, polo became a fashionable sport among aristocratic men and women. The potter captured these two vigorous players and their fine horses at the gallop.

Jiu-Hwa Upshur Collection; photo by John Nystuen

Jiu-Hwa Upshur Collection; photo by John Nystuen

Tomb Guardians. Since Han times, guardians were placed in pairs at tomb entrances. From the fifth century on, as a result of influence from West Asia, where lions were sacred royal beasts, these guardians took the form of ferocious lions and man-lions, as in this pair.

another to include foreign grooms, entertainers, dancers, and musicians in their entourage. Foreign fashions became fads and foreign ways such as drinking grape wines and playing polo became fashionable.

A burgeoning middle class competed with the court and nobility for luxury goods. Central Asian horses were great status symbols. Judging from the numerous models of horses found in tombs, many people owned them. People loved expensive and exotic items, such as jewelry and gems from India and gold and silverware from western Asia, for their non-Chinese shapes and decorative motifs, their foreign ideas, and the foreign persons represented on them. Much of T'ang life can be reconstructed from the numerous pottery replicas of people, animals, and objects buried to serve the dead in the next world.

T'ang cosmopolitanism hinged on the dynasty's military power and the increase in international trade. Skillful military strategists, the early T'ang generals subdued the nomads from Manchuria westward to central Asia and posted garrisons at important points in the interior to maintain peace and secure trade. A strong martial spirit drew recruits to the army. The T'ang also produced several famous female warriors. T'ai-tsung's sister commanded troops and campaigned alongside him. Another young woman, Hua Mu-lan, disguised herself as a man and answered the call to arms for her aged father. According to tradition, she revealed her identity only years later at an audience before the emperor. A famous ballad celebrated her going to war:

In the eastern market she bought a fine horse,
In the western market she bought saddle and blanket,
In the southern market she bought bridle and reins,
In the northern market she bought a long whip.
At dawn she set out from her parents' house,
At dusk she camped at the Yellow River shore.
She did not hear her father and mother calling to
their daughter;
She only heard the hissing voice of the Yellow River's
flowing waves.
At sunrise they set off and left the Yellow River,
At dusk they camped beside the Black Water.
She did not hear her father and mother calling to
their daughter;
She only heard the Hunnish horsemen shout across the
hills of Yen.
Ten thousand li she rode on many duties,
Borders and mountains crossed as swift as flight.
Through the northern night there sounded out the kettle-
drum,
In the winter daylight soldiers' armour gleaming. . . .

The flourishing international trade also contributed to the prevailing cosmopolitanism. The increased volume of trade and the need for a more efficient medium of exchange than metal coins brought about money drafts, the precursor of paper money. Invented in 811, they had the picturesque name of "flying cash."

T'ang international relations were of two kinds. One was between powerful China, under the Son of Heaven, and its dependent and subservient vassal states, particularly the various kingdoms of Korea, the many tribal states of the north and northwest, and Tibet. The presence of Chinese garrisons and the advantages of trade no doubt helped to maintain the overlord-vassal relationship between China and its small neighbors. China maintained equal relations with India, Persia, and the Byzantine Empire. T'ai-tsung and Harsha exchanged ambassadors, and China had diplomatic relations with the Sassanian dynasty of Persia for several centuries. The western limit of the Chinese world was the Byzantine Empire—Fu Lin to the Chinese. T'ang histories recorded four embassies from Byzantium, probably sent to enlist Chinese military aid against rising Muslim power. No Chinese embassies were sent to Byzantium.

The Chinese government first heard about Islam in 638, when T'ai-tsung received an appeal for help from the king of Persia for aid against the advancing Arab

Muslims. T'ai-tsung did not deliver military assistance, because of the distance and because at the time he had barely consolidated his own empire. Early in the eighth century, as Muslim armies advanced on central Asia and Afghanistan, the Buddhist states, which were sometimes Chinese vassals, sent urgent appeals to China for help. From the Muslim side, Caliph Walid also sent an ambassador to the T'ang court to urge against intervention. China did nothing to hinder the Arab advance. In 751 a Chinese garrison was routed by the army of Caliph Abul Abbas of the Abbasid caliphate in a battle near Tashkent, the only time the Chinese and the Arabs were engaged in hostilities. Soon afterward, Lady Yang's favorite began a rebellion, and the remaining T'ang garrisons were recalled from central Asia. The caliph even sent an army to help the Chinese defeat the rebels. Although the rebellion was crushed, the weakened T'ang government could not reassert its power in central Asia, and Muslim rule was established there.

The Apogee of Buddhism

Buddhism came of age in China during the early T'ang. Patronized by the court and supported by all elements of society, it served the ordinary people with festivals, lectures, and charitable activities. After the greatest Buddhist pilgrim, Hsuan-tsang, returned to China from India laden with precious manuscripts, he spent his remaining years translating them into Chinese. He was an indefatigable worker who alone was responsible for translating works equivalent to twenty times the volume of the Bible. The outpouring of religious works won Buddhism the respect of intellectuals. Hsuan-tsang also brought back many "genuine relics" of the Buddha, which became objects of veneration for millions of the faithful, in the same way that "relics" associated with Jesus, the prophets, and saints were venerated by Christians.

As Chinese Buddhist leaders studied the voluminous religious writings, several distinctively Chinese Mahayana Buddhist schools emerged. Three remained most important. T'ien-t'ai, begun about 600 and named after a famous monastery, reflected the Chinese tendency toward synthesis and harmony in the way it organized the vast body of Buddhist literature and recognized the validity of each sutra in its place. In this way, T'ien-t'ai muted the conflicts that had risen between different Indian schools of interpretation. This sect appealed primarily to the educated.

The Pure Land sect was named after the "Pure Land" or Western Paradise that the masses of Mahayana believers strove to achieve. It taught that salvation, or rebirth in the Pure Land, could be attained by faith, expressed through calling the Buddha's name. It appealed mostly to the common people, and thus had many followers.

The Ch'an (Zen in Japan) sect began in China in the sixth century. It was introduced by a semilegendary Indian missionary, Bhodidharma, who reputedly meditated for nine years facing a blank wall before he achieved enlightenment. Ch'an's antischolastic emphasis and stress on meditation and intuitive enlightenment derived at least in part from philosophical Taoism, as did its love of nature and simplicity. Together with Taoism, Ch'an Buddhism was a major inspiration to artists and poets.

Buddhism reached its high-water mark in the early T'ang. Persecution in the mid-ninth century marked the beginning of its decline. Confucians criticized Buddhism on several scores: it promised people what they could not have; it encouraged people to make donations they could ill afford; and its encouragement of celibacy undermined the social order and teachings of filial piety. Confucians also attacked the Buddhist church for its wealth, its tax-exempt status, and the unproductive life of its monks and nuns. Some of the criticisms were justified, but others were xenophobic and nationalistic, as Han Yu's memorial illustrated.

Courtesy of the Royal Ontario Museum, Toronto, Canada

A T'ang-Era Camel. The Chinese buried models of houses, animals, and utensils with their dead, in the belief that they would need these things in the afterworld too. Pottery models of camels, the chief means of long-distance overland trade, are commonly found in T'ang-era graves.

Buddha Is Highly Overrated

*Now Buddha was a man of the barbarians who did not speak the language of China and wore clothes of a different fashion. His sayings did not concern the ways of our ancient kings, nor did his manner of dress conform to their laws. He understood neither the duties that bind sovereign and subject, nor the affections of father and son. If he were still alive today and came to our court by order of his ruler, Your Majesty might condescend to receive him, but it would amount to no more than one audience in the Hsuan-cheng Hall, a banquet by the Office for Receiving Guests, the presentation of a suit of clothes, and he would then be escorted to the borders of the nation, dismissed, and not allowed to delude the masses. How then, when he had long been dead, could his rotten bones, the foul and unlucky remains of his body, be rightly admitted to the palace? Confucius said: "Respect ghosts and spirits, but keep them at a distance!"**

Han Yu (786–824) was the author of this diatribe. He was a famous scholar-official and a staunch defender of Confucianism. He vehemently opposed Buddhism as an alien faith inimical to both Confucianism and Chinese society. The quotation was part of a memorial he presented to the emperor to oppose a planned ceremony in the palace to honor a supposed relic of the Buddha. Han Yu's rhetoric shows that he was opposed to Buddhism both because it was superstitious and because it originated outside China (he also opposed Taoism). The emperor, who was a devout Buddhist, was so enraged by the memorial that he exiled the author. Later Chinese hailed Han Yu as the early leader of the Confucian revival, and the memorial just quoted as the opening salvo of that movement.

*William T. de Bary, ed., *Sources of Chinese Tradition* (New York: Columbia University Press, 1960), vol. 1, p. 373. Reprinted with permission.

Rivalry between Buddhism and Taoism on occasion led to persecution of one faith or the other; in one instance, both religions were targeted at the same time. The most severe persecution of Buddhism occurred between 841 and 845, under a pro-Taoist emperor. The persecutions, however, were chiefly aimed at religious property and members of the clergy, and unlike religious persecutions in Christian Europe, they seldom bothered individual believers.

Buddhism's decline during the later T'ang was also attributable to competition from revitalized Confucianism. International developments also contributed. After the eighth century, Muslim armies seized territories from northwest India through Afghanistan and central Asia—lands that had hitherto been Buddhist. As a result, Chinese Buddhists were no longer able to maintain their contacts with their fellow religionists in India. Intellectually isolated, Chinese Buddhism ceased to be a vital religion.

In restoring the examination system, the T'ang monarchs gave emphasis to Confucian political ideology at the expense of Buddhism. Thus Confucianism became the basis of education and once again began to dominate intellectual life. Ironically, Buddhism contributed to its own intellectual decline by endowing Confucian schools to educate poor boys.

Zoroastrianism and Islam also entered China during this period; the former through Persian traders and later refugees from Muslim invaders. The son of the last Sassanian king was given a commission in the T'ang army. However, unlike the larger Persian refugee community in India, whose members retained their faith and remained a distinct group called the Parsees, the Persians in China were soon assimilated. Reputedly, many Muslim troops sent by the Caliph to assist in putting down the rebellion against Ming-huang did not return home. They married local women and settled down in northwest China, founding the Muslim community there. Similarly, in the Roman Empire soldiers stationed in such far-off provinces as Dacia (Romania) and North Africa had settled and intermarried with local women. Before the end of T'ang, sizable settlements of Muslim traders had also been established in southern Chinese ports, most notably Canton. The Chinese government allowed them to elect their own leaders and to live by their religious laws.

The Golden Age of Poetry and Sculpture

The T'ang was a great creative epoch. Many fields of art flourished, but above all it was remembered as a golden age of poetry. About 3,000 poets from this period are known to us, and several of them are considered unsurpassed. One of the best loved was the romantic Li Po, who relished good wine with or without company, as he wrote in "Drinking Alone by Moonlight":

A cup of wine, under the flowering trees;
I drink alone, for no friend was near.
Raising my cup I beckon the bright moon
For he, with my shadow, will make three men.
The moon, alas, was no drinker of wine;

Courtesy of Jiu-Hwa Upshur

Buddhist Cave Temple. The giant Buddha and attendants are part of a cave temple complex that dates to the T'ang dynasty and is located near the capital city, Loyang. The figures show Greco-Roman-Gandharan influence.

Listless, my shadow creeps about at my side.
Yet with the moon as friend and the shadow
as my slave
I must make merry before the Spring was spent.

To the songs I sing the moon flickers her beams;
In the dance I weave my shadow tangles and breaks.
While we were sober, three shared the fun;
Now we are drunk, each goes his way.
May we long share our odd, inanimate feast,
And meet at last on the Cloudy river of the sky
(The Milky Way).

According to popular legend Li drowned as he leaned out of a boat to embrace the moon during a drinking party with his friends. Great portraitists and painters of landscape also distinguished the age, but few of their works on paper and silk have survived.

Buddhist art and sculpture also reached maturity under the T'ang. Many consider this the great age of sculpture, which until the flourishing of Buddhism had been a relatively minor art form in China. In addition to monumental sculptures preserved in the rock cave temples, artisans also produced small metal images of the Buddha and bodhisattvas, thousands of which survive. The T'ang Buddha images reflect Chinese humanistic interest—they are lifelike and intimate and mirror contemporary concepts of beauty.

Because of the power and prestige of the T'ang, their artistic forms became an international style that spread to Korea, Japan, and other lands. The imperial ambitions of the early T'ang, which led to Chinese control of central Asia, also caused Chinese Buddhist art to move westward, back along the same routes into central Asia. In the early twentieth century, at Tunhuang and further west, Western scholar-explorers discovered long-sealed Buddhist cave temples that had been forgotten or buried for centuries in sand. The paintings and sculptures show that for a thousand years this area was a melting pot where Gandharan, Indian, central Asian, and Chinese styles met and synthesized. Archaeologists have coined the name Serindia for this now desolate area.

Secular sculpture also flourished. The most spectacular are the monumental human and animal figures that lined the path to the artificial earthen mounds that covered the imperial tombs. More than a thousand years later, they are vivid reminders of the power of the ruling house. The six relief sculptures of T'ai-tsung's battle chargers that guarded his tomb, with inscriptions that recount their deeds and wounds, tell poignantly of the close relationship between the man and his horses. T'ang tombs yielded tens of thousands of ceramic sculptures of horses, camels, grooms, officials, and entertainers that are minor masterpieces of the anonymous sculptors of the age. The countless other artifacts excavated from tombs, made of silk, jade, bronze, and other metals and materials all testify to the great prosperity and high artistic standards of that era.

China Partitioned: The Sung and Nomadic Dynasties, 960–1279

*The [enemy's] heavy soldiery is entirely concentrated in the eastern capital. Having repeatedly suffered severe defeat, their morale has been destroyed. Within and without they are shaken and in alarm. According to intelligence reports I have heard, the enemy intends to abandon his baggage and hastily flee across the river. Moreover, now the loyalist guerrillas are responding to the changed situation. The officers and men are obeying orders. Heaven determines the course of human affairs in its own time . . . success is within our grasp. [Such] a time will not come again. The opportunity was hard [to come by] and can be lightly lost. . . . It is only for Your Majesty to desire it.**

*Edward Kaplan, "Yueh Fei and the Founding of the Southern Sung" (Ph.D. diss., University of Iowa, 1970), pp. 434–435.

So urged Yueh Fei, the most successful general of the Sung dynasty and one whose memory as a great patriot is revered by Chinese to the present. Yueh was hoping to stiffen the ruler's resolve and win support for his successful campaign to oust nomadic invaders from North China and regain lost lands. The emperor responded as follows:

> From the moment military operations began, We knew things must end with peace negotiations. . . . Military force was unavoidable, [but] how could we gain pleasure from offensive warfare? During this dynasty, [Emperor] Chen Tsung kept the peace with the Khitan for over one hundred years and the people did not know soldiers. Though [Emperor] Shen Tsung [the predecessor of the emperor who wrote this reply] talked of war and trained soldiers, actually he never used them. From the beginning until the present, We have thought only of peace. As We loved the people of north and south equally, We have taken the road of accommodation to defend them. (Kaplan, pp. 557–558)

Yueh Fei failed to win his emperor's support, and all the military advantage his army had gained was lost. The

Map 6.5 The Sung and Its Neighbors. The Sung dynasty never ruled the entire Chinese world. During the first part of the dynasty (960–1125), called the Northern Sung in retrospect, powerful nomadic states, the Liao and the Hsi Hsia, constantly menaced China.

emperor's speech characterized the policy of the entire Sung dynasty toward the nomadic invaders—avoid war almost at any cost and buy peace whenever possible. The Sung was the most pacifist dynasty in Chinese history. Its love for peace and abhorrence of war was in part responsible for the loss of North China to several nomadic groups and later South China to the Mongols.

A Checkered History

The closing decades of the T'ang dynasty were wracked by civil wars brought on by power struggles between ambitious generals and mutinous troops. They continued for half a century after the T'ang ended in 907. While China was fragmented, much as it had been after the fall of the Han, the nomads once again began moving southward and attacking Chinese lands.

The Sung dynasty was born out of a mutiny. In 960 an adventurer who had recently proclaimed himself emperor in North China appointed a capable young general named Chao K'uang-yin commander-in-chief of an expedition against the nomads. His officers and men did not like their assignment and felt no loyalty toward the government, particularly after the emperor died and left an infant on the throne. They mutinied and hailed Chao their emperor; thus a new dynasty, the Sung, was born. Such "elections" of emperors by rebellious troops had been frequent in the Roman Empire and in post-T'ang China; they had usually led to more violence and bloodshed. The Sung was an exception, for soon after unifying the country the new emperor removed from their military commands those officers that had raised him to the throne. He did it, however, with tact and generosity, rewarding them with titles and pensions.

Chao K'uang-yin, Founder of the Sung Dynasty. Although this portrait shows him wearing civilian clothes, Chao K'uang-yin still looks the part of a powerful general. Most of his successors, however, showed no military aptitude and let the army decline.

National Palace Museum, Taiwan, Republic of China

Domestically the Northern Sung enjoyed peace and prosperity. Even in its smaller territory, the population, over 100 million in 1114, surpassed peak Han and T'ang figures. Cities grew, as did an urban middle class. The printing press, now in wide use, made books cheap and commonly available, and literacy became widespread. For the first time, many men of middle class or humbler origins could afford to study for the examinations and realistically aspire to join the civil service.

The Sung government, pacifist and humane, was dominated by civilians. The two political parties, called the Conservatives and Innovators, settled their differences on social and economic policies through political and philosophical debates. The losers lost their jobs but never their heads. Kaifeng, a city south of the Yellow River, became the Northern Sung capital. Changan and Loyang, despite their fine strategic locations, would never be capitals of China again. Centuries of wars and invasions had so depleted the economy in their vicinities that they could no longer support a central government, and lack of good water transportation made it too difficult and expensive to provision those cities. In contrast, Kaifeng was located in a rich agricultural plain and was easily reachable by canal from the south. However, it lacked natural defenses and was vulnerable to cavalry attacks from the north.

Although the dynasty was founded by a general, it produced no distinguished warrior rulers. Sung emperors were instead known for their patronage of the arts and connoisseurship, and several were accomplished artists. Such cultured and art-loving rulers were ill-equipped to deal with the military and diplomatic needs of the time. In 1127 nomads captured Kaifeng and carried the artist emperor, his heir, and 3,000 members of his court into captivity in the steppes, where they were subjected to numerous indignities, as this victor's account relates:

> The two commoners [of the Sung, former Emperor Hui-tsung and his son Emperor Ch'in-tsung] were presented [to the Court of the nomadic Chin state, whose emperor] bestowed the title of Duke of Stupid Virtue to the father and the title of the Marquis of Double Stupidity to his son. . . . On the xxx day of the sixth month of the eighth year [1134] . . . the Imperial Decree ordered the six

How to Prevent Coups d'état

In the first year of his reign [960] the new Emperor summoned all his military officers—the men responsible for the mutiny to which he owed his throne—to a banquet. When the company had drunk deeply and were in cheerful mood, the Emperor said:

"I do not sleep peacefully at night."

"For what reason?" inquired the generals.

"It is not hard to understand," replied the Emperor. "Which of you is there who does not covet my throne?"

The generals made a bow and all protested:

"Why does Your Majesty speak thus? The Mandate of Heaven is now established; who still has treacherous aims?"

The Emperor replied: "I do not doubt your loyalty, but if one day one of you is suddenly roused at dawn and forced to don a yellow robe [official robe of an emperor], even if unwilling, how should he avoid rebellion?"

The officers all declared that not one of them was sufficiently renowned or beloved for such a thing to happen, and begged the Emperor to take such measures as he thought wise to guard against any such possibility. The Emperor, having brought them to this point, promptly made his proposal known:

*"Life is short. Happiness is to have the wealth and means to enjoy life, and then to be able to leave the same prosperity to one's descendants. If you, my officers, will renounce your military authority, retire to the provinces, and choose there the best lands and most delightful dwelling places, there to pass the rest of your lives in pleasure and peace until you die of old age, would this not be better than to live a life of peril and uncertainty? So that no shadow of suspicion shall remain between prince and ministers, we will ally our families with marriages, thus, ruler and subject linked in friendship and amity, we will enjoy tranquility."**

All carried out their parts of the bargain. There never was a mutiny during the Sung dynasty.

*C. P. Fitzgerald, *China: A Short Cultural History,* 3d ed. (New York: Praeger, 1976), p. 382.

daughters of the Duke of Stupid Virtue to be the wives of members of the Imperial Household.

In 1127 Sung loyalists put another son of the captive emperor on the throne in South China and set up the Southern Sung (1127–1279), with Hangchow south of the mouth of the Yangtze river, as capital city. Marco Polo later described Hangchow as far superior to Venice. In retrospect, the earlier period when Kaifeng was the capital city is called the Northern Sung. The new Sung emperor abandoned his captive relatives, made peace with the northern invaders, and agreed to the watershed of the mountains that divided the Yellow and Yangtze Rivers as their boundary. Everyone then settled down to enjoy the pleasures of peace, and culture flourished as never before.

Soon the fearsome Mongols rose over the steppes and began to cast a dark shadow over the Southern Sung. It was only a matter of time before the Sung, along with everyone else in the way, were swept away by Mongol power. Sung strategists even invented a new weapon—gunpowder-filled bamboo tubes launched rocket-fashion—to defend against Mongol attacks. The Mongols proved to be good students of military science, however, and soon incorporated the gunpowder rockets into their arsenal. The Sung were pushed ever southward, until the last emperor drowned off the coast of Canton in 1279 as his few remaining ships were being overwhelmed. By this time Kubilai Khan, grandson of the feared Genghis Khan and himself a great warrior, was well established in Peking as emperor of the new Yuan dynasty.

Difficulties in the Pursuit of Peace and War

Since antiquity, Chinese statesman had debated the merits of a defensive versus an offensive strategy against the nomads. The Sung opted for defense for two reasons. First, there had been a decline in martial spirit among the Chinese. The great aristocratic families of the Han and T'ang eras who had played a prominent part in the military had been decimated by the wars of the later T'ang period. By contrast, Sung leaders were literati with distinctly unmartial tastes and interests, and the ideal gentleman was an unathletic scholar. Whereas T'ang ladies rode, hunted, and played polo, Sung court ladies began to bind their feet because small, dainty feet became fashionable.

The second reason for the Sung's defensive stance was the ruling house's deliberate strategy of subordinating the military to civilian control and reducing the feeling of esprit de corps among the soldiers. Thus officers were rotated among different units to prevent them from developing a spirit of camaraderie. The Sung rulers also discouraged respect for military service. This disdain was evident in a saying coined at that time: "You don't use good iron to make nails, you don't use good men to make soldiers." Indeed, soldiers were often used like prisoners to perform manual labor, and were sometimes tattooed on the face to prevent desertion. The objective of the Sung's military policies was to prevent mutinies, and in that sense the policies were successful. No mutinies or revolts occurred under the Sung, but their army was also too weak to protect the empire.

Not surprisingly, the Sung produced few great generals. The most famous general was Yueh Fei, who lived in the twelfth century. Operating mainly on his own, Yueh achieved impressive successes in recovering recent territorial losses to the nomadic Chin dynasty in North China. The peace party at court, however, fearful and jealous of his popularity, had Yueh arrested and then murdered in prison. The court quickly concluded a treaty with the Chin, conceding the entire Yellow River valley.

The Sung strategy for survival was to rely on diplomacy. Whereas nation-states that were equals in international status developed in Europe after Charlemagne, no similar evolution took place in East Asia. Under the powerful Han and T'ang dynasties, the tradition of a single powerful state surrounded by satellites had evolved. But the Sung rulers were was compelled to share with other states territories that had formerly been part of the Han and T'ang Empires. After early efforts failed to recover sections of North China from a nomadic state called the Liao, the Northern Sung government concluded a peace treaty with it that not only acknowledged its loss of territory, but also agreed to pay the Liao an annual tribute or "brotherly gift" of 100,000 ounces of silver and 200,000 bolts of silk. After several decades, the Liao demanded an increase of 100,000 units in each category and the Sung government gave in rather than risk a military confrontation.

Anxious to share such good fortune, the Tibetan rulers of Hsi Hsia, another border state in an area once part of the Han and T'ang Empires, also threatened war and ended up getting annual gifts of 200,000 units each of silver and silk from the Sung. These agreements left no doubt who was the "younger brother" or the lesser nation in the relationships. Likewise, the Southern Sung paid a tribute in silver and silk to the Chin, successors of the Liao in North China, and formally acknowledged the Chin's status as overlord. In another reversal from the Han and T'ang model, the Sung emperor addressed the nomad ruler as his "uncle." By accepting such treaties, the Sung rulers had submitted to terms that Han and T'ang emperors would have regarded as shameful and intolerable. Yet the Sung considered the payment of tribute or bribe the lesser evil than war. Thus they were in no position to help in the last decades of the eleventh century when three embassies from the Byzantine Empire sought military help against the invading Turks.

Because of its constant need to raise money to pay tribute and maintain the army, the Sung government encouraged international trade and taxed it for revenue. Chinese

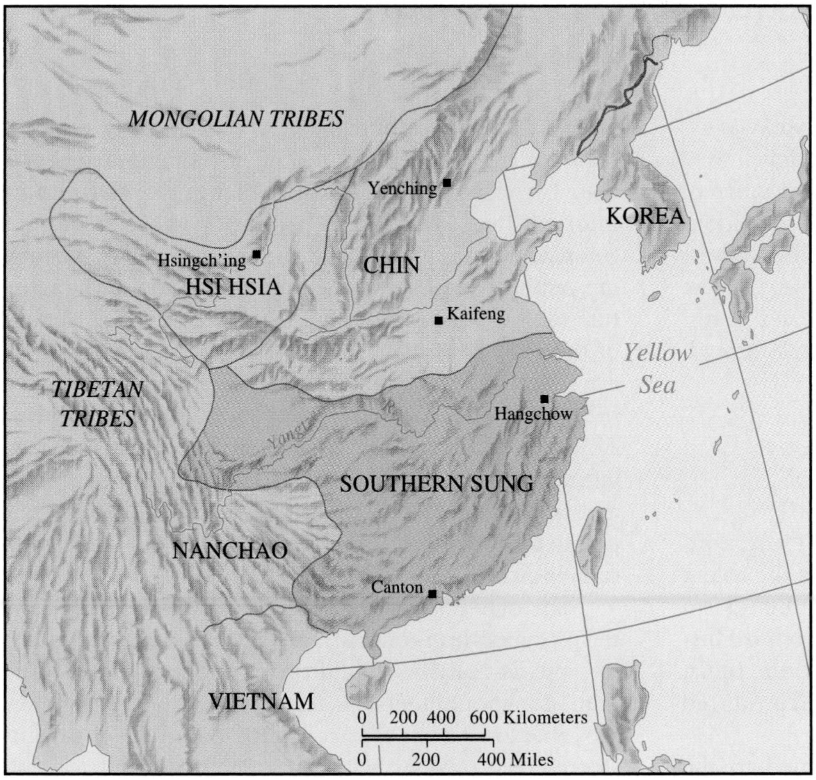

Map 6.6 The Southern Sung. After the loss of North China, the Sung government moved its capital to Hangchow, south of the Yangtze River. It was pushed ever southward and destroyed by the Mongols in 1279. The period between 1127 and 1279 is called the Southern Sung.

National Palace Museum, Taiwan, Republic of China

Two Ladies Enjoying the Cool Air. This thirteenth-century painting on silk shows a garden scene, with two elegantly dressed ladies holding fans.

ceramics, desired everywhere from Japan to Egypt, was exported in large quantities. Assembly-line techniques were developed to speed up ceramic production, and different types of ware were produced to suit the tastes of various customers, as determined by market research. Since hostile nomadic states blocked access to the west by land, Chinese traders worked to develop sea trade with Japan and Southeast Asia. Trade with western Asia was conducted through the Arabs, who dominated the Indian Ocean.

Dynamic Neo-Confucianism and Stagnant Buddhism

Buddhism, already in decline during the late T'ang, continued to wane as an intellectual force among the ruling classes of China. A reason was the collapse of Buddhism in India during the eleventh century, owing to the Muslim invasions. Denied intellectual stimulus from India, Chinese Buddhists created no new schools and produced no additional translations of the scriptures.

Sung governmental policy also contributed to the decline of Buddhism. To address the perennial budget crunch caused by tribute payments and the cost of maintaining a large standing army, the government raised revenue by selling ordination and other priestly certificates. Prior to this, governments had insisted that the sangha (monastic community) maintain its standards by examining candidate monks on their understanding of the scriptures before issuing them ordination certificates. The end of the religious exams and the sale of ordination certificates not only corrupted the priesthood but also contributed to a decline in the doctrinal vitality of Buddhism. Although the Ch'an sect, which emphasized intuitive enlightenment, and the Pure Land sect, which stressed faith and prayer, remained popular, neither was interested in points of doctrine. Neither offered an intellectual counterpoint to revived Confucianism.

The only noteworthy development in this period was the metamorphosis of Maitreya, the Buddha of the Future, into the fat Laughing Buddha, surrounded by many children, commonly found in temples and domestic shrines. He came to embody all that was to be desired—prosperity (represented by a fat belly), many children, and contentment. As a poem commonly associated with him says:

The big belly is capable to contain, it contains all
the things under Heaven which are difficult to
contain.
The broad face is inclined to laugh, to laugh at the
laughable men on earth.

The Confucian revival begun in the late T'ang reached its high point during the Sung period, when the best minds turned to the classical literature of antiquity. Although several Confucian schools emerged, the Neo-Confucian school led by Chu Hsi (1130–1200) eventually prevailed and was acknowledged as orthodox. Neo-Confucianism remained the official interpretation of the master's philosophy in China, Japan, and Korea until the late nineteenth century. Chu Hsi and his followers claimed that earlier Confucians had misunderstood the real meaning of the master, which they had rediscovered.

Neo-Confucianism was the great intellectual contribution of the Sung. Its distinctive feature was its ethical character. It condemned the otherworldliness of Buddhism and insisted that human fulfillment in this life is possible through self-cultivation. It accepted a supreme controlling force in the universe and believed that this force is expressed through the five chief virtues, namely, benevolence, righteousness, reverence, wisdom, and sincerity. It accepted the goodness of human nature and explained that evil resulted from the neglect of this nature. However, Neo-Confucianism failed to provide an answer to the problems of injustice, nor did it explain why humans were born with varying fortunes. This is perhaps why Buddhism, which did explain such matters, continued to have a mass following.

Since Chu Hsi and other Neo-Confucians came from the ranks of scholar-officials, it is not surprising that much of their writing dealt with political philosophy and with policies intended to bring about the well-being and moral betterment of the people. As one famous Sung scholar-official put it: "The true scholar should be the first to become anxious about the world's troubles and the last to enjoy its happiness." Neo-Confucians advocated a benevolent and paternalistic government where morally upright officials advised the hereditary monarch. From late Sung to the end of the nineteenth century, the school curriculum and examinations were based on Chu Hsi's interpretation of Confucianism. The triumph of Neo-Confucian orthodoxy during the last 700 years of imperial China largely explains the stability and conservatism of Chinese society until the twentieth century.

Courtesy of the Minneapolis Institute of Arts

Ceramics for Export. Chinese ceramics were widely exported during the Sung and were treasured from Japan to Egypt. Green glazed wares, called celadon, were especially prized in the Middle East, where people believed that poisoned food could be detected if served on them.

Age of Refinement in Culture and the Arts

The Sung period was noted for its cultural refinement. From emperor down, great and powerful men patronized the arts. The Sung ideal gentleman was a scholar-statesman, and most distinguished scholars and artists were also officials. Their output in historical, literary, and philosophical writing was prodigious. The printing press made their works, along with encyclopedias and other multivolume books, widely available.

Religion no longer dominated art in Sung China. No new monumental Buddhist shrines comparable to those undertaken during the T'ang and earlier eras were constructed during the Sung. Artworks were enjoyed for their aesthetic and not religious worth. Some of the greatest painters in Chinese history worked during the Sung period. Landscape painting flourished, and while some artists represented nature as a whole, others made intimate studies of a branch of flowers, a bird, or a spray of bamboo to depict nature in microcosm. Ceramics ranked highest among the minor arts. The technique of high-fired, hard-glazed porcelain was fully developed and the words *porcelain* and *china* became synonymous. From this time ceramic wares replaced lacquer and metal articles for daily household utensils. New glazes and forms were invented, ranging from the refined and sophisticated pieces produced for the court to various folkware pieces for ordinary use. Potters also turned out sturdy items that would withstand the sea or land journey to Japan, Southeast Asia, the Middle East, and North Africa.

In the daily life of all classes, tea drinking, which had begun in the T'ang, became more common. The tea bush grows in the temperate climate of southern China, and the development of that region resulted in the spread of tea cultivation and drinking. With the completion of the

LIVES AND TIMES ACROSS CULTURES

Companionable and Bossy Wives

Educated Sung families emphasized the training of daughters as well as sons, and the biographies of the era feature many accomplished literary women. Educated girls were desirable wives because they were intellectually compatible with their husbands and good teachers to their children. While some marriages achieved this ideal, others did not, as the two following contemporary accounts show. The first is from the autobiography of Li Ch'ing-chao (1081–1140). Both her parents were distinguished scholars and she herself was famous for her prose and verse. In the second excerpt, a man writes about his sister-in-law.

> *When we were married in 1101, my husband was twenty-one and was still a student at the National University. Both our families being poor, we lived a very frugal life. On the 1st and 15th of every month, my husband had leave of absence from the university to come home. He would very often pawn his belongings to get 500 cash, with which he would walk to the market at Hsianag-kuo Monastery and pick up rubbings of ancient stone inscriptions. These, together with some fresh fruits and nuts, he would carry home and we would enjoy together the edibles and the ancient rubbings, forgetful of all our troubles in the world. . . .*
>
> *When my husband became prefect of two prefectures, he spent practically all his income on books and antiques. When a book was bought, he and I would always read it together, mending the text, repairing the manuscript, and writing the captions. Every evening we studied together till one candle was burned up. In this way our collection of books surpassed all other collections in the country because of this loving care which my husband and I were able to give to it. We were resolved to grow old and die in such a little world of our own.**

> *Tsung-shu was quick-witted from youth and knew how to read. When she came of age, she married the scholar Tung . . . . Tung was weak and timid, Shu arrogant and overbearing. She bossed him around as though he were a servant. Unsatisfied with him she became depressed and fell ill. In the winter of 1126 . . . Tung died. In the following year Shu followed her mother to Nanyang, where she ate, drank, and amused herself without any sign of grief . . . . [Later her father proposed a new marriage for Shu] mentioning Wang Yueh as a possibility. Shu said, "I've already been troubled once in my life by a literary official and have no desire to repeat the experience. I'd be satisfied with a military officer." So she married Mr. Hsi.***

*Hu Shih, "Women's Place in Chinese History," in Li Yu-ning, ed., *Chinese Women through Chinese Eyes* (Armonk, NY: M. E. Sharp, 1992), pp. 9–10.

**Patricia Buckley Ebrey, *The Inner Quarters: Marriage and the Lives of Chinese Women in the Sung Period* (Berkeley: University of California Press, 1993), pp. 160–161.

Grand Canal during the Sui dynasty, cheap waterborne transportation brought tea and other southern commodities to the north. Teahouses sprang up in all towns and cities as social gathering places. The Sung court consumed 60,000 pounds of many varieties of tea annually for various purposes, including official gifts. Government offices served tea, and officials attending meetings were served teas of their choice. Tea often replaced alcoholic drinks at social occasions, and the well-to-do vied with one another to serve tea in the most attractive porcelain cups.

The peace of the Sung period was purchased at a high price, and this perhaps explains why so many people were determined to enjoy it at all levels. Hangchow and other cities were famous for their restaurants, tea and wine houses, and pleasure quarters. There was a mood of resignation even as people pursued their pleasures. As a poet of the Southern Sung wrote:

> *Beyond the hills, more blue hills; tall buildings are backed by taller.*
> *When, here on the West Lake, does singing and dancing cease?*
> *So heady is the warm breeze that pleasure-seekers, quite drunk,*
> *Forget their southern exile, and take Hangchow for Kaifeng.*
> *[Hangchow, capital of the Southern Sung, was built around the shores of the scenic West Lake.]*

As the Mongol forces advanced inexorably southward during the thirteenth century, the impending end must have been apparent. As a T'ang poet had written:

> *The last glow of sunset, for all its boundless beauty,*
> *Portends the fast approach of darkness.*

Two Sinicized States

*At daybreak each morning, with the beating of a drum, the headmaster and the instructors of the academy assemble the students in the courtyard. After making a bow to the instructors, the students enter the hall, where lectures and discussions on the classics take place. They study, deliberate, and counsel and assist one another to reach a full understanding of the relationships between ruler and minister, father and son, husband and wife, elder brother and younger brother, and friend and friend. For days and months, they work and rest together as one body to train themselves until they become new men. It is from these students that the future loyal ministers and the future filial sons are produced in prolific number to serve the state and their families. Indeed, never before in the history of our country have we witnessed such a splendid success in nurturing loyal officials and filial sons as we see now.**

*Peter H. Lee and William T. de Bary, eds., *Sources of Korean Tradition,* vol. 1: *From Early Times through the Sixteenth Century* (New York: Columbia University Press, 1997), p. 298.

This passage, written in the early fifteenth century, describes the curriculum for the young men studying at the Korean government-run Royal Confucian Academy, located adjacent to the Shrine of Confucius in the capital city, Seoul. Like the state university established by the Han Chinese government in the second century B.C.E., the academy trained civil servants by teaching them the Confucian classics, with emphasis on moral teachings, especially the five cardinal human relationships.

Korean culture fused Chinese learning with its own native traditions. This is apparent even in Korea's founding myths. In one myth, Kija (Chi-tzu in Chinese), a relative of the last king of the Shang dynasty, fled his native land with 5,000 followers in the twelfth century B.C.E., when the Shang ended; he then founded a new state in Korea. This story parallels Aeneas's flight from burning Troy and later founding of Rome. A second influx from China came during the end of the Chou dynasty in the wars that preceded unification by the Ch'in. The first Korean state was created in the second century B.C.E., in northwestern Korea, where Chinese influence was strongest. It was called Chosen, the name still often used for present-day Korea. The second founding myth tells about the mating of a tiger and a bear, which produced a human son called Tan'gun, who founded the Korean state and taught the people the arts of civilization.

The dichotomy between Chinese influence and indigenous Korean traditions persists. Despite Korea's transformation into a Sinicized state, it retained distinctive cultural characteristics, and Koreans resisted Chinese political domination. For example, written Chinese was the only script used in Korea up to the thirteenth century, even though spoken Korean belongs to the Altaic linguistic group, which is related to Japanese but not to spoken Chinese. A phonetic alphabet suitable for transcribing spoken Korean was invented in the thirteenth century; yet such was the prestige of written Chinese that the Korean alphabet was not adopted officially until the mid-twentieth century. Chinese vocabulary is so integral a part of Korean that even now Koreans must learn written Chinese. The number of Chinese characters Koreans know remains the measure of the level of their education. It is not possible to distinguish a Korean from a Chinese by personal names.

Korea

Situated on a peninsula on the northeastern tip of mainland China adjacent to Manchuria but separated from China by a mountain range and the Yalu River, Korea is about the size of Minnesota. The ancestors of Koreans migrated to the peninsula from Manchuria and North Asia starting around 2000 B.C.E.; the migration of peoples continued well into historic times. A wave of Chinese immigrants, fleeing the wars of the late Chou era,

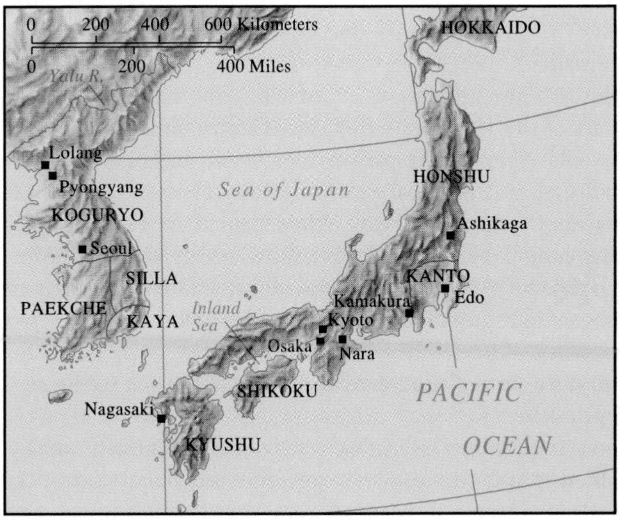

Map 6.7 Early Korea and Japan. Both came under the cultural influence of China.

Buddhist Pagoda. Buddhism became pervasive in Korea and was indistinguishable from Chinese Buddhism. This small pagoda, built during the Koryo dynasty, follows Chinese architectural style.

brought knowledge of bronze and iron making and other advanced technologies to the peninsula. By the third century, a northern Chinese state had extended some control over northern Korea. In 194 B.C.E., Koreans under Chinese influence established the first Sinicized state, called Chosen, in northern Korea, with its capital near modern Pyongyang.

Northern Korea was conquered by Emperor Wu of the Han dynasty in 108 B.C.E., and was organized into four commandaries (provinces) within the Han Empire. By 75, however, only one commandary, called Lolang, remained under Han control. Lolang prospered as a flourishing outpost of Han civilization and remained a part of the Han and its successor states until 313 C.E.

The Han conquest was important to Korea for both cultural and political reasons. Many Han-era tombs excavated near Pyongyang (then capital of Lolang, now the capital of North Korea) show strong Chinese influence. The Han conquest also stimulated the Koreans to organize regional states, which emerged during the first century B.C.E. The three largest ones contended for mastery until one unified the entire peninsula in the seventh century.

Sinicization in all three states had proceeded rapidly, all adopting Chinese-style governments, legal codes, tax systems, state universities to teach Confucianism and Chinese history, and Buddhism as the officially favored religion. All three kingdoms also became tributary states of China. However, because Korean society was more tribal and aristocratic than Chinese, government positions were determined by one's "bone rank," or birth. Thus schools and examinations were limited to the elite few, and the closely knit aristocrats monopolized power for centuries.

The reunification of China in the sixth century had a strong impact on Korea. The confident founders of the Sui and T'ang dynasties, hoping to emulate their illustrious Han predecessors, attempted to reconquer Korea. It would also allow China to outflank the nomads to the north. For these reasons the Chinese governments launched successive campaigns to conquer Korea between 589 and 659. Chinese threats speeded Korean unification under the Silla dynasty, which offered determined resistance to China and compelled the Chinese to withdraw in 668. Although the Silla kings accepted the status of vassals to the T'ang empire, they nevertheless enjoyed autonomy in their government.

The Silla dynasty was overthrown by the Koryo dynasty (918–1392), from which the name Korea derives. The Koryo remained vassals to the Sung and to the nomadic dynasties that ruled North China. The same nomadic groups who raided and conquered China raided and made vassals of Korea, the most ferocious being the Mongols. In one raid alone in 1254, the Mongols reportedly carried off 206,800 male Korean captives. In 1258 Korea surrendered completely to Mongol rule. The Mongol overlords retained the Koryo kings as puppets, married them to Mongol princesses, and frequently required them to live in the Mongol capital Tatu (Peking). Mongol exactions in wealth and human resources, including the lost Korean lives among those forced to serve in Kubilai Khan's two failed attempts to conquer Japan, took a cruel toll on the population. It is no wonder then that when the Mongols were driven out of China, their Koryo henchmen were ousted from Korea as well.

From the seventh to the seventeenth century, unified Korea increasingly resembled China. Korean governmental, legal, financial, and educational systems were all modeled after the Chinese. Thousands of Koreans continued to study in China, so that intellectual trends and styles in the two countries remained indistinguishable.

Vietnam

Like Korea, Vietnam is a close neighbor of China. It is separated from the southern Chinese province of Kwangsi by low mountains and jungles. Because the earliest Vietnamese histories were written by Chinese, and because of China's influence in the making of Vietnamese civilization from early times, Vietnamese history and culture must be looked at against a Chinese background.

Movable Type: Korea's Contribution to the World

In the third year [1403], King T'aejong remarked to the courtiers around him: "If the country is to be governed well, it is essential that books be read widely. But because our country is located east of China beyond the sea, not many books from China are readily available. Moreover woodblock prints are easily defaced, and it is impossible to print all the books in the world by using woodblock prints. It is my desire to cast copper type so that we can print as many books as possible and have them made available widely. This will truly bring infinite benefit to us." In the end, the king was successful in having copper type cast with the graphs modeled after those of the Old Commentary on the Book of Odes *[one of the Confucian classics] and the* Tso Commentary *[a book explaining one of the classics], and that is how the typecasting foundry became established in our country.**

Movable, metallic type was first developed in Korea in the thirteenth century. This was a great improvement on the woodblock method of printing developed earlier by the Chinese. The fifteenth-century Korean king described here is sponsoring book printing because a Confucian state had an obligation to promote scholarship, and concomitantly good government. Movable type spread from Korea to Japan and China, and thence westward from China.

*Peter H. Lee, and William T. de Bary, eds., *Sources of Korean Tradition,* Vol. 1: *From Early Times through the Sixteenth Century* (New York: Columbia University Press, 1997), pp. 305–306.

As in Korea, the historic period for Vietnam began toward the end of the first millennium B.C.E. At that time a people called the Yueh lived in coastal China from the southern bank of the Yangtze River southward to the Red River valley of northern Vietnam. They practiced slash-and-burn agriculture and made bronze artifacts. Toward the end of the third century B.C.E., the newly unified China under the Ch'in dynasty conquered and annexed what is now South China and the Red River valley in northern Vietnam. The Chinese called the Red River region Nan-Yueh (South Yueh) and governed it from Hanoi. Turned around and pronounced in the local manner, Nan-Yueh became Vietnam.

When the Ch'in dynasty fell, northern Vietnam came under a secessionist Chinese state centered at Canton. In 111 B.C.E., shortly before conquering Korea, emperor Wu of the Han dynasty reconquered and annexed northern Vietnam up to roughly the seventeenth parallel and organized the region into three commandaries (provinces). They remained part of China until 939 C.E.

Upper-class Vietnamese assimilated Chinese culture, but some resisted Chinese rule. When the Chinese governor killed a troublesome lord as an example to others in 39 C.E., his widow and her sister (called the Trung sisters) took up his cause, proclaiming themselves queens and leading a revolt that lasted for three years. Later Vietnamese honored them as national heroes. Before the tenth century, twelve separate Vietnamese uprisings against China occurred, propelled by nationalistic or anti-Chinese feelings, and fueled by local grievances. During the T'ang dynasty, China renamed Nan-Yueh An-nan, meaning the "pacified south." Pronounced An-nam in the local dialect, this remains the name for northern Vietnam.

In 939 Vietnamese forces defeated the Chinese army and established an independent dynasty. Except for short intervals of Mongol invasions in the thirteenth century and Chinese control for several decades in the early fifteenth century, Vietnam has retained its own government since that time, although like Korea it acknowledged China as overlord until 1885. At home the Vietnamese ruler called himself emperor, but when he addressed the Chinese ruler, whom he called lord, he referred to himself as subject and vassal king.

Under Chinese rule, Vietnam benefited from rapid progress and technological innovation. Chinese-designed irrigation works made possible intensive rice culture in the Red River valley. China also introduced efficient bureaucratic administrative machinery that replaced the rule of old feudal chieftains. Confucianism became the foundation of the governmental, educational, and moral systems, and Mahayana Buddhism became the influential religion. The Chinese administration collected taxes, demanded corvée labor from Vietnamese males, and drafted them for the military.

Upper-class Vietnamese, like their Korean counterparts, meticulously copied Chinese social customs and cultural norms. The Vietnamese adopted the same surnames and given names as the Chinese and wrote in the

CONNECTIONS IN MIGRATION

The Mariners of Oceania

The Austronesian-speaking peoples originated in what is now South China, in an area near the ancestral homelands of the Vietnamese, Thais, and Khmers, to whom they are related. The domestication of such food sources as yams, rice, taro, pigs, and chickens provided a substantial and relatively stable food supply and allowed these peoples to migrate easily to other areas.

Austronesian-speaking peoples developed maritime technology that enabled them to travel and settle throughout the Pacific and Indian oceans. They were not the first settlers of the lands in and around these large bodies of water, but they were the most far-ranging. One group settled in Taiwan. From there a second group settled in the Philippines, then spread aggressively to other areas. Relying on outrigger canoes and stilt houses, the western Austronesians populated the islands that are today Indonesia and the mainland area of Malaya, where they became known as Malays.

Others moved east from the Philippines, sailing to Papua New Guinea and the surrounding islands, where earlier settlers had developed agriculture and a dense population. This Austronesian group, mixing with the Papuans, became the Melanesians. Another group went east to Tahiti to become the Polynesians, then expanding east to Easter Island, north to Hawaii, and south to New Zealand. For the western group, there was at least one further move west, from Borneo across the Indian Ocean to East Africa and Madagascar.

Austronesian navigators relied on a complex variety of navigational techniques and an adventurous mentality. Once new areas were populated, however, the long-distance voyages ceased.

Austronesian mariners carried to their destinations not only their own culture but also elements of culture they had borrowed. One spectacular example is the sweet potato, which Polynesian migrants found in South America, carried west across the Pacific, and used extensively in the settlement of New Zealand.

---

1. Visit http://leahi.kcc.hawaii.edu/org/pvs/, the site of the Polynesian Voyaging Society. What is the main goal of the society? How do members conduct their research? What techniques do they believe that the ancient Polynesians used to navigate the open oceans? What were the main migration routes in Polynesia? What is the Hokule'a?

2. Go to InfoTrac and enter "Oceania" for journal name using PowerTrac. Look through the list of articles from Oceania and pick three that examine migration in the region. For each article answer the following questions: Exactly who is migrating? Why did they migrate? What was the origin and destination? How did the migrants accomplish the task? What were the long-term results of the migration?

same language, although in time they created new words that were different from Chinese. They wore similarly styled clothing, used chopsticks in eating food of a cuisine closely related to that of southern China, made ceramic wares similar to those of China, and built and decorated their houses in like manner.

Despite Chinese cultural influence, a Vietnamese self-consciousness and national identity emerged, due to several factors. Ancient cultural patterns from prehistoric times linked Vietnam to Southeast Asia. Vietnam's distance from the center of China's political power and its strategic insignificance to China made Chinese intervention less likely than in the case of Korea. Vietnam's frontier location between the Chinese world to its north and the Indianized states to its south and southwest allowed it to draw from two major cultures and sharpened its self-consciousness. This national consciousness was strengthened by struggles against Chinese domination and by Vietnam's southward expansion against the Indianized Champa and Khmer states.

Japan: The Merging of Chinese and Native Cultures

Because We had heard of the great Sui empire of propriety and justice located in the west, We send tribute. As barbarians living in an isolated place beyond the sea, We do not know propriety and justice, are shut up within Our borders, and do not see others. . . .

Our queen has heard that beyond the ocean to the west there is a Bodhisattva sovereign who serves and promotes Buddhism. For that reason, We have been sent to pay her respects. Accompanying us are several tens of monks, who have come to study Buddhist teachings.

. . .

The emperor of China greets the Wo [another name for Japan] empress.

Your envoys . . . have arrived and made their report.

Having been pleased to receive the command of Heaven to become emperor, We have endeavored to extend virtue everywhere, irrespective of distance.

*We are deeply grateful that the Wo empress—residing in the seas beyond—bestows blessings on her people, maintains peace and prosperity within her borders, and softens manners and customs with harmony.**

*Delmer M. Brown, ed., *The Cambridge History of Japan,* vol. 1: *Ancient Japan* (Cambridge: Cambridge University Press, 1993), pp. 182–183.

These are two early accounts of the first Japanese embassy sent to China in 607 by Prince Shotoku, regent of Japan, acting on behalf of Empress Suiko. The first is from the official history of the Chinese Sui dynasty and tells the event from the Chinese point of view. The second is from *Nihonji,* an official history of Japan written in 720 and represents the Japanese perspective. Both accounts agree that it was Japan that took the initiative of seeking knowledge from China.

Geography and Early History

The four main islands of Japan and the many smaller islands are located in northeastern Asia, separated from the mainland by the Sea of Japan and the East China Sea. Japan is roughly the size of California, is larger than Great Britain, and only slightly smaller than France.

There are several similarities between the British Isles and Japan. Both are separated from the continent by sea, which gave them comparative freedom from the wars and invasions that periodically swept the mainland. Compared with the English Channel that separates Britain from France, the seas that separate Japan from China and Korea are much more formidable, being 250 miles wide at the narrowest crossing point. Thus, historically, the Japanese were more isolated from mainland Asia than the British were from Europe.

Only about 20 percent of the land surface, mostly along the coast and river valleys, is level enough for cultivation. The rest of the land consists of mountains covered with forests. Scenes of natural beauty abound; one of the most beautiful is Mount Fuji, whose peak is a perfectly shaped, snow-covered volcanic cone more than 12,000 feet high. Although arable land is scarce, Japan has temperate weather and abundant rainfall, allowing intensive agriculture, with double-cropping in the southern islands. The main cereal crop is rice, grown in irrigated fields. The surrounding seas are rich in fish, shellfish, and edible seaweed, which provide protein in the diet.

Japanese written records date from about 500 C.E., but archaeological evidence and Chinese written records indicate that Japanese culture had been evolving for several millennia prior to that time. By the third century C.E., the Japanese were building huge earthen mounds up to 120 feet high, surrounded by moats and guarded by clay figures of animals and warriors, some riding horses. Those mounds were burial places for important people. We can infer from the size of the mounds and from artifacts they contain that society was highly aristocratic and that mounted aristocrats wielding iron weapons could mobilize the large workforce that was necessary for building the impressive mound tombs. The people of this tomb culture, as the era was called, in increasing contact with peoples on mainland Asia, would last into the seventh century and develop into the fully historic civilization of Japan.

The earliest Japanese written records pertaining to its origins are two works called *Kojiki (Records of Ancient Matters)* and *Nihonji (Chronicles of Japan),* written in 712 and 720 C.E., respectively. Both open with the mythological "age of the gods," a dimly remembered past reshaped to glorify the ruling family and to create a false picture of long-centralized rule and antiquity so the Japanese might enhance their self-image vis-à-vis China and its much older culture. As the *Nihonji* described in the opening passage of this chapter, Amaterasu, the Sun Goddess and founder of the sun line, sent her grandson, Ninigi, from heaven to rule the southern island of Kyushu with the imperial regalia. All three items in the regalia had special significance in early Japan. The bronze mirror was a symbol of Amaterasu, but in general mirrors, many imported from China, were treasured and frequently found in the burial mounds. The iron sword was a symbol of power to the warrior aristocrats, and swords are also found in the burial mounds. The curved jewel probably derived from the shape of bear and other animal claws and were used as amulets; such jewels have also been found in burial mounds in Japan and Korea.

According to the same creation myth, Ninigi's great-grandson overcame other deities and founded the Japanese state in Yamato around the Nara plain, not far from present-day Osaka, in 660 B.C.E. This part of the myth is probably a glorified account of how the Yamato sun-worshipping clan fought and defeated other clans and their patron deities and expanded its power. If so, the Japanese rulers are similar to the Greek heroes of the Trojan War or the chiefs of the Aryan invaders of India, who were also deified by posterity. Chinese records indicate that the Yamato state subdued areas hitherto dominated by "hairy men" (presumably the proto-Caucasian first inhabitants of the islands called Ainu) and became increasingly powerful. Although the Yamato clan dominated Japan at

Haniwa. Pottery warriors and horses are frequently found guarding the grave mounds of Japanese rulers that date to the early centuries C.E.

the beginning of its historic period, the islands were actually ruled by semiautonomous clans, each worshiping its own deified ancestors but acknowledging the supremacy of the sun goddess and her descendants.

This body of myths was later given the name of Shintoism (Way of the Gods) to distinguish it from Buddhism and Confucianism. Shinto myths thus reflected the political supremacy of the sun goddess clan and the subordination of other local cults. The deified ancestors of the subordinate clans were given less important places in the pantheon. Ancestors, awe-inspiring objects, and emperors, called *kami,* were all considered superior and were objects of reverence and worship.

Primitive Shinto, like other shamanistic beliefs, emphasized harmony with nature but had no philosophy, theology, or clear moral code. Most rites involved reverence to the memory of dead family members and clan ancestors. Shrines were simple structures made of wood and frequently rebuilt. Worshippers who attended rites at the shrines bowed, clapped their hands to arouse the spirits' attention, and joined in processions. They also offered wine, food, the first catch or fruit of the season, and the firstborn child (symbolically). Shintoism had no notion of guilt or sin, but stressed ritual purity. Association with birth, death, sickness, and the like brought on ritual impurity, which could be removed with exorcism and cleansing ceremonies. Ritual cleansing involved bathing, which might explain the Japanese preoccupation with bathing and physical cleanliness since early times. Similarly, the official religion of ancient Rome stressed the observance of rituals such as purification and expiation and offered little ethical instruction.

The Adoption of Chinese Civilization

Japanese life was greatly altered by Chinese culture between the sixth and ninth centuries. Much impressed by the might of the Sui and T'ang dynasties, Japanese aristocrats cultivated a strongly Chinese style of life, built a powerful Chinese-style state, and absorbed Chinese art and learning. The year 552 is the traditional date for the formal introduction of Buddhism and the start of the heavy influx of Chinese culture in Japan. Buddhism, then at its height in China and already Sinicized, served as the vehicle for the introduction of many aspects of both Indian and Chinese culture that would transform Japan. Chinese influence spread at a rapid pace for the next three centuries and transformed Japan from a primitive to a sophisticated culture.

Three factors explain the great eagerness of the Japanese to learn from the continent beginning in the sixth century. First, the Yamato rulers had found the existing hereditary clan government, which resembled that of the Germanic tribes of Roman times, inadequate for their expanded needs. They were therefore anxious to learn about more advanced concepts and methods from the continent. Second, by the sixth century the Japanese had attained a cultural level that enabled them to appreciate what China had to offer. Third, starting late in the century, China was again unified and entering a great era under the Sui and T'ang dynasties, thereby offering a successful model worthy of emulation.

Although an empress occupied the Japanese throne at this important time, the actual ruler was her nephew and regent, Prince Shotoku (ruled 573–621). This remarkable man was the chief architect of the great changes that would transform Japan. Legend says that Shotoku was born holding a statuette of the Buddha. He was not only a devout Buddhist, but also a learned theologian. By the time he came to office, many Chinese and Korean Buddhist missionaries were already at work in Japan, and their activities had provoked a heated controversy among the ruling aristocrats. Some were faithful to the traditional Shinto beliefs, while others enthusiastically converted to Buddhism. In 592 Prince Shotoku's pro-Buddhist faction won control of the court, and with their victory, Buddhism was established as the official faith.

Buddhism was an attractive new force in Japan. Some, like Prince Shotoku, studied its teachings, but most early converts were attracted more by Buddhism's elaborate rituals and ceremonies and magnificent art and architecture than by its theology. They were also impressed with the supposed magical powers of the new religion, or the prospect of gaining personal salvation. The eagerness of many to embrace Buddhism must have been inspired, at least in part, by the desire to partake in the material benefits it brought to Japan.

Early Japanese Buddhism was an extension of T'ang Chinese Buddhism. This was evident in temple and monastic architecture (the best extant examples of the T'ang style are found in Japan) and in the early Japanese Buddhist sects. Those architects and craftsmen who built the early temples were probably Chinese and Korean immigrants, and some of the sculptures and decorations they used to adorn the temples were imported from China or Korea. In time Japanese artisans would imbue their works with a uniquely Japanese spirit. All six Buddhist sects in early Japan were Chinese in origin. The most popular, the Tendai sect (T'ien-t'ai in China), appealed to well-educated upper-class Japanese, just as it had to a similar class in China.

Imperial Household Agency, Tokyo

Prince Shotoku and His Two Sons. This posthumous portrait shows Japan's revered ruler and his sons in Chinese-style court robes.

Though a devout Buddhist, Shotoku turned to Confucianism for organizing the government. In 604 he issued a document called the Seventeen Article Constitution, which contained guidelines on morals and ethics for the government and society. An important goal of the constitution was to transform Japanese government into a centralized monarchy by stripping power from the hereditary clans. Except for Article 2, which enjoined all to respect the Three Jewels of Buddhism, the articles embraced Confucian principles and Chinese governmental practices. Article 16 enjoins in part:

> Let the people be employed [in forced labor] at seasonable times. This is an ancient and excellent rule. Let them be employed, therefore, in the winter months, when they are at leisure. But from Spring to Autumn, when they are engaged in agriculture or with the mulberry trees, the people should not be so employed.

This passage refers to the ancient Chinese practice of levying able-bodied males to labor on government projects. The implementation of such a practice on a national level was new to Japan (no one knows precisely how labor was recruited and organized to build the mound tombs).

Prince Shotoku also adopted the Chinese calendar. In doing so he was also embracing the Confucian world order and indicating his acceptance of Confucian ideas about the relationship between heaven, earth, and humans. China required all vassal states to accept its calendar, but Japan did so voluntarily and did not become a Chinese vassal state. He also copied the Chinese court rank system and established Chinese-style government offices.

Shotoku also broke ground in another area. In 607 he organized an embassy to China to learn from the Chinese; later he sent two more. Thirteen more embassies were sent after Shotoku's death, making a grand total of sixteen between 607 and 838. These embassies were major undertakings; each was equipped with four ships carrying between 500 and 600 promising and eager young men chosen from good families. They included junior government officers, Buddhist monks, scholars in Chinese literature, painters, and musicians, among others. These youths remained in China, some for ten years or more, to learn as much as they could in their chosen fields. After returning to Japan, they worked in important positions or taught their skills to others. The voyages were also full of hazards because sailing ships had to cross open seas with no compasses. (The Chinese had invented the first magnetic compass in the fourth century B.C.E., but did not use it in navigation until between 850 and 1050; subsequently, the instrument was widely adopted by other peoples.) The sustained commitment to send numerous embassies showed remarkable farsightedness on the part of Japan's government leaders. The embassies were extremely successful and helped to bring about one of the greatest technology transfers in premodern times. In addition to the officially sponsored students, others were sent by Buddhist monasteries or went under private auspices with trading ships.

In 645 Chinese-trained officials with the goal of transforming Japan into a miniature T'ang China pushed Prince Shotoku's policy to its logical conclusion. A new set of laws, called the *Taika* (Great) Reform, made the ruler, now titled *tenno* (meaning heavenly emperor, a Chinese-sounding title), head of a theoretically centralized empire. The Taika Reform abolished private land ownership, made the emperor the theoretical owner of all land as in T'ang China, and instituted a Chinese-style tax system. Officials with Chinese titles assisted the emperor in administration, using Chinese bureaucratic practices, rituals, and ceremonies. Like China, the country was divided into provinces and counties, which were given Chinese-sounding names. The officials also promulgated a law code, sections of which were copied verbatim from the T'ang code.

Japanese women lost ground as a result of the Taika Reform. In compliance with Chinese notions of propriety, women were gradually barred from the imperial succession. As a result Japanese society was transformed from one based on a mixture of matrilineal and patrilineal principles in which both men and women could succeed to political power (Amaterasu, a goddess, was the founder of the sun clan), to an exclusively patriarchal one. Whereas between 592 and 770 half the rulers were women, after 770 women were shut out from the succession. A desire to conform to Chinese standards was one reason for the change. Another was the behavior of the last reigning empress, who virtually handed over the reins of government to her favorite, a Buddhist monk, rumored also to be her lover. He became so powerful that people feared he planned to usurp the throne. After she died, government leaders determined to forestall a repetition of her disastrous reign by barring women from the succession.

Until 710 Japan had no permanent capital city. This was partly due to the rudimentary nature of the government and to Shinto notions of purity, that death was defiling; so that at the death of an emperor, his residence was abandoned or destroyed, and the residence of his successor became the new seat of government. Thus buildings, including Shinto shrines, were simple and impermanent. These ideas did not apply to Buddhist temples and monasteries, which were grand, beautiful, and built to last.

To symbolize the adoption of T'ang-style centralized government and display the grandeur of the court, a capital city was laid out at Nara in 710. A number of beautiful Buddhist temples already stood in the vicinity. Two and a half by three miles square, Nara was conceived as a scaled-down Changan, capital of T'ang China;

its streets were laid out in a grid pattern with a magnificent palace at the northern end and many temples scattered throughout. The most spectacular temple in the city was called the Todai-ji (Great Eastern Temple); its main hall, built in the eighth century, was the largest wooden building in the world. It housed a fifty-three-foot bronze statue of the Buddha that weighed over a million pounds. In 752 when the temple was formally dedicated, 10,000 monks, including some from China, Korea, and India, attended the celebration. Neither the grand Buddha hall nor the great Buddha statue has survived. Many other great temples were built in the eighth and ninth centuries with the support of the court and aristocratic families.

Nara ceased being the capital after 794; as a result, few buildings were added after that date. Thus it remains a T'ang period city, more so than any city in China. The emperor built a new capital called Heian some distance away in order to escape the domination of the powerful Buddhist monasteries at Nara. It was later called Kyoto (which means capital city) and remained the imperial capital until 1867. Somewhat larger than Nara, it, too, was planned as a scaled-down version of Changan. The four centuries between 794 and 1185 are called the Heian Age, which was characterized by refined and sophisticated culture.

Departures from Chinese Models

Even as the Japanese struggled to duplicate Chinese culture, many things remained different. The Japanese economy was less developed than that of China. Shintoism continued to be important despite the popularity of Buddhism, because even a devoutly Buddhist emperor remained a Shinto high priest and carried out a heavy schedule of Shinto rituals, assisted by the Office of Shinto Deities.

Japanese society also remained sharply differentiated according to hereditary class. Thus, while Japan duplicated China's state university and examination system, both institutions were reserved for the sons of the aristocracy, as they were in Korea. Government posts remained hereditary despite their Chinese-sounding titles.

Some of the ambitious measures of the Taika Reform were abandoned or modified after a trial period, because conditions in Japan did not allow their operation. The most drastic reform had been over land ownership and taxation. The reformers had attempted to adopt the T'ang "equal-field" system. Judging by surviving records, Japanese leaders during the Nara and early Heian periods made heroic efforts to carry it out, with considerable success in some areas. Even in T'ang China, with its considerable bureaucratic machinery and experience, the equal-field system had broken down after a hundred years; small wonder it could not be sustained in Japan.

The Heian period was one of general economic expansion, but the central government did not benefit. Aristocratic families evaded taxes and Buddhist institutions did not pay them. Possessing the capital and manpower to bring new lands into cultivation, the aristocrats gradually gained control over increasing tracts of land. While they thrived and grew rich, the revenue-starved central government became steadily poorer, and its remaining officers had less and less work to do. Meanwhile the remaining small landowners and free peasantry were saddled with the entire burden of the land tax. To escape the crushing taxation, many peasants placed themselves and their land under the protection of a lord or monastery, working for their patrons for a fee less than the tax bite.

By about the tenth century, ceremonial duties were all that were left for the emperor and atrophied central government to perform. But whereas a Chinese royal house that had become irrelevant would be overthrown, such was the prestige of the imperial line and respect for hereditary rights in Japan that no one attempted to replace the dynasty.

Instead of supplanting the imperial family, the most powerful and wealthy court family in Heian, the Fujiwara, simply married into it. The period between the ninth and twelfth centuries is called the Fujiwara centuries because that clan dominated the government through having a monopoly of supplying empresses and consorts to the emperors and princes. In this way, the imperial government became a sham headed by emperors who were puppets of the Fujiwara family. When a child emperor ascended the throne, his maternal uncle or grandfather, a Fujiwara, naturally became regent. When the emperor grew up and married, his empress and concubines were also Fujiwara women, perhaps the daughters of his mother's brother, the regent. Thus there was no reason for the regent to give up his power, even after the emperor became an adult. As soon as the son of a Fujiwara empress was old enough to sit through state ceremonies, the emperor was prevailed upon to retire so that the regency cycle could begin once again.

The Fujiwara were very wealthy because they owned numerous tax-free estates, but by the twelfth century they became decadent and their power faded. Other clans rose to power but let the Fujiwara continue to dominate the imperial family through the web of intermarriage between the two clans.

Language and the Arts in the Nara and Heian Periods

The court and nobility dominated culture and the arts during the Nara and Heian periods. Since Japan had no written language, it borrowed Chinese writing. This posed problems since Chinese and Japanese belong to

Courtesy of Madoka Niwa

Ho-odo (Phoenix Hall). This elegant complex of lakeside garden buildings was created in the eleventh century at Heian (later called Kyoto), capital of Japan. The architecture and landscaping were inspired by China's T'ang dynasty. Similarly, the rich sculpture and artworks that adorn the interior evoke the Chinese Buddhist vision of the Paradise of Amida Buddha.

separate linguistic families, Sinitic and Altaic, respectively, with quite different grammar and syntax. Eventually, the Japanese incorporated Chinese words into their vocabulary and invented a system of syllables that permitted them to reflect the Japanese grammatical structure and to write Japanese words that had no Chinese equivalents. Initially, however, the Japanese were forced to read, write, and compose entirely in Chinese, and Chinese was used exclusively in all early books by Japanese authors, as well as in all government records and documents. However, mastery of written Chinese gave educated Japanese a distinct advantage, for it enabled them to draw on the entire corpus of Chinese literature, the treasures of a 2,000-year-old civilization. Similarly, educated Romans' knowledge of Greek gave them access to the literature of ancient Greece.

Since the Chinese were keenly conscious of the importance of history, the Japanese naturally adopted the same attitude; like the Chinese they preserved historical records and compiled dynastic histories. The Japanese also honored the Confucian moral code, looked up to Chinese sages and heroes as role models, and revered learning.

After the ninth century the Japanese were mature enough to innovate and depart from Chinese models. At this time a distinctly Japanese style began to emerge. A phonetic script, *kana*, was developed for writing Japanese. While men of the upper classes continued to write in Chinese according to Chinese conventions, noble ladies, who did not have to pursue an equally strict educational curriculum, learned to write in Japanese, using *kana*. The result was a flowering of Japanese literature written by women. Lady Sei Shonagon's *Pillow Book* was a journal of court life that painted a picture of sophisticated people preoccupied with good taste and manners even in religion. The outstanding work of the period was Lady Murasaki's *Tale of Genji*. It portrayed a decadent court society of cultivated but effete men and women from the emperor down who followed an elaborate dress code and valued the ability to write poetry more than government.

Such literary works indicate the growth of a native culture. They suggest a parallel with medieval Europe, where the clergy and government officials wrote in Latin, while popular literature was written in vernacular tongues. While Heian Japan and medieval Europe owed their cultural heritage to China and Rome respectively, each developed distinctive characteristics. In its gradual evolution of feudalism, Japan was definitely departing from the contemporary Chinese model of the Sung dynasty and evolving its own unique culture.

Early Feudal Japan

In contrast to Europe, where feudalism declined with the rise of national monarchies, in Japan feudal institutions replaced national institutions after the eleventh century. The emperors reigned but no longer ruled. They were replaced by the provincial lords, some of whom were descended from the old clan aristocrats, while others came from court families who had earlier left the capital. These lords managed the estates, supervised the peasants, and fought local wars against one another or the retreating Ainu. Some still acknowledged vassalage to great court families such as the Fujiwara and remitted part of their in-

Elegant Court Life

*A preacher ought to be a good-looking man. It is then easier to keep your eyes fixed on his face, without which it is impossible to benefit by his discourse. Otherwise the eyes wander and you forget to listen. Ugly preachers have therefore a grave responsibility. . . . If preachers were of a more suitable age I should have pleasure in giving a more favorable judgement. As matters actually stand, their sins are too fearful to think of.**

*About the twentieth day of the second month the Emperor gave a Chinese banquet under the great cherry-tree of the Southern Court. . . . The guests [royal princes, noblemen, and professional poets alike] were handed the rhyme words which the Emperor had drawn by lot, and set to work to compose their poems. It was with a clear and ringing voice that Genji read out the word "Spring" which he had received as the rhyme-sound of his poem. [After the party Genji spent the night with a lady of the court.] Suddenly they saw to their discomfiture that dawn was creeping into the sky. . . ." Tell me your name," he said. "How can I write to you unless you do? Surely this is not going to be our only meeting?" She answered with a poem in which she said that names are of this world only and he would not care to know hers if he were resolved that their love should last till worlds to come. It was a mere quip and Genji, amused at her quickness, answered, "You are quite right. It was a mistake on my part to ask." And he recited the poem: "While I still seek to find on which blade dwells the dew, a great wind shakes the grasses of the level land."***

Lady Sei Shonagon and Lady Murasaki were contemporaries who lived around 1000; both came from the Fujiwara clan and moved in court circles. The former wrote a book of sketches about court life, manners, and morals and the latter a novel about the romantic life of a prince. Both works are masterpieces of prose written in kana, and both paint clear, wonderful pictures of the refined and effete life of the court in Heian.

*Lady Sei Shonagon, *The Pillow Book,* quoted from W. G. Ashton, *History of Japanese Literature* (New York: D. Appleton, 1899), p. 116.

**Lady Murasaki, *The Tale of Genji,* trans. Arthur Waley (New York: Modern Library, 1960), pp. 210–214.

come to them, but less so with time since they no longer needed protection from the imperial government.

Mounted warriors dominated Japan's feudal society. Each aristocratic warrior was attended by small retinues of squires, clad in light armor made of metal, fabric, and leather, which was superior to that worn by contemporary European knights. Armed with bows and arrows and curved swords made of the finest tempered steel in the world by Japanese smiths, they resembled the knights of medieval Europe. A Japanese knight was called either a *samurai,* which means a "servant" (to a lord), or a *bushi,* which means "noble warrior." A feudal relationship, also resembling that in Europe, existed between lord and samurai and often continued for generations. The lord provided his knights with income derived from his agricultural estates. In return, the samurai was expected to serve his lord with absolute loyalty and die in his cause.

The samurai code of conduct, called *bushido* (way of the warrior), did not idealize samurai women, who were expected to be brave and to die rather than submit to shame, but they could inherit property, and some were quite successful in managing estates. Samurai also took pride in their ethic of living a hard, Spartan life. They shunned luxury and were expected to face pain and death with indifference.

The feudal period in Japan was punctuated by many small conflicts between competing warrior cliques. In the twelfth century these culminated in two major wars between rival clans, both descended from junior branches of the imperial line. They had early left Kyoto to make their fortunes in the provinces. Tales from these wars have provided materials for countless plays and stories popular to later generations.

The final victor was a lord named Minamoto. He had the emperor appoint him "Barbarian-Quelling Generalissimo" and delegate to him supreme military authority. In Japanese, the shortened version of the title was *Shogun,* a name the hereditary military dictators used until the mid-nineteenth century. The Minamoto chose Kamakura, a seaside town near present-day Tokyo, as the seat of the Shogunate. Kamakura was located in the productive Kanto plain, where many Minamoto estates were located.

LIVES AND TIMES ACROSS CULTURES

Japanese Adaptations

Japan owed many of its cultural developments to China and to India via China. The transformation of the Indian Dhyana school of Buddhism to Ch'an in China, then to Zen in Japan is a good example. Tradition says that in 520 C.E. the Indian master Bodhidharma came to China to preach a religious discipline aimed at tranquilizing the mind of the practitioner so that he can devote himself to exploring his own inner consciousness. The goal is to attain serenity and peace amid a turbulent world. As it developed in China, Ch'an was influenced by philosophical Taoism, with its emphasis on spontaneity and naturalness.

Ch'an's introduction to Japan coincided with the establishment of military-dominated regimes called the shogunate. In Japan, the sect became known as Zen, a variant pronunciation of the Chinese word. The shoguns patronized Zen partly because it was not dominated by the old court aristocrats as the other Buddhist schools were. In addition, its teachings could be adapted to the culture and code of conduct of the warriors who formed the backbone of the shogunate. Its close association with the military class infused Zen with a martial spirit, and it became especially influential with the Japanese military. During the strife-filled feudal period, however, people in many other walks of life were also attracted to Zen.

The rise of Japanese feudalism brought an increasing segregation of the sexes and sequestration of women. Thus the easy social intermingling between men and women described in Lady Murasaki's and Sei Shonagan's books became history. With the seclusion of respectable women, men could only socialize freely with entertainers and courtesans. This situation had a parallel in ancient Athens, where respectable women were practically cloistered in their own homes, and professional "companions" (*hetairai*) provided physical and intellectual stimulation for men at dinner parties.

Like everyone else in hierarchically structured Japan, the courtesans were segregated in the *Yoshiwara* or "Flower District" of town and were strictly ranked. The *geisha,* which means "art person," stood on top. Like an Athenian hetaira, a geisha spent a long apprenticeship learning literature, song, dance, conversation, and the art of pleasing men. She was a fashion setter in her gorgeous clothes and jewelry and was waited on by maids. She entertained at lavish parties for her male customers, rarely granting her sexual favors except by arrangement. Some eventually became concubines to important men, others retired to teach young aspirants.

The shogunal dynasty called its government the *bakufu*, which means "tent government," that is, a military administration in contrast to the civil government in Kyoto and theoretically subordinate to it.

The Kamakura Shogunate lasted for a century and a half, outlasting the Minamoto line that had established it. In a typically Japanese fashion, another feudal clan, the Hojo family, married a daughter to the Minamoto Shogun and then eliminated the Minamoto line. It then installed a nonentity as Shogun and ruled the country as shogunal regents. By the thirteenth century, Japan had a very confusing government structure, with an emperor who was the puppet of the Fujiwara clan. That clan supervised a sham government in Kyoto, while in Kamakura a puppet Shogun presided over the bakufu, which was really ruled by the hereditary shogunal regent, a man of the Hojo clan.

In the mid-thirteenth century, for the first time in its history, Japan was faced with a terrifying foreign threat: the Mongols who had conquered much of Asia and Europe and intimidated the rest. In 1266, Kubilai Khan sent envoys to Japan demanding submission. The bakufu refused, and it meant war. In 1274 an invasion force of 25,000 Mongols and their Korean subjects landed at Hakata Bay in northern Kyushu. The Mongols were accustomed to massed cavalry tactics, while the samurai fought in individual combat. After an inconclusive battle, the Mongols reembarked in the face of a coming storm and sailed back to Korea, suffering heavy storm-inflicted losses en route; total casualties amounted to a third of the invading force.

Certain that the Mongols would return, the bakufu assembled a large force and erected a wall around Hakata

Bay. When the Mongols returned in 1281 with 140,000 men and a huge armada, the wall restricted the Mongol cavalry, while small, and easily maneuverable Japanese crafts inflicted heavy damage on the large Mongol ships in the confined space of the bay. In the same way, Athenian ships had the advantage over those of the invading Persians in the Bay of Salamis in 480 B.C.E. Then a devastating typhoon struck, wrecking the Mongol fleet and marooning their soldiers. The invading force lost between 60 to 90 percent of its men. The Japanese attributed their salvation to divine intervention in the form of *kamikaze,* or "divine wind," just as the English later thanked God for the storm that destroyed the Spanish Armada. The Mongols never returned, although the bakufu continued the mobilization for two decades just in case.

The strain of the Mongol invasion and the cost of preparedness sapped the strength of the bakufu. The joy of deliverance soon evaporated, and since there were no spoils to share, many of the samurai faced financial hardship. In any case, after several generations the personal bonds that had tied the samurai to the bakufu were wearing thin. The end came in 1333, with the extermination of the Hojo family by a rebel force. With that came also the end of the first phase of feudalism in Japan.

Religion and Social Life during the Early Feudal Era

During the twelfth and thirteenth centuries, cultural changes were also reshaping Japan. The Japanese began to alter Buddhism to reflect the outlook of their feudal society. While the Buddhist sects of the Nara and Heian eras survived and continued to serve the elite, new sects imported from China or formed in Japan emerged that better served the needs of the warriors and the ordinary people. One new sect was the Pure Land, introduced from China in the twelfth century. By offering salvation to the faithful in the blissful Pure Land of Amida Buddha (Japanese shortened form for Amitabha Buddha), it gave hope to the masses and became immensely popular among them. It allowed the faithful to acquire salvation simply by repeating Amida Buddha's name in faith and sincerity. In the thirteenth century, a Japanese priest began an offshoot called the True Pure Land, which discarded most of the scriptures and appealed to ordinary people by repudiating clerical celibacy and encouraging priests to live among the congregation. The True Pure Land went so far as to assert that a single sincere act of calling the Buddha's name was sufficient for salvation. Its simplicity contributed to its popularity, making the True Pure Land the largest branch of Japanese Buddhism, followed by the Pure Land sect.

The Zen sect, which is the Japanese pronunciation of the Chinese word Ch'an (meditation), was introduced to Japan at the end of the twelfth century. It especially suited the needs of the samurai because it emphasized simplicity and discipline, rather than scholastic studies, and reinforced the idea of physical discipline and mental toughness extolled by the bushido code. Thus Zen became the sect of the warrior caste of feudal Japan; and with their support, it achieved great prestige and influence.

Zen also helped shape the Japanese aesthetic sense and to synthesize the refined artistic vision of Sung China with the Japanese love of the simple and tranquil. Tea drinking, newly popular in China, was introduced to Japan at this time, at first for medicinal use. As in China, tea soon became a national drink, and in the hands of Zen aesthetes, it evolved into the tea ceremony, which became an art and a unique style of social intercourse. Imported Sung ceramic ware was favored for the tea ceremony; surviving specimens are among Japan's loveliest cultural treasures.

A monk named Nicheren (1222–1282) founded a popular Buddhist sect, named after himself. A fiery street preacher who militantly opposed the other Buddhist sects, he chauvinistically insisted that Japan was the land of the gods and that Japanese Buddhism was the only true Buddhism. Nicheren's sectarianism and nationalism, as well as his emphasis on congregational worship and reading the scriptures in Japanese translation, in some ways resembled Protestant Christianity that later developed in Europe.

Buddhist religious fervor, so strong at this time, was reflected in many new temple buildings and religious sculptures; the most famous is the monumental bronze Kamakura Buddha, cast in the mid-thirteenth century. The temples that still stand show strong Sung influence, a reflection of the pervasive cultural contacts that continued between China and Japan. Many translations of Buddhist works were written in kana, reflecting the popularizing of Buddhism.

The peasants lived in simple two-room huts, clustered in villages. A few could afford wooden floors, but most simply covered the dirt floor with straw mats. They wore clothes made from the fiber of a perennial hemp plant called ramie; less frequently, they wore clothes made of silk. Cotton cloths were first imported from Korea in the fifteenth century. By the sixteenth century, cotton was grown, spun, and woven in Japan. Although rice cultivation was widespread, most of the crop was turned over to the lord. Peasants ate inferior grains such as millet, roots, and wild grass seeds.

While the medieval peasant was largely self-sufficient, he did trade his surplus and items he made such as vinegar and wines for salt, pottery, and iron tools in the local markets, usually held three times a month. Peasants with the same skills formed guilds. Metal coins, mostly minted in China, were increasingly used in trade; in time peasants began to commute their dues in cash also.

1 C.E.	Ajanta and other cave excavations begin in India Buddhism arrives in China King Kanishka calls Fourth Buddhist Council Gandharan and Mathuran art styles
	Paper invented
	Three Kingdoms and era of disunity in China Spread of Buddhism
	The Gupta dynasty Revival of Hinduism in India Buddhist cave temples begin in China
500	
	Yang Chien reunifies China, Sui dynasty Grand Canal in China
	Harsha rules in India Founding of T'ang dynasty Hsuan-tsang goes to India
	Confucian revival
	Muslims invade India
750	
	Golden age of Chinese poetry: Li Po
	Printing invented
	Northern Sung dynasty Liao, Chin, Hsi Hsia states in North China Neo-Confucianism gains; Buddhism declines in China Chinese examination system fully developed
1000	Turkish Muslims conquer North India; Rajput resistance
	Southern Sung dynasty Porcelain manufacture perfected Gunpowder invented
	Mongols conquer the Southern Sung
1300	

Farm women did most of the planting, threshing, and milling and took goods for sale in the markets. They also formed guilds for recreation and for work associated with festivals. Religious festivals, organized around local shrines, provided villagers with plays and dance performances.

Summary and Comparisons

This chapter discussed the second imperial age in India and China. The Gupta dynasty and later King Harsha brought much of northern and central India under their rule during the fourth, fifth, and early seventh centuries. Under their rule, India enjoyed unprecedented prosperity and cultural advancement; it is the classical era of Indian art and architecture. Buddhism reached its apogee and began to show signs of decline, while a revived Hinduism began to assume its final form. Disunity again prevailed in India after Harsha's death in 648; divided India could not resist the waves of Muslim invasions that began in 712. Muslim rule now prevailed in most of northern India. Southern India, though divided, escaped Muslim invasions.

The Gupta era also saw the peaceful spread of Indian religions and culture throughout most of mainland and island Southeast Asia, from Burma to present-day Indonesia. Buddhist and Hindu missionaries and Indian merchants ushered most of the region into the historic era, as Indian influences blended with local traditions to form distinctive cultures.

After three centuries of divisions and nomadic invasions, China's second imperial age was politically successful and enduring. During the Sui and T'ang dynasties, Buddhism, entering via the Silk Road, became fully Sinicized. Although the Sung dynasty was militarily weak and unable to rule all Chinese-popluated lands, it continued the cultural growth of the preceding era. Unfortunately, the pacifist Sung succumbed to formidable nomadic invasions. Muslim invasions severed the close link between India and China contributing to the decline of Buddhism in China.

Chinese political and cultural influence spread to Korea and Vietnam beginning with the Han dynasty and accelerated in the second imperial age. The Korean and Vietnamese civilizations at this time were scarcely distinguishable from the Chinese, but in time, both merged foreign influences with native traditions.

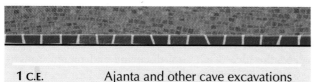

Japan entered its historic age around 500 C.E. under heavy Chinese and Sinicized Buddhist influence. Unlike Korea and Vietnam, Japan was not under Chinese political dominance but freely emulated China's more advanced culture. It too, in time, combined native and imported traditions to form a refined culture and combine titular imperial rule with warlord dominance and feudal institutions.

In both India and China, northern regions suffered invasions after the fall of their respective first empires, and, in both, invasion brought new ideas. The Greeks who settled in Afghanistan and northwestern India introduced their artistic styles to adorn Buddhist worship sites while the Greek-influenced Buddhist missionaries introduced Greco-Indian art to China. Both cultures were enriched as a result. The Muslim invaders that entered India after 712 brought monotheistic religious ideas irreconcilable with Hinduism and Buddhism; their invasions therefore caused fissures that persist on the Indian subcontinent to this day. In contrast, although China's post-T'ang nomadic invaders were unstoppable, they were culturally backward; unlike the highly advanced Arab and Turkic Muslims who invaded India, they were not literate and lacked higher religions. Moreover, their small numbers made them easily assimilable. Each group eventually lost martial prowess, failed to sustain a distinct identity, and ultimately added little to the Chinese civilization that absorbed it.

Though Indian culture had penetrated Southeast Asia in earlier times, its greatest impact in the region occurred during and after the Gupta period. Likewise, while China began its rule over parts of Korea and Vietnam during the Han dynasty, the gradual absorption of China's culture continued under the more advanced T'ang and Sung eras. Japan accepted Chinese culture just as Southeast Asia absorbed that of India; in both cases, the process was voluntary, not the result of political control.

Selected Sources

Arthaud, J., and B. Groslier. *Angkor.* 1957. A richly illustrated book on Angkor, with good text.

*Brazell, Karen, tr. *The Confessions of Lady Nijo.* 1973. This memoir of a Japanese court lady, long lost and rediscovered in 1940, recreates aristocratic life of the fourteenth century.

"Buddha in the Land of Kami." Films for the Humanities. Video on interactions between Buddhism and Shintoism in Japan between the seventh and twelfth centuries.

Carter, T. F. *The Invention of Printing in China and its Spread Westward.* Rev. ed. 1955. Chronicle of an event of vast world importance.

*Chang, K. C. *Food in Chinese Culture: Anthropological and Historical Perspectives.* 1977. Fascinating and entertaining account of Chinese food and eating habits from antiquity to the present.

*Ch'en, Kenneth. *Buddhism in China: A Historical Survey,* 1964. A comprehensive and readable survey of the evolution of Buddhism in China to the twentieth century.

China Central T.V. and Central Park Media. *The Silk Road.* 1982. A series of six 55-minute films, each devoted to a portion of the ancient Silk Road.

*Coedes, G. *Indianized States of Southeast Asia.* Ed. Walter F. Vella. Trans. Sue Brown Cowing. 1968. Deals with the multifaceted influences of India on the region through 1,500 years.

Deuchler, Martina. *The Confucian Transformation of Korea.* 1992. On Korea between the tenth and fourteenth centuries.

Devahuti, D. *Harsha: A Political Study.* 1970. A detailed study of India in the sixth and seventh centuries and of Harsha's accomplishments.

Ebrey, Patricia B. *The Inner Quarters: Marriage and the Lives of Chinese Women in the Sung Period.* 1994. A recent study of women and domestic life.

Ebrey, Patrica B., and Peter N. Buckley, eds. *Religion and Society in T'ang and Sung China.* 1993. A useful collection of articles by nine experts in this period of Chinese history.

Farris, William W. *Heavenly Warriors: The Evolution of Japan's Military, 500–1300.* 1991. On the early phase of Japan's warrior culture.

Gernet, Jacques. *Daily Life in China on the Eve of the Mongol Invasions, 1250–1276.* Trans. H. M. Wright. 1962. A good book on an often overlooked subject.

Hall, D. G. E. *A History of South-East Asia.* 2d ed. 1964. A comprehensive and authoritative book.

Hansen, Valerie. *Changing Gods in Medieval China, 1127–1276.* 1990. Interesting look at religion, especially folk religion.

Jaschid, Sechin, and Van Jay Symond. *Peace, War, and Trade along the Great Wall: Nomadic-Chinese Interaction through Two Millennia.* 1989. Pathbreaking study of interactions between China and Inner Asia.

Lane-Poole, Stanley. *Medieval India under Mohammedan Rule (A.D. 712–1764).* Reprinted 1979. A comprehensive account of Muslim conquerors and rulers.

Lo, Kuan-chung, or Shih Nai-an. *All Men Are Brothers.* Trans. Pearl S. Buck. 1933. A popular Chinese novel about a band of Robin Hood–like men and women during the Sung dynasty who took the law into their own hands for just causes.

*Lady Murasaki. *The Tale of Genji.* Trans. A. Waley. 1935. Japan's greatest novel on courtly life.

Packard, Jerrold M. *Son of Heaven: A Portrait of the Japanese Monarchy.* 1987. Traces the world's longest-reigning royal house from its beginning to the present.

Puri, B. N. *India under the Kushanas.* 1965. A good survey of the Kushan era.

Quaritch Wales, H. G. *The Making of Greater India.* 1951. A concise but comprehensive treatment of the spread of Indian culture throughout Southeast Asia.

Reischauer, Edwin O. *Ennin's Travels in T'ang China.* 1955. T'ang China as observed by a Japanese Buddhist monk.

*Samson, George. *A History of Japan to 1334.* 1954. First of a three-volume work on Japan by a recognized authority.

Sato, Hiroaki, trans. and ed. *Legends of the Samurai.* 1995. This book deals with the Japanese military elite from earliest times to the eighteenth century.

*Available in paperback.

*Schafer, Edward H. *The Vermilion Bird: T'ang Images of the South.* 1967. An interesting account of southern China and Southeast Asia.

*———. *The Golden Peaches of Samarkand: A Study of T'ang Exotics.* 1983. An interesting book about the unusual things most history books leave out.

Sinor, Denis, ed. *The Cambridge History of Early Inner Asia.* 1990. This work by a number of specialists has several chapters on China's nomadic neighbors.

Smith, Vincent A. *The Oxford History of India.* 4th ed. Ed. Percival Spear. 1981. A part of this authoritative book deals with the period this chapter discusses.

Steinhardt, Nancy C. *Chinese Imperial City Planning.* 1990. A comprehensive survey through the ages.

Stierlin, Henri. *The Cultural History of Angkor.* 1979. Profusely illustrated, this short but interesting text deals not only with the Khmer culture, but also those of Burma, Thailand, and Champa.

Swann, Peter. *Art of China, Korea, and Japan.* 1963. A good, short, and well-illustrated book that integrates history and art.

*Tinker, Hugh. *Southeast Asia: A Short History.* 2d ed. 1990. Good, short introduction.

Twitchett, Denis, and John K. Fairbank, eds. *The Cambridge History of China.* Vol. 3: *Sui and T'ang China, 589–906.* Part 1. 1979. Many experts contributed to this authoritative volume.

Waley, Arthur. *The Poetry and Career of Li Po.* 1958. Waley brings to life a wonderfully eccentric man and his great work.

Whitfield, Susan. *Life along the Silk Road.* 1999. Recreates lives of people, from princesses to laborers, along the greatest trade route in history.

*Wriggins, Sally H. *Xuanzhang, A Buddhist Pilgrim on the Silk Road.* 1996. An engaging account of the travels of China's most famous pilgrim to India and back.

Wright, Arthur F. *The Sui Dynasty: The Unification of China, A.D. 581–617.* 1978. Excellent portraits of two men who ruled China around 600 C.E.

———. *Buddhism in Chinese History.* 1959. A good book for both students and specialists.

*Wu, Cheng-en. *Monkey.* Trans. Arthur Waley. 1943. A sixteenth-century novel of how a supernatural monkey and other beasts helped Hsuan-tsang get Buddhist scriptures from India. Chinese children love it as fairy tale and adults as satire.

Internet Links

Ancient Japan
http://www.wsu.edu:8080/~dee/ANCJAPAN/ANCJAPAN.HTM
This site includes material on all aspects of ancient Japan, including the influence of Chinese culture, the role of Buddhism, the Nara and Heian periods, and cultural and social history generally.

The Diary of Lady Sarashina (1009–1059)
http://history.hanover.edu/texts/diaries/diaryall.htm
The text of the memoir of an eleventh-century Japanese court lady.

Gupta Dynasty: Golden Age of India
http://www.med.unc.edu/~nupam/Sgupta1.html
This site offers excellent short texts on the kings of the Gupta dynasty, keyed to illustrations of contemporary coins.

History of Korea
http://violet.berkeley.edu/~korea/history.html
This homepage contains links to additional pages pertinent to all eras of Korean history. See especially "Ancient History (pre-918 A.D.)," and "Koryo Dynasty (918–1392)."

Murasaki Shikibu (973/8–aft.1014)
http://home.infi.net/~ddisse/murasaki.html
This site is devoted to all aspects of the study of Lady Murasaki's masterful *Tale of Genji.*

The Sung Dynasty (A.D. 960–1279)
http://www.cohums.ohio-state.edu/deall/jin.3/c231/handouts/h11.htm
An outline indicating general characteristics, governmental change, literary and artistic trends, and the emergence of Neo-Confucianism.

The T'ang Dynasty (A.D. 618–907)
http://www.cohums.ohio-state.edu/deall/jin.3/c231/handouts/h9.htm
A handy outline of political, economic, and cultural developments in the era.

Vietnam History
http://www.viettouch.com/vietnam_history.html
This very informative site offers an objective survey of Vietnamese history and culture from ancient times to the present. Good graphics, including an elaborate timeline with hyperlinks to more detailed discussions of specific eras.

Cultural Borrowing and Cultural Isolation

There are three religious groups here, the panc-h'i *[pandits or brahmans] or learned men, the Buddhist monks or* ch'u-ku, *and the Taoists or* pa-ss'u.

James P. Holoka and Jiu-Hwa L. Upshur, eds., Lives and Times: A World History Reader, vol. 1 (St. Paul: West Publishing, 1995), p. 278.

Cavalry warfare in Eurasia came about through a long process of historical evolution. . . . Horsemanship was practiced by Indo-European peoples of the Ukrainian steppes as early as 4000 B.C.E. . . . It is likely that the horse had been domesticated in China during the Neolithic era (circa third millennium B.C.E.) when it was harnessed to the chariot as well as used as a draft animal. . . . Chinese records indicate that the Di [a nomadic people living to the northwest of China] rode horses as early as the Spring and Autumn era (722 to 481 B.C.E.). By the time of the Warring States (403 to 221 B.C.E.), the nomadic use of mounted men had become a form of warfare so powerful as to inspire emulation.

Adam T. Kessler, Empires beyond the Great Wall: The Heritage of Genghis Khan (Los Angeles: Natural History Museum of Los Angeles County, 1993), pp. 17–18.

The first cultures evolved and advanced in isolation mainly through independent invention. For example, agriculture appeared in three widely separated parts of the world (West Asia, China, and the Western Hemisphere) at about the same time, each based on different crops (grain/rice, maize/potatoes). Likewise many early cultures independently invented the technique of firing utensils made of clay to make pottery.

With the passage of time, travel, trade, and warfare brought peoples of different cultures together. Diffusion—the passing of ideas, technologies, and languages from one culture to another—became increasingly frequent. The two passages quoted above prove this point. The first was written by a twelfth-century Chinese visitor to Angkor, capital of ancient Cambodia. Situated in Southeast Asia, ancient Cambodia (also called the Khmer state) was ideally located to benefit from traders, missionaries, and settlers from China to the north and India to the west. Although the writer remarked on the presence of Taoist priests from China, Hinduism and Buddhist became the primary religions of that land, with Buddhism finally triumphing. The second passage shows the importance of warfare in affecting technology transfers. When the Di, a nomadic neighbor of the Chinese, learned horse riding, they were able to menace the Chinese more powerfully, compelling them to adopt cavalry in warfare in self-defense.

Another example of war as an important catalyst of diffusion can be seen in the spread of iron weapons. The Hittites were the first people to use iron weapons and became feared widely as a result. In self-defense their neighbors and victims hastened to learn the new technology and make their own iron weapons. Eventually, the technology of making weapons and agricultural implements from iron spread throughout Europe, Asia, and Africa, and iron replaced bronze as the primary metal.

Wars and conquest also spread cultures and ideas. For example, through conquest, the more advanced Chinese spread their culture to Korea and Vietnam. On the other hand, the less cultured Roman conquerors became admiring students of the sophisticated Greeks they subjugated. The Mongols eventually adopted the religions, written languages, and technologies of their different victims, and as a result lost their homogeneity and unity.

Commerce and group migration have also been important vehicles for the spread and diffusion of cultures. In the case of commerce, Greeks trading with the Phoenicians in the eastern Mediterranean adopted the Phoenician alphabet. Chinese traders and Buddhist teachers brought the Chinese writing system to Japan. The Silk Road, a major commercial route across Eurasia, introduced new religions, crops, technologies, art forms, raw materials, and finished products to different cultures across two continents. Indian merchants and other travelers by sea brought the sciences, mathematics, and writing of India's ancient civilization to the peoples of Southeast Asia. Oceans prevented dissemination from Eurasia to the Amerindian civilizations until the end of the fifteenth century. Ironworking was not independently invented in the Americas.

Group migration is another important means of diffusion. From earliest times, people have moved from one region to another in search of land and resources, as conquerors, or in flight from enemies. In Italy, the immigration of the Etruscans from Asia Minor around 900 B.C.E. and of the Greeks after 700 resulted in rapid advances in technology and art throughout the peninsula. In Africa, when the Bantu migrated into the central and southern part of the continent, they brought their own language and customs, which in time were adopted by local peoples. The spread of the Indo-European languages is another example of this type of diffusion. This language system originated in the steppe heartland of Eurasia; the migrating tribes who moved into other parts of Europe and Asia spread their language. As a result, nearly all the languages from northern India to Ireland belong to the Indo-European family and are related.

It is important in studying world history to understand that most civilizations were the amalgamation of indigenous and borrowed elements. Chapters 6 and 7 prove how true this was throughout classic Mesoamerica, the Amerindian empires, the early African kingdoms, Southeast Asia, and Japan. During more recent centuries, as means of transportation and communication have expedited contact between societies, diffusion has increasingly become the predominant mode of cultural change. As the world becomes more interconnected, so too the speed and extent of cultural borrowings and exchanges will increase.

Developing Civilizations

7

At the same time that the city [Cuzco] was being peopled, our Inca [Manco Capac] taught the Indians those occupations which appertain to a man, such as breaking up and cultivating the ground, and sowing corn and other seeds, which he pointed out as fit for food and useful. He also taught them to make ploughs and other necessary instruments, he showed them the way to lead channels from the brooks which flow through the valley of Cuzco; and even instructed them how to prepare the sandals which we now wear. On the other hand, the Queen employed the Indian women in such work as is suitable to them, such as to sew and weave cotton and wool, to make clothes for themselves, their husbands, and children, and to perform other household duties. In fine, our princes taught their first vassals everything that is needful in life. . . .

*The Inca Manco Capac, in establishing his people in villages, while he taught them to cultivate the land, to build houses, construct channels for irrigation, and to do all other things necessary for human life; also instructed them in the ways of polite and brotherly companionship, in conformity with reason and the law of nature, persuading them, with much earnestness, to preserve perpetual peace and concord between themselves, and not to entertain anger or passionate feelings toward each other, but to do one another as they would others should do to them, not laying down one law for themselves and another for their neighbours. He particularly enjoined them to respect the wives and daughters of others; because they were formerly more vicious in respect to women, than in any other thing whatever.**

*Ynca Garcilaso de la Vega, *First Part of the Royal Commentaries of the Incas* [1609], ed. and trans. Clements R. Markham, vol. 1 (London: Hakluyt Society, 1869), pp. 65–69.

This passage belongs to a foundation legend centering on the achievements of the first Inka, Manco Capac. Especially notable is the concern shown for the status and equitable treatment of women, something not evident in any of the patriarchal societies contemporary with the Inka around the world.

This chapter returns to Amerindian civilizations and African cultures taken up in Chapter 1. It is instructive in looking at these non-Eurasian civilizations to consider the concepts of cultural isolation and cultural borrowing discussed in the previous Comparative Essay.

The Amerindian civilizations that had already been established in Mesoamerica and the Andes continued to develop on an increasingly sophisticated course, particularly in engineering, mathematics, astronomy, and the decorative arts. Down through the years some scholars have claimed that Egyptians or Phoenicians or early Japanese or Chinese or some other Eurasian group had somehow crossed the ocean and created these civilizations. A few even professed to find evidence of extraterrestrials landing in Peru. However, most scholars view the Amerindian civilizations as completely indigenous.

In comparison with the Amerindian civilizations, the cultures of sub-Saharan Africa, although separated from Eurasia by an ocean of sand, showed some signs of Eurasian influence. East Africa had close relations with Egypt because of the Nile, and proximity to commercial traffic on the perimeter of the Indian Ocean meant more substantial contacts in general with Eurasia. On the other hand, cultural diffusion into western Africa before the advent of Islam was slight. The Bantu culture that spread into southern Africa showed the least evidence of diffusion.

Mesoamerican Civilization

Our first father-mothers . . . were simply made and modeled, it is said; they had no mother and no father. . . . No woman gave birth to them, nor were they begotten by the builder, sculptor, Bearer, Begetter. By sacrifice alone, by genius alone they were made, they were modeled by the Maker, Modeler, Bearer, Begetter, Sovereign Plumed Serpent. And when they came to fruition, they came out human:

They talked and they made words.
They looked and they listened.
They walked, they worked.

They were good people, handsome, . . . Thoughts came into existence and they gazed; their vision came all at once. Perfectly they saw, perfectly they knew everything under the sky, whenever they looked. The moment they turned around and looked around in the sky, on the earth, everything was seen without any obstruction. . . .

They understood everything perfectly, they sighted the four sides, the four corners of the sky, on the earth, and this didn't sound good to the builder and sculptor. . . .

And so the Bearer, Begetter took back their knowledge: . . . They were blinded as the face of a mirror is breathed upon. Their eyes were weakened. Now it was only when they looked nearby that things were clear.

*And such was the loss of the means of understanding, along with the means of knowing everything. . . .**

**Popol Vuh,* trans. Dennis Tedlock (New York: Simon & Schuster, 1985), pp. 165–167.

This Maya creation story resembles explanations of the origins of humankind in other cultures. Unlike many of these other accounts, however, there is no "fall," as in the Judeo-Christian tradition, nor are men and women created as limited toys for the gods to enjoy, as in several Asian traditions. In the Maya version, human beings are made perfect and through no lapse of their own are later made imperfect. The stress on knowledge and on perception is also notable and well suits a people who made great innovations in mathematics, astronomy, and engineering.

In Chapter 1 we discussed the Olmec, the parent culture of Mesoamerican civilization. After 400 B.C.E. Olmec society began to lose its vigor, and other cultures arose. The three most notable were the large urban culture centered on Teotihuacán, the mathematically and astronomically sophisticated Maya culture, which lasted almost 2,000 years, and the Aztec state, Mesoamerica's culminating Amerindian empire.

Urban Splendor: Teotihuacán

Teotihuacán arose in an arid valley approximately thirty miles northeast of present-day Mexico City. In 100 B.C.E. the area was a cluster of villages; by 200 C.E., massive public buildings had been laid out. Centuries of prosperity followed, and by 500 Teotihuacán, now a grid-shaped metropolis of 200,000, had become one of the largest urban centers of the world. One reason for Teotihuacán's preeminence was a reliable water supply. Although located in an arid climatic zone, the city was centered on a dozen large, permanent springs in an area of rich volcanic soil. Like the inhabitants of the Tigris-Euphrates valley earlier, the Teotihuacanos used terracing, canals, and other water-saving methods to produce abundant food crops that supported a large population.

The reconstructed center of the city gives some idea of its size and shape. Ceremonial buildings, ball courts, and two great pyramids, the largest almost 600 feet square, sit along a central avenue extending almost three miles. Less dramatic, but equally important to archaeologists, are the remains of some 3,000 other structures within the city. Most of these were multifamily dwellings; typically, each structure featured a patio and a cement foundation with an elaborate drainage system.

Another factor in Teotihuacán's rise to prominence was its control of the obsidian trade between highland Mexico and the gulf coast. Teotihuacán built up a substantial industry for producing obsidian tools, and its artisans also manufactured pottery and other items for large-scale export.

It is unclear how far the Teotihuacanos extended their rule from their valley. Some authorities claim that it expanded hundreds of miles to the east into Maya territory; others maintain that Teotihuacán's influence was commercial and cultural, but that political control reached only into neighboring valleys.

For many Mesoamericans, Teotihuacán was a focus of pilgrimage and worship, for it was there that their ancestors emerged from the underworld. Much of Teotihuacán religion was directed to worship of a "Great Goddess," a female divinity who provided the springs of water. Her images depict her gesturing outward, with water, seeds, and flowers issuing from her body and her clothing. Another powerful symbol of water and fertility was the Feathered (or Plumed) Serpent, the fanged, feather-collared serpent who is depicted undulating on seashell beaches. The Serpent was also a manifestation of the planet Venus, the morning and evening star, the Teotihuacán deity of warfare and blood sacrifice.

Teotihuacanos, living in a generally barren wasteland, were undoubtedly anxious about the permanence of their existence, and devised practices to help the Great Goddess keep Teotihuacán well-watered. Mesoamerican astronomers for many centuries carefully recorded the appearance of Venus as the morning and evening star. Calculating that Venus had a 584-day cycle and that five of these cycles corresponded to eight 365-day years, they formulated an almanac of 2,920 days. Apparently, a warrior cult found in Teotihuacán and other Mesoamerican cultures used the phases of Venus to find the most propitious times to undertake what some modern investigators have termed "star wars," campaigns conducted to secure sacrificial prisoners. These prisoners were executed in great public ceremonies, providing the blood "soul" that turned into water, thus sustaining Teotihuacán; Teotihuacán paintings depict red drops of blood from dead and dying prisoners literally turning into blue drops of water.

Although early Teotihuacán art rarely depicted military themes, after 500 C.E. there were more and more allusions to warfare, and archaeologists have found the remains of a great wall. At this same time, the Teotihuacán trading area began to contract. The population

Temple of the Sun. The city of Teotihuacán flourished in the central highlands of Mexico about 500 C.E. The enormous Temple of the Sun, pictured here, is larger than any of the famous Egyptian pyramids at Giza.

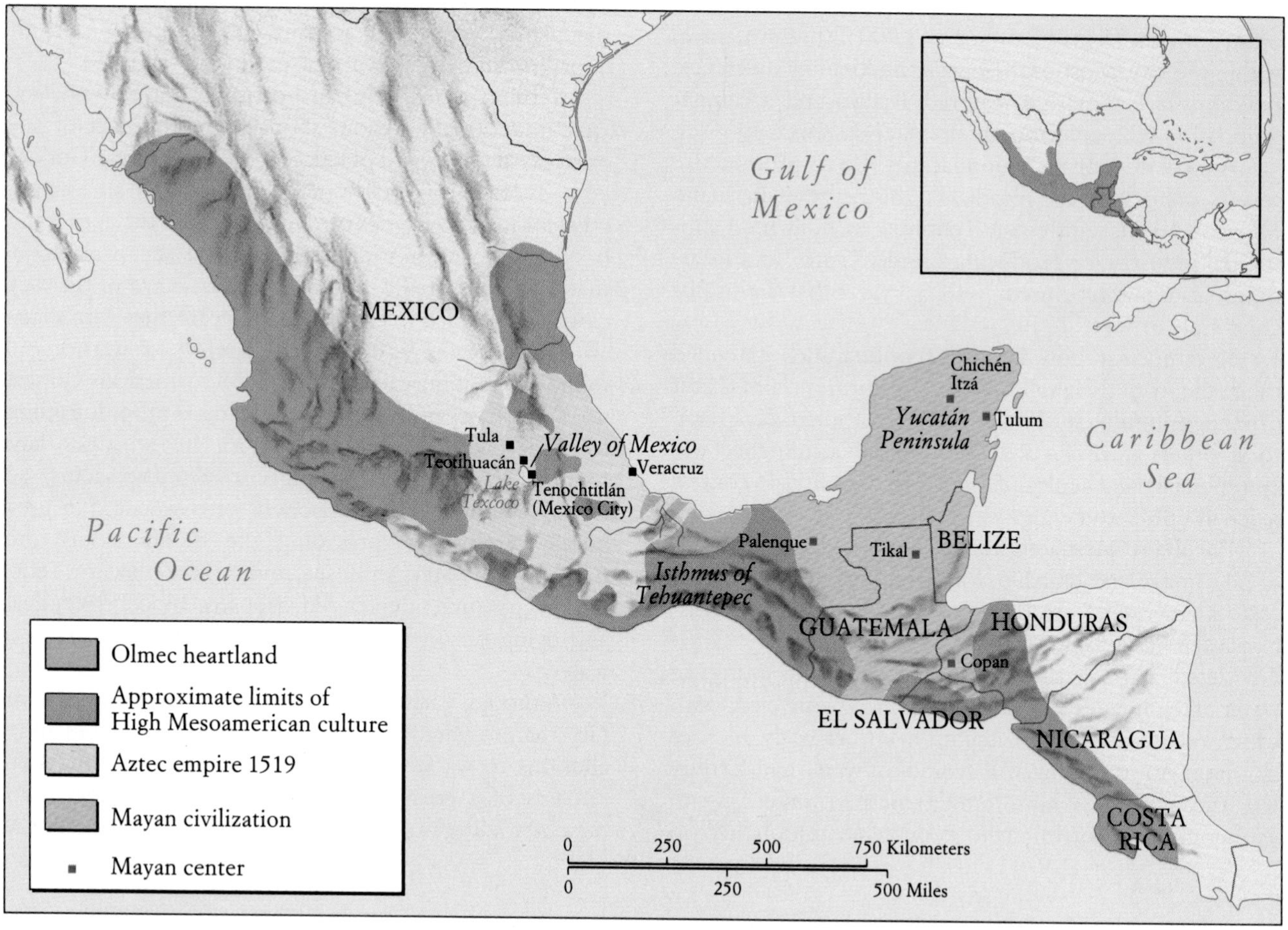

Map 7.1 The Development of Mesoamerican Civilization. Present-day Mexico and Central America were home to several advanced civilizations. The architecture, art, and religion of Teotihuacán influenced the region for centuries. The Maya civilization added greatly to the sophistication of Mesoamerican architecture, mathematics, astronomy, and the calendar.

of Teotihuacán declined dramatically, and by 800 C.E. people had abandoned the city and settled in the outlying villages. Scholars have proposed many reasons for the end of Teotihuacán civilization, including environmental degradation, revolt, and invasion. When the Mexica (Aztecs) came wandering into the valley centuries later, only the crumbling mounds of the great city remained; so impressive were even the ruins, however, that the awed visitors said it must be Teotihuacán, in their language "the Abode of the Gods."

The Integration of Mesoamerican Civilization: The Maya

More is known about Maya civilization than about either the Olmec or Teotihuacán cultures. Maya culture survived, even if somewhat transformed, until after the Spanish conquest, and four million persons still speak Maya today. Although scholars have deciphered Maya writing, overzealous Catholic missionaries, trying to annihilate the pagan past of the Maya, left only three preconquest Maya books intact, together with fragments of a fourth. Several postconquest Maya books, among them the *Popol Vuh,* are also of great value in understanding the Maya. Glyphs (inscriptions on rocks) have survived in great numbers. Archaeologists at first thought that most of them did little more than depict stylized human figures, list names and dates, and make a brief reference to some important event. New discoveries, especially tombs containing murals, pottery, and jewelry, now make it clear that the Maya artisans often portrayed individual Maya rulers realistically.

The Maya lived in dense rain forest lowlands in present-day northern Guatemala and in neighboring Belize, Mexico, and Honduras. Their staple food was maize, and it had long been thought that they practiced exclusively slash-and-burn agriculture, a technique that wasted land and produced a relatively low yield, thus supporting only a small population. However, aerial surveys have revealed "unnatural" tracts of land under the jungle canopy. On-site investigation proved that the Maya in fact had employed a second type of agriculture. They built canals in swampy areas alongside raised plots of earth, which drew moisture from the canals by capillary action. The maize and vegetables were fertilized with swamp lilies (depicted on many Maya statues and monuments) dredged from the drainage ditches. The high yield of the raised-field system could support a population of millions.

By 700–800 C.E.—the approximate era of Muhammad, Charlemagne, and the T'ang dynasts—Mayan civilization was at its height. It was composed of about twenty-five independent city-states led in size by Tikal and Copan with perhaps 30,000 inhabitants each. Each city had a number of satellite towns and villages. These city-states traded with—and made war on—each other via a complex river system supplemented by roads built by forced labor. The city-states were characterized by a highly stratified society in which royal dynasties supported by priests and warrior nobles ruled over farmers, artisans, and traders.

Compared to their Mesoamerican predecessors, the Maya had easy access to an enduring building material—limestone. They built colossal tomb-pyramids, some 250 feet high, topped by temples and palaces made of limestone. In the larger Maya cities, these impressive buildings, interspersed with walled ball courts, were surrounded by hundreds of smaller mounds supporting thatched private dwellings. The tops of the great pyramids were often connected by wide causeways, over which marched sumptuous royal and religious processions, watched by the massed populace far below. The huge city of Tikal was thirty-two square miles in area, spreading out from six temple complexes.

Unlike their Olmec predecessors and the Andean Amerindian cultures, the Maya developed a written language, one that was so difficult to translate that it eluded experts for generations. Some have claimed the decipherment of Maya writing is a feat that ranks with the unraveling of the "double helix," the DNA code. Steles recording the triumphs of Harvest Mountain Lord between 143 and 156 C.E. are the earliest dated writing so far deciphered in the Western Hemisphere. Unfortunately, surviving Maya writing is limited mainly to astronomical almanacs and to glyphs on steles proclaiming genealogical and political propaganda about each city's royal dynasty. The bark books that might have furnished evidence about the economic, legal, and literary aspects of Maya civilization have perished through natural decay or by destruction from European invaders.

The crowning glory of Maya civilization was the full development of a mathematics-calendar system that was among the most advanced in the world at that time. This complex calendar was initially devised about 600 B.C.E. by the Zapotecan and Olmec cultures in south-central Mexico, and spread across the region. The Maya used a base-20 mathematics system, with a dot for units and a bar for fives. It included a sign for zero, a mathematical tool of enormous power. Chinese, Indian, and Muslim mathematics all made use of the zero, while the Romans, in contrast, had no zero, which made their calculations cumbersome at best.

The Mesoamerican calendar, as the Maya fully developed it, was extremely complicated: a 260-day year (thirteen twenties) ran parallel to a solar year (eighteen twenties plus five days that were considered ill-omened). Once every 18,980 days, almost exactly 52 years, the 260-day year and the solar year coincided and the cycle began again; that date was one of great ceremony. Of greater significance in dating and understanding Mesoamerican civilization is the Long Count, a Maya linear calendar. The Maya believed that, after several earlier creations and destructions, a new creation had occurred on August 13, 3114 B.C.E. that was to end no earlier than 4772 C.E., and according to some extremely advanced Maya calculations, perhaps not for 142,000,000,000,000,000,000,000,000,000,000,000,000 (nonillion) years.

The Maya needed an elaborate calendar because the extensive astrological observations and mathematical calculations on which it was based helped them propitiate the gods who demanded appropriate recognition every day of the year. The Maya pantheon contained a host of gods, many of whose functions are not well understood at present. Each day had a name associated with two gods, one from the 260-day ritual calendar and one from the 365-day solar calendar. The pairings of these gods changed daily throughout the fifty-two years it took the two calendars to come back to their starting point. The attributes of each god determined the characteristics of the day. It was no simple matter for an individual to get safely through a given day. He had to know not only the names of the two gods controlling the day but also the relations between the gods and thus what had to be done to placate them. The Maya were obsessed with "good" and "bad" days; according to one of the surviving guides to good and bad days, the bad far outnumbered the good, and on those bad days special care was required in the performance of daily labors.

The religious mainstay of the Maya people was the ruler, who performed the key ceremonies that perpetuated the order of the universe, visible and invisible. The lord, usually male but occasionally female, was divine, or descended from gods. The lord, especially in the role of chief priest, bound together the nine levels of the

The Life-Giving Blood of Monarchs. These carvings illustrate a Maya ceremony in which rulers gave their blood to ensure divine favor for their kingdom. On the left, a queen pulls a rope braided with thorns through her tongue. On the right, she hallucinates, seeing the Vision Serpent, who disgorges a warrior of the Venus cult. (Based on an interpretation by Linda Schele.)

underworld, the earth, and the three levels of heaven and made it possible for the people to communicate with their ancestors and the gods. Upon the lord's death, elaborate state ceremonies prepared for his journey into the underworld. At the same time, intense ceremonies marked the ascension of the new lord, because the people of the city-state were in terrible danger until a lord was in place to maintain the universal order.

Like many premodern cultures, the Maya believed that their gods required humans to practice rituals of sacrifice, thereby feeding the gods and recognizing their role in maintaining the universal order. A key sacrifice was human blood. In many cultures, such as those of the ancient Hebrews, the Greeks, and the Romans, the gods were satisfied by the blood of animals.

It was not so in Mesoamerican civilization. The key sacrificial act of Maya culture was the frequent shedding of royal blood to properly connect the people of the state with the gods. In public ceremonies the lord pushed a sting-ray spine through his penis or scrotum, while his consort pulled a thorn-embedded rope through a hole in her tongue. Maya nobility also shed their blood. This bloodletting not only fed the gods, but also enabled the practitioner to hallucinate, bringing forth the Vision Serpent. The Serpent in turn brought forth such images as Venus warriors and ancestors, who answered questions about the future. Hallucinogenic enemas were another way to contact one's ancestors.

Although Maya city-states waged wars of conquest against each other at times, often Maya wars were ritualistic, designed to capture the rulers of another state rather than destroy the adversary's city. The Maya had adopted from Teotihuacán the Venus warrior cult, which specialized in securing captives for sacrifice in Maya religious and political rituals. The blood of these captives apparently played a supplemental role in the rituals of the Maya.

Some were tortured for years to give blood at many ceremonies, and a captive of high standing, perhaps a ruler, was killed at the accession ceremonies of the Maya monarchs. The number of victims was quite low, however, compared to the mass butchery of the Aztecs (see below).

The Maya version of the sacred ball game appears to have become more complex and deadly compared to Olmec practice, although the rules are still not known. Clad in protective padding, Maya rulers are often depicted playing ball against a captive leader in a T-shaped court flanked by steep temple walls or stone bleachers. Apparently the captive leader, after losing the ritual ball game, was bound to a rubber ball and dropped from the high temple walls or bounced down the stone steps.

The Maya looked on the afterlife as a dangerous, but survivable, experience. The souls of living humans, nobles and commoners alike, were portrayed as being transported in huge dugout canoes across the water of life, paddled by the gods. As death approached, the dugout slowly sank, dropping the souls into Xibalba, a fearsome underground realm with the overwhelming stench of rotting corpses and disease, peopled with death gods, creatures with overpowering putrid breath and stupendous farts, out to kill human souls. Many souls never returned from that dread place, but the Maya had hope. Previously, ball-playing Hero Twins had fooled the not-too-bright death gods and had been reborn and returned as ancestors. Reigning monarchs claimed their predecessors had returned; ordinary Maya hoped their souls, too, would outwit the demons and return as ancestor spirits to advise their descendants.

As archaeological discoveries in the last few years have shown, not all Maya cities centered on astronomy, religion, and war. At Cancuen ("Place of Serpents"), in the jungles of Guatemala, archaeologists have uncovered the splendid palace of King Tah ak Chaan, covering the area of two football fields with 170 high-ceilinged rooms arranged around eleven courtyards. The surrounding city was apparently a prosperous center of commerce and crafts located on a navigable river. There is no evidence that the city's rulers engaged in major wars with neighbors.

Between 800 and 900 Maya civilization in the heartland of Guatemala began to decline. About 1100 there was a revival, mixed with outside influences, centered at Chichen Itza and Uxmal in drier Northern Yucatan, reaching its peak about 1300. After 1400 decline again set in, hastened by plagues, disastrous weather, recurrent warfare, and the lack of a effective central authority. When the Spanish arrived in 1517, Maya civilization, now almost 2,000 years old, was in a state of collapse.

Mesoamerican Imperialism: The Aztecs

As Maya civilization was fading in Guatemala and the Yucatan, a new Mesoamerican group, the Aztecs, became dominant in the highlands of central Mexico, scene of the Teotihuacán culture. The Aztecs, who usually called themselves Tenocha or Mexica, were a nomadic tribe from the north that straggled into the Valley of Mexico and tried to find a place to settle on the shore of Lake Texcoco. For several generations the Aztecs led miserable lives as mercenaries or provided cheap labor for the settled tribes. Then, in 1345, fleeing from an enemy, the Aztecs took refuge on several marshy islands in the lake. According to their legends, when they arrived on the largest island they saw an eagle perched on a cactus with a serpent in its mouth. The eagle commanded the Aztecs to build temples and to feed the sun with the blood of sacrificed victims.

From their island base, the Aztecs created a formidable empire. At first they continued to serve as mercenaries, but in 1428, allied with two other towns, they destroyed their former employers and seized a base on the mainland to supplement their main island, Tenochtitlán. The Aztecs soon dominated their allies and moved into the areas that offered the greatest economic rewards.

By 1500 the Aztec Empire stretched from the Pacific Ocean to the Gulf of Mexico, controlling 28 million people. By then Tenochtitlán and other nearby islands had fused into one great capital city, with an estimated population of 400,000. Another million Amerindians lived in fifty or more city-states in the surrounding Valley of Mexico.

Tenochtitlán was an engineering marvel. The Aztecs built a dam to control the lake level and constructed two aqueducts to bring fresh water from the mainland to supplement the springs on the islands. To supply food for Tenochtitlán, the Aztecs expanded upon the Maya system of hydraulic agriculture, draining swamp land and creating artificial islands to grow food for the city. Three great causeways, the longest more than five miles long, linked Tenochtitlán to the mainland. The city itself had wide avenues, imposing temples and other public buildings.

Tenochtitlán could not be fed from its islands alone, and the Aztecs waged war to secure tribute in both food and luxury goods, as well as to obtain victims for their sacrificial rites. They carried on substantial trade with states that were still independent; merchants were an essential part of the Mesoamerican economy, as they had been since Olmec times. The Aztec language, Nahuatl, became the standard language of the area they controlled, probably from commercial convenience.

Despite this economic reliance on other areas, the Aztecs never completely centralized their government. The Aztec state combined direct control over Aztec areas with indirect control over nearby vassal states. At the center was the emperor, a reincarnation of the sun god, who lived in opulence surrounded by a harem of concubines, a bevy of servants, and a battery of state officials. His governors, who administered the city of Tenochtitlán and the incorporated provinces, acted as rulers themselves as they held court, conducted religious ceremonies, collected taxes, and imposed regulations.

The rest of the empire was essentially a league of tribute-paying city-states. Although the Aztecs built strong fortresses here and there, they generally did not maintain garrisons in conquered territories. If the flow of required tribute diminished, the Aztecs sent out their army composed of imperial troops and allied forces, sometimes accompanied by local militia, and subdued the territory again.

In its exploitative aspects, the Aztec Empire resembled the Roman Empire; but whereas the Roman Empire provided the subject people with many benefits, the Aztecs gave their subjects few benefits and many burdens. Consequently, Aztec vassals were constantly looking for a way to topple their overlords.

With such restless subjects, and since war was essential to their economic system and religion, Aztec society stressed the virtues of the warrior, and the Aztec nobility was one of military service. Although the son of a noble had many advantages, and it was certainly easier for him to rise than it was for the son of a commoner, he did not inherit his father's position or distinctions, which had to be earned. As in Republican Rome and imperial China, but unlike most premodern cultures, it was possible for commoners to earn distinction in war and rise to power.

Aztec society was not entirely organized on a military basis. Priests, who could be female as well as male, had a separate hierarchy, as did those merchants who engaged in long-range trade. The commoners, of course, formed the bulk of the population, and they owned their personal possessions but not the land they worked. Beneath them was a large group whose legal status was about halfway between an indentured servant's and a slave's. For some, this status was temporary, until some debt was paid or some criminal punishment worked off; for others, it might be permanent. In either case, children born to members of this class were free commoners.

Women traditionally had respected status in Aztec society. The early Aztecs had stressed matrilineal descent, and women could own and inherit property, make contracts, sue in court, divorce their husbands, and under certain circumstances, remarry. Motherhood was honored.

As the Aztecs became more imperialistic, however, patrilineal concepts began to emerge, and female roles began to alter. The Aztecs brought in polygamy among the upper classes to balance the excess of male over female mortality brought about by war. Aztec women were encouraged to bestow sexual favors on warriors, and women captured on campaign were given to the victorious soldiers.

Aztec religion focused on nourishing the sun, which in return furnished the light necessary for life. The food

Reconstructed View of Tenochtitlán. Built on islands in a lake, the Aztec capital, in the heart of present-day Mexico City, was surrounded by water.

CONNECTIONS IN CULTURE

Cahokia: Mound Building Center in North America

In addition to the pyramids found in Mesoamerica, Amerindians in North America also built impressive mounds. From as early as 2500 B.C.E., the inhabitants of the Mississippi Valley built earthen mounds as ceremonial centers. These mounds, constructed at key points throughout the woodlands of this great river system, marked centers of population and of political and commercial power. The Amerindian people who built them did not leave written records, but they left a rich archaeological record. The mound builders are known to archaeologists as the Mississippians, and it is assumed that they were the ancestors of the Amerindian peoples encountered by French visitors in the late seventeenth century.

Throughout the Mississippi basin, trading networks and river transport using rafts and canoes facilitated long-distance trade from as far away as the Rocky Mountains, the Great Lakes, and Florida. Mound centers served as junctures for trade of mica, galena, copper, marine shells, and other ceremonial and trade goods. The mound-building culture was a river-basin civilization, relying on a network of tributaries and waterways.

The largest mound center is Cahokia, located on the Mississippi River by modern East St. Louis, Illinois. (Other major mound centers were in present-day Oklahoma, Alabama, and Georgia.) Cahokia was active from 700 C.E. to 1250 C.E. At its height, Cahokia had an estimated population of 15,000 to 38,000 people. The center mound, a huge, earthen "platform mound," was the third-largest structure in the Western Hemisphere: it covered 15 acres and was surrounded by more than 100 smaller mounds. A wooden palisade two miles in circumference enclosed the center and included a watch tower every 70 feet. The platform mound had a rectangular base topped with a series of flat tiers. Large and ornately decorated wooden buildings were built on the highest tier and served as elite homes, palaces, and temples. Such platform mounds were usually situated around a large plaza. Cahokia also contained a ball court and a large circle of wooden posts that served as a ritual calendar for tracking solar events. Artisan communities that used such imported goods as marine shells, copper, and nonlocal stones in their creations were found in the central area.

Cahokia's location probably accounted for its prosperity. It was situated at the juncture of different ecological zones in a productive agricultural region. Maize, squash, and beans were the mainstays of the diet, supplemented by hunting, fishing, and the gathering of local plants. Cahokia's position on the Mississippi River between the mouths of the Missouri and Ohio Rivers allowed easy north-south trade. The substantial trade in precious stones from the Rocky Mountains (brought down the Missouri River by traders) would have made the location particularly beneficial.

---

1. The official web site for the Cahokia Mounds State Historic Site is at http://medicine.wustl.edu/~mckinney/cahokia/cahokia.html. Take the site tour. What are the most intriguing aspects of the central palisade? The stockade? "Woodhenge"?

2. Enter the search term "Cahokia" in the InfoTrac Subject Guide. Find two scholarly articles on Cahokia. What are their main findings? Does this information repeat what you have already learned about Cahokia, or is some or all of it new? Do the articles give you a deeper understanding of Cahokia and the Mississippian culture?

for the Sun God was human hearts, extracted from the living chests of sacrificial victims. As was true at Teotihuacán and in the Maya culture, the need for human victims spurred the Aztecs to make war in order to obtain captives, but the Aztecs took this practice much farther than their predecessors. They not only gathered captives from war, but also forced vassal states to pay tribute in the form of human beings. Precise numbers of those sacrificed are notoriously unreliable, but there is evidence that the Aztecs sacrificed as many as 20,000 victims in one celebration, and Moctezuma II claimed that when he came to the throne in 1502, he sacrificed 40,000 persons. Other gods, hundreds of them, controlled other facets of the world and received a diversity of offerings. To honor the god of planting and springtime, for example, the priests flayed sacrificial victims and then wore the newly removed skins for their rituals. Other offerings, however, might include flowers, music, and dancing.

Like the Maya, the Aztecs were obsessed with good and bad days, signs, portents, and divination. In their mind, the world was in delicate balance, and only continual human sacrifices at their religious ceremonies kept the universe operating and prevented the dark forces from destroying everything.

The Aztecs rewrote history to mask their barbarian origins and their ignominious first century in the Basin

An Aztec Poet Sings

I, the singer, I make a poem
That shines like an emerald
A brilliant, precious and splendid emerald.
I suit myself to the inflexions
Of the tuneful voice of the tzinitzcan. . . .
Like the ring of little bells,
Little golden bells. . . .
A scented song like a shining jewel,
A shining turquoise and a blazing emerald,
*My flowering hymn to the spring.**

This poem not only provides a great deal of information about Aztec technology, but it also suggests the continuing fascination with colors that is a mark of modern Mexican esthetics. On the technological side it shows the use of metals to make bells, and even more, it shows that the Aztecs knew how to make an alloy that would produce a bright, cheerful sound, which is far more difficult than simply casting the metal. A *tzinitzcan* was probably some sort of xylophone.

*John H. Cornyn, "Aztec Literature," in *XXVIIe Congrès International des Americanistes* (Mexico, D.F., 1939), vol. 2, pp. 328–331.

of Mexico. They claimed kinship to the Toltec, a culture that preceded them. They promoted some of the Toltec gods—especially the plumed serpent god, Quetzalcoatl, and the storm god, Tlaloc.

Aztec metalwork was primarily artistic, not utilitarian. The Aztecs used gold, copper, silver, tin, and alloys, including bronze, and their metalwork, based on Toltec models, was superb. The main Aztec concentration in their art was the carving of massive stone statues, bigger than those of their predecessors, intended to last for eternity. Their literature, too, mostly in the form of poetry, was extraordinarily rich.

Andean Civilization

In districts where the quantity of water for irrigation was small, they [the Inka] divided it proportionately (as they did with everything they shared out) so that there would be no dispute among the Indians about obtaining it. This was only done in years of scanty rainfall when the need was greatest. The water was measured, and as it was known from experience how long it took to irrigate a fanega *[1.6 acres] of land, each Indian was accordingly granted the number of hours he needed for the amount of land he had, with plenty to spare. Water was taken by turns, according to the order of the plots of land, one after another. No preference was given to the rich or the nobles, or to favorites, . . . or to royal officials or governors.**

*Garcilaso de la Vega, *Royal Commentaries of the Incas, and General History of Peru,* trans. Harold V. Livermore (Austin: University of Texas Press, 1966), vol. 1, p. 248.

In this passage Garcilaso de la Vega depicts the essential justice of Inka rule in Peru. De la Vega, through his mother, was a second cousin of the last two Inka rulers.

The Inka Empire was the last, and by far the greatest in population and extent, of a series of Amerindian cultures that had flourished in Peru and the Andes for more than 3,000 years. In Chapter 1 we discussed the Chavin culture, the first civilization to appear in this area. Many cultures followed the Chavin in this area in the centuries after 200 B.C.E. In this section we will discuss the Moche, a culture just now coming to the attention of the world through a number of archaeological projects. We will then turn to the Inka, whose engineering skills and thoroughgoing economic and political restructuring programs were unique to Amerindian experience.

The Artistry of the Moche Culture

The Chavin culture that faded out in the last centuries B.C.E. was succeeded by the Moche society, which dominated the Peruvian coast and the nearby hill country between 100 and 700 C.E., the same time as Teotihuacán and the apex of Maya culture. In Eurasian terms, the Moche were active from the height of the Roman Empire to the height of the Carolingian Empire, and from the end of the Han to the beginning of the T'ang dynasty. Little was known about the Moche until the past decade, when archaeologists made a series of important discoveries bearing on this major Amerindian group.

As in Mesopotamia, the Moche maintained their population in their arid coastal climate by inheriting and expanding an elaborate irrigation system that provided food supplies sufficient to support cities of more than 50,000. Their diet consisted of maize, beans, avocados, squash, peppers, potatoes, and peanuts, along with llamas, guinea pigs, and fish, a diet more nutritious than that of many modern South Americans. Their society, like most of the others in Andean and Mesoamerican civilization, was apparently rigidly hierarchical, in which warrior-priest kings, a warrior-priest nobility, and male and female priests lived in splendor while the masses worked. The newly discovered tombs of the elite are crammed with splendid artifacts demonstrating advanced techniques in textiles, pottery, and jewelry and depicting elaborate religious ceremonies. No examples of writing have come to light; it appears that the Moche, like all Andean civilizations and early Mesoamerican cultures, did not have a written language.

As in Mesoamerica, Moche art and architecture centered on religion. Like Mesoamericans, the Moche based their religion on waging war to obtain prisoners whose blood sacrifice was needed to ensure fertility of their land. Warrior-priests, assisted by other priests, conducted these rituals on immense pyramids and platforms that were the center of urban complexes. There is considerable evidence that the Moche warriors relied heavily on bluster and on jangling noises to intimidate their enemies. The Pyramid of the Sun was among the world's largest buildings; built from over 100 million adobe bricks, it was 135 feet tall and covered 12.5 acres. It served as an administration building and a mausoleum as well as a temple.

The Moche culture is notable for the skills of its artists. Although few textiles have survived, those that have are of high quality. Moche potters produced a variety of ceramics, including ritual goblets for religious ceremonies. They created pottery and three-dimensional clay sculptures that depict the life of commoners as well as kings; one can see the misery of tortured captives and the joys of sex and of chewing coca leaves. These potters also worked with low-relief designs and painted complex scenes of important rituals on their pottery.

The Moche were especially skilled and imaginative jewelers, working with smelted gold, silver, and platinum and with jade and turquoise. They used the lost-wax method to create three-dimensional metal castings with interchangeable parts. The artists also employed imaginative gilding techniques to make nonprecious metals, especially copper, look like gold. To adorn the bodies of the elite, Moche crafts workers created necklaces of gold and silver beads shaped like human heads with inlaid mother-of-pearl jaguar teeth, gold ear and nose plugs, gold protective plates for buttocks and chest, silver-copper alloy ritual masks, and hammered gilded copper masks and helmets. Many other objects such as scepters and spearheads were also cast in precious metals or copper.

Moche political power faded about 700, and for several hundred years various empires dominated sections of the Andean uplands, extending their power down to the adjacent coast. Meanwhile, urban states continued to

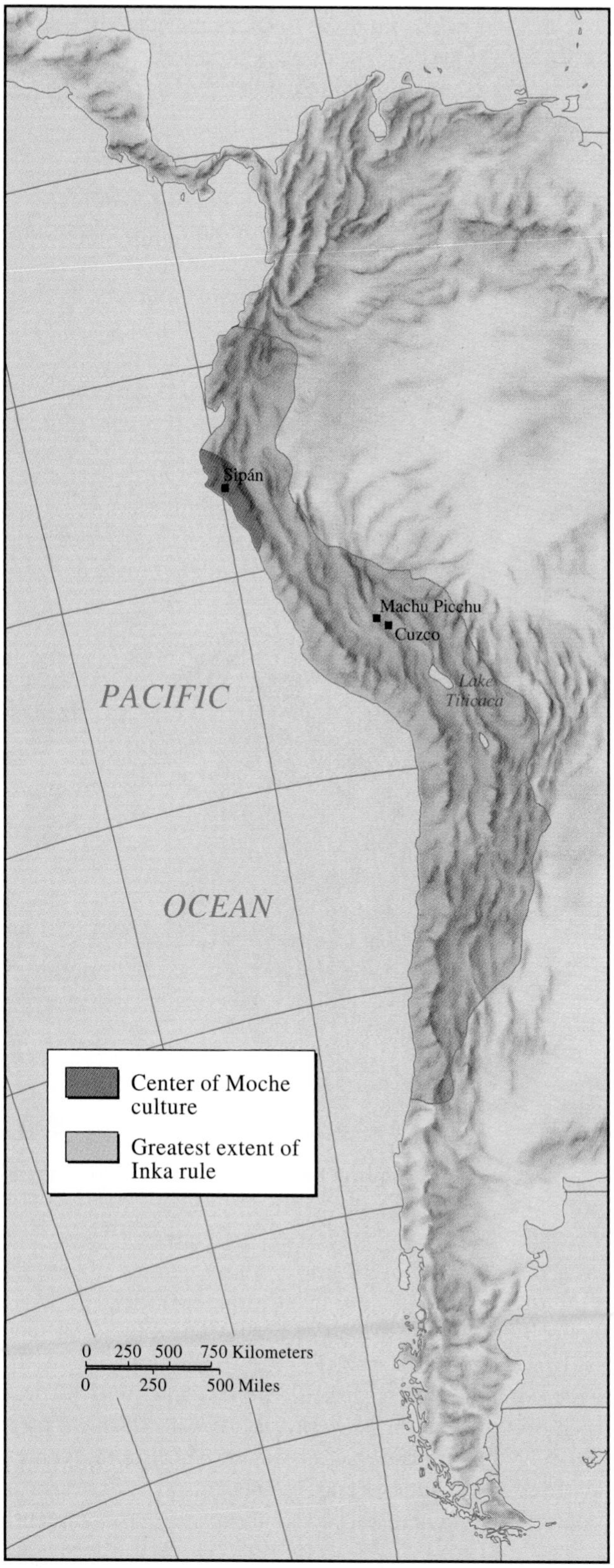

Map 7.2 The Development of Andean Civilization. Over the centuries, highly developed but nonliterate cultures evolved in the area of present-day coastal Peru, Ecuador, Bolivia, and Chile. The Moche culture featured monumental architecture and intricate work in precious metals. After 1200, the Inka, from their capital at Cuzco, began to dominate the Andes region; within about three centuries they had conquered a vast domain underpinned by a centralized administration, state socialism, and an extensive, well-engineered highway network.

LIVES AND TIMES ACROSS CULTURES

Women and Religious Rituals

In 1991, after the three royal tombs at Sipán had been excavated, the tomb of a woman who served as the Priestess of the Sacrifice Ceremony was excavated approximately fifty kilometers south of Sipán . . . [at] San José de Moro. . . . It had a room-sized burial chamber . . . which contained multiple individuals and great quantities of associated grave contents.

The woman was buried with a metal goblet the size and form of the one used in the Sacrifice Ceremony, and she had a pair of large plumes made of a silver-copper alloy, which were identical to those that characterize the headdress of the Priestess. . . .

*The fact that the Sacrifice Ceremony was so widespread in both time and space strongly implies that it was part of a state religion, with a priesthood in each part of the kingdom composed of nobles who dressed in prescribed ritual attire. When members of the priesthood died, they were buried at the temple where the Sacrifice Ceremony took place, wearing the objects they had used to perform the ritual. Subsequently, other men and women were chosen to replace them, and to perform the same ceremonial role.**

Like the priestesses of classical Greece or the Vestal Virgins of Rome, women in Moche society held positions of authority and prestige within the system of religious observances and rituals, as the evidence of wall paintings (as seen here) and goods found in graves of priestesses show.

*Walter Alva and Christopher B. Donnan, *Royal Tombs of Sipán,* 2d ed. (Los Angeles: University of California Press, 1994), pp. 223, 225.

Painting by Felix Caycho, © Gonzalo de Reparaz.

A Moche Priestess (far left) Presides at a Sacrifice Ceremony.

flourish on the north coast of Peru. Chan Chan, the capital of a secondary state, had over 50,000 inhabitants. Its wide, straight streets divided the city into ten districts, each of which had massive protective walls thirty to forty feet high and ten feet thick and its own ceremonial center, an unusual and unexplained design for a city. The era of political fragmentation ended abruptly in the fifteenth century, however, when a highland people, the Inka, burst upon the region.

Amerindian Social Engineering: The Inka

The Inka came late to the Peruvian scene. Because they, like their predecessors, were nonliterate, little is known of them before the Spanish came, and what is known generally concerns the period after 1438. Inka oral tradition, which the Spanish recorded, went back to a king who ruled about 1200. All that is certain is that the Inka started their rise to power from the city of Cuzco, in the Andean highlands northwest of Lake Titicaca. For two hundred years, they expanded slowly at the expense of their neighbors.

Then under their Inka (ruler) Pachacutec (reigned 1438–1473), the Inka people flashed like a meteor across Andean civilization. Within two decades Pachacutec and his son, Thupa Yupanki, conquered dozens of other peoples in the Titicaca Basin and the adjacent highland river systems. The more the Inka prevailed, the more manpower and supplies became available to them. Success bred success, and the Inka conquered to the north as far as present-day Quito, Ecuador, and took control of the older cultures on the Peruvian coast. After Thupa Yupanki (reigned 1471–1493) came to the throne, he smashed uprisings in some of the newly acquired territory and then moved south, adding much of present-day Bolivia and the northern part of Chile to the empire. Wayna Qhapaq (reigned 1493–1525) spent much of his reign consolidating the empire, marching his army from Chile to the rain forests of the upper Amazon and on to Ecuador to put down rebellions, extending the northern limits of the empire slightly in the process.

Christopher B. Donnan, Fowler Museum, University of California Los Angeles

Moche Warrior Ear Ornament. This piece of jewelry, made of gold and blue-green mosaic pieces, depicts a warrior holding a war club in his right hand. It was found in one of the royal tombs at Sipán.

The new empire, essentially acquired in fifty-five years, dwarfed any state hitherto created in the Andes and Peru. Inka emperors ruled some 12 million people patchily distributed in a domain stretching about 3,000 miles from north to south. They had done this without wheeled transport, draft animals, a system of writing, and with only occasional use of copper tools and weapons. Ruling from the highland capital at Cuzco, the Inka called their empire *Tawantinsuyu,* the Land of the Four Quarters, in reference to the four major divisions of their realm.

The Inka had an empire, but with it came a major problem. How, as a tiny minority of perhaps 70,000, could they rule millions of recently conquered peoples scattered across a difficult terrain? To accomplish this, Inka authorities carried out a comprehensive restructuring of much of Andean society. They relocated populations, reordered the economy, constructed an extensive transportation network, and inculcated a state religion. This program was carried out most thoroughly in the older parts of the empire in the central Andes and on the Ecuadorian and Chilean frontiers was influenced by the sophisticated cultures along the Peruvian coast.

Inka planning began with their campaigns of conquest. Inka leaders saw to it that ethnic Inka males were not wasted in nonmilitary tasks or unnecessary combat. In the early days, as much of the military supplies as possible were carried by llamas and Inka women; later, members of conquered groups hauled the goods. The Inka took over other peoples as much as possible by negotiation and bravado, massing their men in a show of force to overawe their opponents and get their peaceful submission. If a group held out in a siege or in other ways fought back, the Inka, like the Mongols or Alexander the Great, massacred the population or deported them as a warning to others. To garrison the frontiers and to watch areas considered likely to rebel, the Inka settled groups of soldiers conscripted from other parts of their empire to remain as alien watchdogs.

The Inka needed reliable stocks of food and other materials to supply their armies, a difficult proposition considering the patchy pattern of settlement and production in their empire. Upon conquering a territory the state claimed control over all its resources, including human labor. In each locality, Inka authorities divided the land into three portions, one each for the sun (the state religion), the state, and the community. Laborers from the community worked Inka state and sun agricultural land as they had worked the lands of their former rulers. The state, with many construction projects on its agenda, wanted the general population to be well fed and self-supporting so they could produce healthy youngsters for the labor force; accordingly, the Inka sometimes gave back part of the conquered land to the community in exchange for *mit'a,* special labor for road building and other state projects.

To increase food production the Inka, combining economic sophistication with military prudence, carried out a massive resettlement program. Before the Inka conquest, local feuds in many areas had forced the local populations to stay out of the more fertile, but more dangerous, valleys where maize could be grown. They lived and fortified themselves on the more defensible ridges, raising potatoes. Having brought peace along with their conquest, Inka authorities moved families from the fortified ridge-top towns—thus reducing the chance of effective revolt—and settled them in new, smaller villages down in the nearby valleys, in order to expand the production of maize. Thus most agricultural families retained their households and remained in a familiar neighborhood near their old town, but became more productive. Some women in the agricultural communities wove cloth from wool supplied by the state, other individuals made rope or utilitarian pottery or collected honey and feathers.

With staple food production stabilized, even increasing, the Inka then designated certain families or groups in every locality to specialize in producing other sumptuary products such as fine textiles, elaborate metalwork, and imperial Inka pottery. Other groups were relocated to the eastern slopes to raise more cotton, cacao, and coca. The alien military colonies that watched the unreliable groups and garrisoned the frontiers were usually held responsible for producing special products. Some young women were selected to reside at the ceremonial centers in the new Inka towns in segregated quarters out of public sight. They wove cloth and brewed beer for religious ceremonies, and were later married to men designated by the state. Other individuals were taken to Cuzco to be servants or concubines for the royal and noble families; some of these individuals rose to positions of prominence.

Like the Persians and Romans, the Inka developed an elaborate road system to move military forces quickly around the empire, transport their food supplies where needed, and in general tie their widespread domains together. Using the forced labor of their subjects the Inka supervised the construction of two main roads, one on the coast and one in the highlands, that ran the length of their empire. With only humans and llamas to traverse them, the roads were only twenty-five feet wide, but well engineered. They were built upon strong foundations and laid along efficient gradients, passing across suspension bridges, through tunnels, and over mountains. Those north-south trunk roads were connected with lateral east-west main roads at major cities; a network of secondary roads tied many villages in the empire to the system. Forced labor gangs built almost 20,000 miles of roads and thousands of rest stations a day's walk apart. Runners stationed at convenient intervals carried government messages throughout the breadth of the empire. In their engineering prowess the Inka were typical of Andean culture, which had already developed an elaborate system of irrigation canals along the coast.

To tie supplies and the road network together, the Inka, directing masses of special mit'a labor, built a series of new towns on the new transportation grid and built hundreds of warehouses outside each town. They reserved the land nearest town for the production of state-owned food, storing it in the warehouses. These storehouses did much more than feed the armies. The Inka used the stored food to support local officials, mit'a laborers, persons traveling on government business, those attending state ceremonies, special craft workers, areas suffering from crop failures, and other projects. Although Inka storage facilities were built along the highways, they were intended mostly for local or regional use. With transport limited to humans and llamas, it was impossible to bring a steady supply of goods from long distance to Inka armies in garrison or on campaign. The Inka could only hope that if they were efficient in producing supplies and storing them in large amounts everywhere in the realm, their armies could be fed and their empire preserved.

As might be expected, the elaborate Inka system of economic and social controls was administered by an extremely hierarchic and bureaucratic government. As in other cultures, the choice of a new Inka was no easy decision. Since each reigning Inka had several wives and a number of concubines, the path to the succession was sometimes disputed by rival claimants. Oral tradition told of crimes and civil wars as rival claimants battled for the throne, until a new divine Inka, Son of the Sun, established his claim. The deceased rulers were believed to be intermediaries with the gods, and their mummified remains were brought forward to partake in religious ceremonies and be consulted by priests on important matters. The male relatives of each departed Inka were entitled to all the wealth that ruler had accumulated during his reign, in part to support that royal corpse in imperial style for eternity. As time went by, the number of royal households supporting imperial mummies had, naturally, increased, and each new Inka was faced with a need to accrue riches during his reign so that his descendants could maintain his corpse with becoming grandeur. This need for each Inka to find new wealth was one of the motives for Inka expansion.

Beneath the eccentric world of the Inka royalty, the machinery of government ran fairly smoothly. The upper nobility, composed of the Inka's blood and adopted relatives administered the four quarters and the provincial subdivisions of the empire. In much of the Inka domain, local bureaucracy was set up on a numerical rather than a

Inka Record Keeping. Inside a government storage complex, the Inka (emperor) Thupa Yupanki receives a report from a *khipu kamayog* (records keeper) holding his knotted rope ledger.

geographic basis. The top local official administered 10,000 families; under him ten officials administered 1,000 families, and so on down to the most minor official, who administered five families. To supply the huge number of officials necessary to run such an elaborate governmental system, the state employed some lesser Inka nobility, but it drew most of these officials (as had ancient Rome) from the traditional leaders of the group to be governed. The cooperating elite received honors and valuable state goods from the Inka. They could pass their office and status on to their children if the Inka found them sufficiently efficient and trustworthy. This practice of having the local elite carry out Inka authority among their people was another method designed to hold the loyalty of conquered peoples and their leaders.

Inka local authorities strictly regulated the private lives of their subjects. They tried to impose their language, Quechua, on their subjects and did not allow individuals to travel far from their homes. Even marriage, which was obligatory, was, in theory, arranged by the government.

The lack of a written language did not handicap the government because the census and storehouse records vital to proper administration were kept on ***khipus***. A khipu was a rope from which hung a collection of strings with knots tied into them to record numbers. Different knots and different textures and colors of the strings coded the data to various subjects and purposes; one khipu could very well have recorded as much information as a modern ledger.

The Inka used religion as another means to unify the state. Cuzco and the new towns built by the Inkas were used to stage elaborate ceremonies that indoctrinated their subjects in the state religion while also allowing their subjects to worship their traditional gods. The Inka encouraged, perhaps required, the people of the nearby communities to come to the new towns for religious ceremonies that sometimes lasted for days. While in town the attendees were housed, fed, and provided with beer, and sometimes given clothing and sandals—all at state expense.

The Inka religion contained a creator god, and in its early stages sparingly featured human sacrifice. The primary focus of public worship, however, was the Sun God, along with the god of rain and thunder. Inka religion included animism as well, with practically every geographic feature having resident spirits and each family and each individual having a guardian spirit. The Inka religion had doctrines of sin and confession and taught a belief in personal immortality. The Inka had oracles, looked for omens, and practiced divination, but unlike the Maya were not obsessed with lucky and unlucky days. The wealthy sacrificed grain or killed llamas in the ritual, and the poor sacrificed guinea pigs. Human sacrifice took place at times, although they never attained anything like the Aztec volume of victims.

Despite their elaborate administrative and engineering systems, the Inka had major problems. Given the primitive level of transport and communication available to them, Inka rulers still found themselves too far from the extremities of the empire to rule effectively. Some scholars maintain that the cumbersome state bureaucracy employed by the Inka retarded economic development, as compared to a money-based market economy.

Perhaps the greatest problem in the Inka state was its capricious system of succession. Under the rule of the three great Inka monarchs the empire was spared strife over the succession, but in 1525, when Wayna Qhapaq died, two of his sons claimed the throne. For seven years, civil war ravaged the empire, while a plague caught from the Europeans spread throughout the Inka world, killing many. When the Spanish arrived in 1532, they found the Inka state already in advanced decline.

African Cultures

*The king . . . was naked, wearing only a garment of linen embroidered with gold from which hung four fillets on either side; around his neck was a golden collar. He stood on a four-wheeled chariot drawn by four elephants; the body of the chariot was high and covered with gold plates. The king stood on top carrying a small gilded shield and holding in his hands two small gilded spears. His council stood around similarly armed and flutes played.**

*I, 'Ezana, king of Axum . . . made war upon Noba [Nubia], for the peoples had rebelled and had boasted of it. Twice and thrice they had broken their solemn oaths, and had killed their neighbors. And as I had warned them, and they would not listen, I made war on them. They fled without making a stand, and I pursued them for 23 days, killing some and capturing others . . . burnt their towns, both those built of bricks and those built of reeds, and my army carried off their food and copper and iron . . . and destroyed the statues in their temples, their granaries, and cotton trees and cast them into the Seda [Nile]. And I planted a throne at the place where the rivers Seda and Takkaze join.***

*Robert W. July, *A History of the African People* (New York: Scribner's, 1970), p. 48.
***The Horizon History of Africa* (New York: American Heritage, 1971), p. 80.

The preceding passages give glimpses into the wealth and power of the King of Axum (in present-day northern Ethiopia) where a large empire of enormous military and commercial power flourished contemporaneously with the Roman Empire around 350 C.E. The account of King 'Ezana's military victory over Nubia was inscribed on a stele (carved stone pillar) at his capital in Axum. Axum was one of many empires that emerged in Africa, some of which dated from early historical times. These states were as varied in organization as the landscape from which they arose. The following section will give a general overview of the geographic and social diversity in Africa. Then, a number of the cultural and political systems that existed from approximately 900 to 1600 will be described; the discussion will begin with the civilizations in North Africa and Ethiopia and will continue geographically from western to central, then from eastern to southern Africa.

Geographic and Social Diversity in Africa

The continent of Africa, an area more than three times larger than the continental United States, exhibits enormous geographic and cultural diversity. Scholars estimate that there may be as many as 1,000 different ethnic groups speaking almost as many languages in Africa. Linguists have classified this multitude of languages into four major phyla or categories. Although human life probably first emerged in Africa, climatic extremes and infertile soil have kept human societies from prospering in much of the land area. Sitting directly on the Equator, much of central Africa is subtropical, and there are vast arid areas in the north and in the south. Sparse rainfall, droughts, and resulting famines have been common in Africa since the beginning of recorded history. For example, along the 1,200-mile Niger River in West Africa rainfall averages between eight and twenty inches in a good year; the lack of rain has impeded population growth in many areas. Deforestation and overuse of the soil since ancient times have contributed to making much of the terrain inhospitable.

Save for the tropical rain forests, the central sections of the continent receive the most rainfall and are therefore the most conducive to agricultural development; however, these areas are infested with the tsetse fly. The fly carries the trypanosomiasis parasite, deadly to both humans and cattle, the main source of livelihood for many African societies. Humans, especially those living along fertile river banks, must also cope with other debilitating and often deadly diseases, including river blindness, malaria, and bilharzia (a parasitic disease transmitted to humans by river snails). African societies have generally adjusted to these diseases and climatic conditions by living within the constraints imposed by nature; or as one Swahili proverb put it, "Do not borrow off the earth, for the earth will require its own back with interest."

Owing to these basic ecological problems, some African peoples led a nomadic existence based on herding sheep, goats, or cattle. In many herding societies, such as the Masai in present-day Kenya, the number of cattle he owned determined a man's status within the community. Cattle were also used as a medium of trade and given as a "bride price" to a young woman's family upon her marriage. Although herding societies often looked down upon the settled, farming communities, economic exchanges of goods (animals, hides, or ivory for sugar and other commodities) between the two were nonetheless commonplace.

In some areas, specific ethnic groups monopolized professions; for example, in land-locked present-day Mali, the Fulani, who are herders, use the banks of the Pondo River as pasture, while the Bambara farm along the river and still others are fisherfolk. However, most African peoples worked in mixed economies as both farmers and

LIVES AND TIMES ACROSS CULTURES

Folk Wisdom

Throughout history, riddles and proverbs have been popular forms of "folk wisdom" in Africa and the rest of the world. Folk wisdom amuses, teaches moral lessons, and tests mental quickness. Among the Yoruba of West Africa, storytellers often asked riddles to attract the attention of audiences before a performance. For example, a storyteller might pose the following riddle:

Question: *We call the dead—they answer.*
We call the living—they do not answer.
Answer: *Dry, dead leaves; fresh tree leaves.*

Proverbs are also popular in most African societies. As the wisdom of proverbs is often universal, it is not surprising that many African proverbs have equivalents in the Arab and Western worlds. Some examples of African proverbs and their equivalents from other cultures are:

Mouth not keeping to mouth, and lip not keeping to lip, bring trouble to the jaws. (Yoruba-West Africa)
Talk is silver, silence is gold. (Western)

He fled from the sword and hid in the scabbard. (Yoruba)
Out of the frying pan, into the fire. (Western)

The tar of my country is better than the honey of others. (Moroccan North Africa)
There is no place like home. (Western)

An old cat will not learn how to dance. (Moroccan)
You can't teach an old dog new tricks. (Western)

If music changes, so does the dance. (Hausa—Central Sudan)
What is written on the forehead, the eye must see. (Arabic)
Keep up with the times, or what must be, must be. (Western)

herders. As in Central and South America, traditional farmers in Africa frequently used the slash-and-burn technique to clear plots of land. They then cultivated the plots for several years; after the soil ceased to be productive, they abandoned the fields and the entire cycle was repeated elsewhere. The slash-and-burn technique contributed to the nomadic existence of many African peoples and also led to further degradation of the soil.

Kinship relationships were extremely important in African societies, and high value was placed on marriage and children. Lineages, or lines of descent, determined crucial matters such as inheritance and identity. As in Indian and Arab societies, marriage involved the entire extended families, not just two individuals as in much of the West. Most African societies were polygamous and patrilineal (descent follows through the father); however, some were matrilineal (descent follows through the mother).

Although the organization of living space, building materials, and architectural styles found in Africa were as diverse as its climate, African villages and homes reflected the high value and emphasis placed on communal relationships. In contrast to the rather private closed-in buildings and rooms found in much of West Asia or Europe, many African homes and public buildings were tightly grouped in circular or irregular patterns and were circular in shape. Circular, communal storage granaries were often clustered around the villages, and were often built beside or on top of homes or on stilts to protect them and to keep out the damp, insects, and vermin. Whereas the centralized governments of ancient Egypt and many Asian empires controlled the collection and storage of basic foodstuffs, in most of sub-Saharan Africa food storage was organized on a local level. The villagers constructed and maintained collectively owned granaries; in some areas separate granaries were built for men and women.

Most Africans used mud brick, straw, clay, and wood to build their homes, generally reserving stone construction for public or monumental buildings. Clay gave artists greater freedom for artistic expression and ease in constructing contoured, free-form designs than did stone or brick; clay was also resistant to the extremes of temperatures, particularly heat, found in much of Africa. Great care was lavished on the upkeep of the clay walls. As early as the fourteenth century the famous traveler Ibn Battuta remarked on the beauty of the decorative ornamentation on the buildings of African towns and villages. Decorative shapes and designs varied tremendously. The one-story, one-room circular homes grouped around larger communal buildings in much of Mali were fairly typical, but homes with straw roofs and monumental entrances were also found in Mali and the Cameroons. In Mauritania and East Africa stone buildings with elaborate interior designs were common.

Historically, the region above the Sahara Desert, extending from present-day Morocco in the west to Egypt in the east, was Mediterranean in orientation. The great Carthaginian Empire flourished in present-day Tunisia, and much of North Africa had been part of the empires of Egypt and later of Rome. Farther south, however, the historical ties with Mediterranean cultures became tenuous.

Islamic North Africa

Western and northern Africa and Egypt, however, had also been connected by trade routes with Saharan and central African societies. The Berbers, who since ancient times have lived in large areas of North Africa, generally controlled these caravan trails. Their origin is unknown, and they speak their own distinct language. As the Muslims spread across Egypt and all of North Africa in the seventh century, the Berbers converted to Islam, but maintained their own language and ethnic identity.

Except for Morocco, the Islamic societies that had been established in North Africa were all incorporated into the Ottoman Empire in the sixteenth century. Governors who were either appointed directly by the sultan or were local rulers who pledged their loyalty to Istanbul ruled these North African provinces. Although trade continued with sub-Saharan states, the northern sectors of Africa remained tied culturally, religiously, and politically with the Arab world and the Ottoman Empire.

The Berber rulers in Morocco, meanwhile, resisted most Portuguese and Spanish territorial onslaughts and at the same time expanded southeastward. In 1590, under Sultan Mansur, Moroccan forces armed with cannon attacked the declining Songhai Empire (present-day Mali), whose soldiers were equipped only with spears

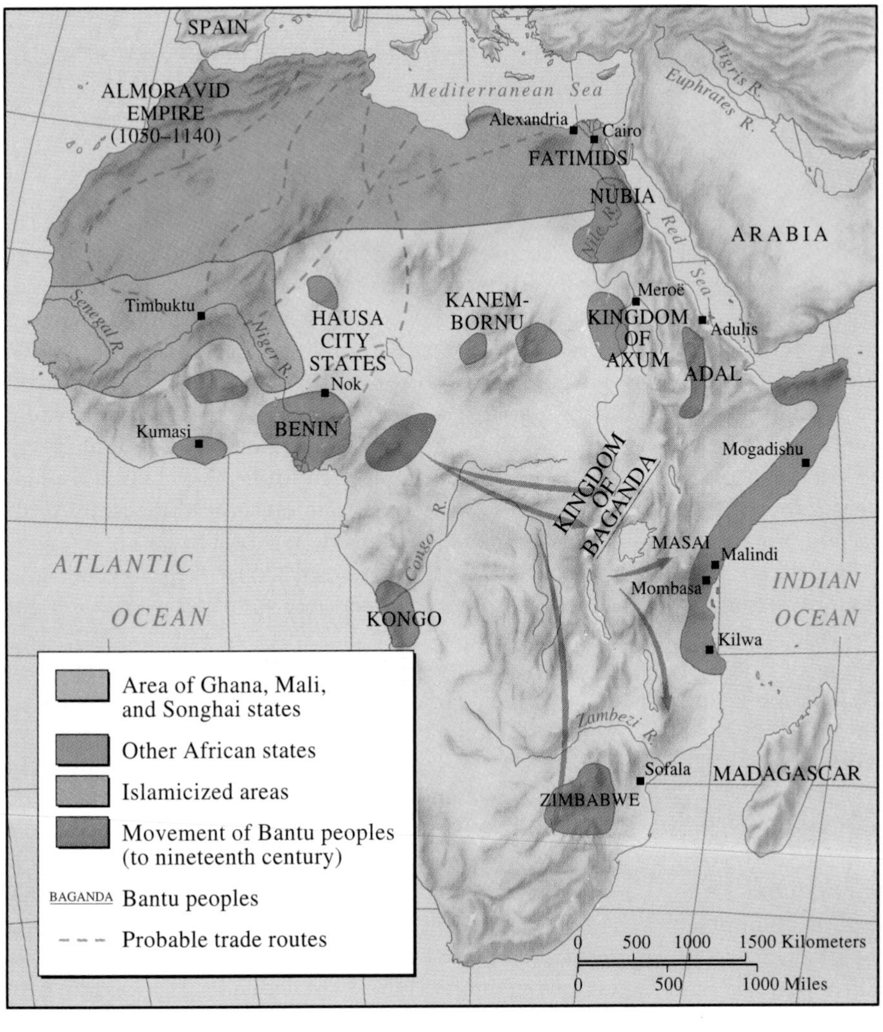

Map 7.3 Africa, 900–1500. Many great empires or kingdoms, such as Ghana in West Africa, Axum in the east, and Zimbabwe in the south, flourished throughout the African continent from 900 to 1500. In North Africa, the majority of the population converted to Islam.

Werner Forman Archive/Art Resource

Courtesy of Janice Terry

Axum Stelae in Ethiopia. These are only a few of the more than 1,300 stelae found at Axum in Ethiopia. Although most of the inscriptions have not yet been translated, the monoliths indicate that the Axum architects were well advanced and that the city must have had elaborate stone palaces and public buildings.

and bows and arrows; the power and wealth of that once great state came under direct Moroccan control.

Thus, despite its ties with the Mediterranean world, North Africa also retained links with central and southern portions of the continent by exchanges of goods, peoples and ideas. Similar interrelationships existed between the great kingdoms in Egypt, the Sudan, and Ethiopia.

Christian Ethiopia

In keeping with the patterns noted in the comparative essay on empires, the most sedentary populations, and ultimately the most highly advanced empires in Africa, tended to develop around the major rivers that provided consistent sources of water and fertile land. As noted in Chapter 1, the early empires of Egypt and the Kushites in the Sudan both arose along the banks of the Nile.

From 300 B.C.E., however, the Kushite kingdom with its capital at Meroë (in present-day Sudan) began to decline. As Egypt declined in military and economic importance under Roman rule, the demand for iron ore from the Kushite kingdom dropped, and its economy suffered. The Kushite kingdom was also weakened by attacks from surrounding desert tribes and, most crucially, by Axum, a new rival economic and military power based in Ethiopia.

In 700 B.C.E. Semitic tribespeople from Yemen, in the southern Arabian Peninsula, moved across the Red Sea to the eastern coastal regions of Africa. They gradually migrated to the Ethiopian highlands, possibly to escape the malaria-infested coast. The new immigrants intermarried with the indigenous population and transmitted their skills in dry stone building and hillside terracing.

From the assimilation of the Semitic and indigenous populations came a unique society with its own language, Ge'ez; though Ethiopians issued documents in Greek as well. The synthesis of African and Arabian peoples in Ethiopia is analogous to the assimilation of peoples in the Hellenistic world and the emergence of Swahili culture along the coast of East Africa.

The new Ethiopian kingdom, with its capital, Axum, in the highlands, and a port, Adulis, on the Red Sea, was in an advantageous position to benefit from increased sea trade in the region. As trade along the Red Sea prospered, Axum emerged as a major trading center for eastern Africa, the Nile, and southern Arabia. To protect both the sea and land trading routes, Axumite kings conquered large sections of Ethiopia, and by the fourth century C.E. had overwhelmed the Kushite kingdom's capital city of Meroë.

Although the early Axum rulers were animists, the empire became Christian in the fourth century, after decades of contact with the Christian world through Byzantium and the Coptic Christians in Egypt. A Syrian Christian was instrumental in converting King 'Ezana, who, like other imperial rulers in Rome and Asia, encouraged or forced the religious conversion of his subjects. Thus, the empire became predominantly Christian many years before much of Europe. However, the decline of Byzantium and the Muslim conquest of Egypt and North Africa in the mid-seventh century cut off Axum from the Mediterranean world, and the Christian kingdom gradually lost its importance as a trading center and became increasingly isolated.

As the commercial power of Axum faded, people migrated to the nearby high plateaus intersected with mountains and deep gorges, which provided ideal terrain for well-defended fortresses. Here in Ethiopia they created a Christian kingdom under the *negus* or emperor, and Ge'ez remained the language of the Coptic (Christian) Ethiopian church.

Haroldo and Flavia de Faria Castro/FPG International

Churches at Lalibela in Present-Day Ethiopia. Some of the many churches at Lalibela are free-standing, while others are carved into the sides of cliffs, as shown here.

The series of spectacular churches carved into solid rock at Lalibela are monuments to the artistic energy and religious fervor of the people. Constructed about 1181 by King Lalibela, the churches attested to his deep-seated religious devotion. Ethiopian tradition holds that one of the most remarkable of these churches was built in one day by fervent believers assisted by angels. In many ways these monuments are reminiscent of the Gothic cathedrals produced during an era of similar fusion of church and state in Europe. The development of the Ethiopian Christian kingdom in relative isolation from outside forces was made possible by its unique terrain and was in marked contrast to the extensive exchanges and assimilation of peoples in central and southern Africa.

By the sixteenth century, Muslim armies from Arabia, which already controlled most of the coastal regions of the Horn of Africa, began to attack Christian Ethiopia. Early in the sixteenth century, a local military ruler, Ahmad ibn Ghazi (reigned 1506–1543), organized forces that threatened the very survival of Ethiopia. Known as Gran, or left-handed, Ahmad instilled his forces with a fervent belief in *jihad* (holy war) and brought most of Ethiopia under his control. To save his government, the Ethiopian emperor Lebna Dengel (reigned 1508–1540), who claimed direct descent from King Solomon and the Queen of Sheba some 2,500 years earlier, appealed to the Portuguese for help.

The emperor's appeal fell on receptive ears. The Portuguese and Ethiopian cultures were both headed by devoutly Christian absolute monarchs hostile to the Muslims. In addition, the Portuguese had long been fascinated with Ethiopia, which they believed might house the famed realm of Prester John. The myth of this fabled Christian kingdom and the mystery of its exact location had created lively debate in Europe; Mongolia, China, and India had been suggested as possible locations. When these possibilities had been discarded, Portuguese adventurers began to search for Prester John's mythical kingdom in Ethiopia. Most were initially disappointed by the poverty of Ethiopia and dismayed by many of its religious customs. Nevertheless, the riches of Ethiopian religious art and architecture impressed the Portuguese missionary Father Alvarez. Alvarez's books on Ethiopia described these finds and excited even more interest among Europeans in the remote African kingdom.

In response to Emperor Lebna Dengel's appeal, Portugal sent an expeditionary force under the command of Dom Christoval da Gama to rescue the Christian kingdom from its many enemies. In 1529, however, da Gama was surrounded by Muslim forces, taken captive, and decapitated. Da Gama's death marked the apex of Muslim power in Ethiopia, which waned after the death of Ahmad the Grand. In the remote mountains of northern Ethiopia, the emperors attempted to continue their absolute rule, but internal political rivalries, religious disputes, and Muslim opposition weakened their power. Although Ethiopia's relative isolation prevented it from keeping pace with the commercial and political growth of other, wealthier kingdoms in central and western Africa, its difficult terrain made it almost impossible for outside forces to conquer it.

The Bantu

As early as 200 B.C.E., peoples from the present-day Nigeria-Cameroon border began a migration that was to change central and southern Africa. Like other groups around the world, these people called themselves simply "the people," or Bantu. Although scholars disagree as to the exact size and chronology of the Bantu migrations, they followed along the northern and eastern edges of the tropical forest and then south along the western coast. Future linguistic and anthropological studies will provide additional information on the Bantu origins.

Originally fisherfolk, the Bantu also grew crops such as yams and sorghum and hunted small game. In East Africa cattle were and, in many regions, still are the basis of the social-economic organization. Some Bantu groups like the Tutsi adopted cattle as the basis of their economic livelihood but did not worship the cattle or consider them sacred. While many Bantu peoples specialized as either agriculturalists or pastoralists, most practiced a mixed economy based on agriculture and herding.

In spite of the enormous diversity of the Bantu peoples throughout central and southern Africa, Bantu societies manifested certain common characteristics, and along with languages based on common linguistic roots, they shared folklore and oral historical traditions and similar pottery-making techniques. Lacking a written language, Bantu elders, like Greek epic poets before Homer, passed on long, involved stories of the history and culture from generation to generation.

Iron implements came into use among the Bantu by 300 B.C.E. The Nok, who lived in the region between the Benue and Niger rivers in present-day Nigeria, were apparently the first people in West Africa to use iron-making technology. As noted in Chapter 1, the Bantu peoples may have gained their knowledge of iron working and the lost-wax process for bronze casting from the Kushites, who migrated west from the Nile valley as their empire declined. It is also possible that ironworking among the Bantu occurred spontaneously through independent invention; archaeological exploration in western Africa may yield more answers to these questions in the future.

As Bantus put iron spears and hoes to use, they increased their food supply, thus creating larger, healthier populations. The increase in population undoubtedly put additional strain on the available arable land, which was quickly exhausted by the slash-and-burn technique

© Dirk Bakker/National Museum Logos; courtesy of Detroit Institute of Arts

Nok Terra Cotta Sculpted Head. This highly stylized sculpture, typical of the Nok civilization, was found at a tin mine in northern Nigeria. The Nok flourished from 500 to 200 B.C.E. Centuries later, African art had a profound influence on twentieth-century abstract artists.

© Dirk Bakker/Museum of Ifé Antiquities; courtesy of Detroit Institute of Arts

Ife Bronze Figure of an Oni. The Ife, from present-day Nigeria, made exquisite bronzes with details so fine that experts believe they may depict actual historical figures, even though African art is generally abstract or symbolic in nature. The oni was the leader of the Ife; this piece (c. 1500 C.E.) shows the leader bedecked in elaborate jewelry, royal insignia, and headdress.

of the Bantu farmers. In addition, the influx of migrants seeking relief from the growing aridity of the Saharan regions put pressure on the Bantu. With plenty of available land southward, they began to migrate into central Africa along the Congo River. From there they apparently moved along the Zambezi and ultimately reached the eastern African coast and southern Africa, perhaps as early as the third or fourth century C.E.

These migrations, each of which may originally have numbered only a few hundred people, continued over hundreds of years. A superior iron technology enabled the Bantus to dominate groups in central and southern Africa. Temperatures of above 1,500 degrees Celsius are needed to melt iron ore, and the Congo, with hardwoods that burned very hot, allowed for the production of particularly fine high-grade iron. The Congo became a leading center for iron production. Numerous smelting furnaces remain scattered throughout central and southern Africa, but as caches of iron ingots have not been found, it appears that the crude iron metal was immediately made into hoes, other implements, and weapons.

With a few exceptions, such as the Pygmies in the equatorial forest, the Bantus successfully assimilated with other indigenous peoples. As a result, the Bantu language, like Indo-European in Eurasia or Nahuatl in Mexico, became the prototype of hundreds of central and southern African languages. Similarly, Bantu cultural and social mores spread throughout the territories, much as Olmec cultural innovations spread throughout Mesoamerica. The Bantu diffusion was based not so much on military or even technological superiority; rather it emerged from their creation of settled agricultural communities, which attracted and culturally overwhelmed the nomads and hunters of central and southern Africa. These numerous Bantu societies were the direct ancestors of the multitudinous ethnic groups that the Europeans encountered in the nineteenth century and are scattered from Nigeria in West Africa, north into the forest and south to the Congo, and to the Indian Ocean in East Africa.

Bantu societies had a complex system of belief in the supernatural and an extremely wide range of means of worship and of ways of dealing with the supernatural. Many believed in nature spirits and in the power of the ancestors, who gave identity and onward movement to life. The ancestors were believed to be responsible for transmitting the accumulated wisdom of the society; for example, passing on the knowledge of iron smelting.

Many Bantu societies, as well as other West African ethnic groups, had a belief system based on a supreme god or higher deity. Some in West Africa, such as the Yoruba, who belong to a Bantu-related linguistic group, had an extremely complex cosmology with a pantheon of gods and goddesses. The Yoruba believed that the God Oduduwa sprinkled sand on water and then released a chicken that scratched the sand, thereby creating the first land on earth; the Yoruba city of Ife, founded about 850 C.E., was believed to have been built on the site of creation. According to Yoruba history, Oduduwa had sixteen sons from whom the Yoruba royalty and *oni* (king) were descended. Building on the Nok knowledge of carving, Yoruba artists at Ife created elaborate bronzes and carved stone sculptures of the royal rulers.

In many Bantu societies, worship involved the use of highly sophisticated and finely wrought carved masks or fetishes, used in a complex system of rituals that often involved dance. Just as some Christians considered icons as aids for spiritual devotion, so, too, did many Bantu peoples consider masks and other carved objects as a means of approaching the supernatural. Specialized experts, or medicine men and women, and diviners often assisted in these rituals and were viewed as intermediaries between the supernatural and the physical world. Many Amerindians had similarly complex cosmologies and ceremonial rites.

The family was the basis of Bantu societies and economies. As one proverb taught, "A man outside his clan is like a grasshopper without wings." Nuclear clusters of related families formed villages and clans. Much as Amerindian societies did, Bantu societies lived in balance with nature; when the population grew too large or the arable land was exhausted, Bantu clans had to migrate elsewhere. Most Bantu societies were organized around the village and were patriarchal and polygamous, although a few were matriarchal.

Many Bantu societies were organized along age sets or age grades in which work, social life, and political responsibility were meted out on the basis of age. Age grades were divided along gender lines from the youngest boys and girls, to those who had reached puberty, to the elders, who had the most responsibilities and authority. When they reached puberty, young boys and girls often underwent extensive rites of initiation to mark their membership in the adult community. The Kikuyu in Kenya divided the male population among boys, warriors, and elders. Work was strictly defined along gender lines, with farming and cooking often considered "women's work" and hunting and martial arts "men's work." The elders in Bantu societies were highly respected for their knowledge and experience.

Bantu societies were often extremely democratic in that adult men had rights of full participation in the governing of the societies. Bantu governmental systems lacked uniformity and ranged from the highly organized monarchy of the Baganda to the decentralized systems of the Kikuyu. The non-Bantu speaking Igbo in southern Nigeria were organized into councils that conducted affairs of state and made political and economic decisions on the basis of consensus. The Igbo placed high value on the work ethic, rewarding those who prospered and contributed to the society. The Ganda had a highly institutionalized monarchy in which the kings were viewed as divine in the same way that the ancient Egyptians and Romans, among others, had deified their rulers. Many of the centralized monarchies established a feudal system of patron-client relationships with other groups who paid tribute or were treated as vassals or held as slaves. In contrast, the Kikuyu never had kings or even chieftains, but lived in scattered homesteads in the Kenyan highlands and relied upon the extended family to act as the major governing force.

As in India, the extremely damp and humid climate of central Africa has militated against the preservation of wood and straw architecture and carvings, and the lack of good building stone limited stone architecture. Nevertheless, some stone constructions—like those of Zimbabwe—do remain as evidence of the Bantu achievements; these will be described later in this section.

Successor States: Kingdoms of Gold and Salt

Less accessible to the Mediterranean civilizations were the states of Ghana (flourished 500–1250), Mali (1250–1450), and Songhai (1450–1600). These wealthy and elaborately organized kingdoms are often referred to as successor states because each built on the ruins and contributions of its predecessor. Located on savannas (grassy plains with scattered trees), these states were originally based on wealth secured from the trade of salt and gold.

Published memoirs in Arabic by Muslim travelers, various works by Europeans, oral traditions, and archaeological and anthropological studies have all contributed to our knowledge about these kingdoms. Firsthand written accounts by contemporaries tend to be more common in the kingdoms under Islamic rule, where literacy in Arabic was fairly widespread among the elite. Many of the non-Muslim kingdoms, lacking written languages, relied on oral traditions to transmit knowledge of historical

The Epic of Askia Mohammad

A man came who was wearing beautiful clothes.
He was a real man, he was tall, someone who looked good in white clothes, his clothes were really beautiful.
One could smell perfume everywhere.
He came in to sit down next to Kassaye.
They chatted with each other, they chatted, they chatted.
He said to her, "It is really true.
"Kassaye, I would like to make love with you.
"Once we make love together,
"You will give birth to a boy,
"Whom Si will not be able to kill.
"It is he who will kill Si and will become the ruler."
Kassaye said to him, "What?"
He said, "By Allah."
She said, "Good, in the name of Allah."
Each night the man came.
It is during the late hours that he came,
Each time during the coolness of the late evening,
Until Kassaye became pregnant by him.
Kassaye carried her pregnancy.
Kassaye had a Bargantche captive.
It is the Bargantche woman who is her captive, she lives in her house, and she too is pregnant.
They remained like that.
Kassaye kneeled down to give birth.
The captive kneeled down to give birth.
So Kassaye, Kassaye gave birth to a boy.
The captive gave birth to a girl.
Then Kassaye took the daughter of the captive, she took her home with her.
She took her son and gave it to the captive.
So the people left for the palace.
They said to Si:
"The Bargantche captive has given birth."
He said, "What did she get?"
They said, "A boy."
He said, "May Allah be praised, may our Lord give him a long life and may he be useful."
Then they were thoughtful for a moment.
They got up and informed him that Kassaye had given birth.
They asked, "What did she get?"
They answered, "A girl."
He said, "Have them bring it to me."
They brought it to him, he killed it.
*It is the boy who remained with the captive and Kassaye.**

This is a portion of the long, oral epic tracing the history of the great Songhai ruler, Askia Mohammad Touré. By the trick described here, Askia Mohammad was saved from death; he ultimately surmounted his humble upbringing, defeated his family's enemies, and became ruler over a vast empire in West Africa. At its zenith, this kingdom covered over 400,000 square kilometers of territory.

**The Epic of Askia Mohammed,* narrated by Nouhou Malio, in John W. Johnson, Thomas A. Hale, and Stephen Belchers, eds., *Oral Epics from Africa: Vibrant Voices from a Vast Continent* (Bloomington: University of Indiana Press, 1997), pp. 127–128.

and social events; recent scholarship indicates that many of these oral traditions are as accurate and detailed as the written records. Like written accounts, oral renditions often exaggerated the glory and power of victorious, successful rulers.

Muslim traders referred to ancient Ghana as the Land of Gold. The gold was mined in Upper Volta and in parts of present-day Guinea and Mali; the salt came from remote regions of the Sahara, where in some places it was so common that it was used as building blocks for houses. The rulers of Ghana, Mali, and Songhai became rich as the middlemen for this vast trade. They had the valuable gold and salt brought to central depots where the goods were loaded on camels in huge Berber-run caravans that traversed the Sahara to the Mediterranean coast. The salt was then sold around the Mediterranean.

The Ghanaian kingdom rose to power by 500 C.E., reaching its peak in 1050. Its founders were the Soninke people, but because all Ghanaian kings took the name "Ghana," little has been ascertained about individual leaders. Oral traditions held that there had been twenty-two kings before the rise of Islam in 622. By the eighth century Muslim writers were already describing the richness of the kingdom. By 1000 the Ghanaian kings ruled over extensive vassal states that paid tribute and were controlled by an army at least 200,000 strong, recruited from among those same vassal states. Ghana was a classic trading state, and its cities, like Kumbi Saleh, Gao, and the fabled Timbuktu became exceedingly rich. As in similar feudal kingdoms elsewhere, internal strife and uprisings by vassal states undermined the central authority of Ghanaian rulers, who by 1250 succumbed to the Mali kingdom founded by Sundiata (reigned 1234–1255).

By this time, Islam had already begun to make a profound impact on the West African kingdoms. As Islam had spread across northern Africa during the eighth century, traders and nomads had brought the new religion with them to West Africa. In general, throughout Africa, Islam made the greatest impact in urban areas, where Muslim traders often resided. Islam had a wide appeal because of its relatively direct theological precepts and its openness to all converts. There were also undeniable commercial benefits to be derived from alliances with the rest of the Muslim world. As a result, the ruling black aristocracy often converted to Islam, while the people in rural areas generally remained committed to the religions of their ancestors. However, converts to Islam often maintained many of their old religious and cultural practices along with their Islamic beliefs.

With the conversion of the ruling elites, Islamic and Arabic cultural and religious beliefs were gradually merged with the indigenous cultures of West Africa. The ties with Islam provided the elites with further commercial and intellectual contacts with the vast and, at that time, powerful Islamic world. As in Europe, the conversion of a feudal leader often meant the ultimate conversion of the people under his rule; as Christianity spread with the conversion of key leaders, so did Islam and Islamic culture in Africa.

Mansa Kankan Musa (reigned 1312–1337) was the best known of the powerful leaders of Mali; Muslim historians were lavish in their praise of his leadership. In 1324–1325, he made a famous pilgrimage to Mecca with an entourage of five hundred slaves, each with a golden staff; the slaves drove hundreds of camels loaded with some four tons of gold. According to contemporaries, Musa and his entourage spent gold so freely that they depressed the price of gold on the Cairo exchange for decades. Mali, however, soon fell to the same sorts of internal rivalries and uprisings that had destroyed the Ghanaian kingdom. The nomadic Taureg attacked and finally occupied Timbuktu in 1433–1434.

By the mid-fifteenth century, the growing Songhai kingdom, founded by Sunni Ali (reigned 1469–1492), had largely supplanted Mali. Ruling from the city-state of Gao, in present-day Mali, the Songhai spread their authority far across western Africa and into the Sahara. Sunni Ali extended and consolidated the empire, dividing it into provinces under appointed officials and creating a navy to patrol the Niger River. The empire reached its zenith under Askia Muhammad Touré, known as Muhammad the Great (reigned 1493–1528). Like his predecessors, however, Muhammad failed to solve the problem of succession. Threatened by military attacks from Morocco in the late sixteenth century and weakened by internal rivalries, the Songhai kingdom collapsed. With the arrival of western explorers, slave traders, and merchants, the great savanna empires were supplanted by African peoples from the coast and forest regions or by Europeans.

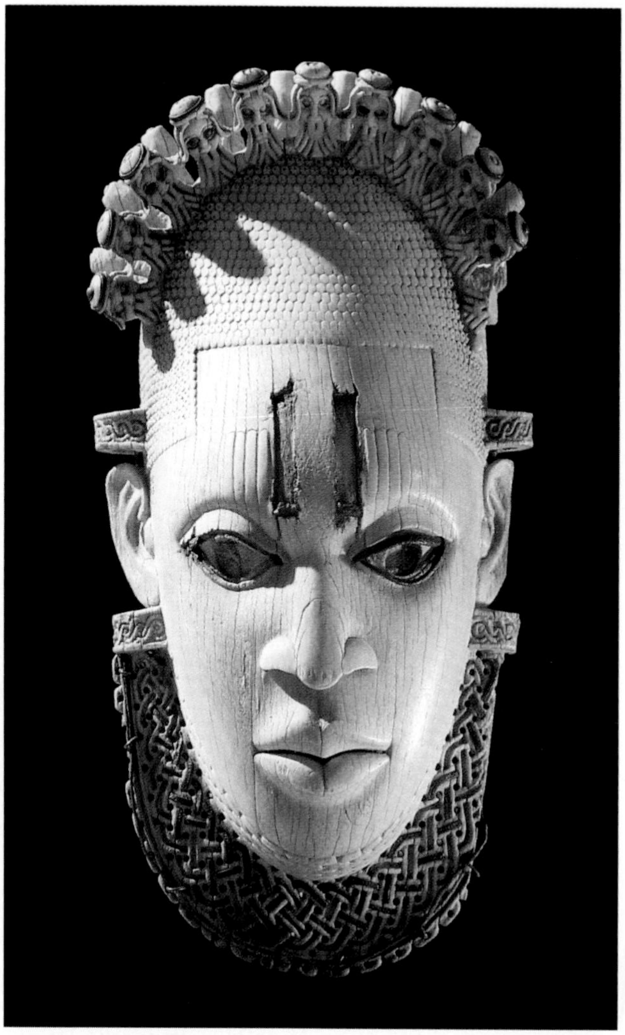

Werner Forman Archive, British Museum/Art Resource

Ivory Mask of a Benin Queen. Such intricately carved sculptures symbolized royal power and glory. The heads carved on the crown represent Portuguese invaders.

As in European feudal kingdoms, the society in these savanna kingdoms was strictly regulated according to class. As in most preindustrial societies, the ruling monarchs controlled much of the wealth and the majority of the people remained pastoralists or small farmers. Vassal states were forced to pay tribute and to provide "volunteers" for the army upon demand. The rich elites and rulers held slaves, but in contrast to slavery elsewhere, the numbers

Smithsonian Institution, National Museum of African Art, gift of David R. Markin

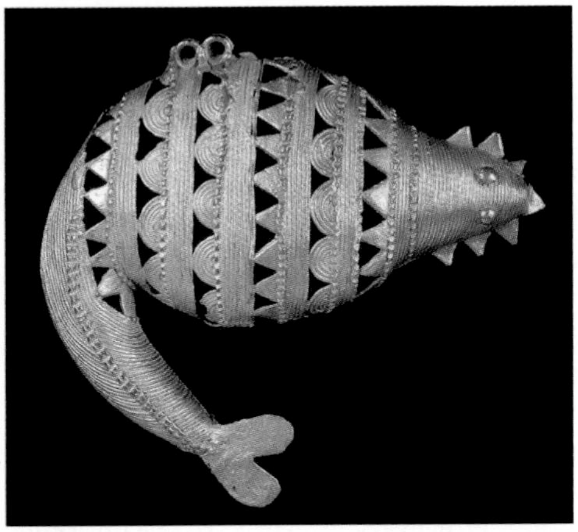

Courtesy of the trustees of the Wallace Collection

Gold Ornaments. In addition to trading in gold, Africans also created intricate golden jewelry and objects for their own pleasure. This golden mask and curving fish reveal a high level of expertise and creativity.

were small and slaves were considered as humans, not merely property. Especially in Muslim areas, they often worked as household servants, not as field laborers.

As in China and the Muslim world, the ruling aristocracy patronized the arts. As previously noted, African artists excelled in sculpture, and many brilliant examples of their craft in stone, wood, and bronze survive. The Nok in northern Nigeria and the Ife and Benin, forest peoples, were expert artisans. The Nok were known for their finely wrought terra cotta sculptures and beadwork. Nok terra cotta humans tend to be highly stylized, while sculptures of animals are highly realistic; Nok sculptures, some of which are almost life size, are finely detailed and often show elaborate hairstyles and beaded jewelry. Many Benin bronzes utilizing the lost-wax method still exist; it is not known whether this technique was indigenous, the product of independent invention, or a cultural exchange from the Nile where the technique was also employed.

Both Mansa Musa and Muhammad the Great brought scholars from Mecca to encourage science and education. Their actions demonstrate how the annual pilgrimages to Mecca facilitated the assimilation and spread of arts and sciences throughout the Islamic world; the annual pilgrimage was undoubtedly a major contributing factor to the strength of Muslim societies. In addition, Muslim pilgrims brought back goods and ideas that were fused with indigenous cultures when the pilgrims returned to their homes, and both ideas and cultures were assimilated and transmuted. Hence, Arabic language words or expressions and Islamic practices are still common among many contemporary West African societies.

Prosperous West African Kingdoms

In common with the kingdoms of gold and salt, other West African states had highly centralized political systems and economies based on trade and agriculture. The Oyo and Benin Empires were ruled by "divine kings," whose welfare was often thought to determine that of their kingdoms. The status of these kings was so high that their subjects sometimes feared that an ailing, sick king meant that the state would weaken and probably die. The Oyo Empire prospered under a series of dynamic kings until the eighteenth century. In conquered areas, village chieftains reported to palace chiefs appointed by the king, who, together with other notables, assisted in his administration.

Benin, perhaps the most powerful kingdom of the centralized states, was already a powerful kingdom by 1300. Under Ewuare the Great (reigned c. 1440–1473), the prosperous kingdom extended from the port at Lagos to the Niger. Although the economies of the western and central African kingdoms had long been indirectly connected with Europe through trade with North Africa and the Muslim world, Benin, a center for overland and sea trade, was one of the first West African kingdoms to come into direct contact with European traders and explorers.

Portuguese traders described Benin city as a large fortified stronghold at least twenty-five miles in circumference. While the *oba* (king) of Benin and his court resided in a lavish palace decorated with bronze plaques, most of the populace lived in mud houses covered with palm leaves. The city was divided by broad streets and connected to the coast by a good road. Portuguese travelers reported that there were no beggars in Benin, as the king and government officials cared and provided for the poor.

Both the Oyo and Benin societies assimilated and extended the artistic traditions of the earlier Ife kingdoms of western Africa. Benin artists were particularly renowned for their highly realistic bronze sculptures made with the lost-wax process. They also excelled in wood, ivory, and terra cotta sculpture. The oba and notables adorned their dress with finely crafted gold and ivory ornaments. At ceremonial functions, the oba wore robes decorated with red coral beads and carved ivory masks attached to his belt; ivory had religious symbolism and indicated the ruler's divine aspects. Ivory carvings were often handed down to royal successors as a symbol of kingship. As in the Ottoman, Safavid, and Chinese Empires, the rulers subsidized a lively court art. By controlling the craft guilds, Benin kings guaranteed their acquisition of the finest art works in bronze, gold, and ivory.

Strong kings, assisted by councils of notables, also led the Akan states, in present-day Ghana. Some of these kings were advised by priests in a type of theocratic government. These states were all dependent upon agriculture for revenues, but they also engaged in trade; the most profitable items were gold and kola nuts. The Ashanti, who moved from the interior into the coastal area of present-day Ghana, were the most powerful of the Akan people. Leading strong military forces, the Ashanti kings soon subjugated the peoples living along the coastal regions; by gaining control over the trade routes for gold from the savanna regions they became both rich and powerful.

The Ashanti excelled in making finely wrought and lavish gold objects. The kings held a monopoly over gold nuggets and crafted pieces; the people could own only gold dust. Ashanti kings appeared at state functions dressed in golden hats, bracelets, necklaces, and even gold-decorated sandals. Europeans were so impressed by these displays of wealth that they called the region the Gold Coast. The Ashanti were also known for handwoven cloth known as *kente*. Kente cloth is woven into long strips, which are then sewn together; originally only chiefs and notables wore the kente. Much as clans in Scotland have

Bridgeman/Art Resource

Benin Bronze. *Above:* The oba, flanked by two attendants, wears the dress, collar, and anklets signifying his high rank. *Below:* Ivory and brass leopards were symbols of royalty.

Bridgeman/Art Resource

A Strong Muslim Kingdom in Africa

Our Sultan Haj Idris . . . sought to follow the example of our Lord and Master Muhammad.

So also his exploits when he fought the Barbara, till the earth in its fulness became too narrow for them and the desert too small for them.

So he made the pilgrimage and visited Medina. . . . He was enriched by visiting the tomb of the companions of the prophet Muhammad . . . and he bought in the noble city a house and date grove.

Among the most surprising of his acts was the stand he took against obscenity and adultery, so that no such thing took place openly in his time.

He built the big town near Damasak and made four gates in the town and placed a keeper in charge of each gate and quartered there a detachment of his army. He ordered all his chiefs who were powerful and possessed of a defense force, to build houses and leave part of their equipment there as for instance, the horses, and quilted-armor . . . and coats of mail.

Among the gifts with which God had endowed him, was an impressive appearance. All his followers, small or great, never felt contented except in his presence. Even though he sent large armies in one direction and went in some other direction with a small force himself, his captains were not content to go without him.

*Such is the account we have given of the character of our Sultan and his wars in the time when he was king. We have written it after there has passed of his reign twelve years.**

Idris ibn Ali, or Idris Alooma, was the powerful African king of the Bornu kingdom from 1570 to 1602. He was a devout Muslim who extended the faith and his realm through negotiation and military conquest. At the peak of its power, the Bornu kingdom centered on Lake Chad and stretched far into present-day Libya. Many of the exploits and extensive experiences of ibn Ali were recorded by Ahmad ibn Fartua in his *History of the First Twelve Years of Mai Idris Alooma.*

* *The Horizon History of Africa* (New York: American Heritage, 1971), pp. 236–238.

their own tartans, Ashanti royal families had their own designs, usually in bright greens, reds, blues, and gold.

The States of Central Africa

Like many states in West Africa, the Kongo kingdom along the Congo River and the Lunda state were well organized politically and economically. The Kongo capital was on high ground more than 100 miles inland from the coast. Following a matrilineal line, the Kongo kings were often succeeded by their sisters' sons. King Nzinga Nkuwu (reigned 1506–1543), baptized Afonso, was one of the first African monarchs converted to Christianity by Portuguese missionaries.

Afonso I learned to read and write Portuguese and sent a number of officials, including his son Dom Henrique, to Portugal for education and religious training. As his numerous letters to the Portuguese king indicate (see Chapter 9 on the slave trade), Afonso considered himself an equal to European monarchs. Although he adopted Christianity and European dress and habits, Afonso was clearly not a puppet or vassal of the Portuguese. Indeed, the Kongo kingdom governed more people and territory than Portugal. Afonso's alliances and agreements with the Portuguese were made on the basis of equality, and he exercised strict administrative controls over both commerce and the slave trade.

As the foregoing description indicates, the societies in western and central Africa had developed their own unique and durable political organizations long before the advent of European exploration. Trade between African states and the Europeans was initially established on an equal footing and for mutually beneficial economic reasons. During this era, most African states, with some exceptions such as the king of the Kongo, retained their own unique traditional religious beliefs and effectively ignored or resisted attempts by European missionaries to gain converts for Christianity.

Commercial Wealth in East Africa

The fusion of cultures was perhaps nowhere more apparent than in East Africa. Along the coastal regions of Ethiopia and Somalia (the Horn of Africa), and southward along the Kenyan and Tanzanian coasts, city-states based on commerce and trade evolved as the dominant

Good Eating in Mogadishu

*We sailed fifteen nights and arrived at Mogadishu, which is a very large town. The people have very many camels. The merchants are wealthy . . . the Sultan of Mogadishu is called Shaikh by his subjects . . . by race he is a Berber. He talks in the dialect of Mogadishu, but knows Arabic. When a ship arrives, it is the custom for it to be boarded by the Sultan's sanbuq [little boat] to enquire whence it has come; they also inquire the nature of the cargo . . . The food of these people is rice cooked with butter . . . with it they serve side-dishes, stews of chicken, meat, fish, and vegetables. They cook unripe bananas in fresh milk, and serve them with a sauce. They put curdled milk [yoghurt] in another vessel with peppercorns, vinegar, and saffron, green ginger and mangoes, which look like apples but have a nut inside. Ripe mangoes are very sweet.**

This passage is from a firsthand account of Mogadishu, written in 1331 by Ibn Battuta, the famous fourteenth-century traveler from Morocco. In over thirty years, Ibn Battuta traveled some 75,000 miles—more than three times the distance covered by Marco Polo—visiting China, Ceylon, Turkey, North and East Africa, and Mecca in Arabia. Ibn Battuta had a keen eye for the smallest detail, and his diaries are full of colorful details about the diet, dress, habits, and culture of the peoples he observed.

**The Horizon History of Africa* (New York: American Heritage, 1971), pp. 161–162.

200 B.C.E. **1 C.E.**	Indians sail to Southeast Asia
	Indian influence in Java, Sumatra, Malaya, Burma
	Bantu migrations
	Moche culture rises in Peru
	Teotihuacán begins era of full flowering in Mesoamerica
500	Indian influence in Burma, Thailand, Malaya
	Chinese trade in Southeast Asia
	Maya civilization at its height
	Prince Shotoku's regency in Japan
	Japanese embassy to China
	Kingdom of Axum begins
	Silla unifies Korea
	Spread of Islam in North and East Africa
	Khmer Empire
	Angkor Wat, Borobodur, Pagan built
	Koryo dynasty in Korea
	Feudal Japan, code of Bushido
1000	Lady Murasaki, *The Tale of Genji*
	Thais form a state
	Shogunate in Japan
	Maya revival in Yucatán
	Kingdoms of Salt and Gold predominant in West Africa
	Mongols conquer Korea, Southern Sung, Pagan
	East Africa city-states
	Stone complexes in Zimbabwe
	Mansa Kankan Musa leader of Mali
1350	Rise of the Aztecs
	Inka Empire expands under Thupa Yupanki
	Moctezuma II becomes ruler of Aztec Empire
1500	

political and economic structures. Owing to the close geographical proximity to the Arabian Peninsula, East African coastal towns had ancient trading ties with Yemen, Persia, and other parts of the Middle East; later they developed commercial contacts with the Greeks and the Roman Empire. Animal skins, ivory, gold from Zimbabwe, and slaves were traded for spears, porcelain, and beads.

By the eighth century, Muslim merchants had begun trading with these coastal cities. Although the Christian kingdoms in Nubia and Ethiopia fought tenaciously against the Muslims, the expansion of Islam along the coastal regions was essentially peaceful. Muslim traders

Zimbabwe. This photograph shows a conical tower and the high circular walls around parts of the vast Zimbabwe complex. The fine granite surface of the walls was likely added by Bantu builders after 1000. Much of the surrounding district still awaits excavation.

from Arabia and Persia began to settle in the port cities of East Africa, known to the Arabs as the Land of Zanj. Not surprisingly, Muslim sources tend to emphasize the dominance of Muslim culture and governors over these city-states. Because the indigenous Bantu peoples lacked a written tradition, sources describing the extent of their economic and political organization are far fewer than Muslim ones. Information comes from either oral traditions or from written accounts by outsiders.

It is apparent, though, that the Muslim/Arab migrants assimilated with the Bantu majority. As these traders intermarried with the indigenous African population, a unique culture was created through assimilation and diffusion. Swahili, an African language infused with many Arabic and Persian words, became the language of trade and intercommunication, and Islam became the dominant religion. It is not always clear from available sources whether these city-states were governed by migrants from Arabia or the Persian Gulf or by indigenous Muslim ruling dynasties.

This new culture prevailed along the coast from present-day Somalia to Tanzania in the cities of Mogadishu, Merca, Brava, and many others, which enjoyed the economic wealth brought by trade. Ivory, gold, and slaves were the primary commodities. By the tenth century, merchants from the Persian Gulf and Oman dominated economic life, extending their trading empire to include the large island of Madagascar and the Comoro Islands. From 1095 to 1291, the Christian Crusaders, avid for riches to take back to Europe, increased the demand for gold and ivory, which came from central Africa through eastern Africa to the eastern Mediterranean, where the Crusaders had established independent feudal kingdoms (see Chapter 8). Gold was brought from Zimbabwe through the port of Sofala to Kilwa in present-day Tanzania. Muslim sources refer to Sofala as the capital of Zanj, or "land of the Bantu," which indicates that Bantu peoples from central Africa had already settled along the southern coast by 900.

Numerous mosques and public buildings along the eastern African coast attest to the wealth of these city-states. Dating from the thirteenth century, the great mosque in Kilwa clearly demonstrates the preeminence of Islamic architectural forms and designs. Many of the mosques and public buildings that remain are remarkably similar to those constructed by the Umayyads and Abbasids in earlier centuries. (See Chapters 5 and 8.)

Inland Cities in Southern Africa

The commercial cities of the coastal regions were linked economically and socially with a series of inland cities ruled by various Bantu societies. Iron production and copper and gold mining provided the economic basis of these cities. They had a flourishing trade with the coastal regions, but it is not yet known whether the merchants who conducted this trade came from the inland cities or the coast.

The massive complex at Zimbabwe is one of the most extensive of these Bantu cities and served as the capital of several Bantu rulers. It includes a hill complex with a huge granite hall, a great enclosure with thirty-foot-high walls and a valley complex. The great enclosure may have housed the rulers' wives, but the purpose of the conical stone tower in its center is unknown. These enormous ruins attest to the architectural skills of the Bantu people. Carbon dating of materials from Zimbabwe reveals that construction probably began around 200 C.E., but most of the buildings left today date from after 1000. Although Europeans originally thought the stone walls were fortresses, these massive complexes were actually built as displays of wealth and power, not for military purposes. It is also thought that the complex had religious importance as a sacred place where one could communicate with the ancestors.

Although the Zimbabwe complex is the most impressive of these Bantu constructions, more than 150 similar ones are scattered along the Zimbabwe-Mozambique border, but only about a dozen have been excavated. The gold jewelry and carved objects found in the Mapungubwe burial mound in northern South Africa indicate the wealth of the society and demonstrate the skill of its artisans. As archaeological research continues in Zimbabwe, more details about the economy, culture, and political and social life of the society will be revealed.

Summary and Comparisons

The cultures in this chapter range from indigenous to derivative in their relationship to Eurasia. In Mesoamerica, the Teotihuacanos, Maya, and Aztecs were the cultural descendants of the Olmec, just as the Babylonians, Assyrians, and Chaldeans had followed the Sumerians. In a larger context, however, Mesoamerican culture as a whole derived little from the Amerindian culture in Peru and the Andes. Contact with Eurasia was nonexistent or insignificant before 1500.

The Mesoamerican cultures that developed after the first century C.E. were essentially clusters of city-states. These states were sometimes aggregated by conquest into larger entities, like the Aztec Empire of the early sixteenth century. The major cities of Mesoamerica usually centered on monumental religious buildings in the shape of flattened pyramids flanked by sacred ball courts. Governments, too, were religion-based, with a single ruler supported by a military elite and a priestly caste that controlled the lower orders. The people of Mesoamerica increasingly turned to human sacrifice to preserve a sense of universal order.

Developmentally, Mesoamerican culture is a paradox: it became quite sophisticated intellectually, employing advanced mathematics and a complex calendar; yet, like the Andean culture, it was technologically backward, lacking metal weapons, the wheel, large draft animals, and heavy transportation. Invading Europeans took full advantage of these deficiencies.

The Inka Empire in the Andean highlands was quite unlike Mesoamerica. A descendant of earlier affluent cultures, the Inka Empire was the most centralized state up to that point in history. A divine emperor presided over a highly structured society, allocating all land, resources, and labor.

Although facing the same problems as the Mesoamericans, the Inka built a remarkable network of roads and supply stations that helped to keep the far-flung empire together. Inka agents collected food into public warehouses and dispensed it, along with clothing and beer, at holidays and state occasions. Sun worshipers, the Inka escaped the bloody religious practices common in Mesoamerica.

The young cultures of sub-Saharan Africa represent various mixes of indigenous and borrowed elements. Before Islam arrived after 700, sub-Saharan Africa was home to indigenous cultures unaffected by Mediterranean influences. Ethiopia saw early development because of its access to the Mediterranean via the Nile River. Here there arose an Axum-Kushite trading empire based on Coptic Christianity. However, this empire was cut off from the rest of Christian civilization by the Muslim conquest of North Africa.

In the sub-Saharan savanna of West Africa, a succession of powerful kingdoms—especially Ghana, Mali, and Songhai—arose between the fourth and sixteenth centuries. Based on the salt and gold trade, they built an urban existence on a firm agricultural base. Though illiterate, they were strong politically and militarily. Their ironworking was either a product of independent invention or an import from the Mediterranean. Islam increased its presence in the region after the seventh century.

A third cultural center was the east coast of Africa, where city-states had profited from trade around the Indian Ocean since Greek and Roman times. Here Muslim/Arab culture mixed with indigenous Bantu culture: one major example was the evolution of the Swahili language.

Central and southern Africa saw the Bantu pervade the lower third of the African continent just as Indo-Europeans had peopled Eurasia. By about 1000, the Bantus, metal-working farmers and herders, had developed at least one major urban center in the Zimbabwe area.

Selected Sources

Bauer, Brian S. *The Development of the Inca State.* 1992. The new standard treatment.

Bovill, Edward W. *The Golden Trade of the Moors: West African Kingdoms in the Fourteenth Century.* 2d ed. 1995. A lively account of Saharan trade routes and the Sudanic kingdoms of West Africa.

Carlson, John B. "Rise and Fall of the City of the Gods." *Archaeology* 16,6 (1993): 58. A look at the Venus warrior cult that provided captives for religious rituals at Teotihuacán.

Carrasco, David. *Moctezuma's Mexico: Visions of the Aztec World.* 1992. A look at Aztec society and culture.

———, ed. *The Oxford Encyclopedia of Mesoamerican Cultures.* 3 vols. 2000. A comprehensive guide to 700 years of history in Mexico and Central America before, during, and after the coming of European invaders.

Coe, Michael D. *Maya.* 3d ed. 1985. The standard work on Mayan historical development.

*———. *Breaking the Maya Code.* 1992. The story of the century-long struggle to decipher the meaning of the Maya glyphs.

*Collins, Robert O., ed. *Problems in African History: The Precolonial Centuries.* Vol. 1. 1992. Includes many subjects for classroom discussion: Bantu origins, slavery, women, and trade, among others.

D'Altroy, Terence N. *Provincial Power in the Inka Empire.* 1992. Reveals the inner political, social, and economic workings of the Inka Empire by studying their operation in a key province.

Davies, Nigel. *The Toltecs.* 1977. A study of the civilization that linked Teotihuacán with the post-classic Maya and the Aztecs.

Fash, William L. *Scribes, Warriors, and Kings: The City of Copán and the Ancient Maya.* 1991. A comprehensive view of one of the great Maya cities and a general survey of current scholarship on the Maya.

"The Glories of Ancient Benin." Films for the Humanities. A short video on the founding of Benin in West Africa, with scenes from the Museum and Palace of Porto-Novo.

Hamdun, Said, and Noel King, eds. *Ibn Battuta in Black Africa.* Rev. ed. 1994. Ibn Battuta's fascinating firsthand narrative of his travels in West and East Africa.

Henderson, John S. *The World of the Ancient Maya.* 1981. Profusely illustrated, focuses on the arts.

The Horizon History of Africa. 1971. A lavishly illustrated account of Africa with many excerpts from primary sources.

Inca. 1995. An informative Time-Life videocassette.

July, Robert W. *A History of the African People.* 4th ed. 1992. A good survey of historical developments throughout Africa.

Kellogg, Susan. *Law and the Transformation of the Aztec Empire.* 1995. Discusses the interface of two legal systems.

"The Lost City of Zimbabwe." Films for the Humanities. Video on the continuing restoration of this great African city.

Malpass, Michael. *Daily Life in the Inca Empire.* 1996. A comprehensive account.

Markman, Roberta H., and Peter T. *The Flayed God: The Mythology of Mesoamerica.* 1992. A combination of original text and contemporary commentary that leads the reader into the mythology of the Mesoamerican cultures.

"Maya Lords of the Jungle" [1980]. British Broadcasting Corporation/Public Broadcasting Associates. This installment of the *Odyssey* program concentrates on agriculture and trade patterns.

Meyer, Karl E. *Teotihuacán.* 1980. An overview of the culture.

Munro-Hay, Stuart. *Aksum: An African Civilization of Late Antiquity.* 1992. A scholarly account of the ancient kingdom in present-day Ethiopia.

Patterson, Thomas Carl. *The Inca Empire: The Formation and Disintegration of a Pre-Capitalist State.* 1991. A special point of view.

Prospouriakoff, Tatiana. *Maya History.* 1993. A well-written alternative to Michael Coe's standard account.

Schele, Linda, and Mary Ellen Miller. *The Blood of Kings: Dynasty and Ritual in Maya Art.* 1986. Text and pictures combine to give the reader insight into Maya religious and dynastic beliefs.

Sharer, Robert J. *Daily Life in Maya Civilization.* 1996. A comprehensive discussion of the topic.

Sweetman, David. *Women Leaders in African History.* 1984. This comprises short biographies of twelve African women, from ancient Egypt to colonial times.

The World Atlas of Architecture. 1984. Lavishly illustrated and fascinating descriptions of building techniques and styles around the world from earliest times to the twentieth century. Includes chapters on African and Mesoamerican civilizations.

*Available in paperback.

Internet Links

Civilizations in Africa
http://www.wsu.edu:8080/~dee/civafrca/civafrca.htm
This homepage contains links to information on many African cultures, their literature, art, religion, and language. Provides excellent chronological and geographical aids as well.

The Inka Trail and Machu Picchu
http://www.raingod.com/angus/Gallery/Photos/SouthAmerica/Peru/IncaTrail.html
This virtual journey to the city of Machu Picchu includes breathtaking photographs and an interactive map.

Lords of the Earth
http://www.mayaLords.org/
This homepage contains links to extensive pages on Maya, Aztec, and Inka civilizations. Excellent photographs and text.

Mystery of the Maya
http://www.civilization.ca/membrs/civiliz/maya/mminteng.html
This site, superbly produced by the Canadian Museum of Civilization, offers readable text, helpful "Slide Shows," a timeline, hyperlinks, and other aids for the study of Maya civilization.

National Museum of African Art Collections
http://www.si.edu/nmafa/exhibits/beninsp.htm
Includes a section devoted to "The Ancient West African City of Benin, A.D. 1300–1897."

Zimbabwe Slide Show
http://www.mc.maricopa.edu/academic/cult_sci/anthro/lost_tribes/zimbabwe/index.html
A series of twenty-three high-quality slides of the ruins at Zimbabwe, with concise commentary.

COMPARATIVE ESSAY 6

The Development of International Trade

An old merchant said to a person who wanted to find out the truth about commerce: . . . "Buy cheap and sell dear."

The merchant who knows his business will travel only with such goods as are generally needed by rich and poor. . . . Likewise, it is more advantageous and more profitable for the merchant's enterprise, if he brings goods from a country that is far away and where there is danger on the road. . . . They get rich quickly.

Ibn Khaldun, *The Muqaddima: An Introduction to History,* trans. Franz Rosenthal (Princeton: Princeton University Press, 1967), pp. 310–311.

"The business of America is business."

Calvin Coolidge

"What's good for General Motors is good for America; What's good for America is good for General Motors."

Attributed to Charlie "Engine" Wilson, General Motors Corporation, although his actual words were slightly different.

Ibn Khaldun's observations about commerce and trade are as true today as when he wrote in the fourteenth century—a time when international commerce was beginning to flourish. In the twentieth century, industrialists and leaders (like American president Calvin Coolidge or Charlie Wilson of General Motors) have also recognized the important relationship between economic prosperity and national well-being. For centuries, rulers have sought to increase the wealth of their realms; commerce and trade have frequently made major contributions to the growing power of empires and nation states.

By 1500 a well-developed international trade was being carried on among the major civilizations of Africa, Europe, and Asia. From that time to the present, international trade has been a crucial global driving force. Trade among diverse and far-flung parts of the world was made possible by the development of revolutionary advances in the sciences, technology, transportation, and finance that began about five hundred years ago. Since then advances in transportation and communications have shrunk the world to a global village.

It was not always the case. Although international trade had been important for several thousand years before 1500, trade volume grew slowly, and was often subject to interruptions and disruptions caused by wars and politics. Viewing history over the span of several thousand years, we can discern three broad cycles in the rise and fall of trade among civilizations: The first cycle lasted between approximately 500 B.C.E. and 400 C.E., the second cycle spanned between around 600 and 1200, while the third and most recent one began around 1500 and continues to the present.

Cycle 1: International trade in luxury goods or essential raw materials evidently began earlier than 500 B.C.E. In very ancient times, intricate and interlocking trade routes connected civilizations in Eurasia and Africa. For example, a semiprecious stone called lapis lazuli mined in high altitudes in Afghanistan has been found in tombs of ancient Egyptian rulers. During the Bronze Age, tin from Cornwall in Britain may have been traded as far as the eastern Mediterranean. Recent X rays and other tests suggest that Chinese silk fibers were also used in the cloth that wrapped ancient Egyptian mummies over 3,000 years ago. Similarly, when a Chinese general arrived in northwest India in the second century B.C.E., he found that Chinese silks were already available in India. They evidently had reached India via southwestern China and Burma.

These trade routes were regularized and expanded by the Hellenistic kingdoms in Egypt and western Asia, the Roman Empire, the Mauryan Empire in India, and the Han Empire in China. Along these routes people, goods, and ideas intermingled and cosmopolitan towns grew up to provide housing, food, places of worship, and recreation for the merchants.

By 400 C.E. violent invasions disrupted much of this Eurasian trade. The collapse of the Roman and Han Empires had by then reduced the Pax Romana and Pax Sinica to mere memories.

Available technology determined the mode of long-distance trade. Goods were hauled by carts where roads permitted and on pack animals such as oxen, mules, horses, and camels where roads were poor. The animals' carrying capacity severely restricted the quantity of goods that could be carried, so trade was often limited to luxury items. Water transport was always more efficient and much cheaper than land transport. For example, a ten-foot boat could carry as much weight as thirty pack horses. However, the vagaries of wind, storms, piracy, and the lack of navigational charts and compasses hampered shipping. Therefore most ancient sailing ships avoided open seas and hugged coasts, undertaking long-distance sea voyages in stages. Hull, mast, and sail design were primitive compared to those of later sailing vessels and limited the size of waterborne cargoes. As a result boats, too, tended to carry luxury items.

The high cost of transportation ensured that the most costly goods—silk, spices, precious metals, and gems—traveled the longest distances. Most of the cargo carried in ancient trade, both overland and seaborne, went from Asia to Europe. In exchange, Asian producers received silver and gold from Europeans. Large quantities of Roman coins have been discovered in many Indian towns, suggesting that they might have been so common as to be circulated as the local currency. Thus European rulers from the Roman Emperor Augustus on bemoaned the loss of precious metals to Asian lands for ephemeral luxuries such as silk fabrics.

The Western Hemisphere was not involved in the intercontinental trade until the arrival of Europeans at the end of the fifteenth century. Within the region, the lack of any pack animals other than llamas, which would only carry small loads, and the absence of suitable water routes limited commerce. Thus trade between cultures in the Americas was limited to what could be borne on the backs of porters and by canoes along river routes.

Throughout the ages, the wealthy have been major consumers of the goods obtained by long-distance trade. Governments fostered trade by building and maintaining roads and ports and by suppressing piracy; they also derived revenues by taxing commerce. Some governments, most notably Islamic dynasties of West Asia, including the later Ottoman and Safavid Empires, encouraged trade through tax incentives and by inviting outside traders into their realms. In China the Han and T'ang governments encouraged foreign traders to settle in their empire by providing them with residential quarters and places of worship. Successive Chinese dynasties also established markets with the nomads beyond their borders, on the correct assumption that trade was preferable to war.

Cycle 2: The reestablishment of a unified government in China in the sixth century and the gradual restoration of peace and order in Europe following the "dark age" of the barbarian invasions at the fall of the Roman Empire led to a revival of international trade. By the twelfth century, a new cycle of trade peaked. Land and water routes extended from China to western Europe and North Africa, connecting eight overlapping trade zones. The linchpins that linked these zones were Changan in northern China and Canton on the South China coast, Calicut in India, Samarkand in Central Asia, Baghdad in West Asia, Cairo (then called Fustat) in northern Africa, Constantinople at the entrance of the Bosporus in the eastern Mediterranean, and Venice in Italy.

Although governments were more fragmented during the second cycle than the first, international trade flourished perhaps even more than during the previous one. Improved transportation technology was the main reason for this increase. The increased volume of trade satisfied the demands for Asian goods that the Crusaders had stimulated among Europeans since the twelfth century. In East Asia after about 1000, economic advances in Japan and the Sung dynasty's encouragement of exports to raise revenue for defense against the Mongols led to a vibrant international trade in that region.

The second golden age of trade was disrupted in the thirteenth century when nomadic people called the Mongols rudely erupted across Eurasia, causing enormous havoc to lives and material culture. However, Mongol rulers later promoted commerce, especially in luxury goods. Thus the Pax Tartarica, or "Mongol peace," followed the devastation of the Mongol conquests.

In the fourteenth century, a plague or "Black Death" swept Europe and West Asia and also devastated China and India. It wiped out as much as a third of Europe's population and perhaps as much as half the population of India. Recurrent warfare in western Asia, in addition to the high taxes exacted on transit trade by the newly established Ottoman Empire, contributed to the further disruption of trade between western Europe and India and China. As a result, supplies became irregular and prices rose.

Cycle 3: The third era of intercontinental trade began in the fifteenth century. The impetus came from the newly centralized European states, which adopted policies that led to the development of a new international trading pattern. As a result of advances in the sciences and technology, Europe was propelled to the forefront of world trade. Portugal and Spain developed new trade routes that bypassed the old land and water routes and in the process opened up a new era of world trade.

Three Continents: Conflict and Commerce

8

The life story of Shagarat al-Durr—slave, wife of one Sultan, stepmother of another, ruler of a dynasty, and murderer—reads like a script for a Hollywood adventure film. Shagarat al-Durr, whose name means "tree of pearls," entered the lavish Mamluk court in Egypt as a slave during the thirteenth century and subsequently married the Sultan. After his death (of natural causes), Shagarat concealed his demise for three months so that her stepson could return from greater Syria and take the throne. However, Shagarat quickly became disenchanted with him, had him murdered, and proclaimed herself ruler. Encouraged to legitimize her position by marrying, Shagarat took a new husband, with whom she shared power for several years, until it was rumored that he planned to take another wife. Shagarat retaliated by having him murdered. But this assassination so enraged Shagarat's many enemies that they conspired to have her assassinated (she was beaten to death with heavy, wooden bath clogs). Her body was thrown from the palace tower to be devoured by dogs. The remains were ultimately buried in a grandiose tomb that Shagarat had built for herself. The memory of this remarkable woman lives on in present-day Cairo, where there is still a street named after her.

Shagarat al-Durr is one of a number of powerful, and sometimes ruthless, women who became politically powerful during an era of empires and absolute rulers. The period 1100–1500 was one of great disruption in the eastern Mediterranean. In West Asia, the Abbasid caliphate ruled over a vast, powerful, and prosperous Islamic state. This golden age of Islam marked a high water point for Islamic sciences, arts, and literature.

The turbulence of the Crusades, coming in the aftermath of the collapse of a unified Islamic empire, lasted several centuries. But those disruptions pale when compared with the havoc wrought by Mongol and Turkish onslaughts across Eurasia in the thirteenth and fourteenth centuries. The Mongol invasions devastated central and West Asian societies, many of which never recovered their former glory or power. The consolidation of Mongol rule in Asia, however, restored trade relations between that continent and Europe.

Another important event of this convulsive period was the creation of the Ottoman state by the Turks of the Anatolian Peninsula. Making effective use of artillery and firearm-bearing infantry, the Ottomans, like the Mongols before them and others after them, created "gunpowder empires." With their technological military superiority, the Ottomans conquered the Balkans and captured Constantinople, thus ending the 1,000-year-old Byzantine Empire.

This period also marked the second cycle of flourishing trade; war and commerce brought the large populations of Europe and Asia into direct contact (as described in the preceding comparative essay). At the beginning of this period, trade between the West and the East flourished amid general prosperity and continued even in times of bitter warfare.

The Golden Age of Islam

The Caliph himself, surrounded by his chief ministers and favorite slaves covered with gold and jewels, resembled a planet amidst a galaxy of stars.

Eunuchs, black and white, with inferior officers of the number of eight thousand, served as a foil to these gems. Silk-and gold-embroidered tapestries, numbering thirty-eight thousand pieces, ornamented the palace walls, and on a curious tree of gold and silver were perched a variety of birds whose movements and notes were regulated by machinery.

*Twenty-two thousand carpets covered the floor, and there floated on the broad stream of the Tigris, before the windows of the palace, thousands of vessels, each splendidly decorated; while a hundred lions, in charge of their keepers, lent a contrast to the glittering scene.**

*Abufelda, "The Caliph of Baghdad receives an Ambassador from Greece," in Rhoda Hoff, *The Arabs: Their Heritage and Their Way of Life* (New York: Henry Z. Walck, 1979), pp. 19–20.

This description gives some indication of the richness and splendor of the Abbasid court in Baghdad during what has become known as the golden age of Islam in the eighth and ninth centuries. During the golden age, Islamic society, which was known for its tolerance and intellectual dynamism, achieved a high level of cultural and artistic production. Many Islamic scientific, philosophic, architectural, and artistic creations subsequently formed the basis for scientific and artistic developments in surrounding societies and in the Western world.

Life under the Abbasids

The second Abbasid Caliph, Abu Jafar (reigned 754–775), better known as al-Mansur, established a new fortress capital on the Tigris River, at the site of the village of Baghdad. This circular, walled complex took some 100,000 workers over four years to construct. At its zenith in the ninth century, Baghdad, with a population variously estimated at 800,000 to 2 million, rivaled Constantinople as the largest city of the age. Officially known as Madinat al-Salam (City of Peace), Baghdad became the fabled city of *The Tales of the Arabian Nights*, a collection of highly romanticized and exaggerated stories based on court life under the Abbasids.

Baghdad was dominated by a massive palace that housed the caliph and the administrative complex. With its advantageous location on the Tigris, the capital dominated the trade routes and was a major entrepôt for commerce from the West and East. Thus under the Abbasids the center of Islamic power shifted eastward from Damascus to Baghdad in present-day Iraq.

Under Caliph Harun al-Rashid (reigned 786–809) and his son Mamun (reigned 813–833), the Abbasid Empire reached its zenith of power and wealth. As in the Chinese empires, the government was highly centralized. A grand vizier and an advisory council administered the extensive Abbasid Empire. Taxes were collected for different categories of landowners, and a separate tax was levied on non-Muslims, who did not pay the *zakat*, or Islamic alms, or serve in the army. During the long reign of Harun al-Rashid, the Arabs began to tire of military service, and Turkish forces began to command the military. As the empire declined, they became the masters where once they had been slaves. Similar takeovers by mercenary forces had contributed to the downfall of the Roman Empire.

Abbasid wealth rested primarily upon agriculture and trade efficiently administered by a series of able, dynamic caliphs and advisors. An extensive highway network expedited trade, while a well-organized postal system enhanced communications and also facilitated intelligence gathering; reportedly, old women were particularly able agents. Most of the international trade was with China and India; Muslim traders brought textiles, paper, and porcelains from China and other parts of Asia along overland routes through Samarkand.

Because the Abbasids had the political and social support of the Iranian provinces, Persian influences were particularly strong, and Abbasid rulers often sought to copy the habits and cultural tastes of the old Persian Empire. Under the Abbasids, expert artisans, both from local areas and from other parts of Asia, produced finely decorated porcelains, carpets, jewelry, metal and inlaid wood products, and innumerable luxury items. Court life under the Abbasids was so lavish that Harun al-Rashid's wife Zubayda reputedly wore shoes studded with jewels and hosted feasts where the food was served on golden plates. Zubayda was typical of upper-class women who lived extravagant lives and sometimes wielded political power. The great majority of the population, however, consisted of peasant farmers and women who not only worked long hours in the fields, but also kept house and raised children.

With enormous power and wealth at their disposal, the Abbasid caliphs became famous patrons of intellectuals and artists. Under Abbasid rule, Baghdad became a center for learning and the arts. Although Muslim sources make little mention of the event, Charlemagne sent a mission in 797 to secure safe passage for Christian pilgrims to Jerusalem. After his delegates returned with stories about the untold wealth of Baghdad, the city became a symbol for the glories of the Muslim dominions.

Abbasid Decline

By the ninth and tenth centuries, the once mighty Abbasid caliphate was showing signs of decay. A major problem was that its rulers were constantly threatened by rival dynasties from within the empire, as governors appointed from Baghdad sought to establish their own dynasties. In general, the more distant a province was from Baghdad, the more likely it was to become independent. In the future, the vast Ottoman Empire would have similar problems controlling its provincial governors.

Weakened by the growing economic strength of rival Muslim rulers in North and West Africa, the rulers in Baghdad turned increasingly to Persian and Turkish

Map 8.1 The Abbasid Empire. At the zenith of its power, the Abbasid caliphate based in Baghdad included much of Arabia, present-day Iran, and Afghanistan. Rival Islamic regimes ruled Egypt and North Africa.

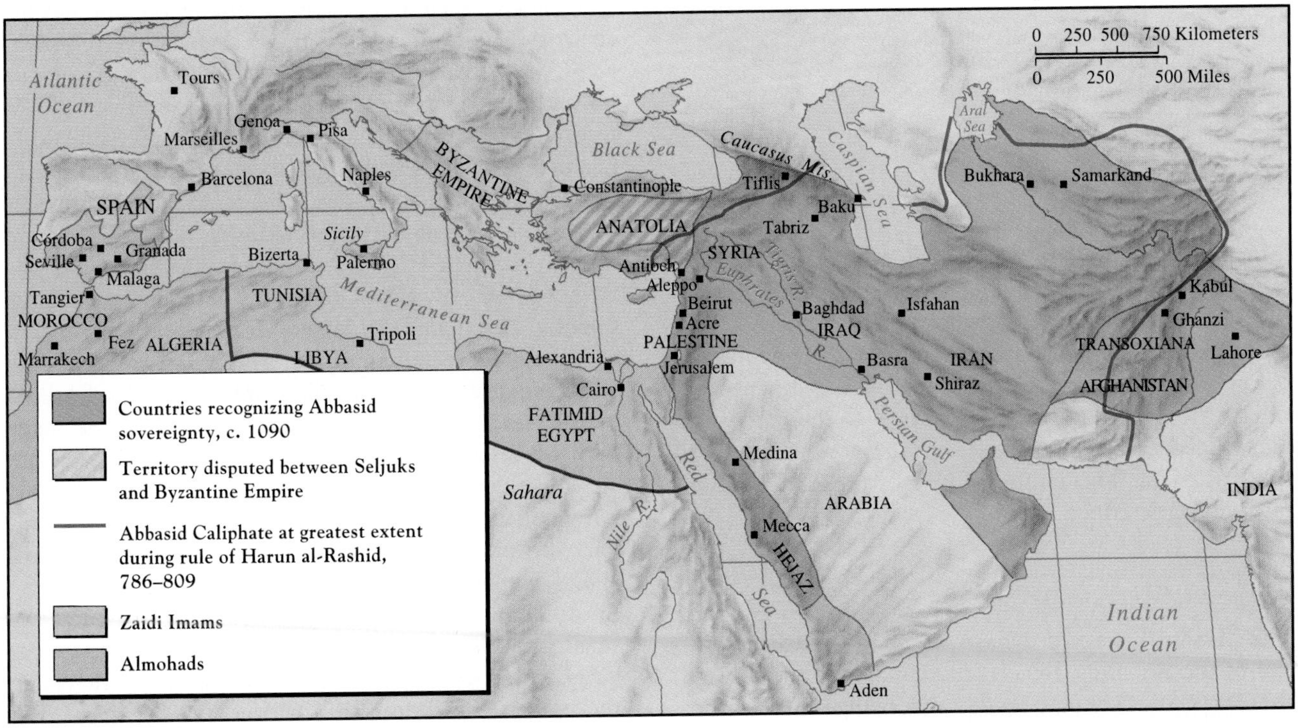

The Good Life in Baghdad

When I wandered about the city after a long absence, I found it in an expansion of prosperity. Affluence is abundant among the upper rank. . . . This may be seen in the case of their purchase of arms inlaid with gold, ornamented vessels, and splendid furniture. They cover their walls with embroidery and silk brocade, and take an interest in planting flowers in their gardens, even to the extent that they have rare flowers brought to them from India.

They indulge in luscious food to the point of buying game and fruit out of season. . . . When it is hot they place their chairs among water gushing from statues of lions and among forms of birds and apples which they chisel in marble. When their bodies have obtained sufficient water to refresh the soul, they place fans on the ceiling. . . .

*They indulge in clothes and ornamentation and in riding horses with silk brocade and heavy finery of silvery, to a degree which no affluent nations before them have reached.**

These excerpts from a letter by an Arab nobleman visiting Baghdad to his father in the latter part of the eighth century give some indication of the vast wealth and luxury of life in the Abbasid capital.

*"Muslim Culture in Baghdad," trans. John Damis, in Ilse Lichtenstadter, *Introduction to Classical Arabic Literature* (New York: Schocken Books, 1974), pp. 357–362.

leaders for military and political support. The power of Baghdad was also undermined by religious schisms and the weakness of the caliphs, who preferred the pleasures of the court to administrative or military duties. Empires before and after the Abbasids have been weakened by rulers who have preferred opulent lives to the hard work of administering vast territories or the rigors and perils of the battlefield. The actual collapse of the Abbasid Empire will be described later in the chapter.

The Glories of Muslim Spain

The Muslim Umayyad dynasty in Spain rivaled the glories of the Abbasids. By 710 the Umayyads had crossed the Strait of Gibraltar, and, after being ousted from Damsacus by the Abbasids, established a rival caliphate in 756; the new Umayyad Empire included Spain and western North Africa (present-day Morocco and Algeria). Under Caliph Abd al-Rahman I (reigned 756–788), who had escaped the Abbasid takeover in Damascus, the Umayyads ruled until 976 from al-Andalusia in southern Spain. Subsequent Muslim rulers continued to govern parts of Spain until their final defeat by the Christian forces of King Ferdinand and Queen Isabella in 1492.

Córdoba, the capital of the Umayyad Empire in the West, became one of the richest cities in Europe and exported goods to the East and West. Education was highly valued, and Abd al-Rahman III (reigned 912–961) established dozens of free schools and libraries. He also encouraged Jewish scholarship at a time when minorities were vigorously persecuted in the rest of Europe. Thus Muslim Spain became a dynamic center for the arts and sciences.

While Jews were suffering persecution at the hands of Christians in most of Europe, Spanish Jews lived in relative harmony with Muslims; many adopted Arab names and spoke Arabic. A noteworthy Spanish Jew who made valuable cultural contributions was Rabbi Musa bin Maymun, also known as Moses Maimonides (1135–1204), who spent most of his adult life in Egypt. As court physician to the Egyptian sultan Salah ed-Din (reigned 1174–1193), Rabbi bin Maymun wrote treatises based on empirical methods that criticized the still authoritative opinions of classical Greece. Subsequently, he wrote *The Guide for the Perplexed,* a philosophical interpretation of Judaism for those seeking a rational basis for their faith. His openness to Aristotle antagonized more traditional Jews, but Christian thinkers such as Thomas Aquinas soon adopted his analysis of the connection between revelation and reason.

Unfortunately, the Umayyads' political and military power did not match their cultural renown. The Muslim territories under Umayyad authority were continually plagued by civil wars in which local provincial governors or military commanders established rival governments. To save the empire, successive caliphs recruited outside forces, many from Africa; however, these mercenaries founded their own rival kingdoms in Africa, which frequently threatened Umayyad domination in Muslim Spain. To protect the empire from rival Muslim forces and from attacks from hostile Christian armies, fortified towns were built along the coastal areas. These ruins may still be seen along the coasts of Spain and Portugal.

By the end of the eleventh century, the Muslim Empire in Spain was clearly on the retreat in face of the military advances by the famous Spanish Christian hero, al-Cid, who also fought as a mercenary with Muslims. By the fifteenth century, Muslims in Spain held only the small kingdom around Granada, where the highly secular Nasrid rulers built lavish pleasure palaces that remain the epitome of "Moorish" (Moroccan) architecture in the West. After years of fierce fighting, the forces of Queen Isabella and King Ferdinand defeated the Nasrids and entered Granada in January 1492. As Boabdil, the last Muslim monarch in Spain, looked down on his lost capital and wept, his mother allegedly said, "You weep like a woman for what you could not hold as a man." Boabdil escaped into exile, and several centuries of Muslim rule in Spain came to an end. For Christendom, the conquest of Granada with its great al-Hambra palace in some ways compensated for the earlier loss of Constantinople to the Ottomans in 1453.

In face of massive persecutions by the Spanish monarchy and Catholic church, Muslims and Jews either converted or fled to the relative safety of Muslim-dominated territories in Africa or the eastern Mediterranean. Many of those immigrants were merchants or highly skilled artisans whose exodus promoted the cultural and economic development of the Ottoman Empire. Their departure also impoverished Spain, hereafter the home of a small, wealthy elite and a large, poor peasantry. Although the Spanish monarchs swiftly moved to eradicate all traces of Muslim domination, the centuries of Muslim presence had made an indelible mark on the culture of the Iberian Peninsula, and Muslim/Arab artistic styles are still readily recognizable in the music and much of the architecture and language of Spain and Portugal.

The Better Half

*Women are superior to men in certain respects: it is they that are asked in marriage, desired, loved and courted, and they that inspire self-sacrifice. . . . An indication of the high esteem in which women are held is that if a man be asked to swear by God to distribute his possessions all that comes easily to him, but let him be asked to swear to put away his wife, and he grows pale, is overcome with rage, protests, expostulates, gets angry and refuses—God created a child out of a woman without the intervention of any man, but He has never created a child out of a man without a woman.**

This passage is from an *adab,* or graceful, sophisticated essay, by Abu Uthman 'Amer ibn Bahr al-Faqaimi al-Basri al-Jahiz (d. 869.) Al-Jahiz, the grandson of a black slave, lived from the gifts of rich patrons in the Abbasid caliphate; he is reputed to have written more than 200 books.

*Al-Jahiz, "Women's Superiority to Men," trans. D. M. Hawkes, in *The Islamic World,* ed. William H. McNeill and Marilyn Robinson Waldman, (New York: Oxford University Press, 1973; reprint, Chicago: University of Chicago Press, 1983), p. 131.

Islamic Theology, Philosophy, and Science

Abbasid and Umayyad rulers actively supported philosophers and theologians. Islamic intellectuals were particularly instrumental in preserving and subsequently translating Greek works into Arabic. Had Islamic writers and thinkers not recognized the importance of keeping classical thought alive, many of the books and writings of Greek philosophers that were to form the basis of much subsequent European intellectual development might well have been lost forever. Since Islam had not separated the functions of government and religion, Islamic philosophers were also keenly interested in exploring the relationship between the spiritual and the so-called rational worlds.

Influenced by Plato and Aristotle, Ibn Sina (Avicenna, 980–1037) emphasized that prophecy could be based upon the intellect as well as upon the emotions. Another renowned philosopher, Ibn Rushd (Averroes, 1126–1198) also argued for the necessity of harmonizing revelation and reason. Ibn Rushd, known as "prince of the learned," was an Islamic judge who served in Córdoba and Seville and for a short time also acted as court physician. As a Muslim renaissance man, Ibn Rushd wrote on subjects as diverse as Aristotle, medicine, and astronomy.

By contrast, Muhammad al-Ghazali (1058–1111) argued that the spiritual, even mystical, qualities of revelation were far more important. Orthodox Muslim theologians generally agreed with al-Ghazali's approach, and Ibn Rushd's works were eventually labeled heretical. Indeed, al-Ghazali became one of the most widely read and cited of all philosophers in the Islamic/Arab world.

Islamic rulers were also enthusiastic patrons of scientific endeavors. Under the Abbasids, Baghdad became a major scientific center, much like Hellenistic Alexandria under Ptolemaic rulers. Translating voluminous materials into Arabic, Islamic scientists preserved both the Greek traditions and Persian and Indian texts. Arab mathematicians studied and enlarged upon Indian traditions of numerical reckoning, including the concept of zero. Arab scholars were particularly interested in geometry and astronomy and were especially advanced in the development of navigational devices such as the astrolabe. They also made substantial progress in the study of optics.

Arabic astronomers were familiar with the works of Indian and Persian scientists as well as treatises from the Greek. They were particularly influenced by the Ptolemaic (earth-centered) system and were keen observers of the

CONNECTIONS IN FAMILY

Women in Judaism, Christianity, and Islam

A man takes a wife and possesses her. She fails to please him because he finds something obnoxious about her, and he writes her a bill of divorcement, hands it to her, and sends her away from the house.
—The Torah, Deuteronomy 24:1

Let a woman learn in silence with full submission. I permit no woman to teach or to have authority over a man; she is to keep silent. For Adam was formed first, then Eve; and Adam was not deceived, but the woman was deceived and became a transgressor. Yet she will be saved through childbearing, provided they continue in faith and love and holiness, with modesty.
—Bible, 1 Timothy 2:11–15

Men are the protectors
And maintainers of women,
Because Allah has given
The one more (strength)
Than the other, and because
They support them from their means.
Therefore the righteous women
Are devoutly obedient, and guard
In (the husband's) absence
What Allah would have them guard.
—Qur'an 4:34

Under the three major monotheistic religions, men and women were equal in the sense that both could achieve spiritual salvation. However, the social order of all three societies was based on the superior status of men. The excerpts from Jewish, Christian, and Muslim holy texts above are examples of the patriarchal nature of all three religions and the dominance of men in leadership roles in both community and family life. Judaism and Islam both reflected the tribal mores and traditions of the eastern Mediterranean and Arabian Peninsula. As Christianity evolved, it was heavily influenced by the chauvinism prevalent in Hellenistic society. Paul's letter to Timothy, cited above, reflects the male-dominated society in which they lived.

Judaic and Islamic laws meticulously spelled out women's rights and obligations. Christian beliefs and traditions tended to be less legalistic, but as in Judaism and Islam, men were generally the only accepted interpreters of theological questions, religious practice, and worship. Only men held the leadership positions of rabbi, priest, or imam. More liberal interpretations of women's roles and their inclusion as ministers in many Protestant Christian denominations or as leaders for Jewish services evolved during the modern era.

In many respects, the introduction and spread of Islam under the Umayyad and Abbasid caliphates brought greater equality for women than they had known previously in Arabic society. The *Shari'a,* the system of laws and social standards based on the Qur'an and the Hadith (recorded sayings of the Prophet), formally specified the rights and limitations of women, particularly women's marital and financial rights, as noted above. Marriage in Islam was a civil contract, unlike the religious contract in Christianity. The Islamic contract specified a dowry given by the bridegroom, which remained the female's property. Muslim women also had the right to own property and to inherit. In contrast, until recent times, women in Western, predominantly Christian societies had few rights to property ownership, and upon marriage, a woman's property became her husband's.

Women were expected to be obedient to their husbands. Early Judaic society was polygamous; in Islam, a man was allowed up to four wives, provided he could treat them equally. However, a woman could specify in the marriage contract that her husband was not to take additional wives. In actual practice, few men could afford the financial burden imposed by multiple marriages. All three religions discouraged divorce; in Islam, specific laws regulated divorce proceedings that were easier for men than for women.

All three religions emphasized the role of women as mothers and as caregivers for the family. In Judaism, the religion of the children followed that of the mother. In Islam, children followed the religion of the father. In contrast, in Christianity, children followed the religion of either parent.

---

1. Since its inception, Islam has spread to many areas in which different legal and cultural traditions developed regarding women. After the 1979 Islamic revolution in Iran, the rights of Iranian women regarding social behavior and dress were strictly regulated; however, they had equal political rights and played an important role in the *majlis,* or Iranian parliament. Visit http://www.aiwusa.org/, http://www.womensnet.org.za/news/show.cfm?news_id=367, and http://www.uri.edu/artsci/wms/hughes/reform.htm. What were the nature of restrictions on Iranian women? How have these changed as a result of the elections in the 1990s and in present-day Iran?

heavens and climatic changes. New tables were developed on the basis of observations, particularly of solar and lunar eclipses. By 1259, in the reign of Hulagu, Muslim scientists had established what was perhaps the first professional observatory, with over a dozen full-time astronomers. Many stars are still known by their Arabic names, and remains of the Muslim observatory built at Samarkand by the grandson of Timurlane still exist.

In the field of medicine, Muslim doctors not only translated Greek medical writings, but also wrote treatises on problems as diverse as kidney stones, smallpox, nutrition, and the relationship between the psyche and the body. In the eleventh century, Ibn Sina, a prolific writer in scientific subjects as well as in philosophy, wrote a fourteen-volume work, *The Canon of Medicine,* and a twelve-volume one, *The Book of Healing.* In Seville, the doctor Abu L-Ala Ibn Zuhr or Avenzoar (d. 1130) was known for his clinical diagnoses and was far ahead of his time in advocating medical experimentation. The Ibn Zuhr family carried on the tradition of medicine for five generations. A son, Abu Marwan (d. 1161), a friend of Averroes, wrote a manual of medical technique.

Writing in both Hebrew and Arabic, Rabbi bin Maymun (Maimonides), became so famous that reputedly an Iraqi doctor traveled to Egypt to hear him lecture. The scientific achievements of Rabbi bin Maymun show the relatively open nature of Muslim society during this golden age. Likewise, the ease with which many Muslim intellectuals and scientists moved from place to place attests to the overall unity in culture, language, and society even in the far reaches of the Muslim world.

Hospitals also flourished under Islamic rule; Arabic speaking doctors became renowned for their work in ophthalmology, surgery, pharmacology, and human anatomy. Islamic inventors were also fascinated with mechanical devices. In the book *Automata,* or *The Book of Knowledge of Ingenious Mechanical Devices,* written about 1206, the inventor Ibn al-Razzaz al-Jaziri drew designs for dozens of whimsical contraptions. His inventions, reminiscent of Archimedes' creations in Hellenistic times, range from devices for pumping water to automatic washbasins. As none of these devices is extant, it is not known whether the designs were ever actually constructed or were merely the fantasies of a creative mind.

Islamic scientists also devoted considerable efforts to trying to turn base metals into valuable gold or silver (alchemy), just as did many in medieval Europe. Alchemy proved to be a scientific dead end, but in the process of experimenting, Islamic scientists gained some valuable skills.

Major Architectural Achievements

Early Islamic architects quite literally built on the foundations of Byzantine or Persian edifices, and they rapidly altered these earlier forms into a unique style. Mosques were initially constructed around a large open courtyard with a fountain where the faithful could wash before prayers. Simple, unadorned loggias and halls, used for community gatherings that helped bond the society together, surrounded the courtyard. In the central hall, a *mihrab* (prayer niche), pointed east toward Mecca, the direction for the faithful to pray. Minarets, or towers, for calling the faithful to prayer were constructed above the roof of the main halls.

As the Islamic communities grew richer, they ornamented their mosques and public buildings with elaborate designs, often based on various calligraphic renditions of verses from the Qur'an. The Great Mosque at Damascus and the Dome of the Rock and the al-Aqsa Mosque in Jerusalem are among the most important of the surviving early Islamic monuments. Built over an earlier Christian basilica, the Great Mosque in Damascus had a huge great hall and splendid mosaics depicting trees and village scenes. The Dome of the Rock in Jerusalem, completed in 691, is octagonal in plan and is decorated in sumptuous blue-glazed tiles and topped with a dome that was later covered in gold. Owing to decay caused by climatic extremes and destruction by conquest, few of the great architectural monuments built by the Abbasids in Baghdad remain.

Illustration from a Manuscript of al-Jaziri's *Automata.* This ingenious mechanical device measured the amount of blood lost by a patient during bloodletting. As the blood flowed into the bowl, the weight caused the pulley to move the two scribes, who then noted the amount on the tablet.

Robert Harding Picture Library

The Ibn Tulun Mosque. This mosque in Cairo, completed in 879, is typical in its large, open courtyard for the faithful. The small central building (left) contains a fountain used for ablutions before prayer. The square minaret (right) is similar to brick towers found in pre-Islamic Mesopotamia. Today the Ibn Tulun mosque is a quiet oasis in Cairo, one of the world's largest and busiest cities.

The Ibn Tulun mosque in Cairo is an outstanding example of Mesopotamian work. Ibn Tulun was appointed governor of Egypt in the mid-ninth century by the Abbasid caliph, but he soon established an independent regime. A great patron of the arts, Ibn Tulun financed numerous buildings and developments in Cairo. The Mosque bearing his name was built between 876 and 879 and is noted for the huge central courtyard—for centuries second in size only to the courtyard surrounding the Ka'bah in Mecca—and for its simplicity of design. The minaret of Ibn Tulun is unusual because it is square and has an outside staircase, recalling the ancient ziggurats of Mesopotamia.

The caliphs in Muslim Spain were also enthusiastic builders. Begun in 785, the Mosque at Córdoba underwent numerous alterations and additions, including the building of a Christian church in the center of the mosque following the Christian conquests of the fifteenth century. The Holy Roman Emperor Charles V, generally no lover of the Muslim world, is reputed to have said of this addition, "They have taken something extraordinary and made it ordinary." The Córdoba mosque has a huge central dome with a "forest" of horseshoe arches in two tiers in what was an original development in Islamic architecture. The Great Mosque at Qairawan (Kairouan) in Tunisia has a similar "forest" of marble columns within the main hall.

In Spain, the al-Hambra, or Red Castle, and the summer palace, the Generalife, are the most elaborate and best known of the Muslim monuments that still survive. Built during the fourteenth century, these pleasure palaces have highly sophisticated systems of water fountains, gardens, and ornately decorated and ornamented salons. They are indicative of the secular nature of the Nasrid regime; mosques were added almost as afterthoughts. Sporting lavish stucco decorations throughout and an outstanding "court of the lions," the al-Hambra, in particular, remains among the most famous and best-preserved examples of secular Islamic architecture.

Islamic Literature and the "Lively Arts"

In addition to their work in philosophy and theology, Muslim writers developed a lively literary tradition as well. Muslims universally regarded the Qur'an as the highest achievement in the Arabic language. Hence, early Arabic writers used the flowing cadences and style of the Qur'an as the model for both prose and poetry.

In pre-Islamic Arabia, poetry had long been regarded as the ultimate literary form, and long narrative poems were passed down through the generations by oral transmission. After the advent of Islam, a strong written tradition developed, and poets enjoyed lavish court patronage under both the Umayyads and the Abbasids. Thus poetry continued as the most highly esteemed creative form in Islamic societies.

Political and historical events were popular subjects for early Muslim writers. Poets were often employed to glorify conquests or to vilify political opponents of particular rulers. For example, the renowned classical Arabic poet, known by the irreverent pen-name al-Mutanabbi, or "The Pretender to Be a Prophet" (915–965), wrote in praise of one ruler:

Whither do you intend, great prince? We are the
herbs of the hills, and you are the clouds:
We are the ones time has been miserly towards
respecting you, and the days cheated of your presence.
Whether at war or at peace, you aim at the heights,
whether you tarry or hasten.
Would that we were your steeds when you ride forth,
and your tents when you alight!

Al-Mutanabbi's motto was, "Live honorably or die heroically."

Often written in the vernacular, love poems were also extremely popular. For example, the twelfth-century Córdoban poet Ibn Quzman, who came from a noble Arab family, was noted for mixing colloquial Andalusian language with classical Arabic. Ibn Quzman was a master storyteller who successfully blended irony, cynicism, and dramatic language in a manner similar to European writers such as Dante and Boccaccio.

In the Arab world, music was closely linked to poetic traditions, and under the court influences of the Umayyads and Abbasids, Arabic music gradually fused with the musical traditions of the Byzantines, the Syrians, and other Eastern empires. Caliphs patronized musicians and the very popular poet-singers. In Baghdad, Caliph Mamun had many Greek classical essays on music translated into Arabic; these formed the foundation for scholarly works on nomenclature and musical modes.

Based largely on quarter tones, Arabic music stressed melodies with complex nuances and ornamentation. A number of Arabic instruments influenced Western instruments. The lute was derived from the *'ud,* a pear-shaped stringed instrument, various percussion instruments from the drums, and the medieval rebec from the *rababah,* a single-stringed instrument played with a bow. Arabic musicians also played a wide variety of flutes and the *ganun,* a trapezoid-shaped stringed instrument similar to the zither. Musicians in Spain incorporated both Arabic and Western musical forms into their work; later, returning crusaders also brought Arabic musical instruments and songs back to Europe.

In the Spanish courts of Córdoba and Granada, singers elaborated romantic themes, which were then copied and

The Great Mosque, Córdoba. The Great Mosque (left) was begun by the Umayyad prince Abd al-Rahman I. The horseshoe pillars form a forest of marble and decorated stucco. By placing the arches in two layers, one above the other, the architects achieved the illusion of greater height. Similar horseshoe designs were used in the mosque of the puritanical Islamic ruler Ibn Tumert (right) in the remote, high Atlas mountains in present-day Morocco. The Córdoba mosque has been enlarged several times and remains one of the outstanding architectural achievements of the Islamic world.

© Paul Almasy/Corbis

Courtesy of Janice Terry

The Court of the Lions at the al-Hambra. This courtyard is a cool, shady spot that reverberates with the sound of falling water from the fountain. The al-Hambra complex is the epitome of lavish court architecture in Islamic Spain.

expanded by the romantic troubadours in Europe. "Moorish" traditions, or musical traditions transferred from Morocco, are still found in the popular flamenco music of Spanish Gypsies. Depictions of musicians and dancing groups were also popular subjects for artists and potters in the Iberian Peninsula and Persia (present-day Iran).

During the Islamic golden age, potters were well known for their sophisticated glazes, particularly the lusterware technique. Because Muslim tenets disparaged the depiction of the human form as encouraging idolatry, Muslim artists became experts in the application of geometric patterns and "arabesques," ornate designs of plant forms in interlaced patterns, and in the use of Qur'anic inscriptions or other written forms to decorate their creations. The beautiful and elaborate penned writing called calligraphy was a highly prized skill that was amply rewarded by court patrons. Persian influences during the Abbasid caliphate prompted depictions of human forms in manuscripts and in painted miniatures portraying court life or favorite legends and stories. Poetry and architecture, however, remained the most esteemed artistic endeavors.

The Crusades

*O race of Franks . . . race chosen and beloved by God! From the confines of Jerusalem and from Constantinople a grievous report has gone forth . . . that a race from the kingdom of Persians, an accursed race, a race utterly alienated from God . . . has invaded the lands of [Eastern] Christians and has depopulated them by the sword, pillage, and fire. . . . The labor of avenging these wrongs [is placed] . . . upon you. . . . Enter upon the road to the Holy Sepulchre; wrest that land from the wicked race, and subject it to yourselves. . . .**

*Robert the Monk, "The Speech of Pope Urban II at Clermont," trans. D. C. Munro, *Translations and Reprints from the Original Sources of European History,* rev. ed. Series I, vol. 1, no. 2 (Philadelphia: University of Pennsylvania Press, 1902), pp. 5–8.

As Pope Urban II gave his rousing speech in the city of Clermont, France, in 1095, the crowd shouted, "It is the will of God! It is the will of God!" Much to Urban's surprise, his call for the Christian world to unite and attack the Muslim "infidel" in the Holy Lands received a tremendous response. Many devoted believers were deeply committed to securing the holy sites for the Christian world. Urban's speech, given in response to an appeal from the Byzantine emperor for troops to assist him against the Muslims, helped initiate the Crusades, a series of Christian military expeditions against the Muslims in the eastern Mediterranean. The Crusades worsened European-Muslim relations by intensifying religious fanaticism and fostering long-lasting, deep-seated cultural prejudices. They also had a profound effect on East-West commerce. They initially disrupted trade patterns, but eventually boosted Western desire for Eastern commodities, a desire that would strongly affect the history of the world in the centuries to come.

Crusading Zeal

There were four main reasons for the Crusades. First, the pope hoped to unite the entire eastern Mediterranean and the divided Christian faith under the banner of the Latin church. Second, the Italian city-states, with their large navies, hoped for commercial gains and were therefore keen supporters of the Crusades. Third, the Byzantine Empire was in a severe decline and could no longer act as a buffer between the Muslim East and the

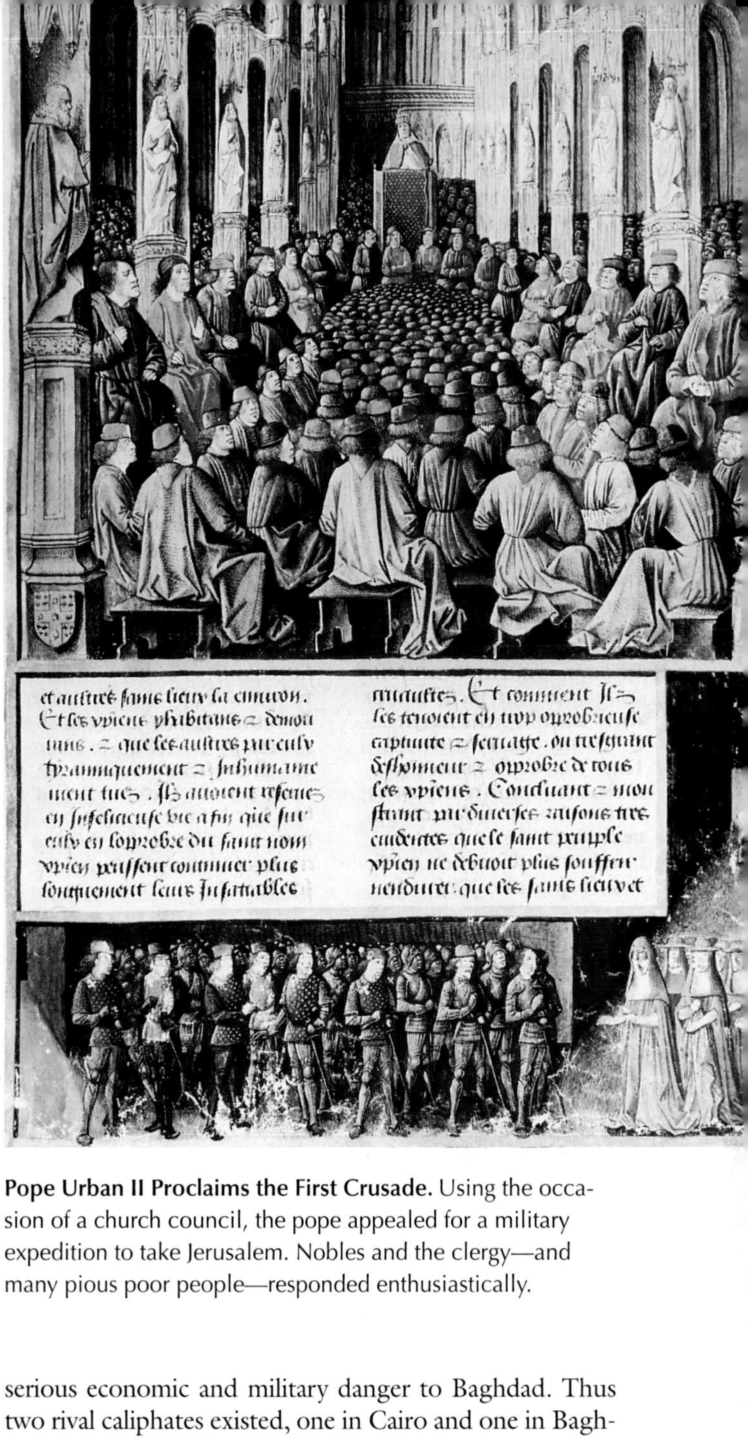

Pope Urban II Proclaims the First Crusade. Using the occasion of a church council, the pope appealed for a military expedition to take Jerusalem. Nobles and the clergy—and many pious poor people—responded enthusiastically.

Catholic West. Finally, the Seljuk Turks, declining in military power, were no longer able to ensure the safety of the Christian pilgrims visiting the holy sites.

By 1097 some 30,000 knights, primarily Frankish and German, were ready to conquer the "infidel" and secure the Holy Land for Christendom while reaping their share of booty and glory. They were preceded by a Peasants' Crusade, a band of land-hungry peasants who journeyed east, only to have their hopes deflated in an alien land; the survivors quickly returned home.

The Divided Muslim World

Initially, the crusaders met with military success largely because of the political weakness of the Muslim/Arab world at the end of the eleventh century. The pressures of the religio-political schisms that had arisen within the Abbasid Empire in the tenth and eleventh centuries had undermined the strength of the Muslims to resist outside attacks. Local rulers in North Africa and central Asia all at one time or another pulled free of Abbasid control while rival Turkish and Iranian forces usurped the power of the Abbasid caliphs. Under the *atabeg* system, slaves (atabegs) acted as tutors to the royal princes and subsequently rose to key positions; often, however, the one-time slaves overthrew their former masters. The atabegs then hired new slaves as tutors for their sons, and the entire system repeated itself. The atabegs and Turkish mercenaries often joined forces to take control from the Abbasid rulers. In 861, Caliph Mutawakkil (reigned 847–861) was assassinated by Turkish mercenaries, who continued to put puppet caliphs in power. At one time, three blind former Abbasid caliphs were reduced to begging on the streets of Baghdad.

By 945, following the takeover of Baghdad by the Iranian-based Buyids in 932, the Abbasid caliphate had effectively ceased to exist. Although Baghdad technically remained the center of the caliphate, the empire was increasingly ruled by various Persian and Turkish forces. Just as strong rulers in European nations competed for control or dominance over the papacy, so, too, did regional rivals within West Asia and Africa compete for control over the caliphate.

Ultimately, the rival Fatimid caliphate in Cairo challenged the preeminence of the caliphate in Baghdad. The Fatimids, adherents of the Shi'i branch of Islam, claimed descent from the seventh Imam and Fatima, the Prophet's daughter and wife of Ali. After becoming the dominant military force in North Africa, the Fatimids conquered Egypt in the second half of the tenth century. They moved their capital to the newly built city of Cairo and from there proceeded to take southern Syria by 969, thereby gaining control over two of the key trading routes in the Muslim world. They then established bases in northern Syria and Damascus and subsequently posed a serious economic and military danger to Baghdad. Thus two rival caliphates existed, one in Cairo and one in Baghdad, each dedicated to the eradication of the other.

Fatimid economic strength was based primarily on the sale of agricultural products and gold, purchased by European merchants. Under the Fatimids, Cairo became an economic and cultural center. Great builders, the Fatimids used the money from agricultural productivity and commerce to construct numerous mosques, public buildings, and, in particular, al-Azhar University. Established in 972, al-Azhar is the oldest active university in the world and has been a major theological center for the training of Islamic theologians until the present.

With the expansion of the Seljuk Turks out of Anatolia (present-day Turkey) in 1037, the fragmented political situation in West Asia became even more complex. The Seljuks replaced the old order in Baghdad with their own form of loosely associated kingdoms, each allied to

LIVES AND TIMES ACROSS CULTURES

Schools and Universities

In early societies, education of the youth was the responsibility of parents, who generally trained their children from very early ages in the skills and crafts that they themselves followed. But as societies evolved, the education of youth became more systematized and formalized. Ruling families and wealthy elites often hired private tutors to teach their children, particularly sons, reading, writing, mathematics, martial arts, and other skills needed by future leaders. In the Roman empire, Pliny the Younger put up "matching funds" for a school in his hometown so that students would not have to travel far from home.

In ancient Egypt, as well as in the Christian and Islamic worlds, temples, churches, or mosques were centers for formalized education. The curriculum stressed theology, religious law, and spiritual matters. In Islamic societies this involved the memorization of the entire Qur'an, often at a very early age. One of the first universities in the world, al-Azhar, was established by Islamic rulers of Egypt in the 900s. Its original goal was to train young men in theology and legal studies. Over the centuries al-Azhar has remained one of the preeminent universities in the Islamic world and its curriculum has been expanded to educate present-day students, including women, in a broad range of skills, including engineering and medicine.

Formal education was generally reserved for boys. Some societies, as in ancient Greece, actively discouraged teaching girls to read and write. In most societies only girls from privileged families were educated at home, and the curriculum often focused on the so-called feminine skills of weaving, music, and household management. Corporal punishment was common; flogging was the traditional means of punishment in Europe, and the bastino, a whip cracked over the bare feet of students, was used in much of Africa and western Asia.

a specific family. This governmental structure contributed to further political disarray. After conquering most of Persia and Mesopotamia, from 1084 to 1117, the Seljuks moved into Syria, where they clashed with the Fatimids.

Acting out of self-preservation, the local rulers aligned with whatever side appeared the stronger at the time. To add to their problems the Fatimids were plagued by the same difficulties the Abbasid Empire had faced; namely, numerous mercenary elements, particularly Berbers, within the army and a firmly entrenched atabeg system. The Fatimids' war against Byzantium in 1055 further weakened the Fatimids.

In 1060 the Mamluks, former Turkish slaves from central Asia, rebelled in Cairo, hastening the collapse of the Fatimid dynasty. That rebellion provided the signal for separatist movements throughout the empire. Syria became the battleground of local rival forces. Leaders in Damascus played off Berber forces within the army who, in turn, threatened the Fatimid rulers. Religious minorities, including the Druze, Maronites, and Alawites, proceeded to create their own governments in Syria. In present-day Lebanon and Syria, these minorities continue to be political forces and sometimes rivals for power. Local emirs, whose feudal domains resembled those in Europe, also sought to expand at each other's expense.

The Seljuks sometimes persecuted and extracted heavy taxes from Christian Arab minorities—a reason why some Arab Christians initially were eager to assist the crusaders. European Christian pilgrims to the holy places in Palestine were also poorly treated by the Seljuks, who charged high tariffs and made it difficult for the pilgrims to enter. Under the Seljuks, merchants also found it increasingly difficult to conduct business. Torn by civil strife, the area became unsafe for travelers and merchants. Those who were brave enough to attempt the journey inland were often heavily taxed in every village; each emir wanted to obtain his share of the wealth that passed through his area. Lacking any central control, each local ruler was free to do as he pleased.

By the late eleventh century, on the eve of the Crusades, Syria was in the throes of political collapse and economic stagnation. The Byzantine Empire and the ambitious mercantile Italian city-states had already taken advantage of this political weakness to attack along the frontiers of the Islamic Empire. Thus, when the call for the Crusades went out and it became obvious that the crusaders had a good chance of acquiring footholds along the eastern Mediterranean, the Italian city-states were prepared—for a price—to offer their services to the crusaders. Italian merchants, ready to deal with Christians or Muslims, soon followed the knights.

The Crusader States

Moving into Asia, the heavily armed crusaders met little unified opposition. Wearing red crosses on their chests, they assembled in Constantinople, crossed Anatolia, and reached Antioch in the fall of 1097. In June 1098, with the aid of the large Christian Armenian population, they captured the city. After a brief respite they moved quickly down the coast and took Jerusalem in 1099. The crusaders massacred the civilian population of Jerusalem—mostly eastern Christians and Jews. It was reported that human blood ran knee-deep. Many Jews were herded into the central synagogue, which was then burned to the ground. Following this massacre, the knights gathered at the Church of the Holy Sepulchre where, after some debate, they proclaimed Godfrey of Bouillon, a French nobleman, as king. Godfrey continued the war against the Muslims and extended Christian-held territory. About 3,000 knights remained around Jerusalem, more settled in Antioch, and a small group in Edessa. Successive European rulers continued to enlarge their territory. By 1123, the crusader states reached their zenith, controlling the Syrian coastal regions and Palestine. However, people in the nearby predominantly Muslim and Arab provinces in Arabia and Iraq were not greatly affected by the Crusades and viewed the wars as frontier skirmishes along the fringes of the Islamic world.

In the areas controlled by the crusaders, the ruling barons organized their states into feudal domains based on familiar European patterns. Each fief, granted to favorites and to those knights who had rendered particular

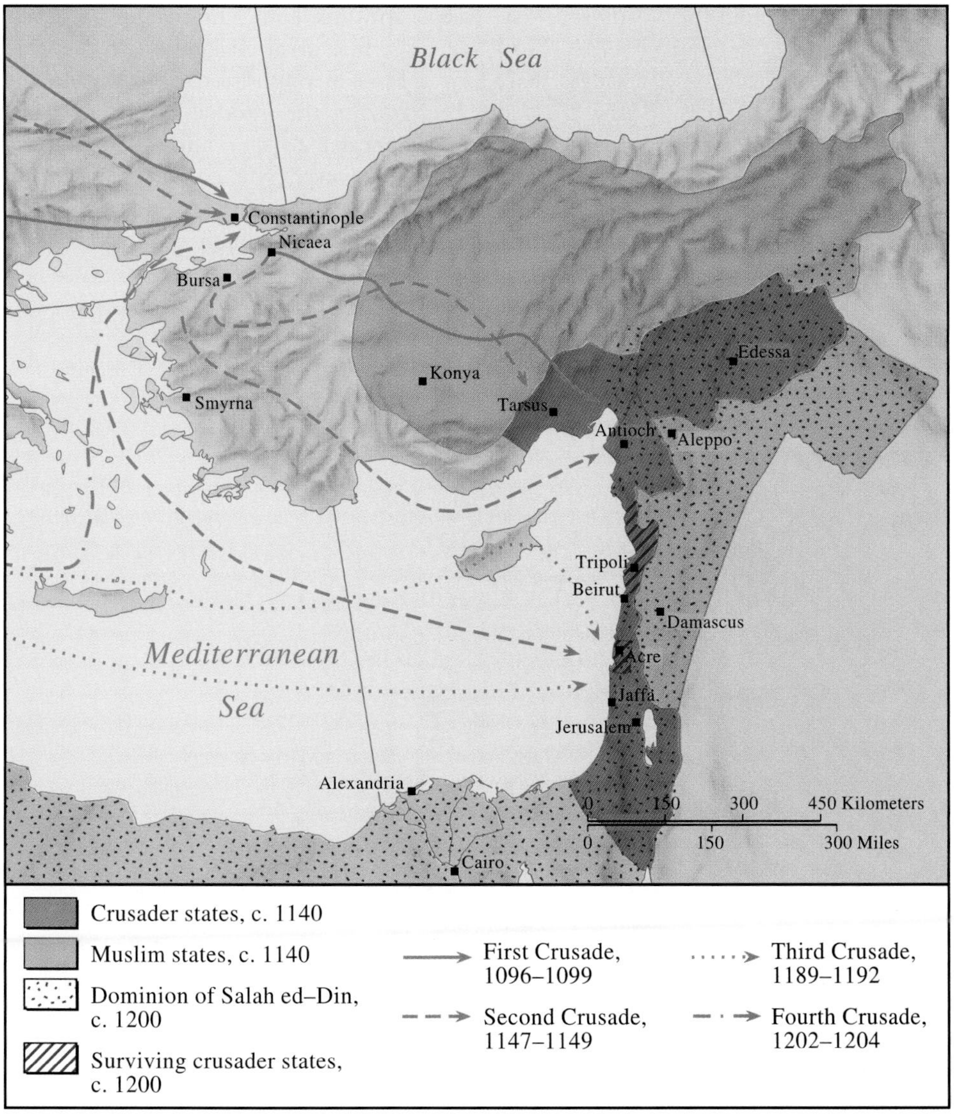

Map 8.2 The Crusader States and Empire of Salah ed-Din. Although the first two Crusades relied on overland routes, later crusaders traveled east primarily by sea. At their greatest extent, the crusaders' holdings formed only a small coastal strip amid extensive Islamic territories, and by 1190 they were rather easily retaken by Salah ed-Din.

service for the crown, became more or less an independent entity. The controlling barons were only loosely tied to each other by the common threat of attack by the Muslims. Each lord was responsible for the defense of his own land, but on the occasion of a severe attack, the lords united forces. To protect their territories, the crusaders built imposing fortresses or castles, which were imitations of those in Europe. Scattered on hilltops in West Asia, many of these still survive as the main physical remains of the Crusades.

The European feudal system was superimposed upon the existing Arab village system. As the two structures closely resembled each other, the native population was little affected. Under both methods, the people rendered tribute to a lord or emir; they also had specific military obligations to fulfill in time of war.

Under the crusaders, agriculture remained the backbone of the state economy; cereals and fruits were the main crops. The crusaders attempted to enlarge the already existing industries such as sugar refining, soap making, and glassblowing. Jewelry making continued to flourish in Jerusalem.

Despite their apparently sound economy, the crusader states were in a precarious position. Both the church and the military orders, such as the Templars, were exempt from taxation. In addition, the various Italian city-states, which often provided both the financial backing and sea transport for the crusaders, enjoyed special extraterritorial rights. The small crusader states were dependent upon these Italian city-states for protection and for banking and finance. Indeed, the Italians were the major financial beneficiaries of the Crusades. Finally, the crusaders expended considerable energy and money on fighting one another and in repelling attacks from Muslim/Arab forces. The pressures of internal divisions, coupled with external threats from the surrounding Muslim territories, made it impossible for the Frankish crusader states, hemmed in by their geographic position, to have either security or a sound economy.

Muslim Counterattacks

The Muslim community did not sit back and let the crusaders have free political and commercial movement. Each petty emir fought tenaciously to keep his sovereignty. Strong warriors, often of Turkish origins, emerged to counterattack against the crusader kingdom. Zengi (reigned 1127–1146), the Turkish emir of Mosul (in present-day Iraq), and his son Nur-ed-Din (reigned 1146–1174) were the first great challengers to the crusaders. Faced by a Muslim opposition from the north, the crusaders, recognizing the internal divisions within the Muslim world, appealed to the Fatimid kingdom in Egypt for assistance. However, Nur ed-Din managed to outmaneuver both the Fatimids and the crusaders and succeeded in placing one of his own supporters, Salah ed-Din

Quala'at al-Husn (Krak des Chevaliers). When the crusaders captured this old Arab fortress in present-day Syria, they enlarged it along the lines of European military structures. The vast outer wall protected the castle, a church, and numerous other buildings. Situated on high ground above surrounding valleys, the castle, in its ideal defensive position, can be seen from miles away.

Coping with Rude Franks

*Everyone who is a fresh emigrant from the Frankish lands is ruder in character than those who have become acclimatized and have held long association with the Moslems. Whenever I visited Jerusalem I always entered the Aqsa Mosque, beside which stood a small mosque which the Franks had converted into a church. When I used to enter the Aqsa Mosque, which was occupied by the Templars, who were my friends, the Templars would evacuate the little adjoining mosque so that I might pray in it. One day I entered this mosque, repeated the first formula, "Allah is great," and stood up in the act of praying, upon which one of the Franks rushed on me, got hold of me and turned my face eastward saying, "This is the way thou shouldst pray!" A group of Templars hastened to him, seized him and repelled him from me. I resumed my prayer. The same man, while the others were otherwise busy, rushed once more on me. The Templars again came in to him and expelled him. They apologized to me, saying, "This is a stranger who has only recently arrived from the land of the Franks and he has never before seen anyone praying except eastward." Thereupon I said to myself, "I have had enough prayer." So I went out and have ever been surprised at the conduct of this devil of a man, at the change in the color of his face, his trembling and his sentiment at the sight of one praying toward the qibla [toward Mecca].**

Muslims called the crusaders "Franks," or those from the west or foreigners. To the average Muslim the Franks seemed remote and even barbarous. The Templars were a Christian religious and military order created to protect visiting pilgrims. In his autobiography (published as *Memoirs of an Arab-Syrian Gentleman)* Usamah Ibn-Munquidh wrote a highly personal account of his relations with the crusader knights; his memoirs are an insightful look at the clash of two cultures. In the above excerpt, Usamah Ibn-Munquidh describes his encounter with some knights when he attempted to pray at the al-Aqsa mosque in Jerusalem.

*William H. McNeill and Marilyn Robinson Waldman, eds., *The Islamic World* (New York: Oxford University Press, 1973; reprint, Chicago: University of Chicago Press, 1983), p. 188.

(Saladin, reigned 1174–1193) in charge of Egypt. Salah ed-Din, of Kurdish origins, moved swiftly to unite the Muslims and to lead the attack against the crusaders. His actions ended the Fatimid Shi'i domination and returned Egypt and the surrounding territory to Sunni rule. The battle of Hittin on July 4, 1187, ended any chance of crusader expansion into the heartland of the Arab world. On the offensive, Salah ed-Din continued to attack the crusaders' strongholds and eventually took Jerusalem in 1187.

The loss of Jerusalem provoked the Third Crusade, which attracted the flower of European knighthood, including King Richard the Lion-Hearted of England, Holy Roman Emperor Frederick I (Barbarossa), and Philip II of France. After Frederick drowned in Asia Minor in 1190, the other two kings quarreled, and Philip returned to France. Although Richard secured a truce that allowed Christians access to Jerusalem, the Third Crusade failed to defeat Salah ed-Din militarily. Salah ed-Din often pardoned his enemies, let captured prisoners go free, and provided lavish hospitality for Christian leaders. His honesty and chivalry earned him the respect of both Muslims and Christian crusaders.

The failure of the Third Crusade foreshadowed the demise of the crusader states. As Christian control over the Holy Land lessened, Pope Innocent III called for new attacks on Egypt, the Muslim power base since Salah ed-Din. The pope hoped to regain the holy places and to reunite Eastern Orthodox and Roman Catholic Christians. When the Venetians demanded exorbitant fares for transporting the Christian armies, however, the crusader knights agreed to conquer Zara, a city on the Adriatic coast, for the Venetians. In spite of the pope's arguments that Christians should not attack other Christians, the crusaders took Zara in 1202. In 1204, when a deposed and disgruntled Byzantine emperor promised them enormous payments if they would restore him to his throne in Constantinople, the crusaders seized the Byzantine capital. When the emperor failed to deliver on his promises, the crusaders looted the city and established the short-lived Latin Empire of Constantinople (1204–1261).

At Grips with the Infidel

*I was at my father's side during the battle of Hittin, the first I had ever seen. When the king of the Franj found himself on the hill, he and his men launched a fierce attack that drove our own troops back to the place where my father was standing. I looked at him. He was saddened; he frowned and pulled nervously at his beard. Then he advanced, shouting "Satan must not win!" The Muslims again assaulted the hill. When I saw the Franj retreat under the pressure of our troops, I screamed with joy, "We have won!" But the Franj attacked again with all their might, and once again our troops found themselves grouped around my father. Now he urged them into the attack once more, and they forced the enemy to retreat up the hill. Again I screamed, 'We have beaten them!' But my father turned to me and said, "Silence! We will have crushed them only when that tent on the hill has fallen." Before he had time to finish his sentence, the king's tent collapsed. The sultan then dismounted, bowed down and thanked God, weeping for joy.**

In this firsthand account, Salah ed-Din's son describes the fierce battle of Hittin, where his father defeated the crusaders.

*Amin Maalouf, *The Crusades through Arab Eyes* (New York: Schocken Books, 1987), pp. 192–193.

Although the crusaders ostensibly reunified the Christian world, in fact they embittered the Eastern Orthodox Christians. The schism, or division, between Eastern Orthodox churches and the Roman Catholic church widened, and persists today, despite twentieth-century attempts by the Roman Catholic popes and Eastern patriarchs to heal the wounds.

The attack on Constantinople discredited both the papacy and the crusading enterprise. It also crippled the Byzantine Empire so badly that the Byzantines proved unable to withstand later Ottoman Turkish expansion into southeastern Europe.

Renewed political divisions in the Muslim world after Salah ed-Din's death in 1193 enabled the crusaders to reestablish control over much of the territory they had lost. By the mid-thirteenth century, however, continued attacks by the Mamluk rulers from Egypt placed the crusader states once again on the defensive. After a protracted defense, the last crusader territory, Acre, fell in 1291.

Cultural and Commercial Exchanges

Although the Crusades were aggressive militaristic ventures, they produced a number of long-lasting cultural exchanges. The Muslim world introduced the crusaders to a wide range of new foods and luxury items, including silks and brocades, perfumes, and soaps. Some crusaders became so attracted to the different way of life that they joined it, intermarrying and becoming assimilated with the indigenous populations. Those who returned to Europe introduced the new commodities, particularly textiles, to their homelands. In a comparable fashion, republican Roman soldiers who had served in the Hellenistic East brought aspects of that life home.

Seeing the demand for these items, the Italian traders were not content to confine their activities simply to supplying the crusader states; instead, they sought to establish direct trade with the whole Muslim world. Such contacts with the Muslims gave the Italians a chance to tap into the land and sea trade routes to India, central Asia, and East Asia.

Eyewitnesses related with some surprise that trade continued across the frontiers even in times of open warfare. Salah ed-Din encouraged this trade, and various treaties between the Muslim state and the crusaders ensured free passage of goods. Even after the crusaders were ousted from the region, the Italian merchants continued their lucrative trade, which profited the Italian city-states and provided the economic basis for the artistic achievements of the Italian Renaissance.

The most important item of trade between the East and West were spices, especially cinnamon from India, cardamon from Aden, and ginger and pepper from Indonesia. Although the crusader states raised cotton for export, Egyptian cotton was also in high demand, as were Egyptian linen and dates. Precious stones, particularly coral from Ceylon and pearls from the Persian Gulf, were desirable luxury items. Porcelain from China was shipped to Egypt via Aden. Silks and brocades manufactured in Syria were major trading items, as were metal goods from Mosul and Cairo. Damascus was a key center for industry and commerce and profited as a stopping point for pilgrims on their way to Mecca. Jerusalem remained important solely for its religious monuments and as a seat of government.

On the negative side, the era of the Crusades intensified religious animosities between the Christian and Muslim worlds; to some extent these have persisted until the present. The Crusades also fostered further religious disputes between Roman Catholic and Eastern Orthodox Christians. As previously noted, many indigenous eastern Christians suffered persecutions at the hands of both Latin

Christians and the previously usually tolerant Muslims, who came to view them as collaborators with the crusaders. In actuality, in spite of having been under Muslim control for over 400 years, nearly half the Arab population along the eastern Mediterranean was Christian when the crusaders arrived. Outraged by the excesses and massacres committed by the crusaders, many eastern Christians subsequently converted to Islam; still others converted to avoid persecution by zealous Muslim leaders. As a consequence, the Crusades ironically proved instrumental in making the eastern Mediterranean predominantly Muslim.

The Mongol Conquest of Eurasia

Then in 1206, the Year of the Tiger, after Chinggis had unified the people of the felt-walled tents, they assembled at the source of the Onon river. There they hoisted the white banner with nine pennants and gave Chinggis the title "Khan". . . . And having finally imposed order on the Mongolian tribes, Chinggis Khan issued a decree:

"I wish to bestow favours on all those who have served me in establishing this nation. I shall make you all commanders of units of a thousand men."

So he decreed, naming ninety-five trusted companions to command ninety-five thousand men. Then he issued a further decree:

"I have appointed ninety-five men—including my sons-in-law—to be commanders over ninety-five thousand.". . .

*And he added: "At the time when I, protected by Eternal Heaven, was setting the entire nation in order, you were my eyes and ears. The entire nation shall be divided between my mother, my brothers, my sons and myself. The people of the felt-walled tents shall be divided and the people of the wooden-doored dwellings shall be separated according to their tribes. And let no one presume to countermand my orders!"**

*Urgunge Onon, trans., *Chinggis Khan: The Golden History of The Mongols,* rev. by Sue Bradbury (London: Folio Society, 1993), pp. 102–103.

This passage recounts how Genghis Khan became ruler of all Mongols in 1206, organized his men into thousand-man units, and rewarded his faithful lieutenants and relatives with commands and the promise of a share of his conquests. Genghis Khan was one of history's most feared conquerors—his name conjured up terror through much of Europe and Asia. The path of the Mongol army in the thirteenth century was strewn

Map 8.3 The Mongol Empire under Genghis Khan. Genghis Khan and his immediate successors conquered a huge empire that stretched from Korea to the shores of the Black Sea. The conquests brought the Mongols unprecedented wealth, but at the expense of terrible destruction and millions of slaughtered victims.

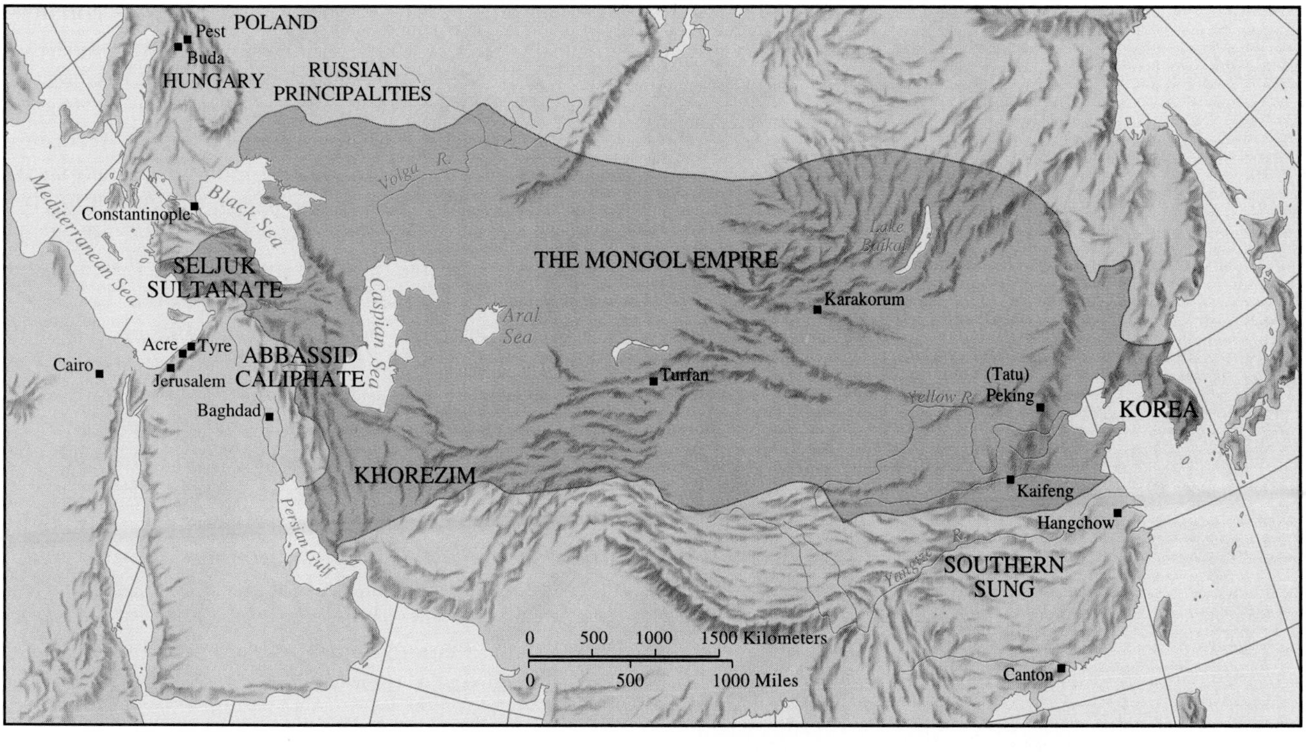

with unprecedented death, devastation, and suffering. Erupting out of the North Asian steppes, the Mongols conquered China, central Asia, Persia, and Russia, creating the largest land empire in Eurasian history. As a result, to this day, Mongols hold him in the deepest reverence. Mongol legend says that he will return and once again lead them to greatness.

Genghis Khan, the World Conqueror, 1155–1227

The Mongols originally roamed the steppes south of Lake Baikal in present-day Russia. They hunted and herded and, when possible, raided the settled peoples nearby for loot. Mongol custom dictated that men obtain wives from outside their own tribe. A man could have as many wives as he could afford but accorded preeminence to the first wife. Custom prescribed that the heir marry all his late father's wives except his own mother, and that brothers marry their widowed sisters-in-law. Tribal wars to gain territory, seize cattle and horses, and capture slaves and wives were endemic. Mongols worshiped a great god and spirits; shamans or priests interpreted the spirit world for them. Until the thirteenth century, the Mongols had no written language.

Genghis's given name was Temuchin; he was the oldest son of a minor Mongol chief. At age nine, his father took him to the camp of his mother's tribe to arrange a marriage with the chief's daughter, named Borte, then ten years old. En route home, his father was poisoned by an enemy and died. The next few years were full of hardships for Temuchin, his mother, and brothers, because they were cast out by the dead chief's clan. He was hardened by the struggle of these years, claimed his bride, and, with his father-in-law's support, began to rebuild his tribe.

Genghis Khan. Genghis Khan was a powerfully built man with alert eyes and a luxuriant beard, as seen in this idealized portrait by a Chinese artist.

The Hulton/Deutsch Collection

Soon after his marriage, an enemy raided Temuchin's camp and captured his wife and animals. By the time he rescued her from her abductor, she was the mother of an infant boy. Temuchin named him Juji which means "guest" in Mongol, an indication of his doubtful paternity. Borte bore him three more sons. They and Juji would be their father's principal heirs. Temuchin so distinguished himself as a leader in war and in organization that he was acclaimed Genghis Khan (Universal Ruler) by the Mongol tribes in 1203.

It was Genghis's good fortune that the traditionally powerful states that surrounded Mongol territory were suffering from internal divisions at the time of his rise. The Chin Empire, to which Genghis was initially vassal, was situated to the south of the Mongols. Since its victory against the Sung in the mid-twelfth century, the Chin had ruled all North China. Chin prosperity peaked in the late twelfth century, the result of a succession of good harvests and the heavy tribute in silks and silver that it received from the Southern Sung government annually. Its decline began in 1194 when the Yellow River burst its dikes, flooded large areas, and then changed its channel to the sea. Years of famine followed. Government currency manipulations added to the economic chaos. By the thirteenth century, the Chin dynasty was in irreversible decline. Because the Chin were conquering nomads themselves, they had no deep roots in China, and despite partial Sinicization did not enjoy the full support of their Chinese subjects. Even in decline, however, the Chin remained a major power. According to the census of 1195, the Chin Empire had a tax-paying population of 48.5 million and an army of over 500,000, including 120,000 cavalry troops. In addition, the Chin possessed impressive defenses in the Great Wall and numerous heavily fortified cities.

Two other states bordered Mongol lands, the Kara-Khitai to the west and the Hsi Hsia to the southwest. The Persian Empire and the caliphate of the Abbasids were located further west. Both had been weakened by domestic dissent and by the schism and struggles between the Sunni and the Shi'i branches of Islam.

Fired by ambition to rule the world, and backed by his warriors, Genghis began his conquests. Even though the Mongol population was minuscule compared with that of the opposing states, the Mongols' control of the interior line of communications prevented their enemies from coordinating their defenses or forming alliances

Mongol Captives. These prisoners are placed in cangues (neck pillories) as they are led off by their captors. Mongols massacred millions of their captives, drove them in front of their assault troops as moat fillers and cannon fodder, or enslaved them.

with one another. Nevertheless, Genghis Khan's victories over all his enemies were spectacular feats of generalship.

Genghis began by attacking the Hsi Hsia, a Buddhist nation situated in northwestern China next to the borders of Tibet, and the weakest of his three neighbors. Its people were proto-Tibetans called Tanguts. He had little difficulty ravaging the Hsi Hsia countryside, but suffered considerable losses at first because his soldiers had no experience in storming walled towns. Accounts say that Genghis took his first walled town by cunning and ruse. He sent a message to the defending commander that he would raise the siege and retire in return for a ransom of 1,000 cats and 10,000 swallows. The astonished defendants complied. Then Genghis ordered his men to tie tufts of cotton wool to the tails of the animals, set them afire and release them. The frightened birds flew to their nests and the cats ran back to their lairs, and in so doing setting innumerable blazes in the town. Amidst the resulting confusion, the Mongols stormed the walls and captured the town. Later, Genghis used more traditional methods to take walled towns by employing siege engineers whom he had captured. In 1209 the Hsi Hsia surrendered, acknowledged Genghis as overlord, and agreed to pay him tribute.

In 1211 Genghis Khan declared war on his next enemy, the Chin. His army of 150,000 ravaged the northern Chinese countryside, leaving famine and pestilence in its wake. Only the few towns that surrendered without resistance were spared. Captured civilians were driven in front of Mongol troops as cannon fodder or as filling for moats. Any town that resisted was razed and its people put to the sword. In six months, ninety towns lay in ruins. The Chin capital, located near present-day Beijing (Peking), fell in 1215 and was systematically looted and then torched. It burnt for a month and then lay in complete ruin. The booty was sent to Mongolia by caravan. "Useful" men such as artists, craftsmen, engineers, astrologers, and philosophers were spared but taken captive. Some women became slaves or concubines; all others were massacred.

One of the captives from the Chin court who was spared was the scholarly Yeliu Chu-ts'ai. He was a nomad by descent but was a fervent admirer of Chinese culture. A professional astrologer, he became a powerful advisor in the Mongol court. He had the unique distinction of successfully dissuading Genghis from committing some of his worst atrocities. A typical nomad, Genghis hated and despised sedentary people and decided to order the extermination of all people in conquered northern China so that their farmland could be turned into pasture for Mongol horses. Chu-ts'ai made a calculation of the annual taxes the victims paid and noted that the sum was greater than could be produced by the same land used for grazing. The appeal to Genghis's greed succeeded, and the people were spared.

Mongol Terror

"The Tangqut are a powerful, good and courageous people, but they are fickle. Slaughter them and take what you need to give to the army."

That summer Chinggis Khan pitched his camp on the Snowy mountain. He sent soldiers out against those of the Tangqut people who had rebelled against him. . . . The whole tribe was completely wiped out. Then he showed favour to Bo'orchy and Muqali, saying: "Take what you want, until you can carry no more. . . . Make their fine sons follow behind you, holding your falcons. Bring up their daughters to arrange your wives' skirts". . . .

By plundering the Tangqut people, by making their leader [who had surrendered to the Mongols] change his name [to humiliate him] before he suffocated him, Chinggis Khan destroyed the mothers and fathers of the Tangqut even to the seed of their seed, until they were no more.

Then he issued a decree saying:

"While we eat, we will talk of our victory, how we finished them off and saw them die. And we will say to ourselves: 'That is the end. They are no more.'"

*Because the Tangqut people made promises they did not keep, Chinggis Khan had hunted them down a second time. On his return, on the 12th day of the 7th lunar month in the Year of the Pig, 1227, he died and was taken up to Heaven, and many of the Tangqut slaves were given to the Lady Yisui [one of his wives who accompanied him on his last expedition].**

This is the chilling account of how Genghis Khan dealt with the Tanguts who had dared rise up against the Mongols after surrendering to them. Genghis Khan used terror and extreme brutality as a means of psychological warfare, killing millions in the process.

*Urgunge Onon, trans., *Chinggis Khan: The Golden History of The Mongols*, rev. by Sue Bradbury (London: Folio Society, 1993), pp. 152–154.

The remnant Chin government entrenched itself in the well-defended city of Kaifeng and the war dragged on. After conquering Manchuria in 1216 and Korea in 1218, Genghis put deputies in charge of the Chin campaign and turned west. In 1218, he destroyed the Buddhist kingdom called Kara-Khitai to unblock his route west. After annexing the territory of the Kara-Khitai, Genghis's empire touched that of the Khorezim Empire, which included modern Persia and part of Afghanistan and central Asia and was populated by Christians and Muslims. Between 1219 and 1221, he attacked the larger army of the Khorezim with his force of 200,000 soldiers. As in China, the Mongols committed wholesale butcheries, sparing no civilians except those useful to them, whom they deported to Mongolia. Much of central Asia and northern Persia were systematically laid waste and depopulated. For example, Genghis reputedly massacred 700,000 people at Merv, sparing only 80 craftsmen. A small group of Turkic tribesmen nearby, the ancestors of the Ottoman Turks, were among the few who escaped. They fled westward to Asia Minor, where they were given asylum by the Seljuk Turks. Mongol armies advanced as far west as the Christian kingdom of Georgia in the Caucasus and to the Crimean Peninsula on the Black Sea, but did not consolidate these far-flung conquests until a later time.

In 1223 Genghis began his homeward trip. He was infuriated that the Chin still resisted and that the Hsi Hsia were in revolt. In 1226 he once again took the field against the Hsi Hsia, repeating atrocities against them. Their capital city, Ninghsia, did not fall until 1227, after Genghis' death. According to his wish, the entire population of the city and most of the people of the kingdom were put to the sword. According to Chinese records, only 1 percent of the people survived. The Hsi Hsia written language was lost, and their irrigation works were wrecked or abandoned because not enough people were left to work them. The fields were choked by sand and the land became desert. The region never regained its population or prosperity.

Genghis Khan's Heritage

Genghis died in 1227 at seventy-two, the result of falling from a horse while hunting. The guards who escorted his cortege back to Mongolia left nothing but death behind, for any living thing unlucky enough to have en-

LIVES AND TIMES ACROSS CULTURES

Treasures from Royal Tombs

Across the ancient world from Egypt to China, many cultures held that people needed in the next life the material goods they had enjoyed while alive. Thus surviving relatives buried treasured items with their loved ones. Royal tombs were therefore packed with artifacts, and, because this was common knowledge, they have been the targets of tomb robbers and treasure hunters from antiquity up to the present. Archaeologists, too, search for ancient royal graves, but with the goal of learning about ancient times. They have made spectacular finds since the late nineteenth century and their quest continues.

In 1829 a seven-year-old German boy, Heinrich Schliemann, was given a copy of the *Iliad.* He became convinced that the events described by Homer were real and not mythology and devoted his later life to finding Mycenae, home of the Greek king Agamemnon, and Troy, the city Agamemnon's victorious men destroyed. Schliemann's boyhood dream came true in the 1870s when he made the spectacular discoveries of both Mycenae with its royal tombs, and the Troy of the *Iliad* with its hoard of treasures. His finds also transformed the Trojan War, about 1200 B.C.E., from myth to history.

In 1922 an English Egyptologist, Howard Carter, found the tomb of King Tutankhamon ("King Tut") of Egypt, who died around 1350 B.C.E. Although it had been looted in antiquity, thousands of treasures, including a solid gold sarcophagus and the mummified body of the king remained intact, making this discovery one of the most spectacular from ancient Egypt.

In 221 B.C.E. Ch'in unified China, inaugurating the imperial era. Giving himself the title of First Emperor, this megalomaniacal ruler began to construct a huge mausoleum for himself, which he reputedly furnished with fabulous treasures. It was looted after his dynasty fell in 206 B.C.E., but till now the huge mound that surmounts the tomb had not been excavated. However, farmers drilling a well in the 1970s discovered huge underground pits surrounding the mound that yielded over 7,000 life-sized pottery horses and men intended to guard the ruler in death.

In 1227 Genghis Khan, the ruthless and fearsome Mongol conqueror, died while campaigning. His remains were returned to Mongolia for elaborate burial with vast treasures, reputedly including the crowns of seventy-eight subjugated rulers. The site's exact location remains unknown, and several recent expeditions have failed to locate it.

Numerous known tombs as well as those still awaiting discovery will furnish work for generations of future archaeologists and scholars.

countered the procession was slaughtered. Finally, at home in Mongolia, he was buried on top of Mount Burkan-Kaldun, a site he had loved since his youth. He is still revered by his people as Genghis the Heaven-Sent, and many Mongols hold the messianic hope that one day he will rise again and lead them to new glory.

To his immediate successors Genghis left two main legacies, as conqueror and as a law-giving administrator. As a conqueror he had no peer and laid the groundwork for the largest land empire in the world. Like Alexander the Great, he was a military genius. However unlike Alexander, who neglected to consolidate his conquests, Genghis and his successors were superb adapters and improvers of selected existing government and military practices. For example, centuries earlier the Chinese had packed gunpowder in bamboo tubes and propelled them as missiles. In resisting the Mongols, the Southern Sung replaced the bamboo tubes with cast-iron barrels, thereby inventing the first cannon in warfare. Mongols quickly adopted cannons in besieging walled cities, with devastating effect. Cannons quickly spread to Europe and were in use there by the early fourteenth century.

Genghis was also a master of other aspects of warfare. He inspired fanatical devotion and loyal service from a group of outstanding generals. His cavalry were the most skilled horsemen in the world. He was meticulous in doing all the necessary groundwork before embarking on a campaign. Well served by spies, he gathered information about his enemies. He also accumulated needed supplies and provisions and protected his lines of communications. Genghis was also a master of psychological warfare. To inspire terror and demoralize his enemies into surrender without resistance, he deliberately committed acts of cruelty of the greatest magnitude and spread tales of the bloody orgies his men had reveled in during previous campaigns. He made terror a system of government and a method of diplomacy. Any foe that dared resist him found no mercy; any city that loosed one arrow against his forces could expect all its inhabitants (except those whose skills he could use) to be massacred. Thus he ensured success. His career brought glory to Mongols but slavery and ruin to millions of others. As a Muslim poet lamented, no survivors were left to weep for the dead in his path. The devastation caused by his campaigns disrupted the economies and the trade routes across Asia for a generation.

Genghis looked on the empire he conquered as clan property, so clan members and his supporters formed the ruling class. To improve communications and administration, he supervised the invention of an alphabet for the Mongol language, based on the Turkic Uighur script. He set up an efficient postal system that sped information and government business across the far-flung empire. He promulgated the first written law code for Mongols called the Yasa. It decreed religious toleration, exempted the clergy from taxation, forbade washing and urinating in running water (which shows how precious water was to nomads), and prescribed the death penalty for spying, desertion, theft, adultery, and butchering animals in the Muslim manner. He further ordered that no future decrees of Mongols could conflict with the Yasa.

Genghis also created an administrative structure to rule his empire, and since few Mongols had the requisite skills or inclination for the undertaking, he employed conquered peoples, such as Yeliu Chu-ts'ai. After an area was fully subdued, he would even permit the remaining population to return and rebuild their cities so that they could begin paying taxes to him. To his subjugated populace, Genghis was surely the most frightful and monstrous curse imaginable. The Chinese had never suffered such barbarities; few of the Buddhist Hsi Hsia people survived, and the Muslim and Christian peoples were cruelly battered. It is no wonder that the Christian Europeans called him the Scourge of God.

Genghis Khan's measures succeeded in the short term, and his heirs continued to expand the empire he created for half a century. In the long term his plans failed because his people could not combine their pastoral way of life with the needs of governing sedentary populations. Most opted to change, became sedentary, were corrupted by the luxuries they enjoyed, and adopted the religions of their conquered subjects.

Mongol Domains under Genghis Khan's Heirs

Near death, Genghis Khan assembled his sons and grandsons. His eldest son, Juji, had predeceased him. The sons of Juji and the surviving three sons of Genghis and Borte were his heirs. Juji's sons received Russia, the westernmost of the conquered lands, located farthest from home, according to Mongol custom. This area was the least well defined; its western limit was described as the point "as far as the soil has been trodden by the hooves of Mongol horses." Juji's sons became known as khans of the Golden Horde. The second son, Chagatai, received central Asia; Ogotai, the third son, received Chinese Turkestan, while Tului, the youngest son, received the homeland, as well as North China. Genghis designated Ogotai to succeed him as grand khan, subject to confirmation by an assembly of Mongol leaders.

Two years after Genghis's death, the assembly met in Karakorum in Mongolia and formally elected Ogotai the second grand khan. After forming an alliance with the Southern Sung, Ogotai and Tului then resumed the war against the Chin. When Kaifeng was captured in 1233, its last ruler committed suicide and all North China fell under Mongol rule. The Mongols and the Southern Sung soon disputed over the division of spoils. In 1235 Ogotai declared war against the Southern Sung, which was not totally subdued until 1279.

Earlier the Mongols had conquered Manchuria and forced the submission of Korea. Koreans were assessed an annual tribute of 10,000 pounds of cotton, 3,000 bolts of silk, 2,000 pieces of gauze, and 100,000 large sheets of paper. Otter skins were later added. Between 1217 and 1258, the Mongols repeatedly invaded and ravaged Korea, carrying off prisoners and looting the land. For a time the Korean kings of the Koryo dynasty sought safety on an offshore island, but eventually they had to submit. Many Koreans were later impressed to serve in Kubilai Khan's forces that invaded Japan.

In 1237 a major force set out to conquer Europe to secure the patrimony of Juji's sons. Led by another of Genghis's grandsons, Batu, it swept across Russia and captured Moscow, Kiev, and other principal cities. The fall of Kiev ended the Kievan (or Ukrainian) phase of Russian history. The Mongol juggernaut then advanced through Poland, East Prussia, and Bohemia and swept into Hungary, seizing the cities of Buda and Pest on the Danube River. By the end of 1241, Mongol forces had advanced to the border of the Holy Roman Empire and were at the northern coast of the Adriatic Sea.

Unable to unite against the mighty foe, the rest of Europe was saved in 1241 by Ogotai's death. This event forced the Mongol princes and generals to rush back to their homeland to elect a new grand khan, and the threat to Europe ended. Batu withdrew his forces to the lower Volga Valley, where they remained and created the khanate called the Golden Horde. Europeans had ruefully learned that Mongols were not the people of Prester John, the legendary Christian king of the east, in whom they had hoped to find an ally against the Muslims.

Ogotai's early death and the lack of an obvious leader and heir almost caused a civil war among the Mon-

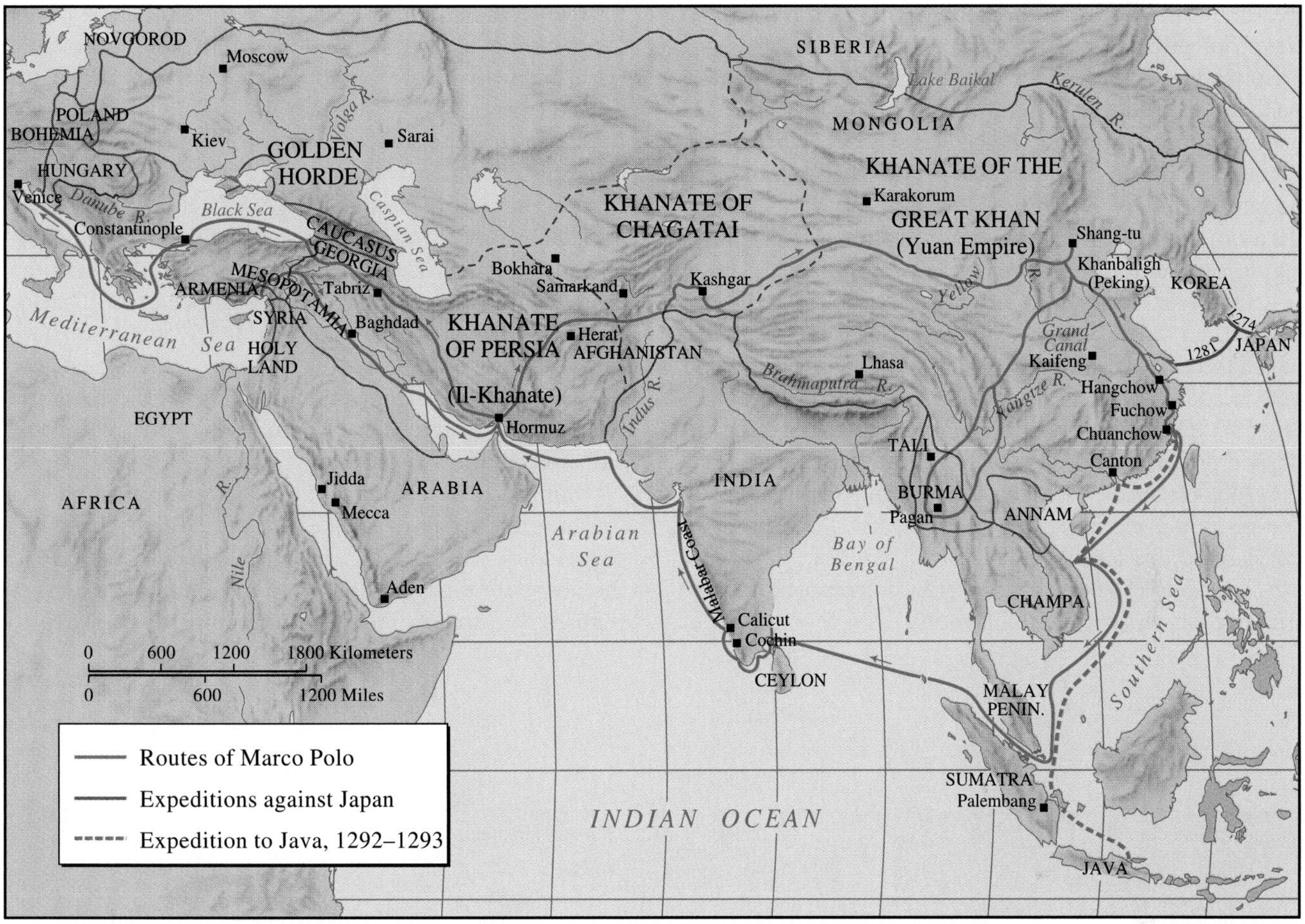

Map 8.4 The Mongol Empire in 1255. Genghis Khan's successors added to his extensive conquests to create the largest land empire the world had ever seen, stretching from Korea in the east to the heart of Europe. Mongol military force held the empire together under a great khan from the house of Genghis.

gols. His widow temporarily assumed the regency while different factions of Genghis's family vied for power. Not until 1246 did the assembly elect Ogotai's son the third grand khan, but he was immediately challenged by rival claimants. Civil war was averted only because the new grand khan died within two years of his election.

To ensure a peaceful succession, the assembly now turned to the house of Tului, Genghis's youngest son. It elected Mongke, Tului's eldest son, the fourth grand khan. Mongke was an able general and made the conquest of the Southern Sung his first priority. He personally directed the campaign and took his younger brother Kubilai with him. He appointed another younger brother, Hulagu, to conquer West Asia, while leaving the youngest, Arik-Boke, in charge of Mongolia.

Mongke's sudden death while campaigning in China brought about civil war. He had intended Arik-Boke to succeed him as grand khan, but Kubilai disagreed. In 1260 he convened an assembly in China that elected him fifth grand khan. Contending that an assembly convened outside the Mongol homeland was invalid, Arik-Boke called a rival assembly at Karakorum, the capital of the whole empire, which elected him grand khan. In the civil war that followed, the descendants of Ogotai and Chagatai supported Arik-Boke, while Hulagu declared for Kubilai. Fighting lasted for four years, with Kubilai the victor. He pardoned his brother, but hostile feelings between various branches of the family survived the protagonists, and some Mongols never recognized Kubilai as the legitimate grand khan. With Kubilai's election, the unity of the Mongol Empire ended forever.

Kubilai Khan's Empire

In 1260 Kubilai Khan established his capital at Peking, the former Chin capital that his grandfather had destroyed. He chose Peking because Karakorum in Mongolia was too far from major population centers and therefore no longer feasible as capital of the entire empire. He called the city Tatu, or Great Capital in Chinese; in Mongolian it was called Khanbalik, city of the khan.

Kubilai Khan resumed the conquest of the Southern Sung for several reasons. In Mongol eyes the success of a ruler was measured by how much new territory and wealth he could bring to his people, and southern China was a rich prize. For decades the Southern Sung government had assiduously developed trade with Southeast Asia, another source of wealth that Mongols would be happy to tap. Conquest of the south would also bring valuable political benefits, for although Kubilai ruled northern China, the traditional heartland of Chinese civilization, control of all Chinese territories would confer legitimacy and remove a possible source of danger.

Conquest of the south proved to be slow and arduous. The terrain was unsuited to Mongol cavalry operations, which forced Kubilai to develop an infantry force, employ new weapons and tactics, and create a navy to counter the Sung navy. Hulagu helped by sending Arab engineers, who devised powerful catapults capable of throwing huge rocks over long distances, flame throwers, fragmentation bombs, and other war machines that could breach the formidable defenses of Sung fortress cities.

The Southern Sung resisted with determination. One strategic city in central China withstood a Mongol siege for five years before it finally fell. Fear and hatred of the Mongols also served to rally the people around the Sung government, which enjoyed wide support as the legitimate dynasty.

Despite its resistance, the end of the Southern Sung was only a matter of time. In 1259 the Mongols destroyed the southwestern kingdom of Tali, in present-day Yunnan province. Mongol conquest of Tali had sent many of its inhabitants fleeing southward, where they found a home in modern Thailand, calling themselves the Thai, or free people. Control of Tali allowed the Mongols to attack the Southern Sung with two pincers. The capital city, Hangchow, surrendered in 1276 without the slaughter that had characterized the fate of many other cities that had resisted the Mongols.

Sung loyalists continued to resist while retreating ever southward. During its last decades, the Sung throne was occupied by young boys, hardly the dynamic leaders that the desperate times needed if the fortunes of the dynasty were to be revived. The last Sung emperor drowned in

Mongol Forces Using New Weaponry. Quick to learn about new military technology, Mongols effectively used catapults, cannon, and other weapons to attack the walled cities of their enemies, as depicted in this later Persian miniature painting.

1279, as his last ships were overwhelmed. A few loyalists fled to Annam, Champa, and Thailand. In 1271 Kubilai Khan had already adopted a Chinese dynastic name, Yuan, meaning the first. This dynasty ruled China until 1368.

Kubilai also consolidated Mongol dominion in Korea. The heir to the Korean throne became hostage in his court; later this Korean prince was married to one of Kubilai's daughters. Marriages between Korean kings and Mongol princesses was continued by Kubilai's successors. In time the Korean royal family became a mere branch of the Mongol ruling house. At least once a year a Korean tribute mission would travel to Tatu, and a Mongol garrison was stationed in Korea, controlling it with an iron hand.

In his last years, Kubilai attempted to establish control over the many states of Southeast Asia. He first sent envoys to the states to demand submission and tribute. If a state refused, he would declare war to force it to submit. Annam (present-day northern Vietnam) submitted voluntarily in 1265, sending tribute and receiving in return a calendar from Kubilai (from early times a symbol of political submission to Chinese overlordship). Later, when the king of Champa (present-day central and southern Vietnam) refused to become the great khan's vassal, Kubilai decided to punish him. To do so, he demanded that Annam cooperate with him and allow Mongol troops passage on the route south. When the King of Annam refused that demand, he too found himself the target of Mongol attack. When the Mongol expedition arrived at Hanoi, they found that the Annamese king had fled. Mongol troops soon bogged down in Annam and Champa. The terrain was unsuitable for cavalry action, and Mongol warriors fell prey to tropical heat and diseases, while their morale plummeted in the face of guerrilla attacks.

Despite the difficulties the Mongols experienced in securing and holding Annam and Champa, the government of these states also realized the high cost of resistance. In compromise they submitted to Mongol overlordship and agreed to send tribute regularly; in return, Mongol forces would withdraw from their territories. After the Mongols ravaged Pagan in present-day Burma (Myanmar), the Burmese also accepted Mongol overlordship. Next Mongol envoys were dispatched to Ceylon and the Malabar Coast to demand tribute. In the case of Ceylon, they were also in search of Buddha's relics, for by now Kubilai and many of his followers had converted to Buddhism. Kubilai's last tribute-enrolling expedition was dispatched to Java in 1292. It consisted of 1,000 ships, a 20,000-man army, one year's provisions, and 40,000 ounces of silver for expenses. It was a costly failure.

Kubilai's inconclusive and stalemated campaigns against his cousin Khaidu Khan in central Asia ultimately brought a mutual recognition of the legitimacy of each other's dominion. Kubilai conceded he could not control central Asia, while Kaidu agreed not to make incursions into China. Kubilai's house had now become primarily a Chinese dynasty, identifying with some aspects of China's distinctive history and traditions. Other branches of Genghis's family went their separate ways.

The Last Mongol Conquests in West Asia and Russia

In 1255 Mongke had sent his brother Hulagu with a large army to West Asia, to destroy the fortress of the Assassins and to bring about the submission of the caliph. Entrenched in their almost impregnable fortress of Alamut and other strongholds south of the Caspian Sea for over a century, the Assassins, members of a heretical Muslim sect, had been a great menace to both Muslim rulers and the crusaders. (They were called the Hashishans, because of the use of hashish in their rituals; the word *assassin* is a corruption of *hashishan.*) It took the Mongol army three years to wipe out the Assassin forts and to kill their leader, called the "Old Man of the Mountain."

Hugalu next demanded that the caliph submit to Mongol overlordship, and when he refused, the Mongols besieged Baghdad. The fall of Baghdad in 1258 was followed by six days of pillage and massacre. The Caliph Musta'sim was captured, forced to reveal where his treasures were hidden, and then killed. Then the Mongols overran Mesopotamia and Syria up to the Mediterranean coast, completing the conquest of West Asia begun by Genghis Khan.

Hulagu was poised to attack Egypt in 1259 when he received news of Mongke's death. He left the command of his front forces to a general and returned to participate in the succession struggle. The battle at the Spring of Goliath (A'in Jalut) in present-day Israel in 1260 was a turning point in the history of Mongol conquests. Here, in Hulagu's absence, the Mamluk rulers of Egypt decisively defeated the Mongol forces and shattered the spell of their invincibility. When Hulagu was ready for another test, he found out too late that Mongol instructors sent by the khans of the Golden Horde (who had turned Muslim) had taught the Mamluks Mongol cavalry tactics. Thus ended Mongol dreams of further westward conquest.

Egypt and North Africa were thus saved from Mongol invasion. Egypt would continue to be a powerful bastion against the Mongols, and because Baghdad was under Mongol control, Egypt also became the political center of Islam. Hulagu supported Kubilai, acknowledged the latter as Great Khan, and was in turn recognized as the il-khan, or regional ruler, of western Asia from Persia westward.

India was the only major area in Asia not conquered by the Mongols. It was saved for two reasons. First, the Delhi Sultanate that controlled northern India possessed a powerful army and was acquainted with Mongol fighting methods. Second, Genghis Khan's descendants became preoccupied with wars among themselves, sapping them of the manpower necessary to invade India.

From the middle of the thirteenth century to its end, the rulers of the Golden Horde, already masters of a realm that extended from the steppes of southern Russia to central Asia, launched great drives to conquer Poland and Lithuania. Although they failed, the region was widely devastated and depopulated. Afterwards the Polish government called in German settlers to the area; their descendants accounted for the ethnic German minority in the region that persisted to the twentieth century.

By the late thirteenth century the conquests of the Mongol people were over and Genghis Khan's realm had lost its unity in the civil wars between his descendants. The next phase of Mongol rule would be consolidation, followed by rapid decline. These topics will be discussed in the next section.

The Mongol Legacy

Within the bounds of this royal Park there are rich and beautiful meadows, watered by many rivulets, where a variety of animals of the deer and goat kind are pastured, to serve as food for the hawks and other birds employed in the chase, whose pens are also in the grounds. . . . Frequently, when he [Kubilai Khan] rides about this enclosed forest, he has one or more small leopards carried on horseback, behind their keepers; and when he pleases to give direction for their being slipped, they instantly seize a stag, goat, or fallow deer, which he gives to his hawks, and in this manner he amuses himself.

*In the centre of these grounds, where there is a beautiful grove of trees, he has built a Royal Pavilion, supported upon a colonnade of handsome pillars, gilt and varnished. . . . The roof, like the rest, is of bamboo cane, and so well varnished that no wet can injure it. . . . The building is supported on every side like a tent by more than two hundred very strong silken cords. . . . The whole is constructed with so much ingenuity of contrivance that all the parts may be taken apart, removed, and again set up, at his Majesty's pleasure.**

*Marco Polo, *The Travels of Marco Polo,* ed. Manuel Komroff (New York: Boni and Liveright, 1928), pp. 106–107.

Marco Polo's description of Kubilai Khan's pavilion and hunting park at his summer capital Shangtu (the Xanadu of Samuel Coleridge's poem) is quite revealing about the grandson of Genghis Khan. On the one hand, he continued his nomadic heritage, living in a pavilion that is a glorified tent and enjoying his hunting. On the other hand, his lifestyle was already modified by his contact with the settled civilization of his Chinese subjects. Genghis Khan had moved from one encampment to another; Kubilai Khan traveled among several capital cities. While his grandfather hunted in the wild, Kubilai sometimes hunted in an enclosed artificial game park. And whereas his forefathers lived in tents made of felt and animal hide, his tent was made of fine fabric, and its opening was fastened by silken cords. The rapid assimilation by some Mongols to the life modes of their sedentary subjects became a source of tension between them and their compatriots who abided by the nomadic way of life, and ultimately contributed to the speedy collapse of their empires.

After the heroic phase of conquest was over, Genghis Khan's grandsons were faced with ruling large agricultural and urban populations of many different cultural backgrounds. Since the Mongol rulers were warriors inexperienced in the complex tasks of government, they needed to enlist the aid of their non-Mongol subjects in order to govern. In time, each ruler inevitably identified with the interests and needs of the people he ruled. Additionally, the center of the empire, present-day Mongolia, was insignificant economically and culturally compared with several of the conquered parts. Thus, when Mongol rulers were pulled several ways by the competing interests of their different subjects, the Mongol way often lost. Nonetheless, the heirs of Genghis who ruled large parts of Europe and Asia left a lasting impact. The four Mongol states were:

1. The Yuan dynasty (1279–1368), ruled by Kubilai Khan and his descendents, controlled China, Mongolia, and peripheral lands.
2. The Il-Khanate of Persia (1256–1349) was built by Hulagu Khan and his descendants.
3. The Khanate of the Golden Horde on the lower Volga River was created by the house of Juji; it broke up in the fifteenth century and remnants were completely subjugated by the Russian state in the sixteenth century.
4. The Khanate of Chagatai in central Asia was controlled by the family of Chagatai; its western part was incorporated into Timurlane's empire after 1370.

The Yuan Dynasty

Kubilai Khan (reigned 1260–1294) was the first Yuan emperor of China and Mongolia and overlord of Korea and much of Southeast Asia. He was also the first great khan not acknowledged by all Mongols. As the fifth great khan, he claimed to be ruler of the whole Mongol world and overlord of the other khanates. He was in reality the emperor of China, the largest and wealthiest part of Genghis Khan's empire, but nevertheless not the khan of the entire Mongol world. In crowning himself emperor of China, Kubilai can be compared with Charlemagne, who had been crowned in 800 by the pope as Emperor of the Romans of the West. As emperor of the Yuan dynasty, Kubilai ruled from his capital Tatu (Peking), shifting the axis of the Mongol Empire. As a result Mongolia became a mere province of his expanded Chinese empire.

When conquering the Southern Sung, Kubilai's legions did not pillage and massacre to the same extent that the warriors of Genghis had done earlier. Nevertheless, it was as conquerors that the Mongols ruled reunified China. The people of the Yuan Empire were divided into four hierarchic classes. On top were Mongols, followed by Persians, Arabs, Turks, and other non-Chinese minorities (called light-color-eyed people). Then came the northern Chinese, which included the assimilated nomads who had earlier settled in the region. The southern Chinese, the most recently conquered, came last.

Since most Mongols had neither the inclination nor training to staff and maintain an administration, Kubilai relied heavily on non-Mongols to run the imperial bureaucracy. He and his heirs never trusted the Chinese, however, so they turned to Persians, Arabs, and other central Asians of the Muslim faith. Ahmad, Kubilai's long-time minister of finance, was a central Asian Muslim. Muslims usually served as "tax farmers" (people who collected taxes and kept a percentage of the total amount collected) and finance administrators for the Yuan rulers, and they enriched themselves in the process. Ahmad, for example, was notoriously corrupt and was hated for the merciless way he collected taxes for his master. Kubilai also hired a few Europeans, of whom Marco Polo is the best known.

Kubilai favored Muslims and other non-Chinese for several reasons. As a small minority of foreigners, they were easy to control and utterly dependent on their Mongol masters. Muslims were active in the international trade, both overland with West Asia and by sea with Southeast Asia and India. Since Mongols benefited from international trade, they rewarded the Muslims who were active in it. Finally, whether consciously or not, the Mongols used the Muslims as scapegoats to divert Chinese anger from themselves—an endeavor that was partially successful. Chinese writings of this period were bitter about the excesses and financial manipulations of the Muslim officials and merchants.

The non-Chinese staff of the Mongol rulers was still inadequate to administer China, so Chinese were recruited to fill numerous subordinate positions, where they were carefully watched by their Mongol supervisors. All state documents had to be written in Mongol, a language the Chinese were not allowed to learn. When finally the Confucian civil service examinations were re-

National Palace Museum, Taiwan

Kubilai Khan Hunting. This detail of a large painting shows Kubilai Khan, clad in a dragon robe and ermine coat and mounted on horseback, with a female companion. It was painted in 1280 before he became too obese to ride.

instituted, half the top degrees had to be awarded to Mongols, regardless of qualification.

Yuan economic policy was designed to produce revenue for the Mongol ruling class and not to promote general well-being. It favored trade, since trade brought revenue and rare luxuries for the rulers and their allies. The Yuan government made sure that the roads were kept open and safe for travelers so that international trade flourished, and luxury goods were traded among the Mongol realms. To the extent that agricultural prosperity underpinned international commerce and increased tax revenue, the Mongol government fostered agricultural recovery, but it did not allow the peasants to benefit. Thus the prosperity observed by Marco Polo was superficial and enjoyed only by the ruling groups, merchants, and privileged foreigners. To most Chinese the Yuan era was a period of unparalleled degradation. Millions were pauperized and an unprecedented number of people became slaves. Northern China was especially devastated and depopulated; even in southern China, which had escaped the worst Mongol depredations, vast acreages were turned into pasturage and parkland for the Mongol lords.

The Bitter Pill of Foreign Rule

*According to our Great Yuan system, people are reckoned in ten classes. First, officials; second, clerks . . . seventh, craftsmen; eighth, "entertainers" [actors, prostitutes]; ninth Confucian scholars; tenth, paupers. . . . Ah! how low! Those who are sandwiched under the "entertainers" and above the "paupers" are the Confucian scholars of today! The Emperor, feeling sorry for these people, ordered that two school professors be installed for each circuit and district in the Chiangnan provinces. . . . These school officials look noble but are actually debased. Their salaries are not even sufficient to save them from cold and hunger. The worst among them have sunken faces, needle-sharp Adam's apples, and firewood-like bones.**

This passage, written by a scholar who lived through the fall of the Southern Sung into the Yuan dynasty, describes the suffering of the scholars during Mongol rule and their pitiful, poverty-stricken state. Although the Yuan codes did not in fact classify people into these ten classes, the bitter statement indicates how the once respected Confucian scholars had fallen from the pinnacle of society to among the poorest and most despised.

*Sherman E. Lee and Wai-Kam Ho, *Chinese Art under the Mongols: The Yuan Dynasty (1279–1368)* (Cleveland: Cleveland Museum of Art, 1968), p. 77.

Kubilai, like his forebears, was tolerant of any religion that helped promote obedience and stability. He protected Christians, befriended Muslims and Taoists, and above all paid honor to Buddha. He particularly favored Tibetan Buddhism, partly because the Tibetan Buddhist clergy identified him with the Boddhisatva of Wisdom and portrayed him as a universal Buddhist emperor that all must obey. The magic and rites of Tibetan Buddhism, which somewhat resembled the Mongols' traditional shamanism (animism and belief in magic), were easy for Mongols to relate to. Thus the Mongols of the homeland became Buddhists of the Tibetan church.

Kubilai Khan died in his eightieth year. In death as in life, he was pulled between the two worlds he dominated. He was not buried in a sumptuous mausoleum in the manner of Chinese rulers. Rather, his remains were returned to Mongolia and laid to rest near those of his grandfather and father. A Mongol assembly in Tatu ratified his appointment of a grandson (since his favorite son and heir had predeceased him) as next emperor and great khan.

Kubilai ruled long and accomplished much. He maintained the Mongolian Peace (Pax Mongolica), under which his realm began to recover. His cosmopolitan court opened up East and West to each other, and his lavish patronage of the arts led to wide interchanges of ideas. These positive achievements must be weighed against the misery of the great mass of his subjects. His successors were lesser men who did not share his vision. Thus the Pax Mongolica did not measure up to the sustained and genuine accomplishments of either the Pax Romana or Pax Sinica that more than a thousand years earlier had given the world so much.

The Yuan dynasty did not long survive Kubilai's death. Power struggles quickly divided the royal family. In the twenty-six years between 1307 and 1333, seven rulers occupied the throne, none surviving beyond age thirty-five. Many of the early deaths were due to palace coups and murderous intrigues, but some can be attributed to diseases caused by excessive indulgence. Mongols loved a strong drink called ***koumiss*** made of fermented mare's milk. Kubilai's father and other kinsmen had died early from alcohol-related causes. Kubilai himself drank heavily and excessively in his old age, and suffered from diseases associated with alcoholism; he was also extremely fat. In their love of strong alcoholic drinks Mongols are akin to the ancient Macedonians; Philip II and Alexander the Great both loved strong drink and feasting, and were likely alcoholics.

Other factors also contributed to the downfall of the Mongols. The government became increasingly extortionate and inefficient, and natural disasters contributed to a worsening economic situation. As famines spread, so did peasant revolts. South China led in uprisings against Mongol rule. In 1368 troops of a southern-led rebel movement captured Tatu. The remaining Mongols fled northward back to the steppes.

The Il-Khanate of Persia

Hulagu was invested by his elder brother Kubilai Khan, as il-khan, or regional ruler, and settled down to rule Persia and part of Mesopotamia. In the continuing power struggle between Genghis's descendants, Hulagu and Kubilai, brothers who ruled empires with sedentary populations, were allied against the Golden Horde of southern Russia and the Chagatai khans of Turkestan, who upheld the traditional nomadic Mongol way of life. The Golden Horde, now Muslim, was also allied with the Egyptian Mamluks. Thus the il-khans' lands were ringed by hostile neighbors.

Persian Muslims were most numerous among Hulagu's subjects. Just as Kubilai favored foreigners and minorities to staff his administration, Hulagu employed Jews, Christians, and Buddhists to run his government and had many Chinese soldiers in his army. Hulagu died in 1265 at age forty-eight. He had held to his Mongol faith, although his principal wife was a Christian and his son and successor was also married to a Christian, the daughter of the Byzantine emperor.

Hulagu's son was confirmed by Kubilai as il-Khan of Persia, but Kubilai could not provide effective military support for the il-khans because their territories were separated by the hostile Chagatai khanate. Faced with the Mamluks, the il-khan turned to the non-Muslim West for assistance. He sent ambassadors to the pope and to European monarchs to offer alliances against the Mamluks and even promised to support the return of Jerusalem to Christian rule should they succeed in ousting the Mamluks from Palestine. But by now crusading zeal had gone out of the Europeans, who moreover remembered earlier Mongol savageries against them. The proffered alliance was declined.

Around 1300 the il-khan announced his conversion to Islam and changed his title to sultan, in the Muslim fashion. In so doing he also renounced his vassalage to the great khan (ruler of Yuan China), because he was not a Muslim. The conversion showed a growing identification with the subject Persians and was also a political tactic aimed at weakening the alliance between the Golden Horde and the Mamluks by depriving them of a religious reason to oppose the il-khanate in Persia. The conversion also ended the favored status of the minority religious groups. The Buddhists in the il-khanate fared worse as a result of their ruler's conversion: they were persecuted as polytheists; some were forcibly converted to Islam. Civil wars between members of the ruling house ended the dynasty in 1349.

Like Yuan China, Persia under the il-khans was superficially prosperous. Merchants benefited from the international trade that passed through their land. A luxury-loving court and aristocracy encouraged crafts and certain cultural activities, especially painting and architecture. Meanwhile the peasants and ordinary people were burdened with crushing taxation and financial mismanagement. Many peasants, in addition, had their fields and crops regularly destroyed by the Mongol nomad lords who made their annual migration north and south through the countryside. Finally the il-khans resorted to printing paper money with no backing (as the Yuan government had also done with similar results) and brought on financial ruin.

The Golden Horde

The westernmost part of Genghis's empire, ruled by the descendents of Juji and called the Khanate of the Golden

A Mongol Feast. Hulagu, the younger brother and ally of Kubilai Khan in the succession struggle, was rewarded by Kubilai with the appointment as il-khan, or regional ruler of Persia and western Asia. In this picture, Hulagu is seated with another Mongol potentate at a feast before a battle with the Mamluks of Egypt. They are surrounded by standing and kneeling servants.

Mongol Rule through Victims' Eyes

The Mongols rank high among the most ruthless conquerors and exploitative rulers the world has seen. They used armies of occupation to rule and mercilessly exploit conquered lands. The following quotation is from the *Chronicles of Novgorod, 1016–1471,* written by monks of that Russian city, which was spared because it paid human and material tribute to the Mongol rulers. It recounts the terror tactics the Mongols used to conquer their enemies, putting to death the inhabitants of whole towns that dared resist.

> *[In 1238] foreigners called Tartars came in countless numbers, like locusts, into the land of Ryazan . . . and thence they sent their emissaries to the Knyazes [leaders] of Ryazan . . . demanding from them one-tenth of everything: of men and Knyazes and horses—of everything one tenth. And the Knyazes of Ryazan . . . without letting them into their towns, went out to meet them. And the Knyazes said to them: "Only when none of us remain then all will be yours.". . . The Tartars took the town on December 21 . . . and they killed the Knyaz and Knyaginya, and men, women, and children, monks, nuns and priests, some by fire, some by the sword, and violated the nuns, priests' wives, good women and girls in the presence of their mothers and sisters.**

*Robert Michell and Nevil Forbes, trans., *The Chronicle of Novgorod, 1016–1471,* vol. 5 (London, 1914), pp. 81–84.

Horde, stretched from the Carpathian Mountains and the northern shores of the Black Sea across the Caspian Sea to the Aral Sea. Unlike the Mongol rulers of China and Persia who adopted some of the sedentary ways of their subjects, the Mongols on the Eurasian steppes maintained their ancestral nomadic habits, assimilating the indigenous nomads.

The Khans of the Golden Horde ruled southern Russia from Sarai, their capital city on the lower Volga River. Because they were furthest from the Mongol homeland, they were the first to go their own way. After successful campaigns to the north and west from 1240 to 1242, they received the submission of all Russian princes, who were required to go to Sarai to tender personal homage and to offer tribute in gold, silver, fur, cattle, and young men and women slaves.

The khans found indirect rule lucrative and effective. They appointed one Russian ruler grand prince and authorized him to keep the other rulers in line. The position of grand prince was not hereditary, however, and since the khan could invest any Russian prince with the position, he was able to sow dissension among the Russian princes and promote loyalty and subservience to himself. The princes of Moscow gradually proved their loyalty to the Golden Horde, and therefore won continued confirmation as grand princes. In this way Moscow became second only to Sarai in importance during the Mongol period. Mongol expeditions periodically burned towns and ravaged crops to punish disobedience and to instill fear.

Mongol power lasted in Russia without effective challenge until 1380, when the prince of Moscow defeated the Mongols in the major battle of Kulikovo. Although weakened, Mongol authority continued for another hundred years. Finally in 1480, Ivan III, Prince of Moscow, renounced his and Russia's allegiance to the khan. The Golden Horde split up, and after the sixteenth century, in a reversal of events, the rulers of Russia would absorb the Horde's successor states one after another into the Russian Empire. Russians called the descendants of the Mongols Tartars.

Two major factors account for the longevity of Mongol power over Russia. One was the disunity among the Russian princes, who succumbed to the Mongol policy of divide and rule. Since Russia was simultaneously threatened by Lithuanians and Germans to the west, Mongol overlordship even afforded some Russians a measure of protection against their western enemies. Another reason was Russia's relative cultural backwardness compared with China and Persia, so that the Russian way of life was less a model for Mongol emulation than Chinese and Persian ways. Thus Mongols in Russia remained distinct and did not assimilate.

In the fourteenth century, the Golden Horde converted to Islam. This act placed an insurmountable barrier between the Mongols and their Christian subjects. It raised the Russian struggle for independence into a crusade for Orthodox Christianity, and allowed Russians to turn to their religion for identification and consolation. This religious difference continued to accentuate the division between Russian and Mongol and later prevented the full integration of Mongols into Russian life.

The Khanate of Chagatai

The region including present-day Chinese Turkestan and the central Asian republics of the former Soviet Union was assigned to Chagatai, Genghis's second son. It consisted of landlocked steppe grasslands and was home of mostly Turkish-speaking nomads. There were few cities that could provide wealth, but the khans were able to draw substantial revenues from international luxury trade along the famed Silk Road that passed through their territory.

The Chagatai Khanate was surrounded by the three empires ruled by other branches of the Genghis clan: Yuan China, the Il-Khanate of Persia, and the Golden Horde of Russia. Since it could not expand outward, its leaders turned their energies inward, concentrating on destructive and complicated dynastic struggles and civil wars. Because the civil wars concerned the descendants of Genghis Khan, they often drew in other branches of the clan, and because its geographic position was central to the whole Mongol imperial structure, politics in the Chagatai Khanate came to have consequences for the Mongol Empire as a whole. The bitter wars, especially those against Kubilai Khan, helped destroy the already shaky structure of the Mongol Empire.

The Chagatai Khanate broke up in the fourteenth century. The peoples in the western portion embraced Islam. Mongols from the eastern part allied with the remnant Yuan Mongols who had been expelled from China. They reverted to the ways of their ancestors, staging plundering raids against the Chinese. This was a fatal mistake, because whereas China was weak and divided at the time of the first Mongol incursions, it was now united and strong under the new Ming dynasty. In revenge, a Chinese army hammered into Karakorum in 1388 and burned to the ground what remained of the once grand capital. The Chinese then chased the Mongols further northward and smashed their last pretense of power. By the fifteenth century, only memories and legends remained.

The Empire of Timurlane

In 1369, as the Chagatai Khanate was breaking up, a Turkish leader established himself in Samarkand and began a career of conquest as remarkable and terrible as that of his ancestor Genghis Khan. Known in the west as Timurlane or Tamerlane (Timur the Lame), he first consolidated his power over central Asia and conquered Persia and Mesopotamia. He next defeated and captured the Ottoman sultan (descended from the Turks who fled Genghis Khan and finally settled in Anatolia), invaded the realm of the Golden Horde, and turned north, briefly occupying Moscow. He next proceeded southward and eastward, marched through Afghanistan and descended on India, sacking Delhi in 1399. After a massacre that lasted for three days, he left India, taking with him large numbers of captives. Complete anarchy desolated northern India in the wake of his depredation. He was planning to attack China when he died in 1405 at the age of seventy.

Although a devout Muslim, Timurlane was regarded as another scourge of God by Christians and Muslims alike, because he plundered and slaughtered his way across Eurasia, massacring Muslims, Christians, and Hindus indiscriminately. His men relished cruelty and reenacted some of the worst atrocities committed by Genghis

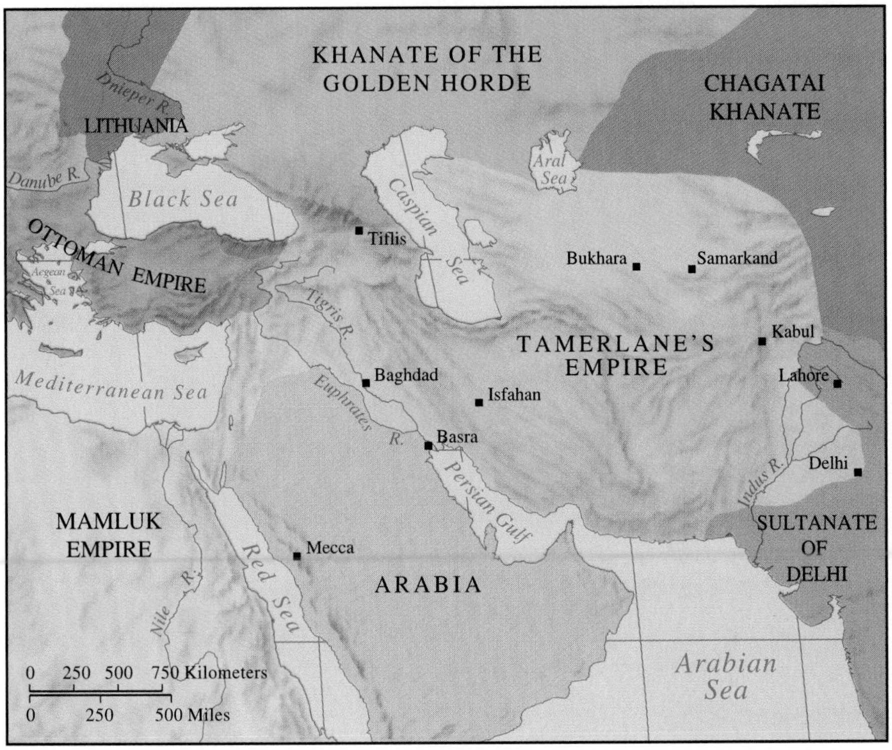

Map 8.5 Timurlane's Empire. Timurlane subjugated twenty-seven states, and his empire stretched from India to Anatolia. His dream of creating a lasting empire was not realized, however, because he left no capable heir.

Khan, such as building pyramids from the severed heads of captives. He left depopulated lands in his wake. Some, such as Mesopotamia, would never recover fully, because his men irrevocably wrecked the irrigation system that had sustained the population. On the other hand, he was the lavish benefactor of Samarkand, capital of his short-lived empire, where he brought the loot of continents and the captives of many lands, to build and decorate a city he never found time to live in.

Unlike Genghis, who consolidated his conquests and left an empire to his heirs, Timurlane moved too quickly to forge an enduring empire. His empire split up and collapsed after his death. His was the last assault of the Mongol era.

The Legacy of Mongol Imperialism

The Mongol invasions had both negative and positive long-term results. In the short term there was destruction and devastation wherever Mongol armies had swept through. The population of China was reduced by half as a result of the massacres and other horrors that the invaders inflicted. Similar drastic population declines took place in Persia and other lands they conquered and ravaged.

Everywhere Mongol rule contributed to the brutalizing of society; some of the barbarous practices they introduced persisted after their collapse. For example, when the first Chinese emperor of the succeeding Ming dynasty died, a large retinue of his concubines was killed to serve him in the next world. Since such inhuman practices had died out in China over 2,000 years earlier, their revival can be attributed to precedents recently introduced by the Mongols.

Mongol rule was blatantly racial and helped define Chinese national consciousness. Mongol discrimination against Chinese was especially humiliating to the scholar-gentry. The fact that foreigners had collaborated in the Mongol rule of China brought about the isolationist and antiforeign policies of the succeeding dynasty. Such policies were in marked contrast to the confident cosmopolitanism of the earlier Han and T'ang eras. In Persia the rule of the il-khans helped solidify modern Persian boundaries and sense of identity.

In Russia, where overthrow of the Mongol yoke resurrected an independent nation, the centuries of humiliation served to forge a national, religious, and racial consciousness among the Russian people. Mongol domination cut Russia off from Europe, turned it inward,

Timurlane's Tomb. Timurlane was buried in his capital, Samarkand. Although he spent little time there, the city benefited enormously from the loot he sent back from all the lands he conquered and ravaged.

Ric Ergenbright/Corbis

and isolated it from the advances brought about by the Renaissance. Subsequent Russian fear of the "yellow peril" can be traced to Mongol rule. Mongol destruction of the Grand Duchy of Kiev and occupation of southern Russia turned Russia's power center northward to Moscow, whose rulers rose to power as servants to the khans and then led the liberation of Russia from the Mongol yoke.

The Mongol conquest brought about the spread of the Turkish ethnic/linguistic group throughout West Asia. Turks had played a role in West Asia since the ninth century, but Mongol rule gave them an unprecedented opportunity to expand. The first people conquered by Genghis, the Turks far outnumbered and were more advanced than the Mongols; as a result they were coopted into Mongol armies and administration. The Turkish Uighur script was adopted to make Mongol a written language. Later, most Mongols began to speak Turkish, which became the dominant language across the Eurasian steppes. By the fourteenth century the peoples of the Chagatai Khanate and the Golden Horde thought of themselves as Turks rather than Mongols. Only the small remnants who were chased back to Mongolia by the Chinese retained their Mongol identity, although that was also altered by conversion to Tibetan Buddhism. In Mongolia a modified Tibetan script was adopted for the alphabet, replacing the Uighur one.

The Mongol conquests reshaped religious patterns in Asia. Though they initially put Islam on the defensive, Mongols in western Asia soon embraced the religion of their subjects, with several important consequences. One was the end of Arab dominance of the Muslim world. Arab leadership was replaced by that of the Turks. Another was the collapse of Asian Christianity, both Nestorian and Catholic. The Nestorian Christian church, found across Asia from Syria to China, had roots that went back for centuries. Both Kubilai's and Hulagu's chief wives were Nestorian Christians, as were many other Mongols and Turks. Their faith did not survive the tumult of events, except in small pockets. The Catholic West's rejection of an alliance proffered by the il-khans resulted in the collapse of a Western Christian bridgehead in the Holy Land, which was conquered by Muslim Mamluks. Buddhism was wiped out in central Asia, but the Tibetan branch of Buddhism was accepted by Mongols of the homeland when Kubilai patronized that church. Mahayana Buddhism remained dominant in China.

The postconquest Pax Mongolica revived commercial and cultural exchange across Eurasia; travelers and their goods moved in safety as never before. Europeans, who had become addicted to the luxury products of Asia long before the Mongol invasions, were again able to acquire such products.

The demand for luxury goods stimulated the creativity of craftsmen. For example, the best cobalt was mined in Persia, and the best porcelain was made in China. During the Yuan, Persian cobalt was brought to China and was used by Chinese potters to decorate ceramics. The result was the blue and white china of that era that is still considered unsurpassed in the world. Chinese called the cobalt-decorated porcelains "Mohammedan blue wares." Turks, Egyptians, and Europeans marveled at the thin, translucent Chinese porcelains. They snapped up these Chinese exports and later learned to make porcelains themselves. Early Turkish porcelains made in Isnik and European porcelains such as Delft ware showed distinct Chinese influence. Persians adapted Chinese portrait painting techniques to produce miniature paintings.

New Dynasties in West Asia

*History makes us acquainted with the conditions of past nations as they are reflected in their national character. The writing of history requires numerous sources and much varied knowledge. Historians . . . have committed frequent errors in the stories and events they reported. This is especially the case with figures, either of sums of money or of soldiers. . . . They offer good opportunity for false information. A hidden pitfall in historiography is disregard for the fact that conditions within nations and races change with the change of periods and the passage of time. When politically ambitious men overcome the ruling dynasty and seize power, they inevitably have recourse to the customs of their predecessors and adopt most of them. At the same time, they do not neglect the customs of their own race. This leads to some discrepancies between the customs of the new ruling dynasty and the customs of the old race.**

*Ibn Khaldun, *The Muqaddimah [Introduction to History]*, trans. Franz Rosenthal (Princeton: Princeton University Press, 1969), pp. 11, 24–25.

Born in Tunisia in 1332, Ibn Khaldun, who studied the patterns of change in civilizations over long spans of time, was a pioneer in the study of the philosophy of history. His analytical yet encyclopedic studies are early examples of rational attempts to trace patterns of change while centering on human beings as the main instruments of change. In the passage quoted here, Ibn Khaldun could well have been describing the world in which he lived. During Ibn Khaldun's lifetime, sweeping changes and military upheavals transformed the old Islamic/Arabic empires and brought about the emergence of several new competing centers of power.

After the disruptions caused by the Crusades and the Mongol invasions, West Asia split into three rival political entities: the Persians in present-day Iran; the Mamluks in

Egypt, who had repelled the invading Mongols and thereby fell heir to a major portion of the old Islamic Empire; and the Ottomans in present-day Turkey. With some variations, these divisions have persisted until the present.

The Flowering of Islamic Culture in Persia

In Persia and Iraq, the Mongol ruler Hulagu had established the il-Khanate dynasty, which had practiced religious toleration. Although the early il-Khanate rulers had favored Buddhism, the majority of their subjects remained Muslim. In hopes of converting the il-Khanate to Christianity, several popes sent missions to the capital of Tabriz, but these attempts failed. Over successive decades, il-Khanate rulers intermarried with Persian or Turkish Muslims, converted to Islam, and adopted the Persian language, known as Farsi (the Persian word for "Persian").

During the Arab conquests, Persian culture and language had been preserved and, as noted in the discussion of the early Islamic empires, had influenced many Islamic/Arab cultural forms, including art, architecture, and literature. Persian writers, particularly Firdawsi (c. 920–1020) in the *Shahnama* (Book of Shahs), helped to glorify and popularize Persian history. Just as Homer's *Iliad* and the Chinese Book of History relate tales from the mythological and ancient past, so too does the exceedingly long, 120,000-line *Shahnama* chronicle Persian history. The hero, Rustam, with his trusty horse Rakhsh, slays enemies, falls in love, mistakenly kills his own son, and lives over 500 years. This massive epic remains one of the greatest Persian cultural achievements.

As a result of the Mongol conquest, Persia had been freed from Arab domination, and it subsequently continued to develop along separate linguistic, political, and cultural lines. Persian became the language of the court and later heavily influenced literary Turkish. The il-Khanate introduced Chinese and Indian cultural influences and thereby freed Persian artists and scholars from some of the more puritanical constraints of Islamic/Arab culture. For example, the depiction of the human form, discouraged by strict adherents to Islam, became fairly commonplace among Persian artists. The vibrant Persian literary tradition, which developed separately from the Arabic tradition, furthered the division between the two societies, as did the continued predominance of Shi'i practices and interpretations of Islam among most Persians.

Persian poetry exemplifies these new influences. Persian poetry had already been heavily influenced by Sufism, or Islamic mysticism, which was generally frowned upon by Sunni Muslim communities. Sufis advocated using a variety of modes, including dance, music, poetry, and song, to attain unity with God.

Under the il-Khanate rulers, Persian poetry developed in several innovative ways. New meters and subject matter were introduced, as were rhyming couplets. As a result, Persian poetry—and, for that matter, other cultural fields—became more varied than the Arabic forms, which tended to remain static and traditional. Persian poets composed long epic and lyrical poems celebrating love, wine, women, and song. Rhyming quatrains such as these from *The Rubaiyat* by Omar Khayyam, who was also a noted astronomer, remain among the most widely read and quoted poetical works in the world.

Here with a little Bread beneath the Bough,
A Flask of Wine, a Book of Verse—and Thou,
Beside me singing in the Wilderness—
Oh, Wilderness were Paradise enow!

. . .

The moving finger writes; and, having writ,
Moves on: nor all your piety nor wit
Shall lure it back to cancel half a line,
Nor all your tears wash out a word of it.

Following the collapse of the il-Khanate and the chaos of Timurlane's invasions, a powerful new dynasty, the Safavids, emerged in Persia. The Safavids perpetuated and augmented the Persian cultural identity. The dichotomy between Persian and Arab societies—although both remained Islamic—has persisted until the present.

The Mamluk Dynasties

With the destruction of the Islamic state in Baghdad, Egypt became another center for Muslim cultural expression under the patronage of the new Mamluk dynasties. The first Mamluks, mostly of Turkish and Mongol origins, were former slaves and professional soldiers. These slaves were brought from outside Muslim territory to huge slave markets in Syria and Egypt where rulers who had themselves been slaves purchased them. The new owners educated the Mamluks (literally, those possessed or owned) and then freed them in a formal ceremony. The newly freed slaves were given a state subsidy and entered the service of ruling households. The slaves became the masters following the collapse of the descendants of Salah ed-Din's dynasty.

The Mamluks did not follow the principle of hereditary succession. A son did not inherit his father's position; instead, power was passed on to new slaves who had been raised to become generals or administrators. Although this process ensured a degree of upward mobility and a constant infusion of new, ambitious leaders, it also frequently led to bloody struggles for power. Indeed, the average reign of a Mamluk sultan was only six years. Throughout history, dynasties and governments have struggled with the problems posed by rules of succession and the passing on of leadership (see Comparative Essays 4 and 5).

The first twenty-four Mamluk rulers were known as the Bahri (river rulers); they were followed by a succession of so-called Burji (tower Mamluks), who took their name from having been quartered in the towers of the Citadel fortress, overlooking the city of Cairo. The Burji Mamluks were predominantly Circassian (a region in the Caucasus) in origin. The Mamluks successfully maintained Egyptian control over the Syrian provinces and, under Baybars (reigned 1260–1277), succeeded in driving the crusaders out of the region. Crucially, they also succeeded in repelling four major invasions by the Mongols. Unable to extend his authority over North Africa, and with a keen sense of power politics, Baybars established alliances with potential enemies, including Sicily, Seville, and the Turks.

Mamluk government was based on a strictly hierarchical, feudal system of allegiance of vassals to higher-ranking officials. In addition to their obvious military prowess, the Mamluks were also known for their cruelty and corruption, and as zealous converts to Islam were not as tolerant of minorities as their predecessors. Essentially foreign rulers, the Mamluks excluded most Egyptians from positions of authority, and many never learned Arabic.

The Mamluks sought to legitimize their rule by fervent support of Islamic institutions. Although many of them were not personally religious, the Mamluks gave sanctuary to the exiled Abbasid caliph (Islam's spiritual leader) from Baghdad. Successive caliphs had no real power, but the presence of the caliphate in Cairo gave the Mamluks legal authority throughout much of the Islamic world. The acceptance of Mamluk authority by the holy cities of Mecca and Medina provided a further stamp of legitimacy.

By protecting the trade routes and encouraging commercial activities, the Mamluks made Egypt the most prosperous Islamic state during much of the fourteenth and fifteenth centuries. Because the Mamluks were

A. F. Kersting

Courtesy of Janice Terry

Mausoleum of Qait Bey (reigned 1468–1495). The mausoleum includes a fountain and a monastery, as well as the tomb chamber. Ornate stonework domes (above) were literally the crowning glories of Mamluk tombs. Like many Mamluks, Qait Bey was a great builder, and more than a dozen monuments by his architects remain in present-day Cairo. Qait Bey had been a slave purchased for about $130; an outstanding soldier, he worked his way to the commanding position and ultimately became a renowned Mamluk sultan.

A Fable

*Fairuz [the intelligent hare] watches the king of the elephants entering the lake and seeing the reflection of the moon . . . He notices the movement of the moon's image . . . Hanging like a canopy over the scene is a deep blue sky with a golden moon.**

The book of fables, *Kalila wa Dimna,* is a fascinating example of the transfer of culture from one society to another over hundreds of years. Originally written in Sanskrit, the book is a collection of fables much like those of Aesop or the French tales of Reynard, the wily fox. These fables all teach basic lessons of ethics and behavior. *Kalila wa Dimna,* named after the two jackals who are the heroes of the stories, was brought to Persia in the sixth century. Ibn al-Muqaffa translated it into Arabic in the 700s. The stories were still popular during the reign of the Mamluks; a lavishly illustrated copy from 1354 has survived, and it reveals the timeless quality of these tales. The manuscript also demonstrates the skill and sophistication of the artists who worked under Mamluk patronage.

**Kalila wa Dimna,* from a fourteenth-century manuscript, ed. Esin Atil (Washington, D.C.: Smithsonian Press, 1981), p. 42.

Bodleian Library

Mamluk Painted Manuscript. This painting depicts the fable of the clever hare and the king of the elephants. The hare tricks the elephant into thinking that the moon, shown in the reflection of the water, is talking to him.

keen patrons of the arts, they encouraged artisans, particularly metalworkers and textile manufacturers, to settle in their territories, often providing them with substantial financial rewards. However, Mamluk attempts to monopolize the trade in luxury goods and heavy taxation ultimately caused many merchants to shift their activities away from Egypt.

The Mamluks supported building trades and social welfare projects. Many of the medieval monuments remaining in the modern city of Cairo date from the period of Mamluk rule. In addition to huge complexes of hospitals, schools, and mosques, they erected massive mausoleums for themselves and their wives and children. The great Islamic university, al-Azhar, and other Islamic schools prospered under Mamluk patronage. Scholars from throughout the Islamic world flocked to Egypt, which became a center of intellectual activity.

The life of Ibn Khaldun, the best-known of these scholars, demonstrates the overriding cultural unity of the Islamic world, a unity that overcame continual political upheavals and divisions. At various times in his life, Ibn Khaldun worked in his native Tunisia and in Morocco, Granada (the last Arab stronghold in Spain), and Egypt. He was sent as an emissary to negotiate with the King of Castile in Spain, and he even met with Timurlane after the fall of Damascus. Not surprisingly, Ibn Khaldun's historical studies deal extensively with the problems of establishing good governments and the negative effects created by political rivalries.

Despite the insights of Ibn Khaldun, the Mamluks continued their perpetual infighting, which seriously undermined their power and made them increasingly vulnerable to outside threats. Failing to forge a united front, the Mamluks fell in 1517 to the superior political and military organization of the Ottoman Turks.

The House of Osman

As the nomadic Turkish tribes converted to Islam, they devoted their traditional warrior way of life to protecting

Islam from internal and external threats. Turkish warriors, adherents of Sunni Islam, viewed themselves as the "guardians" of Islam and fought tenaciously along the religious frontier between Islam and Christianity, particularly against the Byzantine Empire. Known as *ghazis,* these warriors amassed booty and slaves in their fights against the enemies of Islam, and many of their leaders established separate emirates (principalities). One of the Turkish emirs, Osman (reigned 1299–1326), was the founder of one of the greatest world empires, the Ottoman Empire (*Ottoman* is an Italian corruption of Osman). Between 1300 and 1320, Osman, leading his ghazi warriors personally into battle, began to extend his authority from his capital at Bursa out into the Anatolian Peninsula.

Clearly, the army was a key institution in the creation of the Ottoman Empire. Originally, the army was composed mostly of volunteers from the nomadic Turkish tribes, but as it grew, recruitment and organization of the army were formalized. As Osman's power increased, other ghazis, attracted by the promise of wealth, joined him. These Islamic warriors were guided by a strict code of behavior, similar to the European knights' code of chivalry.

The creation of the *janissary* corps (from the Turkish term *yeni cheri,* or new soldiers) was a uniquely Ottoman military innovation. Male child slaves taken from predominantly Christian communities under Ottoman control became janissaries, trained from childhood to become professional soldiers. The janissaries learned Turkish, became Muslims, and owed loyalty only to their immediate superiors and to the Ottoman rulers. Like the professional warriors in ancient Sparta and the samurai

Map 8.6 Ottoman Empire in 1461. From its small territory in central Anatolia, the Ottoman Empire had defeated the old Byzantine Empire, making Istanbul its new capital. From there the Ottomans conquered much of the rest of the Anatolian Peninsula and the Balkans, known as Rumeli.

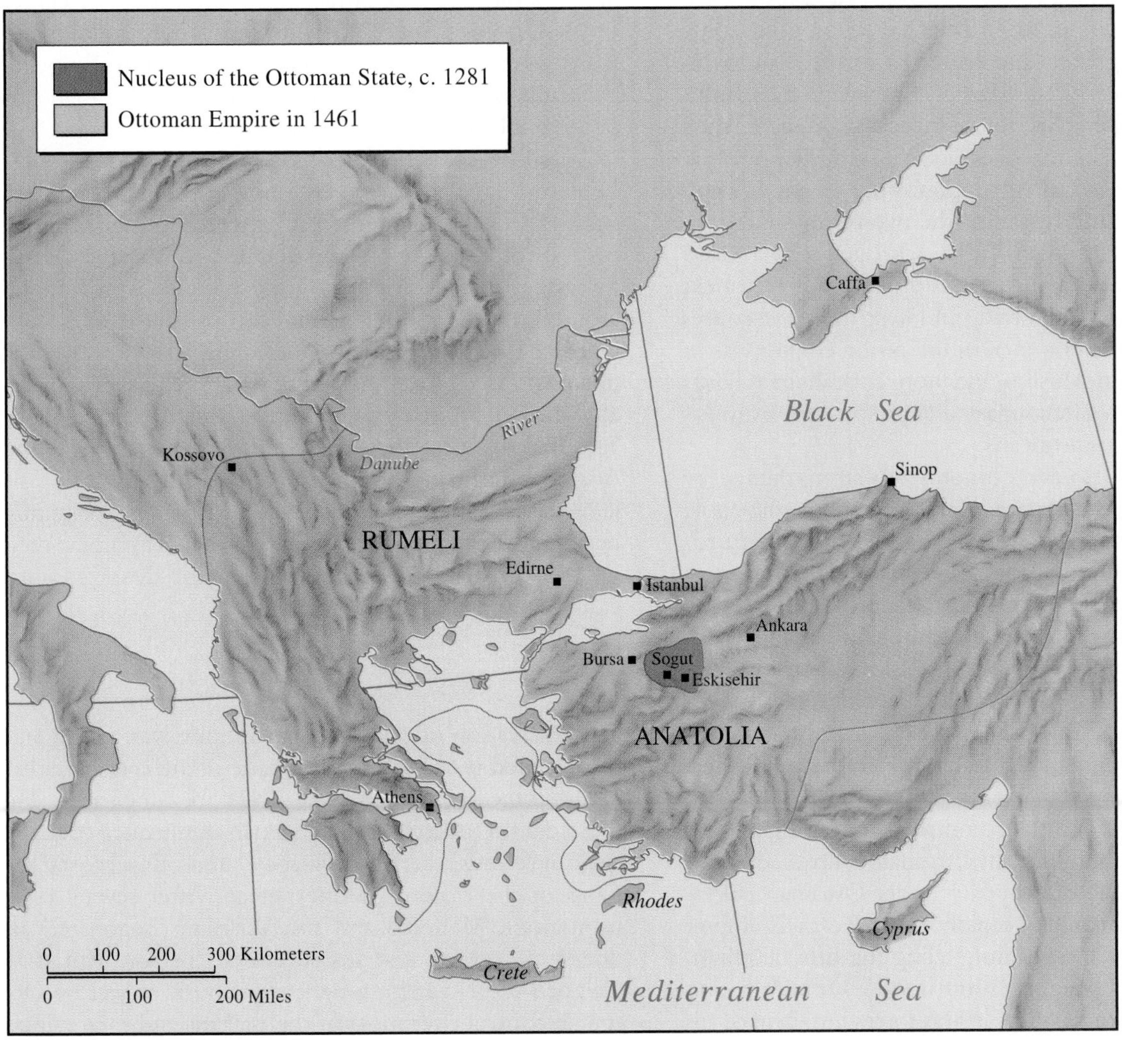

warriors in Japan, the janissaries became known for their fighting zeal and professionalism. They lived, ate, and fought together and became a highly cohesive force. Janissaries did not marry until they retired from active military service, and even after marriage often continued to take their meals with their colleagues.

When the empire was at its zenith, the janissaries were a key force in the extension and power of the state. As the sultans became weaker and less dynamic, however, the janissaries often revolted against them. Not infrequently, the sultans, like Roman emperors under the control of their personal bodyguards, ruled only at the pleasure of the janissaries, who had the power to oust or even to assassinate them. But the potential threat of the janissary forces was not evident during the early centuries of Ottoman rule. Wisely, Osman and his son Orhan (reigned 1326–1360) willingly accepted outside recruits and formed alliances with Greeks in the captured territories. Such alliances, often reinforced through marriage (for example, Orhan married the daughter of a Greek noble), helped the Ottomans to consolidate their conquered territories.

Ottoman rulers gave land to soldiers as a reward for bravery and success on the battlefield; as a result, some soldiers held huge fiefs and retired as wealthy landowners who frequently hired overseers to manage their holdings. Similarly, the collection of taxes was often "farmed out" to professional tax collectors, a system that resulted in pervasive abuses and corruption. Booty from war and tax revenues on land remained the two major sources of income for the Ottoman Turks, who generally looked down on business and trade. Although the Ottoman government encouraged trade and kept the trade routes in good repair, the commercial life of the empire was in the hands of non-Muslim and non-Turkish merchants and artisans, who often amassed large fortunes from lucrative trade with Europeans.

The whole Ottoman economy was strengthened by the booty gained in warfare. Merchants and craftspeople joined together in *akhis*, which were similar to the European guild. Often members of the guilds were also members of the same *sufi* or mystical Islamic order. Hence, the religious and economic institutions were highly cohesive. The Ottomans followed the Islamic precept of allowing freedom of worship for all "people of the Book." Through the "millet" system (the Islamic system for governing religious minorities), they granted considerable autonomy to the many heterogeneous religious and ethnic groups under their control. For example, the large Jewish community in Ottoman-controlled lands enjoyed considerable prosperity under Ottoman rulers.

The Ottoman sultans rapidly expanded their empire at the expense of Byzantium. Taking the title of sultan, by 1362 Murad I (reigned 1360–1389), Orhan's young warrior son, had successfully led his forces into Thrace (in present-day Greece and Turkey) and took Adrianople, which became the new Ottoman capital of Edirne. Pushing his army further into the Balkans, at Kosovo in 1389 Murad decisively defeated the Serbian rulers but lost his life in the process. The military defeat at Kosovo is still remembered by the people of contemporary Balkan nations. Through the marriage of his son Bayezid to the daughter of a leading emir in Anatolia, Murad nearly doubled Ottoman holdings in Asia.

Bayezid (reigned 1389–1402) immediately sought to consolidate his own position. He had his only brother—a possible rival—killed, thereby establishing a tradition: for the next several hundred years, new Ottoman sultans had their siblings assassinated or imprisoned within the imperial palaces. Having secured sole possession of the leadership, Bayezid then moved to avenge his father's death with further victories in Europe. He surrounded Constantinople and closed the Bosporus and the Dardanelles.

In face of this renewed threat to Christian authority over Constantinople, rulers in Europe, particularly Sigismund, the king of Hungary and later Holy Roman Emperor, were roused to action. Bayezid forsook the siege of Constantinople to meet the crusading Christian forces at Nicopolis in 1396. Attacking directly into the center of the Ottoman forces, the Europeans were routed, and many were taken as slaves or held for ransom. Enjoying the fruits of victory, Bayezid was the first Ottoman sultan to establish the trappings of a royal court.

Had Bayezid concentrated on the Balkan territories, he might have continued to enjoy unparalleled military success; however, he aimed to extend Ottoman control over all of Asia Minor, and this led to disaster. As his forces began attacking rival Turkish emirates in Asia, he aroused the anger of Timurlane. At the battle of Ankara in 1402 Bayezid's army was defeated, and he was taken prisoner. Placed in a cage as a prize of war, Bayezid probably died en route to Timurlane's capital of Samarkand. The Balkans were lost, but Timurlane turned over the Anatolian territories to Bayezid's sons. After swearing allegiance to Timurlane as his vassals, the sons promptly began fighting among themselves. When Timurlane died in 1405, his loosely fashioned empire dissolved into competing, rival local emirates.

The Conquest of Constantinople

The restoration of the Ottoman Empire was a long and complicated process. After a decade of internecine fighting, Mehmed I (reigned 1413–1421) became sultan. He created a fleet to challenge Venetian dominance over the Aegean Islands, the Anatolia coast, and other coastal regions of the eastern Mediterranean. After several confrontations, Mehmed and the Venetians negotiated an uneasy peace. He and his successor, his son Murad II (reigned 1421–1451), fought tenaciously to restore Ottoman control over most of the Balkans and even raided into Hungary. Known for his piety and adherence to the ghazi warrior traditions, Murad attracted a loyal following of old Ottoman families. He resumed the siege of Constantinople but was forced to lift it in face of renewed revolts in Asia Minor.

Under Murad's patronage, Turkish arts flourished. A new literary tradition glorifying the warrior ethos of the early Ottomans developed and gained popularity. Like the Roman Emperor Diocletian and the later Holy Roman Emperor Charles V, Murad twice announced his retirement for a life of study and contemplation, but attacks by Hungarian and Balkan leaders, who apparently thought the empire would collapse with Murad's departure, impelled his return to the battlefield.

Under Murad's leadership, Ottoman forces easily conquered Serbia, Bosnia, and parts of Greece. Many Eastern Orthodox Christians willingly aligned with the Ottomans who, unlike the Roman Catholic Hungarian leaders, were relatively tolerant of adherents to the Eastern Christian rites; some even sent their sons as hostages to the sultan, and others willingly converted to Islam.

When Murad II died in 1451, his son, Mehmed II (reigned 1451–1481), became the new sultan. Competent and well educated, Mehmed knew several languages and was a student of philosophy. All Ottoman rulers were skilled in a trade, and Mehmed was an accomplished gardener who worked in the royal gardens for relaxation between battles. He was also an efficient administrator who

Mehmed II. In this portrait by the Turkish artist Sinan Bey, Mehmed II is depicted not as an able military commander but as a cultured gentleman. An expert gardener, Mehmed was known for his love of flowers; here he enjoys the scent of a favorite rose blossom.

Giraudon/Art Resource

950	Fatimid caliphate established in Cairo
1000	al-Azhar University established Arab scholars and scientists: trigonometry, geometry Ibn Sina (Avicenna) Rise of the Seljuk Turks
1100	Crusaders conquer Jerusalem Trade between Europe and Asia increases Salah ed-Din reconquers Jerusalem Genghis Khan leads the Mongols Ibn Rushd (Averroës) Rabbi Musa bin Maymun
1200	Mogols conquer northern China, Russia, eastern Europe Kubilai Khan ascends Mongol throne Marco Polo visits China Mamluks rule in Egypt and Syria Mongols convert to Buddhism and Islam
1300	Ottomans conquer Anatolia Omar Khayyam, *The Rubaiyat* Timurlane conquests Mongol Yuan dynasty ends in China
1400	Ottomans capture Constantinople al-Hambra (Red Castle) Ivan III renounces allegiance to the Golden Horde

established highly centralized systems of taxation and bureaucracy.

Upon accession to the throne, Mehmed II immediately launched his plans for a total assault on Constantinople. He assembled a fleet at Gallipoli and amassed a huge supply of armaments, including cannon, gunpowder, timbers, and bows and arrows. Although the Mongols, as previously mentioned, had primitive cannon, the Ottomans effectively utilized forged metal cannon to gain strategic advantages over their enemies and thereby became one of the first "gunpowder empires."

To assist in taking Constantinople, Mehmed II constructed Rumeli Hisar, a massive fortress on the European shore of the Bosporus opposite the fortifications built by his great-grandfather. He then had siege cannon moved into position, and when all the preparations were in order, the actual siege began, in April 1453. It lasted fifty-four days. Mehmed even had ships hauled up a wooden ramp to the Golden Horn in order to bombard the city from all directions. With the city completely surrounded, Emperor Constantine called for help from Rome, but by this time most of the Byzantine citizens preferred the toleration of the Ottoman Muslims to the noted intolerance of the Roman papacy.

Finally, on May 29, 1453, the city walls were breached and the Ottoman forces entered the fabled city. After three days of pillage, Mehmed entered the city and proclaimed Istanbul (the Turkish name for the city) the new Ottoman capital. Eyewitness accounts relate that Mehmed was much taken with the glory of the city and was determined to create an even more glorious capital for himself.

Mehmed II, now "the Conqueror," encouraged artisans and merchants from around the world to settle and work in Istanbul and embarked on an ambitious program to make the city a capital worthy of the new Ottoman Empire. For the Christian world, the fall of Constantinople marked the end of the old Roman Empire and the beginning of an era of Ottoman Muslim control over the eastern Mediterranean.

Summary and Comparisons

The spectacular military and political success of the Muslims from the seventh century onward produced an era of affluence and cultural achievement known as the golden age of Islam. It reached its zenith under the Abbasid caliphs in Baghdad at the time of the early medieval period in western Europe. Assimilating many diverse peoples, a new Islamic/Arabic amalgam developed in culture and the arts. Muslims acted as a conduit for the transmission of Greek and Roman learning to later generations. The T'ang dynasty in China, the Guptas in India, and the Ghanaian kingdoms in West Africa fostered similar cultural contributions.

Schisms fragmented the Abbasid Empire into rival components. Earlier empires in the region had been weakened and torn apart by similar problems. The coastal areas along the eastern Mediterranean fell to a small army of Christian crusaders from Europe.

The Crusades were launched by European Christians of the Roman Catholic church to end Muslim control of the Holy Land and establish European-style feudal kingdoms in the eastern Mediterranean region. Ultimately, the Crusades failed, but they contributed to the rising prosperity of the Italian city-states by spurring European demand for Asian goods and thus promoting international trade. On the negative side, the Crusades caused tension and mutual intolerance between Christians and Muslims.

In the early thirteenth century, Genghis Khan led the Mongol nomads out of the grasslands north of China to create the largest land empire in history. For millions of people in Korea, China, Persia, the Arab world, Russia, and eastern Europe, the Mongol conquest was a cataclysmic event that brought death and destruction; it also cut off Russia from the rest of Europe.

The empire of Genghis Khan remained essentially united until his grandson's generation, when, as in so many earlier empires, civil wars led to its collapse. With little culture and no tradition of settled government, the Mongol rulers recruited foreigners to control their empires. As in the Roman and other earlier empires, when the Mongol rulers became corrupt and decadent, their subject peoples rose up and overthrew them. The Mongols of the heartland and those who ruled China became Buddhists; the others converted to Islam.

Mongol rule did have some beneficial effects, including international trade in luxury items and security for merchants under the Pax Mongolica. But slavery and oppression remained the lot of the Mongol subjects; unlike the Romans and Muslims, the Mongols did not grant citizenship to conquered peoples or generally assimilate them. In marked contrast to earlier empires in Egypt, Mesopotamia, India, and the Western Hemisphere, the Mongol Empire did not bequeath many monuments or enduring cultural achievements to future generations.

Mongol invasions did not destroy the culture or religious zeal of the Muslims. Under Mongol and later Safavid rule, the Persians established their own linguistic and cultural traditions, with strong influences from Chinese, Indian, and Sufi (Islamic mystical) traditions.

The Mamluks, former slaves, established their own dynasties in Egypt and greater Syria. They helped to preserve Islamic traditions and encouraged architecture and the arts, but, as with so many dynasties around the world, political disunity led to their defeat.

Beginning in the thirteenth century, the Turkish leader Osman and his successors extended Ottoman control into Europe and across Anatolia, forming a frontier society based on a strict adherence to Islam. Despite a temporary setback at the hands of Timurlane in Asia, by the mid-fifteenth century the Ottomans controlled most of the Balkans and Anatolia. In 1453, Mehmed II conquered Constantinople, destroying the last vestiges of the Byzantine Empire. Like the Chinese in the Sui and T'ang Dynasties, the Ottomans established a highly centralized government with rule emanating from the top down and following a dynastic line through the ruling family. Many empires in the ancient world had been organized along similar principles.

Selected Sources

Allen, T. T. *Mongol Imperialism.* 1987. A study of the overall effects of Mongol rule.

*Babinger, Franz. *Mehmed the Conqueror and His Time.* 1978. A colorful account of the outstanding Ottoman leader.

Chambers, James. *The Devil's Horsemen: The Mongol Invasion of Europe.* 1979. A good, short account of the origins and results of the Mongol incursion into Europe in 1241.

De Hartog, Leo. *Russia and the Mongol Yoke: The History of the Russian Principalities and the Golden Horde.* 1996. A good, recent book on how the Mongols dominated Russia.

Esposito, John L., ed. *The Oxford History of Islam.* 2000. An excellent, up-to-date reference work, with chapters on culture, art and architecture, the sciences, and philosophy during the golden age.

*Fletcher, Richard. *Moorish Spain.* 1993. Short introductory text with emphasis on cultural and social life.

*Grousset, René. *The Empire of the Steppes: A History of Central Asia.* 1970. Trans. Naomi Walford. A classic study of nomadic peoples and empires from the ancient Huns on.

*Hart, Henry. *Venetian Adventurer.* 1956. Good biography of Marco Polo.

*Hillenbrand, Carole. *The Crusades: Islamic Perspectives.* 1999. A lavishly illustrated reader, with discussions of the socio-economic and military effects of the Crusades on Christian-Muslim relations.

Kwanten, Luc. *Imperial Nomads: A History of Central Asia, 500–1500.* 1979. A study of the influence of nomads, especially Turks and Mongols, on the civilization of China, Persia, and Russia.

Langlois, John D., Jr., ed. *China under Mongol Rule.* 1981. A collection of articles on many topics.

Lister, R. P. *Genghis Khan.* 2000. A vivid, short biography.

*Maalouf, Amin. *The Crusades through Arab Eyes.* 1987. A highly readable account of Arab/Islamic reaction to the crusaders, with descriptions of how the Arabs overcame political divisions to oppose the European invaders.

Mernissi, Fatima. *The Forgotten Queens of Islam.* 1993; reprinted 1997. An insightful look at numerous powerful women in the early Muslim empires.

Nicolle, David. *The Mongol Warlords.* 1990. On the rise and rule of the Mongols.

Ratchnevsky, Paul. *Genghis Khan: His Life and Legacy.* 1991. Well-written, based on the latest scholarship.

*Riley-Smith, Jonathan, ed. *The Oxford Illustrated History of the Crusades.* 1995. An excellent, recent account, with superb photographs, maps, and chronologies.

*Rossabi, Morris. *Khubilai Khan: His Life and Times.* 1988. The only English-language biography of the first Mongol ruler of China, and a good one. It brings to life the man and his times.

———. *Voyage From Xanadu: Rabban Souma and the First Journey from China to the West.* 1992. This is a tale of a trip that was the reverse of Marco Polo's journey.

Twitchett, Denis, and John K. Fairbanks, eds. *The Cambridge History of China.* Vol. 6: *Alien Regimes and Border States, 907–1368.* 1994. This comprehensive and authoritative book is written by many experts.

*Available in paperback.

Internet Links

Abbasid Caliphate (Baghdad): 750–1258
http://www.northpark.edu/acad/history/WebChron/Islam/Abbasid.html
A helpful chronology of political and cultural events and trends; part of the online "WebChronology project."

Chronology of the Crusades
http://www.wcslc.edu/pers_pages/m-markow/sscle/ssclechr.html
A quite detailed listing of the year, season, month, and often day of important events. "While by no means complete, this list of significant dates can serve those who start a quest for understanding the crusades."

Empires beyond the Great Wall: The Heritage of Genghis Khan
http://vvv.com/khan/
Based on a special exhibit at the Royal British Columbia Museum in 1995, this website features concise texts and some graphics "representative of the rich cultural heritage of Inner Mongolia." Includes biographical information about Genghis Khan.

The Fall of Constantinople, 1453
http://www.greece.org/Romiosini/fall.html
An excellent, accurate, and lively account by Dionysios Hatzopoulos, professor of Classical and Byzantine Studies at the University of Montreal.

Medieval Sourcebook: Al-Makrisi: Account of the Crusade of St. Louis
http://www.fordham.edu/halsall/source/makrisi.html
A lengthy extract from an important early Arab source for this Crusade.

Medieval Sourcebook: Marco Polo: The Glories of Kinsay [Hangchow] (c. 1300)
http://www.fordham.edu/halsall/source/polo-kinsay.html
A good extract from Marco Polo's *Travels,* recounting his impressions of a major city in the empire of Kubilai Khan.

COMPARATIVE ESSAY 7

European Imperialism through the End of the Seventeenth Century

I came to get gold, not to till the soil, like a peasant.

Hernán Cortés (William Prescott, *The History of the Conquest of Mexico* [Chicago: University of Chicago Press, 1966], p. 47)

Tell me, by what right or justice do you hold these Indians in such a cruel and horrible servitude? On what authority have you waged such detestable wars against these peoples, who dwelt quietly and peacefully on their own land? Wars in which you have destroyed such infinite numbers of them by homicide and slaughter never before heard of? Why do you keep them so oppressed and exhausted, without giving them enough to eat or curbing them of their sicknesses from the excessive labor you give them, and they die, or rather, you kill them, in order to extract and acquire gold every day?

Fray Antonio de Montesinos (George Sanderlin, ed., *Bartolomé de Las Casas: A Selection of His Writings* [New York: Knopf, 1971], p. 81)

Not only have [the Indians] shown themselves to be very wise people and possessed of lively and marked understanding, prudently governing and providing for their nations . . . and making them prosper in justice; but they have equalled many diverse nations of the world, past and present, that have been praised for their governance, politics and customs, and exceed by no small measure the wisest of all of these, such as the Greeks and the Romans, in adherence to the rules of natural reason.

Bartolomé de Las Casas (Lewis Hankey, *All Mankind Is One* [De Kalb: Northern Illinois Press, 1959], p. 77)

Cortés's statement, made to the secretary of the governor of Hispaniola, aptly describes the motive that drove him and other Spanish adventurers beyond the coast into uncharted territory, risking their lives and doing battle with Indian forces many times larger than their own. The conquistadors not only seized the treasures they found, but enslaved the Amerindians and compelled them to work in the mines for their further enrichment and that of their masters. Fray Antonio de Montesinos's sermon, part of which is quoted above, initiated the Dominican campaign against slavery. Influenced by what he heard, Las Casas joined the order in 1511 and took the lead in the effort to arouse the conscience of Spain. In his many writings he attempted to refute the argument that the Amerindians were inferior and should be considered as the natural slaves of the Spaniards. Las Casas's plea before the King was so eloquent that new laws were passed in 1542, resulting in the amelioration of the lot of the Amerindians.

The urge of strong and dynamic states to subjugate weaker ones dates back to the earliest civilizations. The word "imperialism," which is used to designate this drive, suggests the use of force to establish and maintain domination. The forms of imperialism varied from region to region, depending on the nature of the governments involved and the level of civilization of the conquered population. In some instances foreign rule was exercised through local tribal chiefs. In others it was administered directly through colonial administrators. The motives for expansion were mixed, but political, economic, religious, and strategic interests were the most important.

During the early modern period, imperialism was largely, but not exclusively, a European phenomenon. Prior to the eighteenth century, several major Asiatic states also dominated weaker neighbors. In 1453 the Ottoman Turks breached the walls of Constantinople, completing their conquest of the thousand-year-old Byzantine Empire. Early in the sixteenth century they conquered Syria, Palestine, and Egypt, creating a state that stretched from the Danube to beyond the Nile and posing a major threat to western Europe. In China the Ming emperors' expansion to the northwest was primarily defensive in nature, designed to forestall renewed Mongol invasion. More impressive were their great maritime expeditions that ventured thousands of miles south and west into the Indian Ocean, the Persian Gulf, and the Red Sea. These voyages, however, were intended essentially to proclaim the resurgence of China, to promote commerce, and to gain geographic knowledge. As the Chinese established no overseas naval bases and planted no colonies, the early expeditions had no lasting effect. Issuing from central Asia, the Moghuls embraced the Islamic religion and invaded India, uniting the country's many petty principalities. Babur, the founder of the Moghul dynasty, and his descendants established an empire that, at its peak, embraced almost the entire subcontinent.

In the late fifteenth century, Europeans embarked on an exploratory burst that changed the course of history. By then improvements in navigational techniques and ship design had made possible long ocean voyages. Then, too, the centralized monarchies could look outward, having attained relative internal peace and stability and possessing the material resources to carry through large-scale enterprises. Portugal, a seafaring nation with a long Atlantic coastline, began the process of opening new worlds to Western peoples. A series of Portuguese expeditions slowly inched along the west coast of Africa and rounded the Cape of Good Hope before a fleet, captained by the intrepid Vasco da Gama, reached India in 1498. The fear that Portugal would dominate the sea lanes spurred Spain to underwrite Columbus's famous journey to find a new route to the Far East. By the seventeenth century other nations, notably England, France, and the Netherlands, had entered the scramble for overseas empires, establishing footholds in Africa and parts of Asia and annexing large territories in the Western Hemisphere.

The desire for profit was the dominant motive for overseas exploration. Monarchs funded exploratory voyages, hoping to find new sources of gold and silver. Merchants and traders also had reason to look abroad. For centuries Asia had supplied Europe with luxury goods and spices, essential for the preservation of food and in pharmaceutical products. The cost of Asian goods was exorbitant because each intermediary who handled them took huge profits. Thus western European commercial interests were anxious to bypass the middlemen and go directly to the source.

Competing European powers tried, usually unsuccessfully, to gain effective control over high-priced commodities. For example, the Dutch jealously guarded their monopoly over nutmeg from the Dutch Indies, even going so far as to treat the seeds with lime to prevent their propagation elsewhere. Ultimately the English were able to break the monopoly and established nutmeg plantations in the Caribbean.

Although the importance of religious zeal has probably been exaggerated by historians, it certainly ranks high among the reasons that drove Europeans across the seas. The crusading impulse against non-Christians was still very much alive in the fifteenth century, particularly among the Spanish and Portuguese whose commitment to Catholicism had been reinforced during the reconquest of the Iberian Peninsula. The Iberian nations spearheaded the movement to convert heathens and to identify supposedly lost Christians in the east who might serve as allies against Islam. Christian missionaries had little success in Asia because the adherents of Hinduism, Buddhism, Islam, and Confucianism resisted conversion. On the other hand, Spanish and Portuguese missionaries were much more successful in the Western Hemisphere, where they compelled the surviving indigenous Amerindians to abandon their traditional faiths. France, regarding itself as the "eldest daughter of the Catholic church," sent missionaries to Indochina and other areas of the world. Although not as zealous to win over converts, Protestant Netherlands and England used their colonies to rid themselves of religious dissenters.

The lure of adventure was another factor prompting Europeans to probe the unknown. They yearned to see for themselves the distant lands and cultures that so differed from their own. Stories abounded about the existence of exotic lands in Asia, popularized by early travelers like Marco Polo, and about the mythical Christian kingdom of Prester John in Africa.

Finally, national rivalry also stimulated imperialism. In the seventeenth century, the English, Dutch, and French governments joined in the search for trade and empire partly because of nationalistic hostility toward Spain and Portugal. Not only did they compete against one another for new lands, but they frequently intruded into the overseas colonial possessions of Spain and Portugal.

Several different patterns of European colonization emerged during this period. The first and oldest form was the fortified trading post, initially established by the Portuguese and later emulated by other European powers in Africa and East Asia. As European states expanded, they often conquered territories possessing the desired commodities. For example, Spain seized control of the gold and silver supply of Mexico and Peru, the Dutch took over much of the spice trade by conquering most of the East Indian islands, and many of the imperial European nations annexed sugar-producing regions in the Caribbean and Brazil. When there were not enough indigenous laborers to work the sugar plantations, black slaves were imported in large numbers from Africa, thereby altering the racial composition of many parts of the Western Hemisphere.

Beginning in the seventeenth century, the English and the French, in particular, created "new Europes," or areas in which a flood of European immigrants replaced the small local populations. Colonies of settlements were established for various economic, political, and religious reasons. The English, Dutch, and French created such colonies on the eastern coast of North America. Spanish and Portuguese settlers had come a century earlier, and in spite of their scant numbers had succeeded in transplanting key aspects of European culture to Latin America. Western Europeans did not attempt to form settlements in Asia, where the dense population provided sufficient labor for their economic exploitation.

Emerging Global Interrelations

9

Wednesday, November 28, 1520, we debouched from [the Strait of Magellan, at the tip of South America], engulfing ourselves in the Pacific Sea. We were three months and twenty days without getting any kind of fresh food. We ate bisquit, which was no longer bisquit, but powder of bisquit swarming with worms. . . . It stank strongly of the urine of rats. We drank yellow water that had been putrid for many days. We also ate oxhides . . . and sawdust from boards. Rats were sold for one-half ducados apiece, and even [then] we could not get them. [But the worst was that] the gums . . . of some of our men swelled [from scurvy], so that they could not eat under any circumstances and therefore died. . . . Had not God and His blessed mother given us . . . good weather we would have all died of hunger in that exceeding vast sea. Of a verity I believe no such voyage will ever be made again. . . .

*On Monday, September eight [1522] we cast anchor near the quay of [Seville, Spain] . . . with only [twenty-one] men and the majority of them sick. . . . Some died of hunger; some deserted . . . and some were put to death for crimes. . . . We had sailed fourteen thousand, four hundred and sixty leguas [about 40,000 miles] and furthermore completed the circumnavigation of the world from east to west. . . . Tuesday we all went in shirts and barefoot, each holding a candle, to visit [shrines]. . . .**

*Antonio Pigafetta, in Charles E. Nowell, ed., *Magellan's Voyage around the World* (Evanston, IL: Northwestern University Press, 1962), pp. 122–124, 259.

The (appropriately named) Portuguese ship *Victoria,* which limped into the harbor near Seville on September 6, 1522, with its sick and ragged surviving crew, had made history by circumnavigating the globe. Although the expedition's commander, Ferdinand Magellan, did not live to savor the triumph, his crew had done what no humans had done before.

Magellan's expedition was the culmination of a century of European voyages of discovery that had begun with Prince Henry the Navigator of Portugal. The European appetite for adventure and taste for the luxuries of Asia dated back to the First Crusade (1096–1099); Marco Polo's accounts of his travels in the thirteenth century had also created great interest in Asian lands far removed from Europe. But not until the fifteenth century did advances in shipbuilding and navigational knowledge permit oceangoing vessels to sail around the Cape of Good Hope and across the Indian Ocean to Asia. At the end of the century, Christopher Columbus sailed across the Atlantic and stumbled onto a "New World" in the Western Hemisphere while seeking an alternative route to Asia. Magellan proved the existence of such a route by sailing around South America, past Cape Horn, and across the Pacific to Asia.

Whereas major civilizations had developed in relative isolation from each other in the preceding 5,000 years, the voyages of discovery of the fifteenth and sixteenth centuries began to meld the world into an interrelated whole. The earth today is truly an interdependent "global village."

This chapter begins with a discussion of the highly centralized and powerful Ottoman and Safavid Empires, based in western Asia, and their interactions and confrontations with one another and with Europe. Commercial interactions between Asian empires and Europe had fueled Europeans' appetites for Asian luxury goods and also helped to foster the new intellectual and artistic climate of the Renaissance, which began in Italy and spread through the rest of Europe. Following a description of the Renaissance, this chapter will trace the development of centralized monarchies in Europe and the religious and political changes brought about by the Reformation.

The chapter will then examine how European horizons in the fifteenth century expanded to include—for Europeans—the newly discovered continents of Africa south of the Sahara and North and South America. The impacts of the slave trade on African societies and the Western Hemisphere will be described. The chapter closes with a discussion of the creation of colonial empires by Europeans in the Western Hemisphere.

The Rival Ottoman and Safavid Empires

The Sultan was seated on a rather low sofa, not more than a foot from the ground and spread with many costly coverlets and cushions embroidered with exquisite work. Near him were his bow and arrows. His expression . . . is anything but smiling, and has a sternness which, though sad, is full of majesty.

The Sultan's head-quarters were crowded by numerous attendants, including many high officials. All the cavalry of the guard were there . . . and a large number of Janissaries. . . . The Sultan himself assigns to all their duties and offices, and in doing so pays no attention to wealth or the empty claims of rank. . . . He only considers merit and scrutinizes the character, natural ability, and disposition of each.

The Turks were quite as much astonished at our manner of dress as we at theirs. They wear long robes which reach almost to their ankles, and are not only more imposing but seem to add to the stature; our dress, on the other hand, is so short and tight that it disclosed the forms of the body, which would be better hidden.

*What struck me as particularly praiseworthy in that great multitude was the silence and good discipline. . . . Each man kept his appointed place. . . . The officers . . . were seated; the common soldiers stood up. The most remarkable body of men were several thousand Janissaries, who stood in a long line apart and so motionless that . . . I was for a while doubtful whether they were living men or statues.**

** The Turkish Letters of Ogier Ghiselin De Busbecq,* trans. Edward S. Forster (Oxford: Clarendon Press, 1927), pp. 58–62. Another brief excerpt of the letters can be found in Peter N. Stearns, ed., *Documents in World History,* vol. 2 (Oxford: Clarendon Press, 1988), pp. 73–77.

In these words, the imperial ambassador for the Holy Roman Empire described the court of Suleiman the Magnificent, the ruler of the Ottoman Empire. While Christian Europe was entering a period of religious turmoil (discussed later in the chapter), Suleiman's empire and its powerful rival, the Safavid state in Persia, were both in the ascendant. Indeed, the Ottoman Empire profited from Christian turmoil and dynastic rivalries, extending its rule into central Europe and advancing to the gates of Vienna. Religious differences also existed in the Islamic world, however; the Ottoman and Safavid states were sectarian as well as political rivals. Although Ottoman taxation of international trade helped to stimulate European interest in developing new trade routes to Asia, the two Muslim empires were far too strong in this period to feel adverse effects from European expansion.

Ottoman Territorial Expansion and Government

Immediately following the conquest of Constantinople in 1453, the Ottoman Sultans moved to extend their control over the Balkans. Aided by the rugged terrain in the region, the predominantly Christian but politically divided Balkan peoples repelled Ottoman advances until late in the sixteenth century. Papal calls for crusades against the Ottomans were ignored as Europeans, more interested in economic gains than religious confrontations with the Muslim Ottoman government, sought to establish commercial and political relations.

Sultan Selim I (reigned 1512–1520) sought territorial gains in the east and south. After successfully thwarting the threat of expansion by the Safavid emperors in Persia, in 1517 Selim routed the Mamluks in Egypt and gained control of Palestine and Syria. The defeat of the Mamluks gave the Ottomans control over most of the Arab world, including the key Muslim cities of Mecca, Medina, and Jerusalem. The Ottoman rulers moved the caliphate to Istanbul and assumed leadership over the Sunni Islamic world. They now viewed themselves as the guardians of Islam and the military might of their empire as the Sword of Islam. Later, the sultans also took the title of caliph.

Ottoman expansion continued during the reign of Suleiman the Magnificent (reigned 1520–1566), when

Map 9.1 Ottoman Expansion. The Ottomans expanded rapidly throughout the fifteenth and sixteenth centuries, conquering vast territories around the Black Sea, in the Balkans, and in the Arab provinces along the eastern Mediterranean and North Africa.

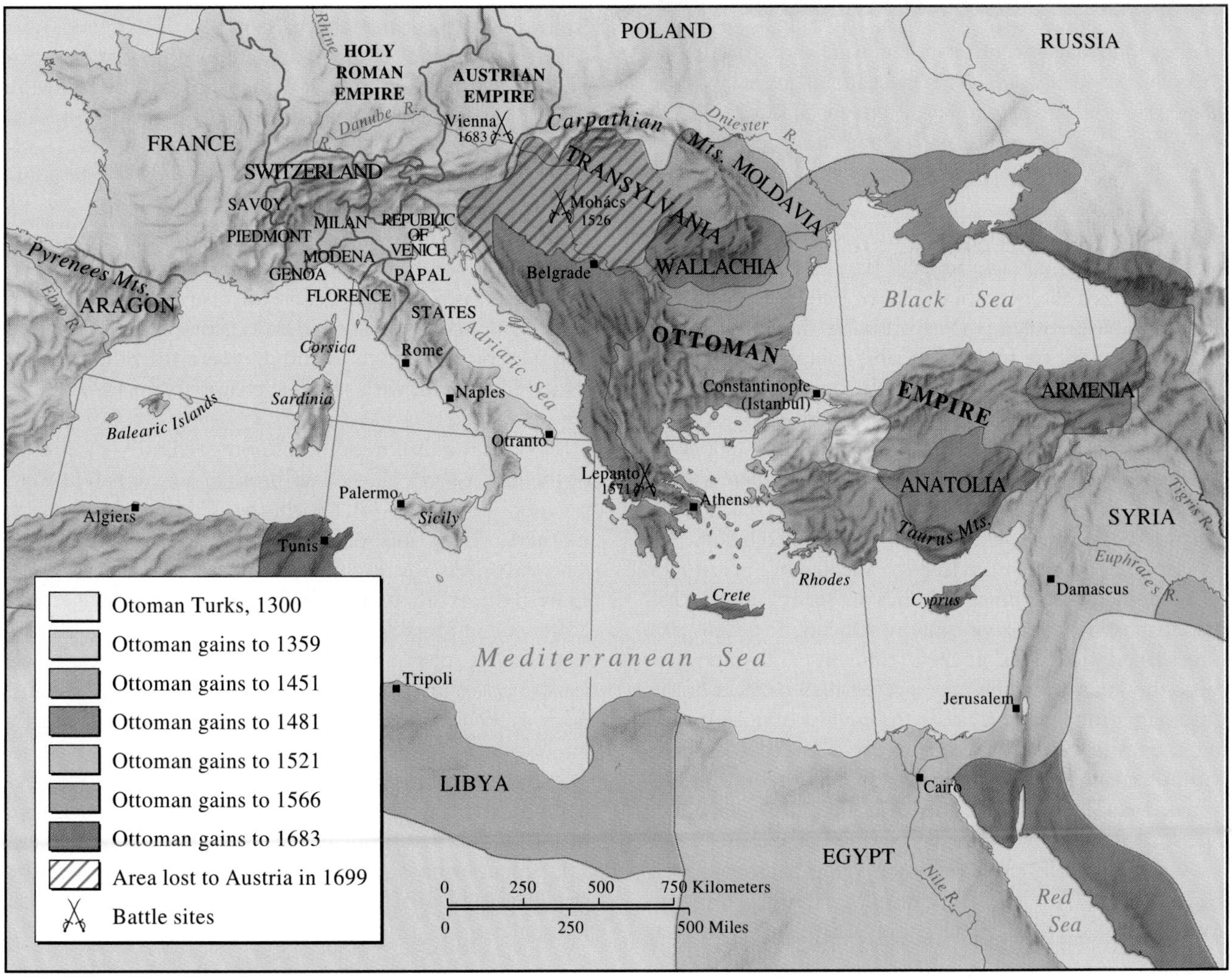

Topkapi Palace Museum, Istanbul. Photo © Giraudon/Art Resource

Suleiman the Magnificent. Here Suleiman, who wrote poetry under the pen name *muhibbi,* or beloved, is flanked by two guards. He is clad in a fur-trimmed ceremonial kaftan; the white turban was worn by all early Ottoman sultans.

the empire reached the apex of its power. Suleiman brilliantly led his armies against rulers in central Europe and in 1521 seized the Serbian capital of Belgrade. In an age of mighty kings, Suleiman was probably the most powerful and dynamic. He was a successful military commander and a clever diplomat; competing European powers, such as France, sought and secured his protection. By exploiting the rivalry between the Austrian Habsburg emperors and the French kings, Suleiman's forces conquered most of Hungary. His political alliance with the French soon expanded into mutually beneficial economic relations.

In 1529 Suleiman laid siege to Vienna, but because of overextended communication lines and heavy rainfall that made transporting heavy cannon difficult, the Ottoman forces failed to take the city before the onset of winter. Because the Janissaries (the elite, professional soldiers of the Ottoman army) and the cavalry refused to campaign during the winter months, Suleiman was forced to retreat without taking the Habsburg capital. Reportedly, the Ottoman army left behind sacks of coffee, a new product that soon gained popularity among the Europeans.

At its height in 1566, Suleiman's empire incorporated Hungary and the Balkan Peninsula; extensive territory around the Black Sea; the entire Anatolian Peninsula; Arab territories bordering the eastern Mediterranean and the Red Sea; Egypt and the northern Sudan; most islands in the eastern Mediterranean, including the strategic islands of Rhodes and Crete; and the coastal areas of North Africa east of Morocco.

Like many emperors in other powerful empires before him, Suleiman failed to leave a worthy successor to his throne. Influenced by his most beloved wife, Hurrem Haseki ("the Joyous One"), to make her son the successor, Suleiman had his favorite and more able son killed, just as rulers in China and the Roman Empire had killed members of their own families in order to ensure their own power or the succession of particular favorites. Following Suleiman's death in 1566, Hurrem Haseki's son succeeded to the throne as Selim II, but this alcoholic, nicknamed The Sot, proved unworthy of his capable and abstemious father. Ottoman military and naval supremacy waned under his rule, and at the Battle of Lepanto in 1571, the navies of the Habsburgs and the Italian city-states crushed the Ottoman fleet. This defeat marked the beginning of a military decline that lasted more than 200 years.

The administration of the Ottoman Empire, like the Safavid in Persia and the earlier T'ang in China, was highly centralized. The Sultan acted as the supreme political, religious, and military ruler, subject only to divine law. Below him, the grand vizier and the divan (imperial council) were responsible for political and economic administration. Ottoman administration was highly complex and required a multitude of bureaucrats, drawn from an elite whose prestige was based on ownership of land and booty acquired in military campaigns. They were responsible for matters as diverse as the translation of documents to the supervision of the vast royal palace complex of Topkapi in Istanbul, where the Sultan maintained his harem, with separate chambers for his mother, wives, children, and servants.

Without a firm tradition of primogeniture (succession of the eldest son), all the half-brothers in the harem were potential candidates for the throne. Consequently, wives, mothers, sisters, and sons often intrigued to gain the sultan's favor. As the example of Hurrem Haseki demonstrates, the mothers and favorite wives of sultans could exercise considerable political power. When the sultans were strong rulers, the harem did not pose a threat to effective government. For example, the first ten sultans, from 1299 to 1566, all led their military forces directly into battle and were personally in charge of military strategy and governmental policy. Indeed, the personal dynamism and strength of the first Ottoman sultans were major factors in Ottoman expansion. However, the less able sultans who succeeded Suleiman frequently became virtual prisoners of the royal court, the harem, and the Janissaries.

Elegy for Suleiman the Magnificent

That master-rider of the realm of bliss
For whose careering steed the field of the world was narrow.

The infidels of Hungary bowed their heads to the temper of his blade,
The Frank admired the grain of his sword.

He laid his face to the ground, graciously, like a fresh rose petal,
The treasurer of time put him in the coffer, like a jewel.

May the sun burn and blaze with fire of your parting;
In grief for you, let him dress in black weeds of cloud.

Weeping tears of blood as it recalls your skill,
May your sword plunge into the ground from its scabbard.

May the pen tear its collar in grief for you,
*The standard rend its shirt in affliction.**

This elegy was written by Muhammad Baki (1527–1600), one of the greatest Ottoman poets. It is a lyrical idealization of the imperial ruler, much in the vein of the celebrations of great rulers as mighty heroes in ancient Greek and Latin poetry.

*Wayne S. Vucinich, *The Ottoman Empire: Its Record and Legacy,* trans. Bernard Lewis (Princeton: Van Nostrand, 1965), pp. 146–147.

Like the Safavids in Persia, Ottoman rulers placed the major provinces under appointed governors who ruled for about two years. As authorities in Istanbul correctly feared, provincial governors often tried to establish their own bases of authority. Generally, the central Ottoman government retained tight controls over its Anatolian territories, which lay close to Istanbul. The more distant European and Arab territories tended to enjoy more autonomy.

The administration was financed through new wealth acquired from the expansion of the empire and from taxes. The collection of taxes was assigned to "tax farmers," who collected as much as possible from a given territory in return for a percentage of the total amount collected. As in Rome and China, tax farming became a source of abuse and corruption within the empire.

Founded by the military, the Ottoman Empire remained dependent upon the army, which, like the government, was rigidly structured. The Janissaries, along with the cavalry, were the backbone of the military. They quickly adapted to the use of European military technology, especially siege and field artillery, and became a major military force of the age.

In this Islamic empire, the Sheik al-Islam was responsible for religious life, and since there was no separation of civil and religious law, he served as supreme judge, handing down *fatwas,* or legal opinions. In the provinces, *qadis* (judges) appointed by Istanbul joined with local experts in religious law to settle legal disputes. They also served as overseers of such charitable religious endowments as orphanages, soup kitchens, and hospitals.

Social and Economic Life in the Ottoman Empire

During the golden age of the empire under Suleiman, Ottoman society was remarkably open. The Ottomans did not see fit to settle Turkish tribes throughout their empire; most Turks remained peasants scattered in remote and poor agricultural villages throughout the Anatolian Peninsula. Ottoman rulers initially made no attempt to impose the Turkish language or customs on their subjects or to force non-Muslims to convert to Islam. On the contrary, Ottoman society allowed diversity, and considerable "upward mobility" occurred. Under the *millet* system, religious and ethnic minorities retained their own educational, religious, and judicial institutions, and enjoyed considerable economic autonomy in return for the payment of an additional tax. Arabs, Armenians, Christians, and Jews were able to reach the highest levels of society, and some served as advisors and doctors to the sultan himself. Only the sultanate was denied them, for it was solely reserved for the heirs of the Osman rulers. This open society, remarkable for the age, was one of the sources of Ottoman strength.

The Ottoman Empire was at the center of a lively international trade from East to West and West to East that persisted despite rivalries among Western and Eastern monarchs. Istanbul and Cairo became major centers on the route between India and Europe. Slaves, gold, and ivory were transported from sub-Saharan Africa through Cairo to European markets. New foodstuffs like potatoes, tomatoes, and tobacco came from the Western Hemisphere into the

Asian Art Museum of San Francisco, Avery Brundage Collection B65P6

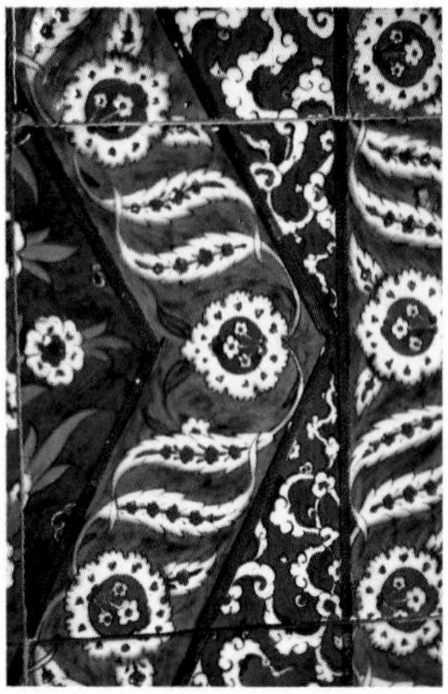

Courtesy of Janice Terry

Chinese and Ottoman Blue and White Porcelain and Tiles. Chinese decorated porcelains were widely exported to Moghul India and the Ottoman Empire. Pieces like this large dish (top) influenced Ottoman artisans, who were known for their manufacture of vivid blue tiles (left). These tiles have retained their lustre for more than 300 years.

Ottoman Empire and into Asia. Coffee from Ethiopia and Yemen was traded to Europe. Coffeehouses became major gathering spots for the elite in Ottoman, Safavid, and European cities. The use of tobacco quickly spread from Europe to the Ottoman Empire, where pipe smoking became a common practice among both men and women.

Despite the rich trade that passed through the empire, the Ottoman elite, reflecting the values of a still predominantly agrarian society, held commerce, banking, and most manufacturing businesses in low esteem. As a result, they permitted and encouraged subject peoples (such as Armenians) and foreigners to organize and maintain these economic activities. Under the system of capitulations, which had also been used by the Mamluks and the Safavids, foreign Christians living in the empire were given freedom of activity and were exempted from Ottoman taxes and laws. When the empire flourished, these special privileges fostered international trade and increased revenues, but as the empire declined and European nations grew stronger, the capitulations enabled Europeans and minorities to dominate economic life.

Ottoman authorities encouraged international trade across their domains in part, of course, to benefit the imperial treasury. Taxes on trade had often gone uncollected in the Arab provinces in the period of political instability before the Ottomans conquered them. The Ottoman government began to collect these taxes with more efficiency, and in some cases raised them. Traders in turn raised prices, which angered European consumers, especially those at the end of the line. Consequently, the newly centralized and energetic nations became increasingly eager to find new trade routes to Asia.

Cultural and Artistic Achievements

The noteworthy cultural achievements of the Ottoman Empire began at the top. According to custom, Ottoman Sultans were all trained in a craft, and some achieved considerable artistic and literary skill. Suleiman, for example, was an accomplished goldsmith. Ottoman Sultans were great patrons of the arts; and as in most Islamic societies, literary skills, especially the ability to write poetry, were much admired. An accomplished poet in his own right, Suleiman strongly supported the cultural life of Istanbul in an effort to make his court the most splendid of the age. The Turkish language continued to develop, borrowing many words from both Arabic and Persian. Some poets wrote in Turkish and Arabic. Turkish historians chronicled the development of the empire and the exploits of the military, and although most literature was highly derivative of Persian or Arab forms, a lively folk literature continued to flourish.

Like many imperial rulers, Suleiman was also a great builder. He financed the construction of monumental buildings, many designed by Sinan, one of the most prolific architects of all time. Originally a slave from the conquered Greek provinces, Sinan was recruited as a Janissary and became a military engineer. His skills attracted the attention of the sultan, who enlisted him as the royal architect. Living to the (at the time) incredible advanced age of ninety-nine, Sinan designed buildings to commemorate Ottoman imperial power. His massive, interconnecting buildings surmounted by domes became the hallmark of Ottoman architecture throughout the empire. Although the Suleimaniye complex of mosque, schools, hospital, bath, shops, and cemetery in Istanbul is the largest of Sinan's creations, the Selimiye Mosque in Edirne, outside Istanbul, finished in 1575, is generally considered his masterpiece.

In the fine arts, Ottoman artisans synthesized earlier Islamic/Arab designs and techniques with Chinese and

European motifs and crafts. They decorated Sinan's structures with Isnik (named after a Turkish city) tiles whose glazed surfaces contained painted floral designs. Clearly an imitation of Chinese porcelains, these tiles still retain their crystal-clear coloring. Such glazing techniques and designs were copied in much of Europe. Ottoman artisans also produced textiles, silver work, bookbindings, and calligraphy of remarkable beauty and luxury. The Ottomans were known for their woven textiles and carpets. "Oriental" carpets from Turkey and Persia became popular decorative items among wealthy classes around the world. Although Ottoman culture, like Roman culture, has been criticized for its lack of originality, the synthesis of disparate cultural ideas and motifs from West and East enabled Ottoman artisans to fashion unique objects of remarkable beauty.

The Imperial Safavids

During the sixteenth and seventeenth centuries the Ottoman Empire's chief rival in the Muslim world was the neighboring Safavid Empire centered in Persia (present-day Iran). The Safavid realm differed from that of the Ottomans in two major respects. First, it was based upon Shi'i Islam rather than on Orthodox Sunni Islam. Second, the Safavids maintained and reinforced the separate identity of Persian society and language. In contrast, the Ottoman Empire sought to assimilate many new cultural styles while retaining cultural pluralism. The Ottomans made no attempt to impose their language or values over the diverse peoples they ruled. In particular, the Arabs, the single largest linguistic and ethnic group within the empire, were allowed to retain their linguistic and cultural identity.

Founded by Shah Isma'il, who ruled from 1500 to 1524, the Safavid Empire reached its zenith under Shah Abbas the Great (reigned 1587–1629), an autocrat who ruled with an iron hand. He killed or blinded three of his five sons and, like Suleiman the Magnificent, left no able successor. In the Safavid Empire, as in most other empires, whenever the central authority was strong, the local chieftains remained submissive, paid taxes, and rendered homage to the shah. Whenever the shah or central

Map 9.2 The Ottoman and Safavid Empires. By 1689 the Ottoman Empire had reached its zenith and included most of the Arab provinces of the eastern Mediterranean, the holy cities of Mecca and Medina, and most of North Africa. However, the Safavid Empire, with its glorious capital at Isfahan in Persia, competed for control in the region; despite many wars, neither empire could conquer its rival.

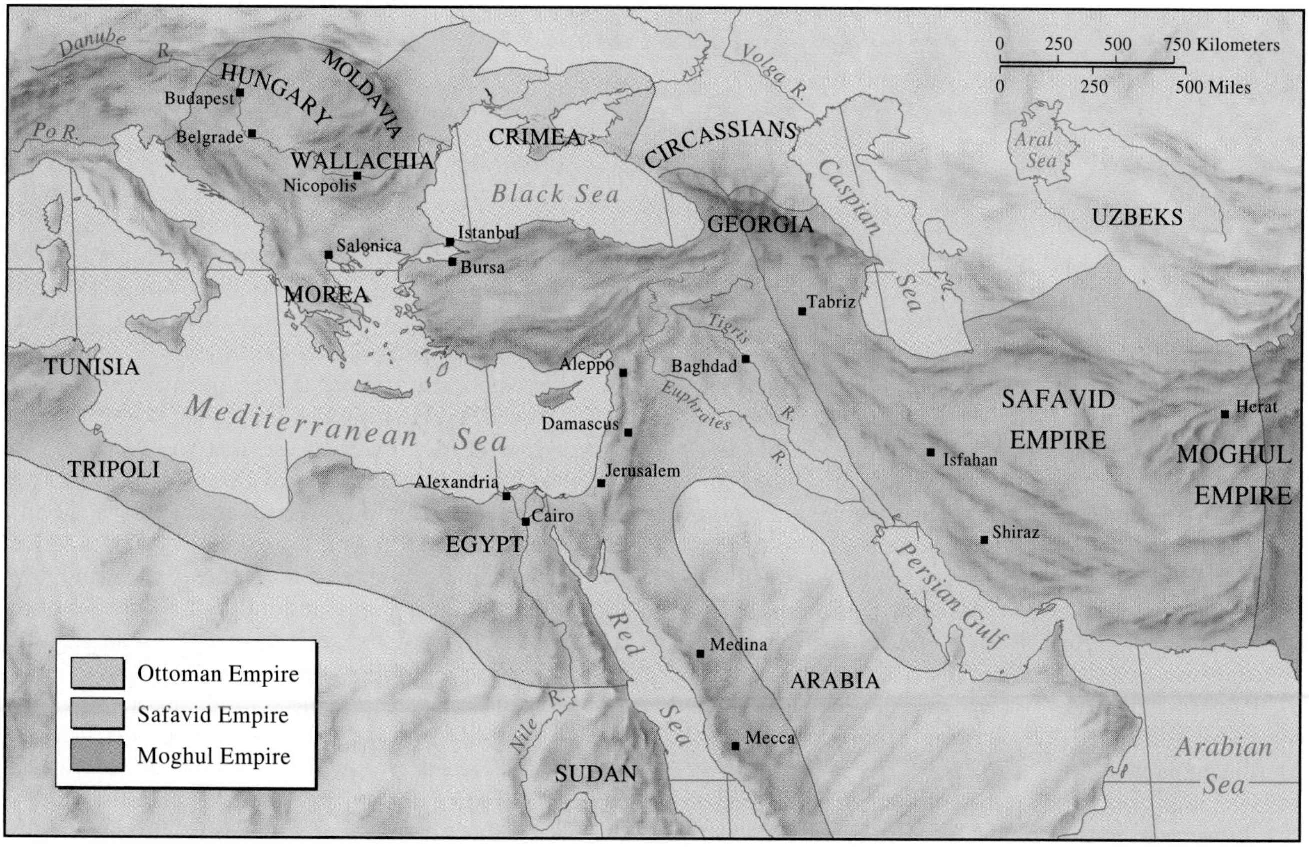

The Safavid Shah Writes to His Ottoman Rival

Shah Isma'il of Persia to the Ottoman Sultan Selim [c. 1514]:

Now to begin: Your honored letters have arrived one after another. . . . Their contents, although indicative of hostility, are stated with boldness and vigor. The latter gives us much enjoyment and pleasure, but we are ignorant of the reason for the former. . . . In the time of your late blessed father . . . when our royal troops passed through the lands of [eastern Anatolia] . . . complete concord and friendship was shown on both sides. . . . Thus now, the cause of your resentment and displeasure yet remains unknown. If political necessity has compelled you on this course, then may your problems soon be solved.

Dispute may fire words to such a heat
That ancient houses be consumed in flames.

The intention of our inaction in this regard is twofold:

(1.) Most of the inhabitants of the land of Rum are followers of our forefathers. . . .

(2.) We have always loved the . . . Ottoman house. . . . Nevertheless, there is no cause for improper words: . . . At this writing we were engaged upon the hunt near Isfahan, we now prepare provisions and our troops for the coming campaign. In all friendship we say do what you will.

Bitter experience has taught that in this world of trial

*He who falls upon the house of Ali always falls. Kindly give our ambassador leave to travel unmolested. . . . When war becomes inevitable, hesitation and delay must be set aside, and one must think on that which is to come. Farewell.**

In this letter Shah Isma'il of Persia very diplomatically, but firmly, expressed his views on the conflict between the Safavid (Persian) and the Ottoman Empires. Between them, these two great Muslim empires dominated much of the eastern Mediterranean and West Asia from the fifteenth to the nineteenth centuries and were almost continually in a state of war with one another. Although neither succeeded in destroying the other, the perpetual conflicts drained the economic and military strength of both, thereby contributing to their downfalls.

*William H. McNeill and Marilyn Robinson Waldman, eds., *The Islamic World* (New York: Oxford University Press, 1973; reprint, Chicago: University of Chicago Press, 1983), pp. 342–344.

authority was weak, the local rulers assumed more power. One of Shah Abbas's first moves in consolidating his power was to curb the influence of the local chieftains.

The populace of Safavid Iran consisted largely of peasants who lived in small rural villages. There were a few nomadic pastoralists as well as a small urban middle class that engaged in cottage industries and trade. In this predominantly rural setting, the Safavid government was organized along feudal lines, and officials acquired fiefs from the shah in return for services to the central government. The Safavids divided their territories into provinces, placed under the administration of appointed governors. The shahs also depended upon the *ghulams*, or slave elite. Obtained mainly from central Asia, these slaves were converts to Islam and gradually achieved prominent positions in the royal court, thereby following a tradition in other Muslim empires.

The mullahs, or Shi'i clergy, also exercised considerable power within the empire; like the feudal landowners, the mullahs tended to be more powerful whenever the shah was ineffective. Their authority was particularly strong in rural areas, where the peasants looked to them for both religious and political guidance.

Taxes, land, and commerce were the major sources of wealth in the Persian economy. Crown lands were owned directly by the royal court to use as it wished; as in the Ottoman Empire, state lands were given as payment or rewards to officials or army officers, generally for a specific time, after which they reverted to the crown to be parceled out again at the pleasure of the court. Some land was owned directly by religious authorities; the revenues from these lands provided the mullahs with an independent source of income and also helped to finance mosques, religious schools, and welfare projects for the poor.

The manufacture and sale of textiles, particularly silk fabrics and carpets, was a major source of Safavid income. Soon after coming to power, Shah Abbas added the silk-producing areas in the north to his empire. Although Abbas did not directly confiscate the land, the sale of silk became a royal monopoly. Anxious to expand the silk industry, Abbas encouraged foreign traders and Christian communities, particularly the Armenians, who formerly had been silk producers, to settle in his domain. Although earlier Safavid rulers had persecuted religious minorities and forced religious conversion to Shi'i Islam by sword, Abbas was known for his relative tolerance. To some extent, his more liberal policies regarding the Armenians and other Christian minorities, who dominated the silk manufacturing and commercial trade with the West, were motivated by economic considerations.

To strengthen the Persian economy, Shah Abbas established a new Safavid capital in Isfahan, situated at an intersection of key trade routes. He moved a number of Armenians into a new community on the outskirts of the city and provided interest-free loans for them to rebuild their houses and businesses. As a result of Shah Abbas's tolerance and patronage, Isfahan quickly became a world center for trade in luxury textiles.

In search of new markets, Shah Abbas sent emissaries with samples of luxurious silks to Venice, Spain, Portugal, Holland, Russia, and Poland. Foreign traders were encouraged to establish businesses in Persia by special financial inducements, including tax breaks. These privileges contributed to an economic boom from which the royal court benefited. As early as 1617, agents from the English East Indian Company arrived along the Persian Gulf and petitioned the shah for permission to trade. By the middle of the seventeenth century, Bandar Abbas on the Persian Gulf had become a major seaport for trade with Europe. The Safavids also enjoyed a lively trade through northern routes with Russia. Trade through the northern provinces often continued even during periods of open warfare with the Ottoman Empire.

Control of the silk trade provided the Safavid rulers with the economic means to extend their control over all of Persia. As was true for the sultans in the Ottoman Empire, when the central authority of the Shahs was strong, the special privileges for foreign communities were not a threat. However, as subsequent Safavid leaders became weaker, and the European nations strengthened and augmented their global power, these privileges enabled foreign governments, acting in support of their subjects, to undermine the central government and to dominate Persia.

Architecture, the Fine Arts, and Literature in Persia

Literature, painting, music, and architecture flourished under the Safavids. Like imperial rulers in China, Egypt, Rome, and elsewhere, the Safavids encouraged and patronized the arts. The new capital of Isfahan became a glittering cultural center; as the Persians said, "Isfahan is

The Textile Museum, Washington, D.C., 1985.5.1, Ruth Lincoln Fisher Fund

Persian Silk Robe. This elaborate brocaded taffeta robe in rich blues, oranges, and gold shows the floral designs favored by high-ranking Safavid courtiers.

half the world." Shah Abbas ordered numerous mosques, inns, schools, and baths built in Isfahan and along the important trading routes. His Shah Mosque in Isfahan with its ornate tile work, large entrance facades, and bulbous dome epitomizes Safavid architecture at its best. Safavid artists also continued to excel in painting complex miniatures on paper and ivory. Many such miniatures adorned and illustrated Persian manuscripts.

The Safavids and the aristocrats were conspicuous in their love of luxury items. They lived lavishly and wore ornate silk and gold-brocaded attire. Persian artisans were noted for their skills in weaving gold brocade and large, extremely fine carpets. Many weavers of carpets were women and children. European traders often commented on the conspicuous consumption of Safavid lifestyles. Nonetheless, the Safavids were early believers in recycling. Every seven years the used clothes from the royal court were burned and the gold and silver threads collected for use in new garments. For relaxation, the upper class enjoyed games such as chess (a Persian invention) and polo. The entire population participated in religious festivals marking the Shi'i calendar, particularly services commemorating the death of Ali (the Shi'i believe that the ruling authority of the Muslim community should have passed through Ali's descendants) and the martyrdom of his son, Husayn. Husayn's death was reenacted in protracted and moving passion plays.

Indeed, much Safavid literature was devoted to religious themes, and the Safavids financed numerous religious schools that reinterpreted and reinforced Shi'i theological tenets. Religious differences between the Shi'i Safavids and Sunni Ottomans were one of the sources of conflict between the two empires. In contrast to the religious written works, romantic love poetry continued to be highly popular, and Persian poets and poetry dominated and influenced literary life in both the Ottoman and Moghul Empires. Like the Ottoman sultans, Safavid rulers also encouraged writers to immortalize their military and political achievements in long histories and biographies.

Wars between the Rival Empires

Throughout their long histories, the Ottomans and Safavids were rivals for control over the territories around the Tigris-Euphrates Valley (present-day Iraq). As Sunni Muslims, the Ottomans also clashed with the Shi'i Safavids over domination of Islamic territories and interpretations of basic Islamic doctrines. The long struggle drained both of needed military power and resources.

Safavid Mosque. The Shah Mosque in Isfahan is one of the glories of Safavid architecture. The mosque is covered in ornate, vivid blue tiles.

© Sue Pashko/Envision

Neither delivered a fatal military blow to the other, but debilitating intermittent warfare made both increasingly vulnerable to other outside enemies.

The conflicts began when Suleiman's father, Selim I, initiated a "holy war" against the Shi'i and the Safavid dynasty. In 1514 Ottoman forces equipped with cannon decisively defeated the Safavids in the northern provinces of present-day Iran, but Selim failed to follow through on his victory. Suleiman continued the struggle by launching several campaigns against the Safavid ruler, Shah Tahmasp, who employed a policy of "scorched earth" as a defensive measure, thereby forcing the Ottomans to bring all their supplies with them. Suleiman successfully conquered the major northern city of Tabriz, but found it costly to maintain its control. In 1555 his difficulties holding the northern territories forced him to arrange a treaty with the Safavids. Suleiman retained Iraq, with the major trading center of Baghdad and a port on the Persian Gulf, but had to withdraw from the northern Persian provinces.

The Safavids countered Ottoman power by allying with the Habsburgs, the major Ottoman enemy in eastern Europe. Taking advantage of the power vacuum following Suleiman's death, Shah Abbas occupied present-day Iraq and parts of the Anatolia Peninsula. By 1623 the Ottomans, now strengthened by internal reforms, took advantage of Safavid weakness after Shah Abbas's death to oust the Safavids from these territories. A peace treaty between these two mighty empires in 1639 established boundaries that approximate those of present-day western Iran.

In spite of several attempts to implement internal reforms, the Safavid Empire never regained the power wielded by Shah Abbas. As a consequence, it was ill prepared to meet the challenges of expansionist neighbors. By the eighteenth century, tribes from Afghanistan began to expand into Safavid territories and by 1722, Afghan forces took Isfahan. Safavid weakness allowed Ottoman forces then to move into northern Persian provinces. Under Shah Tahmasp II, the Safavids unsuccessfully counterattacked the Afghan forces. The assassination of Nader Shah in 1747 ended the Safavid dynasty. With the collapse of effective centralized government, numerous rival local rulers vied for political and military control until the Qajar dynasty emerged as the dominant power in 1794.

The Culture of the Renaissance in Europe

If then we are to call any age golden, it is beyond doubt that age which brings forth golden talents in different places. That such is true of our age, he who wishes to consider the illustrious discoveries of this century will *hardly doubt. For this century, like a golden age, has restored to light the liberal arts, which were almost extinct: grammar, poetry, rhetoric, painting, sculpture, architecture, music . . . and all this in Florence. Achieving what had been honored among the ancients, but almost forgotten since, the age has joined wisdom with eloquence, and produce with the military art . . . and in Florence it has recalled the Platonic teaching from darkness into light.**

*Letter of Marsilio Ficino to Paul of Middleburg, trans. M. M. McLaughlin, in *The Portable Renaissance Reader* (New York: Viking, 1953), p. 79.

In this excerpt, the Florentine philosopher Marsilio Ficino (1433–1499) expresses his joy at living in a time of intellectual revolution, sparked by a reawakened interest in the values and culture of ancient Greece and Rome. Ficino and his contemporaries scorned what they perceived as the ignorance and barbarism of the "dark ages," the thousand years between the collapse of the Roman Empire and their own era, to which they applied the term *Renaissance,* meaning "rebirth" in French. They believed that they were living in a "golden age" that had broken abruptly with the immediate past.

Although Renaissance thinkers were aware of the contrast between their own and the medieval period, they failed to appreciate the full dimensions of their age. To them, the revival of cultural antiquity was the outstanding characteristic of their progressive era. Yet artistic creativity was only one aspect of the Renaissance. In fact, changes affected every element of European society—political, social, and religious as well as cultural. Nor did the Renaissance develop in complete isolation from the era that preceded it. Indeed, the Renaissance continued many trends of medieval civilization. The difference lay in the faster pace of change, not in the creation of something entirely new.

This is not to say that there were no differences in attitude between the Middle Ages and the Renaissance. The medieval cultural perspective had centered on theology, with emphasis on God's will, human sinfulness, and heavenly existence after earthly life. That outlook permeated all intellectual life: education, philosophy, theology, art, and architecture. Medieval religion had firmly rejected life in this world as evil, useless, and perilous to the salvation of the soul. Abandoning secular culture in favor of a monastic life seemed to many the surest way to gain salvation and please God. During the Renaissance, however, thinkers, writers, and artists made man, not God, the chief center of interest. They glorified the human body as beautiful and the human intellect as capable of unlocking the deepest mysteries of nature by rational processes. Renaissance thinkers known as humanists argued that God in fact wanted men to engage in political and civic life, to create and discover, and to marry and have families. In short, fulfillment within the secular sphere was in accord with God's will. Thus a major innovation of the humanists was to reconcile the new urban culture and life with Christianity and the possibility of salvation.

The Origins of the Renaissance: Italian Literature and Humanism

The Renaissance was an age of rapid transition, linking medieval to early modern ways of life. The chronology of the Renaissance raises some problems for historians in deciding when it began and how long it continued. Most accept early fourteenth century as the start and mid-sixteenth century as the end. The Renaissance began and took shape in Italy before spreading across the Alps.

There are many reasons why Italy was the birthplace of the Renaissance. For one thing, the survival of Roman artistic and architectural heritage and the continued use of Latin had kept memories of classical civilization alive. Italy also had profited from both Islamic and Byzantine cultural influences. Trade remained important in Italy, which gave rise to early modern capitalism, and furnished the material resources for cultural development. Less feudal than northern Europe, Italy enjoyed renewed vigor in its urban centers in the wake of the Crusades. Political developments fostered the growth of independent city-states, and prominent commercial cities like Genoa, Venice, and Milan competed with one another in cultural as well as commercial affairs. These cities gave rise to an affluent, middle/upper class with the leisure for education and a sense of political responsibility. Such individuals sought models of civic duty, social responsibility, and governmental values. The urbanized, sophisticated world of ancient Greece and Rome provided just such models in an extensive body of literature and art. Thus, the humanists returned to classical literature and found inspiration there for an active life of political involvement and reasoned analysis of morals and beliefs.

The early Renaissance in Italy during the fourteenth century centered on a few eloquent writers from Tuscany (the area around Florence) who stimulated interest and delight in the physical world. Francesco Petrarca, or Petrarch (1304–1374), sometimes called the father of humanism, idolized the ancient Roman authors and emulated their literary compositions and writing styles; he also adopted the ancient writers' secular outlook on life in his own works. Petrarch as a man of letters gained enduring fame from his poetry, written in the Tuscan vernacular. A keen observer of nature, he wrote tender sonnets and exquisite odes in celebration of his burning love for Laura, a married woman whom he adored at a distance. Although Petrarch expresses real love for a living woman and rhapsodizes over her physical features, his devotion to her is essentially spiritual, so that a conflict between body and mind underlies his poems. Being

LIVES AND TIMES ACROSS CULTURES

Racy Tales

Renaissance writers, with their interest in describing society as they observed it, tended to be tolerant of human behavior. The following racy passages illustrate how far Renaissance society had departed from Christian moral restraint.

The first excerpt centers on an adulterous relationship. A young wife, Petronella, tells her lover, Gianello, to get into a tub when her husband returns home unexpectedly. Petronella explains that she has sold the old tub to a man who is inspecting it from the inside. Gianello leaps out of the tub and expresses satisfaction with it, except for an area that is coated with a hard substance. The wife tells her husband to climb into the tub to scrape it off.

> *While she was busy instructing and directing her husband in this fashion, Gianello, who had not fully gratified his desires that morning before the husband arrived, seeing that he couldn't do it in the way he wished, contributed to bring it off as best he could. So he went up to Petronella, who was completely blocking up the mouth of the tub, and in the manner of a wild and hot-blooded stallion mounting a Parthian mare in the open fields, he satisfied his young man's passion, which no sooner reached fulfillment than the scraping of the tub was completed, whereupon he stood back, Petronella withdrew her head from the tub and the husband clambered out.**

* Giovanni Boccaccio, *The Decameron,* trans. G. H. McWilliam (London: Penguin, 1995), p. 494.

The second excerpt contains a wife's justification for taking on a lover.

> *As you can see, Lusca [her maid], I am young and vigorous, and I am well supplied with all the things a woman could desire. In short, with one exception I have nothing to complain about, and the exception is this: that my husband is much older than myself, and consequently I am ill provided with the one thing that gives young women their great pleasure.***

The third excerpt describes a young man's clumsy and crude efforts to seduce a noble Parisian lady.

> *"Would you like a bolt of bright crimson velvet, striped with green, or some embroidered satin, or maybe crimson? What would you like—necklaces, gold things, things for your hair, rings? All you have to do is say yes. Even fifty thousand gold pieces doesn't bother me. . . ."*
>
> *"No. Thank you, but I want nothing from you."*
>
> *"By God," said he, "I damned well want something from you, and it's something that won't cost you a cent, and once you've given it you'll still have it, every bit of it. Here"—and he showed her his long codpiece—"here is my John Thomas, who wants a place to jump into."****

** Ibid., p. 534.

*** François Rabelais, *Gargantua and Pantagruel,* trans. Burton Raffel (New York: Norton, 1990), p. 201.

ambitious and desiring fame and fortune, he struggled against the medieval notion that God wished men to renounce the material things of this world. Petrarch's work thus exemplifies the typical Renaissance propensity to elevate the secular.

The new interest in worldly life that marks Petrarch's thought is evident also in the work of his friend, Giovanni Boccaccio (1313–1375), the first great Italian prose writer. His *Decameron* is concerned with everyday life, portraying people from all social classes, often with a strong satirical flavor. With Boccaccio, the lustfulness and earthy wit of the lower classes enter serious literature during the Renaissance. In contrast to Dante's *Divine Comedy,* the *Decameron* is sometimes termed the "Human Comedy."

Although many humanist literary works were written in Italian, most writers maintained that the Latin of Cicero was the supreme literary language. Shunning "corrupt" medieval Latin, they found in classical literature a purity of style, form, and eloquence absent from most medieval literature, and they argued that to speak and write correctly one should imitate the ancients.

Petrarch, for example, developed the finest Latin style of his age. Succeeding Renaissance writers and scholars, stimulated by the migration of Byzantine scholars who had begun to flee Constantinople before its fall in 1453, promoted the study of Greek.

An important aspect of humanist activity was the recovery of manuscripts of classical literary, scientific, and historical works. Searchers discovered many Latin manuscripts in European monasteries and churches. Increasingly, during the fifteenth century, Greek history and literature became available in the West as humanists obtained copies of Greek manuscripts through contacts with Byzantine scholars. Manuel Chrysoloras, a Byzantine diplomat, began a regular course of lectures on Greek in Florence in 1397; his grammar textbook gained wide circulation (it was used by Erasmus, discussed later in this section) and in 1471 became the first Greek grammar to be printed.

The recovery of so many texts gave rise to modern textual criticism, including the disciplines of paleography (the analysis of manuscripts and the handwriting in which they are transcribed) and philology (the critical study of language and literature). Dictionaries, grammars, indices, and commentaries were produced, and the texts of ancient authors were put on a sound footing by scholars who collected and compared manuscripts. From their careful textual studies, the humanists learned how to assess authenticity, showing, for example, that the "The Donation of Constantine," used by popes to support their territorial sovereignty over Rome and its environs, was in fact a forgery written 400 years after the Roman emperor's death.

The spread of classical learning was accelerated by print. The use of movable type to print books, a momentous innovation for Europe, though known earlier in China and Korea, is attributed to Johannes Gutenberg of Mainz about 1450. The mass production of texts that printing facilitated soon made the cultural heritage of the classical world and, with it, the Renaissance widely available in Europe.

Classical texts were the basis of humanistic elementary and secondary education; the curricula included literature, mathematics, music, science, and athletics. In contrast to medieval scholars, teachers and students achieved a direct familiarity with classical Greek authorities in most subject areas. Students who received such classical training excelled in law and theology, or became secretaries for princes, prelates, and town councils.

Renaissance historians modeled their work on the classical authors, producing histories of their city or state, rather than the universal histories or annalistic accounts favored by medieval scholars. They departed from medieval precedents in emphasizing politics and stressing the role of human motives over divine intervention. Renaissance historians were also more critical in their evaluation of source materials.

The Genius of Petrarch

*[Petrarch] dwarfs his precursors in every respect: he was an immeasurably greater poet and greater man than any of them; his horizons were wider and his influence, never cramped within the limits of town or province, extended over most of Western Europe; he had the vision and the ability to unite the two existing strands of humanism, the literary and the scholarly, and to combine aims which reached for the moon with the capacity for painstaking research; he went further than anyone else in trying to revive within the framework of a Christian society the ideals of ancient Rome, and his attempts to get close to the great figures of the past, and indeed to rival their achievement, though flirting with the vainglorious, unleashed passions and ambitions which were to reanimate the whole cultural legacy of the ancient world and bring it to bear upon contemporary modes of thought and literature.**

Petrarch is the archetypal figure of the humanist as scholar poet. While he assembled a personal library of thousands of manuscripts, with special emphasis on his beloved Cicero, he was no mere antiquarian book collector. He read with intensity and absorbed the thought of the classical authors to his very marrow.

*L. D. Reynolds and N. G. Wilson, *Scribes and Scholars: A Guide to the Transmission of Greek and Latin Literature,* 2nd ed. (Oxford: Clarendon Press, 1974), pp. 113–114.

The philosophers of the Renaissance were proponents of the new humanist outlook. Unlike the Scholastics of the late Middle Ages, they tended to prefer Plato to Aristotle because of the former's superior literary style and the more mystical nature of his thought. Marsilio Ficino translated into Latin all the works of Plato as well as many commentaries on his philosophy. Renaissance Platonists drew on Plato's fascination with numbers and harmonies to promote interest in geometry and mathematics. Ficino and the brilliant young scholar, Giovanni Pico della Mirandola (1463–1494), also held that humans were free, perfectible individuals, with social responsibilities and a dignity derived from their position midway between the material world and the spiritual

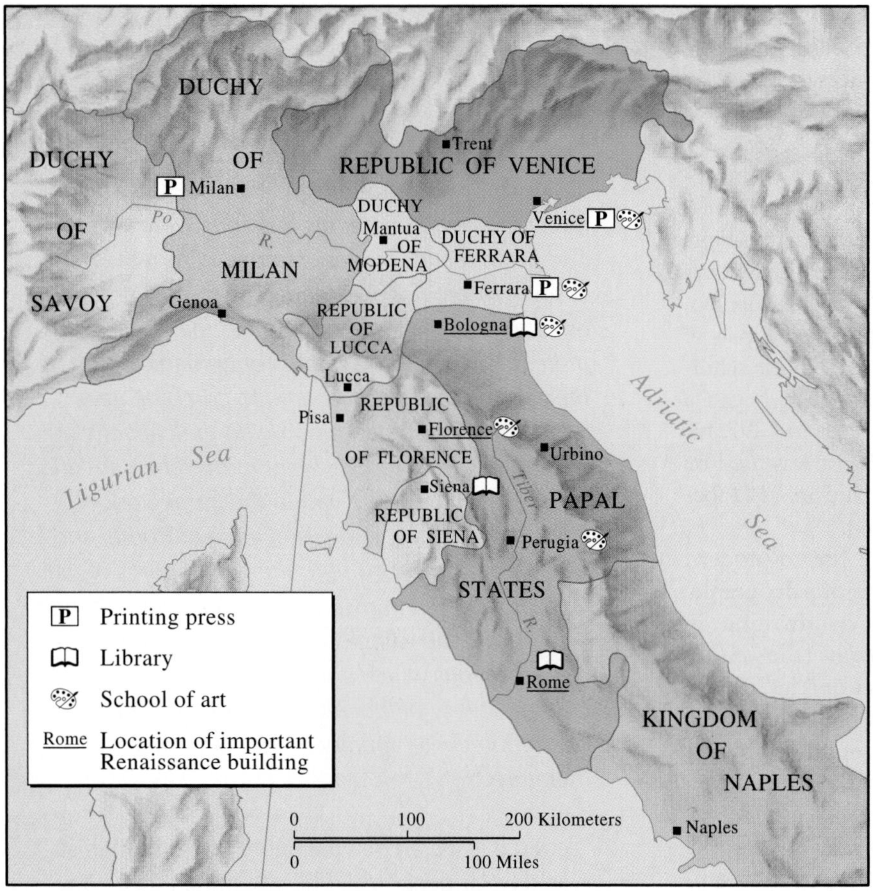

Map 9.3 Renaissance Italy. The commercial vitality and political disunity of northern Italy stimulated cultural creativity. Prosperous towns patronized and promoted artists and scholars. A remarkable number of Italian cities contributed significantly to Renaissance thought, literature, and art.

God. Pico's "Oration on the Dignity of Man," delivered in Rome in 1486, was a manifesto of humanism:

> O unsurpassed generosity of God the Father, O wondrous and unsurpassed felicity of man, to whom it is granted to have what he chooses, to be what he wills to be! The brutes, from the moment of their birth, bring with them . . . from their mother's womb all that they will ever possess. The highest spiritual beings [angels] were, from the very moment of creation, or soon thereafter, fixed in the mode of being which would be theirs through measureless eternities. But upon man, at the moment of his creation, God bestowed seeds pregnant with all possibilities, the germs of every form of life. Whichever of these a man shall cultivate, the same will mature and bear fruit in him. If vegetative, he will become a plant; if sensual, he will become brutish; if rational, he will reveal himself a heavenly being; if intellectual, he will be an angel and the son of God. . . . Who then will not look with awe upon this our chameleon, or who, at least, will look with greater admiration on any other being? (A. R. Caponigri, trans., *Giovanni Pico della Mirandola: Oration on the Dignity of Man* [Chicago: Regnery, 1956], pp. 8–9).

Renaissance Art in Italy

During the fourteenth century, Renaissance painters and sculptors, like Italian writers, drew inspiration from classical models. They could do so partly because Roman antiquities (monuments and ruins) were unusually numerous and near at hand and partly because Gothic art, popular elsewhere in Europe, had penetrated only slightly into Italy.

Art in the Middle Ages tended to be subservient to the church and its purposes. The object was to emphasize spiritual aspiration at the expense of physical beauty. Italian painting, usually religious figures against solid backgrounds, had been stiff and flat, with the human form covered almost entirely with clothing. In short, the art of the Middle Ages had tended to ignore nature and the physical features of the human figure, because these were thought to be sources of evil and corruption that distracted from the contemplation of God. Renaissance artists, by contrast, following the lead of the humanists, depicted a world in which nature, human beauty, the family, and even fame were pleasing to God. Because human beings were to fulfill themselves as Christians in this world, the things of this world were now, in wonderful detail, suitable subjects for artists.

A serious difficulty in the imitation of nature in painting was the simulation of movement and depth on a flat surface. A late medieval painter, the Florentine Giotto di Bondone (1266–1337), overcame this obstacle by discarding the flat forms, aloof figures, and formal compositions of the Byzantine style that had dominated Italian painting. Allegedly able to draw a fly so realistically that viewers attempted to brush it away, he skillfully contrasted light and shadow to create an illusion of depth that made his human figures look solid and round. Among the artists influenced by Giotto was Tomasso Guidi (1401–1428), better known as Masaccio. He employed the laws of atmospheric perspective to show objects receding into a background and to make figures appear round and truly three-dimensional. Although only twenty-seven when he died, Masaccio's innovations inspired succeeding generations of painters, including Michelangelo and the other giants of the High Renaissance.

The first of these was Leonardo da Vinci (1452–1519), who more than any other person of his age personified the Renaissance ideal of versatility. As an artist, he was keenly interested in the natural world and was a masterly portrayer of human psychology and personality. *The Last Supper* is a careful study of the emotions that each of Jesus' disciples was likely to have expressed on that occasion. In the *Mona Lisa,* he skillfully employed light and shadow and perspective to make the figure fully human, enigmatic and mysterious, and forever fascinating.

The most popular of the Renaissance painters, Raphael Sanzio (1483–1520), excelled in composition and use of soft colors. His *School of Athens* is a symbolic and allegorical portrayal of the classical philosophers Plato and Aristotle with their students. Raphael was best known for his many Madonnas, which are warm, pious, and graceful.

Michelangelo Buonarroti (1475–1564) considered himself a sculptor first of all, but as painter he was unsurpassed in technical excellence and grandeur of conception. He painted with a sculptor's eye and made the muscular male figure his ideal of beauty. His most ambitious project, perhaps the greatest single achievement in Renaissance art, was the painting of the frescoes covering the ceiling of the

The School of Athens. In this painting, Renaissance master Raphael presented his version of the humanist ideal of classical antiquity. Many Greek and Roman cultural heroes are depicted in the dress of sixteenth-century Italians in a setting of Renaissance architecture and sculpture. At the center of the composition, framed by the arch, Plato and Aristotle are deep in discussion.

Vatican Museums

Scala/Art Resource, New York.

The Fall. In this scene from the Sistine Chapel, Michelangelo depicts the expulsion of Adam and Eve from the Garden of Eden.

Sistine Chapel in the Vatican. This masterpiece, which required four years to complete, often with the artist lying flat on his back on a scaffold, depicts nine scenes from the Old Testament, from the creation to the flood.

Sculpture followed a parallel course to painting in its development. The first major artist in this medium was Donato di Niccolï di Betto Bardi, known as Donatello (c. 1386–1466). He drew on models of classical antiquity for inspiration, traveling to Rome to study ancient art remains. His studies included anatomy and the human body, and he employed models. Donatello's *David,* the first nude statue of the Renaissance, is graceful, well proportioned, and superbly balanced.

Michelangelo brought to sculpture the same scientific accuracy, endowment of life, and deep emotion that distinguished his paintings. His statues, whether standing like *David* or seated like *Moses,* show dramatic and emotional postures and expressions. His absolute mastery of sculptural technique powerfully served the Renaissance glorification of man. Especially moving is his exquisite *Pietà,* which depicts a grief-stricken Mary looking at the dead body of Jesus lying across her lap.

Michelangelo's later works exemplify an important change that took place in the art of the sixteenth century. His later sculptures show an exaggeration, elongation, and distortion that heightens their emotional and religious qualities. For example, his crowded *Last Judgment* painting on the Sistine Chapel's end wall is full of violence, tragedy, and horror, in contrast to the classical harmony and restraint of the ceiling figures.

Architects, though slower in exploring new directions, were still more strongly influenced by classical models. In his church designs, Filippo Brunelleschi (1377–1446) combined the Romanesque cruciform floor plan with such classical features as columns, rounded windows, and arches. His greatest triumph was the cupola (dome) atop the Florence cathedral, which echoes both Rome's Pantheon and Constantinople's Hagia Sophia.

The Renaissance Outside Italy

A great watershed in western European literature and thought was the spread of the Renaissance outside of Italy between 1490 and 1530. Italian humanists accepted positions as secretaries and diplomats with northern kings and princes. Scholars from the north studied in Italy and returned home to write and teach humanism. Northern universities incorporated humanist studies into their curricula, and humanist historians used their critical skills in writing the histories of northern lands.

Italian humanism, fostered in the republics and communes of Italy, had a strong civic strain that was believed to be acceptable to God and quite consistent with Christian life. In northern Europe, humanists wrote less about civic and political duty and more about personal morality, though they still drew heavily upon both Christian and pagan (that is, non-Christian Greek and Roman) authors. Although they stressed the Bible and the words of the church fathers over classical writings, northern humanists believed that by absorbing the wisdom of both, they could improve individual morality and revitalize and purify contemporary social and religious life. Nevertheless, like their Italian predecessors, northern humanists also believed, as Thomas More (1478–1535) said, that education in Latin and Greek "doth train the soul in virtue." More, who was a lawyer and diplomat (even becoming lord chancellor of England) as well as a humanist, is best known for his *Utopia*. The *Utopia* contrasted the evil conditions of sixteenth-century Europe with an idealized, peaceful, and prosperous society living communally in accord with reason and Christian values.

The foremost northern humanist was Desiderius Erasmus (c.1466–1536), a native of Rotterdam. His wit, marvelous writing style, and extensive travels earned him international renown and ensured that his works would be "best sellers." Erasmus formulated a humanist religion of simple piety and noble conduct based on a belief in human dignity and free will. He embraced the naturalism, tolerance, and humanitarianism he found in classical writings and used his formidable satiric power to oppose war, violence, ignorance, and irrationality. His *Adages* collected apt sayings from classical Latin writers and the *Praise of Folly* attacked the pedantic dogmatism of scholars and the ignorance of the masses. Erasmus's fresh edition of the Greek New Testament became the basis of various translations into the vernacular languages.

In areas of Europe outside Italy, vernacular literatures, already developing in the thirteenth century, now registered remarkable achievements. In England, Geoffrey Chaucer (1340–1400) made the East Midland dialect the ancestor of modern English. His highly entertaining *Canterbury Tales* are filled with realistic and humorous portrayals of men and women from various social classes and occupations.

By the fifteenth century, humanist stimulation had fostered a quickening of literary achievement in western Europe. In France, François Rabelais (1490–1553) produced a prose masterpiece, *Gargantua and Pantagruel*, that glorified the human and the natural, rejected Christian doctrine and morality, and satirized scholasticism, bigotry, and church practices with bawdy humor. At the abbey where many of the book's episodes occur, the only rule is "do what you will." A little later Michel de Montaigne (1533–1592) introduced the essay as an important literary form. His great collection of *Essays* is a kind of extended intellectual autobiography, ranging over a wide variety of topics in an engaging conversational tone. Characteristic of Montaigne's essays is a healthy skepticism regarding human opinions, doctrines, institutions, and customs, as in the following passage from "On Cannibals":

> I am not so anxious that we should note the horrible savagery of these [cannibalistic] acts as concerned that, whilst judging their faults so correctly, we should be so blind to our own. I consider it more barbarous to eat a man alive than to eat him dead; to tear by rack and torture a body still full of feeling, to roast it by degrees, and then to give it to be trampled and eaten by dogs and swine—a practice which we have not only read about but seen within recent memory, not between ancient enemies, but between neighbors and fellow-citizens and, what is worse, under the cloak of piety and religion—than to roast and eat a man after he is dead. (J. M. Cohen, trans., *Michel de Montaigne: Essays* [Harmondsworth: Penguin, 1958], p. 113.)

For the most part, the golden age of Spanish literature came somewhat later than that of France. Miguel de Cervantes's (1547–1616) *Don Quixote,* sometimes regarded as the greatest novel ever written, is a rich depiction of human nobility and folly. Cervantes ridicules the nobles' pretensions to be champions of honor by recounting the adventures of a Spanish gentleman who, after reading too many chivalric romances, becomes a wandering knight. Imagining windmills to be giants and inns to be castles, the hero (mis)behaves in accord with those (mis)perceptions. His squire, Sancho Panza, is, by contrast, a practical man untroubled by romantic dreams and content with the simple creature comforts of eating, drinking, and sleeping.

England's literary developments were contemporary with those of Spain and were most impressive in drama. William Shakespeare (1564–1616) drew themes and story lines from Greek and Roman literature and from English history. Extremely adept in the use of language and the analysis of character, he showed a deep understanding of human potential, both for good and for evil. The following is an example:

> What a piece of work is a man! How noble in reason! How infinite in faculty! In form and moving how express and admirable! In action how like an angel! In apprehension how like a god! The beauty of the world! The paragon of animals! (*Hamlet* 2.2.315–319.)

In an ironic vein reminiscent of Greek tragedy, Shakespeare's heroes are responsible for their own dilemmas and suffer by their own sins and mistakes. His strongest plays express bitterness and overwhelming pathos, as the characters conduct a troubled search into life's mysteries. Of these plays, the later ones present an overall view of the universe as benevolent and just, despite individual tragedy and grief.

Northern Renaissance art represented physical and emotional reality by use of detail, careful observation of nature, and skill in the technique of foreshortening. Jan van Eyck (1370–1440) capitalized on the advantages of oil paints, excelling in the painting of portraits in which the subjects seem to live and breathe; each detail, from a blade of grass to the hair of a dog, is meticulously rendered. Albrecht Dürer (1471–1528) studied the human form carefully and gave attention to both detail and harmonious composition in woodcuts, engravings, and paintings. He admired Martin Luther (see the next section) and often chose biblical themes for his work. Many of his pieces have a pervasive somber and often gloomy quality. The great Spanish painter, Doménikos Theotokópoulos

(1541–1614), known as El Greco from his birth on the island of Crete, was an avid admirer of Michelangelo. He used severe colors and elongated features to express Spanish religious zeal in his powerful and emotional paintings. His greatest work, *The Burial of Count Orgaz,* conveys the Catholic spirit of communion among God, saints, and humans.

Architects outside Italy continued to use Gothic techniques in building both churches and secular structures, but as they reached the structural and decorative limits of the Gothic, they began to employ the classical Greco-Roman style revived by fifteenth-century Italians. Those Italian influences are especially evident in central France's Loire Valley chateaux, country houses for French kings, nobles, and wealthy townspeople.

Women and the Renaissance

In the Renaissance, as in earlier periods of European history, education and intellectual professions were accessible almost exclusively to males. Laws were designed to keep women in a subservient role. As a rule they could not hold public office, testify in a court of law, make their own wills, or buy and sell property. Most women from the nobility and wealthy merchant class had few career options: they either entered into arranged marriages or became nuns. A few women, however, did receive schooling based on the revival of classical learning during the Renaissance; they were typically daughters of aristocrats or royalty instructed by fathers or husbands or by private tutors.

Despite the restrictions imposed by male-oriented societies, some females achieved personal and intellectual fulfillment. Christine de Pizan (1365–c. 1430), for example, was the first woman known to have made her living as a professional writer. In 1390, the death of her husband, a secretary at the court of the French king (Charles V), left her with three children, her mother, and two brothers to support. To do so, she developed her skills in a variety of genres: love poetry, literary criticism, histories of eminent women, political theory, religious meditations, a biography of King Charles V, and poetry written for aristocratic patrons; her last work was a poem celebrating the victory of Joan of Arc at the siege of Or-

Melancholia I. The melancholy figure by Albrecht Dürer sits amid symbols of the new learning of the sixteenth century, suggesting that greater knowledge does not necessarily produce happiness. If meant as a self-portrait, it is a very early example of the "tormented artist" theme so familiar in modern times. The work shows the exquisite detail that a master engraver could achieve.

léans during the Hundred Years' War (see the next section). She also penned a fascinating autobiography entitled *Christine's Vision*.

Even for learned women, a life of scholarship did not combine easily with wifely duties and maternal obligations of child bearing and rearing. Ginerva Nogarola (c. 1417–1468) and Cataruzza Caldiera (d. 1463), both of whom showed exceptional promise as young women, abandoned their studies and writings altogether after they married and bore children. Described by some humanists as a prodigy, Cassandra Fedele (1465–1558) married reluctantly at age thirty-three and continued her scholarly work only haphazardly, failing to complete any of the three major works she had planned.

There were a few exceptions, however, when privileged women were able to study, write, marry, and have children. Marguerite of Navarre (1492–1549) was one of the greatest women literary writers of the sixteenth century. Although a poet of unusual sensitivity, her fame rests on her principal prose work, the *Heptameron,* a collection of short stories modeled on Boccaccio's *Decameron.*

Some women found themselves in conflict with their family and society as they followed a literary career outside of marriage. Constanza Barbaro (born c. 1419), daughter of a Venetian humanist, became a nun so that she could devote all her time to study. Isotta Nogarola (1418–1466) was probably the best known among women writers who created their own cloistered world. She was trained by a private tutor and at age eighteen started a correspondence with male humanists in Verona. Though her letters show great promise and were praised by some, others advised her that she would have to "become a man" if she wished to continue her career as a writer. Isotta decided against both the alternatives of married life and the nunnery and lived as a recluse in her mother's home, producing some fine Latin verse and an important theological tract.

Women who aspired to paint had to overcome the same disadvantages as those drawn to the intellectual movement. Still, many succeeded in earning a living by selling their works to, or accepting commissions for portraits from, wealthy patrons. Levina Bening Teerline (c. 1520–1576) was invited by Henry VIII to come from Flanders to paint miniature portraits. The English monarch was so delighted with her paintings that he paid her a life annuity of £40, then a generous sum. The portraitist Sofonisba Anguissola (c. 1535–1625), the daughter of an Italian noble family, drew a similar commission from Philip II of Spain, who rewarded her lavishly with a pension, a dowry on her marriage, and appointment as lady-in-waiting to the court.

During the Baroque phase of the Italian Renaissance, Artemisia Gentileschi (1593–c. 1652), trained by her father and other artists, achieved a reputation on a par with that of Leonardo Da Vinci and Michelangelo. She often chose women for her subjects: for example, the biblical heroines Susannah and Judith beheading Holofernes. In another medium Properzia de' Rossi (c.1500–1530) was singled out by the biographer Vasari for the excellence of her relief sculptures in the Church of St. Peter in Bologna and for her great versatility: "[she was] skilled not only in household matters . . . but in infinite fields of knowledge. . . . She was beautiful and played and sang better than any woman in the city." Few women of the Renaissance were able (or allowed) to be so multitalented.

Uffizi Gallery/Art Resource

Sofonisba Anguissola, *Self-Portrait.* Anguissola belonged to a noble Italian family in Cremona. Her father encouraged her to study painting, and her work for Philip II of Spain won her many honors and privileges, including the position of lady-in-waiting to the court.

European Nation-States and the Reformation

[At the Diet of Worms in 1521, the spokesman said:] "Martin, how can you assume that you are the only one to understand the sense of Scripture? Would you put your judgment above that of so many famous men and claim that you know more than they all? You have no right to call into question the most holy orthodox faith,

instituted by Christ the perfect lawgiver, proclaimed throughout the world by the apostles, sealed by the red blood of the martyrs, confirmed by the sacred councils, defined by the Church in which all our fathers believed until death and gave to us as an inheritance, and which now we are forbidden by the pope and the emperor to discuss lest there be no end of debate. I ask you, Martin—answer candidly and without horns—do you or do you not repudiate your books and the errors which they contain?"

*Luther replied, "Since then Your Majesty and your lordships desire a simple reply, I will answer without horns and without teeth. Unless I am convicted by Scripture and plain reason—I do not accept the authority of popes and councils, for they have contradicted each other—my conscience is captive to the Word of God. I cannot and I will not recant anything, for to go against conscience is neither right nor safe. God help me. Amen." [In the earliest printed version the words "Here I stand. I cannot do otherwise," were added.]**

*Roland H. Bainton, *Here I Stand: A Life of Martin Luther* (New York: Mentor, 1958), p. 144.

This exchange was the culmination of a sequence of events that produced the Protestant Reformation, a broad revolt against the medieval church. Although religious dissent was the root of the problem, the Reformation was also intimately bound up with political, social, economic, and intellectual matters. Within a generation of Luther's defiant act, many Europeans had set up separate religious organizations outside the Catholic church, ending the centuries-long religious unity of western Europe. Although the various Protestant denominations disagreed among themselves on minor theological points, they were firmly united in their opposition to Catholicism. The confrontation inspired a long period of bloody strife that would profoundly affect Western civilization.

The Reformation was closely associated with the formation of powerful national states in western Europe, a process that had begun some two centuries earlier. The pride, power, and resources of these states found expression in various forms of political and commercial rivalry, including developing trade overseas (see the following sections). The emergence of these nation-states of western Europe will open this section.

The Centralization of Western European Monarchies

The High Middle Ages had witnessed the resurgent power of the monarchy in Europe as the prelude to the development of the modern state. However, the troubles of fourteenth- and fifteenth-century Europe—civil and foreign wars, economic depression, and the plague—undid much of the earlier work of consolidation. The powers of government came to be divided between the king and his semiautonomous vassals, the great nobles of the realm. Royal vassals maintained private armies, dispensed justice in the courts, and served as advisors and royal officials. The nobles were monarchs in miniature, often having the power of life and death over the people in their territories. As a result, a country like France was not a single nation under one king; rather, it was a mosaic of principalities, each with its own ruler. At times of a major threat, vassals would sometimes temporarily join forces under their king.

For the peasants or serfs, it made little difference whether they were exploited by king or duke, because life close to the soil was harsh in either case. For dwellers in manufacturing and trading towns, the situation was less clear. The city fathers longed to win self-rule and, to that end, liked to play one great lord off against another or against the king. At the same time, however, those who aspired to trade over larger areas found the political fragmentation of their country a hindrance.

The trend towards decentralization was dramatically reversed during the second half of the fifteenth century with the emergence of strong, ambitious kings in France, England, and Spain. They ended internal disorders in their lands, reduced the power of the nobility, and extended greater control over their subjects. The achievements of these "New Monarchs" served as examples for lesser kings to follow.

Several factors led to the recovery of the monarchy in western Europe. As already noted, in the centralized states around the world, the European kings needed to generate an assured source of income sufficient to create an army and a bureaucracy under their control. The new towns provided a potential source of new money. In a mutually beneficial arrangement, the kings granted the towns privileges and rights in return for money payments to the royal treasury. In this way, towns and monarchs became allies against the great lords, who often sought to encroach on the independence of both. These arrangements not only reduced the kings' dependence on the great nobles but resulted in the growth of semi-independent towns in early modern Europe.

With the new revenue, the kings moved to abandon feudal levies and create a powerful army. In the traditional feudal levy, vassals supplied forces for temporary service, but so long as the great nobles controlled the military, the king's power was limited. Accordingly, the monarchs began to build up armies of paid soldiers commanded by loyal officers who were willing to follow orders and even make war on the nobles, if necessary.

The kings further strengthened their position through marriages calculated either to neutralize powerful antagonists or to add territory to their own realm. No less important was the development of bureaucracies. Civil servants attached to districts collected taxes and administered in the king's name. Kings selected their officials from outside the nobility and paid them in money and in small, scattered estates instead of huge blocks of territory. In this way, the kings ensured that the officials would be dependent on them and thus loyal to the crown.

In France, the first of the New Monarchs, Louis XI (reigned 1461–1483), inherited a realm devastated by the Black Death and the Hundred Years' War (1337–1453). The latter was a debilitating struggle fought between the English and the French, and among the French, over a maze of feudal claims and commercial competition. At a dark moment for France, a young woman, later known as Joan of Arc (1412–1431) changed the course of the war. Believing herself to be acting at God's urging, she persuaded Charles VII (reigned 1422–1461) to appoint her to a military command. Her prestige reached its height in 1429 when she succeeded in relieving the besieged city of Orléans and cutting a path for Charles to Rheims, where he was properly crowned in the place and manner of his ancestors. Joan, who was later captured and executed, came to symbolize the French national spirit.

Louis XI was nicknamed the "Spider," in part because his misshapen body appeared spiderlike, but more because he devised political traps and plots reminiscent of a spiderweb. He attracted the loyalty of the lesser nobility and employed many of them as royal officials. Louis used the army to expand royal power within France, and in a series of adroit, if underhanded, moves, he suppressed the great nobles, already weakened by losses during the Hundred Years' War. At the same time, he curbed town autonomy and asserted administrative control over the provinces. He seldom convened the Estates General, France's rudimentary representative assembly. By his death in 1483 Louis had united France, strengthened its economy, and laid the foundations for royal absolutism.

Like France, fifteenth-century England was wracked by factionalism, which culminated in a civil war (the War of the Roses, 1455–1485) between the great feudal families of Lancaster and York. The civil war ended in 1485 when Henry Tudor, the foremost surviving Lancastrian, seized the crown as Henry VII (reigned 1485–1509) and married Elizabeth of York, the leading Yorkist claimant, thereby uniting the two feuding groups. With peace temporarily assured, Henry set out to centralize his power. He drew his officials from the ranks of the lesser gentry and townsmen and seated many of his councilors in Parliament, where they could manipulate matters to the king's liking. Henry received such ample revenues from customs duties on increased international trade and from fines derived from active law enforcement that he needed to summon Parliament only once in the last twelve years of his reign. He supplemented traditional English law with Roman law for many purposes. Roman law, formulated to govern a far-flung empire, favored central authority over the rights of aristocrats and common people alike and helped Henry legally justify seizing the lands and revenues of "overmighty subjects." At his death in 1509, Henry left a powerful monarchy to his son, Henry VIII.

Events in the Iberian Peninsula paralleled those in France and England. Beginning in the eleventh century, the salient feature of Iberian history was the Christian *Reconquista* (Reconquest) against the Muslims, who controlled most of the peninsula. By the mid-fifteenth century, the three kingdoms of Aragon, Castile, and Portugal dominated the peninsula. Portugal was the first national state to emerge in Europe. There the House of Avis centralized royal administration by suppressing revolts of nobles and executing many of their leaders. Partly as a result of this centralization, Portugal was the first European nation to use its resources to expand overseas (discussed later in this chapter).

The marriage of Ferdinand, King of Aragon (reigned 1479–1516), to Isabella, Queen of Castile (reigned 1474–1504), in 1469 united their two realms into the Kingdom of Spain. Ferdinand and Isabella moved against the nobles, who objected to any increase in the crown's power and opposed the introduction of Roman law, which the royal couple supported. They forged alliances with the towns, ostensibly to combat bandits but actually to counter the power of feudal levies. The Cortes, the representative assembly dominated by the nobility, steadily lost power.

The desire to consolidate their strength led the Spanish rulers to establish the Inquisition, a tribunal for the detection and punishment of heresy. It operated as an agency of the state, free from papal or church control. Ferdinand, who was not religious, did not hesitate to use it as well as an instrument to enforce civil despotism; in particular, to suppress rebellious churchmen and nobles. Most of the inquisition's fury, however, was aimed at achieving religious uniformity. Its officials energetically and carefully examined the religious purity of all, searching for blasphemers and heretics. The officials conducted trials and passed sentence, often gathering information and confessions through torture. The state then executed those found guilty. When Ferdinand and Isabella conquered Granada (1492), the last Muslim outpost on the peninsula, they ordered all unconverted Muslims and Jews to leave the country with only what they could carry. The confiscated property of the religious exiles, coupled with the profits from discoveries overseas, greatly enriched the crown.

The Background of the Protestant Reformation

The Reformation, the religious upheaval that splintered the Roman Catholic church, took place during the sixteenth and seventeenth centuries, at the same time that centralized monarchy was on the rise in western Europe. Earlier, in 1054, Christianity had split into two main branches, the Eastern or Orthodox church, which prevailed in the Byzantine Empire, and the Western or Roman Catholic church, which was dominant in central and western Europe. In the High Middle Ages, the popes had succeeded in centralizing the administration of the church under their control, permitting them to impose religious uniformity and to exercise a potent influence on European political life. The Catholic church reached the height of its power under Pope Innocent III (reigned 1198–1216). Laxity and worldliness characterized Innocent III's successors, weakening the papacy's moral authority and opening the way for increasing defiance and contempt. Papal power eroded at the same time that the prestige of the new national states was on the rise.

The turning point in papal history occurred when the strong and consolidated monarchy of France challenged the secular pretensions of the papacy. The result was the humiliation of the pope, Boniface VIII (reigned 1294–1303), in 1303 and the removal of the papacy to Avignon, in southern France, two years later. From 1305 to 1378 the popes resided at Avignon, where, to all appearances, they became tools of French interests and, consequently, objects of suspicion and hostility to France's enemies. The long period of papal exile at Avignon, known as the Babylonian Captivity, was a minor scandal compared to what followed during the next half century.

Pope Gregory XI (reigned 1370–1378) ended the Babylonian Captivity when he moved back to Rome, where he died in 1378. The cardinals met and, amid scenes of mob violence, first elected an Italian pope, Urban VI (reigned 1378–1389), who publicly scolded them for their worldliness and attempted to reduce their revenues. Most of the cardinals thereupon withdrew from Rome, declared Urban's election invalid because it had been held under threat of violence, chose a Frenchman as Pope Clement VII (reigned 1378–1394), and settled with him at Avignon. To the bewilderment of conscientious Christians, there were now two popes, one at Rome and the other at Avignon, each with competing systems of church administrations, courts, and taxation. Corruption and financial abuses worsened as each pope, seeking to oust the other, became more involved than ever in politics. At the urging of bishops and powerful laymen, a church council was summoned with the object of ending the schism.

The second church council, held at Constance (1414–1417), reunited the Catholic church. The delegates deposed the rival popes and elected a new pope, Martin V (reigned 1417–1431). Radical elements wanted to go further and strip away papal powers and have councils govern the church, but the efforts of these conciliarists were thwarted by papal intransigence and by their own inability to agree. In the meantime Martin and his successors tried to win over the temporal rulers in western and central Europe who had initially supported the conciliarists. The popes achieved their objective, but only after permitting the monarchs to assume more control over the church in their respective countries. Before the end of the fifteenth century, the papacy had once again asserted its dominance over the church, although it was unable to recapture the spiritual and moral leadership it had formerly enjoyed. The price for the papacy's triumph was high. Preoccupied for many years in combating the conciliarist movement and practicing power politics, the popes showed little interest in undertaking the reforms that sincere Christians were demanding.

A number of abuses had arisen in the church in the fourteenth and fifteenth centuries. Simony, the sale of church offices, was one such problem. Some 2,000 church offices were for sale, and the resulting revenues formed a significant part of papal income. A case in point was the Archbishop of Mainz, who paid the astronomical sum of 30,000 ducats for his office—equivalent to fifteen years' salary for a mid-level functionary in the papal bureaucracy. Another serious problem was pluralism, where one individual held several church offices at the same time. Priests and bishops often hired stand-ins to fulfill their duties. In Germany in 1500, more than 90 percent of the parishes were served by part-time priests. The practice of nepotism, giving lucrative church offices to relatives of the higher clergy, was widespread. Churchmen, from the highest rank to the lowest, were frequently affected by the secular spirit of the Renaissance and showed more interest in worldly pleasures and pursuits than in attending to their spiritual responsibilities. Popes led a life of luxury rivaling that of the secular rulers of their time. The church's ever-growing fiscal demands, together with the immorality and secular interests of the clergy, aggravated the resentment and sense of alienation felt by many Christians.

When church leaders did not initiate reform, some priests and laity on the local level tried to make changes, while in other areas, secular princes led popular reform movements. Appealing to scriptural precedents, the life of Jesus, and the activities of the early church described in the Book of Acts, most reformers demanded back-to-basics change. Such was the general situation on All Saints' Eve, 1517, when Martin Luther made his famous demand for reform of church practices and doctrines.

Martin Luther Breaks with the Church

Martin Luther was born in 1483 at Eisleben in Saxony (central Germany), the second son of a moderately prosperous miner. To please his father he went to the University of Erfurt in 1505 to study law. That same year, according to his account, he was caught in a fearsome thunderstorm

Library of Congress

Luther before the Diet of Worms, 1521. Luther was resolute in his defense, partly because of the support he received from Germans of all classes. His journey to Worms was made triumphant by the acclamation of cheering crowds who lined the road.

and thrown to the ground by a flash of lightning. Following his miraculous survival, which affected him emotionally, he entered an Augustinian monastery at Erfurt, where he was ordained a priest in 1507. He returned to the university and became a doctor of theology. From 1511 until his death thirty-five years later, he served as professor of theology at the newly founded University of Wittenberg.

Luther's growing reputation as a biblical scholar masked his torment about gaining God's grace and his own salvation. Beyond scrupulous monastic observance, he had been diligent in confessing his sins, praying, and fasting. Yet performing good works, as commanded by the church, did not give him the comfort and spiritual peace he was seeking. Through the study of the Bible he found the answer to his dilemma in one of St. Paul's letters to the Romans, especially in the phrase "the just shall live by faith." It dawned on him that people could be saved only by repenting their sins and throwing themselves on God's mercy and accepting His grace. Salvation was a gift from God as a reward for faith in His mercy and could not be earned by doing good works. This doctrine struck at the heart of orthodox Catholic belief, which held that only through the sacraments of the church could sinners be redeemed and made worthy of salvation. Luther was at first unaware of the conflict. He thought he was simply giving more emphasis to the Bible in Christian education. Only after he was drawn into the indulgence controversy did he realize the revolutionary implications of his religious views.

According to Catholic teaching, an indulgence was supposed to remit punishment in purgatory for sins for which insufficient penance had been done while on earth. It was granted on condition that the sinner was repentant and was willing to perform some pious deed such as going on a crusade or a pilgrimage. By the sixteenth century, however, the practice had become perverted. Church agents made extravagant claims, implying that indulgences secured total remission of sins, on earth and in purgatory, without bothering to mention the acts of contrition and confession demanded of every sinner as a prerequisite for forgiveness. An indulgence, so it was advertised, guaranteed swift entry in heaven for the purchaser himself or for a loved one in purgatory. As one hawker put it: "As soon as the coin in the coffer rings, the soul from purgatory springs." Many flocked to buy indulgences; the huge sums collected went either into the pockets of leading political and church officials or to Rome to pay for such papal projects as Saint Peter's basilica.

Luther was outraged to see poor people being deprived of their hard-earned money under false pretenses. He objected to the sale of indulgences on the grounds that the pope had no control over purgatory and, most important of all, that it did not mandate repentance as a condition for forgiveness of sins. On October 31, 1517, Luther posted a list of ninety-five theses (statements of error) on the church door at Wittenberg. His purpose in doing so was to challenge the defenders of indulgences to a debate. Luther had expected reaction to be confined to the university community, but to his surprise printed copies of his theses circulated throughout Germany, arousing widespread public interest. To the consternation of church authorities, the sale of indulgences fell off sharply.

As Luther was forced by critics to define his theological position, it became increasingly apparent that his beliefs were sharply at odds with those of the Catholic church. In 1520 Pope Leo X (reigned 1513–1521) condemned Luther's teachings and ordered him to recant within two months or face excommunication. Luther responded by publicly burning the document. The pope then formally excommunicated Luther and called upon the Holy Roman Emperor, Charles V, to punish him as a heretic. But Luther had become a national figure, and the German princes did not feel he could be condemned without a hearing.

In the spring of 1521 Luther, under the protection of an imperial safe conduct, appeared before Charles V at a diet (meeting) at Worms. There he refused to recant unless it could be proved that his writings were contrary to Scripture. Branded an outlaw with a price on his head, he traveled home with the assistance of agents of Frederick, elector of Saxony, under whose protection he would remain for the rest of his life. In 1522 Luther returned to Wittenberg where he gathered his supporters and established the first Protestant church.

The rapid spread of Lutheranism was in marked contrast to other reform movements, which had failed to divide the church. Luther was a brilliant theologian and possessed nearly every quality essential to a revolutionary leader. He also enjoyed advantages that had been denied to his predecessors. First, his revolt against Rome occurred when the church was in a state of decline and was being strongly criticized from within. The abuses resulting from the Great Schism and a series of worldly Renaissance popes had lowered public support for the church. Meanwhile, the writings of Erasmus and other humanists generated a critical spirit that challenged many accepted beliefs. Erasmus's scholarly edition of the New Testament (1516) and the publication of the writings of the church fathers, including all of Jerome's letters, in the vernacular, coupled with other humanist texts, revealed that some church doctrines had shaky foundations. Second, the invention of the printing press allowed for the mass production of books, including the Bible, at relatively low cost. Published materials thereafter became available to larger numbers of people, permitting the rapid spread of new ideas. Third, an unusual political situation existed in Germany. Charles V, the Holy Roman Emperor, was committed to maintaining an alliance with the papacy and also wanted to extend his authority over Germany. About half of the 300-odd German rulers supported Lutheranism as a way to resist Charles V. Some among them may have been moved as much by material considerations as by religious concerns. By adopting Lutheranism, the princes could confiscate the rich and extensive Catholic holdings in their domains. Finally, the rising capitalistic classes, finding Catholicism incompatible with the practices of trade and banking, were willing to push for a system that suited them better.

Many of Luther's early followers broke away from his guidance. The largest group to do so was the Anabaptists, a radical religious sect whose social ideas included a refusal to bear arms and the abolition of private property. Luther disavowed them because, apart from sharp religious differences, his views on the social order were extremely conservative. The humanists, who had scorned and ridiculed church practices, hailed Luther for his efforts to restore the purity of Christianity. But the humanists, placing unity ahead of doctrine, wanted to reform the church from within, not start a new religion. When Luther refused to patch up his differences with Rome, most of them, including Erasmus, decided to remain within the Catholic fold. In 1524–1525 the Peasants' Revolt had far more serious consequences. Thousands of downtrodden peasants in southwest Germany, seeking relief from economic and manorial burdens, revolted against their landlords. At first, Luther had shown considerable sympathy for the commoners' cause but, when they resorted to violence, endangering the fabric of society and the structure of the state, he called for their suppression. The princes did so with unspeakable cruelty, causing Lutheranism to lose much of its appeal among the poor of southern Germany.

Luther saw himself not as a social and economic reformer but as a restorer of true doctrine and practices of the early Christian church. In final form, Luther's religion differed from the Catholic church in a number of important ways. Luther believed that salvation came through faith in God rather than through good works, sacraments, and rituals. The true church, he contended, consisted of all believers and not just an organization of ecclesiastics; thus he eliminated the hierarchy of pope, cardinals, and bishops and reduced the importance of the clergy. For Luther, ultimate authority rested with the Scriptures, not with church traditions and papal pronouncements. Of the seven Catholic sacraments, he retained only baptism and communion, the two found in the Bible. He abolished monasteries and the celibacy of the clergy. Luther himself married a former nun, by whom he had six children. He replaced the Latin liturgy with a German service that included Bible reading and the singing of hymns. So that the Bible would be available in German, Luther translated both the New and Old Testaments. Finally, unlike Catholicism, Luther gave the state supreme authority over his church except in matters of doctrine.

The spectacular progress of Lutheranism troubled Charles V, who sought to find an accommodation that would prevent Germany from being divided by religion. His political skirmishing with the Lutheran princes only intensified matters, however, and led to open war in 1546, the same year that Luther died. Although Charles was determined to crush the Lutheran states, he was unable to intervene forcefully because of his preoccupation with wars against the French and the Turks. With neither side able to gain a clear advantage, the Peace of Augsburg in 1555 ended the nine-year conflict. By this compromise sovereign princes and cities were given the right to decide between Catholicism and Lutheranism; subjects who objected to their ruler's choice would be permitted to emigrate. The peace of Augsburg left Lutheranism firmly entrenched in the northern half of Germany. From there it spread to Scandinavia and to the Baltic lands under the control of Sweden. Lutheranism would also have a great influence on all subsequent Protestant movements.

Protestant Reformers after Luther

Luther may have been the first to revolt against the established church, but others soon followed. Ulrich Zwingli (1484–1531) led a reform movement in Zurich, Switzerland, that incorporated many of Luther's teachings. Zwingli believed in the supreme authority of Scripture and simplified church services, taught justification by faith instead of good works, and opposed clerical celibacy. But he went beyond Luther in considering baptism and communion to be merely symbolic ceremonies. These doctrinal differences proved irreconcilable and marked the first in a long series of Protestant schisms. Zwingli also maintained that the church needed to take the lead in imposing Christian discipline on civil life. The Swiss confederation of cantons could not agree on which church to follow, so it allowed each canton to make its own decision.

The reform tradition that Zwingli started in Zurich was carried on by John Calvin (1509–1564) in Geneva a generation later. Calvin, who next to Martin Luther was the most celebrated Protestant leader of the sixteenth century, was born in the French town of Noyon, the son of a prosperous lawyer. His heart was set on becoming a priest, but at his father's insistence, he abandoned theology for law. Early in life he associated with followers of Luther and about 1534 converted to Protestantism. Forced into hiding to avoid persecution, Calvin fled to Switzerland and settled in Geneva where, as a dynamic agent of change, he rose to become virtual dictator of the city.

Calvin outlined his religious views in *The Institutes of the Christian Religion,* published in 1536 when he was only twenty-six. The book was a clear, logical, and superb synthesis of Protestant theology. On the surface Calvin's beliefs resembled those of Luther. He accepted the sinfulness of humans and their impotence to save themselves, denied the value of good works as a means of salvation, regarded the Bible as the sole authority in matters of faith, and rejected all the Catholic sacraments except baptism and communion. But Calvin's differences with Luther were significant enough to rule out collaboration between the two. Calvin favored suppressing anything that was not clearly sanctioned in the Bible, which he regarded as the supreme authority in every aspect of life. Luther, regarding the Bible as a vehicle for Christ's teachings, permitted anything that it did not specifically forbid. Far more than Luther, Calvin stressed the omnipotence of God. Calvin accepted Luther's concept of salvation through God's grace, but believed more strongly than the latter that this priceless gift was granted only to some men. According to Calvin, people were condemned to live in perpetual sin as punishment for Adam and Eve's fall from grace. But God through his infinite mercy had chosen some human beings to be saved and had damned all the rest to suffer in hell. Men and women could do nothing to change their fate, which was predestined before they were born. The doctrine of predestination was at the core of Calvin's theology. The doctrine itself was not new, but Calvin's emphasis on it was. Luther's belief in justification by faith implied divine predetermination, but he was too consumed with other matters to follow through. Calvin, with his rigorous logic, was driven to carry the doctrine to its ultimate conclusion.

Logically, one might think that if individuals could have no effect on their destiny, they would be indifferent about their personal conduct. Calvin took another position on that point, however: although people had no sure way of knowing who would be saved and who would be damned, those living in accordance with God's will could take it as a hopeful sign. Even if a pious life did not ensure salvation, an immoral life proved that one was not among the chosen. Calvin's doctrine had an enormous appeal. It gave believers a powerful motive to do God's work in order to convince themselves that they would be saved.

Calvinism was not confined to Switzerland. Geneva became a training center for Calvinist preachers who came from many parts of Europe. Impelled by a sense of militancy and dedication, they returned to promote Calvin's teachings in their homeland. Calvinism triumphed in Scotland under the leadership of John Knox (c. 1510–1572), in the German Palatinate, and in the Dutch Netherlands, where it played a major role in overthrowing Spanish tyranny. It gained many converts in England (Puritans) and a vigorous following in France (Huguenots), Bohemia, and Hungary. From Europe Calvinism made its way to America, where it contributed significantly to the growth of constitutional government.

The act that sparked the English Reformation had little to do with Calvinism or church doctrine, however. The king, Henry VIII, wanted to annul his marriage to

LIVES AND TIMES ACROSS CULTURES

Life in Geneva and Venice in the Sixteenth Century

Under a constitution Calvin helped write, Geneva became a theocratic republic in which the administration of church and state were closely interwoven. Calvin's objective was to transform the city into his version of the ideal Christian community. Ruling with the assistance of a council known as the Consistory, he considered it his duty to supervise every aspect of the city's life and to enforce God's will. Guided by the Bible, laws were passed forbidding such things as idleness, dancing, frivolous pastimes, card playing, profanity, adultery, and marriage to Catholics. There were instructions for the way people dressed, on how women were to arrange their hair, even for the selection of names for infants. Calvin demanded sobriety, regular church attendance, hard work, frugality, and pursuit of a trade. Secret agents were on the lookout for wrongdoing.

Calvin had no tolerance for human weaknesses, and even common sins were punished with unprecedented rigor. The most notorious example of Calvin's harshness was the execution of Michael Servetus, a Spanish refugee, for publicly denying the doctrine of the Trinity. Gradually, as the more liberal-minded people left the city and were replaced by zealots from all over Europe, the character of the city changed. In 1546 John Knox reported that Geneva was the most perfect community of Christ seen anywhere on earth since the days of the apostles.

In many ways unique among Italian cities, Venice stood in sharp contrast to Geneva. Built almost exclusively on trade and shipping, Venice was a rich, highly cultural and cosmopolitan city. It was governed by a hereditary oligarchy of wealthy merchants comprising only about 2 percent of the population. Although members of this aristocracy, as they styled themselves, tolerated no opposition, they ruled wisely and did much to improve the economic welfare of the disenfranchised masses.

Venice was untroubled by internal disorder, social tensions, or party factionalism. Travelers were struck by the paradoxical nature of the city. On the one hand, they saw a city that projected a sober image of republican restraint and judicious modesty, founded on the principles of equality, magnanimity, domestic harmony, and justice for all of its citizens. On the other hand, they reported that Venice was a pleasure-seeking community—full of festive people, indulgent of gambling, of roisterous parties, of the theatre, and of lax sexual mores. As early as the fourteenth century Petrarch noted with disapproval his impression of the city: "Much freedom reigns there in every respect, and what I should call the only evil prevailing—but also the worst—far too much freedom." Freedom was possible because there was no opposition to the government; and there were few grounds for criticism because the government had adopted progressive social policies and secured boundless wealth.

Laws in Venice were enacted without reference to God's will. In fact the government was anticlerical and as a rule ignored interdicts issued by the papacy. During the Counter-Reformation the papacy rejuvenated the Inquisition as a means to maintain orthodoxy and effectively extend the church's power in the Catholic world. Most Catholic countries rallied behind this institution without reservation. However, Venice, long impervious to papal influence, adopted a middle position, designed to contain heresy without compromising the authority of its secular government or severely restricting rights traditionally enjoyed by its citizens.

his wife, Catherine of Aragon, by whom he had only a daughter, Mary. Although England had no law that barred a woman from the throne, Henry and his advisors felt that the country should be ruled by a male. While divorce was contrary to church law, ecclesiastical authorities sometimes allowed marriages to be annulled, especially when monarchs were involved. The problem in this case was that Catherine was the aunt of the powerful Holy Roman Emperor, Charles V, whose troops not only controlled Rome but held the pope captive. Henry was not a patient man; when the pope delayed acting on his request he turned to the compliant Archbishop of Canterbury, Thomas Cramner, who granted the annulment in 1533. The following year Parliament passed the Act of Supremacy, which repudiated papal primacy and declared the king head of an independent Anglican church. In this capacity, Henry subsequently dissolved the monasteries and enriched his treasury with their great wealth.

Despite his break with Rome, Henry continued to think of himself as a devout Catholic. The official theology of the Church of England made few departures from Catholicism. When Henry died in 1547, his nine-year-old son, Edward VI, ascended the throne. During the regency government of the youth, Protestants gradually moved Anglican doctrine closer to mainstream Protestant tenets through the Book of Common Prayer. When Edward died without an heir in 1553, the crown passed to Mary, a devout Catholic, who dedicated herself to restoring the Roman Catholic church in England. Persecution of Protestants during Mary's rule earned her the nickname "Bloody Mary." In 1558 the childless Mary died unexpectedly, and the crown went to her Protestant half-sister, Elizabeth, who quickly restored the Anglican church and declared herself its governor. During her long reign (1558–1603), Elizabeth successfully steered a middle course between Roman Catholicism and Calvinism. The Anglican church's beliefs were spelled out in a modified Book of Common Prayer and in the Thirty-nine Articles, published in 1563.

A great upheaval, such as the Protestant revolt, was bound to produce extremist groups. The most radical among the reformers were the Anabaptists, the ancestors of the modern Mennonites and Amish. They generally came from the lower classes and stressed a literal interpretation of the Scripture, seeking a return to the simplicity of primitive Christianity. The name *Anabaptist* meant "baptize again," and came from their rejection of infant baptism and their belief that only adults capable of free choice should be baptized. Adults who had been baptized as children had to be rebaptized. Generally the Anabaptists rejected any association between church and state, refused to recognize civil authority when it conflicted with their religious ideals, and favored the creation of egalitarian communities like those of the early Christians. Because they posed a religious and political threat to established society, they were intensively and cruelly persecution by both Catholics and Protestants.

The aim of early Protestant movements was to modify rather than reject the medieval church. All, to varying degrees, retained features of the old Roman church, but their sharp differences could not be harmonized. By the middle of the sixteenth century, Protestantism had triumphed in nearly half of Europe and the existence of the Catholic church itself seemed threatened.

Women and the Reformation

Women showed as much interest in the Reformation as did men. For most women, exposure to Protestant doctrines came through their husbands or fathers. Some, inspired by what they heard and anxious to promote their new faith, did so in ways open to them. Anabaptist women were allowed to preach and administer baptism, and, occasionally, zealous wives of evangelizers were active alongside their husbands from the pulpits. However, larger Protestant groups, as with Catholics, closed the ministry to women. As John Calvin put it: "The custom of the church . . . may be elicited first of all from Tertullian [church father, c. 160–230], who held that no woman in church is allowed to speak, teach, baptize or make offerings; this in order that she may not usurp the functions of men." Apart from the lack of theological training, women serving conspicuously in nontraditional roles would have been objectionable to most men.

The most common venue in which women conveyed their views and feelings was the home. Here they discussed doctrinal matters and instructed occasional visitors and friends on the virtues of their new faith. Some educated women composed hymns or wrote devotional works. Married women taught their children the catechism, pronounced prayers, and sang hymns. There were even instances of noblewomen pressuring their husbands into converting to their faith.

The Reformation affected women not only through new religious ideas but also through institutional and political changes. Protestant reformers stressed the value and sanctity of marriage, challenging the medieval tendency to denigrate women and encourage celibacy. Luther considered marriage a divinely ordained union and a natural vocation for women. Although he and other Protestant reformers exalted the state of marriage and urged that husbands treat their wives in a kindly manner and share authority with them within the household, they nevertheless insisted that women remain subject to men in that union. Convinced that women's primary duty was to obey their husbands and bear children, the reformers did not want them to serve as ministers or hold too many public responsibilities. A strong patriarchal family seemed indispensable to the social stability of the state.

Laws regulating marriage were quite equitable: if a marriage failed, women had the same right as men to divorce and remarry. Unlike Catholics, who permitted only separation from bed and board, Protestant reformers allowed divorce under circumstances such as abuse, abandonment, or adultery. Still, the various Protestant denominations discouraged the breakup of families, permitting divorce only after all efforts to reconcile had failed. Even "liberated" women rarely sought divorce, which was apt to leave them without financial support.

The closing of convents in Protestant territories imposed a cruel hardship on many nuns. Some married or returned to their paternal homes, but most were left alone to face the hazards of life. They took whatever employment was available; some found no work, while others, in desperation, even turned to prostitution.

Protestant leaders, eager to increase biblical literacy and make individuals better Christians, encouraged education for women and men alike. They established schools for both sexes at the primary and secondary levels, as well as academies and colleges to train pastors and male lay church workers. Education gave women an opportunity to find employment as teachers or become authors. Although illiteracy remained pervasive in Europe, a base for expanding educational opportunity had been laid: it proved to be one of the most enduring legacies of the Reformation.

The Roman Catholic or Counter-Reformation

Rome responded hesitantly and slowly to the Protestant challenge and to calls for changes from within. But as hopes for reconciliation dimmed and Protestantism continued to make gains, the Catholic church launched a vigorous counterattack on a number of fronts, a response termed variously the Catholic Reformation or Counter-Reformation. First and foremost, success in halting the spread of Protestantism and reclaiming lost lands depended heavily on reform within the Roman Catholic church. Long before Luther acted at Wittenberg, many sincere and devout Catholics, disturbed at the deterioration of the church, had urged that a general council be held to carry through needed reforms. The popes had resisted summoning a church council, in part because they were mindful of the efforts of the conciliar movement in the fifteenth century to strip them of their authority. Ultimately, however, the pressure for reform became too

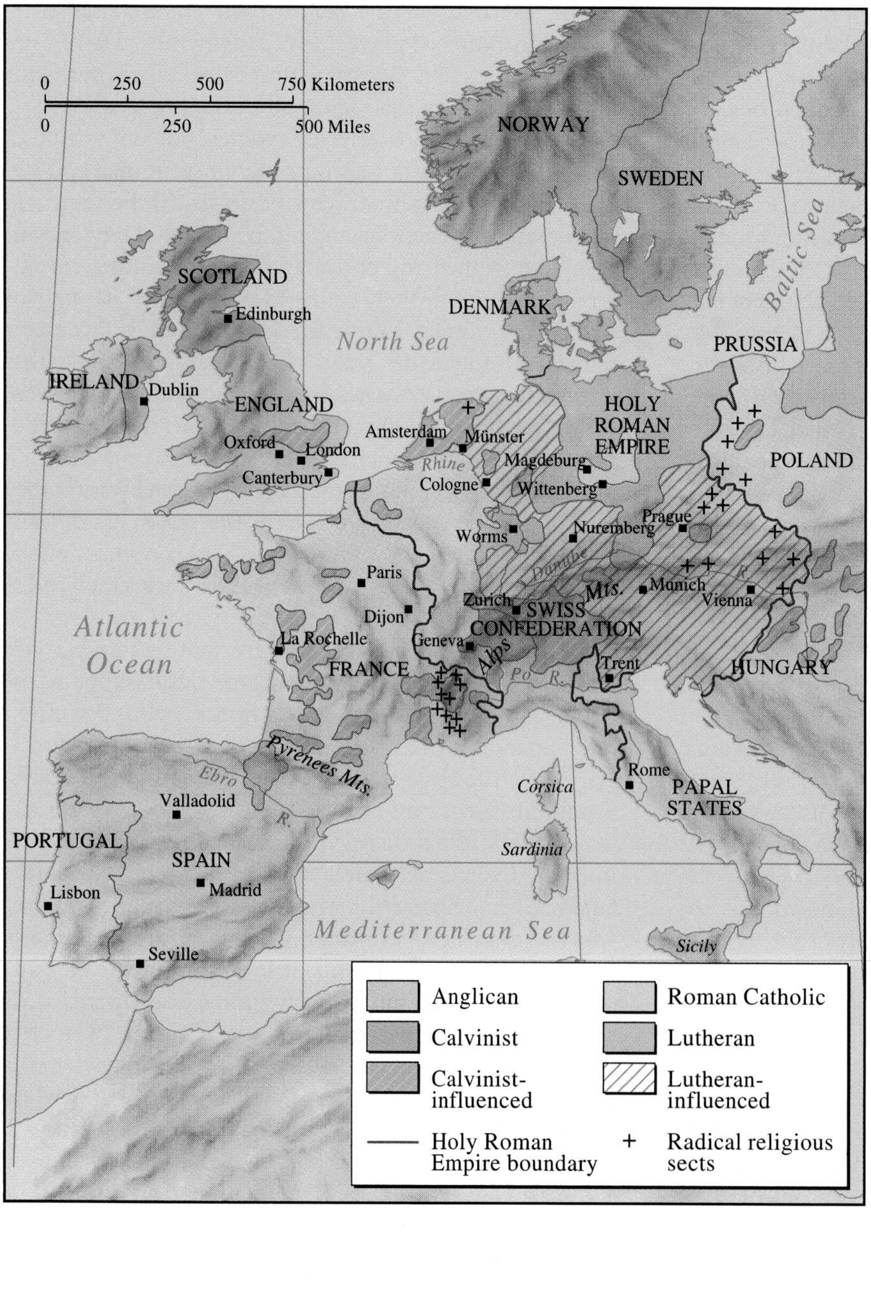

Map 9.4 Catholics and Protestants in Europe by 1560. Reformation religious upheavals affected most of Europe, with Protestant faiths predominant in the north. Protestantism also made substantial headway in France, the Habsburg dominions, southern Germany, and Poland, but these areas eventually reverted to Roman Catholicism.

great, and Pope Paul III (reigned 1534–1549) called for a church council.

The most important work of the council, which met at Trent, in northern Italy, between 1545 and 1563, dealt with doctrinal matters. All doctrines, especially those under Protestant attack, were reaffirmed. They were set out in clear and precise terms and their differences with Protestantism were specified. The council also outlined a comprehensive program of reform. It condemned such corrupt practices as simony, pluralism, and nepotism and made provisions for better discipline and higher educational standards among the clergy.

Besides reforming itself, the Catholic church took measures to halt the spread of Protestant beliefs. The council instituted the Index of Forbidden Books—a list of books, periodically revised, that Catholics were forbidden to read. The council also revived and extended the Inquisition to combat heresy and the practice of witchcraft. The work of the Council of Trent created a foundation on which a new, more vibrant Catholic church could be built.

The most effective single weapon of the Catholic church in battling the Protestants was the Society of Jesus, popularly called the Jesuit order. Founded by Ignatius Loyola (1491–1556), a Basque noble and former soldier, the order was modeled on military lines, highly disciplined, and devoted to actively promoting and defending the teachings of the church. Applicants for membership were carefully screened, and those selected had to pass rigorous training and a long apprenticeship. When found ready, they were sent to whatever field seemed most in need of their services.

The Jesuits were effective missionaries, carrying the gospel to nations as far away as China, Japan, and South America. Some became priests and from the pulpits preached simple sermons that stressed morality. As confessors and advisers to kings and princes, they were able to influence state policy to the benefit of Catholicism. They won their greatest fame, however, in the field of education. In Europe the Jesuits built schools or took over existing ones and in many areas were the dominant force in education. Their results were impressive. Through their dedication and zeal, they played a key role in holding southern Germany and France and in bringing Poland and much of Hungary back to Catholicism.

The zealous efforts of the Catholic church to stamp out Protestantism led to bitter religious wars in the late sixteenth century and first half of the seventeenth. England experienced an attempted invasion by Catholic Spain in 1588, and heavy sectarian fighting occurred in the Netherlands, France, and elsewhere in Europe (see Chapter 11). In Germany the Peace of Augsburg proved to be only an uneasy truce. The growing tensions finally erupted into a destructive conflict, known as the Thirty Years' War, which began in 1618 and continued until 1648. Over time, every major power became involved in the struggle, and the character of the war changed from religious to political. Protestant and Catholic armies, mostly composed of mercenaries, crisscrossed the German landscape, wreaking havoc.

The stalemated Thirty Years' War ended in 1648 with the Treaty of Westphalia. Most of the contending major powers demanded and received grants of territory as compensation for their efforts. Politically the settlement practically dissolved the Holy Roman Empire, though it continued to exist as a formal entity. Each German prince was recognized as a sovereign ruler, free to govern his state without interference by the emperor. The key religious clause accorded Calvinist rulers the same right to determine the religion practiced in their territories that Catholic and Lutheran princes had enjoyed since 1555. All in all, Germany was the big loser. Perhaps 300,000 soldiers and civilians were killed during campaigns, and several times that number died from malnutrition and disease. The damage wrecked the economy of the German states and caused many Germans to migrate to North America.

The Treaty of Westphalia, like the Peace of Augsburg, did not quell religious enmities. Religious strife continued to plague Europe, but on a far smaller scale than in the previous century. By regenerating itself and taking the offensive, the Catholic church had staged a strong comeback, stemming the Protestant tide and even winning back some lands that seemed irretrievably lost. But it could not regain domination over all of Western Christendom. After 1648 the religious map of Europe would not change appreciably.

European Expansion

Beginning in the fifteenth century the new European monarchies, which, as discussed earlier in this chapter, had achieved a high degree of national unification, embarked on five centuries of expansion that brought European power to every continent on the globe. Most of the indigenous societies around the world felt the impact of this movement in one way or another. Some were relatively untouched; many were profoundly altered; a number were destroyed. In the process Western society would itself feel the impact of other cultures.

European overseas expansion occurred for numerous reasons. The new national states of western Europe were now sufficiently centralized to support and finance exploration and expansion. Technological advances in navigational systems and ship design enabled sailors to undertake longer voyages. Moreover, Europeans had visions of wealth; gold, pepper, ivory, and slaves from Africa were all valued commodities on world markets. European governments and merchants were also eager to find alternative ocean routes so they could avoid the high import taxes imposed by the Ottoman Empire on goods coming overland from Asia by caravans. For Spain and Portugal, religion also played a role. After the long struggle (*Reconquista*) that ended Muslim supremacy of the Iberian Peninsula, the devoutly Christian rulers of Spain and Portugal were eager to dominate the Islamic states in North Africa and to convert non-Christians. Some Europeans even dreamed of forging links with the legendary African kingdom of the Christian leader Prester John.

Portugal was the first to move. With a long maritime tradition and an advantageous geographic position on the Atlantic, Portugal was the first European nation to look for a seaborne route to tap the wealth of the Atlantic Islands, Africa, and (hopefully) Asia. Beginning in the 1430s, Prince Henry (later called the "Navigator" by the English), the brother of the king of Portugal, used the royal treasury to finance voyages of discovery down the African coast; by 1498 the Portuguese were in Asia. In 1492, with the voyage of Columbus, Spain moved westward to the Americas. A century later, England, France, and the Netherlands joined in. The text will take up European expansion in the context of the cultures of each geographic area the Europeans entered; this chapter will discuss Africa and the Western Hemisphere, and Chapter 10 will deal with Asia.

African Kingdoms, European Contacts, and the Slave Trade

Your people . . . seize many of our people, freed and exempt men; and very often it happens that they kidnap even noblemen and the sons of noblemen, and our relatives, and take them to be sold to the white men. . . .

And as soon as they are taken by the white men they are immediately ironed and branded with fire, and when they are carried to be embarked, if they are caught by our guards' men the whites allege that they have bought them but they cannot say from whom. . . .

*And so to avoid such a great evil we passed a law so that any white man living in our Kingdoms and wanting to purchase goods in any way should first inform three of our noblemen and officials of our court . . . who should investigate if the mentioned goods are captives or free men. . . . But if the white men do not comply with it they will lose the aforementioned goods.**

*A letter by King Afonso of the Kongo to the King of Portugal, October 18, 1526, in *Horizon History of Africa* (New York: American Heritage, 1971), p. 334.

In this letter in 1526, King Afonso, a convert to Christianity, complains of the excesses of European slave traders in his Kongo Kingdom. The slave trade became an important aspect of a dynamic and complex situation in Africa during the period from the fifteenth to the seventeenth century. The Portuguese moved down the West African coast and eventually to southern and eastern Africa, beginning the trade for the riches of those regions. In the fourteenth century, when Europeans first began to make extensive contact, many societies in West Africa had been, in economic terms, nearly as prosperous as those in most of Europe. The slave trade substantially altered that balance. As it turned out, the greatest wealth for European traders was to be found in the labor of human beings. The slave trade devastated many regions of Africa; it also profoundly changed the Western Hemisphere (see the following section). The ensuing discussion will focus on a number of African societies beginning about the fifteenth century, when European explorers and traders began to have extensive contact with local African rulers and peoples.

European Entry into Africa

In the early fifteenth century, the Portuguese began to move into Africa. Portugal's first target was Morocco, where it conquered small coastal areas. During the next half-century the Portuguese worked down the West African coast to Angola. The voyages of Bartholomeu Dias in 1487–1488 and Vasco da Gama in 1497–1499 opened up the Cape of Good Hope and East Africa to Portuguese traders and explorers; in 1498 da Gama arrived in India (see Chapter 10). At the East African city-state of Malindi, a king seated on a bronze chair and wearing an ornate robe trimmed in green satin greeted da Gama. The leaders of Malindi welcomed an alliance with the Portuguese as an aid in their commercial rivalry against traders in Mombasa.

Traders and adventurers, the Portuguese were not initially interested in founding colonies in Africa. However, they did establish fortified trading posts at strategic ports along the western and eastern coasts. Fort Sao Jorge was established at Elmina on the west coast in 1482. In 1576 it was followed by Luanda, which became a major center for the transport of slaves from Angola. Along the East African coast the Portuguese extracted tribute from the local rulers of Kilwa and later extended their domination over the older commercial city-states of Malindi and Mombasa.

African forces from the interior frequently attacked the Portuguese enclaves, limiting Portuguese domination to the coastal regions. Mombasa resisted for so many decades that the Portuguese nicknamed it the Island of War. In 1592 the Portuguese finally seized Mombasa and largely destroyed local opposition. Afterward they built a new outpost, called Fort Jesus, which still stands as evidence of Portuguese presence in Africa.

CONNECTIONS IN MIGRATION

Encounters, 1400–1600

In the years from 1400 to 1600, a new system of global migration brought transoceanic movement of growing numbers of people. Voyagers, as they moved across the surface of the globe, sought adventure and achievement. Whatever their motives for traveling, they encountered new individuals and new groups that were distinct in stature, dress, skin color, language, religion, and customs. Each party decided how to act toward and how to view the other, choosing between emphasizing differences or similarities, unity or division.

How does one respond when encountering a new and different person for the first time? Is the person to be treated as a friend and equal or as a person alien in nature and hostile in motive? Are there yet other choices? Can one view another as friendly yet alien? As equal yet hostile? The early modern age of new connections raised these questions repeatedly.

Traders and adventurers captured people they met, and they themselves were sometimes seized. But there were also efforts to establish mutually beneficial trade and communication agreements.

Male travelers and merchants sometimes established ports and trading outposts, settling down to start families with local women; this gave emphasis to alliance and shared values. Yet, in cases where these same men later denied rights or inheritance to their wives or children, they were emphasizing hierarchy and differences among groups of people, rather than commonality. Sexual relations were a statement of dominance as much as a statement of sharing.

Many of these new encounters took place along two great bodies of water. The Indian Ocean had been crossed many times in earlier centuries, and its land margins had become a largely Muslim region. The arrival of European Christians added a new element of conflict. People of the East African port of Kilwa were surprised by the arrival of the Portuguese in 1498 but knew who they were. The Atlantic Ocean, in contrast, was a new area of oceanic contact in which most of the connections were mediated through the religion and culture of Christianity.

How can you know what people felt when they encountered each other in the fifteenth and sixteenth centuries? The historian's principal approach is to sift evidence from primary documents, such as the statements and the images that people constructed.

---

1. Go to Unit 2 of the Migration CD to find such primary documents. Read through all the documents in the unit. Find five that are of special interest to you, including at least one dealing with each of the following regions: Asia, Africa, and Latin America. For each document, answer these questions: How did the two sides view each other? How did preexisting attitudes shape the encounter? What was the power relationship between the two sides, and did the more powerful party take advantage of its superior power?

Although the Portuguese struggled to monopolize the African trade routes and the access they provided for the Asian trade, they were quickly challenged by the Spanish, Dutch, English, and other European powers. By 1630 English traders were operating along West Africa; the French and Dutch soon followed them. The Swedes and Danes also competed for territorial footholds in Ghana, or the Gold Coast. The Dutch proved a particularly formidable rival, and by 1610 they had effectively ended Portuguese dominance in the Indian Ocean. These rival European powers build many forts and military installations along the West African coast; these installations were intended primarily to defend the nation's trading interests against competing Europeans, not as protection against the African states.

As Portuguese naval power waned in the seventeenth century, first Mombasa and then other East African city-states revolted. Mombasa requested aid from fellow Muslims, most notably from the *imam* (leader) of Oman, on the Arabian coast. The Omanis, who had a long naval tradition, quickly responded and after several failures succeeded in ousting the Portuguese from Mombasa in 1698 and subsequently from neighboring East African city-states. The Omanis then established a Muslim empire in coastal East Africa that lasted into the nineteenth century.

Dutch Settlements in South Africa

In 1652, at Table Bay in South Africa, the Dutch founded Africa's first European settlement. Originally,

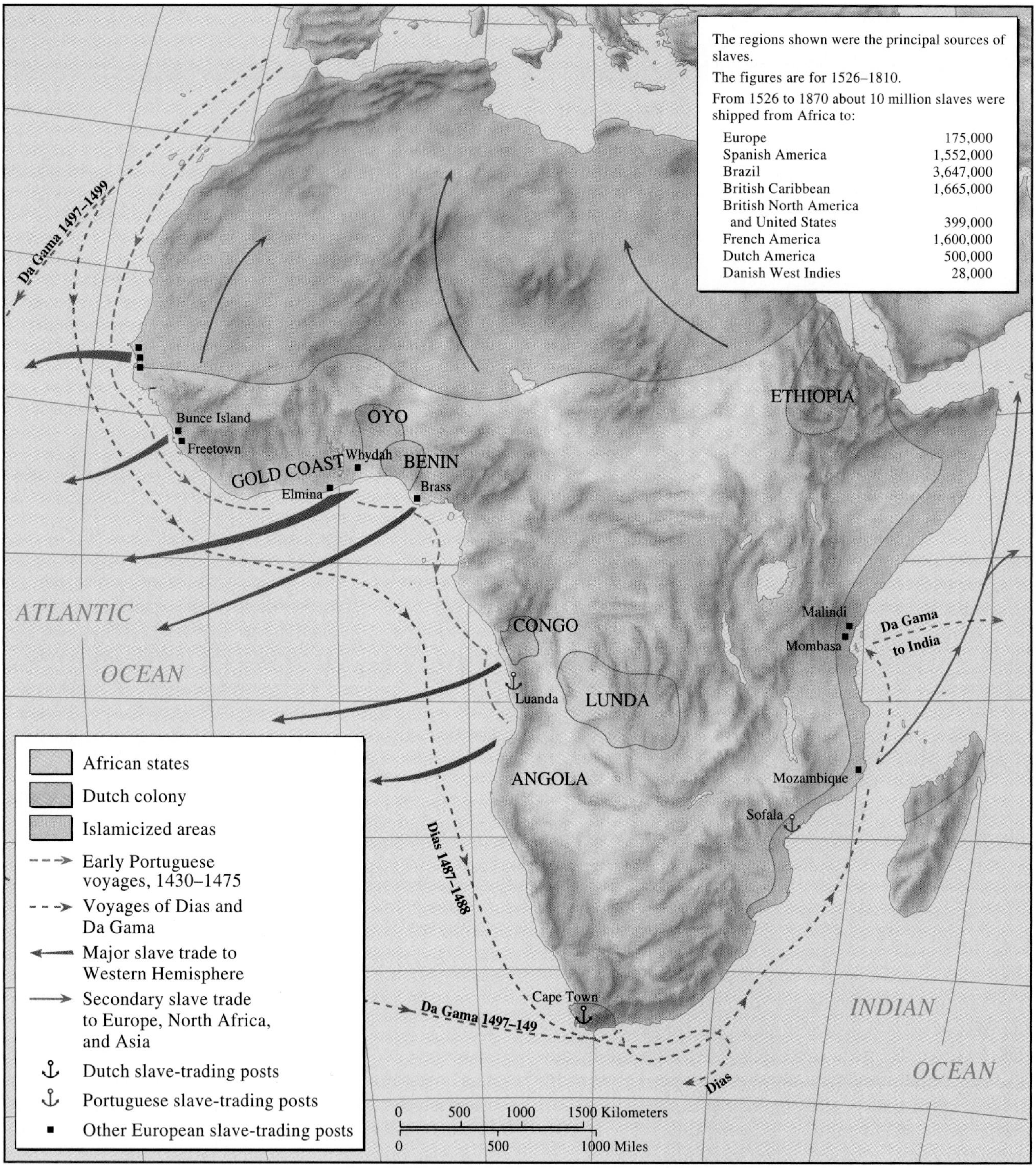

Map 9.5 Africa, 1500–c. 1750, and the Slave Trade. By the sixteenth century, Islam had spread throughout much of North and East Africa, while many independent kingdoms and city-states continued to prosper. Along the African coasts, European explorers also founded small trading posts, where the slave trade flourished as growing numbers of Africans were transported as slave labor for plantations in the Western Hemisphere.

the settlement was intended as a reprovisioning station for ships of the Dutch East India Company undertaking the long voyage between Europe and Asia; it was not meant to be an outpost for further Dutch settlement or colonial expansion. However, the persistent need for fresh food supplies led the Dutch East India Company to bring in colonists to establish farms in South Africa in 1657. Slaves were then brought in as forced laborers.

As the colony expanded, the Dutch attacked the indigenous Khoi, who were forcibly dispersed. The colonists recruited single Dutch women so that the predominantly male population of the colony could marry Europeans. French Huguenots who fled the persecution of Louis XIV reinforced the Dutch settlers. These frontier farmers, who called themselves both Boers (farmers) and Afrikaners, were strict Calvinists. Their descendants continued to dominate South Africa well into the twentieth century.

The Boers viewed black Africans as inferior human beings and used their strict Calvinist tenets to justify their attitude of racial superiority. They established a system of strict social and racial stratification in which the Dutch Boers were placed at the top, followed by later Asian immigrants and coloreds (people of mixed race), with blacks at the bottom. This racial hierarchy based on white European domination continued into the 1990s. Racism, the belief in the superiority and inferiority of differing peoples based on race, was not, however, confined to the Dutch in South Africa. It was common in European and American societies and was frequently used to justify the enslavement of African peoples.

Memoirs of a Slave

The first object which saluted my eyes when I arrived on the coast was the sea, and a slave ship which was then riding at anchor and waiting for its cargo. These filled me with astonishment, which was soon converted into terror when I was carried on board. I was immediately handled and tossed up to see if I were sound . . . and I was now persuaded that I had gotten into a world of bad spirits and that they were going to kill me. Their complexions too differing so much from ours, their long hair and the language they spoke (which was very different from any I had ever heard) united to confirm me in this belief. . . .

*I now saw myself deprived of all chance of returning to my native country. . . . I became so sick and low that I was not able to eat. . . . In a little time after, amongst the poor chained men I found some of my own nation. . . . I inquired of these what was to be done with us; they gave me to understand we were to be carried to these white people's country to work for them.**

The slave trade persisted for centuries. In the above excerpt, Olaudah Equiano, from present-day Nigeria, described his reactions to being captured and taken into slavery. Equiano was taken to the West Indies, Canada, England, and the United States; he was freed in 1766 and became a spokesperson for the antislavery movement (see Chapter 11). His memoirs offer a moving testimony to the human cost of slavery and its disruption of African society.*

*Olaudah Equiano, in *Modern Asia and Africa,* ed. William H. McNeill and Mitsuko Iriye (New York: Oxford University Press, 1971), pp. 82–84.

The Slave Trade in Africa

The slave trade was a key factor of European expansion and had disastrous results for African peoples. As in many other societies and cultures, slavery had very deep roots in Africa and was known in antiquity. Africans had enslaved other Africans, and, although there were Qur'anic injunctions against such practices, Islamic societies in Africa had perpetuated the system. It persisted throughout Africa and especially in the Sudan in the ninth century, and it was practiced in other parts of the continent as well. African slaves could be found throughout the Islamic world, in India, and perhaps also in China prior to European expansion into these areas. Slavery in Africa and the Islamic world was not based on race or religion, however. Animists, Christians, and Muslims in Africa and elsewhere had historically enslaved members of their own and other religions. As in most civilizations up to this time, Africans acquired slaves from raids or victories in wars. In African and Islamic cultures, slaves were generally treated as part of the family and were integrated into the larger society. Most such slaves in the Islamic world served as domestic servants, concubines, or slave-soldiers.

The extensive trade in African slaves by the Western nations between the late fifteenth and the nineteenth centuries severely affected the social, cultural, economic, and even political life of the African societies. Although experts disagree on how adversely this trade affected African development, none deny its social and economic

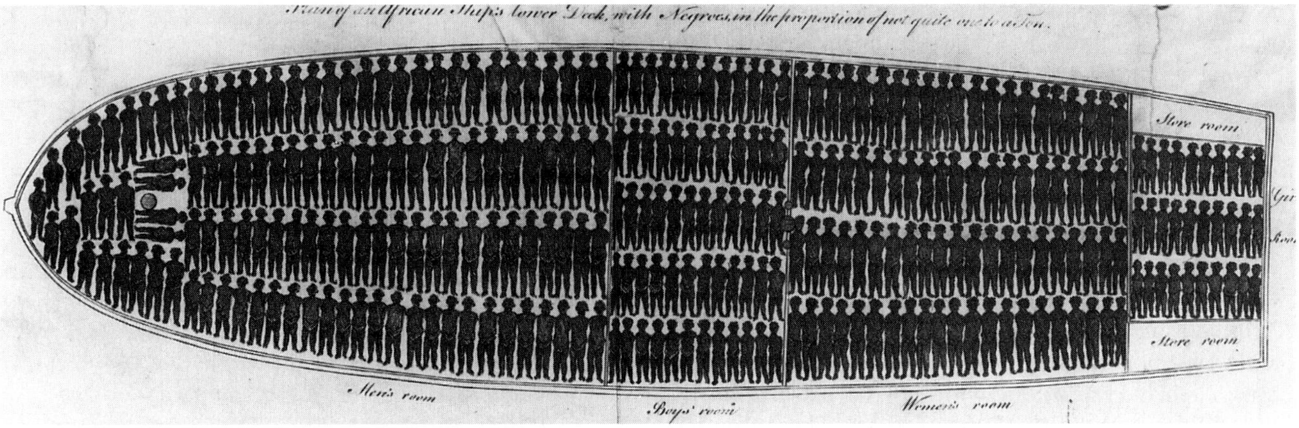

Historical Society of Pennsylvania, Pennsylvania Abolition Society Papers

Slave Ship. This diagram shows how slaves were "packed" into ships for the long and often fatal journey to the Americas. Crowded on and below decks, slaves frequently died of asphyxiation, thirst, and disease during the long Atlantic crossing.

consequences. Although Muslims and Europeans took some African slaves for sale in Europe, the Canary and Madeira Islands, Muslim North Africa, the Ottoman Empire, and Asia, the vast majority of those taken by the Europeans and their African allies were sent to the Western Hemisphere for sale.

In contrast to the work of slaves in other societies, the overwhelming majority of slaves in the Western Hemisphere was used as agricultural workers on vast cotton, tobacco, or sugar plantations or as laborers in copper and silver mines. As only able-bodied men and women were suitable for such hard labor, most slaves taken from Africa were young males from fifteen to thirty years of age. Although experts disagree on the exact numbers, it appears that between 10 and 15 million Africans were forcibly removed from their homelands to become slaves in the Americas; in addition, possibly several million more were killed or died during armed raids to secure the slaves, and the forced marches and brutal conditions to which the captives were subjected.

The first African slaves were shipped from Spain to Latin America in 1501. By 1518 Spanish slave traders had established direct trade routes between Africa and the Americas. Recognizing the enormous profits to be made in this human traffic, the Portuguese, English, French, and Dutch also engaged in the slave trade. For the most part, European slave traffickers did not capture the slaves, but paid professional African slave traders, or local political leaders, to secure slaves from the interior and to bring them to ports or marshaling yards on the coast. They were then herded into ships for the long voyage to the Western Hemisphere.

Although their African owners or rulers sold some slaves as punishment, most were captured through wars and raids. Slave hunting was a violent activity. Able-bodied men and women were torn from their villages, shackled in chains, and fastened together in long lines by strips of rawhide. These long human chains were then forcibly marched to either the East or West African coast, where European traders purchased them. Many slaves died of abuse or committed suicide before they ever reached the coasts. Others (at least 15 percent) died of inadequate food or diseases in the overcrowded, vermin-infested ships that transported the slaves to the Americas. Slave revolts were not uncommon, particularly among Muslim Africans, especially after they reached the Western Hemisphere.

African leaders who cooperated with European slave traders became rich from the slave trade. They coveted European armaments with which to extend their authority. The Songhai leaders in northwest Africa, for example, sold slaves for horses and guns. On Goree Island off the coast of present-day Senegal, one of the major trading depots for the traffic in human beings, West African women, who often engaged in commerce, controlled the sale of slaves brought from the interior regions. Likewise, some Muslim African traders became wealthy from the slave trade in East Africa and the Sudan. On the other hand, some African leaders sought to stop or to contain the trade. The obas in Benin banned the export of males from their territories until the end of the seventeenth century. King Afonso I in the Kongo also protested the trade and made numerous attempts to control and to curtail it.

In Angola, where the Portuguese were particularly active, Africans fiercely opposed the slave trade and foreign intervention. The Portuguese had made considerable inroads into Angola during the reign of weak monarchs, but in 1623–1624 Nzinga Mbandi ascended to the throne. As strong a ruler as Cleopatra of Egypt or Catherine the Great of Russia, Nzinga was an astute diplomat and politician. Forbidding her subjects to call her queen, Nzinga took the title king and promptly launched a lifelong struggle against the Portuguese. She joined forces with the Dutch against the Portuguese and lured Portuguese slave-soldiers to desert by promising them freedom and land. In spite of several uneasy treaties with the Portuguese, she continued fighting them until her death in 1663. No strong ruler followed Nzinga. As a result, the Portuguese were able to prevail, and slave raids increasingly decimated Angolan villages.

While coastal areas of Africa frequently prospered because of the slave trade, many villages, farms, and political institutions in the interior were weakened or destroyed. Damage to the cultural and economic life of African societies varied greatly from region to region. The forced removal of vital segments of their populations had lasting impact on some African societies. Many major states, however, particularly West African states like Benin, survived the attacks. Most African states remained independent of outside rule until the nineteenth century (see Chapter 13).

One of the most abusive and inhumane enterprises shared between Africa and the West, slavery spread throughout much of the Western Hemisphere in the following century. Slavery profoundly altered traditional social, economic, and political patterns in both Africa and the Western Hemisphere.

European Colonial Empires in the Western Hemisphere

*Strange people have come to the shores of the great sea [the Caribbean]. . . . Their trappings and arms are all made of iron; they dress in iron and wear iron casques on their heads. Their swords are made of iron; their shields are iron; their spears are iron. Their deer carry them on their backs wherever they wish to go. Those deer, our lord, are as tall as the roof of a house. . . . The strangers' bodies are completely covered, so that only their faces can be seen. Their skin is white, as if it were made of lime. They have yellow hair, though some of them are black[-haired]. Their dogs are enormous, with flat ears and long dangling tongues. . . . Their eyes flash fire. [Referring to a gun:] a thing like a ball of stone comes out of its entrails; it comes out shooting sparks and raining fire. The smoke that comes out has a pestilent odor, like rotten mud. . . . If the cannon is aimed against a mountain, the mountain splits and cracks open.**

*Miguel Leon-Portilla, ed., *The Broken Spears: The Aztec Account of the Conquest of Mexico,* trans. A. M. Garibay and L. Kemp (Boston: Beacon Press, 1969), pp. 30–31.

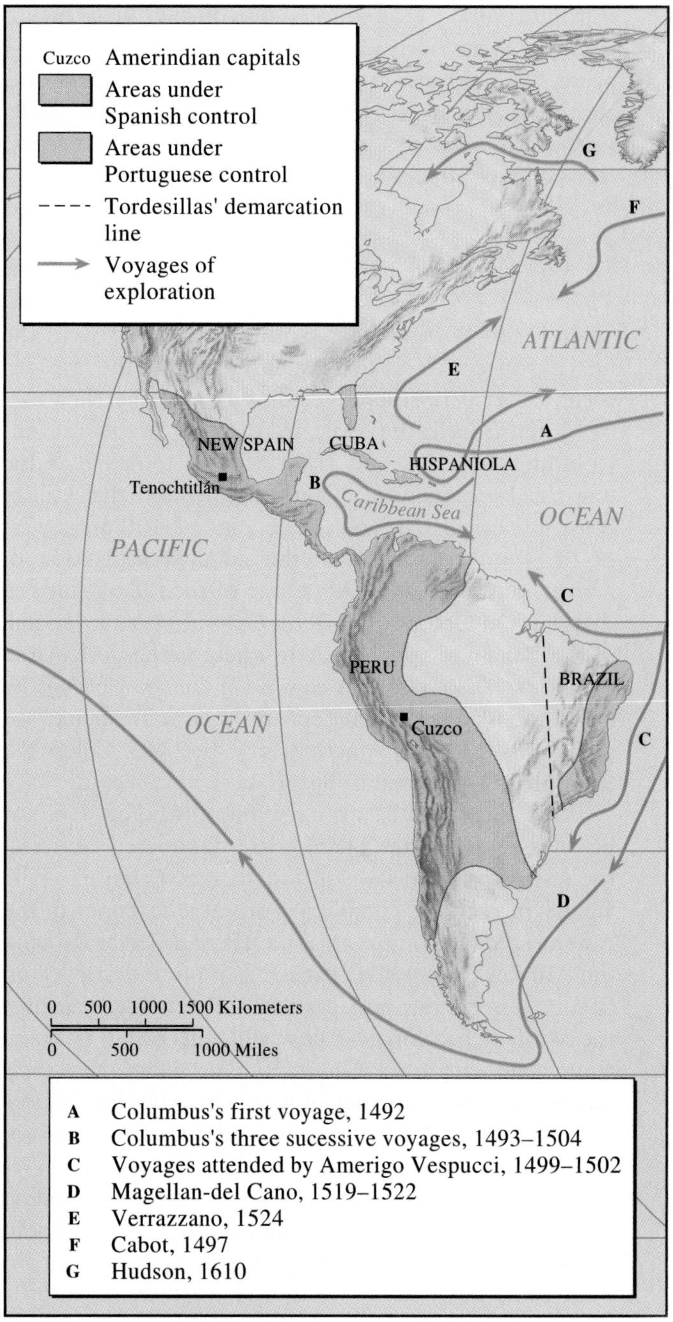

Map 9.6 The Western Hemisphere, c. 1600. After a century of exploration and conquest, Spain had created a huge colonial holding, based in large part on the ruins of the Aztec and Inka Empires. The Portuguese were beginning to create a major colony in Brazil.

This vivid description of the Spanish arrival in Mexico was in a report given to Moctezuma, the Aztec ruler, by his spies who observed the landing and advance of the Spaniards in 1519. The presence of the Spanish in the heartland of Mesoamerican civilization was but one aspect of a remarkable phenomenon, the expansion of

European power around the globe during the sixteenth century. As has been seen in the previous section, Europeans were already constructing fortified trading posts along the African coast and building up the slave trade. Europeans were also appearing on the shores of Asia (see Chapter 10).

Early European Exploration of the Western Hemisphere

Spanish and Portuguese explorers and settlers were the first Europeans to make a lasting impact on the Western Hemisphere. Christopher Columbus, an Italian financed by Queen Isabella of Castile, led the way. By sailing west, Columbus hoped to find a shorter route to Asia than the one the Portuguese were pursuing around the African coast. He calculated Japan to be about 2,400 miles west of the Canary Islands (off the northwestern coast of Africa), putting Asia within range of the sailing ships of that day. On October 12, 1492, Columbus made landfall in the Bahamas, approximately where he had calculated Asia to be. Assuming that he was off the coast of Asia he called the islands the "Indies" and their inhabitants "Indians" (in this text, Amerindians). In 1493 Columbus triumphantly returned to Spain.

In January 1492, just a few months before Columbus's first voyage, the Spanish had conquered Granada, the last Muslim enclave on the Iberian Peninsula. The victory marked the completion of seven centuries of the *Reconquista* (Reconquest) of the Iberian Peninsula from the Muslims, a crusade that left a profound impact on Spanish institutions and practices. The struggle against the Muslims had forged a powerful partnership between church and state in Spanish society. The end of the *Reconquista* left a large number of men who were looking for new and profitable adventures and for new areas for Christianity to conquer.

During the quarter-century after Columbus's landing in the Bahamas, the Spanish occupied the major Caribbean islands. They found that European crops and domestic animals could thrive in the Western Hemisphere. Eventually it became clear that the islands could produce valuable crops of sugar and tobacco. These products, however, required constant attention and thus a large labor force.

To get this labor, the Spanish instituted the *encomienda* system, in which the Spanish king gave individuals control over Amerindian lands and villages. The *encomiendero* had the right to force the Amerindians under his control to work in his mines and fields. This brutal labor system and the ravages of new diseases from Europe, plus secondary factors, killed nearly all of the Amerindians in the Caribbean. Deprived of a native work force, the Spanish imported large numbers of black slaves from Africa.

To avoid confrontation, the Spanish and Portuguese negotiated a treaty to divide the Western Hemisphere between them. Under the Treaty of Tordesillas in 1494, the pope selected a line of longitude in which Spain received everything west of the line and Portugal everything east of it. The treaty technically gave Asia, the East Indies, and Brazil to Portugal, while everything else in the Western Hemisphere went to Spain. In 1500 Pedro Cabral landed in Brazil and formally claimed the area for Portugal. Brazil eventually became a major sugar-producing area.

Meanwhile, Europeans were readjusting their thinking about the nature of the lands that Columbus had found. After two voyages to the Western Hemisphere in which he visited much of the eastern coast of South America, Amerigo Vespucci claimed in 1501 that he had seen a "new land . . . a continent." In 1507 cartographers putting out a new map labeled the area representing present-day Brazil "America" in his honor.

By the early sixteenth century it was becoming clear that Asia was far away from Europe, with the new "America" in between. In 1513 Vasco Núñez de Balboa crossed the Panamanian isthmus and saw what he called the South Sea (the present-day Pacific Ocean), a sea that ships might sail on to Asia if a way could be found to get through or around America to enter it. Various European expeditions searched for a "Passage to India," a water route around or through America that led to Asia. They all failed, confirming the dismaying proposition that America was an unbroken barrier that extended northward and southward from the Caribbean to the stormy and icy waters of the Arctic and Antarctic seas.

In 1519 the Spanish government dispatched an expedition under Ferdinand Magellan to find a passage to Asia that would justify a Spanish claim to some of the southeast Asian Spice Islands held by the Portuguese. Magellan fought his way for thirty-eight days through a stormy water passage (later called the Straits of Magellan) at the tip of South America. Afterwards, Magellan pushed across the enormous stretches of Balboa's South Sea, which Magellan termed the Pacific (from Latin for "calm") Ocean. His men died from lack of water and ate rats to survive. In 1521 he reached the Philippines, where he was killed in a skirmish. His navigator, Juan Sebastián del Cano, and one surviving ship pushed on across the Indian Ocean, reaching Spain in September 1522, three years after their departure. This first circumnavigation of the globe was one of the great epics of human bravery and was the high mark of the age of European exploration. The discoveries of Magellan and del Cano demonstrated that Asia was too far away, and the trip too dangerous, for a successful trade route westward to Asia. Although holding on to the Philippine Islands,

Spain would have to derive its main colonial wealth from the Western Hemisphere, not the Eastern.

Spanish Conquests in Mexico and South America

Great wealth was not long in coming to the Spanish. For years Spaniards had heard tales of Amerindian empires of gold and silver on the mainland of present-day Mexico. In 1519 Hernán Cortés organized an expedition of 11 vessels, 550 men, 16 horses, and 10 cannon, and sailed from Cuba to the Mexican coast. Marching inland, Cortés swiftly reached the outer fringes of the Aztec Empire.

Aided by large forces of Amerindian allies disaffected by the parasitic rule of the Aztecs, Cortés and his tiny band of Spaniards defeated the Aztecs and conquered Mexico. The key reasons were clear. Cortés himself gave much credit to his Amerindian allies, both as warriors and porters. The Tlaxcalans, armed with razor-sharp obsidian weapons, were especially effective. The Spanish firearms and cannon, as well as metal armor and weapons, totally outclassed the Aztec's stone-age weapons and cotton armor. In battle the Spanish horses and huge mastiffs, which were unknown to the Amerindians, often unnerved them. Cortés also capitalized on prophecies in Mexican folklore that seemed to foretell his coming.

Disease was perhaps the greatest ally of Cortés. An epidemic of smallpox saved Cortés from an Amerindian revolt in 1520. Since Amerindians did not have natural immunities to the many diseases the Europeans carried, including smallpox, measles, and influenza, the ravages of these diseases continued unabated. When Cortés landed, there were about 28 million persons in the Mexican heartland. Fifty years later the population had plummeted to 3 million. By 1620 only 1 million Amerindians lived in the area. As a result of the massive depopulation, Amerindian culture in the Western Hemisphere was substantially demolished.

In 1532 the Mexican story was repeated in Peru when Francisco Pizarro led a force of 170 men into the Andes, looking for the gold and silver of the Inka Empire. Inka rule centered in the mountains of present-day Peru, Ecuador, Bolivia, and northern Chile. Like the Aztecs, the Inkas had only lately come to power (see Chapter 7). By the time the Spanish arrived, the Inkas ruled about 8 million persons living in an area about half the size of the Roman Empire at its height. The Inka

The Conquest of Mexico. This Amerindian painting depicts several of the techniques by which the Spanish triumphed. Although the painting does not show the firearms of the Spanish, it pictures their horses, war dogs, and many Amerindian allies. The Amerindians on both sides are equipped with black, razor-sharp obsidian, whose lethal effects are apparent.

Stock Montage

state was a rigid autocracy in which all power focused in the person of the ruler, the Inka; this proved to be a fatal weakness.

Finding this highly structured civilization divided by civil war and racked by an epidemic, Pizarro captured, imprisoned, and murdered the Inka ruler Atahualpa and destroyed every element of the Inka leadership; by 1533 he had gained control over the empire.

The *conquistadores* in Mexico and Peru were well rewarded for their ruthless daring. They robbed the Amerindians of their gold and silver objects and then searched for deposits to mine. In both Mexico and the Andes they found substantial supplies of gold and huge amounts of silver. Their search for precious metals and other opportunities for wealth took them into the southern third of the present-day United States, throughout Central America and across much of South America outside Brazil. A very rich lode was discovered at Cerro Potosí in Bolivia in 1545, which supplied enormous quantities of silver to the Spaniards. Potosí had a population of 160,000 persons in 1650, when the silver mine was at its most productive. It shrank to a minor town of 8,000 persons by 1825, when the mine had been largely depleted.

To exploit the wealth of the Inka Empire, the Spanish instituted a forced labor regime that was, if anything, more brutal than those in Mexico or the Caribbean. Inka rulers had demanded *mit'a* (forced labor) from their subjects. The Spanish claimed that their own demand for forced labor was an extension of the mit'a; under the Inkas, however, mit'a demands were harsh, but could be met without starvation and other ills that became prevalent under the Spanish. The dangerous and arduous labor in the mines killed many Amerindians. Coupled with recurrent epidemics, the Andean population declined in the same proportion as in Mexico, with the same devastating cultural results.

It is likely that the Amerindians gave their conquerors syphilis in exchange for the terrible plagues that had been let loose among them. Syphilis raged for decades as an epidemic, mortal disease in Europe. Eventually it became a slow-acting but still immensely dangerous disease.

In the middle of the sixteenth century, the Amerindians were proclaimed subjects under the protection of the crown. As such they could no longer be legally enslaved, but many were still worked to death in the mines, businesses, and fields of their Spanish overlords. Over time, racial interrelationships created many individuals of mixed ancestry called *mestizos,* who eventually formed a major element in the Latin American population.

Based on the toil of this Amerindian and *mestizo* work force, fleets carried enormous wealth in silver, hides, gold, dyes, cacao, and quinine from the mainland of the Western Hemisphere to Spain. The Spanish monarchy, from its share of the precious metals and from taxes, received 40 percent of the value of these shipments. Two fleets from Spain carrying food, clothing,

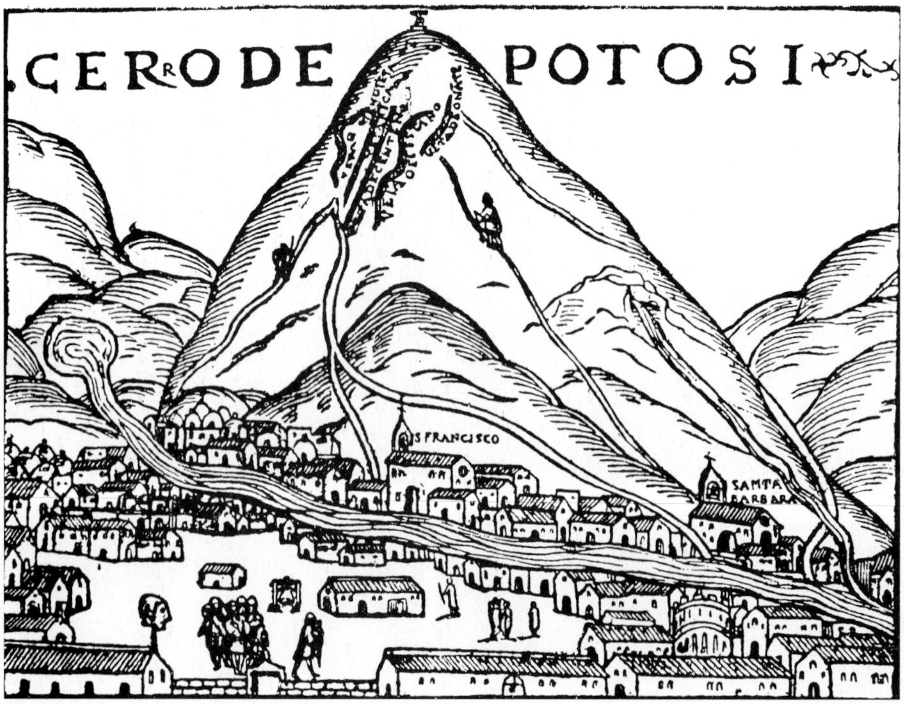

Stock Montage

The Mountain of Silver at Potosí. This 1553 woodcut shows the main fruit of Pizarro's conquest of the Inka Empire. The silver mines and smelteries at Potosí (in present-day Bolivia) yielded the Spanish about $1 billion in silver during the colonial period. The woodcut omits the deaths of tens of thousands of Amerindian workers.

wine, tools, household items, and a few settlers sailed to the Western Hemisphere annually, but the goods sent over were inadequate for the colonial population.

The Spanish and Portuguese, in name at least, made their colonies Roman Catholic. In many areas church teachings mixed with indigenous Amerindian and African religious practices. Some of the Spanish religious leaders went to great lengths to destroy all remnants of the Amerindian heritage on the grounds that their pre-Conquest culture was based on devil worship, sodomy, and cannibalism. A Spanish bishop destroyed all the pre-Conquest Maya books that he could locate because they contained aspects of the old religion. Of the hundreds of Maya books that once existed, only four survived to modern times. In many areas Catholic churchmen were responsible for exploration and settlement. Some priests also led the fight for more humane treatment for the Amerindians.

Several aspects of the Western Hemisphere were transmitted to Europe. Foods such as potatoes, maize, several varieties of peppers, tomatoes, chocolate, and many others became a part of the European diet; maize became a staple in China.

Rival Empires in the Western Hemisphere

By the middle of the sixteenth century, the Spanish and Portuguese had used the Western Hemisphere as an arena to create enormous colonial empires. Unlike the collection of fortified coastal towns and trading depots set up by the Portuguese in Africa and Asia, the Spanish colonies constituted a territory many times larger than Spain itself. Portugal created an equivalently huge colony in Brazil.

During most of the sixteenth century, while the Spanish and Portuguese exploited the riches of Latin America, the English, French, and Dutch, preoccupied with religious wars and other domestic problems, stayed home. Late in the century, however, these nations were ready to compete with the Spanish and Portuguese; in particular, they had devised effective economic incentives to foster their own colonialism. The Spanish and Portuguese had allowed a small percentage of their business community to monopolize opportunities abroad, thus limiting available investment resources. In contrast, the English, French, and Dutch governments encouraged merchants and bankers to invest in overseas commerce by granting charters to new "joint stock" companies specializing in trading and colonization. Participants in joint stock companies had their risks limited to the proportion of their investment; this restricted liability encouraged smaller investors to put their money in new overseas companies. Investment was further encouraged by easier access to marine insurance. The wealth brought into Europe from the Western Hemisphere later helped to fuel further European expansion into Asia (see Chapter 10).

At first the northern nations concentrated on finding a share of the Asia trade. During the sixteenth century, despite the discouraging news of earlier explorers,

Forced Labor in Peru, 1652

*According to His Majesty's warrant, the mine owners on this massive range have a right . . . to 13,300 Indians in working and exploitation of the mines. It is the duty of the Corregidor of Potosi [governor] to have them rounded up and to see that they come in from all the provinces. . . . These Indians are sent out every year under a captain. . . . This works very badly, with great losses and gaps in the quotas of Indians, the villages being depopulated. . . . After each has eaten his ration, they climb up the hill, each to his mine, and go in, staying there from that hour until Saturday evening without coming out of the mine; their wives bring them food, but they stay constantly underground, excavating and carrying out the ore from which they get the silver. They all have tallow candles, lighted day and night; that is the light they work with, for as they are underground, they have need of it all the time. The mere cost of these candles used in the mines . . . will amount every year to more than 300,000 pesos, even though tallow is cheap in that country, being abundant; but this is a very great expense, and it is almost incredible, how much is spent for candles in the operation of breaking down and getting out the ore.**

The above description of forced Amerindian labor in silver mines provided insight both into the working conditions for the miners and attitudes of Spanish observers. This report revealed rather more concern over the cost of candles than for the health or well-being of the Amerindian workers.

*"The Potosi Mine and Indian Forced Labor in Peru," in Antonio Vasques de Espinosa, *Compendium and Description of the West Indies,* trans. C. U. Clark (Washington: Smithsonian Institution, 1942), pp. 623–625, in Peter N. Stearns, ed., *Documents in World History,* vol. 2 (New York: Harper & Row, 1988), pp. 83–84.

LIVES AND TIMES ACROSS CULTURES

New Stuff on Your Plate

We have already seen two important results of European conquests in the Western Hemisphere: one was the migration of millions of Europeans and Africans to the Americas, and the second was the spread of diseases, especially smallpox, which decimated the Amerindian populations. A third effect was the reciprocal introduction of new foods. Europeans brought with them both field crops and livestock. Wheat now supplemented the indigenous maize, and citrus fruits and grapes also enjoyed local success in the Americas. On the other hand, cash crops like sugar, rice, bananas, and tobacco (indigenous) enriched the landowning elite in the Americas.

Before Columbus, the Amerindians had domesticated only dogs, turkeys, ducks, alpacas, and llamas—none of which provided much food or hauling power. Worst of all, the Amerindians had few animals that could turn grass into meat. The European introduction of sheep, goats, swine, cattle, and horses varied the diet of many and furnished powerful draft animals. Later, horses, cattle, and sheep became the basis of full-scale Amerindian herding and riding cultures among, for example, the Navaho and the Apache.

At the same time, Amerindian field and tuber crops had a tremendous impact in Europe after 1500. Maize and potatoes spread through the Eastern Hemisphere, superseding indigenous staples because they supplied more nutrients per hectare.

The potato, native to the cool valleys of the Andes, adapted very readily to temperate northern Europe, providing the dietary mainstay from Ireland to Russia. The Dutch peasant family portrayed in Van Gogh's *The Potato Eaters* could just as well have been Peruvian. Maize, native to warm Mesoamerica, was adopted in much of southern Europe; its cultivation in Africa increased steadily till, by the 1990s, it had become the leading consumer crop on that continent. Maize and sweet potatoes became major crops in Asia, surpassed only by rice and wheat. Other Amerindian foods that proliferated around the world were tomatoes, squash, certain beans, and peanuts. Manioc (cassava) was an important food crop, first in Brazil and later in Africa.

Enormous economic consequences flowed from the improvement of diet ensured by maize and potato farming. In the British Isles, for example, the new crops spurred population growth, thereby furnishing both the labor and the consumer basis for the Industrial Revolution.

many northern Europeans hoped that a water route to Asia might yet be found somewhere in the northern latitudes. Beginning in 1497 English, French, and Dutch expeditions hunted for a "Northwest Passage" around North America, but to their dismay found the northern seas clogged with impenetrable ice. However, the explorers did learn that the northern parts of North America contained valuable timber and furs and that the North Atlantic teemed with fish.

As hopes of finding a northern route to Asia faded, the northern European nations turned their attention to the Western Hemisphere. Since Spain and Portugal monopolized the wealth of the most valuable parts of the Americas, England, France, and the Netherlands had to fight their way in. In the beginning this meant smuggling goods and slaves into the Spanish colonies; the Dutch were particularly active in this. Soon the interlopers were attacking Spanish and Portuguese ships laden with wealth bound for Europe. Pirates, both freelance "buccaneers" and marauders secretly outfitted by European governments, pillaged the "Spanish Main," raiding Spanish silver fleets and attacking Caribbean ports.

By the mid-seventeenth century, the English, French, and Dutch were strong enough to attempt the conquest of the Spanish and Portuguese colonies in the Western Hemisphere, as well as in Africa and Asia. The Spanish and Portuguese held on to their main possessions in the Americas, but the newcomers did capture a number of small islands in the West Indies, turning them into agricultural plantations for growing sugar and tobacco. To work the crops, the English, French, and Dutch shipped in slaves from their trading posts in West Africa. The constant importation of slaves into the European plantation colonies quickly transformed the racial composition of the eastern fringe of the Western Hemisphere, replacing the original Amerindian population with a few Europeans and masses of black slaves.

During the seventeenth century the northern European states established new colonies on the east coast of North America. The Dutch, Swedes, and French were primarily interested in developing a lucrative fur trade with the Amerindians, but their colonies proved to be only modestly profitable, considering the cost of maintenance and defense. To cut down on costs, they brought over a few farmers to provide food.

In 1607 the English established a new kind of colony on the east coast of North America. In such colonies, often termed "New Europes," large numbers of European settlers landed, killing off or driving out the Amerindian inhabitants and setting up replicas of European society. The English authorities had originally hoped to trade with the Amerindians for skins and furs, as the French and Dutch were doing. Failing that, they wanted to find or grow the products that had made the Spanish and Portuguese rich: gold, silver, silk, spices, and tea. They had other motives as well: outflanking the Spanish; converting Amerindians to Christianity; and removing from England some of its criminals, paupers, unemployed, religious dissenters, and political unreliables. English leaders believed that the work of these people would be profitable to the merchant trading companies. Encouraged by such "boosters" as Richard Hakluyt and with varying degrees of pressure by the government and the trading companies, more than 100,000 settlers came to English North America by the middle of the seventeenth century.

To the disappointment of the English investors, many of the colonies produced little in the way of Asian

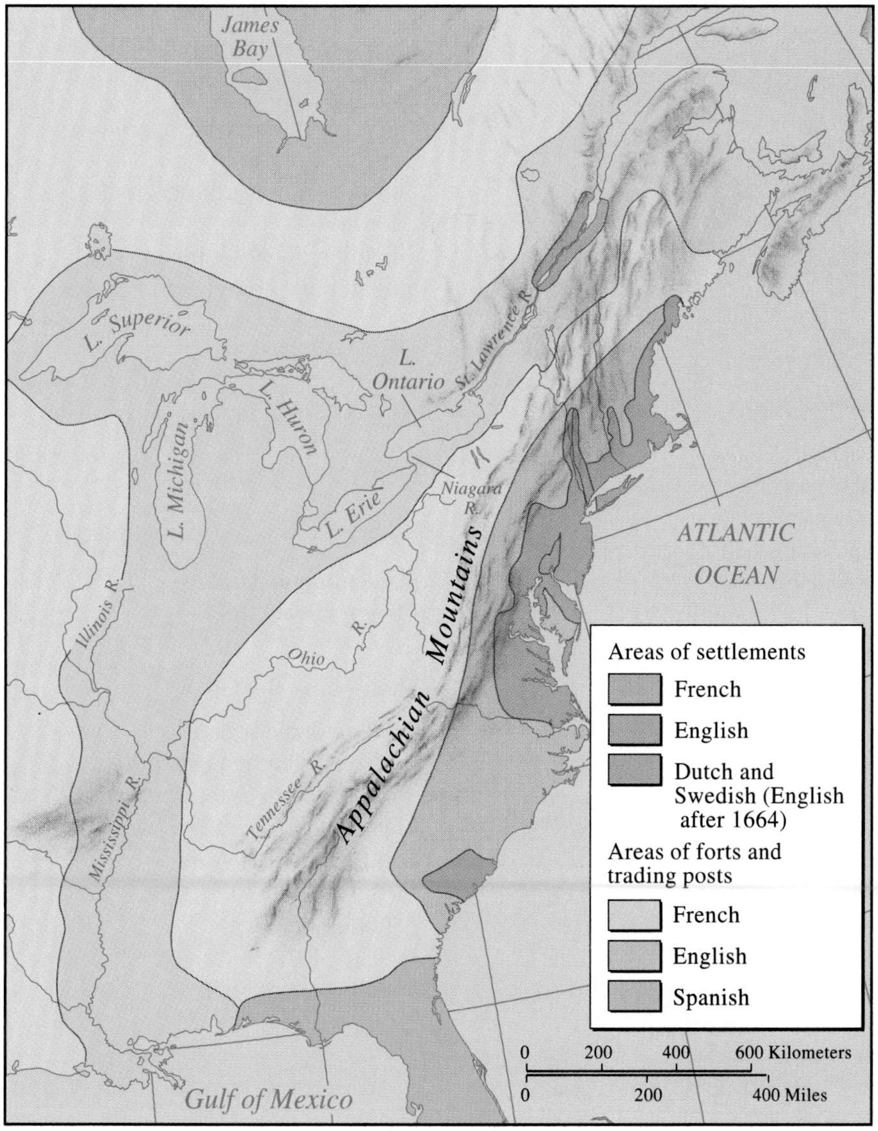

Map 9.7 European Holdings in North America, c. 1685. After nearly a century of activity in North America, the French and the English had secured very disparate colonial holdings. The French presence centered on fur and deerskin trading posts radiating from a small settlement in Quebec. The English controlled an area smaller in extent but greater in population, dominated by family farms.

Corbis-Bettmann

Slavery in Virginia. In 1619, at Jamestown, England's Virginia colony, a Dutch ship has landed with the first blacks offered for sale. The Virginians stare at the strangers, trying to gauge the economic and social consequences of purchasing them. Their decision to buy slaves radically transformed the racial composition of the Western Hemisphere.

and Latin American wealth. North of Chesapeake Bay, the natural products were timber, fish, grain, and meat; only the first was wanted in England. The foodstuffs, however, could be sent to the Caribbean, allowing the planters there to keep their slaves at work exclusively growing sugar and tobacco. From the Chesapeake southward, the English had more luck: Here settlers could grow tobacco and (later) rice, indigo, and cotton—all valuable products. Slave traders brought in slaves from the Caribbean and from Africa to raise these products; as a result some areas from the Chesapeake southward rapidly took on the brutal economic and social characteristics of the plantation culture of the Caribbean and Brazil.

1300	Petrarch and the Italian Renaissance The Black Death Renaissance in northern Europe
1450	Johannes Gutenberg's printing press Benin kingdom in West Africa End of Muslim rule in Spain Voyage of Christopher Columbus
1500	Centralization of western European monarchies Leonardo da Vinci Michelangelo Buonarroti Desiderius Erasmus Beginnings of the Safavid Empire Voyages of Balboa and Magellan Martin Luther's ninety-five theses Spain conquers Aztecs and Inkas Ottoman Turks conquer Arab territories Suleiman the Magnificent Suleimaniye complex in Istanbul John Calvin Afonso I, king of the Kongo Henry VIII Roman Catholic Reformation Slave trade in Africa Queen Elizabeth I Shah Abbas the Great
1600	William Shakespeare British and French establish colonies in North America Miguel de Cervantes, *Don Quixote* The Thirty Years' War "King" Nzinga in Angola Ashanti kingdom Louis XIV, the Sun King Dutch make settlement in South Africa
1700	

By the mid-seventeenth century, the center of economic power in Europe had shifted from the Iberian to the North European nations. Having sufficient power and economic stability, these nations created, enlarged, and protected their colonial empires. Increasingly efficient in mercantile and banking affairs, they augmented the profits obtained from their colonies and avoided dissipating their wealth in European wars. Many English and Dutch families became wealthy from overseas trade, and company investors plowed profits from their colonial enterprises into new manufacturing and trading projects in Europe (see Chapter 11).

Summary and Comparisons

The fifteenth, sixteenth, and seventeenth centuries were marked by the rise and fall of absolutist states. The Ottoman and Safavid Empires were flourishing; several of the Atlantic-facing nations of Europe were building up centralized monarchies; and the papacy was beleaguered. The Renaissance reissue of classical histories and biographies gave some new perspective to this process. Largely as a result of European exploration and expansion, the Aztec and Inka Empires in the Western Hemisphere were overthrown.

Authoritarian government was well established in the Ottoman and Safavid Empires. Although old enemies, these empires were remarkably similar. Each was highly centralized politically and economically, and their cultural and social life shared a common Islamic heritage. Differences did exist, however, because the Ottoman Empire adhered to Sunni Islam while the Safavids were ardent believers in Shi'i Islam.

As a leading military power in the eastern Mediterranean, the Ottomans successfully absorbed the Balkans, Hungary, and the Arab lands of the eastern Mediterranean and North Africa. Ottoman attempts to take Vienna and to destroy Safavid power failed. The Ottoman Empire reached its zenith under Suleiman the Magnificent, a great patron of the arts, but steadily declined in world status afterwards.

The Safavid Empire entered its golden age under Shah Abbas, who created a new, glorious capital at Isfahan and made Persia a cultural center. Control of the silk industry provided the Safavids with economic wealth and enabled them to become patrons of the arts. Like the Ottoman Empire, the Safavids encouraged trade with European nations and granted special privileges to European traders. Both the Safavids and the Ottomans also maintained economic links with Asia, where other centralized empires flourished during the sixteenth and seventeenth centuries.

During these centuries European societies also underwent profound changes. In Europe, the otherworldly orientation of the Catholic church gave way to a secular outlook in thought and in art. Spurred on by refugee scholars who fled Ottoman advances in the eastern Mediterranean, Italy became the center of a remarkable intellectual, literary, and artistic reawakening called the Renaissance. Deriving inspiration from recently recovered manuscripts by classical authors of Greece and Rome, and from contacts with Islamic scholars, humanists produced superb works in history, philosophy, and philology. Drawing from nature, painters and sculptors now concentrated on capturing and interpreting the world about them. By the sixteenth and seventeenth centuries, the practices and perspectives of the Italian Renaissance also spread into western Europe. Vernacular literature flourished, and humanism became a strong force. France, England, and Spain enjoyed golden ages of literary productivity, particularly in drama.

During the fifteenth and sixteenth centuries national monarchies also developed in western Europe. These national monarchies established territorial unity and centralized governmental functions, and their monarchs overcame the opposition of the nobles by allying with towns and relying on advisers and bureaucrats from outside the aristocracy. Expanding centralized monarchies also had impacts on the relationships of European governments with the Catholic church.

The Protestant Reformation of the sixteenth century had several causes. A weakened papacy lowered popular support and abuses of simony, indulgences, and pluralism stirred reformers to action. Luther and Calvin led the movement to break with the Catholic church and to establish Protestant Christianity. Within the Roman Catholic church, humanists and clergy led reforming activities, and Pope Paul III made reform a churchwide activity. The Council of Trent reaffirmed traditional Roman Catholic doctrines and sought to eliminate abuses. Religious wars disrupted European societies until 1648, when the Treaty of Westphalia recognized both Protestant and Catholic states in Europe.

The newly unified European states along the Atlantic Ocean had also amassed the economic resources and technology necessary to explore new trade routes. Spurred on by Ottoman taxes on goods from Asia, and to some degree by a desire to make converts to Christianity, they began to search for routes to Asia that they could control. In the process they explored much of the globe and brought European power not only to Asia but to Africa and the Western Hemisphere as well.

The Portuguese, Dutch, French, and English all established trading routed along the coasts of Africa. The Portuguese were initially strongly entrenched in both West and East Africa, but they gradually lost their favored positions to the Dutch and English.

In East Africa, indigenous African and Arab opposition drove out the Portuguese, who had been weakened by Dutch naval victories in the Indian Ocean. In South

Africa, the Dutch established a permanent colony based on the racial supremacy of the white Boers. This initially small colony would have many long-term ramifications for the history of South Africa.

Finally, the slave trade, which lasted some 400 years, affected all of Africa. Millions of Africans were shipped by force to the Americas. Although some Africans cooperated and benefited from this trade, many, like "King" Nzinga of Angola, fought against it. The slave trade had many disastrous results on individual African societies, particularly in the interior of the continent. In spite of the negative impacts of the slave trade, most of Africa remained independent and continued to develop under its own political and cultural institutions until the nineteenth century.

During this era, Spain led the European expansion across the Atlantic and established a vast empire, exceedingly rich in silver, in Mexico and South America. In the course of this conquest, the great majority of Amerindians died from European diseases. Europeans also transformed the Caribbean into sugar and tobacco plantations worked by black slaves who lived and died under brutal conditions. Portugal established a similar plantation-based economy in Brazil. Three key characteristics of Iberia—paternalistic government, aristocratic privilege, and mercantilist economics—were essentially replicated in Latin America, but in this case imposed on populations who were predominantly Amerindian and black. Amerindian and black culture—especially food, clothing, textiles, music, and speech—modified the lifestyles of Europeans, both in Latin America and elsewhere.

In the seventeenth century, the French, Dutch, and English also became active overseas. Although they failed to find passages to Asia through the Arctic ice, the northern European states did establish colonies on the Atlantic seaboard of North America and used the wealth from these colonies for financial and industrial developments in Europe. Thousands of Europeans settled in North America, displacing and often massacring the Amerindians. These colonies began to exhibit more liberal social, political, and religious values and practices than Europe.

These major upheavals mark the beginning of a remarkable five-century period in which some European nations extended their power into four other continents. In the process they destroyed or profoundly altered many indigenous cultures in the Western Hemisphere and also in Africa and Asia. As a result of these developments, the center of political and economic power shifted from Mediterranean to Atlantic societies.

Selected Sources

Adas, Michael, ed. *Technology and European Overseas Enterprise: Diffusion, Adaptation, and Adoption.* 1996.

*Atil, Esin. *The Age of Sultan Suleyman the Magnificent.* 1987. Lavishly illustrated discussion of art, crafts, and culture during the zenith of Ottoman power.

Augustijn, Cornelius. *Erasmus: His Life, Works and Influence.* Trans. J. C. Grayson. 1991. Presents a balanced account of Erasmus's life and works.

*Bailyn, Bernard. *Origins of American Politics.* 1970. Examines colonial roots of American political theory and practice.

*Balewa, Abubakar Tafawa. *Shathu Umar.* 1967. A novel about the life of a slave by a former prime minister of Nigeria.

Barber, Noel. *The Sultans.* 1973. Readable account of the Ottoman Empire, based on the lives of the Sultans.

Benesch, Otto. *The Art of the Renaissance in Northern Europe.* 1965. Well-illustrated presentation relating northern European art to contemporary trends in thought and religion.

Bethell, Leslie, ed. *Colonial Spanish America.* 1987. *Colonial Brazil.* 1988. Both books contain essays concerning Latin America from the conquest to independence. Noted authorities write about rural society and the hacienda, urbanization, and Amerindian cultures matters.

*Bouwsma, William J. *John Calvin: A Sixteenth-Century Portrait.* 1988. An essential biography of Calvin.

Boxers, Charles R. *Four Centuries of Portuguese Expansion, 1415–1825.* 1969. Overview of Brazil within the context of the Portuguese Empire.

Braudel, Fernand. *The Mediterranean and the Mediterranean World in the Age of Philip II.* Abridged 1992. Excellent background for understanding Spain and Spanish transplantations in the Americas.

Brown, Judith C., and Davis, Robert C., eds. *Gender and Society in Renaissance Italy.* 1998. A useful collection of essays on the interplay between gender and society.

*Costain, Thomas B. *The Moneyman.* 1947. Historical novel on the life of a French merchant.

Cutter, Donald C. *Quest for Empire: Spanish Settlement in the Southwest.* 1996. An overview of Spanish policies.

Ferro, Marc. *Colonization: A Global History.* 1997. A good general account.

Fuentes, Carlos. *The Buried Mirror: Reflections on Spain and the New World.* 1992. Excellent introduction to Spain and the Americas; beautifully crafted with prints, maps, and artwork.

*Goodwin, Godfrey. *A History of Ottoman Architecture.* 1971; reprinted 1992. Includes hundreds of illustrations and dozens of floor plans for mosques, government complexes, and homes; also a particularly informative chapter on Sinan, the noted Ottoman architect.

"Gorée: Door of No Return." Films for the Humanities. A moving historical description of Gorée, a slave-trading center in West Africa.

Green, Guy, dir. *Luther.* 1974. Stirring film interpretation of Luther's reforming activities.

Grimm, Harold J. *The Reformation Era: 1500–1650.* 2d ed. 1973. Focuses on the religious issues and personalities of the Reformation era.

*Haring, Clarence H. *The Spanish Empire in America.* 1975. An authoritative study that is sympathetic to the Spanish.

*Available in paperback.

*Hodgson, Marshall G. S. *The Venture of Islam: The Gunpowder Empires and Modern Times.* Vol. 3. 1974. Scholarly analysis and truly global approach to the confrontation of Islamic states, including the Ottoman and Persian Empires and Muslim India, with the West.

*Innes, Hammond. *The Conquistadors.* 1969. A lively, beautifully illustrated account.

Jensen, De Lamar. *Reformation Europe.* 1992. The best one-volume account.

Joffe, Roland, dir. *The Mission.* 1986. A visually spectacular film about a Jesuit mission in the jungles of Brazil and its destruction by the greed of merchants and factionalism within the church.

*Kinross, Patrick Balfour. *The Ottoman Centuries: the Rise and Fall of the Turkish Empire.* 1977. Well-written account of Ottoman history, with good analysis of strengths and weaknesses of the empire.

Labalm, Patricia, ed. *Beyond Their Sex: Learned Women of the European Past.* 1980. Contains a number of useful articles analyzing educational and scholarly roles open to females in Renaissance society.

*Leonard, Irving A. *Baroque Times in Old Mexico: Seventeenth-Century Persons, Places, and Practices.* 1959. A colorful insight into the society and culture of Latin America.

Leon-Portilla, Miguel. *The Broken Spears: Aztec Accounts of the Conquest.* 1962. An enduring classic, employing Amerindian accounts of the fall of the Aztecs.

———. *Pre-Colombian Literatures of Mexico.* 1992. An anthology of poetry and prose, including indigenous accounts of the Conquest.

*Maalouf, Amin. *Leo Africanus.* 1986; reprinted 1992. A novel based on the celebrated traveler's life, with vivid, historically accurate descriptions of Moorish Spain, Timbuktu, and Italy during the Renaissance.

Marks, Richard L. *Cortés: The Great Adventurer and the Fate of Aztec Mexico.* 1993. A biography of the Spanish conqueror against the backdrop of a clash between the Aztec and European civilizations.

Marshall, Sherrin, ed. *Women in Reformation and Counter-Reformation Europe.* 1989. Explores the role and status of women in the Reformation era, and their contribution to spiritual renewal and reform.

*Morison, Samuel E. *Christopher Columbus, Mariner.* 1983. A lively, if traditional, introduction to Columbus.

Oberman, Heiko O. *Luther: Man between God and Devil.* Trans. E. Walliser-Schwarzbart. 1989. Examines Luther and his theology against the intellectual currents of the later medieval world.

*Pernoud, Regine. *Joan of Arc, by Herself and Her Witnesses.* Trans. Edward Hyams. 1969. Powerful biography; also the film *Joan of Arc,* dir. Victor Fleming, 1948, starring Ingrid Bergman.

*Perroy, Edouard. *The Hundred Years' War.* 1965. Combines social and political history with military events.

*Perry, Glenn E. *The Middle East: Fourteen Islamic Centuries.* 3d ed. 1997. Concise overview of the region from early times to the present day.

Ptak, Roderich, ed. *Portuguese Asia: Aspects in History and Economic History, Sixteenth and Seventeenth Centuries.* 1987.

Rubin, Nancy. *Isabella of Castile: The First Renaissance Queen.* 1991. A lively biography of the strong-willed queen.

Sale, Kirkpatrick. *The Conquest of Paradise: Christopher Columbus and the Columbian Legacy.* 1990. A fervent exposition of the concept that a sickly, dispirited post-Black Death Europe essentially destroyed the environment, native population, and indigenous culture of the Americas.

Shaffer, Peter. *The Royal Hunt of the Sun.* 1981. A moving play depicting the story of the capture, imprisonment, and execution of the Inka emperor by Pizarro.

Sobel, Dava. *Galileo's Daughter.* 1999. Based on the surviving letters of his illegitimate daughter, a cloistered nun in Florence, this study reveals much about Galileo the man, accenting his struggle to reconcile his scientific discoveries with his beliefs as a good Catholic.

*Stone, Irving. *The Agony and the Ecstasy.* 1961. An historical novel based on Michelangelo's life; also the basis for a movie of the same title.

Suleiman the Magnificent. 1987. This one-hour film, produced by the National Gallery of Art, is a colorful, historically accurate account of the Ottoman empire at its zenith.

The Isfahan of Shah Abbas. 1987. This 28-minute film is a stunning visual presentation of Safavid culture with narration by art expert Oleg Grabar.

*Thompson, Vincent Bakpetu. *The Making of the African Diaspora in the Americas 1441–1900.* 1988. Full account of the slave trade and its cultural impacts.

Williams, Selma. *Demeter's Daughters.* 1976. A survey of the various roles of women in British North America, stressing the stories of individuals.

Wölfflin, Heinrich. *Classic Art: An Introduction to the Italian Renaissance.* 3d ed. 1968. Brief, comprehensive, well-illustrated introduction to this large topic.

Wood, Betty. *The Origins of American Slavery: Freedom and Bondage in the English Colonies.* 1997.

Zili, Madeline C. *Women in the Ottoman Empire.* 1997. A scholarly study of the lives of women over the many centuries of Ottoman rule.

Zophy, Jonathan W. *A Short History of Reformation Europe.* 1997. A concise, readable overview of the period. Tailored for students who have not had much exposure to the subject.

———. *A Short History of Renaissance Europe.* 1997. Like its above companion, a useful introduction for the beginning student.

Internet Links

1492: An Ongoing Voyage

http://www.ibiblio.org/expo/1492.exhibit/Intro.html

This virtual exhibit, sponsored and maintained by the Library of Congress, "examines the first sustained contacts between American people and European explorers, conquerors and settlers from 1492 to 1600."

The Beginnings of European Slave Trade

http://www.wsu.edu/~dee/DIASPORA/SLAVE.HTML

This concise account is one segment of the excellent "African Diaspora" website at Washington State University.

Discovery and Reformation Reader
http://www.wsu.edu:8080/~dee/refread.html
This site features good, concise biographies of Luther and Calvin together with key selections from their works.

Italian Renaissance Reader
http://www.wsu.edu:8080/~dee/renread.html
A helpful collection of short biographies (Leonardo Da Vinci, Machiavelli, Pico della Mirandola, Michelangelo), selected texts, and good illustrations.

Safavid Iran: A Persian Empire
http://www.smcm.edu/academics/aldiv/art/webcourses/arth100/empire/Safavids/safhm.html
This website contains basic information on Safavid Persia, with good illustrations, biographical sketches, and a glossary of terms.

Asia in the Early Modern Era

10

All the face of the earth, so far as we could see, was covered with people, troops of horses, elephants, etc., with innumerable flags small and great, which made a most gallant show; for it is the custom of every great man to go with a great many of these flags carried before him.

*Then thousands of horsemen going breadthwise; then came about 19 or 20 elephants of state with coverings and furniture; most of them of cloth of gold, the rest rich stuff, velvets, etc.; some of them carrying a flag with the king's arms, which is a tiger crouching with the sun rising over his back. . . . Then came the king himself mounted on a dark gray horse, and with him Mahabat Khan. A little distance behind rode his eldest son Dara-Shikot all alone, all the rest of the lords on foot, before and behind, and on each side of him. All this moving in one, on so many huge elephants [that it] seemed like a fleet of ships with flags and streamers. So that all this together made a most majestical, warlike and delightsome sight.**

*Peter Mundy, *The Travels of Peter Mundy in Europe and Asia, 1608–1667*, vol. 2, (Cambridge: Hakluyt Society, 1907–1936), p. 188.

This awestruck description was written in 1632 by Englishman Peter Mundy after the Moghul Emperor Jahangir's entry into Ahmadabad. The great splendor of the Moghul court reflected the wealth of India and led Europeans to call the Moghul emperors Great Moghuls. Rulers have always tried to impress the world with pomp and circumstance; in seventeenth-century India with horses, elephants, and many retainers; in the modern West with jet planes, helicopters, and fleets of limousines. Such showmanship is designed to inspire awe and obedience.

Similar accounts by Westerners record the court splendors of Ming and Ch'ing China and Tokugawa Japan, whose leaders ruled more people and wealthier territories than their European counterparts. This is why European adventurers and traders fought to control new trading routes to Asia.

This chapter describes the last great imperial age in Asia, when India, China, and Japan experienced political success and cultural flowering. Southeast Asia continued to be influenced culturally by China, India, and West Asia and remained politically divided. During this period, European voyages to find a direct sea route to Asia culminated in Vasco da Gama's arrival in India in 1498 via the southern tip of Africa and the Indian Ocean. Europeans were happy to be granted permission to trade in India, China, and Japan by those countries' powerful governments. The Portuguese mercantile empire in Southeast Asia, where no strong governments existed, eventually failed for lack of manpower. In time the Netherlands dominated trade in Southeast Asia, while Spain colonized the Philippines and England focused on India.

This chapter continues to examine the Moghul Empire that unified India for the first time in almost 1,000 years. By securing almost 200 years of peace, it allowed Indians to evolve an Indo-Islamic style of art and to attain great heights in other cultural areas. The chapter also looks at the Ming and Ch'ing dynasties, under which China enjoyed great economic prosperity and a final flourishing of traditional culture and arts. It concludes with Japan, which emerged from civil war to achieve unity under feudal warlords called shoguns.

Early European Colonization of Southeast Asia

*From ancient times the country of Siam was known as Shahru'n-nuwi, and all princes of these regions below the wind were subject to Siam. . . . And when the news reached Siam that Malaka was a great city but was not subject to Siam, the [king] sent an envoy to Malaka to demand a letter of 'obedience': but Sultan Muzaffar Shah [reigned 1446–1459] refused to own allegiance to Siam. The Raja of Siam was very angry and ordered an expedition to be made ready for the invasion of Malaka. . . . [Later] the men of Siam arrived, and they fought with the men of Malaka. After a long battle, in which many of the soldiers of the Raja of Siam were killed, Malaka still held out and the Siamese withdrew. . . .**

*From the *Sejarah Melayu* (Malay Annals), in *Asia on the Eve of Europe's Expansion,* eds. Donald F. Lach and Carol Flaumenhaft (Englewood Cliffs, N.J.: Prentice-Hall, 1965), pp. 86–87.

The *Malay Annals* tell this story of how the city of Malacca came to be founded (near the tip of the Malay Peninsula opposite Sumatra) in the early fifteenth century. The *Annals* are a mixture of myths and oral history and provide a rare indigenous account of the early greatness of the city. Malacca was a center of trade for China, the East Indies, India, and West Asia, and, after the coming of Europeans, for Europe as well.

A Kaleidoscope of States and Cultures

Southeast Asia is a rich mosaic of many peoples and cultures. Blessed with varied natural resources, it was since early times the destination of traders and immigrants from India and China, and later also from West Asia. Each group brought along its culture, language, technology, and religion, contributing to a melting pot.

Few indigenous writings describe conditions in Southeast Asia, especially the islands, prior to the coming of Europeans. Thus scholars must reconstruct the history of the region from a combination of external written sources, mainly Chinese, incidental local inscriptions, traditional accounts, and oral history and corroborate them with archaeological evidence.

Mongol invasions launched from China during the late thirteenth century are a good point of demarcation. As elsewhere in continental Asia, Mongols established overlordship over the mainland states. They destroyed the Burmese kingdom and its capital city Pagan. After the Mongol era, several petty Burmese states fought one another and fought periodically with neighboring Siam. Mongol invasions into southwestern China had accelerated the southward migration of the Buddhist (mainly Theravada) Shan or Thai people into Thailand. The Thais defeated the Khmers and in 1350 established a state, Siam, whose capital city was Ayuthia (named after Ayodhia in India, the legendary capital of King Rama of the *Ramayana* epic). Though culturally influenced by India and Khmer, the Thai gradually developed a national art style no longer dependent on Gupta Indian and Khmer models. Many monuments and great quantities of elegant religious sculptures survive from post-fourteenth-century Siam, but few written records remain because a Burmese invasion destroyed Ayuthia and its perishable contents in 1767. In 1782 King Rama I founded a new Siamese dynasty with its capital city at Bangkok. His descendants escaped European colonization and rule the country to the present.

The Mongols were unable to dominate island Southeast Asia, as their expensive failed attempt to conquer Java in the 1290s proved. Afterward a new Javanese commercial empire was established over Borneo, Sumatra, the Malay Peninsula, and parts of the Philippines and lasted for about 100 years. In the early fifteenth century many Malay and island East Indian states accepted Chinese suzerainty in the wake of the massive naval expeditions commanded by Ming admiral Cheng Ho (discussed later in this chapter). Rising Arab commercial power centered in Malacca in Sumatra led many states in the region to accept Islam, with rulers adopting the new religion to facilitate trade with Muslim Indians and Arabs. When the Portuguese under Alfonso d'Albuquerque first came to Southeast Asia, they found no powerful empires in the region but a mosaic of many faiths and numerous petty states.

Southeast Asia: Magnet for Europeans

When the first Europeans, Portuguese explorers, sailed around the coast of Africa in the fifteenth century in search of a direct route to Asia, they found strong governments in parts of India, China, and Japan. Too weak to attempt establishing territorial bases on mainland Asia, the Portuguese were grateful to be allowed to trade. However, island Southeast Asia's political fragmentation and desirable products made the region easy prey for European domination.

Once established in Asia, the Portuguese carefully guarded charts of the navigation routes and defended their trading posts against other European nations, forcing them to seek other routes. Thus England's King Henry VII commissioned John Cabot (or Giovanni Caboto) to find a northwest passage to Asia by following the American coast northward along the Atlantic Ocean in 1497. Cabot failed, but in 1519 Spain's Ferdinand Magellan rounded the tip of South America and in 1521 reached a chain of islands that the Spanish later named the Philippines, after King Philip II of Spain. Spain later colonized the Philippines not because the islands possessed many valuable products but because Chinese sailing junks had been trading there for centuries. Control over the islands gave Spain access to goods made in China and Japan. Spain ruled the Philippines until it was ousted by the United States at the end of the nineteenth century.

In the seventeenth century, for economic, religious, and nationalistic reasons, England and the Netherlands challenged Portuguese and Spanish dominance of the Asian trade. A small nation that lacked the population to sustain its Asian enterprise, Portugal encouraged its men stationed overseas to marry local women. Their sons, raised as Catholics, supplied some of the needed manpower. Portugal also recruited displaced samurai from Japan to serve in its garrisons. Despite these measures, Portugal could not successfully defend its empire after the sixteenth century and lost its holdings in Ceylon, Taiwan, and the East Indies to the Dutch. The Dutch prevented England from establishing a firm foothold in Southeast Asia until the nineteenth century, forcing the English to concentrate their energies on commercial and later territorial expansion on the Indian subcontinent.

Portuguese and Spanish Empires

The rise of the Ottoman Empire and political changes in Persia during the fifteenth century disrupted established overland trade routes to the east (see Chapter 9), forcing Europeans to seek alternative sea routes to India and East Asia. Technological improvements in shipbuilding and the adoption of the compass in navigation during the fifteenth century made the long sea voyages possible. With its advantageous location along the Atlantic Ocean, Portugal under Prince Henry the Navigator took the lead in sponsoring voyages of exploration. At the same time that the Portuguese were developing a slave trade in Africa, they were also heading east across the Indian Ocean in search of spices and other exotic goods. In 1497 four Portuguese ships led by Vasco da Gama (1469–1525) left Lisbon and sailed down the west coast of Africa, around the Cape of Good Hope, and across the Indian Ocean, arriving at Calicut on the west coast of India in 1498. In 1508 another Portuguese squadron under Alfonso d'Albuquerque (1453–1515) sailed for Southeast Asia. He built permanent fortified stations at Aden near the mouth of the Red Sea, Ormuz near the mouth of the Persian Gulf in East Africa, Goa on the west coast of India, and in 1511 at Malacca, on the Malay Peninsula. Strategically located to control trade between East and South Asia, Malacca was also a center of trade within Southeast Asia.

The voyage of da Gama and others began a century of Portuguese domination of Southeast Asia. Albuquerque became the first governor-general of a string of fortified trading ports of Portugal's newly established trading empire, administered from Goa. Later Portuguese commanders established additional outposts on the coast of India, on Ceylon (Sri Lanka), and the Sunda Isles and Malacca in Southeast Asia. They fought some local rulers and formed alliances with others for control of the lucrative trade in spices and other exotic and precious goods either produced in Southeast Asia or obtainable there. Other intrepid Portuguese sailors ventured to China and Japan, briefly establishing and manning an outpost on the Chinese island of Taiwan (which Portuguese explorers named Ilha Formosa, or beautiful island). In the mid-sixteenth century, the Chinese government granted Macao, a small peninsula in southern China near Canton, to Portugal for a trading base, but excluded them from other Chinese ports.

Zealous Catholics and fanatically anti-Muslim, the Portuguese carried their hatred for Muslims (who had ruled their homeland for several centuries) to Asia, where to their horror they found many Muslim communities. Catholic missionaries followed in the wake of the explorers and introduced Christianity to the region.

Portugal reaped immense wealth from its Asian trade. Malacca, the linchpin to its trading empire, was guarded by 200 intrepid Portuguese soldiers and 300 adventurous civilians. For much of the sixteenth century, the Portuguese government derived immense wealth from this domination. To ensure a steady supply of the spices, they made some of the weak local rulers vassals and compelled them to pay tribute in the desired items. Annually, a fleet of up to twenty *carracks,* or sailing ships, plied the ocean lanes between Portugal and Asia. On the outward voyage, they carried silver, glass, linens, woolen textiles, and metal manufactures for sale in Asia, and returned to Lisbon laden with pepper, spices, nutmeg (highly prized and expensive in Europe because it was believed to enhance male sexual powers), other spices, precious stones, porcelains, and silks. Portugal also controlled interisland trade throughout the region and collected tolls. Portuguese ships engaged in piracy in areas not under their control. By the late sixteenth century, however, the Portuguese commercial empire was declining because of inadequate manpower and shipping technology that lagged behind new advances made by the Dutch.

Spain also sought to engage in the Asian trade, but because Portugal closely guarded its trade lanes across the Indian Ocean, the Spanish had to discover a different route to the East. This quest culminated in Ferdinand Magellan's voyage in 1519 through the straits at the tip of South America (thereafter named after the explorer) into the Pacific Ocean (see Chapter 9). He reached an archipelago in 1521 and named one of the islands St. Lazarus (the chain of islands was renamed the Philippines in 1542). Although Magellan was killed, one of his ships returned to Spain in 1522 via the Indian Ocean and Africa, the first to circumnavigate the globe.

Spain easily established control over the numerous petty states of the Philippines. Most of its people were preliterate and were followers of animistic religions. Spanish missionaries eventually Christianized most Filipinos, except for the inhabitants of Mindanao and the

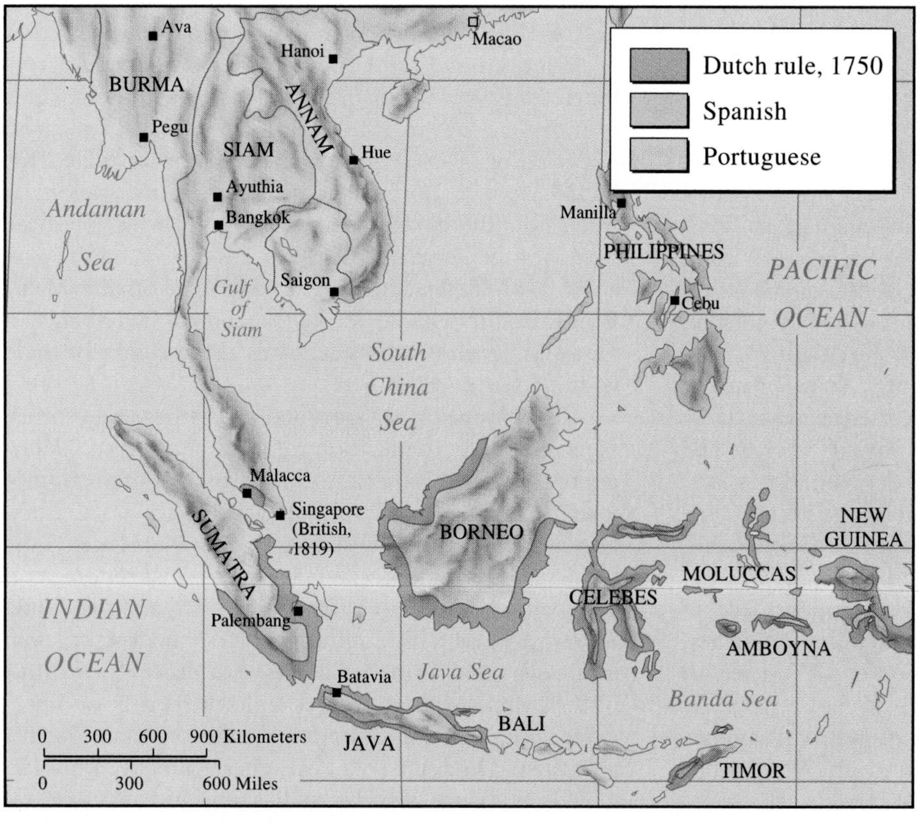

Map 10.1 Southeast Asia, c. 1750. Early European empires in Southeast Asia focused on trade and were mainly interested in the spices that had made the islands famous. By the mid-seventeenth century, the Portuguese had been largely expelled from their trading outposts in the region, replaced by the Dutch in the East Indies. Spain ruled the Philippine Islands. Indigenous states, many of them vassals to China, ruled mainland Southeast Asia.

Sulu islands who retained their Muslim faith. Spain also introduced distinctively European clothing styles and Christian names to the Filipinos, making them closer culturally to Spaniards and Latin Americans than to other Asians.

Spanish rule of the Philippines followed precedents and patterns set in Spanish America. From the capital at Manila, a governor supervised many provinces. Land was granted to a privileged class of Spaniards and local chiefs, who ruled over the peasants in a feudal fashion. The Catholic church dominated religious life. It also provided education, from village schools for boys and girls, convent schools to daughters of the elite, and the College of St. Thomas in Manila for select young men. Founded in 1619, the latter was the first university in Southeast Asia; as St. Thomas University, it remains one of the most prestigious universities in the Philippines.

Although plantations were developed for commercial crops such as tobacco and hemp, Spain did not undertake major economic development of the islands. The port of Manila served an important function as the hub and entrepôt of trade between China, Spanish America, and Spain. Chinese sailing junks, which had been coming to the Philippines since the first millennium to trade with local peoples, now brought silks, tea, porcelain, and other Chinese and Japanese goods to Manila for the Spanish and Spanish-American market as well. From Manila they were shipped across the Pacific to Acapulco in Mexico. There they were carried by porters across the isthmus to Vera Cruz and other ports on the Atlantic coast, where they were loaded onto ships that sailed across the Atlantic to Spain. Thus Spain was able to obtain East Asian goods despite the Portuguese stranglehold on the Pacific-African route.

Spain paid for its imports from China and Japan mainly with silver mined in Mexico and Peru, minted as coins or in bars. The high-quality Spanish coins were widely accepted throughout Southeast Asia, Japan, and China. Many Chinese middlemen settled in Manila to participate in this trade. From Spanish America new crops such as maize, tobacco, sweet potatoes, potatoes, and peanuts were brought to the Philippines, whence they were introduced to China and Japan, with important and lasting impact. So secondary were the products of the Philippines that only one "Manila galleon" carrying local products sailed annually from the islands to Spain.

In 1580 Spain annexed Portugal. This event motivated the Dutch, who were in revolt against Spain, to expand their anti-Spanish activities to include attacks on Portuguese outposts and commercial interests. When the Spanish Armada that set out to conquer England was destroyed by storm in 1588, the era of Portuguese and

Catholic Cathedral. This Baroque cathedral in Cebu City was one of many built by the Spanish when they ruled the Philippines.

CONNECTIONS IN CULTURE

Coffee and Tea

Tea and coffee have ancient origins, and over the centuries their appeal has become global. The story of how they were introduced to new lands shows the power of trade from ancient to modern times.

Tea is native to Szechuan in western China, where inhabitants first felled trees to strip them of leaves. They would then make a drink by pouring boiling water over the dried, processed leaves. Beginning from the Han dynasty, cultivation and drinking of tea spread to all of China, and teahouses became prominent in Sung times. Tea use spread west across the steppes among nomads and other peoples. The Hindi and Arabic words for tea, *sha,* and the Russian word, *chai,* are borrowings from the Chinese *cha,* as is the English word *tea,* which derives from the pronunciation of the word according to a southern Chinese dialect.

Coffee originated in the Ethiopian region of Kaffa, from which it takes its name. By the fifteenth century, coffee drinking had expanded to the north. Coffee (sweetened with sugar) and coffeehouses became common throughout the vast Ottoman Empire. In Safavid Iran, coffee (consumed unsweetened) dominated, but tea (sweetened) was the beverage of choice in the north.

European visitors to the Indian Ocean region began purchasing both coffee and tea in the sixteenth century. Dutch merchants purchased coffee at Mocha, in Yemen. They began growing it in Ceylon and, around 1700, in Java. Coffee production began in the early eighteenth century in Brazil and the Caribbean. Coffee consumption spread much further: Jean-Baptiste Point du Sable, the Haitian merchant whose trading post on the Chicago River formed the nucleus of modern-day Chicago, traveled home almost every year to buy a supply of coffee from his mother's plantation.

English and Dutch merchants bought tea from China, and, in the nineteenth century, began developing plantations in Ceylon, India, and Java. Tea was such a popular beverage in British North America that the colonists' grievance against tariffs charged on tea by the British governent contributed to the war of independence. Thereafter, Americans remained drinkers of coffee, while in England coffee lost its dominant place to tea at the end of the eighteenth century. In Iran and Russia, a similar shift from coffee to tea occurred in the nineteenth century.

Production, marketing, and consumption of these beverages shifted and expanded repeatedly. Tea production remained concentrated in Asia, and coffee production became worldwide. Asian coffee, especially from Java, dominated the eighteenth century but was displaced by Latin American coffee in the nineteenth and early twentieth centuries. In the mid-twentieth century, coffee production grew to major importance both in East Africa, its original home, and in western Africa.

---

1. Tea has had a special social significance in many cultures. To explore the nature and meaning of the Japanese tea ceremony, go to http://www.geocities.co.jp/Hollywood/6036/. What is the purpose of the tea ceremony? What are its typical characteristics? What is the significance of the hanging scroll? In what ways is Zen Buddhism involved?

2. Enter the search term "tea ceremony" into your favorite Internet search engine. You should be able to find sites detailing, at a minimum, the Chinese and Russian tea ceremonies, and perhaps those in other countries as well. In what ways are they similar to the Japanese tea ceremony? In what ways do they differ?

Spanish naval supremacy ended. By the time Portugal recovered its independence in 1640, its Asian commercial empire had all but collapsed and could never be revived.

Dutch and English Empires

During the seventeenth century the Portuguese were supplanted in much of Asia by the Dutch and English. The Dutch first appeared in Southeast Asia in the late sixteenth century. Needing money to support their war of independence from Spain, they attacked the Spanish-Portuguese trading posts whenever possible and traded with Asians wherever they could. An early example of commercial espionage occurred in 1595, when a Dutchman who had spent some years in service of the Portuguese in Goa and other parts of Asia published a manual on sailing to the eastern seas. Armed with this "inside" information, a Dutch expedition immediately set sail for Southeast Asia. It was welcomed by some local rulers who wanted assistance in ousting the unpopular Portuguese. Some Muslim rulers were happy to conclude treaties with the Dutch for the additional rea-

How the Dutch Eliminated the English from the East Indies

[Through three treaties, concluded in] 1613, 1615, and 1619 . . . it was agreed, that in regard of the great blood-shed and cost, pretended to be bestowed by the Hollanders, in winning of the trade of the Iles of the Molluccos, Banda, and Amboyna, from the Spaniards and Portugals, and in building of Forts for the continual securing of the same, the said Hollanders therefore should enjoy two thirds parts of that trade, and the English the other third; and the charges of the Forts to be maintained by taxes and impositions, to be levied upon the merchandise. Wherefore, in consequence of this agreement, the English East India Company planted certain factories for their share of this trade, some at Molluccos, some at Banda, and some at Amboyna. . . .

Upon these islands of Amboyna, and the point of Seran, the Hollanders have four Forts; the chief . . . at Amboyna [with] . . . four bulwarks . . . upon each of which six great pieces of ordnance mounted, most of them of brass. The one side of this castle is washed by the sea, and the other is divided from the land with a ditch of four or five fathoms broad, very deep, and ever filled with the sea. The garrison of this Castle consists of about two hundred Dutch soldiers, and a company of free burgers. . . . The English lived, not in the Castle, but under the protection thereof, in a house of their own in the town; holding themselves safe, as well in respect of the ancient bonds of amity between both nations. . . . They continued here for some two years, conversing and trading together with the Hollanders, by virtue of the said treaties. . . .

[On the] fifteenth of February, 1622 . . . they [the Dutch] sent for Captain Towerson, and the rest of the English that were in the town, to come to speak with the governor of the Castle: they all went. . . . Being come to the governor, he told Captain Towerson, that he himself and others of his nation were accused of a conspiracy to surprise the Castle, and therefore, until further trial, were to remain prisoners. Instantly they . . . took the merchandise of the English Company . . . and seized all the chests, boxes, books, writings, and other things in the English house. . . . The same day also the Governor sent to the two other Factories in the same island, to apprehend the rest of the English there. . . .

*[All prisoners were tortured and condemned to death] all protesting their innocence. . . . [Despite] the manifold testimonies of their innocence by their own writings before their death, devout and deep protestations at their death. . . . At the instant of the execution, there arose a great darkness, with a sudden and violent gust of wind and tempest; whereby two of the Dutch ships, riding in the harbour, were driven from their anchors, and with great labour and difficulty saved from the rocks. . . . Forthwith also fell a new sickness at Amboyna, which swept away about a thousand people, Dutch and Amboyners: in the space wherein, there usually died not above thirty at other seasons. . . . These signs were by the Amboyners interpreted as a token of the wrath of God for this barbarous tyranny of the Hollanders.**

This is a survivor's account of the Dutch massacre of English traders at Amboyna in 1622. It shows the cutthroat nature of Anglo-Dutch trade rivalry in the East Indies. Unable to retaliate, the English withdrew from trading in the East Indies, conceding a monopoly to the Dutch.

*Samuel Purchas, *Hakluytus Posthumus or Purchas His Pilgrimes,* vol. 10 (Glasgow: MacLehose and Sons, 1905), pp. 508, 510, 516–517.

son that unlike the Portuguese, the Dutch had no interest in converting local peoples to Christianity.

These developments brought a lucrative trade to Dutch merchants. Between 1595 and 1601, sixty-five Dutch ships sailed for the East Indies under various commercial companies. In 1602, the newly formed Dutch government granted a charter to the United Dutch East India Company and gave it monopoly rights to trade, make treaties, and establish forts in lands bordering the Indian and Pacific Oceans. With capital of

6.5 million guilders, this company was the largest commercial enterprise to date in the world. Stocks sold to private shareholders soon soared in price as enormous profits poured in. Dividends averaged 37 percent annually, and in some years went as high as 75 percent.

To monopolize the spice trade, the Dutch launched a systematic war of attrition against the Portuguese, which culminated in the siege and fall of the Portuguese stronghold of Malacca in 1640. Portuguese commerce in Asia, long since in decline, would be miniscule from now on. A similar fate had earlier befallen the English in Southeast Asia. Beginning in 1600, the English East India Company had also sought a share in the lucrative spice trade of the East Indies. Initially, when they were both interlopers, the English and Dutch had cooperated against the Portuguese, but as Portuguese power waned, the two newly emerging commercial powers became bitter rivals. The massacre of the entire staff of an English trading post by the Dutch in 1623 ended English trade in the East Indies. In 1658 the Dutch expelled the Portuguese from Ceylon, a valuable way station and the sole producer of cinnamon. With the capture of Ceylon, the Netherlands gained control of the entire lucrative spice trade from Asia to Europe—a control they would maintain for the next century and a half.

The Dutch Asian administrative and governing headquarters were located at Batavia (present-day Jakarta), a port on the northwestern coast of the island of Java. Batavia was an entrepôt of intra-Asian trade from Japan to Persia and the clearinghouse of Asian goods shipped by the Dutch to Europe. The port was guarded by a great fortress, manned by 1,200 Dutch soldiers and Japanese mercenaries. The governor-general and an advisory council, appointed by the East India Company and only indirectly responsible to the Dutch government, supervised trade, defense, and administration.

Like the Portuguese before them, the Dutch in the seventeenth century were mainly interested in trade and not colonization or direct territorial control. Dutch ships, now the best in the world, patrolled the sea lanes and controlled strategically important ports. They eliminated rivals, exacted a tariff on all traffic, and maintained the Dutch monopoly on the spices that all Europeans sought. They intervened in local wars to ensure that friendly rulers stayed in power and acquired territory only when trade demanded territorial control.

Interestingly, the Dutch in Batavia and other ports in Asia tried to maintain their accustomed northern European mode of life even in the tropical climate: they wore

A Dutch Couple at Batavia Harbor. This painting by Aelbert Cuyp shows a Dutch couple in heavy European clothing despite the tropical climate. The man points to Dutch East India Company ships in Batavia (Jakarta) harbor, while a Javanese servant in European clothes shades the couple with a parasol.

An Oppressive Agricultural Policy

The coffee-plant, which is only known on Java by its European appellation, and its intimate connexion with European despotism, was first introduced by the Dutch early in the eighteenth century, and has since formed one of the articles of their exclusive monopoly. The labor by which it is planted, and its produce collected, is included among the oppressions of forced services of the natives, and the delivery of it into the government stores, among the forced deliveries at inadequate rates . . . [after 1809] this shrub usurped the soil destined for yielding the subsistence of the people, every other kind of cultivation was made subservient to it, and the withering effects of a government monopoly extended their influence indiscriminately throughout every province of the island.

In the Sunda districts, each family was obliged to take care of one thousand coffee plants; and in the eastern districts, where new and extensive plantations were now to be formed, on soils and in situations in many instances by no means favourable to the cultivation, five hundred plants was the prescribed allotment. No negligence could be practised in the execution of this duty: the whole operations of planting, cleaning, and collecting, continued to be conducted under the immediate superintendance of European officers, who selected the spot on which new gardens were to be laid out, took care that they were preserved from weeds and rank grass, and received the produce into store when gathered. . . .

A government of colonial monopolists, eager only for profit, and heedless of the sources from which it was derived, sometimes subjected its native subjects to distresses and privations, the recital of which would shock the ear of humanity. Suffice it to say, that the coffee culture in the Sunda districts has sometimes been so severely exacted, that together with the other constant and heavy demands made by the European authority on the labour of the country, they deprived the unfortunate peasants of the time necessary to rear food for their support. Many have thus perished by famine, while others have fled to the crags of the mountains, where raising a scanty subsistence in patches of gaga*, or oftener dependent for it upon the roots of the forest, they congratulated themselves on their escape from the reach of their oppressors. Many of these people, with their descendants, remain in these haunts to the present time: in their annual migrations from hill to hill, they frequently pass over the richest lands, which still remain uncultivated and invite their return; but they prefer their wild independence and precarious subsistence, to the horrors of being again subjected to forced services and forced deliveries at inadequate rates.**

This account of the forced delivery of coffee to the Dutch East India Company on Java is a scathing indictment of the cruelty of a colonial administration that was motivated purely by profit. During his short tenure as Lieutenant Governor of Java under a British administration, Sir Stamford Raffles, the author of this account, reformed some of the abuses of Dutch rule.

*Thomas S. Raffles, *The History of Java*, vol. 1 (1817); reprint ed. by John Bastin (Kuala Lumpur: Oxford University Press, 1965), pp. 125, 129–130.

heavy woolen clothes, seldom bathed, lived in Dutch-style houses with windows tightly closed, ate heavy European meals, and drank large quantities of gin, beer, and wine. Many died prematurely. Few bothered to learn the native languages and instead learned a form of debased Portuguese that remained the international trading language of Southeast Asia for a long time. Because few women came from the Netherlands to the East Indies, many Dutch men formed unions with local women. In fact, a shortage of Dutch immigrants of either sex led the company to encourage Chinese and Japanese immigrants; the business acumen of Chinese merchants and the fighting qualities of Japanese samurai were especially appreciated. New Japanese laws cut off fresh supplies of Japanese immigrants in the early seventeenth century, but a large influx of southern Chinese refugees fleeing the Manchu conquest of China in the late seventeenth century spurred the economic development of Java. The Netherlands also established an outpost on Taiwan, ousting the Portuguese garrison, and held it until they were expelled in the mid-seventeenth century by China. Local peoples on southern Taiwan respect the geckos (a tropical lizard), because, as

Ingo Jezierski/APA Photo Agency

Raffles of Singapore. Sir Thomas Stamford Raffles acquired Singapore for Great Britain in 1819, thus securing a major trading center and British dominance of trade between the Indian and Pacific Oceans.

the story goes, they alerted Chinese forces of a Dutch night attack by squawking loudly.

By the late seventeenth century, British power had overtaken the Dutch. Nevertheless, Dutch control continued in Java, where they established plantations to grow export-oriented commercial crops; the most important were coffee (introduced from Arabia), sugarcane (from China), indigo (for dye making), and, later, tea (also from China). The Netherlands either established direct rule or began to exert strong political supervision over local rulers to ensure the success of the plantations. Many local rulers saw mutual benefits to be derived from plantations and willingly joined forces with the Dutch authorities to exploit the peasants, sometimes requiring them to grow cash crops rather than the food they needed, as shown by Raffles's account quoted in the preceding box.

Anglo-Dutch colonial rivalry continued throughout the eighteenth century. Together with France, the Netherlands fought against Great Britain during the American War of Independence. Although Britain lost its North American colonies, it emerged from the war as the dominant naval power, with overseas interests that shifted from North America to Asia. In 1793, war broke out between revolutionary France and its subordinate ally, the Netherlands, against Britain and several other European powers. To deprive France of the benefits of the Dutch Empire, Britain seized Dutch outposts and colonies throughout the world: the Cape of Good Hope and Malacca in 1795, Ceylon in 1796, and finally Java in 1811. Sir Stamford Raffles, a rising young administrator of the British East India Company, ruled Java and other Dutch possessions in the East Indies between 1811 and 1816 and instituted many liberal reforms, including the ending of forced delivery of cash crops. A keen amateur antiquarian, Raffles commissioned the first archaeological survey of Borobodur.

To Raffles's intense chagrin, the valuable former Dutch possessions in the East Indies were returned to the Netherlands in 1816 in the territorial settlement that ended the Napoleonic Wars. To compensate, Raffles purchased Singapore for Britain from a Malay prince in 1819. Situated at the southern extremity of the Malay Peninsula, Singapore, then a fishing village, possessed a wonderful deep-water port and was strategically located to control trade between the Indian and Pacific Oceans. Under British rule, it attracted many Chinese settlers, and as a free port it became a thriving entrepôt of international trade, supplanting Malacca. It also became a major British naval base.

From Singapore, Britain developed control over Malaya, but except for a part of the island of Borneo it stayed clear of island Southeast Asia. With its huge naval base in Singapore, Britain controlled the eastern approaches to the Indian Ocean and thus maintained its preeminent trading position in East Asia.

Life in Southeast Asia

Life varied so much in the diverse region that few generalizations are possible. Most people were subsistence farmers; fishing produced food that supplemented the diet. A benign tropical climate made living relatively easy and clothing uncomplicated. Most people wore a blouse and, below the waist, a sarong or a wrap, made of locally woven or traded cotton or silk cloths. Locally made tie dyed and intricately woven cloths, called *ikat,* were also made into the simply tailored blouses and sarongs. Housing was also simple; most houses had open sides to allow ventilation, and were raised on stilts to avoid insects and flooding.

Many island Southeast Asians were unwilling to work under the onerous conditions imposed by European commercial farming. Some ran away from the exactions of European and local rulers, causing labor shortages. To rectify the problem, the British encouraged Chinese and Indians to immigrate to their colonies. Accustomed to a more rigorous and competitive life, Chinese and Indian immigrants were willing to endure

© Photobank, Singapore

Singapore's Busy Harbor. This 1846 picture of Singapore shows a thriving port with many ships dotting its harbor. It had been a mere fishing village when a British colonial official, Sir Stamford Raffles, purchased the land from a Malay ruler in 1819.

the discipline of plantation farming or mining. Many also had good business acumen, and thus rose to dominate commerce throughout the region.

While most Filipinos became Roman Catholics, other Southeast Asians remained Buddhists and Muslims, with a small pocket of Hindus on Bali in the East Indies. Chinese immigrants remained Buddhists and Confucians, while most Indian immigrants were Hindus. The different religious groups tended to live in separate communities, the life of each dictated by its religious and social practices.

The Moghul Dynasty

The emperor [Akbar] came to Fatehpur. There he used to spend much time in the Hall of Worship in the company of [Muslim] learned men and shaikhs . . . continually occupied in discussing questions of religion. . . . The learned men used to draw the sword of the tongue on the battlefield of mutual contradiction and opposition, and the antagonism of the sects reached such a pitch that they would call one another fools and heretics. . . .

[Then he had] Samanas [Hindu or Buddhist ascetics] and Brahmans . . . [bring] forward proofs, based on reason and additional testimony, for the truth of their own, and the fallacy of our religion, and inculcated their doctrine with such firmness and assurance that they affirmed mere imaginations as though they were self-evident facts. . . . [They also] instructed His Majesty in the secrets and legends of Hinduism, in the manner of worshipping idols, the fire, the sun and stars, and of revering the chief gods of these unbelievers, such as Brahma. . . .

Sometimes . . . His Majesty listened the whole night to Shaikh Taj ud-din's Sufic obscenities and follies. The shaikh, since he did not in any great degree feel himself bound by the injunctions of the law, introduced arguments concerning the unity of existence, such as idle Sufis discuss, and which eventually led to license and open heresy. . . .

Learned monks also from Europe, who are called Padre . . . brought the Gospel, and advanced proof of the Trinity. His Majesty firmly believed in the truth of the Christian religion. . . .

*Fire worshippers also came from Nousari in Gujarat, proclaimed the religion of Zarathustra as the true one, and declared reverence to fire to be superior to every other kind of worship. They also attracted the emperor's regard, and taught him the peculiar terms, the ordinances, the rites and ceremonies of [Zoroastrianism].**

*William T. de Bary, ed., *Sources of Indian Tradition,* vol. 1 (New York: Columbia University Press, 1958), pp. 432–434.

Emperor Akbar, third ruler of the Moghul dynasty, was raised as a Sunni Muslim. Open-minded on religious matters, he summoned teachers of other religions, including Hindus, Buddhists, Jains, Christians, and Zoroastrians to the Hall of Worship in his new capital city, Fatehpur Sikri, to discuss and debate their religious teachings. Akbar eventually proclaimed a Divine Faith, based on what he considered the best of Islam and Hinduism, but did not enforce it among his subjects. Akbar's radical religious ideas scandalized orthodox Muslims like Bada'muni, the author of the passage quoted above.

The Moghul dynasty (1524–1857) ruled most of India efficiently in the sixteenth and seventeenth centuries and nominally until 1857. It is called the Moghul, or Mughal, a corruption of Mongol, because the Moghuls came from central Asia and were descended from Timurlane, and more remotely from Genghis Khan. Like the Mongols, they were expert horsemen and professional raiders, adventurers, and conquerors. Babur, founder of the Moghul dynasty, had reputedly been inspired to conquer India from stories he had heard about Timurlane's exploits in that land.

Many surviving documents show that the Moghul dynasty is important for several reasons. It unified India for the first time since Harsha nearly 1,000 years earlier, and its administrative framework became the basis of government for the British and later for independent India. The dynasty provided several capable rulers who were lavish patrons of art, sponsoring major monuments and works of art. Akbar, the greatest Moghul emperor, achieved a degree of religious reconciliation between Hindus and Muslims; in contrast, earlier Muslim conquerors had typically opposed Hinduism and pursued a divisive religious policy.

Rise and Fall of Moghul Rule

India was divided and turbulent in the early sixteenth century. North India and the Deccan were ruled by Muslim dynasties, mostly of Afghan origin. In Rajasthan in the west, Rajput nobles (Hindus and professional warriors) battled one another and the Muslims. Hindu dynasties controlled South India. Central Asia, too, had been in chaos since Timurlane's death in 1404, and had been the battleground between his numerous descendants.

The founder of the Moghul dynasty was born in 1483, the son of the ruler of a small central Asian state called Ferghana, north of the Hindu Kush Mountains. He was named Babur, which means panther in Turkish. A great deal is known about him because of details he provides in his *Memoirs,* a book of considerable literary merit. Only eleven when he inherited a very shaky throne following his father's death, Babur struggled for the next twelve years against many dangers.

In 1504 Babur was driven out of central Asia. He then seized the throne at Kabul in Afghanistan, where he planned to build his fortune in India. In 1524 he set out for India with 12,000 soldiers and camp followers. Two years later he met the Afghan king of Delhi at the Battle of Panipat, the historic battleground in the gap between the mountains and desert fifty miles north of Delhi, where the fate of India had already been decided more than once. Although outnumbered ten to one, Babur had cannons and guns (acquired from the Ottomans) that his adversaries did not have. The battle ended with the enemy in rout and the Afghan king dead. Babur entered Delhi and Agra and was proclaimed emperor of Hindustan. A prize of the battle was the Koh-i-nor (mountain of light) diamond, one of the world's largest and now part of the British crown jewel collection.

Babur had a hard time persuading some of his followers to remain in India through the torrid North Indian summer instead of returning to Kabul with the loot. To alleviate the effects of the fierce heat, he immediately laid out gardens and fountains and planted trees in Delhi and Agra. His successors continued to do so and have left a legacy of beautiful Moghul gardens in many North Indian cities. Seeking to enlarge his domains, Babur subdued some of the Rajputs and was beginning to create administrative offices when he died suddenly in 1530.

Humayun (reigned 1530–1556) succeeded his father, but possessed none of Babur's abilities; he drank to excess and was addicted to opium. As a result Humayun lost most of his patrimony to the Afghans, and ten years after inheriting the throne, had been reduced to a fugitive. It was up to his son Akbar (reigned 1556–1605), who had many of the great qualities of his grandfather, to turn the family's fortunes around.

Partly because his youth was spent in wandering and adversity, Akbar never learned to read. But he had a keen intellect and inquiring mind; he collected an extensive library of books in several languages and during his spare moments had others read books to him. Fatherless at thirteen, he took up the immense responsibility of recovering his family's fortunes. In 1557 he met the Afghan king at the Second Battle of Panipat. The Afghans had a huge army with 1,500 war elephants, but their forces dissolved in confusion when their leader became injured. After this victory Akbar was able to regain Delhi, Agra, and the rest of Hindustan and then reconquer Afghanistan. He devoted the remaining years of his reign until his death in 1605 to building a stable administration.

Europeans, who began arriving in India during the early Moghul dynasty, called its rulers the Great Moghuls. This title is an apt description, because until the end of the seventeenth century most Moghul rulers were talented men. Akbar was succeeded by his son Jahangir (reigned 1605–1627), also a good ruler. Jahangir's son, Shah Jahan (reigned 1627–1657), is best remembered for building the Taj Mahal, a mausoleum for his favorite wife, Mumtaz Mahal, which remains an architectural wonder of the world. But Shah Jahan lived too long for some of his many sons' ambitions. One of

Michael Holford, Longton, Essex, England

Fatehpur Sikri. Emperor Akbar built this new capital, where he ruled for fifteen years, to commemorate the birth of his son Jahangir. This view shows the elegance of Moghul architecture.

them, Aurengzeb, revolted in 1657, seized the throne, and proclaimed himself emperor. In action reminiscent of the Ottoman sultans, Aurengzeb (reigned 1659–1707) then killed his brothers. He imprisoned his father in a suite of rooms in the palace with a view of the Taj Mahal and later buried him beside his mother. Shan Jahan had planned to build another mausoleum for himself beside that for his wife. The civil war and fratricide that brought Aurengzeb to power were but one instance of the bloody politics of the Moghul royal family, where sons often revolted against fathers and family members murdered each other for possession of the throne.

Although Aurengzeb was a capable ruler, his strictly pro-Muslim and anti-Hindu religious policy put the clock back on the development of better relations between the two religious groups. He surrounded himself with religious bigots, and harshly persecuted Hindus. He restored discriminatory and humiliating taxes on Hindus and razed many of their temples, thus re-igniting bad relations between members of the two faiths. The Hindus were provoked to revolt, and the ensuing wars permanently weakened the empire. Wars of succession plagued his heirs. In 1739 the Persians invaded and took Afghanistan, and even captured and looted Delhi, taking with them the fabled jewel-encrusted peacock throne of the Moghuls.

The Moghul Empire lost all effective power after 1760. North India was invaded by Afghans, and over much of the subcontinent Hindus, Muslims, and Sikhs (a new religious group begun in India in the sixteenth century) contended for control. Indians call the century after 1760 the Great Anarchy or Time of Troubles. Order was only restored with the consolidation of British power. Some Indians who opposed British rule during the Indian Mutiny in 1857 used the figurehead Moghul then reigning in Delhi as a symbol for their rebellion. When Great Britain suppressed the mutiny, it deposed the Moghul emperor, ending the dynastic era of Indian history.

Moghul Absolutism

Akbar created an absolute government that endured for two centuries, an accomplishment that made him one of

Brooklyn Museum of Art, gift of Mr. and Mrs. Robert L. Poster, 87.234.7

Jahangir with a White Falcon. Jahangir, an avid hunter and patron of the arts, is shown with his falcon. This portrait is a typical miniature watercolor in the Moghul court style.

the great rulers of Indian history. In theory the Moghul emperor's power was unlimited; his word was law and he commanded the military directly. As caliph (secular ruler of a Muslim state), his only restraints were to obey the Qur'an and Islamic tradition. The early Moghul emperors exercised their power wisely and were dedicated to improving the lives of their subjects.

Because of the foreign origins of the dynasty, a large portion of the bureaucracy and military that maintained the Moghul government was foreign also, as had been true of the earlier Yuan Mongol Empire of China and the il-khanate that ruled Persia. Maintaining military power was essential, so every official had to be enrolled in the military. The state maintained a large army, partly commanded by the emperor himself. Vassal chiefs, such as the Rajputs, provided supplemental levies. Aside from ships to keep coastal areas free of pirates, the Moghuls had no navy. Even after Akbar's reforms opened public service careers to Hindus, the Moghul bureaucracy remained tilted against indigenous Indians. Seventy percent of the high imperial officers were Persians and central Asians, the remainder equally divided between Indian Muslims and Hindus. However, these foreigners were expected to remain in India and could not take their wealth out of the country. In later times the proportion of Indians increased.

The keystone of Akbar's statesmanship was his conciliation of his Hindu subjects. Like many other successful rulers, Akbar was a good listener, chose his advisors based on ability, took advice on its merit, and paid attention to detail. He often put on disguises and mixed with the people to learn their points of view. Akbar married Hindu Rajput princesses, one of whom was the mother of his successor, raised many Hindus to positions of power, and abolished the special taxes levied on them. He also encouraged members of his court and other high-ranking Muslims to marry Hindus. However, these intermarriages did not produce genuine cultural fusion because Hindu women were merely transferred to Muslim households, whereas Muslim women seldom married Hindu men. As before, leaders of the various religious communities administered civil laws according to the tenets of their respective religions—Islam, Hinduism, or one of the other religions. The *ulema,* or Muslim theologians, interpreted Islamic civil and criminal law.

The principal functions of the Moghul government were the collection of taxes, maintenance of order, enforcement of the law, building and maintenance of roads and bridges, and encouragement of cultural life by court patronage. It did not concern itself with irrigation works and water conservancy or with relief for those in distress. Nor did the government remit taxes even during famines, which caused enormous hardships. During the widespread famines of 1594–1598 and 1630–1632, desperate people even resorted to cannibalism.

Since the Moghul emperor was the sole source of power, the whole government moved with him wherever he traveled. According to custom, the emperor presented himself before the public at least once daily, usually at sunrise. He spent most of the morning holding public audience, receiving petitions, and giving orders. Other business was conducted in a more confidential manner with his ministers and advisors.

The emperor supervised a centralized administration with ministers who controlled the secretariat and other government bureaus. Much of the imperial service was borrowed from Persia, including the ranking system of thirty-two grades. The official language was Persian. Because good communications were vital to effective government, the early Moghuls built and maintained a system of roads that linked parts of the empire to the two capitals, Delhi and Agra. Rest houses along the roads provided for the needs of people on government business and the postal service.

As in the Ottoman, Manchu, and Russian Empires, land under direct imperial rule was divided into provinces, districts, and subdistricts down to the village. The efficient revenue system devised by the early Moghuls persisted to British times. For most Indians the payment of land taxes was their main contact with the government; custom duties, import and transit dues, and tolls on domestic trade provided minor sources of revenue. A detailed land register, including the type of crops grown, was compiled under Akbar and became the basis of taxation, which was usually set at a third of the gross product. In addition to land taxes imposed on the centrally governed parts of the empire, a tribute was levied on the territories ruled by local princes, such as the lands under the Rajputs. The bulk of tax revenues went to the imperial treasury. After paying for the military and bureaucracy, the remaining funds were spent on erecting imposing buildings, entertainment, and luxurious living by the rulers.

Akbar insisted on paying official salaries in cash, so that all revenue went to the central treasury, which then disbursed all payments. As administrative efficiency deteriorated under later rulers, officials came to be assigned the revenues from various lands in lieu of salaries. Here again, the Moghuls and the Ottomans followed similar patterns.

Whereas the divided state of India prior to Moghul rule produced chaotic coinage systems, Akbar centralized the mint and struck gold, silver, and copper coins. In purity of metal, constancy of weight, and artistic merit, they were in general superior to coins struck by European rulers of the same era. Most of the gold and silver used for coinage came from the Americas and Africa to pay for Indian goods desired by Europeans.

Society and Economy under the Moghuls

Much is known about the lives of Moghul emperors and aristocrats from their own memoirs and from accounts by European ambassadors, merchants, and missionaries. The emperors lived and entertained lavishly, supported by over a hundred offices and workshops that looked after their boats, horses, elephants, dogs, and other animals, and made many luxury items for their households. The imperial harem reputedly had as many as 5,000 women, each with a separate apartment and an allowance. The women were looked after by eunuchs and protected by female guards. A number of the ladies of the imperial

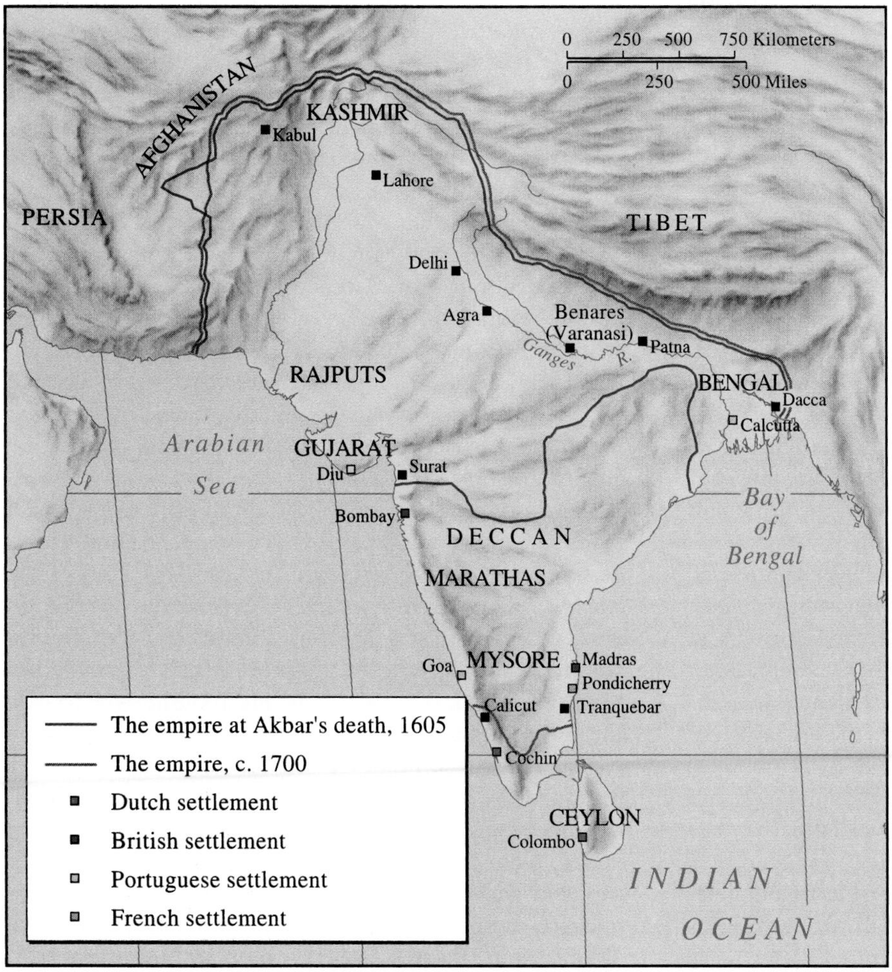

Map 10.2 The Moghul Empire. The seventeenth century was the great age of the Moghul Empire. Under talented rulers and able generals, the empire expanded until it included all of the Indian subcontinent except for Cape Comorin in the extreme south, as well as part of present-day Afghanistan. Moghul power and wealth became legendary in Europe.

MacQuitty International Collection

Empress Mumtaz Mahal. The famous Taj Mahal was built as the resting place of this beautiful empress.

family—consorts, mothers, sisters, and daughters—managed their own estates, painted, wrote poetry, and patronized the arts. After Akbar's reign a unique problem confronted the sisters and daughters of the emperors. Because civil wars and revolts killed many of the males of the imperial clan, and men outside the imperial clan were considered beneath the princesses for marriage, few suitable husbands could be found and many of the princesses did not marry.

Several Moghul queens and princesses influenced state affairs; the most powerful was Persian-born Nur Jahan, the daughter of a courtier. She married a Persian nobleman at seventeen and had a daughter by him. Later her husband rebelled against Emperor Jahangir and was killed. She was brought to court, where the emperor became infatuated with her and made her his principal wife. Nur Jahan was noted for her beauty, intellect, and patronage of the arts. She achieved great influence over her husband, and successfully schemed to influence the succession, marrying her daughter to one of her husband's sons and a niece (Mumtaz Mahal) to another (his successor Shah Jahan).

Moghuls traveled in great style and liked to hunt along the way, as the following description of Shan Jahan's trip in 1633 illustrates:

> A city of canvas, 100,000 horsemen, 50,000 men on foot, as many functionaries, slaves, and eunuchs, the whole retinue of the Queens, Princesses, and favourites escorting them. The elephants sniffed the snow of the passes. At night, in front of the master's pavilion, a giant beacon signalled the sovereign will that moved this tumultuous mass, the soul of the horde. They traveled by short stages. There were two camps, so that one was always pitched on the arrival of the train. On the road they hunted the wild boar, the tiger, the lion even . . . by means of nets, of armies of beaters, or of a donkey drunk with opium that served as a bait.

Such expeditions resembled military campaigns, and are similar to the arena "hunts" staged by the Roman emperor Commodus. Beaters enclosed a huge tract of land and drove the animals into ever-smaller areas for the slaughter. Once, in the seventh year of his reign, Jahangir hunted for eighty consecutive days. At age forty-seven he had a scribe list all the animals he had personally killed; the number totaled 17,167. The roundups also captured primitive jungle-dwelling people, who were sold as slaves. Other favored sports were polo, pigeon flying, and wrestling. Like the Romans, the Moghuls also loved to watch animal combat, the favorite being elephant fighting. Popular indoor games included cards and chess. Akbar had a large chess board of marble squares laid out on a palace floor and used dancing girls as chess pieces.

Like the ancient Macedonian rulers and their Mongol ancestors, many Moghul rulers and noblemen drank strong alcoholic spirits, sometimes mixed with hemp and opium. Babur's *Memoirs* reveal how he loved to lie in the shade of trees in a state of intoxication with his boon companions. Several Moghul princes died young of alcohol-related diseases. Aurengzeb differed from most of his relatives by strictly observing the Islamic prohibition against alcohol.

Although nobles imitated the ruling house in lavish living and entertaining, ordinary people, Hindus and Muslims alike, rarely engaged in heavy drinking. Their lives were enlivened by special events such as weddings, fairs, and religious celebrations. Hindus enjoyed pilgrimages to sacred shrines, which, since Akbar's reign, did not require payment of a special tax. He abolished the levy on the ground that no one should be taxed for worshiping God, although some of his officials lamented the loss of revenue from its abolition. Muslims made the *hajj,* or pilgrimage, to Mecca, by sea in large sailing vessels, and the needy often received imperial financial assistance for their trip. For fear of revolts during his absence, no emperor undertook the pilgrimage. Rulers sometimes got rid of troublesome ministers by sending them to Mecca.

A small middle class of merchants worked hard and lived frugally. Most commerce was in Hindu hands. Muslims who came to India with the Moghuls considered themselves the ruling class and disdained commerce. The Islamic rule against charging interest for loans also discouraged Muslims from trading.

Tradition prevailed in the villages, and agriculture followed its age-old pattern, relying on the monsoon rains. Most farmers engaged in subsistence agriculture and crafts, but commercial crops such as cotton, mulberry trees (for silkworms), sugar cane, spices, and indigo (for dyeing textiles) increased in importance due to domestic and foreign demand. Although most farmers were free, some became serfs when they could not repay their debts. Most artisans were poor, working under contract. The economic condition of most Indians deteriorated during the late Moghul period.

Slavery was permitted under both Hindu and Muslim law. Some crimes were punished by enslavement of the perpetrator. Debtors could be enslaved until they worked off their debt, and thus resembled indentured servants. Some poor parents sold their children into slavery. Other slaves were captured tribal people, who were looked upon as being beyond the pale of civilization. A regular slave trade brought additional slaves from East Africa. Most slaves performed domestic duties.

Specialized artisans were dependent upon the patronage of the emperor and the nobles. Foreigners with special skills were welcomed and came from many Asian and European lands; Persians were most especially skilled in rug-making, which became an important industry in India and remains so to the present. India was best known for cotton textiles, and the Western names of many types of cotton cloth, such as calico, dungaree, muslin, madras, and cambric were of Indian origin. European travelers in Moghul India marveled that every part of India excelled in some kind of textile making, including an extensive silk industry; one traveler estimated that the province of Bengal alone produced 2.5 million pounds of silk, mostly for local consumption, but also for export. Markets for Indian cotton cloths ranged from Southeast Asia to Arabia, east Africa and Egypt, and Europe. In addition, India exported pepper, indigo, opium and other drugs, saltpeter for gunpowder, and various luxury handicrafts. Indians imported horses from central Asia, porcelain from China, bullion and costly knickknacks from Europe, and other luxuries such as coral, amber, and gems. After about 1620, Indians began to cultivate tobacco and took up smoking, both the crop and the habit introduced by Europeans. Many great cities thrived on trade. Unlike the Safavids in Persia, the Moghuls did not play an active role in developing commerce and did not rely on its taxation as a key source of revenue.

Rulers and nobles took pride in patronizing learning and establishing or endowing schools, usually associated with mosques, where boys and sometimes girls received an elementary education. Sons of Hindu farmers and craftsmen received a rough primary education given by local brahmans in vernacular languages. Learned men called *pandits* (compare the English word *pundit*) taught the sons of the upper castes in Sanskrit such subjects as logic, law, and grammar. Daughters of the imperial and noble families were privately educated; some, like men, were patrons of the arts, while others wrote poetry and prose, though mostly anonymously.

The condition of women varied, depending on religion and class, but generally it deteriorated during this era. The Islamic *purdah* kept Muslim women secluded or heavily veiled in public. While Hinduism did not require the veiling of women, the practice became common among high-caste Hindu women in North India. Muslim law allowed daughters to inherit property, but Hindu law generally forbade daughters from inheriting landed property to prevent the transferring of the joint family's land to another family. In both communities a daughter joined her husband's family upon marriage. Early arranged marriages were common, especially for girls who were expected to be virgins at marriage and chaste afterward. Hindu parents also had to provide dowries for daughters. Except for aristocrats, most Hindus were monogamous; in contrast, Muslim men could have several wives and concubines. Divorces were almost unknown among Hindus but were allowed among Muslims. Muslim widows were allowed to remarry, but Hindu widows were discouraged from remarrying, and the practice of *suttee* (or *sati*, the suicide of a widow on her husband's funeral pyre) was encouraged among high castes in certain communities, for example, the Rajputs. Members of both faiths relied on astrology for guidance before making important decisions such as marriage.

Diverse and Divisive Religions

The religious situation in Moghul India was complex. More than three-fourths of Moghul subjects were Hindus. Hindus lived by caste rules and tended to look at Muslims and followers of other religions as members of castes. The ranks of the minority Muslims were continually swelled by immigrants from Persia and central Asia and by Hindu converts, mostly from lower castes; these converts tended to retain their former ways of living. In time Hindus and Muslims shared many tastes and habits.

Most Indian Muslims were Sunnis and were concentrated in the northwest and along the western coast of the Indian subcontinent, where Arab traders had settled and intermarried with Hindus. However, most immigrants from Persia were Shi'i Muslims. There were also Muslims in northeastern India and scattered throughout the subcontinent. Many Moghul rulers were eclectic in their religious practices. Akbar was religiously tolerant. He allowed his Hindu wives their own places of worship in the palace, and he also forbade the destruction and desecration of Hindu temples and allowed new ones to be built. For his personal and political needs, Akbar synthesized what he thought were the best elements of Hinduism and Islam and proclaimed a state religion called Divine Faith, with himself as its chief interpreter and head.

Divine Faith taught people to pursue virtue. From Islam, it borrowed the idea of one god and no priesthood, but it rejected the Muslim belief in a last judgment in favor of the Hindu idea of the transmigration of souls. It also borrowed many Hindu ceremonies. This syncretic religion failed to gain the support of the people, but many Hindus honored Akbar for the generosity of his intentions. Conversely, many orthodox Muslims bitterly resented his religious ideas and regarded his Divine Faith as a heresy. Like Akhenaton's religious innovations in ancient Egypt, Divine Faith did not survive its founder. Aurengzeb ended Moghul religious tolerance and persecuted Hindus.

Sikhism, another religion that began during the early sixteenth century, also stemmed from the desire to find common ground between Hinduism and Islam. Guru Nanak (1469–1538), founder of Sikhism, taught about the one loving god, whom he called the True Name, did not care about one's caste or creed, but demanded goodness and charity. He rejected asceticism, an established clergy, and vegetarianism, commanding Sikhs (disciples) to live healthy, clean lives. Nanak wrote poems and hymns that were later collected in the Granth, the sacred book of Sikhism, which is honored in the Golden Temple, a holy shrine in the city of Amritsar.

Nanak was followed by ten gurus. The first gurus won the respect of the Moghul emperors by their saintly lives. The fifth Guru, Arjan (1581–1606), backed the losing side in a Moghul war of succession, refused to pay a fine exacted by the winner, Emperor Jahangir, and was tortured and executed. Before his death, Arjan told his

Krishna and Radha in the Rain. This eighteenth-century miniature painting depicts a favorite Hindu subject—the god Krishna and his lady, Radha.

A Moghul Pleasure Garden

One of the great defects of Hindustan being its lack of running-waters, it kept coming to my mind that waters should be made to flow by means of wheels erected wherever I might settle down, also that grounds should be laid out in an orderly and symmetrical way. With this object in view, we crossed the Jun-water to look at garden-grounds a few days after entering Agra. These grounds were so bad and unattractive that we traversed them with a hundred disgusts and repulsions. So ugly and displeasing were they, that the idea of making a char-bagh in them passed from my mind, but needs must! as there was no other land near Agra that same ground was taken in hand a few days later.

*The beginning was made with the large well from which water comes from the hot-bath, and also with the piece of ground where the tamarind-trees and the octagonal tank now are. . . . Then in that charmless and disorderly Hind, plots of garden were seen laid out with order and symmetry, with suitable borders and parterres in every corner, and in every border rose and narcissus in perfect arrangement.**

Not much remains of Babur's Persian gardens in Agra. When he died, his remains were taken to Kabul, via a road he had ordered built and planted with shade trees (sections of which remain). Humayun's troubles gave him no opportunity to build, but he did plan a noble mausoleum for himself at Delhi that his son completed. It was the model on which the plan of the Taj Mahal was based.

**Memoirs of Babur*, trans. A. S. Beveridge (New Delhi: Oriental Book Reprint Corporation, 1979), pp. 531–532.

followers to arm themselves and organize into a disciplined movement. After this episode relations between the Sikhs and the Moghul government continued to deteriorate, and Sikhs became implacably opposed to Islam. Arjan's successors instilled in Sikhs a belief that they were an elect group and organized them into a fighting brotherhood with an initiation and a distinctive dress. Most early Sikhs were from Punjab in northern India and some were converts from the Hindu kshatriya (warrior) caste, which made their transition into warriors an easy one. Thus Sikhism failed to reconcile Hinduism and Islam and has continued as a separate religion. Sikhs and Hindus were on amicable terms and often intermarried.

Artistic Fusion in Architecture and Painting

Early Moghul rulers were patrons and connoisseurs of the arts and lavish builders. They attracted artists and artisans from many lands, who worked alongside their Indian counterparts. The interactions of these artists produced a sophisticated common culture and a new style called Indo-Islamic that is a fusion of many elements and traditions.

Akbar and Shah Jahan were the great builders among Moghuls. They left their monuments in the magnificent forts, palaces, and mosques of red sandstone and white marble in the cities of Agra, Delhi, and Fatehpur Sikri. Agra was Akbar's capital city during most of his reign. Starting in 1558, he built a fort and palaces and surrounded them with a massive wall, all made from local red sandstone. Eleven years after the start of his building activities in Agra, Akbar began a new capital at Sikri. As his son Jahangir said in his memoirs:

> My revered father, regarding the village of Sikri, my birthplace, as fortunate to himself, made it his capital, and in the course of fourteen or fifteen years the hills and desert, which abounded in beasts of prey, became converted into a magnificent city, comprising numerous gardens, elegant edifices and pavilions, and other places of great attraction and beauty. After the conquest of Gujrat, the village was named Fatehpur (the town of victory).

The fifteen years that Akbar ruled from this "rose-red city" marked the zenith of his reign. Then he resumed his residence in Agra. Except for occasional visits by later emperors, Fatehpur Sikri has remained deserted but intact, protected by the dry climate and the absence of portable treasures.

Moghul rulers built many mausoleums; the most famous was the Taj Mahal, built by Shan Jahan for his favorite wife at Agra. It took 20,000 men seventeen years to complete. Since Akbar's reign artists, architects, and craftsmen from central Asia, Persia, Arabia, and elsewhere had been working in India. With their Indian colleagues, they gradually synthesized their various traditions into an eclectic Moghul style, epitomized in the Taj Mahal. It commemorated the emperor's devotion to his wife and the zenith of Moghul power.

Mausoleum for an Empress. The Taj Mahal, built of white marble and a masterpiece of Indo-Islamic art, was the mausoleum of the beautiful empress Mumtaz Mahal, wife of Shah Jahan. Surrounding the reflecting pool is a Persian formal garden with cypresses, flowering trees, and flower beds.

In addition to architecture, the Moghuls left a rich legacy in the visual arts. Moghul painting had its origin in Persia, whose painters had earlier learned their skills from China via the Mongols and the Timurids. Babur encouraged Persian painters to settle in India and commissioned them to paint portraits, documents of state occasions, and landscapes. Indian painters soon assimilated Persian techniques and by Akbar's reign the majority of court painters were Hindus. They fused Sino-Persian and Muslim artistic traditions with the Hindu-Buddhist tradition of India and created two distinctive schools, the Moghul and Rajput.

The Moghul school concentrated on court life and the illuminating of manuscripts, while the Rajput school emphasized scenes from the Indian classics and domestic subjects. Both schools excelled in painting miniatures. The Moghul school reached maturity under Jahangir, a great connoisseur and accomplished critic of painting. He invited Jesuit artists to his court to teach the painting techniques of Italian Renaissance masters. Jahangir said in his *Memoirs:*

> As regards myself, my liking for painting and my practice in judging it have arrived at such a point that when any work is brought before me, either of deceased artists or of the present day, without the names being told me, I say on the spur of the moment that it is the work of such and such a man. And if there be a picture containing many portraits, and each face be the work of a different master, I can discover which face is the work of each.

Calligraphy, or the art of penmanship, which was highly esteemed in China, Persia, the Arab world, and India, was closely associated with Moghul painting. Painters and calligraphers often worked side by side, and, as in Chinese paintings, many pictures had space reserved for calligraphic inscriptions. The art of illuminating manuscripts (similar to the tradition established in medieval European monasteries) also flourished.

Numerous minor arts thrived. Artisans created decorative relief carving on stone or marble and latticework screens to shield ladies from public view and to filter strong light. Those that survive in Agra and Fatehpur Sikri continue to filter the bright light of the hot Indian summer and still give cooling relief. Indian craftsmen who did mosaic work and inlay decoration acquired familiarity with an Italian form of inlay called *pietra dura:* semiprecious and precious stones were cut into thin slivers and imbedded into sockets prepared in the marble to form patterns and pictures. Lapidaries (those who cut and polish gem stones) and jewelers benefited from the Moghul love of pomp and display, for both men and women wore extravagantly rich jewels and clothes. The rich clothes, sumptuous jewels, and lavish furnishings of the Moghul court dazzled early European visitors, and their descriptions gave Europeans visions of India's fabulous wealth. Europeans referred to the emperor as the Great Moghul; the word *mogul* (Anglicized form) entered English as an epithet for a powerful man, though a business entrepreneur rather than a ruler.

The Ming Dynasty

*From time immemorial whenever emperors and kings have ruled over the universe, the Middle Kingdom has always been considered the center of government, from which the emperors and kings rule over the barbarians. The barbarians are left outside but they are subject to the Middle Kingdom. It is unheard of that barbarian tribes have ever come to rule the universe.**

*Albert Chan, *The Glory and Fall of the Ming Dynasty* (Norman, OK.: University of Oklahoma Press, 1982), p. 378.

This ringing statement was the rallying cry of Chu Yuan-chang, founder of the Ming dynasty (1368–1644), who welded together many of the disparate groups that had risen against the tyrannical rule of the Mongols. When the last Mongol emperor fled his capital, Tatu, to his ancestral homeland beyond the Great Wall in 1368, all China was once again ruled by Chinese. The Ming government emulated many Han and T'ang institutions and policies and invoked their memory.

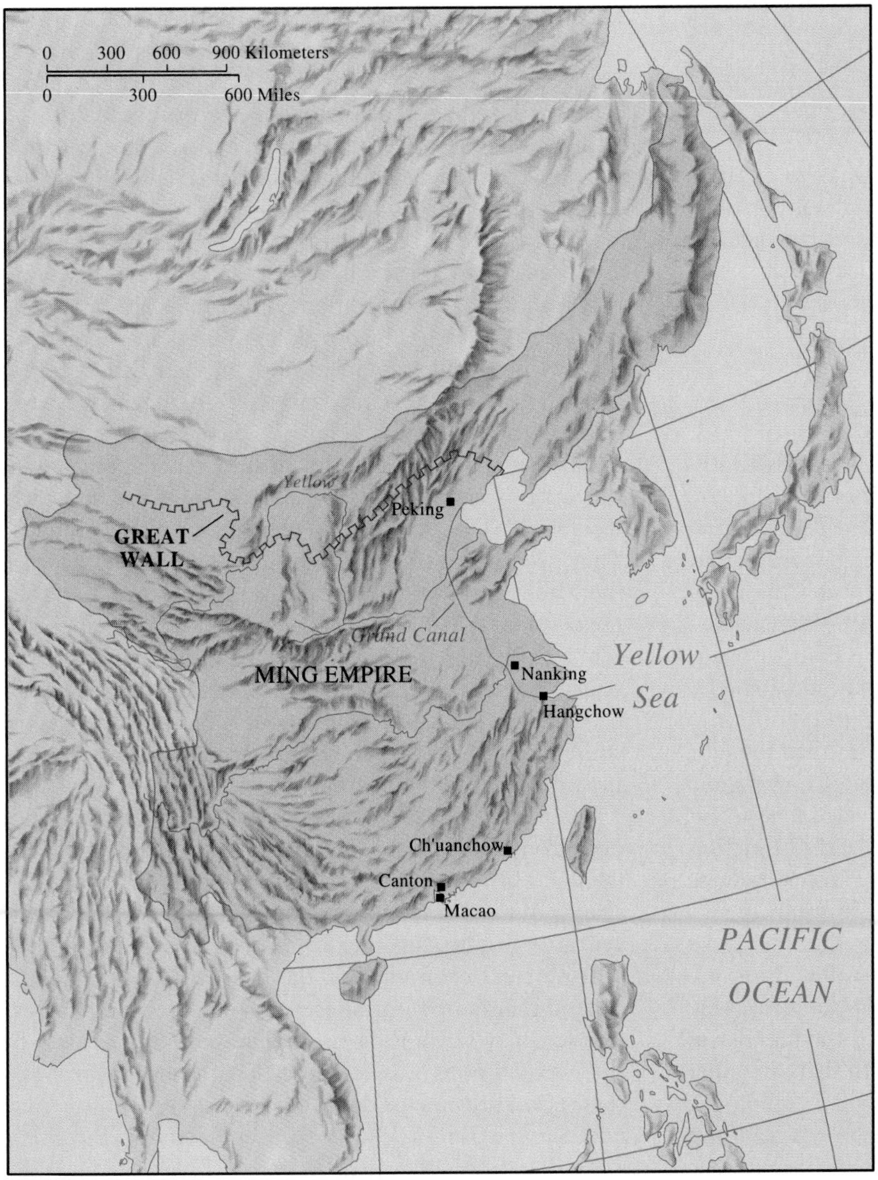

Map 10.3 The Ming Empire. The Ming dynasty ruled over all lands inhabited by Chinese people. Early Ming military campaigns and naval expeditions reestablished Chinese prestige and ensured Chinese suzerainty throughout most of the region. The northern nomads, however, continued to pose a threat, which prompted major reconstructions of sections of the Great Wall.

National Palace Museum, Taipei, Taiwan

Emperor Hung-wu, Founder of the Ming Dynasty. Chu Yuan-chang (who reigned under the name Hung-wu) was the second commoner to found a dynasty in China. His humble origin and physical ugliness (not evident in this formal portrait) contributed to his paranoia as a ruler.

Ming History

The last three decades of Mongol rule (1330s–1360s) were marked by murderous palace intrigues and by civil and military collapse. Merciless taxation, neglect of water conservation for agriculture, and natural disasters drove desperate peasants to revolt. One rebel was Chu Yuan-chang, who at age sixteen had lost both his parents and most of his relatives to drought-induced famine. To survive, he abandoned his small family farm and joined a Buddhist monastery, but the monastery, too, ran out of food, and he was reduced to beggary. Chu then joined a secret society dedicated to driving out the Mongols and distinguished himself in military action. In 1356 his forces captured Nanking, a city of great wealth and historic importance on the southern bank of the lower Yangtze River, and there he set up a rudimentary government.

In 1368 Chu proclaimed himself the Hung-wu ("Bounteous Warrior," reigned 1368–1398) Emperor and founded a dynasty called the Ming or "brilliant." He thus became the second commoner (after the founder of the Han) to rise to the Chinese throne. In that same year the last Mongol emperor fled to Mongolia, ending the Yuan dynasty. During the next fourteen years, Ming armies brought all China under control. Further, they campaigned deep into Mongolia, burnt Karakorum (Genghis Khan's capital), nearly reached the shores of Lake Baikal in present-day Russia, and ventured westward to central Asia. Not since the T'ang had Chinese arms reached so far and been so successful. Korea and states in central and Southeast Asia once again acknowledged Chinese suzerainty. Hung-wu built a wall twenty miles long and sixty feet tall around his capital at Nanking, making it the largest enclosed city in the world.

Although he had little formal education, Hung-wu was an intelligent man who clearly understood the needs of his subjects. He not only restored the pride of the Chinese but also labored to rebuild their prosperity. His character also had a dark side: he was suspicious, despotic, cruel, and increasingly paranoid in his later years, especially after the deaths of his wife and eldest son. When it was revealed after his death in 1398 that he had passed over his capable fourth son, the Prince of Yen, the experienced commander of a large army stationed near the former Yuan capital, Tatu, in favor of his eldest grandson, a youth of sixteen, China was plunged into a three-year civil war. When the Prince of Yen captured Nanking, the young emperor disappeared in the ensuing confusion (he escaped disguised as a monk; several decades later he was identified by an aged eunuch and was allowed to live out his life in obscurity).

The Prince of Yen became Emperor Yung-lo (reigned 1402–1424). A powerful general and forceful ruler, he personally led five expeditions into Mongolia and humbled the Mongols. Using a political crisis in Vietnam as pretext, his army conquered and annexed that country. His most spectacular exploits were seven huge naval expeditions led by a eunuch admiral, Cheng Ho; the expeditions were made possible by advances in shipping since the Sung dynasty, including the development of compartmentalized, water-tight ships and the magnetic compass. They proclaimed the resurgence of Chinese power under the Ming, enrolled vassal states, and promoted trade. In their wake the Ryukyu Islands, Champa, Cambodia, Siam, and states in Borneo, Java, Sumatra, Malacca, Sri Lanka, South India, and others sent tribute. Cheng also had a secret mission: to find out whether the missing young emperor had fled abroad. Never before or since has the Chinese navy attained such power.

Chinese naval dominance of the Indian Ocean lasted only from 1405 to 1433, ending as suddenly as it had begun. The expeditions sent by Emperor Yung-lo were sharply different in motive and nature from European ventures that began later in the century. Being largely self-sufficient economically, the Chinese did not seek to expand their empire or to establish colonies, naval bases, or even new trading partners. The primary purpose of these expeditions was to show the flag and display the power and prestige of the Ming empire. When it proved necessary to use force to obtain submission to the Ming

China's Brief Maritime Supremacy

The largest ocean vessel was about 500 feet in length and 211.5 feet broad. The first expedition consisted of 27,000 men and 62 large vessels, each of which carried about four or five hundred people, valuable gifts of silk, embroideries, and curiosities, as well as all the necessary provisions. . . .

The fleet set sail from Liuchia Ho on the Yangtze estuary [on a southward course. After passing] . . . the Malacca Straits it entered the Indian Ocean. Its object was to reach the country of Kuli, the present Calicut on the Malabar coast of India, which was then the focal point of all sea routes in the Indian Ocean, and held the key position between many states in Southern Asia and the Near East. . . . For some years Kuli had maintained very amicable relations with China. On account of its frequent delivery of tribute to the Ming court, Cheng Ho was authorized to entitle the chief, Sami, king of Kuli. Cheng Ho handed Sami the imperial gifts and Sami in return gave a great celebration for their visit. . . .

Two years later, the expedition sailed homeward. As the fleet passed by Chiu Kang . . . present Palembang [on Sumatra in Indonesia], it encountered the fleet of a powerful Chinese pirate named Ch'en Tsu-i who had for years been a threat to the voyagers passing the Malacca Straits. . . . After a major sea battle, Ch'en's fleet was badly defeated. More than five thousand of his crew were killed, ten of his vessels were burned, seven others damaged and Ch'en . . . was captured alive. The victory undoubtedly gave great prestige to the . . . Ming dynasty in Southern Asia.

*On their way back the whole expedition visited Java [where a civil war was raging. Cheng intervened on behalf of the rightful ruler and] . . . raised the heir of the East King to regain his kingdom. In the summer of 1407, Cheng Ho returned to Peking and reported to the Emperor.**

Cheng Ho's fleets roamed Southeast Asia and the Indian Ocean as far as East Africa, attesting to China's advanced maritime technology and its dominance of the seas. The Ming government did not establish naval bases or plant colonies, however. Later it discontinued the expeditions for political reasons; China never recaptured world naval supremacy. Portugal and Spain became the leading naval powers later in the fifteenth century.

*Kuei-sheng Chang, "Chinese Great Explorers: Their Effect upon Chinese Geographic Knowledge prior to 1600" (Diss., University of Michigan, 1955), in James P. Holoka and Jiu-Hwa L. Upshur, eds., *Lives and Times: A World History Reader,* vol. 1 (Minneapolis/St. Paul: West Publishing, 1995), p. 358.

emperor's claim of suzerainty, Cheng Ho landed troops and intervened in the affairs of numerous minor states.

The expeditions also collected strange and exotic products to flatter the emperor and entertain the court. For example, a giraffe was brought back from Africa and presented to Yung-lo with the suggestion that it was the *chi-lin* of Chinese mythology, a fabulous beast said to come down to earth when a sage ruled. The emperor welcomed the strange gift but dismissed the suggestion. The civil service opposed such extravagant and largely futile expeditions because they produced few tangible results and were commanded by eunuchs who were personal servants of the emperor and not members of the bureaucracy. After Cheng Ho's death, the officials conveniently "lost" the navigation charts. Thus China left exploration to European nations.

Yung-lo's reign was also notable for great public works projects. The silted-up Grand Canal was dredged, facilitating north-south trade and improving drainage, transport, and food distribution. The eastern section of the Great Wall was rebuilt to guard against nomad incursions. Yung-lo was anxious to leave Nanking, where unpleasant memory of his usurpation lingered, and to return to the north, where his power base lay. He therefore built Peking, near the site of the Yuan capital, which had been flattened to obliterate the hated Mongol rule from memory. Most of the great palaces and temples in Peking that survive today date from his reign. He also chose a valley near the city to build his mausoleum. Peking was a bad choice for a capital for two principal reasons. First, situated only 40 miles south of the Great Wall, it was vulnerable to attacks by nomads. Second, the capital was located on a dry, infertile plain, and the nearby region was not productive enough to support the city's population. Thus resources of the prosperous south had to be diverted to Peking.

Yung-lo's successors were mostly undistinguished and often grossly incompetent. For example the Emperor

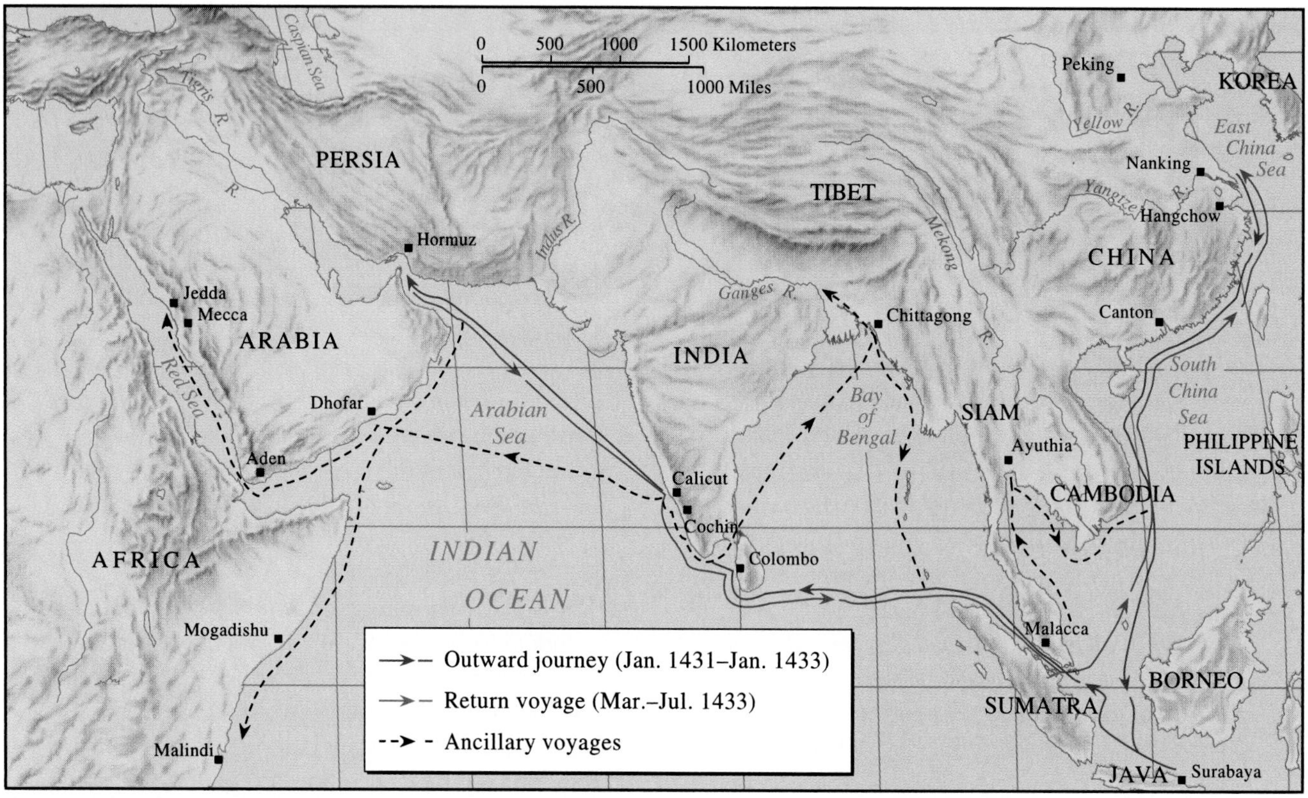

Map 10.4 Chinese Sea Voyages during the Ming Dynasty. In the early fifteenth century, large Chinese naval expeditions reached the Red Sea and East Africa. But China planted no colonies and established no naval bases in this area. After the return of the last expedition in 1433, China lost interest in overseas explorations.

Wan-li (reigned 1572–1620) ascended the throne at age eight, led a debauched life surrounded by eunuchs and palace ladies, and indulged in drinking and opium smoking. For years he avoided meeting with officials and conducted the business of government through eunuch intermediaries. By the end of his unfortunately long reign, thousands of official posts were vacant because he refused to appoint replacements. The dynasty nonetheless survived because of the strength of the bureaucracy and the durability of tested institutions. In time, however, the toll of misgovernment mounted. By the early seventeenth century, decline was all too apparent, and a natural disaster drove the disaffected peasants to revolt. Most Chinese interpreted these disasters as symptomatic of the dynasty's loss of the mandate of heaven, or authority to rule. In 1644 Peking fell to a rebel army; to avoid capture, the last Ming emperor killed his wife and daughters and committed suicide.

An Autocratic Government and a Conservative Military

Ming government was consciously patterned after that of the T'ang but was more autocratic, for several reasons. One is the disappearance of the great families of the Han and T'ang dynasties. Another is the dominance of a nonhereditary civil service, recruited through the rigorous examination system, but consisting of men with no independent power base. A third was the legacy of absolutist Mongol rule. After discovering a planned attempt by the prime minister on his life, Emperor Hung-wu abolished the office and concentrated all power in his own hands, assisted by a Grand Secretariat and various ministries in the central government. The empire was divided into fifteen provinces and subdivided into counties, which have largely survived to the present. All officials belonged to a strictly ordered bureaucracy.

Emperor Hung-wu sternly ruled over his officials and ruthlessly punished disloyalty or disobedience. Although his successors continued his autocratic practices, they discarded his unequivocal admonition that "eunuchs should not be allowed to interfere with affairs of state; death to the offender," because the rise of eunuchs to power had been traditionally associated with dynastic decline. In contrast, the usurper emperor Yung-lo executed many officials who had been loyal to his nephew. He also distrusted his relatives, who might do to his descendants what he had done to his nephew. Accordingly, he gave his relatives and in-laws honors and lavish stipends, but no political positions or power. He turned to eunuchs—for example, appointing the eunuch Cheng Ho admiral of his fleet. Most eunuchs came from poor families and were despised by officials and the people alike for their profession. In revenge, many eunuchs ruthlessly enriched themselves and when possible humiliated the officials.

Yung-lo's eunuchs served him loyally, but the self-indulgent later Ming emperors who feared criticism by the bureaucracy undercut it by entrusting authority to eunuchs and tolerating their abuses of power. A prominent eunuch who fell from power in 1510 owned coins and bullion totaling 251 million ounces of silver, twenty-four pounds of unmounted precious gems, over 7,000 pieces of precious-stone jewelry mounted in gold, 500 gold plates, two suits of armor in solid gold, and several mansions. He had amassed all this wealth in one lifetime. The power of eunuchs demoralized the civil service and contributed to the fall of the dynasty.

Despite the corruptions that eventually weakened the dynasty at the top, China was relatively well governed during this period. The greatness of the Ming dynasty was largely due to its able and dedicated bureaucracy recruited through impartial examinations, which drew the most talented men to public service.

The military constituted the largest component of the Ming government and consumed most of its revenue. In practices similar to their Ottoman contemporaries, Emperor Hung-wu allotted state land as farms to his million-plus soldiers. After the initial expense of setting up the farms, the emperor boasted that it cost the treasury nothing to maintain the army. In fact, the treasury had to allocate ever-increasing sums to subsidize an army that increased to 4 million men.

Military service became hereditary and was not esteemed. Officers' sons became officers once they passed a relatively easy examination on military techniques and rudimentary book learning. There was little innovation in military technology, particularly in firearms, during this dynasty, and China began to fall behind the West militarily. By the seventeenth century, the army was unable either to put down peasant revolts or to ward off nomadic incursions.

The Economy, Society, and Educational System

Much of China, especially the north, was ravaged and depopulated when the Ming dynasty was first established. Although early figures are only estimates, the population of China was probably around 150 million in the early thirteenth century, on the eve of the Mongol invasion of North China. By 1368 the population was reduced to about 60 million, down to the T'ang level. It recovered to approximately 100 million by 1500, and then rose steadily to around 200 million by 1600. Even more telling was the distribution of the population. Whereas numbers were about evenly divided between the north and south in the early Sung, the brutal Mongol conquest of the north and the bubonic plague (which was at least as terrible in China as in western Europe) reduced the population of the north during the Yuan dynasty to less than a quarter (some say as little as a tenth) of the land.

Emperor Hung-wu, the son of a poor farmer, was particularly solicitous of farmers. He took his heir on visits to farms to show them the farmers' hard life, once lecturing him in the following words:

> Now, you see the hard life of these people. They hardly ever leave their fields, and their hands are always on the plow. They work hard throughout the year, and hardly ever take any rest. They live in crude straw huts, their clothes are made of rough cloth, and their food consists of unrefined rice and vegetables. Nevertheless the government depends chiefly on them for revenue. I wish therefore that in your daily life you shall remember the hardships of the farmers. When you exact anything from them, be reasonable and use what you receive from them with great care, so that they may not have to suffer from hunger and cold.

Courtesy of Jiu-Hwa Upshur

Ming Dynasty Great Wall. The continuing need to defend its territory against Mongol raids led the Ming government to rebuild parts of the Great Wall. This section protected the capital city, Peking.

The Temple of Heaven. The Chinese emperor performed many ritual duties, the most important being the worship of heaven at the Temple of Heaven in Peking.

Early Ming rulers took vigorous and effective measures to repopulate the north by emancipating slaves and encouraging refugees to settle on confiscated Mongol estates as freehold farmers. They remitted taxes and provided land grants, free seeds, tools, and animals. These measures led to the reinvigoration of the economy during the first century of the dynasty. Later rulers forgot the founder's admonitions and led ever more extravagant lives that caused general economic misery.

To stimulate agricultural production, the government also undertook major projects in hydraulic engineering. It built a sea wall that protected the coast between Shanghai and Hangchow (south of the Yangtze River) to prevent floods by storm tides. Improvements in printing allowed the government to offer farmers agricultural and technical manuals that further contributed to greater productivity.

Farmers took up the cultivation of mulberries and the raising of silkworms even more than before. Silk production became widespread in all provinces, especially those south of the Yangtze River and techniques improved greatly; Nanking and Soochow were the best-known silk manufacturing centers. Women and girls were trained for raising silkworms; men, women, and children were employed in silk manufacturing. As before, Chinese silks were sought after in many lands. After the opening of direct sea trade with Europe, southern coastal cities prospered because they became the principal ports of export. Just as several different types of cotton cloth were named after Indian towns, many varieties of silk were named after their places of production in China; for example shantung, honan, and satin. Cotton cultivation and manufacture also became widespread, but unlike India, China produced cotton textiles mainly for affordable domestic consumption.

New food crops stimulated population growth. Maize, sweet potatoes, peanuts, and (despite official discouragement) tobacco were introduced from the Americas by the Spaniards via the Philippines. However, the potato, the least nutritious staple food, which became important in Europe in the eighteenth century, never became popular in China. As a result of the new foods, the late Ming Chinese were among the best-fed people in the world, consuming on average more than 2,000 calories a day in a wide variety of grains, vegetables, fish, and meats. Beneficial dietary practices, such as a preference for hot cooked foods and an insistence on drinking tea and boiled water, promoted public health and productivity.

While the population was predominantly rural, the number of town dwellers grew steadily. Peking had over 700,000 registered citizens, while Nanking and Hangchow had over a million people each. Soochow, China's most populous city, had over 2 million. Soochow and Hangchow were manufacturing and cultural centers as well as resort cities for the rich. The popular saying "Above are the Halls of Heaven; here below, Soochow and Hangchow" suggests the pleasures afforded by each of these cities. Slavery existed, but the Ming code was more humane to slaves and gave them greater protection than had the Han and T'ang codes. Prisoners of war were the major sources of slaves early in the dynasty; certain political prisoners were enslaved, and poor parents could sell their children into slavery. On numerous occasions, however, the government intervened to free children sold into slavery by poor parents or during famines.

Another indicator of prosperity was the stable currency. During the Southern Sung and Yuan dynasties inflation had undermined paper currency. Although paper money still continued to circulate and was even required for payment of certain taxes, silver became the preferred medium of exchange. Trade with Europe generated a favorable balance for China, as the Europeans paid for the goods in silver, the basis of China's currency.

Intermediate-sized manufacturing and market towns proliferated, many with over 100,000 people. Ching-te-chen was a prime example of a market town and surrounding district devoted to a single product—porcelain manufacturing. By the mid-Ming era it had a population of almost a million people and nearly 3,000 factories making porcelains that were sought after worldwide. A fifteenth-century poet described the scene created by all the burning kilns:

> Like a glowing cloud arising from a crimson city,
> it is transformed into a piece of beautiful silk; or
> like the sun arising from a violet sea, its brilliant
> rays spread all over.

Or, as a Jesuit missionary said more prosaically:

> The finest specimens of porcelain are made from clay found in the province of Kiam [Kiangsi, where Ching-te-chen is located] and these are shipped not only to every part of China but even to the remotest corners of Europe, where they are highly prized by those who appreciate elegance at their banquets rather than pompous display.

Porcelain production was highly specialized and technically advanced. Division of labor and assembly-line techniques expedited and accelerated production. For a moment China seemed on the verge of an industrial revolution, but then Chinese technology stagnated, while that of less advanced Europe caught up and forged ahead. Why China failed to make the transition to industrialism is not clear, but the explanation must lie partly in the nature of Chinese government and society, which esteemed book learning that emphasized such subjects as philosophy, literature, and history and denigrated the sciences. An abundant labor force and a moral code that disdained the profit motive and the merchant class channeled creative minds away from scientific and technological fields. The conditions that prepared western Europe for the industrial revolution will be explored in Chapter 11.

Next to textile and porcelain in importance were the metal, lacquer, and paper industries, the last supplying the needs of the growing reading public. Up to the end of the Ming, more books had been published in China than in the rest of the world combined.

In many cities and towns, many types of artisans plied their trade; some were itinerant artisans who moved from place to place. Not only did some cities specialize in certain products, but within cities shops engaged in the same business or craft grouped together. As in medieval European towns, many street names identified the trade conducted there; for example, Scissors Lane, Lane of Oil Manufacturers, and Handkerchief Lane. Nanking had forty streets and lanes named after trades and crafts.

Although officially merchants as a class ranked low in the Chinese social system, they nevertheless became very important. The growth of cities, commerce, and industry led to the development of an urban middle class of shopkeepers, wholesalers, manufacturers, and artisans with a sophisticated lifestyle. They demanded paintings and decorations for their homes and required places of pleasure and entertainment for their leisure hours. Beginning in the sixteenth century, coastal cities prospered from growing trade with Europe; from Europeans the Chinese learned to enjoy luxury items such as clocks and other mechanical devices, enameled decorative articles, and woolen textiles.

Whereas the tone of society under the Han and T'ang dynasties was aristocratic, that of the Ming was

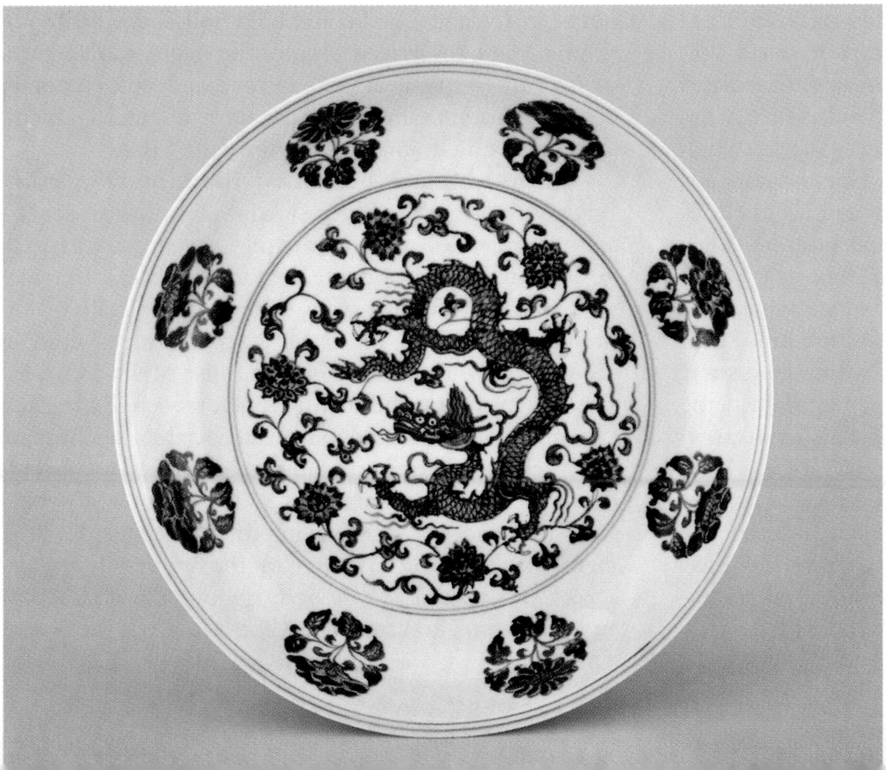

National Palace Museum, Taipei, Taiwan

Blue-and-White-Dragon-Decorated Dish. Ceramic art reached great heights under the Ming dynasty, and Ming porcelains were prized around the world. This dish, made for the Chinese court, is decorated with a dragon, symbol of royalty.

decidedly bourgeois. The growing egalitarianism or leveling of society owed in part to government policy, which deliberately favored ordinary citizens and broke up large estates. The spread of education, made possible by growing prosperity and advances in printing, favored the middle class.

Education had suffered sadly under Mongol rule. To remedy this situation, and to provide the state with a pool of well-educated talent, Hung-wu founded the most extensive public education system in premodern China. He encouraged village elementary schools, and ordered each county to maintain at least one school where the state provided financial support for some students. After matriculating, the best graduates from these schools then attended the state university in the capital city as honor students. Educational reforms particularly benefited those who lived in the prosperous south. Millions of families were able to educate their sons, who in turn could advance up the social ladder by passing the examinations.

Two years after the founding of the dynasty, Hung-wu restored and improved the examination system, which remained essentially unchanged to the end of the nineteenth century. Those who passed the county examination were called Cultivated Talents, a degree comparable to the modern B.A. Recipients of this degree were exempted from corvée labor and entitled to wear distinctive robes. Those who passed the provincial examination were called Elevated Men, a degree equivalent to the M.A., and were entitled to take the metropolitan examination. Held triennially in Peking, this examination, like all exams, required mastery of the Confucian classics. About 300 men passed the metropolitan examination each time it was administered; those who passed were further tested in the palace and ranked.

Men who passed these additional tests received a degree similar to the modern Ph.D. and were called Presented Scholars. Those with first, second, and third places acquired the status of national heroes, and their families and communities shared in their reflected glory. High scorers received appointments to the Hanlin Academy, where they perfected their scholarship and acquired familiarity with government functions and business. They were then selected to fill vacancies in important posts. Men without degrees could hold only minor administrative and clerical jobs; no civil service position in the ladder of promotion was given to anyone without a degree. While individual family fortunes rose and fell with the success of its sons, the scholar-gentry class as a group dominated society. There were no schools for girls. With society esteeming education, girls from educated families received an education at home from their mothers and teachers. Many biographies of famous men cite their mothers as their first teachers. Ming histories and biographies list many famous women painters and writers.

The examination system had both strengths and weaknesses. When Jesuit missionaries came to China in the late sixteenth century, they reported on the Chinese method of selecting officials with wonder and unconcealed admiration. After Yung-lo forbade imperial clansmen to hold positions of power, examinations served as the only recognized road to high government service, status, and social esteem; this system constantly added new blood to the corps of the elite. More than half of all doctoral degree holders throughout the dynasty came from families that had not produced any degree holders for three generations. A geographical quota system of degree holders ensured that government positions would be distributed nationally.

A major disadvantage of the system was the restrictive nature of its curriculum. It was confined to the mastery of Confucian classics, along with approved commentaries by scholars from the Sung neo-Confucian school. This narrow focus curbed individual creativity and discouraged the investigation of science and technology.

Vibrant Culture and Arts

Scholarship thrived during the peaceful centuries of Ming rule. The state officially sponsored some scholarly endeavors, especially those in historiography, the most esteemed field of study. Scholars wrote local histories and gazettes (over 1,000 have been preserved), poetry, and prose. They also produced substantial numbers of collected writings; the 1,500 that survive possess considerable literary distinction. The Ming craze for anthologies proved fortuitous, for thousands of books that otherwise might have perished were thereby preserved.

The Ming era was noted for drama. During the preceding Yuan dynasty, Chinese scholars had been forced out of government and could hold only subordinate positions. Some took to writing for the stage as a new form of expression. Drawing on history and contemporary life, they made drama a popular form of entertainment. This interest in drama persisted into the Ming.

Chinese theaters resembled those of Elizabethan England; both used a three-sided stage with no scenery, and regardless of the time the play was set, actors were gorgeously attired in contemporary costumes. For reasons of propriety casts were either entirely male or entirely female. Even today, all stage costumes used in modern theatrical production are those of the Ming period. As in many other cultures, actors were designated "mean" people and held the lowest social status. Because of actors' poor moral reputation, their sons were forbidden to sit for the examinations.

The novel was another important literary development of the Ming. Written in the mode of popular speech, it was enjoyed by both poorly educated people and scholars. The first great Ming novel was Lo Kuan-

Courtesy of Jiu-Hwa Upshur

Ruins of the First Jesuit-built Church in China. Only one side remains of the church built in the late sixteenth century in Macao by Jesuit missionaries.

chung's *The Romance of the Three Kingdoms.* Set in the waning years of the Han dynasty in the third century, it was the story of politics, war, and intrigue and is considered seven parts history and three parts fiction; it gave readers the color that formal histories lacked. Lo reputedly also wrote another novel, *All Men Are Brothers.* Its heroes are a band of men and women, who, like England's folk hero Robin Hood, were driven to banditry by corrupt government officials. Although set in the Northern Sung era, the novel undoubtedly was intended as a criticism of the corrupt government of the late Ming. Both novels have supplied plots for countless later Chinese plays and operas and remain immensely popular to the present.

The Golden Lotus, of unknown authorship, is Ming China's third great novel. Focusing on domestic life in an upper-middle-class provincial household, it is the first novel to give female characters, who are depicted with skill and sympathy, equal importance with males. The *Golden Lotus* paints an exceedingly frank picture of human relationships and offers explicit descriptions of the sexual lives of the characters.

Early Contacts with Europeans

In 1515 the Portuguese arrived at the southern Chinese port of Canton. The Ming government greeted them with the same hospitality and tolerance that earlier Chinese governments had shown to peaceful Persian, Arab, and Malay merchants. However, the violent and bigoted conduct of Portuguese sailors soon convinced Ming officials that the Portuguese were little better than pirates and should be dealt with as such. Their appearance and conduct led ordinary Chinese to call the Portuguese "devils," an epithet that was soon applied to all Europeans.

Despite their repugnance for Portuguese merchants, the Ming nevertheless desired to engage in profitable trade and formulated a plan to deal with them. In rules promulgated in 1557, the government allowed Portugal to establish a trading station at Macao, situated at the tip of the Pearl River estuary, not far from Canton but sufficiently remote from China's other major cities to make aggression difficult. As a further protection, the Chinese built a wall across the peninsula, separating Macao from the rest of China, and guarded the wall with a strong garrison.

A mutually profitable trading pattern evolved at Macao. The Portuguese eagerly purchased tea, porcelain, silks, spices, lacquerware, and other luxury items from China and shipped them to Europe. Each round trip from Lisbon required two years, a voyage so rigorous that half the crew did not live to return. Some ships were lost, but both merchants and rulers profited enormously. One Portuguese writer declared in 1541 that a piece of Chinese porcelain was worth several slaves. European royalty and aristocrats eagerly snapped up the porcelain and other luxury goods, and in time began to order specially decorated chinaware, silk embroideries, and other items from Chinese workshops.

After 1571 between thirty and forty Chinese sailing junks annually brought porcelain, silks, and other products to Spanish-controlled Manila, where they were shipped to Mexico and transferred to other ships bound for Spain. Dutch sailors, who first arrived at Macao in 1602, behaved as abominably as had the Portuguese, and the Ming government reacted by closing the entire Chinese coast to them. However, the Dutch established a base in northern Taiwan, an island outpost of Ming China. Between 1604 and 1656 more than 3 million pieces of Chinese porcelain were imported to the Netherlands by the Dutch East India Company. Neither the English nor the French played an important role in trade with Ming China.

When Catholic missionaries arrived in China, they found that the traders had given Europeans a bad reputation among the Chinese. Thus when the Jesuit Francis Xavier, who spent many years proselytizing in India, the East Indies, and Japan, arrived in China, he was denied permission to land and died on an island off Macao while waiting for a favorable ruling. In 1583 another Jesuit missionary, Matteo Ricci, received permission to build a church near Canton. Twenty years elapsed before Ricci obtained permission to proceed to Peking. Meanwhile he established a high reputation among Chinese scholar-officials as a mathematician, astronomer, cartographer, and clockmaker. Until his death in 1610, Ricci wrote treatises explaining the Christian religion in Chinese and also translated Chinese classics into Latin. He converted a number of respected officials to Catholicism.

Ricci was followed by other learned missionaries of the Jesuit order, who introduced aspects of the culture of Renaissance Europe to China. Some Jesuits served the Ming government in various nonreligious capacities in order to gain protection for their brethren who worked as missionaries in the field. In 1611 the Ming government appointed Jesuits learned in astronomy to reform China's calendar. After successfully making these reforms, one of them was named director of the prestigious Bureau of Astronomy. A late Ming observatory built in Peking by the Jesuits remains standing. Confronted by rebels, the government even prevailed on one Jesuit to cast 200 cannons for the Ming army. Having little choice, he eased his conscience by naming each piece after a saint. On the whole, the Jesuits did much to change the unfavorable view of Europeans that the sailors and merchants had created. Significantly, Chinese records refer to the missionaries as men from the western oceans and not as devils. Grateful for their services, the Ming government granted the Jesuits a piece of land outside Peking for a mission home, church, and cemetery.

The Ch'ing (Manchu) Dynasty at Its Height

On hunting expeditions, as on campaigns, one must look after the officials and men in the retinue. In hot weather, when possible [there should be] cold drinks ready by the roadside to refresh the marchers—iced water, or herbal wines, or plum cider. When it was snowing, I used to send guards officers over to the camel drovers' tents with food and charcoal, so that hot meals could be prepared for the carters who had not yet arrived, and they could rest up. . . . So planning and attention to details are essential, and the advice of the veteran commanders should always be considered. . . . For my part, I reviewed the campaign instructions of my ancestors' victories and combined them with the demands of this new campaign. . . .

Giving life to people and killing people—those are the power that the emperor has. He knows that administrative errors in government bureaus can be rectified, but that a criminal who has been executed cannot be brought back to life any more than a chopped string can be joined together again. He knows, too, that sometimes people have to be persuaded into morality by the example of an execution.

*On tours I learned about the common people's grievances by talking with them, or by accepting their petitions. In northern China I asked peasants about their officials, looked at their houses, and discussed their crops. In the South I heard pleas from a woman whose husband had been wrongfully enslaved, from a monk whose temple was falling down, and from a man who was robbed on his way to town of 200 taels of someone else's money that he had promised to invest—a complex predicament, and I had him given 40 taels in partial compensation. But if someone was attacked in an anonymous message, then I refused to take action, for we should always confront a witness directly; and if someone exaggerated too stupidly, then too I would not listen.**

*Jonathan D. Spence, *Emperor of China: Self-Portrait of K'ang-hsi* (New York: Vintage, 1975), pp. 16–18, 31, 43.

Emperor K'ang-hsi (reigned 1661–1722), the longest-ruling emperor in Chinese history and one of the greatest, wrote the above passages about war, justice, and administration. Like Louis XIV of France and Akbar of Moghul India, he inherited a shaky government, which he consolidated into a powerful, autocratic state. He bequeathed to his son the largest, most prosperous dominion of the time. A man of keen intellect, a capable general, and an indefatigable administrator, K'ang-his, in his personal qualities and rule, exemplified autocracy at its best. This was in sharp contrast with the capricious and self-indulgent rulers of the late Ming dynasty that the Ch'ing replaced.

The Consolidation of Ch'ing Rule

The Ming was overthrown and replaced by the Ch'ing dynasty in 1644. As Ming authority tottered, rebellions swept the countryside. A combination of accidental circumstances, superior organization, and effective leadership brought to power the Manchus, a nomadic people from northeastern China called Manchuria. Originally forest dwelling vassals of the Ming, the Manchus claimed descent from an earlier nomadic group, the Jurchens of the Chin dynasty that ruled North China in the twelfth century. Living in frontier communities intermixed with the Chinese, they learned agriculture and Chinese ways. Just as the Mongols had relied on the organizing and military genius of Genghis Khan, the Manchus owed their rise to the skills of Nurhachi (1559–1626), a petty chief who defeated rival nomads and proclaimed himself Khan in 1616, establishing his capital at Shenyang (later also called Mukden, which later became the secondary capital of the Manchu dynasty). His work was continued by his son, Abahai (1592–1643), who subdued Korea and conquered all Ming territories northeast of the Great Wall and all eastern Mongol tribes. In 1635 Abahai adopted the dynastic name of Ch'ing (pure) to signal his ambition to rule all China.

Although they patterned their state after the Chinese model, Nurhachi and Abahai organized the Manchus into an efficient fighting machine through the banner system, which enrolled all men for compulsory military service in one of eight banners. As non-Manchus were conquered and incorporated into the Manchu state, Manchu males were freed from the pursuit of agriculture and trade and restricted to fighting and administration in the same manner as the ancient Spartans; the conquered peoples worked their lands, as the helots had worked for the Spartans. As the Manchus expanded their power, eight Mongol and eight Chinese (Han) banners were added.

Nurhachi and Abahai adopted the traditional Chinese bureaucracy to rule their expanding state, and recruited Chinese to fill many posts. Because many Chinese admired the good discipline of the Manchu troops and recognized the Manchu leaders' keen appreciation of Chinese civilization, increasing numbers of Ming officials and officers defected to the Manchus. Thus the rise of Manchu power was clearly different from that of the Mongols.

Courtesy of Jiu-Hwa Upshur

Temple to Taiwan's Tutelary Deities. This temple to honor the local guardian deity was built in Taipei during the Ch'ing dynasty. It enjoys a constant stream of worshippers daily.

However, the Manchus became a national dynasty by accident. In 1664 rebel forces captured Peking and subjected it to a reign of terror. With the last Ming emperor dead, a loyal Ming general asked the Manchus for help in expelling the rebels, and opened the gates of the Great Wall to let their army in. Their combined armies defeated the rebels, captured Peking, and installed the son of Abahai on the throne. Manchus thus claimed to be the avengers of the last Ming emperor, whom they buried with honor, and liberators of the people. Most northern Chinese preferred the Sinicized Manchus to the rapacious and destructive rebels and accepted their rule with little resistance. However, Ming supporters in South China resisted the conquerors for several decades.

In 1661 the first Manchu ruler on the Chinese throne died while still a young man; he was succeeded by his seven-year-old son, K'ang-hsi, in part because the boy had survived smallpox, a dreaded childhood disease. One of the great sovereigns in all Chinese history, K'ang-hsi was raised by his devoted grandmother. However, until the mid-nineteenth century, no woman was permitted to act as regent, and she made no attempt to influence the government. K'ang-hsi's uncle acted as his

Emperor K'ang-hsi. This monarch enjoyed one of the longest reigns in Chinese history. The Ch'ing dynasty reached its zenith under his capable rule.

regent and wisely retained most of the Ming administration intact, weeding out the corruption.

K'ang-hsi had awesome physical and intellectual abilities. Accomplished in Chinese and Manchu, he also learned Latin, music, the sciences, and higher mathematics from his Jesuit tutors. He was a careful and decisive general and took personal charge of the campaigns to subjugate South China. In 1683 a naval expedition to Taiwan defeated the last Ming loyalist general and brought that island under Ch'ing rule. All China was now under firm Manchu grip, but two bitter campaigns in South China left southern Chinese–Manchu relations embittered throughout the dynasty.

The father of fifty-six children born to his empress and twenty-nine consorts of varying ranks, K'ang-hsi was plagued in his later years by intrigues among some twenty sons who vied for the succession. Chinese emperors had one empress at any time but could have many consorts of varying ranks. The empress was generally chosen by the parents of the reigning emperor, often in consultation with high officials. She had many ceremonial duties. Han Chinese dynasties practiced primogeniture, preferring the eldest son of the empress. Manchu custom also preferred sons born by the empress, but not necessarily the eldest one. Unlike the Ottoman and Moghul dynasties, no wars or succession plagued the Ch'ing dynasty. K'ang-hsi's final choice was his fourth son, whom he said most resembled him, who ruled as the Emperor Yung-cheng (reigned 1723–1735). Vigorous and capable, Yung-cheng worked as hard as his father. He personally led campaigns, maintained government discipline, and sternly punished corruption. Already forty-five when he ascended the throne, he had a relatively short reign.

Yung-cheng's son, the Emperor Ch'ien-lung (reigned 1735–1796), ruled for sixty years and abdicated in 1796 out of filial piety, so as not to exceed his revered grandfather's reign. Like his father and grandfather, Ch'ien-lung was an accomplished man of letters, patron of the arts, and dynamic military commander. He personally led military expeditions to the north and west, where he crushed Mongol power and brought Tibet and part of central Asia under Chinese control. In 1792 a Ch'ing army marched into Nepal, inflicting an unprecedented defeat on the Gurkhas (later renowned as warriors for the British Empire) and ensuring the submission of Nepal as a Ch'ing tributary state.

The three great early Ch'ing monarchs ruled for almost a century and half. Under them traditional Chinese civilization achieved a last great flowering, and Chinese power and prosperity overawed neighboring peoples. Prolonged peace, increased food production (including government-sponsored introduction of early-ripening strains of rice from southern Indochina), and improved public health (including widespread smallpox inoculations for children with serum from infected cows) resulted in steady population growth. By the end of the eighteenth century, China's population had reached the saturation point for a preindustrial economy. Jesuit missionary reports on the luxury and elegance of Chinese court life and the justice of their governmental system made China the model for the European Enlightenment intellectuals and made Confucius their patron saint. By the time Ch'ien-lung's reign drew to a close, however, the dynasty had passed its zenith. During the next century the Ch'ing dynasty

The Education of a Prince

[His] training began at home, under the personal direction of his father. It consisted largely of private tutorials—a confrontation between father and son. . . . Later Ch'ien-lung paid tribute to [his father] Yung-cheng's untiring and detailed direction of his studies. . . . From nine sui *[eight years] on Ch'ien-lung was a school boy. He began classes in the classics and history and later, from the age of fourteen* sui *[thirteen years] in composition. The classes were first held at home [under a] highly respected tutor. . . . With Yung-cheng's assumption of power, Ch'ien-lung's education became more intensive, more highly structured, and less isolated . . . in a Palace School for Princes [that his father had established]. . . .*

Class hours were long, from 5:00 A.M. to 4:00 P.M., and the school operated throughout the year. Only five official holidays were recognized: New Year's Day, the Dragon Boat Festival, Mid-Autumn Festival, the emperor's birthday, and the prince's own birthday. . . . Classroom procedures appear to have differed according to the needs of individual students and both individual instruction and small group study sessions were employed. The princes learned to read by rote. . . .

*None of the princes enrolled was exempted from attendance, and if the emperor learned of any inexcusable truancy he would have the culprit punished regardless of his age, marital status, or accumulated official honors. Even on days when a prince was in attendance at court he was expected to proceed to the school directly upon being relieved.**

This account of the future Emperor Ch'ien-lung's schooling (his father had not been designated crown prince when it began) shows the rigorous attention early Ch'ing rulers paid to the education of their sons. The strict training produced conscientious rulers that served the dynasty well for almost two centuries.

*Harold L. Kahn, *Monarchy in the Emperor's Eyes: Images and Reality in the Ch'ien-lung Reign* (Cambridge: Harvard University Press, 1971), pp. 116, 118–119.

rapidly declined, and China was almost destroyed by the growing power of the West.

The Manchu Government: Traditions Continued

The Ch'ing maintained the government and bureaucracy they had inherited from the Ming with a minimum of changes. They retained the three-tier examination system for recruiting scholar-bureaucrats, with its geographical quotas and educational requirements, but liberalized it to admit previously ineligible groups. Bannermen, however, were allowed to take special, less rigorous exams. The Manchus represented only about 2 percent of the population, but preferential treatment allowed them to hold 10 percent of all official appointments. Although Han Chinese officials held most provincial and county government positions, they shared positions equally with Manchus at the top levels of the central government. Statutes required that the emperor's top advisors include equal numbers of bannermen and Han Chinese, and each government ministry had dual Manchu and Han Chinese ministers and vice-ministers. This system, called dyarchy, produced a collegial form of government; it also maintained a system of checks and balances.

The Manchus enacted laws aimed at preventing their total assimilation by the Han Chinese. One law prohibited intermarriage between bannermen and Han Chinese, another stipulated that all official documents be bilingual (a written script, derived from the Mongol alphabet, was invented for writing Manchu in the early seventeenth century). Although the ban on intermarriages persisted until the last years of the dynasty, bilingualism ended once the Manchus learned Chinese. All instruction in the palace school was in Chinese by the early eighteenth century, with the result that most Manchus quickly lost facility in their own language.

The three great early Ch'ing emperors exercised power more forcefully and decisively than their weak and self-indulgent Ming predecessors. As a secretary of the Grand Council (the highest advisory body to the emperor) wrote: "Ten or more of my comrades would take

Palace Museum, Beijing

National Palace Museum, Taipei, Taiwan

Royal Favorites. Each emperor had one empress and also consorts of various ranks. On the left is a portrait of Emperor Yung-cheng's consort, painted in the Chinese manner. On the right is an oil painting of Hsiang Fei, a Turkic Muslim consort of Emperor Ch'ien-lung, dressed in European armor; this painting is attributed to the Italian Jesuit Giuseppe Castiglione.

turns every five or six days on early morning duty and even so would feel fatigued. How did the emperor do it day after day?" Such a government worked well so long as the ruler was capable and hardworking. Unfortunately, Ch'ing monarchs of the nineteenth century, like the Spanish Habsburgs, French Bourbons, and Moghuls ruling during the same period, lacked the ability that distinguished their forebears.

Because they embraced Chinese culture and values, conciliated all classes among the Chinese, and created an essentially humane and fair government, the Manchus were successful where the Mongols had failed. In contrast to the Mongols, who only cared about their luxuries for themselves, the Manchus built granaries to control famine, subsidized local schools and academies to propagate classical learning, sacrificed to local deities and heroes, bestowed honors on the aged and virtuous, and commissioned top scholars to compile the official history of the Ming dynasty. Thus early Ch'ing was one of the best periods in Chinese history.

The dynasty was ultimately sustained by its military might. The 169,000 banner forces that wrested control of China in 1644 were concentrated in the capital and its environs, in strategic spots in the northwest to prevent nomad invasions, and in key metropolitan centers. Commanding officers were drawn from the Banner aristocracy. As Manchu power grew, additional Chinese levies (around 500,000 men), called the Green Standard Army, were put on garrison duty across the land. Early Ch'ing monarchs labored to keep up the fighting spirit and readiness of the banner armies. Like their Ming predecessors, they purchased artillery from the Portuguese and put Jesuit missionaries to work casting cannons. Artillery played an important role in campaigns against the Mongols and ensured the final destruction of their nomadic power. While cannons were incorporated into

Ch'ing military strategy, Manchu troops continued to rely on archery and swords and did not adopt muskets. No advances were made in military technology in the seventeenth and eighteenth centuries, while Europeans were rapidly forging ahead, with disastrous consequences for China in the nineteenth century.

The Final Flowering of the Traditional Economy and Society

The transition from Ming to Ch'ing was the least disruptive major dynastic change in Chinese history. However, as conquering rulers, they ordered Han Chinese men to adopt Manchu hair fashion—shaving the front part of the head and wearing a long queue in the back—and to wear a tight-fitting Manchu-style robe with side slits designed originally to facilitate mounting horses (in contrast, Chinese men in Ming times had worn their long hair knotted on the crown, and had worn loose-fitting long robes). Han women, however, continued to wear their long skirts with jackets and vests, and upper-class women bound their feet, as their standard of beauty dictated (despite early Ch'ing government efforts to stop the custom), which distinguished them from Manchu women who had unbound feet and wore one-piece long dresses with side slits originally designed for riding on horseback.

Sweet potatoes, maize, and peanut, introduced during the Ming dynasty, became basic crops by the mid-Ch'ing. Rice dropped from about 70 percent of the total national staple output in the late Ming to about 36 percent in the nineteenth century. It became the staple diet of the wealthy, as sweet potatoes and maize became staples for the poor. These new crops transformed agricultural life and resulted in a population explosion, from around 150–200 million in early Ch'ing to about 450 million in the mid-nineteenth century.

Map 10.5 The Ch'ing Dynasty at Its Height. At its maximum extent, around 1775, the Ch'ing Empire controlled more lands than any other empire in Chinese history and was surrounded by vassal states from Korea to Siam (present-day Thailand).

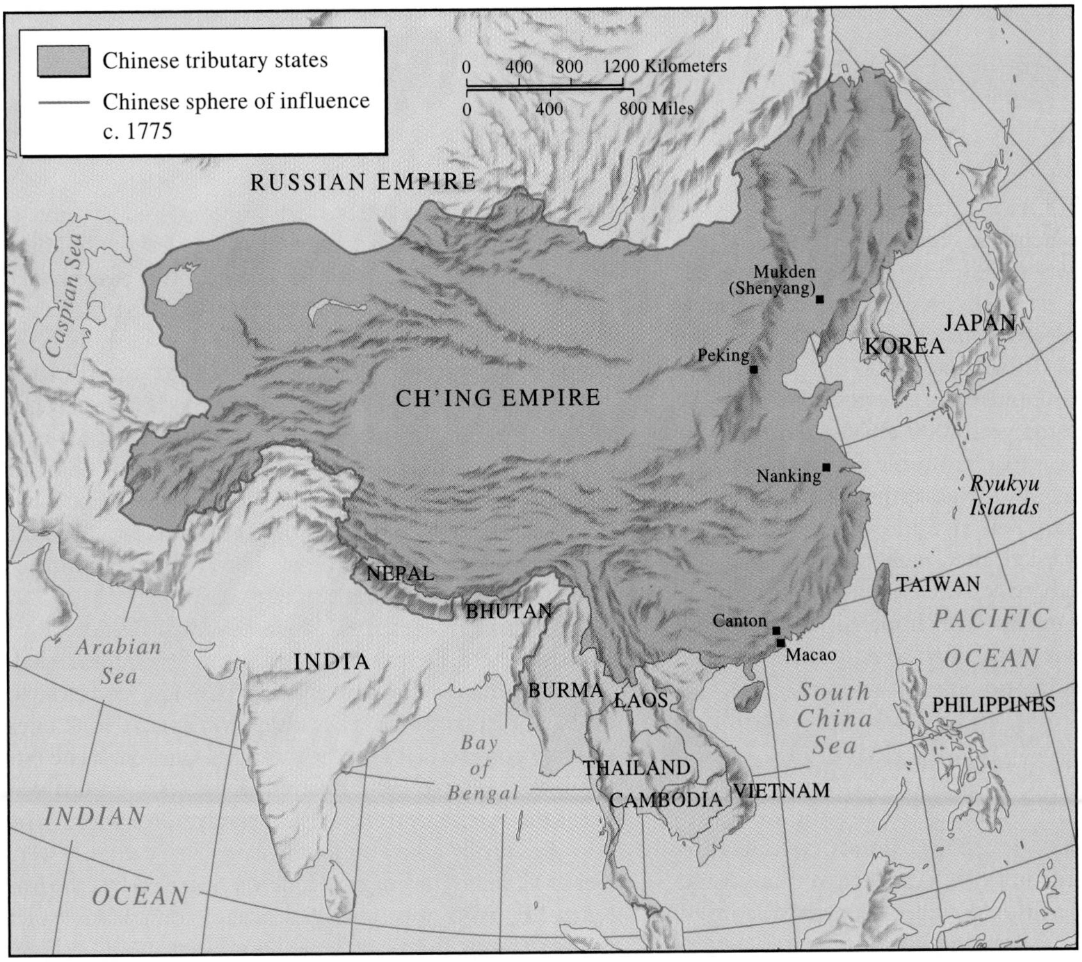

Food for an Emperor's Table

Main course dishes:
- *A dish of fat chicken, pot boiled duck, and bean curd*
- *A dish of swallows' nests and julienned smoked duck*
- *A bowl of clear soup*
- *A dish of julienned pot-boiled chicken*
- *A dish of smoked fat chicken and Chinese cabbage*
- *A dish of salted duck and pork*
- *A dish of court-style fried chicken*

Pastries:
- *A dish of bamboo-stuffed steamed dumplings*
- *A dish of rice cakes*
- *A dish of rice cake with honey*

Pickles:
- *Chinese cabbage pickled in brine*
- *Cucumber preserved in soy*
- *Pickled eggplant*

Rice:
- *Boiled rice**

This menu for Emperor Ch'ien-lung's dinner in 1754 shows the emperor ate well but not extravagantly. It was a typical good Chinese meal and demonstrates the Sinicization of the Manchus in contrast with the earlier Yuan rulers' preservation of Mongol eating habits.

Good cuisine was considered one of life's pleasures. Many cookbooks from the Ch'ing period survive, and many famous chefs left their names to their special dishes. Several regional cuisines rose to prominence, and famous restaurants and eating clubs in major cities catered to the eating fancies of the rich; some also had take-out and delivery services and rented out chefs for special occasions to clients. Small eateries and mobile snack stands were everywhere in cities and villages.

*K. C. Chang, ed. *Food in Chinese Culture* (New Haven: Yale University Press, 1977), p. 282.

Ch'ing policy prohibiting the migration of Han Chinese into Manchuria kept the region sparsely settled and much of the land virgin. Elsewhere in China, the expanding population stripped forests, plowed marginal lands, and colonized areas that had hitherto been the homes of aboriginal tribal peoples. The government failed to adjust to population growth. Whereas the county magistrate in the year 1000 governed an average of 80,000 people, he was responsible for over 250,000 in mid-Ch'ing. Inevitably, the government became more remote for the ordinary person. Similarly, the number of doctoral degrees awarded after each triennial examination did not increase between the eleventh and the nineteenth centuries; thus in late imperial China many brilliant and ambitious young men were doomed to frustration, a dangerous situation for any regime.

Missionaries, Foreign Relations, and Trade

Jesuit missionary activities, begun during the Ming dynasty, increased under the Ch'ing. Jesuits continued to head the Board of Astronomy, which forecast eclipses and issued calendars. One tutored young Emperor K'ang-hsi in Western sciences and learning. Others worked as cartographers, interpreters, court painters, and architects; several Jesuits even designed and supervised the building of a villa outside Peking for the emperor that resembled a scaled-down Versailles. Such activities won favor for their brothers who proselytized in the field. The number of Chinese converts to Christianity grew to an estimated 150,000 in the mid-seventeenth century. Jesuit successes were due in part to their acceptance of so-called Chinese rites. They allowed Chinese converts to honor Confucius and to practice ancestor worship, reasoning that they were secular rites and did not contradict monotheistic Christian beliefs. Thus Chinese converts could continue to behave as good, moral Chinese.

Christian influence in China began to decline when Franciscan and Dominican missionaries arrived and challenged Jesuit concessions allowing Chinese converts to maintain their customs. They even proclaimed that Confucius had gone to hell since he was not a Christian. The bitter dispute between the different missionary groups was called the Rites Controversy; it generated 262 books. The pope was finally called on for a ruling. Two cardinals were sent to China to investigate. One was received by emperor K'ang-hsi, who was outraged that a European leader would presume to rule on what his subjects should believe.

In 1715 the pope decided against the Jesuits and decreed that Chinese practices of honoring Confucius and ancestor worship were incompatible with Catholicism. Henceforth, all Catholic missionaries embarking for China were required to vow not to permit Chinese rites (this ban was not lifted by the Vatican until the 1930s). K'ang-hsi retaliated by drastically restricting all missionary activities and severely limiting all missionaries from entering China in the future. When the pope dissolved the Society of Jesus in 1773, two centuries of Catholic missionary activity came to an end. Of the 500 Jesuits sent to China during that time, 80 substantially contributed to cultural exchange. The Jesuits not only aided the Chinese in astronomy and calendar making but also conducted geographical explorations and compiled a detailed atlas of China, the first showing longitudes and latitudes, though they diplomatically placed China at the center of the world. Jesuit translators also provided the Chinese with European works on geometry, trigonometry, physiology, geography, and other subjects.

The Jesuits also successfully introduced Europeans to the riches of Chinese culture. In 1688 they presented the pope with translations of more than 400 Chinese works in Latin and other European languages, exposing Europeans to the riches of Chinese philosophy and literature for the first time. Great scholars and thinkers such as Spinoza, Leibnitz, Goethe, Adam Smith, Voltaire, and Diderot became admirers of Chinese culture. They were particularly impressed with the Chinese rational approach to government and of the separation of church and state. In art, the Rococo movement reflected Chinese influence: Chinese gardens became a rage (for example, Kew Garden, outside London, was built in the Chinese style) as did Chinese porcelains and artworks.

In the long run, the Jesuits were more successful in presenting Chinese civilization to the West than vice versa, for several reasons. First, as men of religion rather than the sciences, they influenced China only in those facets of European civilization to which the Chinese were receptive, such as astronomy and cartography. Second, most Chinese scholars were ethnocentric, which impeded their reception of alien cultures. Few scholar-bureaucrats could be convinced that they could learn from a culture they deemed inferior. Opportunities for those Chinese who did see profit in Western study ended with the dissolution of the Jesuit missions in the eighteenth century.

In dealing with European states, the early Ch'ing emperors shared the world view of their Ming predecessors and relied on Ming precedents in their foreign relations. They assumed Chinese cultural and diplomatic superiority, a position totally intolerable to European monarchs. The Ming dynasty had created a Reception Department in charge of its extensive network of tributaries (many had been enrolled by Cheng Ho during his naval expeditions). The Ch'ing modified the Reception Department, giving it charge of the tributaries from southern and eastern Asia, plus the Western countries, and added a Court of Colonial Affairs to deal with the peoples of Inner Asia. The latter defined the tribal territories of Mongols and other nomads, regulated their relations with the court, arranged marriage alliances between tribal chieftains and members of the imperial clan with such success that after the mid-eighteenth century, the nomads ceased to be a source of trouble.

In its trade policy, the Ch'ing government continued the Ming's quarantine that restricted the Portuguese to Macao. Canton was later opened to trade with all Western countries. Here, the government licensed a number of Chinese merchant houses and granted them a monopoly in foreign trade. Correspondingly, Western commercial companies from thirteen countries established "factories," or trading agencies, subject to Chinese regulations. Factory offices were located along the riverfront outside of Canton.

Trade steadily increased, and until the closing years of the eighteenth century, the balance remained in China's favor. Exports consisted of porcelains, tea, silks, and various handicrafts, all in great demand in the West. China's self-sufficiency and small demand for European manufactured goods limited imports to such luxuries as furs from Siberia and North America and clocks, mechanical items, and art objects from Europe. The balance was made up in silver, the basis of Chinese currency.

Anxious to gain the privilege of trade, the Portuguese and Dutch did not object to being enrolled as Chinese tributaries. Between 1655 and 1793, seventeen European missions traveled to Peking bearing tributes, and the leaders of sixteen of them performed the ritual of three kneelings and nine *kowtows* (touching the ground with one's head) before the emperor. Only the British refused to kowtow. An embassy sent by the government of King George III and led by Lord Macartney, arrived in China in 1793. Great Britain, now the major world sea power and China's main trading partner, sought to establish formal diplomatic relations and to negotiate a new and less restrictive trading agreement.

China refused to change the established mode of international relations, continued to treat the British diplomats as tribute bearers from a vassal state, and after entertaining them lavishly, sent them home empty-handed. Although sorely disappointed, the British were too involved in European wars to press the Chinese. Macartney, however, note that China was behind Europe technologically and predicted that it would be easy to defeat.

China's relations with Russia were an exception to this pattern in that the two nations treated each other as equals. Russian ambassadors performed the kowtows before the Chinese emperor, while Chinese ambassadors saluted the tsars according to Russian court protocol. Since the sixteenth century, Cossacks had spearheaded the Russian advance eastward across Siberia in pursuit of furs, especially sable. They arrived at the Amur River in northern Manchuria at the same time as the Manchus rose to power. Preoccupied with consolidating their power in China, the Ch'ing government endured Cossack raids without retaliating. After quelling a revolt in South China, K'ang-hsi turned his attention to Russian. He was anxious to come to terms with the Russians so that the yet unsubdued western Mongol tribes would not ally themselves with Russia. Two Jesuit priests acted as interpreters for the Ch'ing delegation and also as mediators between the two camps. The Treaty of Nerchinsk in 1689 and another treaty concluded in 1714 defined the boundaries between the two empires and regulated trade and other relations. These treaties were written in five languages—Chinese, Russian, Manchu, Mongol, and Latin; the Latin version served as the official text.

The Last Great Era of Traditional Culture and the Arts

Since the Ch'ing rulers admired Chinese civilization, cultural life experienced little disruption with the transfer of power from Ming to Ch'ing. Early Ch'ing emperors patronized artists and artisans, as did wealthy scholars and merchants, most notably the flamboyant millionaire salt merchants of Yangchow on the lower Yangtze River, a city noted for its eccentric artist colony and beautiful gardens.

A Floral Study. This painting on silk is one of a set of twelve by the famous eighteenth-century female painter, Yun Ping. She came from a family of noted painters, married a painter, and shared his studio. She painted in the antique academy style first developed at the Sung dynasty court. Her works were much sought after in her lifetime and commanded high prices.

Painting, considered the most important form of artistic expression, continued along the styles established since the Sung dynasty with some modifications on perspective introduced by Jesuit court painters. Just as the Moghul emperor Jahangir patronized European artists to teach Renaissance art forms to Indians, Emperor Ch'ien-lung employed Jesuit artists to introduce new techniques to the Chinese. The most notable Jesuit painter was the eighteenth-century Italian Giuseppe Castiglione (better known as an artist by his Chinese name Lang Shih-ning). Dozens of Castiglione's paintings, many documenting Emperor Ch'ien-lung's military campaigns and hunting expeditions, others portraying the monarch's favorite ladies, horses, and dogs, survive in Chinese and Western museums and private collections.

Scholarly pursuits also continued along traditional lines. Historians wrote many local histories. Scholars also made significant contributions in historiography and philology and compiled and published major dictionaries and encyclopedias. In the 1770s a government board published a monumental work called the *Complete Writings of the Four Treasuries* (classics, histories, philosophies, and belles lettres). It consisted of all major works published to date and came to 36,000 volumes. They were so expensive to print that only seven complete sets were made; fortunately, several have survived. The benefits of this monumental effort are obvious, but the Emperor Ch'ien-lung also had a dark motive for sponsoring the project—to expurgate from the collected writings derogatory mentions of the Manchus and other dynasties with nomadic origins. About 3,000 works were tampered with and some works by Ming authors were suppressed altogether.

Poets, essayists, and novelists continued to work in the Ming tradition. *The Dream of the Red Chamber* is the most noted novel of the Ch'ing. It focused on women, as did many other popular novels. The admired women in these novels are described as "literary and talented," because they studied the classics, wrote poetry, painted, and played musical instruments. Although precise figures are not available, more women received an education than in previous eras. An anthology of Ch'ing women poets made in 1831 had 933 names, while a supplement made in 1835 listed an additional 513 names. A collection of song writers had 783 female composers who wrote 22,045 songs.

The theater remained popular. Both the Peking opera and regional style operas presented historical stories and stories taken from popular novels, through a combination of singing, dancing, and acrobatics. Storytellers in tea houses in villages and towns also retold these stories. Operas were patronized by everyone from emperors to common people. Other popular modes of

LIVES AND TIMES ACROSS CULTURES

Marriage Customs in India and China

In India since medieval times, arranged marriages between children became common in well-to-do families. The bride's parents had to provide her with a dowry and to pay for the festivities, often incurring heavy debts to do so. The marriage was solemnized by a brahman priest according to the Vedas. The first part was held in the bride's parents' home when her father formally gave her to the groom, who promised not to be false to her in respect to the three goals of life—piety, wealth, or pleasure. The newly wed couple then returned to the groom's home to perform further rites. The proceedings lasted for about a week before the marriage was consummated. The solemnity of the ceremony indicated the importance, sanctity, and binding nature of marriage to Hindus. Divorces were virtually forbidden among the upper castes but were permitted by custom among the lower castes. The ideal marriage was monogamous; though rulers and some rich men took secondary wives, the senior wife was held in the highest respect.

Likewise, in China marriages were arranged by family elders, often with the help of go-betweens, and involved contracts specifying the number and value of presents from the groom's family and the bride's dowry; the husband generally managed his wife's property, but to her benefit and that of her children. The prospective bride and groom did not see each other until the wedding, generally when the couple were in their late teens. The marriage ceremony was secular in nature, and no priests officiated. On the wedding day the groom's party traveled to the bride's home to escort her to his home, where the wedding ceremony consisted of obeisance by the two before the groom's ancestral shrine and his parents, followed by feasting. The pair subsequently returned to the bride's home to pay honor to her ancestors' shrine and her parents, followed by festivities hosted by her family. As in India, the bride lived with her husband's family. Divorces were permitted, under more lenient terms when initiated by the husband, but family and societal pressure made them rare. A man could have only one legal wife at a time, but was allowed to have concubines if his financial position permitted, especially if the wife was childless.

recreation were religious and folk festivals, many of which featured distinctive foods and drinks.

The Chinese and other East Asians followed the lunar calendar and did not have a seven-day week. Thus there was no regular days of rest on Sundays. Holidays followed cycles of the moon or some other form of rotation. The most important holidays were the lunar New Year, which was celebrated for fifteen days until the first full moon of the first month and climaxed with the lantern festival. Other popular festivals were holidays to visit ancestral graves in the spring, the Dragon Boat festival on the fifth day of the fifth month, a lovers' festival on the seventh day of the seventh month, and a mid-autumn full moon festival to celebrate the harvest. Gift giving, visiting friends and families, and special foods were associated with each holiday. Some holidays were specific to a profession; for example, Confucius's birth was celebrated in schools and fishermen honored the goddess Ma-tsu of the sea. Others were local in nature. Tobacco smoking through long pipes, introduced by Westerners during the Ming dynasty, and taking snuff, a powdered tobacco, had become very prevalent among both men and women.

Families celebrated betrothals, weddings, births of children, and birthdays, especially those of old people. Social etiquette segregated upper-class men and women in most entertainments and parties. When the emperors K'ang-hsi and Ch'ien-lung celebrated their birthdays in old age, they sometimes invited old men from throughout the empire to attend an elaborate banquet at the palace where they were served by the emperors' sons and grandsons. In cities men had added opportunities of visiting pleasure quarters and being entertained by singing girls and prostitutes. Dominos, playing cards, and *mah jong* were popular gambling games. People also wagered on various contests, the most popular being cricket fights and kite flying contests.

Imperial patronage and general prosperity also led to a flowering of many minor arts, most importantly ceramics.

National Palace Museum, Taipei, Taiwan

Snuff Bottles. Tiny bottles, often beautifully decorated, held snuff, which men and women enjoyed. These three eighteenth-century examples are of painted enamel on copper, a technique introduced by Europeans (note the European figures on the center bottle).

Porcelains produced from the K'ang-hsi reign to the latter part of the eighteenth century provided a dazzling grand finale to the cavalcade of several thousand years of the Chinese potters' art. An extremely wide variety of porcelains produced in imperial and private kilns catered to the tastes of Chinese, other Asians, and Europeans. On the one hand, the craze for porcelains led to the establishment of pottery works in Europe based on information provided by the Jesuits. On the other hand, Chinese fondness for European novelties resulted in the adoption of European methods of decoration and designs in Chinese ceramics. For example, the Jesuits introduced a rose pink color in Chinese porcelain decoration. Pieces so decorated became popular from the Yung-cheng reign onward and are called "famille rose" in the West but "foreign colors" in China. Ch'ing ceramics are prized in public and private collections the world over.

Although most artisans were men, women and girls continued to be important in the textile industries. Even girls in rich households were taught to sew and embroider, which were considered feminine accomplishments. Women also helped their husbands and sons run family businesses, farm women labored alongside the men, and poor women worked as maids, nurses, and governesses and in such "women's professions" as midwifery.

A Centralized Feudal State in Japan

[In 1534] there appeared off our western shore a big ship. No one knew whence it had come. It carried a crew of over a hundred whose physical features differed from ours, and whose language was unintelligible. . . . In their hands they carried something two or three feet long . . . made of a heavy substance. . . . To use it, fill it with powder and small lead pellets. . . . Grip the object in your hand, compose your body, and close one eye, apply fire to the aperture. Then the pellet hits the target squarely. The explosion is like lightning and the report like thunder. . . . This thing with one blow can smash a mountain of silver and a wall of iron. If one sought to do mischief in another man's domain and he was touched by it, he would lose his life instantly.

Lord Tokitaka saw it and thought it was the wonder of wonders. . . . Thus, one day, Tokitaka spoke to the two alien leaders through an interpreter: "Incapable though I am, I should like to learn about it." Whereupon, the chiefs answered, also through an interpreter: "If you wish to learn about it, we shall teach you its mysteries."

*Tokitaka procured two pieces of the weapon and studied them, and with one volley of the weapon startled sixty provinces of our country. Moreover, it was he who made the iron-workers learn the method of their manufacture and made it possible for the knowledge to spread over the entire length and breadth of the country.**

*As described by Nampo Bunshi, "Teppo-ki," in *Sources of Japanese Tradition*, ed. William T. de Bary (New York: Columbia University Press, 1958), vol. 1, pp. 308–312.

This account of the introduction of firearms by Portuguese traders to Japan was recounted sixty years after the event by a descendant of the southern Japanese lord in whose domain the first Portuguese ships had landed. Japanese lords immediately appreciated the significance of firearms and widely adopted them for use

Courtesy of the Freer Gallery of Art, Smithsonian Institution, Washington, DC: Purchases F1965.23 and F1965.22

Screens Showing Europeans. Richly painted screens decorated the interiors of wealthy Japanese households; during the seventeenth century, European subjects were popular. The upper one of this pair shows curious Japanese watching Portuguese sailors and priests as they walk along a street. The lower one depicts a Portuguese ship.

against their local enemies. As a result, Japanese battle tactics and castle construction were revolutionized. Firearms also were important in the wars that unified Japan in the late sixteenth century.

Although Europeans did not attempt to conquer Japan, their success in establishing control over strategic points in Southeast Asia and the proselytizing success of Catholic missionaries in Japan inspired alarm in Japanese leaders. They feared Europeans lest they might be tempted to conquer Japan, and lest Japanese Catholic converts declare allegiance first to the pope. These fears and domestic political reasons propelled early-seventeenth-century leaders of the newly unified Japan to expel most foreigners, ban Christianity, and severely restrict the outside contacts of Japanese.

The Building of a Centralized Feudal State

The Kamakura shogunate ended in 1336. It had controlled Japan since the twelfth century, but had been fatally weakened by costly military expenditures to halt the invading Mongols. General Ashikaga Takauji established his family as hereditary shoguns in 1338. Although the Ashikaga shogunate lasted until 1573, it exerted effective central control only for a brief initial period. Then civil wars broke out between the *daimyo* (literally meaning "great name," but referring to the feudal lords; in feudal Europe and Japan only the lords and knights had surnames). The imperial court at Kyoto remained impotent.

Although the Ashikaga period was marked by a long succession of civil wars, it was also a time of rapid cultural and economic development. Increasing yields in the rice crop fueled an expanding economy. In the growing towns, specialized artisans organized in guilds similar to their counterparts in Europe, specializing in paper, textiles, metal wares, and art objects. Trade flourished, especially with China. Japan imported copper coins, books, and artworks from China and exported copper, painted folding fans, screens, and, most importantly, swords. The shogunal government, daimyo, and Buddhist monasteries

© Nicholas Krestof/NYT Pictures

Ear Mound in Kyoto. Unable to bring home the decapitated heads of their Korean victims, Hideyoshi's soldiers cut off their ears and noses, showed them off as trophies, and then buried them in ear mounds like this one in Kyoto, the imperial capital. It reputedly contains the ears of more than 40,000 victims. Several other mounds are found in daimyo domains.

all participated in a lucrative trade with China. To facilitate trade the Ashikaga shoguns acknowledged the Ming emperors as overlords and were in turn invested as "kings of Japan." Other Japanese turned to piracy, which the ineffectual shoguns were powerless to control. Cultural contact with China ensured the growing importance of Zen Buddhism, tea drinking, the tea ceremony, flower arranging, and landscape gardening.

In the midst of these civil wars, the first Europeans, with their novel firearms, arrived in Japan. The warring daimyo immediately appreciated their importance and began first to purchase and then to manufacture their own. The winning side in a battle fought in 1575 had 38,000 soldiers and 10,000 matchlocks.

The advent of firearms hastened the process of unification, led by three successive leaders. Oda Nobunaga (1534–1582), a daimyo from near Kyoto, quickly grasped the importance of learning about new weaponry from the Europeans. He treated Christian missionaries cordially, because he and others had noticed that Portuguese traders tended to land in the domain of those daimyo who were friendly toward missionaries. He also adopted firearms and other Western battle tactics, built himself a virtually impregnable fortress, destroyed his monastic and secular enemies, and ended the Ashikaga shogunate. Oda was assassinated in 1582 before he could consolidate his work.

In the chaos of the civil wars, the strict hereditary social ranks lapsed and talented men of humble birth rose to power. The rise of Hideyoshi (1536–1598) was the prime example and without precedent in Japanese history. Born in such a humble family that he had no surname, he rose to power by sheer ruthlessness and ability. Five years after Oda's death, he had consolidated power by killing Oda's young heirs and crushing all foes. After that he adopted the grand surname of Toyotomi, meaning "wealth of the nation!" Subsequently, he ordered a national land survey, assigned fiefs to his supporters, confiscated all weapons from peasants, and, ironically, fixed all people in their social positions and occupations. Ambitious for more conquests and eager to find fresh outlets for his warriors, Hideyoshi set out to conquer the world—meaning China. Before he could attempt to conquer China, however, he had first to control Korea. With an army of 150,000, he overran Korea in 1592, but then was turned back by a Ming army. With Korean "turtle ships," the world's first metal plated wooden vessels, harassing his supply line, he was forced to retreat. Hideyoshi resumed his attack in 1597, but the invasion was abandoned upon his death the following year. The horrors inflicted on Korea by the invading Japanese left a lasting scar on the victim nation. As much as a third of Korea's population may have perished as a result of the invasion.

Hideyoshi did not have a son until late in life, and had designated a nephew as his heir. When a son was finally born to him, he forced his adult nephew to commit suicide and named his son as successor. As death drew near, he appointed a council of five regents to rule on behalf of his young son. He hoped the regents would check one another's ambitions, thereby enabling the boy to escape the fate of Oda's heirs.

One of the five regents was Tokugawa Ieyasu (1542–1616), a daimyo who did not participate in the Korean campaigns and took advantage of them to expand his power. From his formidable castle at Edo (now the Emperor's palace in modern Tokyo), Tokugawa's forces won the power struggle against his rivals, and he took the title of shogun in 1603. He then killed all Hideyoshi's heirs, organized the government, and enacted new laws that ensured the survival of his family as shoguns until 1868.

To make sure that his heirs to the shogunate would have unrivaled wealth and unchallenged power, he reserved for his family one-quarter of the arable land of Japan, mainly around Edo and Kyoto, as well as all major ports. He surrounded his domains with land awarded to relatives and allies. He ordered many castles torn down and forbade the daimyo to build and even repair old ones without his permission.

Ieyasu required all daimyo to spend alternate years in residence at Edo, and in the off years to keep their principal wives and heirs at the shogun's capital. Like Louis XIV of France, he encouraged the daimyo to build splendid residences, surround themselves with large and sumptuous retinues, and live in lavish style in Edo; many became impoverished courtiers as a result. To forestall plots against the shogunal government, he created a secret service that watched for weapons and scrutinized the secret movements of daimyo wives. To ensure intellectual orthodoxy, Ieyasu encouraged Neo-Confucian studies, banned Christianity, and expelled most foreigners, thereby isolating Japan from a potentially dangerous outside world.

After Ieyasu had done all he could to make his government secure, he retired in 1605 in favor of an adult son. However, he retained the reins of government behind the scene until his death in 1616. In like manner, the second shogun retired in favor of his son. By this means, the younger man learned his job under an experienced father's tutelage. Thus the Tokugawa line was secured. Other laws ensured stability and prevented ambitious officials from seizing power from weak shoguns. As a result, Japan enjoyed two and a half centuries of peace.

Japan Becomes Isolationist

Christian missionaries made an even more powerful impact on Japan than on China. Christianity was introduced to Japan by Francis Xavier, a close friend of Ignatius Loyola, founder of the Society of Jesus. Called the "apostle of the East," Xavier was active in Japan from 1549 to 1551. To many Japanese the Christianity preached by the Jesuits seemed a variant on Buddhism. Noting the deference Portuguese merchants paid to the priests and their tendency to visit ports where missionaries were welcome, many daimyo welcomed the missionaries in order to obtain European goods, especially weapons. Some even converted to Catholicism for that reason and ordered their subjects to do likewise, in the same manner as in Europe where rulers held the power to choose their subjects' religions.

In his attempt to win more Japanese converts, Xavier left Japan for China; he believed that Japanese respect for the Chinese was so great that success in China would lead to massive conversions in Japan. As in China, the Jesuits' success roused the jealousy of the other missionary orders, notably, the Franciscans and Dominicans. By 1582 Christian missionaries had won 150,000 converts in Japan, and by 1615 perhaps as many as 500,000.

Such large numbers of converts caused a backlash among many Japanese, some because they were offended by the Christian intolerance for existing religions. Some Buddhists opposed the Christian missionaries on religious principles. Most important, many Japanese leaders equated missionary activities with the expansionist policies of European nations, and they doubted the political loyalty of Japanese converts. Thus Hideyoshi banned Christianity in 1587, but did not strictly enforced his edict. In 1612 all Japanese converts were ordered to renounce Christianity on pain of death, and European missionaries were either expelled or executed. Until 1660 numerous military expeditions searched the countryside for Christian communities, and tens of thousands were killed; as a result, only small clandestine Christian communities on Kyushu island survived.

Portrait of Tokugawa Ieyasu. This formal portrait of the elderly founder of the Tokugawa shogunate shows a still-imposing man.

Tokuawa Art Museum, Nagoya, Japan

LIVES AND TIMES ACROSS CULTURES

Determining Political Succession

Succession within the ruling family marked all dynastic rule. Although most cultures had laws regarding succession, some had no clearly defined and accepted practices.

The Moghul dynasty had no definite rules of succession among an emperor's sons by his different wives. Aging Moghul emperors were often challenged by their impatient and ambitious sons; the many revolts and civil wars over succession contributed significantly to weakening the dynasty. For example, the emperor Aurangzeb (reigned 1659–1707) successfully revolted against his father Shah Jahan, imprisoned him for the last seven years of his life, and then murdered his brothers, who had supported their father. As one historian wrote, "his life would have been a blameless one, if he had had no father to depose, no brethren to murder, and no Hindu subjects to oppress." The wars of succession and massive revolts that broke out after Aurengzeb's death ended effective Moghul power.

In China the Ming dynasty strictly followed the practice of primogeniture, and after the successful revolt by the Prince of Yen, fourth son of the founding emperor, no succession struggles marred the dynasty. The Ch'ing dynasty did not follow primogeniture and allowed the ruling emperor to chose among his sons. The nation learned of the choice of the great K'ang-hsi (reigned 1662–1722) only after his death in his final valediction: "My Fourth Son Yin-chen—Prince Yung—has a noble character and profoundly resembles me; it is definite that he has the ability to inherit the empire. Let him succeed me to the throne and become emperor."

In Japan Tokugawa Ieyasu ensured the stability of the shogunate he had founded by choosing an adult son, Hidetada, to succeed him as shogun in 1605. As Ieyasu's biographer stated: "Ieyasu accomplished two things in transferring the shogunal title to Hidetada. First, he established the principle that the shogunal title was the hereditary possession of the Tokugawa family. . . . Second, he shifted a host of tedious administrative and judgemental matters onto Hidetada's shoulders." Ieyasu lived for eleven years after the formal transfer of power. This pattern was repeated by Hidetada with his own son, by which time the line was secure.

In its zeal to isolate Japan from Europe, the Tokugawa shogunate expanded the ban on missionaries to include all Spanish, Portuguese, and English traders as well. The Dutch alone were allowed to send two ships yearly to Nagasaki, because they were not Catholics and had not attempted to convert the Japanese; however, the few Dutch who resided in Japan lived in virtual imprisonment on an offshore island. Remarkably, a small number of Japanese continued to learn Dutch and to translate Western books on mathematics, the sciences, and medicine into Japanese during the centuries of isolation. As one late-eighteenth-century Japanese said with admiration:

> In Holland . . . they consider astronomy and geography to be the most important subject of study because unless a ship's captain is well versed in these sciences it is impossible for him to sail as he chooses to all parts of the world. Moreover, the Dutch have the excellent national characteristic of investigating matters with great patience until they can get to the very bottom. For the sake of such research they have devised surveying instruments as well as telescopes and helioscopes with which to examine the sun, moon, and stars.

The isolation of Japan intensified in 1636 when an edict prohibited all Japanese from leaving Japañ and those already abroad from returning. Chinese ships were allowed to trade in Japan under license, however, and brought in limited knowledge about the West. To prevent clandestine departures, shipbuilders were allowed to construct only coastal vessels. Those Japanese already abroad were forbidden to return, the sizeable Japanese communities scattered about Southeast Asia were isolated from their homeland, and Japanese trade with Southeast Asia and Europe came to a virtual end. Western interest in Japan soon faded. As a result of this isolation, although the Japanese were as advanced as Europeans in many fields in the sixteenth century, they were well behind the West in technology and industry by the nineteenth.

Feudalism under the Tokugawa Shogunate

Economic growth continued throughout the Tokugawa era. Unlike Europe, where economic growth and political changes in the late Middle Ages had brought feudalism to an end, in Japan, the Tokugawas imposed a centralized and rigidly ordered feudal state and society after they had reunified the country. Unlike Confucian China, where the four hierarchic social classes (scholar, farmer, artisan, and merchant) were fluid and legally not hereditary, in Neo-Confucian Japan (Chu Hsi's Neo-Confucian teachings were proclaimed orthodox in Tokugawa Japan), the four classes (with the samurai replacing the scholar class) were rigidly divided and hereditary. Japanese social stratification more resembled European social classes under feudalism than Hindu castes, because in both Europe and Japan the divisions were not religiously based, as castes were under Hinduism.

Atop the social structure were the daimyo and their retainers, the samurai, who accounted for about 7 percent of the population, or 2 million people (out of a total of approximately 30 million people at the height of the shogunate, a larger proportion than the aristocracy in feudal Europe). Their incomes were measured in rice equivalents, based on assessments made on the farmers. All samurai bore surnames, lived under a strict code of honor, wore distinctive clothing, were entitled to wear two swords, and were forbidden to engage in manual labor or commerce. They congregated in castle towns of the daimyo or in Edo.

Most daimyo provided schools for educating samurai boys. Their curriculum was divided between the martial arts and the Confucian classics. There were no schools for daughters of samurai. They were taught the womanly arts, including flower arrangement, etiquette and the social graces, music, and practical matters of housekeeping by their mothers and visiting female teachers. Few women learned more than rudimentary Chinese writing; like aristocratic ladies of the Heian age, samurai women of the Tokugawa period learned to write in Kana, the Japanese syllabary form. Samurai were enjoined to be frugal and live hard Spartan lives. With the passage of time, they also took to the same leisure pursuits as townspeople, such as visiting brothels and theaters. Living on fixed incomes, many fell into debt.

Whereas in European feudal society serfs cultivated the land for aristocratic landowners and lived clustered around manors, the bulk of the Japanese were tax-paying peasants (about a quarter were tenants) living in villages and enjoying a large measure of self-government. Some richer peasants, who were descended from samurai but whose ancestors had opted to farm when Hideyoshi allowed them a choice, even bore family names. Many villages had their own schools, often associated with Buddhist temples, and literacy among peasants was high.

Rice was the primary crop, followed by other cereals such as wheat, barley, and millet. Three plants were grown for giving material for textiles: hemp for a linen-like cloth for outer clothing, cotton for daily clothes (at

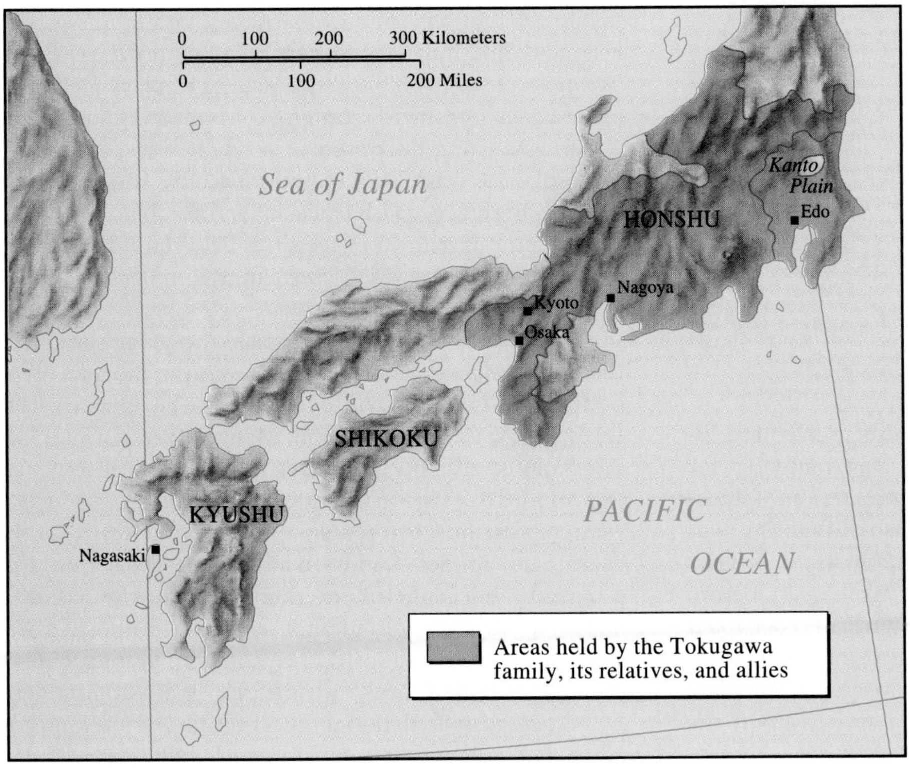

Map 10.6 Japan under the Tokugawa Shogunate. The house of Tokugawa, with its relations and allies, controlled most of the cultivatable lands and cities of Japan and devised laws that restricted the other daimyo. This ensured a period of peace for two and a half centuries.

How to Live and Die with Honor

When they were all seated in a row for final despatch, Sakon turned to the youngest and said: "Go thou first, for I wish to be sure that thou doest it right." Upon the little one's replying that, as he had never seen seppuku *performed, he would like to see his brothers do it, and then he could follow them, the older brothers smiled between their tears: "Well said, little fellow. So canst thou well boast of being our father's child." When they had placed him between them, Sakon thrust the dagger into the left side of his abdomen and said: "Look, brother! Dost thou understand now? Only don't push the dagger too far, lest thou fall back. Lean forward, rather, and keep thy knees well composed." Nicki did likewise. . . . The child looked from one to the other, and when both had expired, he calmly . . . followed the example set him on either side.**

The code of honor that governed the lives of samurai dictated that one take one's own life when necessary. This famous true story tells of two young brothers who failed in their attempt to assassinate Tokugawa Ieyasu to avenge wrongs he had inflicted on their father. They were condemned to death, but in recognition of their courage and filial piety, he commuted their sentence to suicide, or *seppuku.* Their youngest brother, only eight years old, was also sentenced to die, in accordance with Japanese tradition (were he allowed to live, he would have to avenge his brothers' deaths). This touching tale tells of how the two older brothers taught the youngest to die like a samurai.

*Inazo Nitobe, *Bushido: The Soul of Japan* (New York: Putnam, 1905), p. 121.

first imported from Korea, grown and manufactured locally after the seventeenth century), and mulberry for silkworms and the luxury silk fabrics. As in China, women were key to the textile industry. Tailoring was simple and was done by women of the household. Garments were merely tacked together, taken apart before each laundering, and resewn afterward. Preoccupied with cleanliness, families either had their own bathhouse or frequently used the communal ones. Woven straw mats covered floors, and shoes were removed upon entering the house.

Farmers paid between 40 and 60 percent of the estimated rice crop in taxes, in addition to other dues and corvée labor. Since taxes increased more slowly after the first half of the seventeenth century than did productivity (partly due to crops introduced from the Americas), so the farmers' standard of living rose.

Unlike the Chinese, who divided the family land among all sons, the eldest son inherited the paternal farm, while younger sons were forced to become farm laborers or to drift to cities. Many families practiced infanticide, euphemistically called "thinning out" (girl infants were more likely to be killed). Abortion was also practiced. In hard times farmers sold extra daughters into what amounted to slavery in the brothels. However, a girl in a brothel or entertainment house could be redeemed either by a patron, to become his wife or mistress, or by her parents. Young women who had worked in brothels or as entertainers were often in demand as wives upon returning to their villages because of their "education" and experiences in the big outside world.

Most accounts about farmers were written by unsympathetic city dwellers who depicted them as crude yokels, or by samurai who portrayed them as near-criminals bent on cheating the samurai out of their rice stipends, or as feckless people prone to rioting. Records show that there were around 1,500 peasant revolts during the Tokugawa era. Most were minor and involved local grievances or were protests against high taxes and other hardships. Leaders of failed peasant revolts were cruelly punished.

Entertainment for country people evolved around family celebrations such as marriages, community projects, and Buddhist and Shinto religious holidays. Early Tokugawa laws prohibited the staging of plays for farmers lest they become discontented from seeing luxurious upper-class living portrayed in plays. Besides, attending performances wasted their time. The law was soon relaxed, however, because it was unenforceable. Watching the sumptuous daimyo processions between Edo and the feudal domains provided free entertainment for those living en route.

Pilgrimages were very popular; the great shrine to the Sun Goddess Amaterasu at Isé was the most favored destination. It was the ambition of most Japanese to visit Isé at least once in his lifetime. Many villages formed Isé associations; all who paid dues were eligible to enter a drawing each year for a trip to the shrine. Those who went represented the whole village and returned with charms and amulets for all. In addition to the shrine, Isé provided a full range of entertainments for the pilgrim, including brothels, restaurants, *kabuki* and puppet theaters, and souvenir shops. Other popular pilgrimage destinations included a hike up the slopes of Mount Fuji.

Cities prospered during the centuries of Tokugawa peace. Edo had almost a million people by the early eigh-

Newark Museum/Art Resource

Buddhist Religious Procession. This eighteenth-century woodblock print shows many participants marching toward a Buddhist temple outside Kyoto, watched by spectators crowded on balconies. Religious festivals featuring parades, theatrical performances, and feasts provided entertainment for all.

teenth century, Osaka and Kyoto each had about 300,000. Merchants, artisans, and laborers thronged to the cities to serve the needs of the rulers and one another.

The socially lowly but economically well-off merchants dominated urban culture. Their wealth made them the objects of both envy and hate by the samurai; many samurai became indebted to merchants. Several groups of merchants were conspicuously successful, the *sake* (the ubiquitous rice wine) dealers, the rice exchangers, shippers, and pawnbrokers. Successful merchant families formed diversified business empires. The house of Mitsui, a modern giant conglomerate, had its roots in the Tokugawa period. It began with a woman and her sons who became sake merchants, pawnbrokers, and drapery shop owners. Many merchants attributed their success to frugal living and a good work ethic. One merchant house broke down the reasons for its success as follows: early rising, 10 percent; devotion to family business, 40 percent; working after hours, 16 percent; thrift, 20 percent; and good health, 14 percent. It then warned its members against:

1. Expensive food and women; silk *kimonos* every day.
2. Private carrying-chairs for wives; music or card lessons for marriageable daughters.
3. Drum lessons for sons of the house.
4. Football, miniature archery, incense appreciation, poetry contests.
5. Renovations to the house, addiction to the tea ceremony.
6. Cherry-blossom viewing, boat trips, daily baths.
7. Spending nights on the town, gambling parties, playing indoor games.
8. Lessons, for townsmen, in sword drawing and duelling. . . .
9. Sake with the evening meal, excessive pipe-smoking, unnecessary trips to Kyoto.
10. Sponsoring charity wrestling; excessive contributions to temples. . . .
11. Familiarity with actors and pleasure districts.
12. Borrowing money at more than 8 percent per month.

Despite such warnings, townspeople flocked to the kabuki theater, which featured real-life dramas, presented on revolving stages. Wealthy men went to quarters where *geisha* entertained them with witty conversation, song and dance, just as the hetaerai in Periclean Athens did. (This was the only situation in an otherwise segregated society where men and women mingled socially.)

Artisans also congregated in cities. They were organized into guilds similar to those in Medieval Europe. Boys were apprenticed to learn a craft at a young age. Apprentices lived in the homes of their masters for seven to eight years learning their trade and serving their masters with filial respect. They were expected to serve their

Werner Forman Archives/Art Resource

Swordsmith's Workshop. Swordsmiths were the most highly regarded artisans because they made weapons for the samurai. This woodblock print shows the many steps in making a sword.

masters for six months to a year after completion of their apprenticeship. Then they could become journeymen or set up independent businesses. Like their European, Indian, and Chinese counterparts, people of the same trade tended to live together in the same quarter of the town, which often bore their trade names. People of the same trade also shared a protective deity in the Buddhist or Shinto pantheon and celebrated the same festivals.

Some trades were more prestigious than others. The sword makers were among the most respected, not surprising in a warrior culture. Among workers in the same trade, those who worked for the shogun or daimyo also enjoyed greater prestige. Except for the textile industry, most trades were male preserves. Tradesmen paid taxes. Laborers such as porters and servants ranked below artisans, and were numerous in all cities and towns.

Numerous publishing houses flourished, printing a wide range of books including history, poetry, religious commentary, guide books to amusement quarters, and stories that portray characters set in contemporary Japan. Woodblock prints, called *ukiyo-e* (pictures of the floating world because Buddhism taught that the pleasures of the senses were transitory and therefore floating), depicted famous actors, beautiful geisha, and scenic spots. The prints became the popular art of the day because they were less expensive than original paintings. It was the first Japanese art form esteemed in the West and influenced late-nineteenth-century European artists. Ceramic art also flourished, initially under the impetus of Korean potters brought back by Hideyoshi's soldiers. Local potters supplied utilitarian vessels for daily needs and esthetically refined pieces for tea ceremonies.

In cities and the countryside, among all social classes, men were legally superior to women, and marriages were arranged for both parties. The bride normally went to live with her husband's family, where she was strictly subordinated to her mother-in-law; her status improved after she had born male children. A family that had no son might adopt a son-in-law into the family. In this situation, the roles were reversed. Except among the daimyo, who might have concubines, marriages were monogamous.

Strains in the Late Tokugawa Era

By the eighteenth century, changing economic, social, and cultural conditions had put the rigid political structure of the Tokugawa shogunate under stress. Even in isolation the Japanese economy had outgrown its feudal restrictions. Paper money and drafts of credit were used in business transactions, rice exchanges at Edo and Osaka quoted daily fluctuating prices, and wealthy merchants, such as the house of Mitsui, dominated commerce. The samurai and daimyo, who lived on fixed incomes calculated in measures of rice, found themselves in straitened circumstances in an increasingly affluent world, and many became indebted to merchants. Some daimyo tried such temporary and arbitrary remedies as enacting laws that canceled their debts to the politically impotent merchants. Others married their sons to rich merchants' daughters for their large dowries. Such measures, however, could not solve the fundamental economic problem, which was that the feudal restrictions had put the economy in a straitjacket.

Although the Tokugawa shoguns gave no political power to the emperors, they did treat them with greater respect and dignity than had previous shoguns and thus inadvertently raised them to the status of potential political rivals. In encouraging Neo-Confucianism with its emphasis on the study of history, the shogunate revived interest in the emperor and the cult of the monarchy. Japanese learned that the emperors had once actually

1300	Ashikaga shogunate begins in Japan
	Ming dynasty begins in China
1400	Ming capital established at Peking
	Chinese naval expeditions to South and Southeast Asia
	The Portuguese arrive in India
1500	Portuguese establish a trade empire in Southeast Asia
	Moghul conquest of India
	Guru Nanak founds Sikhism
	Portuguese establish trade with China
	The Portuguese introduce Christianity and firearms to Japan
	Akbar rules India
	Era of great Chinese opera and novels
	The Spanish rule in the Philippines
	Jesuit missionaries arrive in China
	The Dutch establish a trade empire in the East Indies
1600	Tokugawa shogunate begins in Japan
	Japan expels foreigners
	Neo-Confucianism adopted in Japan
	European trade in China restricted to Canton
	Ch'ing (Manchu) dynasty begins in China
	Taj Mahal built in India
1700	Ts'ao Hsueh-chin, *The Dream of the Red Chamber*
	Effective Moghul rule ends in India
	Christian missionary activity ends in China
	British embassy sent to China
	Great Britain acquires Ceylon
1800	Great Britain purchases Singapore

ruled, and some began to believe that they should rule again. Still others developed an interest in Shintoism.

The economic changes, social developments, and intellectual turmoil of the late Tokugawa period all point to the increasing strains to the shogunate. Japan was outgrowing its feudal constraints and was on the threshold of entering the modern age. The pervasive ferment beneath the surface calm made Japan much more receptive to change in 1853, when Western nations forced it to open, than China was in the nineteenth century.

Summary and Comparisons

This chapter looked at Asia region by region from the fourteenth to the eighteenth centuries. In the thirteenth century, much of mainland Southeast Asia came under the domination of Kubilai Khan's branch of the Mongol Empire, though the islands escaped conquest. After the fall of the Mongols, Ming China dominated many parts of the region through its preeminence on land and sea. From the sixteenth century on, island Southeast Asia, lacking any strong, unified governments, attracted European traders and empire builders drawn by its many precious raw materials and products, especially spices, and its potential as an entrepôt for trade with China. Portugal's short-lived control of strategically located ports ended in the sixteenth century, to be succeeded by the Dutch Empire based on Java. Spain colonized the Philippine islands and converted the majority of their peoples to Catholicism. Elsewhere Islam continued its peaceful conversion in Malaya and present-day Indonesia. Buddhism, too, continued to thrive.

Powerful empires ruled in India and China during the early modern era. The Moghul dynasty, with its great administrators, avid builders, and generous patrons of the arts, unified India after centuries of division. Though Muslims, many Moghul rulers allowed their majority of Hindu subjects considerable religious freedom. The empire declined rapidly in the eighteenth century, formally ending in 1857. Portuguese sailors, the first Europeans to reach India, were supplanted by the English, who eventually also replaced the Moghuls as India's ruling power.

In 1368 a Chinese-led revolt expelled the Mongols and created the Ming dynasty. The capable early Ming emperors repaired China's shattered economy, repopulated the land, and restored Chinese pride. Well-educated Ming bureaucrats gave China three centuries of stable government at home, while Ming military and naval power secured many vassal states on China's periphery.

In 1648 a frontier people, the Manchus (or Ch'ing), superseded the Ming dynasty after its long decline. Already deeply influenced by Chinese civilization, the Manchu rulers preserved earlier governmental institutions and patronized learning and the arts. As elsewhere in Asia, Portuguese sailors were the first Europeans to reach China and were eventually restricted to one port, Macao. China enjoyed a favorable balance of trade with Europe because of the appeal of luxury products like silk and porcelain. As in India, Jesuit missionaries converted few but earned deep respect as learned men and cultural ambassadors.

In Japan, after a long period of civil chaos, the Tokugawa shogunate inaugurated a centralized and bureaucratic feudal government in 1603, with the emperors remaining as impotent figureheads. Troubled by the early successes of Catholic missionaries in winning converts and the dangers of European weapons in the hands of potential dissidents, the Tokugawa shogunate banned Christianity and closed Japan to the world in the early seventeenth century. This arrested political and social development and helped to perpetuate the Tokugawa shogunate for two and half centuries.

The Moghul dynasty in India, the Ming and Ch'ing dynasties in China, and the Tokugawa shogunate in Japan all established unified, prosperous, and long-lasting regimes founded on military strength and cultural advancement. All three stimulated intellectual growth and cultural flowering. The Moghuls and Manchus were both outsiders whose language and religion differed from those of the people they conquered. However, while the Moghuls retained their Muslim faith and the Persian language, the Manchus quickly began to speak Chinese and abandoned shamanism for Buddhism and Confucianism. Thus Moghuls introduced another cultural element into India, while the Manchus continued the development of Chinese culture. By contrast, the Ming and Tokugawa were both indigenous rulers. However, the Tokugawa family was of noble lineage, while the founder of the Ming dynasty came from poor peasant stock and rose through his ability alone.

Unlike the other regions discussed in this chapter, Southeast Asia lacked political and cultural unity, having been heavily influenced by Indian and Chinese cultures. Further complexity ensued as the era progressed. China retained its political influence over parts of mainland Southeast Asia, while European nations built trading and territorial empires in the islands. In the religious realm, Islam continued its spread over the Indonesian islands and in Malaya, while Catholicism became predominant in the Philippines.

Selected Sources

Allan, John, T. W. Haig, and H. H. Dodwell. *The Cambridge Shorter History of India*. Part II: *Muslim India*. 1958. A concise and authoritative account of Muslim rule from the thirteenth century to the end of the Moghul Empire.

Allyn, John. *The 47 Ronins*. 1970. In this true story, a group of eighteenth-century samurai avenge the wrong their lord has suffered.

Babur. *Babur-Nama (Memoirs of Babur)*. Translated by Susannah Beveridge. 1922, reprinted 1970. Fascinating, frank autobiography by an empire builder, keen observer, and lover of nature.

Bernier, Françoise. *Travels in the Mogul Empire A.D. 1656–1668*. 2d ed. Translated by Irving Brock. 1968. First-hand account by a Frenchman.

Berry, Mary E. *Hideyoshi*. 1982. A biography of Japan's sixteenth-century unifier.

Beurdeley, Cecile. *Giuseppe Castiglione: A Jesuit Painter at the Court of the Chinese Emperors*. 1971. A beautifully illustrated book on Jesuit influence on Chinese art.

Boxer, C. R. *The Christian Century in Japan, 1549–1650*. 1967. On the rise and fall of Catholicism in Japan.

———. *Four Centuries of Portuguese Expansion, 1415–1825*. 1969. A comprehensive survey.

Chaudhuri, K. N. *Trade and Civilization in the Indian Ocean: An Economic History from the Rise of Islam to 1750*. 1985. Explains how the trade, religion, and cultures of many peoples influenced this region.

Cooper, Michael, ed. *They Came to Japan: An Anthology of European Reports on Japan, 1543–1640*. 1965. Interesting accounts of Japan by contemporary Europeans.

Gascoigne, Bamber. *The Great Moghuls*. 1971. Well-written text with lavish illustrations.

Grewal, F. S. *The Sikhs of the Punjab*. 1998. Traces Sikhism from its beginnings to the present.

Hall, D. G. E. *A History of South-East Asia*. 3d ed. 1968. A standard survey of the whole region.

*Huang, Ray. *1587, A Year of No Significance: The Ming Dynasty in Decline*. 1981. Using an unusual approach, Huang has crafted an engrossing book on the personality of the Emperor Wan-li and the politics of the late Ming.

Hucker, Charles O. *The Traditional Chinese State in Ming Times, 1368–1644*. 1961. A concise, clear summary.

Lall, Janardan S. *Taj Mahal and the Glory of Mughal Agra*. 1982. Wonderful color photos make this volume the next best thing to visiting Agra; well-written text.

Lane-Poole, S. *Babar*. 1957. A fine biography drawing heavily from Babur's memoirs.

*Levathes, Louise. *When China Ruled the Seas*. 1994. A lively account of the era of Chinese naval supremacy in the fifteenth century.

Michael, Franz. *The Origins of the Manchu Rule in China*. 1942. Study of the Manchus from tribal nomads to great power.

Mote, Frederck, and Denis Twitchett, eds. *The Cambridge History of China*. Vol. 7, part 1: *The Ming Dynasty, 1368–1644*. 1988. The definitive reference book on the period.

Nishiyama, Matsunosuke. *Edo Culture: Daily Life of Diversions in Urban Japan, 1600–1868*. 1997. An important work on popular culture and daily life.

Reid, Anthony. *Southeast Asia in the Age of Commerce, 1450–1688*. Vols. 1–2. An authoritative treatment of the impact of early Western trade.

*Available in paperback.

Sheldon, C. D. *The Rise of the Merchant Class in Tokugawa Japan, 1600–1868.* 1958. How the merchants rose to importance despite restrictions placed on them by a feudal government.

Shelov, J. M. *Akbar.* 1967. A fine biography.

*Spence, Jonathan. *Emperor of China: Self-Portrait of K'ang Hsi.* 1974. The life and policies of a great ruler in his own words.

*———. *The Memory Palace of Matteo Ricci.* 1984. A richly descriptive book on a great missionary and the China he worked in around 1600.

Totman, Conrad D. *Tokugawa Ieyasu: Shogun.* 1982. Good biography of the powerful founder of the last shogunate.

———. *Early Modern Japan.* 1993. A well-written history of events from the reunification of Japan to the end of the Tokugawa shogunate.

*Ts'ao Hsueh-ch'in. *The Dream of the Red Chamber.* Translated by C. C. Wang. A perennially popular love story set in a large and aristocratic eighteenth-century household in China.

Waldron, Arthur. *The Great Wall of China: From History to Myth.* 1990. Good short book on the political and strategic reasons for building the walls and how they affected the lives of Chinese and nomads.

Wu, Silas. *Passage to Power: K'ang-hsi and his Heir Apparent.* 1979. A moving book on a great monarch and his problems with his sons.

Wurtzburg, Charles E. *Raffles of the Eastern Isles.* 1954. Well-written biography of Britain's great empire builder in Asia.

Internet Links

1681: Revolt of the Three Feudatories Is Suppressed

http://campus.northpark.edu/history//WebChron/China/3Feudatories.html

A useful, brief treatment of this important event in the reign of Emperor K'ang-hsi.

Feudal Japan

http://www.wsu.edu:8000/~dee/FEUJAPAN/CONTENTS.HTM

This very detailed website, a part of the "World Cultures" project, contains information on political developments, religion, art, and music, as well as links to illustrations, bibliographies, other Internet resources, and a helpful "Glossary of Japanese Terms and Concepts."

First Battle of Panipat; Babur Rules the Whole of North India; 1526–1530: Reign of Babur

http://www.itihaas.com/medieval/babur.html

These webpages provide concise accounts of these topics in the career of Babur. An online production of "India-World."

The History of the Philippines

http://www.ualberta.ca/~vmitchel/

This site presents succinct accounts of the history of the Philippines, including "Beginnings of the Archipelago," "Discovery of the Philippines," "American Era," and "Republic of the Philippines."

Ming China: The Ming State; The Decline of the Ming

http://www.wsu.edu:8001/~dee/MING/STATE.HTM

These webpages furnish good, accurate surveys of the history of Ming China.

COMPARATIVE ESSAY 8

The Global Impact of Industrialization

The basis of the industrial revolution was the application of steam power to machinery for purposes first of production and then of transport. . . . This transformation of industrial life—which began in England in the later eighteenth century— . . . spread eastward into Europe. Its impact and repercussions varied according to the conditions and character of each country. . . . The chief way in which industrialism affected government and politics was in its conferring new wealth and power upon the growing middle class . . . and in its creation of a new industrial proletariat.

David Thomson, *Europe since Napoleon* (New York: Knopf, 1964), pp. 95–97.

A further consequence is a greed for material possessions, leading certain members of the new generation into reprehensible practices. Corrupt officials, untrustworthy doctors, dishonest engineers are all too common. . . . This generation is in many ways the first which earns its living by industry and commerce alone and which meets the expenses of contemporary life without the benefit of a private fortune: it is thus inclined to increase its profits by any means available. . . .

Abd al-Fattah Subhi Wahida, "On the Eve of the Industrial Era," in Anouar Abdel-Malek, ed., *Contemporary Arab Political Thought* (London: Zed Books, 1983), pp. 31–32.

The British historian David Thomson describes the sweeping economic and social changes—some positive, some problematic—wrought by industrialization. In contrast, the Egyptian writer Abd al-Fattah Wahida warns of the dangers that industrialization and changing economies pose to traditional societies.

Whatever one's assessment of the overall results of industrialization, there is no doubt that the Industrial Revolution ranks with the Agricultural Revolution as one of the greatest turning points in human development. The continuing progress and spread of the Industrial Revolution have been and continue to be key agents in global integration. It has fundamentally changed the mode of production from dependence on human and animal labor to machines powered by wind, water, coal, petroleum, natural gas, and more recently, nuclear energy.

As noted above, the Industrial Revolution began in the mid-eighteenth century in England, where inventors developed steam power to create cheap and ever-more efficient energy sources to increase productivity. Why did the Industrial Revolution first occur in England? The answer is that only England (later called Great Britain), and later other parts of western Europe, had the prerequisites—economic, intellectual, political, and legal—necessary to bring about the changes.

First, economic conditions: England had most of the essential raw materials for beginning an industrial revolution: abundant water that could be harnessed, coal, iron ore, and wool. It also had an adequate but not overly abundant labor supply. (Ancient Egypt, China, India, and Rome all had an abundance of labor, many of whom were forced to work for the state. This availability of cheap labor may well have smothered the incentive to invent labor-saving devices.)

Second, the intellectual climate: The Reformation of the sixteenth and seventeenth centuries also gave impetus to the scientific and intellectual revolution. In Protestant England, both the liberation of intellectual activities from the control of a restrictive church and the work ethic taught by the Calvinist-influenced Protestant church contributed to the quest for knowledge and wealth creation that fueled the Industrial Revolution. The age of the Reformation was followed by the Age of Reason that reigned in Europe during the seventeenth and eighteenth centuries. The intellectual climate of this era encouraged scientific inquiry and experimentation, which led to innovations in manufacturing and agricultural production. James Watt, a Scotsman who invented the steam engine, is an example of an inventor whose practical application of theoretical formulations led to a major industrial advance.

Other inventions revolutionized the traditional textile industry with labor-saving machines that vastly increased productivity. Improvements in farming increased food production. English farmers invented farm machinery that pioneered new methods of plowing and adopted new crops that provided a surplus food supply to feed a growing urban population. For example, "Turnip" Townsend, an English gentleman farmer, discovered that it was no longer necessary to leave a third of the fields fallow every third year. Instead, those fields could instead grow turnips without depleting the soil. Turnips were a good feed for cattle, which as a result no longer had to be slaughtered in the fall because of lack of food to tide them through the winter. This discovery improved soil management and animal husbandry and increased meat supply. These innovations enhanced productivity, reduced costs, and decreased labor needs. The surplus rural workers then migrated to cities, where they found jobs working in the new factories.

Third, political conditions: People with money are more likely to invest it in wealth-producing enterprises if the political order will protect their investment. In traditional societies where arbitrary governments could confiscate commercial profits at will, people tended to hide their money or spend it on nonproductive activities. In Great Britain and France in the eighteenth century, the governments gave support for and developed partnerships with traders in overseas commercial ventures. When the Industrial Revolution began in those countries, the governments likewise encouraged investment in industry.

In Great Britain, as a result of the Glorious Revolution of 1689 and several centuries of struggle with the crown, Parliament emerged supreme. The limiting of the powers of the monarch and the civil rights guaranteed to all Englishmen by the Bill of Rights, which the Glorious Revolution brought about, protected the people from arbitrary taxation and expropriation of their properties. These freedoms and the liberal political climate in Great Britain allowed entrepreneurs to invest in new industrial and commercial enterprises. This situation was in marked contrast to the earlier political order, which allowed fewer opportunities and guarantees for innovations and investment. The spread of constitutional government and legal protections for citizens to western European countries ensured their peoples similar freedoms, and created conditions conducive to the spread of the Industrial Revolution.

Fourth, the legal framework: Legal structures are closely connected to political conditions. Parliamentary rule and political reforms resulted in the creation—first in Great Britain, then in other European countries— of the legal framework and institutions that protected and regulated private enterprise. Modern law codes enhanced the climate conducive to private investment. In Great Britain, the law of primogeniture that gave the eldest son the bulk of the family inheritance also encouraged younger sons to enter business in order to gain enough money to enjoy the high standard of living that they were reared in but could not otherwise maintain. Younger sons from the aristocracy and gentry were thus disproportionately responsible for the enterprises that fueled the expanding economy of Britain during the Industrial Revolution.

The Industrial Revolution affected virtually all aspects of life in Europe and then around the world, transforming the technology and the economy wherever it spread. Steam energy made it possible to develop large manufacturing facilities in iron, steel, and textiles. This led manufacturers to undertake worldwide searches for the raw materials such as iron ore, coal, copper, petroleum, rubber, and cotton needed to produce a wide variety of products. Merchants sought to enlarge old markets and discover new ones for their mass-produced goods. The need for raw materials and new markets and the accelerating pace of inventions (for example, electricity, the internal combustion engine, and, later, atomic energy and the computer) provided motivation for the industrialized nations to take over territories in imperial conquests worldwide.

In addition, many of the inventions brought by the Industrial Revolution resulted in more effective and lethal weapons, making modern warfare more destructive than had been conceivable in earlier times. The fall of traditional empires and the beginning of a new global order hastened global integration and the spread of the Industrial Revolution in the late twentieth century.

Mass production lowered the price of consumer goods and enabled more people to enjoy the basic comforts of life. The Industrial Revolution and the accompanying scientific and medical advances also changed demographic patterns by lowering infant mortality rates and lengthening life spans; it has produced the population explosion that is yet unchecked in parts of the world. Industrialization also contributed to ecological problems, including air and water pollution and the destruction of rain forests and wetlands.

Cities, some so large that they are called megalopolises, developed because of the technologies generated by the Industrial Revolution. They are vastly larger than any earlier urban centers. In Great Britain, for example, whereas there was only one city with a population over 100,000 in 1700, there were thirty by World War I. Many of the new industrial cities mushroomed from villages or farmlands, changing the landscape. This process began in western Europe; it, too, spread throughout the world.

The Industrial Revolution has profoundly altered the lives of all peoples. It has made the pace of daily life more disciplined because the time clocks of the factory shift have replaced the seasonal rhythms of the farm. The problems and pressures that had always plagued urban life—crime, pollution, overcrowding—were also magnified.

Exploitation of workers in factories and in the mines and on the plantations and farms that produced the crops that supplied the industrial raw materials, was another evil that resulted from the Industrial Revolution. This problem was especially acute during the early stages of the Industrial Revolution and led to the formation of new social theories and political ideologies designed to transform governments and alter the relationship between workers and capitalists. Marxism is the best-known economic and political ideology spawned by the Industrial Revolution. It advocated violent political revolution to bring about social and economic change, and explained most historical changes as economically motivated.

The process of industrialization continues, as do the problems that remain unsolved, including the depletion of natural resources, population explosion, and pollution. Although some fear that industrialization will destroy traditional customs and values, most peoples in nonindustrialized countries still seek the economic benefits that industrially developed nations enjoy.

The West: 1600–1800

11

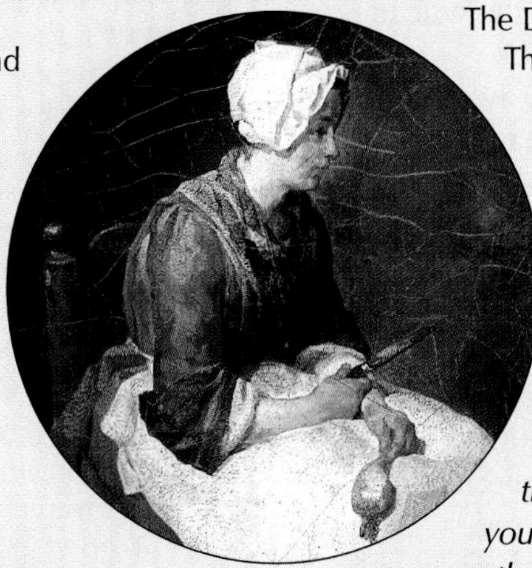

Silly, you men—so very adept
at wrongly faulting womankind,
not seeing you're alone to blame
for faults you plant in woman's mind.
After you've won by urgent plea
the right to tarnish her good name,
you still expect her to behave—
you, that coaxed her into shame.
You batter her resistance down
and then, all righteousness, proclaim
that feminine frivolity,
not your persistence, is to blame.
When it comes to bravely posturing
your witlessness must take the prize;
you're the child that makes a bogeyman,
and then recoils in fear and cries.

It's your persistent entreaties
that change her from timid to bold.
Having made her thereby naughty,
you would have her good as gold.
So where does the greater guilt lie
for a passion that should not be:
with the man who pleads out baseness
or the woman debased by his plea?
Or which is more to be blamed—
though both will have cause for chagrin:
the woman who sins for money,
*or the man who pays money to sin?**

*Sor Juana de la Cruz, "Recondillas," trans. Alan S. Trueblood, in *A Sor Juana Anthology* (Cambridge, Mass.: Harvard University Press, 1988), pp. 111–113.

These lines were written, not by a worldly-wise woman of the viceregal court in Mexico City, but by a Hieronymite nun, Sor Juana Ines de la Cruz, at the end of the seventeenth century. That a cloistered nun wrote poetry and drama may seem surprising. However, the convent was a woman's only alternative to marriage and offered a place for learning and study as well as religious devotion. An early representative of a developing feminist consciousness, Sor Juana poignantly satirized and lambasted patriarchal Spanish and Mexican society. She provides a glimpse into the structure of colonial society and the role of the church.

In the period covered in this chapter, western Europe witnessed controversy over the nature of government and the role of the sovereign. Increasingly absolutist regimes culminated in the reign of Louis XIV of France. By contrast, in Great Britain constitutional institutions flourished and became the model of government in political struggles from the late eighteenth century on. The period also saw philosophical and intellectual excitement generated by scientific discoveries and the advent of the Enlightenment intellectuals who deified reason as the arbiter of human progress. Several authoritarian monarchs in central and eastern Europe claimed they were guided by the "enlightened" dictates of reason, not tradition, in governing.

This chapter also surveys new forms of Western civilization in Latin America and British North America, especially the constitutional government of the newly independent United States of America. It concludes with the emergence of global trade relations and the onset of the Industrial Revolution.

Absolutism and Constitutionalism in Europe

To assign the right of decision to subjects and the duty of deference to sovereigns is to pervert the order of things. The head [of the nation] alone has the right to deliberate and decide, and the functions of all the other members consist only in carrying out . . . commands. . . . [In a well-run state] all eyes are fixed upon [the monarch] alone, all respects are paid to him alone, everything is hoped for from him alone; nothing is expected, nothing is done, except through him alone. His favor is regarded as the only source of all good things; men believe that they are rising in the world to the extent that they come near him or earn his esteem; all else is cringing, all else is powerless. . . . *

*Louis XIV, "Lessons in Kingship," from his *Memoirs,* trans. H. H. Rowen, in *From Absolutism to Revolution* (New York: Macmillan, 1963), pp. 26–27.

Although Louis XIV (1643–1715) of France may never have spoken the words often attributed to him, "*L'état c'est moi*" (I am the state), his principle of government, stated above, conforms to the sentiments they expressed. As previously noted (see the section on The Centralization of Western European Monarchies in Chapter 9), the so-called New Monarchs had wanted to continue the work of centralizing governments in sovereign territorial states, but were interrupted by the troubles of the fourteenth and fifteenth centuries. This process was thus concluded only in the first half of the seventeenth century, the beginning of the age of absolutism. Although absolutism first appeared in the Iberian states, France under Louis XIV produced its most admired and emulated model.

England ("Great Britain" after the 1707 union of England and Scotland) charted its own course, ultimately embracing the principles of constitutionalism under a sovereign legislature and furnishing the archetype of good government for the United States and other British possessions. This section explains the development of absolutism and constitutionalism in western Europe; a subsequent section of this chapter takes up constitutionalism in the United States.

The Foundations of Absolutism

In the early centuries of modern Europe, absolutism, at least in theory, vested ultimate power in a hereditary monarch, who claimed a God-given right to rule. In practice, however, absolutism in Europe, as in China, was seldom arbitrary. Although the monarch was not subject to any earthly authority, particularly any institution of popular representation, he had to respect the laws of God and the laws of nature.

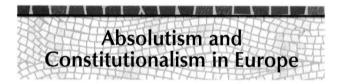

Royal absolutism drew theoretical justification from many sources, including the scriptural teaching that God sanctified the "divine right" of kings. According to this notion, a hereditary monarchy with its inference of unquestioned obedience on the part of subjects was the only divinely approved form of government. The French bishop Jacques Bossuet (1627–1704), a court appointee of Louis XIV, asserted that kings were justified in exercising absolute power because they derived that power by divine right, that is, directly from God. As God's representative on earth, the monarch's judgment was law and he was accountable to no man. According to Bossuet, whoever challenged the king was in reality challenging God Himself. Many other contemporary political theorists like Thomas Hobbes (1688–1789) of England agreed that a single, absolute authority was needed to impose order on all the people of the state. In Hobbes's view, all people are naturally selfish and ambitious, and unless restrained by strong government would engage in "war of all against all." It was also widely believed that people born to high station were inherently better equipped for ruling. Legal scholars justified royal absolutism by pointing to the example of the ancient Roman emperors.

There were also practical reasons for the success of absolute monarchies. After the century of upheavals accompanying the split in the Christian church, the public was ready to support strong leaders who could ensure order and stability. The Reformation had strengthened the monarchs by weakening or eliminating papal interference in the secular affairs of their states.

Finally, economic developments during the seventeenth century fostered the growth of royal absolutism. Absolute monarchs needed money to sustain their powerful governments; mercantilism, the prevailing economic doctrine in Europe, produced that wealth. Under mercantilism the government supervised all forms of economic activity in order to increase national wealth and thus make the state more powerful in relation to its neighbors. Governments that practiced mercantilism granted trading companies monopolies in various parts of the world, encouraged the expansion of industries and the establishment of new ones, regulated production, erected high tariff barriers on imports, and built navies to protect trade. Some countries established overseas possessions with a view to exploiting them for their benefit. Accordingly, the mother country tried to retain exclusive trading rights with its colonies as a means of acquiring cheap raw materials and assuring markets for its manufactured goods. The aim of mercantilists was to accumulate wealth, ultimately at the expense of other states.

The Eclipse of Spain

The Spanish Empire was the first European state to embrace fully the tenets of absolutism and mercantilism. Toward the end of the fifteenth century Ferdinand and Isabella had arranged the marriage of their daughter Joanna to the Habsburg Archduke Philip of Austria. The offspring of this union succeeded to the Spanish throne in 1516 and three years later became Holy Roman Emperor as Charles V. The most powerful man in Europe, Charles was the formal leader of the decentralized Holy Roman Empire and ruler over a conglomerate domain that included Castile and Aragon, Naples and Sicily, the Spanish Empire in America, Austria, Bohemia, the Free Country of Burgundy, Luxembourg, and the Netherlands.

Arriving in Spain in 1517, Charles did not endear himself to the people in the early years of his reign. Brought up in the Low Countries, he spoke no Spanish and initially installed his Flemish entourage in key government positions. The Spaniards at first regarded him as a foreign prince who taxed them to support policies in which they had no interest. In 1520 Spanish resentment against the government flared into open revolt, beginning in Toledo and spreading to other cities in Castile. By the end of 1521 the uprising had been suppressed and the monarchy was never again threatened under the Habsburgs. Although the monarchy had become absolute in theory, Charles never sought to impose a centralized imperial system lest he offend his subjects. He did his best to avoid his previous errors, respecting the traditional rights and liberties of his subjects, keeping the administration in Spanish hands and identifying himself with Spanish interests. His devotion to his duties and his robust defense of Catholicism gradually won him the loyalty of his subjects. In 1556 Charles abdicated in favor of his son Philip, to whom he bequeathed most of his empire.

Philip II (reigned 1556–1598) firmly believed in his divine right to govern Spain as an absolute ruler, accountable to no one save God. He developed an elaborate bureaucracy, but was determined to maintain close supervision over his possessions and to make all the major decisions himself. In 1580 he made good his claim to the Portuguese throne, defeating in battle his most serious rival, and uniting the Iberian peninsula under one sovereign. With Portugal's vast overseas domains added to the Spanish Empire, Philip could justly claim to rule more of the earth's surface than any previous sovereign in history. The heavy flow of precious metals, tobacco, cocoa, indigo and sugar from the Americas, to say nothing of the expanding colonial market, greatly enriched the Spanish treasury. Yet all the incoming revenue was never enough to meet the needs of the Spanish government.

A substantial part of the government's income went to pay for the cost of Philip's imperial wars. Philip's devotion to the Catholic faith influenced not only his personal conduct but his foreign policy as well. His aim was to rid the Mediterranean of infidels and wipe out the Protestant heresy wherever it existed. One of the most glorious moments of his reign occurred in 1571, when his fleet decisively defeated the Turks at Lepanto in the Gulf of Corinth. His religious crusade against the Protestants, however, was much less successful.

Philip became trapped in a quagmire when he tried to reconquer the rebellious Protestants concentrated in the northern part of the Netherlands. These Protestants had declared their independence from Spain in 1581 and formed the United Provinces of the Netherlands. They then invited a staunch Protestant, William the Silent of the House of Orange, to be their chief executive, or

Alinari/Art Resource

Philip II of Spain. Philip's regal bearing, grimness, and projecting jaw are obvious in this portrait by Titian. But Philip was short and fair, not tall and dark as he appears here.

stadtholder (his descendants still reign in the Netherlands). The Dutch developed a navy to prey on Spanish shipping and built up a merchant fleet. The fighting dragged on until 1609 when the weary combatants agreed to a truce. The United Provinces, commonly called the Dutch Republic, had won their independence. The Spanish retained control of the southern provinces (present-day Belgium).

One of Philip's major ambitions was to bring England back into the Catholic fold. He first married Queen Mary of England, the daughter of Henry VIII and Catherine of Aragon. Mary was a devout Catholic who fervently attempted to undo the Protestant course her father Henry VIII had set, but she ruled for only five years and died childless. Philip hoped to continue his influence over England by gaining the hand of Mary's half-sister and successor, Elizabeth I. However, Elizabeth rejected his marriage proposal, as she did all others. Other differences arose, particularly Elizabeth's assistance to the Dutch rebels and her support of English privateers preying on Spanish treasure ships returning from the Americas. His patience exhausted, he made plans to invade England. For that purpose he assembled about 20,000 soldiers and 130 ships, the greatest display of naval power the world had ever seen. Sailing from Lisbon, the Spanish Armada swept into the English Channel late in July 1588. Just as the smaller but faster and more maneuverable Japanese ships had wrought havoc on larger ships of the Mongol invaders, English warships inflicted heavy damage on the Spanish Armada. And just as the typhoon destroyed most of the crippled Mongol fleet, storms around the British Isles sank most of the remaining Spanish vessels. The defeat of the Armada safeguarded England from invasion and probably ensured the survival of the Dutch Republic. In more general terms, it dealt such a blow to Philip's navy that maritime leadership passed increasingly to the English. During the first half of the seventeenth century Spain would also lose its lofty position as the dominant continental power, a status that France would assume.

Philip II was followed by weak, self-indulgent rulers with little capacity for government. Since the Spanish monarchs' powers were absolute, weak rulers and poor leadership at the top paralyzed the government. Spain's faltering economy was its greatest underlying weakness, however. Spain itself had little mineral wealth and its poor soil inhibited agricultural production. In these circumstances it desperately need to develop its industries and create a balanced trade pattern, but such practical business moves clashed with the dominant Spanish nobility's notions of chivalry. In addition, Spain's century-long involvement in most European wars had severely strained the Spanish economy, which never fully recovered. Spain was thus beset by economic stagnation and government mismanagement. Only the annual arrival of treasure-laden ships from its American colonies prevented fiscal collapse.

The Pinnacle of Royal Absolutism: France under Louis XIV

In France the move toward more efficient absolutism was threatened by a religious war that lasted nearly thirty years. Despite state-sponsored persecution, Calvinism had grown steadily in France in the sixteenth century, attracting the rising middle class and nearly half the nobility, many of whom resented the centralizing tendencies of the monarchy. Although the Calvinists, nicknamed Huguenots, probably comprised no more than 12 percent of the total population, their wealth and influence made them disproportionately powerful. Distrust between Catholics and Protestants deepened, breaking out into an armed conflict in 1562. The war was fought with unusual savagery. In 1589 the Protestant leader, Henry of Navarre, proclaimed himself Henry IV (reigned 1589–1610) after his Catholic foe was assassinated. Nevertheless, the fighting continued until 1593, ending only after Henry converted to Catholicism. The next year he was officially crowned king of France, the first in the line of Bourbons. To ensure internal calm, Henry issued the Edict of Nantes in 1598, granting Huguenots freedom of worship and equal civil rights. This landmark decree was the first admission by a major European government that two religions could coexist without endangering the state. Henry spent the ensuing decade restoring royal power and rebuilding French prosperity.

The assassination of Henry IV by a religious fanatic left control of the government in the hands of his power-hungry and politically inept widow, Marie de Medici, who acted as regent for the new king, nine-year-old Louis XIII (reigned 1610–1643). The queen mother's misrule plunged the country into a new and prolonged period of disorder as greedy and ambitious courtiers and nobles exploited the state and feuded with one another. Once Louis XIII grew to manhood he threw off the domination of his mother and in 1624 made cardinal Richelieu his principal minister. With the unfailing support of the king, Richelieu pursued a twofold policy: to exalt royal authority at the expense of the nobility and to restore French prestige by undermining the Habsburgs.

Richelieu died in 1642 and Louis XIII followed him to the grave six months later. Richelieu's successor, an Italian-born cardinal named Jules Mazarin, remained in office on the accession of Louis XIV (reigned 1643–1715), then a child of five, until his own death in 1661. Mazarin carried forward Richelieu's policies of protecting the monarchical structure and waging war against the Habsburgs. But the nobility regarded him as a foreign upstart and the bourgeoisie resented the high taxes he imposed to continue the war with Spain. The upshot was a serious rebellion from 1648 to 1653. The civil war, known as the Fronde, was a last-ditch effort to reverse the drift toward an absolute monarchy. But divisions and mistrust among the Frondeur leaders doomed the uprising and left the monarchy stronger than ever by reinforcing the public's belief that only an absolute ruler could maintain peace and security. Mazarin's domestic triumph was followed by a diplomatic victory that concluded the long war with Spain and marked the end of Habsburg leadership in Europe

Louis assumed personal control of his government at Mazarin's death in 1661. The king's first public act was to summon the heads of the government departments and announce to them that henceforth he would personally take on the duties of chief minister. A profound believer in his divine right to rule, Louis saw himself as the best person to decide on the needs and interests of the state.

Louis XIV. This 1701 portrait of Louis by Hyacinthe Rigaud (1659–1743) shows the king in his later years. Pose, costume, and setting all bespeak the radiance of the Sun King, model of all absolute monarchs.

Louis was diligent and conscientious, and he was blessed with a robust constitution that enabled him to endure the most stringent of schedules. Building upon the work of Richelieu and Mazarin, Louis moved ruthlessly to crush any challenge to his authority. He expanded the duties of intendants, royal agents sent to the provinces to supervise and to direct the activities of local officials, many of whom had purchased or inherited their offices. By means of a *lettre de cachet,* an administrative order bearing the royal seal, disobedient subjects were arrested and, without benefit of a trial, were sent into exile or imprisoned indefinitely.

For Louis, religious uniformity suited his concept of absolutism—"one king, one law and one faith." In 1685 Louis revoked the Edict of Nantes, which had been the basis for religious toleration. Under pain of imprisonment or torture, some Protestants converted to Catholicism, others practiced their religion in secret, but most fled abroad, taking with them their wealth and skills as professionals and businessmen, to the detriment of France.

Influenced by painful childhood memories of the Fronde, Louis considered the aristocracy to be the greatest threat to his own despotic rule. While allowing the nobles to keep their economic and social privileges, he excluded them from the leading government offices. Instead Louis staffed his administration with educated men of middle-class background who were entirely dependent on his favor. Prominent among Louis's ministers was Jean Baptiste Colbert, controller-general of finances.

LIVES AND TIMES ACROSS CULTURES

The Pageantry of Versailles

Since his youth Louis had disliked Paris, the seat of the French monarchy, for, among other things, its narrow streets and turbulent crowds. Accordingly he decided to use his father's hunting lodge as a base on which to construct a new residence outside of Paris that would impress the world with its splendor. Work on the palace ran from 1668 till 1702, though the court moved into it in 1682. Louis employed the best talent to design and decorate the palace. Some 35,000 men worked on the royal residence, the grounds, and the canals that supplied the water for the many fountains.

The finished structure was a quarter of a mile long and could house 10,000 people. It was surrounded by acres of gardens, lakes, fountains, and more than 300 kinds of trees brought from all over France. The interior, though lacking in sanitary conveniences, radiated opulence on a grand scale, furnished as it was with mosaics, paintings, statues, and mirrors. At night, thousands of candles set in immense chandeliers or in massive candlesticks lighted the hallways or ballrooms.

From 1682 on, the king lived and worked at Versailles, isolated from his subjects, with his every whim attended to by an army of servants. Each year France's higher nobility were expected to spend time at court. Here Louis dispensed favors and occupied them in idle pursuits, thus further neutralizing them politically. The once proud nobles were reduced to contemptible parasites, frittering their lives away in intrigue and in search of pleasure. A ritual of daily ceremonies centering on the king evolved, from the moment he rose until he retired. Nobles vied with each other to hand Louis his shirt in the morning or to be allowed to hold a candlestick while he climbed into bed. Despite the superficial and stilted atmosphere of Versailles, it evoked the envy of other kings and princes of Europe, some of whom built smaller versions of the palace and tried to imitate the court life and etiquette of the "Grand Monarch."

As a mercantilist he was committed to government control and encouragement of industry. His ministry built roads and canals and regulated prices, wages, and the quality of goods. It protected French industry with high tariffs, reduced local tolls to strengthen the domestic market, and promoted France's trade with Europe and its expanding overseas empire. Colbert made no fundamental change in government finances, but by eliminating much corruption, expanding the economy, and keeping taxes high, he was able to increase revenue. Although Louis had more wealth at his disposal than his predecessors had ever dreamed of, it was never enough to meet royal expenditures for wars, building projects, and maintenance of the court.

Just as Charles V and Philip II of Spain had earlier waged wars of aggrandizement, Louis fought four wars to enhance French power between 1667 and 1713. To prevent French domination and to ensure a balance of power among the many separate states, much of the rest of Europe, led by the Dutch and the English, formed alliances to resist his ambitions. By the end of his reign Louis had added some territory to his northeastern frontier and had placed a Bourbon on the throne of Spain, but at a heavy cost in French lives and treasure.

Louis chose the sun as his emblem and called himself the "Sun King," likening himself to the sun around which everything else orbited. He moved to Versailles, where he built, at tremendous cost, a huge palace as a monument to his vanity. To extol the achievements of his reign, the king became the main patron of all the creative arts. His reign coincided with a renaissance of French culture as he established academies (for painting, sculpture, architecture, and music), in addition to subsidizing and honoring a galaxy of artists. In the second half of the seventeenth century, France produced some of the greatest poets and dramatists in its history. But government sponsorship and supervision of the arts had its negative side. Censorship was freely exercised, inhibiting the development of the artists' individuality and reducing them to adjuncts of the government, which used their works to glorify the king and the state.

As Louis was the most admired and emulated monarch in Europe, French culture had an enormous impact on the Continent. The artistic and literary styles of prominent

Giraudon/Art Resource

Royal Palace at Versailles. This 1688 painting shows the palace of Versailles as the king arrives in pomp and circumstance at the gates (bottom). Note the geometrical layout of the vast palace and its grounds.

French painters and writers were slavishly copied. French etiquette, taste, cuisine, and fashion became the fad among the elite. All educated Europeans learned French, which replaced Latin as the language of diplomatic exchange.

Classicism and the Spread of French Cultural Influences

The dominant artistic style at the start of Louis's reign was the baroque, which originated in Italy and was inspired by the Counter-Reformation. Baroque emphasized or exaggerated certain features of Renaissance art. Its artists favored massiveness, lavish decorations, bright colors, and the impression of turbulence to dazzle the spectator. The Flemish artist Peter Paul Rubens (1577–1640) was perhaps the most popular painter of his era. His compositions, marked by swirling lines, figures in intense movement, rich colors, and opulence, are masterpieces of the baroque style. The new musical form, the opera, invented by the Italian composer Claudio Monteverdi (1567–1643), clearly illustrated the baroque passion for pageantry and exaggerated emotion. The theatrical effects of baroque art harmonized the purpose of both ecclesiastical and secular authority: the former saw it as an affirmation of a revitalized Catholic church and the latter as reflecting the wealth and power of absolute monarchs.

The wife of Henry IV, Marie de Medici, had introduced the baroque style to France. It reached its apogee with the construction of the magnificent palace at Versailles. But baroque, for reasons described immediately below, did not come close to achieving the same degree of popularity in France as it did in the other Catholic countries of western Europe.

Louis XIV's insistence on order, restraint, and balance, which he presumed were ideal principles of human behavior in any age, led to the development of classicism, a new aesthetic style. French artists looked to Greek and Roman models for their order and appeal to reason, and imitated their style and subject matter. The work of Nicholas Poussin (1594–1665), a painter primarily of pastoral scenes, is explicitly in the French classical tradition with reminders of Greco-Roman architecture and the balance and order of the landscapes. The tragedian Jean Racine (1639–1699), the most famous writer in the court of Louis XIV, wrote in regular, rhythmic verse, and drew on Greco-Roman mythology for his plots. His heroes and heroines were figures of classical nobility, wrestling with the conflicting claims of duty, honor, and love (or lust). French courtiers liked to see themselves in the noble figures of Racine's plays. In contrast, the French comic playwright Jean Molière (1622–1673) used classical dramatic forms to satirize all classes of French society. His plays remain popular and continue to be produced to this day.

Classicism seemed to many to be a new kind of civilization, but, in fact, it was artificial, lacked warmth and spontaneity, and stifled freedom of expression. Nevertheless it endeared itself to the aristocracy because of its elegance and predictability. Like many aspects of French culture, classicism spread to virtually all parts of Europe.

The Rise of Constitutionalism in England

While Richelieu and Mazarin were laying the foundations of absolutism in France, England was in the grip of a constitutional crisis. The accord between parliament and the monarchy, which had been a characteristic of Tudor rule, broke down with the accession of the Stuart dynasty. A struggle ensued that gradually turned into a conflict to determine whether sovereignty should repose in parliament or the crown. The issue was settled after the Glorious Revolution of 1688 with parliament emerging as the dominant partner in government. Thereafter the monarch was limited in power and subject to control by the House of Commons, the elected house of Parliament.

England had flirted with absolutism under the strong-minded Tudors (1485–1603). But the autocratic rule of the Tudors differed considerably from the absolutism of the Bourbons in France. The Estates General (France's parliament) had only advisory powers and so lacked the means to stem absolutism. In England Parliament emerged from the Middle Ages as an integral part of the machinery of government; its consent was required to give legality to royal acts. By controlling taxation and limiting the income of the ruler, Parliament could influence royal policy.

The Tudors, however, were able to avoid parliamentary interference by finding other ways to replenish their financial resources when regular taxation proved insufficient for their needs. The Tudors were skillful rulers who usually got what they wanted without alienating public opinion or creating constitutional crises. They made no effort to supersede Parliament or flout common law. Instead they worked patiently to establish cordial relations with Parliament, consulting it on major issues, controlling its membership, and respecting the laws of the land. Their success was in no small part due to the fact that their policies coincided with the best interests of their subjects. Tudor rule was absolute, but it was also popular and constitutional.

England attained stability, greatness, and cultural maturity during the long reign of Queen Elizabeth I (reigned 1558–1603), the last of the Tudors. She dominated the English scene in the second half of the sixteenth century just as Philip did in Spain. After the country had shuttled between Protestantism and Catholicism, Elizabeth's compromise settlement of the religious issue was approved by the bulk of the English population. As reestablished, the Anglican church was Protestant in its theology, but much of its ritual and ecclesiastical organization remained Catholic in form.

Elizabeth pursued an active foreign policy and dared the vengeance of the world's strongest power. Her navy's dramatic victory over the Spanish Armada in 1588 secured England and opened the way for her country's domination of the seas. She sent an ambassador to the Moghul court in India to begin trade between the two realms, and granted a charter to the English East India Company, allowing it to monopolize trade in India and points east. She also established relations with the rulers of Russia and authorized the formation of the Muscovy Company, the first in western Europe to trade with Russia.

The Elizabethan Age was also noted for its cultural attainments. The extensive repertoire of historical plays, tragedies, and comedies of William Shakespeare (1564–1616), the greatest English writer, played in the Globe Theater in London alongside those of many other great authors. Music also flourished. English composers wrote religious music for the Protestant liturgy and secular music, to which many of Shakespeare's sonnets were sung.

Elizabeth never married, and after her death in 1603 the crown passed to her cousin, James Stuart, King of Scotland, who became James I (reigned 1603–1625) of England. James was warmly welcomed by his new subjects, but his popularity gradually evaporated. He had a better than average education, knew several languages, and was versed in theology, but, for all his learning, he lacked political wisdom. From the outset he failed to understand that the English Parliament, unlike the weak legislature of Scotland, was a strong institution with a definite role in national government. He unwisely claimed to hold by divine right powers that the Tudors had exercised only by carefully managing Parliaments. By rejecting the Tudor appearance of sharing sovereignty, he gave the impression of defying established law. Parliament retaliated by using its control of the purse strings to defy the king. A wise ruler probably could have undone the damage of James's reign, but his son and successor, Charles I (reigned 1625–1649), was inept and stubborn, so the tension between crown and Parliament continued unabated and even grew worse. In 1628 Parliament, in return for a grant of money, obtained the king's agreement to a statement known as the Petition of Right. In particular, it prohibited the king from imposing taxes without parliamentary consent and from arbitrarily imprisoning people. Like the Magna Carta of the thirteenth century, this parliamentary initiative was a landmark attempt to limit royal authority.

Charles ignored the conditions of the Petition of Right, and when Parliament protested, he dismissed it and for eleven years ruled without a Parliament. But severe religious troubles and a shortage of money forced him to reconvene it, and angry parliamentarians took advantage of his troubles to extort concession after concession. Finally,

Charles would concede no more, and following fruitless negotiations, a civil war broke out in 1642.

In the ensuing bitter struggle, parliamentary forces led by a stern parliamentary general, Oliver Cromwell, carried the day. Convicted of treason, Charles was executed in January 1649. Cromwell proceeded to establish a Commonwealth, in theory a republic but in practice a military government. England, it turned out, had merely exchanged one type of tyranny for another. Although Cromwell made England a ranking power in Europe once more, at home his conflict with Parliament and his implementation of what today would be called blue laws offended English moderates. His death in 1658 left the country without a strong leader. By 1660 the republican experiment had clearly failed and the country was eager for a change. Parliament, viewing the return of the monarchy as the only solution, invited the son of the beheaded Charles to return from exile.

The new king, Charles II (reigned 1660–1685), soon realized that absolutism was incompatible with England's national mood and therefore resorted to subterfuge and political patronage in dealing with Parliament. His use of favors and bribes to gain parliamentary support for his policies led to the development of two political groups. Those inclined to defend the Anglican church and to allow the monarchy relatively broad latitude came to be called Tories (Irish robbers) by their opponents. The other faction, derisively nicknamed Whigs (Scottish cattle thieves), favored the subordination of the crown to Parliament and religious toleration of "Dissenters," that is, non-Anglican Protestants. These factions were not yet true parties, because they did not see themselves as actually taking power and because they lacked organization and discipline.

Animosity among the different religious groups in England persisted after the Restoration and brought on another constitutional crisis. Parliament, dominated by Anglican Protestants, placed various restrictions on the rights of the Catholic minority, including barring them from public office. Charles II, who never felt secure about his position, did not reveal that he was a Catholic until he was on his deathbed, but his brother and successor James II (reigned 1685–88) practiced his Catholicism openly. Furthermore, he dismissed Parliament when it refused to repeal laws that discriminated against Catholics, appointed Catholics to high positions, and issued a Declaration of Indulgence that gave religious freedom to all religious denominations. Many thought, with some justification, that James was going to restore Catholicism as the state religion and was also out to establish an absolute monarchy.

When a son was born to James's Catholic wife, the prospect of a Catholic dynasty galvanized parliamentary leaders of both factions to offer the throne to Mary, James' daughter by a previous marriage, who was a

British Museum

The Execution of Charles I, January 30, 1649. In an age of absolute monarchy, the execution of the English king stunned Europeans. But Charles's refusal to accept the sovereignty of parliament left Cromwell little choice. Charles was condemned to death on the fifth day of his trial. His courage in the face of death evoked widespread admiration and somewhat mitigated his misdeeds.

Protestant. Mary accepted after parliament agreed to make her husband, William of Orange, chief magistrate of the Dutch Republic, her co-ruler. In 1688 William and a small expeditionary force landed in southwest England and moved slowly toward London, gathering support along the way. In panic, James and his family fled to France.

The Triumph of Parliament

The essentially nonviolent events of 1688, known as the Glorious Revolution, marked the final stage of Parliament's triumph over the monarchy. By assuming the authority to depose and appoint monarchs, Parliament had dealt a powerful blow to the concept of the divine right of kings.

Further developments consolidated Parliament's position. Early in 1689 William III (reigned 1689–1702) and Mary II (reigned 1689–1694) jointly accepted the throne from Parliament on terms later embodied in the Bill of Rights. This important document asserted and extended the civil rights of the English people and laid down the principles of parliamentary supremacy. Another law granted freedom of worship to non-Anglican Protestants and marked the first step toward religious toleration in England.

Mary had no children, and those of her sister and successor Queen Anne (reigned 1702–1714) had died young, a situation that prompted Parliament to provide in advance for a peaceful, Protestant succession. The 1701 Act of Settlement barred James II's Catholic descendants from the throne and specified that royal succession should ultimately pass to Anne's Protestant relatives, the rulers of the German state of Hanover. As it happened, this was the

The Bill of Rights

And thereupon the said lords spiritual and temporal and Commons . . . for the vindication and assertion of their ancient rights and liberties declare:

1. The pretended power of suspending laws, or the execution of laws, by regal authority, without consent of parliament, is illegal.

2. That the pretended power of dispensing with laws, or the execution of laws, by regal authority, as it hath been assumed and executed, is illegal. . . .

4. The levying money for or to the use of the Crown by pretense of prerogative, without grant of parliament, for longer time or in other manner than the same is or shall be granted, is illegal.

5. That the right of the subjects to petition the king, and all commitments and persecutions for such petitioning are illegal.

6. That the raising or keeping a standing army within the kingdom in time of peace, unless it be with consent of parliament, is against law.

7. That the subjects which are Protestants may have arms for their defense suitable to their conditions, and as allowed by law.

8. That elections of members of parliament ought to be free.

9. That the freedoms of speech, and debates or proceedings in parliament, ought not to be impeached or questioned in any court or place out of parliament.

10. That excessive bail ought not to be required, nor excessive fines imposed nor cruel and unusual punishments inflicted. . . .

13. And that for redress of all grievances, and for the amending, strengthening, and preserving of the laws, parliament ought to be held frequently.

*The said lords spiritual and temporal, and commons assembled at Westminster, do resolve that William and Mary, prince and princess of Orange, be, and be declared, king and queen of England, France, and Ireland, and the dominions thereunto belonging, to hold the crown and royal dignity of the said kingdom and dominions to them and the said prince and princess during their lives.**

Like the Magna Carta, the Bill of Rights was largely specific and negative and did not deal in broad generalities of political theory. Nevertheless, the Bill established the essential principles underlying limited monarchy and remains the closest thing to a formal constitution that the British people have. It also served as an inspiration for republican government. The first ten amendments of the U.S. Constitution (1791) and much of the French Declaration of the Rights of Man (1789) owe a debt to the English declaration of 1689.

*Edward P Cheyney, *Readings in English History* (Boston: Ginn, 1922), pp. 545–547.

last artificial change in the succession of the British monarchy; the descendants of the House of Hanover have reigned to the present. Two events during Queen Anne's reign need to be mentioned. She was the last sovereign to veto an act of Parliament; and in 1707 Parliament passed the Act of Union that joined England and Scotland, creating the Kingdom of Great Britain.

During the half century following the Glorious Revolution, special circumstances influenced the evolution of the relationship between the still influential sovereigns and the newly powerful Parliament. A cabinet of ministers developed from the old privy council of high officials chosen by the king to advise him on policy. Beginning with William III, monarchs began to choose ministers from the party that controlled a majority in the House of Commons. Both William and Anne were powerful sovereigns, appointing and dismissing ministers and actively participating in cabinet meetings.

The accession of the Hanoverians to the British throne put control of the cabinet into the hands of Parliament. George I (reigned 1714–1727) and George II (reigned 1727–1760) were not very interested in English affairs and rarely attended cabinet meetings. In their absence Sir Robert Walpole, the most influential minister between 1721 and 1742, began to chair cabinet meetings and to act as intermediary between the king and cabinet. Thus he became the first (prime) minister, although the title of prime minister did not become official until later. Thereafter, it became traditional for the monarch to appoint as head of the cabinet the acknowledged leader of the strongest party in the House of Commons. In this way, although the cabinet ruled in the monarch's name, its policies were subject to the approval of Parliament. Walpole resigned when he was defeated in Parliament in 1742. His action established the principle, now practiced in all cabinet-style governments the world over, that a ministry must resign when it ceases to command the confidence of the elected house.

Early in his reign, British-born and British-educated George III (reigned 1760–1820) succeeded in subverting the growing power of cabinet government. Later, however, the disasters associated with the years of George's rule (loss of the thirteen American colonies and a huge increase in the national debt) and his periodic lapses into insanity eroded royal influence and enabled the cabinet to regain the initiative. Ever since, the task of governing Great Britain has belonged to the prime minister and his or her cabinet colleagues, subject to the approval of Parliament.

Life in England in the Era of Constitutional Development

England's dynamic development in many areas, which had begun in the great Elizabethan age, continued in the seventeenth and eighteenth centuries. The English people enjoyed a government that was the most efficient in Europe and, after the Glorious Revolution, the freest as well. The events of 1688 vindicated parliamentary government, the rule of law, and the right of revolt against tyranny.

Except for the decades of the mid-seventeenth century, when Puritans ruled and banned the theater and

Map 11.1 Europe, c. 1715. The Habsburg Empire dominated central Europe. The Bourbon dynasty ruled both France and Spain but was forbidden to unify the two nations. In northern Germany, the Hohenzollerns were consolidating their disparate lands in a strong centralized state.

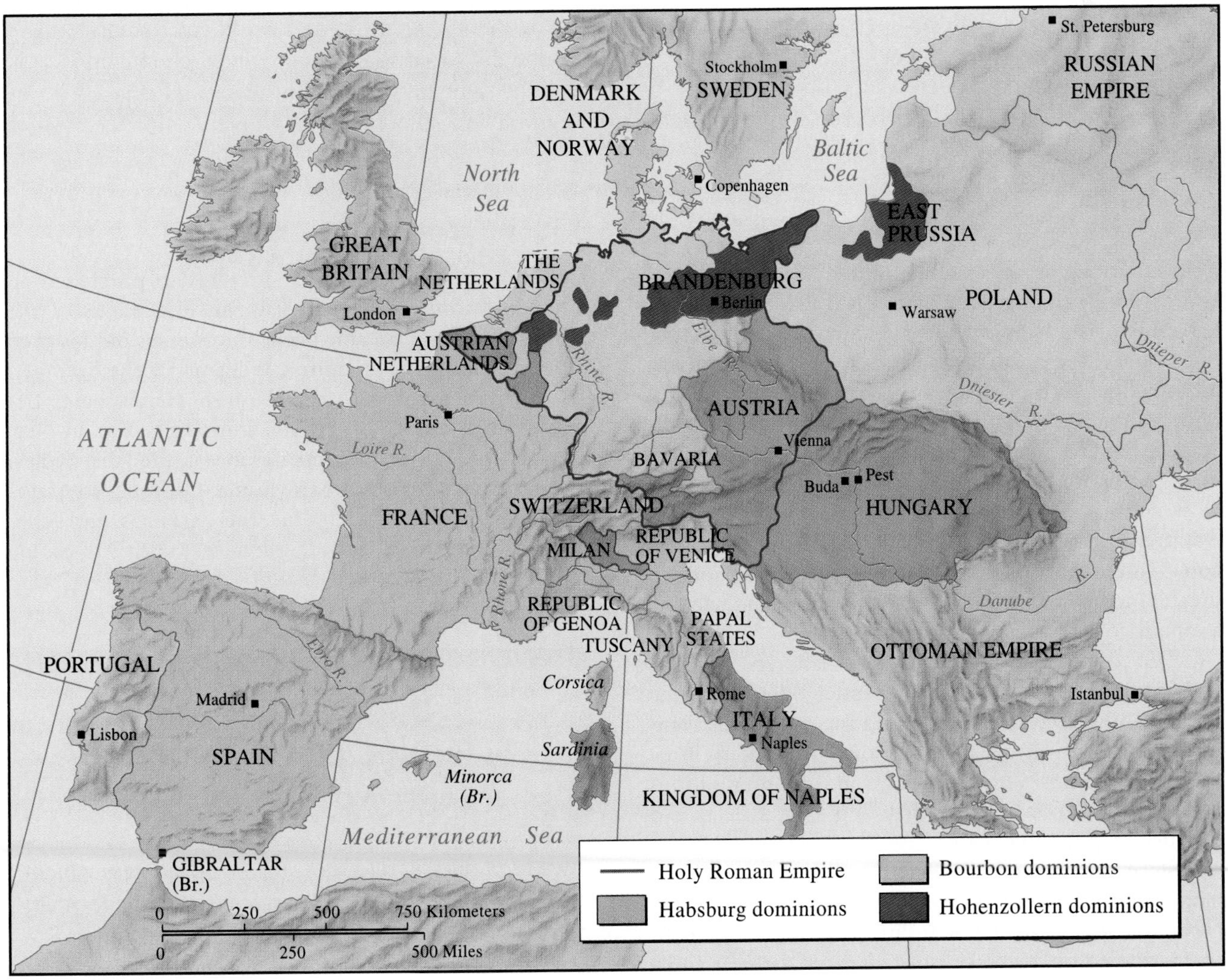

LIVES AND TIMES ACROSS CULTURES

Inventing Childhood

Until the seventeenth century, children were generally treated as "miniature adults." At a very young age children entered the workforce, with sons often helping their fathers in the fields or with the animals, and daughters assisting their mothers in household chores or gardening in the family vegetable plot. Well into the twentieth century, children in poorer countries followed these age-old patterns. Clothing and items for children were no more than small replicas of those worn or used by adults.

Across cultures and times toys were universal. Early toys were limited to simple dolls, balls, tops, or carved animals. Toy horses have been uncovered at archeological sites of the ancient Egyptians in Africa, the Chinese in Asia, and Navaho in the Western Hemisphere. But in eighteenth-century Europe, particularly England, as more and more consumer goods were manufactured at decreasing costs, a myriad of items were created solely for children. Parents eagerly bought children's books, games, elaborate dolls, and intricately wrought mechanical toys to amuse their sons and daughters. Some playthings were gender oriented, with dolls for girls and toy soldiers and trains for boys. Others, such as board games, kites, and the hobbyhorse, were for children of either gender.

By the twentieth century, throughout the industrialized world, entire industries revolved around the manufacturing of ever more complex toys, bicycles, skate boards, educational materials, and athletic equipment for the "children's market." Entire theme parks and restaurants catered to children and their parents, and the mass media produced myriads of films, cartoons, and programs aimed solely at children. As a result, childhood became commercialized throughout the industrialized world and parents around the world sought to provide their children with the same toys and highly advertised videos, "spin-off" playthings, and diversions.

most entertainments as sinful, cultural life was vigorous and urban life flourished. London had half a million inhabitants by the end of the seventeenth century. It was the capital city, a cultural center, and a hub of commerce. Most people lived in villages and hamlets, pursuing not only farming but a flourishing cottage industry of crafts and small-scale manufacture. The medieval open-field method of farming had been replaced by enclosed farms, worked by independent freehold and tenant farmers. Adult males who paid forty shillings in rent or taxes could vote in parliamentary elections. However, a much greater income was required before a man could become a candidate for Parliament.

The countryside also had its poor laborers, paupers, and wandering craftsmen, tinkers, and gypsies. Everyone hunted and snared small game, and the poor and adventurous poached on lands that belonged to the well-to-do. Because roads were very rough and communications poor, few common folk traveled, and local dialects and traditions tended to persist.

Since the days of Elizabeth I, adventurous Britons had sought their fortunes abroad and then returned home to enjoy them. Thomas Pitt, who went to India to trade, rose to be governor of Madras for the East India Company, returned to Great Britain and purchased an estate and won a seat in Parliament. His grandson, the Earl of Chatham, became prime minister, as did his even more famous great-grandson, William Pitt the Younger.

Many emigrated to the Western Hemisphere. Between 1630 and 1640, 20,000 Puritans settled in New England and about the same number in the West Indies, while Quakers went to Pennsylvania, Catholics to Maryland, and Anglicans to Virginia, the Carolinas, and other colonies. Many went as indentured servants or to escape criminal punishment.

Intellectual and Scientific Developments: The Age of Reason

If we limit ourselves to showing the advantages which have been extracted from the sciences . . . the most important of them perhaps is to have destroyed prejudice and reestablished . . . human intelligence formerly compelled to bend to the false directions forced upon it by . . . absurd beliefs . . . the terrors of superstition and the fear of tyranny.

*We may observe that the principles of philosophy, the maxims of liberty, the knowledge of the true rights of men and of their real interests have spread in too great a number of nations, and control in each of them the opinions of too many enlightened men, for them ever to be forgotten again.**

*M. J. de Caritat, Marquis de Condorcet, "Esquisse d'un tableau historique des progrès de l'esprit humain," in O. E. Fellows and N. L. Torrey, eds., *The Age of Enlightenment: An Anthology* (New York: Appleton-Century-Crofts, 1942), pp. 623, 626.

This optimistic account of "the progress of the human spirit" sums up some of the deepest convictions of the eighteenth-century West: the liberating impact of science and reason on the human mind, the importance of human rights, and the inevitable triumph of freedom in the world. The author of these impassioned sentiments, the Marquis de Condorcet (1743–1794), was an enlightened aristocrat and a disciple of Voltaire, the most famous social philosopher of the era. A strong believer in freedom and progress, Condorcet was an admiring student of the experiment in free government undertaken by the United States of America. Ironically, he died a victim of the political terror that accompanied the struggle for survival in the French Revolution. Yet this tract, written shortly before his tragic death, indicates that Condorcet died still confident that in the long run, the political promise of that age of intellectual enlightenment would be realized. The following pages discuss the scientific revolution from which the Age of Reason sprang and thereafter focus on the Enlightenment in Europe and in the European possessions overseas. The section concludes with a summary of developments in the arts during this innovative period. Later sections of this chapter will trace the impact of the Scientific Revolution and the Enlightenment on new forms of Western culture evolving in Latin America and British North America.

The Scientific Revolution

The scientific revolution, contrary to the normal meaning of the word revolution, did not involve rapid, explosive overthrow of traditional authority. Rather, it was a complex movement characterized by gradual and piecemeal change. What was revolutionary was the birth of a new science culture that transformed Europe into a dynamic, rational, and materialistic society.

Beginning in the sixteenth century and reaching full bloom late in the seventeenth, the scientific revolution produced dramatic advances in anatomy, astronomy, physics, and mathematics. Ultimately, rational scientific thought spilled over from pure science into other areas of Western life, notably politics, economics, art, philosophy, and religion.

The evolution of science is best seen against the backdrop of earlier eras in history. In the late Middle Ages, intellectuals had assumed that the universe was the orderly creation of God and that its laws could be explained by rational analysis. They developed in rudimentary form the principles of the scientific method and made crucial advances in mathematics and physics.

The Renaissance witnessed commercial and geographic expansion, which created a demand for more precise instruments of navigation. The resultant technology, in turn, made more accurate measurements possible, something that was central to the new scientific age. The printing press, invented during the second half of the fifteenth century, deserves much credit for later scientific advancements. It facilitated the rapid dissemination of ideas and enabled scientists to profit from each other's work.

Despite such advances, however, Aristotelian concepts still dominated European scientific thinking during the Renaissance. Aristotelian physics posited a world in which all matter was arranged in a hierarchy according to the quality of its substance. Smoke and fire were seeking out their "natural" place in the hierarchy as they moved upwards into the heavens; the same was true as a stone fell to earth or water moved downhill. The different forms of matter had innate properties: smells, sounds, numbers, moods, colors. The entire universe was seen to be alive and arranged in a hierarchy determined by the quality of the material. Such Aristotelian principles were adapted to Christianity by medieval thinkers who argued that the higher an object was located on the hierarchy, the closer its nature was to God.

Ptolemaic astronomy fit in very well with Aristotelian physics because it placed the most important objects in the universe—the earth and humans—in the center of the picture. Christian astronomers then arranged the sun, moon and planets in an ascending order to God, based on the nobility of their matter.

The medieval/Renaissance hierarchical worldview reinforced the reigning social and political order: members of the nobility were thought to be better than anyone else, regardless of their intellectual, social, or economic abilities. They were by nature more fit to rule because of the composition of their matter. Members of other social strata, including even the wealthy merchant class, were considered unfit for political power because their matter was inferior to that of the aristocracy.

Between 1500 and 1750, scientists developed a new method of inquiry—the "scientific method." Observation and experimentation were followed by rational interpretation of the results. The Englishman Sir Francis Bacon (1561–1626) and the Frenchman René Descartes

(1596–1650) rejected traditional abstract approaches and insisted on more empirical methods of discovery. Bacon urged the use of direct observation and collection of data. This emphasis on empiricism, beginning with observable data and building general truths on this foundation, became one of the hallmarks of the new science. Descartes stressed rational understanding as the guarantor of truth. The French philosopher's famous assertion "I think, therefore I am" was the first link in a chain of rational proofs that accounted for the existence, progressively, of humanity, God, and God's universe.

A wide range of sixteenth-century studies that today would fall into the category of magic also helped to create an environment that encouraged exploration and experimentation. The common belief in astrology, which explained earthly affairs by the motions of stars and planets, contributed to interest in astronomy. Alchemy stressed a mystical search for ultimate truth, but alchemists also used laboratory equipment and conducted chemical experiments. Mystical studies of Neoplatonism and of the Jewish religious book, the *Kabbala,* led to a broadening interest in the characteristics of nature and also emphasized the importance of numbers in understanding the way the world worked, a mathematical approach that modern science utilized. The scientific revolution emerged from this stimulating intellectual world.

The New Scientists

The leaders in this scientific revolution included Copernicus, Kepler, Galileo, and Newton. Nicholas Copernicus (1473–1543), who revealed the basic structure of the solar system, is sometimes called the Columbus of the scientific revolution. A Polish churchman with a purely theoretical understanding of astronomy, Copernicus questioned the orthodox Ptolemaic view that the earth stood at the center of the cosmos. In *On the Revolutions of the Heavenly Spheres* (1543), Copernicus declared that the sun was the true center and that the stars and planets orbited around it. The earth, Copernicus dared to suggest, was merely one planet moving around that solar center. His investigations suggested that mathematics is the language of the universe. Johannes Kepler (1571–1630), a German astronomer, offered a much more detailed and exact account of the laws of planetary motion, demonstrating that the planets moved in elliptical orbits around the sun.

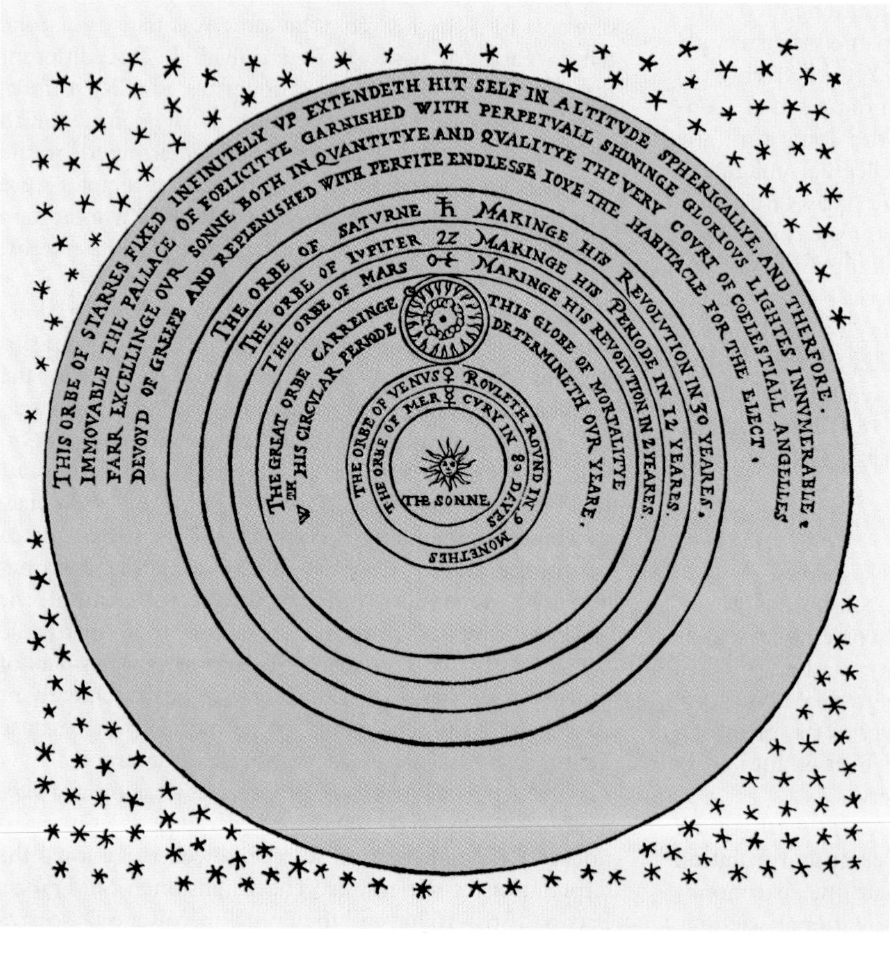

The Copernican View of the Universe. The Englishman Thomas Digges created this schematic representation of the universe thirty years after Copernicus's book appeared in 1543. The sun is in the center, the earth is the third planet out from it, and the moon revolves around the earth.

Bridgman/Art Resource

The Trial of Galileo. This painting shows the trial of Galileo by the Inquisition, a rare case of ecclesiastic persecution of a scientific revolutionary. The trial, climaxing in Galileo's coerced recantation of the Copernican worldview, became the symbol of resistance to the new scientific understanding of the universe.

Galileo Galilei (1564–1642), a brilliant Italian student of physics and astronomy, made major contributions in both areas. In physics, he challenged Aristotle's theory that objects fall at velocities proportional to their weight. His experiments demonstrated that larger objects did not fall faster than smaller ones; "noble" objects fell at the same rate as a lowly cannon ball made out of lead. He established a universally applicable mathematical formula for the acceleration of falling bodies. Galileo replaced Aristotle's qualitative view of the universe with a quantitative one.

In astronomy, Galileo reinforced Copernicus and Kepler's sun-centered theory of the universe by using a telescope, a device newly developed in the Netherlands, for direct astronomical observations. His examination of the moon (see the accompanying box) was a blow to Ptolemaic heavenly hierarchies; instead of a smooth, radiant, material holding one of the noblest objects in its appropriate place in God's celestial hierarchy, Galileo found ordinary matter like that on earth, piled in random peaks and valleys. These revolutionary views brought Galileo a summons from the Inquisition, which forced him to recant his scientific beliefs; however, his ideas long outlived the power of his persecutors.

Once the Aristotelian and Ptolemaic systems were discredited, the question remained: What could explain the workings of the universe? A century and a half after Copernicus, Isaac Newton (1642–1727) tied the achievements of his predecessors together with his crucial formulation of the law of gravity. Gravity was a powerful force that could not be seen, smelled, or heard, yet it exerted a pull on every object in the world. In his *Mathematical Principles of Natural Philosophy* (1687), Newton asserted that every particle of matter in the universe attracts every other particle with a force that varies with the size of the objects and the distance between them. Thus this single force affected everything, from planets in space to apples falling from trees. Newton also explored the nature of light and the laws of optics and defined the general laws of motion in terms of inertia; he declared that for every action there is an equal and opposite reaction. As a result of his long dedication to science, Newton became one of the most honored of all the founders of the scientific revolution. Working separately toward similar ends, Copernicus, Galileo, and Newton had constructed a new, coherent, and increasingly accurate picture of the physical universe.

Gradually, the universe came to be seen as an immense and intricate machine that operated according to mathematically formulated laws. Many believed that all matter was composed of atoms, tiny particles whose mass, motion through space, and encounters with other atoms explained everything that happened in nature. To help in these explorations, Francis Bacon advocated the creation of large, state-supported research institutions and correctly predicted that future generations would

The First Human Eye to Look upon the Mountains of the Moon

About ten months ago, a report reached my ears that a certain Fleming had constructed a spyglass by means of which visible objects, though very distant from the eye of the observer, were distinctly seen. . . . I succeeded in constructing for myself so excellent an instrument that objects seen by means of it appeared . . . over thirty times closer than when regard[ed] with our natural vision. . . .

*Now let us review the observations made during the past two months. . . . Let us speak first of [the] surface of the moon. . . . I distinguish two parts of this surface, a lighter and a darker. . . . From observations of these spots repeated many times, I have been led to the opinion and conviction that the surface of the moon is not smooth, uniform, and precisely spherical, as a great number of philosophers believe it . . . to be, but is uneven, rough, and full of cavities and prominences, being not unlike the surface of the earth, relieved by chains of mountains and deep valleys. . . .**

Vivid reports like this account of Galileo's discoveries both challenged traditional religious belief that the entire universe was perfect—except for the earth—and fueled the desire for further discoveries about the nature of the universe. Modern societies continue to be fascinated by the formation of the universe and the composition of distant planets. Thus the quest for more knowledge continues in the space explorations of the contemporary era.

*Galileo Galilei, "The Starry Messenger" in Stillman Drake, ed. and trans., *Discoveries and Opinions of Galileo* (New York: Doubleday, 1957), pp. 28–29, 31.

acquire greater mastery of the material environment than humanity had ever achieved before.

The Enlightenment

The Age of Reason reached its climax in the intellectual movement known as the Enlightenment, a ferment of new ideas important in the growth of modern social, economic, and political thought. The Enlightenment's origins can be found in several major cultural strands from previous centuries, including the Renaissance humanists' reverence for the classics, reactions against the religious intolerance of the Reformation, the impact of the age of discovery, and, above all, the scientific revolution.

Classical education and its emphasis on the literature of the Greeks and Romans, which had been preserved by the Islamic states, provided models for Enlightenment thinkers. French radicals and American revolutionaries alike fancied themselves heirs to that "republican virtue" that had flourished in Rome before the Caesars rose to power. Enlightenment intellectuals also reacted against the widespread religious bigotry that gained momentum during the wars of the Reformation. The new writers demanded not only an end to sectarian intolerance, but a more secular society in general.

Expanded contacts with other cultures, from the Americas to Asia, and the establishment of European empires overseas also influenced writers during the Enlightenment. Eighteenth-century European thinkers were impressed by a wide range of non-European cultural achievements, especially the ancient learning of Confucian China and the native wisdom of preliterate Amerindian cultures. Educated Europeans did not yet know much about these far-flung societies, but the little they did know led them to the recognition that no single continent or culture held a monopoly on truth and encouraged them to develop a greater degree of toleration.

New discoveries in a broad spectrum of scientific fields—biology and chemistry as well as physics and astronomy—also profoundly shaped the thought of the age. Scientific societies such as the British Royal Society were founded to bring scientists and interested laypersons together. Popular books, available to the literate upper classes, explained the scientific worldview. During the Enlightenment many lay people dabbled in science just as earlier Europeans had patronized the arts during the Renaissance.

Enlightenment writers, influenced by the new thinking about the physical universe, applied the scientific method to the social as well as the natural world. Some posited that human nature was as susceptible to controlling laws as any other part of nature. As the first step in uncovering these laws, Enlightenment thinkers used reason as a means to analyze and expose faults in traditional social institutions. In so doing, they challenged many of the injustices and weaknesses of the ancien régime, as society in this period was later called. Some writers began to dream of a perfect society of the future, designed according to scientific principles, in which all human beings would live a better life. The application of scientific principles to the study of society formed the foundations of the modern social sciences, including political science and economics.

The scientific revolution involved a dangerous political corollary: if nature was not ordered hierarchically, then neither was society. No group or class was "better" than another and should not be favored by laws. Nor should any group monopolize political power because of an accident of birth. The idea spread that society and government should be a meritocracy, where persons were judged by their achievements not their social background.

The Philosophes

Although the Enlightenment was an international movement, its center was in France, or, to be more precise, in Paris, where its ideas found expression in a unique group of writers known as the *philosophes.* This French word does not denote professional or academic philosophers, but rather social critics who relied on rational analysis to solve the concrete problems of their time.

The philosophes wrote mainly for the aristocracy and the bourgeoisie. Gradually, the ideas of the Enlightenment filtered down to the working classes. Progressive aristocrats, who were eager to keep up with the latest ideas, mingled with the philosophes in a distinctive Enlightenment institution, the salon. At these elegant social gatherings, literary readings, serious conversations, and sparkling wit were to be expected. The salons were often hosted by rich, cultivated women who facilitated the exchange of ideas and introduced various intellectuals to one another.

The writings of the philosophes reached a wide audience among the middle class, who were wealthier, better educated, and more self-confident than ever before. Middle-class readers could identify with the ideas of the philosophes and delighted in their criticism of the gross inequalities of the old regime. Many of the philosophes were of bourgeois origin, and their writings reflected the values and attitudes of their class. Nothing was sacred to these men of letters, who in calling for an intelligent program of reform, held up to public ridicule the stupidity, irrationality, unfairness, and hypocrisy of many existing traditions.

The most successful and famous of the philosophes was François Marie Arouet (1694–1778), better known by his pen name, Voltaire. He wrote on many subjects and in almost every literary form, including history, philosophical fiction, drama, poetry, popular science, and essays on social questions. Voltaire's voluminous private correspondence alone fills almost ninety-eight volumes. Guests flocked to his home to enjoy good food, wit, and wisdom. A passionate reformer, he turned the sharpest edge of his sword against the Catholic church, frequently mocking its superstition and hypocrisy. Voltaire was no revolutionist, believing that society's evils could be eradicated peacefully through an appeal to common sense and enlightened thinking. As he put it, "the more enlightened men are, the more they will be free." The most widely read of his many books was the comic novel *Candide* (1754), which ridiculed snobbish aristocrats and hypocritical churchmen.

Voltaire. The son of respectable middle-class parents and the graduate of a Jesuit school, Voltaire had been intended for the law but instead chose to be a writer. He became the most famous and influential of all the philosophes.

Jean-Jacques Rousseau (1712–1778) was an emotional, deeply serious critic of the social order, occupying a position among writers that was second only to Voltaire's. Rousseau's best known works are *The Social Contract, Confessions* (autobiographical), and *Emile,* in which he opposed rote learning and championed the development of the individual's innate capacities. Rousseau believed that humans were basically good but that they had become corrupted by the progress of civilization. In contrast to his fellow philosophes, he held that intuition and emotion were far better guides to the truth than reason. Unlike Voltaire, Rousseau did not achieve wealth or widespread

A Medieval Solution to the Problem of Earthquakes

The University of Coimbra had pronounced that the sight of a few people ceremoniously burned alive before a slow fire was an infallible prescription for preventing earthquakes; so when the earthquake had subsided after destroying three-quarters of Lisbon, the authorities . . . could find no surer means of avoiding total ruin than by giving the people a magnificent auto-da-fé.

*They therefore seized a Basque, convicted of marrying his godmother, and two Portuguese Jews who had refused to eat bacon with their chicken; and after dinner Dr. Pangloss and his pupil, Candide, were arrested as well, one for speaking and the other for listening with an air of approval. . . . They were then marched in procession . . . to hear a moving sermon followed by beautiful music. . . . Candide was flogged in time with the anthem; the Basque and the two men who refused to eat bacon were burnt; and Pangloss was hanged. . . . The same day another earthquake occurred and caused tremendous havoc.**

In Candide, Voltaire used the historic Lisbon earthquake of 1755 as a means to assault medieval views, anti-Semitism, and the Catholic church. The "crimes" mentioned included violation of dietary and marriage laws (although a godmother is, of course, no blood relation) and the too-free speech for which the philosophes themselves were often punished. To Enlightened thinkers, the practices of much organized religion seemed superstitious, fanatical, and absurd.

*Voltaire, *Candide: or Optimism,* trans. by John Butt (Baltimore: Penguin Books, 1947), pp. 36–37.

critical acclaim in his own lifetime, but his political ideas, which will be discussed later, had great impact on the course of the French Revolution.

Another leading figure of the Enlightenment was Denis Diderot (1713–1784), chief editor of a multivolume *Encyclopedia* (1751–1772) to which most of the philosophes contributed. Diderot wanted the reference work to sum up and popularize eighteenth-century learning. Thus he sought to apply the methods of science and reason to every area of human knowledge. Although neither the church nor the state was directly attacked, the articles contained veiled criticisms that did not always escape the censor's wrath. Diderot constantly faced the dangers of official censorship and suppression, but he overcame all obstacles and carried the work through to completion.

The role of religion and the existence of a divine being were two of the major questions pondered by Enlightenment writers. Many philosophes became deists and some even moved toward atheism. Deists believed in a rational God who, after creating the world and the laws governing it, refrained from intervening in human affairs. Many also rejected the sectarian divisions between Catholics and Protestants, arguing that all Christians, Muslims, and Buddhists had access to God as they understood the divine being. Public profession of atheism was rare in the eighteenth century, but by 1800 a famous scientist told Napoleon that he had no need of the "hypothesis" of God's existence to explain the universe.

Enlightenment writers also debated the condition of women in society. For centuries women had been regarded as inferiors and denied an education and a professional career; if married, they enjoyed few property rights and could be abused with impunity by their husbands. Although leading writers of the period occasionally decried the legal inferiority of women, they retained the traditional view of women and expected men to dominate marriage and family life. Diderot, who regarded his mistress as his intellectual equal, was among the few to actively support women's rights. He called for improved educational opportunities for women and favored reforms that would accord them the same legal status as men. By the mid-eighteenth century, perceptions began to change as wealthy women organized fashionable salons where the enlightened gathered for free and open discussions. More and more learned women challenged the popular view of their gender. They insisted that women were by nature the equals of men and had been made subservient by artificial laws and institutions. In *Vindication of the Rights of Women* (1792), Mary Wollstonecraft (1759–1797) provided an eloquent statement of female emancipation. Writing at the time of the French Revolution, Wollstonecraft called for a revolt against the tyranny of men and the recognition of women as in every way their equals.

Weary of corrupt absolute monarchies, Enlightenment writers believed that humans, being rational and virtuous, could devise a system of government that was both efficient and benevolent. John Locke (1632–1704), an English philosopher, refuted the defense of divine right and substituted a political theory of his own. He boldly stated that all people are born with equal rights to life, liberty, and property. He argued that the only legitimate government—which could be a constitutional monarchy or an assembly of elected representatives—was one formed by mutual consent between the ruler and the ruled. People invested the government with limited powers in return for the safeguard of their inborn rights. If the government violated the social contract, it forfeited the loyalty of its subjects and could be overthrown. The revolutionary idea that governments were responsible to the sovereign people found an eloquent advocate in Jean Jacques Rousseau.

In *The Social Contract* Rousseau, in the Lockean tradition, insisted that a government was legitimate only if it had the consent of the governed. He shared the Enlightenment's antipathy for restrictions on individual freedoms, but more than any reformer of his time, he was concerned with the rights of society as a whole. He portrayed the state as a corporate body of citizens whose individual aims must be subordinated to the "general will." This general will always represented what was in the best interest of the entire community and everyone living within it. Those unwilling to conform to the general will must be compelled to do so. Thus Rousseau's doctrine of the general will provided justification for unrestrained government suppression of individual freedoms.

The French aristocracy's resistance to absolute monarchy is symbolized by Baron de la Brède et de Montesquieu (1689–1755). Although an admirer of the British political system, Montesquieu denied that there was a single perfect form of government that was suitable for all people. His solution for avoiding tyranny was a system of checks and balances rather than a social contract. The powers of government should be divided equally among the executive, legislature, and judiciary; each would perform its own functions but be capable of being checked by the other two. This principle was incorporated into the Constitution of the United States and to the present day continues to have a profound effect on the development of liberal democracies throughout the world.

The Enlightenment's faith in reason also led to pressure for social reforms. The philosophes abhorred slavery and the callous treatment of the criminally insane. But nothing stirred them more profoundly than the cumbersome, antiquated judicial procedures and the torture of prisoners. In a legal treatise entitled *Crimes and Punishments,* Cesare Beccaria (1735–1794), an Italian jurist, appealed for the application of reason to the administration of justice. He argued that the aim of punishment was not to extract vengeance but to reform the perpetrators and prepare them for reintegration in society. He maintained that the criminal codes should be clear, that penalties should be applied equally to all classes of society, and that punishments should not only be swift and sure but proportionate to the crime. Widely acclaimed, Beccaria's book was translated into other languages and promoted the cause of penal reform in a number of European countries.

Some philosophes in search of a better life sought to apply the methods of natural law to the study of economics. Rejecting the mercantilist theories that had been held for centuries, early writers concluded that the economy operated best when it was left to its own devices. The most able proponent of the new laissez-faire school was Adam Smith (1723–1790), whose monumental study, *The Wealth of Nations,* published in 1776, became a bible for bourgeoisie capitalism. Smith asserted that a natural law of supply and demand formed the basis of all economic exchanges. If the economy were left free of government regulation, it would respond naturally to public demand, supplying what the people wanted at a price they were willing to pay. Such free-market policies, which were to be widely abused by industrialists in subsequent centuries, would result, according to Smith, in a steady growth in the wealth of all nations. In the twentieth century, the free trade, capitalist, or free enterprise systems of many nations, from the United States to western Europe to Japan, still reflect some of these ideas.

The Arts in the Age of Enlightenment

Enlightenment painting and literature were less innovative than the scientific and social thought of the period, although some new forms and styles emerged. Aristocratic patrons and small, elite groups continued to dominate much of the artistic life during the eighteenth century, but the newly affluent middle class was beginning to demand a role in cultural life and would have an important impact later. Music of the period, performed in large opera houses and concert halls, reached larger numbers of people than ever before. The development of a wider audience was particularly important for the long-term future of the arts.

Neoclassical and rococo styles predominated in the arts during the century. Neoclassicism was a refinement of the classical styles of the past, which required the artist to adhere to the rules and models of the ancients. In contrast, rococo art was light, elegant, and highly decorative. Named for the stone and seashell (*rocaille* and *coquille*) motifs used in its room decorations, the rococo style was lighter than the previous baroque style and more informal than neoclassical.

The growing interest of the middle classes in art led to several major changes in artistic themes and approaches.

Interest in the "common people" as opposed to the aristocracy was expressed in paintings of peasants or working people. The depiction of common people often stressed their dignity, piety, and warmth. The English artist William Hogarth (1697–1764) produced satirical printed etchings of the poorest and most disaffected groups with such subjects as *The Harlot's Progress* or *Gin Lane*, which sold many copies.

Middle-class tastes had the greatest impact on prose fiction. The first modern novels, *Robinson Crusoe* by Daniel Defoe (1661–1731) and *Tom Jones* by Henry Fielding (1707–1754), attracted widespread audiences who delighted in the adventurous and even bawdy humor of these novels. *Evelina* by Fanny Burney (1752–1840), one of many female novelists, detailed a girl's discovery of high society. Fictional works like this and shorter stories appeared in many women's magazines, which catered to middle-class preferences for stories stressing feeling and morality.

Perhaps the greatest artistic achievements of the eighteenth century came in music. The German states, particularly Austria, produced many brilliant composers who decisively shaped classical music. From Bach to Mozart, it was one of the great ages in the history of music.

Johann Sebastian Bach (1685–1750) spent a quiet life creating religious music for German church congregations; his compositions embody the very spirit of the Age of Reason. George Frederick Handel (1685–1759), Bach's contemporary, produced dramatic compositions of instrumental and choral music.

Two other Germans, Joseph Haydn (1732–1809) and Wolfgang Amadeus Mozart (1756–1791), dominated the musical world during the second half of the century. Haydn enjoyed the patronage of Austrian royalty and produced an immense volume of compositions. Mozart was a child prodigy who dazzled courtly audiences with his virtuoso playing skills; as an adult, he also earned a more precarious living by composing operas and symphonies and died in debt at the age of only thirty-five. Haydn and Mozart helped to develop the modern symphonic orchestra, and Mozart's operas, especially the often-performed *Marriage of Figaro*, combined comic and tragic themes with intricate composition in works that transcend the age.

The Kitchen Maid. This depiction of a humble servant at work by Jean-Baptiste Chardin (1699–1779) and similar paintings lent a dignity to the respectable bourgeoisie and hard-working lower classes that was often lacking among Europe's rulers in the eighteenth century.

Eastern Europe and the Age of Enlightened Despotism

It is certain that among troops one cannot see their equal in the world in beauty, propriety and order; and although along with marching, parading, manual dexterity and the like, goes much that is affected and forced, these are accompanied by so many useful and proper things which belong to the craft itself, that one must say, that not the least thing is missing in the Army and the troops. . . .

All this the King directs, solely and by himself, and besides this he works on public affairs, private affairs, economic affairs and the affairs of his domain with such seriousness that no thaler [Prussian money unit] can be spent without his signature.

*He who has not seen it can not believe that one man in the world, of whatever intelligence, could expedite and do by himself so many different things, as one sees this King expedite daily; for which he uses the morning from 3 o'clock to 10 o'clock, but then spends the rest of the day with military exercises. . . .**

*Max Schilling, *Quellenbuch zur Geschichte der Neuzeit,* trans. George L. Morse (Berlin: 1890), p. 299.

So wrote the Austrian ambassador in 1723 about the Prussian army and the character of Frederick William I, who built the Prussian army into a superb fighting force. A firm believer in absolutism and descendent of a series of competent and hard-working Hohenzollern rulers, Frederick William once declared "Salvation belongs to the Lord; everything else is my affair." Similarly, in the seventeenth and eighteenth centuries the Austrian House of Habsburg rebuilt its fortunes under several able rulers, and isolated and backward Russia emerged as a major power once its own monarchs, most notably Peter the Great, achieved absolute power. All these monarchies sought to follow the pattern set by Louis XIV of France in building and strengthening the machinery of a centralized royal government and in the trappings they instituted at their royal courts.

Enlightened Despotism

In the mid- to late eighteenth century, European absolutism displayed a special set of characteristics that historians now refer to as "enlightened despotism." Inspired by the writings of the Enlightenment philosophes, some monarchs embraced enlightened despotism as a means of reconstructing and strengthening their states during an era marked by recurrent wars.

Enlightened despots believed their own interests could best be served by dynastic internal reforms. Measures designed to promote the development of the economy not only increased the wealth of their subjects but also provided the treasury with more revenues to finance larger armies. By curbing the power of the nobility and church, by building up a corps of trained and salaried officials, and by rationalizing administrative procedures, these monarchs were able to strengthen the central government and increase its efficiency. Other reforms, such as the granting of religious toleration, instituting progressive legal and judicial systems, and improving public health and education, generated greater public support for their rule.

Enlightened despots differed from old-style absolutist monarchs primarily in attitude and style. Enlightened despots rarely spoke of their divine or hereditary right to rule. Instead they focused on their paternalistic roles as heads of state. Denying that the masses were capable of ruling themselves, they claimed their paternalistic government best served the interests of all. Realistically, few enlightened despots actually achieved what they claimed. Collectively, they ignored the philosophes' demand that they accord social equality and individual rights to their subjects, and they refused to institute reforms that damaged their own interests. Of the handful of rulers who embraced the concept of enlightened despotism, the three most outstanding were Joseph II of Austria, Frederick the Great of Prussia, and Catherine the Great of Russia.

Habsburg Revival and Austrian Absolutism

The Thirty Years' War (1618–1648) that ended Europe's religious wars shattered the power of the Habsburg dynasty in central Europe. Surprisingly, however, the Holy Roman emperors of the Habsburg dynasty improved their status during the late seventeenth century and rebuilt their multinational empire. The architect of this revival was Emperor Leopold I of Austria (reigned 1658–1705). A contemporary of Louis XIV, Leopold was an unaggressive, extremely religious prince who had none of the Sun King's self-confidence or skill at public relations. Nevertheless, with the help of brilliant generals, Leopold built up his army and used it to turn back the last great Ottoman invaders of central Europe and to drive them out of Hungary. He then added these new possessions to Austria and Bohemia (modern Czech republic). Thus strengthened, he reclaimed authority over the German states vested in his role as emperor, and Austria resumed its position as a great power in Europe.

Leopold and his successor Charles VI (reigned 1705–1740) strove to implement centralized absolutist rule, but their efforts were imperfectly realized because of the complex political conditions in central Europe. Unlike Louis XIV, who drew on the French bourgeoisie

Voltaire and Frederick II at the Royal Palace of Sans Souci in Potsdam. Although Frederick appointed Voltaire a chamberlain with a generous pension, relations between the two were difficult because both were by nature prickly and self-centered.

to assist him in building his centralized absolutist state, the Habsburg had to rely on the aristocracy, including the non-German Hungarian and Bohemian nobility, as the basis of their power. They had to turn to the aristocrats in part because the Habsburg domains were economically less advanced than France and had few large towns. Large estates owned by conservative aristocrats and worked by serfs predominated in the countryside of the Habsburg possessions. To win the support of the aristocrats, the Habsburgs allowed them to increase their traditional control over their peasant populations, which in effect diluted royal power and enhanced aristocratic influence in the empire. Powerful provincial assemblies and deep ethnic divisions between the majority Germans and the minority populations of Magyars (Hungarians), Italians, Czechs, and other Slavs also militated against absolutism and allowed for particularism.

The most sincere and least successful of the enlightened despots was Joseph II of Austria (reigned 1780–1790). His cautious mother, Maria Theresa (reigned 1740–1780), had made reforms during the previous reign without offending vested interests. Joseph was well meaning but lacked political wisdom. As a doctrinaire reformer, he was intent on sweeping away anachronistic institutions and creating new ones based on the philosophes' highest ideals of justice and reason, regardless of whether they fitted local requirements. In centralizing the administration of the far-flung Habsburg territories, he curtailed the authority of local assemblies and tried to undermine the power of the nobility. He subordinated the church to the state, stripping it of much of its wealth, ending its control of education, legalizing civil marriages, and granting religious toleration. He made the judicial system more uniform, irrespective of local needs. He made school attendance mandatory for seven years, but did not provide the funds for schools or teachers. He freed the serfs, without making work arrangements for their livelihood. "Joseph always wishes to take the second step before he has taken the first," was the perceptive observation of Frederick the Great. Joseph's reforming whirlwind frightened and alienated almost every segment of society, especially the church and the aristocracy. In the end, most of his reforms failed or fell short of their goal, and he died a broken and disillusioned man at age forty-nine. He summed up his career in an epitaph he composed for himself shortly before his death: "Here lies a prince whose intentions were pure and who had the misfortune to see all his plans miscarry." Most of his reforms were rescinded by his cautious brother and successor Leopold II (reigned 1790–1792).

Hohenzollern Power and Prussian Absolutism

The Hohenzollern dynasty in Prussia provides the most spectacular example of the rise of absolutism in central and eastern Europe. In 1648 the princely House of Hohenzollern governed a string of scattered lands that stretched across northern Germany. The Elector Frederick William I (reigned 1688–1740) wisely used his limited resources to build a powerful and disciplined army, and under his successor the army became the fourth largest in Europe and one of the best. He and his successors also established an efficient governmental bureaucracy.

Collectively, the army and the bureaucracy proved useful instruments that made possible Hohenzollern territorial expansions in the wars of the eighteenth century. Both were staffed by Prussian aristocrats, known as the Junkers, who loyally supported the monarchy in return for increased authority over the peasant populations on their estates. The Junkers remained the backbone of Hohenzollern power until World War I. In 1701 the Hohenzollern rulers acquired the title of king. They then proceeded to transform Berlin, their capital city, into a great metropolis.

To some, Frederick II (reigned 1740–1786), known as Frederick the Great, was the quintessential enlightened despot. This remarkable ruler loved art, literature, and music and was a fervent admirer of the French philosophes, in particular Voltaire, whom he invited to his court. Frederick was a hard worker and called himself "the first servant of the state." Like China's Emperor K'ang-hsi, he rose before dawn and labored at his desk until evening, when he turned to cultural pursuits. No aspect of his government escaped his attention. He visited each part of his kingdom annually and bombarded distant officials with correspondence, periodically sending royal agents to report on their activities. During his rule the Prussian civil service set the standard for efficiency and honesty throughout Europe.

A believer in mercantilism, Frederick tailored his economic and agricultural policies to achieve national self-sufficiency. He also saw to the codification of laws, improved the administration of justice, and extended religious toleration to all except Jews. Torture was eliminated except in cases of murder and treason. He paid judges adequate salaries, thereby reducing the need for them to accept bribes. Under Frederick, justice was made not only simpler and less burdensome but also uniform across his domains.

For all his enlightened reforms, Frederick applied the laws of reason to statecraft only when it suited his interests. He spoke about the value of public education but provided little funding for it. He defended the hierarchical social order and rigidly defined the legal status of the different classes. Because he depended on the aristocracy for service in the army and bureaucracy, he refrained from abolishing serfdom, even though he declared the institution an abomination. He granted only limited freedom of speech and of the press.

Frederick's foreign policy was based on power politics and not on the humanitarian and pacifist ideals of the philosophes. Without any legal or moral justification, he invaded and annexed the rich Austrian province of Silesia, thereby provoking the long and bloody War of the Austrian Succession (1740–1748). Eight years later he was compelled to fight a second conflict, the Seven Years' War (1756–1763), at the end of which he was again allowed to retain his ill-gotten gain. In 1772, in collaboration with Russia and Austria, he participated in the first partition of Poland. He gained West Prussia, which linked East Prussia with the main body of the Hohenzollern state. Thus under his rule Prussia more than doubled in size and population. With its efficient government, sound economy, and superb army, Prussia was the dominant power in central Europe at the time of Frederick's death.

Autocracy in Russia

Strong government was not new to Russia. The Principality of Moscow, the precursor of modern Russia, had an autocratic tradition that reached back hundreds of years. During the fifteenth century, Moscow expanded in every direction. Building on the achievements of his predecessors, Moscow's Prince Ivan III (reigned 1462–1505) subjected other Russian princes to his rule and transformed the principality of Moscow into the state of Russia. He tripled the territory under his control by annexing several Russian principalities and conquering Novgorod and various Lithuanian-held lands. In addition, he repudiated Mongol authority and stopped tribute payments.

Ivan also identified Russia as the cultural heir of the Byzantine Empire, which had recently been conquered by the Ottoman Turks. He made the Russian church independent of Constantinople and established it as the defender of the true Orthodox faith. The church promoted unity among Slavic Christians and hoped that a strong Moscow might overthrow the Mongol domination.

Ivan III's marriage to Zoe, niece of the last Byzantine emperor, and his adoption of the Byzantine imperial emblem, the double-headed eagle, added political prestige to his military-based state. He now termed himself tsar (caesar or emperor) of all the Russias. Just as Charlemagne considered himself heir to Roman tradition, Ivan saw himself as the successor of the Byzantine emperors and regarded Moscow as the new center of Orthodox civilization, replacing Constantinople.

Ivan III's grandson, Ivan IV (reigned 1533–1584), called Ivan the Terrible, expanded and centralized the Russian state. He won control of the entire Volga River, gained an outlet on the Baltic Sea, and launched expeditions into western Siberia. To weaken the power of the hereditary nobility, Ivan granted newly conquered lands in the form of nonhereditary military fiefs, thus producing a lesser nobility built on service, who in time became the most powerful class in the state. To ensure a supply of workers for those lands and to keep peasants where they could be taxed, Ivan passed a series of laws binding formerly free Russian peasants to the soil for life. Thus serfdom, which had disappeared in England and in other parts of Europe, became a new and permanent institution in Russia.

The autocracy of Ivan III and Ivan IV was followed by the "Time of Troubles," a period of anarchy characterized by popular revolts and invasions by the neighboring states of Sweden and Poland. A new royal dynasty, the house of Romanov, emerged in 1613 and ruled Russia until the revolution of 1917. The first three Romanovs supervised an expansion of the bureaucracy and foreign trade, and most importantly, Russian expansion eastward across Siberia to the Pacific. Nevertheless, throughout the seventeenth century Russia continued to be plagued by peasant and cossack rebellions and by a great schism that split the Russian Orthodox church. Thus, at the beginning of the 1680s, Russia remained a huge backward state at the eastern edge of the European world. It needed a dynamic leader to harness its potentials and transform it into a European power.

Ascending the throne at the age of ten, Peter I (reigned 1682–1725), called Peter the Great, was a

Corbis-Bettmann

The Building of St. Petersburg. Absolute monarchs demonstrated and enhanced their power by building lavish palaces and even whole cities. Here Peter the Great supervises construction of his new capital. Peter, who had worked with his hands in his youth, was a harsh taskmaster, but the city he built is considered by many to be the most beautiful in Russia.

major architect of Russian absolutism. He was a human whirlwind, shaking up backward, traditional Russia as it had never been before and would not be again until the twentieth century. Peter was huge, standing nearly seven feet tall. Although ill-educated, uncouth, and often brutal, he was nevertheless intelligent, practical, and open to new ideas and possessed an incredible capacity for work. His goal at the outset was to increase his political and military power and bring Russia up to date with the West. In 1697–1698 he traveled through Germany, the Netherlands and England, observing western practices, technology, and institutions. His return was followed by an imperial policy of westernization that touched almost all phases of Russian life.

For Peter, modernization meant not only introducing new ideas and procedures but also attacking reactionary attitudes. He banned beards and ordered his courtiers and officials to wear Western dress instead of the traditional long robes. Women were summoned to court from their domestic seclusion and encouraged to mingle socially with men. Stressing the need for education, he founded schools and institutions of higher learning. He brought in Western technicians in large numbers to help operate new state-subsidized industries, which he protected with mercantilist policies. He adopted a bureaucratic system that in many ways resembled that of Louis IV, to make his authority more absolute. Peter deprived the aristocrats of what political power they had hitherto enjoyed, but rather than reduce them to an idle class, as in France, he compelled them to serve in the government or the army. When the church came out in opposition to some of his reforms, he abolished the office of patriarch and assumed control of religious affairs through an appointed board, the Holy Synod. Moreover, he built a sizable fleet and reorganized the army on the Prussian model.

In foreign affairs, Peter did not achieve all of his objectives, but at least he made Russia a major power. His most important military engagement was a long-drawn-out war against Sweden, from which Russia acquired immense territory, allowing it access to the Baltic Sea. Peter immediately proceeded to build a new capital, St Petersburg, at the cost of many thousands of workers' lives. He called it his "window on the west." By moving the capital away from isolated Moscow, he opened Russia further to western European trade and cultural influence.

Peter did not really change Russia internally, for few of his reforms survived him. The succession of rulers who followed him were weak or inept. Thirty-seven years would pass before another ruler left an imprint on Russia.

Many historians have viewed Catherine II (reigned 1762–1796), later called Catherine the Great, as another example of an enlightened despot. As such, she owed her reputation more to skillful self-advertising than to her record of accomplishments. A German princess, she came to the throne through a coup in which her husband, Peter III (reigned 1762), was overthrown and subsequently murdered. A crafty ruler, Catherine fancied herself an intellectual, wrote plays, and corresponded with French philosophes. Few of her enlightened ideas, however, were translated into social deeds. Catherine realized early in her reign that the necessary conditions for implementing Enlightenment ideas were not native to Russia. She did, however, carry through such reforms as she thought were politically feasible. She founded orphanages, hospitals, and schools for privileged children and encouraged trade by abolishing internal tolls. Her reforms, such as they were, ended after a violent serf uprising—an episode reminiscent of the abortive slave revolt against Rome led by the gladiator Spartacus in 70 B.C.E. There had been a steady deterioration in the conditions of the serfs so that when Emelian Pugachev, an illiterate cossack, sounded the call to arms in September 1773 they flocked to his banner by tens of thousands. The rebellion became widespread and threatened Moscow before it was crushed. Thereafter the serfs were reduced to the level of chattel slaves with no legal rights against their landlords.

Like Frederick the Great, Catherine pursued an expansionist and unscrupulous foreign policy. As she remarked, "If I could live for two hundred years, all of Europe would be brought under Russian rule." She waged two wars against the Ottoman Empire that gained the north shore of the Black Sea and warm-water—but virtually landlocked—ports. Through three partitions of Poland (1772, 1793, and 1795) Catherine acquired about two-thirds of the once huge Polish state, pushing Russia's western boundary deep into central Europe. Catherine's conquests earned her the title "the Great" and enhanced Russia's position as a great European power.

Catherine the Great as an Equestrian. Catherine, aware she was not beautiful, surrounded herself with handsome young men. She had twenty-one known lovers, the last after she had turned sixty. As each paramour dropped from favor, he was rewarded with a title, estate, serfs, and money—reputedly based on his sexual performance.

Giraudon/Art Resource

The Development of Latin American Culture

If [entrance to the city of Cuzco] is not granted at once, I shall not delay for an instant my entrance with fire and sword. . . . I am the only one who remains of the royal blood of the Incas, kings of this kingdom. I have decided to try all means possible that all abuses . . . may cease. . . . My desire is that [tyrannous local officials] shall be suppressed entirely; . . . and that in each province there may be a [governor] of the same Indian nation and other persons of good conscience. . . . It is indispensable that in this city a royal audiencia *shall be erected, where a viceroy shall reside as president in order that the Indians may have nearer access to him. I wish to leave to the King of Spain the direct rule which he has had in his possessions. . . . This . . . is not against God or the King, but against the introduction of bad laws.**

*José Gabriel Túpac Amaru, in Lillian E. Fisher, *The Last Inca Revolt, 1780–1783* (Norman, OK.: University of Oklahoma Press, 1966), pp. 96, 122.

This is a statement of José Gabriel Túpac Amaru, a descendant of the Inka rulers and the leader of the Amerindian revolt in the Andes, 1780–1783. His words and even his name are a microcosm of eighteenth-century Latin America. His conquered people had been suffering for two and a half centuries under brutal abuses, especially a forced labor system that amounted to slavery. He was determined to destroy the system of local government that fostered this oppression and to give Amerindians a larger role in the political system. Yet at the same time he was also a product of the pervasive impact of Spanish culture in Peru. This mestizo rebel was a devout Catholic, a believer in the justice of the Spanish monarchy, and a firm supporter of the viceroy's rule in Peru, as long as it was supervisory and did not support corrupt and exploitative local officials. Túpac Amaru's rebellion was crushed, and his life ended in an agony of torture and dismemberment.

In the early eighteenth century, 3 million inhabitants of European descent and millions of mixed ancestry lived in Latin America and British North America. European settlers arriving in the Western Hemisphere naturally expected to live in much the same way as they did in their homelands. However, as they experienced the new environment, they dropped or modified inappropriate European practices and adopted new ones more suitable to their current surroundings. This section discusses Latin America, the first part of the world where Western culture as it emerged differed markedly from that of Europe. The next section will take up yet a different version of Western culture, that which evolved in British North America.

A Multiracial Society

The greatest difference between Western civilization as it developed in Latin America compared to Europe was the unique multiracial situation that developed in the Western Hemisphere. The Spanish and Portuguese controlled three-quarters of that hemisphere, an area some forty times larger than their homelands, but only small numbers of Iberians, at first mostly men, settled in the vast conquered areas. By the eighteenth century these whites—Peninsulars (aristocrats from Spain) and Creoles (aristocrats of Spanish descent born in America)—comprising only 2 percent of the population, owned virtually all the mines, ranches, plantations, and manufacturing establishments in the hemisphere. Protected by special privileges and powers, isolated in small groups by great distances and difficult terrain, the elite were surrounded and outnumbered by Amerindian peons, mestizos, African slaves, and mulattos, whose forced labor was the foundation of the economy.

Map 11.2 Spanish and Portuguese Possessions in the Western Hemisphere, 1784. The colonial empires of Spain and Portugal are shown at their greatest extent. Over the next forty years, nearly all this territory was lost to independence movements and the expanding United States.

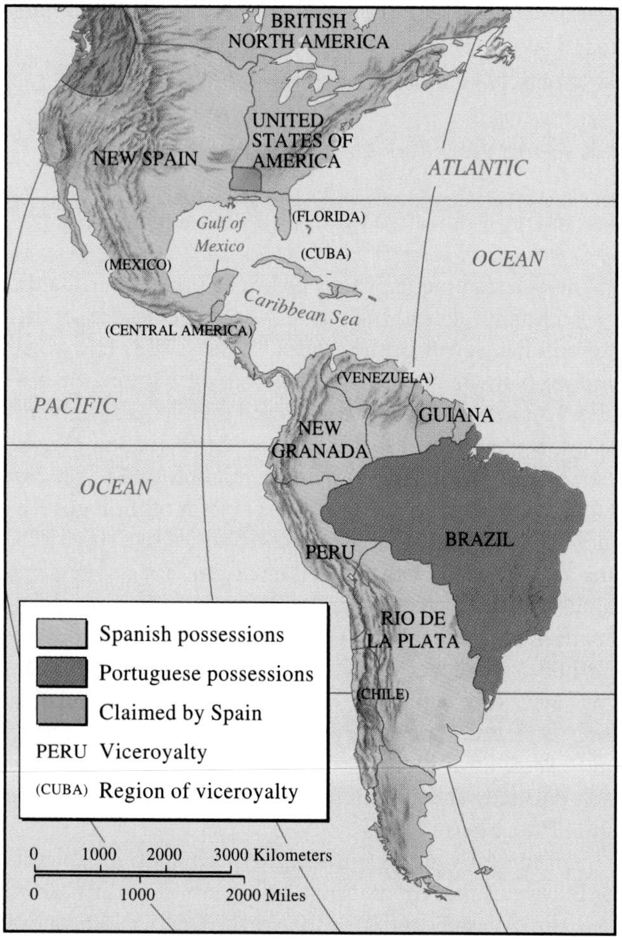

Amerindians remained in the majority in some areas, and throughout the colonial period were the largest single racial group in Latin America. Mestizo descendants from white-Amerindian unions were in the majority in some areas. There was an extensive mulatto (descendants of white and African American unions) population throughout the Caribbean and Brazil.

The realities of multiracial living brought about a somewhat more relaxed attitude about race in Latin America than in Europe or in British North America. The status of the large and increasing mestizo population was in general worked out by a rough color code. A few individuals from wealthy and accomplished families were accepted as members of the white ruling class despite their mixed Amerindian ancestry; others of mixed blood became a part of the small middle class. Some mestizos and lower-class Iberian immigrants filled the need for merchants and artisans.

The Life of the Masses in Latin America

Whatever their ancestry, more than 90 percent of the population—blacks, mulattos, Amerindians, and most mestizos—toiled for the few. Initially, many Amerindians were enslaved; later, the Spanish crown and the Catholic church held that the Amerindians were free subjects of the crown, to be treated as dependent minors. They could be parceled out to work for the benefit of whites, but only on a limited basis, and were to receive religious and vocational instruction. In actuality, whites often worked their "dependents" severely. Masters forced the Amerindians under their control to work in mines and factories, on ranches and farms, and as porters and construction laborers. Often separated from their families, Amerindians frequently labored under brutal conditions that brought premature death. They sometimes rose in revolt, but the uprisings were always crushed. However, by the eighteenth century the more brutal forms of exploitation had disappeared, and the mass of Amerindians and mestizos had become peons, bound to the land by insurmountable debts for shelter, food, and clothing. The local officials who supervised the Indian villages in rural areas often violated the legal rights of the

CONNECTIONS IN MIGRATION

Forced Migration, 1600–1800

The progress of the early modern era depended heavily on exploited labor. In northwestern Europe, many of the poor worked as indentured servants. In northeastern Europe, serfs were bound to the land, and in Russia they could even be sold. In the Christian and Muslim regions of the Mediterranean and the Black Sea, slaves served as domestics or laborers; in the Ottoman Empire, there was even an elite corps of slave soldiers. In the Americas, many Amerindians were either enslaved or forced to work in mines in Peru and Mexico. The economy of parts of the newly colonized Western Hemisphere grew rapidly, thanks to the forced migration of Africans. These men and women worked on plantations (especially those cultivating sugar, tobacco, and indigo), in mines, and as transport, construction, and domestic workers. In 1600, Africans were a small minority among the world's slaves; by the eighteenth century they were a clear majority. In these two centuries, 10 million Africans crossed the Atlantic to the Americas, in comparison to the 2 to 3 million Europeans who migrated during the same period. These two immigrant groups made their impact on the Americas and on each other.

Relatively densely populated, western Africa was the main supplier of slaves to purchasers from Europe and America. The number reached approximately 100,000 persons per year in the late eighteenth century. As a result, the population of West Africa and western central Africa declined for over a century, beginning about 1730. The wars stimulated by the taking of captives for sale into slavery divided and weakened African societies.

Men were taken in larger numbers, so American slave populations were mostly male, while in regions of Africa, the populations consisted of more adult women than men. Enslaved children died at a high rate from exposure and disease. The growing practice of enslavement increased the number of people held in slavery in Africa as well as in the Americas. Large numbers of East Africans were captured and sold into slavery in western Asia. This slave trade lasted for more than one thousand years.

By about 1800, antislavery movements were growing in Europe. Serfs were emancipated. The last country to do so was Russia in the mid-nineteenth century.

1. Explore Unit 6 of the Migration CD. What do the documents indicate about the extent of the spread of slavery? Under what conditions were slaves typically forced to live and work? Did they have any rights?

2. Also visit http://www.fordham.edu/halsall/med/lewis1.html to gain a better understanding of the practice of slavery in the Middle East. How was slavery justified by Muslims? What were the conditions of slavery there? What were the prospects for escaping slavery?

Amerindians by seizing their land and levying fraudulent taxes. These magistrates were the oppressors challenged so vehemently by Túpac Amaru.

Blacks fared even worse than the Amerindians. Whereas most Amerindians at least lived a family life in their villages and continued to practice many aspects of their traditional culture, blacks were torn away as individuals from their home and culture, shipped across the ocean along with other suffering strangers, and put to grueling labor in a strange new land. Since males greatly outnumbered females, most could not even establish families. By law, they held a dual status: as human beings, they were entitled to humane treatment; as slaves, they were chattel, like livestock. In practice, most masters treated their slaves as personal property rather than as human beings. Many slaves were simply worked to death or to incapacity and then replaced by new slaves brought in by the efficient slave-trading companies.

There were a few ways out of slavery. Portugal in particular had provided relatively liberal laws that allowed Brazilian slaves to buy their freedom, and masters found few legal obstacles if they wished to free a slave. In fact, however, few slaves could accumulate the price of freedom, and few masters freed their slaves. Nevertheless, those blacks and mulattos who did gain their freedom legally found that, unlike the situation in British North America, their race was not an absolute barrier to rising in society. Black artisans and mechanics often found acceptance, especially in areas where there were few skilled white workers. In parts of Brazil, where black slaves and freemen overwhelmingly outnumbered whites, even a small degree of white ancestry gave some mulattos the social status of whites.

Blacks resisted their enslavement in several ways. Slaves in the Caribbean sporadically rose in revolt, but always unsuccessfully. Some individuals escaped into unsettled areas, and occasionally runaways banded together and successfully held out against whites, as the Maroons did in the interior of Jamaica. Brazilian slaves often fled into the vast jungle interior. In the seventeenth century, runaway blacks set up the state of Palmares, which lasted thirty years before it was destroyed.

Mercantilist Theory and Spanish American Reality

Like the other colonial powers, the Spanish government followed mercantilist economic doctrine, closely regulating its American colonies until well into the eighteenth century. The crown permitted a group of private companies in Seville and Cadiz to monopolize commerce with Spanish America, while at the same time the Casa de Contratación, the government bureau that managed the economic life of the colonies, collected the crown's share of taxes and monopolies. The Portuguese monarchs were not as rigid as their Spanish counterparts and allowed merchants in Portuguese ports to send their ships to any port in Brazil.

Under the protection of the Spanish navy, two annual convoys stopped at three Caribbean ports in Spanish America, picked up the cargoes waiting there, and then returned to Spain. The Spanish government apparently believed that the convoy system may have been necessary to protect the cargoes of gold and silver. However, forcing all the exportable products scattered across Spain's vast American domains to be gathered at only three ports made it extremely difficult for producers (in most of South America in particular) to get their goods to Spain. By the eighteenth century the convoy policy was strangling Spanish American exports.

Imports posed, if anything, an even greater problem. Under mercantilist doctrine, colonists were to consume the products of the mother country or products from other parts of the world supplied by the ships of the mother country. Colonists were not to buy goods from foreign ships and were not allowed to produce items—metalware, textiles, and wine, for example—that competed with those of the mother country. That was the theory; in fact, by the eighteenth century, Spain was no longer able to supply products needed for everyday life in its colonies. The colonists, desperate for affordable European products, welcomed British, Dutch, and French smugglers. They began to produce their own textiles, metalware, and wine, while Amerindians provided woven goods, pottery, and basketry. The upper classes, however, continued to demand high-quality goods made in Europe.

Church and State in Spanish America

Ministering to the spiritual needs of the millions living in the huge area across the ocean was the responsibility of the Roman Catholic church's widespread colonial orga-

The Rise and Fall of Empires. This seventeenth-century painting of Cuzco, Peru, the capital of the former Inka Empire, depicts the Church of Santo Domingo and a Dominican monastery rising over the ruins of Coricancha, the golden Temple of the Sun.

nization. The Spanish monarchy selected all clerical officials in America up to the rank of archbishop. Since the church, like the state, reflected the class structure of the time, nearly all the top ecclesiastical appointments (ten archbishops and thirty-eight bishops) went to Spanish aristocrats. Most of the clergymen on the parish or local levels were Spaniards of common origin.

The most important responsibility of the church in Spanish America was to convert the Amerindians. Franciscan and Dominican missionaries accompanied the early conquistadores and converted millions of Amerindians, sometimes forcibly. In the more remote areas, this clergy, now joined by the Jesuits, often replaced the conquistadores as frontiersmen, setting up missions in previously unconquered territories. With the help of army detachments, they rounded up the nearby Amerindians and brought them in to work for the missionaries and to receive Christian instruction and baptism.

The regular clergy were followed by the secular clergy and by the religious orders of nuns. The new orders were specifically sent to organize local parishes, build schools and universities, and found hospitals, orphanages, and poor houses. Bishops erected cathedrals and other religious edifices with money contributed by rich laity and the government. Many of these buildings were of outstanding architectural and artistic beauty.

As in Spain, Roman Catholicism was the only faith tolerated. The Holy Office (the Inquisition) punished blasphemy by fines and flogging. Unrepentant Protestants, Jews, and atheists faced exile or burning at the stake, although executions were quite infrequent compared to Europe. Amerindians were not subject to the jurisdiction of the Holy Office.

Many abuses and problems attended the transplanting of the Catholic church to the New World. By the eighteenth century the church had accumulated enormous wealth; that and the huge size of the church organization made corruption inevitable. The Spanish American Catholic church was burdened with idle clerics who congregated in the cities for sumptuous and sometimes debauched living. Up to one-half of city property in the Americas was owned by the church or by the religious orders. The orders often competed with the laity in banking and commerce, taking advantage of their special exemptions from taxation and economic regulation.

The church also faced great problems in the countryside. Many dedicated clerics served their mestizo and Amerindian parishioners faithfully by their teaching, vocational instruction, and spiritual guidance. Some, however, were uneducated and avaricious, exploiting Amerindian labor as brutally as the secular landlords did, while exacting high fees for administering the sacraments and saying mass. Many Amerindians and blacks learned only the external, ceremonial aspects of their new faith. Ironically, some clergy encouraged the exploitation of black slaves in their efforts to protect Amerindians from enslavement and mistreatment.

The Granger Collection

Antonio de Mendoza, Viceroy of New Spain, 1535–1551. As agents of the Spanish crown, viceroys exercised great power in the Americas. They were, however, somewhat restricted by competing colonial institutions and by the king's own inspectors.

The political situation in eighteenth-century Spanish America was complex. Up to the middle of the eighteenth century, the administration of Spanish America reflected that of Spain, coupled with some unique features. In Spain the traditional privileges of the nobility and churchmen placed some limits on the power of the monarchy. In America, however, the monarchs had virtually unlimited sovereignty, since the popes had awarded them the Americas as their personal property. With little competition from the aristocrats and the clerics, the kings quickly set up *cabildos* in Spanish America to buttress royal authority. The cabildo was an appointed city government that administered the surrounding countryside. It was the center of a complex control system that enabled the power of the king to fan out over the islands, jungles, plains, and highlands of

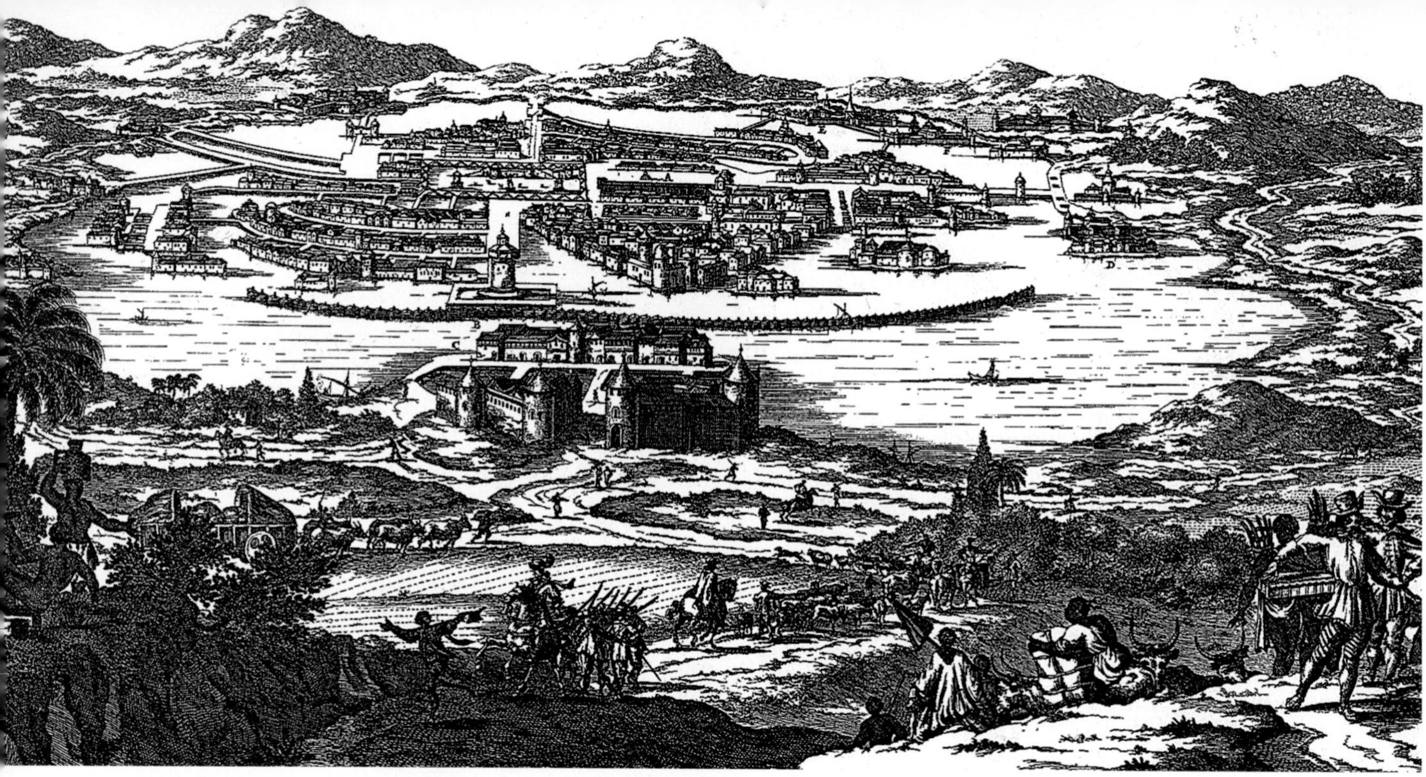
Stock Montage

Mexico City, 1673. Tenochtitlán, conquered by the Spanish 150 years earlier, was built in the middle of Lake Texcoco on an artificial earthen base intersected with canals. The new Mexico City was clearly Mediterranean in its architecture. The approaches to the causeways were protected by turreted fortifications.

the sprawling region. The Spanish monarchs appointed a Council of the Indies and gave that body the authority to act for the king on matters of economic policy, justice, military affairs, and religion.

Viceroys, representing the king in New Spain (Mexico, the Caribbean, and Central America) and Peru (Spanish South America), had great power over local appointments, administration, finance, and the military forces. Their authority was subject to review, however, by judicial-consultative bodies known as *audiencias* and by inspectors sent from Spain. The viceroy also supervised a hierarchical network of officials, including the regional presidents and captains-general, the provincial governors, and local officials. Spain gave most of the important governmental positions to Peninsulars, slighting the Creoles. Only four of the 170 viceroys who governed Spanish America during the colonial period were Creoles. By the early eighteenth century some Creoles were beginning to think of themselves as Spanish Americans rather than as Spaniards and resented the Peninsulars' monopoly of political power and aristocratic privilege. The Creoles, in their turn, were contemptuous of lower-class Iberian immigrants and the mestizo middle class.

Spanish American Culture: Derivation and Innovation

The church controlled education at all levels, and academic training was reserved for the upper and middle classes, who considered it unnecessary and even dangerous to educate the masses. As a result, 90 percent of Spanish Americans remained illiterate. Most women, even of the upper class, were not taught to read and write and were trained only in domestic and social skills.

Until the mid-eighteenth century, intellectual and artistic developments followed the lead of Iberia, which emphasized Aquinas and the scholastics. Innovative thought was discouraged by the Inquisition, with its Index of Prohibited Books. Most Spanish American writers concentrated on literary genres favored in Spain: chivalric romances, lyric poetry, and devotional literature.

However, a few Spanish American writers of the sixteenth and seventeenth centuries contributed to Western literature. These often employed traditional epic and romance formats to portray the struggles between the Spaniards and the Amerindians. An example is the first literary work concerning the Americas, *La Araucana,* an epic poem by Alonso de Ercilla y Zúñiga (1569–1589), which celebrated the heroic resistance of the Araucanian Amerindians of southern Chile.

The greatest poet of Spanish America may well have been Sor Juana Inés de la Cruz (1651–1695), a highly intelligent woman interested in science, mathematics, and writing. Refused admission to the University of Mexico because she was a woman (despite her offer to wear men's clothes!), she went into a convent at sixteen, where she wrote exquisite drama and love poetry while pursuing her studies in other subjects. Her superiors later put a stop to her writing; she sold her enormous library and devoted herself to charity until she died at forty-four.

Histories of the conquest were popular in both Europe and America. Bernal Díaz del Castillo (c. 1492–c. 1581), one of Cortés's soldiers, wrote an influential book entitled *The Discovery and Conquest of Mexico.* Another widely read book on the conquest was the *Royal Commentaries of the Incas,* by Garcilaso de la Vega (c. 1540–1616), son of a Spanish father and an Inka princess. European and Spanish American readers were also interested in descriptions of the Western Hemisphere's strange flora and fauna, such as the *General and Natural History of the Indies* (1535), by Gonzalo Fernández de Oviedo (1478–1557).

By the late eighteenth century, the scientific revolution and the Enlightenment had a widespread impact on Latin America. The ideas of Copernicus and Newton, Bacon and Descartes were taught in Latin America's two dozen universities, particularly those in Mexico City and Lima. Some Spanish American colonists, like their counterparts in the British colonies, corresponded with European scientific societies. Religious toleration remained a problem in Catholic Latin America because the Inquisition could still persecute those advocating radical ideas.

Latin America also became strongly influenced by the social theories of the Enlightenment. Colonial newspapers expressed concern over political abuses, voiced demands for economic and social changes, and spread the ideas of the philosophes. The same new ideas were being discussed by mestizo groups in colonial "economic clubs" and by aristocrats in traditional social gatherings called *tertulias.* No representative assemblies existed in the Latin American colonies, but individual, enlightened Bourbon rulers encouraged social reform. The Enlightenment's belief in reason and social progress and its willingness to challenge traditional authority contributed to the outbreak of the Latin American wars of independence in the early nineteenth century.

Cultural Evolution and Political Independence in British North America

[British] America is formed for happiness, but not for empire: in a course of 1200 miles I did not see a single object that solicited charity; but I saw insuperable causes of weakness, which will necessarily prevent its being a potent state; . . . it appears to me very doubtful . . . whether it would be possible to keep in due order and government so wide and extended an empire; . . . fire and water are not more heterogeneous than the different colonies in North America.

*Nothing can exceed the jealousy . . . they possess in regard to each other. . . . In short, such is the difference of character, of manners, of religion, of interest of the different colonies, that . . . were they left to themselves, there would be a civil war, from one end of the continent to the other; while the Indians and Negroes would, with better reason, impatiently watch the opportunity of exterminating them all together. . . . [There] will never take place a permanent union or alliance of all the colonies. . . .**

*Andrew Burnaby, *Travels through the Middle Settlements in North America,* 2nd ed. (Ithaca: Cornell University Press, 1960), pp. 110–114.

The Reverend Andrew Burnaby, traveling in British North America in the middle of the eighteenth century, was not the only European who foresaw chaos rather than unity for an area so different from Europe. To eyes such as Burnaby's the diversity of British North American society appeared to be a prescription for perpetual disorder. What many observers failed to comprehend at that time, however, was that the heterogeneous, often antagonistic collection of inhabitants that made up British North America were learning how to deal with each other; in the process they were creating a new, more dynamic form of social and political stability.

The Multiracial Basis of British North America

British colonial settlements east of the Appalachians were established more than a century after those in Latin America. The land area and population (about one million) of British North America were both about one-tenth of those of Latin America. Most of British North America had a temperate climate and relatively fertile soil.

In the course of a century and a half of colonial development, settlers in British North America had departed further from European culture than Latin Americans had in almost three. As in Latin America, Europeans arriving in British North America were confronted by Amerindians. The Amerindians were too few in number and too volatile in culture to provide the large sedentary work force as had the conquered Aztec and Inka people for the Spanish Empire. By the eighteenth century, Europeans settling in North America had virtually exterminated the Amerindians living east of the Appalachians or driven them across the mountains. Thus, before the huge importation of black African slaves began in the eighteenth century, British North America, unlike Latin America, was by population an offspring of Europe.

The status of blacks in British North America varied more than in Latin America. Despite the regimentation and brutality inevitable in slave labor, particularly on the rice plantations of South Carolina, slaves in British North America enjoyed a higher standard of living and lived longer than slaves in Latin America. Slaves in North America also had more family life as the proportion of

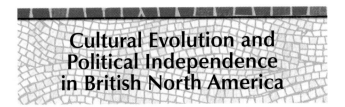

Slavery in British North America. This 1700 woodcut for a tobacco label depicts white planters at their ease in the shade, while black slaves toil in the tobacco fields under the hot sun.

women relative to men rose through generations of natural increase.

Despite less burdensome living conditions, blacks in British North America, because of their race, were at a greater economic and social disadvantage than Latin American blacks. Northern European settlers had stronger racial prejudices than did Iberians. Slaves were seldom freed, and the few who were had difficulty acquiring property, especially land, or jobs as artisans or mechanics. Free blacks were restricted to the most menial and poorly paid tasks. In contrast to Brazil, racial bias was so strong in British North America that a person with even a small percentage of black ancestry was legally classified by law as black.

A New Economy and Society for the Common Settler

English monarchs began the process of colonial development by granting extensive blocks of land to individual favorites, reserving to the crown a portion of the rent money and all income from precious metals. Grantees were to set up companies, find investors, and put some of England's surplus labor to work on the east coast of North America. These commodity companies were expected to produce profitable commodities that other European nations were finding—spices, silk, precious metals, and sugar. To the chagrin of the English government and the dismay of the grantees and investors, the colonies in North America turned out to be virtually devoid of traditional colonial riches. Furs were lucrative, but most of the fur-bearing animals were in the northern interior of the continent, an area predominantly under the control of the French before 1763. As it turned out, British North America north of the Chesapeake produced only foodstuffs and a few products of secondary value.

The scarcity of valuable commodities in British North America brought about a radical departure from European economic and social conditions. Abandoning the company/worker format, the English government and its aristocratic grantees began to encourage common folk to settle in North America. The grantees made money by charging the settlers for passage expenses and by dividing up their huge holdings into rental plots.

Unlike Spain, England did not restrict settlement to members of the state church; troublesome English Protestant minorities were often encouraged to emigrate to North America, and some colonies admitted Catholics and Jews. Protestants from the continent were also encouraged to settle. As a consequence, hundreds of thousands of settlers—individuals, families, and religious groups—came to British North America, quadrupling the population between 1700 and 1740.

Most settlers when first arriving undoubtedly believed that society as they knew it in Europe would be replicated in British America. The aristocrats would continue to own the land and the common folk would rent and work it. This idea turned out to be quite erroneous. In fact, absentee landlords found it difficult to collect rent, and some settlers simply seized crown and grantee lands and claimed "squatter's rights"—ownership on the basis that they had improved the property by erecting buildings and tilling the soil. Rather than try to police their distant property, the crown and the grantees found it easier and more profitable to sell off their land in small parcels at affordable prices.

The seller with cheap land was met by the settler with money to pay for it. From its earliest history British North America differed from Europe in having a chronic labor shortage. Although the immigration numbers are impressive, there were nonetheless not enough workers to meet the demands of colonial development. Employers began to abandon European-level wages and indentures (contracts obligating persons to labor for another for a specified period of time) and to compete with each other for scarce labor. By the early eighteenth century employers were offering wages that were so high that commoner families, who would have been lifetime laborers in Europe, had an opportunity in a short time to save enough money to buy land. In most of British North America, high wages continued to be available to white immigrants, but the rice, indigo, and tobacco planters in the southern colonies solved their labor shortages by importing large numbers of black slaves.

As a result of the land and labor situation, by the early eighteenth century, an economic and social revolution was under way. Most commoner families in British North America—unlike their European and Latin American counterparts—owned property or paid a nominal rent. As a consequence, a high percentage of white settler families achieved a rough-and-ready economic security and some measure of social respectability. Compared with the situation in Latin America and Europe, class lines were more fluid in British North America. The mild deference that colonists of the "middling sort" and "lower sort" paid to those of the "better sort" by no means resembled the servile fawning often found in Europe. Individual wealth and merit rather than inherited titles now often determined social status.

Although more numerous than in Latin America, European women in British North America were nevertheless in short supply. This circumstance marginally improved their condition compared with Europe. Although in the colonies, as in Great Britain, the common law defined a married woman as being subject to her husband's authority, the scarcity of women enabled them to make prenuptial agreements giving them some control over their property if widowed. The labor shortage also meant that wives often helped their husbands in business; they sometimes also ran businesses inherited from their husbands.

In contrast to Latin America and Europe, many white families in British North America were able to improve their social standing. With no aristocratic monopoly of property, it was relatively easy for commoners to obtain land, the traditional measure of social status. Laborers who acquired their own farms or shops thus found themselves in the middle class. Those of the middle class who accumulated extensive land or commercial property—or who rose to distinction as professionals, particularly lawyers and clergy—became the gentry, although they were looked on as country bumpkins by European aristocrats.

By the eighteenth century, British North America had developed an extensive international trade along mercantilist lines. The colonists were required to send "Enumerated Articles"—furs, lumber, molasses, naval stores (turpentine, pitch, tar, masts, spars), tobacco, rice, and indigo—to Great Britain, or via Great Britain to other destinations. The northern colonies had built an extensive merchant marine to carry their grain, meat, and fish to the West Indies and the Mediterranean. Colonists north and south had begun to produce iron and iron products, but since they competed with British iron, the British government soon regulated their production. Like their Latin American counterparts, colonists were often forced to sell low and buy high and consequently turned to smuggling.

Great Britain placed fewer controls on its colonies than Spain did on hers. The government restricted trade with the colonies to English (and after 1707 also Scottish) and colonial ships, but it did not limit the trade to a few companies, allowing individual ships to sail in and out of any port. In addition, products not on the Enumerated Articles list could be sold anywhere in the world without regulation.

Religious and ethnic diversity was another distinctive characteristic of British North America. Before 1750, there were English-speaking Anglicans, Congregationalists, Presbyterians, Catholics, Baptists, and Quakers. From continental Europe came Dutch, German, and French Reformed; German, Dutch, and Swedish Lutherans; German Moravians, Mennonites, Dunkers, and Schwenkfelders; and Portuguese-speaking Jews.

Despite the fact that established churches were in place in most colonies by the eighteenth century, efforts to enforce religious uniformity failed in British North America. The English Act of Toleration in 1689 acknowledged England's religious divisions by giving some religious rights to Congregationalists, Presbyterians, and Baptists. About the same time, the English government forced the Congregationalist colonies to allow Anglicans to worship without penalty. Actually, conditions in British North America did more than English laws to encourage diversity. Most colonies needed settlers and unofficially tolerated thousands of adherents of other religions fleeing religious persecution, economic dislocation, and war. Often the new dissenters settled in such numbers that it was impractical for adherents of the established churches to control them or drive them away. Some colonies were founded to protect religious dissenters, further encouraging religious diversity. Catholics, banned from worshipping in England and most colonies, were tolerated in Maryland through most of its history. Catholics and all Protestant groups had full rights in Pennsylvania. Rhode Island went farther, granting full religious freedom to Christians, Jews, and Muslims. Thus, in the early eighteenth century, British North America moved steadily in the direction of complete religious freedom, which in Europe only a few reformers advocated.

A New Political Process

As Iberian monarchies imposed their tradition of expensive, centralized government on Latin America, so too the English government set up its particular brand of frugal, partially decentralized government in its colonies.

The Granger Collection

New England Town Meeting. Although such an intense encounter was exceptional, this public forum is evidence of the new political process under way in British North America.

In England, the lesser gentry had long represented the royal government in local affairs, sparing the crown the expense of a large set of appointed officials. In the colonies, the English government sent a governor only, whose function was to work with an assembly that represented the colonial gentry, who in most colonies also constituted the local government.

The governor of a colony had the power to appoint from the ranks of the colony's gentry a few executive officials and a council, which also served as the upper house of the colonial legislature and performed certain judicial functions. The governor could control the procedures of the assembly and veto its acts. His position was severely weakened, however, because the British government—to save expense—had given the assembly the power to pay the governor's salary from taxes laid on the colonists. Unlike Latin America, the colonists paid no tax money or royal "fifths" to the crown. Nevertheless, many colonial gentry, like many Creoles in Latin America, chafed at what they saw as excessive power wielded by outsiders or by the mother country.

Much of this was soon to change. Partly as a result of broad-scale economic and social change, a new political process, quite unlike anything in Europe, was evolving. Because of the widespread incidence of property holding in British North America, many white males had access to political power. In Great Britain, one of the few nations having some semblance of government by consent, only adult males who owned property and belonged to the state church could vote. This restricted political participation to about 5 percent of the adult males.

When these requirements were brought over to British North America, however, they produced radically different effects in a population where landholding was more widespread with each passing decade. An estimated one-half of the adult white male colonists could vote in the early eighteenth century, and the proportion continued to rise. Many colonists also met the much higher requirements for holding office. Still, only about 10 percent of the eligible voters took advantage of the opportunity. Most had little appreciation for voting practice or its potential. The New England tradition of the local town meeting was a major exception. By and large, however, colonial voters served as no more than a check, occasionally turning out an incompetent gentleman officeholder.

The Enlightenment in North America

By European standards, British North America was as much a wasteland intellectually and culturally as it was geographically. The French scientist the Comte de Buffon and his followers at one time claimed that all species, including humans, degenerated in the New World environment. Certainly, colonists of all class levels, busy exploiting the land's resources, gave little time to the development of scholarship, arts, or letters. Nonetheless, a significant start toward a popular rather than an elite culture had been made. Impelled by the Protestant emphasis on Bible reading and the usefulness of education, many men and some women in British North America learned to read and write. The resources and density of population of the New England towns and the Atlantic seaports provided the means and the will to support schools. Here perhaps two-thirds of the males and one-third of the females were literate by the early eighteenth century, a far higher percentage than anywhere else in the world. To be sure, higher education lagged far behind the great learning centers of Europe and Latin America, but a beginning had been made. By the early eighteenth century, three private colleges, beginning with Harvard in 1636, offered a traditional curriculum designed to train ministers. Seven more colleges would soon be founded.

As it had in Latin America, by the mid-eighteenth century the Enlightenment began to nourish intellectual activity in British North America. Colonial scientists made significant contributions to the fields of biology, physics, astronomy, and other sciences. In the New World, as in the Old, educated persons dabbled in science and met in societies to debate the latest experiments and discoveries.

Benjamin Franklin (1706–1790), the multitalented printer from Philadelphia, is a good example of Enlightenment thinking in North America. One of the founders of the United States, Franklin was noted for his keen enthusiasm for scientific investigations. He experimented with electrical energy and made such practical contributions as the Franklin stove and the lightning rod. Franklin was the founder of a philosophical society, a journal, and an academy that subsequently became a major university. Like a dozen other colonists, Franklin was elected to the Royal Society in Britain.

The political, economic, and social ideas of the Enlightenment also found a warm welcome among the colonists, whose elected legislative assemblies gave them more political power than most Europeans. Merchants and farmers who had come to find greater economic opportunity in North America favored free enterprise. Although religious hatreds remained widespread on the local level, many early American leaders were firm believers in religious tolerance.

Thomas Jefferson (1743–1826), a Virginia landowner, was a latter-day Renaissance man who exemplified the application of Enlightenment thought to political theory and practice. His commitment to political rights and popular sovereignty still lives in the Declaration of Independence and the Bill of Rights. Like Franklin, Jefferson was an avid student of the physical sciences and was also a noted architect; he corresponded with European writers on subjects ranging from science to economics. He was a strong believer in religious toleration and in greater social equality. He opposed slavery of blacks, but failed to support immediate freedom for slaves, preferring a program of gradual emancipation and emigration of blacks to Africa or elsewhere.

Colonial Unrest and Colonial War

After 1763 the British government took the position that the colonists had not borne their proportionate share of the costs of the war against the French and had become too autonomous in their mercantilist relationship with the mother country. Consequently, the British government required the colonists to provide private quarters for the British garrisons and to pay new taxes created by Parliament and enforced by the king. The government imposed new trade regulations and enforced existing ones more stringently. Finally, the government prohibited settlement across the Appalachian Mountains, fearing that settlers would interrupt the deerskin and fur trades and provoke unnecessary wars with the Amerindians. These new policies shocked many colonists in British North America, who had begun to take autonomy in their local affairs for granted. Because of the new restrictions and exactions, discontent and hostility spread quickly among the colonists in much of British North America during the 1760s. At first the colonists confined their actions to securing the repeal of the new laws and regulations. Colonial lawyers and journalists turned a significant portion of the informed public against the British policies. The colonists' most effective tactic, however, was refusal to sell colonial products to British merchants and to buy British goods. As the colonists had hoped, financially strapped British businessmen persuaded Parliament on several occasions to repeal the offending taxes or regulations.

During the late 1760s and early 1770s, tensions steadily mounted. Radical colonists had begun to question the fundamental constitutional relationship between the colonies and Great Britain. Some denied that Parliament could legitimately regulate colonial affairs and argued that the king was only a symbol of unity and had no constitutional authority to enforce Parliament's policies. By 1774 a number of disruptive incidents instigated by the colonists had provoked the British government into repressive acts. In response, anti-Parliament colonials created the Continental Congress, composed of representatives from the older thirteen colonies (but not the new colonies of Florida and Quebec). The Congress met in Philadelphia and announced a new economic boycott enforced by local vigilante groups. The Congress also encouraged the colonies to organize, equip, and train companies of local militia.

In April 1775 British troops clashed with militia companies at Lexington and Concord, Massachusetts, inaugurating seven years of warfare. Despite the outbreak of fighting, most colonists were still loyal to Great Britain and respected the crown as a symbol of unity. However, George III rejected an appeal by colonists for local autonomy inside the British imperial system. As fighting continued, sentiment crystallized around complete separation from Great Britain. On July 4, 1776, the delegates of the Continental Congress signed a Declaration of Independence stating the reasons for their action.

During the ensuing war for independence, each side enjoyed distinct advantages and suffered from major problems. The British were clearly superior in conventional military forces. They had a winning tradition, a well-trained army, money to buy supplies and allies, and a navy that could land troops wherever desired, giving the British the military initiative. However, Great Britain also faced a new and difficult kind of war. The colonists fought a war of attrition against the large army that their opponents had to deploy across an area four times the size of Great Britain. Communication across the Atlantic was so slow that by the time orders arrived they were often no longer relevant. Supplies and reinforcements frequently were late and inadequate. The British won battles, but the colonists continued to resist, and the British lacked the troops and allies to garrison the hostile countryside. The rebel commander, George Washington, although losing battles, kept his army intact, providing a rallying point for continued resistance.

"It Is the Will of Heaven for Our Two Countries to Be Sundered Forever"

Yesterday the greatest question was decided which ever was debated in America, and a greater, perhaps, never was nor will be decided among men. A resolution was passed . . . "that these United Colonies are, and of right ought to be, free and independent States. . . . " You will see in a few days a Declaration setting forth the causes which have impelled us to this mighty revolution, and the reasons which will justify it in the sight of God and man. A plan of confederation will be taken up in a few days.

*When I look back . . . and recollect the series of political events, the chain of causes and effects, I am surprised at the suddenness as well as the greatness of this revolution. Britain has been filled with folly, and America with wisdom. . . . Time must determine. It is the will of heaven for our two countries to be sundered forever. It may be the will of Heaven that America shall suffer calamities. . . . But I submit all my hopes and fears to an overruling Providence, in which, unfashionable as the faith may be, I firmly believe.**

John Adams wrote these observations in a letter to his wife Abigail on July 3, 1776, where he expressed a mixture of satisfaction and trepidation. He, as much as any man in America, had brought independence about. The history of independence movements is often a record of heroic idealism on the part of men and women of firm conviction. Though the conditions of revolutions vary from case to case, the willingness to engage, as Jefferson put it, in "dangerous and fateful action" is a common denominator for all of them. The result has been a realignment of political power around the world and also the creation of an enduring creed of liberty and resistance to oppression. That the ideals expressed in that creed have not always been achieved does not diminish the importance of the struggle to realize them.

*John Adams, from Henry S. Commager and Richard B. Morris, eds., *The Spirit of 'Seventy-Six: The Story of the American Revolution as Told by Participants* (New York: Harper & Row, 1967), pp. 320–321.

Although distance, area, time, and sporadic aid from France favored them, the rebels also faced huge problems. Many colonists remained loyal to the crown, and rebel leaders quarreled incessantly, despite Benjamin Franklin's admonition "We must all hang together or we will all hang separately." The rebels were underfinanced, lacked soldiers willing to abandon cover and fight the British in the open, and were frequently distracted by trouble with the Amerindians. Slowly and painfully, they built a regular army that could fight in the open and reinforce local militias.

By 1777 neither side had made much headway in overcoming their problems. The British controlled only a strip of territory from Philadelphia to New York and had surrendered an army at Saratoga, while Washington and other rebel commanders had difficulty in keeping their fighting forces assembled. As time passed, each side doubted that their supporters could sustain the sacrifices necessary to outlast the enemy and win the war of attrition.

Beginning in 1778, events in Europe transformed the colonial war in the New World. The French, who had been rebuilding their army and especially their navy, watched with interest as Great Britain exhausted itself in North America. Capitalizing on the jealousy and fear of other European powers toward the British, France succeeded in isolating Great Britain diplomatically. Hearing the news of the British defeat at Saratoga, France, followed by Spain and the Netherlands, declared war on Great Britain. The colonial war in North America now expanded to India and the Caribbean. The French gave their most effective aid to the rebels in 1781, when a French army and fleet combined with Washington's army to capture Cornwallis's army at Yorktown, Virginia.

In 1781 the British government, unable to crush the rebellion, gave up their rebellious colonies in North America in order to concentrate their forces in a successful defense of their Caribbean and Indian possessions. At the Peace of Paris in 1783, Great Britain recognized the independence of the United States of America, ceding to the new nation the area south of Canada and east of the Mississippi, except for Florida and the Gulf coast, which went to Spain.

The United States of America

During the first half century of its independence the United States expanded and prospered. The population increased fivefold, and the key aspects of the colonial economy—foodstuffs, fishing, and the maritime trade—continued to flourish. Americans also made a small beginning in manufacturing. An enormous innovation was brought about by a simple technological invention. The cotton gin enabled Americans to grow abundant supplies of short-fibered cotton as the basis for mass-producing cheap cotton clothing. The enormous demand in Europe soon made cotton the most valuable American commodity: as some enthusiastic southerners put it, "Cotton is king!" The huge size of the new nation also placed a premium on improving transportation and communication. Americans, with heavy financial backing from British investors, were in the forefront of constructing or improving canals, roads, steamboats, and, eventually, the railroad and telegraph systems.

Society and politics in the United States continued the trends already under way in the colonial period. The percentage of those owning property continued to rise, as did the general standard of living. The passage of time, plus the libertarian influence of the Enlightenment, eased religious animosities and began to create an atmosphere of toleration. Ethnic and religious hostilities persisted, but they lessened as individuals of different backgrounds began to associate and intermarry. Most white Americans learned to read and write, and women rapidly closed the literacy gap between themselves and men. Many colleges opened, mostly sectarian and primarily for men. Some schools reflected the influence of the Enlightenment as they introduced courses in mathematics, science, foreign languages, and history.

Men of property still dominated politics as they had in colonial times, and the officers of the new nation came from the ranks of the upper class. However, the organized political party and the rapid abolition of state religious and property qualifications for voting gradually placed political power in the hands of the mass of white males.

The greatest political achievement of the new nation was the Constitution of 1787 and the Bill of Rights of 1791. These documents fashioned a federal republic in which the national government controlled diplomacy, war, peace, interstate and international commerce, the army and navy, and Indian affairs. The states retained control of the bulk of everyday affairs, including civil and criminal law, education, health and safety, and the militia. The Bill of Rights promised an open, liberal society that would tolerate freedom of religion, speech, and the press. Further, it guaranteed procedural protections and a fair trial for those accused of crime. Most whites did not interpret these provisions as applying to blacks or Amerindians. Nevertheless, the principles of the American revolution, as expressed in the Declaration of Independence, the Constitution, and the Bill of Rights inspired many French revolutionaries in 1789.

The British Surrender at Yorktown, Virgina, October 19, 1781. The victory over the British by rebel colonial forces, aided by French army and navy units, opened the way for independence. In this detail from John Trumbull's somewhat overdramatized painting, General O'Hara, representing the absent General Charles Cornwallis, formally capitulates to General Benjamin Lincoln, representing George Washington.

John Trumbull, Yale University Art Gallery, Trumbull Collection

Despite its internal prosperity, the United States was an insignificant military power. After 1792 it became enmeshed as a minor party in the long struggle between Great Britain and France. While some Americans were making great sums of money supplying the belligerents, others had their ships seized and some crewmen imprisoned or pressed into naval service by the British and the French. Beyond the Appalachians, the Spanish and British intrigued with the Amerindians and harassed settlers, jeopardizing American interests in the region. When diplomacy and embargo failed to protect its commerce, the United States declared war on Great Britain in 1812, but the struggle was inconclusive.

Although it had great problems in defending its overseas trade, the United States rapidly expanded across the North American continent between 1803 and 1826. U.S. military forces crushed the Amerindians, who thereafter ceased to be a serious obstacle to white expansion. Although the United States failed to take Canada in the War of 1812, it acquired Louisiana and Florida by negotiation, extending its territory to the Rocky Mountains. Beyond the Rockies, the United States laid claim to the Oregon territory from the Rocky Mountains to the Pacific coast.

Despite growing freedom and prosperity in the United States, unresolved problems threatened the unity of the republic. Economic competition between regions had become acute by the 1820s. Many northerners favored a protective tariff to build up American industry and create a home market for agriculture. Most southerners, on the other hand, wanted free trade so they could keep their costs of production down and sell their cotton, rice, and tobacco abroad without fear of foreign tariff retaliation.

The economic competition between north and south was exacerbated by another issue, slavery. Although slavery was declining in the north, the cotton economy had fixed it firmly into the social, cultural, and ideological fabric of the southern states. An increasing number of individuals, mostly in the north, wanted either to restrict slavery to the south for economic reasons or to abolish it for moral reasons. By mid-century, the earlier optimism that the United States was blending its disparate ethnic and social elements into a harmonious society began to fade in the face of increasing sectional rancor.

The Global Contest for Empire and the Onset of the Industrial Revolution

The separating distance was growing less and less. A hundred paces now! Would that grim line of redcoats never fire! Seventy-five!! Fifty!! Forty!! . . . "Ready!—Present!—Fire!!! . . . the British volleys crashed forth, from right to left, battalion by battalion, all down that thin red line.

The stricken front rank of the French fell before these double-shotted volleys almost to a man. When the smoke cleared off the British had . . . closed up some twenty paces . . . reloading as they came. And now, taking the French in front and flanks, they fired as fast as they could, but steadily and under perfect control. The French on the other hand, were firing wildly, and simply crumbling away under that well-aimed storm of lead. . . . In a vain, last effort to lead them on their officers faced death and found it. Montcalm, . . . told he had only a few hours to live, replied, "So much the better, I shall not see the surrender of Quebec."

*Wolfe, with three bullet wounds, also lay dying. "They run; see how they run!" a subordinate shouted. "Who run?" Wolfe demanded, like a man roused from sleep. "The enemy, sir. Egad, they give way everywhere!" Wolfe, turning on his side, murmured, "Now, God be praised, I will die in peace."**

*Thomas Wood, *The Passing of New France,* pp. 137–148 passim; *The Winning of Canada,* pp. 138–139. Both in George M. Wrong and H. H. Langton, eds. *Chronicles of Canada,* vols. 10, 11 (Toronto/Glasgow: Brook, 1914–1921).

On September 13, 1759, on the Plains of Abraham outside the fortress city of Quebec in New France (Canada), the British army led by James Wolfe defeated the French forces of Louis de Montcalm and delivered French North America to Great Britain. Coupled with victories over the French in the Caribbean and India, the conquest of New France gave Great Britain colonial supremacy and dominance of the global trade network. This worldwide confrontation between Great Britain and France had been building throughout the eighteenth century as the great age of seaborne discovery was coming to a close and the age of industrialization was dawning.

Exploration in the Pacific, Competition in North America

In the seventeenth and eighteenth centuries, Europeans continued to expand their knowledge of the world, chiefly through explorations by sea. Commercial gain was as usual the main motive, but there was also a thirst for scientific knowledge that was typical of the Age of Newton. As the explorers discovered areas of the world previously unknown to Europeans, Western traders followed close behind.

Although the Europeans explored the Indian Ocean and other regions, they concentrated on the Pacific during the eighteenth century. The new chronometer, which allowed navigators to calculate the correct longitude in determining a ship's location, was a major aid in

Mansell Collection

The West Meets the Pacific. Captain James Cook's reception by the peoples of the Pacific varied as widely as the different cultures he visited. Overawed by his vessels, most groups received him peacefully, but he eventually lost his life in Hawaii during a skirmish with islanders. Here Cook lands in the New Hebrides in 1774. A salvo of greeting—and intimidation—stuns a few Hebrideans, but most, though excited, stand their ground. Cook holds a palm frond as a symbol of peace.

the exploring enterprise. Led by the greatest explorer of the age, Captain James Cook (1728–1779) of Great Britain, European ships stopped at Tahiti, Hawaii, and other islands of the central and south Pacific. Following up on earlier sightings and shipwrecks, Dutch and British explorers, chiefly Abel Tasman and Cook, found a landmass large enough to be classified as a continent; it was later named Australia (Southern Land). Coastal eastern Australia was blessed with a moderate climate that proved suitable for European settlement. Farther south, Europeans began to detect the frozen continent of Antarctica. In the offshore waters they found sources of future wealth in the whales and seals, whose oil and pelts were in great demand, particularly in China.

Europeans also explored the North Pacific and its North American and Asian shorelines, finding more whales and seals, as well as sea otters, a new source of wealth. In 1728 Vitus Bering (1680–1741), a Danish explorer in the employ of Peter the Great, found that Asia and North America were separated by a body of water. By 1779, when Cook was killed in a skirmish with the Hawaiians, little was left for Europeans to explore by sea, although the interior of most of the continents still remained unknown to them.

During the eighteenth century, several nations competed vigorously for control of the remote but lucrative furs on the Pacific coast of North America. The Spanish set up missions and forts along the Pacific coast in California and made claims northward as far as Alaska; there they were soon challenged by Russian traders from Siberia looking for sea otter and seal pelts. By the 1790s both Great Britain and the United States were also asserting claims in the Pacific Northwest, based on competing trading posts.

Competing Colonial Systems

The overseas dominions of Spain, Portugal, and the Netherlands expanded only marginally during the eighteenth century. Except for its movement north along the California coast, Spain was too weak to do more than doggedly hold on to its sprawling possessions. The Portuguese, having lost most of their Asian empire to the Dutch, concentrated on expanding their "second empire" in Brazil. They grew tobacco and sugar in the tropical north, importing ever-larger numbers of slaves from their African possessions. An economic boom came with the discovery of gold and diamonds in Brazil's interior. In the early nineteenth century, as the gold rush faded, the Portuguese turned to producing coffee in Brazil's temperate southern uplands.

About 1650 it appeared that the Dutch might carve out the greatest European overseas empire, but despite having the largest seventeenth-century merchant marine and navy, the Dutch fell victim to their homeland's small size and vulnerable location. They lost three naval wars

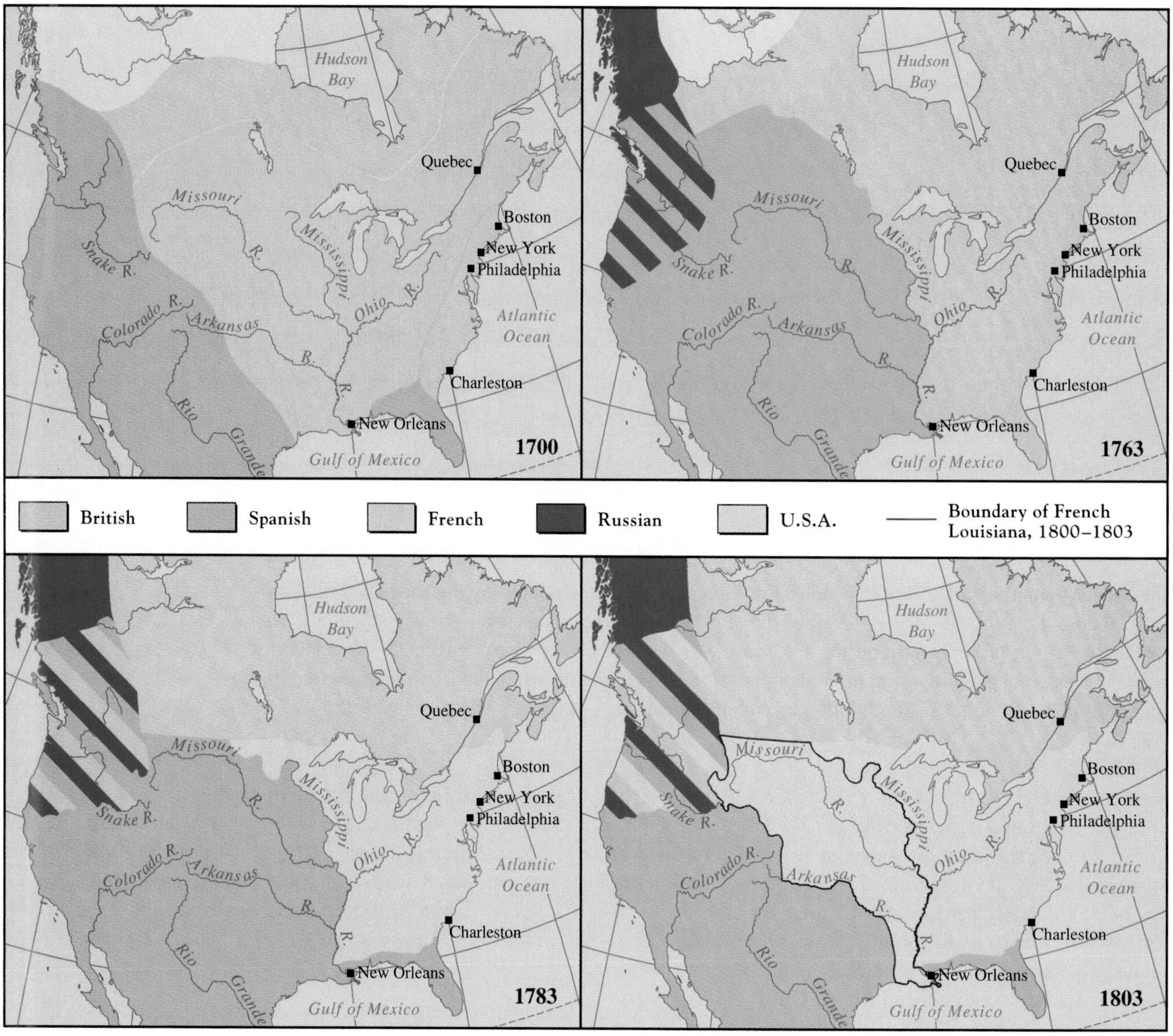

Map 11.3 North America, 1700–1803. These four maps illustrate the British triumph in the struggle for North America and the expansion of the United States at the expense of Great Britain, France, and Spain.

with the English in the late seventeenth century while at the same time fighting a series of wars against France. Despite these problems, the Dutch in the eighteenth century still held sugar islands in the Caribbean, slave-trading posts on the African coast, settlements at the southern tip of Africa, cinnamon and tea plantations on Ceylon, and clove and nutmeg production in Indonesia; and after 1677 they slowly took control of the pepper and coffee areas in Java and gained footholds in the spice islands. During much of their expansion, the Dutch employed the classic divide-and-conquer technique, already used to great effect by the Spanish and other Europeans on the Amerindians and soon to be employed by the British and French in India.

During the eighteenth century, Great Britain and France increased their efforts to control the lucrative colonial trade, redirecting more and more of their economic and military resources from traditional contests on the European continent to new struggles overseas. By mid-century, the fighting in India and the Western Hemisphere had acquired a tempo quite different from that of wars and diplomacy in Europe.

In contrast with the relatively static Portuguese, Spanish, and Dutch colonial regimes, the British and French aggressively expanded their overseas power. In the process, they became embroiled in a long series of international struggles for colonial and continental supremacy (1689–1815). Louis XIV, for example, was as aggressive overseas as he was in Europe; France acquired additional possessions in the Caribbean and trading posts in India.

In North America French pioneers pushing out from New France laid claim to the enormous Mississippi–Missouri–Ohio–Great Lakes basin extending from the Appalachians to the Rocky Mountains and from the Great Lakes to the Gulf coast between Florida and Mexico; they named the whole vast region Louisiana. Meanwhile, French and British traders competed for the profitable far northern fur trade. By 1702 the French had erected a chain of forts from the Great Lakes down the Mississippi to the Gulf coast.

The French now threatened the Spanish possessions in Cuba and Mexico and the British colonies on the Atlantic seaboard, and both nations responded. The Spanish set up several posts in Texas to protect Mexico and one at Pensacola to shield Florida and Cuba. After 1713, however, the new Bourbon dynasty in Spain became an ally of France and later aided the French by attacking settlements in the southern British colonies. The English launched a counteroffensive and conquered Nova Scotia and Newfoundland, prime bases for fishing. British expansion in the Caribbean enabled them to break Spain's trade monopoly with Spanish America.

By the 1750s the British and French were in a critical phase of a worldwide struggle that focused on India, the Caribbean, and North America. In India, British and French trading companies were interested in expanding beyond their original assortment of coastal trading posts. The Indian subcontinent produced valuable spices and textiles, and its huge population was at once a source of cheap labor and an opportunity for profitable taxation. It was also a prospective captive market for European goods that could reverse the drain of European silver going to pay for Indian products. The European-owned East India companies were interested in controlling blocks of territory, where labor could be efficiently organized to produce a higher output of spices and textiles. This arrangement had long been typical of European colonization in the Western Hemisphere, and the Dutch were emulating it in Indonesia.

By the mid-eighteenth century, the French and British India companies saw their chance. As the Moghul dynasty

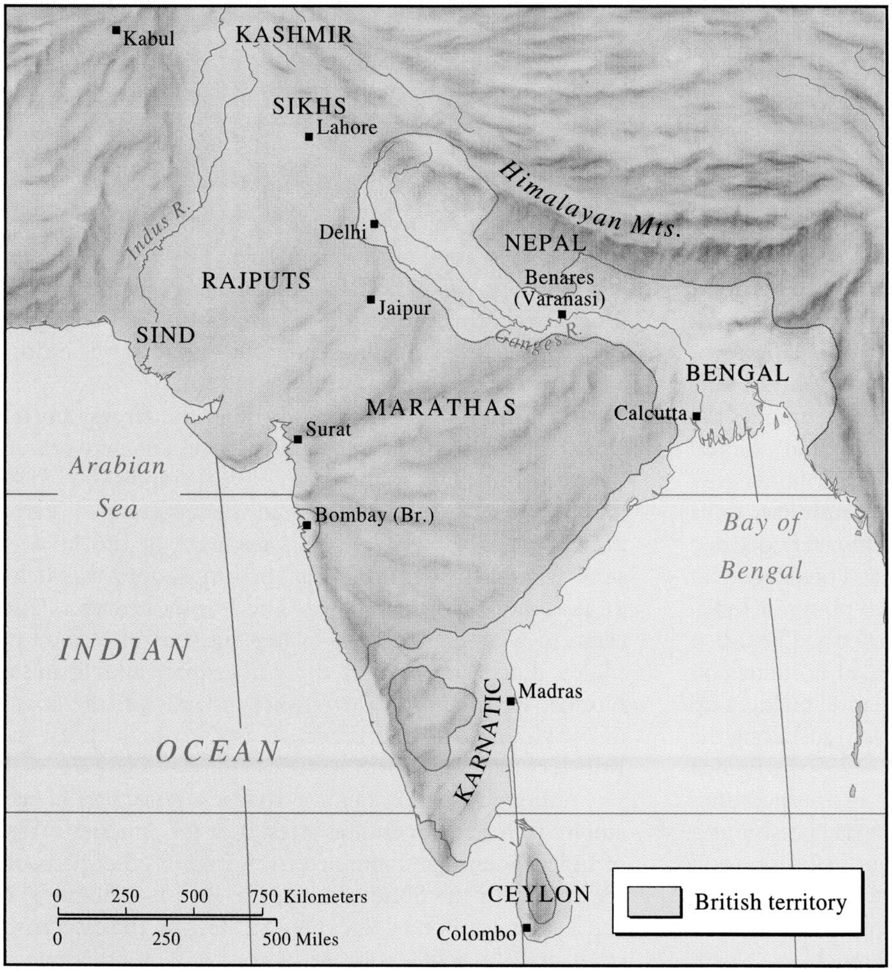

Map 11.4 British Empire in India, c. 1800. After the disintegration of the Moghul Empire and the defeat of France in India in the eighteenth century, Great Britain emerged as the dominant power in India. Further conquests and alliances with Indian princes during the nineteenth century consolidated British supremacy on the subcontinent.

National Portrait Gallery, London

Triumph in India. This scene depicts the aftermath of the battle of Plassey, June 23, 1757, which opened India to British conquest. Robert Clive meets with Mir Jaffar, whose treachery secured the British victory. The imperialist strategy of divide and conquer succeeded as well in India as elsewhere.

of Muslim emperors rapidly dissolved under numerous rebellions and outside attacks, each national trading company supported certain Indian princes against others in return for help in destroying the competing trading company. Once it had eliminated its European rivals, the surviving company could then exploit rivalries among the Indian potentates and expand its economic and political controls over India. By 1751, even while their home governments were at peace, the French and British East India companies were at war. The issue was ultimately decided by the British capture of the key post at Pondicherry in 1761, which effectively eliminated French power in India.

As in India, fighting between the French and British in North America in the mid-1750s preceded hostilities on the Continent. The French took the initiative, building up their military forces in New France (Canada) and along the Great Lakes to the Ohio Valley. In 1754–1755 the French and their Amerindian allies defeated two expeditions mounted against Fort Duquesne (present-day Pittsburgh).

In 1756 a general conflict broke out in Europe and merged with the world war for colonial supremacy already in progress. With France preoccupied on the continent, the British fleet cut off the French in North America and methodically conquered New France. In 1759 James Wolfe defeated the main French army at Quebec, and his successors captured Montreal in 1760. Meanwhile, British naval expeditions wrested away nearly all of the French islands in the Caribbean.

By 1763 Great Britain controlled the largest European colonial empire and the most profitable network of overseas trade; by contrast, the colonial empire of France had been almost totally destroyed. In the Treaty of Paris in 1763, Spain received Louisiana west of the Mississippi, giving it, with its earlier holdings, approximately 40 percent of North America. The British, however, laid claim to New France (thus taking full control of the fur trade), Louisiana east of the Mississippi, and Spanish Florida. Restricted to a few fishery islands off the coast of Newfoundland, the French ceased to be a threat to British colonies in North America.

Although Great Britain was to lose a major part of her empire in North America as a result of the American War of Independence, it continued to expand in other parts of the world. In the South Pacific, the British established a penal colony at Botany Bay (now Sydney) on the east coast of Australia in 1788, soon to be followed by other penal settlements. No other European power considered Australia worth contesting, and Great Britain thus added an entire continent to its dominions.

To the British, however, gaining full control of India was of far greater importance than developing Australia. The process of conquest began in 1757 when Robert Clive defeated a large Indian army at Plassey, obtaining the province of Bengal in northeast India for the British East India Company. Between the 1780s and the 1820s, the efficient and well-equipped forces of the British East India Company seized large additional territories, giving Britain effective control of the subcontinent.

Besides taking over India and Australia, the British made one more major expansion of their colonial empire, seizing some colonies of the Dutch. During the 1790s, revolutionary France had made the Netherlands a satellite. This gave the British, persistent foes of Revolutionary and Napoleonic France, an opportunity to conquer Dutch possessions that threatened British trade routes to India and East Asia. By 1815, the British had taken over Mauritius Island (from the French), Cape of Good Hope in South Africa from the Dutch, and Ceylon. By the 1820s a major British base at Singapore at the tip of the Malay Peninsula controlled the trade route to East Asia.

The Developing Global Economy

As European explorers charted the world's waterways and fought for footholds and colonies, they built up a global network of seaborne commerce that brought ever-increasing prosperity to Europe. Portugal, Spain, the Netherlands, Great Britain, and France added an extensive colonial commerce to their trade on the continent. Including the smaller colonial trading interests of Hamburg and the Baltic states of Denmark, Sweden, and Prussia, eighteenth-century overseas commerce now rivaled in value the traditional trade patterns inside Europe. Two-thirds of Great Britain's trade now involved areas outside Europe.

Three major trade patterns dominated overseas commerce. The oldest originated when the Spanish began importing gold and silver from Spanish America. The Spanish sent most of these precious metals to Great Britain, France, and the Netherlands in exchange for manufactured products. The Dutch, French, and British then carried this bullion to China and India to exchange for silk and cotton textiles, tea, and spices, which they brought back and sold to Europeans. The new trade routes and the influx of gold and silver from the Western Hemisphere weakened the Ottoman Empire financially as the importance of the overland routes it controlled lessened.

Plantation agriculture in the Western Hemisphere and Asia formed the second, and, by the eighteenth century, most valuable, international trading pattern. Europeans had transformed much of the Atlantic coast of the Americas into plantations. The plantation zone extended 5,000 miles from Chesapeake Bay in North America south through the Caribbean islands and down the northern coast of Brazil. Planters produced a variety of valuable fibers, foodstuffs, drugs, and forest products desired in Europe. Sugar imports alone equaled in value the entire Asian trade. In addition, the Dutch shipped to Europe a variety of commodities from their rapidly developing East Indian plantation system. In a subpattern of this trade, North Americans shipped furs, lumber, and naval stores to Great Britain and France.

The growing commerce in plantation products from the Americas made a third pattern—the trade in slaves—increasingly lucrative. The grueling work under tropical or subtropical conditions and the constantly expanding plantations required a continual flow of fresh labor, and the trade in black African slaves grew increasingly efficient. During the eighteenth century, some 60,000 slaves annually were imported into the Western Hemisphere from Africa. The Portuguese, Dutch, and French had successively taken over the largest share of the slave trade, but by the mid-eighteenth century the British and New Englanders dominated the slaving business outside Brazil, which was supplied by the Portuguese.

The three global trade patterns brought immense prosperity to a few European seaports. Great Britain became the world's foremost overseas trading nation after 1763, and London the world's greatest port, growing rich on Caribbean sugar, Indian cotton, and many other products. Liverpool and Glasgow were fast rising to commercial prominence through their trade in slaves, furs, and tobacco. Until 1763 the overseas trade of France rivaled that of Great Britain in value, with Bordeaux and Nantes prospering from the slave trade, sugar, and Asian goods. Amsterdam, enjoying immense profits from the slave and spice trades, continued to be one of the greatest commercial centers in Europe, although the overall value of Dutch trade had slipped behind that of Great Britain and France. Lisbon and Cadiz were still prosperous cities, although the early colonial trade supremacy of the Iberian states had gone.

The merchants of the great trading centers exerted increasing economic and political power. They had superior management and marketing skills, a knack for cooperating with the banking interests to secure capital and credit, and a sharp eye for technological improvements. Their interests and needs increasingly influenced politics and diplomacy, including decisions on peace and war. Merchants also plowed some of their profits into new manufacturing enterprises, fueling the major socioeconomic transformation known as the Industrial Revolution.

The Beginnings of the Industrial Revolution

Modern industrial society first took shape in Great Britain in the mid-eighteenth century. The changes that industrialization brought were so momentous that historians speak of a "revolution"—not a political upheaval but an "industrial revolution." This revolution may be likened to an explosive chemical reaction. Industry became possible only in the presence of certain essential components: specifically, adequate natural resources and labor, sufficient economic demand, accumulations of capital, technological advances, and entrepreneurship. In the eighteenth century more of these elements were present in Great Britain than elsewhere.

The basic raw materials, iron ore and coal, were found in substantial quantities in central and northern England, either near each other or near water. Entrepreneurs thus found it relatively cheap to bring coal and iron ore together for industrial purposes. The distances from the manufacturing centers to the cities and ports of Great Britain were short, enabling manufactured products to reach both domestic and foreign markets expeditiously.

Another essential element in the Industrial Revolution was increased agricultural production. Eighteenth-century improvements in crop rotation, soil fertilization, and animal breeding boosted British agricultural output, thus increasing the food supply and stimulating a rapid growth in population. The expanding consumption of potatoes, which were more nutritious than corn, led to an increased and healthier population. More efficient agriculture also freed manpower for industrial work. At the same time, landowners were enclosing village lands, dispossessing many peasants and causing them to look for work in the new factories.

The demand for goods that accompanied the increase in population further stimulated industrial production. The prosperity accumulated during centuries of overseas trade also spurred demand; and Great Britain, with its large overseas empire, was the most prosperous nation in eighteenth-century Europe. Improved roads and canals and the absence of internal tolls and tariffs facilitated a profitable flow of goods; after the union of England and Scotland, Great Britain was the largest free trade area in Europe.

Profit from commercial and colonial enterprises also generated investment capital. Great Britain's excellent banks, including Europe's strongest financial institution, the Bank of England, had large amounts of capital to invest. As with the joint-stock companies of an earlier era, limited liability laws also encouraged speculation by re-

Profiles in Human Misery. By the eighteenth century, the Atlantic slave trade had reached its peak, yielding vast profits to Europeans active in that trade. The brutal inhumanity of the slave ships is graphically portrayed here.

The Granger Collection

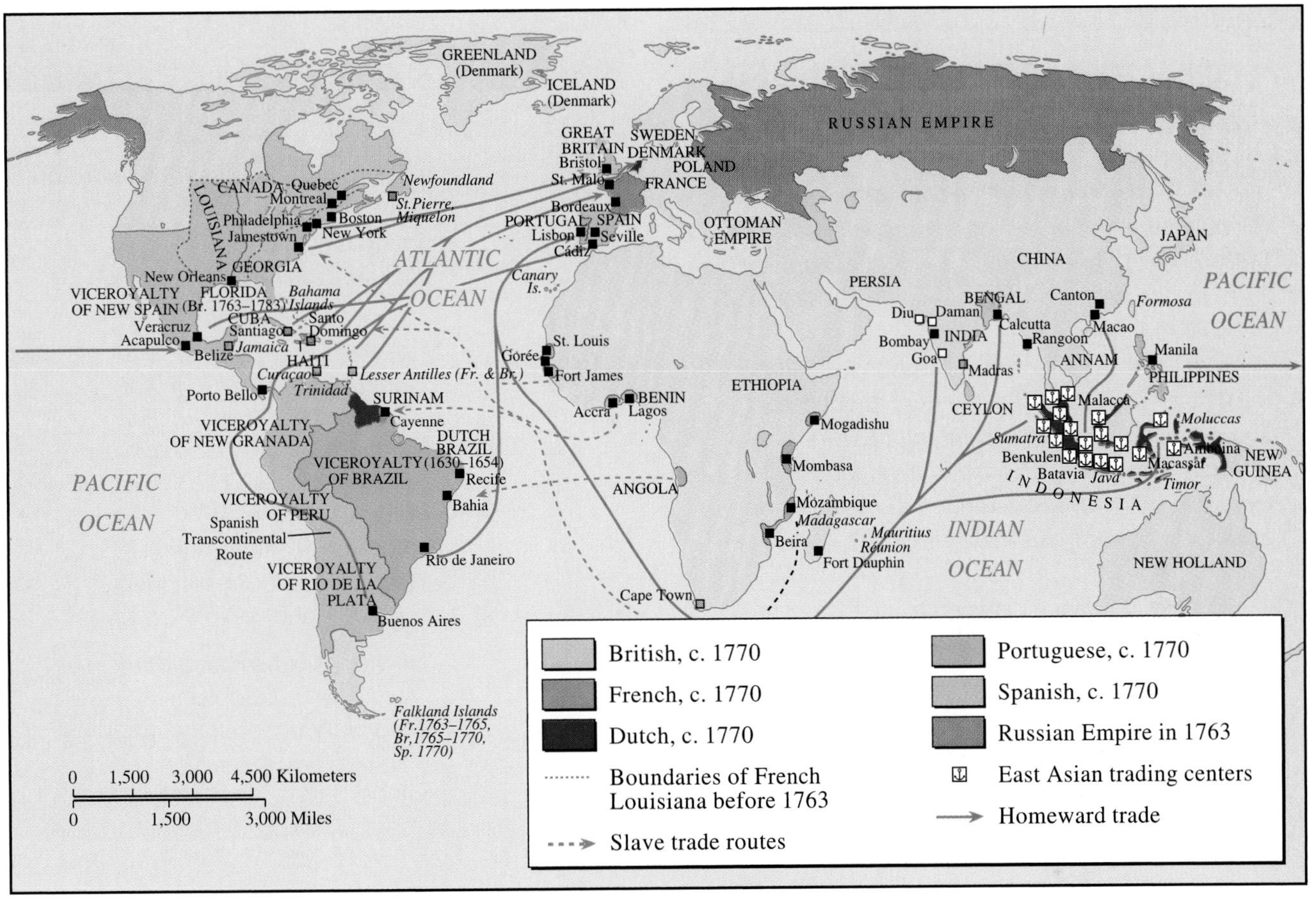

Map 11.5 European Colonial Empires and Global Trade Patterns, c. 1770. After 300 years of exploration and trade outside their continent, European nations had made massive changes around the globe. Nearly all of the Western Hemisphere had come under their control, and they had built up an extensive network of trading centers along the African coast and across much of South and Southeast Asia. Products from four continents poured into the Atlantic ports of five European nations, to be consumed or resold to the rest of Europe. In addition, an enormous trade in African slaves, along with pockets of European settlement, was transforming the Americas racially. The interior of Africa, the Islamic world, and East Asia, at this time lightly touched, faced the power of the European onslaught in the next century.

stricting an investor's obligation for a firm's debts to the amount of his own investment.

The availability of new sources of energy was a key component in the onset of the Industrial Revolution. The steam engine provided the essential source of power. Steam had long been used in a limited way for pumping water out of coal mines, but in the 1760s a Scottish mechanic, James Watt, designed steam-powered engines efficient enough for other industrial uses. In partnership with Matthew Boulton, an English entrepreneur, Watt produced engines that could do the work of up to twenty horses—the origin of the "horsepower" rating. By the early nineteenth century, steam had replaced water mills as the chief energy sources of the booming Industrial Revolution.

Under these favorable conditions, technological advances in industry came rapidly. Inventors and technicians developed new machines specifically to solve recognized industrial problems. Developments in one industry also expanded the technological base from which other entrepreneurs might borrow, furthering even more industrial growth. Additionally, the weakening of the power of the guilds allowed much more rapid innovation than the conservative artisans would have permitted.

Entrepreneurship was another essential catalyst for industrial expansion in Britain. The profits to be made attracted ambitious and ingenious men to industry. The law of primogeniture, which turned a family's entire landed estates over to the oldest son, and the relative lack of prejudice against being "in trade" sent well-educated, self-confident younger sons into business. Such men made a paying proposition out of the new technology and activated the machinery of the Industrial Revolution.

Making Hay while the Sun Shines: Supply and Demand in Industry

We wish you to drop the Sattinets, they are not new here and only fit for two months sale. The Buff stripes . . . are not fine enough for People of Fashion. . . . Arkwright must lower his Twist and he must spin finer. . . .

*We want as many spotted muslins and fancy muslins as you can make, the finer the better. . . . You must give a look to Invention, industry [that is, industriousness] you have in abundance. We expect to hear from you as often as possible and as the sun shines let us make the Hay.**

This correspondence between a late-eighteenth-century British merchant and a manufacturer illustrates how industrial manufacturing in the cotton textile business responded to public demand. When fickle public taste demanded certain dress fabrics, technology was expected to deliver the goods. The entrepreneurial spirit of the early Industrial Revolution is well expressed in the concluding phrase.

*Correspondence between Samuel Oldknow and his London agents, in Charles Wilson, "The Entrepreneur in the Industrial Revolution in Britain," in Sima Lieberman, ed., *Europe and the Industrial Revolution* (Cambridge, Mass.: Schenkman, 1972), p. 385.

New Industries

The evolution of cotton textile manufacturing well illustrates the dependence of industries on sources of power like the steam engine. Indian imports had already created a growing demand for cotton cloth; Parliament, however, had prohibited the importing of cotton textiles to protect British wool producers, most of whom were peasants with spinning wheels and looms in their cottages. To satisfy the demand for cotton, eager (and sometimes unscrupulous) entrepreneurs like Richard Arkwright imported raw cotton and began to produce cotton cloth in Great Britain, inventing new machinery in the process.

As the market for cotton fabrics grew, technicians devised machinery to speed up both the spinning of cotton thread and the weaving of the threads into cloth. The new machines, too big and costly for cottage industry, had to be housed in large sheds—the first modern industrial factories—and were driven first by water power and later by the new steam engines.

1500

Copernicus, *On the Revolutions of the Heavenly Spheres*
Philip II of Spain
Galileo Galilei

1600

Garcilaso de la Vega, *Royal Commentaries of the Incas*
Romanov dynasty in Russia
René Descartes
Louis XIV of France
Palace of Versailles built
Harvard University founded
Casa de Contratación

Newton, *Mathematical Principles of Natural Philosophy*
The poetry of Sor Juana Ines de la Cruz
Glorious Revolution in England

1700

Peter the Great begins Westernization of Russia
Daniel Defoe, *Robinson Crusoe*
Johann Sebastian Bach
The philosophes
Frederick the Great

Battle of Plassey
Voltaire, *Candide*
Captain James Cook
James Watt's steam engine

1775

Benjamin Franklin
American Revolution
Adam Smith, *The Wealth of Nations*
Catherine the Great of Russia
Destruction of Poland
Thomas Jefferson
The British colonize Australia
U.S. Constitution and Bill of Rights
Joseph II of Austria
Wolfgang Amadeus Mozart
The cotton gin

1800

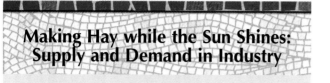

The immense success of this new industrial system may be measured by the growth of the cotton industry. In 1770 Great Britain had only a handful of cotton manufacturing plants and exported few cotton textiles. By 1830 cotton cloth not only sold widely in Great Britain but also accounted for 45 percent of all its foreign exports, much of it going to protected markets in the British colonies.

Two other industries that were essential to the exploitation of new techniques in many areas of the economy were coal and iron production; both experienced major advances in the eighteenth century. England had burned off much of its forest cover by early modern times and had begun to use coal instead of wood for home heating and for some industrial purposes even before 1700. In the eighteenth century British coal miners developed a number of advanced techniques for extracting coal from greater depth. Steam power was particularly valuable for pumping water out of the deeper shafts of the mines.

Iron production also increased in this first century of the Industrial Revolution. Iron manufacturers learned to use coke (made from coal) instead of expensive charcoal (made from wood) for smelting high-grade iron. Ironmasters like John Wilkinson also learned to work iron precisely and to apply it to many new purposes, from bridges to steam engine boilers.

Summary and Comparisons

Europeans found religious and historical justifications for the absolutist form of government, in part built upon the national-state structure of the preceding era. Charles V and Philip II made the Spanish-Habsburg Empire the foremost absolutist state in Europe in the sixteenth century and imposed a mercantilist economic system on the Spanish Empire. However, Spanish treasure was squandered on mostly unsuccessful wars against the Protestant Netherlands, England, and the German states. After Philip II, an exhausted Spain declined to a second-class power.

Royal absolutism reached full bloom during the reign of Louis XIV of France. Louis reduced the once powerful nobles to frivolous courtiers, ignored the Estates-General, and centralized power in his own hands. Practicing mercantilism, Louis's government developed the French economy, fostered overseas trade, and conquered an overseas empire. It also fought wars to replace Spain as the preeminent European nation. Culture and the arts thrived under Louis's lavish patronage, and everything French—from the Versailles palace to fashion—set the style for the rest of Europe.

The English government evolved from absolutism to constitutionalism during this period. Royal power was decisively checked after a bloody civil war, the execution of one king, and the expulsion of another. Parliament emerged victorious, opening the way for constitutional government.

The conviction that a king should act to eliminate injustice and ensure prosperity and stability of the state led to enlightened despotism, epitomized by Frederick the Great. Frederick saw himself as the first servant of the state and responsible for the welfare of the people in his care.

The Age of Reason, or the Enlightenment, grew out of the scientific revolution of the sixteenth and seventeenth centuries, which had begun with Copernicus's heliocentric theory and climaxed with Newton's formulation of the law of gravity. Meanwhile, seventeenth-century philosophers like Bacon and Descartes developed the scientific method. In the eighteenth century, the philosophes made rational critiques of existing social conventions and proposed new political approaches. Voltaire, Diderot, and Rousseau attacked the abuses of the old regime, and John Locke and Adam Smith urged a new order based on political and economic freedom.

The Enlightenment spread to the Western Hemisphere and affected societies around the world. Other European cultural achievements included the development of the novel and art catering to the tastes of the rising middle class. The Western world was on the threshold of major changes.

Between 1648 and 1740, absolutist governments dominated in central and eastern Europe, as they did in France and Spain. The Austrian Habsburg dynasty used absolutist methods to recover from their loss of power in the Thirty Years' War. The Prussian Hohenzollerns joined the front rank of nations with the help of absolutist techniques and an impressive bureaucracy and army.

By the eighteenth century, the Iberian monarchies had firmly implanted Western civilization throughout an area twice the size of Europe. The impact of Western culture varied widely according to region, ranging from strong influence in Mexico and Peru to nonexistent in the Amazon and the southern tip of South America. The impact also varied by social status: the upper classes clung to their Iberian background, while the lower orders were still strongly influenced by their native Amerindian and African cultures. The Iberians established Roman Catholicism as the only faith throughout the colonies. Amerindians "converted" to Catholicism, but on their own spiritual and cultural terms. Three key characteristics of Iberia—paternalistic government, aristocratic social and economic privilege, and mercantilist economics—were substantially replicated in Latin America. Latin Americans also inherited the intellectual, literary, and artistic outlook of Spain and Portugal, though ongoing interaction with Amerindian and African cultures led to new forms of Western civilization.

By the early eighteenth century, the residents of North America had developed a distinct culture that departed more substantially from Europe than did Latin America's. Yet, in some ways, British North America approximated Europe more closely than did Latin America: the area was overwhelmingly European racially and linguistically, and Amerindian culture played an insignificant role. The African impact was also less profound as yet. On the other hand, British North America was fast departing from continental Europe and Latin America in that it demonstrated a strong tendency toward socioeconomic and political liberalization, a tendency that was also getting under way in Great Britain.

Europeans visiting British North America were naturally impressed by the differences rather than the similarities. They commented on the strange landscape, the raw look of both cities and farms, and the lack of monuments or any sign of a living, visible past. They were discomfited by the restless moving about of the population and the cacophony of ethnic groups and religious sects. Above all, Europeans were struck by the individualism at all levels of society and by the absence of servility among the middle and lower orders of whites. Europeans attributed these characteristics to the general prosperity of the population, to education, and to the weakness of the class system. Most visitors went home dismayed by the brawling confusion and the social dislocation, but a few enthusiasts felt they had seen the future of Western civilization.

After 1763 the British attempted to rein in their North American colonists and subject them to new taxes. The colonists resisted and in 1775 fighting broke out; compromise failing, the colonists declared their independence in 1776 and a war of attrition ensued. France and other nations entered the war against Great Britain and in 1783 the British recognized the independence of the United States of America.

A liberal federal republic, the United States enjoyed, in spite of a number of national problems, a vibrant economy and both population and territorial growth. Most of its white citizens owned property, were literate, and participated in politics. By the middle of the nineteenth century, however, dissension between the northern and southern sections brought fears of disunity.

From the late seventeenth to the early nineteenth century, Europeans expanded their knowledge of, and controls over, more of the world. Though they charted the Pacific and discovered Australia, their greatest interest was in the interior and northwest coast of North America, where several European nations competed for beaver, seal, and otter pelts. The fur trade, however, was only a minor part of an emerging global economy that combined the products of Asia and the Americas and the labor of Africa into enormous wealth for the seafaring powers of Europe and their Atlantic port cities.

While the Spanish, Portuguese, and Dutch were struggling to retain their empires, the French and British rapidly expanded their colonial possessions. The two nations fought each other in North America and India with increasing intensity throughout the first half of the eighteenth century, with the British emerging triumphant in 1763. After Spain was reduced to impotence in India and the Caribbean, Great Britain was by far the greatest colonial power in the world.

The Industrial Revolution was a crucial event in world history, with far-ranging socioeconomic consequences on both sides of the Atlantic. It resulted from a mix of natural resources, an expanding labor force, growing economic demand, the accumulation of investment capital, technological ingenuity, entrepreneurial leadership, and a progressive mindset. Unprecedented manufacturing expansion, first in Britain, thereafter in continental Europe and the Americas, produced new industries and new sources of energy, including iron, coal, textiles, and the steam engine itself in the later 1700s and earlier 1800s. As we shall see in Chapter 12, many nations in Europe and in the New World followed Great Britain's lead.

Selected Sources

Adam, Antoine. *Grandeur and Illusion: French Literature and Society, 1600–1715.* Translated by Herbert Tint. 1972. Good Survey of the intellectual history of the age; section on classicism particularly well done.

*Artz, Frederick B. *The Enlightenment in France.* 1968. A brief survey of the movement in the land of the philosophes.

Ashton, T. S. *The Industrial Revolution, 1760–1830.* 1968. The English origins of the modern industrial system.

Bannon, John Francis. *The Colonial World of Latin America.* 1982. A useful introduction to Spanish America and Brazil.

*Bernard, Paul P. *Joseph II.* 1968. A concise and balanced treatment of the ill-fated monarch.

Bethell, Leslie, ed. *Colonial Spanish America.* 1987. *Colonial Brazil.* 1988. Both books contain essays concerning Latin America from the conquest to independence. Noted authorities write about rural society and the hacienda, urbanization, and Amerindian cultural matters.

Brading, D. A. *The First America: The Spanish Monarchy, Creole Patriots, and the Liberal State, 1492–1866.* 1990. Stresses the development of an American identity in such Creoles as Simón Bolívar and José de San Martin. Provides good background for the postindependence period.

Braudel, Fernand. *The Mediterranean and the Mediterranean World in the Age of Philip II.* Abridged 1992. Excellent background for understanding Spain and Spanish transplantations in the Americas.

*Available in paperback.

*Bridenbaugh, Carl. *Myths and Realities: Societies of the Colonial South.* 1952, reprinted 1963. A well-written survey of the British North American colonies that most resembled the Caribbean and Brazil.

*Commager, Henry S., and Elmo Giordanetti. *Was America a Mistake?* 1967. A fascinating collection of eighteenth-century attacks on, and defenses of, the New World.

Commager, Henry S., and Richard B. Morris, eds. *The Spirit of 'Seventy-Six: The Story of the American Revolution as Told by Participants.* New York: Harper & Row, 1967. An excellent collection of contemporary documents.

*De Madariaga, Isabel. *Russia in the Age of Catherine the Great.* 1981. Meticulously researched biography, sympathetic to Catherine.

*Dumas, Alexander. *The Three Musketeers.* 1844. Famous novel of swashbuckling seventeenth-century soldiers. There are also film versions.

Eccles, William J. *France in America.* 1972. The best study; concise and well written.

Fuentes, Carlos. *The Buried Mirror: Reflections on Spain and the New World.* 1992. Excellent introduction to Spain and the Americas; beautifully crafted with prints, maps, and artwork.

Gardner, Brian. *The East India Company: A History.* 1971. An engagingly written survey of the rise and fall of the greatest trading company in British history.

Gooch, G. P. *Louis XV: The Monarchy in Decline.* 1956. A highly respected study.

Goubert, Pierre. *Louis XIV and Twenty Million Frenchmen.* Translated by Ann Carter. 1970. An analysis of French society under the Grand Monarch.

Hamish, M. Scott. *Enlightened Despotism.* 1990. A good, recent survey of the subject.

Henry, John. *The Scientific Revolution and the Origins of Modern Science.* 1997. A brief survey of the key aspects of the Scientific Revolution.

*Hofstadter, Richard. *America at 1750: A Social Portrait.* 1971. Incomplete at Hofstadter's death, an insightful presentation of society in British North America.

Jensen, Merrill. *The Founding of a Nation: A History of the American Revolution, 1763–1776.* 1968. A long but well-written survey that stresses the complexity of the period.

Kitson, Michael. *The Age of Baroque.* 1966. Beautifully illustrated history of art in Europe in the seventeenth and eighteenth centuries.

*Koyre, Alexander. *From the Closed World to the Infinite Universe.* 1968. Expanding knowledge of the universe, from Copernicus through Newton.

Leonard, Irving A. *Baroque Themes in Old Mexico: Seventeenth-Century Persons, Places, and Practices.* 1966. Although somewhat dated, still an exceptional undergraduate resource. The chapter-length biographies shed much light on class, race, culture, and upper-class mores and ideas.

Lynch, John. *The Spanish-American Revolutions, 1808–1826.* 1973. The best synthesis of a sprawling subject.

Martin, Luis. *Daughters of the Conquistadores: Women of the Viceroyalty of Peru.* 1983. An informative survey, with applications to all of Latin America.

*Massie, Robert. *Peter the Great.* 1980. Highly readable, Pulitzer Prize–winning account.

*Parry, J. H. *Trade and Dominion: The European Overseas Empires in the Eighteenth Century.* 1971. The standard account, stressing the European impact on the colonies.

*Pushkin, Alexander. *The Captain's Daughter.* 1836. Various editions. A colorful Russian novel, set against the Pugachev rebellion.

*Rabb, Theodore K. *The Struggle for Stability in Early Modern Europe.* 1975. Brief, sweeping survey of the "crisis of the seventeenth century," to which absolutism provided partial solution.

*Read, Conyers. *The Tudors: Personalities and Practical Politics in the Sixteenth Century.* 1969. Biographical sketches of the Tudor rulers.

Ritter, Gerhard. *Frederick the Great.* 1968. A useful assessment by a leading German scholar.

Sobol, Dava. *Galileo's Daughter.* 1999. Letters of Galileo's illegitimate daughter, a cloistered nun, reveal much about his struggle to reconcile his scientific discoveries with his Catholic faith.

Trueblood, Alan S., ed. and trans. *A Sor Juana Anthology.* 1988. A bilingual collection with a helpful historical introduction.

*Voltaire, François Marie Arouet de. *Candide or Optimism.* 1759. Many editions. Satirical novel highlighting foibles and hypocrisies of eighteenth-century European and colonial life.

*Wolf, John B. *Louis XIV.* 1968. Monumental biography of the Sun King.

Internet Links

Catherine the Great
http://www.fordham.edu/halsall/mod/18catherine.html
Selected primary sources bearing on the character and career of the enlightened Russian empress.

The Decline of the Holy Roman Empire and the Rise of Prussia, 1700–1786
http://www.fordham.edu/halsall/mod/hre-prussia.html#Frederick II (1740–1786): Memoirs
A short anthology, including revealing pieces from the letters and memoirs of Frederick II himself and from his "Essay on Forms of Government."

Duc de Saint-Simon: The Court of Louis XIV
http://www.fordham.edu/halsall/mod/17stsimon.html
Fascinating passages from the memoirs of a courtier who lived at Versailles for many years.

Nicolas Copernicus: From The Revolutions of the Heavenly Bodies, 1543
http://www.fordham.edu/halsall/mod/1543copernicus2.html
Selections from Copernicus's famous work presenting his theory of the heliocentric nature of the solar system.

Philosophers (Björn Christensson's Guide to Philosophy)
http://sunsite.informatik.rwth-aachen.de/phil/filosofer/philosophers.html
This website includes brief biographies and links to other resources for such Enlightenment figures as Berkeley, Hobbes, Hume, Kant, Leibniz, Locke, Rousseau, and Voltaire.

Steam Engine Library
http://www.history.rochester.edu/steam/
A collection of (complete) books and other historical documents relating to the history of the steam engine.

Tables Illustrating the Spread of Industrialization
http://www.fordham.edu/halsall/mod/indrevtabs1.html
Eight chronological tables showing changes in manufacturing production, railway lines, illiteracy, and population in a number of key countries that underwent industrialization.

Was the American Revolution a Revolution?
http://odur.let.rug.nl/~usa/E/revolution/revoxx.htm
A superb overview of competing theories about the American Revolution, with links to well-chosen primary and secondary sources.

COMPARATIVE ESSAY 9

Nationalism: An Emerging Global Force

Our country is our Home; the house that God has given us. In laboring for our own country on the right principle, we labor for Humanity.

Giuseppe Mazzini

Foreigners often compare the Chinese with loose sand because we lack a sense of national cohesiveness. . . . The reason that we have been so long unsuccessful in resisting foreign oppression is because we have not awakened to our dire plight and have not organized our whole race. . . . However, when we do link up and bind together all our 400 million people, then we will not find it difficult to resist foreign aggression.

Sun Yat-sen on his principle of nationalism

Nationalism emerged as a potent force after 1815. Addressing their fellow citizens, the Italian nationalist Giuseppe Mazzini (1805–1872) and the Chinese nationalist Sun Yat-sen (1867–1925) both exhorted them to unify, but they put forth two quite different arguments to justify their calls for national unity. Mazzini used the argument—albeit mythological—that the nation had always existed and was a divine creation. In contrast, Sun Yat-sen stressed that national unity was a prerequisite for the Chinese to maintain their independence and to prevent domination by foreign powers. Numerous nationalist leaders popularized both points of view during the nineteenth and twentieth centuries.

Nationalism may be defined as an emotional loyalty of a people to a given state. The building blocks that help people forge a common national identity include a common language, traditions, history, economic interdependence, belief in a common political and judicial system, hope for a glorious future, and sometimes religion. Although religion has been a unifying force in some nations, in others, such as Ireland, India, and Lebanon, religious or confessional differences have led to long, protracted civil wars and political strife.

Until the end of the nineteenth century, nationalism was a particularly strong force in Europe and the Americas, after which it spread throughout Asia, the Middle East, and Africa. As a worldwide phenomenon, nationalism impelled countless wars of independence and led to the creation of almost 200 separate nations by the end of the twentieth century.

The French Revolution and the Napoleonic wars accelerated the development of modern nationalism, which was also heavily influenced by romanticism. The process began with the transformation of the Estates General into the National Assembly; this new institution represented not three separate classes but the entire nation. The revolution also led to the abolition of class privileges, the destruction of the old, chaotic, provincial government administrations, and, most importantly, the creation of a centralized national governmental system. A constitution made France, like the United States, a nation of free citizens protected by law. The broad participation of the general public in both politics and the armed forces increased the emotional involvement of citizens in the future of their own nations.

Although most political colonial leaders in the United States and Latin America shared the basic ethnic characteristics and cultural values of their European rulers, they nonetheless ousted those rulers when they were perceived to have become both unresponsive and tyrannical. Similarly, during the Napoleonic wars, conquered peoples throughout Europe were willing to pay high costs in life and money to preserve their national and cultural identities. In Spain and Prussia, citizens made enormous sacrifices to throw off alien French rule.

After 1815, national minorities in the polygot Habsburg and Russian Empires and oppressed nationalities in Ireland and the Belgian Netherlands all sought to shake free of foreign domination. In part, both Germany and Italy, as emphasized by Mazzini, were molded into unified nations by recalling—or creating sometimes highly romanticized or mythical—common histories.

There was also a nationalistic awakening among the subject peoples of the Ottoman Empire. In the Ottoman Empire, religion and ethnic-cultural differences as well as dissatisfaction with the increasingly corrupt and ineffectual government led to the growth of separate nationalist groups, first among the Greeks and then among the Arabs, Kurds, Armenians, and others.

In much of Asia and Africa, nationalism was rooted in opposition to Western imperialism and colonial domination. Many Asian and African nationalist leaders were Western-educated and had personally observed the power of nationalism as a driving force in Western nations. For example, the Indian National Congress, the oldest and most powerful nationalist organization in India, was founded in 1885 by British-educated Indians and some Englishmen. Because shared ideals could best be communicated in a common language, the early publications of the Indian National Congress were in English, the unifying language of many educated Indians until the present day. Similarly, in Africa, the Kenyan nationalist leader Jomo Kenyatta and Tanzanian leader Julius Nyerere were both influenced by Western education.

When Sun Yat-sen, father of the Chinese Republic, founded the United League (forerunner to the Kuomintang, or Nationalist Party) in 1905, he made nationalism the first principle of the party's ideology. As noted above, Sun explained that without the glue of nationalism, the Chinese people were like sand, ineffective and doomed to outside domination.

Threats of foreign domination often galvanized nationalist movements. In Japan, already homogenous because of geography and a common history, strong nationalist feelings were easily spread when Western nations threatened economic and cultural domination.

Although nationalism helped to create cohesive unified nations and to provide for conquered people to throw off foreign domination, it also had a number of negative ramifications. The desire for national glory often led to territorial expansion at the expense of neighboring states, thereby inciting major wars. Thus nationalism was a major contributing factor to both World War I and World War II. Nationalism manifested itself in the most brutal form in the totalitarian states that emerged after World War I, in which citizens were taught to worship the state as an end in itself. If the state could do no wrong, it followed that it had the right to expand, even at the expense of other nations. Mussolini, Hitler, and Stalin all manipulated nationalist feelings to exploit popular support and to justify the oppression of their own citizens and the conquest, or even extermination, of other peoples.

Finally, nationalism has also contributed to the continued oppression of national minorities, leading to abuses of human rights and to massacres and the "ethnic cleansing" of rival ethnic or national groups, as in the cases of nations as diverse as India and Sri Lanka in Asia, the states of the former Yugoslavia in Europe, and Rwanda in Africa.

The Modernization of the Western World

12

It was then that M. de Launay [commander of the forces of the Bastille] asked the garrison what course should be followed, that he saw no other than to blow himself up rather than to expose himself to having his throat cut by people, from the fury of which they could not escape; that they must remount the towers, continue to fight, and blow themselves up rather than surrender.

The soldiers replied that it was impossible to fight any longer, that they would resign themselves to everything rather than destroy such a great number of citizens, that it was best to put the drummer on the towers to beat the recall, hoist a white flag, and capitulate. The governor, having no flag, gave them a white handkerchief. An officer wrote out the capitulation and passed it through the hole, saying that they desired to surrender themselves and lay down their arms, on condition of a promise not to massacre the troops: there was a cry of "Lower your bridge; nothing will happen to you! . . ."

*As soon as the great bridge was let down . . . the people rushed into the court of the castle and, full of fury, seized on the troops of Invalides [probably a unit of handicapped soldiers]. . . . Several of these soldiers, whose lives had been promised them, were assassinated; others were dragged like slaves through the streets of Paris. Twenty-two were brought to the Grève [a square in the city], and, after humiliations and inhuman treatment, they had the affliction of seeing two of their comrades hanged. . . . De Launay, torn from the arms of those who wished to save him, had his head cut off under the walls of the Hôtel de Ville [city hall]. . . . De Losme-Salbray, his major, was murdered in the same manner. . . . The head of the Marquis de Launay was carried about Paris by the same populace that he would have crushed had he not been moved to pity. Such were the exploits of those who have since been called the heroes and conquerors of the Bastille.**

*E. L. Higgins, ed., *The French Revolution as Told by Contemporaries* (Boston: Houghton Mifflin, 1938), pp. 98–100.

The above account by eyewitnesses describes the fall of the Bastille, an imposing medieval fortress once used as a royal prison and a hated symbol of Bourbon despotism. On July 14, 1789, a large crowd, composed mostly of skilled artisans and small shopkeepers, marched to the Bastille in search of arms for protection against a possible counterrevolution. The governor barred the gates and, fearing an attack, ordered his men to fire into the crowd. Enraged by the death of ninety-eight of its members and the wounding of many others, the mob assaulted the fortress and gained entrance after the governor had been persuaded to surrender. The event was an expression of the people's power and provided a catalyst to the French Revolution.

The French Revolution destroyed the old regime and introduced a new era that promised to realize the ideals of the Enlightenment. This chapter focuses on the period from 1789 to 1914, when several powerful trends changed the course of Western history. The French Revolution and the Napoleonic Wars that followed led to other upheavals throughout Europe and to independence movements in Latin America. In the United States the cultural animosity between the northern and southern regions culminated in a civil war lasting four years. The victory by federal forces created an indissoluble union that provided a secure foundation for a constitutional republic. At the same time, the Industrial Revolution spread outside Great Britain and altered European and North American society. New concepts of economics and political theory, such as Karl Marx's socialist ideology, emerged in response to the new economic and social conditions brought on by the revolutionary ferment of the nineteenth century and by the spread of industrialization. The chapter concludes with a survey of nineteenth-century cultural and intellectual developments.

The French Revolution and the Napoleonic Era

The path leading to the scaffold was extremely rough and difficult to pass, the King [Louis XVI] was obliged to lean on my arm, and from the slowness with which he proceeded, I feared for a moment that his courage might fail; but what was my astonishment, when arrived at the last step, I felt that he suddenly let go my arm, and I saw him cross with a firm foot the breadth of the wood scaffold. . . . I heard him pronounce distinctly these memorable words "I die innocent of all the crimes laid to my charge; I pardon those who have occasioned my death; and I pray to God, that the blood you are now going to shed may never be visited on France."

*He was proceeding, when a man on horseback, in the national uniform, waved his sword, and . . . the executioners . . . seizing with violence the most virtuous of Kings . . . dragged him under the axe of the guillotine, which with one stroke severed his head from his body. . . . The youngest of the guards, who seemed about eighteen, walked round the scaffold; he accompanied this monstrous ceremony with the most atrocious and indecent gestures. At first an awful silence prevailed; at length some cries of "Vive la République!" were heard. By degrees the voices multiplied, and in less than ten minutes this cry, a thousand times repeated, became the universal shout of the multitude, and every hat was in the air.**

*Abbé Edgeworth, *Memoirs* (London: Hunter, 1815), pp. 84–87.

This gruesome scene, vividly depicted by a contemporary English observer, was the product of a historical movement inspired, not by a conspiracy to institute a new order, but by men who favored reforming the system. It began with an attempt to solve the financial crisis and then escalated to an attack on the political and social institutions. These economic, political, and social forces converged at a moment when the authoritarian system, its foundations eroded by decades of neglect, inefficiency, and corruption, was ready to succumb. Like the movement of a clock pendulum, the revolution passed through various stages, becoming more extreme and reaching the high tide of radicalism in 1793–1794 before a revulsion in public opinion led to the return of moderate rule. The years of revolutionary activity witnessed the abolition of the monarchy, the end of feudalism, the proclamation of religious and individual freedom, and the legal equality of all Frenchmen. The revolution ended when Napoleon Bonaparte overthrew the government in November 1799 and established a dictatorship.

The French Revolution was one of the pivotal events in the history of the modern European world. It not only repudiated what we now know as the old regime in France but prepared the way for the transformation of Western society. Indeed, even generations later it would inspire uprisings and colonial struggles for independence in Africa and Asia. This section will focus on the period of the revolution and the career of Napoleon Bonaparte.

The Old Regime

The origins of the French Revolution are much disputed among contemporary scholars. If France had been a backward country whose people were brutally governed and miserable, the explanation would be relatively simple. As it happened, France was the center of the Enlightenment, its culture was widely imitated and admired in Europe, it was wealthy, and its underprivileged classes enjoyed a higher standard of living than their counterparts in neighboring states. But it was precisely because they were better off and better informed that they were less willing to tolerate the inequities in the existing institutions.

On the eve of the revolution, France had a population of some 27 million people. The central feature of the government was the absolute monarchy, which had reached full development during the reign of Louis XIV. The king appointed all the high officials in the government, and he alone was responsible for the conduct of the state's foreign policy. As the monarchy was based on the concept of divine right and not on the consent of the people, the king's will was law. The Estates-General, the rough equivalent of Great Britain's Parliament, had not been summoned since 1614 and was, for all intents and purposes, obsolescent. The law courts were riddled with corruption and favoritism. The judges of the supreme courts, the *parlements,* were aristocrats who had bought or inherited their offices. They were mainly interested in using their position to enrich themselves. In cases brought by commoners, the judges always favored their own kind. The inequities inherent in the French system, tolerated in the past, encountered increasing resistance as the ideas of the Enlightenment gained strength.

By custom and law, everyone in France belonged to one of three distinct orders or estates: the clergy made up the first estate; the nobility the second; and everyone else the third. The church in France was practically a state within a state, and, although it was attacked by the philosophes for promoting superstition and impeding reform, it still exerted great influence among the masses. Served by about 130,000 clergymen, it owned about 10 percent of the land. Its annual income, derived from its landed property, tithes levied on crops, and other sources, was immense, estimated to have been half as much as that of the government itself. The church paid no taxes but periodically made a "free gift" to the state—a contribution that was considerably less than direct taxes would have been. A major source of weakness in the church was its deep social divisions. The upper church officials—archbishops, bishops and abbots—came from the ranks of the aristocracy and lived and upheld the values of their class, while often ignoring their spiritual responsibilities. In contrast, the parish priests and monks were commoners by birth and usually poor. They resented the lifestyle of the upper clergy and served and identified with the interests of the lower classes.

The aristocracy comprised about 2 percent of the population, roughly 400,000 persons, and owned between 20 and 25 percent of the land. They enjoyed special privileges, not the least of which was exemption from direct taxation. The nobility did not form a cohesive social unit but rather varied in fortune and prestige. The one thing that bound them together was a desire to maintain their privileges and regain the political power they had lost under Louis XIV. During the reign of the indifferent Louis XV their aggressiveness in defense of their ancient rights paid off. In the second half of the eighteenth century, the top-level bureaucratic administrators, once drawn mainly from the middle class, were recruited, almost without exception, from the ranks of the nobles. Not content with their virtual monopoly of the highest offices in the government, they looked forward to the day when they would again rule France, just as their ancestors had done in the Middle Ages.

Below the privileged classes stood the commoners—primarily bourgeoisie or middle class, urban workers and peasants—who comprised about 97 percent of the total population. The upper segment, because of their wealth and education, were the middle class, a varied group that included merchants, bankers, industrialists, intellectuals, professional men, and skilled artisans. Although the bourgeoisie did not face the kind of hardships that the laborers or peasants did, they resented more keenly the abuses of the old regime. What they found especially intolerable was the snobbery of the aristocracy and the second-class status assigned to them by the monarchy. The avenues of social advancement, once open to bourgeoisie who purchased an office that carried with it noble status or gained a high-level position in the army or government, were now full of obstacles because of the aristocratic resurgence. Undoubtedly the desire for social and political advancement was the basic reason why some members of the bourgeoisie challenged the old order. They wanted privileges based on birth abolished and careers opened to talent. For others, imbued by a sense of justice, the motive was more noble. They longed to end royal absolutism and reform France in accordance with the just and rational outlook of the philosophes.

The prosperity of the bourgeoisie was not shared by the petty artisans or unskilled laborers who were concentrated in the major cities, particularly Paris. During the half century before the revolution, prices for consumer goods rose by 65 percent, while wages increased by only 22 percent. Thus workers usually lived on the edges of starvation. The economic depression that gripped France in the late 1780s intensified their suffering and fueled their resentment against the government.

The peasants who tilled the soil made up at least four-fifths of the French population. They enjoyed a unique status in Europe. Serfdom had largely disappeared in France, and peasants owned 30 to 35 percent of the land. Nevertheless, most of their income was siphoned away by feudal and manorial dues, church tithes, and royal taxes. The economic conditions of the peasants

Giraudon/Art Resource

Marie Antoinette with a Rose. This portrait of the French queen by Marie Louise Elizabeth Vigée-Lebrun captures her beauty, vivacity, grace, and unbending will but masks her impetuosity, immaturity, and lack of education and tact. All her adult life she behaved like a spoiled teenage princess, wasted huge sums on gambling and shopping, especially for jewelry, and sought relief from the stilted atmosphere of the court by engaging in frivolities unbecoming to a queen. Beloved at first by the people, she soon became an object of intense hatred.

worsened during the last decades of the old regime because of poor harvests and high inflation. Yet they remained essentially traditional in outlook, merely desiring relief from taxation and an opportunity to own their land or, if they already did, extend their holdings.

The Last Days of the Old Regime

The glory and prestige that had marked the Bourbon monarchy during the age of Louis XIV began to fade with his passing. Although his heirs lived in great style and claimed to rule by divine right, they were weak and allowed power to slip from their hands. Louis XV (reigned 1715–1774) was intelligent enough, but he was indolent, fickle, pleasure loving, and uninterested in the affairs of state. While seeking new ways to alleviate his boredom, Louis permitted the woman of his current fancy to influence state policy. His haphazard and irresponsible conduct of foreign policy dragged the country into two wars, the last of which, the Seven Years' War, ended in a shattering defeat and the resultant loss of Canada and French India. The immense cost of prosecuting these wars, added to the profligate extravagance at the royal court, cut deep into the nation's finances. Louis left a legacy, best encapsulated in an expression erroneously attributed to him, "*Après moi, le déluge.*"

The new king, Louis XVI (reigned 1774–1792), was twenty years old, well meaning, moral and anxious to disassociate his reign from that of his discredited late grandfather. But he was also dull and indecisive, lacked intellectual gifts, and suffered from the reflected unpopularity of his Austrian-born wife, Marie Antoinette. The queen's few good qualities were overshadowed by her extravagance, insensitivity, indiscretion, and intrusion in politics. Too often the king ignored the advice of his councilors lest he be subjected to his wife's scorn and ridicule.

Louis XV had made little effort to correct the abuses of the old regime, which had grown more serious by the time his successor ascended the throne. Apart from the mounting social unrest, the government faced a deepening financial crisis. Already high in 1774, the debt would triple over the course of the next fifteen years—largely as a result of France's participation in the American War of Independence. France was a wealthy country, but the crux of the problem was that royal expenditures exceeded income. The only way to remedy the shortfall was to make all classes pay their fair share of taxes. But the nobility and clergy refused to give up their ancient privileges and Louis XVI lacked the backbone to override them. His successive controller-generals had no alterative but to borrow money to cover the deficit. By 1788 half of the state's annual revenue went to service the interest on the accumulated debt of nearly 4 billion livres. In desperation Louis tried to impose a tax on all landowners, but he was challenged by the parlements, which insisted that such a reform required the consent of the Estates-General. Louis's plan to set up new courts to replace the parlements foundered because of popular opposition, leaving him with no option but to summon the Estates-General. The aristocracy was certain that it could control this body and through it protect its privileges and weaken the monarchy. It miscalculated badly.

Forging a New Order: The Moderate Stage

The election of the representatives to the Estates-General took place amid widespread economic suffering. A severe recession had caused a wave of bankruptcies, and unemployment reached staggering levels in the cities. In large parts of the country, hail and drought had reduced the harvest. By the spring of 1789, grain prices had doubled. Because the lower classes spent as much as two-thirds of their income on food, these increases had a particularly devastating effect on their living standards. Riots swept across the country and mobs attacked granaries and bakeries.

In May 1789, one week after a particularly severe riot in Paris, Louis XVI formally opened the proceedings of the Estates-General. Before the delegates turned to the work at hand, a sharp debate broke out over the method of voting. According to tradition, the three estates met separately and voted as individual bodies; that is, each estate cast one vote. Such a system ensured that the privileged estates could always outvote the third estate two to one. The third estate, with its double membership, reinforced by some reform-minded clergy and aristocrats, wanted the three estates to meet as a single body and vote by head. The first and second estates naturally resisted this demand, and a deadlock ensued. The haggling went on for six weeks until finally the third estate took a momentous step. Insisting that it was the only true representative of the nation, it proclaimed itself the National Assembly on June 17 and invited the other estates to join its sessions. When the members of the third estate assembled for their daily debates on June 20, they found the doors of their chamber locked. Carpenters were preparing the hall for a royal speech to be delivered two days later, but the deputies believed that they had been deliberately locked out in an attempt to send them back home. They angrily withdrew to a nearby indoor tennis court where they vowed never to disband until they had given France a constitution. The Tennis Court Oath marks the beginning of the French Revolution. It was an assertion that sovereign power resided with a new body that had no legal authority.

What had begun as an aristocratic struggle to undermine the monarchy had taken an unexpected turn. The nobles became more concerned at the defiant behavior of the third estate, which they saw as a threat to their privileged status. They immediately reversed their longstanding position and joined hands with the king in an effort to stop the incipient social revolution. At the royal session on June 23, the king came down on the side of

Fall of the Bastille. On July 14, 1789, a mob stormed the Bastille to obtain the arms cached inside. Prison guards panicked and fired into the crowd, killing nearly a hundred. In this painting, a mutinous detachment of French soldiers, supported by cannon, joins the assault. Soon after, the commander of the fortress surrendered on condition that he and his men be spared. Once inside, the frenzied crowd disregarded its pledge and butchered the commander and several other members of the garrison, placing their heads on pikes and parading them through Paris. The fall of the Bastille demonstrated vividly that the king had lost control of the city.

Réunion des Musées Nationaux/Art Resource, NY

Charlotte Corday. This portrait by Jean-Jacques Hauer was painted in the prison of the Conciergerie shortly before its subject was executed.

the nobility, directing the estates to meet separately. The third estate, however, would not budge from its declared purpose. Royal regiments were within call, but the king characteristically vacillated when confronted with a tough decision. On June 27, on learning that a majority of the clergy and some aristocrats had joined the National Assembly, Louis conceded defeat and directed the three estates to sit together and vote by head. His action implied recognition of the right of the National Assembly to act as the highest sovereign power in the nation. The leadership of the revolt had now passed from the aristocracy to the bourgeoisie who represented the masses in the National Assembly.

The king's concession did not reduce the level of tension in Paris. Angry over the increasing cost of food and terrified by the royal regiments concentrating in the vicinity of the city, mobs rioted and broke into gunsmith shops and public buildings in search of arms. Three days of wild disorders culminated with an attack on the Bastille. The day on which the Bastille fell, July 14, is a national holiday in France, celebrated as the birth of freedom and justice.

The disturbances in Paris coincided with a movement in the countryside known as the Great Fear. During the spring of 1789, there were numerous peasant demonstrations sparked by the economic crisis. Galvanized by these mounting disorders, the National Assembly hastily abolished the old feudal privileges, serfdom, ecclesiastical tithes, and all forms of personal obligations formerly imposed on the third estate. It proclaimed the principles of equal taxation and civil equality.

These social changes were supplemented in August by legal guarantees embodied in the Declaration of the Rights of Man and the Citizen. Echoing the U.S. Declaration of Independence, the document proclaimed that men were born and remained free and were equal in rights. It was framed to apply not only to French citizens but to all humans, regardless of their national origin. The universality of the declaration was a challenge to the old regimes throughout Europe and subsequently became a rallying point for champions of human rights around the world.

The king's delay in ratifying the social changes and the Declaration of the Rights of Man and the Citizen fueled rumors that he was planning to use troops to undo the work of the revolution. Amid widespread uncertainty, a large mob of Parisian women marched eleven miles to the royal palace at Versailles and demanded that the price of bread be lowered. The king yielded, and to further appease the women, he agreed to return with them to Paris. After arriving in Paris, the king and his family were installed in the old Tuileries palace. A few weeks later, the National Assembly followed the king to the city. Both the assembly and the king were now subject to the pressure of the Parisian populace.

In Paris the National Assembly, now called the National Constituent Assembly, continued the work of drawing up the constitution. Guided by the philosophes' principles of humanity, rationality, and efficiency, it enacted a series of sweeping reforms that were later incorporated into a single document known as the Constitution of 1791. One of the major undertakings of the assembly was to reorganize the whole ecclesiastical system after it confiscated church property and abolished tithes. To this end, the assembly promulgated the Civil Constitution of the Clergy, which was designed to maintain the clergy and subordinate the church to the state. Clergymen were to be paid by the state and, like other public servants, were to be elected by those they served. Since the pope was denied any authority over the French church, he was left with no choice but to condemn the Civil Constitution. This turned the majority of pious Catholics against the revolution.

In reshaping the government, the Constituent Assembly had confirmed the transferal of power from the privileged orders to the educated bourgeoisie. The constitution preserved the hereditary monarchy, but the authority of the king was reduced in accordance with Montesquieu's formula of "separation of powers." The king still controlled the army and navy and directed for-

LIVES AND TIMES ACROSS CULTURES

Charlotte Corday and the Murder of Marat

On July 9, 1792, Charlotte Corday, a tall, strikingly attractive young woman of twenty-four, boarded a coach for Paris. Born to a noble but poor family in Caen, she was a fanatical follower of a revolutionary faction (Girondins) vying with the more radical elements (Jacobins or Montagnards) for control of the government. Her mission in Paris, which she undertook without anyone's knowledge, was to murder Jean-Paul Marat, whom she had been told was an enemy of freedom and the cause of many of France's woes. Implacable and vengeful, the forty-nine-year-old Marat had been in the forefront of those demanding the execution of the king. Editor of *L'Ami du Peuple (Friend of the People),* he attacked a wide range of targets whom he considered enemies of the revolution.

On arriving in Paris, Charlotte took a room in a hotel and then purchased a sharp dinner knife for two francs. On the evening of July 13 she went to Marat's house and gained entry on the pretext that she had important information, which she could only convey to him in person. She found him soaking in a high-walled copper bath, seeking relief from a painful and unpleasant skin disease, which he had contracted hiding in the sewers of Paris. She gave him a report of what was happening in her home town, revealing the names of men she claimed were plotting against the Jacobins. Marat picked up a nearby pen and began to copy down the names, commenting, "In a few days I will have them all guillotined." Before he could say another word, Charlotte pulled out the knife from the top of her dress and plunged it into his heart. Marat's scream alerted his staff, who ran into the room and captured Charlotte before she could escape. At her trial she did not seek to evade the consequences of her deed and went to her death cheerfully under the illusion that she had saved France from the horrors of a civil war.

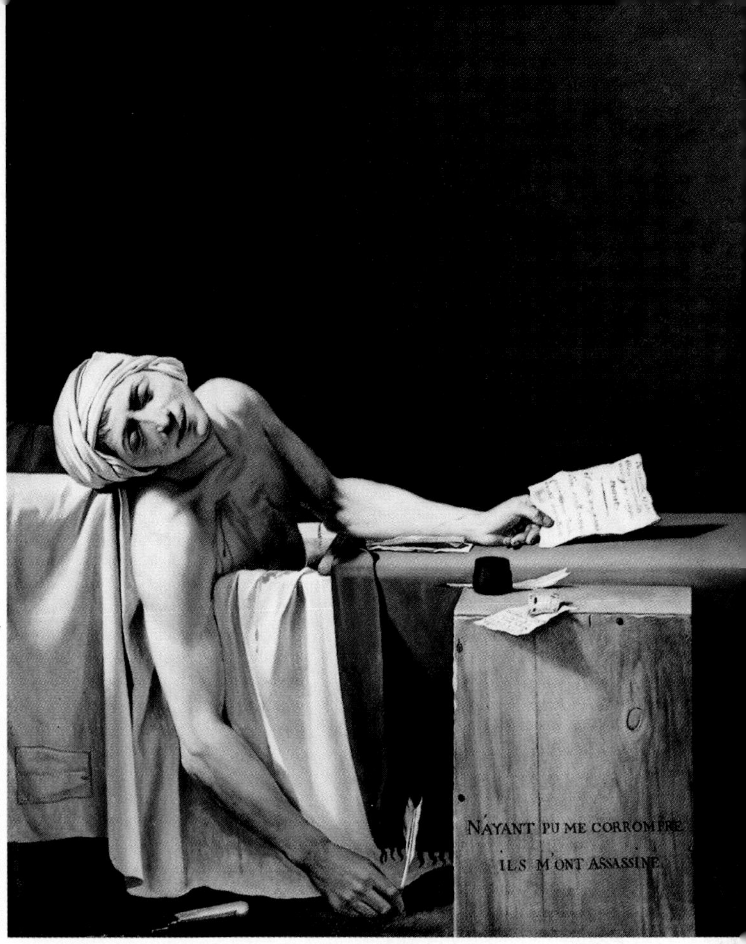

Réunion des Musées Nationaux/Art Resource, NY

The Death of Marat by Jacques Louis David. This awe-inspiring painting is David's tribute to a martyred hero. Marat's fatal wound is visible on his upper body, as his arm, pen in hand, dangles over the bath tub, symbolizing his devotion to the people.

eign policy, but most of the authority over internal affairs was now in the hands of a single Legislative Assembly, which controlled both taxes and expenditures. Suffrage was indirect. Males over the age of twenty-five paying taxes equivalent to three days' wages could vote for electors who chose the deputies. The property requirements for an elector were so high that probably no more than 70,000 Frenchmen had the means to qualify. Nevertheless, the new French political system was more democratic than that of any other European state.

In June 1791 the king, unreconciled to the reforms forced upon him, secretly fled Paris with his family. He hoped to rally loyal supporters in the northeast and to return to power with the support of those European governments alarmed by the revolutionary changes. He was recognized at Varennes near the Belgian border, however, and sent back to Paris under armed guard. After considerable debate, the deputies voted to retain the monarchy, and when Louis showed himself to be penitent, he was reinstated. In the fall of 1791 the Constituent Assembly disbanded and declared the revolution at an end. Thus far the revolution had ended feudalism, established individual rights and liberties and legal equality, undercut the power of the church, and lessened the authority of the king.

Though launched with great expectations, the constitutional monarchy lasted less than a year. Its demise propelled the revolution from a moderate to a radical stage. The failure of the new system was principally due to three reasons. First, the king was unwilling to accept the modest

Both photos: Bibliothèque Nationale de France, Paris

The Guillotine. In keeping with eighteenth-century enlightened thinking about the need to eliminate the torturous punishments practiced during the *ancien régime,* the guillotine was devised as a swifter, more certain, and thus more humane method of execution. As Dr. Joseph-Ignace Guillotin (1728–1814) said when recommending its adoption to the National Assembly, "The mechanism falls like thunder; the head flies off, blood spurts, the man is no more." Though the "machine" is named for the doctor, it was in fact designed and fabricated under the direction of a Dr. Louis, the secretary of the French Academy of Surgery.

role he had been assigned under the constitution. Second, the poorer classes in the cities felt cheated by the changes, which had primarily benefited the middle class and the peasants. The bourgeoisie had in effect replaced the aristocracy as the ruling class; the peasants had been freed of feudal obligations, and many of them owned property. Third, the outbreak of war in the spring of 1792 created tension and hysteria. The events in France had alarmed the European monarchs, who feared the spread of revolutionary ideas to their own lands. At the same time, the émigrés (nobles who had fled France) stoked the fires by calling for the destruction of the revolution. Under these circumstances the Austrian and Prussian monarchs publicly supported the use of armed force to restore royal absolutism in France. This move was seen in France as an insult and a threat, and the new Legislative Assembly reacted by declaring war on April 20, 1792.

France was woefully unprepared for war, and early military reverses aroused fear and disturbances in Paris. In August a hysterical mob stormed the Tuileries, convinced that the king was in league with the enemy. The royal family sought refuge in the halls of the Legislative Assembly. Fearful of the mob, the legislators deposed the king and ordered the election of an assembly to draw up a republican constitution. The abolition of the monarchy marked the beginning of the violent phase of the revolution.

From the Reign of Terror to the End of the Revolution

Although the new assembly, called the National Convention, was composed mostly of moderates, its leadership was dominated by Jacobin or left-wing elements. The National Convention held its first session on September 20, 1792,

Robespierre's Theory of Revolutionary Government, 1793

We shall first outline the principles and the needs underlying the creation of a revolutionary government; next we shall expound the cause that threatens to throttle it at birth.

The theory of revolutionary government is as new as the Revolution that created it. It is as pointless to seek its origins in the books of the political theorists, who failed to foresee this revolution, as in the laws of the tyrants, who are happy enough to abuse their exercise of authority without seeking out its legal justification. And so this phase is for the aristocracy a mere subject of terror or a term of slander, for tyrants an outrage and for many an enigma. It behooves us to explain it to all in order that we may rally good citizens, at least, in support of the principles governing the public interest.

It is the function of government to guide the moral and physical energies of the nation toward the purposes for which it was established.

The object of constitutional government is to preserve the Republic; the object of revolutionary government is to establish it.

Revolution is the war waged by liberty against its enemies; a constitution is that which crowns the edifice of freedom once victory has been won and the nation is at peace.

The revolutionary government has to summon extraordinary activity to its aid precisely because it is at war. It is subjected to less binding and less uniform regulations, because the circumstances in which it finds itself are tempestuous and shifting, above all because it is compelled to deploy, swiftly and incessantly, new resources to meet new and pressing dangers.

The principal concern of constitutional government is civil liberty; that of revolutionary government, public liberty. Under a constitutional government little more is required than to protect the individual against abuses by the state, whereas revolutionary government is obliged to defend the state itself against the factions that assail it from every quarter.

*To good citizens revolutionary government owes the full protection of the state; to the enemies of the people it owes only death.**

Strongly influenced by Rousseau's writings, Robespierre was convinced that only through him could the ideals of the revolution be achieved. His obsessive vision of an ideal republic made him indifferent to the human costs of creating it. In this excerpt from a speech he delivered to the National Convention on December 25, 1793, he justifies the extreme steps taken by the revolutionary government as necessary to ensure the survival of liberty.

*George Rudé, ed., *Robespierre* (Englewood Cliffs, N.J.: Prentice Hall, 1967), pp. 58–59.

the very day that French troops at Valmy halted the enemy. Free to turn to other matters, the convention formally established a republic and debated the fate of the king. Found guilty of treasonable communication with the enemy, Louis was sentenced to die under the guillotine, now the official instrument of execution. The king's execution on January 21, 1793, sent tremors throughout the capitals of Europe. Ten months later his wife would follow him.

At the time of Louis's death, both external and internal troubles were threatening to destroy the radicals and the revolution itself. After Valmy, French armies took the offensive and occupied the Austrian Netherlands, the Rhineland, and Savoy. However, reverses followed in the spring of 1793 when Great Britain, Spain, Portugal, and several lesser states joined Austria and Prussia in a formidable coalition against France. To make matters worse, a revolt erupted in the Vendée, a region southwest of Paris, where the peasants had remained faithful to the church and the monarchy. The revolution spread to Bordeaux, Lyons, Marseilles, and other important cities.

In April 1793 the National Convention created a Committee of Public Safety with almost unlimited authority to deal with the new perils facing the republic. The most influential member of the twelve-man committee was Maximilien Robespierre (1758–1794), a provincial attorney and rabid exponent of Rousseau's concept of democracy. The committee instituted a reign of terror against a wide range of people perceived to be enemies of the revolution. No dissent was tolerated. All suspected political enemies and all opponents of government policies were imprisoned or guillotined.

While the Committee of Public Safety was ruthlessly crushing its internal foes, the defense of the republic against its external enemies was entrusted to Lazare Carnot, a brilliant soldier and administrator. With the full support of the committee, he mobilized the entire nation for war, instituting universal conscription and placing vital industries under state control. He raised a huge army of keen young conscripts in place of a relatively small army of uninspired riffraff and mercenaries. His officer corps consisted of men who had risen to their position through merit rather than birth. This energetic policy turned the tide. French troops not only hurled back the forces of the coalition but invaded neighboring nations.

Beyond surmounting the crises and saving the revolution, the committee wanted to make France even more democratic. Robespierre and his associates sought to create a "Republic of Virtue" in which citizens, uncorrupted and fervently dedicated, would practice exemplary behavior. To keep the cost of living down, the committee imposed wage controls and set prices for essential commodities. It abolished imprisonment for debt, slavery in the colonies, and primogeniture. All titles were eliminated, and "citizen" and "citizeness" became the proper form of address. A new "rational" standard of weights and measures, the metric system, was established. It proved so convenient that most of the nations of the world eventually adopted it.

Pushing beyond political and social changes, the ruling Committee of Public Safety launched a movement to de-Christianize France. Churches were converted into temples of reason, where deists like Robespierre and his associates could worship the Supreme Being. A new calendar was introduced that eliminated Sundays and all church holidays and designated the birth of the republic, rather than the birth of Christ, as the beginning of Year 1. It was never popular with the masses, however, and was quietly shelved in 1806.

The work of the committee ended abruptly when Robespierre and his close supporters were overthrown. The republic that Robespierre created bore no resemblance to the utopian one he had tried to establish at the outset. It was in fact a brutal dictatorship, supported by only a small minority of the population and sustained through censorship and terrorist methods. Certain elements in the National Convention, fearing that they would become Robespierre's next victims, denounced him when he made an ill-tempered speech before the convention and stampeded the other members into ordering his arrest. He was executed on July 28, 1794, along with his closest collaborators.

The fall of Robespierre sparked a reaction against the excesses of the Terror, known as the "Thermidorian Reaction" (Thermidor was the month of July in the new revolutionary calendar). The change in public attitude led to a relaxation of tensions, and the government returned to moderate constitutionalism dominated by the urban middle class. The Terror was discontinued, freedom of speech and the press were restored, Catholic churches were reopened, and a laissez-faire economy was reinstated. Finally, the convention drew up a new constitution that provided for an executive board of five directors and a two-house legislature. In October 1795 the National Convention dissolved itself to give way to the new government.

The new regime, called the Directory after its executive board, inherited a sagging economy and other problems from the National Convention. Badly divided and burdened by a war, the government was unable to respond effectively to the task at hand and thus aroused much internal unrest and disorder. It was forced to rely on the army to crush insurrections in Paris and to deal with a dangerous royalist threat. French military reverses in Italy and Germany bred still more popular discontent with the Directory. The unstable internal conditions and collapsing economy, together with the army's defeats, provided an opportunity for Napoleon Bonaparte, a rising, popular general, to seize power.

Women and the French Revolution

The revolution did not afford women the same opportunities and benefits as men. Yet from the outset women of different backgrounds had taken an active role in the revolution. They organized political clubs, were present during the storming of the Bastille, engaged in street demonstrations, and, in their famous march to Versailles, forced the royal family to return to Paris. A few like Jeanne Roland, the wife of a government official, moved close to the center of political power and helped shape policy for their revolutionary factions.

In the emerging new order, women became more militant as they were no longer content to make vague statements about equality. In a spate of pamphlets, feminists called for suffrage, equal partnership in marriage, greater access to education, and better-paying jobs. In 1790 a small group founded the *Cercle Social* (social circle), which launched a campaign to end sexual inequality. Among the great figures of the period, none was more vocal in advocating women's emancipation than the Marquis de Condorcet. He refuted many of the traditional arguments against women and insisted that they should have the same political rights as men, that domestic authority should be shared, and that positions should be opened to both sexes. But his was virtually a lone voice in the wilderness.

The various legislative assemblies, for all their talk of equality and civil rights, were not keen on lifting restrictions against women. On the few occasions when the matter of granting women political rights arose, it was greeted with widespread ridicule and disbelief. Deputies left no doubt that the social role of women was to stay home, obey their husbands, raise the children, and keep out of public affairs. Only minor concessions were made, although they did improve women's private life. Piecemeal legislation between 1790 and 1794 guaranteed the right of women to share equally with male heirs, set the age of majority for women the same as for men (twenty-one), and admitted women as witnesses in civil suits. Moreover, women were to have the same standing as men in divorce cases as well as a voice in the administration of their own property and in the rearing of their children. Unfortunately, most of these gains were rescinded by Napoleon's codes a decade later and were not reinstated until the twentieth century.

The Rise of Napoleon

Napoleon Bonaparte (1769–1821) owed his rapid rise to good fortune and ability rather than to social position or wealth. He was born in 1769 on the French-controlled island of Corsica, the son of an impoverished noble of Italian origin. He studied at military academies in France and at the age of sixteen became a sublieutenant of artillery. Without a title or a powerful patron, Napoleon would not have risen high in the army of the old regime, but the downfall of the monarchy, the flight of many royalist officers, and the European war threw open the gates of opportunity. A general by the time he was twenty-five, he received his first battlefield command two years later in 1796 when he was put in charge of the French army in Italy.

Napoleon's brilliance as a tactician, thoroughness in planning his campaigns, and ability to make quick decisions and inspire his troops led to a series of spectacular victories. Once the war was over in Italy, he returned to France, where he had become a national hero. Anxious to increase his newly won popularity, he decided on a campaign to Egypt, then part of the Ottoman Empire, in order to destroy British commerce and naval predominance in the Mediterranean and ultimately British power in India. Along with his army, Napoleon took many scholars to study the culture of ancient Egypt. Although his forces initially enjoyed military success against the divided government in Egypt, the British fleet dealt him a decisive defeat at the battle of the Nile. Napoleon's dreams of conquering the eastern Mediterranean were crushed. Hearing of French defeats in Europe, he left for France, leaving most of his army stranded in Egypt.

The short-lived conquest of Egypt by French forces had more dramatic consequences in Europe than in the Ottoman Empire. The chance discovery of the Rosetta Stone during the campaign provided the key to deciphering ancient Egyptian hieroglyphics. Travelers' memoirs and scholarly studies of the culture of ancient Egypt excited enormous curiosity among Europeans. This interest later stimulated a lucrative tourist trade as Europeans and Americans traveled to the eastern Mediterranean to see the wonders of the ancient world. As for the Egyptians themselves, a few members of the upper class were influenced by the ideas of the French Revolution and Western scientific developments; however, most Egyptians who came into contact with the French were repulsed by the drunken behavior of the soldiers and resented Napoleon's imperialistic aggression in their country.

Arriving in France in October 1799 Napoleon was greeted with a hero's welcome. The people had heard only of his victories in Egypt and were convinced that he was the man of the hour. Within a few weeks of his return, he joined a conspiracy that was plotting to overthrow the unpopular Directory. On November 9, with the aid of loyal troops, Napoleon compelled the legislators to resign and to turn power over to him and his group.

The coup d'état was soon followed by the promulgation of a constitution that established a dictatorship under the guise of parliamentary government. Napoleon took the title "first consul" (recalling the chief magistrate of republican Rome) and, as chief executive for ten years, held the reins of power. Two other consuls shared the executive but possessed only nominal authority. By means of a plebiscite, the public overwhelmingly endorsed the constitution. Weary after ten years of chaotic revolutionary experiment, the French turned to a strong man whom they believed would restore civil and economic order and guarantee the gains of the revolution.

The Consulate

Napoleon brought to completion the centralizing process begun by Richelieu and Mazarin and provided France with an honest and efficient government. Although he professed to sympathize with the principles of the French Revolution, he was above all a realist, not an ideologue. He continued certain reforms of the revolution that were popular with the nation and that also served his own purpose. On the other hand, he reversed some of the revolutionary gains by suppressing all forms of free expression and by instituting a new form of absolutism. He truly believed that political and social liberties would undermine good government and lead to anarchy. His regime had many of the characteristics of enlightened despotism, which France had eluded in the eighteenth century.

Napoleon wanted to end the war with the other European nations so that he could consolidate his position at home. A combination of brilliant military maneuvers and skillful diplomacy broke the coalition by 1801, leaving Great Britain alone at war with France. Exhausted and isolated, the British were receptive to peace overtures and the following year signed the Peace of Amiens.

Napoleon's Views on Religion

Conversation with General Gourgaud, August 28, 1817:

*"I have been reading the bible," [said the Emperor]. "Jesus should have been hanged like scores of other fanatics who posed as the Prophet or the Messiah. . . . I prefer the religion of Mohomet: it is less ridiculous than ours."**

Conversation with General Bertrand, March 21, 1821, followed by the latter's comment:

*"I am very glad that I have no religion," the Emperor remarked. "I find it a great consolation, as I have no imaginary terrors and no fear of the future. . . . " In actual fact the Emperor died a theist, believing in a rewarding God, the principle of all things. Yet he stated . . . in his will . . . that he had died in the Catholic religion because he believed that to be [the right thing to do in terms of] public ethics.***

Conversation with Comte Roederer, August 18, 1800:

*"Morality? There is only one way to encourage morality and that is to reestablish religion. Society cannot exist without some being richer than others, and this inequality cannot exist without religion. When one man is dying of hunger next door to another who is stuffing himself with food, the poor man simply cannot accept the disparity unless some authority exists which tells him 'God wishes it so. There have to be both rich and poor in this world: but in heaven things will be different.'"****

Napoleon understood that France was fundamentally Catholic and that reconciliation with the church would be beneficial both to the people and for his own policy. Personally irreligious, he pretended to be a Catholic in France and a Muslim while he was attempting to establish control over Egypt, and he once claimed that if he had occasion to govern a nation of Jews he would rebuild Solomon's temple.

*G. Gourgaud, *St. Helena Journal, 1815–1818,* trans. S. Gillard (London: Bodley Head, 1932), p. 259.

**General H. G. Bertrand, *Napoleon at St Helena: Journal of General Bertrand* (Garden City, N.Y.: Doubleday, 1952), pp. 133, 181.

***M. Vitrac, ed., *Autour de Bonaparte: Journal du Comte P. L. Roederer,* trans. M. Hutt (Paris: H. Daragon, 1909), pp. 18–19.

For the French it was a generous settlement, allowing them to retain most of their European conquests.

The short period of peace enabled Napoleon to concentrate on achieving domestic and financial stability. One of his chief concerns was to heal the breach between church and state that had been created by the Civil Constitution of the Clergy. After protracted negotiations he concluded an agreement, the Concordat of 1801, with Pope Pius VII (reigned 1800–1823). Under the terms of the Concordat, the pope agreed to give up all claims to church property confiscated during the revolution (which the state had broken up and sold mostly as small plots to the peasants) and to allow the state to appoint French bishops. In return, the state recognized Catholicism as the religion of the majority of French citizens and agreed to pay the salaries of the clergy. Napoleon thus not only removed a counterrevolutionary threat, but earned the gratitude of pious French Catholics and owners of former church property.

The Consulate also put the economy on a sound basis. The national debt was handled by issuing bonds bearing 5 percent interest to replace the various existing obligations. In 1800 Napoleon established the Bank of France (on the model of the Bank of Great Britain) for the purpose of lending money to businessmen as well as freeing the government from reliance on private credit. These measures, together with the systematization of tax collection and strict economies in all branches of government, made it possible to balance the budget in 1801–1802. Within two years Napoleon had succeeded in solving the financial problem that had precipitated the revolution and continued to vex the various governments throughout the 1790s.

Napoleon's most enduring domestic achievement was the codification of the laws. In the 1790s the revolutionary governments had taken the first steps in this direction, but it remained for Napoleon to bring the work to completion. The First Consul introduced the civil code in 1804, the first of five codes collectively called the Code Napoleon. The Code Napoleon preserved many of the revolutionary principles such as equality of all men before the law, religious toleration, equality of inheritance, abolition of serfdom, and the right to choose one's occupation. Still, in some respects the code was more reactionary than the laws of the revolutionary era. For example, it discriminated against illegitimate children, protected the interests of the employer by outlawing trade unions and strikes, and subordinated wives to the authority of their husbands. Whatever its faults, the code was an enormous improvement over what had existed before the revolution. Outside of France it greatly influenced the legal systems of Italy, Belgium, parts of Germany, Spain, a number of Latin American nations, and even Louisiana.

Like Caesar Augustus, Napoleon sometimes undermined the institutions he professed to be upholding.

His primary concern was to strengthen his regime, not preserve the ideals of the Enlightenment and the French Revolution. That was apparent when he founded the Legion of Honor to reward civil as well as military merit. All decorations and symbols for meritorious service had been abolished during the revolution, but Napoleon recognized that everyone loved distinctions. In creating an aristocracy of merit he would add luster to his rule as well as bind the recipients closer to his person. In overhauling the educational system, Napoleon followed a similar pattern. He made provisions for a nationwide system of public education, creating a network of primary and secondary schools and institutions of higher learning. However, Napoleon's aim was not so much to bring literacy to the masses as to groom competent administrators and instill moral and patriotic values in the citizenry.

Napoleon undoubtedly would have fulfilled the philosophes' ideal of an enlightened despot, but the reforms that he instituted in France were achieved at the high cost of suppressing liberty and restoring absolutism. Yet he enjoyed popular support from all classes except the diehard royalists and left-wing republicans. As a rule, his subjects were prepared to accept restriction of individual freedoms in exchange for order, prosperity, and the security of property.

Napoleon's Empire: From Triumph to Collapse

In 1802 Napoleon, taking advantage of his rising popularity, declared himself first consul for life. His ambition increased with each addition to his power, and in 1804 he crowned himself Napoleon I, Emperor of the French. Fearful of Napoleon's imperial designs on central Europe, Great Britain declared war on France once again in 1803. Britain was soon joined by the other continental powers. British warships under Lord Nelson (1758–1805) annihilated a French fleet off Cape Trafalgar on October 21, 1805, forcing Napoleon to postpone his scheme for invading Great Britain indefinitely. However, on land, where Napoleon could display his genius as a military commander, it was a different story. Between 1805 and 1807 he defeated in succession Austria, Prussia, and Russia, thus becoming the virtual ruler of continental Europe.

Napoleon extended to conquered lands the reforms he had already instituted in France. New legal codes were introduced, class distinctions abolished, peasants freed

Coronation of Napoleon and Josephine. Jacques Louis David's painting shows Josephine kneeling to be crowned empress by Napoleon. Moments earlier, Napoleon, defying tradition, had seized the crown from the pope and placed it on his own head. The pope resignedly accepted the indignity and paid the emperor back in kind by withdrawing while Napoleon read the constitutional oath.

The Granger Collection

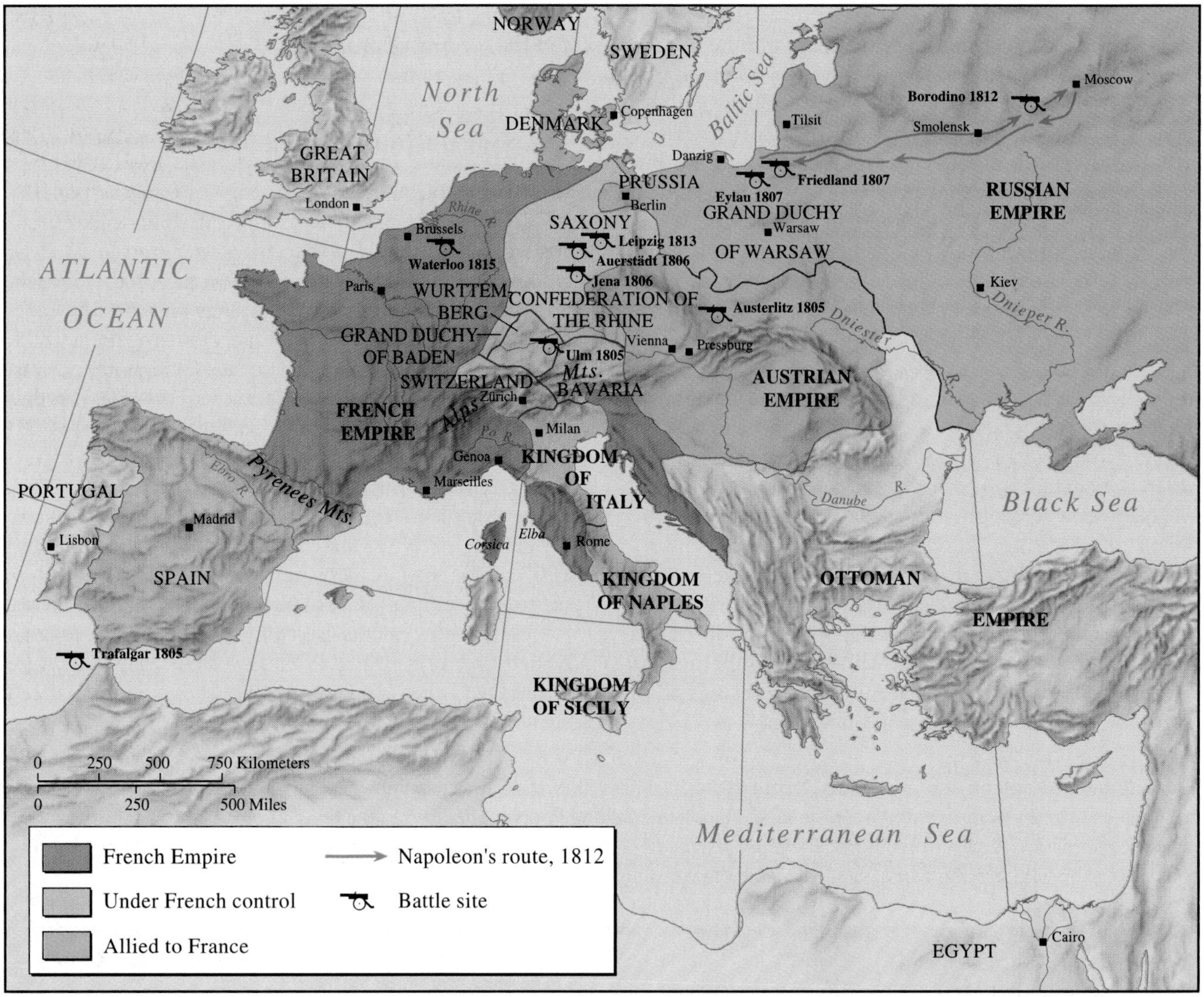

Map 12.1 Napoleon's Grand Empire. Besides pre-1789 France, Napoleon's empire included Belgium, the Netherlands, German lands to the Rhine and eastward to Hamburg, Italian towns down to Rome, Corsica, and the Illyrian provinces (in present-day Yugoslavia). Surrounding the empire were satellite states: the Confederation of the Rhine, the Grand Duchy of Warsaw, the Kingdom of Naples, Switzerland, and Spain. To the north and east were the allied states of Prussia, Austria, Russia, and Denmark.

from serfdom, and the church subordinated to the state. The middle classes in these territories initially welcomed the French as liberators, but they became less enthusiastic when they discovered that Napoleon's imperial rule also brought political repression and financial exploitation.

By 1808 Napoleon was at the apex of his power, but British resistance had not been broken. Napoleon's inability to knock out Great Britain, the main obstacle to his dream of complete hegemony over Europe and the world beyond, led him to resort to economic strangulation. In laying down his new policy, called the Continental System, Napoleon prohibited the nations of continental Europe from importing British goods. He calculated that by depriving the British of their main export market, he would ruin their trade and commerce and ultimately secure an advantageous peace. The Continental System hurt Great Britain economically but failed to cripple it, principally because its sea power enabled it to develop new markets overseas and smuggle goods to old customers on the Continent. At the same time, his ban caused widespread antagonism to Napoleon's regime on the Continent. A heavy strain was placed on the economies of European nations dependent on Great Britain, not only for cheap manufactured goods, but also as a market for their food and raw materials. Many ships lay idle in ports, hundreds of industries closed down and unemployment rose sharply.

The Continental System not only produced economic distress in Europe, but Napoleon's attempts to enforce it also caused him unexpected difficulties. When Portugal, as an old ally of Great Britain, defied the Continental System in 1807, Napoleon's army poured into the Iberian Peninsula and entered Lisbon without resistance. French troops remained in Spain to protect the lines of communication and supply and ignored official requests to withdraw. Determined to retain control over Spain, Napoleon ousted the Bourbon dynasty and appointed his older brother Joseph to the vacant throne. His action provoked a popular uprising throughout Spain. The Spanish rebels waged guerrilla warfare against the French troops in the spirit of a holy war. The Peninsular War dragged on, draining Napoleon's treasury and tying down 400,000 French troops. "It was the Spanish ulcer," Napoleon later complained, "that ruined me."

Napoleon's assessment may have been an overstatement, but there is no doubt that his disastrous campaign into Russia in 1812 marked a crucial turning point in his fortunes. An almost exclusively agricultural country, Russia had suffered extreme economic distress when it was no longer able to exchange its surplus grain for British manufactured products. Weary of the hardships caused by the Continental System, the Russian tsar, Alexander I (reigned 1801–1825), decided to open his ports to British ships. Napoleon, rather than see his system collapse, decided to punish the tsar.

In June 1812 Napoleon began the long march into Russia with an army of 600,000 men, the largest yet assembled under a single command. Reluctant to face Napoleon in a single great battle, the Russians retreated steadily inland, destroying homes and burning crops as they withdrew. Napoleon advanced over 500 miles before he fought a major engagement, at Borodino, about 75 miles from Moscow, on September 7. Both sides suffered heavy losses, but the French won out and a week later entered Moscow. Almost immediately a fire broke out and destroyed much of the city, leaving the invaders to face a Russian winter without housing and supplies. Napoleon waited five weeks for a surrender that never came, and it was not until October 19 that he ordered a retreat along the same route. The delay had catastrophic consequences. Lack of food and an early, severe winter turned the withdrawal into a rout. Discipline broke down and the once proud Grand Army dissolved into a horde of desperate fugitives struggling to stay alive. When the French army regrouped near the Russian border in mid-December, it contained about 50,000 men. The rest, over half a million, had died of battle wounds or frost or famine or had been captured by pursuing Russians.

The defeat destroyed the myth that Napoleon was invincible, and one by one the European nations joined against him in another formidable coalition. After a complex ebb and flow of military victories and defeats, Napoleon was driven back into France in 1814 and agreed to abdicate. He was exiled to the Mediterranean island of Elba, but returned to France in 1815 and resumed imperial power for a last brief interlude of glory known as the Hundred Days. At the Battle of Waterloo on June 29, 1815, he was decisively beaten by a combined Anglo-Prussian military force led by the "Iron Duke," the British Duke of Wellington. Forced to abdicate once more, Napoleon was sent to a lonely exile on the bleak Atlantic island of St. Helena, where he died in 1821.

Napoleon's defeat can be attributed to a number of interrelated factors. Perhaps his greatest mistake was to neglect his navy, which prevented him from striking directly at Great Britain and effectively enforcing the Continental System. Other factors include the sheer exhaustion of France after twenty years of almost uninterrupted warfare, the backlash in Europe against his rule caused by growing nationalism, and his massive ego, which betrayed him into undertaking unsound schemes such as the invasion of Russia.

Napoleon's career has been the subject of endless debate. Determining the balance between good and harm done by Napoleon is difficult. He was in many ways a thorough reactionary, and the cost of his wars in terms of death, destruction, and human misery was incalculable. Throughout his career he remained convinced that the end justified the means. Yet his accomplishments in the sphere of domestic reform cannot be matched in any other comparable period in French history. His major legal and administrative reforms survived his fall and became part of the machinery of government and society, not only in France but in many other European nations as well. Perhaps the best brief characterization of Napoleon is that of the eminent French historian Alexis de Tocqueville: "He was as great as a man can be without virtue."

Reform and Revolution in the Nineteenth Century

The Kings of Württemberg and Denmark arrived before any of the others . . . but the ceremony which by its pomp and splendor was evidently intended to crown the series of wonders of the Congress was the solemn entry of Tsar Alexander and the King of Prussia. . . .

From the moment Vienna assumed an aspect which was as bright as it was animated. Numberless magnificent carriages traversed the city in all directions [the imperial stables held fourteen hundred horses at the disposal of the royal guests]. . . . The promenades and squares teemed with soldiers of all grades, dressed in the varied uniforms of all the European armies. Added to these were the swarms of the servants of the aristocracy in their gorgeous liveries. . . . When night came, the theatres, the cafés, the public resorts were filled with animated crowds, apparently bent on pleasure only. . . . In almost every big thoroughfare there was the sound of musical instruments discoursing joyous tunes. Noise and bustle everywhere. . . . Hence it is not surprising that the extraordinary expenses of the fêtes of the Congress, during the . . . months of its duration, amounted to forty millions of francs.

Doubtless, at no time of the world's history had more grave and complex interests been discussed amidst so many fêtes. A kingdom was cut into bits or enlarged at a ball; an indemnity was granted in the course of a dinner; a constitution was planned during a hunt; now and again a cleverly placed word or a happy and pertinent remark cemented a treaty. . . . *

*Comte A. de la Garde Chambonas, *Anecdotal Recollections of the Congress of Vienna,* ed. Comte Fleury (London: Chapman and Hall, 1902), pp. 1–3, 12, 29.

In the autumn of 1814, a brilliant gathering of kings, princes, and statesmen assembled in the animated capital of the Habsburg Empire to draw up a peace settlement. As host to the treaty makers, the Austrian government sponsored extravagant festivities, operas, and balls. For ten months, rulers and diplomats, when not dining or dancing, worked to remake the map of Europe. As a rule, they tried to restore conditions as they had been before the French Revolution. They took precautions against a possible renewal of French aggression, returned legitimate monarchs to their thrones whenever feasible, established a balance of power in Europe, and set up a mechanism to crush revolutionary outbreaks at their source before they could spread.

In the aftermath of the Congress of Vienna, most European regimes pursued conservative policies. Monarchies, supported by the aristocracy and clerical hierarchy, resisted the demands of the bourgeoisie and workers for constitutional government or national independence. The inevitable clash between the proponents of the old order and those of change produced a rash of revolutions in Europe in the decade after 1820. The continental powers, in particular Austria, played a central role in preserving the status quo. By maintaining stability and suppressing dissent at home they were able to shore up less secure authoritarian regimes elsewhere. The revolutions were stamped out nearly everywhere in Europe. This was not the case in Latin America, however. Restless South Americans, inspired by the American and French revolutions and benefitting from liberal versus conservative struggles in Europe, seized the opportunity to secure their independence and founded new nations.

By mid-century, however, new historical trends—nationalism and industrialization—had changed the social and economic conditions of life. New political philosophies challenged the traditional systems of governance. The revolutions of 1848, though they failed to curtail the abuses of absolutist governments, were harbingers of more effective and permanent reform movements to follow.

Restoration and Conservatism versus Reform and Revolution

At the Congress of Vienna, the delegates of the major powers—Great Britain, Austria, Russia, and Prussia—formed an inner circle and decided the most important questions,

Giraudon/Art Resource

The Congress of Vienna. This watercolor by J. B. Isabey shows a gathering of the statesmen of Europe, dressed in old and contemporary styles, to hammer out a peace settlement. In fact, the major decisions were made by a few men, often at social events. Metternich, in white breeches, stands in front of a chair at left.

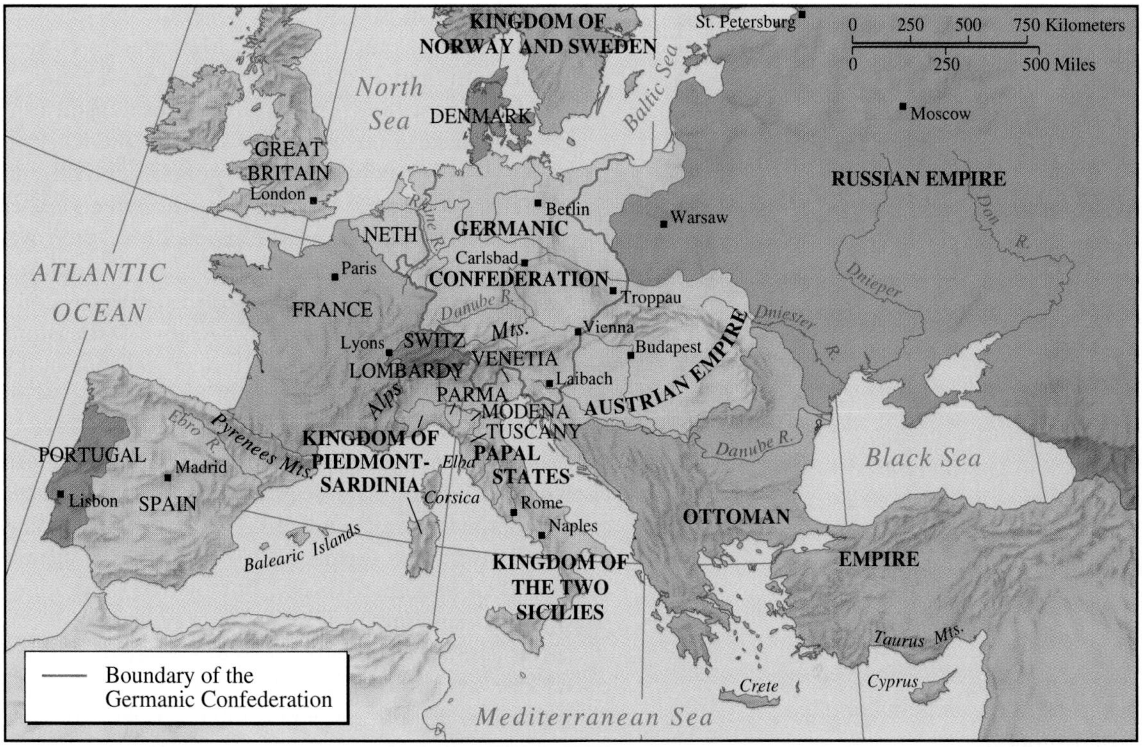

Map 12.2 Europe after the Congress of Vienna. The boundaries established at the Congress of Vienna were intended to prevent any one state from dominating continental affairs. France was reduced to its pre-1792 borders. Great Britain, despite its key role in overthrowing Napoleon, received only a few naval bases. The Netherlands acquired Belgium, and Prussia gained the Rhineland and much of Saxony. Russia obtained Finland and considerable Polish territories.

rarely bothering to consult with the representatives of the lesser states. Prince Klemens von Metternich (1773–1859), the foreign minister of Austria, dominated the inner circle. Metternich was determined to inaugurate an era of stability in Europe by suppressing liberal ideas and restoring the balance of power.

The first objective of the peacemakers was to guard against renewed French aggression. France's boundaries were pushed back essentially to where they had been before the outbreak of the revolutionary wars. To contain France within its frontiers, strong buffer states were established around it. Next, Metternich and his colleagues tried to restore the status quo before the French Revolution, returning legitimate monarchs to their thrones and establishing a balance of power in Europe. The Bourbon monarchy, for example, was restored to the French throne in the person of Louis XVIII. The Congress of Vienna also made every effort to distribute the spoils of war fairly among the victors or to compensate them for lost territory; thus some territories came under foreign domination once again.

Although the representatives at the Congress of Vienna could not undo the impact of the French Revolution and the era of Napoleon, they did formulate a settlement that helped to preserve the general peace in Europe for almost a century; in that sense the Treaty of Vienna stands as one of the better treaties of the modern era. At the same time, by ignoring democratic and nationalist sentiments, the statesmen at Vienna opened the door to popular unrest and revolution in some European nations. After 1815, many Europeans were determined to regain the social and political advantages they had lost at Vienna; others, once again living under alien governments, were equally determined to throw off foreign domination.

On the heels of the congress, Austria, Russia, Britain, and Prussia joined in the Quadruple Alliance, committing themselves to police the peace settlement for twenty years and to meet regularly to discuss common problems. Metternich was determined to use the league as an international police force to suppress liberal and nationalist movements before they could lead to general war. In 1818 France, having shown good behavior, was admitted into the group, which then became the Quintuple Alliance. This instrument to regulate international conduct, known as the "Concert of Europe," was in some ways a forerunner of the League of Nations.

Metternich's Conservative Credo

There is besides scarcely any epoch which does not offer a rallying cry to some particular faction. This cry, since 1815, has been Constitution. But do not let us deceive ourselves. . . . Everywhere it means change and trouble. . . .

Governments having lost their balance, are frightened, intimidated, and thrown into confusion. . . .

We are convinced that society can no longer be saved without strong and vigorous resolutions on the part of the Governments. . . . By this course the monarchs will fulfill the duties imposed upon them by Him who, by entrusting them with power, has charged them to watch over the maintenance of justice and the rights of all. . . .

The first principle to be followed by the monarchs . . . should be that of maintaining the stability of political institutions. . . .

The first and greatest concern for the immense majority of every nation is the stability of the laws. . . .

Let them be just, but strong: beneficent, but strict.

Let them maintain religious principles in all their purity. . . .

*In short, let the great monarchs strengthen their union, and prove to the world that if it exists, it is beneficent, and ensures the political peace of Europe . . . that the principles which they profess are paternal and protective, menacing only the disturbers of public tranquility.**

Metternich's statement of his political principles, written in 1820 at the request of Tsar Alexander I, was designed to justify his policy and refute the ideas that had spawned the revolution.

*Richard Metternich, ed., *Memoirs of Prince Metternich*, vol. 2 (New York: Harper, 1881), pp. 322–337.

During its early years, it functioned successfully, stamping out popular uprisings in Naples, the Kingdom of Sardinia, and Spain. The system was weakened in 1824 when Great Britain, to protect its vital interests, withdrew from the alliance (see the next section).

After 1815, most European governments followed policies that were compatible with Metternich's conservative ideas. In France, the monarch, Charles X (reigned 1824–1830), in a bid to restore royal absolutism, canceled the constitution instituted by his predecessor, Louis XVIII. His action set off a popular uproar, and angry Parisians erected barricades in the streets. After three days of fierce fighting, the rebels drove the royal troops from the city, prompting Charles to abdicate. Representatives of the people offered the crown to Louis Philippe, the Duke of Orleans and a relative of the Bourbons, who promptly accepted it. In open defiance of the settlement of 1815, a popular revolt had driven a legitimate monarch from the throne.

The French rebellion of 1830 sparked revolutions elsewhere in Europe. The Belgians overthrew Dutch rule and established an independent constitutional monarchy. The Poles were less fortunate in their struggle against Russia. They fought heroically, but by 1831 the much stronger Russian army had broken their resistance.

After 1830 Metternich's system operated with reduced effectiveness. France, like Great Britain, became committed to a more moderate foreign policy. In contrast, Austria, Prussia, and Russia were firmly resolved to prevent any more breaches in the Vienna settlement. In 1833 they formally pledged to render joint assistance to any monarch threatened by revolution. The forces of nationalism and democracy, however, reinforced by new ideologies, were too powerful to be repressed for long.

Revolt and Independence in Latin America

The aftershocks of the French Revolution and the era of Napoleon were also felt in Latin America. At the beginning of the nineteenth century, Spain, with its huge block of possessions in the Western Hemisphere, rivaled Great Britain as a major European colonial power. The Spanish Empire in America, however, along with Portugal's, soon crumbled under the twin pressures of upheavals at home and revolt in the colonies.

For centuries, Spanish and Portuguese colonists had chafed under economic deprivations, and many Creoles had resented the political power of the Peninsulars sent to govern them. Influenced by the republican political principles instituted in the United States of America and by the reforms of the French Revolution and Napoleon, some Creoles hoped to create comparable liberal institutions in Latin America, at least for the upper classes. Some of the more radical wanted to disestablish the Roman Catholic church and tax or confiscate its property. Few gave much thought to the needs of the masses of workers and peasants.

The revolutionary era was launched, however, not by Creoles but by black slaves and mulatto freemen. In the 1790s, black slaves in the French Caribbean colony of Saint Dominique (Haiti) revolted and drove out

Giraudon/Art Resource

Delacroix's *Liberty Leading the People.* Liberty, personified as a composed and rational goddess holding the tricolor aloft, is uniting workers and bourgeoisie against the forces of political reaction. The artist intends to glorify the July Revolution in Paris in 1830 and to inspire future revolutionaries. The painting also exemplifies the link between the romantic movement in the arts and the political movements of liberalism and nationalism from 1820 to 1850.

white authority. Toussaint L'Ouverture, the rebel leader, created a disciplined army and fended off attacks by other European nations and revolts by mulatto factions. He abolished slavery before the republican government of France belatedly terminated it in all French possessions. Napoleon, however, flirting with thoughts of recreating the old French empire in the Western Hemisphere, decided to restore white rule in Haiti and the old plantation system in the French Caribbean. He sent an army to subdue Haiti, but the climate, yellow fever, and the resistance of blacks destroyed the French in a struggle punctuated by racial massacres. L'Ouverture was captured, however, and died in a French prison. In 1804 Jean Jacques Dessalines proclaimed the independence of the new nation of Haiti, proclaiming himself emperor. The success of the blacks of Haiti disturbed conservative nations in general and slaveholding nations in particular. Haiti was shunned in diplomatic circles for decades.

The main struggle for Latin American independence began in 1807–1808. When Napoleon deposed the Bourbon monarchy in Spain, royal authority throughout Spanish America weakened. Argentina removed itself from royal control in 1810 and formally proclaimed independence in 1816. Rebels in Venezuela pronounced their liberation in 1811. Simón Bolívar (1783–1830), a Venezuelan aristocrat who had taken an oath to free his country from Spain, became the hero of Latin American independence movements. For seven years Bolívar's fortunes fluctuated from splendid victories to humiliating defeats and exile. Finally, his forces decisively defeated the Spanish in Colombia in 1819 and in Venezuela in 1821. The triumphant rebels hailed him as "Liberator." Meanwhile, in 1817, José de San Martin made a spectacular surprise crossing of the high Andes passes from Argentina into Chile and drove out the Spanish in 1818. With the aid of the British and Chileans, he built a navy and in 1821 landed in Lima, Peru, the heart of the Spanish authority in South America. Bolívar moved south in 1822 through Ecuador to join forces with San Martin against the remaining Spanish army. San Martin returned to Argentina, and Bolívar,

The Granger Collection

The Liberator. This portrait of Simón Bolívar depicts a remarkable man. On a dozen battlefields, he liberated one-third of South America from Spanish rule.

taking command of the combined armies, crushed the last remnants of Spanish authority at Ayacucho, Peru, in 1824. Ironically, it was victory over the Inkas in the same Andean highlands three centuries earlier that had given the Spanish control over most of South America.

The Spanish were not the only threat to the South American revolutionaries. Conservative nations in Europe had smashed a liberal revolution in Spain in 1822 and restored the deposed monarch. Some of these nations also considered sending troops to Latin America to eradicate the rebellion there against the Spanish monarchy, and perhaps pick up some territory of their own in the Americas. The British government, however, opposed European intervention, realizing that independence had opened up an entire continent to trade and investment. Since the British navy could block any expedition across the Atlantic, the invasion scheme was dropped. Wishing to strengthen its own influence in the hemisphere, the United States, after consulting with Great Britain, issued the Monroe Doctrine (1823) to voice its opposition to European interference. However, the attitude of that weak nation was virtually irrelevant at the time.

Whereas independence movements in South America had essentially been struggles among members of the European-descended upper classes, Mexico's path to independence was marked by class revolution and even race warfare. Various Creole groups and Peninsulars engaged in confused maneuverings from 1808 until 1810, when the upper classes were confronted by an uprising of mestizo and Amerindian peasants initially led by Father Miguel Hidalgo under the banner of the dark-skinned Virgin of Guadalupe. Hidalgo's demands for civil rights for the peasants alarmed the upper classes; liberal and conservative Creoles joined to crush the rebellion, and the revolutionary movement dissolved into guerrilla warfare. The 1820 liberal revolution in Spain inspired conservative Mexican Creoles to rebel. Agustín de Iturbide, a military adventurer, drew up the Plan of Iguala, which called for independence and promised something for all the elite groups in Mexico, without basic social and economic change. Iturbide had such overwhelming support that the Spanish were forced to concede the independence of Mexico in 1821. Social revolution was to recur in Mexico, however, as the twentieth century would show.

Compared with the wars and revolutions in Spanish America, Brazilians won their independence from Portugal relatively easily. While the Portuguese royal family was ruling in exile in Brazil, it opened the territory to free trade, encouraged immigration and industrial production, and formally confederated Brazil with Portugal as a joint kingdom. After King John VI returned to Portugal in 1820, leaving his son Pedro as regent, the Portuguese legislature began to strip Brazil of its status and repealed John's reforms. The exasperated Brazilians persuaded Pedro to support a break with Portugal and to proclaim an independent state in 1822. Portugal capitulated and recognized Brazilian independence in 1825. By that year the only European colonies remaining in the Western Hemisphere south of Canada were the Caribbean islands (except Santo Domingo) and a few small enclaves on the coasts of Central and South America.

By the 1830s nineteen new states had emerged in Latin America. Although each had its distinct social and political personality, their similarities, especially their common colonial heritage, far outweighed their differences. These new nations were dependent on the export and sale of agricultural and mineral raw materials. They imported manufactured goods from European nations and also became indebted to them for investment capital. Their own industrial output was low, and their outmoded production techniques, still dependent on cheap hand labor, resembled those of central and eastern Europe.

Despite these economic negatives, Latin America nonetheless had significant economic attractions, although not necessarily of benefit to the general population. The area contained abundant raw materials, and in some areas there were large populations that could be turned into lucrative markets. Latin American govern-

Bolívar Ponders a Suitable Government for Spanish America

The diversity of racial origin will require an infinitely firm hand and great tactfulness to manage this heterogeneous society, whose complex mechanism is easily . . . disintegrated by the slightest controversy. . . .

It is a marvel that the [federal] prototype in North America endures so successfully and has not been overthrown at the first sign of adversity or danger. . . . But . . . never . . . compare the position and character of two states as dissimilar as the English-American and Spanish-American. We [are] not prepared for such good. . . . Our moral fiber [does] not . . . possess the stability necessary to derive benefits from a wholly representative government. . . .

*Thus I recommend . . . the study of the British Constitution . . . for that body of laws appears destined to bring about the greatest possible good for the peoples that adopt it; but . . . I only refer to its republican features; and indeed can a political system be labeled a monarchy when it recognizes popular sovereignty, division and balance of powers, civil liberty, freedom of conscience and press, and all that is politically sublime? . . . [It serves] as a model for those who aspire to the enjoyment of the rights of man and who seek all the political happiness which is compatible with frailty of human nature.**

Writing in 1819, when the future of the independence movement was still in doubt, Simón Bolívar recommended a house of representatives elected by a restricted franchise and a hereditary senate of specially trained and educated members. He also suggested an elected chief executive, reelectable for long terms, and an independent judiciary. Influenced by his readings in Enlightenment thought and by the limitations placed on him because he was a Creole, Bolívar was a radical, demanding equality before the law. He favored limiting political power to the middle and upper classes for the foreseeable future until the masses were educated and their economic condition uplifted. By 1826 the final divisive struggle for independence and the rampant factionalism after independence had made Bolívar more conservative. He created a government for Bolivia that resembled the authoritarian state under Napoleon.

*"Address to the Second National Congress of Venezuela," trans. L. Bertrand, in *Selected Writings of Bolívar,* ed. Harold A. Bierck (New York: Colonial Press, 1951), pp. 174–197, passim.

ments augmented these economic opportunities by offering tax breaks and other investment incentives. With the British in the vanguard, Europeans began to invest heavily in Latin America during the nineteenth century. European businessmen combined labor-saving technology with cheap labor to create enormously profitable plantations and mines and later factories, roads, railroads, telegraph networks, and petroleum refineries.

The social and political characteristics of the Latin American states also reflected colonial conditions. Rich property holders and the Catholic church continued to wield economic and political power in Spanish America; they were now joined by the national military establishments of the new nations. Independence brought few economic improvements for the masses, who continued to work for the elite. Like the eastern European peasantry, the peons received little pay and lacked decent housing, adequate food, proper sanitation, and basic education.

On paper, the constitutions of Spanish American states were influenced by revolutionary France and the United States. They set up liberal republics with elected officers, civil liberties, equality before the law, and varying degrees of religious toleration. In reality, however, these ideals were difficult to realize in societies composed of a tiny elite at the top and an impoverished and uneducated mass at the bottom. Civil rights were not extended to the masses, and political involvement was limited to a few opportunistic individuals and cliques. Politics was often tainted by fraud and corruption, and elections were frequently overturned by the armed forces, who installed dictators. Two groups emerged in most nations—the conservatives and the liberals: the conservatives stood for preserving the prerogatives and powers of the upper classes and the church, whereas the liberals wished to break down these privileges so that the small, mostly mestizo, middle class could share economic and political power.

1848: The Year of Revolutions

In 1848 an outburst of revolutionary activity occurred throughout much of Europe. Among the major European powers, only Great Britain and Russia were relatively unaffected. The causes of the upheavals varied, but economic distress, nationalism, and liberalism were all potent factors.

As in the past, upheavals in France stoked the fires of revolution through the rest of Europe. A severe economic crisis in 1846–1847 increased working class opposition to the monarchy and led to a protest campaign that culminated in the overthrow of Louis Philippe. For the second time in a generation, constitutional monarchy had failed in France. In the last days of February 1848 political power passed to a provisional government that proclaimed France a republic and ordered the writing of a new constitution. The government was dominated by moderate elements, but included several socialists led by Louis Blanc, who organized national workshops to provide employment for the poor. The national workshops were public projects that never developed into self-supporting industrial enterprises as Blanc had intended; instead, they degenerated into a straight dole for unemployed workers.

Map 12.3 Latin America in the First Half of the Nineteenth Century. The nations of Latin America appeared in two basic stages. Ten nations achieved independence from Spain and Portugal between 1810 and 1822. The rest appeared when regional issues in the infant nations resulted in secessions between 1825 and 1844.

In April the French voters elected a Constituent Assembly that was much more conservative than the provisional government. One of the first acts of the new Assembly was to dissolve the workshops. Violent reaction to this legislation was brutally crushed and thousands of rebels were executed or deported to penal colonies overseas.

By the autumn of 1848, the Assembly had completed a constitution for the Second French Republic. It declared property inviolable and scrapped a proposed "right to work" clause. It acknowledged free speech, freedom of the press, and security from arbitrary arrest. It provided for a president vested with strong executive

Map 12.4 Principal Centers of Revolution, 1848–1849. The uprisings all over Europe in 1848 ultimately failed, not only because of the strength of the conservatives but also because hostile national minorities fell out with each other and antagonisms developed between the anticapitalist urban workers and the bourgeoisie. The reactionary regimes responded quickly and quenched the flickering flames of liberty and nationalism in the insurgent countries.

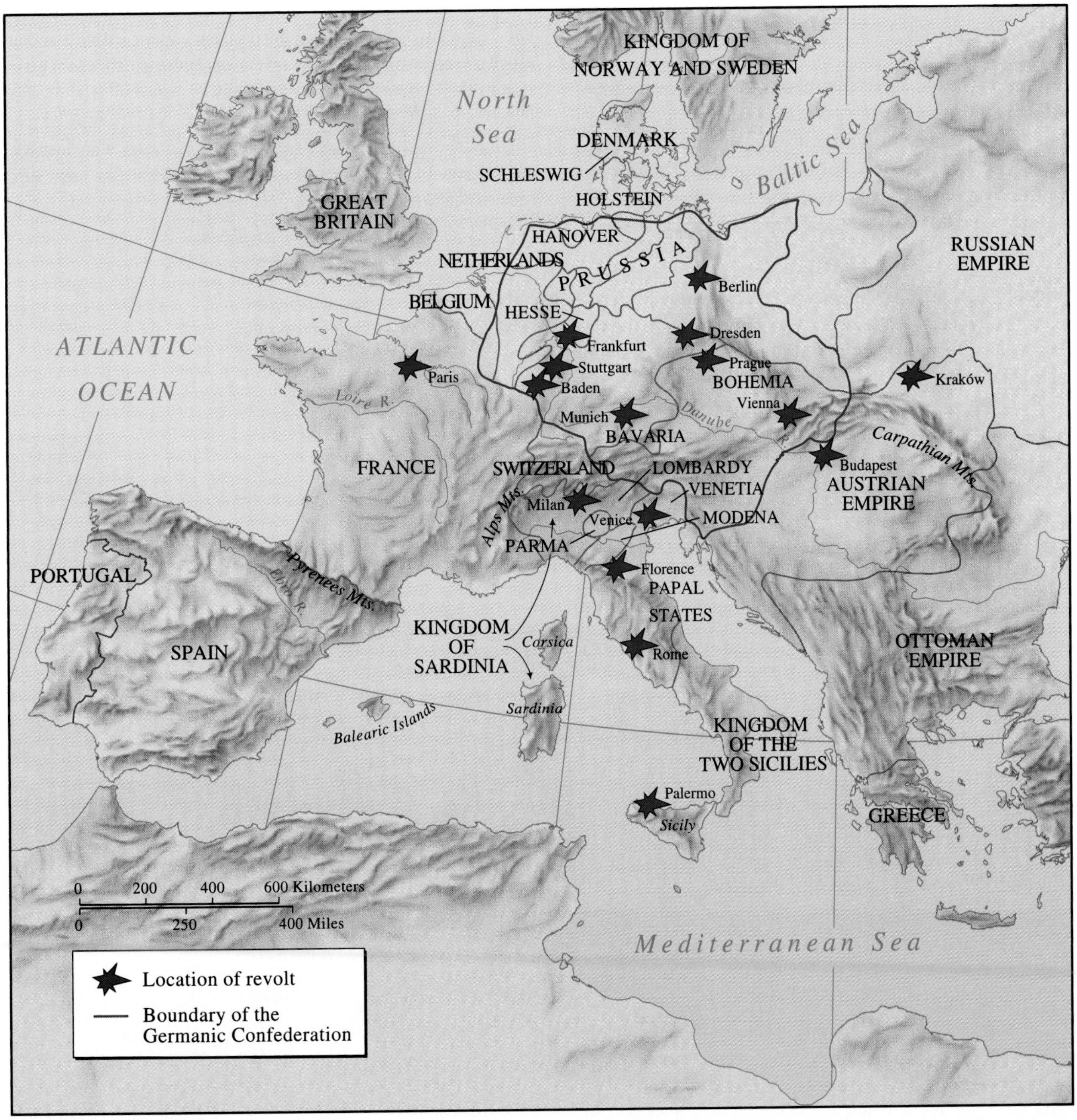

powers and a single legislative body elected by universal male suffrage (women continued to be excluded from the political process). Thus France emerged from the 1848 revolution as a middle-class rather than a worker's republic.

Reforms in France inspired groups in Prussia and Austria to demand more representative governments and the abolition of remaining feudal practices. In western Europe, where constitutional government had already been achieved, liberals wanted political power extended to all classes. A general economic crisis heightened the tensions of 1848 and fed popular discontent.

The revolutions of 1848 did not spring only from demands for political and economic reforms. Nationalistic ideals inspired Germans and Italians, who were divided among many political entities, to make a bid for national unity. Nationalist fervor also provoked the subject peoples of the Austrian Empire to seek political independence.

Inspired by noble aims, the revolutionary movements of 1848 began with great promise, but in most cases ended in defeat and disappointment, particularly in central and eastern Europe. The revolutionaries gained the upper hand in the opening stages because the European governments were reluctant to use their superior armed forces.

Another element explaining the failure of the revolutions was the disintegration of the alliance between middle-class liberals and urban workers. In general, the various groups seeking political concessions made uneasy allies. The middle class favored reforms that would give them a fair share of political control but were unsympathetic to the workers' demands for social and economic change. Finally, long-established ethnic rivalries often divided nationalist movements in central Europe. Eventually, the reactionary governments regained the initiative and moved quickly. Using military force, and often playing one ethnic group off against another, the established order crushed the uprisings.

Although the 1848 revolutions failed to achieve many of their goals, they left their mark on Europe. France adopted universal male suffrage; serfdom was abolished in the Austrian Empire; and parliaments were established in all the German states, though most were not democratic. After 1848 many reformers became convinced that violence was not the best way to reshape society and placed their faith in the British example of gradualism and peaceful change. Others, most notably the Marxists (see next section), continued to struggle for revolutionary transformation of existing political and social systems.

Revolutionary Fighters Resisting Royal Forces, Berlin, March 18–19, 1848. Most of the insurgents were artisans, but merchants and students also participated in the fighting. The victorious Berliners forced King Frederick William to go through a grotesque ceremony of saluting the corpses of slain revolutionaries. Recalling the incident in later life, Frederick William remarked, "We all crawled on our bellies."

Corbis-Bettmann

Nationalism and Political Conflict in the West: 1848–1914

Standing erect, his gaze firmly fixed on those who were awaiting him, the image of venerable nobility, the aged monarch [William I] ascended the dais where he would be crowned. . . . There he stood on the very place once occupied by Louis XIV's chair of state, dressed in the uniform of his First Regiment of Foot Guards, adorned with the ribbon of the Order of the Black Eagle as well as a number of other orders, . . .

The Crown Prince energetically commanded, "Remove your helmets to pray!", whereupon Rogge, the court chaplain, recited the liturgy according to Prussian military usage, followed by a performance of a soldier's choir. . . .

*Then Bismarck, his face pale, wearing tall riding-boots so that he looked like a giant, bowed deeply before the approaching Emperor. On his shoulders he wore the epaulettes of a lieutenant-general, for he had just been promoted to that rank. In his left hand he held his massive helmet, in his right hand the coronation charter, which he read. . . . Then I heard the Grand Duke von Baden shout in a loud voice. "His Majesty Wilhelm the Victorious, long may he live!" Three times a thundering "Long live the Emperor!" issued from innumerable throats . . . ; flags fell, sabers were drawn from their sheaths, helmets were waved in the air. Again and again the soldiers roared "Hurrah's," almost drowning out the three regimental bands playing "Hail to thee in the victor's wreath!" as loud as they could.**

*Wilhelm Stieber, *The Chancellor's Spy: The Revelations of the Chief of Bismarck's Secret Service* (New York: Grove, 1979), pp. 211–212.

This scene in the Hall of Mirrors in Versailles on January 18, 1871, marked the culmination of the German people's quest for a unified German Empire. It also symbolized the replacement of France by Germany as the most powerful continental European nation. A decade earlier the Italians had also realized their dreams for national unification. Similarly a number of Christian Slavic peoples in the Balkan Peninsula achieved nationhood at the expense of the crumbling Islamic Ottoman Empire. However, the nationalistic aspirations of the Slavs in the Austro-Hungarian Empire remained unfulfilled. Non-Russians in the Russian Empire likewise remained victims of the official policy of Russification.

Newly unified Italy and Germany, together with Great Britain and France as well as the multinational Austro-Hungarian and Russian Empires, shared in varying degrees the social problems caused by the Industrial Revolution. At the same time, the better-educated and increasingly vocal populations in these states demanded political reforms. This section will explore these major themes.

The Second Napoleonic Empire

France continued its turbulent quest for a viable political structure throughout the nineteenth century. When the 1848 revolution overthrew the Orleanist monarchy of Louis Philippe, a Second Republic was briefly established, but it in turn was overthrown in an almost bloodless coup by the popularly elected president, Louis Napoleon Bonaparte. In 1852 Bonaparte established the Second Empire, giving himself the title of Napoleon III (reigned 1852–1870); all his actions were then duly ratified by a plebiscite. Although the governmental structure during the early years of the Second Empire retained the outward forms of a parliamentary system, the emperor had almost unlimited authority, controlling the army, foreign affairs, legislation, and finance. The Legislative Assembly, which was elected by male suffrage, lacked the power to initiate or amend bills. It could only vote for or against the emperor's proposals, and elections were often rigged to return government-sponsored candidates.

Napoleon III did much to develop the French economy and industry, to beautify Paris, and to make France the cultural center of Europe. Eager to emulate the military glory and conquests of his uncle, Napoleon I, he engaged in an active foreign policy, which initially was successful. He joined Great Britain and the Ottoman Empire against Russia in the Crimean War (1853–1856), fought alongside the British against China (1858–1860), and battled the Austrians (1859) to help the Italians in their drive for national unification.

Up to 1860 most Frenchmen did not object to Napoleon III's benevolently despotic government, which offered them order, prosperity, and glory. After 1860, however, his popularity and authority began to crumble, as a result of successive failures in foreign policy. His attempt to create an empire in Mexico was a fiasco that eroded his prestige and damaged French interests, as did the diplomatic setbacks he then experienced in German affairs. Napoleon countered with wide-ranging concessions in an attempt to save his tottering throne. Under the new, "liberal" phase of his empire, Napoleon relaxed press censorship, legalized strikes, and even allowed an opposition to form in the Legislative Assembly. As of 1870 France under Napoleon III apparently remained the leading power on the European continent.

The Triumph of Nationalism in Italy

Italy had not known national unity since the fall of the Roman Empire. It was a patchwork of petty states, or as

Scala/Art Resource

Victor Emmanuel and Garibaldi at the Bridge of Teano in 1860. This romanticized painting shows Garibaldi selflessly turning over his conquests to Victor Emmanuel, even though the armies of the two men had confronted each other at the brink of civil war only a short time before. Garibaldi yielded rather than allow his personal ambitions to thwart the unification of Italy.

Metternich had once contemptuously remarked, "a geographical expression." The revolutions of 1848–1849 had failed to unify Italy, leaving Austria more firmly entrenched in the north. After these events, the prospect of Italian national unity seemed more remote than ever. Yet not everything had been in vain. Sardinia, a kingdom comprised of Piedmont and the island of Sardinia, emerged from the conflict with an enhanced prestige because of its liberal constitution and its gallant stand against Austria. More and more Italian patriots looked to the ruler of Sardinia, Victor Emmanuel II (reigned 1849–1878), as the natural leader. Victor Emmanuel was neither inspiring nor a first-class statesman, but he had a good deal of common sense. He showed much wisdom when he selected as his prime minister Count Camillo di Cavour (1810–1861), who was to play a vital role in the unification drama. Cavour, a practitioner of cool, tough-minded statecraft, dominated Italian politics from 1852 until his premature death in 1861. In the early years in office, he strengthened Sardinia with numerous domestic reforms that made it the model Italian state.

The main barrier to Italian unity was Austria, which controlled Lombardy and Venetia in the northeast and dominated the Italian reactionary states. Cavour realized that Sardinia was too small to tackle Austria without al-

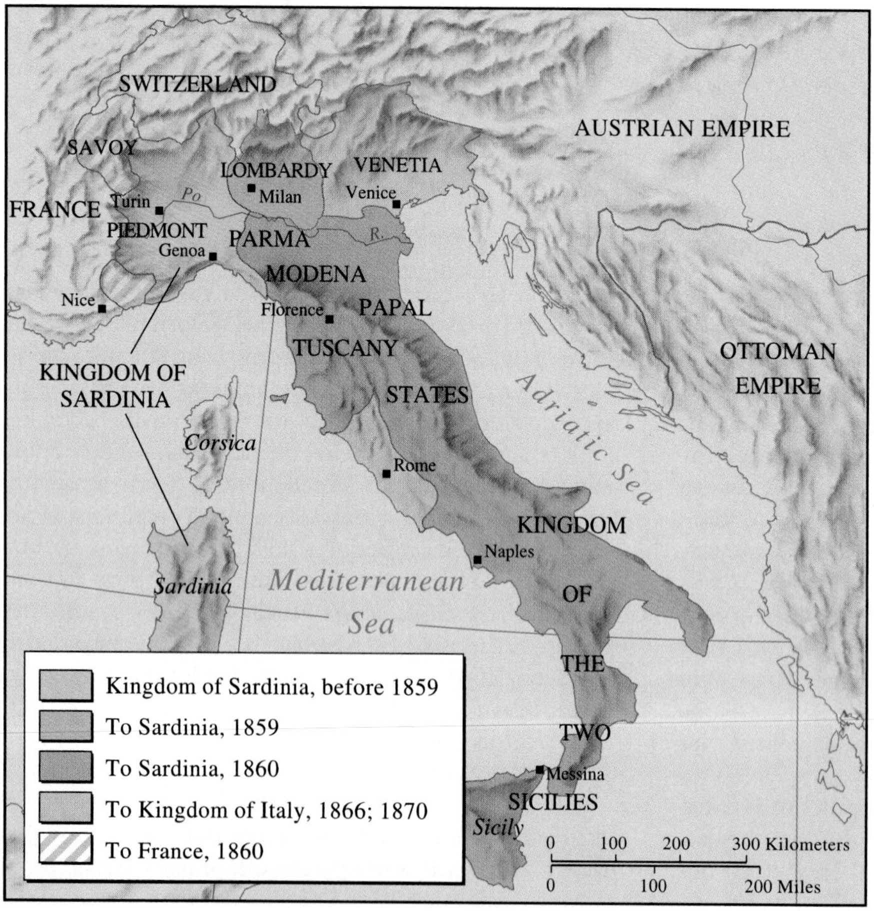

Map 12.5 The Unification of Italy. With the help of France, Sardinia (which included Piedmont) acquired Lombardy in a war against Austria in 1859. Soon afterward, revolutionaries seized power in Modena, Tuscany, Parma, and Romagna (one of the papal states) and voted to join with Sardinia. The nationalist movement spread south and culminated in a new Italian state that included all of the peninsula except Venetia and Rome. Italy received Venetia as a reward for being Prussia's ally in the Seven Weeks' War and took possession of Rome in 1870 when France withdrew its garrison.

Garibaldi Calls on Italians to Fight for Unity

Italians! . . . It is the duty of every Italian to succor [the Sicilian rebels] with words, money, and arms, and above all, in person. . . .

The misfortunes of Italy arise from the indifference of one province to the fate of others.

The redemption of Italy began from the moment that men of the same land ran to help their distressed brothers. . . .

Let the inhabitants of the free provinces lift their voices in behalf of their brethren, and impel their brave youth to the conflict. . . .

A band of those who fought with me the country's battles marches with me to the fight. Good and generous, they will fight for their country to the last drop of their blood, nor ask for other reward than a clear conscience.

"Italy and Victor Emmanuel!" . . .

At this cry . . . the rotten Throne of tyranny shall crumble . . .

*To arms! Let me put an end, once and for all, to the miseries of so many centuries. Prove to the world that it is no lie that Roman generations inhabited this land.**

*"Proclamation for the Liberation of Sicily," Public Documents, The Annual Register, 1860 (London, 1861), pp. 281–282; in Perry M. Rogers, ed., *Aspects of Western Civilization: Problems and Sources in History,* 2d ed. (Englewood Cliffs, N.J., 1992) 2.225–226.

Giuseppe Garibaldi, the author of this manifesto issued from Sicily in 1860, was a romantic adventurer and the embodiment of Italian military nationalism, as Cavour was its civilian genius. The self-educated Garibaldi was a sailor in his youth and in 1833 joined the cause of Italian unity. He was condemned to death and fled to Latin America, where he was involved in civil wars in Brazil and Uruguay. He returned to Italy during the revolutions of 1848 and fought for Sardinia against Austria.

In 1849 Garibaldi and a volunteer legion tried but failed to defend a republican uprising in Rome against French and Austrian forces; once again he fled for his life, this time to the United States, where he became a citizen. In 1854 he returned to Sardinia. After turning over his forces to Victor Emmanuel in 1861, Garibaldi temporarily retired. In 1862 and 1866 he raised a third and a fourth set of volunteers and twice marched on Rome with the goal of incorporating it into the Italian kingdom. He was defeated both times, first by Victor Emmanuel (who did not want to antagonize the French), then by papal and French forces; taken prisoner twice and released twice. In 1870 Garibaldi, now sixty-three, and his two sons fought as volunteers in the French army against Prussia. In the years before his death in 1887, he became a supporter of socialism.

lies. Thus he sought to gain favor with Great Britain and France by participating on their side in the Crimean War. Subsequently, he met Napoleon III and promised to cede the Sardinian provinces of Nice and Savoy to France in return for his help in a future war against Austria.

With French military aid assured, Cavour provoked Austria to declare war on Sardinia in 1859. Napoleon, true to his word, quickly moved his troops into Italy and, along with the Sardinians, drove the Austrians out of Lombardy. French military and economic costs were high, however, and Napoleon, without consulting Cavour, concluded a separate peace in which Austria gave up Lombardy but not Venetia. The Sardinian leaders considered the settlement inadequate, but their disappointment was only temporary. Sardinia's victory over Austria had spurred nationalistic uprisings that expelled unpopular rulers from the small states on the upper peninsula and brought all of northern Italy except Venetia into union with Sardinia. In return for Napoleon's acquiescence to the union, Cavour turned over Nice and Savoy as called for in the original agreement.

At this point a firebrand nationalist, Giuseppe Garibaldi (1807–1882), decided to complete the unification process. He raised a volunteer army and headed for Sicily, where a revolution had broken out against the reactionary Bourbon ruler of the Kingdom of the Two Sicilies. Garibaldi landed on the island on May 11, 1860, with 1,000 untrained volunteers (later called the Thousand) dressed in bright red shirts. Gathering strength as he campaigned, Garibaldi and his Red Shirts first conquered Sicily (see the accompanying box) and then crossed over to the mainland. He advanced on Naples, the capital of the kingdom, and, with the Bourbon ruler in flight, entered the city to the joyful acclaim of the populace. Garibaldi threatened to create a crisis when he proposed to march on Rome. Such a move, Cavour believed, was bound to offend France, which since 1849 had stationed a garrison in Rome to protect the pope. To head off Garibaldi, Victor Emmanuel personally led an army south and on the way seized all the papal lands save for Rome and its environs. Just north of Naples, he met Garibaldi, who agreed to give up his command and turn over his conquests. On March 17, 1861, the Kingdom of Italy was proclaimed, with Victor Emmanuel as king. When Cavour died three months later, only Venetia and Rome remained outside the new nation.

Cavour's political heirs completed Italian unification. During the Seven Weeks' War (Austro-Prussian War) in 1866, Italy allied itself with the victorious Prussians and gained Venetia. The outbreak of the Franco-Prussian War in July 1870 compelled Napoleon to recall the French troops from Rome. On September 20, 1870, Italian troops took possession of Rome, except for the few square miles enclosing the Vatican City. Rome was annexed to Italy and became its capital.

The Unification of Germany

Germany, like Italy, had not been a unified state in modern times. German unification came about in a manner strikingly similar to the process that created the Kingdom of Italy. It was essentially the work of one man, who led the strongest and most prosperous of the interested states. The process was achieved in stages through a combination of complex political maneuvering and war. Here, too, the chief victim was Austria, which was ejected as completely from Germany as it had been from Italy.

During the revolutions of 1848, liberal nationalists from the various German states had met at Frankfurt and attempted to create a unified Germany. Their effort was unsuccessful. In 1849 the conservatives regained power throughout Germany, dismissed the Frankfurt Assembly, and nullified its acts. In the aftermath of this failure, frustrated nationalists rejected vague abstractions and misty romantic ideals in favor of cynical realism and power politics. They had been influenced by Cavour's commonsense approach and became convinced that only Prussia was strong enough to play the role Sardinia had assumed in bringing about Italian unity.

Throughout the middle decades of the nineteenth century Prussia's economic infrastructure—industry, banking system, roads and railroads—grew by leaps and bounds. As a result, Prussia became the strongest of the German states, now joined in the *Zollverein* (customs union). In contrast, Austria, which had been excluded from the Zollverein, lagged behind in economic development; this undercut its traditional titular leadership of the German Confederation, a league created chiefly to provide a means of common defense against foreign attack.

During the 1860s the Hohenzollern ruler, King William I of Prussia (reigned 1861–1888), wished to build up the Prussian army. Stung by a recalcitrant Prussian legislature that opposed the new taxes needed to raise the requisite revenues, William was on the verge of abdicating when he appointed Otto von Bismarck (1815–1898) as minister-president. A consummate practitioner of *Realpolitik* (the pursuit of policy by any means), Bismarck, later known as the Iron Chancellor, stated bluntly how he proposed to conduct state business: "The great questions of the day are not to be decided by speeches and majority resolutions . . . but by blood and iron." When parliament continued to resist the proposed taxes, Bismarck ordered them collected anyway. By successfully defying parliament, Bismarck severely undermined the ideals of constitutionalism and liberalism and ensured that the monarchy and the military would dominate Germany's political life for decades to come.

Bismarck engineered three wars to complete German unification under Prussian leadership. The first was a short war against Denmark, in which Prussia and Austria fought together to prevent the Danes from annexing the duchies of Schleswig and Holstein, which had a large German population. After Denmark's defeat, Austrian and Prussian troops occupied the two duchies. Problems in setting up the administration of Schleswig and Holstein prompted Bismarck to harass Austria and maneuver it into declaring war against Prussia. Prussia had new and better weapons

The Iron Chancellor. Otto von Bismarck was a political genius who dominated European politics for three decades. A realist concerned with the application of power without scruple or sentiment, he believed his foremost duty was the pursuit of the reasoned interest of the state.

The Granger Collection

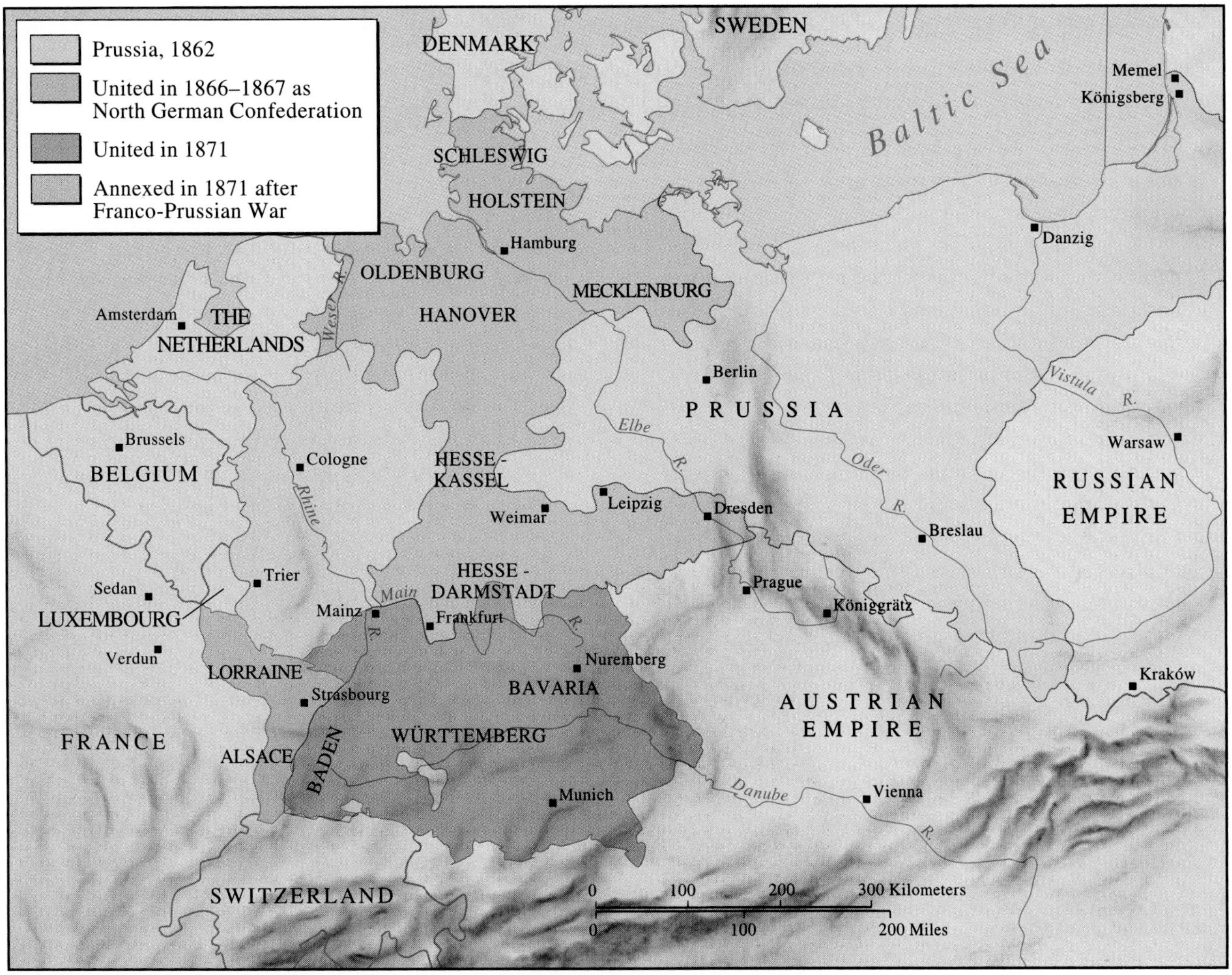

Map 12.6 The Unification of Germany. Prussia, under Bismarck's leadership, unified Germany in three stages. In 1864 Prussia and Austria defeated Denmark over the Schleswig-Holstein issue. Prussia then crushed Austria in a short war in 1866 and then set up the North German Confederation, headed by the Prussian king. Following Prussia's victory over France, the South German states joined the North German Confederation, which, together with Alsace and Lorraine, completed the formation of the German Empire.

and a superb railway system that transported troops and supplies to any front with unprecedented speed. Victory came so quickly that the Austro-Prussian conflict was known as the Seven Weeks' War.

In the treaty that followed the war, Prussia gained territory in north Germany that closed the gap between Prussia's eastern and western provinces and added 5 million people. The treaty also dissolved the German Confederation and excluded Austria from German affairs in the future. In its place Bismarck welded the twenty-two German states north of the Main River into the North German Confederation under Prussian domination. German unification remained incomplete, however, because the four Catholic states of South Germany remained outside. These giant steps toward German unification squelched liberal parliamentary opposition to Bismarck's extraconstitutional methods.

To induce the South German states to join a Prussian-dominated Germany, Bismarck needed a common enemy to unite them. France, led by the vainglorious Napoleon III, was the obvious choice. Bismarck's opportunity came when the vacant Spanish throne was offered to Prince Leopold of Hohenzollern, a distant relative of King William I. Alarmed at the prospect of being encircled by Hohenzollerns, Napoleon protested so vehemently that William persuaded Leopold to withdraw his candidacy. Not content with his diplomatic victory, Napoleon sent his ambassador to the bathing resort of Ems to seek assurances from William that Leopold's candidacy would not be renewed in the future. William firmly but politely

"Preserve, Protect, Defend"

I hold, that in contemplation of universal law, and of the Constitution, the Union of these States is perpetual. . . .

It follows from these views that no State . . . can lawfully get out of the Union . . . that resolves and ordinances to that effect are legally void, and the acts of violence, within any State or States, against the authority of the United States, are insurrectionary or revolutionary.

*I therefore consider that, in view of the Constitution and the laws, the Union is unbroken; and to the extent of my ability, I shall take care, as the Constitution itself expressly enjoins upon me, that the laws of the Union be faithfully executed in all the States. . . . You have no oath registered in Heaven to destroy the government, while I shall have the most solemn one to "preserve, protect and defend" it.***

The mystic chords of memory, stretching from every battle-field, and patriot grave, to every living heart and hearthstone, all over this broad land, will yet swell the chorus of the Union. . . .

*First Inaugural Address, March 4, 1861, in Roy P. Basler, ed., *The Collected Works of Abraham Lincoln,* vol. 4 (New Brunswick, N.J.: Rutgers University Press, 1953), pp. 264–268 passim.

Four score and seven years ago, our fathers brought forth on this continent, a new nation, conceived in liberty, and dedicated to the proposition that all men are created equal.

Now we are engaged in a great civil war, testing whether that nation, or any nation so conceived and so dedicated, can long endure. . . .

*We here highly resolve that these dead shall not have died in vain—that this nation, under God, shall have a new birth of freedom—and that the government of the people, by the people, for the people, shall not perish from the earth.*****

In these famous addresses, and in many other communications in the first half of the Civil War, Abraham Lincoln, employing both reason and emotion, stressed the nationalist concept of the indissoluble union as the main reason for fighting the war. Later, as in his Second Inaugural, Lincoln, perhaps because of the enormous suffering embodied in the conflict, took the more radical position that slavery, or possibly God's punishment of both sides for permitting slavery, was the basic cause of the war.

**Gettysburg Address, November 19, 1863, in Roy P. Basler, ed., *The Collected Works of Abraham Lincoln,* vol. 7 (New Brunswick, N.J.: Rutgers University Press, 1953), p. 23.

refused the French request and later wired an account of the interview to Bismarck, who was in Berlin. Bismarck saw an opportunity, as he described it, to "wave a red flag" before "a Gallic bull." He edited the king's telegram, which has become famous as the Ems Dispatch, to make it appear that the French ambassador and the Prussian king had insulted each other, and then leaked it to the press. The public in both nations were furious, but the French were more openly belligerent and the French government declared war first, in July 1870.

As Bismarck had anticipated, the Franco-Prussian War brought the divided Germans together. Portraying the struggle as a national war and whipping up patriotic sentiment, Bismarck drew in the South German states, and the combined German armies poured into France in three great columns. The battle-tried Prussians overwhelmed the poorly prepared and badly led French troops. Within six weeks the Germans encircled the main French army, commanded by Napoleon himself, and compelled it to surrender. They went on to lay siege to Paris, which was starved into submission on January 28, 1871.

Ten days before Paris capitulated and the French acknowledged defeat, William I was proclaimed German Emperor in the palace at Versailles. The new empire included the states of the North German Confederation, the South German states, and the former French provinces of Alsace and part of Lorraine, which were ceded to Germany by the peace treaty that formally ended the war in 1871.

The United States Creates an Indivisible National Union

At the time Latin Americans were expressing their sense of nationalism by winning independence, citizens of the United States, who had become independent two generations earlier, were beginning to confront the contradictory concepts of nationalism embodied in their federal form of government. Intensifying cultural animosity between the northern and southern regions of the country brought about decades of political, economic, and racial strife during the middle of the nineteenth century, culminating in a brutal civil war. Out of this turmoil came a new, more active sense of nationalism in the minds of most Americans. By the turn of the century, many Americans would express their sense of nationalism in the same kind of superior, jingoistic terms that were commonplace among the other great powers, drawing the United States into the worldwide imperialist competition of that era.

From its inception, the Constitution of 1787 contained a deep ambiguity about the nature of the government of the United States. Men of equal talents and insights, such as Thomas Jefferson and Alexander Hamilton, could, and increasingly did, see their federal, two-level form of government quite differently. Some, increasingly centered in the southern states, believed that the separate states were the sovereign entities in the union. The states had created the national government and the states could dissolve it, or, failing that, individual states could withdraw from union with other states. In this view the great bulk of the regulation of personal behavior and property rights, so-called domestic matters, rested in the hands of the states. Radical thinkers along this line, such as John C. Calhoun, believed that the national government was in effect merely an "agent," an employee whose duty was to protect the domestic institutions of the individual states, particularly slavery. The authority of the national government was limited to a few areas where the collective authority was more effective than that of individual states: diplomacy and treaties, war with foreign states, fiscal and monetary policy, and interstate commerce.

At the same time, some Americans, increasingly centered in the North, had come to believe that the American people as a whole, not the states, had created the union. The states collectively could not dissolve it, nor could individual states secede from it. (Such "unionists," while tending to give greater scope to the power of the national government, agreed with their constitutional opponents that most personal and property concerns, as well as civil rights and liberties, were essentially in the domain of state authority; by and large, Americans did not look to the national government to regulate domestic matters until the twentieth century.)

This great difference in constitutional outlook intensified the economic and social differences that increasingly divided the United States into two distinct cultural regions after 1820. At first the focus of the struggle was economic, centering on the protective tariff, which many Southerners viewed as an unconstitutional policy to enrich the North and impoverish the South. Then, after the tariff issue was to some extent compromised, the focus turned to the issue of the enslavement of African Americans in the southern states, a domestic institution that raised a gamut of constitutional and moral issues.

During the 1850s, Southerners and Northerners increasingly saw the other region as a hostile aggressor; many Southerners feared that the northern majority wanted to destroy slavery and bring on a race war; many Northerners believed there was a slave power conspiracy to extend slavery into the North and throughout the Western Hemisphere.

In the months after Abraham Lincoln was elected president in November 1860 on an antislavery platform, eleven southern states seceded from the union and

The Aftermath of Battle. Confederate dead piled up at Antietam, Maryland, indicate the terrible losses of the Civil War. Out of this carnage a new, stronger union was forged.

Library of Congress

formed a new government, the Confederate States of America. Lincoln, a unionist, believed that secession was fundamentally unconstitutional and that, in more general terms, state sovereignty concepts represented a threat to the survival of constitutional republics everywhere. He called on Americans to take up arms to force the secessionist states back into the union.

In the Civil War (1861–1865) that followed, the United States conquered the Confederate States, thus creating an indissoluble union that provided a secure foundation for a constitutional republic. The growing perception among U.S. citizens that the United States was a single national entity is shown by the shift between the 1870s and the 1890s from the plural verb reference to the nation ("The United States are determined to proceed in this matter") to the singular verb ("The United States is determined to proceed in this matter").

Although the Civil War brought a unified nation, the United States had not yet become a centralized nation or a truly liberal nation. During the Civil War and the period of Reconstruction that followed (1865–1877), the national government took over a number of governmental powers previously exercised at the state level, especially in protecting the rights of African Americans; after 1877, however, the national government exercised less power in regulating the conduct of citizens. As civil and political rights continued to be reserved for adult white males, the United States was not yet a truly liberal republic, although it was more democratic than any of the major states of the late nineteenth century. Although the unification of the United States into a truly national state had major long-range consequences in world history, it had little effect in Italy or Germany, where the final stages of national unification were just getting under way.

Austria-Hungary and Russia: Multinational Empires

Not all national groups succeeded in their quest for self-determination. Most dissatisfied groups lived as subjects of either the Austro-Hungarian or Russian Empires. The frustrations of the ethnic and religious groups in the Austro-Hungarian Empire contributed to international instability and helped to cause World War I.

In the aftermath of the revolution of 1848–1849, the new Habsburg emperor, Francis Joseph I (reigned 1848–1916) of Austria, and his advisors had attempted to quell ethnic unrest by tightening and centralizing the government's absolutist control. These measures, however, only provoked sharp nationalist resentment, most of all among the Magyars (Hungarians), the largest non-German group.

Austria's embarrassing defeat by Prussia in 1866 made clear that the continuation of the Habsburg monarchy depended on the goodwill of the Magyars. Thus an *Ausgleich* (Compromise) was reached in 1867; the Magyars were recognized as equal partners with the Germans within the empire, thus transforming the Habsburg Empire into the Dual Monarchy of Austria and Hungary. The two parts of the empire shared the head of the House of Habsburg as the sovereign and the ministries of foreign affairs, defense, and finance. Otherwise, each unit was autonomous, with its own constitution, parliament, and official language.

The new settlement satisfied the wishes of the Magyars, but it offered few concessions to the other subject nationalities, who together made up a majority in each half of the Dual Monarchy. Although Austria attempted to make concessions to satisfy some of the demands of its non-German peoples during the next half century, the dominant Magyars made no pretense at conciliating their subject Slavic peoples in Hungary. The Austro-Hungarian Empire survived, sustained by the loyalty of its army, the support of the Catholic church, and the deep-seated veneration its people felt for the long-reigning emperor. Ethnic discontent within the empire, however, remained a time bomb waiting to explode.

Compared with Austria-Hungary, the Russian government had tighter and more effective control over its minority ethnic groups, in part because Great Russians remained the overwhelming majority of the population. Russian conquests during the eighteenth and nineteenth centuries had incorporated into the empire Poles, Jews, Finns, Turkic Muslims, and other nationalities. Tsar Alexander III (reigned 1881–1894), adopting the motto "autocracy, orthodoxy, and nationalism," carried out a vigorous policy of Russification of minority groups. For example, Finns were deprived of their constitution and Finnish was replaced by Russian in schools. Constantine Pobedonostsev (1827–1907), procurator of the Holy Synod (chief lay official of the Russian Orthodox church), and a trusted advisor of Alexander III, used coercive and often brutal methods to convert the subject peoples to Russian Orthodoxy. The Jews suffered severely from periodic state-encouraged pogroms (mob attacks on persons and property) that killed many and forced tens of thousands to seek asylum in the United States and elsewhere.

Austria-Hungary and Russia were rivals in the Balkans, where both hoped to acquire territory at the expense of the rapidly weakening Ottoman Empire. The fate of the Ottoman Empire, then known as the Eastern Question, will be taken up in Chapter 13. Russia was eager to gain warm-water ports and access to the Mediterranean. Austria particularly feared Russia's claim to be the protector of Slavs under Ottoman rule. In 1877 Russia intervened to counteract Turkish atrocities against Christians in Bulgaria, and within months its soldiers were on the verge of overrunning Istanbul, the Ottoman capital. In the Treaty of San Stefano, the Ottoman Empire agreed to the creation of a large autonomous Bulgarian state under Russian protection, and gave complete independence to Romania, Serbia, and Montenegro.

Greatly alarmed at the expansion of Russian power, the other major European nations convened an international conference, the Congress of Berlin (1878), to reconsider the Treaty of San Stefano. The ensuing Treaty of Berlin confirmed the independence of Serbia, Romania, and Montenegro. Russia gained Bessarabia and several districts in the Caucasus, and Austria received the right to administer two Ottoman provinces, Bosnia and Herzegovina. Independent Bulgaria was reduced by two-thirds and deprived of access to the Aegean Sea. In a separate treaty, Great Britain received Cyprus from the Ottoman Empire, and in return pledged to aid the sultan if he were attacked.

The Treaty of Berlin aggrieved Russia and Bulgaria and reduced the Ottoman Empire's European holdings to small, exposed fragments. Because the newly independent states had disputed boundaries and ethnic minorities within their territories, the Balkans remained an unstable region, a hotbed of militant nationalism, seething with intrigues, rivalries, and disorders. The Balkans became known at that time as the Tinderbox of Europe, and have remained so to the present day.

European Political Developments to 1914

Nationalism was not the only major catalytic agent affecting Europe in the nineteenth century. Several western European nations developed democratic political systems and institutions. In Great Britain an evolutionary process of peaceful political reforms forestalled the revolutionary upheavals that periodically afflicted the Continent. Still, that nation remained a virtual oligarchy as late as the middle of the nineteenth century. In the aftermath of the Great Reform Bill of 1832 (which enfranchised more males and reformed parliamentary districting), only one adult male in eight could vote for members of the House of Commons; Parliament remained essentially an undemocratic body. From 1832 to 1867 the landed gentry and the upper middle class worked together to control the government, and there was little to choose between the two national parties, the Conservatives and Liberals.

As the old-guard politicians began to pass from the scene, their place was taken by men of widely different temperament and values. The second generation of political figures, who emerged during the reign of Queen Victoria (reigned 1837–1901), was dominated by William Gladstone (1809–1898), the Liberal leader, and his Conservative counterpart, Benjamin Disraeli (1804–1881). The two men alternated in the office of prime minister, and their personal rivalry stimulated reform. The practice of purchasing commissions in the armed forces was ended; the secret ballot was introduced; and corruption at the polls was suppressed. The Second and Third Reform Bills (1867 and 1884, respectively) extended suffrage to practically all adult males. Henceforth the industrial proletariat would share political power with the other groups.

There was a lull in domestic activity after the departure of Gladstone and Disraeli, but at the start of the twentieth century the reigning Liberals initiated a bold program of social change. The Liberal party devised legislation that deprived the House of Lords of the right to veto measures approved in the lower chamber (the House of Commons) in three successive sessions. Known as the Parliament Act, it was another step toward democratic

An Argument for Reform

I take my stand on the broad principle that the enfranchisement of capable citizens, be they few or be they many—and if they be many so much the better—give an addition of strength to the state. The strength of the modern state lies in the Representative System . . . and of the State of this country in particular. . . .

I say this is not a perfect bill with regard to the franchise. . . . No, Sir; ideal perfection is not the true basis of English legislation. We look at the attainable; we look at the practicable; and we have too much of English sense to be drawn away by those sanguine delineations of what might possibly be attainable in Utopia, from a path which promises to enable us to effect great good for the people of England. . . . *

Prime Minister William Gladstone made this speech when he introduced the Franchise Bill (Third Reform Bill) of 1884. When it passed, 2 million more voters, mainly agricultural workers, were added to the register, so that four out of five adult British males could participate in elections. Gladstone's speech shows both his belief that governments based on broad popular support made a modern country strong, and his pragmatism as a politician—he went after the attainable rather than dreaming about the perfect state. These characteristics made him a great British leader.

**Hansard's Parliamentary Debates,* 3d ser., vol. 285 (London, 1884), p. 107.

government, granting the elected representatives of the people the final decision in legislative matters.

The Liberals, who prided themselves on ameliorating inequality, were much less accommodating to women. Women marched, staged hunger strikes, assaulted politicians, and employed other tactics to draw public attention to their demand for voting rights. The Liberal leadership was unsympathetic, however, partly because the suffragists resorted to violence and partly because these women dared to reject the Victorian idea of separate spheres for men and women. The government's attitude changed during World War I, when women played an active and significant role in the war effort. In 1918 the franchise was extended to all men over twenty-one and all women over thirty. Ten years later British women secured the vote on the same terms as the men.

In France, Napoleon III's defeat in the Franco-Prussian War ushered in a new era. News of his catastrophic surrender in 1870 at Sedan triggered a riot in Paris that swept away the Second Empire. A republic was proclaimed, and survived by default because the monarchists, who dominated the Constituent Assembly, were divided over which claimant to put on the throne.

The constitution of the Third French Republic set up a government that resembled the British, substituting a figurehead president for a constitutional monarch. Unlike the British two-party system, French politics was characterized by a large number of loosely organized political factions. Since no one group commanded a majority in the Chamber (lower house), all ministries were necessarily weak and unstable coalitions subject to frequent changes. Nevertheless, in its turbulent early history, the Third Republic crushed the revolt of the radicals in the Paris Commune, overcame the threat of a takeover by a colorful general, survived scandals, and made France a secular state. During the years from 1910 to 1914 France was more stable than it had been at any time since 1871. The republic was achieving unity in time to meet its greatest challenge.

Italy was a constitutional monarchy whose political situation resembled that of France. Most Italians were illiterate and poor, and until 1912 most males were ineligible to vote. Mass corruption at the polls made a sham of elections, and the weak political parties produced by the voting were unable to govern effectively or to solve the nation's pressing social and economic problems.

Suffragists Escorted by Police in 1914 after a Demonstration outside Buckingham Palace. When arrested and put in jail, many suffragists (called suffragettes at the time) went on hunger strikes. The government, anxious not to have them die in jail, adopted so-called cat-and-mouse tactics. Kept in jail until they were exhausted, the suffragists were released, allowed to recover, and then arrested again.

The Hulton/Deutsch Collection

Culver Pictures

Workers Stage a Triumphant March. This photograph shows workers parading through the streets of Odessa carrying banners and a portrait of Tsar Nicholas II after the government bowed to a nationwide demand for a constitution.

In central Europe, the governments of the German and Austro-Hungarian Empires were a compromise between democratic and authoritarian principles. The constitution of the German Empire provided for a federation of twenty-five states under Prussian leadership. The upper house of the bicameral legislature consisted of appointed members who represented the states. The *Reichstag* (lower house) was elected by universal male suffrage, but it was essentially a consultative body. Unlike government ministers in Great Britain or France, the German chancellor was responsible not to parliament, but to the emperor, who appointed and could dismiss him. Bismarck was the author of this system, and it reflected his autocratic philosophy and his conviction that a strong centralized monarchy was the best guarantee of unity for the new German nation. He was, however, perceptive enough to understand that to govern effectively he needed the participation of political parties, which he attempted to control. When the Social Democratic party, chief critic of the government, won a resounding victory at the 1912 election, strong demands rose for constitutional reform and democratic changes. The outbreak of World War I, however, put a temporary halt to the calls for reform.

Ethnic problems limited political change in the Austro-Hungarian Empire. Reforms in the Austrian half of the empire did give the non-Germans many rights and culminated in universal manhood suffrage in 1907, with the result that they gained a majority in the *Reichsrat* (parliament). Parliamentary debates were so heated, however, that they frequently degenerated into fist fights and unruly demonstrations, which made it impossible for the legislature to carry on business. The emperor had to resort to his emergency powers and rule by decree, sometimes for years at a stretch. Chaos and deadlock in Austria seemed to indicate that political democracy could not function in a nation of such diverse and divided peoples. In Hungary, the Magyars made no effort to conciliate the Slovaks, Rumanians, Serbs, Croatians, and other subject minorities. Although they comprised less than half of the total population, the Magyars monopolized almost all the seats in parliament. The result of this repressive policy was persistent restlessness and disaffection among the non-Magyar peoples. The Serbs and Croats in particular clamored for union with independent Serbia and turned increasingly to their co-nationals outside the empire for support.

In Russia, Alexander III's successor, Nicholas II (reigned 1894–1917), could not maintain the tight lid on antigovernment sentiments. Political parties were formed, including the Constitutional Democratic (Cadet) party, which favored peaceful reforms and constitutional monarchy, and the Marxist-oriented Social Democratic party. The Social Democrats split in 1898 into two factions, one moderately reform-minded and the other revolutionary. Later these two factions became solidified as the *Mensheviks* (minority), who advocated a broad democratic party that included other socialists, while the *Bolsheviks* (majority) preferred a small, tightly knit party under authoritarian leadership. Directed by Vladimir Ilyich Ulyanov (1870–1924), whose underground alias was Lenin, the Bolsheviks insisted on immediate dictatorship of the proletariat, ruling out cooperation with socialists and the liberal bourgeoisie.

Antigovernment groups asserted themselves in 1905 when the Japanese badly defeated Russia's army and sank its navy during the Russo-Japanese War (see Chapter 13). Widespread demonstrations, a general strike, and mutiny among some military units compelled Nicholas to agree to undertake reforms. He promised to adopt a constitution, guarantee individual freedoms, and extend legislative authority to a Duma (parliament) that would be elected by a broad suffrage.

Any hopes for a constitutional monarchy in Russia were dashed, however, after the tsar made peace with Japan and regained his authority. Nicholas proceeded to reinstate his autocracy, rescind most reforms, and reduce the Duma to a mere consultative body. A ruthless secret police sent most political opponents either to jail or to Siberian exile. A few, like Lenin, fled abroad. To make matters worse, the royal family came under the spell of a power-hungry illiterate monk, Gregory Rasputin, who wielded an evil and corrupting influence over national policy. Repressive, inefficient, and corrupt, the tsarist government drifted toward catastrophe.

The Spread of Industrialization and the Appearance of Industrialized Society

*At the face the cutters had gone back to work. They often shortened their lunch time so they wouldn't stiffen, and their sandwiches, eaten in ravenous silence so far from the sun, seemed like lead in their stomachs. Stretched out on their sides, they hacked harder than ever, obsessed by the idea of filling as many carts as possible. . . . They no longer felt the water that was trickling over them and swelling their limbs, or the cramps caused by their awkward positions, or the suffocation of the darkness in which they faded like plants that have been put into a cellar. Yet as the day went on, the air became more and more unbreathable, heated by the lamps, by their own foul breaths, by the poisonous firedamp fumes. It seemed to cling to their eyes like cobwebs, and it would only be swept away by the night's ventilation. Meanwhile, at the bottom of their molehill, under the weight of the earth, with no breath left in their overheated lungs, they kept hacking away.**

*Émile Zola, *Germinal* [1885], trans. S. Hochman and E. Hochman (New York: New American Library, 1970), p. 42.

This description of men at work in a nineteenth-century coal mine was written in 1885 by Émile Zola, a French novelist famous for his on-the-spot research and realism. Working men and women like the ones he described labored through exhausting days under brutal conditions during the early stages of the Industrial Revolution. They, as much as the inventors or the shrewd business entrepreneurs, were integral parts of that revolution.

The diffusion of industry triggered the most astonishing economic expansion the world had ever seen. As a result, the Western nations in a short time acquired more material wealth than any earlier civilization. The Industrial Revolution also produced a whole new society. In addition to stimulating rapid growth of population and large cities, it significantly intensified the differences among social classes. The breakdown of the family and a growing sense of alienation among many people in modern society were side effects of such change. This section will survey the expansion of industrialization in Continental Europe and the Americas in the nineteenth century. It will further examine the socialist theories of Karl Marx, and discuss the rise of big business, the emergence of severe social problems, and the reforms undertaken to remedy those problems.

The Spread of Industrialization

From its origins in Great Britain in the eighteenth century, the Industrial Revolution spread to continental Europe, the Western Hemisphere, and Asia in the nineteenth century, as new methods of production were adopted in France, Belgium, the German states, the United States, and Japan. By 1900 industrialization had also taken hold in southern and eastern Europe, and in some Latin American countries. In these newer industrial nations, capital was sometimes provided by government or by foreign loans rather than by local investors.

Meanwhile transportation and communication revolutions continued apace, as steam power contributed to the new ways of traveling and communicating among cities, nations, and continents. The steam locomotive in particular revolutionized passenger travel and freight haulage. George Stephenson's *Rocket,* the first practical locomotive, took to the rails in Britain in 1830, chugging along at twelve miles an hour. Within forty years, 900,000 miles of track crisscrossed western Europe, and the United States and Canada laid rails from the Atlantic to the Pacific.

Robert Fulton's paddle-wheel steamboat, the *Clermont,* first sailed on the Hudson River in the United States in 1807. Shortly after mid-century, screw propellers and more efficient steam engines led to regular transatlantic voyages. By 1900 iron and steel steamships with ten or twenty times the carrying capacity of wooden sailing ships plied the sea lanes of the world.

The new methods of production and transport and the new society they created spread from one European nation to another during the 1800s. Belgium, building on manufacturing traditions going back to medieval times and on large deposits of coal, became the Continent's first industrialized nation. Belgian industrialists produced large quantities of iron and cotton textiles and the first complete railroad network on the Continent. France began industrialization during the French Revolution and the Napoleonic era. Standardized weights and measures, a national investment bank, an excellent system of roads, bridges, and canals, and the world's best engineering school—the Polytechnic in Paris—made France an industrial power.

Germany's political division into dozens of separate small states seriously hampered industrial growth during the first half of the nineteenth century. Industrial products often had to cross several tariff barriers to reach larger international markets through North Sea and Baltic port cities. In 1818, however, the North German customs union, or Zollverein, established a "common market" of German states. Political unification under Prussian leadership in 1871 made the new German Empire a leading industrial nation. By 1900, Germany was overtaking Great Britain as Europe's most productive industrial power.

Governments played a part in bringing the Industrial Revolution to many European countries by sponsoring protective tariffs, subsidies, and large-scale capital investment. However, several factors limited industrialization in parts of the Continent: southern Europe lacked capital as well as essential natural resources (iron and coal); eastern Europe was relatively poor and technologically backward and lacked a large, aggressive commercial middle class.

Nowhere were such problems more important than in Russia under the Romanov tsars. This backward colossus of eastern Europe had never developed a large, dynamic middle class, and the absence of commercial wealth severely limited Russia's fund of private investment capital. Count Serge Witte, minister of finance to Alexander III and Nicholas II between 1892 and 1903,

Corbis-Bettmann

The *Great Eastern*. This early oceangoing steamship combined sails and steam power. Shown here in 1850 setting sail for Great Britain with the French Atlantic cable, the vessel illustrates nineteenth-century advances in both transportation and communication.

was instrumental in bringing Russia into the industrial age. He promoted the development of the railway system, particularly the enormous Trans-Siberian railroad that linked European Russia with the Pacific across nine time zones. He encouraged industry through government subsidies, protective tariffs, and guaranteed dividends. By placing Russia on the gold standard, Witte attracted much foreign capital, especially from France. Between 1885 and 1900 Russia's index of industrial production tripled: the nation ranked fourth among the world's iron producers and second in petroleum production, an increasingly important power source.

Industrialization also began to spread to the new American republics in the nineteenth century. This was particularly true of the growing North American powerhouse, the United States, which benefited from vast natural resources, including iron, coal, and petroleum. The United States moreover had a fast-growing population, in part because waves of immigrants were arriving from Europe and elsewhere. Investment capital, much of it initially supplied by Great Britain, was relatively plentiful. As in Great Britain, government played a secondary role in U.S. industrialization, although Congress did enact protective tariff laws for American industry and made land grants to railroads. Flamboyant and shrewd entrepreneurs such as Andrew Carnegie, John D. Rockefeller, and Edward H. Harriman built successful financial empires as they led America's industrial growth.

By 1900 the United States, already a leader in agricultural production, had become the world's largest industrial producer. As railroads spanned the continent, great industrial cities had spread from New England across the Midwest. U.S. exports challenged European goods on the world market. Latin America especially was coming under the economic influence of industrialized North America.

Some Latin American nations also began to develop industry in the later nineteenth century. As in North America, a combination of natural resources with foreign capital—first from Great Britain, later from the United States—fueled industrialization in these nations. Nitrates in Chile, tin in Bolivia, and the discovery of petroleum in Mexico at the end of the century all drew eager foreign investors. Argentineans enjoyed a boom based on producing and processing wool, beef, and wheat and other agricultural commodities.

By and large, however, industrialization proceeded at a slower pace in Latin America than in North America or Europe. One reason was the widespread poverty and consequent lack of both domestic demand and domestic capital. Most Latin American nations followed their traditional pattern of exporting raw materials and agricultural products to developed nations in Europe and North America. Rather than constructing industrial economies of their own, they imported manufactured goods from abroad.

New Industries in the Nineteenth Century

The industrial system first formulated in the eighteenth century expanded in new directions during the nineteenth. While industrialists continued to mine coal and produce iron and textiles in increasing quantities, entrepreneurs set up steel and chemical manufacturing combines, generated hydroelectric power, and sponsored amazing advances in transportation and communication.

Steel, a much stronger and more flexible material than iron, became cheaper to produce when technicians learned to combine iron with carbon and such alloys as tungsten or manganese. It was used in a wide variety of products, from sewing machines to ocean-going steamers to superstructures for skyscrapers made possible by the new elevator technology. The Eiffel Tower in Paris was a spectacular example of a tall structure made of steel.

The use of chemicals in industry also increased dramatically. Scientists created artificial dyes for synthetic textiles and adapted alkalis for a range of products from textiles to soap. Whole new industries appeared as chemical industrialists and technologists spearheaded the development of photography and the manufacture of cheap paper for magazines and newspapers.

In the later nineteenth century, inventors like Thomas Edison harnessed electricity for industrial purposes. Water and steam turbines made possible the generation of large quantities of electrical power. The new energy source was soon powering trolley cars and lighting cities with the incandescent lamp. Even more striking, electricity made possible virtually instantaneous communication, when Samuel Morse tapped out the first telegraph message (from Washington to Baltimore) in 1844. Undersea cables linked Great Britain with continental Europe in the 1850s, Europe with North America in the 1860s. Telegraph lines soon joined the cities and nations of the whole world.

Other technological breakthroughs heralded some of the mass-produced manufactured products of the twentieth century. The development of the combustion engine, for example, inaugurated the automobile age. New techniques of petroleum refining would make gasoline and diesel fuel available for cars and trucks. New metal alloys made possible better and more varied tools as well as machine parts. The creation of rayon fabrics and chemical dyes in the laboratory led to the use of synthetic materials in the manufacture of clothing. The canning of food, perfected by the mid-nineteenth century, transformed food preservation; refrigeration, invented in the second half of the century, would revolutionize food storage in the twentieth century.

The Rise of Big Business

The Industrial Revolution had begun in Great Britain in the government-regulated environment of mercantilism. Many of the entrepreneurs who guided the early stages

The Crystal Palace. This towering structure of steel and glass was the center of the first "world's fair," or industrial exposition, held in London in 1851. Built of prefabricated girders and plates, easily assembled and disassembled, the Crystal Palace symbolized both the remarkable advance of industrial technology and Great Britain's leading role in the Industrial Revolution.

of industrialization felt this government paternalism was a hindrance rather than a help. They agreed with Adam Smith, the eighteenth-century founder of modern economics, that free competition at home and free trade abroad would lead to a great increase in the wealth of nations. Accordingly, these early industrialists agitated for an end to mercantilist economic controls, and in the early nineteenth century their efforts began to pay dividends. Great Britain, the leader in the Industrial Revolution, also became the first country to adopt free trade. Soon other governments ceased to support the traditional monopolies and allowed freer competition in major markets.

From the 1820s into the 1870s, free competition came to dominate much of the European economy. Old and new power sources, industries, and manufacturers competed freely. In cloth making, coal mining, and other industries, thousands of small to medium-sized firms competed for business in a relatively unregulated market. "Competition," business leaders commonly asserted, "is the life of trade and the law of progress."

The new system, like the old, entailed difficulties, however. Competition could be brutal and often led to bankruptcies. Many firms went under, especially during the periodic business depressions of the nineteenth century; business owners were sometimes saddled with lifelong indebtedness. In time, some businessmen began to wonder if limited or controlled competition might better serve their interests.

Not all industries had competition. For instance, city governments often granted monopolies to public utilities and urban streetcar lines. In central and eastern Europe as well as in Japan, the national governments frequently capitalized and owned railroads. Inventors who obtained a patent on a key part or process could enjoy a de facto monopoly in many parts of Europe.

In the last quarter of the nineteenth century, however, monopolies began to appear in other areas of the

CONNECTIONS IN MIGRATION

Global Economy, Regional Migration

In the course of the nineteenth century, industrialization changed the world economy. If one thinks of industry primarily as factories, then it was centered in western Europe and North America. But if one thinks of industry not only as inventions and factories but also as obtaining raw materials, developing a transport system, and procuring labor for every stage of production, then it included most areas of the world.

Wherever labor was needed for industrial development, factory owners recruited wage workers, settlers, or contract laborers. If we traced the movement of laborers around the world in the nineteenth century, it would be easy to identify those places where labor was most needed.

Short-distance migrants went from rural areas in Europe and the United States to nearby industrial cities. For example, migrants to the Rhine Valley helped create the great industrial center known as the Ruhr and expanded the commercial center of Amsterdam.

Long-distance migrants sometimes sought industrial work in distant cities. Such was the case of the German and Irish migrants to Baltimore and Boston. More commonly, long-distance migrants of the nineteenth century went to fields, mines, and construction sites. Scandinavian migrants went as wage laborers to farmlands in the North American Midwest. Migrants from India went as indentured workers to mines and plantations in Mauritius, South Africa, Malaya, Fiji, and the Caribbean. Chinese and Indian migrants to Malaya were attracted by the work in tin mines and on rubber and palm oil plantations; migrants to Thailand worked on rice farms.

A third category of laborers—transportation workers—enabled the factories and fields to remain in contact. The new transportation infrastructure included roads, bridges, wagons, canals, steamships, port facilities, and railroads. Creation of this transportation network required increased industrial output to create shipyards, railroad cars, digging equipment, and explosives.

Construction of a canal required years of work by hundreds or thousands of laborers. Coming from near and far, they lived at the work site and moved on at the job's completion. Canal building expanded in the early nineteenth century in England, the Low Countries, and the United States. In China, the earlier centuries of canal construction laid the groundwork for a wave of expansion. The greatest engineering project of the nineteenth century was the construction of the Suez Canal, which opened new shipping lanes between Europe and Asia in 1869.

---

1. Explore Unit 8 of the Migration CD-ROM. Where and in what ways was migrant labor used around the world? What were the typical living and working conditions of these migrants once they reached their destinations? What was the range of economic activities in which they were engaged? How did these migrations and the vast social and economic changes of industrialization affect women? What role did slavery play in the economic growth of the nineteenth century?

industrial economy. New methods of controlling the market were established by businesses themselves. Two innovative types of "industrial combination" were the corporation and the cartel. A corporation was formed by the merger of several smaller industrial firms into a single gigantic company. Aggressive entrepreneurs would buy out weaker rivals, strengthening their own position against other competitors, which might then be absorbed in their turn. Such an industrial combination might include a number of firms in the same line of business; horizontal combinations such as the Nobel Dynamite Trust Company in Europe and Andrew Carnegie's U.S. Steel Corporation in the United States controlled manufacturers of the same product.

Another form of industrial amalgamation was the vertical combination of companies in related businesses, often stages of the same process. An impressive combine engineered by German industrialist Albert Krupp illustrates this form. Krupp began as a steelmaker, but then bought up iron and coal mines and such user enterprises as railway manufacturers, shipyards, and the arms factories for which Krupp industries became famous.

In a cartel, by contrast, companies did not merge, but simply formed a loose alliance based on a cartel agreement. Major manufactures, for example, might form a cartel and agree to fix minimum prices. They would then divide the market among themselves or set a maximum total output and then agree on quotas for each member. Such agreements undercut free competition as effectively as monopolistic industrial combinations. Giant corporations could easily manipulate the market for whatever they produced. Attitudes toward cartels varied. In Great Britain and America, they were often considered illegal "conspiracies in restraint of trade," but in Germany they were legally enforceable accords.

Social Classes in the Industrial Age

Although the society that emerged under the impact of the Industrial Revolution showed continuities with the past, it also differed in several key respects. Population growth, urbanization, and class conflicts, for instance, were not new; yet all three greatly intensified during the eighteenth and nineteenth centuries.

The rapid population growth of the last three centuries is one of the most striking features of modern history. The following figures give a sense of this population explosion. The population of Great Britain, for instance, probably around 5 million in 1710, had increased to 9 million by 1800 and to 32 million by 1900. Moreover, the population of Russia, the largest of the great powers, nearly tripled in the nineteenth century, from 36 million to 100 million people. Western Hemisphere populations grew even more rapidly. The population of the United States, less than 4 million in 1790, was pushing 100 million by 1900.

This sudden population surge had a number of causes. The Industrial Revolution, for example, created many new jobs, making it possible for young people to marry earlier and have more children. Innovations in agricultural techniques and such new crops as the potato supported increasing numbers of people. Then, too, modern medicine and sanitation increased life expectancies by lowering the rates of death from infectious diseases like smallpox and tuberculosis.

The population increase gave the Western world many more workers to mine ores, lay rails, and labor in factories. Many more people began to live in modern industrial cities. Rapid development transformed villages into towns and towns into cities. Workers flocked to the cities seeking jobs in the new factories, which employed both adults and children.

The industrial cities of the nineteenth century were overcrowded and filthy with polluted water and thick industrial smoke. Factories were the scene of many industrial accidents. Workers lived in slum tenements, where whole families were jammed into a single room. The slums were fertile breeding grounds for crime and disease. Industrial depressions threw many out of work. North America's industrial working class, like Europe's, suffered brutal hardships in the early stage of industrialization. As late as 1900, New York's Hell's Kitchen matched the horrors of London's East End slums.

If not the most comfortable places to live, nineteenth-century cities were certainly the most exciting. In cities could be found shops, theaters, cafés, horsecars, and later the electric tram, gas and then electric lights, and the telephone. The charms of earlier periods and the wonders of the new age were concentrated in London, Paris, New York, and Buenos Aires, the capitals of the new industrial civilization.

Before the Industrial Revolution, social divisions had traditionally been based on race, religion, lineage, and legal rankings. In the new industrial society, however, class distinctions corresponded more directly to position in the economic structure. By expanding the

Coketown

*It was a town of red brick, or of brick that would have been red if the smoke and ashes had allowed it; but as matters stood it was a town of unnatural red and black like the painted face of a savage. It was a town of machinery and tall chimneys, out of which interminable serpents of smoke trailed themselves forever and ever, and never got uncoiled. It had a black canal in it, and a river that ran purple with ill-smelling dye, and vast piles of buildings full of windows where there was a rattling and a trembling all day long, and where the piston of the steam-engine worked monotonously up and down like the head of an elephant in a state of melancholy madness. It contained several large streets all very like one another, and many small streets still more like one another, inhabited by people equally like one another, who all went in and out at the same hours, with the same sound upon the same pavements, to do the same work, and to whom every day was the same as yesterday and tomorrow, and every year the counterpart of the last and the next.**

The above description of "Coketown," an English industrial city, is from Charles Dickens's novel of the Industrial Revolution, *Hard Times* (1854). This perceptive author vividly depicted many of the problems of urban, industrialized society, including air and water pollution, the ugliness of early industrial cities, and the psychologically crushing monotony of labor controlled by the rhythm of the machines and the discipline of the factory whistle.

*Charles Dickens, *Hard Times for These Times* (New York: New American Library, 1961), pp. 30–31.

opportunities to accumulate great wealth, the Industrial Revolution increased the disparity between the upper and lower classes. The magnitude of the economic changes affected the social order, promoting tensions and even class conflict.

European society was dominated by a small, wealthy elite comprising the landed aristocracy and the commercial and financial magnates of the upper middle class. Although not as powerful as in the past, the aristocracy continued to enjoy status and financial stability throughout most of the nineteenth century. Land maintained a high value, but increased competition from cheaper overseas grain and a reluctance to change the old ways reduced profits. As their income from land declined, some aristocrats were able to make the transition to modern capitalist agriculture or industrialization. The new economy created a group of aggressive and vigorous entrepreneurs who amassed vast fortunes that enabled them to gain control over their nation's economy and government. Increasingly, they established common bonds with the aristocracy. Their sons were admitted to the elite schools that formerly only the children of the aristocracy had attended. Sometimes the wealth of business tycoons and noble titles came together through mutually advantageous marriages. More and more, wealthy industrialists purchased landed estates in the country and emulated the manners and attitudes of the aristocracy. During the latter part of the nineteenth century, the aristocracy and the upper middle class became indistinguishable.

Standing below the wealthy elite were mid- and lower-level bourgeoisie. In the mid-level middle class, such traditional groups as lawyers, physicians, and relatively prosperous businessmen were joined by new groups created by the expansion of industry. These included upper management and the new professionals such as architects, scientists, engineers, and accountants. Small shopkeepers, along with teachers, nurses, and white-collar employees—clerks, secretaries, salespeople, and lower bureaucrats—formed the lower middle class. Although their lifestyles varied somewhat, mid-level and lower bourgeoisie shared the same values and attitudes. They were active churchgoers and professed to follow Christian moral strictures, strove for greater status and income, and understood the importance of science and progress.

The vast majority of Europeans, about 80 percent, still earned their livelihood through physical labor. Many of them were landowning peasants, sharecroppers, and agricultural workers. The latter lived in extreme poverty; their wages averaged less than half the salary of factory workers. The living conditions of the first two groups ranged from deep poverty in much of southern and eastern Europe to relative prosperity in western Europe. These country people were socially conservative and remained loyal to regional customs and old social and religious authorities. They resented government exactions, including high taxes, but resorted to open rebellion only in the hardest of times.

During the latter part of the nineteenth century, urban workers constituted the largest single social group in most western and central European nations. The urban labor force was even more diverse than the middle class. At the top of the hierarchy were the highly skilled workers—machine tool specialists, shipbuilders, metal workers—who were reasonably well off, enjoying steady employment and wages that were at least twice as high as those in industries requiring little or no skill. These workers had middle-class aspirations and sought good housing and education for their children. Those toiling in semiskilled occupations such as masonry, carpentry, and bricklaying earned about a third less money than the skilled workers. The lowest wages went to the unskilled workers, including domestic servants and the day laborers who had no regular employment.

The standard of living for the urban working class advanced after 1870. During the last three decades of the nineteenth century, new industrial and agricultural techniques kept the price of clothing, shoes, and food down, while real wages rose by 37 percent. Many workers earned wages above the subsistence level. This meant that they now could afford to buy more clothes, move into better housing, and add meat, dairy products, and vegetables to a diet that previously had consisted almost entirely of bread and potatoes. Life expectancy among members of the lower class increased, slowly at first and then more rapidly.

Although some of the patterns of industrial society in Europe were repeated in the Americas, the class divisions and problems of the masses of people in the new nations across the Atlantic were significantly different. Notable differences also existed between the class structures of North and South America.

In Latin America landed aristocrats remained very powerful, owning vast farms and much of the mineral wealth. Landless peasants, including Amerindians, blacks, and mestizos, continued to be bound to the owners of the landed estates by peonage. An urban middle class, however, emerged in the cities of South America. This business bourgeoisie included many exporters of the agricultural products and raw materials of the great landowners. An urban working class was also recruited to build and operate seaports, railways, and similar facilities connected with the export industries. These workers, often immigrants from Europe, began to organize unions and to become politically active by the end of the nineteenth century.

North American social patterns evolved along different lines. In the United States, the landed gentry of the South and the cattle barons of the West never gained the national preeminence enjoyed by the aristocracy in Europe or Latin America. The pre–Civil War black slaves became tenants and sharecroppers after the war. Immigrant farmers often suffered great hardships on the frontier, but did not become the sort of tradition-bound peasantry found in Europe or Latin America. During the nineteenth century, the middle class gradually became the ruling elite. With the great industrial expansion of the post–Civil War period, business leaders acquired enormous wealth, political power, and social prestige. Although some condemned the wealthiest as "robber barons" for their aggressive and often shady tactics, others hailed them as "captains of industry" for their resourcefulness and success.

Women's Work and the Family

The Industrial Revolution and the subsequent movement of large numbers of people to the cities had a significant impact on the life of women and their place in the labor force. Traditionally, members of a household had clearly defined duties based on their age, gender, and position in the family. In rural areas the men worked in the fields as the chief family wage earner. The wives managed the home, raised the children, and in addition engaged in seasonal work such as tending to a garden or working in the fields at planting or harvest time. Single women were sometimes employed as seamstresses, weavers, or domestics; all or part of their wages supplemented their parents' income.

In the second half of the nineteenth century the emergence of large industrial plants and big businesses, together with the expansion of government services, opened new employment opportunities for women. They were hired to work in such heavy industries as mining and metalwork as well as in the textile mills and the garment industry. Unskilled women were paid higher wages than they could have received elsewhere, but they labored long hours in unhealthy and dangerous conditions at wages lower than those paid to adult male workers. They were often excluded from highly skilled and better-paying jobs and were seldom allowed to join early labor unions. In Germany and Great Britain, laws were passed to limit the exploitation of women (and children) in the factories and mines, but these were not enforced and had only marginal impact.

Besides manual work, many women found careers in teaching, nursing, and other white-collar positions. Many of these became rapidly identified as female occupations. The new positions, except for teaching and nursing, required few skills and minimal training. The work was routine and boring, and the wages were low, because employers assumed that their women employees had other sources of income. Women who supported themselves independently had a difficult time finding jobs that paid an adequate wage.

As a rule, women in the new occupations were young and single, and many were from rural areas, drawn to the city both to find higher-paying jobs and to escape parental supervision. For the single woman away from home, lonely, and unable to earn enough money to support herself, the logical move was to find a husband, but marital aspirations were not always fulfilled. In the absence of supervision by parents, the local community, and the church, premarital sex, illegitimate children, and common-law marriages increased dramatically. Because there were always more women seeking employment than there were jobs available, some were forced to enter prostitution or to exchange sexual favors for food in time of scarcity.

Most women did marry, however. A substantial number withdrew from the regular labor force after the birth of their first child but did not stop working altogether. While rearing their children, they favored part-time work that could be pursued at home, often an extension of their household duties. Such work could involve animal husbandry, sewing gloves or clothing, taking in infants to nurse, washing clothes, or assisting their husband in his profession. Work of this type was an important contribution to the family economy.

For a woman, marriage meant that she no longer had to contribute part of her wage to her parents' household. When women married, they transferred to another family and assumed new responsibilities, but they carried the practices and values of their mothers with them. Although women were denied suffrage and were inferior under the law, they tended to prevail in the domestic sphere. The key to their power lay less in the management of household duties than in control of the purse strings. Women kept household accounts, purchased food from the marketplace, made financial decisions, and in some cases even determined the weekly allowance their husbands received.

Marx Predicts the Triumph of Socialism

While revolutions and independence movements were altering political conditions in the early nineteenth century, industrialization was profoundly changing economic and social conditions. From its very beginning, the Industrial Revolution had transformed the lives of the working masses. Workers no longer practiced skilled crafts in small shops or their own cottages. Instead, they labored for long hours in large factories or mines. Women and children were widely employed in factories, especially in the booming textile industry, where alertness and dexterity were more important than physical strength. Women and even small children could thus add a few shillings a week to an impoverished family's income. Their earnings hardly offset the suffering caused by long hours and poor working conditions in the early industrial age.

Marx Exhorts the Masses to Revolt

The history of all hitherto existing society is the history of class struggles. . . .

In the earlier epochs of history, we find almost everywhere a complicated arrangement of society into various orders, a manifold gradation of social rank. In ancient Rome we have patricians, knights, plebeians, slaves, in the Middle Ages, feudal lords, vassals, guild-masters, journeymen, apprentices, serfs . . .

The bourgeoisie has subjected the country to the rule of the towns. It has created enormous cities. . . . Just as it has made the country dependent on the towns, so it has made barbarian and semi-barbarian countries dependent on civilized ones, nations of peasants on nations of bourgeois, the East on the West. . . .

We have seen . . . that the first step in the revolution by the working class, is to raise the proletariat to the position of ruling class, to win the battle of democracy. . . .

In the most advanced countries the following will be found pretty generally applicable:

1. *Abolition of property in land. . . .*
2. *Graduated income tax.*
3. *Abolition of all right of inheritance.*
4. *Confiscation of property of emigrants and rebels.*
5. *Centralization of credit in the hands of the State. . . .*
6. *Centralization of the means of communication and transport in the hands of the State.*
7. *Extension of factories and instruments of production owned by the State; the bringing into cultivation of waste lands. . . .*
8. *Equal liability of all to labor. . . .*
9. *Combination of agriculture with manufacturing industries; gradual abolition of the distinction between town and country. . . .*
10. *Free education for all children in public schools. . . .*

The proletarians have nothing to lose but their chains. They have a world to win.

*Working men of all countries, unite!**

In *The Communist Manifesto,* Karl Marx and his collaborator, Friedrich Engels, outlined their program for worldwide revolution and a future socialist society. Although the *Manifesto* appeared too late to have an impact on the revolutions of 1848, it became one of the most influential tracts of all time, providing direction for twentieth-century revolutionaries from Russia to China to Cuba. Marx's ideas for revolution and radical change were the direct opposite of Metternich's support for conservative, divine-right monarchy and political stability. The struggle between conservatives wishing to maintain the status quo and revolutionaries seeking to change societies along radical lines has continued to be a major trend throughout the twentieth century.

*Karl Marx and Friedrich Engels, *The Communist Manifesto* (New York: Modern Reader Paperbacks, 1968), pp. 2–62.

Industrial working conditions and the political revolutions that had rocked the Western world stimulated innovative thinkers to formulate new theories about economics and society. Socialism, which developed in reaction to the abuses of the Industrial Revolution, was among the most radical of the new doctrines. Although socialist thinkers did not always agree, most advocated abolishing private ownership of the means of production—factories, raw materials, agricultural land, and means of transportation—in favor of some form of public ownership.

Socialism was especially attractive to the educated people of middle-class origin, who had been dismayed and infuriated by the poor working conditions and low wages in the newly industrialized Western nations. Although some socialists attempted to rally peasants in overwhelmingly agricultural nations like Russia, their central concern was with the factory hands, railroad employees, miners, and other workers in the fast-growing industrial sector of the economy. At this time, socialist leaders were not concerned with the poor peasants and miners in Asia, Africa, or South America, the majority of whom came under Western imperial domination and worked for companies owned or dominated by Westerners.

Living in a time of sweeping economic change, Karl Marx (1818–1883), perhaps the most influential social theorist, believed that economic forces shaped the course of history. For Marx, how people earned their living determined how they lived, what they believed, and what role they played in history. Although Marx did not discount the importance of religion, politics, or nationalism, he argued that economic forces such as labor, capital investment, economic booms, and depressions were the primary forces shaping human events. According to Marx, economic forces had always created two conflicting social groups—the "haves," who owned the means of production, and the "have nots," who were forced to sell their labor to the haves in order to survive. Class conflict ultimately was the most important factor in human history. Marx foresaw a worldwide revolution that would end class conflict and create a society in which the means of production were owned by all. In addition, he believed that religion and nationalism were "opiates" used by the ruling classes to keep the impoverished masses drugged and too passive or preoccupied to revolt against the capitalist system.

Other socialists, including Robert Owens and the Fabians in Great Britain, strongly disagreed with Marxian analysis, and by the end of the nineteenth century, many had abandoned Marx's revolutionary ideology. They pointed out that, contrary to Marx's prediction, the living standard of the workers was steadily improving and the bourgeois state was gaining in strength as it became more democratic. Instead of trying to overthrow the state, many socialists sought to cooperate with capitalist and nationalist political parties to move the state in the direction of socialism in a moderate step-by-step fashion.

Stock Montage

Karl Marx and His Wife. Marx, by far the most influential socialist thinker of the nineteenth century, saw history as a series of class struggles that would end when the proletariat overthrew capitalism and established a classless society. This photograph, taken around 1860, shows him living in exile in a suburb of London, where he spent his days in the British Museum working on *Das Kapital.*

Industrialization and Social Reforms

As industries spread across Europe and North America, workers everywhere experienced the same problems of low wages, poor working conditions, and long hours. They tried to improve their lives by forming labor unions and using collective bargaining and strikes as their weapons. They also sought political action to improve their lot and joined Marxian and other socialist movements. Still others became anarchists in the belief that all governments were evil and should be abolished through violence.

In nations where there was a trend toward representative institutions, governments often responded to worker needs by enacting reforms that forestalled revolution. In Great Britain the great Reform Act of 1832 ushered in an era of government commissions to study abuses, which were followed by reforms enacted by Parliament. Great Britain led the way in abolishing slavery in its colonies, lowering food costs by introducing free trade, and enacting laws that reduced working hours and improved working conditions. Government inspectors enforced the expanding network of laws that checked abuses. Other laws established free and compulsory education, legalized unions, and improved public health. The era of reform in Great Britain reached a climax with the victory of the "New Liberals" in the election of 1905. They believed in using the power of the state to aid the underprivileged. During the next decade, with the support of the newly formed Labour party, the New Liberals enacted the Workers' Compensation Act, the Old Age Pension Act, and the National Insurance Act, and others that laid the groundwork for a welfare state. A progressive income tax and a heavy tax on unearned income exacted money from the rich to pay for the welfare programs. Such measures would become commonplace in industrialized nations in the twentieth century.

As we have seen, the Industrial Revolution had begun later in Germany than in Great Britain, but once under way, it progressed with astonishing speed. A Socialist Democratic party was formed in Germany to champion the cause of workers. Chancellor Bismarck, who equated socialism with anarchy, outlawed the Socialist Democratic party. At the same time, however, he sponsored a paternalistic social reform program designed to undercut the appeal of the socialists. In the 1880s, parliament passed laws providing for compulsory sickness benefits and accident and old age insurance that were the most comprehensive to date.

In France the heavy indemnity paid to Germany and the loss of Alsace-Lorraine resulting from the Franco-Prussian War of 1870–1871 had retarded its economic growth. The working class was smaller and less influential than its British and German counterparts with the result that French political authorities were slow to come to grips with the social and economic problems of the industrial age. Nevertheless, during the generation after 1871 successive governments enacted laws that legalized labor unions, protected workers and permitted them to strike, and introduced social and accident insurance. However, the ruling class drew the line at the advanced legislation the workers called for. In reaction, an important segment of workers embraced the revolutionary doctrines of syndicalism (from the French word *syndicat*, meaning "trade union"). The goal of the syndicalists was to make trade unions the most powerful institution in society, replacing the state as the owner and operator of the means of production; they intended to do so through strikes and violence. But most workers and socialists were prepared to operate within the parliamentary process. In 1905 various groups combined to form the United Socialist party, which immediately controlled a significant block of seats in the National Assembly (lower house), where social welfare measures comparable to those in Germany and Great Britain soon won passage.

The last major European country to industrialize, Russia, was also most backward in social reforms. Rapid industrialization brought to the Russian working class the same extreme hardships and miseries so common in western Europe. But as the workers had no political representation and were not permitted trade unions, they had no effective way to voice their discontent. The government did try to improve their lives with new laws, but did not have an adequate bureaucracy to enforce them. Russia's numerous peasants lived in dire misery as well. They were burdened with high taxes and heavy redemption payments for their plot of land when they won emancipation from serfdom. Farming methods were primitive, though still effective enough to yield surpluses for exportation (something the Soviet system consistently failed to achieve). Reforms introduced after 1905 legalized trade unions, reduced the workday, and began an insurance program for factory workers; furthermore, they cancelled the remaining redemptive payments for peasants (allowing them to own their land outright) and assisted them with credit. An additional purpose of the reforms—to create grassroots support for the throne—was thwarted by the assassination of their author, Peter Stolypin (1863–1911), and by the outbreak of World War I.

In the United States, where the ethos of the rugged individual was prevalent, collective forms of action developed more slowly than in Europe. In the later nineteenth century, farmers' organizations were moderately effective, but labor unions were only just beginning to organize. Only the skilled craft unions had made much headway in wresting concessions from employers. Not until well into the twentieth century did American labor unions become an effective factor in improving working conditions of the labor force.

Western Cultural and Intellectual Trends

The voyage of the Beagle *has been by far the most important event of my life, and has determined my whole career. . . . The glories of the vegetation of the Tropics rise before my mind at the present time more vividly than anything else; though the sense of sublimity, which the great deserts of Patagonia and the forest-clad mountains of Tierra del Fuego excited in me, has left an indelible impression on my mind. . . . Many of my excursions on horseback through wild countries, or in the boats, some of which lasted several weeks, were deeply interesting: their discomfort and some degree of danger were at that time hardly a drawback, and none at all afterwards. I also reflect with high satisfaction on some of my scientific work, such as . . . the discovery of the singular relations of the animals and plants inhabiting the several islands of the Galapagos archipelago, and of all of them to the inhabitants of South America.*

*As far as I can judge of myself, I worked to the utmost during the voyage from the mere pleasure of investigation, and from my strong desire to add a few facts to the great mass of facts in Natural Science. But I was also ambitious to take a fair place among scientific men,—whether more ambitious or less so than most of my fellow-workers, I can form no opinion.**

*Francis Darwin, ed., *The Life and Letters of Charles Darwin,* vol. 1 (New York: Appleton, 1887), pp. 82–83.

The nineteenth century witnessed a tremendous advance in the extent of scientific knowledge. The career of Charles Darwin is one of the best examples of that advance. His service for five years as a naturalist aboard the HMS *Beagle* laid the foundations for the great works on natural selection and evolution that he wrote later in his career. Meticulous observation, constant study, and a fearless readiness to follow the evidence wherever it might lead enabled Darwin to revolutionize our view of life on the planet and earned him "a fair place among scientific men."

This section looks at some of the main cultural and intellectual currents in the West in the nineteenth century, when Europeans and Americans were increasingly prosperous, free of major wars, and expanding their global empires. Although movements like romanticism

LIVES AND TIMES ACROSS CULTURES

Classical Greece: A Perennial Source of Inspiration

The rich legacy of classical Greece has been a perennial source of inspiration to the Western world, during the Romantic era as in other periods. Knowledge of Greek and Roman history, literature, philosophy, and art formed a common bond among educated people in Europe and the Americas.

Two examples from the rich repertoire of poetry of the Romantic period well illustrate the legacy of Greek civilization. John Keats (1795–1821) was the son of a stable keeper. Apprenticed to a surgeon, he abandoned a medical career to write poetry. Keats suffered from ill health worsened by caring for a dying brother and an unhappy love; he died while convalescing in Rome. His odes rank among the most tender of Romantic poems. The "Ode on a Grecian Urn" was inspired by the timeless beauty of ancient Greek painted pottery he had seen in the collections of the British Museum. Its last stanza is quoted below.

O Attic shape! Fair attitude! with brede
Of marble men and maidens overwrought,
With forest branches and trodden weed;
Thou, silent form, dost tease us out of thought
As doth eternity: Cold Pastoral!
When old age shall this generation waste,
Thou shalt remain, in midst of other woe
Than ours, a friend to man, to whom thou say'st,
"Beauty is truth, truth beauty,"—that is all
Ye know on earth, and all ye need to know.

The second selection is from a long poem, *Don Juan,* by Lord Byron (1788–1824). Born to a noble family, Cambridge-educated, and widely traveled, Byron wrote prolifically while leading a notoriously dissolute life. Like many other Englishmen of his time, Byron passionately championed the cause of Greek independence against the Ottoman Empire. Byron died of malaria while in Greece during its war of independence.

The mountains look on Marathon—
And Marathon looks on the sea;
And musing there an hour alone,
I dream'd that Greece might still be free;
For standing on the Persians' grave,
I could not deem myself a slave.

Byron is referring to the Persian invasion of Greece and the victory won by democratic Athens against a force two or three times its size at the Plain of Marathon in 490 B.C.E.

and materialism and towering intellects like Darwin threatened most of the cherished beliefs and values of this immensely successful society, intellectual and artistic rebellion was actually a sign of strength. Nineteenth-century society in Europe and the Americas was powerful and confident enough to tolerate the heretical ideas of its most gifted citizens, who were free to follow the advice of the poet William Blake: "Drive your cart and your plow over the bones of the dead." In so doing, they enriched our intellectual lives.

The Romantic Movement in Literature, Art, and Music

In the late eighteenth century, the Enlightenment gradually gave way to romanticism, a movement that stressed that the empathetic and intuitional faculties ("emotion") could give insights unobtainable by the logical faculties ("reason"). Aristotle's assertion, dear to the philosophes, that "man is the rational animal" was answered by Wordsworth's romantic declaration that "our meddling intellectual misshapes the beauteous form of things: we murder to dissect."

In the late eighteenth century, some writers began to rebel against the rigid rules for writing laid down by seventeenth-century classicism and eighteenth-century neoclassicism. They felt an urge to express their emotional responses in literature, rather than offering only rational analysis, balanced judgments, or sardonic wit. These new writers became known as *romantics,* a name derived from "Romance," the medieval tale of adventure, love, and often magic and fantasy.

Romantics felt out of place in the new industrial society of nineteenth-century western Europe. As an expression of this discontent, romanticism offered new ways of writing, painting, and composing music, but also challenged the basic attitudes of Europeans toward society and themselves. Strong feelings stood at the center of the romantic worldview. Personal love in particular dominated romantic poetry, plays, and fiction, and the love poem became a primary romantic form.

Romantic poets favored short lyric poems over long epics or philosophical poems. They also invented their own forms of poetry or drama instead. Many rejected the old-fashioned "poetic" language prescribed by classicists, insisting on words used by real people, especially humble country people rather than educated city folk. This tendency was present already in the work of the Scottish poet Robert Burns (1759–1796):

O, my luve is like a red, red rose,
That's newly sprung in June.
O, my luve is like a melodie,
That's sweetly play'd in tune.

As fair art thou, my bonie lass,
So deep in love am I,
And I will luve thee still, my dear,
Till a' the seas gang [go] dry.

These writers often "romanticized" settings like North Africa, the Arab world, or even the forests of the New World, as well as colorful past periods of history, like the medieval era or the Renaissance. *The Hunchback of Notre Dame* (1831) by Victor Hugo (1802–1885) and *Ivanhoe* (1819) by Sir Walter Scott (1771–1832), for example, illustrate the enthusiasm for medieval times.

The heroes of romantic poetry, plays, and prose fiction tended to be rebels, outcasts, great lovers, wanderers in the world, and bearers of dark secrets; they were supreme egoists, glorifying the individual at the expense of society. Some romantic writers were themselves rebels: the romantic poet George Gordon, Lord Byron (1788–1824), lived a scandalous life, engaged in radical politics, and died while still young, in the Greek War of Independence from Turkey.

Nature was another powerful theme in romantic writing; poets like William Wordsworth (1770–1850) felt an almost mystical communion with trees, fields, streams, mountains, and oceans, as in these lines from his moving ode, "Intimations of Immortality from Recollections of Early Childhood":

And O, ye Fountains, Meadows, Hills, and Groves,
Forebode not any severing of our loves!
Yet in my heart of hearts I feel your might;
I only have relinquished one delight
To live beneath your more habitual sway.
I love the Brooks which down their channels fret,
Even more than when I tripped lightly as they;
The innocent brightness of a new-born Day
Is lovely yet;
The Clouds that gather round the setting sun
Do take a sober colouring from an eye
That hath kept watch o'er man's mortality;
Another race hath been, and other palms are won.
Thanks to the human heart by which we live,
Thanks to its tenderness, its joys, and fears,
To me the meanest flower that blows can give
Thoughts that do often lie too deep for tears.

When I Was Young

(1)

All thoughts, all passions, all delights,
Whatever stirs the mortal frame,
All are but ministers of Love,
And feed his sacred flame.

Oft in my waking dreams do I
Live o'er again that happy hour,
When midway on the mount I lay,
Beside the ruin'd tower.

The moonshine, stealing o'er the scene,
Had blended with the lights of eve;
And she was there, my hope, my joy,
My own dear Genevieve!. . . .

(2)

Verse, a breeze 'mid blossoms straying,
Where Hope hung feeding, like a bee—
Both were mine! Life went a-maying
With Nature, Hope, and Poesy,
*When I was young!**

These extracts from poems by the English romantic poet Samuel Taylor Coleridge develop a number of typical romantic images. The first poem is dedicated to the "sacred flame" of romantic love. The second begins with "verse" or "poesy" (poetry)—one of the arts most influenced by romanticism. Both conjure up romantic natural scenes: a moonlit mountain with ruined tower, a breeze-blown flower. Youth, also a major romantic enthusiasm, is implied in the first and emphasized in the second extract. Such phrases as "Nature, Hope, and Poesy" almost sum up the emotional creed of the romantic poets.

*Samuel Taylor Coleridge, "Love" and "Youth and Age" in Arthur Quiller-Couch, ed., *The Oxford Book of English Verse* (Oxford: Clarendon Press, 1953), pp. 670, 673.

Courtesy of the Museum of Fine Arts, Boston, Henry Lillie Pierce Fund, 1899

J. M. W. Turner, *Slave Ship*. This painting depicts slavers, confronted by a coming typhoon, throwing overboard the dead and the dying. As was typical of romanticists, Turner made no pretense of adhering to rigid form and precise draftsmanship. Instead, through the clever interplay of light and color, he created strange misty landscapes or seascapes, allowing his objects to meld into their surroundings.

Like Rousseau—a precursor of the movement—romantic writers preferred the natural world to the artificial sophistication of cities.

The supernatural, dismissed as superstition by eighteenth-century "enlightened" thinkers, found an important place in the romantic view of life. Johann Wolfgang von Goethe (1749–1832), Germany's greatest writer, brought the Devil himself on stage in his *Faust* (1808). The original "Gothic" novels were full of haunted castles and other horrors, as in *Frankenstein, or the Modern Prometheus* (1818) by Mary Shelley (1797–1851), whose husband was the romantic poet Percy Bysshe Shelley (1792–1822).

Painters, like writers, rejected the classical rules for the arts, using richer colors and deeper shadows than neoclassical artists. They aimed for violent motion instead of balance, often in past times and "exotic" locales; an example is *The Entrance of the Crusaders into Jerusalem,* a painting by the French artist Eugene Delacroix (1799–1863) (see also his *Liberty Leading the People,* reproduced earlier in this chapter). J. M. W. Turner (1775–1851), the English painter of seascapes, produced dazzling swirls of color in sunsets and storms at sea.

As musical composers, romantics turned away from the rules of composition developed over the past two centuries, preferring to let strong feeling and free-flowing musical imagination give their work its conviction. French composer and conductor Hector Berlioz (1803–1869) created a rich integration of orchestra with solo and choral voices in his *Romeo and Juliet* and *The Damnation of Faust.*

The romantic ego is also realized in the heroic symphonies of Ludwig van Beethoven (1770–1827), as well as in the brilliantly melodic piano compositions of Frederic Chopin (1810–1849), a Pole who lived in Paris. Virtuoso soloists and famous conductors were hailed as archetypal artistic geniuses; Italian concert violinist and composer Nicolò Paganini (1782–1840), for instance, played so brilliantly that his audiences sometimes burst into tears, yet lived so colorful a life that some said he had bought his talent by selling his soul to the Devil!

Taken as a whole, the romantic movement signified a deep cultural revolt with long-range consequences. Romantic artists—and many of their readers—felt out of place in the new industrial society of nineteenth-century Europe. They had no use for science, preferring to be entranced by the beauty of nature rather than analyzing it. The primacy of the emotions had superseded the glorification of reason. The romantics were early explorers of cultural alienation and nonrationalism, both of which would haunt the modern world throughout the nineteenth and twentieth centuries.

Materialism and Realism in Philosophy and Literature

As romanticism began to fade about the middle of the nineteenth century, materialism, a new view that had its roots in the physical sciences rather than the arts, emerged. Many scientific discoveries contributed significantly to knowledge of the physical universe and added to the prestige of the scientific approach to understanding the world. Scientists explored the structure of matter. The molecular theory explained solids, liquids, and gases (understood to be the three states of matter) in terms of clumps of atoms called molecules in rapid motion. Soon after 1900, subatomic physics penetrated the structure of the atom and revealed miniature solar systems of protons, electrons, and neutrons. Nineteenth-century scientists also developed the cell theory of living tissue. Cells—which had been found in plants as early as the 1600s—were discovered in animals as well. Life itself, it seemed, had a purely material basis. Scientists also formulated the germ theory of the causation of disease: Louis Pasteur (1822–1895) and others discovered that tiny organisms, which they called germs, were the cause of many diseases. Medicine was thus put on a truly scientific basis.

The resurgence of the sciences in the nineteenth century also produced new "isms." One, materialism, was the philosophical belief in matter as the basic causal agent in the universe, to the virtual exclusion of spiritual things. To some extent, this rejection of the ancient, universal belief in a spiritual world beyond this material realm came from both scientists and philosophers. Geologists, for instance, asserted that the earth had not been created by divine decree a few thousand years ago, as Old Testament chronology would have it. Rather, the globe had taken millions of years of slow development to reach its present state.

To the most thoroughgoing materialist philosophers, the cosmos had no place for spirit. Religion was an illusion. God was made in man's image, to serve human psychological needs in times of trouble. The human soul was no more than an individual personality and would die along with the body.

Positivism, an outgrowth of materialism, was primarily concerned with how people could know the truth about the world. Positivists believed that scientific methods should be applied in all academic disciplines. By counting and calculating, by accumulating hard data, historians and economists, like physicists or chemists, could go beyond vague impressions and arrive instead at objective knowledge. Love and appreciation of artistic or natural beauty were merely subjective illusions. As for religion, positivists maintained that Christ was at best a wise teacher and perhaps no more than a myth, like Apollo or Zeus. Systematic biblical criticism and the fledging discipline of archaeology were stimulated by this attitude. For much of the second half of the nineteenth century, materialism and positivism were enthusiastically supported by many advanced thinkers.

These materialist and positivist trends are best illustrated by the French thinker Auguste Comte (1798–1857), also known as the founder of modern sociology. Comte's "positive philosophy" defined three stages in attempts to understand the world. Early humanity, Comte said, made sense out of the world by supposing gods, spirits, or other humanlike supernatural creatures to be in charge of nature. Later, gods were replaced by principles—philosophical abstractions—governing nature, like the purposive force in nature proposed by Aristotle. Finally, modern empirical science had enabled humans to draw "positive" conclusions about the world from the observation of the material world itself. For Comte and his successors, the last-named way alone was the road to truth.

In the second half of the nineteenth century, painters and novelists often reflected the current fascination with the material world. Reacting vigorously against romantic "prettifying" of the natural world, "realists" insisted on depicting life as it really was. Gustave Courbet (1819–1877), for instance, painted a peasant funeral in meticulous detail, from the bored priest and expectant gravedigger to the country people gossiping throughout the service in the background. He said he did not paint angels because he never saw one.

One group of realist painters who emerged in France in the 1870s, the impressionists, dedicated themselves with scientific zeal to recreating the impact of light and color on the human eye—painting an "impression" of reality rather than the subject itself. Their investigations of light led them to break up subtle shades of color into basic primary colors and set these pigments side by side on the canvas, allowing the eye of the observer to do the mixing. The result was a rough, unfinished-looking picture if one stood close to it, but a brilliant composition if viewed from the proper distance. Claude Monet (1840–1926) found in the shifting reflections of light off water-lily pools or the Seine River an ideal subject for experiments in the impact of light on the human optic nerve.

Realist writers were as strongly influenced by scientific trends as romantics had been by love and nature. Later nineteenth-century novels bring society to life with remarkable vividness and sociohistorical accuracy. Emile Zola (1840–1902) produced a series of novels about all levels of French society in the last third of the century, treating such grim subjects as alcoholism, prostitution, and the tragic impact of a miner's strike. In England, Charles Dickens (1812–1870) portrayed with meticulous detail such characters as Oliver Twist and David Copperfield against the background of industrial England, especially gritty, lower-class London. Readers of *War and Peace* (1865–1872) by Leo Tolstoy (1828–1910) and *Crime and Punishment* (1866) by Fyodor Dostoyevsky (1821–1881) learn an immense amount about both the aristocracy and the lower classes of Russia. The realist style continued to be cultivated in the early twentieth century, for example, in the work of the Egyptian novelist Naguib Mahfouz (see Chapter 14).

"Survival of the Fittest" in Science and Society

While romanticism and materialism in general challenged the values of nineteenth-century Europeans, Darwin's exploration of the origins of humankind had especially disturbing effects. Charles Darwin (1809–1882), an English naturalist, set out to account for the infinite variety of species of living things. After long years of studying fossils, animal breeding, and hybrid plants around the world, Darwin published *On the Origin of Species* (1859) and *The Descent of Man* (1871), books as important in the history of science as Newton's *Principles of Natural Philosophy* 200 years earlier.

Darwin declared that all species, including humans, were the product of a long biological evolution involving two crucial factors: variation and competition for survival. All individual members of a given species, Darwin said, differed from one another, and these variations in characteristics could be passed to their offspring. There was never enough of the necessities of life for all living creatures. The result was "natural selection," an intense struggle for existence in which those individuals who had the characteristics best fitted for the particular environment survived. These survivors then passed on their particular characteristics to succeeding generations.

In time, unsuitable variations disappeared and a new species, better adapted to its environment, took shape. This Darwin called the "survival of the fittest." For example, the fastest gazelles would escape the tiger, until speed became a primary characteristic of the species. The human race itself, Darwin declared, was also the product of an evolutionary process. Accordingly, both humans and modern apes were descended from common primate ancestors that lived millions of years ago.

Claude Monet, *La Grenouillère*. Impressionist painters like Monet found as much challenge in the new urban industrial world of steam and power as in the quiet countryside. Their real subject—the play of light on matter—also had a scientific role in the later nineteenth century.

Facts Which Cannot Be Disputed?

(1)

*The main conclusion arrived at in this work, and now held by many naturalists who are well competent to form a sound judgment, is that man is descended from some less highly organized form. The grounds upon which this conclusion rests will never be shaken, for the close similarity between man and the lower animals, in embryonic development, as well as in innumerable points of structure and constitution . . . are facts which cannot be disputed.**

(2)

*Mr. Darwin . . . declares that he applies his scheme . . . of natural selection to man himself, as well as to the animals around him. Now, we must say at once that such a notion is absolutely incompatible not only with . . . the word of God . . . but . . . with the whole . . . moral and spiritual condition of man. . . . Man's derived supremacy over the earth . . . man's gift of reason; man's free will and responsibility; man's fall and man's redemption; the incarnation of the Eternal Son; the indwelling of the Eternal Spirit—all are equally and utterly irreconcilable with the degrading notion of the brute origin of him who was created in the image of God. . . .***

Charles Darwin, in the first extract, claimed the scientific evidence of embryology and anatomy supported his view that human beings had evolved from "some less highly organized form" of life. Bishop Samuel Wilberforce, a leading opponent of Darwinian evolution, responded by pointing in horror to the "moral and spiritual" implications of evolution. Darwin's "facts which cannot be disputed" convinced the large majority of biologists, yet are still debated today, mostly because of the religious and moral implications that so disturbed Wilberforce.

*Charles Darwin, *The Descent of Man,* in *Darwin,* ed. P. Appleman (New York: Norton, 1979), p. 196.

**Samuel Wilberforce, review of *Origin of Species,* in B. D. Henning et al., *Crises in English History, 1066–1945* (New York: Holt, 1957), p. 451.

Social Darwinists took the scientific concept of survival of the fittest from the world of nature and applied it to human society. For example, they used the theory to account for the fierce, fang-and-claw competition among businessmen and to explain the dominant position of the middle class. They defended the new wave of European imperial conquest (see Chapter 13) as the triumph of the superior—more fit—white race. War itself could be seen as an inevitable form of natural selection.

Many people opposed Darwinism. The theory of a struggle for survival, of "nature red in tooth and claw," had little in common either with the Enlightenment vision of a system of harmonious natural laws or with the romantic emphasis on the beauty and divinity of nature. Further, Christian morality was affronted by the efforts of social Darwinists to justify war and unbridled competition as socially healthy for the species despite the pain inflicted on the individual.

Most disturbing to nineteenth-century sensibilities, however, was Darwin's contention that human beings were only very clever animals. Evolution seemed to deny religious notions of the "soul" and a divinely created universe; science seemed to dethrone human reason from its central place.

Darwin helped launch a powerful new secularism around the globe. This amoral outlook, especially attractive to intellectual and political leaders, displaced traditional ideas of man's place in the universe. The new ideology, stressing concepts of intrinsic inferiority and superiority, was to have important repercussions in the twentieth century.

The Development of Culture in the Americas

The cultural life of the new American nations followed its own course in the nineteenth century, although it continued to be heavily influenced by Europe. Both romanticism and literary realism, for instance, had their devotees across the Atlantic. The American poet and short-story writer, Edgar Allan Poe (1809–1849), displayed the romantic's fascination with the emotions, the supernatural, the bizarre, and the macabre, as in this passage from his short story, "The Tell-Tale Heart," in which a madman murderer describes the moments just before his grisly crime:

> I scarcely breathed. I held the lantern motionless. I tried how steadily I could maintain the ray upon the eye. Meanwhile the hellish tattoo of the heart increased. It grew quicker and quicker, louder and louder every instant. The old man's terror *must* have been extreme! It grew louder, I say, louder every moment!—do you mark me well? I have told you that I am nervous: so I am. And now at the dead hour of the night, amid the dreadful silence of that old house, so strange a noise as this excited me to uncontrollable terror.

In the later years of the nineteenth century, American authors like Hamlin Garland (1860–1940) depicted with uncompromising realism the drab loneliness and hard work as well as the strength of spirit of midwestern pioneers and farmers. The muckraking social novels of Frank Norris (1870–1902), which exposed the seamier side of American business and politics, were directly influenced by the works of Zola.

Nineteenth-century American painters were mostly influenced by European artists. The seascapes of Winslow Homer (1836–1910) have a strongly romantic feeling for nature. The impressionist Mary Cassatt (1845–1926) was so deeply involved in French impressionism that she moved permanently to Paris. Distinctively American subjects did attract some artists, however, including the romantic painters of the Hudson River school and George Catlin (1796–1872), who painted American Indians.

The United States in its first century also produced some "isms" of its own. The transcendentalist movement of the pre–Civil War period showed a distinctively American confidence in the divine essence of each individual. Henry David Thoreau (1817–1862) and Ralph Waldo Emerson (1803–1882) preached freedom, individual conscience, and self-reliance as typically American virtues. During the Gilded Age of American industrial growth after the Civil War, William James (1842–1910) expounded another characteristically American philosophy: pragmatism. James defined the truth of an idea in terms of its practical usefulness. Truth, he said, is what works—an idea that suited many people in the bustling, not overly idealistic United States of his time.

Some of the United States' most famous writers were striking individuals not easily classified according to European literary trends. *Moby Dick* (1851) and other novels of the sea by Herman Melville (1819–1891) explored fundamental aspects of individual experience. The humorous narratives of life along the pre–Civil War Mississippi and on the western frontier by Mark Twain (Samuel Clemens, 1835–1910) had no parallel in Europe. The exquisite lyrics of Emily Dickinson (1830–1886) explored her own soul and the spiritual dimensions of simple things. The passionate *Leaves of Grass* (1855) by the poet Walt Whitman (1819–1892) hymned the potential greatness of a whole people, as in these lines from his "When Lilacs Last in the Dooryard Bloom'd":

Lo, body and soul—this land,
My own Manhattan with spires, and the sparkling and hurrying tides, and the ships,
The varied and ample land, the South and the North in the light, Ohio's shores and flashing Missouri,
And ever the far-spreading prairies cover'd with grass and corn.

Although Latin American scholars and writers drew heavily on European cultural sources, they used these to help them achieve their own cultural and intellectual independence from the Old World. An underlying concern of much of this writing was the desire to explore and establish a genuinely Latin American culture, distinct from those of Europe and the United States. By condemning their European ancestors and glorifying their Amerindian ones, by evoking such clearly South American phenomena as the gaucho of the pampas, these writers strove to achieve a sense of their own cultural uniqueness. Latin American men of letters also frequently combined literature with political affairs or even armed struggle. José Marti, for example, Cuba's most honored writer, was a poet who died fighting in Cuba's rebellion against Spain in the 1890s.

Although romanticism had a longer and deeper influence in Latin America than in North America, it was adapted to local cultural needs. South American writers had little enthusiasm for the towering romantic ego of Byron or for the supernaturalism of the Gothic romance. They seized on the romantic glorification of freedom, the primacy of emotion, and the superiority of the primitive over the artificial or sophisticated. Glorifying the free life, for instance, the Argentine poet José Hernandez

Corbis-Bettmann

Emily Dickinson. The American poet is depicted here as a young woman. Despite a narrowly circumscribed life in the small town of Amherst, Massachusetts, Dickinson's creative genius could encompass the broadest of human concerns.

1775	
	The French Revolution Napoleon Bonaparte Robert Fulton's steamboat
	Ludwig van Beethoven
1815	Battle of Waterloo Congress of Vienna Latin American independence movements: Simón Bolívar
	Romantic poetry: Wordsworth The Great Reform Act in Britain Samuel Morse and the telegraph Revolutions of 1848 Karl Marx, *Communist Manifesto*
1850	Second French Empire: Napoleon III Henry David Thoreau, *Walden* Charles Darwin, *On the Origin of Species* Unification of Italy U.S. Civil War Charles Dickens Leo Tolstoy, *War and Peace* The unification of Germany The Paris Commune
1875	Impressionist painting: Claude Monet Gladstone and Disraeli dominate British politics
	Thomas Edison and electric light Louis Pasteur and germ theory Tsar Alexander III
	The internal combustion engine
1900	Euclydes da Cunha, *Rebellion in the Backlands*
	John D. Rockefeller
	Mary Cassatt, American impressionist painter
1920	

(1834–1866) praised the freedom-loving gaucho, the cowboy of the pampas. Mexican poets honored the memory of the ancient Aztecs, and Brazilians celebrated their Amerindian ancestors.

Realism, naturalism, and positivism also appeared in Latin America in the last decades of the century. Writers documented the worst abuses of the old Spanish colonial regime and the materialistic inhumanity of the Industrial Revolution in western European nations. Chilean realist Alberto Blest Gana depicted a money-grubbing society in novels like *Arithmetic in Love* (1860). The Brazilian novelist Euclydes da Cunha (1866–1909), in his *Rebellion in the Backlands* (1902), powerfully evoked primitive backwoodsmen in revolt against an oppressive government.

Summary and Comparisons

The French Revolution was a great watershed in European history. Like the Protestant Reformation, it inaugurated widespread changes in Western society. Though the underlying causes of the French Revolution are difficult to disentangle, its immediate source was the growing national debt, which in turn triggered the collapse of the old regime. The pre- and early revolutionary phase was dominated by the aristocracy, seeking to retain privileges and political authority at the expense of the monarchy. Initially the nobles scored a victory when they forced the king to summon the Estates-General in the spring of 1789, but they lost the initiative to the middle class, which transformed France into a constitutional monarchy.

The threat of counterrevolutionaries and a war with the rest of Europe propelled into power the radical Jacobins, who abolished the monarchy and imposed a reign of terror. A reaction followed, as the middle class made a short-lived attempt to reassert its authority. The revolution ended in November 1799 when Napoleon Bonaparte established a military dictatorship.

In many ways Napoleon emulated the best features of enlightened despotism and continued reforming France: finances were put on a sound footing, laws were codified, and the educational system was reorganized. But politically he was a reactionary, reinstituting the very sort of absolutist state the French people had rebelled against. Napoleon moreover indulged his natural instincts for conquest and glory. He did not massacre innocent civilians and raze towns in the manner of Genghis Khan or Timurlane, but his victories were achieved at a high cost in blood and treasure. Those who initially welcomed him as a liberator soon realized they had exchanged one absolute ruler for another. Although he came closer than any man to imposing a political unity on the European continent, he was ultimately defeated at Waterloo.

In the aftermath of Napoleon's downfall, a mood of uneasiness and disillusionment—like that following the Thirty Years' War—permeated Europe. This pessimistic outlook was in part attributable to the peace settlement reached at Vienna in 1815. Metternich, the dominant voice both then and for many years after in European politics, was determined to destroy the forces of nationalism and liberalism released by the French Revolution. He created a system that kept such movements in check, but advocates of radical change again burst forth in the revolutions of 1830 and 1848.

By contrast, Latin American nationalists succeeded in ousting the Spanish and Portuguese and created new independent states. In the first three decades of the nineteenth century, colonists in part of the Caribbean and throughout Latin America won independence. Though most of the new nations were liberal republics, they maintained their common colonial culture in which a small elite controlled the masses and a stagnant but potentially rich economy.

Back in Europe, the revolutions of 1830 succeeded only in the countries where the insurgents formed a large segment of the population. In the revolutions of 1848, the liberals fought for constitutions while revolts in eastern Europe for a time threatened the conservative Habsburg Empire. The failure of the 1848 revolutions heightened the nationalism at work around the world in the second half of the nineteenth century.

In the United States, nationalism was expressed through a momentous civil war that clarified the nature of the American union. The constitution of 1787 was fundamentally unclear as to whether the government of the United States was a confederation of sovereign states or a perpetual union. Economic and cultural differences between the northern and southern sections of the country, especially regarding the enslavement of African Americans, imperiled the young nation. To defend slavery, eleven southern states seceded in 1860–1861. In the ensuing civil war, the state sovereignty doctrine was defeated, and the United States entered the twentieth century as an indissoluble union.

Even more dramatically than in the United States, nationalism in Italy and Germany involved a forcible union of disparate elements into centralized states. The process of political unification in Italy was piloted by Cavour with the Kingdom of Sardinia as its focus, and in Germany by Bismarck under Prussian hegemony. Independence for many Christian peoples in the Balkans, formerly subjects of the Ottoman Empire, marked another victory for nationalism. Not all peoples realized their nationalistic dreams, however, most notably Slavic subjects in the Austro-Hungarian Empire and non-Russians in the Russian Empire. The frustrations of those still denied freedom, and the instability in the new states created a volatile political climate in eastern Europe.

Another continent-wide trend during this era was the development of democratic institutions, smoothly and through an evolutionary process in Great Britain and in lurches and amidst turmoil in France. Germany and Austria-Hungary made concessions to democratic institutions, but their governments retained authoritarian characteristics. Russia remained a despotic empire into the twentieth century and had no meaningful representative institutions.

The Industrial Revolution was as significant in the advancement of humanity as the development of agriculture during the Neolithic period. It began in Great Britain with the widespread use of mechanical power in factories and spread first to the European continent and then to the United States, with far-reaching economic and social consequences. Steam power was harnessed to new forms of transportation, the railroads and steamships, and electrical energy to new means of communication, especially the telegraph.

During this era, many socialists advocated public ownership of the means of production to ensure a more even distribution of wealth and improvements in the living standards of the poor. Followers of Karl Marx believed that class struggle would lead to a world revolution and the seizure of power by the proletariat and an eventual classless society.

The Industrial Revolution transformed Europe's economic institutions. The new business leaders opposed government economic controls and succeeded in destroying the mercantilist system. The unfettered free competition of the mid-nineteenth century, however, gave way after 1870 to a new form of control of the economy by giant corporations and cartels.

Industrial society had several striking features. The population explosion multiplied the sheer number of Western people. An unprecedentedly high proportion of them lived in the new industrial cities. Finally, the middle class became the dominant element in Western society and the industrial masses emerged as a challenging new force. In all these ways, industrialism fostered new European and American societies during the late eighteenth and the nineteenth centuries.

The culture of the nineteenth century was complex and often challenged conventional beliefs and values. Romanticism in the first half of the century and materialism and Darwinism in the second half pervaded the European mind. In the Americas, these and other themes influenced the cultures of the new nations.

Romanticism in literature, painting, and music asserted the superiority of the emotions over reason and exalted nature, underdeveloped cultures, faraway places, and colorful periods of the past. Romantic artists also rejected the classical rules for the arts, insisting instead on the free play of the imagination. As a cultural revolt, romanticism expressed a growing alienation from the vulgarities of nineteenth-century industrial civilization and once more stressed emotion over intellect.

Materialism concluded from the progress of the physical sciences that only the material world existed. Dismissing religion as an illusion, this world view insisted on positivistic knowledge, derived exclusively from empirical observation. Realists attempted to describe this material world in paint or prose. Impressionists tried to paint light as the eye sees it, naturalists like Zola to describe human beings as mere biological organisms, without spiritual or moral dimensions.

Charles Darwin explored the animal origins and instinctive drives beneath human reason. Darwinian evolution stressed the struggle for existence and the transformation of all living creatures through natural selection. His theories led to an intense and unending intellectual debate. As a rule, scientists supported Darwin in contrast to most theologians and the devout, who decried the idea of any direct relationship between man and higher primates as a repudiation of the account of the creation in the biblical book of Genesis.

The cultural history of the Americas reflected both European influences and New World concerns. The growing United States produced some writers influenced by romanticism and realism, but also gave birth to such distinctive schools of thought as transcendentalism and to such unique talents as Mark Twain, Emily Dickinson, and Walt Whitman.

Latin American culture in the nineteenth century struck closer to European models, from romanticism to naturalism and positivism. But Latin American writers used these forms and ideas to define the uniqueness of their culture, lauding freedom and their Amerindian heritage and condemning their Spanish colonial past and the industrializing present.

Selected Sources

Bloom, Harold, and Lionel Trilling, eds. *Romantic Prose and Poetry.* 1973. A good, representative reader.

Bosher, J. F. *The French Revolution.* 1988. A superb recent study of the revolution.

*Brinton, Crane. *The Anatomy of Revolution.* 1938, revised ed. 1965. Useful comparison of English, American, French, and Russian revolutions. A good starting point for the understanding of revolution.

*Chevalier, Louis. *Laboring Classes and Dangerous Classes in Paris During the First Half of the Nineteenth Century.* 1981. Working-class misery and resentment in the early Industrial Revolution.

Clark, Kenneth. *The Romantic Rebellion: Romantic versus Classic Art.* 1973. Well-written and illustrated essays on important artists by a leading art historian.

*Crankshaw, Edward. *Bismarck.* 1981. A lively, rather critical account of the Iron Chancellor.

*Dickens, Charles. *A Tale of Two Cities.* 1859. Numerous editions. Colorful, sometimes moving novel based on the French Revolution. Skillfully captures the atmosphere of the revolution.

Doyle, William. *The Oxford History of the French Revolution.* 1989. Latest insights into a major event in world history. The author rejects the theory of a bourgeois revolution, arguing that this group and the aristocracy shaped similar views and interests in the pre-1789 era.

Droz, J. *Europe Between Revolutions, 1815–1848.* 1968. An overview of the period.

*Eiseley, Loren. *Darwin's Century: Evolution and the Men Who Discovered It.* 1958. Thoughtful and readable account of the early evolutionists.

*Herold, J. C. *The Age of Napoleon.* 1963. A well-written popular history.

*Howard, Michael. *The Franco-Prussian War.* 1961. A fascinating and meticulously researched study by a leading British military historian.

Korg, Jacob, ed. *London in Dickens' Day.* 1961. Brief contemporary glimpses of everyday life, from pubs to clubs, parks to prisons.

Landes, David S. *The Unbound Prometheus.* 1969. Survey of industrial development from the eighteenth to the twentieth centuries, especially good on technology.

Levy, Darline G., et al., eds. and trans. *Women in Revolutionary Paris, 1789–1795.* 1979. A useful collection of documents on women in the era.

*Lichtheim, George. *Marxism: An Historical and Critical Study.* 1982. Excellent critique of nineteenth-century Marxism.

*Lindemann, Albert S. *A History of European Socialism.* 1983. Particularly good on comparison of socialist and syndicalist movements.

*Marx, Karl, and Friedrich Engels. *The Communist Manifesto.* 1848. Many editions. Brief presentation of Marx's view of history.

The Molly Maguires. Ritt, Martin, dir. 1970. Film about a workers' rebellion in the Pennsylvania coal fields, with vivid images of life in the mines and company towns.

Norton, Rictor, ed. *Gothic Readings: The First Wave, 1764–1840.* 2000. Contains many Romantic instances of the gothic subgenre.

*Palmer, R. R. *The Age of Revolutions.* 2 vols. 1964. Interesting thesis that the French Revolution was part of a general revolutionary movement in the West, by one of the foremost scholars in the United States.

Popkin, Jeffrey D. *A Short History of the French Revolution.* 1997. A well-written survey, with a discussion of the various interpretations of the origins of the revolution and its broader impact.

Porter, Glenn. *The Rise of Big Business, 1860–1910.* 1973. Good survey of big business in the United States.

Ruis, Eduardo del Rio. *Marx for Beginners.* 1976. Humorous yet informative cartoon book with historical overview. See also *Trotsky for Beginners* and *Cuba for Beginners.*

*Available in paperback.

Schama, Simon. *Citizens: A Chronicle of the French Revolution.* 1989. An excellent study of the revolution from a sociological vantage point.

Smith, Denis Mack. *The Making of Italy, 1796–1870.* 1968. A scholarly overview of the Italian problem in the nineteenth century.

*Stavrianos, Leften S. *The Balkans, 1815–1914.* 1962. Good survey of the troubled area.

*Stearns, Peter. *1848: The Revolutionary Tide in Europe.* 1974. A sound general study, with special emphasis on social conditions.

*Sutherland, D. M. G. *France, 1789–1815.* 1985. An interpretation of the revolutionary period, stressing the connection between social and political conflict.

*Tolstoy, Leo. *War and Peace.* 1865–1869. Numerous editions, complete or abridged. Classic novel about Napoleon's invasion of Russia. (Also a film.)

Ward, Barbara. *Nationalism and Ideology.* 1966. Puts modern nationalism in the broadest context of evolving human loyalties.

Wheen, Francis. *Karl Marx.* 1999. A richly entertaining biography that humanizes the father of historical materialism.

Internet Links

Abbé Sieyes: What Is the Third Estate?
http://www.fordham.edu/halsall/mod/sieyes.html
A quintessential statement of the principles of the liberal phase of the French Revolution: "The Third Estate embraces . . . all that which belongs to the nation; and all that which is not the Third Estate, cannot be regarded as being of the nation."

Documents of German Unification, 1848–1871
http://www.fordham.edu/halsall/mod/germanunification.html
Important documents by J. G. Droysen, Friedrich Wilhelm IV, Otto von Bismarck, and Helmuth von Moltke.

The Guillotine Headquarters
http://www.logp.dk/guillotine/
Everything you always wanted to know about the guillotine: who invented it, how it was constructed, on whom it was used. Many graphics.

Impressionism (Web Museum, Paris)
http://www.oir.ucf.edu/wm/paint/glo/impressionism/
Useful information about the artistic movement and its major proponents; exceptionally clear graphics.

The Karl Marx and Friedrich Engels Internet Archive
http://csf.colorado.edu/mirrors/marxists.org/archive/marx/index.htm
A very extensive website, including biographical materials, letters, images, and online editions of *The Communist Manifesto* and all of *Das Kapital* in English translation.

Maximilien Robespierre: Justification of the Use of Terror
http://www.fordham.edu/halsall/mod/robespierre-terror.html
This selection from Robespierre's "On the Moral and Political Principles of Domestic Policy" is a stirring call to arms against the abuses of the *ancien régime.*

Napoleonic Literature
http://www.napoleonic-literature.com/
This extensive website offers a wealth of information: complete texts, images, chronologies, and bibliographies.

Romantic Circles: Scholarly Resources
http://www.rc.umd.edu/reference/
Offers "a set of online research tools . . . for the study of the younger romantics . . . and their cultural contexts." Includes texts of Lord Byron, John Keats, Mary W. Shelley, Percy B. Shelley, and Mary Wollstonecraft, with links to resources for such other romantics as Blake, Coleridge, and Wordsworth.

British History: The Reform of Parliament, 1750–1832
http://www.spartacus.schoolnet.co.uk/PRparliament.htm
This site offers biographical accounts of dozens of reformers, politicians, writers, and artists, together with details of specific events and parliamentary reform acts.

Total War

The great strides which civilization makes against barbarism and unreason are only made actual by the sword.

Heinrich von Treitschke, *Politics,* vol. 1 (New York: Macmillan, 1916), p. 65.

The first shock at the news of war—the war that no one, people or government, had wanted— . . . had suddenly been transformed into enthusiasm. There were parades in the street, flags, ribbons, and music burst forth everywhere, young recruits were marching triumphantly, their faces lighting up at the cheering.

Stefan Zweig, a noted Austrian literary figure, describing the scene in Vienna on the outbreak of war in August 1914. Marvin Perry, Joseph R. Peden, and Theodore von Laure, eds., *Sources of the Western Tradition,* vol. 2 (Boston: Houghton Mifflin, 1987), p. 231.

In three days, on a front of about 200 yards, we lost 909 men, and the enemy casualties must have amounted to thousands. The blue French cloth mingled with the German grey upon the ground, and in some places the bodies were piled so high that one could take cover from shell fire behind them. . . . Don't ask about the fate of the wounded! Anybody who was incapable of walking to the doctor had to die a miserable death; some lingered in agony for hours, some for days, and even for a week. . . . There are moments when even the bravest soldier is so utterly sick of the whole thing that he could cry like a child.

Richard Schmeider, a German student in philosophy writing from a trench near Vaudesincourt, March 13, 1915. Perry M. Rogers, ed., *Aspects of Western Civilization,* vol. 2 (Englewood Cliffs, N.J.: Prentice Hall, 1992), pp. 284–285.

However much we may sympathize with a small nation confronted by a big and powerful neighbor, we cannot in all circumstances undertake to involve the whole British Empire in a war simply on her account.

British Prime Minister Neville Chamberlain in a broadcast to the nation during the crisis over Czechoslovakia. Neville Chamberlain, *In Search of Peace* (Freeport, N.Y.: Books for Libraries Press, 1971), p. 175.

The decade before World War I witnessed a surge of militarism in Europe. This attitude was particularly strong in Germany, where writers like Heinrich von Treitschke gloried warfare as a great adventure that was essential to human progress. In August 1914 the citizens of the belligerent nations, conditioned by years of nationalistic propaganda, greeted their respective government's declaration of war with almost carnival gaiety, cheering and showering flowers and gifts on soldiers departing for the front. After trench warfare set in at the close of 1914, the rapturous mood turned first to disillusionment, then to bitterness as the fighting dragged on for four years, exacting a horrendous toll in human lives. It was the haunting memories of the slaughter in World War I that led statesmen in western European democracies, such as Neville Chamberlain, to embrace a policy of conciliation with Hitler and Mussolini in the 1930s that came to be known as "appeasement."

The wars of both 1914–1918 and 1939–1945 were fought as much at home as at the front. The term *total war* emerged during World War II and is traditionally associated with the two global wars of the twentieth century. Broadly defined, total war required a belligerent nation to mobilize all its resources, both human and material, for the purpose of waging war.

Under these criteria, it would seem that instances of total war predate the twentieth century and that some earlier military conflicts had key features of total war. As an aggressor nation, the ancient Mongols, no less than the modern Nazis, practiced total war against an enemy by organizing all available resources, including military personnel, noncombatant workers, intelligence, transport, money, and provisions. More recently, during the French Revolution, the government in Paris introduced conscription, took control of industries vital to the war effort, managed the economy, and restricted individual rights.

Conversely, targets of aggression were compelled to wage total war to survive as nations or to stave off annihilation. During the Third Punic War, the entire population of Carthage was involved in a desperate effort to resist the Roman siege. Noncombatants toiled feverishly to forge new weapons of war and to strengthen the defenses of the city, while the women gave their hair to be made into strings for bows and catapults. Similarly, the city of Tyre did all it could to resist the siege of Alexander the Great but failed.

The spread of the Industrial Revolution in the nineteenth century revolutionized weapons, tactics, and the ability of nations to mobilize their resources. The totality of warfare was foreshadowed in the U.S. Civil War and in the Franco-Prussian War and the subsequent siege of Paris (1871). In each case, combatants and noncombatants became indistinguishable in the face of the threat to their survival.

When opposing coalitions proved unable to end the war quickly, World War I added a number of novel features to the practice of total war. For the first time governments attempted to integrate completely all elements of a nation in arms, making the home front an integral part of the fighting front. Belligerent nations not only had to put huge armies in the field but also had to devise the means to supply them with weapons, ammunition, replacements, clothing, and food. Simply to remain in the war required a national commitment on a scale never before contemplated. To that end, the government had to control and manage the economy and maintain the nation's morale and its will to go on fighting. The degree to which the belligerent governments succeeded in harnessing their resources varied from nation to nation, but few people were not affected by the war.

Among the most important changes the war imposed on civilians was the great increase in the power of the state to exercise control over all aspects of political, economic, and social life. All able-bodied men, sometimes even those in war-related industries, were drafted into the army. Governments temporarily set aside free market capitalism and moved toward planned economies. They set up agencies to convert industrial machines to military production, allocate raw materials, ration food supplies and essential materials, regulate wages and prices, and nationalize transportation systems and vital industries. Some governments sponsored scientific research and efforts to devise synthetic substitutes for some goods that were simply unattainable. Industries called upon women to replace the men sent to the front.

As the war dragged on with no end in sight, warring governments resorted to propaganda to maintain civilian morale and generate enthusiasm for the war. One way to do this was to foster hatred for the enemy. Both sides portrayed the other as the lowest form of vermin, guilty of heinous crimes and entertaining diabolical war aims. Moreover, the need for national unity precluded dissent of any kind. Thus all governments accompanied their propaganda with censorship.

World War II required an even greater commitment on the part of the belligerents. Fighting was more widespread, weapons more destructive, and civilians more directly exposed to the war. Victory was likely to go to the side better able to mobilize its home front.

As was the case in the 1914–1918 conflict, the power of the central government after 1939, even in democracies, expanded over all facets of national life. Since many of the World War II leaders had gained experience in administration during World War I, they were able to avoid many of the mistakes of the earlier conflict. For example, at the beginning of World War II, they established the full set of regulations that had only come in the last stages of World War I. Once again a national system of rationing, allocation of raw material, and price controls was set up to put the economy under government direction. Women left their homes to work in factories or serve in the armed forces. Propaganda was used to greater effect in the second conflict than in the first. As the struggle took on ideological overtones, warring powers mobilized the press, radio, and film to whip up national sentiment. Science played a crucial part in the war. Scientists were active in all fields, devising ways to escape damaged submarines, planning precision bombing, and improving weapons.

After 1945, nuclear weapons, with their capacity to destroy the world in a matter of hours, if not minutes, made the concept of total war obsolete. As nations stockpiled arsenals of ever more powerful nuclear weapons, the former balance between nations became a balance of terror. A sardonic acronym for this grim "balance of terror" was MAD (Mutually Assured Destruction). Yet these awesome weapons have led to less rather than more death and destruction in recent decades. They have forced nations to seek alternatives to war, or at worst, less destructive forms of warfare to attain their goals. Since World War II, limited, rather than total, warfare has become the norm between nations unable or unwilling to resolve their differences at the negotiating table.

The Race for Empire and World War I

13

CAUSES OF IMPERIALISM AND THE PARTITION OF AFRICA

Imperial Motivations
Europe Partitions Africa
African Resistance
The Boer War

WESTERN IMPERIALISM IN THE MIDDLE EAST AND ASIA

Ottoman Reforms and Territorial Losses
The Eastern Question
Imperial Gains in Asia
India: The Jewel in the Crown of the British Empire
Protecting India: Imperialist Confrontations in Asia
British Settlement of Australasia
The European Onslaught on the Ch'ing Empire in China

JAPAN AND THE UNITED STATES BECOME WORLD POWERS

Japanese Imperialism
The Rise of the United States
The United States Becomes an Imperialist Power
The Caribbean Becomes a U.S. Lake
The United States and Canada
U.S. Expansion in Asia

THE CAUSES AND COURSE OF WORLD WAR I

The Underlying Causes of the Conflict
Bismarckian Diplomacy
The Post-Bismarck Era
Conflicts and Compromises, 1907–1914
Archduke Francis Ferdinand's Assassination Leads to War
The Controversy over Responsibility
Stalemate on the Western Front
The Eastern Front
The War outside Europe
The Home Front
Women and the War
American Entry and the Collapse of the Central Powers

POSTWAR SETTLEMENTS AND THE INTERWAR YEARS

The Paris Peace Conference and the Versailles Treaty
The Settlements with the Other Central Powers
Evaluation of the Peace Treaties
The League of Nations
Germany under the Weimar Republic
The Quest for International Security
The Victorious Democracies in the 1920s
The Great Depression

SUMMARY AND COMPARISONS

Take up the White Man's burden—
Send forth the best ye breed—
Go bind your sons to exile
To serve your captives' need;
To wait in heavy harness,
On fluttered folk and wild—
Your new-caught, sullen peoples,
Half-devil and half child.

Take up the White Man's burden—
Have done with childish days—
The lightly proffered laurel,
The easy, ungrudged praise.
Comes now, to search your manhood
Through all the thankless years,
Cold, edged with dear-bought wisdom,
*The judgment of your peers!**

*Rudyard Kipling, *Rudyard Kipling's Verse: Definitive Edition* (New York: Doubleday, 1940), p. 321.

In "The White Man's Burden," Britain's best-known imperialist writer, Rudyard Kipling, represented empire building as a duty, a thankless job, rather than as a naked expression of economic and political power. Kipling earnestly believed in the mission of the white races to bestow the blessings of their higher culture and superior civilization on "backward" societies. He called upon the United States to join Great Britain in this vast civilizing movement. Given that the United States' population had surpassed Great Britain's and its industrial strength was increasing at an unprecedented pace, he felt the time had come for Americans to shoulder the responsibility of a great nation and accept their destiny.

Western, industrialized nations entered the twentieth century confident of their scientific, technological, and cultural superiority. By the end of the nineteenth century, the industrialized nations had become imperialistic, and successfully moved to extend their domination over Africa, Asia, and Latin America. But World War I ended the industrialized world's boundless faith in its own superiority and irrevocably changed the course of history around the world. Attitudes about the continued progress of Western civilization were permanently changed, and society at large no longer believed in the absolute ability of rational thought, as manifested in science and technology, to solve all human problems.

The cost of the war in human and financial terms far exceeded anyone's predictions. Western imperial powers, shaken by the war, would never recover total control over their far-flung territories. Likewise, political and economic systems, particularly in the West, were permanently altered. This chapter begins with a discussion of the causes of imperialism and traces the pattern of Western and Japanese imperialism around the world. It then describes the course of World War I and the far-reaching impacts of the war. Finally, postwar developments in the Western democracies and the worldwide financial crisis of the Great Depression will be described.

Causes of Imperialism and the Partition of Africa

At midday on Tuesday, June 22, 1897, Queen Victoria of England, Defender of the Faith, Empress of India, ruler of the British Dominions beyond the Seas, arrived at St. Paul's Cathedral to thank God for the existence of the greatest Empire ever known.

The representatives of an imperial caste awaited her there. Bishops of the Church of England fluttered hymnal sheets and remembered half a century of Christian effort—the suppression of slavery, the conversion of heathen tribes, mission stations from Niger to Labrador. Generals and admirals blazed with medals and remembered half a century of satisfactory campaigning. . . .

*There were poets, musicians, and propagandists. . . . Behind these marshals, soldiers from every part of the Queen's Empire honored the royal presence. The Chinese from Hong Kong wore wide coolie hats. The Zaptiehs, Turkish military policemen from Cyprus, wore fezzes. The Jamaicans wore white gaiters and gold-embroidered jackets. There were Dyaks from Borneo, and Sikhs from India, and Canadian Hussars, and Sierra Leone gunners . . . and Maltese, and South Africans, and a troop of jangling Bengal Lancers. . . . [These soldiers represented] nearly 400 million subjects living in all five continents, honoring a thousand religions, speaking a thousand languages—peoples of every race, culture, stage of development.**

**The Horizon History of the British Empire* (New York: American Heritage, 1973), pp. 9, 11.

This account of the Diamond Jubilee, a ceremony celebrating the sixtieth year of the reign of Queen Victoria, describes the high-water mark for the British Empire, the largest and most powerful imperial power of the age. In the nineteenth century a new form of imperialism swept the world. This new imperialism, or extension of one nation-state's domination or control over territory outside its own boundaries, differed from the empires of the fifteenth and sixteenth centuries in that the industrialized nations of the Western world did not generally seek to colonize or to settle territories with their people; rather, they sought to control faraway lands for a complex variety of economic, political, national, and social reasons.

Imperial Motivations

Nineteenth-century imperialism built on many of the same foundations as the earlier imperialism, but its impact on societies and economies around the world was much more intrusive and in many cases more disruptive. This was particularly true in Africa, where the firepower of Western armies and navies overwhelmed the swords and spears of non-Western peoples. Western steam-powered gunboats, rifled artillery, and machine guns could dominate any area of the world. Railroads and river streamers, built by local labor but owned by the Western interests or nations, could transport valuable commodities and raw materials from remote inland regions to industrial centers; conversely, these same transport systems could carry manufactured goods to new markets around the globe. New telegraph lines laid overland and under oceans facilitated rapid communications that previously might have taken months. From modern ports in Africa and Asia, the new oceangoing ships, made of iron and powered by steam-driven screw propellers, carried larger cargoes to their destination faster and more safely than the old wooden sailing ships. Engineers designed and Egyptian laborers dug and constructed the Suez Canal, and later the United States constructed the Panama Canal. These new canals enabled navies and shipping lines to cut in half the length and time of the journey from Great Britain to India or New York to San Francisco.

New economic forces also propelled imperialism. The industrialized nations constantly sought new markets and cheap raw materials. They needed supplies of coal, iron ore, copper, other industrial ores, and (later) rubber and petroleum. As domestic markets in industrial nations became saturated, manufacturers looked for new markets abroad. Nigeria, Egypt, China, and India, with large and growing populations, offered enticing possibilities to industrialists looking for new purchasers of their manufactured goods. These nations also offered a potential supply of cheap labor. In the late nineteenth and early twentieth centuries, as labor unions in the West grew and secured higher wages and better working conditions, many industrialists sought to evade higher costs by transferring their businesses abroad where labor was largely unorganized and where people in need of jobs would accept poor working conditions and low wages.

Some economists such as J. A. Hobson (1858–1940) and Marxists such as V. I. Lenin argued that it was inevitable that the capitalist, industrialized nations would become imperialistic. Hobson and Lenin, among others, stressed that capitalists constantly sought to increase their profits, and as these profits grew, large amounts of capital became available. Thus fortified, capitalists would seek to extend their economic control over the markets, resources, and labor of the rest of the world. This analysis intrigued many Western intellectuals, but, with the possible exception of Japan, the capitalist dynamic does not seem to have been the major, overwhelming factor behind imperialism in the nineteenth century.

Some industrialists even opposed their governments' annexing of new colonies on the grounds that they were too expensive and troublesome. At the same time, many people with no economic interest at stake favored imperialism. In Great Britain, for example, support for imperial expansion tended to be bipartisan; both the conservative and liberal parties—in spite of differing economic policies and outlooks—backed imperial endeavors. Although economic considerations were and still are major factors for imperialism, it is simplistic to attribute all of nineteenth-century imperialism to economic motivations. For example, economic reasons cannot explain why France, one of the least industrialized great European powers, more than doubled its imperial holdings between 1815 and 1870 or took over the landlocked, impoverished regions in Africa.

Certainly, the quest for empire led to a marked increase in nationalist rivalries among European powers. Nationalism, particularly for the average citizen of industrialized Western nations, was a major motivating factor behind imperialism. The desire of industrialized nations to have the biggest and most powerful empire often led them to acquire new territories even when they provided no economic benefit, as, for example, in the case of the French takeover of Chad in Africa, which proved an economic drag on the French economy.

Nations in the late nineteenth century also seized areas for strategic reasons, especially to provide naval bases to protect the sea lanes between the key colonies and the colonial powers. The Hawaiian Islands, the Suez Canal, and Aden on the Arabian coast are examples of such strategic locations. The imperial powers also took the islands in the Pacific and Atlantic oceans for ports and strategic communication lines between the powers and their valuable land territories in Asia, such as India or Indochina.

The desire of nations to impose their culture on others was another major motive for imperialism. With new technology and growing economic and military strength, Western peoples were convinced that theirs was the "best of all possible worlds." They believed that as "superior" people in possession of the best culture, they had been chosen to bring good government, Christian religion, and light to the rest of the world. Most confused scientific and technological superiority with cultural superiority. This misconception—Europeans called it the white man's burden—impelled Western powers to recreate the rest of the world in their own image. As one imperialist writer put it, "We are imperialists in response to the compelling influences of our destiny . . . we are imperialists because we cannot help it."

Westerners evolved two influential doctrines to rationalize their domination over non-Western, nonwhite, and non-Christian civilizations. One was social Darwinism. Some misinterpreted Darwin's theories regarding the survival of the fittest through adaptation to mean that some human groups were intrinsically "fitter" than others. These social Darwinists, typified by the English writer Herbert Spencer (1820–1903), propounded the notion that select human groups would and should flourish and rule over those that were less "fit."

Accepting the misconceptions of social Darwinists, some racists extolled a doctrine of the superiority of the white race. Writers like the English poet Rudyard Kipling (1865–1936) reinforced this belief with emotional and romantic images of whites bringing a better life to their

Stanley and Livingstone. Here the explorer and adventurer Henry Stanley greets David Livingstone, the missionary whom most westerners believed to be lost in central Africa. In this drawing, the artist shows Stanley accompanied by a large entourage of porters carrying guns, supplies, and a huge American flag; in contrast, Livingstone is surrounded by rather bewildered onlookers.

poor, inferior "brown brothers." In effect, most Westerners were sure that their conquests of other peoples conformed to the laws of God and nature. As they saw it, the conquered groups would benefit by being brought under the tutelage of a superior culture and would naturally want to discard their backward ways. Because these inferior peoples were not expected to grasp the essence of Western civilization, they would have to remain under Western rule. Nineteenth-century Westerners were so certain of their superiority that when traveling around the world they tended to see exactly what they wanted or expected to see. Western literature, art, and music depicted the African, Arab, and Asian worlds as exotic, erotic, mysterious, and slightly threatening. To a great extent, many of these "Orientalist" images of Asian and African cultures continue to permeate Western perceptions and culture to the present day.

Nineteenth-century missionaries, explorers, and adventurers were also imbued with attitudes of cultural superiority, and they, too, helped to foster the imperial spirit. The desire to gain converts to Christianity was a key factor in the spread of imperialism. Up to this point the Roman Catholic church had generally taken a far more active and successful role in securing converts than had the Protestant denominations, but this situation changed during the nineteenth century. The aggressive efforts of the French government to spread Catholicism in Africa, Asia, and Polynesia were matched by the vigor with which Protestants from Europe and the United States sought to convert "heathen" peoples under British or U.S. control.

Nineteenth-century Westerners were also interested in exploring formerly inaccessible and remote parts of the globe. In this they were in some ways similar to twentieth-century astronauts. As early as 1788 the British African Association had financed expeditions to West Africa. Ambitious and wealthy Europeans vied to be the first to find the fabled city of Timbuktu or the source of the Nile River. It did not seem important to most of these adventurers that powerful African societies had built Timbuktu or had lived along the Nile River since the beginning of human history. For the most part, historians, and later archaeologists and anthropologists, did not publish serious scholarly studies on African cultural accomplishments until the twentieth century. As a result, most Westerners learned about Africa from the written exploits of explorers like Richard Burton, John Speke, Samuel and Florence Baker, and Henry Stanley, who were all famous for their African journeys.

Explorers also brought back stories of precious metals, valuable goods, and industrial raw materials. Their tales encouraged other adventurers and entrepreneurs to launch enterprises in Africa, South America, and Asia, where many fortunes were made. For example, mining magnate Cecil Rhodes became one of the richest men in the world from his interests in South Africa and Zimbabwe, which he renamed Rhodesia. An astute politician, Rhodes was also instrumental in pushing the

British government to construct a Cape-to-Cairo railroad to connect South and North Africa. Although this dream was never realized, Rhodes succeeded in extending British imperial holdings in eastern and southern Africa. Similarly, a company headed by King Leopold of Belgium came to control the entire Congo River basin. Later, after considerable maneuvering, Leopold, who had run the Congo as a private fiefdom, was forced to turn over control of the Congo state, eighty times larger than Belgium, to the Belgian government. Finally, as new advances in tropical medicine controlled some previously incurable diseases, such as malaria, the African interior became more attractive to European settlers.

Motivated by these diverse factors, the European powers raced to grab territories in a so-called scramble for Africa. Until the late nineteenth century, European holdings in sub-Saharan Africa were restricted to coastal regions in West and East Africa and South Africa. Then, in less than twenty-five years, European nations claimed most of the continent; in 1875 they had controlled less than 10 percent of Africa; by 1900 that percentage had increased ninefold. Great Britain gained almost 5 million square miles; within the British domain, Cecil Rhodes alone controlled almost 3.5 million square miles. By the beginning of World War I, only Ethiopia, which had successfully fought off the Italians, and Liberia, which had been established by the United States and was dominated by U.S. interests, remained independent.

Once the colonies were established, Great Britain and France, the two major colonial powers, adopted radically different policies toward the governing and education of their subjects. British imperialism tended to be based on social exclusiveness. The British did not generally mix or assimilate with the indigenous peoples of their empire. At the same time, the British generally did not attempt to destroy indigenous cultures or languages; they chose instead to train small elite groups for bureaucratic and commercial jobs within the empire. In short, the British tended to believe that foreign peoples could not possibly become "British" in culture or language, and therefore it would be counterproductive to try to assimilate the majority of the peoples under their domination. In the Indian subcontinent, the small number of British working there made such a transformation impossible in any case. The British referred to their imperial policy as "indirect rule."

In contrast, the French believed firmly in the importance of their "civilizing mission." In most of its colonies, France adopted policies of assimilation and encouraged all peoples to learn French culture and language. However, even in places like Algeria, where many French colonists settled for more than a century, assimilation of inhabitants never succeeded, because native Algerians resented the suppression of their local languages, religion, and cultures. Most people in Algeria remained devout Muslims, and Islamic culture persisted.

"Dr. Livingstone, I Presume?"

*[Livingstone:] When my spirits had fallen into utter depression, the good Samaritan was already very near. One morning Suzy came running toward me and breathlessly announced: "An Englishman! I saw him!" and she darted away to meet him. The American flag at the head of the caravan showed the stranger's nationality. When I saw the bales of supplies, the tin wash-basins, the pots and large pans and all the rest, I thought: "There's a traveller who has at his disposal all facilities, not a poor devil like myself. . . . "**

*[Stanley:] I pushed back the crowds, and passing from the rear walked down a living avenue of people, till I came in front of a semicircle of Arabs, in front of which stood a white man. . . . As I advanced slowly towards him I noticed he was pale, looked weary. I would have run to him, only I was a coward in the presence of such a mob—would have embraced him, only, he being an Englishman, I did not know how he would receive me; so I did what cowardice and false pride suggested was the best thing—walked deliberately to him, took off my hat, and said: "Dr Livingstone, I presume?" "Yes," said he, with a kind smile, lifting his cap slightly.***

These firsthand accounts describe the famous meeting in 1871 between the Scottish missionary David Livingstone and Henry Stanley, an American of English birth. At various times in his life Stanley was a journalist, adventurer, businessman, and explorer. Financed by a U.S. newspaper, Stanley set out to find Livingstone, who was supposed to be "lost" somewhere in Africa. In fact, Livingstone was not lost, but was merely out of touch with the Western world.

*David Livingstone, *The Last Journals of David Livingstone in Central Africa* (London: Horace Walles, 1874), in *Africa Then: Photographs, 1840–1918*, ed. Nicolas Monti (New York: Knopf, 1987), p. 21.

**Henry Morton Stanley, *How I Found Livingstone* (New York: Scribner's, 1872), in Christopher Hibbert, *Africa Explored: Europeans in the Dark Continent, 1769–1889* (London: Allen Lane, 1982), p. 288.

Europe Partitions Africa

The scramble to annex African territories often led to intense rivalries among the European nations, but in general, European governments sought, whenever possible, to avoid direct military confrontations in Africa. Instead, they called international conferences, negotiated binational agreements, and used diplomacy to obtain African lands. At the Berlin conference in 1884, fourteen European nations and the United States discussed how to divide Africa; at a second conference in Brussels in 1890 the Western nations agreed to King Leopold's ownership of the Congo. No Africans were invited to attend these conferences at which their lands were parceled out among the European powers.

In a sort of giant monopoly game in which nations "traded" properties, European powers sometimes agreed to establish "spheres of influences" or monopolies over specific African territories. For example, in 1881–1882, France and Great Britain agreed that France should establish control over Tunisia, while the British should control Egypt. In western Africa, European nations expanded their control from coastal port cities northward into the interior; in the process they created long, narrow territorial strips that cut across ethnic lines and often put warring or rival fishing peoples from the coast, agriculturalists from the savanna, and nomads from the arid northern region together under one centralized government. Present-day West African nations, like Nigeria, reflect these anomalies and continue to be troubled by them.

The British and French clashed over control of the Sudan and the vital Nile water resources. After defeating the last of the Mahdist forces, in 1898, General Herbert Kitchener immediately sought to extend British control over the southern portions of the Sudan. Simultaneously, French forces, led by Captain Jean-Baptiste Marchand, who had marched from western Africa clear across the continent, had laid claim to the territory. Kitchener

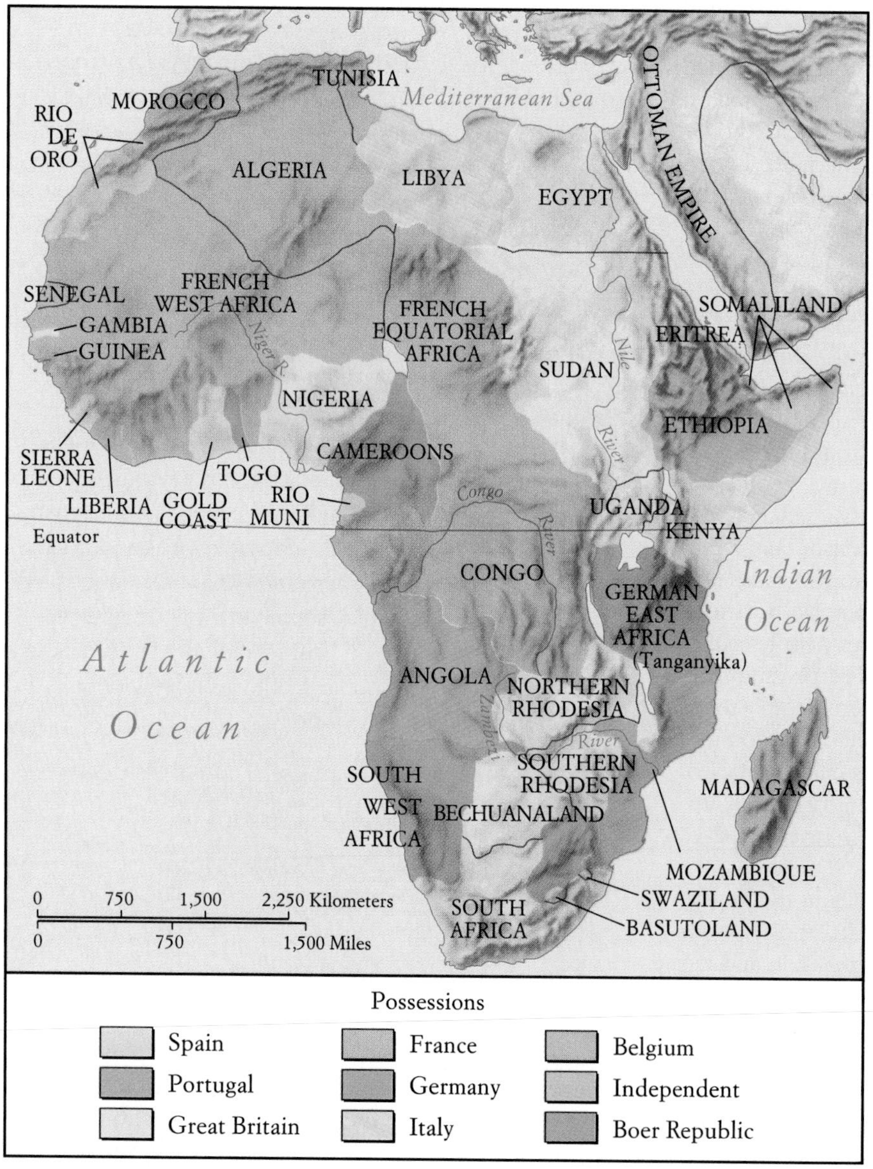

Map 13.1 Africa in 1914, after Partition. Almost all of the African continent was held by European powers by the outbreak of World War I. Great Britain and France held huge contiguous blocks of territory and some smaller possessions as well. Portugal, the oldest colonial power, had consolidated its string of trading posts into three colonies, while the late-arriving Germans and Italians had to settle for small, scattered holdings.

and Marchand met "eye-ball to eye-ball" in the remote Sudanese village of Fashoda, but Marchand was greatly outmanned, and Kitchener held the military balance of power. Seeking to defuse a crisis that threatened to turn into open warfare, French and British diplomats quietly met in Paris and London to settle control over the Sudan. Public opinion during the Fashoda crisis was whipped to a fever pitch; a belligerent music hall song expressed the mood in Great Britain:

We don't want to fight,
But by Jingo! if we do
We've got the ships,
We've got the men
And got the money, too!

World War I might have started in the Sudan had the British and the French come to blows. Those in each country who advocated going to war were known as "jingoists" and a new word for extreme and militant nationalists was added to the English language. Calmer minds prevailed in the Fashoda crisis, and a diplomatic settlement was reached whereby the British gained control over the Sudan and, in compensation, the French secured some small territories in West Africa. Similarly, competition between France and Germany over control of Morocco was settled by diplomacy and negotiations, and Morocco was ceded to France as a protectorate in 1912. Morocco was the last African territory taken over by Europe prior to World War I.

African Resistance

African societies did not accept outside domination without a struggle, and they often launched massive resistance movements against European intervention. Many Muslim African societies in particular led well-organized and effective struggles against foreign invaders. In the early nineteenth century, prior to European domination, a number of Muslim crusaders in West Africa had waged highly successful jihads or "holy wars" against African nonbelievers. One of the most successful of these militant Muslims, a Fulani named Usuman dan Fodio, commanded an empire in northern Nigeria and Cameroon that still existed when the British invaded that region in the 1890s. Usuman's brother, Abdullah, was an intellectual and poet who captured the religious fervor of the movement when he wrote: "The face of religion had become white after its nadir. And the face of unbelief has become black after dawning brightly. And religion is mighty, and on a straight way. Unbelief is in disgrace." The jihads in West Africa presaged Muslim reform and resistance movements in Libya, Sudan, and the Arabian

The Mahdi and General Gordon. The Mahdi, the Sudanese national hero, in an engraving by a European artist; juxtaposed is his archenemy, General Charles George Gordon, a British imperial hero, killed by the Mahdi's forces when they took the city of Khartoum in 1885. The British subsequently determined to avenge Gordon's death by eradicating the Mahdist movement and adding the Sudan to their imperial holdings.

(Left) Mansell Collection (right) Hulton/Deutsch Collection

Local History Museum's Collection, Durban

King Shaka. The Zulu king, Shaka, holds a lance and a large shield. A contemporary of Napoleon, Shaka forged a huge kingdom that opposed the expansion of both the Dutch Boers and the British into southern Africa.

Peninsula of a later era. Likewise, they are analogous to many militant Islamic movements in the contemporary age.

Muslim zealots in Algeria (discussed later in this chapter) and the Sudan led two of the most protracted struggles against European domination. In the Sudan, Muhammad Ahmad Abdullah (d. 1885), who declared himself the Mahdi (rightly guided one), unified Sudanese tribes under the banner of Islam to attack Ottoman, Egyptian, and British invaders. The Mahdi was both a religious and a Sudanese nationalist leader. His forces inflicted several humiliating defeats on the British and in 1885, after a protracted siege, took the Sudanese capital of Khartoum and beheaded the British commander, General George "Chinese" Gordon. Gordon, who had remained in the Sudan in spite of orders to retreat, became a martyr to the British imperial cause, and the British government vowed to avenge his death.

The Mahdi did not live long enough to enjoy or to consolidate the fruits of his victory; he died in 1885. His followers attempted to carry on the struggle but were weakened by drought, economic hardships, and internal divisions. In 1898 the British General Kitchener, a hero of several imperial campaigns, launched the successful invasion of the Sudan that led to the Fashoda crisis. Thousands of Sudanese were killed in the fighting. Kitchener eradicated the Mahdist movement, and the vast Sudanese territories were incorporated into the British Empire.

King Shaka Questions a European Envoy

The King told his visitors about the glories of his realm. His vast wealth in cattle of which they would get an idea on the morrow and the following days. His regiments which were the terror of all his enemies. The magnificence of his capital, Bulawayo. Then he very pointedly asked if Farewell and his companion had ever seen a more orderly governed State than his Zululand, or subjects who were more moral and law-abiding. . . .

*Thereafter he made many inquiries about King George, the size of his army, the nature of his government and country, the size of his capital and the number of his cattle and wives. He applauded the wisdom of his "brother" King in having only one wife. "That accounts for his advanced age; but he would have been wiser still to have none at all like myself."**

This passage from a biography of Shaka describes the first meeting between a British envoy, Lieutenant Farewell, and Shaka, the Zulu king. The meeting took place in 1825.

*E. A. Ritter, *Shaka Zulu* (Harmondsworth: Penguin, 1955), pp. 278–279.

The Ethiopians were more successful in repelling foreign invasions. In 1896 they soundly defeated the Italian invasion forces at Adowa. By cleverly playing off rival European nations, the Ethiopian emperors managed to secure arms and avoid any subsequent partition or takeover of their ancient nation. Ethiopia remained independent until the 1930s, when it fell to a new wave of Italian invaders.

The Zulus in South Africa also resisted foreign domination. In the early nineteenth century King Shaka, the able political and military Zulu leader, led his skilled warriors to subdue other tribes. At its zenith the Zulu kingdom was as large as all of western Europe. Although he often dealt with his enemies in a brutal fashion, Shaka was known for his sound political judgment. The Zulu kingdom expanded at the expense of weaker tribal groups, and for many who came under Zulu domination, Shaka's reign was known as the Mfecane, or "the time of troubles."

As a result of his successes, Shaka had the military power to deal with Western envoys as equals. He ex-

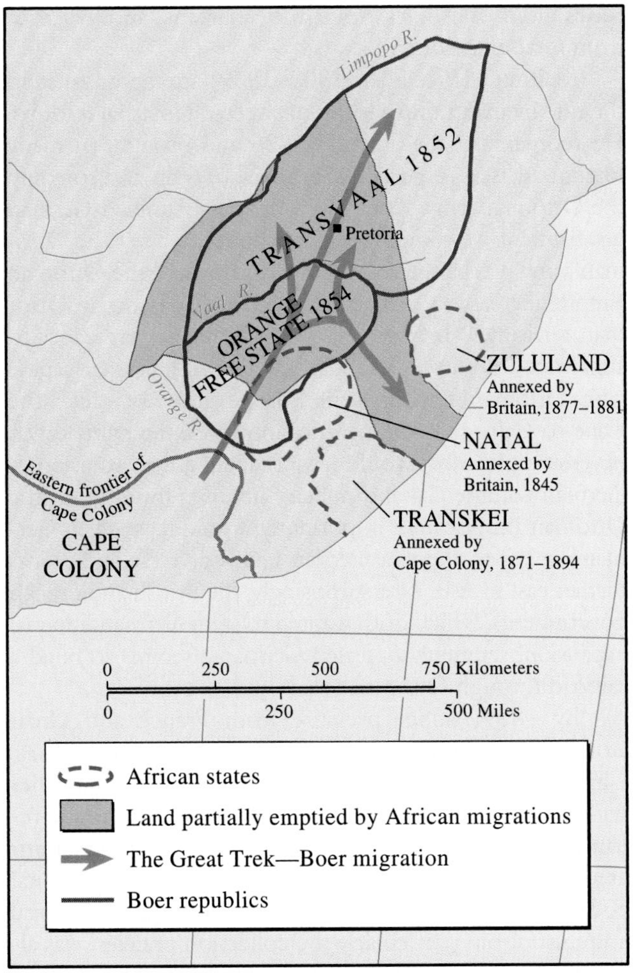

Map 13.2 Conflicting Claims in South Africa. A number of Bantu peoples lived in South Africa, but during the eighteenth century Dutch settlers, known as Boers, moved into the region and struggled with African tribes for control of the land. Then, in the 1800s the British began to incorporate valuable portions of South Africa into their empire. The Boers opposed the British, but were defeated by their enemy's superior military might.

pressed a keen interest in the Western world and was initially eager to establish mutually beneficial ties between his realm and Western nations. Like many absolute rulers, though, Shaka failed to create a peaceable system of succession. Thus, after his assassination by rivals, the Zulu kingdom was torn apart by internal disputes, which in turn weakened its ability to oppose Dutch and British expansion in South Africa.

The Boer War

The major military confrontation in Africa prior to World War I was not between European and African forces but between the British and the Dutch Boers in South Africa. This confrontation led to the Boer War (1899–1902). Great Britain had seized the Cape of Good Hope from the Netherlands in 1806 and gained permanent control of the land in 1815 at the end of the Napoleonic Wars. The Dutch settlers, or Boers (farmers) as they were called, resented both British domination and British emancipation of their African slaves. Seeking to evade British domination, in the 1830s and 1840s the Boers began a Great Trek, or mass migration, out of areas under British jurisdiction. In the 1850s the Boers created two independent nations, the Transvaal and the Orange Free State, which Great Britain did not recognize.

Attracted by fertile agricultural land and the discovery of gold and diamonds, increasing numbers of British settlers moved into the coastal areas and subsequently moved northward. The Boers opposed British expansion, discriminated against English settlers in their midst, and resorted to hit-and-run guerrilla tactics against British garrisons. Earlier these same guerilla tactics had been employed by the Zulu in their long but unsuccessful struggle against the Dutch settlers. Soon a full-scale war was in progress.

British forces, joined by units from Australia and commanded by General Kitchener, crushed the Boers' resistance by destroying their villages and rounding up families from entire districts and putting them into internment camps, thereby cutting off civilian support for the Boer fighters. Kitchener's tactics would subsequently be applied by others confronting guerrilla warfare, such as the French against the Algerians and the United States against the Viet Cong. Although the British failed to secure support from other Western nations in the war, they ultimately defeated the Boers. By 1902 the British had won, and in 1908 they incorporated Boer territories and English colonies in southern Africa into the Union of South Africa, granting it self-government within the British Empire.

Africa was not the only continent to be dominated by Western imperial nations, however. Imperial powers also sought to extend their control over Ottoman territories in western Asia and well as India, China, and Southeast Asia. The next section will describe how Western nations established empires in those far-flung regions.

Western Imperialism in the Middle East and Asia

Education, if it is good, produces perfection from imperfection, and nobility from baseness. If it is not good it changes the basic state of nature and becomes the cause of decline and decadence. This appears clearly among agriculturalists, cattle raisers, teachers, civil rulers, and religious leaders. . . .

This is why every people who enter into decline, and whose classes are overtaken by weakness, are always, because of their expectation of Eternal Grace, waiting to see if perhaps there is to be found among them a wise renewer, experienced in policy, who can enlighten their minds. . . .

*There is no doubt that in the present age, distress, misfortune, and weakness besiege all classes of Muslims from every side. Therefore every Muslim keeps his eyes and ears open in expectation—to the East, West, North, and South—to see from what corner of the earth the sage and renewer will appear and will reform the minds and souls of the Muslims, repel the unforeseen corruption, and again educate them with a virtuous education. Perhaps through that good education they may return to their former joyful condition.**

*Jamal al-Din al-Afghani, "Commentary on the Commentators," in *An Islamic Response to Imperialism: Political and Religious Writings of Sanjid Jamal al-Din "al-Afghani,"* ed. and trans. Nikki Keddie (Berkeley: University of California Press, 1968), pp. 123–129.

As in Africa, the spreading influence of Western politics, economics, and culture also threatened indigenous cultures in the Middle East and Asia in the nineteenth century. This crisis of identity was particularly intense in Islamic societies, where religious leaders and intellectuals grappled with the problems posed by Western mores and culture. In the above excerpt, Jamal al-Din al-Afghani (1839–1897), a Persian who spent most of his academic career in Egypt, described how Islamic societies felt threatened by Western advances. Al-Afghani was one of the many writers who sought to synthesize Islamic and Western cultures. Like many other writers in Asia, he placed particular emphasis on education as a means of spiritual and political renewal.

Ottoman Reforms and Territorial Losses

Western advances and technology particularly challenged the Ottoman Empire. By the nineteenth century the formerly great empire was in serious decline, and Tsar Nicholas I of Russia dubbed it the Sick Man of Europe. Extensive corruption on the highest levels was only one cause of Ottoman weakness. Officials often secured high positions in the bureaucracy, not through ability but by personal connections and bribery. The system of tax-farming, or hiring individuals to collect taxes, had resulted in many of the poorest and least powerful peasants paying absurdly high taxes, while wealthy landowners evaded payment by providing "kickbacks" to key officials or the tax collectors. At the same time, European nations, particularly Russia, the Austro-Hungarian Empire, and even Great Britain and France sought to wrest territories along the Black Sea, in the Balkans, and in Africa from Ottoman control.

Mahmud II (reigned 1808–1839) attempted to stem the tide by instituting a series of sweeping internal reforms. He reorganized the army in 1826 and brought in many foreign advisers, especially Germans, to train and to equip the Ottoman army. After 1870 the newly unified German government welcomed the opportunity to assist the Ottoman army. Exchanges between Germany and the Ottoman Empire increased German influence and presence in Ottoman territories. In particular, the Germans were eager to construct a Berlin-to-Baghdad railroad to link their capital with Ottoman territories in Europe and Asia. Like the Cape-to-Cairo railroad in Africa, however, the railroad was never completed. It would have facilitated the extension of German commercial and military interests throughout the Ottoman Empire and, importantly, would have given Germany access to the vital Persian Gulf waterway and points further east in Asia. Not surprisingly, the British and French governments, which both wanted to stem German imperial expansion, staunchly opposed German attempts to build a railroad through Ottoman territory.

By 1839, under pressure from France and Great Britain, the Ottomans issued the Declaration of the Rose Chamber, which guaranteed the security of minorities within the empire and launched widespread domestic reforms. From 1839 through 1876, Ottoman leaders initiated a series of reforms known as the Tanzimat: new legal codes were devised, education was encouraged, and local administration, particularly the collection of taxes, was altered along Western lines. These reforms were reiterated and widened under another formal declaration in 1856.

However well intended, Ottoman efforts at reform were hampered by two major difficulties: they were instituted from above and did not enjoy grassroots support; and they were often forced on the Ottomans by European nations and were, therefore, based on European political and social institutions. As a result, the reforms failed to take into consideration deep-seated religious and cultural attitudes of the predominantly Islamic population. Consequently, Ottoman reforms during the nineteenth century tended to affect only the minorities, particularly the Christians and Jews within the empire, or the elites in urban centers. Despite support from most of the intelligentsia and elites, who were often Western educated, the reforms had little or no impact on the vast majority of the rural population within the Ottoman heartland of the Anatolian Peninsula or the distant Arab provinces. As a result, the Ottomans were unable to regain their former strength. As the Ottoman Empire crumbled, European imperial powers continued to take over territories in the Middle East and Africa.

The British and French both took Ottoman territories in Africa. In 1830 the French moved into Algeria, which, although nominally an Ottoman territory, had historically been ruled by beys (provincial governors), who exercised considerable autonomy. Under Abdel Kader, a charismatic Muslim political and religious leader, the Algerians tenaciously fought French domination, but by 1847 they were forced to surrender to the superior French forces. Abdel Kader was exiled; he ultimately moved to Syria, where he heroically saved many Christian Syrians during riots in 1860.

Many European nations maneuvered to gain control of Egypt for its strategic geographic location. In Egypt, the French retained cultural and economic ties with Muhammad Ali, a janissary of Albanian origin, who had broken with the Ottomans to establish an autonomous government. When Muhammad Ali, with his newly equipped and trained army, defeated Ottoman forces in several decisive battles and moved to extend his authority over Palestine and Syria, the sultan obtained British and French assistance to perpetuate Ottoman rule in the eastern Mediterranean. In 1840, with French and British assent, Muhammad Ali and his heirs were recognized as the khedives or rulers of Egypt in exchange for withdrawing from Palestine and Syria; they also agreed to nominal recognition of Ottoman suzerainty over Egypt. His heirs continued to act as the real or titular rulers of Egypt until the monarch was overthrown in the 1952 revolution.

Muhammad Ali embarked on an ambitious program of industrial and agricultural development, for which he has often been called the founder of modern Egypt. Subsequent Egyptian khedives continued Muhammad Ali's plans to model the Egyptian economy, educational system, and building programs along Western lines. The Suez Canal was the result of the long-standing cooperation between the French and the Egyptian ruling family.

Ferdinand de Lesseps, a French engineer and financier, had long dreamed of building a canal to connect the Red Sea with the Mediterranean; with the political and financial support of the Egyptian khedive, de Lesseps constructed the canal using Egyptian labor and moneys secured from the sale of private shares in the Suez Canal Company. Although the British initially opposed the construction of a canal, after it was completed in 1869 and began to carry heavy traffic, the British government realized the canal's commercial and strategic importance. When huge expenditures for grandiose development schemes, including the Suez Canal, and personal extravagance by the khedive brought Egypt to the brink of bankruptcy, the British stepped in and took over Egyptian finances.

In 1882, the British military crushed a revolt led by nationalist Egyptian army officers. After some negotiations, the French agreed to the British occupation in exchange for British assent to French occupation of Tunisia in North Africa. Great Britain retained the khedive as the nominal ruler, but through political advisers and a continued military presence, the British controlled the Suez Canal and ruled Egypt. Under Muhammad Ali, Egypt had developed sufficient economic infrastructure to move it close to becoming an industrialized nation. The British, however, were primarily interested in Egypt for strategic reasons and secondarily for its agricultural materials, especially cotton. In an important reversal, they enacted economic restraints that essentially stopped the process toward industrialization; as a consequence of British policies Egypt remained primarily an agricultural country. The loss of Egypt was also a major defeat for the Ottoman Empire and demonstrated its pervasive weakness.

The Eastern Question

To the European powers, the issue of what should become of the ailing Ottoman Empire was known as the Eastern Question. Although the British and French both incorporated former Ottoman provinces into their own empires, they generally acted to keep the Sick Man alive in the eastern Mediterranean. With Austrian support, they protected the Ottoman sultan, not because they were close allies of the Ottomans but because they did not want the Russians to gain territorial advantages in

Abdel Kader. This engraving depicts Abdel Kader, the Algerian leader who struggled against the French occupation of his country for a quarter of a century.

Mansell Collection

the Black Sea or eastern Mediterranean. The British, and to a lesser extent the French, were particularly anxious that Russia, already in control of the northern shores of the Black Sea that had formerly been held by the Ottomans, not secure warm-water ports and control over the vital Dardanelles and Istanbul, which would increase its influence in the eastern Mediterranean. The Austrians, with imperial ambitions of their own in the Balkans, were also anxious to constrain Russian advances. On the other hand, Russia was anxious to see the Sick Man on his deathbed so that it could expand into eastern Europe and the Mediterranean.

Ottoman leaders recognized the intense rivalries among the European powers and frequently played European governments against one another in order to protect their own imperial interests. Ottoman relations with the various European powers regarding eastern Europe, the Black Sea, and the Dardanelles can be divided into three main phases. In the first phase, from approximately 1702 to 1820, the Eastern Question centered primarily on Russian expansion around the Black Sea. Russia successfully moved into the Black Sea region in 1772 and from that time onward looked toward the Mediterranean. Russian aims in the region alarmed Great Britain. When Napoleon conquered Egypt in 1798, the importance of the Middle East came into sharp focus for the British.

In the second phase, as the Ottoman Empire weakened, the interest of European nations turned to the Balkans, whose predominantly Orthodox Christian peoples, often the victims of Ottoman misgovernment, became increasingly nationalistic during the nineteenth century. The Greek Revolution of 1821 marked the beginning of the long and often bloody struggle for independence by the diverse peoples of the Balkans. Although poorly organized militarily, the Greeks enjoyed the support and sympathy of many Europeans, who admired and felt indebted to ancient Greek culture. The poet Byron and many others publicized and worked for Greek independence; indeed, Byron went so far as to enlist in the Greek struggle. The Greek war against the Ottomans dragged on until 1830, when Greece finally secured its independence along with guarantees for protection by the major European powers. Ottoman decay also enabled European imperial powers and ambitious local leaders to increase their power and influence in Ottoman territories. As previously noted, during the 1820s and 1830s Muhammad Ali had established an autonomous government in Egypt.

The third phase of the Eastern Question culminated in the Crimean War (1853–1856). Conflicting French and Russian aspirations over Christian holy sites in Palestine led to bitter disputes; as ruler over the territories and peoples in question, the Ottoman sultan should have settled the issue, but he was far too weak. It was during this dispute, when asked about the weakness of the Ottoman Empire, that Tsar Nicholas I remarked, "We have on our hands a very sick man."

When the dispute remained unresolved, Russia declared war against the Ottomans, and Great Britain and France joined in on the Ottoman side. Although the Russians won several decisive battles, high casualties on all sides, heavy costs, and bad weather combined to make the war increasingly unpopular. During the war Florence Nightingale (1820–1910), shocked by the high death rate among soldiers, personally went to the battlefield. Appalled by the lack of even rudimentary hygienic practices, she instituted modern nursing techniques that drastically reduced the death rate and marked the beginning of the Red Cross. After the death of Tsar Nicholas I, the

Victoria and Albert Museum

Muhammad Ali at the Citadel in Cairo. Once the Mamluks were inside the fortress, they were all massacred by Muhammad Ali's soldiers. The painting shown here depicts Muhammad Ali watching as his enemies are killed.

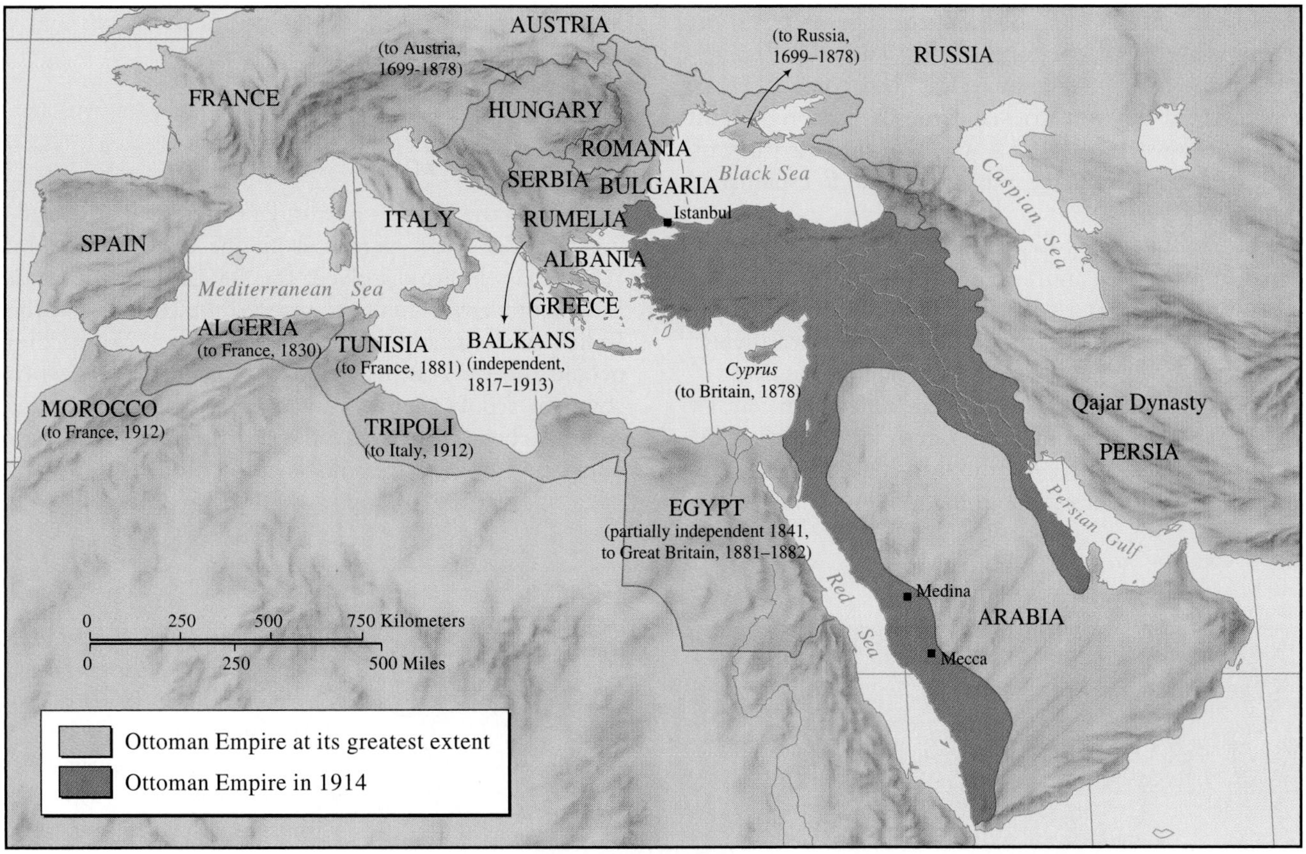

Map 13.3 Ottoman Territorial Losses, 1699–1912. The Ottoman Empire had lost most of its territories by the outbreak of World War I: North Africa to European powers, Black Sea areas to Russia, and the Balkan nations to independence movements. By 1914 the Ottoman Empire had shrunk to a small piece of Europe around Istanbul, the Anatolian Peninsula, the Arab provinces including Greater Syria and Iraq, and the holy cities of Mecca and Medina in the Arabian Peninsula.

new Tsar, Alexander II (reigned 1856–1880), agreed to peace negotiations. Great Britain, Austria-Hungary, and France agreed jointly to guarantee the political independence and territorial integrity of the Ottoman Empire. This great power protection helped the Ottoman Empire to survive until World War I.

Imperial Gains in Asia

At the same time the Europeans were expanding into Ottoman territory, they had also been continuing to extend their influence into the rest of Asia. Compared with the rapid takeover of Africa, European domination over Asia took more than four centuries to accomplish. Europeans initially went to India, China, and Japan to trade. Eventually, however, Western governments began to establish more direct controls over Asian territories. In the nineteenth century, superior British military forces defeated the independent princes of India, while the Russian armies conquered the principalities of central Asia. Persia and the great Chinese Empire, torn by internal disputes, were crumbling under foreign attacks.

The Qajar dynasty, which ruled Persia (present-day Iran) from 1779 to its overthrow in the 1920s, reacted to Western pressures and incursions in similar ways to the Ottoman sultans. Like Mahmud II in the Ottoman Empire, some Qajar shahs attempted internal reforms and supported modernization along Western lines. Western education was encouraged, and elite Iranians traveled, studied, and copied the West. Also like the Ottomans, however, the Qajars were often caught between the conflicting imperial ambitions of the British and the Russians. The Russians sought to expand along their southern border into the potentially rich oil fields of northern Iran. Distribution of crude oil from northern Iran had become a small industry by the end of the nineteenth century. As the industrialized nations converted to the use of internal combustion engines for transport systems, petroleum became a crucial source of energy and, in the twentieth century, was to become a crucial raw material for industries and transportation systems around the world. By 1914, when World War I began, the petroleum industry was already well established in Iran.

Great Britain was also interested in Iran both for the petroleum reserves and in order to maintain a presence in southern Iran as a protective buffer zone for British possessions further east, particularly India. Nevertheless, with its relatively more isolated geographic position vis-à-vis Europe, Persia at the end of the nineteenth century was subjected to less intense Western pressure than the Ottoman Empire. In 1907 the British and the Russians agreed to avoid a direct confrontation by dividing Persia into a Russian sphere of influence in the north and a British sphere of influence in the southeast.

India: The Jewel in the Crown of the British Empire

After 1603 the English East India Company began trading in India under permit from the Moghul Empire. When that empire dissolved, the (by-then) British East India Company virtually completed the conquest of the Indian subcontinent and controlled about 250 million people. In 1857 British control was challenged when company sepoys (native soldiers) rebelled over religious issues. Rebellion then spread in northern India for economic and political reasons and took fourteen months of heavy fighting to suppress. British control was not

A. Soudavar Collection; courtesy of the Freer Gallery of Art, Smithsonian Institution

Fath Ali Shah, Persia. This large painting (shown here in two sections) depicts the Qajar ruler, Fath Ali Shah (reigned 1797–1834), surrounded by his entourage of bejeweled courtiers and royal personages, including several high-ranking women.

again seriously threatened until Mohandas K. Gandhi's civil disobedience campaigns in the 1920s. The British government took control of the Indian territories from the company in 1858, ruling 60 percent of the subcontinent directly and the rest indirectly through Indian princes or maharajahs who were supervised by British representatives. India became the centerpiece of the British Empire, symbolized in the proclamation of Queen Victoria as Empress of India in 1876. A special ministry, the India Office, supervised the governing of the Indian subcontinent.

Control of India brought the British vast wealth, which contributed to a substantial rise in the living standards in England. British- and Indian-owned plantations produced indigo, jute, cotton, and tea. To exploit these products, the British built modern textile and steel mills in India and an extensive railroad network and later trunk roads and telegraph lines. India was perhaps more crucial to Great Britain as an importer of British goods than as a supplier of raw materials, however. Hundreds of millions of Indians bought British manufactured products, which entered India duty-free. Consequently, as in Egypt, British domination impeded the industrialization of India.

Several hundred thousand Britons controlled India, with a population of approximately 350 million in the early twentieth century. With its kaleidoscope of ethnic groups, languages, and religions, India was a geographic expression rather than a unified culture; it was further divided by historic animosities, especially between Hindus and Muslims. Thus the British found it relatively easy to persuade Indians of one background or religious affiliation to help them subdue or control Indians of another sect or group. Nepalese Gurkha troops were generally reliable, and many Bengalis and Sikhs, as well as others, aided British rule and received preferential treatment in return.

India also had a major impact on Great Britain. Events in India affected the lives and livelihoods of millions of Britons who never saw the subcontinent. Hundreds of thousands of Britons served in the military or government, and visited for business or pleasure. Many Indian words—bungalo and pajamas, for example—entered the English vocabulary; likewise, Indian foods such as curry became part of regular British cuisine.

Many Britons felt themselves racially and culturally superior to the Indians, as they did with other Asians and Africans; even the maharajahs were viewed as inferiors, capable of learning only the outer forms of Western culture. Rarely appreciating the philosophical, religious, and artistic contributions of India, British officials diligently sought to eradicate social abuses, especially the subjugated status of women. They eliminated the thuggees (a religious cult whose members killed and robbed as a religious act), banned suttee (the burning alive of widows), and tried to eliminate the practice of child brides. A few sympathetic Britons came to admire Indian culture and learning. After discovering Sanskrit's affinity with European languages, some began its scientific study, initiated archaeological investigations, and undertook the preservation of historic relics. These specialists in ancient Indian culture were called Indologists.

Thus, for Indians, as for Africans, British occupation had mixed results. Prior to British rule, the masses of Indians had lived an impoverished and illiterate life toiling for the benefit of their rulers; now they were often forced to toil for two sets of masters. As India was integrated into the world market economy, landlords planted cash crops, which meant less food. By improving sanitation and introducing public health measures, the British contributed to a population explosion. This further reduced the per capita food supply and contributed to periodic famines. A similar population growth, with parallel economic results, also occurred in Egypt.

Western civilization had a distinct impact on India. The great majority readily accepted Western science and technology, such as railroads and telegraph lines, but only a tiny minority embraced European culture. A few, such as Gandhi, also rejected much Western technology and argued that home-based "cottage industries," such as spinning cotton, would be a better way to raise the economic and social status of the poor. Those that chose to copy the British learned English, attained a rudimentary Western education, and adopted British dress and social customs. A small number of upper-class Indian males attended Western-style universities founded in India or were sent to Great Britain to attend elite schools and universities.

British-educated Indians argued that Great Britain should apply its principles of liberty in India. Some of them formed the Indian National Congress in 1885. At first, the Congress was primarily a debating and lobbying society, but after 1905 it began to organize mass demonstrations and boycotts against the British.

Christian missionaries had been active since the arrival of the Portuguese in 1498, but gained few converts; less than 2 percent of the population was Christian by 1900. A few Western-educated Hindus sought to reform regressive social aspects of Hinduism and organized societies to promote its reform. As in Africa and the Middle East, Muslims in India firmly resisted conversion, but formed organizations for social and political reforms later than the Hindus. Nevertheless, by the early twentieth century, Indian Muslims had also begun to advocate social reforms, Western education, and political organization.

Protecting India: Imperialist Confrontations in Asia

Much of Britain's imperial policy revolved around the protection of India. With that objective in mind, the

Mansell Collection

A Symbol of Imperial Power and Glory. The British monarch was also the emperor of India, and twentieth-century British kings went to India to be so crowned. In this scene at the 1911 *durbar* (court), King George V and Queen Mary, newly crowned king-emperor and queen-empress of India, receive the homage of the Indian princes amid a huge crowd of soldiers and onlookers.

British seized control of such strategic islands and ports as Ceylon (present-day Sri Lanka) and Aden to safeguard the trade routes between the subcontinent and Great Britain. By the end of the eighteenth century the British had eliminated the French threat to India, which was replaced in the nineteenth century by fear of Russian expansion in southern and central Asia.

In 1840 the French annexed Cochin China and by the end of the nineteenth century expanded its control over Cambodia, Laos, and the rest of Vietnam. The French thereby secured rubber, tin, and rice and in the process sought to spread Catholicism and French culture. This revival of French aspirations in Southeast Asia drew a quick British response. To create a buffer zone between India and French-controlled territories in Asia, the British took over Burma (present-day Myanmar) and expanded from Singapore onto the Malay Peninsula. Although conflicting imperial ambitions of the British and French overlapped, they avoided war by using Siam (present-day Thailand) as a buffer between their empires.

To the north and west of India, the British Empire faced the threat of expansionistic tsarist Russia. The Russians had moved steadily in Siberia and the southeastern steppes of central Asia during the nineteenth century and had incorporated the Muslim khanates near the Indian frontier. The Russians were also interested in Afghanistan and Iran as means of access to the Persian Gulf and Indian Ocean. Britain and Russia came close to war over Afghanistan, but the Boer War (1899–1902) and the Russo-Japanese War (1904–1905) forestalled the confrontation.

British Settlement of Australasia

British imperialism in Australia and New Zealand paralleled the pattern in British North America. The British conquered the Maori native population of New Zealand and pushed aside the Australian Aborigine people by the end of the nineteenth century. The British initially used parts of Australia as penal colonies, but most of coastal Australia and much of New Zealand were temperate areas that attracted many settlers from the British Isles and Europe. They originally came for sheep ranching and farming but quickly developed a mixed economy, including mining and manufacturing.

Remembering its North American experience, the British government granted its colonists in Australasia self-rule, unified the six Australian colonies into the self-governing Commonwealth of Australia in 1901, and created the equivalent for New Zealand in 1907. Labor governments brought in the welfare state in both nations, and women secured the vote by the 1890s, much earlier than in Europe or the United States.

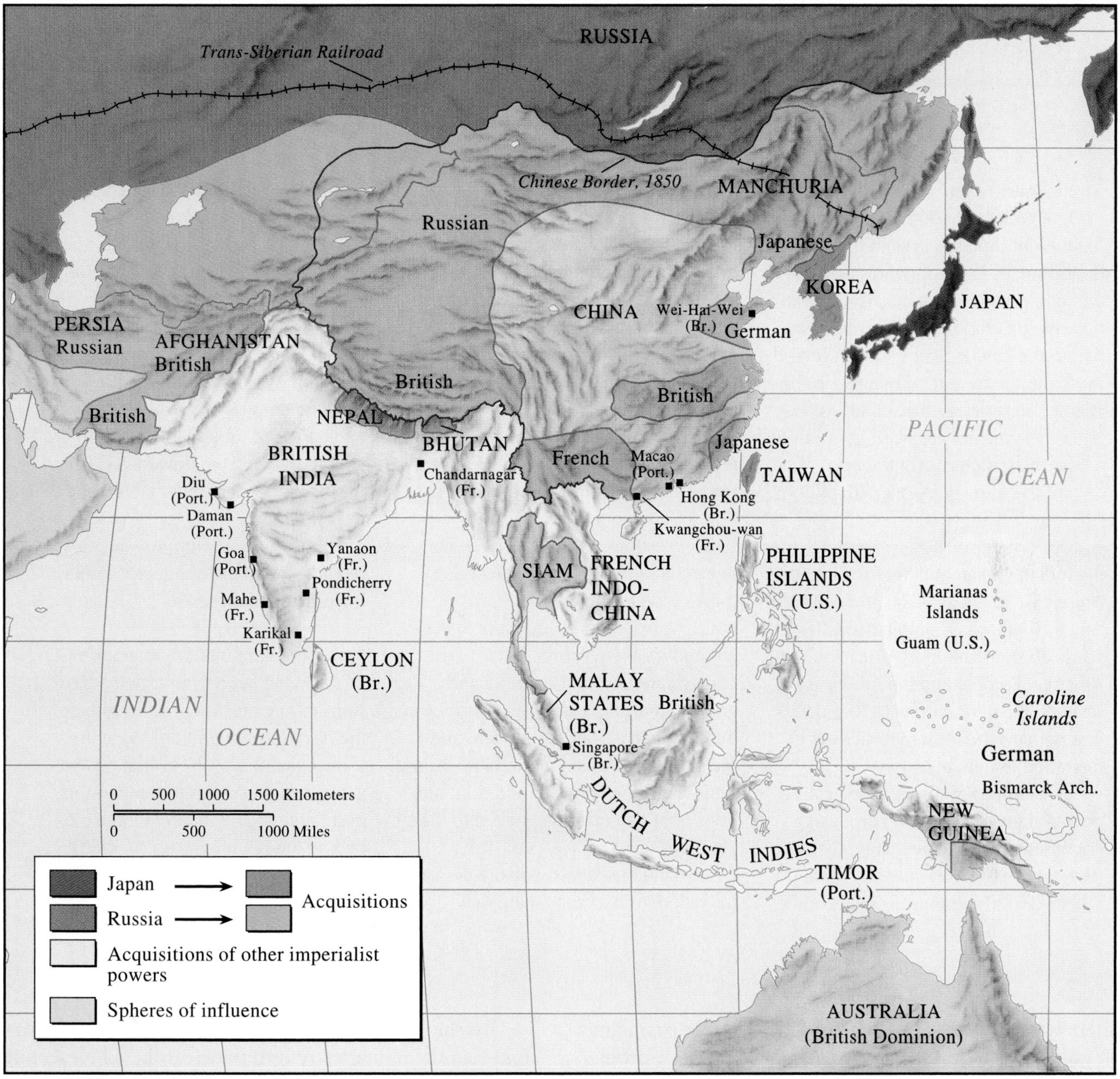

Map 13.4 Asia in 1914. Much of Asia was now controlled by imperial powers. Many areas of South and Southeast Asia were colonial possessions of the European nations and the United States. Independent states like Persia and China came under the control of foreign nations, which divided parts of those countries into their spheres of influence. Japan, the new imperialist power in Asia, had annexed Korea and the island the Japanese called Formosa (Taiwan); Japan also obtained a sphere of influence in China.

Great Britain, Germany, and the United States sought to extend their control over the Pacific, even though the economic value of the scattered islands of the area was slight, and most of them had little strategic value. By 1914 nearly all of the islands and coral atolls in the Pacific Ocean flew the flag of one of the imperialist nations.

The European Onslaught on the Ch'ing Empire in China

As discussed in Chapter 10, the Western nations became rivals for control over the vast Chinese Empire, the one great prize that had eluded them. Whereas Western traders sought tea, silk, porcelain and other commodities,

CONNECTIONS IN MIGRATION

Empire and Migration

In the seventy years from 1850 to 1920, well over 100 million people left their birthplaces in search of better opportunities in other countries. Most of the long-distance migrants, some 60 million, were European. Half of these settled in the United States. Others settled mostly in the Americas, but also in the Pacific, Australasia, Africa, and Asia. Still others moved eastward from Russia across the steppes of central Asia.

At the same time, over 40 million Chinese, Indian, Japanese, and other Asian workers and settlers moved across the Indian Ocean and the Pacific to the Americas, Southeast Asia, and parts of Africa. There was a simultaneous large-scale labor migration in Africa and Latin America, Europe, and the Americas. Overall, the period from 1850 to 1920 was perhaps the most intensive era of migration in human history.

This same era also saw several powerful governments in European countries invade, annex, and otherwise take control of lands in Asia, Africa, and the world's islands. Britain, France, Portugal, Germany, Russia, Japan, the United States, and Italy each expanded its imperial territories.

Empire building and migration were two major processes through which European societies—and societies based on European models—came to dominate the world in the nineteenth and twentieth centuries.

The British Empire, the dominant world power at this time, exemplified the patterns of both empire and emigration. Britain controlled areas known as "settler colonies," to which large numbers migrated from the home country; these colonies included Canada, Australia, New Zealand, and parts of eastern and southern Africa. Britain also consolidated its hold on India and gained control of vast new territories in the Middle East, Southeast Asia, and lower parts of Africa, though few Britons settled in those lands. In addition, millions of British migrants moved to the United States.

What caused this global wave of migration? What created the new empires? Were these two phenomena connected?

Emigration is the story of millions of individuals, whereas empire is the story of a handful of great powers and their societies.

Certainly the expansion of industrialization was important in both migration and empire. Steamships, railroads, and canals required labor for their creation and made the flow of goods and passengers easier. Other factors include the population explosion in many parts of Europe and Asia, improvements in medicine, and the conquest of many once-dreaded diseases.

---

1. Explore Unit 9 of the Migration CD-ROM. What factors contributed to decisions to migrate? What were some of the hazards of migration? What are some examples of the conditions migrants faced when they reached their destinations? Did different groups of people tend to migrate to specific places?

there was little that the Chinese wanted except payments in gold, silver, and furs. Trade with the West was a profitable but minor part of the Chinese economy, and the Manchu or Ch'ing Empire, like the Ming dynasty before it, permitted Westerners to trade only in the Canton area of South China.

In the nineteenth century, several major factors led to the accelerated decline of the Manchu dynasty: dynastic problems of leadership, rapid population increases that led to mass impoverishment and rebellions, spreading addiction to opium (a drug introduced by Westerners), and increasing Chinese resentment of ineffectual Manchu rule. Westerners and the Japanese began to see China not only as purchasers of manufactured goods but also as a source of coal, iron ore, and other industrial raw materials. The Chinese, unaccustomed to borrowing from other cultures, had done little to industrialize or to build up modern armed forces.

By the nineteenth century, powerful European nations had the military strength to defeat the Chinese, but mutual rivalries prevented any of them from annexing major parts of it. In a series of wars beginning in 1839 and ending in 1885, victorious British, French, German, and Russian forces defeated the Chinese Empire. The Chinese government was forced to accept a series of unequal treaties that compelled it to open ports, accept trade on Western nations' terms, permit the import of opium, cede territories, pay indemnities, and establish diplomatic relations with the victors.

The defeated Chinese had to surrender areas in central Asia, Manchuria, and the northeast Pacific coast to Russia. The British took Hong Kong and established a leading role in trade and shipping. France forced China to give up its overlordship of Vietnam, while Japan gained influence in Korea. Loss of territory on the fringes of the empire was secondary, however, compared with three disastrous impo-

E. Duncan, Nemesis Destroying Chinese War Junks, 1841; National Maritime Museum, London

British Warship Destroys Chinese Fleet. This is a battle scene from the First Anglo-Chinese War, 1839–1842.

sitions that the West forced on the Chinese: spheres of influence, fixed tariffs, and extraterritoriality (freedom of citizens of Western countries from Chinese laws). By the end of the century Great Britain, France, Germany, Japan, and Russia had divided most of China into spheres of influences. Each European nation and Japan had the exclusive right to secure and sell materials and commodities, build railroads, and develop ports in its sphere. Their gunboats patrolled the coasts and rivers of China to secure the spheres against competitors and to intimidate the Chinese into compliance. China was saved from partition only by fear among the Western powers and Japan that such attempts would lead to war with one another.

Western nations carved out "concessions" in Chinese ports, where their laws prevailed. Christian missionaries flocked into China to convert the Chinese. As in India, few Chinese converted, but Christian educators became an important force in changing China.

The unequal treaties were a humiliation to the heirs of a proud civilization. Anti-Western sentiment came to a head in 1900, when the Boxers, xenophobic people who practiced shadow boxing and hated Westerners and Westernized Chinese, took control of Peking. Supported by the ruling Dowager Empress Tz'u-hsi, who also hated foreigners, the Boxers besieged the foreign diplomatic section of the city, killing many, until an international relief expedition drove them off. As a result of the Boxer Rebellion, China was forced to pay an indemnity and make other concessions. The accumulated humiliations convinced many Chinese that the Manchu dynasty had to be replaced by a government strong enough to end foreign domination and lift China to equality among nations.

Like the Japanese earlier, progressive Chinese believed that China would have to develop Western technology and educational institutions. Chinese students went to the United States, Europe, and Japan to study, and some of them began to plan a revolution to overthrow the Ch'ing Empire and to establish a republic that would make sweeping changes. The next section will discuss the

Chinese Opposition to the Drug Trade

During the commercial intercourse which has existed so long, among the numerous foreign merchants resorting hither, are wheat and tares, good and bad; and of these latter are some who, by means of introducing opium by stealth, have seduced our Chinese people, and caused every province of the land to overflow with that poison. . . . Moreover, the great emperor hearing of it, actually quivered with indignation, and especially dispatched me, the commissioner, to Canton, that in conjunction with the viceroy and lieut.-governor of the province, means might be taken for its suppression!

Every native . . . who sells opium, as also all who smoke it, are alike adjudged to death. Were we then to go back and take up the crimes of the foreigners, who, by selling it for many years have induced dreadful calamity and robbed us of enormous wealth, and punish them with equal severity, our laws could not but award to them absolute annihilation.

We find that your country is distant from us about sixty or seventy thousand miles, that your foreign ships come hither striving the one with the other for our trade, and for the simple reason of their strong desire to reap a profit. . . .

We have heard that in your own country opium is prohibited with the utmost strictness and severity—this is a strong proof that you know full well how hurtful it is to mankind. Since then you do not permit it to injure your own country, you ought not to have the injurious drug transferred to another country. . . .

Your honorable nation takes away the products of our central land, and not only do you thereby obtain food and support for yourselves, but moreover, by reselling these products to other countries you reap a threefold profit. Now if you would only not sell opium, this threefold profit would be secured to you: how can you possibly consent to forgo it for a drug that is hurtful to men, and an unbridled craving after gain that seems to know no bounds! . . .

*P.S. We annex an abstract of the new law, . . . "Any foreigner or foreigners bringing opium to the Central Land, with the design to sell the same, the principals shall most assuredly be decapitated."**

In a letter that ironically foreshadows the drug problem in the modern West, commissioner Lin Tse-hsu, an official in the Chinese government, wrote to Queen Victoria in 1840 to denounce the British government for permitting its merchants to sell opium to China. Lin's letter is also revealing for its blunt discussion of the economic relationships between China and Great Britain.

**Chinese Repository*, vol. 8 (February 1840), pp. 497–503, in *Modern Asia and Africa*, ed. William H. McNeill and Mitsuko Iriye (New York: Oxford University Press, 1971), pp. 111–118.

emergence of Japan and the United States as major imperial powers and their quest for empire in the Western Hemisphere and Asia.

Japan and the United States Become World Powers

I am willing to admit my pride in this accomplishment for Japan. The facts are these: It was not until 1853 that we began to study navigation from the Dutch in Nagasaki; by 1860, the science was sufficiently understood to enable us to sail a ship across the Pacific. This means that about seven years after the first sight of a steamship, after only about five years of practice, the Japanese people made a trans-Pacific crossing without help from foreign experts. I think we can without undue pride boast before the world of this courage and skill. . . . *

*Eiichi Kiyowka, *The Autobiography of Yukichi Fukuzawa* (New York: Columbia University Press, 1966), quoted in Peter N. Stearns, ed., *Documents in World History*, Vol. 2 (New York: Harper & Row, 1988), p. 60.

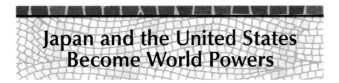

In his autobiography, the noted Japanese educator Yukichi Fukuzawa shows his pride in the rapid industrialization of Japan and its success in adopting Western technology. The founding president of an important university, he had contributed to this progress. As Japan and the United States became world powers in the nineteenth century, their growing pride and worldwide economic interests would cause them first to compete and later to clash over dominance in the Pacific and Asia.

The emergence of Japan as a world power was more disturbing to the Europeans than the rise of the United States. In one generation, Japan succeeded in transforming from a technologically backward state to one of the world's great powers. It then expanded in East Asia at the expense of China, Russia, and Korea and in competition with both the European nations and the United States.

Confronted in the 1850s by U.S. naval power and forced to open its ports and to sign unequal treaties, the Japanese leaders quickly realized that they would lose their independence unless they built up an industrial base and a modern military. Japan's cultural traditions permitted borrowing and adapting from other societies. More than a millennium earlier it had incorporated many aspects of Chinese culture; it now looked to adopt the best from the West.

In 1868 the Tokugawa shogun, whose government could not resist Japan's forced opening, was overthrown by new leaders who proclaimed loyalty to the young Meiji Emperor. They destroyed the power of the old military elite and embarked on a massive program of modernization. Japanese missions were sent to Europe and the United States to study Western technology, education, and government. Industrialists and entrepreneurs were encouraged to establish modern enterprises, becoming the new elite of the nation. Benefiting from government policies, private firms such as Mitsui expanded into zaibatsu, or vast conglomerates. To forestall labor unrest, the government also enacted welfare programs. Importantly, most Japanese workers were intensely loyal to their employers and, in contrast to workers in the West, rarely moved from job to job. In return, companies provided their employees with numerous social and welfare benefits. The Meiji government also established a universal education program that stressed loyalty to the emperor and nation. After studying governmental systems in the West, it adopted a constitution modeled after that of Germany.

By the end of the nineteenth century, Japan had built a powerful industrial base, a modern transportation system, and a large merchant marine. New schools had all but eliminated illiteracy and provided broad technological and vocational education to undergird their industrialization. Modern universities prepared the brightest young men for government service and managerial positions; women's colleges trained young women for modern professions in medicine, nursing, and teaching. Japan also constructed a large fleet of warships like Great Britain's and adopted conscription for an army like Germany's. Japan was the first Asian country that successfully pressured the Western powers to relinquish the unequal treaties.

The Japanese people paid a high price for the government's successes. They were subjected to a grinding discipline of long hours, low pay, heavy taxes, and a standard of living below that of the more affluent nations of the West. As in Great Britain, population increases had made Japan dependent on imported foodstuffs, and Japanese factories needed raw materials from abroad. As in the West, Japan's growing industrial output led it to seek overseas markets where it could sell its goods.

Japanese Imperialism

In an age of imperialism, Japanese leaders sought international recognition through expansion. Japan attacked China in 1894 in a dispute over Korea, a Chinese tributary state, and defeated it easily on land and sea. China was forced to give up overlordship of Korea, which allowed Japan to pursue its aggressive designs there; and to cede to Japan its island province of Taiwan (Formosa). In 1900, Japanese forces joined an international expedition sent to Peking to put down the Boxer Rebellion.

By 1904, Japan was ready to confront Russia. Russia had established a sphere of influence in northeastern China, in a region called Manchuria, where it had a naval base and an extension of the trans-Siberian railroad. Japan launched a surprise attack that destroyed the Russian Far Eastern fleet in 1904 and then drove the Russian army out of southern Manchuria. Later, in the Battle of Tsushima Straits, the Japanese navy inflicted a devastating defeat on the Russian Baltic fleet as it arrived off the Japanese coast. These victories astonished Western observers and earned their respect, but more importantly the Japanese defeat of a major Western power electrified other Asians and gave them hope that Western imperialism was not invincible. In the peace treaty that ended the Russo-Japanese War (brokered by U.S. president Theodore Roosevelt), Russia ceded to Japan southern Sakhalin Island and its spheres of influence in southern Manchuria. It also agreed to keep its hands off Korea. Japan annexed hapless Korea in 1910.

The Rise of the United States

By the nineteenth century, Americans had become one of the most affluent peoples on earth. The United States was virtually self-sufficient in food and led the world in agricultural exports, iron ore and coal output, iron and steel production, and railroad mileage. Its manufacturing output had increased so markedly that it was rapidly catching up to the leading European industrialized nations.

However, the economic boom also created new social problems. Periodic labor strikes and boycotts led to increased unionization among American workers; farmers

Mansell Collection

Technological Imperialism. The Panama Canal, here shown under construction, was the engineering marvel of the early twentieth century. Cut through a mountain range and operated by means of a system of hydraulic locks, it was a much greater technological feat than the Suez Canal, which was essentially a ditch through flat terrain. The Panama Canal, opened in 1919, was the realization of centuries of hope by those in international commerce for a direct connection between the Atlantic and the Pacific.

also organized politically and formed the Populist party to push forward their demands for social change. Racism and opposition to new immigrants from eastern Europe also continued to divide the society. Urban and rural reformers sought to institute welfare projects that were often rejected by the more conservative courts. The Progressive movement, which advocated a number of reform measures, also attracted numerous supporters in the early twentieth century. Progressive leaders wanted to increase the powers of state and national governments while regulating big business and the economy. The progressive movement was instrumental in obtaining the graduated income tax, the regulation of food and drug standards, and in improved public services.

The United States Becomes an Imperialist Power

By 1900 the United States stood on the threshold of great-power status. It was the fourth most populous nation, and its residents were the most literate and longest-lived in the world. In general, the average U.S. citizen's standard of living equaled that of the citizens of the major powers of western Europe. The government, relatively stable, was dominated by white males who enjoyed suffrage and constitutionally protected individual rights.

Despite its self-sufficiency in many areas, the United States was typical of other rapidly industrializing nations in that it increasingly looked overseas for raw materials, consumer products, and markets. Protected by two oceans from would-be enemies, the United States possessed only a small army. However, to protect its expanding overseas commerce, it built the third largest navy in the world. Many Americans opposed overseas expansion, but by 1900 those favoring expansion were in the ascendancy.

The Caribbean Becomes a U.S. Lake

Mexico, the Caribbean, and South America were the first regions to feel the effects of U.S. expansionism. As an imperialist power, the United States was primarily interested in dominating the Western Hemisphere. U.S. policy had three goals: prevent European domination over the Caribbean, obtain land for a canal across Central America, and dominate trade with Latin America and Canada. The United States was able to achieve its goals because no nation in the Americas was strong enough to oppose it, and most European nations, preoccupied with imperialist ventures in Asia and Africa, chose not to interfere with U.S. interests in the Western Hemisphere.

In the five years between 1898 and 1903, presidents William McKinley and the staunch imperialist Theodore "Teddy" Roosevelt took control of the Caribbean. In a "splendid little war" brought on by tensions over Cuba, where declining Spanish power was challenged by local unrest, the United States defeated Spain and forced it to give up Cuba and Puerto Rico, its two last possessions in the New World. Whereas the United States retained Puerto Rico and built naval installations there, it allowed Cuba nominal independence but turned it into an economic and political protectorate, extracting from Cuba a perpetual lease of the strategic Guantánamo Bay for a naval base.

These new bases in Puerto Rico and Cuba enabled the United States to become the major naval power in the Caribbean by 1901. Great Britain agreed to withdraw its naval forces from the Caribbean in return for a U.S. pledge that the British would have unencumbered rights to use any future canal across Central America.

In 1903 the United States supported a separatist movement in the Colombian province of Panama. Once freed, Panama promptly granted the United States the right to complete a canal started earlier and abandoned by a French company, and also granted the United States the further right to control in perpetuity a thirteen-mile strip on either side of the Canal. The new Panama Canal, opened to international traffic in 1914, was an impressive multilock project cut through mountains. U.S. medical authorities also eliminated the scourge of yellow fever in the canal zone

Although many Americans viewed the Caribbean as *mare nostrum,* "our sea," the United States was not completely secure in the Caribbean, as was demonstrated when a combined European fleet led by Germany bombarded Venezuela in 1902 for violating its treaty and defaulting on its loan obligations to them. Fearing more European interference in Latin America, the United States modified its 1823 Monroe Doctrine, which opposed European expansion into the Western Hemisphere. The new Roosevelt Corollary to the doctrine stated that if Latin American nations exhibited "chronic wrong-doing," the United States would exercise international police power and intervene to make financial reforms and restore order. European nations would thus have no legitimate reason to intervene. The Roosevelt Corollary succeeded in its purpose. European nations avoided any future interventions and did not challenge U.S. military control over the region.

The United States increased its share of trade and investment in Latin America through its "Dollar Diplomacy," whereby Latin American governments were pressured to support U.S. business interests in their nations. U.S. businessmen accordingly made extensive investments in Latin American petroleum, copper, coffee, fruit, rubber, tin, sugar, and other products. By 1913 the United States had displaced Great Britain as the leading exporter to Latin America. With many valuable investments and markets, U.S. businessmen were eager to maintain orderly, pro-American governments in power in the region, an example being the compliant dictator Porfirio Diaz in Mexico.

Sometimes having friends in high places was not enough. Thus when periods of disorder swept Latin American nations, the U.S. government would intervene militarily. Between 1903 and 1934 it sent armed forces one or more times into six nations in the Caribbean, occupying three of them for more than a decade.

U.S. wealth and power generated fear and hatred throughout the Caribbean. To many upper-class Latin Americans, Yankee Imperialism by the Colossus of the North was an affront and an injury to their national sovereignty. By openly backing dictators, the United States also became a party to the exploitation of the masses. Consequently, many Latin American reformers and revolutionaries viewed the United States as an enemy to domestic social change and revolution.

The United States and Canada

The United States also periodically showed interest in expansion north of the border. Ever since the War for Independence many Americans wished to bring Canada into the Union. In 1867 the British Parliament passed a bill that united its colonies in North America and the Hudson's Bay Company into a federation called the Dominion of Canada. Through a process called devolution, early in the twentieth century Great Britain allowed Canada to

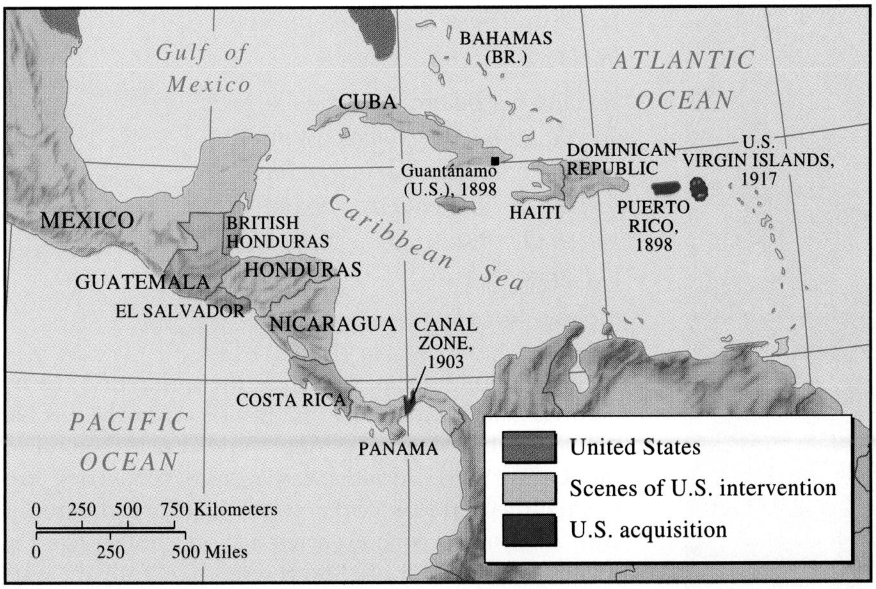

Map 13.5 U.S. Imperialism in the Caribbean to 1934. The United States secured firm control of the Caribbean region during the early twentieth century. By acquiring bases in Cuba and Puerto Rico and controlling the Panama Canal, the United States strategically dominated the region and enforced its supremacy by intervening in or occupying for varying periods most Latin American nations in the area. Some, like Nicaragua, were taken over several times.

assume control of its external affairs. U.S. businesses continued to invest heavily in Canada, accounting for almost one-quarter of its foreign investments in 1914. Great Britain, however, still remained Canada's major trading partner.

U.S. Expansion in Asia

From its inception, the United States had been interested in the China trade. By 1900 the United States had assumed a major role in the Pacific, with possessions that extended from Alaska to Samoa, including a string of island stepping-stones leading from the west coast of the United States through the Hawaiian Islands (annexed in 1898) to the Philippines. Like the Cubans, the Filipinos had begun to fight a guerrilla war for independence from Spain during the Spanish-American War. The United States, for a mixture of strategic, economic, and cultural reasons, refused to allow the Filipinos independence and acquired the islands from Spain at the end of the war. President McKinley even went so far as to announce that God supported U.S. control over the Philippines.

In 1899 Filipino nationalists revolted against U.S. rule and waged a protracted guerrilla war at an enormous human and economic cost; but they lost. The United States established its largest overseas naval base at Subic Bay in the Philippines to safeguard its Asian interests.

Imperialism in Asia. U.S. troops engaged in suppressing the insurrection in the Philippines are shown after a massacre of lightly armed Filipinos. The insurgents had originally been fighting for their independence against the Spanish; when they found that the United States was going to hold the Philippines rather than grant independence, they also fought the Americans, but were eventually defeated.

Culver Pictures

Because the United States was interested in maintaining its share of the China trade, it proposed an Open Door policy of equal trading opportunity for all foreign nations in China in 1899. The European nations and Japan did not formally agree to the Open Door, but for fear of offending the United States, none openly rejected the principle. U.S. businessmen, engineers, and missionaries became increasingly active in China in the twentieth century, and U.S. gunboats patrolled China's major rivers to protect them. Unequal treaties imposed on China allowed Americans to enjoy the same extraterritorial immunity from Chinese laws as did the Europeans. Similarly, Westerners enjoyed immunity from local laws in Persia and the Ottoman Empire.

By the twentieth century, peoples under imperial control began to form political and economic organizations to combat foreign domination and to achieve national independence. Later chapters will describe the mounting opposition by Asian and African peoples to Western and Japanese imperial domination.

The Causes and Course of World War I

In Flanders Fields the poppies blow
Between the crosses, row on row,
That mark our place; and in the sky
The larks, still bravely singing, fly
Scarce heard amid the guns below.

We are the Dead. Short days ago
We lived, felt dawn, saw sunset glow,
Loved and were loved, and now we lie
In Flanders Fields.

Take up our quarrel with the foe:
To you from failing hands we throw
The torch; be yours to hold it high.
If ye break faith with us who die
We shall not sleep, though poppies grow
*In Flanders Fields.**

*John McCrae, *Punch,* December 6, 1915.

This haunting poem, written in the spring of 1915 by a Canadian physician at the front, evokes the terrible loss of life that occurred during World War I (then called the Great War). Months earlier most countries had greeted the outbreak of the war with relief and enthusiasm. Almost everyone expected a short conflict like the Austro-Prussian War of 1866 and more recently the wars in the Balkans. Economists strengthened this line of

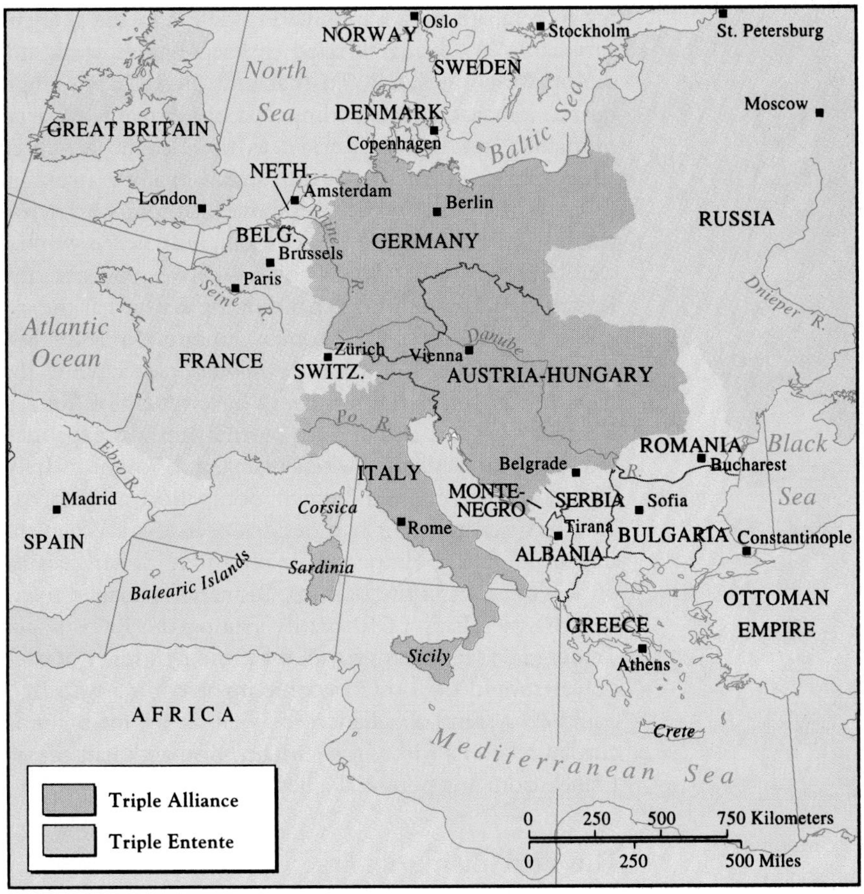

Map 13.6 Europe in 1914. The map shows the alliance systems before the war. Germany, Austria-Hungary, and Italy formed the Triple Alliance, while France, Russia, and Great Britain made up the Triple Entente. Italy refused to join Germany and Austria-Hungary in August 1914, ultimately selling its services to the highest bidder—the Entente.

thinking by predicting that the heavy cost of modern war could not be borne by any participant for very long. No one dreamed that the war would last four years, drain the energies of the belligerents, and ultimately involve many nations outside Europe. Nor did anyone foresee that the war would wreck the order and stability of Europe, leaving its people to face a forbidding future.

The Underlying Causes of the Conflict

The origins of World War I are complex and cannot be explained solely on the basis of the events that immediately preceded it. Fundamentally, the Great War was the product of destructive forces whose roots go far back into history. Among the deeper causes of the war were nationalism, the arms race and militarism, and the alliance system.

Nationalism, with its roots in the era of the French Revolution, had increased significantly during the second half of the nineteenth century. While the Germans and Italians had achieved nationhood, other groups had not. The divisive effect of ethnic nationalism was particularly evident in the Habsburg Empire. The Dual Monarchy of Austria-Hungary kept the Slavs in the empire subordinate to the German Austrians and the Magyars of Hungary. By the turn of the century, Slavic nationalists, having concluded that their people would never acquire equal status, intensified their efforts to secede from the Austro-Hungarian Empire. Such an event would permit some Slavic elements like the Czechs to set up their own independent state and others like the South Slavs (Croats, Slovenes, and Serbs) to join the national state of their kin, Serbia, across the border. Freed from Ottoman rule in 1878, Serbia had dreams of a greater Serbia that would include the South Slavs not only in Austria-Hungary but in Bosnia and Herzegovina as well. Since Serbia was weaker than Austria-Hungary, it launched a covert campaign of agitation and subversion designed to undermine and ultimately destroy the integrity of the Dual Monarchy.

The atmosphere of suspicion and fear after 1870 gave rise to a bitter and costly armaments race. In the name of national security, Western states vied with one another in strengthening their armies and navies. Huge sums were spent on military equipment and ships, and all the major powers, except Great Britain and the United States, adopted conscription. German and Austrian military spending doubled between 1910 and 1914, and the expenditures of other powers increased markedly. By 1914, Germany and France each had about 800,000 men in uniform with millions of trained reservists. The military buildup on land was accompanied by a naval race between Great Britain and Germany. When, in 1906, Great Britain launched a new, superior class of battleships with

Corbis-Bettmann

Powers of Europe and the Balkans. This 1912 cartoon in *Punch* shows the European powers acting in unison to prevent the lid from blowing off the Balkans.

the *Dreadnought,* Germany followed suit. Such contests not only drained national reserves but stirred hostility and distrust.

The arms race also led to growing militarism—a spirit that exalts military virtues and ideals—which conditioned people to view war as a glorious adventure essential to human progress. Such an outlook profoundly affected foreign policy, as political leaders more frequently sought and took the advice of army and naval officials. This was particularly evident during the summer of 1914, when governments, confronted by the inflexibility of their generals, often made decisions based on military rather than political considerations.

Besides strengthening their military capability, the European powers forged alliances among themselves in the hopes of deterring aggression and preventing war. But belonging to an alliance carried unforeseen risks and increased the chances that a local conflict would spread into a general war.

Bismarckian Diplomacy

Chancellor Otto von Bismarck of Germany originated Europe's system of alliances. Fearing that France might try to retaliate for its humiliating defeat in the Franco-Prussian War, Bismarck tried to keep France weak and diplomatically isolated. To that end, in 1873, he engineered a major alliance, composed of Germany, Austria-Hungary, and Russia. Known as the League of Three Emperors, it committed the signatories to maintain friendly neutrality in the event one of them was at war with a fourth power. That combination never worked well because of the growing rivalry between Austria and Russia as each sought to expand in the Balkans at the expense of the declining Ottoman Empire. In 1879 Bismarck negotiated a defensive military agreement, the Dual Alliance, with the Habsburg government of Austria-Hungary. Two years later the partnership was expanded into the Triple Alliance when Bismarck brought in Italy, which deeply resented French occupation of Tunis in North Africa, where it had designs of its own. When the League of Three Emperors finally broke down because of new tensions in the Balkans, Bismarck managed to retain the friendship of Russia by signing the Reinsurance Treaty (1887), which provided for the neutrality of each power should the other become involved in a war. By a complex system of alliances as well as by maintaining cordial relations with Great Britain, Bismarck had cut off France from any potential allies.

The Post-Bismarck Era

After 1890 the alliance system drove Europe toward war rather than preserving the peace. The impetuous new German emperor, Kaiser William II (reigned 1888–1918), dismissed Bismarck, changed the direction of Germany's foreign policy, and allowed the Reinsurance Treaty to lapse. This unexpected turn of events prompted France to solicit the friendship of the Russians, offering, as an inducement, arms and large loans. The resulting rapprochement led to a defensive pact between France and Russia in 1894.

France scored another diplomatic triumph ten years later when it buried its differences with Great Britain and signed the Entente Cordiale. This accord was a friendly understanding to reconcile points of contention and not a formal military alliance. The next logical step for the French was to bring together Britain and Russia, two traditional enemies. The timing was propitious. Badly defeated by the Japanese, the Russians wanted to reestablish their position in Europe. The British, with the threat of Russian aggression in Asia removed, were more concerned about Germany's uncertain aims. The upshot was the Anglo-Russian Entente of 1907. Again, no provision was made for mutual military assistance, but the parties' conciliatory attitude made cooperation easier. The agreement completed the three-power bloc of France, Russia, and Great Britain, which came to be known as the Triple Entente.

Stock Montage

The Last Ride. Francis Ferdinand and his wife, Sophie, have just left the Sarajevo City Hall and taken seats in the rear of a car minutes before their assassination. While on their way to visit a hospital, they were both shot by a young Bosnian who had been stirred to fever pitch by Serbian propaganda.

Conflicts and Compromises, 1907–1914

Between 1907 and 1913 crises resulting from suspicions and national rivalries threatened to embroil the major European powers in a general war. Although in each instance solutions were found and major warfare avoided, these crises tended to solidify the alliance systems and to widen the gulf separating the two camps.

In 1911 Germany protested France's penetration of Morocco, and for a time the two powers stood on the brink of war. The Germans had raised similar objections six years earlier, but an international conference at Algeciras, Spain, had ruled in favor of France. This time the Germans held their ground, and at the eleventh hour the French backed down. They gave the Germans a slice of the French Congo in return for recognition of their rights to Morocco.

The other hot spot was in the Balkans. In 1908 Austrian annexation of Bosnia and Herzegovina infuriated both Serbian nationalists, who hoped to create an enlarged Slavic state, and the Russian government, which had imperial ambitions of its own in the region. When Germany came to Austria's support, Serbia and Russia were forced to yield. In 1912 four Balkan states joined forces to oust the Ottoman Turks from the region in the First Balkan War. They won a succession of victories and were about to overrun Istanbul when the great powers intervened to prevent the total collapse of the Ottoman Empire. At the peace conference, the Ottoman Empire was stripped of all its territory in Europe except Istanbul and its environs. The ink on the treaty was barely dry when the victors clashed over the distribution of the spoils. The Second Balkan War erupted in 1913 and, although it was over quickly, the Balkans remained a politically unstable region.

Rather than inducing the European powers to exercise greater caution, these recurring crises convinced them that they should take all steps to avoid a repetition of past failures. By 1914, national rivalries, sharpened by the feverish arms race, had brought tensions in Europe to a highly combustible state. Only a spark was needed to set off the explosion.

Archduke Francis Ferdinand's Assassination Leads to War

On June 28, 1914, the Archduke Francis Ferdinand, heir to the Austrian throne, and his wife were shot to death as their motorcade drove through the streets of Sarajevo, capital of Bosnia. The assassin, Gavrilo Princip, was the tool of a secret Serbian terrorist society, the Black Hand, dedicated to unifying all South Slavs under Serbian rule. The Archduke became a victim of the Black Hand because it was widely believed that he wanted to place the Slavs on the same autonomous footing as the Germans and Magyars within the Habsburg Empire. Such a policy would have caused the South Slavs in the Austrian Empire to lose their enthusiasm for union with Serbia. The murder plot had been hatched in Belgrade, the Serbian capital, and was the brainchild of the chief of intelligence of the Serbian army. Though not directly involved in the conspiracy, members of the Serbian government knew of it but took no effective steps to foil it or to forewarn Austrian authorities.

The Austrians saw the assassination as a chance to settle accounts with Serbia once and for all. Before taking punitive action, they sought support from their ally, Germany. The kaiser and his advisers believed that Austria required the complete support of Germany if it was to survive as a great power and be an effective partner in

Austria's Reaction to the Serbian Reply

The Austrian Ambassador to the British Foreign Office, July 27, 1914:

The Royal Serbian Government has refused to agree to the demands which we were forced to make for the lasting assurance of those of our vital interests threatened by that Government, and has thus given evidence that it is not willing to desist from its destructive efforts directed toward the constant disturbance of some of our border territories and their eventual separation from the control of the Monarchy. We are therefore compelled, to our regret and much against our will, to force Serbia by the sharpest means to a fundamental alteration of her hitherto hostile attitude. That in so doing, aggressive intentions are far from our thoughts, and that it is merely in self-defense that we have finally determined, after years of patience, to oppose the Greater Serbia intrigues with the sword, is well known to the Imperial German Government.

It is a cause of honest satisfaction to us that we find both in the Imperial German Government and in the entire German people a complete comprehension of the fact that our patience was of necessity exhausted after the assassination at Sarajevo, which, according to the results of the inquiry, was planned at Belgrade and carried out by emissaries from that city; and that we are now forced to the task of securing ourselves by every means against the continuation of the present intolerable conditions on our southwestern border.

*We confidently hope that our prospective difference with Serbia will be the cause of no further complications; but in the event that such should nevertheless occur, we are gratefully certain that Germany, with a fidelity long proven, will bear in mind the obligations of her alliance and lend us her support in any fight forced upon us by another opponent.**

In the days following Austria's ultimatum, Great Britain took the lead among European states in pressing the Habsburg government to refrain from attacking Serbia. In this note, authorities in Vienna seek to justify the coming invasion of Serbia. The Austrians were worried about the attitude of Great Britain, which, as yet, had refused to give any firm pledge to assist the entente in case of war. The hint of full German backing was evidently intended to dissuade the British from abandoning their position of neutrality.

*Max Montgelas and Walter Schücking, eds., *Outbreak of the World War: German Documents Collected by Karl Kautsky*, trans. Carnegie Endowment for International Peace (New York: Oxford University Press, 1924), no. 268, p. 249.

the alliance. They urged the Austrians to take vigorous action against Serbia even though it could lead to a European war. They believed a major war was inevitable and that Germany was in a better position to fight now than it would be in several years when Russia and France would be stronger as a result of army reforms. Fortified by Germany's "blank check," Austria delivered an ultimatum to Serbia, couched in terms calculated to make its rejection certain. The Serbians were unexpectedly conciliatory, but Austria deemed the reply unsatisfactory and on 28 July declared war on Serbia. The Austrians wanted to localize the conflict, hoping that Germany's unqualified support would deter the Russians from helping Serbia.

Within a week, however, Austria's military initiative brought about a general war. Russia, assured of French support, ordered immediate full mobilization because it required more time to get its military machine into operation than did either Austria or Germany. For the Germans, Russia's mobilization was equivalent to an act of war. Germany's Schlieffen plan—devised by Count von Schlieffen, chief of the general staff from 1891 to 1906—envisaged a two-front war against Russia and France. It called for a holding action against the slowly mobilizing Russians while the bulk of the German army drove through Belgium in order to outflank France's frontier defenses, encircle Paris, and fall behind the French forces in the south. The full strength of the German army could then be directed against the Russians. Thus Germany could not permit Russia to mobilize first. When the tsar refused to heed a warning from Berlin to stop military preparations, Germany declared war on Russia on August 1. Two days later, the kaiser's government declared war on France, having concluded that France was almost certain to come to the aid of its Russian ally.

Maps 13.7 and 13.8 Western and Eastern Fronts, 1914–1918. After initial victories on the western front, the Germans became bogged down in protracted trench warfare where little territory changed hands for over three years. On the eastern front, shown on the map below, the German army drove up into Russian territory and inflicted severe losses on the Russian army.

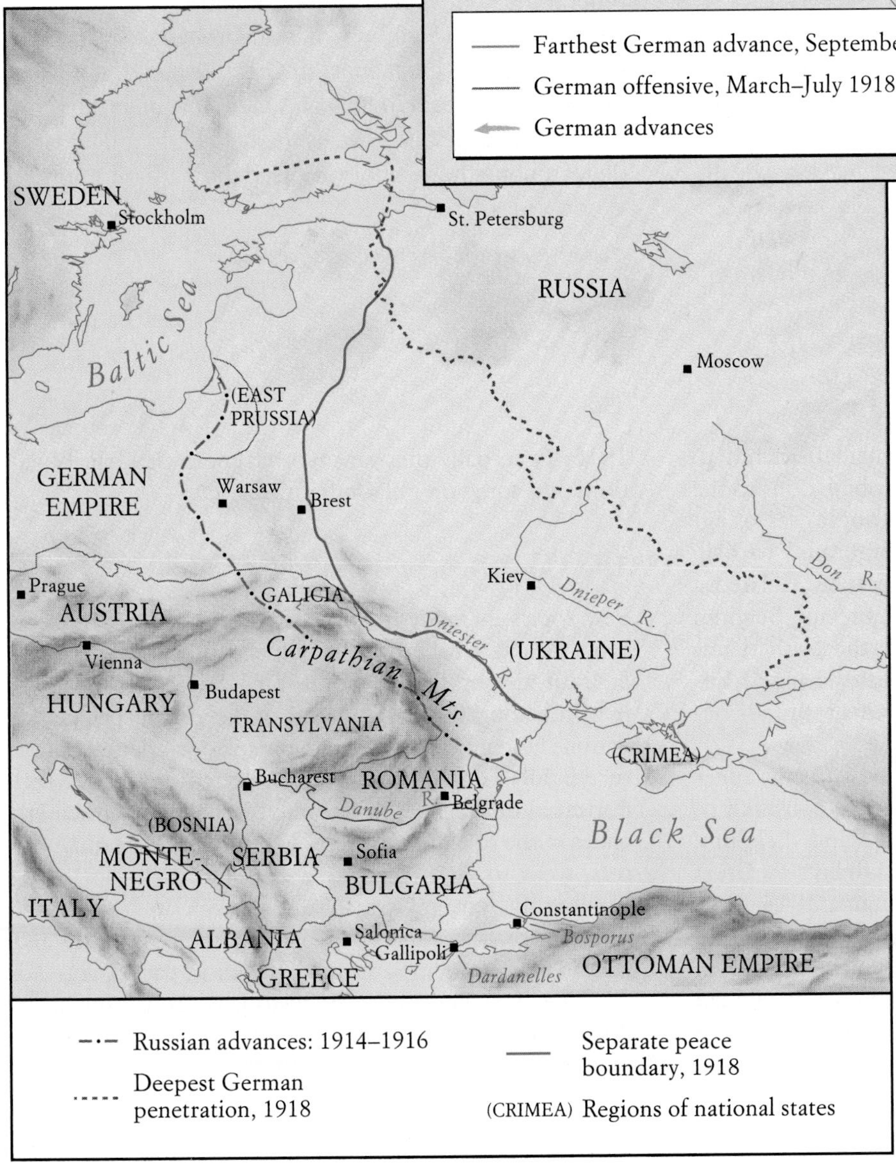

Life in the Trenches

Patriotism, in the trenches, was too remote a sentiment, and at once rejected as fit only for civilians, or prisoners. A new arrival who talked patriotism would soon be told to cut it out. . . . Great Britain . . . included not only the trench-soldiers themselves and those who had gone home wounded, but the staff, Army Service Corps, lines-of-communication troops, base units, home-service units, and all civilians down to the detested grades of journalists, profiteers, "starred" men exempted from enlistment, conscientious objectors, and members of the Government. The trench-soldier, with this carefully graded caste-system of honour, never considered that the Germans opposite might have built up exactly the same system themselves. . . .

*Hardly one soldier in a hundred was inspired by religious feeling of even the crudest kind. It would have been difficult to remain religious in the trenches even if one had survived the irreligion of the training battalion at home. A regular sergeant at Montagne . . . had recently told me that he did not hold with religion in time of war. . . . "And all this damn nonsense, Sir—excuse me, Sir—that we read in the papers, Sir, about how miraculous it is that the wayside crucifixes are always getting shot at, but the figure of our Lord Jesus somehow don't get hurt, it fairly makes me sick, Sir." This was his explanation why, when giving practice fire-orders from the hill-top, he had shouted, unaware that I stood behind him: "Seven hundred half left, bloke on cross, five rounds, concentrate, FIRE!". . . . His platoon, including the two unusual "bible-wallahs" whose letters home always began in the same formal way: "Dear Sister in Christ," or "Dear Brother in Christ," blazed away.**

This passage from the memoirs of a British infantry captain, who later gained fame as a writer, reflects the contempt of fighting soldiers for those who did not serve with them in the trenches. That emotion had no great effect in Great Britain, but it had a major impact in Italy and Germany after the war. The passage also reveals the decline in religious belief among those who witnessed the barbarities of World War I.

*Robert Graves, *Good-bye to All That,* rev. ed (Garden City, N.Y.: Doubleday, 1957), pp. 188–189.

At this point, Italy and Great Britain hesitated to enter the conflict. Italy claimed that its obligations to the Triple Alliance did not include supporting a war of aggression. Great Britain was not legally bound to help France or Russia but did so when Germany violated a long-standing international treaty guaranteeing Belgium neutrality. If Germany could dominate the Netherlands and Belgium, directly across the English Channel, England would be in jeopardy. Hence Great Britain declared war against Germany on August 4.

The two conflicting groups were known as the Allies and the Central Powers. Initially the Allies consisted of Great Britain, France, Russia, Serbia, and Belgium. Japan, partly to honor its treaty commitments to Great Britain, entered the conflict late in August 1914. Italy remained on the sidelines until 1915 when it reversed sides and joined the Allies, as did the United States two years later. Germany and Austria-Hungary were joined by the Ottoman Empire late in 1914 and Bulgaria in 1915. Eventually the war involved more than thirty nations and some 65 million fighting men.

The Controversy over Responsibility

Few topics in modern European history have generated more heated debate than the question of who was most at fault for the outbreak of World War I. Soon after the fighting broke out, the governments of the various belligerent nations hastened to publish diplomatic documents relating to the July crisis in 1914. They selected only those that portrayed their action in a favorable light and cast their enemies in the role of aggressors. The Allies, the eventual victors, went so far as to write a clause in the peace treaty blaming the war on Germany and its associates. Historians began to challenge that harsh assessment in the 1920s and instead apportioned blame to all the initial participants.

The next generation of historians, benefiting from documents made available after World War II, rejected both interpretations. While acknowledging that no nation was wholly to blame, historians judged certain governments and individuals more responsible than others. One thing is certain: Germany urged Austria forward during the critical period, knowing that doing so was likely to lead to a general war. If Germany is to be singled out as the chief culprit, then Austria-Hungry, Serbia, and Russia are not far behind. France follows, with Britain bearing little if any responsibility. To this day there is no consensus on the exact degree to which each power was responsible for the war, in part because information on disputed points is missing. But undoubtedly all the involved nations made errors in judgment during the tense weeks after the assassination, and none, with the possible exception of Great Britain, is entirely free of blame.

Stalemate on the Western Front

Both sides had based their plans on a lightning offensive campaign that would overwhelm the opposition and produce a quick victory. The first phase of the Schlieffen plan worked with almost clockwork precision. The German army smashed through Belgium, poured into northeastern France, and by early September was within forty miles of Paris. In the meantime the French drove into Alsace-Lorraine, only to be hurled back after some of the fiercest fighting in the war. The French redeployed northward and westward to meet the invading Germans. Aided by a small British contingent, they counterattacked along the Marne River. The Germans, who were exhausted and bewildered, were halted and driven back. The First Battle of the Marne dashed Germany's hopes for a quick victory over France and compelled it to fight a protracted war on two fronts.

Thereafter the fighting in the west changed from a war of movement to a war of position. The opposing armies tried to outflank one another but only succeeded in extending the front northward. By the end of 1914 the combatants faced each other along a 500-mile line of trenches from the Swiss border to the North Sea. Flanking movements were no longer possible, and the greatly increased firepower of modern weapons, especially machine guns, and fortified trench networks gave the defense a clear advantage against frontal assaults. Behind barbed wire entanglements, defenders repelled attacking waves with scorching fire, mowing the attackers down in swaths.

Baffled by the new type of warfare, unimaginative generals concentrated men and artillery against a sector of the enemy's line, confident of breaking through and resuming the war of movement. As a result, millions of young men were recklessly squandered in a futile effort to pierce the enemy's defenses. The French army lost 1,430,000 men in various attacks in 1915. The Germans abandoned the five-month siege of Verdun (1916) after their killed and wounded approached 300,000. The French defenders sustained slightly heavier casualties. Over 57,000 British infantrymen were killed or wounded on the first day of the Battle of the Somme (1916), the heaviest loss Great Britain ever suffered in a single day's battle. All this carnage served absolutely no purpose. Despite the introduction of new weapons such as poison gas, flamethrowers, and tanks, the battle lines established at the close of 1914 changed little in three and a half years.

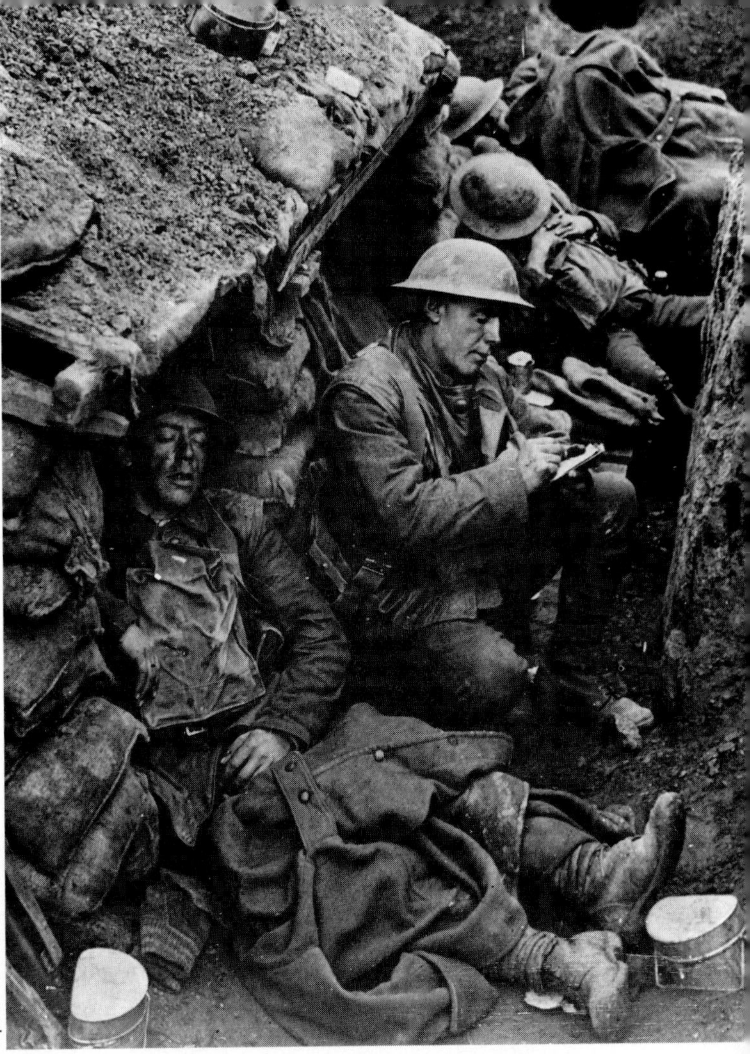

Imperial War Museum, London

Trench Warfare on the Western Front. For nearly four years the two great armies were cramped in a double line of trenches from which futile attacks to dislodge the enemy were repeatedly launched. Life for the common soldier was a hell of boredom in rat-infested trenches, horrifying battle experiences, bad weather, sniper fire, and the loss of comrades. Trench warfare left terrible psychological as well as physical scars on many of those who survived.

The Eastern Front

In contrast to the stalemate in the west, the war in the east was fluid, with frequently shifting battle lines that resulted in huge blocks of territory won and lost. When war began,

LIVES AND TIMES ACROSS CULTURES

The Fighting Goodyears

The subject peoples under the rule of European powers were at war the very moment their mother country entered the conflict in August 1914. While some colonies were unenthusiastic, others like Newfoundland, then part of the British Empire, responded wholeheartedly to the call to arms. The Goodyears were not only proud to be "Newfies," but were among the staunchest British patriots in the colony. Louisa and Joshua had seven children, six boys and a girl. Five of the boys volunteered for the army and the girl, Kate, served in the nursing corps. Raymond, the youngest, wanted to go to war with his brothers, and twice tried to enlist, only to be retrieved each time by his father. Although still slightly underage, he got his wish early in 1916 and in the fall joined the Newfoundland Regiment manning the line outside of Ypres. In his first battle, a shrapnel shell ripped open his waist, killing him instantly. A year later his brother Stan, athletic and deemed indestructible, tempted fate once too often and was killed by an artillery blast while racing through a firefight to bring munitions to his unit near Langemarck in Belgium. The oldest of the brothers, Hedley, who enlisted while still at the University of Toronto, was the third to die. He was reported killed when his unit attacked at the Somme on August 7, 1918, but in fact survived for another week. Huddling in a trench at night, he made a fatal mistake when he disregarded the mythical dangers of three on a match. He shared a light with two Australian soldiers and, as he drew his hand towards his own cigarette, a sniper shot him through the head. The remaining two brothers, Joe and Ken, suffered serious wounds and were invalided home.

For Kate, who attended to the wounded at St. Luke's hospital in Ottawa, and the other surviving members of her family, the war did not end in 1918. Her great-nephew wrote that for the next seventy years the normally reserved Kate would sometimes pause in the midst of a sentence, particularly at the thought or mention of Hedley, whom she adored, as tears welled up unexpectedly in her eyes. Kate Goodyear and millions like her lived with their losses, mindful always of the void that could never be filled, and of what might have been had their loved ones lived to return home.

the Russians completed mobilization quickly and mounted ill-prepared invasions of German and Habsburg territory. With most of the German army tied up in the west, the Russians made unexpected gains, advancing well into Germany's easternmost province. Alarmed German authorities appointed General Paul von Hindenburg (1847–1934) to direct the operations with the brilliant General Erich Ludendorff (1865–1937) as his chief of staff. Although outnumbered, von Hindenburg won major victories, first at Tannenberg at the end of August and two weeks later at the Masurian Lakes. In these two battles the Germans killed or captured 250,000 Russians.

The Russians fared better against Austria, occupying most of Galicia before the arrival of four German army corps from the western front checked their drive. In the spring and summer of 1915 a combined Austro-German thrust forced the underequipped Russians to abandon Galicia and most of Poland and inflicted some 2 million casualties. Remarkably, the Russians not only stayed in the field after these incredible losses but mounted an offensive the following year. They opened a wide gap in the Austrian lines and took several hundred thousand prisoners but were unable to sustain the drive. A German counteroffensive cost the Russians all the territory they had gained and a good deal more. Russia lost another million men and sank into a state of apathy from which it never recovered. These defeats, food shortages, and the inefficiency and corruption of the government bred discontent among the civilian population. In March 1917 popular outbreaks forced the tsar to abdicate, and a provisional government was created. When the government attempted to continue the war effort, it was overthrown by Marxist revolutionaries who immediately negotiated a peace treaty with Germany. In March 1918 Russia signed the Treaty of Brest-Litovsk and dropped out of the war.

The War outside Europe

Although the main battles were fought in Europe there were subsidiary operations elsewhere involving forces from many countries of the world. Instinctive loyalty to Great Britain prompted the self-governing dominions to pledge their support the moment the British government declared war. Canada sent 640,000 men to fight overseas, Australia 329,000, and New Zealand 117,000. As the war expanded, Britain drew on India and other colonies for manpower. For its part France raised 270,000 men from its North African colonies alone. African losses in the various campaigns likely amounted to at least 300,000 men.

Allied command of the seas sealed the fate of Germany's colonies in Asia and Africa. To the Japanese, the war offered an opportunity to consolidate and expand their empire in East Asia. In September 1914 their forces landed on the Shantung Peninsula of China and in a brief, hard-fought campaign took the German port of Tsingtao. The Japanese then forced the Chinese government to transfer to them all German possessions in Shantung, as well as commercial rights in southern Manchuria and elsewhere in China. During November 1914 Japanese soldiers occupied the Marianas, the Marshalls, the Carolines, and other German-held North Pacific islands. South of the equator, New Zealand and Australia had raced ahead of Japan to acquire the German colonial islands of Samoa and New Guinea, respectively.

Similarly, German colonies in Africa fell one by one to the Allies. In 1914 British and French troops seized Togoland and, within a year and a half, the Cameroons. In 1915 Great Britain's dominion of South Africa invaded and occupied German Southwest Africa. In German East Africa, British, Indian, and South African forces took possession of most of the colony, although the resourceful German commander, Lettow-Vorbeck, kept his badly outnumbered army in the field right up to war's end.

The war in West Asia was of greater magnitude and consequence than in Africa. By joining the Central Powers, the strategically located Ottoman Empire posed grave problems for the Allies, particularly Great Britain. In 1915 the British landed an army on the Gallipoli Peninsula with the object of knocking the Ottoman Empire out of the war and bringing aid to the beleaguered Russians. Blunders in planning and execution forced the British to withdraw after suffering heavy losses. The British sustained another major defeat in Mesopotamia, where they had undertaken to advance on Baghdad with insufficient strength. Halted and then surrounded at Kut, British-Indian forces withstood a six-month siege before surrendering in April 1916. Great Britain had more success against the Turks in Syria and Palestine. A British force advancing from Egypt found invaluable allies in the Arabs, who were advised by British officers, including the famous T. E. Lawrence (1888–1935)—later romanticized as Lawrence of Arabia. Roused by the British, the Arabs fought the Turks to secure an independent state after the war. The conquest of Jerusalem and southern Palestine by the end of 1917 was followed by a vigorous drive into Syria in 1918 that led to the capitulation of the Ottoman Empire.

The war outside Europe had wide ramifications. In Asia, Japan's increased power and aggressive policies in China set the stage for future trouble. Within the British dominions, the war had stirred strong national feelings and demands for more say in shaping their foreign policy. Indian nationalists like Mohandas K. Gandhi had backed the British war effort in the expectation that victory would hasten the independence of India. In the Middle East, the Arabs had aided the Allied cause in exchange for freedom. But in the Balfour Declaration of 1917 Britain had pledged to establish a national home for the Jewish people in Palestine, thereby violating promises made to the Arabs (the impact of the conflicting agreements will be described in the next chapter). All these forces set in motion created many problems after the war.

The Home Front

World War I was the first total war in modern history to impose burdens on all the citizens of the participating states. Gone were the days when wars were fought by

Kate Goodyear in Her Nurse's Uniform. Gracious, reserved, and beautiful, she was by all accounts the brightest and most ambitious of all the Goodyears. Defying convention, she left Newfoundland as a young woman to study business at the University of New Brunswick, and later, after the war broke out, trained as a nurse in Ottawa. She was on her way overseas when the armistice was signed.

Courtesy of David Macfarlane, Toronto

professional armies while the average civilians at home went about their usual business.

In August 1914 the belligerents anticipated a brief war and lacked the resources and contingency plans to meet long-term production needs. As the war dragged on, all governments had to confront the vital questions of matériel, food, and manpower. The demands of total war led to the increased centralization of political authority, the imposition of economic controls, and the restriction of civil liberties.

In the euphoria that accompanied the outbreak of war, the general public and all political parties rallied behind their respective governments. In France, the president appealed for a "sacred union" of all French to defend the homeland. The kaiser, in a speech before parliament, exclaimed "I know parties no more. I know only Germans." "I am in perfect union with my united people!" said Tsar Nicholas II. In the name of national security, governments indulged in practices which the press and opposition parties would never have tolerated in time of peace. In Russia progress toward sharing political responsibility ended when the tsar suspended the Duma for the duration of the war. During 1917 and 1918 the Hindenburg-Ludendorff team in Germany had replaced the imperial government with a military dictatorship, controlling diplomatic and economic as well as military policy. Even in France and Great Britain, greater power was concentrated in the hands of the prime minister and the cabinet.

The stress of total war also produced tight control in the economic organization of the belligerent nations. The economy had to be managed so that human and material resources were employed in the most efficient manner. Everywhere priorities were set for military versus civilian needs. Germany, which was short on raw materials, was the first to introduce economic regimentation, establishing a War Raw Materials Department to allocate raw materials on a priority basis. In the United States, Bernard Baruch, a Wall Street financier, was given sweeping powers to harness the nation's industrial capacity. Laws passed between 1914 and 1916 empowered the British government to requisition factories and control production, discard trade union rules, outlaw strikes, and introduce conscription.

The regulation of economic life and the need to maintain the nation's unity and its will to go on fighting placed restrictions upon the freedoms of citizens. All governments, even those of democracies, passed laws to intern people suspected of being enemy agents or sympathizers and prohibited defeatist activities. Houses were searched without warrants, public meetings were prohibited, and persons making antiwar speeches were liable to receive prison sentences.

Along with censorship, all governments actively used propaganda to achieve their goals. Newspapers were censored, and all items that were critical of the government or provided aid and comfort to the enemy were deleted. In trying to win over neutral states, each side tried to discredit the other while trumpeting the righteousness of its cause. Allied propaganda effectively highlighted Germany's brutal conduct in Belgium, sinking of merchant ships, and misusing of civilians in occupied countries. It became common in Great Britain to refer to the Germans as Huns. At home propaganda was designed to breed confidence in victory and to engender hatred of the foe. The German people were shielded from the truth and until practically the end they were told they were winning the war. In the Allied countries, the kaiser was a favorite target of cartoonists. With his spiked helmet and with gleaming eyes and oversized upturned mustache, he was depicted as the incarnation of the devil or as a mad fiend bent on world domination. Such ideas and images deepened hatreds and created illusions that were difficult to set aside when the time came to arrange a peace.

Women and the War

The war provided women with an opportunity to assume new roles and to contribute to the war effort in various ways. In Great Britain newly established women auxiliary forces attracted thousands of volunteers. These women lived in camps, wore khaki uniforms, and drilled, but worked mostly as secretaries and kitchen help. The Russian government organized battalions of women to help maintain order in the cities.

All nations relied on volunteer aides along with professional nurses to serve in understaffed hospitals. Many unpaid volunteer nurses from wealthy families worked side by side with salaried nurses from more modest backgrounds. In an atmosphere where all pulled together for the nation's survival, class divisions were blurred. All toiled long hours to mitigate the sufferings of soldiers under primitive conditions that exposed them to infections and disease. Those in medical facilities immediately behind the front were also exposed to the dangers of artillery bombardment and possible capture. One of the best-known incidents of the war involved a British nurse, Edith Cavell, who worked with the Red Cross in German-occupied Belgium. Tried for helping British and French soldiers caught behind enemy lines to escape, she was found guilty of espionage and shot. The worldwide revulsion that followed provided another propaganda triumph for the Allies.

In the cities, employers were compelled to turn to women as replacements. In some nations special agencies solicited and assigned women for war work. Women by the thousands took over jobs previously denied them. They drove trucks, delivered mail, swept chimneys, and worked in mortuaries and especially in factories. In Great Britain women eventually comprised 60 percent of all those employed in the armament industry. Only a handful of women were employed in the Krupp Armament Works in Germany before the war, but by 1917 their numbers had climbed to 12,000. The percentage of women in the industrial force in Moscow rose from 39.4 percent in 1913 to 48.7 percent in 1917. In rural areas, women managed family farms, plowed the land, and made business decisions.

Although women held all sorts of jobs formerly reserved for men, they were paid less than men doing the same work, and few reached positions of authority. In the munitions factories, for example, women earned only about half of what men received. Some governments tried to intercede on behalf of women workers. In France the government established minimum wages for women in certain industries and then outlawed discrimination on the basis of sex. Although women made more as a result of government regulations, their wages by war's end still lagged behind those of their male counterparts.

The war had an impact on the social behavior of women. Economic independence ensured them the personal freedoms they desired. More women lived on their own. Even their appearance was transformed: they cut their hair, wore shorter skirts and less constraining clothes—many abandoned the corset—went out unescorted in public, and put on makeup, a practice traditionally associated with prostitutes. Women enjoyed greater sexual freedom as well. The high risks for young men going to the front encouraged couples to become intimate more quickly.

Men generally acknowledged the essential contributions women made to the war effort and conceded their right to participate in the political process, a notable reversal of prewar attitudes. In 1917 the provisional government in Russia even allowed women to vote. In February 1918 the British parliament granted the suffrage to women over thirty. Immediately after the war, women in Austria, Germany, and the United States were similarly enfranchised.

Women workers suffered setbacks after the war ended, however, when demobilized soldiers reclaimed their jobs. Nearly all the gains made during the war were reversed. In the postwar period, males reverted to traditional attitudes and demanded that women return to their homes.

American Entry and the Collapse of the Central Powers

The highly touted German High Seas Fleet was reluctant to challenge Britain's domination of the seas. It remained in port except for one sortie in May 1916 when it suffered a defeat in a running battle with a British squadron off the coast of Jutland. Thereafter the Germans relied on a deadly new naval weapon, the submarine, to break the crippling British blockade. As a highly industrial nation, Germany depended on overseas imports of raw materials and especially food in order to survive.

As early as 1915, the German government had declared the waters surrounding Great Britain a war zone in which Allied merchant ships would be torpedoed without warning. In May the British liner *Lusitania,* which was carrying war matériel, was torpedoed with the loss of 1,200 passengers, including more than a hundred Americans. Strong protests from Washington compelled the German government to modify its policy, and the crisis passed. By the beginning of 1917 the Allied blockade was having a serious effect on Germany, strangling its industry and causing widespread food shortages. The German High Command considered defeat inevitable if the war lasted much longer. Thus in a desperate bid to starve Great Britain into submission, the German authorities decided to resume unrestricted submarine warfare, even at the risk of adding the United States to their growing list of opponents. Germany believed, however, that the United States was militarily unprepared and incapable of putting a sizable army in the field before Great Britain was defeated.

The outrage in the United States was great. President Woodrow Wilson (1856–1924) suspended diplomatic relations with Germany but did not immediately ask Congress for a declaration of war. The sinking of several American ships was followed by revelations that Germany was plotting to entice Mexico to attack the United States, promising to restore Mexico's "lost provinces" of Texas, Arizona, and New Mexico in return for its support in case of war between Germany and the United States. Appearing before Congress on April 2, Wilson declared that U.S. intervention would make the world "safe for democracy." Congress approved a declaration of war four days later. Although American troops did not arrive at the front for a year, the United States did supply the war-weary Allies with immediate financial, material, and naval aid.

At first Germany's unrestricted submarine campaign exceeded the expectations of its planners, but as the months passed Great Britain developed increasingly effective countermeasures, including depth charges, hydrophonic detectors, mine barrages, and the convoy system. By the close of 1917, it was clear that the submarine campaign had failed. Facing economic strangulation, Germany was forced to seek a decisive breakthrough on the western front.

In the spring of 1918, with reinforcements from the Russian front, General Ludendorff launched the first of five offensives that nearly won the war for Germany. Ludendorff not only possessed superiority in numbers, but he also counted on new tactics pioneered by General Oscar von Huetier: rather than attack on a broad front after an intense artillery barrage, the idea was to push highly trained shock troops, organized into small fire teams, through weakly defended areas, leaving follow-up units to reduce the strong points. Achieving strategic surprise, Ludendorff pierced the Allied line and within three months stood on the Marne, some forty miles away from Paris. In this crucial hour, the Allies took the long delayed step of creating a unified command under a French general, Ferdinand Foch (1851–1929), to coordinate their operations. Ludendorff's great offensive ultimately stalled owing to the exhaustion of his soldiers and the timely arrival of American forces. The last German offensive in July lacked strength after the initial surge. With the Americans arriving at the rate of 250,000 a month, time had run out for the Germans.

On July 18 the Allies counterattacked along the whole front, driving the Germans back from their gains of the previous spring. On August 8, the "black day of the German army," British tanks smashed through the German lines near Amiens; the Allies now pressed on relentlessly, with the Americans bearing the brunt of the fighting. German morale began to crumble, and on September 29, Ludendorff, almost in a panic, advised the kaiser to seek peace. While Germany entered into negotiations to achieve a cease-fire, its allies dropped out of the war one by one. On November 8 the Allies presented their armistice terms to a German commission. At 11.00 A.M. on November 11, 1918, the guns fell silent on the western front.

The Great War was one of the greatest calamities to befall Western civilization. Not since the Black Death in the mid-fourteenth century had so many people died in so brief a time. The war killed about 10 million soldiers and wounded twice that many. Civilian losses from air raids, bombardments, submarines, and the blockade totaled at least another million. A whole generation of European youth had been wiped out. The war also destroyed the wealth the European states had accumulated during the preceding century and left them heavily in debt. It caused the collapse of the German, Austro-Hungarian, Russian, and Ottoman Empires. It was the beginning of the end of Europe's political domination of the rest of the world.

Survivors of the Great War were left with a sense of despair and futility. The senseless mass destruction of life and property by nations thought to be the most advanced in the world shook the confidence of Western men and women in the basic tenets of rationality and progress. It was hoped that the peace settlements would be the first step in the reconstruction of Europe's social, political, and economic order.

The Mark I. This earliest version of the tank was first used, by the British, at the Somme in August 1916. These armored caterpillars made an unimpressive debut because of mechanical limitations and improper deployment. Still they had immense psychological impact and were used in later battles, though usually with little military effect.

Hulton/Archive

Postwar Settlements and the Interwar Years

*So far as possible . . . it was the policy of France to set the clock back and to undo what, since 1870, the progress of Germany had accomplished. By loss of territory and other measures her population was to be curtailed; but chiefly the economic system, upon which she depended for her new strength, the vast fabric built upon iron, coal, and transport must be destroyed. If France could seize, even in part, what Germany was compelled to drop, the inequality between the two rivals for European hegemony might be remedied for many generations.**

*John Maynard Keynes, *The Economic Consequences of the Peace* (New York: Harcourt, 1920), pp. 35–36.

In this discussion, the leading postwar economist, John Maynard Keynes, inaccurately outlines France's plans to destroy future German power and its attempts to inflict a final defeat on its old enemy at the peace table. Keynes knew little about French policy, and his views were shaped by his own guilt as a pacifist over having participated in Great Britain's war effort. There is no evidence that France was seeking hegemony, revenge, or anything beyond security against a third German invasion. Keynes's book was slanted, but given his international reputation, it was accepted as gospel in English-speaking countries. As a result, Keynes helped to create the myth that the peace settlements were instruments of Allied vengeance that prepared the way for a future war.

The Paris Peace Conference and the Versailles Treaty

In January 1919 delegates of the victorious nations gathered in Paris to decide the fate of Germany and its associates. The Central Powers were not represented, nor was Russia, which had dropped out of the war and

Wilson's Fourteen Points

I. Open covenants of peace, openly arrived at, after which there shall be no private international understandings of any kind but diplomacy shall always proceed frankly and in the public view.

II. Absolute freedom of navigation upon the seas, . . . alike in peace and in war.

III. The removal, so far as possible, of all economic barriers and the establishment of an equality of trade conditions among all the nations. . . .

IV. Adequate guarantees given and taken that national armaments will be reduced to the lowest point consistent with domestic safety.

V. A free, open-minded, and absolutely impartial adjustment of all colonial claims, based upon a strict observance of the principle that in determining all such questions of sovereignty the interests of the populations concerned must have equal weight with the equitable claims of the government whose title is to be determined.

VI. The evacuation of all Russian territory. . . .

VII. Belgium . . . must be evacuated and restored.

VIII. All French territory should be free . . . the wrong done to France in the matter . . . of Lorraine . . . should be righted.

IX. A readjustment of the frontiers of Italy should be effected along clearly recognizable lines of nationality.

X. The peoples of Austria-Hungary . . . should be accorded the freest opportunity of autonomous development.

XI. Rumania, Serbia, and Montenegro should be evacuated, occupied territories restored.

XII. The Turkish portion of the present Ottoman Empire should be assured a . . . sovereignty, but the other nationalities which are now under Turkish rule . . . [should have] autonomous development.

XIII. An independent Polish state should be created which should include the territories inhabited by indisputably Polish populations, which should be assured a free and secure access to the sea. . . .

*XIV. A general association of nations must be formed under specific covenants for the purpose of affording mutual guarantees of political independence and territorial integrity to great and small states alike.**

Wilson knew what he wanted the conference to do, but many of his Fourteen Points were maddeningly vague. He hoped to overcome any problems that arose through the force of his own personal popularity and through the new power of the United States. Wilson relied perhaps too heavily on influencing the other Allied leaders by flexing America's economic muscle. He failed to understand that there were things money could not purchase. Not even a shack had been destroyed in the United States during the war, but in France alone 4,000 towns had been obliterated. For Clemenceau, France's security had no price tag. He proposed to protect France not with vague Wilsonian principles but with practical measures that would cripple Germany.

*Speech of President Woodrow Wilson to a joint Session of Congress, January 8, 1918, *Congressional Record,* 56 (1918), pt. I, 680–681.

was currently in the midst of civil strife. Taking a lesson from the 1815 Congress of Vienna, where the loser (the French) had participated and exploited the divisions among the victors, the Allies decided that they would meet first without the Germans present. The victors would thus agree on the broad outlines of the peace and require Germany to sign that "preliminary" peace before holding a general peace conference with Germany's participation. As matters turned out, the preliminary peace became the final peace, and the Germans never had the opportunity to present their case.

The major decisions in Paris were made by an inner council of four: President Wilson of the United States and Prime Ministers Georges Clemenceau of France, David Lloyd George of Great Britain, and Vittorio Orlando of Italy. In theory, all sovereign states had the same rights. In reality, the lesser states were consulted only in cases involving their direct interests. Since the "Big Four" powers would have the responsibility of carrying out the treaty provisions, their agreement was vital.

The Allied leaders were eager to lay the foundations of a lasting peace, but they differed on the means to achieve their goal. Wilson alone made no territorial or financial claims on the defeated nations. His idealistic vision of a just and enduring peace, embodied in the Fourteen Points, would obviate defeated Germany's desire for revenge and permit the building of a better and safer world order. In November 1918 the Allies had tacitly agreed to make peace on Wilson's terms, excluding only two offending points regarding freedom of the seas and reparations.

Yet when the actual peace negotiations got under way, the Fourteen Points were often conspicuously disregarded. The European leaders, whose people had fought and suffered through a long war, demanded indemnification from the Central Powers. They were bound by secret treaties and agreements, and each had his own ulterior motives. Clemenceau, nicknamed the Tiger, wanted above all to ensure France's security, which he felt could only be accomplished by crippling Germany. He viewed Wilson with extreme cynicism. The Tiger reportedly quipped that since mankind had been unable to keep God's Ten Commandments, it was unlikely to do better with Wilson's Fourteen Points. Besides coveting certain German and Ottoman territories, Lloyd George wanted to prevent any one power from dominating Europe. Orlando concerned himself chiefly with gaining territories from the former Austro-Hungarian Empire. When it became clear that all his demands would not be met, he left the conference in a huff, and the Big Four became the Big Three.

The Paris Peace Conference lasted from January to May 1919 and was marked by bitter wranglings and threats of a breakup. The most serious disagreement was over the future of the Rhineland, German territory on the left bank of the Rhine River. As protection against a new invasion from Germany, Clemenceau wanted the area turned into a buffer zone, preferably under French control. But Wilson, backed by Lloyd George, resisted the demand, and Clemenceau was driven to accept its demilitarized status. One by one, important issues were settled by reconciling clashing viewpoints, and a draft treaty was drawn up and handed to a German delegation.

The Germans protested the severity of the treaty's terms, but the Allies made no substantive changes in the document and warned the Germans that failure to accept it would mean renewal of the war. Germany's delegates signed the treaty on June 28, 1919, in the Hall of Mirrors at Versailles.

The Versailles Treaty weakened but did not destroy Germany as a great state. Still, Germany lost about 10 percent of its population and territory in Europe. It ceded Alsace-Lorraine to France, small areas of land to Belgium and Denmark, and much of Prussia, including a corridor to the Baltic Sea, to Poland. The Saar Valley was placed under international control for fifteen years, after which a plebiscite was to be held to determine whether the population wished to be under France or Germany. Germany gave up all its colonial possessions to the Allies as mandates (trusteeships) nominally under the supervision of the League of Nations. Germany's reparations bill, as determined by an Allied commission in 1921, was set at about $33 billion.

The treaty sought to prevent a resurgence of German militarism by reducing its army to 100,000 volunteers and severely limiting its weaponry and the size of its navy. Germany had to accept the demilitarization and military occupation of the Rhineland. The kaiser and other leaders were to be tried for violations of international law and customs of war. But the kaiser, who had abdicated on November 9, 1918, was not brought to trial. The government of the Netherlands, which granted him sanctuary, refused to allow him to be extradited.

The Settlements with the Other Central Powers

Treaties with the other defeated nations were signed in 1919 and 1920; all were closely modeled on the Versailles pact, with provisions for reparations and reduction of armed forces. The treaties with Austria and Hungary dissolved the Habsburg Empire and created independent Czechoslovakia, Poland, and Yugoslavia from its former domains. Austria was also forbidden to enter into union with Germany. Bulgaria surrendered territory to Romania, Greece, and Yugoslavia, losing its outlet to the Mediterranean.

A first treaty with Turkey in April 1920 stripped it of lands occupied mostly by Arabs and partitioned the Turkish heartland of Anatolia. The harsh terms produced a vehement Turkish reaction, and nationalists found a leader in a World War I hero, Mustafa Kemal (1881–1938), later Atatürk ("chief Turk"), who organized resistance and drove Allied forces from the Anatolian Peninsula. In 1923 the Allies reluctantly negotiated a new treaty, by which Turkey kept all of the Anatolian Peninsula, Istanbul, and the European territory around the city. Turkey under Atatürk also successfully resisted Armenian demands for an independent state carved out of Anatolia.

The Arab territories in the Ottoman Empire were divided as mandates between France and Great Britain, with France receiving Syria, including present-day Lebanon, and Great Britain securing Palestine, Transjordan, and Iraq (these divisions and nationalist reactions to them will be detailed in Chapter 14). Territories in the Arabian Peninsula, including the Muslim holy cities of Mecca and Medina, achieved independence and later formed the Kingdom of Saudi Arabia under Abd al-Aziz ibn Saud.

Evaluation of the Peace Treaties

Few peace treaties in modern times have provoked sharper criticism or controversy than those hammered out in Paris in 1919 and 1920. The treaties were denounced by the defeated nations, as was to be expected. But in the victor nations as well, many critics charged that the Paris settle-

Atatürk Addresses the Turkish Assembly

Let us return to a closer examination of the facts. . . .

Morally and materially, the enemy Powers were openly attacking the Ottoman empire and the country itself. They were determined to disintegrate and annihilate both. . . .

Now, Gentlemen, I will ask you what decision I ought to have arrived at in such circumstances. . . .

1. *To demand protection from England.*
2. *To accept the United States of America as a mandatory Power. . . .*
3. *The third proposal was to deliver the country by allowing each district to act in its own way and according to its own capability. . . .*

The results of the Lausanne Conference, which lasted for eight months in two sessions, are known to the world at large. . . .

The debates were heated and animated. No positive results regarding the recognition of Turkish rights were noticeable. . . .

The Ottoman Empire, whose heirs we were, had no value, no merit, no authority in the eyes of the world. It was regarded . . . as it were, under the tutelage and protection of somebody else.

*We were not guilty of the neglect and errors of the past. . . . It was, however, our duty to bear responsibility for them before the world. In order to procure true independence . . . for the nation we had still to submit to these difficulties and sacrifices. . . . Our greatest strength and our surest point of support was the fact that we had realized our national sovereignty, had actually placed it in the hands of the nation and had proved by facts that we were capable of maintaining it.**

In this speech to the Turkish assembly in October 1924, Atatürk explained how Turkey managed to avoid partition and retain its independence. Once in power, Atatürk embarked on a series of reforms that swept away old Ottoman institutions, including the sultanate and the Islamic institution of the caliphate.

* William H. McNeill and Marilyn R. Waldman, eds., *The Islamic World* (New York: Oxford University Press, 1973; reprint, Chicago: University of Chicago Press, 1983), pp. 432–438.

ments were unduly harsh and violated many of the Fourteen Points. John Maynard Keynes, whose book *The Economic Consequences of the Peace* (1919) shaped public opinion in the United States and Great Britain, asserted that the Versailles Treaty was ruinous, immoral, and unworkable. He likened it to a "Carthaginian peace" (like those ancient Rome dictated to defeated Carthage), arguing that the proposed reparations would cripple Germany's economy and bring economic ruin to Europe.

More recently, some scholars have taken exception, noting that Germany, unlike ancient Carthage, had not been destroyed, but remained politically united, with its industrial strength relatively intact. They claim that Adolf Hitler's rise to power was due less to the Versailles Treaty than to Allied unwillingness to enforce it and point out that had Germany won the war, it would almost certainly have imposed much harsher terms on the Allies. No one can be sure whether a conciliatory peace would have prevented World War II.

A more relevant question is whether a conciliatory peace was possible. Wilson's idealistic vision was ill-suited to the realities of 1919. Moreover, none of the Big Four was a free agent. They were all bound to interpret and execute the will of their public and legislatures back home. Trapped in their own rhetoric and propaganda, they could not disavow the hopes and expectations they had raised at home without creating an electoral backlash that would drive them out of office. The upshot was an unsatisfying compromise between Wilson's high moral principles and Clemenceau's nationalistic aims. It was neither harsh enough to cripple Germany forever, as the French had wished, nor generous enough to conciliate the vanquished in the postwar era.

In short, it is perhaps unfair to judge the peacemakers of 1919 too harshly for the treaty's shortcomings, given the complex and multiple issues that had to be faced and the time limitations and other difficulties under which they worked. It is unlikely that any peace treaty, however carefully drawn, could have preserved the peace. Colonel Edward House, Wilson's chief adviser, summed it up neatly in his diary entry on the day he left Paris: "Looking at the conference in retrospect there is much to approve and much to regret. It is easy to say what should have been done, but more difficult to have found a way

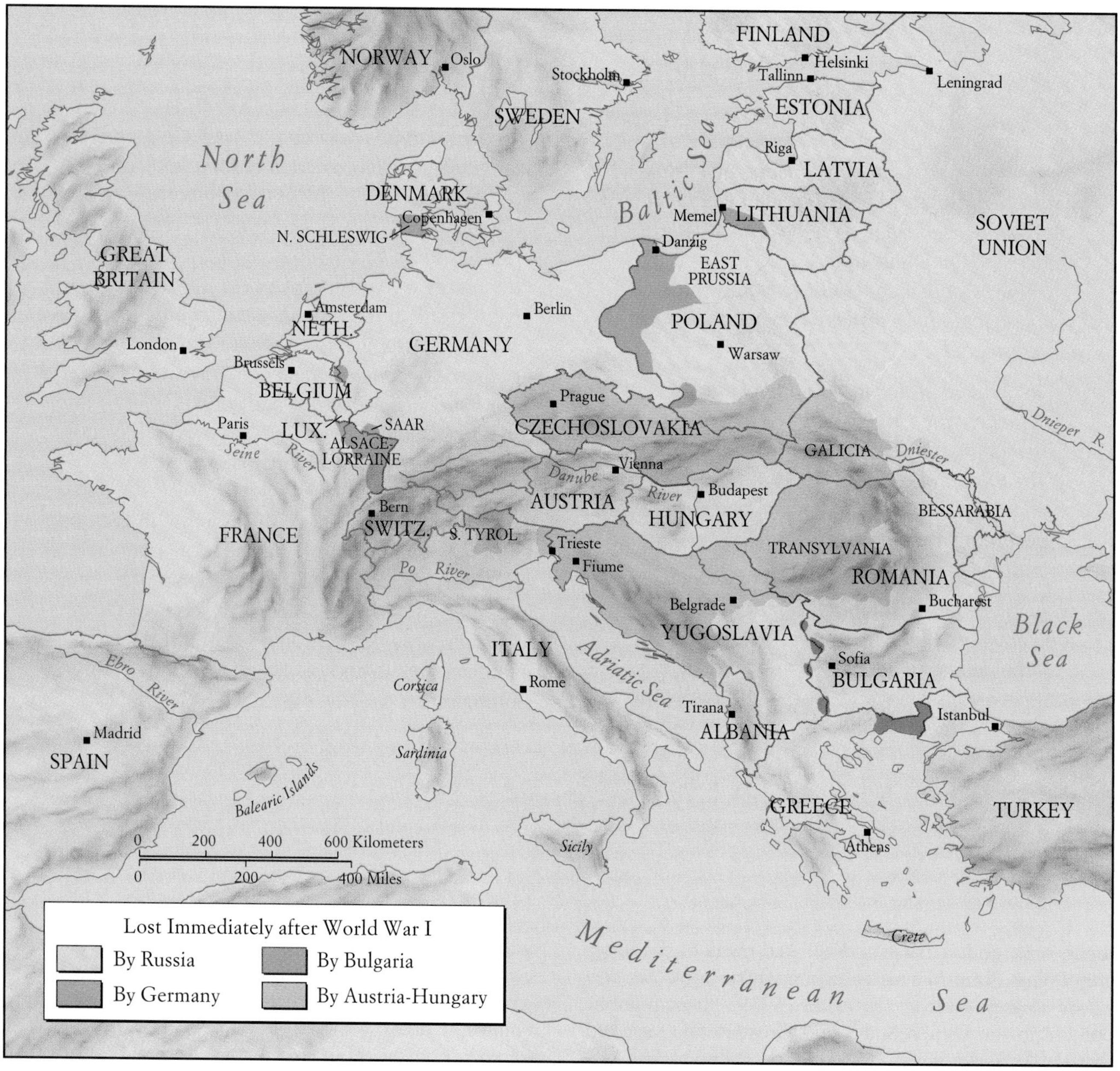

Map 13.9 Europe after 1919. The post–World War I settlements radically altered the map of Europe. Germany had to return Alsace-Lorraine to France, while Bulgaria lost its coastline to Greece. Italy acquired South Tyrol, Trieste, and Istria. The greatest changes occurred in eastern Europe, where seven new, fully sovereign states were created. The Habsburg Empire was broken up, and the independence of Czechoslovakia, Poland, and Yugoslavia was recognized. On the Baltic the subject nationalities of the Russian Empire—namely, the Finns, Estonians, Latvians, and Lithuanians—also gained their independence.

of doing it. . . . While I should have preferred a different peace, I doubt whether it could have been made, for the ingredients of such a peace . . . were lacking at Paris."

The League of Nations

All the treaties contained the covenant (charter) of the League of Nations, Wilson's top priority for postwar rehabilitation. Wilson sacrificed a number of his cherished principles to gain its acceptance, but he was confident that once the League began to operate, it would correct the mistakes and make good the deficiencies in the peace treaties. However, there was no agreement on precisely how the League would do its work.

The League of Nations was established in 1920, with headquarters in Geneva, Switzerland. It consisted of two

Hulton/Deutsch Collection

The League of Nations. The League of Nations was weakened by the refusal of the United States to join and by a lack of commitment on the part of its members. League members struggled but failed to keep the general peace.

deliberative bodies, the assembly and the council. All member nations were represented in the assembly, where each had a vote. The council was made up of the four great powers (Great Britain, France, Japan, and Italy) as permanent members, together with four other nations chosen periodically by the assembly. The third organ, the World Court, with international jurists elected by the assembly, adjudicated international quarrels.

The primary function of the League was to provide the machinery for a peaceful resolution of international disputes. Members had to respect the territorial integrity of other members and seek arbitration should regular diplomatic methods fail to resolve a dispute. If an aggrieved nation deemed the arbitration result unsatisfactory, it could not resort to war until at least three months after the decision had been rendered. Failure to abide by these terms could result in the League imposing economic sanctions against the offender or, if that proved inadequate, taking military action with troops provided by member states.

League membership came from every part of the globe, reaching its peak of fifty in 1924. Tragically, the United States did not join the League. Wilson was unable to allay isolationist fears in the U.S. Senate that membership in the League might lead to involvement in foreign quarrels. Russia, under Bolshevik rule, was kept out until 1934. Nor were the defeated powers immediately permitted to join. Japan, Germany, and Italy later resigned to pursue their respective courses of aggression. Only Great Britain and France remained members throughout the League's existence.

The League was judged to have been a failure because it was unable to prevent aggression and preserve the peace. One cause of the failure can be traced to the peacemakers themselves, who deprived the League of the mantle of impartiality by associating it with the treaties ending World War I. A second factor was the absence of some of the great powers, in particular, the United States, in the international organization. Third, even among the members, there was a reluctance to agree to arrangements that would limit their sovereignty. Last, decisions in the council on crucial issues required unanimity, which was almost impossible to obtain among states motivated more by self-interest than moral considerations.

The League did, however, successfully promote international cooperation in economic and technical areas. It was most effective in social projects such as aiding and settling refugees, providing drugs and vaccines, and generally improving health care in less advanced countries. The World Court successfully mediated a number of disputes between small, weak nations. As a rule, however, large, powerful nations opted to settle disputes on their own terms rather than rely upon decisions by a panel over which they had little control.

Germany under the Weimar Republic

The kaiser's government collapsed just before the armistice and was replaced by a provisional government committed to the establishment of a republic. The men in charge of Germany's affairs held elections for a National Assembly, which met in the town of Weimar and drafted a constitution for what would become known as the Weimar Republic. The democratic constitution, approved in July 1919, provided for a president and a two-house legislature.

The Weimar Republic led a precarious existence from the very beginning. Although the government conformed to democratic principles, conservatives dominated the new republic through control of the army, judiciary, bureaucracy, and educational systems. Antidemocratic elements were strengthened when the government signed the unpopular Versailles Treaty.

Weimar Germany suffered from a troubled economy and the $33 billion reparations bill assessed by the Allied Reparations Commission. The German government, unable to make the scheduled payments, tried to meet its obligations by printing more and more currency. The result was disastrous inflation. The mark fell from 4.2 to the U.S. dollar in 1914 to 62 to the dollar in May 1921 and 270 to the dollar by the end of November. When Germany defaulted on its payments in 1923, France (the chief recipient of reparations) and Belgium retaliated by occupying the entire Ruhr region, the main center of German industry. But the move caused a patriotic reaction in the Ruhr, where the workers engaged in passive resistance, refusing to enter the mines and factories. The 5 million inhabitants of the Ruhr had to be fed and supported; to do this, the German government printed more money, triggering more inflation. By September 1923 the mark had fallen to 100 million to the dollar, by October to more than 1 trillion, and by November to 4.2 trillion. Wages and prices had to be revised daily, even hourly. Like most inflations, it had only a slight effect on the rich, who owned apartment buildings and factories, which retained their value regardless of currency convulsions. It hit the lower middle class hardest, quickly wiping out savings and pensions. These bitter and impoverished Germans later became Hitler's most fanatical followers.

The turning point came in August 1923, when Gustav Stresemann became chancellor of a coalition of moderate parties. He ended the policy of passive resistance in the Ruhr, pledged resumption of reparation payments, and took drastic steps to halt inflation and stabilize the currency. Stresemann worked to restore Germany to equality with the other great powers and to bring about a treaty revision. Two committees of experts were formed to draft a plan to reduce the annual German payment and provide loans to speed up German economic recovery. In 1924 France evacuated the Ruhr.

Stresemann's successful policies restored stability and prosperity to Germany. During the second half of the 1920s, Germany benefited enormously from a massive infusion of foreign investment and loans, mainly from the United States, where the postwar boom had created surplus capital. German industry modernized its equipment and, by adopting methods of mass production and scientific management on the U.S. model, regained the lead in Europe that it had held before the war. The Weimar Republic appeared politically healthy and economically prosperous.

The Quest for International Security

In 1919 most Allied nations felt optimistic about lasting world peace. The task of peacekeeping became a secondary concern as most nations focused on rebuilding their society and economy. The United States rejected the treaty and reverted to isolationism. Great Britain, burdened with economic and imperial problems, wanted to limit its involvement in European affairs and wavered between a stern attitude and leniency toward Germany. Russia under communist rule was an outcast. Thus the responsibility for enforcing the peace and maintaining stability rested primarily with France.

The central concern of the French government was the containment of Germany. France felt deserted by its wartime allies and did not look to the League of Nations as an instrument to preserve peace. Instead it relied on diplomatic and military policies to secure its own protection. It concluded alliances with Poland, Czechoslovakia, Romania, and Yugoslavia in the 1920s, but few French deluded themselves into thinking that they could replace the pre–World War I alliance with Russia as a counterbalance to Germany.

In 1925 Stresemann, now Germany's foreign minister, sought to allay French fears by offering to respect the western frontiers established at Versailles. The outcome of his proposal was the Locarno Pact, signed in December of that year. With Great Britain and Italy as guarantors, France, Germany, and Belgium agreed to respect one another's existing frontiers. Interestingly enough, Germany did not provide the same assurances to Czechoslovakia and Poland on its eastern borders. Still, the Locarno Pact engendered a mood of goodwill and conciliation dubbed the Spirit of Locarno. Germany was now admitted to the League of Nations, ending its period of isolation. At the Washington Naval Disarmament Conference in 1921–1922, the powers established a ten-year naval holiday, during which no new capital warships would be built. Furthermore, they set up a system to limit the size of navies: the British and U.S. navies would be equal, the Japanese navy would be three-fifths that size, and the Italian and French navies one-third the size of the first two.

In 1928 the French foreign minister, Aristide Briand, and U.S. Secretary of State Frank Kellogg prepared a document in which the signatories, which ultimately totaled sixty-two nations, formally renounced war as an instrument of national policy. In reality, the agreement merely fostered the illusion of peace, for no machinery was set up to enforce the ban on war. But on the positive side, the agreement further contributed to the relaxation of European tensions. There followed several additional diplomatic pacts, one of which provided for the evacuation of Allied troops from the Rhineland (completed in 1930, four years ahead of schedule).

Although the second half of the 1920s was an interlude of stability and good feeling, it had produced no real reconciliation. The basic cause of friction remained. Germany wanted to revise features of the Versailles Treaty it found objectionable. The French for their part were haunted by fears of facing a revenge-minded Germany alone and were adamant about collecting their share of reparations to cover the cost of rebuilding their war-ravaged country. Thus the spirit of international cooperation never struck deep roots. It ended abruptly with the advent of the depression.

The Victorious Democracies in the 1920s

The return of peace presented the victorious democracies with social and economic problems of unprecedented magnitude and complexity. These myriad problems could not be solved through conventional methods; they called for vigorous and creative leadership, which was conspicuously lacking. As a result, critics charged that liberal democracy was too slow, obstructive, and inefficient to resolve the urgent postwar problems and espoused totalitarian dictatorships.

Generally speaking, governments on both sides of the Atlantic showed little concern for social reform in the 1920s. The United States resumed "business as usual," viewing the war as an unpleasant interruption. The Republican majority in the Senate enacted Prohibition (against alcohol consumption) and sought to lessen the power of organized labor. In Europe, the focus on achieving economic stability, coupled with resistance by entrenched interest groups, checked any impetus toward social reform. The annihilation of a whole generation of young men in the war had allowed the older generation, fearful of everything from Bolshevism to Americanization, to maintain its hold on business, government administration, education, and the army. In France only the threat of massive strikes prompted the government to enact the eight-hour workday. The sole notable legislative victory in Great Britain was the broadening of the franchise to include women.

Besides destroying a great deal of the housing, industrial plants, and transportation and communication facilities in northeastern France, Belgium, and northern Italy, the war caused a major loss of foreign markets. Conversely, business interests in the United States expanded into overseas markets formerly monopolized by European manufacturers. Great Britain, heavily dependent on foreign trade, suffered grievously and never fully recovered.

The decade following the peace treaties may be divided into two parts. The first period, from 1919 to 1924, was a time of psychic exhaustion and economic hardship mingled with cynicism and a general lack of direction. In multiparty states like France and Italy, the fragility of party coalitions led to notoriously short-lived governments unable to implement long-term economic and political programs. Still, both Great Britain and France, unlike Italy, survived their crises without sacrificing their democratic institutions.

Between 1925 and 1928, western Europe experienced a sort of Indian summer, marked by economic recovery and political stability. Europe's share of total world production returned to prewar levels, monetary systems stabilized, and living standards improved. The United States doubled its industrial production over the decade, and the value of stocks and bonds skyrocketed on the Wall Street stock exchange.

Beneath the surface prosperity of the era, however, important segments of Western society were still mired in poverty. Miners in the United States and elsewhere were badly hurt by the postwar decline in demand for their products. International competition caused agricultural prices to fall, forcing farmers into debt. In France inflation and weak government finance hampered the reconstruction of the devastated regions. In Great Britain massive unemployment remained endemic.

The social customs of the Roaring Twenties, as the press sometimes called the decade, were markedly more liberal than before. Young women in particular broke with traditional social mores and gender stereotypes. Short skirts and bobbed hair were symbols of the greater freedom of women, even in Japan and China, to hold jobs, live independently, and assert their general social and moral emancipation. The automobile liberated "flaming youth" of both sexes to seek entertainment away from home, and drinking, smoking, and recreational sex became chic.

Each nation had its peculiar problems. The United States experienced a "Red Scare," when Marxists and other radicals were harassed, arrested, and, if aliens, deported. A prewar trend toward racism and hostility to recent immigrants resulted in new, tighter immigration laws to limit the numbers of entries into the country. There was also a new wave of anti-Semitism and a resurgence of bigotry against African Americans typified by the revival of the Ku Klux Klan.

Great Britain struggled with the perennial Irish demands for independence. After an unsuccessful Easter Rebellion in 1916, the Sinn Fein (Gaelic for "we ourselves"), or Irish Nationalist party, employed guerrilla tactics and terrorism in an effort to achieve complete independence from Great Britain. Finally, in 1921 the British government signed a treaty with moderate Irish republicans. It divided Ireland into a northern part, Ulster, which was

Devastating Dust Bowl Destroys Crops and Family Farms

In the middle of the night the wind passed on and left the land quiet. The dust-filled air muffled sound more completely than fog does. . . . All day the dust sifted down from the sky, and the next day it sifted down. An even blanket covered the earth. It settled on the corn, piled up on the tops of the fence posts, piled up on the wires; it settled on roofs, blanketed the weeds and trees.

*The people came out of their houses and smelled the hot stinging air and covered their noses from it. And the children came out of the houses, but they did not run or shout as they would have done after a rain. Men stood by their fences and looked at the ruined corn, drying fast now, only a little green showing through the film of dust. The men were silent and they did not move often. And the women came out of the houses to stand beside their men—to feel whether this time the men would break.**

John Steinbeck in his moving novel, *The Grapes of Wrath,* vividly describes the dust bowls of Oklahoma that destroyed crops and forced farmers to travel west to California in search of better lives.

*John Steinbeck, *The Grapes of Wrath* (1939; reprint, Baltimore: Penguin, 1979), pp. 3–4.

predominantly Protestant and remained united with Great Britain, and a self-governing dominion called the Irish Free State, comprising the remainder of Ireland. In 1937 the Irish Free State gained complete independence and changed its name to Eire. The division of Ireland created a problem that persists to the present.

French policy was dominated by the quest for security against Germany. Accordingly, France maintained a large standing army and formed military alliances. It also built a massive row of fortifications, called the Maginot Line, across its eastern frontier as an impregnable barrier against German invaders.

All in all, the latter part of the 1920s encouraged many people to face the future with optimism. The physical damage to property had been largely repaired, immediate postwar problems had been solved, unemployment had been reduced, and increased harmony characterized international relations. The prosperity evident in most European countries, however, rested on a shaky base, dependent as it was on the continued voluntary flow of funds from the United States to Germany.

The Great Depression

The roots of the global depression of the 1930s lay in the fundamental financial weaknesses of the postwar world. Because the economies of most African, Asian, and Latin American nations were tied to those of the industrialized Western nations, they, too, felt the impact of the economic crisis. The Great Depression, which began in the United States in 1929, soon spread around the world, creating a crisis for all and an opportune climate for the rise of totalitarian dictators in the 1930s.

The United States emerged from the war as the richest nation in the world, having converted itself from a net debtor to a net creditor. With its mass markets and rapid technological advances, profits and production reached new heights over the next decade. During the economic boom, many individuals speculated in the soaring stock market, often on credit and amassing debts far beyond their ability to pay. In 1929 there was an economic slowdown. An exceptionally good harvest in Europe cut demand for American agricultural products, decreasing the purchasing power of U.S. farmers. Simultaneously there was a reduction in exports of American raw materials and fuels. Overproduction led to depressed prices and unemployment. As a reflection of the slumping economy, the stock market was hit by a wave of panic selling on October 24, 1929. As the value of stocks tumbled, many investors panicked and rushed to sell, thereby causing further drops in prices. Those who could not repay their debts lost everything; demand for goods dropped, and overstocked factories closed, throwing many workers out of jobs. Because the unemployed could not afford to purchase goods, a vicious cycle of further surpluses and factory closings was set in motion. Consequently, the economies of even unindustrialized countries like China, which were largely dependent on supplying raw materials and agricultural goods to the industrialized world, were severely undermined.

By 1931 the full effects of the depression in the United States were evident in Europe. The most immediate result was the withdrawal of American capital, which caused banks and businesses to fail. Throughout the world, trade declined and unemployment rose. A few figures give an indication of the impact caused by the economic collapse. By 1932, production in France was down 28 percent from predepression levels, in the United States 30 percent, and in Germany 50 percent. A quarter of all U.S. workers were unemployed, and the percentage was even higher in Germany. In the United States the shantytowns filled with jobless people were called "Hoovervilles," after President Herbert Hoover.

The Great Depression, or world slump, shook the governments of the Western world and Japan. While the United States and Great Britain responded to the economic crisis within the framework of their democratic institutions, other nations, such as Germany, turned to totalitarian solutions. The United States took effective countermeasures to combat the depression after President Franklin Roosevelt (1882–1945) assumed office in 1933. A New York aristocrat with a keen sense of humor, Roosevelt, although crippled by polio, had enthusiasm and determination. With the help of his politically concerned and active wife, Eleanor, and a team of reforming advisers dubbed the "brain trust," he immediately launched his New Deal.

The New Deal was a comprehensive program of national planning, economic experimentation, and innovative reforms that went far toward pulling the nation out of the depression. New laws and government bureaus provided relief payments for the hungry, low-cost mortgages, business loans, public works jobs for some of the unemployed—especially the young—and assistance for hard-hit farmers. Additional legislation monitored business and finance to prevent a repetition of the stock market collapse. Wages, hours, and conditions of labor were also regulated by new laws similar to those already enacted in many European nations. Most important, the New Deal began to build a welfare state in the United States by instituting the Social Security system.

Unlike the United States, Great Britain, France, and other Western democracies did not respond vigorously to the depression. The Conservative government in Great Britain tried to get by with the "dole," relief payments for unemployed workers, and subsidies to farmers. In France, the socialist premier Léon Blum tried to end the economic crisis by introducing reforms reminiscent of the New Deal, but his coalition government did not survive long enough to make a difference.

Latin America felt the crisis very severely because its economies were heavily dependent on exports. Likewise, global demand for Japanese exports dropped 50 percent from 1929 to 1931. Farmers were particularly affected by falling prices, and unemployment reached an all-time high. The Japanese people blamed the politicians and the rich bankers and industrialists for the economic crisis, and many argued that only an authoritarian regime headed by the military could solve the problems. As a result, Japanese democracy, which was not deeply rooted, collapsed. Although Japan was among the first industrialized nations to recover from the depression, conservative military and authoritarian forces gained widespread popularity and support as a direct consequence of the crisis. In foreign policy, these groups advocated conquest and expansion to solve Japan's economic and population problems.

Library of Congress

A Homeless Family during the Depression. The abject poverty and misery of the underprivileged are vividly captured in this portrait taken during the depression. Note that the woman and her children are living in a tent.

The Great Depression was the primary cause or catalyst of the radical swings from liberal and leftist governments to rightist, totalitarian, or authoritarian regimes in much of Europe, Japan, and Latin America. These totalitarian regimes adopted radical measures to remedy the problems caused by the economic disaster; in Hitler's Germany and elsewhere, the totalitarian rulers seemed more successful than the democratic ones in achieving economic recovery. Furthermore, the Great Depression reinforced demands by nationalists in West and East Asia and Africa for both economic and political independence. The Soviet Union pointed to the depression as seeming proof of the inherent weaknesses of the capitalist system. Antiimperialist struggles, revolutionary Marxism in the Soviet Union, and the emergence of totalitarian regimes during the interwar years will be described in the next chapter.

1775	
	Britain settles Australia
	King Shaka's Zulu kingdom Greek war of independence Muhammad Ali in Egypt Britain settles New Zealand Ottoman Empire declining Britain defeats China in Opium War Abdel Kader in Algeria
	Decline of the Manchu dynasty
1850	United States opens Japan
	Christian missions in Africa Direct British rule in India
	Opening of the Suez Canal Meiji Restoration; modernization of Japan European partition of Africa
	African resistance to imperialism
	Beginning of shifting European alliance systems Stories of Rudyard Kipling
	Spanish-American War; United States annexes Philippines United States proposes "Open Door" policy in China The Boer War The Boxer Rebellion in China
1900	
	The Russo-Japanese War
	Arms stockpiling and war plans by European nations United States domination in Latin America; the Panama Canal World War I
	Paris Peace Conference
1920	
	Formation of the League of Nations The Weimar Republic in Germany
	The Great Depression
1930	

Summary and Comparisons

From 1800 till 1914, European nations, the United States, and Japan dominated Africa, Asia, and Latin America. Demands for raw materials and markets and a variety of strategic, cultural, and nationalistic motives propelled the powerful nations of the world to dominate weaker states and peoples. Twentieth-century imperialism differed from previous conquests in that most imperial powers did not incorporate their new territories into their own states or settle them with colonists; rather, they were more interested in the natural resources, markets, and national glory that empire provided.

European imperialists overran Africa in one generation. Although Africans resisted conquest and often revolted against European domination, European military superiority was too great. Through international conferences and diplomacy, the European nations avoided conflict with one another as they partitioned the continent.

Similarly, the weakened Ottoman Empire, in spite of internal reforms, lost territory to Russia and western European nations. The Persian Empire under the Qajars was threatened by Russian and British expansion. In Asia, Great Britain was chiefly concerned with controlling India. Meanwhile, European powers defeated the Chinese Empire, dividing it into spheres of influence where the victors monopolized raw materials and markets and generally exercised control over Chinese internal affairs.

By adopting Western technology and modern military techniques, Japan also became an imperialist power. Japan expanded in East Asia by defeating Russia and China. The United States, already a major economic power, also became imperialistic. Beginning in 1898, it took military and economic control of the Caribbean and extended its economic domination over South America and Canada, while annexing the Philippines. Thus, by the first decade of the twentieth century, most of Africa, Asia, and Latin America had come under either direct or indirect imperial domination.

During the years before 1914, nationalism, the arms race, and the system of alliances all contributed to rising international tensions. None of the participating powers wanted a general war, but it is equally true that none did all they could to prevent the conflict. The assassination of the Archduke Ferdinand by a Serb nationalist provided the spark for the war. Taking for granted the complicity of the Serbian government, Austria declared war against its neighbor. When that happened, the system of alliances and the exigencies of military planning and mobilization schedules instantly dragged the major European powers, save one, into the conflict.

In August 1914 the belligerents went into battle confident that the war would be over in a few months.

The French attack broke down completely, while the Germans almost reached Paris before they were halted. A stalemate ensued, and both sides dug in for a long period of trench warfare. In the east the Germans handed the Russians one defeat after another and eventually knocked them out of the war. Unrestricted submarine warfare by Germans against any ships carrying goods to the Allies helped to bring the United States into the conflict. The involvement of the United States counteracted the loss of Russia and helped boost Anglo-French morale. In the spring of 1918 the Germans made a desperate effort to win the war before the Americans could arrive in France in force. When Germany's drive failed, its leaders agreed to an armistice that went into effect on November 11, 1918.

At the peace conference, which met in Paris in the first half of 1919, separate treaties were arranged with each of the defeated nations. Only the winners participated in the discussions at Paris, unlike the earlier Congress of Vienna where the losing French had been allowed to attend. Moreover, at Vienna the issues had been resolved by Europeans alone, whereas at Paris nations from around the world, including the United States and Japan, participated. In 1815 the winners had been very lenient toward the French, but at Paris the Allies came down hard on Germany and its associates, stripping them of much wealth and territory.

Whether the Central Powers were treated unjustly has long been a matter of debate. The purpose of both the Paris and Vienna meetings was to redraw the boundaries of Europe and ensure a lasting peace. In both cases there was no common blueprint and the settlements were decided by the leaders of the great powers. The Congress of Vienna produced an agreement that provided nearly a century of general peace in Europe. In contrast, the Paris accords, far from preserving peace, fostered resentment, particularly in Germany and Italy, and contributed to both the economic depression of the 1930s and World War II.

The return of peace confronted the Western democracies with numerous complex problems, but none as daunting as the Great Depression, which was triggered by the Wall Street crash in October 1929. The West tried various experiments to cope with the depression. The United States abandoned economic liberalism when it embraced the New Deal, opening the way for government participation in the economy. Great Britain declined to put the economy further under state control and essentially left the task of recovery to industry itself.

The French government made many significant reforms, but political instability inhibited economic recovery. The major nations in the West recovered from the depression at varying rates and degrees, but full recovery was not achieved until World War II.

Selected Sources

*Achebe, Chinua. *Things Fall Apart.* 1978. A fascinating novel about the clash between African and Western cultures; by a noted Nigerian author.

Beasley, W. G., ed. *The Rise of Modern Japan: Political, Economic and Social Change since 1850.* 2d ed. 1995. A clear and comprehensive look at Japan's modern transformation.

Brading, D. A. *The First America: The Spanish Monarchy, Creole Patriots, and the Liberal State, 1492–1866.* 1990. Stresses the development of an American identity in such Creoles as Bolívar and San Martín. Provides good background for the postindependence period.

Brittain, Vera. *Testament of Youth: An Autobiographical Study of the Years 1900–1925.* 1933; reprinted 1980. A moving account of what the war meant to an entire generation. See also *Testament of Experience* on World War II.

Carrington, Charles. *Soldier from the Wars Returning.* 1965. Carrington, who was a company officer in World War I, a military historian in the years between the wars, and a general staff officer in World War II, brings multiple perspectives to his study of the war years.

*Collins, Robert O., ed. *Historical Problems of Imperial Africa.* Rev. ed., 1992. An overview of key issues, including education, nationalism, and colonial rule and its impact on African societies.

Dedijier, Vladimir. *The Road to Sarajevo.* 1966. The author had access to Serbian sources and defends the conspirators.

Elegant, Robert. *Mandarin.* 1983. A novel depicting the interplay of traditional and Western culture in late nineteenth-century China.

Eyck, Erich. *A History of the Weimar Republic.* 2 vols. 1962. The best overall study of Weimar.

*Fairbank, John K. *The United States and China.* 4th, enlarged ed. 1983. A good analysis of Chinese history and U.S. involvement in China.

*Fischer, Fritz. *Germany's Aims in the First World War.* 1967. A controversial account, stressing German responsibility in bringing on the war.

*Forbath, Peter. *The River Congo.* 1977. A dramatic account of Western exploration and exploitation of central Africa; with maps and illustrations.

*Forster, E. M. *Passage to India.* 1924. A novel about English men and women in India and their interaction with Indians. Also a film.

Fussell, Paul. *The Great War and Modern Memory.* 1975. A study of the literary tradition of the war and of what the war meant to contemporaries.

*Galbraith, J. K. *The Great Crash.* 1929; reprinted 1979. An account of the Wall Street stock market panic by a well-known economist.

The Grapes of Wrath. John Ford, director. 1940. A dramatic rendition of Steinbeck's famous novel on the Dust Bowl and its human victims.

The Great Depression. Public Broadcasting System. A six-part series with extensive documentary footage and moving narrative.

*Available in paperback.

*Joll, James. *The Origins of the First World War.* 2d ed. 1992. A well-written and capable analysis of the evidence and divergent interpretations of a controversial question.

Keegan, John. *The First World War.* 1999. A lively recent account.

Kerr, Ian J. *Building the Railways of the Raj, 1850–1900.* 1995. An account of the largest transfer of technology in the nineteenth century.

*Kindleberger, Charles P. *The World in Depression, 1929–1939.* 1975. A good survey of the global economic crisis.

Lauderdale Graham, Sandra. *House and Street: The Domestic World of Servants and Masters in Nineteenth-Century Rio de Janeiro.* 1990. A well-written social history.

*Lyons, Alan. *The Versailles Settlement: Peacemaking in Paris, 1919.* 1991. An accurate and insightful study.

Lyons, Michael J. *World War I.* Rev. ed. 2000. A fine overview with an annotated bibliography.

Macfarlane, David. *Come from Away: Memory, War, and the Search for a Family's Past.* 1991. A poignant and well-written account of one family's war.

*Marks, Sally. *The Illusion of Peace: International Relations in Europe, 1918–1933.* 1976. A sound summary of the diplomatic history of the 1920s.

*Miller, Susan Gilson, ed. and trans. *Disorienting Encounters: Travels of a Moroccan Scholar in France in 1845–1846: The Voyage of Muhammad As-Saffar.* 1992. This firsthand account of a visit to France by a Moroccan official provides a rare, unromanticized, and unprejudiced glimpse into Arab/Muslim reactions to the West.

Morgan, C. Wayne. *America's Road to Empire.* 1968. A description of the motives of U.S. imperialism.

*Remarque, Erich Maria. *All Quiet on the Western Front.* 1929. The preeminent novel of the war, distinctly antiwar in tone.

*Taylor, Stephen. *Shaka's Children: A History of the Zulu People.* 1994. A readable narrative about Shaka Zulu and his historical impact on South Africa.

*Tuchman, Barbara. *The Proud Tower.* 1966. In a series of essays, Tuchman evokes the period before the war.

Waley, Arthur. *The Opium War through Chinese Eyes.* 1958. A sympathetic account of China's attempt to deal with opium.

Wohl, Robert. *The Generation of 1914.* 1979. What the war did to the youth of the European nations.

Internet Links

American Life Histories: Manuscripts from the Federal Writers' Project, 1936–1940
http://lcweb2.loc.gov/ammem/wpaintro/wpahome.html
This amazing window into depression-era America offers a rich array of documents "varying in form from narrative to dialogue to report to case history. The histories describe the informant's family, education, income, occupation, political views, religion and mores, medical needs, diet and miscellaneous observations."

Dadabhai Naoroji: The Benefits of British Rule, 1871
http://www.fordham.edu/halsall/mod/1871britishrule.html
An Indian assesses the benefits and detriments of British rule: "The natives call the British system 'Sakar ki Churi,' the knife of sugar. . . . There is no oppression, it is all smooth and sweet, but it is the knife, notwithstanding."

Guide to Japan: Meiji Period, 1868–1912
http://www.japan-guide.com/e/e2130.html
A very useful synopsis of cultural and political trends of the era, with links to online information on the Sino-Japanese War and the Russo-Japanese War.

Scramble for Africa
http://kanga.pvhs.chico.k12.ca.us/~bsilva/projects/scramble/index.html
A clear presentation, with details on such specific individuals as David Livingstone, Cecil Rhodes, and Menelik II and such events as the Boer War and the Fashoda crisis.

The Versailles Treaty
http://history.acusd.edu/gen/text/versaillestreaty/vercontents.html
An outstanding resource, this site contains all 440 articles of the complete treaty, plus maps, illustrations, chronologies, bibliographies, and hyperlinks to additional materials.

World War I: Trenches on the Web
http://www.worldwar1.com/
A fascinating collection of 110 photographs, including weapons and battlefields, both then and now.

COMPARATIVE ESSAY 11

Antiimperialism

There are some who say we have no right in Africa at all, that "it belongs to the natives." I hold that our right is the necessity that is upon us to provide for our ever-growing population—either by opening new fields for emigration, or by providing work and employment which the development of over-sea extension entails. . . . While thus serving our interests as a nation, we may, by selecting men of the right stamp for the control of new territories, bring at the same time many advantages to Africa.

Captain F. D. Lugard, *The Rise of Our East African Empire,* vol. 1 (London: Blackwood, 1893), pp. 379–382, 473, reprinted in Dennis Sherman, *Western Civilization: Sources, Images, and Interpretations,* vol. 2: Since 1660 (New York: McGraw-Hill, 1995), p. 184.

Europe undertook the leadership of the world with ardor, cynicism, and violence. Look at how the shadow of her palaces stretches out ever further! . . . If we want to turn Africa into a new Europe, and America into a new Europe, then let us leave the destiny of our countries to Europeans. . . . But if we want humanity to advance a step further . . . we must invent and we must make discoveries. . . . For Europe, for ourselves, and for humanity . . . we must turn over a new leaf, we must work out new concepts, and try to set afoot a new man.

Frantz Fanon, *The Wretched of the Earth,* trans. Constance Farrington (New York: Grove Press, 1963), pp. 311, 315–316.

In the first passage, Lord Lugard, a British soldier and colonial administrator, justifies Great Britain's quest for empire. Lugard and many others argued that empires were economic necessities for industrialized powers, but that, properly governed, they could also bring benefits to poor, less "developed" peoples. In contrast, Frantz Fanon, a French-educated psychiatrist from the island of Martinique, speaks for the oppressed who struggled to free themselves from imperial domination in the twentieth century. Fanon became an active member of the Algerian Liberation Front (FLN), which fought a long and bloody war to achieve independence from France. Fanon's writings epitomize the often idealistic dreams for the creation of new societies in a postimperial world that many youth in the so-called Third World championed during the era from 1950 through the 1970s.

In the nineteenth century in Asia and Africa, the prospects for successful resistance to Western domination were not promising. The Indians waged an unsuccessful uprising against British rule; similarly, the Boxers in China attempted and failed to expel foreign intruders in 1900. In Africa European forces defeated the followers of the Mahdi in the Sudan and the Zulu in South Africa. Only Ethiopia was able to retain its independence in Africa. Although most of China, Persia, and the Ottoman Empire were not ruled directly by the Western imperial nations, they were indirectly but very effectively dominated by them. During the nineteenth and early twentieth centuries, Japan was the only non-Western nation to transform its economy from an agricultural to an industrial one. After 1895 Japan also emerged as a major imperialist power with a growing empire in Asia.

In the twentieth century, subject peoples adopted new methods to oppose imperial powers and, as a result, overthrew empires to establish many new nations. Paradoxically, the seeds for future independence movements were germinating just as the forces of imperial oppression seemed at their zenith.

In Asia, Africa, and Latin America, societies were subjected to humiliation, economic exploitation, and social and cultural dislocations. However, Western domination also brought some benefits, including improved health care, new education and legal institutions, and modern transportation and communication systems. In the process, societies under imperial control were introduced to such Western concepts as nationalism, individualism, and various forms of parliamentary systems. The elites in many Asian, African, and Latin American societies eventually adopted and adapted these concepts in their struggles against imperialism.

Children of elite families around the world went to school in Europe and North America, where they learned about Western politics, education, and military affairs. They also learned the value of mass political action and propaganda methods. They then adopted these techniques to good effect in their homelands to mobilize the masses and exert political and economic pressure on the colonial governments. At the same time, those with modern education filled the lower-echelon civil and military posts in colonial administrations, thereby gaining the experience needed to run their governments after they achieved independence.

In 1885 Western-educated Indians formed the Indian National Congress to pressure the British government to grant increased self-government, which would lead to independence. Under the leadership of Mohandas K. Gandhi, the Congress developed techniques of strikes, economic boycotts, and nonviolent civil disobedience. Egyptian nationalists used similar methods to oppose the British. Gandhi's tactics of noncooperation and mass campaigning contributed to winning Indian independence. His ideals were later adopted by the leaders of the civil rights movement in the United States and initially by the African National Congress in South Africa. World Wars I and II also weakened the economic, political, and military might of most European nations.

People in many other nations, such as Vietnam, Algeria, Kenya, and several in southern Africa had to resort to armed struggles to achieve independence. In these nations, nationalist leaders used guerrilla warfare tactics and protracted armed rebellions to oust the imperial powers. By the 1970s most nations in Asia and Africa had achieved independence, and by the 1990s even South Africa had achieved full political rights for all of its citizens.

In Latin America many nations continued to struggle against the indirect economic and political domination of the United States. When Latin American nations threatened to move too far outside the orbit of the United States, Washington invoked Theodore Roosevelt's adage, "Speak softly but carry a big stick," intervening militarily or in covert actions in nations as diverse as Chile, Panama, and Grenada.

The Soviet Russian Empire was the last to collapse, but during the 1990s the former Soviet republics finally broke away from Russian domination. The collapse of the Soviet Union was generally bloodless and resulted in a number of newly independent nations in eastern Europe and western Asia. As a result, as the century drew to a close, the traditional imperial systems had been dismantled, and nationalism seemed to have triumphed everywhere.

Twentieth-Century Political and Cultural Ferment

14

INDEPENDENCE MOVEMENTS IN WEST ASIA, AFRICA, AND MEXICO
Three Conflicting Agreements Regarding the Arab World
Modernism versus Tradition
African Revolts against Foreign Domination
The Emergence of African Political Organizations
Social Revolution in Mexico

STRUGGLES FOR INDEPENDENCE IN SOUTH AND EAST ASIA
British Rule and the Birth of Modern India
Indian Nationalist Awakening
A Changing Indian Society
Nationalist Opposition in Southeast Asia
The Chinese Nationalists Triumph
The Twin Challenges of Communism and Japanese Imperialism
A Changing Chinese Society

THE SOVIET UNION, 1917–1939
The Last Years of the Tsarist Regime
The Provisional Government Succeeds the Tsar
Lenin and the Bolsheviks Seize Power
The Bolshevik Regime, 1918–1924
The Deadly Struggle for the Succession to Lenin
The Stalin Dictatorship
Life and Culture in the Soviet Union
Soviet Foreign Policy

TWENTIETH-CENTURY SCIENTIFIC, TECHNOLOGICAL, AND ECONOMIC DEVELOPMENTS
Scientific Advances in the Age of Einstein
Major Trends in Biology, Anthropology, and Psychology
New Trends in Technology
Changing Patterns of Economic Organization
Societal Changes and Women's Rights

TWENTIETH-CENTURY SOCIAL AND CULTURAL PATTERNS
Philosophic Trends: Secularism, Pragmatism, Existentialism
Secularism versus Religion
Social Thought in the Contemporary Era
Modernism and the Arts
Popular Culture

SUMMARY AND COMPARISONS

Late in the evening of the ninth day in his new home, Ford brought a primitive, toylike engine into the kitchen. Its cylinder consisted of a one-inch diameter gas pipe fitted with a piston and connected to a flywheel made from an old lathe. It was Christmas Eve, and as [his wife] Clara bustled about preparing dinner for a host of relatives expected the next day, Henry clamped the engine to the sink. Since the house was on direct current, he was able to split the electric wire and use it to provide a spark. Beckoning to Clara, he had her drip gasoline into the cylinder from a can. As he spun the flywheel, the engine exploded into life. Spurting flame, popping wildly, filling the house with smoke and fumes, it shook the sink and brought coughing protestations from Clara.

*Henry was elated. It was a beginning.**

*Robert Conot, *American Odyssey* (New York: Morrow, 1974; reprinted New York: Bantam, 1975), pp. 145–146.

Henry Ford's home experimentation with the internal combustion engine in 1896 was indeed a beginning. The American industrial genius had soon built factories to mass produce automobiles by the assembly-line method; in 1913, the firm showed a profit of $27 million. But far more significant than the balance sheet of the Ford Motor Company was the all-pervading impact of motorized transport in the twentieth century, on everything from Hitler's blitzkrieg tactics to expressway travel and the modern suburban lifestyle.

The tremendous increase in speed of transportation was paralleled in other spheres of activity; indeed, it has been said that in the past century change itself changed. This has been true in global political developments, with the end of colonialism, the emergence of new nations, and revolutionary changes in government; in the economic realm, with the rise of multinational corporations; in social dynamics, with the alteration of the traditional family structure; in science, with the advent of the atomic (and subatomic) age; in information technology, with the proliferation of computers, electronic mail, and the Internet. And all of this at an astounding pace that has led some to speak of "future shock."

This chapter begins with the story of people living under the sway of imperialism fighting back with increasing determination. For some, as in China, this meant adapting Western science and technology to their own traditional cultures and religions. Others, such as the leadership in Turkey or Iran, rejected their traditional cultures as outdated and oppressive and fully embraced the Western system. Still others, like Gandhi in India, shunned Western scientific discoveries in favor of a traditional, religious way of life. The desire for economic and political independence fueled antiimperialist struggles around the world. This chapter also discusses a number of the major nationalist movements in Africa and Asia as well as the sweeping revolutionary changes in Mexico and Russia. It concludes with an overview of many of the scientific, technological, economic, and cultural developments that have made the twentieth century, for better or worse, an era of rapidly accelerating innovation and achievement.

Independence Movements in West Asia, Africa, and Mexico

- *I am an Arab, and I believe that the Arabs constitute one nation.*
- *The Arabs: All who are Arab in their language, culture, and loyalty.*
- *The Arab Homeland: It is the land which has been, or is, inhabited by an Arab majority, in the above sense, in Asia and Africa.*
- *Arab Nationalism: It is the feeling for necessity of independence and unity which the inhabitants of the Arab lands share.*
- *The Arab Movement: Its motive force is her glorious past, her remarkable vitality and the awareness of her present and future interests.*
- *The Arab National Idea: It is a national idea which proscribes the existence of racial, regional, and communal fanaticism. It respects the freedom of religious observance, and individual freedoms such as the freedom of opinion, work, and assembly, unless they conflict with the public good.**

*"First Arab Students' Congress, 1938," in *Arab Nationalism: An Anthology,* ed. Sylvia G. Haim (Berkeley: University of California Press, 1962), pp. 100–101.

This Arab manifesto of 1938 typifies the ideas and statements of nationalists throughout Africa, Asia, and South America. Emulating the liberal, secular nationalism of the West, Arab leaders and their contemporaries under imperial domination throughout the world at the turn of the century sought to oust the imperial powers and to create independent, progressive nations. By 1900, the various people within the Ottoman Empire—like those under or threatened by imperial domination around the world—had become nationalistic. Because the development of nationalism in West Asia is closely interrelated with World War I and the postwar era, the emergence of national movements and the dismemberment of the Ottoman Empire into a number of separate nations are discussed in its entirety in this section.

Prior to the onset of World War I in 1914, a group of highly Westernized Turkish officials and army officers organized the so-called Young Turk movement to seize control of the authoritarian, corrupt sultanate. In 1908 the Young Turks forced Sultan Abdul Hamid II (reigned 1876–1909) to restore the old constitution of 1876 and to institute reforms. The Young Turks centralized the administration and educational institutions under their control. They believed that by emphasizing the importance of Turkish history, culture, and language, they could save the crumbling empire from final destruction. In reaction to their attempts, Arab nationalist feelings intensified.

The non-Turkish people in the empire, Kurds, Armenians, and especially Arabs, who formed the single largest component of the populace, all opposed the programs to enforce Turkish as the language of the empire or to teach history from a solely Turkish perspective in the schools. Efforts to make Turkish the main language of instruction in schools were particularly unpopular. In the years prior to World War I, both Kurdish and Armenian national movements were crushed, and the Ar-

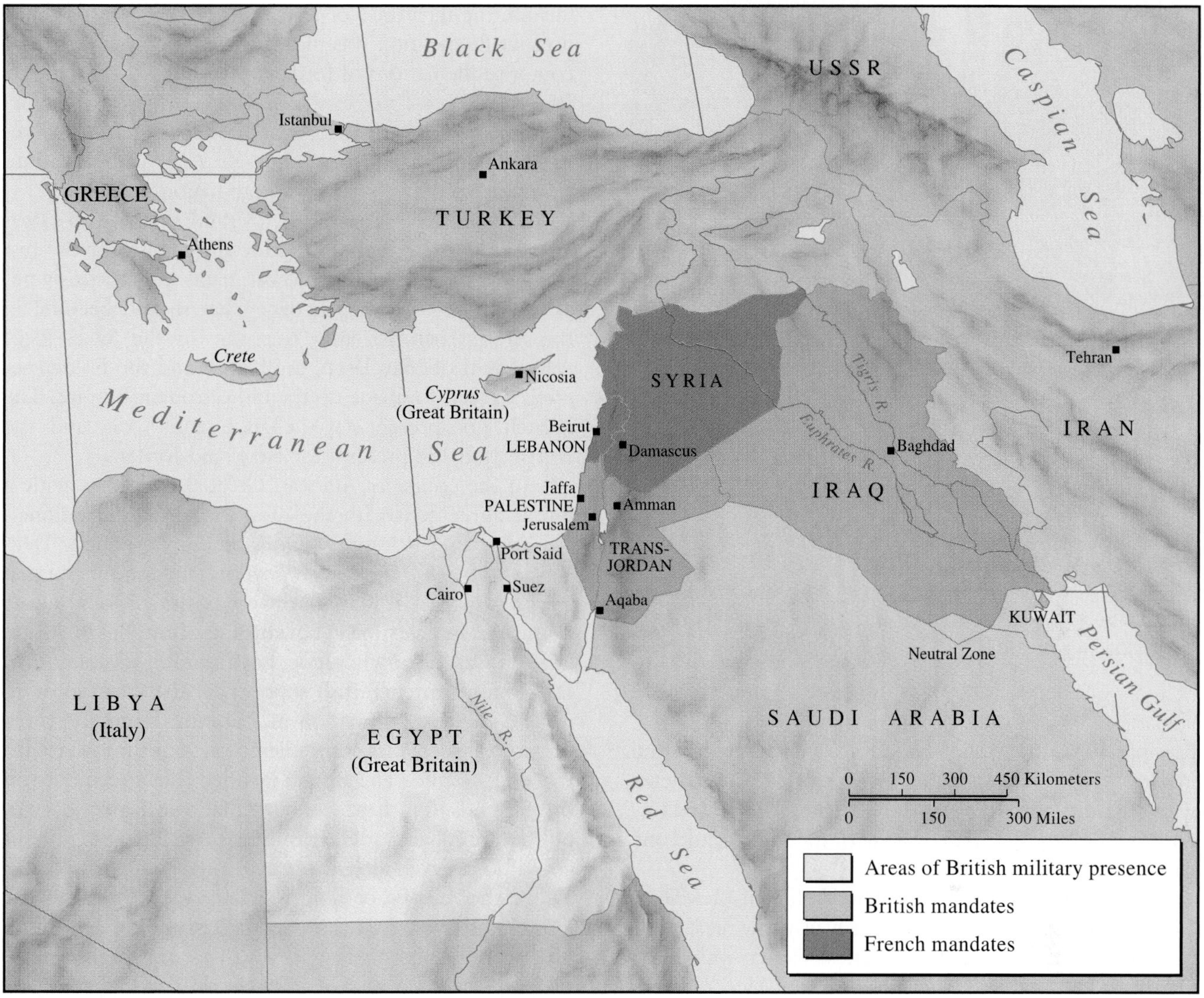

Map 14.1 Spheres of Influence in West Asia after World War I. After World War I the British and French divided the Arab provinces of the former Ottoman Empire into separate states, which they controlled either indirectly or as mandates.

menians suffered from massive persecutions and massacres. When the Young Turks joined the war effort in 1914 on the side of the Central Powers, many nationalists in the region seized the opportunity to further their goals for independent nationhood.

Three Conflicting Agreements Regarding the Arab World

World War I was a decisive turning point in Arab history. The various deals and agreements made by the British government, the Arabs, and the Zionists (Jewish nationalists) during the crucial years of 1914 to 1920 set the stage for many of the problems facing the region and the world until the present day.

The British were interested in the Arab world for military, political, and strategic reasons. They already controlled Egypt with the vital Suez Canal and most of the coastal areas along the Arabian Peninsula, and they wished to secure indirect—if not direct—influence over the Arab territories of the eastern Mediterranean. Recognizing that the Ottoman Empire, which had joined the German side in the war, would be dismembered after the war ended, the British were determined to become the dominant force in the region.

The Arabs also believed Ottoman participation in the war would bring about its final collapse. They saw the war as an opportunity to secure big power support for the creation of an independent Arab nation. Consequently, the British, who were anxious to secure whatever support

Imperial War Museum, London

Emir Faysal. Sherif Husayn's son, Faysal (center), tried but failed to persuade the great powers at the Paris Peace Conference to accept the creation of one independent nation. Lawrence of Arabia (in British military uniform and Arab headdress and standing behind Faysal to his left) had participated in the Arab revolt and acted as an adviser to Faysal at the conference. Subsequently, Faysal, with British support, was made king of Iraq.

possible to assist in the war effort against the Central Powers, therefore negotiated three separate agreements with regard to the Arab territories in the eastern Mediterranean: one with the Arabs, one with the French, and one with the Zionists.

The British negotiated the Sherif Husayn-McMahon Correspondence, the first, and in many ways the most complicated of these agreements, in a series of letters with Sherif Husayn, a key Arab leader in the holy city of Mecca. Henry McMahon was the British high commissioner in Egypt. Sherif Husayn, from the important Hashemite tribe, could trace his ancestry back to the Prophet Muhammad, and he became the self-appointed spokesperson for Arab nationalism. In 1915 Sherif Husayn proposed that the Arabs rise up against the Ottomans and fight on the side of the Allies in the war in exchange for an independent Arab state when the war was over. Husayn proposed that the borders of the new Arab state include all of the Arabian Peninsula and the territories of Iraq and greater Syria to the southern border of what is today Turkey and along the eastern Mediterranean to the Red Sea.

Although the British were delighted with the idea of having yet another ally in the war effort, they did not accept the proposed borders. The British knew there was oil in Iraq, and they had strategic interests in Palestine along the eastern Mediterranean; in addition, the French had imperial ambitions in Lebanon and Syria. Consequently, the British delayed settlements on Iraq and Lebanon. Sherif Husayn agreed in 1916 to raise the standard of revolt in exchange for an independent Arab state that would not include the territories of Iraq and Lebanon. Importantly, no specific mention was made of the territories that now comprise the nations of Jordan and Palestine (present-day Israel), which did not exist as separate entities at the time. It was assumed—at least by the Arabs—that those regions, which were overwhelmingly Arab in population, would be included within the Arab nation.

In June 1916 the Arabs revolted against the Ottoman Turks and fought alongside the British for the rest of the war. The British, however, had simultaneously negotiated with the French over what should become of the Arab territories after the war. In the Sykes-Picot Agreement of May 1916, the British and the French secretly agreed to divide up the old Ottoman Empire. The French got present-day Lebanon and Syria, and the British Iraq and present-day Israel and Jordan.

In the course of the war, Great Britain also made a public agreement with the Zionists, or Jewish nationalists, regarding Palestine. Under the public Balfour Declaration in 1917, the British government announced that it would "view with favor" the establishment of a Jewish homeland in Palestine. The wording of the Balfour Declaration was purposely vague, but the Zionists contended that it constituted British support for the creation of an independent Jewish nation in Palestine. Thus the three wartime agreements contradicted one another over control of Palestine. The British justified the agreements on the grounds that these were pragmatic deals necessary to bolster the Allied war effort and that any conflicting claims could be resolved after the war.

At the Paris Peace Conference the various parties with interests in West Asia came to present their cases. Sherif Husayn sent his son Faysal, who was the great favorite of Lawrence of Arabia, one of the British "advisers" to the Arab war effort. The Arabs were optimistic because President Wilson had strongly supported the idea of self-determination. Sherif Husayn even wrote to President Wilson requesting U.S. support. The Zionists sent the President of the World Zionist Organization, Chaim Weizmann, who had excellent contacts in the West and who had been instrumental in securing the Balfour Declaration, to represent them at Paris. In the end, however, the imperial interests of France and Great Britain triumphed.

Although it was no longer possible in an era of increasing nationalist fervor for the victors to annex lands of defeated powers as colonies, the victorious Western powers sought to retain or expand their imperial influence by devising a stratagem of issuing "mandates" under which the League of Nations would exercise nominal control over territory actually governed by Western nations. As a result, France secured mandates over what is today Lebanon and Syria. Great Britain got control over Iraq and present-day Jordan and Israel. The French also agreed that Great Britain would retain the major interest or "sphere of influence" over the territory of the Arabian

Peninsula that comprises present-day Saudi Arabia. As no one knew there was petroleum in the peninsula, the imperial powers did not demand direct control over the largely desert territory. Thus the Arab world was divided into several states under British or French domination.

The French had a very difficult time in establishing control in their mandated territories and in fact ruled in Syria only by military force. Although the French succeeded in putting down the revolts, the Syrians were never reconciled to the French presence. In Lebanon, the French established a patron-client relationship with the Maronite Christian population, with which they had a long historic relationship; they also gave additional Syrian territory to Lebanon. French policies in Lebanon laid the foundations for the "confessional" system whereby political power was meted out on the basis of one's religious affiliation. As in Ireland, the confessional system has caused many of the on-going problems in present-day Lebanon.

The British decided the fate of their Arab empire at the Cairo Conference in 1921. Led by the then colonial secretary, Winston Churchill, the British decided that the most efficient and cheapest method of rule would be to install, wherever possible, quasi-independent Arab leaders. In spite of a massive rebellion by tribal groups and nationalists in Iraq, the British installed their favorite, Amir (prince) Faysal, as king of Iraq. That monarchy continued to rule Iraq until it was overthrown in a military-led revolution in 1958.

When Egyptian demands for "complete independence" were refused, in 1919 the Egyptians launched a full-scale revolt in which all sectors of Egyptian society participated. When many of the male leaders were jailed and exiled by the British, Egyptian women stepped in to fill leadership roles and to lead the opposition. Finally, in face of continued strikes, riots, boycotts, and protests, Great Britain granted Egypt limited independence under a constitutional monarchy in 1922. However, the British continued to maintain a large military presence along the Suez Canal and directly interfered in Egyptian politics whenever British interests were threatened. The Egyptian monarchy lasted until it was overthrown in a popular revolution in 1952.

In Jordan, which had traditionally been ruled from Damascus as part of greater Syria, the British selected Sherif Husayn's eldest son, Abdullah, to become amir and ultimately king. That monarchy continues to reign; the present King Abdullah was named for his great-grandfather.

The British viewed Palestine as a strategic buffer zone to protect the Suez Canal and therefore installed direct military, political, and economic controls there. At the same time, it attempted to balance the conflicting nationalist demands of the Zionists, who wanted an independent Jewish state, and the Palestinians, who wanted an independent Arab state. When the British gained the mandate over Palestine, the Jewish population constituted approximately 10 percent of the total populace; in spite of Palestinian

Egyptian Women in the 1920s. Egyptian women played an important role in the struggle for independence against the British. During the 1920s they also demonstrated and worked for equal rights, better education, and more political power.

Corbis-Bettmann

Modernism versus Traditional Thought in Islam

Hasan Al-Banna: Spokesperson for Tradition

When we observe the evolution in the political, social, and moral spheres of the lives of nations and people, we note that the Islamic world—and, naturally, in the forefront, the Arab world—gives to its rebirth an Islamic flavor. This trend is ever-increasing. Until recently, writers, intellectuals, scholars, and governments glorified the principles of European civilization, gave themselves a Western tint, and adopted a European style and manner; today, on the contrary, the wind has changed, and reserve and distrust have taken their place. Voices are raised proclaiming the necessity for a return to the principles, teachings, and ways of Islam, and, taking into account the situation, for initiating the reconciliation of modern life with these principles, as a prelude to a final "Islamization."

*The Western way of life . . . has remained incapable of offering to men's minds a flicker of light, a ray of hope, a grain of faith, or of providing anxious persons the smallest path toward rest and tranquillity.**

Taha Hussein: Spokesperson for Modernism

The subject to be treated in this discourse is the future of culture in Egypt. . . . Many people in various parts of the world have found their freedom and independence to be meaningless and unproductive. . . . There is no use in regretting what is past, for we cannot do anything about it.

Like every patriotic educated Egyptian who is zealous for his country's good reputation, I want our new life to harmonize with our ancient glory. . . .

*The controlling factors in Egypt's destiny are its geographical situation, religion, artistic heritage, unbroken history, and the Arabic language. To defend our country, with its geographical situation, against aggression necessitates adopting European weapons and technique. Our religion, I feel, will be best maintained by doing as our ancestors did and keeping it responsive to contemporary needs.***

These excerpts from al-Banna and Hussein typify the arguments over modernism versus traditional thought made by Muslim Arab intellectuals and activists in the twentieth century. Although Western ideas and institutions heavily influenced most anti-imperialist leaders, some, like Hasan al-Banna (1906–1949), rejected Western culture and advocated the creation of a society based on Islam and traditional mores. An Egyptian, Al-Banna established the Muslim Brotherhood, which attracted members throughout the Islamic world. The Brotherhood opposed secular governments and worked for the creation of states based on religious law. Offshoots of the Brotherhood have continued to demand the creation of states based on Islamic law and principles to the present day.

Al-Banna's ideas contrast sharply with the secular approach of another Egyptian, Taha Hussein (1889–1973). Although secular leaders dominated the first generation of nationalists, in the second half of the twentieth century, religious leaders and their followers would become increasingly powerful in Iran, southern Lebanon, and elsewhere in the Islamic world.

*Hasan al-Banna, in Peter N. Stearns, ed., *Documents in World History*, vol. 2 (New York: Harper & Row, 1988), p. 176.

**Taha Hussein, in William H. McNeill and Marilyn Robinson Waldman, eds., *The Islamic World* (Chicago: University of Chicago Press, 1973), pp. 412–421.

Arab opposition, the British permitted increased Jewish immigration. A tricornered struggle among the British, Zionists, and Palestinians for control of the territory continued until the British withdrew, and the Zionists proclaimed Israel an independent Jewish state in 1948.

In those regions not taken over directly by the European imperial powers, independent nationalist leaders rose to power. These leaders differed markedly in their domestic policies and programs for future development. Modernizing approaches were particularly evident in Turkey and Iran, while in Saudi Arabia the government adopted a policy of retaining traditional culture and Islam as the basis of the nation.

Modernism versus Tradition

After the war, Turkey and Iran were led by military dictators committed to destroying old traditional institutions, while Saudi Arabia was led by a monarchy based on tradition and puritanical Islamic law. Both Mustafa Kemal, or Atatürk, father of the Turks (1881–1938), in Turkey and Reza Khan (1878–1944) in Iran were determined to westernize their nations as rapidly as possible. Atatürk toppled the old Ottoman monarchy and successfully led his forces against the Allied attempts to partition Turkey. A popular national hero, Atatürk saved Turkey from foreign domination; he then used his charismatic personality and national reputation to push through a series of sweeping reforms calculated to destroy the last vestiges of the Ottoman Empire and to make Turkey as European as possible. Hating both religion and the Ottoman regime, Atatürk abolished both the sultanate and the caliphate and personally developed a parliamentary constitutional state that by law was secular. Although he forced the creation of a two-party system, in actual fact, Atatürk controlled the political life of the nation until his death in 1938.

Atatürk's reforms also extended into the social sphere. He abolished wearing the fez, the traditional Ottoman headdress for men, and the veil for women and pushed such Western social activities as ballroom dancing. Encouraged by women's movements elsewhere and by Atatürk's social reforms, Turkish feminists organized to demand greater legal rights in the 1920s and even dropped leaflets from an airplane to attract attention to their cause.

Atatürk encouraged the development of modern state-owned industries and changed the Turkish alphabet from the old Arabic script to Western script. Although he was a dictator, Atatürk never amassed a personal fortune and, importantly, he bequeathed a tradition of parliamentary and secular government to Turkey. Atatürk has often been viewed as the personification of a "benevolent" dictator.

Similarly, in 1923 Reza Khan, a professional soldier, overthrew the Qajar dynasty in Persia. He abolished the old monarchy and embarked on a massive program of modernization, which included building roads, reforming the military and financial administration, and encouraging Western, secular education. He, too, attempted to lessen the power of religion and in particular sought to destroy the authority of the mullahs, the established Shi'i clergy. In contrast to Atatürk, Reza Khan amassed a huge personal fortune. He also created a new royal dynasty, the Pahlavi, with himself as the first shah. In 1935 he formally changed the nation's name from Persia to Iran. The failure to establish lasting parliamentary institutions, the attacks against the clergy, and the continuation of the monarchy all had long-lasting impacts on Iranian political and social development.

The political development of Saudi Arabia offers a marked contrast to that of Iran and Turkey. During the nineteenth century, the House of Saud had linked forces with Muhammad ibn Abd al-Wahhab, a puritanical reformer who wanted to purge Islam of worldly deviations

Stock Montage

Mustafa Kemal, or Atatürk. Atatürk traveled widely throughout Turkey to popularize his programs for modernization. As seen here, he sometimes brought a portable blackboard along and used it to teach the new alphabet to villagers in the countryside.

that had crept into the religion over the centuries. As in the early centuries of Islamic development, the merger of a political and military force with religious reform proved a potent combination. As the house of Saud and the Wahhabi followers spread their brand of Islamic puritanism across the Arabian Peninsula, they were repeatedly attacked by tribal rivals and by the Ottomans. The Wahhabi movement was militarily defeated several times, but each time, like the proverbial phoenix, it came back to life stronger than ever.

In Abd al-Aziz ibn Saud, king of Saudi Arabia (reigned 1932–1953), the movement found a charismatic, energetic champion. During the first decades of the twentieth century, Abd al-Aziz ibn Saud steadily enlarged his territories and defeated his rivals. After World War I, he moved against Sherif Husayn, his main rival in the Arabian Peninsula. Sherif Husayn's forces were no match for the committed and zealous Wahhabis, and by 1926 Abd al-Aziz ibn Saud had ousted Husayn's supporters and had taken over the holy cities of Mecca and Medina. King Abd al-Aziz promptly proceeded to forge a kingdom, Saudi Arabia (named after his family), based on strict adherence to puritanical Islam. Although the legitimacy of King Abd al-Aziz's rule rested primarily upon his commitment to maintaining the kingdom as an Islamic state, he did not reject modern technological innovations. He brought cars, radios, and telephones into the kingdom. The first

Chilembwe Rouses His People to Action

You are all patriots as you sit. . . . This very night you are to go and strike the blow and then die. I do not say that you are going to win the war at all. You have no weapons with you and you are not at all trained military men even. One great thing you must remember is . . . love [of] your own country and country men, I now encourage you to go and strike a blow bravely and die.

You must not think that with that blow, you are going to defeat whitemen and then become Kings of your own country, no. . . . I am also warning you strongly against seizing property from anybody. . . . Another order I want you to remember, is about women and young children, do not, in any way, do anything to them, treat them as innocents, what you are to do with them is to bring them over peacefully, and afterwards send them back. . . . Be of good courage, and strike the blow and die. . . . *

John Chilembwe led an abortive revolt against British coffee and tobacco plantation owners in Nyasaland in 1915. Before the battle, Chilembwe delivered the rousing patriotic speech quoted above.

* *The Horizon History of Africa* (New York: American Heritage, 1971), p. 472.

telephone link in the nation was between Abd al-Aziz's palace and his beloved sister's home. With the discovery of huge petroleum reserves in the peninsula and the subsequent influx of large amounts of money after World War II, Saud's kingdom was soon awash with consumer goods. Abd al-Aziz's sons have continued to rule Saudi Arabia to the present day. The kingdom is representative of those states that have attempted to amalgamate modern technology with fundamentalist religion and traditional culture. How successful that amalgamation will prove remains uncertain.

African Revolts against Foreign Domination

As in West Asia, numerous armed revolts against European domination in Africa occurred during the first quarter of the twentieth century. Specific ethnic or tribal groups generally dominated these revolts or religious movements that rallied mass support against foreign occupation. Without exception, the Europeans, with superior military power, were able to defeat these movements, but at enormous human cost to their African opponents. In a very real way, these revolts presaged many of the successful armed struggles launched around the world against imperial domination following World War II.

Like the Boxer Rebellion in China, the revolts in Africa were motivated by distrust and hatred of foreign occupation, anger over the destruction of local economies, and the determination to protect indigenous cultures from destruction. Owing to their relative military weakness vis-à-vis the Europeans, who possessed both technologically superior weapons and the will to use them, all the African revolts against European domination at the beginning of the twentieth century failed. The British succeeded in putting down strong resistance by the Ashanti in the Gold Coast in 1900. The Herero revolts in German South-West Africa (present-day Namibia) from 1904 to 1906 and the Maji Maji Revolt (1905–1907) in German East Africa (present-day Tanzania) are other examples of armed struggles by Africans against European domination. The Germans so brutally defeated these movements that the Herero people were nearly destroyed. The last Zulu revolt in South Africa occurred in 1906, and it, too, was defeated. Likewise, the Portuguese put down widespread rebellions in Angola in 1913, though the Tutsi, cattle-owning people, and the Hutu, mainly farming people, in present-day Burundi and Rwanda continued to resist both the British and Germans from 1911 until 1917.

As in much of the Islamic world, African opposition to foreign domination often took religious forms. For example, John Chilembwe in Nyasaland (present-day Malawi) established his own separatist religious mission. A product of Protestant missionary education, Chilembwe had lived in the United States, where he had become involved in the political activities of African Americans seeking the unity of blacks and a return to Africa. Angered by the favoritism shown to white settlers and increased prices and shortages brought about by World War I, Chilembwe led a rebellion against the settlers and British domination in 1915; his revolt was crushed, however, and Chilembwe was ambushed and assassinated.

In North Africa, resistance movements were able to organize and maintain more protracted and far bloodier struggles. Under the leadership of Muhammad Abd al-Krim, the tribes in the Moroccan Rif Mountains organized an efficient and effective opposition to Spanish domination. In 1921 Krim's forces inflicted a devastating military defeat on the Spanish at Anual; several years of bloody confrontations ensued. Determined to defeat Krim's forces, successive Spanish leaders reinforced their troops. Francisco Franco, the future dictator of Spain, began his rise to power by leading Spanish forces fighting in North Africa.

As Krim's rebellion spread, it was opposed by France, which held the protectorate over the portion of Morocco not held by Spain. Although successful in repelling the weak and dispirited Spanish army, Krim's forces were no match for the French. By 1926 Krim was forced to surrender to them and was sent into exile on the island of Réunion in the Indian Ocean. Moroccan independence from Spain and France would not be achieved until after World War II.

During the 1920s Omar Mukhtar's struggle against Italian occupation of Libya had a similar outcome. The Libyans fiercely opposed the Italian occupation, but, once in power, Mussolini was equally determined to incorporate Libya into his new Italian Empire. Using bases in desert oases, the support of the people, and superior knowledge of the terrain, Omar Mukhtar launched guerrilla warfare against the Italian troops in the 1920s. After suffering several humiliating defeats, the Italians began rounding up Libyans, killing many, placing women and children in concentration camps, cutting off supplies from the outside, and attacking with planes and superior military armaments. In 1931 Mukhtar was captured, summarily tried, and publicly executed by Italian forces. The struggle in Libya presaged similar confrontations against the Italians in Ethiopia in the 1930s, and were an indication of postwar resistance movements against the European imperial powers. Meanwhile, Africans took their nationalist struggles into political arenas as well.

The Emergence of African Political Organizations

As noted in Chapter 13, World War I had a major impact on Africa. Not only had hundreds of thousands of Africans died in the war, but the imperial powers, particularly the British and French, had increased taxes and commercial controls in their African possessions in order to help pay for the war. After the war, the British and French sought to hold on to their African possessions for as long as possible and to make them increasingly profitable. Because these policies stimulated opposition, it can be said that the war hastened the development of African political organizations. Many of the early African political movements were influenced by a pan-African approach and had international components. Three very disparate personalities dominated the pan-African movement, and they adopted widely different approaches to the problems of people of African descent around the world.

Dr. W. E. B. DuBois, an African American, was one of the foremost intellectual leaders of the pan-African movement. Influential in the United States, DuBois organized a pan-African congress in Paris to coincide with the Paris Peace Conference in 1919. He called for improved racial, economic, and political reforms and called attention to the problems facing blacks. Early pan-Africanists had often been influenced by négritude, a literary movement extolling the virtues of black Africa. In a very real way, writers and politicians like Leopold Senghor (1906–1993; see the final section of this chapter) sought to compensate for racism and ethnocentric Western attitudes regarding Africans and African culture.

Initially, DuBois enjoyed the support of Blaise Diagne from Senegal; however, the two leaders disagreed over what course African relations with the imperial powers should take. In short, Diagne and others believed that Africans should seek to attain parity with the Europeans within the imperial framework. The French encouraged this approach by advocating assimilation, and, when that policy was attacked, a program of association. To

Mansell Collection

Abd al-Krim. Abd al-Krim, seated, led a protracted rebellion against the Spanish in the mountains of Morocco but was finally defeated by a combination of Spanish and French forces.

Léopold Senghor with President and Mrs. Kennedy. An early proponent of Senegalese nationalism, Senghor went on to become the first president of independent Senegal. In addition to his political career, Senghor was also a well-known poet.

implement this approach, France granted citizenship to the Senegalese and allowed them to elect a deputy to the French National Assembly. In 1914 Diagne was elected to this post, which he held until his death in 1934. Diagne used his influential position to push for improved relations between the French and black Africa. When DuBois became more strident in calling for African independence and economic freedom, Diagne denounced him for holding pro-Marxist ideas. Diagne continued to believe that only France would give equal political and social treatment to Africans.

A flamboyant Jamaican, Marcus Garvey, was perhaps the most popular pan-African leader. Operating from Harlem in New York City, Garvey campaigned for a return to Africa by all blacks in the Western Hemisphere. African Americans from the United States, the Caribbean, and South America flocked to his calls, but political problems in Liberia, where many African Americans planned to return, prevented a major emigration from the West. Nonetheless, Garvey's political platform and his publication in 1920 of a "Declaration of Rights of the Negro People of the World" influenced a future generation of African leaders, including Kwame Nkrumah of Ghana (formerly known as the Gold Coast).

Other Africans also began to form political organizations aimed at securing independence in specific African nations. For example, in 1917 a number of educated West Africans established the National Congress of British West Africa; led by J. E. Casely Hayford, a journalist and lawyer from the Gold Coast, members of the congress traveled to London in 1920 to demand an elected legislature with the power to impose taxes, equal opportunities for Africans and Europeans in the civil service, the foundation of a university, and autonomy for local chiefs. After some protracted negotiations in the 1920s, the British allowed the creation of some legislative councils, dominated by Europeans, in Nigeria and Ghana.

Anticolonial political organizing began early in South Africa. Established in 1912, the South African Native National Congress was the first political organization of its type in Africa. Later, it changed its name to the African National Congress (ANC) and continued to lead the protracted struggle for African political rights in South Africa. Similarly, in eastern Africa, opposition to land appropriations by whites led to the formation of the East Africa Association and the Kikuyu Provincial Association led by Harry Thuku. The Kikuyu, who were generally farmers, had been particularly affected by white settlers, who in the 1930s began to expand their farms by ousting the Kikuyu from rented land the Kikuyu regarded as their own. The settlers then took on the displaced Kikuyu as hired hands.

None of these political organizations called for complete independence; rather, they all sought to secure domestic reforms and improved economic status. Prior to World War II, African organizations had little success in altering European imperial policies or in improving the day-to-day standard of living in their nations.

While black Africans were expanding their demands, whites in South Africa also organized to perpetuate their dominant social, economic, and political positions. In 1934 the Afrikaners, led by Generals Jan Smuts and James Hertzog, organized the United party. The United party remained the preeminent white political organization until it was superseded by the Afrikaner National party, which adopted even more rigid policies of racial segregation and white supremacy. The tendency toward government policies of racial segregation was apparent even in the United party's 1936 Natives Representation Act. Under this law Africans lost their political rights, but coloureds (people of Asian or mixed racial heritage) kept the right to vote on the common roll in the Cape Province. Thus, while the Union of South Africa allowed for democratic representation of whites, the majority of the nation was denied any political rights. In the decades to follow, segregationist policies were extended and fur-

An African School. Here a teacher instructs boys and girls from Niger in West Africa in an outdoor classroom.

ther entrenched into government policy by the Afrikaner minority.

Social Revolution in Mexico

Unlike events in West Asia and Africa, the revolution that swept through Mexico in 1911 was not a revolt against direct colonial rule; Mexico had been independent since 1821. It was, however, the first social revolution of the twentieth century in which the masses of peasants and urban workers were an active force. It was also the first time in the modern history of the Western Hemisphere other than Haiti that persons of part or full Amerindian descent improved their position in a region where persons of European descent dominated nations.

In 1911, after thirty-four years in power, Porfirio Díaz's dictatorial rule came to an abrupt end in Mexico. The reign of the dictator had touched every aspect of Mexican life. Díaz's policies were designed to achieve political stability by centralizing power and to modernize the economy by building a modern technological infrastructure and increasing exports. In pursuit of these goals, Díaz's regime allowed the *hacendados,* the large landowners, to increasingly take over small farms and Amerindian communal property in order to consolidate large tracts of land for raising products for export, such as sisal, hemp, sugar, and meat. He excluded most of the developing middle class and northern elites from political power and harshly suppressed urban workers who wished to organize for better working conditions and workers' rights. These policies were characterized by the phrase *pan o palo*—"bread or a club."

Foreign capital and finance paid for Mexican modernization, and the Díaz regime allowed non-Mexicans unprecedented holdings in mining, transportation, communications, electricity, and petroleum. By linking local economies to larger markets, modernization also linked the peasantry to the volatile whims of the global market. Railway intrusion into the countryside spurred the commercialization of agriculture; wherever railroads were built, demand for land increased and so did takeovers. The new developments in communications and transportation also gave Díaz stronger political control over larger areas and allowed his rule to reach the farthest corners of Mexico.

As Díaz's regime widened and centralized, it also weakened. When Diaz extended his power to isolated, localized regions, he installed political officials of his choosing, thereby excluding from the power structure, and alienating, local elites who were used to a large degree of self-rule. As a result, coalitions opposed to Díaz's centralization began to form.

Initial opposition arose in the northern section of Mexico, which, ironically, was one of the chief beneficiaries of Porfirian modernization. The north was experiencing an unprecedented growth in economic prosperity, which gave rise to an urban middle class. Both this middle class and the economically powerful desired access to political power.

In 1910 Francisco Madero, one of the northern elite, challenged Díaz, having taken him at his word

Brown Brothers

Mexico's Favorite Revolutionary. The collapse of Francisco Madero's administration sparked unrest in the Mexican countryside. Emiliano Zapata, pictured here, led rebellious Amerindians against wealthy landowners in southern Mexico, making demands of his own for land reform.

when, in an interview with a journalist from the United States, Díaz promised to allow opposition candidates in the upcoming elections. Madero wrote an influential work regarding the elections that promptly landed him in jail as an opposition spokesperson. Madero escaped and fled to San Antonio, where he and his supporters put together a political platform. They issued the Plan of San Luis Potosi, which proclaimed Madero provisional president of Mexico, declared Díaz's rule null and void, and called for an uprising set for November 20, 1910. At this point, no significant mention was made of any social programs or reforms, other than a brief mention of the restitution of illegally acquired lands to the peasantry. Madero's "Revolt from Abroad" prevailed; Díaz fled the country in 1911 with the parting words: "Madero has unleashed a tiger; let us see if he can control it."

Díaz's departure was followed by six years of bloody civil war. Madero became president, but soon fell victim to a counterrevolution by conservative forces, who in turn soon fell to the legendary figures in Mexican history, Pancho Villa and Emiliano Zapata. Villa was a bandit and popular hero of the lower classes in northern Mexico. He was a staunch supporter of Madero, and after Madero's death formed his own "Division of the North" to carry out the revolution. Zapata was a small landowner in the state of Morelos, south of Mexico City. Zapata reflected the agrarian nature of the revolution; he was a leader of *campesinos* (peasants) fighting against exploitation. His Plan of Ayala called for the restitution of lands to all peasants who had suffered losses to large landowners and illegal landgrabbers.

By 1917 the Constitutionalist faction had gained the upper hand in the civil war and convened a constitution-drafting body that contained representatives of most of the competing factions. They produced a constitution that set up the most socially and nationalistically radical basis for government in the Western world. The constitution called for the redistribution of land to the peasantry and to all persons requiring it. Land and subsoil rights (ores, gas, and petroleum) were to be the property of the nation and its peoples. Other provisions guaranteed sweeping workers' rights, including a minimum wage, eight-hour workdays, regulation of child and female labor, safety standards, and the right to strike. The constitution also deprived the Catholic church in Mexico of much of its wealth, power, and influence over the masses.

Most of the bloody revolutionary infighting ended by 1920, and political stability was solid enough for elections to be held. With the end to revolution, reconstruction of the nation began, with a new constitution, a new sense of nationalism, and a new generation of political elites. From 1927 on, the Institutional Revolutionary party (PRI) ruled Mexico, allowing no major formal opposition. The party was not rooted in one political philosophy but rather was composed of all members of the political spectrum and worked solely to perpetuate its own power and rule. One unemployed general snorted that "the revolution has now degenerated into a government."

The revolution did, however, make great strides during the presidency of Lázaro Cárdenas (ruled 1934–1940). His administration bore many similarities to the New Deal programs of U.S. president Franklin Roosevelt. The popular Cárdenas actively sought information about the plight of the Mexican peasantry by visiting villages. He expedited land reform by restoring land to Amerindians and by shifting it from the wealthy *hacienderos* to the destitute farmers. Cárdenas also took an interest in building schools and improving industrial working conditions in the cities. Another development of these years was the nationalization of the railroads and petroleum companies. The government ran the national oil corporation more effectively than foreign owners had run the former private corporations. Though large foreign consumers of Mexican oil in the United States and Europe raised objections, the Cárdenas administration channeled much of the increased flow of oil into important new domestic projects.

Besides changing the social and economic structures of the country, the revolution brought a change in the Mexican self-image. The Latin element in Mexican civilization was emphasized in favor of stressing Amerindian history and culture. Mestizos, after all, were now a major element in the racial mixture of Mexico. Books, paintings, and the mass media featured themes from contemporary Amerindian life and informed the populace about the great achievements of the Aztec and Mayan cultures.

The revolution lost its momentum in the 1940s. Despite land redistribution policies, the *haciendaros* were still in possession of half the cultivable land in the country, while a third of the Mexican people still lived in virtual serfdom. Governmental corruption also impeded many of the reforms initiated by Cárdenas. Nonetheless, Mexico had traveled a long way from the dictatorship of Porfirio Díaz.

In retrospect, the Mexican Revolution appears to have been an indigenous phenomenon. Its leaders sought unique Mexican solutions to Mexican problems; they did so without applying any of the ideologies that motivated many European revolutionaries. From a decade of civil chaos, a consensus among disparate groups and a political party capable of concerted action emerged slowly. The profound changes in economics, society, and culture that the revolution set in motion still remained to be consummated.

As in West Asia, Africa, and Mexico, nationalists in East and South Asia also fought for increased control over their own national identities in the interwar years. The organization of Asian nationalist movements and their conflicts with imperial forces are treated in the next section of this chapter.

Struggles for Independence in South and East Asia

Salt suddenly became a mysterious word, a word of power. The salt tax was to be attacked, the salt laws were to be broken. . . . As people followed the fortunes of this marching column of pilgrims from day to day, the temperature of the country went up. . . .

I went to see Gandhiji [Indians add "ji" to name endings to indicate respect; Gandhiji is thus a respectful way of referring to Gandhi]. . . . We spent a few hours with him there and then saw him stride away with his party to the next stage in the journey to the salt sea.

It seemed as though a spring had been suddenly released; all over the country, in town and village, salt manufacture was the topic of the day. . . . We knew precious little about it. . . . It was really immaterial whether the stuff was good or bad; the main thing was to commit a breach of the obnoxious salt law, and we were successful in that, even though the quality of our salt was poor.

I was arrested on the 14th of April. . . . That very day I was tried in prison and sentenced to six months' imprisonment under the Salt Act.

When I heard that my aged mother and, of course, my sisters used to stand under the hot summer sun picketing before foreign cloth shops, I was greatly moved.

*Many strange things happened in those days, but undoubtedly the most striking was the part of the women in the national struggle. They came out in large numbers from the seclusion of their homes and, though unused to public activity, threw themselves into the heart of the struggle. The picketing of foreign cloth and liquor shops they made their preserve. Enormous processions consisting of women alone were taken out in all the cities; and, generally, the attitude of the women was more unyielding than that of the men.**

**The Autobiography of Jawaharlal Nehru* (London: John Day/Bodley Head, 1941), in *Modern Asia and Africa*, eds. William H. McNeill and Mitsuko Iriye (New York: Oxford University Press, 1971), pp. 224–229.

In his *Autobiography*, Indian nationalist leader Jawaharlal Nehru described his participation in the struggle for independence from British rule. Nehru wrote his *Autobiography* while in British prison during World War II, serving one of several prison terms to which he was sentenced for his involvement in the nationalist movement. For many Asian and African nationalists before and after World War II, a prison sentence was the price they paid for the independence struggle for their homelands.

All of Asia came under some degree of European political and economic domination. In South and Southeast Asia, all nations except Thailand were fully incorporated into Western empires. In the Indian subcontinent and on mainland and island Southeast Asia, militant organizations developed with the primary goal of ousting imperial control and winning national independence.

British Rule and the Birth of Modern India

In Asia as in Africa, Great Britain was not so much concerned with either assimilation or elimination of indigenous cultures as with maintaining control over its territories. While Britain ruled most of India directly, it nevertheless retained many of the native princes or maharajas in power in their ancestral domains. Even in these native states, however, British officials supervised the administration.

Although Great Britain did not work actively to subvert local culture and traditions in India and its other colonial holdings in Asia, British policy did suppress certain local practices such as child marriages. Some traditionalist Hindus objected strenuously to these attempts because they tampered with old traditions and religious rules; others reacted by reexamining their traditions to reform outmoded practices. Although Hindus and Muslims were allowed to retain their religious beliefs in the civil law code, the British administration gradually superimposed British legal concepts in criminal law, and also instituted modern commercial codes. British banking and commercial institutions, modern roads, and the telegraph gradually transformed India and integrated it into a global economy.

As early as the 1830s, British authorities in India had begun to establish modern English-language schools and universities and also encouraged religious institutions and other bodies to open private Western-style schools. These schools educated the children of Hindu upper and middle classes, as well as those who traditionally had no opportunity to obtain an education, notably girls and lower-caste Hindus. Some of the brightest boys went on to attend schools and universities in Great Britain. Civil service exams recruited the best to join the prestigious Indian Civil Service. Upper-caste Hindus who traditionally revered education eagerly grasped these educational opportunities. Many Muslims, however, felt aggrieved because Britons had replaced them as the ruling class. They were thus reluctant to send their children to Western-style schools. As a result, the number of Muslims with a modern education was small in proportion to their total population; consequently, Muslims played a lesser role in the modern sector than their proportional numbers warranted.

British policy tried to maintain a balance and tolerance for all the religions in the subcontinent, particularly Islam and Hinduism. Great Britain did not encourage conversion of members of either religious community to Christianity. Christian religious missionaries made few converts, but medical and educational missionaries were highly successful in introducing modern medicine and technology through education. English was used in the new schools and so became the common language of a growing urban middle class, bridging regional and linguistic barriers among Indians.

Indian Nationalist Awakening

The growth of national consciousness was the most important phenomenon of modern India because it culminated in independence for the subcontinent. It was also the forerunner of other independence movements throughout the colonial world. The Indian National Congress, formed in 1885 by seventy modern educated Indians and Britons, was the first major secular nationalist organization in India. Meeting in annual conventions, the Congress from the beginning had two main goals: developing self-government by means of representative institutions, and promoting educational, social, and other reforms. A modern press in English and vernacular languages began to demand the extension to Indians of the same political rights enjoyed by Britons in their own country, as well as social reforms, including the emancipation of women.

Although membership in the Indian National Congress was open to all, few Muslims joined. As the Congress's lobbying efforts won increasing respect from British leaders, Muslims became fearful of the implications of representative government: as the minority community, they would lose any elections. In 1905 Indian Muslim leaders organized the All India Muslim League, which had the twin goals of representative government and separate electorates for Muslims (that is, Muslims would vote for Muslims for designated Muslim seats in any elections). Although the Congress opposed separate electorates, they were granted to Muslims in 1909 when the British parliament passed the Morley-Minto Reforms, which granted limited suffrage to male Indians and created advisory representative bodies.

As in the African colonies, India also played an important part in the British Empire's war effort during World War I. After the war, Indians demanded increased participation in their own government. In 1919 the British Parliament responded by enacting the Government of India Act, which expanded the franchise (women were granted the right to vote on the same terms as men in 1925) and the powers of the elected legislatures. Separate electorates for Muslims were retained at the insistence of the League. Indian nationalists maintained that the concessions were insufficient and began to agitate for complete independence.

After World War I Mohandas K. Gandhi (1869–1948) reenergized the mass struggle for Indian independence. The son of a prosperous Hindu family and a London-educated lawyer, Gandhi had won great respect among Indians for his use of nonviolent techniques to champion Indian rights against discrimination by whites in South Africa. Returning to India from South Africa in 1915, Gandhi emerged as the spiritual head of the Indian nationalist movement by perfecting the techniques of nonviolent protest and by widening the appeal of Congress to millions of ordinary Indians. Gandhi taught that whatever the grievance, violence was wrong. He also taught Indians that because Indian acquiescence had made British rule possible, Indians could force Britain to leave India if they withheld their cooperation. He therefore organized nationwide nonviolent, noncooperation campaigns similar to strikes that shut down the government and all its services. When the strikes and demonstrations turned violent, Gandhi would call them off, because, he maintained, two wrongs did not make a right. For this reason, some Indians anxious to win independence immediately and at any price accused Gandhi of retarding the achievement of Indian independence.

Gandhi also championed social reforms such as the right of Hindu widows to remarry, the ending of child marriages, and above all the end of untouchability, which made millions outcastes from Hindu society. He sought to attain his goals not by legislation but by his own saintly example and by touching the hearts of friends and adversaries alike. Gandhi also taught his fol-

Gandhi Revitalizes the Congress

Gandhi . . . brought about a complete change in its [the Congress's] constitution. He made it democratic and a mass organization. Democratic it had been previously also, but it had so far been limited in franchise and restricted to the upper classes. Now the peasants rolled in, and in its new garb it began to assume the look of a vast agrarian organization with a strong sprinkling of the middle classes. . . . Industrial workers also came in, but as individuals and not in their separate, organized capacity.

Action was to be the basis and objective of this organization, action based on peaceful methods. Thus far the alternatives had been: just talk and passing resolutions, or terroristic activity. Both of these were set aside and terrorism was especially condemned as opposed to the basic policy of the Congress. A new technique of action was evolved which, though perfectly peaceful, yet involved non-submission to what was considered wrong, and as a consequence, a willing acceptance of the pain and suffering involved in this. . . .

The call to action was twofold. There was of course the action involved in challenging and resisting foreign rules; there was also the action which led us to fight our own social evils . . . which involved the solution of the minority problems, and the raising of the depressed classes and the ending of the curse of untouchability. . . .

*He sent us to the villages, and the countryside hummed with the activity of innumerable messengers of the new gospel of action. The peasant was shaken up and he began to emerge from his quiescent shell. The effect on us was different but equally far-reaching, for we saw, for the first time as it were, the villager in the intimacy of his mud hut and with the stark shadow of hunger always pursuing him. We learned our Indian economics more from these visits than from books and learned discourses.**

Jawaharlal Nehru was Gandhi's disciple, a leader of the Congress, and first prime minister of independent India. Here he commented on Gandhi's effect on both the elite leadership of the Congress and on Indian masses.

*Jawaharlal Nehru, *The Discovery of India,* ed. Robert I. Crane (Garden City, N.Y.: Anchor Books, 1946), pp. 276–279.

lowers the dignity of labor and sought to avoid the abuses of industrial society by advocating handicrafts. He gave up wearing Western clothes, spun and wove cloth for his own clothes, and insisted that all men and women of the Congress do likewise. Thus the spinning wheel came to symbolize the Indian nationalist movement. Later, independent India would reject Gandhi's idyllic notions of a nonindustrial society. Nevertheless, he continued to be revered in India and worldwide as the gentle apostle of peace and as a nonviolent crusader for social change. Because of his exemplary life and the humanitarian causes he championed, Gandhi came to be called the Mahatma (Great Soul). Gandhi's philosophy of nonviolent resistance to wrongs and immoral laws influenced U.S. civil rights leader Martin Luther King Jr. and South Africa's Nelson Mandela.

During the 1920s and 1930s, the Gandhi-led nonviolent protest movements filled British jails and baffled British officials, who had no precedent in dealing with such a saintly adversary. Public opinion forced the British to negotiate and make concessions to Gandhi's demands, thus advancing the Indian nationalist movement. By the mid-1930s Gandhi's massive civil disobedience campaigns against British rule compelled the British government to advance the time frame for its withdrawal from India. As the prospect of independence drew nearer, however, Muslim fear of Hindu domination also intensified. In India communal differences, or identification by religious affiliation, were old and intense, and became more so between Hindus and Muslims as independence drew closer. The tensions arose because all modern Indian nationalist movements sought to establish democratically elected governments after independence. The majority Hindus foresaw political dominance as rightfully theirs, but that prospect frightened the Muslims, who would become a permanent minority under Hindu domination.

During the 1930s the British government conferred with Gandhi in London and held a series of conferences over the timetable and conditions of independence. In

1935 the British parliament passed the India Act, which made India a federation of provinces and princely states under a British-appointed governor-general, who shared power with representatives of a bicameral legislature of elected and appointed members. The franchise was further enlarged, Muslims retained separate electorates, and reserved seats were guaranteed for women, depressed classes, and minority communities. At the national level, this act was the last transitional step before the full attainment of self-government. On the provincial level, an elected government comprised of Indians controlled all affairs, with the British-appointed provincial governor retaining only emergency powers. This plan gave wide powers to the provinces and princely states and was an attempt to reconcile the fears of the Muslims and accommodate the special needs of the princely states. As expected, the elections held under the India Act returned Congress majorities to predominantly Hindu provinces and League majorities to provinces where Muslims predominated.

Mohammed Ali Jinnah (1876–1948), a British-educated lawyer and founder of the Muslim League, led the Muslim community in demanding a separate identity for Muslims. Jinnah epitomized Indian Muslim separateness in a speech he made in 1940 at the annual meeting of the Muslim League:

> Hindus and Muslims belong to two different religious philosophies, social customs, literature. . . . To yoke together two such nations under a single state, one as a numerical minority and the other as a majority, must lead to growing discontent and final destruction of any fabric that may be so built up for the government of such a state. . . . The only course open to us all is to allow the major nations separate homelands for dividing India into "autonomous nation states."

Gandhi and the Salt March. In 1930 Gandhi and his followers participated in the famous Salt March to oppose the British tax and monopoly on salt. Thousands of Indian men and women joined the march in a massive act of civil disobedience and passive resistance against British imperial policies.

www.historypictures.com

Following this speech the Muslim League passed the Pakistan Resolution, which called for the creation of a separate state called Pakistan ("Land of the Pure" in Urdu, the language of many Muslims in northwestern India) in areas of the Indian subcontinent where Muslims formed a majority.

In contrast to 1914, when Indians followed Great Britain to war without protest and made major contributions to the Allied cause, in 1939 the Congress protested India's automatic involvement in World War II on behalf of the British Empire. Congress leaders argued that an India that was itself unfree could not join in the effort to fight against Nazi and Fascist tyranny. They demanded the immediate granting of full independence by Great Britain, and promised that as a free people, they would gladly join in the Allied war effort.

Great Britain responded by dissolving the Congress-controlled provincial governments and imprisoning the key Congress leaders, including Gandhi. Jinnah and the League declared the closing of Congress-dominated provincial governments a "Day of Deliverance and Thanksgiving." The League and the provinces it controlled cooperated with the British war effort, thereby gaining administrative experience and improving the Muslims' political position.

Several British missions came to India to negotiate with Indian leaders during the war. They suggested formulas for power sharing, but all failed because of the irreconcilable differences between the Congress and the League and conflict over the timetable for granting complete independence. Despite these unresolved problems, India and Indians played greater roles in World War II than in World War I. The Indian Army increased from 182,000 men in 1939 to over 2 million in 1945. Indian units served with distinction in North Africa, West Asia, Italy, western Europe, and Southeast Asia and defended India from threatened Japanese invasion. India's abundant resources were also put to full use in aiding the Allied war effort.

A Changing Indian Society

With improved medical care and technology, India's population reached 400 million people by 1945. However, the standard of living for most Indians, especially in the rural sectors where 80 percent of the people lived, remained pitifully low. After particularly severe famines in 1896 and 1901, the British government responded by establishing famine relief funds and by founding agricultural colleges, a department of agriculture, and agricultural cooperative services. It also began various major irrigation projects to bring more land into production and to increase agricultural yield.

The British government also emphasized the need to expand the economy by establishing industries, beginning with textile, iron, and steel industries. The two world wars assisted in rapid industrialization. The development of industries led to legislation to regulate the conditions of labor. India's first Factory Act was passed in 1911. It regulated working hours and conditions for women and children and was the forerunner of other factory legislation that set minimum wages and allowed unions and legalized strikes. The labor movement, however, was hobbled by the abundance of labor, generally poor standard of living, and lack of adequate enforcement.

The status of women steadily advanced. Ameliorative measures included several laws beginning in the early twentieth century to increase the minimum marriageable age for girls (and boys too). In 1923 a Women's Indian Association was founded; it operated children's homes and performed other social services. In 1924 a Birth Control League was established in Bombay. In 1914 the All-India Muslim Ladies Conference was organized; among its goals was the abolition of polygamy. The Women's Suffrage Movement, founded in 1917, reflected the growth of women's political consciousness. As a result of its lobbying and in accordance with a worldwide trend, women gained the right to vote under the same conditions as men in the 1920s, and the India Act of 1935 reserved a number of seats in all legislatures for women. In 1925 a woman activist and poet, Sarojini Naidu, was elected president of the annual meeting of the Indian National Congress (she later became the first woman provincial governor). Other women leaders of international renown followed her. An All-India Women's Conference was established in 1926; it became an auxiliary organization for the Indian National Congress, just as similar women's organizations in Egypt had made important contributions to the nationalist cause.

The changes in women's role in society matched those in the political realm. Women began to come out of seclusion; many entered the professions, especially as elementary school teachers. By the 1940s government agencies recommended that the same educational facilities be provided for both girls and boys. The actual status of women continued to be subordinate, however, because ancient traditions held fast in the conservative countryside.

Both Hindus and Muslims worked to bring about a cultural renaissance in their communities and a general awakening of the nation. The Brahma Samaj (Brahman Society) and Arya Samaj (Aryan Society) were foremost among Hindu organizations in reexamining and reforming traditional Hindu values, while the Aligarh Movement did the same for Islam. They all promoted education, a popular press, and social service. There was a new appreciation of traditional arts, and literature in many vernacular languages flourished. Despite excellent universities and schools, literacy remained low because of poverty and the high birthrate. Yet literacy did rise from 8 percent in 1931 to 12 percent in 1941.

Nationalist Opposition in Southeast Asia

In Burma (present-day Myanmar) as in India, the British faced mounting opposition to their continued imperial domination. Anti-British riots in the 1930s forced the British to separate Burma from India and to grant it limited autonomy. As the Japanese moved closer to occupying Burma during World War II, many Burmese nationalists sided with the Japanese, who, they mistakenly hoped, would grant them full independence.

Similarly, a robust nationalist movement developed in the Dutch East Indies, named Indonesia after independence. In 1908 a largely student-led cultural and religious society became the vanguard nationalist movement against the Dutch, who maintained a highly paternalistic regime there. In 1926 a Communist-led revolt shook Dutch complacency. This revolt was followed by the creation of the Indonesian Nationalist party (PNI) in 1927 by Achmed Sukarno (1901–1970), a Dutch-educated engineer who was known by the single name Sukarno. Like Gandhi in India, Sukarno advocated a policy of noncooperation with the Dutch, who responded by imprisoning him and other PNI leaders in 1929. Sukarno spent thirteen of the next fifteen years in exile or prison. In reaction to Dutch repression, many Indonesians welcomed the Japanese when they invaded the islands in 1941.

Early in the twentieth century, independence movements also emerged in French Indochina, especially in Vietnam. Vietnamese Communists, led by Ho Chi Minh and Vo Nguyen Giap, both committed Marxists, protested French domination. France crushed all pro-independence uprisings and imprisoned or exiled nationalist leaders. After the Japanese occupation in 1941, Ho and Giap organized guerrilla resistance against the Japanese. Later, they used these same techniques against French and U.S. forces. Although none of these movements succeeded, they laid the foundations for protracted but successful struggles for independence after World War II ended.

The Chinese Nationalists Triumph

By the late nineteenth century, many educated Chinese had concluded that, like the Japanese a generation earlier, they would have to adopt Western technology, science, government, and military techniques if the nation was to survive as an independent entity (see Chapter 13). As more Chinese went to the United States, Europe, and Japan to study, many were converted to work toward overthrowing the Manchu dynasty, now widely regarded as incapable of leading them to modern statehood.

Western-educated Dr. Sun Yat-sen (1867–1925) became the leader of an anti-Manchu republican movement that proclaimed a program for the regeneration of China called the Three People's Principles. The principles were nationalism (anti-Manchu dynasty and anti-Western imperialism), democracy, and people's livelihood (social reforms). An uprising in 1911 led to the abdication of the last Manchu boy emperor and the establishment of Asia's first republic. Sun served briefly as president of China, but, lacking a powerful military force, he and his revolutionary organization, renamed the *Kuomintang* (Nationalist party) were unable to hold power, and Sun was forced to resign in favor of a leading general.

The young Chinese republic soon fell into chaos as rival generals or warlords staked out their respective territorial domains, as had occurred after the fall of earlier powerful dynasties in China, and in India following the decline of the Moghul dynasty. The warlords were local leaders, who took advantage of the weakened Manchu dynasty and the infant republic to raise private armies with which they challenged the authority of any central government. Unlike previous eras of chaos, however, it was no longer sufficient for a charismatic leader to assume the mandate of heaven and create a new dynasty. An ideology that could lift China from impotence and fit it into the modern world had become essential. Sun Yat-sen had an attractive ideology but no army. Thus he had been powerless to oppose the warlords until he sought

Sun Yat-sen. Dr. Sun Yat-sen and his wife, Soong Ch'ing-ling from the wealthy Soong family, aboard a ship going to Peking for negotiations with warlord leaders in 1924. Sun was a champion of Chinese nationalists and sought to modernize China while maintaining its rich cultural and historic heritage.

© Eastfoto

Sun Yat-sen's Formula for Revitalizing China

If we today want to restore the standing of our people, we must first restore our national spirit. . . . Therefore, . . . besides arousing a sense of national solidarity uniting all our people, we must recover and restore our characteristic, traditional morality. . . . First comes loyalty and filial piety, then humanity and love, faithfulness and duty, harmony and peace.

*What are the newest discoveries in the way of exercising popular sovereignty? First, there is suffrage, and it is the only method practised throughout the so-called advanced democracies. . . . The Second . . . is the right of recall. . . . These two rights give the people control over officials and enable them to put all government officials in their positions or to remove them from their positions. . . . What powers must the people possess in order to control the laws? If the people think that a certain law would be of great advantage to them, they should have the power to decide upon this law and turn it over to the government for execution. This third kind of popular power is called the initiative. If the people think that an old law is not beneficial to them, they should have the power to amend it and to ask the government to enforce the amended law. . . . This is called the referendum and is a fourth form of popular sovereignty.**

Sun Yat-sen was the founder of the Kuomintang and father of the Chinese republic. Educated in Honolulu and trained as a medical doctor in Hong Kong, Sun Yat-sen devoted his life to making a new China. His vision for China was to combine what he considered to be the best of its traditional morals and virtues with the best democratic methods of government that he had learned from the West.

*Sun Yat-sen, lecture 6, pp. 51–52, 143–145, in *Sources of Chinese Tradition,* ed. William T. de Bary (New York: Columbia University Press, 1960), pp. 771, 773–774.

LIVES AND TIMES ACROSS CULTURES

Nontraditional Schools

Illiteracy has been widespread in poor, premodern nations. During the twentieth century, innovative programs to eradicate illiteracy and other social problems have been tried in China, India, and other countries.

In Ting Hsien (a county in North China near Peking) in the 1920s and 1930s, a successful experiment in mass literacy, improved public health services, and agricultural reform was led by American-educated James Yen and other idealistic men and women with various skills. Because there were few trained teachers in the villages, Yen and his associates promoted a system of "chain teaching" using the "little teacher" method. Their slogan was "each one teach one," whereby schoolchildren would go home and teach their family members. Older students were used as "student guides" or teacher's assistants. As Charles Hayford said in his book *To the People: James Yen and Village China:* "The approach was not to substitute raw talent and unfocused enthusiasm in the role of the professional, but to develop a system in which roles were carefully and creatively designed to be filled by the people available."

Ting Hsien was proclaimed a model county; its successful programs were emulated in other regions. The experiment was halted by the Japanese invasion and World War II and ended after the Communist victory in China in 1949. In 1948 Yen persuaded the U.S. Congress to found the Sino-American Joint Commission on Rural Reconstruction. After 1949 the commission moved to Taiwan, where it oversaw many rural improvement projects and contributed to the Taiwanese "economic miracle." The Philippine government invited Yen to form the Philippines Rural Reconstruction Movement, which became the basis for the International Rural Reconstruction Movement that he headed in 1952.

In India after World War I, Mohandas K. Gandhi advocated "basic schools" in the villages to foster mass education; they were cheaper to establish and operate than conventional schools because they employed local people, who taught village children to read and write and to become skillful in useful, marketable crafts. Gandhi promoted basic schools and village industries to play complementary roles in uplifting the people. It is a testament to his foresight that basic schools continue to operate in every state in India.

and received aid from the new Marxist government of the Soviet Union in 1923, on condition that he accept members of China's infant Communist party into his Kuomintang.

Although he advocated a moderate socialist approach to China's economic woes, Sun Yat-sen also sought to absorb the Chinese Communist party into his own. Because Sun died from cancer in 1925, it is uncertain whether he would have succeeded in the effort. After Sun's death, his brother-in-law (the two men had married sisters of the powerful Soong family), Chiang Kai-shek (1887–1975) became the leader of the Nationalist party. A professional military officer, Chiang was not so firmly committed to democratic institutions and socialism as his mentor had been. Between 1926 and 1928, Chiang built up a modern military force for the Kuomintang and led a military expedition that defeated many warlords and unified China.

Between 1928 and 1937, the Nationalist government modernized and expanded modern education and built industries, roads, and railways. It also implemented numerous reforms, including new legal codes that gave equality to women. The legal reforms were partially aimed at ending the extraterritorial rights wrested from China by imperialist nations on the grounds that Chinese legal codes did not conform with Western standards. The Nationalist government succeeded in regaining tariff autonomy and other concessions from Western nations. However, Great Britain, France, and the United States and increasingly powerful Japan refused to give up their remaining privileges.

The Twin Challenges of Communism and Japanese Imperialism

Although the Nationalist government had instituted some improvements for the middle and upper classes, it failed to implement the type of sweeping agrarian reforms necessary to improve the lot of the Chinese peasants. The Chinese Communists played upon these failures and gained

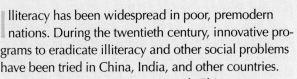

Earl Leaf/Rapho

Mao Tse-tung. A young Mao, left, led the Chinese Communists on the Long March to Yenan and subsequently to victory over the Chinese Nationalist government under Chiang Kai-shek.

peasant support by making violent and dramatic land reforms in areas they controlled, similar to the land reforms made during the early years of Communist power in the Soviet Union. The Kuomintang, determined to prevent the Chinese Communists from gaining power, empowered Chiang to launch all-out attacks on them.

In the 1930s a new leader emerged in the Chinese Communist movement. Unlike many Nationalist leaders and the founders of the Chinese Communist party, who came from middle-class families and had studied in the West or Japan, Mao Tse-tung (1893–1976) was the son of a wealthy farmer, had only attended normal school, and had not been educated in the West. Classical Marxism called for the urban proletariat to wrest power from the bourgeoisie, but China's urban proletariat was too small to play that role. Thus Mao argued that the peasants in China and other agrarian countries held the key to seizing political power.

By 1934, however, the Chinese Communists were clearly being defeated by Chiang. To escape destruction, Mao Tse-tung (Zedong) led the Communists on a 6,000-mile circuitous march from southern China to Yenan in the northwest. The Long March began with almost 100,000 people. One year later only about 20,000 were left, but they included Mao and other key leaders. It was a rare feat of survival and came to symbolize the Communist struggle against the Nationalists. The Communists survived in Yenan thanks to the difficult terrain of that isolated region, and, more importantly, the Sino-Japanese War that began in 1937.

Unlike China, Japan had successfully modernized and westernized its society and economy. It was the first and up to that time the only Asian country to transform itself into a powerful nation. Determined to prove its equality with Western nations, Japan embarked on expansion at the expense of its neighbors (see Chapter 13). By defeating China in 1895, Japan annexed its first colony, Taiwan (Formosa). After defeating Russia in 1905, Japan annexed Korea. When Western nations ceased expanding at China's expense, Japan stepped in to fill the vacuum. A weak and divided China was crucial to the Japanese imperialistic dream of expansion on the Asian continent. Conversely, the threat of Japanese imperialism drove the Kuomintang government to accelerate its program of uniting and strengthening China.

To forestall Chinese unity, Japan invaded and seized northeastern China (called Manchuria in the West) in 1931. Unable to resist Japan unaided, China appealed to the League of Nations and the United States for help, but in vain. Japanese military success in Manchuria doomed both parliamentary government in Japan (because Japanese civilian leaders were less imperialistic than the military but proved unable to control it) and the League of Nations as international peacekeeper. Ultimately, Japan's success encouraged Fascist Italy and Nazi Germany to flout the League of Nations in launching aggressions against other sovereign states.

Militarily, Chiang Kai-shek was correct when he maintained that weak China's only hope of successfully resisting Japan lay in first achieving domestic unity. Thus he saw the destruction of the remnant Communists as his first task; but public opinion was opposed to continuing a civil war in the face of the Japanese threat. The Nationalists were forced to call off the anticommunist campaign and forge a united front with the Chinese Communist party to resist Japan. To the Chinese Communists, war with Japan was their salvation, both because it would end the Nationalist attempt to eliminate them and because they knew that a prolonged war with Japan would weaken the Nationalist army and government.

After 1932 Japan's technologically superior armed forces seized additional territory in North China, and the military-dominated Japanese government became more aggressive toward the Chinese government. Japanese imperialism became the catalyst that fueled Chinese nationalism, while intensifying Chinese nationalism fueled Japanese militarists' demand for a full-scale war to subdue China before it succeeded in unifying. The all-out Japanese invasion of

Mao Explains the Global Nature of Communism

Comrade Norman Bethune, a member of the Communist Party of Canada, was around fifty when he was sent by the Communist Parties of Canada and the United States to China; he made light of travelling thousands of miles to help us in our War of Resistance Against Japan. He arrived in Yenan in the spring of last year [1938], went to work in the Wutai Mountains, and to our great sorrow died a martyr at his post. What kind of spirit is this that makes a foreigner selflessly adopt the cause of the Chinese people's liberation as his own? It is the spirit of internationalism, the spirit of communism, from which every Chinese Communist must learn. . . .

*We must unite with the proletariat of all the capitalist countries, with the proletariat of Japan, Britain, the United States, Germany, Italy and all other capitalist countries, for this is the only way to overthrow imperialism, to liberate our nation and people and to liberate the other nations and peoples of the world. This is our internationalism, the internationalism with which we oppose both narrow nationalism and narrow patriotism.**

In 1939, the Chinese Communist leader Mao Zedong gave a speech in memory of Norman Bethune, a Canadian doctor who had traveled to China to assist the Communist revolution. On this occasion, Mao emphasized the global aspects of the conflict in China.

*Mao Zedong, speech of December 21,1939, in *Selected Works of Mao Tse-tung*, vol. 2 (Peking, 1965), pp. 337–338, reprinted in *Modern Asia and Africa*, ed. William H. McNeill and Mitsuko Iriye (New York: Oxford University Press, 1971), pp. 240–241.

China in 1937 led the Nationalists and the Chinese Communists to abandon their civil war temporarily and form a united front against the Japanese. Japan initially expected to defeat China in six months. Despite heavy losses, China fought on. In 1941, the Sino-Japanese war became a part of World War II when Japan attacked the United States at Pearl Harbor and in the U.S.-held Philippines, as well as British and Dutch possessions in Asia.

A Changing Chinese Society

Much of the chaos China suffered in the nineteenth and early twentieth century seemed a repetition of earlier eras of dynastic change. However, a change in attitude toward science, technology, and values introduced by the West marked this period as different from previous eras.

Western science and technology were irresistible, and China needed to master them to survive. But Western science and technology were premised on Western philosophy, institutions, and values, and China needed to learn them, too. When the 2,000-year-old imperial system collapsed, so did the Confucian philosophy that was its foundation. Although the Chinese often floundered about in their quest for a new and viable political system, all contenders ruled out a return to the monarchial past. Most articulate Chinese wished to establish a modern Western-style government; some advocated a Marxist-type government.

When the Confucian political system fell, so did the other foundations that Confucianism was built upon: submission of youth to age in a patriarchal family, and women to men in society. "Mr. Science" and "Mr. Democracy" became the catchwords of the educated young as they sought to adopt Western individualism and establish a modern civil society. A social and sexual revolution was beginning in China.

Since the nineteenth century, Christian missionaries had been busily trying to convert the Chinese, opening missions, schools, hospitals, and charitable establishments to do so. As in India, however, few Chinese converted to Christianity. Nonetheless, also as in India, Christian schools and hospitals revolutionized Chinese thinking and society. Christian missionaries opened the first schools for girls and spoke out against the ancient and pernicious custom of foot binding for middle- and upper-class girls. Earlier efforts by the Manchus had failed to persuade the Chinese to give up foot binding, but by the early twentieth century the "natural foot movement" was sweeping China.

Not surprisingly, Western-educated young men and women flocked to Sun Yat-sen's revolutionary movement. A women's battalion fought alongside men during the revolution in 1911. A women's delegation demanded equality at the first meeting of the parliament of the republic, but were denied a hearing. Nevertheless, the movement for equality gathered inexorable force,

The Beginning of Women's Emancipation

In my childhood I used to sleep in the same bed with my oldest sister. One night I was awakened by the sound of chirping sobs; I saw her sitting up with the quilt over her shoulders, holding her feet in her hands and weeping, her face streaked with tears. . . . I asked her what was wrong. She replied in a low voice, "My feet have been bound by Nanny Ho. Although during the day it makes walking difficult, I can still bear the pain. But at night my feet get hot under the quilt, and I can't sleep with the cutting pain. What am I to do?" . . .

At daybreak, I went to Mother's bedroom and tearfully told her about Elder Sister's suffering. I earnestly beseeched her to permit Sister to unbind her feet. I also vowed, "I would rather no one showed any interest in me all my life than try to curry favor injuring the body my parents gave me." . . .

My mother put on her clothes and got up out of bed. She patted me on the head and said with a nod, "What you say is quite right. Let's wait for the right opportunity."

*Two years later, the American missionary Dr. Gilbert Reid founded the Society for Natural Feet in Shanghsien Hall in Shanghai. My father was the first to support this, and he sent us the society's rules and regulations and its literature promoting natural feet. I was overjoyed and begged my mother to print hundreds of thousands of copies to distribute all over. I led my aunts and sisters in liberating their feet, and never tired of talking to anyone about the harmful effects of footbinding and the advantages of natural feet, as evident in all the advanced countries of the world.**

Chang Mo-chun (1884–1965) wrote this passage in her autobiography. The daughter of a prominent father and a poet mother, she, like all wealthy girls of her era, was expected to have her feet bound to make her attractive. Her revolt against the time-honored practice had her mother's passive and later her father's active support. Nevertheless, the moving force behind the "natural feet movement" was a U.S. missionary. Chang later joined Sun Yat-sen's anti-Manchu society, participated in the 1911 revolution, and had a long and distinguished career as a women's leader and educational administrator.

*Yu-ning Li, ed. *Chinese Women through Chinese Eyes* (Armonk, N.Y.: M. E. Sharpe, 1992), pp. 125–127.

and women gained legal equality in the new codes promulgated in the 1930s; for example, daughters now had equal inheritance rights with sons. Men and women demanded and won the right to choose their marriage mates and the right to divorce them, and men were no longer allowed to take concubines.

By the early 1920s, almost all Chinese universities had become coeducational, and by the mid-1930s a quarter of college students were females. Increasing numbers of women entered government service, teaching, and the professions. As in India, a lively modern vernacular literature developed to reflect the changes in society. Western literature as well as scientific and technological works were translated into Chinese. Shanghai, the most cosmopolitan city, had a flourishing film industry.

The changes sponsored by the nationalist movement in China mostly affected a relatively small Western-educated or Western-influenced urban middle class. As in India, the new laws and ideas had little effect on the majority of the tradition-bound rural people. Nevertheless, in winning these rights and in obtaining economic independence in the modern cities, many young men and women in the middle class had freed themselves from dominance by the traditional patriarchal family, and as will be seen, they paved the way for more fundamental changes later.

The Soviet Union, 1917–1939

Down in front of the Soviet palace an autotruck was going to the front. Half a dozen Red Guards, some sailors, and a soldier or two, under command of a huge workman, clambered in and shouted to me to come along. . . . A three-inch cannon was loaded. . . . Occasionally a patrol tried to stop us. Soldiers ran out into the road before us, shouted "Stoi!" and threw up their guns.

*We paid no attention. "The devil take you!" cried the Red Guards. "We don't stop for anybody! We're Red Guards!" and we thundered imperiously on.**

*John Reed, *Ten Days That Shook the World* (New York: Random House, 1960), pp. 308–309.

This description by the U.S. revolutionary John Reed captures some of the excitement and energy that spilled out into the streets of Petrograd, the Russian capital, during the 1917 revolution that swept the old regime from power and instituted massive revolutionary changes. The Russian Revolution was one of the major events of the twentieth century and was to have an enormous impact on much of the rest of the world.

Imperial Russia in the middle 1800s was an autocracy, an empire in which the tsar, or emperor, had total power with no restraint from a parliament or constitution. The tsar exercised authority through the nobility, whose wealth came from large estates worked by serfs. By the early nineteenth century, serfdom had disappeared in the rest of Europe but remained entrenched in Russia. As late as 1850, almost half of Russia's population lived in conditions close to those of slavery. Stung by the poor showing of serf-soldiers in the Crimean War and eager to avert a revolution, in 1861 Tsar Alexander II promulgated decrees that led to the emancipation of the serfs. Although liberated from servitude to their noble masters and allotted a small parcel of land, the newly freed slaves gained only limited freedom (as their activities were supervised) and they were burdened with heavy annual "redemption" payments to the government. Emancipation did not transform the peasants into contented, loyal citizens.

The Last Years of the Tsarist Regime

At the dawn of the twentieth century, Russia was the most politically authoritarian and economically backward of the great powers. The Romanov dynasty headed by Nicholas II (reigned 1894–1917) still regarded itself as a divine right monarchy, ruling with the help of a large bureaucracy and an army that could be used against rebellious subjects as well as against foreign enemies. A secret police that had made Siberia notorious as the site of Russian penal colonies kept down dissent.

The people of imperial Russia faced major problems in the last years before World War I. The peasant population increased more than 50 percent between 1861 and 1900, mostly as a consequence of the high birthrate and declining death rate. This meant a reduction in individual peasant land holdings, which were too small in the first instance to maintain a family adequately. In the latter stages of the nineteenth century, Russia experienced the growth of large-scale machine industry, resulting in the emergence of a small, urban working class. Since industrialization was new to Russia, its workers labored under conditions reminiscent of the early factories in Great Britain. In 1904–1905 Russia's imperial designs for expansion into eastern Asia culminated in a disastrous war against Japan, which brought the accumulated troubles to a head. As defeat followed defeat and evidence of inefficiency and corruption in high circles came to light, a wave of strikes, disturbances, and riots swept across the land and blossomed into a full-fledged revolt in 1905.

The tsarist government managed to restore order in the fall of 1905 after agreeing to make constitutional reforms. In October 1905, a month after the Treaty of Portsmouth ended the war with Japan, the tsar issued a manifesto that promised full civil liberties, a constitution, and the creation of a Duma—an elective legislature with the power to enact laws. The October Manifesto was supposed to transform autocratic Russia into a constitutional monarchy. But once the revolutionary crisis had passed, the government returned to its reactionary ways and restricted the authority of the Duma.

World War I hastened the decay that had been eating away at Russia for decades. As described in Chapter 13, the Germans inflicted several crushing defeats on the Russians and sent them reeling back into Russia. In the fall of 1915 Tsar Nicholas II unwisely took personal command of the Russian armies, marking him in the public eye as the cause of Russia's defeats. Effective control of the government fell into the hands of Empress Alexandra and her confidant, Gregory Rasputin, a dissolute and self-proclaimed holy man. Ministers were appointed and dismissed on a word from Rasputin, while inefficiency and corruption in government reached new heights. Fearful for the survival of the monarchy, three members of the high aristocracy murdered Rasputin in December 1916. But by then all public confidence in the tsar had disappeared.

The Provisional Government Succeeds the Tsar

Three years of war had shattered Russia's armies and devastated the home front. Enormous casualties, shortages of food, fuel, and housing, government inefficiency and corruption, and rumors of treason in high places had turned the people against the crown. On March 8, 1917, a spontaneous outbreak of strikes and riots convulsed the capital, now called Petrograd (the new name was meant to replace the German-sounding name of St. Petersburg). Troops ordered to fire upon the crowds chose instead to join them, and in succeeding days demonstrations against the government spread rapidly to other cities. Alone and helpless, Nicholas followed the advice of his generals and abdicated on March 15. Thus the long reign of the Romanovs ended abruptly in a leaderless and nearly bloodless revolution.

Abdication of the Russian Throne

In the midst of the great struggle against a foreign foe, who has been striving for three years to enslave our country, it has pleased God to lay on Russia a new and painful trial. Newly popular disturbances in the interior imperil the successful continuation of the stubborn fight. The fate of Russia, the honor of our heroic army, the welfare of our people, the entire future of our dear land, call for the prosecution of the conflict, regardless of the sacrifices, to a triumphant end. The cruel foe is making his last effort and the hour is near when our brave army, together with our glorious Allies, will crush him.

In these decisive days in the life of Russia, we deem it our duty to do what we can to help our people to draw together and unite all their forces with the State Duma. We therefore think it best to abdicate the throne of the Russian State and to lay down the Supreme Power. Not wishing to be separated from our beloved son, we hand down our inheritance to our brother, Grand Duke Michael Alexandrovich, and give him our blessing on mounting the throne of the Russian Empire. . . .

We call on all faithful sons of the Fatherland to fulfil their sacred obligations to their country by obeying the Tsar at this hour of national distress, and to help him and the representatives of the people to take the path of victory, well-being, and glory.

May the Lord God help Russia.
*March 15, 1917, 3 P.M.**

Nicholas chose to abdicate out of patriotic motives: to avoid the disintegration of the Russian army, which would have led to a humiliating defeat. If his foremost concern had been to preserve his throne, he would have arranged a settlement with Germany and used his frontline troops to crush the internal disturbances. Nicholas also abdicated on behalf of his sick son, passing the crown to his brother Michael. The leaders of the Duma, however, warned Michael that if he accepted the throne a violent rising was certain to erupt and, without reliable troops on hand, they could not guarantee his personal safety. Thereupon Michael renounced the throne.

*"Abdication of The Tsar" in Frank A. Golder, ed., *Documents of Russian History, 1914–1917,* trans. Emanuel Aronsberg (New York: Century, 1927), pp. 296–297.

Nicholas was replaced by a provisional government, headed first by a liberal nobleman, Prince Georgi Lvov, and later by a moderate socialist, Alexander Kerensky. The new regime proclaimed civil liberties, announced plans for social reforms, and promised to summon a constituent assembly. It faced many massive problems, but two stood above the rest—the peasants' hunger for land and the nation's overwhelming desire for peace. Lacking clearheaded leadership, the provisional government failed to address the urgent domestic issues and thereby played into the hands of an emerging Marxist revolutionary group, the Bolsheviks, led by Vladimir Ilyich Ulyanov, better known by his underground alias, Lenin.

Lenin and the Bolsheviks Seize Power

The course of the revolution began to change when Lenin returned to Russia in mid-April 1917. A professional revolutionary since the 1880s, Lenin had spent the war years in exile in Switzerland. There he lived a miserable and lonely existence, all but abandoning hope that he would live to see a socialist state patterned on Marxist ideology. His opportunity came after the sudden fall of the imperial regime. Impatient to return to Russia, he received help from an unexpected source. The German High Command, calculating that Lenin's agitation would disrupt and weaken Russia's war effort, arranged to transport him in a sealed train through Germany and Scandinavia. Back in Russia, Lenin was soon joined by Leon Trotsky (1870–1940), as well as other fellow Marxists, whom the tsar had formerly imprisoned or forced to flee abroad.

The Bolsheviks were a small socialist group, but like the Jacobins in 1792, they alone, in the face of confusion and despair, had a clear program. In speech after speech, Lenin repeated the familiar themes of Marxism; under the benevolence of a Bolshevik regime, he promised, Russia would see the emergence of a new, happy society, resting upon equality, without rich or poor. His promise of land, peace, and bread—three things that the provisional government had been unable to provide—had a

Brown Brothers

Lenin Speaks. V. I. Lenin addresses a rally in Moscow in 1917. In later years Communists, like other totalitarian parties, organized large-scale parades and public spectacles as expressions of solidarity and loyalty to the party.

wide appeal to the land-hungry peasants, the soldiers sick of the war, and the workers threatened with starvation. Throughout the summer of 1917, the Bolsheviks increased their party membership and gained control of the revolutionary councils, or soviets, in Petrograd, Moscow, and other cities and towns. Spontaneously created at the local, provincial, and national levels, the soviets consisted of elected delegates representing soldiers, workers, and peasants. As the war continued to go badly and conditions at home worsened, Lenin demanded that power be transferred to the soviets, which he claimed, with justification, were more representative of the people than the provisional government. Of course, Lenin realized that his party's only chance to gain control of the government was to use force. While he laid plans for an armed insurrection, his lieutenants organized a workers' militia called the Red Guards in Petrograd and other cities.

The Bolshevik takeover proved relatively easy, given the weakness of the provisional government. On the evening of November 6, the Red Guards, supported by sympathetic regular army units, quietly seized railroad and communication centers, post offices, electric power plants, and other key points in Petrograd. At noon the next day they stormed the Winter Palace, seat of the provisional government, and arrested or put to flight all the cabinet ministers. Kerensky escaped in a car borrowed from the U.S. embassy and eventually settled as an exile in the United States. In less than a day the Bolsheviks had successfully carried out their revolution with a minimum of bloodshed.

On the afternoon of November 7, Lenin announced to the National Congress of Soviets (representing local councils from all over the country) in Petrograd that he was transferring sovereignty to that body. Lenin's seemingly selfless display was a mask for his real objective, the dictatorship of the Bolshevik party. He maneuvered the Congress into accepting the Council of Peoples' Commissars as the executive of the new government. The Bolsheviks occupied the top positions in the council. Lenin took the post of chairman with Trotsky in charge of foreign affairs and Joseph Stalin (1879–1953) as commissar for national minorities. Lenin pledged to build a socialist state and to end the war with Germany.

The Bolshevik Regime, 1918–1924

In the first months, the Bolsheviks built the rudiments of a new order, while struggling to hold on to power. A series of decrees nationalized the economy, distributed confiscated land to the peasants, and turned over management of mines and factories to the workers. All imperial institutions were dismantled, and a venomous campaign was unleashed against the church, which the Bolsheviks regarded as an ally of the tsar and an enemy of change. The debts incurred by the tsarist administration were repudiated to the fury of foreign governments that had provided funds to Russia before and during the war.

Confident that a majority of the public would confirm their policies, the Bolsheviks allowed elections for a constituent assembly to be held. To their shock and disbelief, their main adversaries, the Social Revolutionaries, won twice as many seats as they did. But Lenin and his associates had come too far to be thwarted by a mere popular verdict. When the constituent assembly met in January 1918, Bolshevik troops disbanded it as part of a calculated policy to establish a one-party dictatorship. Combating all counterrevolutionary activity was the newly established secret police, familiarly called the Cheka (later known by other names, including the KGB), which would become a dreaded symbol of Bolshevik oppression.

Next to staying in power, Lenin's most cherished goal was to conclude hostilities with Germany. In December 1917 he opened peace negotiations with the Germans, who, realizing Russia's helplessness, demanded, among other things, Finland, Ukraine, Poland, and the Baltic provinces—more than a million square miles of territory, including a quarter of Russia's population, a third of its arable land, and much of its natural resources. Lenin balked at making such concessions, but the resumption of the German advance, coupled with the disintegration of the Russian army, left him no option but to yield. The treaty signed at Brest-Litovsk in March 1918 was a harbinger of the fate of the Allies had they lost the war.

Lenin was not overly troubled at the exorbitant price of peace, trusting that a socialist revolution would soon spread to Germany and invalidate the treaty. But real peace, which Lenin needed to consolidate his regime at home, would prove elusive. No sooner did hostilities against Germany end than Russia sank into civil war.

As 1918 wore on, groups hostile to the Bolsheviks, who now called themselves Communists, emerged from every quarter of Russia. These counterrevolutionaries, collectively called "Whites," were led by former tsarist officers and included members of the outlawed nobility, former landowners, supporters of the tsar, and rival revolutionary parties. The Allies intervened in the civil war. The Japanese occupied Russia's far eastern provinces, while the French, Americans, and British sent supplies as well as troops to aid the White forces. The Allies were eager to see the Whites win, not only to prevent the spread of communism but also because they hoped that under different leadership Russia would reenter the war. To meet the new danger, the Communists hastily formed the Red Army in the summer of 1918. Under the leadership of Trotsky, now war commissar, it became a well-organized and disciplined fighting force.

The conflict was the bloodiest phase of the revolution, with neither side asking or giving quarter and both sides committing the most gruesome atrocities. Although close to defeat in the early stages of the conflict, the Red Army reversed the tide and succeeded in defeating its enemies one by one, until by 1920 its victory was assured. A number of factors enabled the Communists to triumph over seemingly hopeless odds. The Whites were unable to cooperate effectively with each other, partly because of deep political differences and partly because their forces, moving in from the periphery, were separated by vast distances. By contrast, the Communists, single-minded in their sense of purpose, had the advantage of interior lines that allowed them to shift troops rapidly from one front to the other. Finally, the Allies gave the White elements only halfhearted support. Once Germany was beaten, they were less concerned about what kind of regime ruled Russia and withdrew their troops in 1920, except for the Japanese, who stayed in western Siberia until 1922.

The Communists were equally successful in crushing political opposition in the territory under their control. Following a failed attempt to assassinate Lenin, the Communists initiated a "Red Terror" to eliminate suspected counterrevolutionaries and terrorize the rest into accepting their rule. The Cheka, repeating the worst excesses of the French Revolution, brutally carried out its task, summarily executing anyone known or suspected of being hostile to the revolution. The most famous victims were the former tsar, Nicholas II, and his entire family, who were executed in Ekaterinburg. All other political parties were outlawed so that no organized opposition could develop. The Communists had converted Russia into a one-party dictatorship.

At the end of the civil war, the Communists faced probably their most severe crisis. The ravages of a disastrous general war, two revolutions, and a savage civil war were followed by a severe famine. Lenin and his colleagues had exacerbated the hardships during the civil war by seeking to socialize the economy and requisitioning food from the peasants. In most industries and mines, chaos resulted because workers lacked experience in management. The output fell until by 1921 it was only 17 percent of the 1913 level. Many workers moved from cities to rural areas seeking work. Agricultural production also experienced a sharp decline. The practice of requisitioning food so alienated the peasants that many grew only enough food for their own immediate needs. By 1921 only about 62 percent of the farmland was under cultivation. Shortages of grain and manufactured articles caused prices to rise inordinately. Transportation broke down, and the value of exports shrank to a fraction of the 1917 level. Russia, it seemed, was on the verge of a complete collapse.

A mutiny by the sailors at Kronstadt, once the shock troops of the revolution, induced the pragmatic Lenin to make an ideological retreat. In 1921 he adopted the New Economic Policy, better known by its initials as NEP, which was a compromise between socialist and capitalist practices. Lenin spoke of it as "a step back in order to go forward," a temporary measure that would be abandoned as soon as the economy stabilized. Under the NEP the state retained control over large industries, transportation, and foreign trade. It did, however, permit

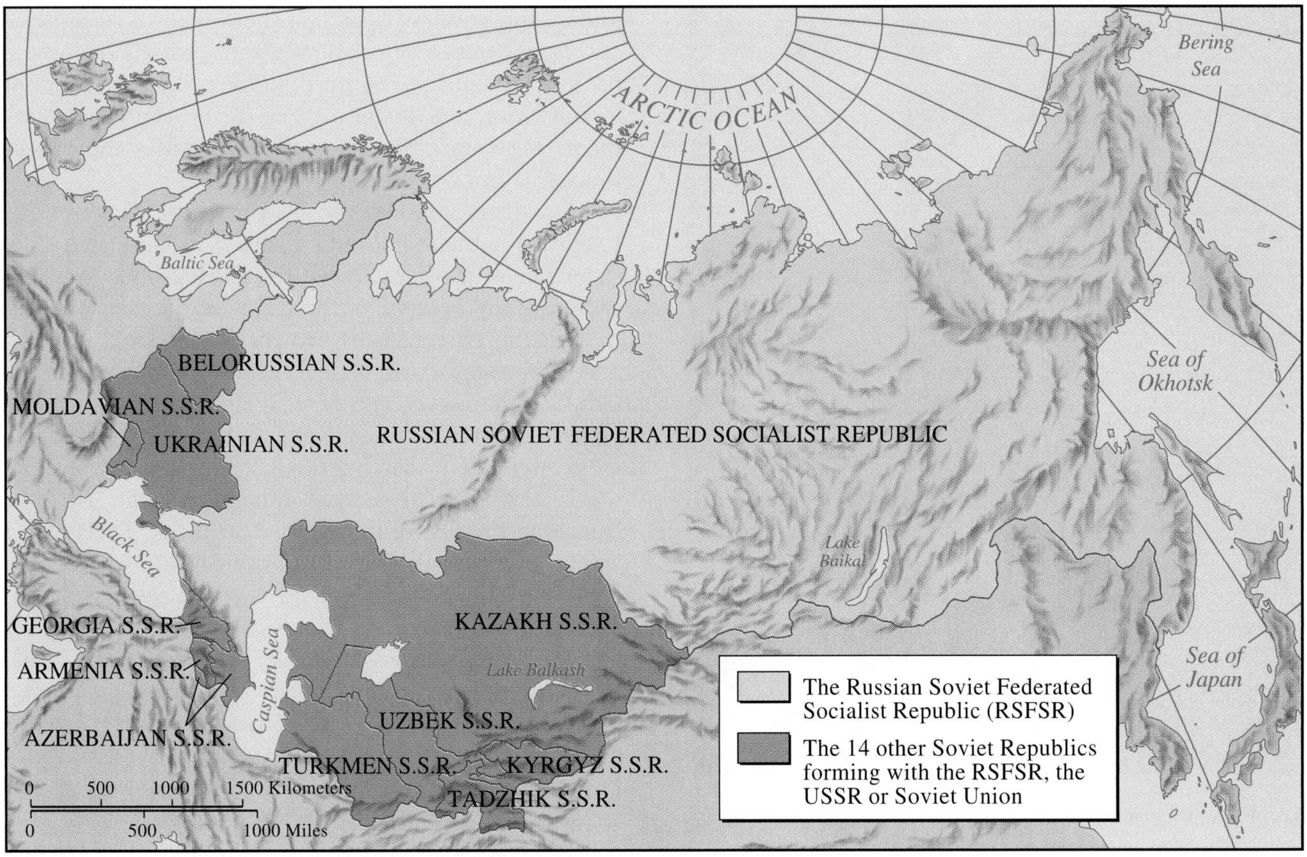

Map 14.2 Union of Soviet Socialist Republics (USSR). Under the 1924 constitution, the USSR became a federated nation of republics that, in fact, had exceedingly limited autonomy. This map shows the various republics with Russia as the dominant power.

private local trade and restored small shops and factories to their former owners. A fixed tax in kind replaced the forcible requisitioning of produce and allowed the peasants to sell their surplus crops on the open market. Concessions were offered to foreign entrepreneurs to exploit mines and oil wells in Russia. By 1927 these measures had restored output in both agricultural and nonagricultural areas to prewar levels. Without the NEP it is doubtful that the Communist revolution would have survived.

While coping with a myriad of problems, the Communists formalized their authoritarian rule in the constitution of 1924. The Soviet Union, or Union of Soviet Socialist Republics (USSR), officially came into being as a federated union consisting of territories, regions, nominally autonomous states, and republics. Originally there were four republics, with Russia the largest and most influential; the number would rise to eleven by 1936, either by carving states out of Russia or by upgrading autonomous areas.

Under a veneer of democratic procedures, the Soviet Union was in fact a dictatorship. The constitution granted the franchise to all productive workers over age eighteen but not to the bourgeoisie or to those closely identified with tsarism and the church. Despite the election of various soviets, congresses, and committees, real power rested with the Politburo, the high command of the Communist party, which made all the major policy decisions for both the party and the government.

The Deadly Struggle for the Succession to Lenin

On January 21, 1924, at about the same time the constitution was promulgated, Lenin died after a series of paralytic strokes that had left him incapacitated. Because Lenin had not designated a successor, a desperate power struggle ensued between Trotsky and Stalin, two of his chief associates. Both men were ardent revolutionaries, but they differed on matters of policy. For example, Trotsky stood for an unceasing effort to promote revolutionary uprisings throughout the world, whereas Stalin maintained that communism must consolidate its power at home before it could be established elsewhere. A gifted orator, intellectually brilliant and idealistic, Trotsky enjoyed a popularity with the public that was second only to

Leon Trotsky. Trotsky organized the Red Army that secured the Bolsheviks' victory in the civil war. Following Lenin's death, however, Stalin outmaneuvered him for control of the party and government and forced him into exile.

Lenin's. Abler than his rival, he disdained petty backstairs maneuvering, and his aloof manner, interpreted as arrogance, often offended his comrades.

Stalin lacked polish and formal education, but he was relentless and cunning, excelled as an infighter, and profited from his position as general secretary of the Communist party. As such, he was able to place his henchmen in key positions so that he essentially controlled the party apparatus by the time Lenin died. Stalin emerged victorious and had Trotsky expelled from the Politburo and the party. Forced to leave the Soviet Union in 1929, Trotsky entered a period of exile that would take him to distant Mexico, where he was assassinated in 1940 by a Stalinist agent.

The Stalin Dictatorship

Stalin's triumph ended whatever democratic practices had existed in the Communist party and government. Lenin had sanctioned police-state methods as a means of survival, but he had permitted freedom of discussion within the party itself. Stalin wanted no rivals who might challenge his scheme to transform the political structure of the country into a personal dictatorship. By a most skillful and ruthless campaign, he forced old Bolshevik adversaries out of key positions and replaced them with his followers in the Politburo, in the party organizations in the cities, and in the organs of the central government. Thereafter, Stalin's advance toward complete authoritarianism was unstoppable.

Stalin proposed to use his power to transform his backward, agricultural nation into a modern industrial state. Lenin had been forced to retreat from socializing the economy because of the chaos of the civil war. Although the NEP had rescued the Soviet Union from a major economic crisis, Stalin remained committed to the old Communist dream of effacing capitalism. In the process he altered the daily life of the Soviet people to a far greater extent than did the first Bolshevik revolution.

In 1928 Stalin marked the end of the NEP by launching the first of three Five-Year Plans. Their object was to eliminate all elements of capitalism, increase agricultural production through mechanized collective farming, and develop large-scale industries. Implementing the first goal meant dispossessing the property of the *kulaks* (prosperous, landowning peasants) and the *nepmen,* who operated small businesses. Simultaneously, the Communists undertook to merge the many small holdings into mechanized state-run farms that were expected to increase productivity significantly. Peasants relocated on the collectives were to share in the profits according to their original (forced) contribution in land and livestock as well as the amount and quality of their work. By and large, though, the peasants cherished their own plots of land and wanted no part of collectivization. Pandemonium broke out in the countryside. Many were killed outright or sent off to forced-labor camps in Siberia. Nevertheless, peasants continued to resist collectivization by burning their crops, smashing their equipment, and destroying their livestock. By 1933 agricultural production had actually declined, and the total number of cattle, sheep, and goats had fallen to half of the 1928 level. In that half-decade, executions and deportations, together with a severe famine, had claimed no fewer than 5 million lives.

The drive to expand Russia's industrial output was more successful. Production quotas were fixed, and plans were laid to accelerate mining operations, extend or improve railways, and rapidly construct power plants, refineries, large factories, and steel mills. The emphasis was on heavy industry, not consumer goods. Such difficulties as shortages of workers, inexperienced management, inadequate equipment, and an inefficient transportation system prevented some of the government's objectives from being met. Even so, between 1928 and 1939 overall production rose sevenfold, a phenomenal achievement. On the eve of World War II, the Soviet Union ranked third among the world's industrial powers, behind only the United States and Germany. Yet Soviet industrial expansion was achieved at a heavy cost. To fund the acquisition of technical exper-

AP/Wide World Photos

Russian Agricultural Workers in the 1930s. This "production meeting" in the open fields reflects Stalin's efforts to increase agricultural production through industrial methods. But agricultural output continued to lag behind projected goals, and many Russian peasants bitterly opposed collectivization.

tise and heavy equipment from the West, the government kept workers' wages low and exported grain at the expense of its ill-fed and often starving population.

The imposition of a socialized economy enabled the state to tighten its grip on the masses. But the hardships caused by Stalin's program provoked opposition even from within his own party. Beginning in 1934, Stalin undertook sweeping purges of his opponents, real or imagined. After initially targeting potential political rivals and other Communist bosses, the purge extended down to the lower ranks of the party and ultimately spread to virtually all branches of government, the army, and the secret police itself. By 1939 millions had been executed, jailed, or sent to forced-labor camps. With the elimination of all rivals, Stalin had cemented his power.

At the height of the terror in 1936, Stalin promulgated a new Soviet constitution that guaranteed universal suffrage, the secret ballot, and freedom of speech, assembly, and the press. As a piece of propaganda, it was very effective, fooling Western liberals ready to be duped. In reality, the new constitution marked no change from Stalin's rule of force. The existence of a one-party system obviously precluded the establishment of democracy.

Life and Culture in the Soviet Union

The creation of a new classless society along Marxian lines meant a repudiation of traditional religious values and social institutions. Once in firm control, the Communists tried to destroy the Russian Orthodox church. They closed churches, confiscated church property, persecuted the clergy, decreed that only civil marriages were legal, forbade religious instruction in schools, and encouraged atheism. But in time it became apparent that the antireligious campaign was counterproductive. Most Russians, especially peasants, were devout Orthodox Christians or affiliated with other religions. Stalin relaxed his campaign in the mid-1930s, in part because he needed the support of the Christian West.

From the beginning, the Bolsheviks aimed to achieve a classless society, rewarding each "according to his needs." That philosophy did not survive the first Five-Year Plan, because economic equality robbed workers of all incentive and kept able individuals from accepting positions of responsibility. The Communists were compelled to return to some of the bourgeois values they had previously denounced. Wage differentials were introduced with factory managers, engineers, and scientists receiving preferential treatment. Even among ordinary workers, those who were especially productive were rewarded with higher wages and paid vacation trips.

Although Soviet society embraced aspects of capitalism, it did develop distinctive features of its own. While the standard of living for workers was far below that of their counterparts in the industrialized West, the Soviet government was unique in guaranteeing the right of employment. The state also provided extensive welfare programs such as free medical care and nurseries for children of working mothers and subsidized housing and food. An extensive program of compulsory free education covering all levels was launched in 1928; it reduced illiteracy from about two-thirds to a fifth of the population. The quality of education was uneven, however. Soviet universities produced good scientists and engineers, but courses in the liberal arts were peppered with propaganda, and the truth was often deliberately distorted. As proponents of equality between the sexes, the Communists granted women the franchise as well as equal educational and professional opportunities. Although women worked in all occupations—from street cleaner to scientist—they rarely reached the highest political or economic positions.

As in education, the Soviet government controlled the arts in order to shape the fundamental beliefs of its subjects. Artists, writers, and composers were expected to conform to Marxian ideology, to serve the interests of the party, and to integrate their work into the everyday lives of the masses. "Art belongs to the people," Lenin remarked, "it must have its deepest roots in the broad masses of the workers. It must be understood and loved by them." Few well-known artists and writers of the older generation were prepared to come to terms with the Communists; most of the disillusioned allowed their creative talents to languish or went into exile. But young artists, who shared the utopian revolutionary zeal of the new regime, put on poetry readings and concerts for workers and created artistic works that extolled revolutionary heroes or glorified the social aims of the government. By and large the literature, art, and music produced, particularly under Stalin, tended to be for propaganda effect and had little creative value.

Soviet Foreign Policy

When the Bolsheviks toppled the provisional government in 1917, they expected anticapitalist revolutions to break out in Europe within a matter of months. As Marxists, they believed in the inevitability of world revolution and in the triumph of the proletariat. Accordingly, they took steps to exploit the unrest caused by the war, inspiring a few futile social uprisings in central Europe. In March 1919 they founded the Third Internationale, known thereafter as the Comintern, which eventually included Communist parties from various parts of the world. With headquarters in Moscow, its avowed purpose was to promote and direct revolutions throughout the world. But the Western democracies survived the trials of the immediate postwar period, and world revolution failed to materialize. The Comintern's policy of subversion only served to create fear abroad and to make the Soviet Union a pariah among nations.

After the advent of the NEP, the Soviet Union adopted a more conciliatory attitude toward the West. Since the Soviet economy could not recover without foreign trade and capital, the Communist leaders were anxious to resume normal relations with the rest of the world. The Western powers, wanting to believe that the new Soviet regime was about to revert to capitalism, responded positively to the friendly overtures. In the early 1920s Russia signed commercial treaties with such countries as Poland, Turkey, and Great Britain. By 1924 most of the powers had recognized the Soviet Union, although the United States held back until 1933.

Cooperation between the Soviet Union and the West broadened after 1928. The success of the first Five-Year Plan depended heavily on Western equipment, machines, and technical experts. The rising threat of Japan and Nazi Germany was another factor in pushing the Soviet Union closer to the Western democracies. To promote friendly relations, Stalin stressed the idea of conciliation rather than world revolution and clamped down on the activities of the Comintern. In 1934 the Soviet Union was admitted into the League of Nations, and the following year it concluded military agreements with France and Czechoslovakia. But the outward collaboration did not dissipate the distrust between the capitalistic states and the Soviet Union. The ideological differences separating them were too great to be bridged by trade agreements or alliance treaties.

Twentieth-Century Scientific, Technological, and Economic Developments

I vow to strive to apply my professional skills only to projects which, after conscientious examination, I believe to contribute to the goal of co-existence of all human beings in peace, human dignity and self-fulfilment.

I believe that this goal requires the provision of an adequate supply of the necessities of life (good food, air, water, clothing and housing, access to natural and man-made beauty), education, and opportunities to enable [people] . . . to work out for [themselves] . . . [their] life objectives and to develop creativeness and skill in the use of hands as well as head.

*I vow to struggle through my work to minimise danger; noise; strain or invasion of privacy of the individual; pollution of earth, air or water; destruction of natural beauty, mineral resources and wildlife.**

*Meredith Thring, "Scientist Oath," in *New Scientist* (1971), reprinted in *From Creation to Chaos: Classic Writings in Science*, ed. B. Dixon (Oxford: Blackwell, 1989), p. 220.

The sentiments expressed in this scientist's version of the Hippocratic oath of medical doctors are certainly praiseworthy, and modern science may rightfully claim to have alleviated much human misery. But science in the twentieth century has also made it possible to unleash previously unimagined destructive forces, such as the atomic bomb, nerve gas, and biological weapons. And, by probing the mysteries of life itself, "genetic engineers" have not only opened new vistas for good, but also posed difficult moral and ethical questions. In short, those who have made the crucial scientific and technological advances in this century have not always had the goals of the "scientist oath" in the forefront of their minds. The repercussions of these advances—for good and for ill—have been profound.

Despite such catastrophes as World Wars I and II, the Great Depression, and the Cold War, there has been outstanding material progress in the present century. The overall economic trend for industrialized, high-income nations has risen to a level of affluence unmatched in history. Scientific and technological advances have yielded a productive capacity unequaled in quantity, intricacy, or quality. Socially, new wealth and the new technology have brought unprecedented levels of health, education, and material welfare to those who can afford it.

This section surveys the progress of knowledge in several branches of scientific study. It also looks at technological advances of the twentieth century and the economic and social changes they have entailed.

Scientific Advances in the Age of Einstein

The scientific achievements of the past century have been enormous. Scientists have split the atom and probed the depths of the human psyche, speculated on the evolution of the universe and learned many of the secrets of life itself. Like the age of Isaac Newton, the century of Albert Einstein has impressively expanded understanding of our world, particularly in the fields of physics and astronomy.

Physicists in the twentieth century have uncovered many mysteries and have begun at least to formulate some answers. Even before 1900, for example, scientific experiments raised seemingly unanswerable questions about the nature of light. Light behaved sometimes as waves, sometimes as though it were quanta (a series of separate pulses of energy). Similar challenges to common sense resulted from exploration of the phenomenon of radiation. In her experiments with radium, Marie Curie (1867–1934) discovered that this rare element lost weight as it gave off radiant energy. Mass was being converted into energy; this defied the traditional scientific distinction between the material and the immaterial.

The theory of relativity proposed by Albert Einstein (1879–1955) challenged scientific common sense even further. Einstein insisted that physical phenomena were not absolute, independent entities, but were relative to one another. The basic nature of anything, he asserted, is fundamentally determined by its relationships to other things. He defined a four-dimensional space-time continuum with length, breadth, depth, and a "fourth dimension"—time.

Physicists formulated broad new conclusions about the relationships of matter and energy. They discovered, for example, that the "indivisible" atom is really composed of still smaller particles, called protons, neutrons, and electrons. Subsequent research multiplied the kinds of particles and offered a much more complex image of their motions; this made the billiard-ball atomic models of the seventeenth century and the crude philosophical materialism of the nineteenth look very simplistic indeed.

The Newtonian vision of a single law of gravity has also been upset by twentieth-century scientists. Einstein suggested that gravity is not a force of attraction linking any two objects but a field of forces through which objects move. This gravitational field affects the motions, not only of material things, but of such manifestations of pure energy as light itself. The work of Curie and others on radiation made it clear that gravity was not the only fundamental force affecting the behavior of the universe. In this century, three basic forces have in fact been distinguished: gravity, the "strong force" holding the atomic nucleus together, and the "electro-weak force" revealed in electromagnetism and radioactivity. The formulation of a "unified field" theory that would reduce these three governing forces to a single underlying principle has been a great, elusive goal of modern physics.

Twentieth-century astronomers have greatly expanded our detailed knowledge of the universe, in part through the development of new instruments for probing the farthest reaches of space. Bigger and better telescopes, including ones stationed in space (outside the earth's atmosphere), gathered in the light of distant, previously undetected stars. After many initial problems that were corrected in a record-setting five days of repairs by crews operating in space, the Hubble Space Telescope in 1994 permitted scientists to see farther into space than ever before and has continued to expand and enrich our knowledge since.

In the aftermath of the Cold War, international, cooperative space probes and shuttles including crews of Americans, Russians, Europeans, Saudi Arabian, and other experts have continued to provide new information about the universe. Many women scientists and astronauts are leaders in these exciting new fields of exploration; in the United States Space program (NASA) women hold key leadership and administrative roles.

Spectroscopes make possible the analysis of light to determine the elemental composition of stars. Radio astronomy facilitates the study of radiation outside the visible spectrum. Space probes took human beings to the moon and have transported cameras to other planets to collect photographic data.

Astronomers have mapped the outer reaches of space and analyzed the flaming interiors of stars. They have discovered that the cosmos is composed of immense collections of millions of stars called galaxies and proposed such intriguing possibilities as "black holes"—burned-out stars with gravitational fields so strong that nothing, not even light, can escape from them.

New cosmological theories about the origin, history, and ultimate fate of the universe have also emerged. The "big bang" theory, for example, asserts that perhaps 15 billion years ago all the matter and energy in the universe was condensed in a single, unimaginably dense "cosmic fireball." This ball then exploded, producing the big bang with which the universe as we know it was born. The history of the cosmos since has been the story of the expansion and cooling of the fragments of matter and energy thus unleashed. Some scientists believe that the expanding universe will gradually run out of energy, until all the stars are burnt out and the cosmos itself is left dead and cold. Others foresee gravity slowly reining in the scattered fallout from the primal explosion and pulling it all back together again. This may in turn be followed by another big bang and another expansion and contraction; ours may thus be a "pulsating" universe, cyclically reborn again and again.

Major Trends in Biology, Anthropology, and Psychology

Charles Darwin's theory of biological evolution through natural selection remains central to twentieth-century biology. However, biologists have modified Darwin's basic evolutionary theory (see Chapter 12); some have argued that evolution is not a process of small changes adding up to large transformations over long periods, but rather of relatively rapid change interspersed with long, static periods of little change in any given species. Botanists and zoologists, especially those seeking to increase and improve the world's food supply, have accelerated the "natural selection" process. Hybrid corn, for example, now produces more than twice the yield in a shorter growing season than was possible fifty years ago.

Major new biological discoveries are revealing much about the genetic base of life and the ecological interaction of many species in a system of related life forms. At the microscopic level, biologists discovered DNA (deoxyribonucleic acid), which controls the chromosomes composing the nucleus of the living cell. DNA molecules twisted around each other in a complicated "double helix" pattern, program living tissue to develop and reproduce itself through cell division—that is, to perform

Repairs in Space. Here astronauts repair the Hubble Space Telescope while in space. These repairs, a technological feat in and of themselves, enabled scientists to receive detailed pictures of objects deep in space. At the turn of the millennium, space continued to be one of the most exciting areas for new scientific discoveries and explorations.

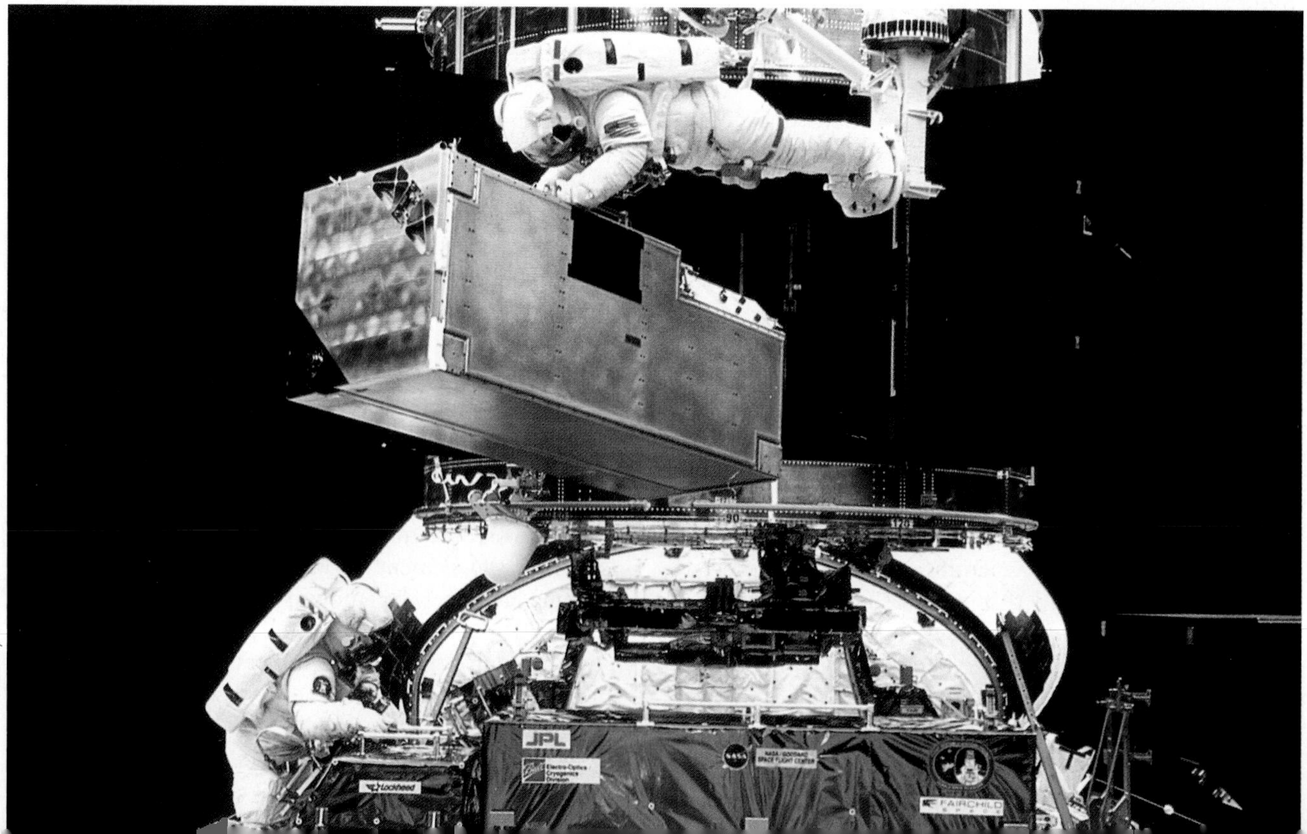

Courtesy of NASA

Corbis-Bettmann

Margaret Mead. Margaret Mead was among the first anthropologists to demonstrate the significance of the environment in shaping and molding the individual. She gained prominence in the late 1920s as a result of her study of Samoan female adolescence. She found that Samoan teenagers differed considerably from their U.S. counterparts but attributed this less to biology than to culture.

all the basic processes of life. Among the results of the Human Genome Project will be a better understanding of the genetic origins of disease and clues to their cures.

At a different level of organization of life, ecologists have studied how species of animals and plants interact with each other and with other aspects of their common environment. Through their discoveries of the interrelatedness of all living matter, ecologists have warned that what humans do to their common environment profoundly affects the lives of other species on the planet.

The science of anthropology developed in the wake of Charles Darwin's discoveries about human biology. Physical anthropologists study the biological differences among the racial subdivisions of the human species. Cultural anthropologists investigate the beliefs and ways of life of peoples who lived in older and simpler forms of society. Some anthropologists work with archaeologists and biologists to learn about our prehistoric ancestors; by piecing together bits of bone and crude stone tools, they have reconstructed the story of early human life on earth. Investigators like the Leakey family—Louis, Mary, and their son Richard—accumulate evidence on the nature and development of prehistoric humanity, and have proved that the human race and its precursors goes back millions of years.

Some anthropologists did field work by living with the isolated, technologically primitive peoples they were studying in order to understand them better and to learn about cultural evolution. Margaret Mead (1901–1978), for example, became famous for her observations about adolescent sexuality and guilt-free sexual practices in some South Pacific island societies. Some anthropologists have also applied their findings to more "advanced" societies, as Mead did when she wrote about the generation gap in the contemporary United States.

Anthropologists seek to judge each society or culture by its own standards, rather than by any supposedly universal set of standards. They contribute to an attitude of cultural relativism now widespread among serious students of history. Many anthropologists argue that norms of right and wrong are specific to a given society, and that cultures and peoples have different but equally valid standards of behavior.

Sigmund Freud (1856–1939), the founder of psychoanalysis, and Ivan Pavlov (1849–1936), the pioneer of behaviorism, originated theories and procedures that provided a fundamental basis for the science of psychology in the twentieth century. Freud explained that all human attitudes and actions are rooted in the unconscious mind. The basic human drive, he believed, is libido, controlling not only the sexual instinct but also a broad range of human desires. Freud further developed and applied his ideas of unconscious instincts shaping thoughts and behavior, and postulated not one but two basic human impulses, a life-affirming urge related to the libido, and a "death instinct" that could drive the human race to destroy itself in holocausts like the First World War. Freud also applied his theories to the most fundamental achievements of the past, explaining religion and civilization itself as products of psychological needs and conflicts.

Several disciples of Freud's developed their own psychological theories, explaining behavior by other unconscious instincts than those Freud had proposed. Alfred Adler (1870–1937), for instance, saw an aggressive urge to achieve superiority as the central human motive and explained many psychological problems as the result of "inferiority complexes." Carl Jung (1875–1961) developed such basic psychological types as "introvert" and "extrovert" and found deep psychological meaning in the symbols of the great world religions. Others, like Freud's daughter, Anna Freud (1895–1982), and Melanie Klein (1882–1960), applied Freudian doctrines to new areas such as the psychoanalysis of children.

Sigmund Freud. This is a drawing of the founder of psychoanalysis by the American modernist Ben Shahn (1898–1969). The picture reflects the feeling many had that Freud saw deeply into what had traditionally been considered the darker side of the human personality.

The chief rival of Freudianism was the behaviorist school founded by the Russian psychologist Ivan Pavlov (1849–1930). Pavlov and his successors, particularly the American B. F. Skinner (1904–1990), explored their subject not in the psychiatrist's office, but in laboratories. They maintained that human actions, like those of other animals, were caused by "conditioned reflexes." Behavior that earns rewards—from nature, from society, from the authority figures of laboratory experimenters—tends to be repeated to earn further rewards. Behavior met by punishment tends not to be repeated and soon disappears. Child rearing, commercial advertising, and government propaganda all depend on such conditioning to manipulate human behavior. For behavioral psychologists, free will is a delusion, and human conduct (response) is shaped, not by unconscious instincts, but by the conditioning impact (stimulus) of the external environment.

New Trends in Technology

Underlying the fluctuations in economic prosperity and the new forms of economic organization in this century was the accelerating advance of technology, especially in heavy industry. Even before 1900, iron and coal were giving way to steel and petroleum as the essential materials of industrialization. Steamships and railroads continued to be the most important means of transportation until World War II, but from then on, automobiles, trucks, and airplanes increasingly replaced them.

Important breakthroughs in manufacturing included the assembly line, automation, and the use of efficiency studies to increase productivity. Henry Ford (1863–1947) used assembly lines to great advantage in his automobile factories. By the 1980s, computer electronics made it possible to put entire manufacturing facilities under robotic controls, all but eliminating the human industrial worker. Efficiency studies, pioneered by Frederick Taylor early in the century, detected wasted time and motion in the plant or office, showing where improvements could be made. All of these developments speeded up the processes of industrial production, making goods less expensive to manufacture and more affordable to purchase.

Americans and Russians became the global leaders in heavy industry. The United States led in the production of oil, steel, and other heavy industrial products for more than half the century. Cities like Pittsburgh and Detroit became internationally known for their steel mills and automobile factories, and forests of oil derricks put Texas on the industrial map. The Soviet Union developed heavy industries after 1928 principally through the large-scale, centralized state planning that was the core of the Soviet system. Hydroelectric dams and industrial complexes like Magnetogorsk, Russia's "steel city," sprang up in impressive numbers beginning in the 1930s. Industrialization also changed the architectural face of modern cities, as twentieth-century builders used structural steel, poured concrete, and plate glass, combined with the electric elevator, to fill cities with skyscrapers.

The development of efficient agricultural equipment—the tractor and various harvesting machines—proceeded rapidly in the twentieth century. The use of chemical fertilizers and insecticides and the perfection of new and inexpensive varieties of seeds produced hardier, more abundant crops, to the point that we may speak of a "green revolution."

Technology brought remarkable transformations in the manufacture of food products and clothing, household implements, and recreational devices. Useful objects of all sorts were now made of plastics (complex organic compounds produced by polymerization), and a broad range of clothing was woven of synthetics or of a mix of synthetic and natural fibers. These artificial "raw materials" enabled manufacturers of consumer goods to fabricate products with the durability, toughness, resistance to heat, and other properties that met the demands of increasingly selective consumers. In western Europe, Japan, and the United States, the new consumer technology produced a culture of waste. Cheap discardable items such as tin, glass, paper, and plastic created a "throw-away" economy.

Twentieth-century technology made a host of labor-saving household appliances commonplace. Though in-

Courtesy of Ford Motor Company

A Ford Model T. Mass-produced automobiles like this famous Ford car gave middle-class Americans a new freedom of movement in the 1920s. These women have paused in their touring to draw water from a well, perhaps to replenish the auto's radiator.

vented earlier, both gas and electric ovens first came into wide use after World War I. Electric washing machines, vacuum cleaners, refrigerators, and freezers (and thus frozen foods) were more recent inventions. Telephones were invented as early as 1876, but were not widely available until after 1900.

The automobile was made economically available to the masses through Henry Ford's assembly-line manufacturing techniques after 1908. In 1913, a million cars were on American roads; by 1970, over a hundred million. Goods were delivered by trucks over networks of highways, and developers laid out business districts and residential areas on the assumption that shoppers and homeowners would own automobiles.

In the affluent West, luxury recreational or entertainment items became virtual necessities. Motion picture theaters spread to countless cities and even small towns beginning in the 1920s. Millions of families bought radios during the first half of the century and televisions in the second half. Whole industries, such as those devoted to musical records, tapes, and compact disks have grown up to satisfy the demands of consumers for entertainment. The United States has been the leader in mass production of consumer goods, although today Japan, western Europe, and the Pacific rim area are striving to overtake it.

Technology advanced at a much faster rate in the twentieth century than in earlier ages. Individual inventions, small in themselves—like the vacuum tube or the microchip—had remarkable consequences in many fields, and the science fiction of earlier times became the hard science of the present.

Medical scientists, building on such earlier discoveries as anesthetics, antiseptics, and the microbe theory of the causation of disease, carried both surgical and chemical medicine to unprecedented levels. Researchers discovered vaccines for yellow fever, tuberculosis, diphtheria, polio, measles, and other diseases. Vitamins and the science of human nutrition provided cures for rickets, beriberi, and similar disorders. Sulfa, penicillin, and many other antibiotic "wonder drugs" saved countless lives.

Surgery also made astonishing advances. The use of X rays greatly improved diagnostic methods, and radiation treatment for various forms of cancer is common. Tissue and organ transplant surgery and the use of surgical lasers became commonplace. Medical scientists devised and improved mechanical support systems for failing lungs, livers, and hearts.

From the 1980s onward, the computer revolution has ushered in major changes in communications, business practices, and human interactions. Computers operate much more rapidly than the human brain, instantly processing immense quantities of information. Computers have been applied to an expanding variety of tasks, from recording airline reservations to guiding artificial satellites and shuttlecraft in their orbits. The Japanese and others "robotized" entire factories with computers. At present, Japanese and American scientists are in a friendly competition to produce even more powerful computers.

Computer technology has enabled societies around the world to store, order, and retrieve vast amounts of knowledge. As the decades pass, raw data piles up in records repositories, on paper and film, on tapes and computer disks. Collections of statistical data alone furnish mountains of information unimaginable in the past. But in many ways, the resulting flood of knowledge has often been overwhelming. The twentieth century has become an age of specialization—a century of experts. As a result, people even in the same society or nation often do not share a common body of knowledge or cultural values. Thus at the very time that technology has made it far easier to transmit and share knowledge, the cultural values and belief systems of many societies have become increasingly fragmented and diverse.

As always, the latest technology was increasingly applied to military weaponry. World War I saw the widespread use of machine guns, submarines, and aircraft as well as the introduction of the flame thrower, poison gas, and tanks. With World War II came amphibious landing craft, radar, and incendiary bombs. Scientists learned to use subatomic particles to split other atoms; the United States won the race to produce the atomic bomb, which was then used to level Hiroshima and hasten the end of World War II. After 1945, scientists expanded the arsenals of the great powers to include napalm, rockets, military helicopters, jet bombers, intercontinental missiles, and laser weapons.

Technology also made the twentieth century the age of flight. In 1903, Orville and Wilbur Wright flew a propeller-driven heavier-than-air craft for the first time. Aviators in small airplanes conducted reconnaissance missions and dog fights in World War I and carried the mails between the wars. In World War II, the multiengine bombing plane came into its own. After the war, jet-propelled airplanes became prevalent in both military and commercial aviation.

Sir Alexander Fleming. The British scientist discovered the first antibiotic, penicillin, almost by accident in 1928. The new drug was a turning point in treating a host of stubborn, often fatal maladies. Here Fleming is shown surrounded by the still rather crude apparatus in use as recently as the 1930s.

Popperfoto

Space exploration began in 1957, when the Soviet Union put the first artificial satellite, called *Sputnik*, into orbit. In 1961, a Russian cosmonaut, Yuri Gagarin, circled the earth in an orbital space vehicle. In 1969, an American astronaut, Neil Armstrong, became the first to set foot on the surface of the moon. In the 1980s, American spacecraft landed on Mars, and Voyager II photographed the outer planets and their moons. The entire age of flight, from Kitty Hawk to the moons of Uranus, has taken place within a single human lifetime.

Twentieth-century technology also brought great dangers. Modern industry polluted the air and water; "acid rain" defoliated large forest areas. Automobiles put a whole society on wheels; yet road accidents also injured millions and killed tens of thousands annually. High technology also raised the specter of earth-orbiting, high-tech "Star Wars" weaponry. Atomic weapons, stockpiled in huge quantities by the superpowers, posed a very real threat of global annihilation.

An especially momentous breakthrough in technology was the peaceful use of nuclear energy, which now produces substantial proportions of the electricity consumed in industrial societies. But this, too, is a mixed blessing. Although atomic power plants provide cheap energy, the peril of accidental damage to reactors and the leaking of radiation is considerable. The explosions at the Chernobyl nuclear power plant in the Soviet Union in 1986 raised radiation levels in many parts of Europe and had dire long-term consequences.

Changing Patterns of Economic Organization

The overall economic picture in the twentieth century has been one of upward surges and downward slides. World War I produced an economic boom that generally lasted through the 1920s; it was followed by the Great Depression in the 1930s. In the United States, World War II brought another great upsurge in production and affluence. After the war, this prosperity spread to western Europe and Japan. In the early 1970s, a huge rise in the price of petroleum triggered a major economic downturn or recession that lasted into the 1980s. Today, recovery from that crisis has meant generally strong economic conditions in most developed nations of the world, which now include nations of the Pacific rim of Asia.

The twentieth century witnessed remarkable changes in the patterns of industrial activity for both management and labor. Already in the 1880s, a fundamental shift had begun with the "managerial revolution." Today, major enterprises are rarely run by their owners. Capitalist ownership of big companies is spread among many stockholders, who may vote on major issues affecting their companies. Professional executives, trained in busi-

CONNECTIONS IN CULTURE

Diasporas and Culture

Modern culture is often defined in national terms: for example, Mexican culture, French culture, or Japanese culture. Yet diasporas—ethnic communities of migrants and their descendants—have stretched across national boundaries, carrying their cultures with them. The diaspora sustains its identity across great distances as its members maintain contacts and a common identity.

Earlier diasporas from Europe and Africa did much to shape nations on both sides of the Atlantic. The Jewish diaspora sustained ties among Jews who settled in Spain, central and eastern Europe, the Middle East, North Africa, and, later, the Americas. The African diaspora brought enslaved workers from the western coast of Africa to Brazil, the Caribbean, and North America. With the expanded migration of the nineteenth and twentieth centuries, new diasporas developed as people left Scandinavia, India, China, the Mediterranean countries, and other regions.

Diasporas can sustain and transport their traditions without formal political recognition. Diasporas generally have no army and no government; they are held together by shared customs. The social and cultural structure of a diaspora is formed in the original homeland. The linkages sustaining diasporas include family, religion, language, occupation, and traditions in dress, music, art, and cuisine.

From the late nineteenth century, a Lebanese diaspora sustained small shops along the coast of Africa, on Indian Ocean shores, and throughout the Americas. The essayist Kahlil Gibran grew up in Boston, and then in New York, yet he wrote *The Prophet,* a Lebanese condensation of modern wisdom, in Arabic. The book, an example of diasporic culture, has since been translated into many languages and published all over the world.

Other major diasporas are those of the Irish, Chinese, and Italians. All three groups sent migrants to the United States, but the Irish also went in large numbers to Australia, the Italians to South America, and the Chinese to Southeast Asia. The Indian diaspora consists of several linguistic and religious groups, such as the Sikhs, a religious group from northern India, or the Tamils, Hindus from southern India. The Caribbean was the destination of diasporas from Britain, Spain, and several parts of Africa. More recently, a Caribbean diaspora has sent millions from the islands to North America, Central America, and Europe. The Jewish diaspora, one of the oldest, was transformed with the migrations to the United States, the expulsion and genocide in Nazi-controlled Europe, and the creation of Israel in 1948.

In every generation, the continued existence of diaspora culture was called into question with the increase of mixed marriages. Would a child assume the identity of its mother's or its father's family? Responding to this threat to their continued existence, some members of diasporas emphasized traditional names, dress, religion, and even cuisine as symbolic badges of identification that also preserved the memory of the homeland. By maintaining cultural identity across national frontiers, diasporas have done as much as nations to create and disseminate culture in the nineteenth and twentieth centuries.

---

1. Open Unit 10 of the Migration CD-ROM. What are some of the factors that can create a diaspora? What are some of the consequences for those who become part of the diaspora? What examples can you find of the continuance of culture in a diaspora?

2. Visit http://www.bh.org.il/, the Nahum Goldmann Museum of the Jewish Diaspora. Examine the exhibitions section. What do the exhibitions tell you about the nature and extent of the Jewish diaspora? To what parts of the globe did the diaspora extend? Now click on "communities." What information and services are provided here? Overall, what are the different ways in which the site seeks to both educate people about the Jewish diaspora and help maintain the diaspora's ties to Jewish culture and religion?

ness schools and moving from one firm to another, control daily operation and long-range planning of their companies. Computer-controlled robotic machinery has replaced many factory workers. A growing percentage of the labor force is now employed in "white collar" office jobs. Automated farms and factories have meant a shortfall in the number of production jobs available and a general change toward employment in service industries.

In the industrialized world, more people have entered "service" occupations, from hotel or restaurant work to jobs in hospitals, schools, and the public sector. Although they use the new industrial technology, from microwave ovens to X-ray machines in their work, these service workers do not manufacture anything.

Despite efforts to restrain the growth of big business in the twentieth century, huge corporations and international cartels, developed during the preceding century, continue to dominate economic life. In addition, such recent innovations as conglomerates, franchising, and multinational corporations have loomed larger on the business scene.

The growth of conglomerates has reflected the increasing complexity of big business. A conglomerate does not bring together production stages in a single process, as old-fashioned vertical combinations did, nor does it unite competitors in the same line of business, as horizontal combinations do. Instead, the conglomerate brings producers in a broad spectrum of different fields under a single corporate umbrella. It might thus buy up firms manufacturing soap flakes, books, and pharmaceuticals, and then perhaps add television stations or vacation resorts to the mix. Such firms sacrifice the expertise that goes with specialization, but they gain economic balance and the freedom to move into profitable areas of investment wherever they might be found.

The trend toward franchising has been particularly strong in service industries. A parent company leases to a local operator the right to use a particular trademark or to sell a particular product. Hotels, fast-food restaurants, automobile dealerships, and real estate companies are often franchise operations. Individuals with limited capital but good knowledge of local business conditions gain from the name recognition, purchasing power, and quality control furnished by the central organization. The McDonald's restaurant chain is perhaps the most visible example worldwide of a successful franchising organization.

Multinational firms have played a big role in post–World War II business life. These huge corporations own and operate subsidiary companies or factories in a number of nations. Such firms headquartered or created in developed Western countries often build factories in less developed lands, where labor is cheap. This practice has also enabled the multinational to avoid tariff barriers, since the goods are not produced inside any such system of protective tariffs. Thus many U.S. factories have been opened in Europe, Asia, and Latin America since World War II. More recently, Japanese manufacturers have begun to set up factories in the United States.

As in earlier periods, governments after World War II continued to play an important part in economic life, both stimulating and regulating business enterprise. In western Europe, North America, Japan, the Pacific rim area, and most of Latin America, private capital still owns most businesses, and private business people make most operating decisions. In the 1920s and 1930s, however, the government of the Soviet Union took over most of that nation's economic institutions in a form of state capitalism. Other eastern European communist nations nationalized many industries in the 1940s and 1950s, when they became client states of the Soviet Union. Western European governments, recovering from World War II, invested public capital to rebuild industry. Newly independent countries like India, which lacked private capital, also established government-run industries and marketing boards to stimulate their economies. Most capitalist nations, in fact, have developed some nationalized industries, from airlines and electronic media to banks or steel mills.

A key feature of twentieth-century government involvement in economic life was central planning. In communist nations, an elaborate bureaucratic structure set goals and allocated resources for all parts of the economy. In western European nations and Japan, government boards now investigate the international market, encourage research in potentially profitable areas, and generally help private capitalists to be competitive. With the collapse of the Communist regimes in eastern Europe in the late 1980s and the disintegration of the Soviet Union, former Communist nations now seek to privatize and move toward full economic integration with their capitalist Western neighbors as quickly as possible. This rapid decline of the communist, state-run economies has resulted in massive social and economic dislocations that will be described in Chapter 17.

At the international level, post–World War II groups like western Europe's Coal and Steel Community helped businesses in member nations to plan and regulate the production of these vital commodities. Another important task of government economic organizations has been to coordinate the roles of private capital and the state. Government regulation in the public interest has extended from labor conditions and the purity of food and drugs to stock market and banking practices, land usage, and pollution control.

Societal Changes and Women's Rights

The material lives of ordinary human beings during the twentieth century have been changed by technological advances but also in many other ways, including the size and distribution of population, the level of health care and education, and the state of public welfare in general.

Population growth has continued at an accelerated pace. World population numbered some 1.5 billion in 1900. Because of technological advances and improved health care, world population in 1990 rose to over 5 billion with almost 2 billion of the world's people in China and India alone. Western Europe had over 350 million inhabitants, and in Latin America, Brazil had a population of more than 150 million, and Mexico almost 89 million, while Asian nations continued to have the largest populations.

In most nations, the population explosion is a huge problem. In the advanced Western states, Japan, and recently the Pacific rim area, however, population has remained relatively stable, growing at a rate of slightly more than one-half of 1 percent a year. In Europe, indeed, many nations have achieved zero population growth (births almost exactly balanced by deaths). The problem has been more serious in Latin America, where the growth rate is

Women Demand the Vote

The only recklessness the Suffragettes have ever shown has been about their own lives and not about the lives of others. It has never been, and it never will be, the policy of the women's Social and Political Union recklessly to endanger human life. We leave that to the men in warfare. . . . There is something that Governments care far more for than human life, and that is the security of property and so it is through property that we shall strike the enemy.

*Be militant each in your own way. Those of you who can express your militancy by going to the House of Commons and refusing to leave without satisfaction, as we did in the early days—do so. Those of you who can express militancy by facing party mobs at Cabinet Ministers' meetings when you remind them of their falseness to principle—do so. Those of you who can express your militancy by joining us in our anti-Government-by-election policy—do so. Those of you who can break windows—break them. . . . And my last word is to the Government: I incite this meeting to rebellion.**

The agitation to secure voting rights for women in Britain entered a militant phase when Mrs. Emmeline Pankhurst founded the Women's Social and Political Union in 1903. As the members of the group adopted drastic measures to publicize their cause, others responded in varied ways, from support to amusement to hostility. Although the suffragists succeeded in raising public awareness of "women's issues," women did not secure the vote in Western nations until after World War I.

*Mrs. Emmeline Pankhurst's Address to Suffragettes on October 17, 1912.

comparable to that in Asia and Africa—between 2.5 and 3 percent a year. At these rates, the estimated world population in the year 2000 was 7 billion people.

The trend toward urbanization is another feature of twentieth-century demographics. Russia, for example, was a nation of peasants in 1900, but by the 1970s 50 percent of the people lived in cities. Most of the worldwide growth in urban population is the result of rural migration, which has brought Egyptian *fellaheen* (peasants) to Cairo, *campesinos* (country folk) into São Paolo, and African Americans from the rural south to Detroit.

Rapid urbanization brought problems in sanitation, health care, education, crime, and especially housing, as slums sprang up around the city centers. Since World War II, some Western governments have built public housing projects or "new towns" to house the urban poor. Small towns have metamorphosed into new cities throughout Europe and the United States. In the United States, the suburb has provided pleasant living areas for middle- and upper-class citizens who work in the cities.

The growth of the welfare state has changed the lives of almost all Western peoples. The goal of welfare legislation has been to provide such goods and services as unemployment relief, child care, public health and geriatric facilities, and low-cost housing to the citizenry. The economic and technological capacities of the industrialized world have brought these goals within reach. In the 1930s, totalitarian leaders attracted support by promising many forms of social services. The Great Depression led democratic governments in Europe and the Americas to offer relief for the unemployed and other forms of "social security." Only after World War II, however, did communism in eastern Europe and welfare capitalism in western Europe, North America, Canada, and Australia bring basic care to most Western people.

The welfare state has its critics. Some believe that too much security makes people less hard working. Others claim that, especially during economic downswings, even wealthy nations simply cannot afford the full range of welfare benefits.

A good education has never been more essential than in the present technologically sophisticated age. Governments the world over have offered more years of formal education and specialized training to their citizens, although some are too poor to live up to their aspirations. In 1900, most European nations provided free elementary education to boys and girls, and two-thirds of the American states had some form of public grade-school education. Today, virtually all North American and European children attend elementary school, as do most Latin Americans. Four-fifths of North Americans, two-thirds of Europeans, and one-third of Latin Americans go on to secondary school. In the United States, almost half the population has access to some sort of higher education. European nations accomplish in their secondary schools what is normally completed in the

United States in the first two years of college. Less than a fifth of the young people in European nations pass the rigorous examinations for college entrance. In Latin America lack of financial and educational resources has held the figure down to 5 percent. Japan and the Asian Pacific rim countries, heirs to centuries-old traditions of respect for learning, have among the best and most rigorous educational systems. These have played a major role in the rise of these nations to economic prosperity.

A striking feature of the expansion of education the world over is its spread across segments of society traditionally excluded from much schooling. Public education means that education is available to the poor as well as to the rich. The relaxation of ancient sexist taboos has given women access to learning at the highest levels in most parts of the world—and to the careers that are open to those with advanced training; however, in poorer nations preference in economic allocations and societal traditions continues to favor men over women. As a result, women in poor nations may receive inferior or little or no schooling, and many are forced to drop out after only two or three years of primary education.

In the West, major changes occurred in the relationships between urban workers and the established middle and upper classes. The urban proletariat organized to improve wages, hours, and working conditions through labor unions and collective bargaining. When the middle and upper classes, anxious to placate unrest, extended the franchise, workers used the vote as a means to further their cause. In Europe, and to a lesser extent in the United States, they supported moderate socialist parties dedicated to bringing public ownership of the means of production by peaceful, constitutional methods. A minority of workers around the world embraced the radical doctrines of revolutionary Marxism, syndicalism, and anarchism. The capitalist leaders of national governments tried to preempt the advance of socialism by enacting significant measures to promote the welfare of the masses.

The status and role of women also changed. By 1900, women in the industrialized world and from the upper classes in the areas under imperial control were already integrating into many phases of the economy and society. In the West, during the nineteenth century, women had been incorporated into the labor force in major industries such as textiles and garment manufacturing. They had also established their claims to professions in teaching and nursing.

Today, women comprise one-third of the work force in western Europe, the United States, and Japan, and almost half in the Soviet Union and Taiwan. Women now enter prestigious legal and medical professions in increasing numbers: one-quarter of the doctors in Great Britain and more than half of those in the Soviet Union are women. Women have succeeded only very slowly in securing top business management positions, however, and continue to be paid less than men. Nevertheless, a trend to equal participation by women in the economic life of the industrialized world has been established.

Simone de Beauvoir with Jean-Paul Sartre. This photo shows two of the most famous proponents of existentialist philosophy; they were close companions for many years.

UPI/Corbis-Bettmann

NOW and ERA. Members of NOW interrupt Senate proceedings in 1970 to demand hearings on an equal rights amendment (ERA). In 1972, with the new feminism gathering momentum, the ERA finally cleared Congress. The amendment was later declared dead when it failed to win the approval of the necessary thirty-eight states.

A variety of factors combined to expand women's roles. Both world wars drew women into heavy industry, replacing men drafted into the armies. Technological advances also played a part. Labor-saving devices freed women from onerous housework and modern contraceptive techniques allowed parents to limit family size. Finally, ideology has also played an important part. Liberals and feminists from industrialized and traditional societies and communist regimes in eastern Europe all supported—or at least paid lip service to—women's demands for equal treatment.

In 1900, only women in Australia and New Zealand had the right to vote. Prior to World War I, British women led the way in demanding voting rights. To bring public attention to their cause, suffragists (those who struggled for women's suffrage) in Britain chained themselves to lampposts, started fires in mailboxes, and smashed department store windows. When jailed, many suffragists went on hunger strikes. These tactics failed to secure the vote, which was granted after World War I largely owing to women's contributions toward the war effort. In 1918, the franchise in Britain was extended to all males over twenty-one and all women over thirty. Ten years later, British women received the vote on the same terms as the men. Women in the United States secured the vote in 1920 and during the interwar years, the vote was extended to women in most European nations, although French and Swiss women did not receive the vote until after World War II.

Similarly, upper- and middle-class women in Africa and Asia led movements to improve the status of all women. Women were particularly active in nationalist movements to secure independence. A women's corps fought in the Chinese nationalist revolution in 1911. In 1919, Chinese female students were active in the May 4th Movement that led to an intellectual revolution. In Egypt, women played a leading role in opposition to continued British domination. In India, Gandhi's passive resistance movement attracted many women followers. In Turkey and Egypt, urban feminists threw off the veil and demanded more social and civil rights. Egyptian feminists, led by Huda Sharawi, joined others at the International Feminist Meeting in Rome in 1923, which was a prelude to many future conferences on the status of women.

After World War II, the role and treatment of women around the world continued to be hotly debated. Simone de Beauvoir (1908–1986), a French novelist and existentialist thinker (see the next section of this chapter), published her ground-breaking book, *The Second Sex*, in 1949

(English translation 1953), and gave intellectual substance to the accelerating quest for fairer treatment of women. In the English-speaking world, which took the lead in the fight for gender equality, the women's liberation movement found provocative, powerfully eloquent, and persuasive voices in books such as Betty Friedan's *The Feminine Mystique* (1963), Germaine Greer's *The Female Eunuch* (1970), and, in a more literary vein, Mary Ellman's *Thinking about Women* (1968) and Kate Millett's *Sexual Politics* (1970); these works provided a catalyst for changing how many women thought about themselves and their role in the family, the workplace, and society in general. Gloria Steinem created an open forum for the airing of feminist concerns by founding *Ms.* magazine in 1972; this periodical, whose circulation rose as high as 500,000, has introduced the work of such important writers as Alice Walker, Erica Jong, and Mary Gordon and has provided a forum where such pressing issues as sexual harassment, domestic violence, and the crisis in child care have been discussed and debated.

In the United States and other Western, industrialized nations, women organized into groups like the National Organization for Women (NOW) to demand and secure equal rights in hiring, pay scales, and laws governing marriage and divorce and for protection against physical assault and abuse. For most of the twentieth century, the struggle for gender equality has been a persistent and ongoing challenge in societies around the world.

Twentieth-Century Social and Cultural Patterns

*The models of development that the West and East offer us today are compendiums of horrors. Can we devise more humane models that correspond to what we are? As people on the fringes, inhabitants of the suburbs of history, we Latin Americans have arrived at the feast of modernity as the lights are about to be put out. . . . We have not been able to save even what the Spaniards left us when they departed, we have stabbed one another. . . . Despite all this, and despite the fact that our countries are inimical to thought, poets and prose writers and painters who equal the best in the other parts of the world have sprung up here and there, separately but without interruption. Will we now, at last, be capable of thinking for ourselves? Can we plan a society that is not based on the domination of others and that will not end up like the chilling police paradises of the East or with the explosions of disgust and hatred that disrupt the banquet of the West?**

*Octavio Paz, *The Other Mexico: Critique of the Pyramid,* trans. L. Kemp (New York: Grove, 1972), pp. viii–x, in Peter N. Stearns, ed., *Documents in World History* (New York: Harper & Row, 1988), vol. 2, p. 190.

This passage by the noted Mexican essayist and Nobel laureate Octavio Paz (1914–1998) describes the problems of many Latin American, African, and Asian writers and artists who have sought to create innovative and unique works of art independent of outside influences. Despite the appearance of a truly global civilization in the twentieth century, cultural and social diversity has been one of the hallmarks of the era. This section will discuss some of the many cultural currents, historical trends, and social developments that have contributed to the modernist revolution around the world.

Philosophic Trends: Secularism, Pragmatism, Existentialism

The most influential philosophical thought, particularly in the Western world, has focused on the material world, on how best to understand and get along in it. Contemporary philosophers have given comparatively little attention to absolute truths or mystical revelations. Instead, such attitudes as secularism, pragmatism, and more formal schools of thought such as existentialism have predominated.

The secular attitudes of later nineteenth-century materialism have spread widely around the world in the twentieth century. Many have come to believe that whereas science has discovered verifiable truths about this material world, religious convictions about the spiritual world are matters of opinion rather than of fact. The real world, for secularists, is the world of matter known to the senses and studied by scientists.

Modern institutions have reflected this prevailing secularism. Most Western democracies have also institutionalized the separation of church and state. Totalitarian countries typically discourage religion, in part because they see it as a rival to their official ideology.

Cultural and moral relativism has also accompanied secularism. Relativists have argued that a particular belief or practice should not be judged right or proper in absolute terms, but only in terms of its own culture. Behavior considered immoral in one society might be quite moral in another. Cultural anthropologists have increasingly endorsed this view. Pragmatists have encouraged a more active, positive attitude toward this world without certainties. For example, John Dewey (1859–1952) insisted on judging ideas by their social usefulness; Dewey's instrumentalism saw ideas as tools, means to an end, valid if and to the extent they worked in society. This pragmatic, can-do attitude, originally associated with optimistic Americans, was widely admired in China after World War I and has become common in many parts of the world.

In contrast, the existentialists reacted against the materialistic or secular world view. Existentialists trace the roots of their world view to such nineteenth-century thinkers as Nietzsche, who proclaimed the "death of God" in the materialistic age. The French writer Jean-Paul Sartre (1905–1980) expressed the existential mood of the mid-twentieth century in his play *No Exit* and novel *Nausea*. Sartre defined existentialism with the pithy phrase "existence precedes essence," meaning that material existence is the fundamental reality, and essences or spiritual beings are only myths. For existentialists, the harshest thing about human existence is its sheer meaninglessness or even absurdity. For a generation that had survived the horrors of the Great Depression and World War II, absurdity and anguish seemed fitting responses to the age.

Secularism versus Religion

Conflict between secularism and religion has been another continuing trend during the twentieth century. Although some devout Christians and Jews in the West attempted to merge religion and secular materialism, others pushed for increased spirituality and greater religious influence in governmental and educational institutions. Fundamentalists have also often opposed what they perceived to be the moral decline and laxity of modern Western society.

Some Hindus in India and Confucians in China also tried to reconcile Western institutions and values with their own religious and moral beliefs. Likewise, modernizers like al-Afghani and Muhammad Abdu in the Muslim world argued that traditional Islam and Western values and technology were not mutually exclusive but could be fused with one another. In contrast, traditionalists in India and the Muslim world not only rejected Western secularism but also severely criticized their coreligionists for accepting foreign secular ideas. The Muslim Brotherhood, which began in Egypt and expanded through much of the Arab world, is one example of a dynamic organization that sought to establish independent governments based on strict, fundamentalist interpretations of Islam. In part, the legitimacy of the Saudi Arabian monarchy has been based upon its strict adherence to puritanical Islamic government and law.

For the first half of the twentieth century it appeared that the Western secularists were the dominant force in the conflict between materialism and spirituality. Initially, even those traditional societies that achieved independence from the imperial powers following World War II adopted Western governmental forms and largely separated the functions of church and state. However, during the latter part of the century, militant Christian, Muslim, and Jewish movements in Iran, the Arab world, India, Israel, and even the United States gained support and influence. Thus no resolution of the conflict over the relative importance and role of religion in all societies has yet been achieved.

Social Thought in the Contemporary Era

Twentieth-century theories about politics and society have drawn heavily on nineteenth-century ideologies: in particular, nationalism and internationalism, conservatism, liberalism, socialism, and communism. Of these, nationalism has undoubtedly had the greatest impact around the world. After World War II, passionate loyalty to individual

Differing Worldviews

The truth is that the contemporary spirit came to an end with the outbreak of the Great War, in other words the moment 20th Century man discovered that the ideals of the revolutionary democrats—who had put their faith in science and believed that world progress was the . . . consequence of scientific advance—were grossly overoptimistic. The Western camp then split into three groups. The first of these turned back to Christianity . . . and can now be called conservative.

The second group is composed of those who, having despaired of democratic ways, turned away from the Church. . . . This group then rallied to the Communist doctrine. . . .

Finally, there is a third group, people whom Christianity and Communism have not been able to satisfy—people who are looking for a solution to that which the church has disdained and the [Communists] left unanswered. In the West, some of them are awaiting a magician who will provide what neither Hitler nor Mussolini could give them. Others turn to existentialism, which, in the end, is not a solution.

Doubtless, the West still possesses considerable intellectual and spiritual resources; but I defy anybody . . . to deny that there is, in the West today, an attempt to go back to first principles in order to make a stand against the prevailing intellectual and moral chaos. Therefore let us not shun our own fundamental origins, made up of faith in freedom, pride in reason and unchanging values.

*Above all, we owe it to ourselves to keep before our eyes the goal we are working towards; namely to serve our society, elevate it, promote its self-awareness and infuse it with the determination to defend its rights and do its duty.**

The above passage, written in 1952 by the Moroccan nationalist, Alal al-Fasi, provides an analysis of how many Third World peoples view the intellectual and cultural crisis of the Western world; al-Fasi and many other writers have attempted to assimilate the ideas of modernization with their own indigenous cultures and traditions.

*Alal al-Fasi, "The Problems of a Contemporary Approach" (1952), in *Contemporary Arab Political Thought,* ed. Anouar Abdel-Malek (London: Zed Books, 1970, rev. 1980), p. 98.

nation-states declined somewhat in Europe but remained exceedingly strong in the Americas and in Third World areas struggling to gain independence. Allegiance of citizens to their nations, newly freed from Western domination, remained a powerful force in Asia and Africa. In contrast, the relative success of international organizations like the United Nations and the Common Market in Europe have encouraged many to adopt more global perspectives in dealing with political, social, and economic issues.

Conservatism, an ideology dedicated to preserving traditional institutions, has sought to defend the best features of ancient political principles and time-tested institutions. Thus religious principles have remained central to its philosophy. However, twentieth-century conservatives have gradually ceased to champion the old monarchies and hereditary aristocracies and have become dedicated to the preservation of the free enterprise, capitalist economic system. In many nations, conservatives have also reluctantly accepted many features of the welfare state.

Liberalism has also retained some of its original ideas while adding new notions. By 1900, liberal doctrine had evolved toward the belief that government should be by and for all people. Concern for the political rights of all led to such major breakthroughs as the American civil rights movement in the 1960s, when the civil disobedience campaign of Martin Luther King Jr. (1929–1968) helped win civil liberties for African Americans. In economic spheres liberals like British economist John Maynard Keynes (1883–1946) advocated government intervention in such times of crisis as the Great Depression of the 1930s.

In the twentieth century, socialism moved in two directions. Western European socialists moved toward social democracy and the democratic welfare state. Prior to World War II and during the Cold War, the Soviet Union, and much of eastern Europe after the war, moved in the opposite direction, toward the totalitarian regimes of communism. As previously noted, the collapse of the Communist regimes in Europe narrowed the differences between eastern and western European economic systems.

Modernism and the Arts

Nineteenth-century romanticism and materialism and certain aspects of non-Western cultures in Asia and Africa have all influenced twentieth-century culture. Each of these factors has enriched the arts in its own unique way.

From romanticism, modern artists inherited an emphasis on the value of the emotions over that of the rational mind. In this tradition, many writers and artists have

Les Demoiselles d'Avignon. This painting, done in 1907, is an early example of the Cubist style. Particularly in the treatment of the faces, it attests to Picasso's interest in African mask-sculptures from the Congo and the Ivory Coast.

The Museum of Modern Art, New York. Acquired through the Lillie P. Bliss Bequest. Photograph © The Museum of Modern Art, New York. © 1998 Estate of Pablo Picasso/Artists Rights Society (ARS)/NY

Frida Kahlo and Diego Rivera. This self-portrait shows Kahlo and her husband Rivera in 1931. Both Rivera and Kahlo were well-known twentieth-century artists. From Mexico, Rivera was renowned for his large, brightly colored, and finely detailed murals. As a socialist, he often used political themes and messages in his work; consequently, his murals were sometimes criticized or even destroyed by political opponents. In contrast, Kahlo's work, as revealed in this portrait, was more self-analytical and emotional in nature.

Frida Kahlo, Frida and Diego Rivera 1931. Oil on canvas. 39 1/2" x 31." San Francisco Museum of Modern Art, Albert M. Bender Collection; gift of Albert M. Bender

Léopold Senghor Laments the Decimation of Africa

Lord God, forgive white Europe.
It is true Lord, that for four enlightened centuries, she has scattered the baying and slaver of her mastiffs over my lands
And the Christians, forsaking Thy light and the gentleness of Thy heart
Have lit their camp fires with my parchments, tortured my disciples, deported my doctors and masters of science.
Their powder has crumbled in a flash the pride of tatas and hills
And their bullets have gone through the bowels of vast empires like daylight, from the Horn of the West to the Eastern Horizon.
They have fired the intangible woods like hunting grounds, dragged out Ancestors and spirits by their peaceable beards,
And turned their mystery into Sunday distraction for somnambulant bourgeois.
Lord, forgive them who turned. . .
My household servants into "boys," my peasants into wage-earners, my people into a working class.
For Thou must forgive those who have hunted my children like wild elephants,
And broken them in with whips, have made them the black hands of those whose hands were white.
For Thou must forget those who exported two millions of my sons in the leperhouses of their ships
Who killed two hundred millions of them.
And have made for me a solitary old age in the forest of my nights and the savannah of my days.
Lord, the glasses of my eyes grow dim
*And lo, the serpent of hatred raises its head in my heart, that serpent that I believed was dead.**

Senghor was a leading spokesperson for an African cultural renaissance and in 1960 became president of independent Senegal. Educated in France, Senghor wrote this poem in French but sought to fuse African and European artistic expressions. This poem also highlights Senghor's sorrow and anger over the tragic impact of Western invasions into Africa and the human tragedy of the slave trade.

*Léopold Sédar Senghor, *Selected Poems,* trans. John Reed and Clive Wake (Oxford: Oxford University Press, 1964), reprinted in William H. McNeill and Mitsuko Iriye, eds., *Modern Asia and Africa* (New York: Oxford University Press, 1971), pp. 280–281.

glorified love, sex, suffering, and violence and have delved deeply into such emotional experiences as dreams, drugs, and madness. Like their romantic predecessors, recent artists have often felt alienated from their own societies. They have also been fascinated by the grimy underside of modern life, vividly depicting criminal, immoral, and hypocritical behavior. Freud's writings led many to seek truth in the depths of the unconscious mind.

Western artists were often heavily influenced by non-Western traditions and styles. Paul Gauguin (1848–1903) left Europe for the South Seas where, with a vision heavily clouded by "Orientalism" or his own version of what traditional societies should be, he wrote that, "I have all the joys of free life, both animal and human. I am escaping from fakery, I am entering into Nature." His brilliantly colored paintings depict lush landscapes and romanticized native women.

Pablo Picasso (1881–1973), the most famous twentieth-century painter, was influenced by African art and owned a large collection of African masks that he used for inspiration. Picasso's most famous style, cubism, divided real objects, as in his naked Ladies of Avignon, into fragmentary shapes, which he then recombined. Many of Picasso's paintings show remarkable parallels to African sculpture. Likewise, African wood carvings influenced the works of the Romanian-born French abstract sculptor Constantine Brancusi (1876–1957) and the British sculptor Henry Moore (1898–1986), best known for his semi-abstract sculptural depictions of the human figure.

Creators of much modern music and dance deliberately attempted to break with traditional Western forms and to suffuse their creations with non-Western themes and modalities. American jazz represented a mixture of African, Latin, and American music. Other musicians such as the Hungarian Béla Bartók (1881–1945) used traditional or "folk" songs as the basis for new renditions. Similarly, modern Arabic singers such as Um Kalthoum or Fairuz adapted Western instrumentation to Arabic improvisational music.

In the field of literature cross-cultural exchanges became commonplace. In Latin America, scholars and writers drew heavily on European cultural sources, but used them to achieve their own cultural statements. Latin American writers often sought to explore and establish a genuinely Latin American culture, distinct from that of Europe.

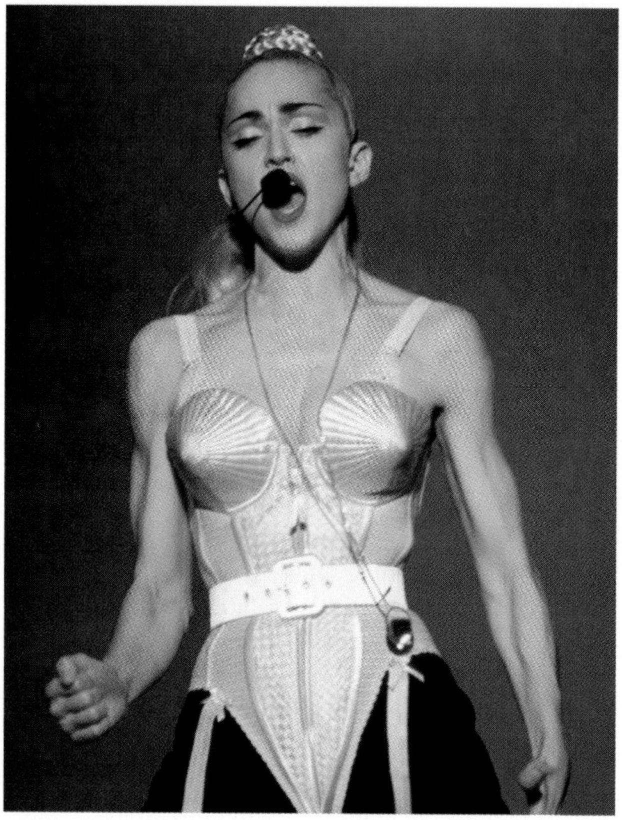
© Neal Preston/Corbis

Madonna. The Material Girl, as Madonna (1958–) was sometimes called, achieved phenomenal success as a rock singer, a field of music traditionally dominated by males. Her popularity was as great in Japan and Singapore as in the United States.

By condemning their European ancestors and glorifying their Amerindian ones, by evoking such clearly South American phenomena as the gaucho of the pampas, these writers achieved a sense of their own cultural uniqueness.

The Egyptian writer Naguib Mahfouz (1911–), used the novel, a Western creation, as his form of expression while describing in vivid terms life in urban Egypt. Léopold Senghor of Senegal, a Catholic married to a French woman, admitted the great influence of Western, particularly French, literature. Yet during the 1930s he led the movement celebrating *Négritude*, or "the sum total of the values of the African world." His poetry focused on Africa, its people and traditions. In addition to being a poet of some renown, Senghor led the nationalist movement in Senegal and was elected the first president of the independent republic in 1960, a position he held till 1980.

Popular Culture

While many artists and writers have gone their own ways in the twentieth century, the rise of the electronic media with their ability to reach large groups of people created a popular culture with a mass following around the world. Sound recording, radio, film, and television brought music, drama, and much more to whole populations on a scale never before imagined.

The history of popular music illustrates how the United States has become the center for much popular culture. Although some of the most successful performers, like the Beatles and the Rolling Stones, came from Great Britain, and many new rhythms and dances such as the tango, samba, reggae, or lambada originated in Latin America or the Caribbean, internationally popular musical forms such as jazz and rock came from the United States. Rock and roll has become the predominant form of popular music around the world. Rock drew heavily on African-American rhythms, as well as on the country and folk music of the rural southern United States. The African-American composer and singer Chuck Berry was a shaping influence on the new form, but Elvis Presley (1935–1977) became the first rock superstar.

Musicians around the world have fused their own traditional forms with elements of Western pop, jazz, and reggae. "Highlife" music by Fela Anikulapo Kuti (1938–1997) and others in Nigeria, and "Rai" from Algeria have become enormously popular among youth in search of their own identities.

Relying on a strong beat, the electric guitar, electronic amplification, and dazzling staging and lighting, rock musicians have sold out their concerts to thousands of fans and circulated millions of copies of their records around the world. Some, like the Jamaican reggae artist Bob Marley (1945–1981), and Bob Dylan (1941–) from the United States, have addressed political controversies and thereby helped to fuel the social protest by youth in the latter half of the twentieth century.

Film and television have also been major factors in creating popular culture. Both as a theatrical form and adapted for the home television screen, moving pictures are the most universally appealing of modern arts. Home videos have made them even more accessible and popular. Film produced its own array of artistic geniuses: director D. W. Griffith (1875–1948) invented many basic techniques of filmmaking, and Charlie Chaplin (1889–1977) brought artistic sensitivity to his portrayal of "the little tramp" victimized by the modern world. Filmmakers like Luis Buñuel (1900–1983) of Spain, Federico Fellini (1920–1993) of Italy, Ingmar Bergman (1918–) of Sweden, Satyajit Ray (1922–1992) of India, Akira Kurosawa (1910–1998) of Japan, and Stanley Kubrick (1928–1999), Martin Scorsese (1942–), Spike Lee (1957–), and Quentin Tarantino (1963–) of the United States have all experimented with new techniques and subject matter. The motion picture also produced a long series of stars whose immense popularity was rooted in personal qualities portrayed on the screen. Marlene Dietrich (1904–1992), John Wayne (1907–1979), Robert De Niro (1943–), Meryl Streep (1949–), and Tom Hanks (1956–) are a few examples.

1885	Indian National Congress
1900	Nationalism in Asia and Africa Freud, *The Interpretation of Dreams* African resistance movements Marie Curie's Nobel Prize in physics Chinese Republic: Sun Yat-sen Díaz dictatorship overthrown Wright brothers at Kitty Hawk Einstein's theory of relativity Assembly-line production Conflicting interests of Arabs and Zionists in West Asia Constitution of 1917 in Mexico The Russian Revolution Du Bois and pan-Africanism Women's suffrage Motion pictures
1920	Rise of Gandhi, Ali Jinnah Atatürk modernizes Turkey Reza Khan Westernizes Persia (Iran) King Abd al-Aziz in Arabia Chiang Kai-shek unites China Stalin in power in USSR Indonesian and Vietnamese nationalism: Sukarno, Ho Chi Minh Institutional Revolutionary party in Mexico Afrikaners in South Africa Stalin's first Five-Year Plan Civil war between Kuomintang and Communists in China Modernism in art: Pablo Picasso, Henry Moore Négritude literary movement: Léopold Senghor Cárdenas reforms in Mexico
1940	Existentialism: Jean-Paul Sartre Television
1950	Rock and roll music DNA research
1960	Novels of Naguib Mahfouz Rise of feminism
1970	

Television, widespread after 1950, opened up new realms of popular entertainment. From radio, television inherited the serial program format, in which the same central characters had new adventures every week. Television evolved the more flexible miniseries form, in which one story, often derived from a successful novel, is told in installments adding up to many hours in length. Films and television both had broad popular appeal, transporting viewers out of their humdrum daily lives into mansions and penthouses, steaming jungles, or distant wars. Torrid love scenes, wild automobile chases, and violence have become parts of the imaginary lives of millions. Fans in Bogotá, Tokyo, and Rome all eagerly watch the latest crisis on *ER, NYPD Blue,* or *Baywatch,* while satellite transmitters provide instant images of events to viewers around the globe.

Finally, the Americanization of popular culture throughout the West and around the globe has been a notable feature of the postwar world. Many social commentators have noted the widespread influence of American jazz, rock and roll music, films, and television programs. However, this popularization of American culture has also been a source of tension as many peoples around the world have sought to maintain their individuality and traditional cultural expressions in the arts, music, literature, architecture, and even dress.

Summary and Comparisons

During the twentieth century, peoples in Africa and Asia organized nationalist revolts against foreign domination. After World War I, despite British promises to support independence, the Arab provinces of the old Ottoman Empire were divided between the British and the French. Atatürk in Turkey and the Pahlavi Shah Reza in Iran led their nations toward independence and westernization. In contrast, leaders like King Abd al-Aziz ibn Saud in Saudi Arabia adopted Western technology and Western material goods, but sought to retain traditional ways and to observe Muslim precepts. This tension between the "modernizers" and "traditionalists" was quite pronounced and sometimes violent.

In Africa, superior European military forces quelled a number of nationalist revolts. India and Southeast Asia, too, witnessed protracted struggles for national independence. In India, Gandhi led the Congress in a struggle of passive resistance against the British.

In China, the Nationalist party embarked on reforms and created the first republic in Asia. However, the Chinese Communist party led by Mao Zedong called for the establishment of a communist regime. In the 1930s, Japan moved to expand its empire into China, launching World War II in Asia.

Thus most nationalist movements in Africa and in both West and East Asia failed to secure complete independence prior to World War II. Sweeping changes in Europe brought about a second global conflict and the ultimate collapse of Western empires.

In the Russian Revolution of 1917, Lenin and the Bolshevik party instituted revolutionary changes to create a socialist state. After Lenin's death, Stalin purged the regime of all rivals, collectivized agriculture, and embarked on an ambitious program to industrialize the Soviet Union; Soviet industrial productivity grew dramatically, but at enormous human cost. The Russian Revolution, like the French Revolution, swept away the old regime, destroyed the power of the church, and altered the fabric of society. In both cases political change outlived social and economic reforms.

During the twentieth century, stupendous and rapid advances were made in all areas of physical science, from astronomy to physics to biology and chemistry. Information gained in the theoretical sciences was applied to medicine, space research, and such fields as psychology, archaeology, and anthropology.

The material lives of most people, especially in the Western world, improved by leaps and bounds. Synthetic materials added to the array of goods; new sources of energy expedited travel and the growth of cities. In many countries heavy smokestack industry gave way to high-tech and service industries. Conglomerates, large corporations, and government-owned enterprises replaced small companies. Wars and changing economic conditions brought women into the workforce and increased demand for political rights and an equitable share of economic prosperity.

Advances in knowledge in many fields globalized twentieth-century cultural life. New ideologies addressed changing conditions around the world. The most influential, rooted in the nineteenth century but maturing in the twentieth, were nationalism, socialism, conservatism, liberalism, and fascism.

Modernism typified twentieth-century artistic developments in painting, sculpture, and music. Rapid communications expedited cross-cultural exchanges of ideas and techniques among many different cultures. Although cultural and economic transmissions had been a constant fact of human history, modern technology and communication systems sped up these exchanges tremendously. Popular culture flourished, with the United States setting trends in music, film, television, "pop" idols, and literature around the world.

Selected Sources

Afigbo, A. E., et al. *The Making of Modern Africa*. Vol. 2, 1986. Timely, scholarly accounts of independence movements throughout the continent.

*Barrett, William. *Irrational Man: A Study of Existential Philosophy*. 1958. Good overview, from nineteenth-century origins to Sartre.

Bass, Thomas A. *Reinventing the Future: Conversations with the World's Leading Scientists*. 1994. Lively interviews with eleven scientists, including biologists and physicists.

The Beatles. *Sergeant Pepper's Lonely Hearts Club Band*. 1967. An album of rock music made popular by this group.

*Borges, Jorge Luis. *Labyrinths*. 1977. Short fictions by the dean of Latin American modernist writers.

Chadha, Yogesh. *Gandhi: A Life*. 1997. A readable biography of a compelling personality.

Chekhov, Anton. *Peasants and Other Stories*. Ed. Edmund Wilson. 1956. Gives insight into the lives and problems of Russian peasants before the revolution.

Conquest, Robert. *The Harvest of Sorrow: Soviet Collectivization and the Terror-Famine*. 1986. Somewhat marred by the author's mistaken belief that the famine in the Ukraine was an attempt at genocide, but it is still one of the best books available on collectivization.

*Crossman, Richard, ed. *The God that Failed*. 1960. Ideological commitment and disillusionment of the left in the 1930s.

Doctor Zhivago. David Lean, dir. 1965. This super-epic film is worthy of Boris Pasternak's novel in following one life through the 1917 revolutions and the civil war. Also see *Lawrence of Arabia* (1962), Lean's epic film of the Arab revolt.

Drees, Willem B. *Beyond the Big Bang: Quantum Cosmologies and God*. 1980. A discussion of the complementary roles of science and religion as guides to an understanding of the nature of the cosmos.

Eisenstein, Sergei M. Films directed by Eisenstein are important not only for their historical elements but also for their cinematic value. Note especially *Potemkin* (1925) on the Revolution of 1905 and *Ivan the Terrible*, Parts I (1944) and II (1945). In the latter, Eisenstein tries to create an analogy between what Tsar Ivan did in the 1500s and what Stalin was doing.

*Fisher, Sydney N., and William Ochsenwald. *The Middle East: A History*. 2 vols. 5th ed. 1997. A readable survey with fine chapters on the region during the nineteenth and twentieth centuries.

*Friedan, Betty. *The Feminine Mystique*. 1963. An influential work that served as a catalyst for the women's movement in the 1960s and 1970s.

*Gandhi, Mohandas K. *An Autobiography: The Story of My Experiments with Truth*. 2d ed. 1940, reprinted 1983. Gandhi's frank account of his life, ideas, and actions.

Gandhi. Richard Attenborough, dir. 1984. An evocative film on the father of Indian independence and the twentieth-century prophet of nonviolence.

"The History of Flight." Video on development of aviation with footage on the Wright brothers and Charles Lindbergh. [Merit Audio Visual.]

Howard, Jane. *Margaret Mead: A Life*. 1984. A readable biography of a leading anthropologist.

Hsu, Immanuel C. Y. *The Rise of Modern China*. 6th ed. 2000. The standard textbook on nineteenth- and twentieth-century China.

*Available in paperback.

The Hunt for Pancho Villa. PBS Video. 1994. Dramatic account of often violent clashes along Mexican-U.S. border during the Mexican civil war.

*Khalidi, R., et al., eds. *The Origins of Arab Nationalism.* 1993. A collection of short essays on Arab national leaders and writers.

Khapoya, Vincent B. *The African Experience: An Introduction.* 2d ed. 1998. A short, engaging overview of African nationalist movements and leaders.

Knight, Alan. *The Mexican Revolution.* 2 vols. 1986. A thorough analysis and definitive account of the revolution from 1910 to the constitution in 1917; Knight argues that the revolution was agrarian and social, begun and sustained by the peasantry.

*Laqueur, Walter Z. *History of Zionism.* 1972. Detailed discussion of the philosophical and historical roots of Jewish nationalism.

Li, Yu-ning, ed. *Chinese Women through Chinese Eyes.* 1992. On and by Chinese women, ancient and modern.

Lion of the Desert. Moustapha Akkad, dir. 1980. An epic film on Omar Mukhtar's struggle against Italian aggression in Libya with Anthony Quinn in the starring role.

*Macfie, A. L. *Ataturk.* 1994. Concise and well-balanced biography of the charismatic Turkish leader.

Mahfouz, Naguib. *Palace Walk.* 1990. *Palace of Desire.* 1991. *Sugar Street.* 1992. The "Cairo Trilogy" of novels by the Egyptian Nobel laureate focuses on family life in Cairo during the twentieth century.

*McLuhan, Marshall. *Understanding Media.* 1965. Pithy commentary on the mass media and their impact on audiences.

"The Meiji Period (1868–1912)." Video on the modernization of Japan prior to World War I. 52 minutes. [Films for the Humanities and Sciences.]

*Nehru, Jawaharlal. *The Discovery of India.* 1946. An Indian nationalist leader and prime minister looks back on Indian history.

Pipes, Richard. *A Concise History of the Russian Revolution.* 1995. An abridgement of the author's two-volume study of the dramatic changes that occurred in Russia from 1917 to 1924.

Reds. Warren Beatty, dir. 1981. An interesting film about the experiences of the American journalist John Reed (see below) during the Russian Revolution.

Reed, John. *Insurgent Mexico.* 1914. The classic journalistic account of the revolution. Reed, who spent a year with Pancho Villa's "Division of the North," presents a sympathetic and engrossing account of the enigmatic Villa.

*———. *Ten Days That Shook the World.* 1919. Sympathetic study by a left-wing U.S. journalist who was in Petrograd during the Bolshevik Revolution.

*Sartre, Jean-Paul. *No Exit and Three Other Plays.* 1955. The existential worldview presented in dramatic form.

Schram, Stuart. *Mao Tse-tung.* 1966. An excellent biography of Mao, excluding his last years.

*Schiffrin, Harold Z. *Sun Yat-sen and the Origins of the Chinese Revolution.* 1970. A good work on Sun's formative years.

*Shattuck, Roger. *The Banquet Years.* 1968. Colorful profile of Paris culture in the Bohemian end-of-the-century years.

*Sheridan, James Z. *China in Disintegration: The Republican Era in Chinese History, 1912–1949.* 1975. On China's struggle toward modern nationhood.

*Sholokov, Mikhail. *And Quiet Flows the Don.* Trans. Stephen Garry. 1934, reprinted 1966. The first volume of the author's epochal narrative of the effect of the Soviet state on the Cossacks.

*Stromberg, Roland N. *After Everything.* 1975. Stimulating, brief survey of cultural trends in the twentieth century.

*Tergeman, Siham. *Daughter of Damascus.* 1994. This highly personal memoir vividly describes family life in an Arab Muslim household during the early part of the twentieth century.

*Trotsky, Leon. *The Russian Revolution.* 1932. A study by one of the major participants; readers should remember that he liked Lenin and loathed Stalin.

Tucker, Robert C. *Stalin in Power: The Revolution from Above, 1928–1941.* 1990. An excellent analysis of the period.

Wolff, Bertram D. *Three Who Made a Revolution.* 1948. A triple biography of Lenin, Trotsky, and Stalin.

Womack, John. *Zapata and the Mexican Revolution.* 1968. The best analysis and interpretation of Emiliano Zapata and the Zapatista movement from 1910 to Zapata's death.

Woolman, David. S. *Rebels in the Rif: Abd el Krim and the Rif Rebellion.* 1968. Dramatic account of Moroccan revolt against the Spanish.

Internet Links

Einstein Revealed
http://www.pbs.org/wgbh/nova/einstein/index.html
This production of "Nova Online" comprises Timeline, Genius, Relativity, Light Stuff, Time Traveler, and Links, featuring excellent texts and graphics.

Ghana: The Growth of Nationalism and the End of Colonial Rule
http://lcweb2.loc.gov/cgi-bin/query2/r?frd/cstdy:@field(DOCID+gh0020)
A concise series of linked texts on the progression in one African country from colonial takeover to independent nation.

Mustafa Kemal (Atatürk), 1881–1938
http://www.ataturk.com/
A helpful collection of online texts and photographs highlighting the Turkish leader's legal, social, economic, political, and cultural reforms during his tenure as president.

Revelations from the Russian Archives
http://lcweb.loc.gov/exhibits/archives/intro.html
A Library of Congress exhibit on The Internal Workings of the Soviet System and The Soviet Union and the United States, from Stalin's takeover through the Cuban Missile Crisis. Excellent photographs of significant persons and documents.

Russian Revolution
http://www.fordham.edu/halsall/mod/modsbook39.html
This site, a subsection of the Internet Modern History Sourcebook, lists links to the best online facilities—text archives, biographies of major figures, etc.—for study of the Russian Revolution.

Sigmund Freud Museum, Vienna
http://freud.t0.or.at/freud/index-e.htm
This site provides a wealth of information: good summaries of Freud's major theories, photographs, and audio-video materials.

Sun Yat-sen: Fundamentals of National Reconstruction (1923 C.E.)
http://acc6.its.brooklyn.cuny.edu/~phalsall/texts/sunyat.html
The founder of the Kuomintang (Nationalist party) enunciates his famous three principles in the history of the Chinese revolution: revolution, democracy, livelihood.

The Interwar Years, World War II, and the Cold War

15

MILITARISM, FASCISM, AND NAZISM
Militarism in Japan
Totalitarian Regimes in Europe
Fascism in Italy
Nazism in Germany
Nazi State and Society
Authoritarian Regimes in the Iberian Peninsula
Personalist Dictatorships in Latin America

AGGRESSION IN ASIA AND EUROPE
Japanese Aggression Against China
Fascist Italy's Aggressions
Nazi Aggression in Europe

WORLD WAR II AND POSTWAR SETTLEMENTS
Japan Launches All-Out War Against China
Axis Advances in Europe
The United States Enters the War
Hitler's "New Order"
The Home Front
The War in North Africa and the Invasion of Italy
Allied Victory in Europe
The Defeat of Japan
Settlements with Germany and Japan

COLD WAR IN EUROPE
The Beginning of the Cold War: 1945–1949
Economic and Political Divisions
Cold War Military Expansion

SUMMARY AND COMPARISONS

Someone was standing up and had begun to talk, hesitatingly and shyly at first. . . . Then suddenly the speech gathered momentum. I was caught, I was listening. . . . The crowd began to stir. The haggard grey faces were reflecting hope. . . . Two seats to my left, an old officer was crying like a child. I felt alternately hot and cold. . . . It was as though guns were thundering. . . . I was beside myself. I was shouting hurrah. Nobody seemed surprised. The man up there looked at me for a moment. His blue eyes met my glance like a flame. This was a command. At that moment I was reborn. . . . Now I know what road to take. . . .

*Hitler's words were like a scourge. When he spoke of the disgrace of Germany, I felt ready to spring on any enemy . . . glancing around, I saw his magnetism was holding these thousands as one. . . . I was a man of 32, weary of disgust and disillusionment, a wanderer seeking a cause . . . a yearner after the heroic without a hero. The intense will of the man, the passion of his sincerity, seemed to flow from him into me. I experienced a feeling that could be likened only to a religious conversion. . . . I felt sure that no-one who heard Hitler that night could doubt he was the man of destiny. . . . I had given him my heart.**

*Perry M. Rodgers, ed., *Aspects of Western Civilization* (Englewood Cliffs, N.J.: Prentice-Hall, 1992), vol. 2, p. 361.

Adolf Hitler possessed an uncanny ability to sway masses with his demonic oratory, not so much by what he said as how he said it. His voice shaking with emotion in the manner of a fanatical fundamentalist preacher, he offered his audience propaganda based on ideals of patriotism, a greater Germany, and race mastery. Many were moved as if by a spiritual conversion, rather than a political experience. The above excerpts by two such converts illustrate this phenomenon.

In the aftermath of the Nazis' rise to power, Germany underwent profound social and political changes. Between the two world wars a similar transformation occurred in Italy and Japan under authoritarian, militaristic regimes. All three countries undertook major shifts in foreign policy as well.

During the 1930s, the aggressive regimes in Japan, Italy, and Germany victimized weak nations to satisfy their appetites for empire and domination. Japan's successful conquest of Manchuria from China in 1931 and the failure of the League of Nations to intervene encouraged further aggressions, culminating in an all-out war against China in 1937. The Sino-Japanese War expanded to World War II in Asia in 1941 when Japan launched attacks on the U.S. naval base in Hawaii and western colonies in Southeast Asia.

In Europe, Fascist Italy attacked Ethiopia and, like Japan, defied the League of Nations. Hitler's annexation of Austria and Czechoslovakia finally discredited appeasement. When he attacked Poland in 1939, Great Britain and France declared war against Nazi Germany. The Soviet Union and the United States later entered the war against the Axis. Despite their initial advantages, the brutality of the Germans and Japanese spurred their victims in Europe and Asia to determined resistance. Finally, the Allies triumphed, but at the cost of tens of millions of lives and devastation on an unprecedented scale.

This chapter will also detail the postwar settlements with Germany and Japan, the emergence of the United States and the Soviet Union as leaders of two antagonistic blocs, and the beginning of the Cold War.

Militarism, Fascism, and Nazism

The best state constitution and state form is that which, with the most unquestioned certainty, raises the best minds in the national community to leading position and leading influence. There must be no majority decisions, but only responsible persons, and the word "council" must be restored to its original meaning. Surely every man will have advisers by his side, but the decision will be made by one man. This principle—absolute responsibility unconditionally combined with absolute authority—will gradually breed an elite of leaders such as today, in this era of irresponsible parliamentarianism, is utterly inconceivable.

As regards the possibility of putting these ideas into practice, I beg you not to forget that the parliamentary principle of democratic majority rule has by no means always dominated mankind, but on the contrary is to be found only in brief periods of history, which are always epochs of the decay of peoples and states.

But it should not be believed that such a transformation can be accomplished by purely theoretical measures from above, since logically it may not even stop at the state constitution, but must permeate all other legislation, and indeed all civil life. Such a fundamental change can and will only take place through a movement which is itself constructed in the spirit of these ideas and hence bears the future state within itself.

*Hence the National Socialist movement should today adapt itself entirely to these ideas and carry them to practical fruition within its own organization, so that some day it may not only show the state these same guiding principles, but can also place the completed body of its own state at its disposal.**

*Adolf Hitler, *Mein Kampf (My Struggle),* trans. R. Manheim (Boston: Houghton Mifflin, 1943), reprinted in Peter N. Stearns, ed., *Documents in World History,* vol. 2 (New York: Harper & Row, 1988), pp. 113–114.

In 1924, in his meandering, often illogical book, *Mein Kampf,* Adolf Hitler set forth his future plans and purposes in explicit detail. In this selection, Hitler describes his concept of dictatorship, which he proposed to put into practice on assuming power.

After World War I a number of governments fell under a variety of dictatorial regimes. Disillusioned by the horrors and unfulfilled promises of the war and fearful of continued economic crises, peoples in Asia, Latin America, and Europe often turned toward opportunist dictators who promised easy answers to the overwhelming problems facing the postwar world. In Latin America, which had a long tradition of military interference in politics, most of these dictators were led by or supported by army leaders. In Japan the militarists, supported by conservative rightist groups, also gradually acquired control over the political system. Likewise, a large number of European nations moved from democratic forms to authoritarian, dictatorial regimes. In contrast to "totalitarian" dictators like Joseph Stalin and Hitler, who sought to control not only the state, but the private lives of its citizens, authoritarian dictators controlled the political institutions of the state, but not necessarily every aspect of the society. This section begins with the emergence of militarism in Japan and then turns to the growing power of the Fascists and Nazis in Europe and concludes with a discussion of the dictators in Latin America.

Militarism in Japan

In Japan the years between 1913 and 1926 are called the period of Taisho democracy, after the reign title of the Taisho emperor. Party government by the winning political parties in the elections became the rule. For many Japanese, the defeat of autocratic Germany and the Austro-Hungarian Empire in World War I proved the superiority of liberal institutions and democratic governments. Western mass culture became popular in urban Japan; young Japanese were attracted to Western music, movies, cafés, and sports. As in Western countries, the "flapper" symbolized the modern young woman (called the *moga* in Japanese, the abbreviation for "modern girl").

Emperor Hirohito (reigned 1926–1989), known in Japan by his reign title, Showa, ascended the throne in 1926. Soon after, Japan began to turn to militarism, ultranationalism, and increasingly more ruthless imperialism. The role of the Showa emperor in these changes is unclear and still debated, but Japanese who favored the changes called the new policy and era the Showa Restoration.

Japan's economy had expanded rapidly during World War I but could not sustain its gains in the postwar years and was severely affected by the Great Depression of 1929. Ordinary Japanese workers and farmers bore the brunt of the hard times. As a result, many Japanese turned against the democratic West and toward ultranationalism and militarism. They blamed their troubles on Western discrimination against Japanese goods and the unwillingness of Western nations to accept Japanese as equals. They were particularly angered by President Wilson's refusal to accept Japan's demand for a clause on racial equality in the Covenant of the League of Nations.

Nationalism and militarism found natural champions in the army and navy, especially among zealous young officers, whose narrow military education had not exposed them to liberal influences from the West. Ultranationalist officers joined organizations such as the Black Dragon Society, which advocated military expansion in continental Asia against China and the Soviet Union. Insisting that they truly represented the imperial will, they claimed that expansion would solve Japan's population and economic problems and that Japan had a mission to dominate Asia. They also maintained that Japan's security had been undermined by the politicians who favored a moderate foreign policy and international cooperation.

The change from a civilian to a military-dominated government occurred without abolishing the Meiji Constitution of 1889, because under that constitution the civil government had no authority over the army and navy, which were commanded by the emperor. As the army and navy defied the civilian government and the emperor did not object, the military gradually gained the upper hand. Middle-level and junior military officers took many policy matters into their own hands and forced their superiors and the civilian leaders to accept the consequences. In some cases, these zealots assassinated superior officers, government leaders, and captains of industry. This outbreak of terrorism culminated in the February Rebellion of 1936 (it occurred on February 26), when fanatical officers assassinated many key government officials. When the courts tried these murderers, the public tended to sympathize with them; when the defendants were sentenced to die, they were viewed as martyrs and became objects of public adulation. As a result of the rebellion, civilian leaders of political parties lost the last vestiges of political influence; the military thereafter dictated foreign policy.

In another form of direct action, the military began to make vital decisions without government authorization. Most notably, on September 18, 1931, army officers launched an all-out offensive against Manchuria in northeastern China. The Japanese army proceeded to conquer Manchuria despite government orders and League of Nations resolutions calling for a cease-fire and restoration of the territory to China. The Japanese public acclaimed the conquest with wild enthusiasm, the cabinet fell, and Japan resigned from the League of Nations. Japan was the first great power to defy the League; its defiance showed that the League could not enforce international law.

The army's triumph against both China and the civilian government marked the victory of pro-militarist forces in Japan. After 1931 censorship laws were enforced with vigor, military police helped ordinary law enforcement officers weed out potential troublemakers, independent-minded professors were dismissed from teaching posts, and their books were banned; hundreds of labor leaders, socialists, and students were thrown into jail. The government revised textbooks to reflect fervent nationalism and used radio and movies to indoctrinate all citizens. Individualism and democracy were denounced, and such previously popular Western practices as ballroom dancing were discouraged as immoral. Ironically, no one demanded the abandonment of Western technology. Even such ancient Confucian virtues as the brotherhood of all humans were reinterpreted to mean worldwide Japanese domination.

Thus Japan's short experiment with some semblance of representative government ended with the triumph of ultranationalist militarism. Most Japanese people, lacking a long democratic tradition, submissively and even enthusiastically embraced the military's dominance over political life. Unlike the Fascists in Italy and the Nazis in

Germany, Japanese militarists won without a mass party, a charismatic leader, or a clearly articulated ideology.

In the late 1930s, Japan signed agreements with totalitarian Germany and Italy, forming an Axis alliance that seemed bent on global domination and that threatened both the Soviet Union and the United States. The Axis alliance soon forced wars on the Western democracies and their empires.

Totalitarian Regimes in Europe

Totalitarian government aimed at total control of society—politics, the economy, and the social lives of the people. The totalitarian leaders of the interwar years had massive bureaucracies and employed modern technologies to exert control more effectively than any absolute monarch or despot of the past. They depended heavily on mass communication—radio and motion pictures—to secure public favor during their rise to power.

In addition, totalitarian regimes relied on their political parties. The Fascists in Italy and the Nazis in Germany were organized political parties before they were governments. They offered uniforms, rallies, careers, and a sense of membership for all, irrespective of class. Above all, totalitarian parties offered a clear political alternative to the disillusioned and demoralized during the interwar era. While fascism in its early existence was really an anti-movement, Nazism drew heavily on the racist nationalism of the late nineteenth century, and communism built on the ideas of Karl Marx. All the totalitarian regimes modified and simplified ideas with slogans and battle cries that aroused mass support. Like nineteenth-century reformers, totalitarian dictators aimed to change society.

Fascism in Italy

Italy under Benito Mussolini (1883–1945) was the first European state to espouse fascism. Mussolini rose to power against a background of government inaction in the face of a collapsing economy, widespread unemployment, and violent social unrest in industrial centers at the end of the war. The son of a blacksmith, Mussolini had embraced socialism as a youth, but broke with the party because of its pacifistic position in 1914. After serving in the army, Mussolini formed the Fascist party (from *fasces,* the bundle of rods with an axe that was the ancient Roman symbol of authority), which at first combined socialist demands with nationalism and anticlericalism. Early electoral setbacks convinced him that he needed to move his party farther to the right.

With increasing financial support from industrialists and large landowners, Mussolini recruited a number of restless and disillusioned men, many of whom were ex-soldiers and unemployed youths. As Il Duce (The Leader), he dressed them in black shirts, subjected them to military discipline, and paraded them through the streets. He had no detailed program or coherent set of principles. Not until after he gained power did his party begin to develop a philosophy to fit its needs. As Mussolini himself admitted, "Fascism was not suckled on a doctrine in advance around a table. It was born of a need for action, and it was action. It was not a party, but in the first two years it was an anti-party and anti-movement."

In his many speeches the charismatic Mussolini told his audience what they wanted to hear, railing against Communists and appealing to the wounded pride of nationalists who felt Italy had been cheated at Versailles. Frequently resorting to violence, Fascists broke up socialist and Communist meetings, smashed their printing presses, broke up strikes, and intimidated workers. The weak Italian constitutional monarchy was unable to stop them. In October 1922 Mussolini, after denouncing the ministry in power, sent his blackshirts to Rome by the thousands to take over the administration by direct action. After they flooded into the city, a bewildered King Victor Emmanuel III (reigned 1900–1946), fearful of civil war, summoned Mussolini and asked him to become the new Italian premier.

Although Mussolini achieved power legally, he had contempt for democratic institutions and wanted to rule Italy as a dictator. Initially, though, he headed a coalition government and made every effort to operate within constitutional limits. He requested and received from parliament dictatorial powers for one year to enable him to restore order. The results were seen almost immediately; strikes were called off or broken up, street fighting subsided, and government services operated with increased efficiency. The public's confidence in Mussolini was evident in 1924 when the Fascists won 63 percent of the vote in the general elections. Backed by a parliamentary majority, Mussolini could proceed to consolidate his authority. In 1925–1926 a series of laws instituted press censorship, forbade strikes, outlawed rival political parties, and gave Mussolini the authority to rule by decree. Like Lenin, Mussolini acted as both chief of state and head of the party that controlled the legislature and administration.

Mussolini further strengthened his position by making peace with the Roman Catholic church. By the Lateran Treaty in 1929, the papacy recognized the Italian state and in turn gained sovereignty over the Vatican City in Rome, received large reparations from the Fascist government for the loss of the papal states (during the unification process), and retained control over education in Italy. Through these concessions, Mussolini gained a freer hand over the political and economic life of the nation. The grateful pope called Mussolini a "man sent by Providence" and generally refrained from criticizing the Fascist regime.

In the early 1930s, Mussolini moved to restructure the nation's economy into a "corporate state." He organized major industries into two dozen "corporations," each run by committees of businessmen, union leaders, and Fascist party officials representing the government. Together the members of the corporations were given the task of determining working conditions, wages, and prices. In general, big business retained a strong voice in these corporations, although Mussolini continued to portray himself as "a man of the people."

During the 1920s and 1930s, Il Duce also surrounded himself with the militaristic pomp that became one of the hallmarks of future totalitarian leaders. Using a variety of "bread and circuses," Mussolini whipped up mass popular support for his regime. The Fascists extolled the glories of ancient Rome. They promised that the Mediterranean would again become an Italian lake and that past victories would be repeated as Italy became an empire once again. Their dreams of reviving the Roman Empire led directly to an expansionist foreign policy in the Adriatic and in North and East Africa.

Nazism in Germany

Next to Russia during the Stalin era, the most vicious and thoroughgoing totalitarian state was Nazi Germany under Adolf Hitler (1889–1945). As a young man, the Austrian-born Hitler tried desperately to become an artist, but he lacked the necessary ability to draw, and the Vienna Academy of Fine Arts rejected his application for admission. Unable to hold a job, he lived like a tramp, eking out a miserable existence from casual manual work and selling postcards. In 1913 he moved to Germany, and when World War I broke out, he joined a Bavarian regiment. Twice wounded in action and decorated, he returned from the front an ardent nationalist. His skill as an orator gradually won him leadership of the National Socialist German Workers' party, familiarly known as the Nazi party, a racist militarist group that opposed the Weimar government. In 1923 Hitler was imprisoned for leading a failed coup, the so-called Beer Hall Putsch, that sought to overthrow the Bavarian government. During his short stay in jail, Hitler wrote the first volume of *Mein Kampf (My Struggle)*, an autobiography that contained his plan to regenerate Germany through the overthrow of parliamentary rule and the persecution of Jews.

In his quest for political mastery of Germany, Hitler used the violent tactics already pioneered by Mussolini in Italy. He terrorized his enemies by using a uniformed

Adolf Hitler and Benito Mussolini. The totalitarian rulers of Germany and Italy both enjoyed reviewing the troops. Militarism was a central feature of most of the authoritarian regimes of the interwar period.

Brown Brothers

paramilitary force of brownshirts. He expertly mobilized public support through mass rallies, radio, and motion pictures. His passionate nationalism and his violent anticommunism made him a favorite with big business, the lower middle classes, and students.

The Nazis made little headway in the 1920s, but the economic crisis that began in 1930 destroyed public confidence in democratic institutions. As unemployment and poverty became widespread, the bewildered Germans began to clutch at ideological straws. In the elections of 1930, the number of Nazi deputies in the Reichstag, the popularly elected house of parliament, rose from 12 to 107. As the Great Depression paralyzed Germany's coalition governments in the early 1930s, the Nazis' strength continued to increase until they became the largest party in the Reichstag. Hoping to exploit Hitler's voter appeal for their own ends, a conservative faction persuaded the aged President Paul von Hindenburg to appoint Hitler chancellor (prime minister) in 1933. These conservatives were neither the first nor the last to be mistaken about Hitler's real intentions.

Nazi State and Society

Within a year Hitler had achieved his purpose of welding Germany into a centralized national state under the control of his party. Since the Nazis were a minority in the cabinet, Hitler requested new elections so that his party could win a parliamentary majority. Before the elections, unknown arsonists set fire to the Reichstag building. The Nazis blamed the fire on the Communists and, on the pretext that stern measures were needed to safeguard the security of the country, persuaded the president to invoke emergency provisions and suspend civil liberties. This enabled the Nazis to legally institute a reign of terror against the opposition, particularly the Communists and socialists. But even intimidation did not produce a clear majority for the Nazis, although they did obtain 44 percent of the popular vote. Nevertheless, the Nazis were able to retain a majority with the support of the Nationalist party, which had garnered 8 percent of the vote. As a next step, Hitler persuaded or coerced two-thirds of the Reichstag to pass the Enabling Act, giving him the power to rule by decree for four years. Within seven weeks Hitler had risen from chancellor to virtual dictator.

Hitler wasted no time in achieving total power. He abrogated the authority of the federal states so that for the first time Germany became a centralized, unitary state. He took control of the press and radio, forbade public meetings, dissolved rival parties, and sought to subordinate religion to the state. Hitler even purged the Nazi party of his rivals and those he did not trust. Particular targets of this "blood purge" were leaders of Hitler's own brownshirts. He appears to have sacrificed them to win the support of Germany's army officers, who feared the growing influence of the Nazi paramilitary force.

After von Hindenburg's death in 1934, Hitler assumed the powers of both president and chancellor under the title *Der Führer* (The Leader). As supreme commander of the armed forces, he required all officers and men to take personal oaths of allegiance to Der Führer. Hitler's deference toward the military kept the army loyal to his regime while he was consolidating his authority.

No action the Nazis undertook would have mattered if they had not been successful in lifting Germany out of the depression. They did so by skillful economic planning, using a mixture of state ownership and free enterprise, and by strong-arm methods. Specifically, the government granted tax relief to industries; it invested in massive public works programs, including the construction of superhighways (*autobahns*), housing projects, and armament production. All this was bankrolled through forced loans from banks and businesses and intricate financial juggling and controls. Because the Nazis lacked an adequate gold supply, they forged agreements with other nations under which Germany's manufactured goods were bartered for raw materials and foodstuffs.

As a result of the government's economic policies, unemployment, which stood at 6 million in 1932, was eradicated less than six years later. Wages were low, however, and the standard of living for average workers rose only slightly. This was because workers were denied collective bargaining powers to win concessions from big business. In 1934 labor unions were abolished and replaced by a National Labor Front controlled by the state. Strikes were forbidden, and disputes with management were referred to a system of enforced arbitration modeled after the one set up by Mussolini in Italy.

Nazi ideology, like that of Fascist Italy, was expansionist and militaristic. It also aimed at reestablishing an old empire or Reich. For Hitler his Third Reich would exceed Germany's previous two and last 1,000 years—the First Reich had lasted 900 years and the Second less than 50. Building up the country's strength was therefore of paramount importance.

Germany's declining birthrate greatly alarmed the Nazi leaders. Their plans called for a population large enough to supply plenty of soldiers in the future and settlers to occupy the new lands they hoped to conquer. Accordingly, they encouraged large families. This mandated that women stay at home rather than go to work. The regime inveighed against women who sought independence and pursued employment in public life traditionally reserved for men. It cultivated the traditional image of women as homemakers, wives, and bearers of children. As an incentive to reproduction, the state provided marriage loans, child subsidies, and generous family allowances. Moreover, it awarded three types of honor crosses to mothers who proved most fertile—gold

A Nazi Rally. The Nazis were masters of propaganda. At gigantic rallies like this one, complete with swastikas, flags, and uniformed party members, Hitler mesmerized vast crowds with his frenzied speeches.

for more than eight children, silver for more than six, and bronze for more than five.

In contrast to Mussolini, whose early Fascist program was not racist, Nazi ideology propounded the myth of the inherent superiority of the Aryan or Nordic race, of which Germans were supposedly the prime example. According to Hitler, Aryan stock over the years had degenerated through intermarriage with other races. Hence the basic aim of Nazi racial policy was to "purify" the German race by weeding out inferior peoples; in particular, Jews, whom Hitler had labeled the cause of all of the nation's ills.

Hitler's SS (*Schutzstaffel*) troops and his secret police, the Gestapo, spread a reign of terror among so-called undesirable elements of the population. They arrested, imprisoned, tortured, and ultimately executed hundreds of thousands of citizens. German Jews were singled out from the beginning. Initially, they were deprived of jobs, stripped of their civil rights, and forced to mark their persons and buildings with a Star of David. Later, they were attacked by mobs, murdered, sometimes compelled to emigrate, and finally imprisoned in slave labor or concentration camps. Dissidents, including religious leaders and leftists who opposed the Nazis, were also imprisoned. After World War II began, the Nazi regime executed these political opponents, along with millions of European Jews, Gypsies, and Slavs—all considered inferior peoples by the Nazis. As the Nazi state began to expand aggressively throughout Europe, these racist policies were implemented in the territories that fell under its control.

All cultural activity was subordinated to the state and its purpose. The Nazis insisted that the new Germany be free of "decadent" cultural influences from the Western democracies. They wanted the masses exposed to ideas and images that glorified the Führer and the party, invited worship of the Fatherland, and called for the destruction of the enemies of the Third Reich. Artists with any sense of creativity and objectivity were blacklisted and left with no choice but to change professions or emigrate. To indoctrinate the nation in their ideology, the Nazis held public spectacles. Hitler copied Mussolini's carefully staged mass rallies and mesmerized the crowds with nighttime "shows," in which he worked his audience into frenzies with promises of future glories. Like all totalitarian regimes, the Nazis sought to control and mold the thoughts of the rising generation. They controlled the school curriculum, falsified textbooks, persecuted teachers who protested, and compelled all youth to join Nazi juvenile organizations such as the Hitler Youth.

The majority of Germans gladly accepted Hitler's authoritarian regime. The new order had ended political instability, solved the unemployment problem, and, to all appearances, was pushing Germany along the path to world power status. When witnessing Nazi horrors, they looked the other way and pretended not to notice what was happening.

Authoritarian Regimes in the Iberian Peninsula

Authoritarian regimes also came to power in the Iberian Peninsula. In Portugal an economics professor, Antonio de Oliveira Salazar (1889–1970), was appointed in the

Giraudon/Art Resource; © ARS, New York/SPADEM, Paris

Picasso's *Guernica*. One of Pablo Picasso's most famous paintings, *Guernica* commemorates the terror and suffering of a devastated town. An ardent supporter of the republican cause, Picasso refused to return to his Spanish homeland as long as Franco ruled.

early 1930s as prime minister by a military junta seeking political and economic stability. Salazar made himself dictator of Portugal and ruled until his death in 1970. In Portugal and Spain, the landowners, high officials in the Catholic church, and army officers tended to support the authoritarian regimes as solutions to social disorder and possible revolution. Peasants, urban workers, and students who tended to support leftist or more progressive forces were kept under careful watch.

In Spain General Miguel Primo de Rivera (1870–1930) ruled during the 1920s. In 1931, after a decade of military rule, liberal leaders won the elections; supported by urban workers, some peasants, and socialists, the newly elected "republican" government enacted a series of social, political, and economic reforms and abolished the monarchy. In 1936 the disaffected old power elites launched a revolt against the new republican government. A career army officer, Francisco Franco (1892–1975), gradually emerged as the leader of these conservatives, or "Nationalists," as they called themselves. The Spanish Civil War between the legitimate republican government and the Nationalists continued from 1936 to 1939.

Liberal and totalitarian regimes in much of Europe took sides in the Spanish Civil War. Many viewed it as the first battle of World War II in Europe. For many Western liberals, Spain seemed the last chance to stop the aggressions of authoritarian and totalitarian regimes. Although democratic governments in Europe and America declared themselves neutral in the Spanish Civil War, liberals, socialists, and others from many Western nations formed brigades of volunteers to fight on the side of the republican government. The Soviet Union sent military advisers and aided the republican government, which included a number of socialist politicians. Much more help poured in for Franco from Mussolini, who sent tens of thousands of troops, and Hitler, who dispatched air support. Hitler saw the war as a testing ground for his newly reequipped military. The German Condor Legion "terror bombed" Guernica and other towns, intentionally causing heavy casualties to destroy civilian morale. Such terror bombing of civilians had been used by the Japanese against the Chinese since 1937 and became common practice during World War II. Franco won the war in 1939, thanks to the substantial aid he received from Germany and Italy. He proceeded to organize Spain along the lines of Mussolini's Italy.

Personalist Dictatorships in Latin America

Dictatorships predominated in Latin America, particularly in the 1930s. By 1930 most Latin American countries had been republics in form for more than a century, considerably longer than most eastern or southern European nations. But democratic forms had often cloaked autocratic regimes. As on the Iberian Peninsula, authoritarian power in Latin America had traditionally been based on the landlords, church, and armed forces, which dominated the backward and poverty-stricken peasant and Amerindian populations. Since the late nineteenth century, however, urban exporters and their foreign customers, often British or American, demanded stable regimes in the interests of commercial development.

CONNECTIONS IN MIGRATION

Murder and Nationhood

The Holocaust of World War II was the most extreme of human massacres. It is, in that sense, a unique case in world history. In response to the inhumanity of what Adolf Hitler called the "final solution," we have learned to express atonement for a collective guilt, remember those lost in the Holocaust, and recognize the heroism of those who sought to rescue its victims.

In another sense, these massacres were not only acts of evil but also an extreme form of nationalism. The idea of the nation, so powerful in the twentieth century, has contradictory tendencies: it emphasizes unity and inclusion of those in the nation, but it draws borders and excludes those outside the nation. As a result, nationalism has often isolated people defined as aliens and expelled them from their homes. At the extreme, nationalist fervor has resulted in mass executions.

The national and international conflicts of the twentieth century include a long list of massacres, such as the slaughter of Armenians in the Ottoman Empire in 1915 and massacres in Cambodia from 1975 to 1979, in Rwanda in 1994, and in various regions of the former Yugoslavia from 1992 to 1999. In all these cases, differences among people mushroomed to a murderous level.

Another set of massacres resulted from colonial conquest and rule. The German repression of the Herero in South-West Africa in 1905 killed most of the population. The 1937 Japanese assault on Nanking, China, led to the death of 300,000 Chinese and the rape of thousands of women. The French repression of a 1947 rebellion in Madagascar killed 80,000.

In each of these cases, the idea of national purity was an excuse for eliminating people who did not fit in with the dominant ethnicity, religion, or ideology.

1. Construct a world map showing major massacres, with dates, in the twentieth century. Where possible, identify the major issue associated with the massacres. You will find help in Unit 11 of the Migration CD-ROM, in Chapter 15 of the text, and on these websites: http://www.remember.org/, http://www.ushmm.org/, http://www.fordham.edu/halsall/mod/nanking.html, http://www.cnd.org/njmassacre/index.html, http://www.cilicia.com/armo10.html, http://www.yale.edu/cgp/, and http://www.usip.org/oc/sr/rwanda1.html.

2. Enter the search term "genocide" in the InfoTrac Subject Guide. Choose "Periodical references" and read at least five articles. What important facts and ideas stand out to you? What can be done to prevent or stop large-scale massacres?

Whether to preserve the traditional order or to encourage commercial growth, military rulers frequently installed the autocratic government required.

In the 1930s and subsequent decades, "personalist" dictatorships, often patterned along the lines of the Fascist regimes in Italy and Spain, flourished, especially in the larger and more developed Latin American nations. By combining welfare programs for the working class with law and order and protective tariffs for business interests, these rulers were sometimes popular with urban workers as well as with business leaders. Examples of such regimes include the Vargas dictatorship in Brazil and the Concordancia government in Argentina.

Getúlio Vargas (1883–1954) seized power in 1930 and dominated Brazilian politics for the next twenty-five years. Vargas made opposition parties illegal, often ruled by decree, and sometimes mobilized the army to impose his will. At the same time, he strengthened Brazilian industry and provided guaranteed employment, wages, and pensions for the urban working classes.

Argentina's Concordancia was an alliance of military men, nationalists, and conservatives who seized control in 1930 and governed through the decade. They ruled by fixing elections and ruthlessly crushing opposition. They also, however, helped Argentine industry to move out of small workshops and into sizable factories, a substantial economic advance. In 1943 a group of military officers, including the future dictator Juan Perón (1895–1974), seized power. Perón, who had observed the Nazi rule in Germany and the Fascist regime in Italy, was elected president in 1946 and 1951. Extremely popular among Argentina's working classes, Perón and his wife, Evita, developed a cult of personality, linking their fate to that of the entire nation. Perón instituted a series of social welfare programs but also accrued a massive public debt. Evita ran her own foundation to provide food and jobs for the urban poor, who repaid her with boundless loyalty. After Evita's death in 1952, there was even a campaign to have her declared a saint. Perón continued to rule until he was ousted in 1955. Perónism enjoyed a brief surge of popularity in the 1970s, but it was quashed by a brutal military dictatorship later in the decade.

Thus, during the interwar years, a wide variety of totalitarian and other authoritarian regimes came to power around the world. The chief totalitarian states were Fascist Italy, Nazi Germany, the Soviet Union under Stalin, and Japan. Less rigorous and bloody were the authoritarian governments of eastern and southern Europe and Latin America.

Aggression in Asia and Europe

I described [Britain's] foreign policy as being based upon three principles—first upon the protection of British interests . . . ; secondly on the maintenance of peace, and, as far as we can influence it, the settlement of differences by peaceful means and not by force; and thirdly the promotion of friendly relations with other nations. . . .

If we truly desire peace it is necessary to make a sustained effort to ascertain, and if possible to remove the causes which threaten peace. . . . We are now engaged upon a gigantic scheme of rearmament . . . , indeed, we were the last of the nations to rearm . . . [but] I cannot believe that, with a little good will and determination, it is not possible to remove genuine grievances and to clear away suspicions which may be entirely unfounded.

*For these reasons, then, my colleagues and I have been anxious to find some opportunity of entering upon conversations with the two European countries with which we have been at variance, namely Germany and Italy, in order that we might find out whether there was any common ground upon which we might build up a general scheme of appeasement in Europe.**

*You know already that I have done all that one man can do to compose this quarrel [between Germany and Czechoslovakia]. After my visit to Germany I have realized vividly how Herr Hitler feels that he must champion other Germans, and his indignation that grievances have not been met before this. He told me privately, and last night he repeated publicly, that after this Sudeten German question is settled, that is the end of Germany's territorial claims in Europe.***

*Prime Minister Neville Chamberlain, *Hansard's Parliamentary Debates*, Commons, 5th ser. (1938), pp. 53, 54, 64, 332, reprinted in George L. Mosse et al., eds., *Europe in Review: Readings and Sources since 1500*, rev. ed. (Chicago: Rand McNally, 1964), pp. 514–516.

***The Times* (London), September 28, 1938, p. 12, reprinted in Mosse et al., eds. *Europe in Review*, pp. 514–516.

The international order built up by the Paris peace treaties broke down in the 1930s as Japan, Germany, and Italy resorted to force to achieve their national goals and settle real or imagined grievances. These statements by the British prime minister, Neville Chamberlain, sum up the reasons Western democracies appeased the aggressor nations. First, although he did not say so explicitly, no major power was willing to assist victims of aggression if that action could lead to war. Second, the Western democracies were militarily weak because they had largely demobilized their armed forces after World War I and were only belatedly rearming in the late 1930s. Third, some leaders, including many in Great Britain, believed that Germany had legitimate grievances, and they assumed that Hitler was a reasonable leader who would keep his promises. In addition, most Western nations feared international communism, and some regarded Hitler and Mussolini as better alternatives, and as bulwarks against Soviet expansion. As we shall see, appeasement encouraged aggressive actions by Japan in Asia, Italy in Europe and Africa, and Germany in Europe that culminated in World War II.

Although no nation fully realized its goals through the Paris peace treaties, Great Britain, the United States, and France were largely satisfied. This was not the case for their allies, Japan and Italy. Italy's ambitions in the Balkans were unrealized, while Japan wanted to further bolster its position in China and the Pacific. Among the defeated nations, Germany was especially bitter at the harsh terms in the Treaty of Versailles. It strongly resented the "war guilt" clause, the heavy reparations imposed, the loss of colonies and territory, and the severe limitations placed on its military establishment. The Soviet Union, a pariah nation now shunned because of its withdrawal from the conflict and its postwar talk of exporting Communist revolution, feared the hostility of the capitalist nations and sought to recover territories lost during World War I.

During the 1920s Great Britain, France, Italy, and Japan dominated the League of Nations, which tried to promote international cooperation and achieve international peace. As previously indicated, some positive steps toward peace were taken: the League mediated peace settlements between minor warring nations; naval powers met in Washington in 1921–1922 and signed a naval limitation treaty; the Locarno Pact of 1925 resolved international disputes, particularly between France and Germany; finally, sixty powers signed the Kellogg-Briand Pact of 1928, committing themselves to renounce war altogether. No general arms limitation agreement was reached, however, and France and the small new nations of Europe, fearful of Germany, built up large armies.

In the 1930s Japan, Italy, and Germany began to use armed force to redress their perceived wrongs and satisfy their territorial ambitions. Great Britain, the United States, and France tried to maintain peace at all costs. They found this could be done only by making repeated concessions to the aggressor states. The result was a pattern of aggression by totalitarian nations and appeasement by the democracies.

Japanese Aggression Against China

Since the late nineteenth century, Japan had sought to expel Western imperialist nations from Asia and to replace them. It had already annexed Taiwan and Korea and established a sphere of influence in China. Japan had joined World War I as Great Britain's ally in order to seize German-held islands in the North Pacific and the German sphere of influence in China; these conquests had been confirmed by the Allies in the Treaty of Versailles. Japan had also forced weak China to make repeated concessions to Japanese commercial and political demands.

In 1928 the Nationalist party, led by Chiang Kai-shek, succeeded in unifying China for the first time since the fall of the Manchu dynasty. As Chiang began to organize China's first modern government, Japan feared the emergence of a strong China that could effectively resist Japanese imperialism. When many nations tried to combat the world depression of 1928 by imposing high tariffs on foreign imports, Japan became even more fearful for its economic well-being in a potentially hostile world. Leaders of the army and navy began to plan the conquest of Asia to secure essential raw materials and markets for Japan's manufactured products.

Japan especially coveted sparsely populated Manchuria's abundant agricultural and mineral resources. As General Tanaka Giichi, prime minister of Japan, purportedly said, "To conquer the world it is necessary to conquer China first, and to conquer China it is necessary to conquer Manchuria and Mongolia first." As long as they could control the local ruler in Manchuria, the Japanese were willing to allow China to maintain a facade of sovereignty over its northeastern provinces. The Nationalist government in China, however, had targeted Manchuria for economic development and was eager to recover rights already lost to Japan. Therefore the Japanese military decided they needed to strike before the Chinese developed a strong defense.

On September 18, 1931, middle-rank officers in the Japanese army stationed in Manchuria staged a bomb explosion on a Japanese-controlled railway outside Mukden, the chief administrative city of the Manchurian provinces. After blaming the Chinese for the Manchurian or Mukden Incident, as it was called, the entire Japanese army in Manchuria, reinforced by Japanese units stationed in Korea, swung into action over a wide front. When the Japanese prime minister and the civilian cabinet tried to control the army during the next months, the minister of war undermined them by declaring that the military was not subordinate to the political authorities. Public support for the army's insubordination led to the fall of the cabinet.

Japanese Advance in Manchuria. The Japanese invasion of Manchuria was well prepared and well coordinated. Ignoring Japanese government orders and League of Nations resolutions, field commanders in Manchuria completed their conquest in 1932. Here a Japanese military unit is on the move.

AP/Wide World Photos

Because the Chinese army would be no match for the Japanese, China appealed to the League of Nations and nations such as the United States that had signed the Kellogg-Briand Pact to resolve the Manchurian Incident. Ignoring the pleas of the League and the U.S. government to cease military activities, the Japanese army completed its conquest of Manchuria in early 1932. Japan then established a puppet regime, called Manchukuo, in the conquered region. The League dispatched a commission headed by the British diplomat Lord Lytton to investigate. Its findings, known as the Lytton Report, condemned Japanese aggression in Manchuria, branded Manchukuo a puppet state, and called on Japan to restore Manchuria to China. When the League Assembly unanimously endorsed the Lytton Report, Japan resigned from the League of Nations. The U.S. government refused to recognize Manchukuo or the territorial changes that resulted from the aggression. Save for these moral sanctions, nothing was done to restrain Japan.

Japan followed up with other acts of aggression against China. In 1932 the Japanese navy opened a second front by attacking Shanghai, China's major port. Japanese warships shelled the city at point-blank range and killed many civilians, but Chinese defenses prevailed and Shanghai did not fall. After this debacle, the Japanese aggressors were uniformly successful. In 1933 they conquered Jehol, a province adjacent to Manchuria, and added it to Manchukuo. Beginning in 1934, Japan launched a simultaneous military and propaganda campaign aimed at creating a second puppet state to comprise all of North China and be called "North-Chinaland."

Realizing that China was not militarily ready to face the Japanese, Chiang Kai-shek sought to gain time by appeasing Japan with piecemeal concessions. Meanwhile, with the help of German advisers, he hurriedly built up his army and air force. He also constructed railroads, roads, and factories in preparation for war. All along, Chiang insisted that China must achieve "unification before resistance." This required that he defeat the Chinese Communist rebels first. Though militarily sound, this strategy was unpopular with many Chinese, who demanded an immediate response to Japanese expansion. In 1935 university students called for the organization of a National Salvation movement to fight Japan. The concept won widespread popular support and eventually forced Chiang to stop his drive against the Chinese Communist forces and to begin talks for the formation of a united front. The hard-pressed Chinese Communists were happy to begin negotiations. The Soviet Union, busily preparing for war against Nazi Germany, also pressed the Chinese Communists to accede to the Nationalist terms. The Soviets recognized that a united China could better resist Japan and thereby ease Japanese pressure on Soviet Siberia.

The prospect of a united China worried Japanese militarists and extremists, who now had great influence in their government. A strong China would foil their dream of controlling Asia. Assassinations of key leaders by junior army officers in the February Rebellion of 1936 had cowed the remaining civilian politicians and allowed the military to dominate the Japanese government. Once in power they sought the international isolation of the Soviet Union and closer collaboration with Germany. To this end they signed the Anti-Comintern Pact with Germany in 1936. When Italy joined a year later, the Axis alliance was complete. While preparing for a possible armed conflict with the United States and Great Britain, General Tojo Hideki (1884–1948), then chief of staff of the Japanese army in China (later prime minister), provoked war with China.

Fascist Italy's Aggressions

Since coming to power in 1922, Mussolini's Fascist government had preached strident nationalism. It bombarded Italians with stirring reminders of the greatness of the ancient Roman Empire and prominently displayed archaeological projects undertaken at government expense. To demonstrate Italy's greatness, in 1935 Mussolini launched an invasion of Ethiopia, one of two independent nations left in Africa and one that had repulsed Italian aggression in 1896. The Ethiopians resisted with all that they had, and Emperor Haile Selassie (reigned 1930–1974) made a moving appeal before the League of Nations on behalf of his country.

The League condemned Italy but took no effective steps to check its aggression. Only an embargo of petroleum to Italy would have stopped Mussolini's war machine, but the economically depressed democracies such as Great Britain and France were unwilling to take that step, and the United States, not being a League member, was not bound by its resolutions. British, French, and U.S. oil companies continued to supply petroleum to Italy. As Japan had shown, a determined power could defy the League and not suffer punishment, and, like Japan, Italy resigned from the League. As the Japanese military had done in Manchuria and Shanghai, Italian planes bombed Ethiopian civilian centers.

In 1936, after a brief, one-sided struggle, Ethiopia was incorporated into the Italian Empire, and Italy's King Victor Emmanuel III was declared emperor of Ethiopia. Two years later, in 1938, Mussolini's forces attacked and conquered tiny Albania, a small Balkan nation Italy had coveted but failed to gain at the Paris Peace Conference.

Nazi Aggression in Europe

Meanwhile Adolf Hitler was implementing his own aggressive foreign policies in central Europe. After coming to power in 1933, Hitler moved quickly to restore Germany's self-confidence and military and economic strength. In defiance of the Treaty of Versailles, Hitler promptly began to rebuild Germany's armed forces. He vigorously demanded that central European territories with large German-speaking populations be incorporated into the Third Reich. He was no less insistent on obtaining living space (*Lebensraum*) for Germans, particularly in Slavic areas of eastern Europe, where German peoples had been settling since the Middle Ages.

Having rearmed Germany and strengthened its industries, Hitler successfully implemented his grand designs between 1936 and 1939. His first move was to send the revived German army into the Rhineland in 1936. Although part of Germany, this important industrial region had been demilitarized under the terms of the Treaty of Versailles and served as a buffer zone between Germany and France. A demilitarized Rhineland gave France a measure of security, but was a galling symbol of Germany's defeat in World War I. German commanders worried that the French would send troops to stop the Germans and enforce the treaty, but Hitler guessed rightly that they would not. Thus Germany remilitarized the Rhineland. Hitler had won his biggest gamble thus far, and his prestige soared. The weakened German high command, which had advised against risking French retaliation by militarizing the Rhineland, was subsequently reluctant to challenge Hitler's judgment.

Great Britain and France had the military power to stop Hitler at this stage, but they did not for a variety of reasons. First, the general populace in both countries genuinely abhorred war. The generation that had suffered from the horrors of World War I was now in power. Governments were also reluctant to increase military spending in the face of many unsolved social and economic problems caused by the depression. Many, especially in Great Britain, felt that Germany had been dealt with too harshly after World War I and thought that the German demands for treaty revision were justified; a few in western Europe and the United States liked Hitler and his policies. Hitler moreover had convinced many that he was a reasonable man with limited goals. Most western Europeans also feared the Soviet Union and viewed a strong Germany under Hitler as a bulwark against potential Soviet aggression and against the feared spread of communism in general.

Although the isolationist-minded United States viewed the advances of the aggressive totalitarian states with misgivings, it adopted no effective policy to counter them. As we have seen, the United States protested the Japanese aggression against China and refused to recognize their conquests. Understandably, the Japanese were unimpressed and undeterred. Most Americans viewed

The Munich Conference. At Munich, Germany, September 29–30, 1938, Neville Chamberlain (here seated to Hitler's right) and other Western leaders tried to avoid war by agreeing to Adolf Hitler's demand to absorb the Sudetenland. Hitler went on to seize the rest of Czechoslovakia, and in less than a year Europe was at war. Ever since, the name "Munich" has symbolized pointless appeasement of an aggressor.

Ullstein Bilderdienst

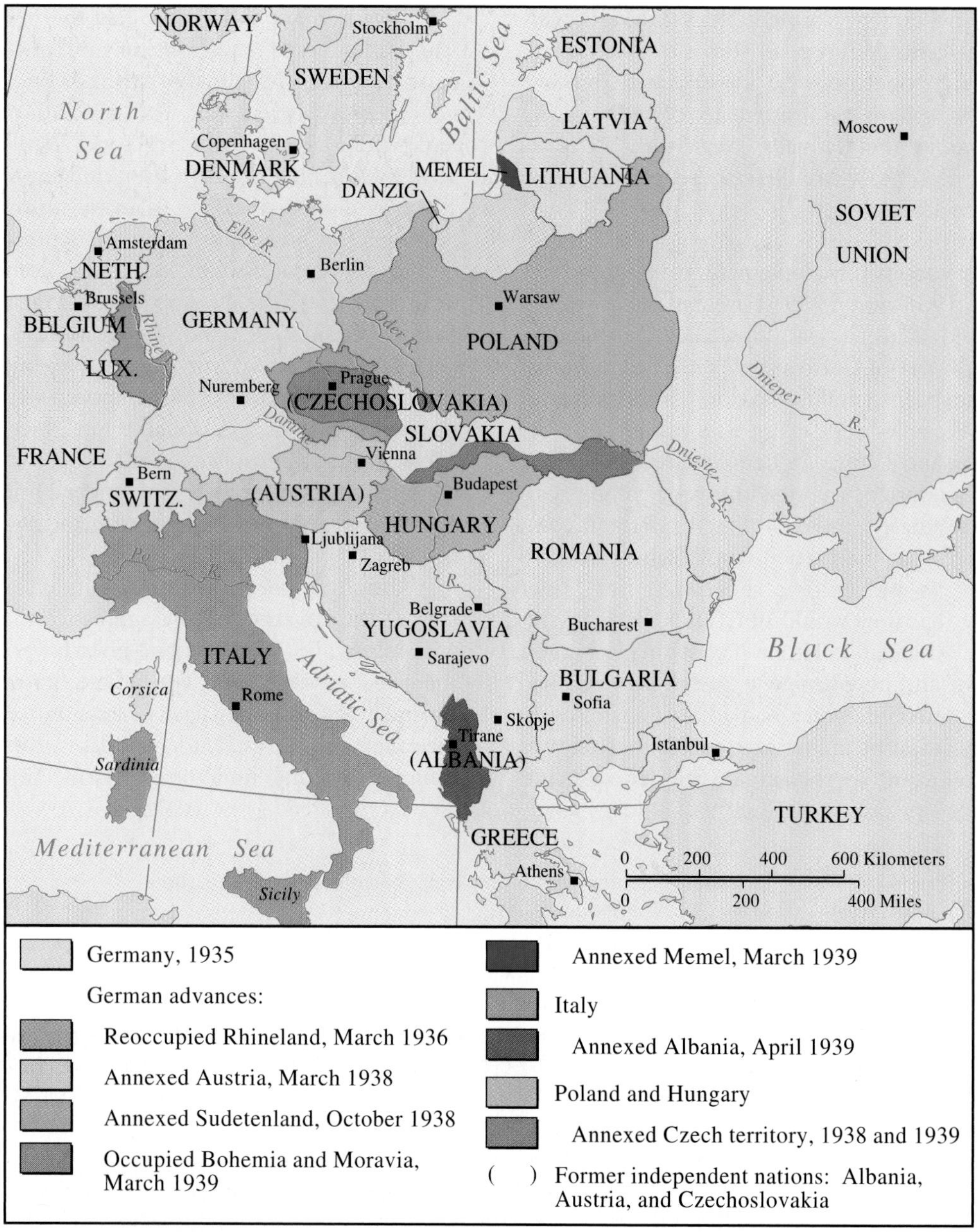

Map 15.1 Central Europe, April 1939. This map shows German gains after three years of aggression and consolidation under Adolf Hitler. Italy, Poland, and Hungary also expanded. Although to this point Hitler had enlarged Germany without war, Great Britain and France were now awake to the futility of appeasement, and Hitler's next aggressive move, against Poland, ignited World War II in Europe.

their participation in World War I as a mistake and did not wish to get embroiled in European problems again. Because they felt that Germany had received harsh treatment at Versailles, most were inclined to be conciliatory to Hitler. They, too, regarded Hitler's Germany as a buffer against international communism. Most Americans devoted their energies to economic recovery from the Great Depression and gave little thought to fascist aggressors. Thus President Franklin Roosevelt's criticism of Hitler's remilitarization of the Rhineland was muted.

Early in 1938 Hitler again violated the Versailles settlement by annexing the German-speaking nation of Austria into his new empire. This move was part of Hitler's ambitious plan to expand Germany by incorporating all adjacent German populations into his Third Reich. Austrian Nazis and many other Austrians supported the century-old notion of greater German unity, and the occupation of Austria was bloodless. The union with Austria, or the *Anschluss*, substantially increased the size and population of Germany.

Having achieved the *Anschluss* without opposition from the Western democracies, Hitler turned his attention to the German-speaking minority in the Sudeten mountain region of Czechoslovakia, which, like Austria, bordered on Germany. Hitler demanded the right to incorporate the Sudetenland into Germany, because 3 million ethnic Germans lived there.

France and the Soviet Union had signed treaties with Czechoslovakia that required them to aid the Czechs in the event of war. Although Great Britain had no treaty ties with Czechoslovakia, it was also concerned about peace in Europe. The democracies' acquiescence in Hitler's dismemberment of Czechoslovakia, a brutal act against a peaceful, sovereign nation, was a shameful episode of appeasement. Many Americans were shocked by what happened to Czechoslovakia, and Roosevelt appealed to Hitler to refrain from attacking other European nations in the future. Hitler ridiculed Roosevelt's appeal and characterized the United States as a degenerate nation that would not fight. Indeed, the U.S. Congress refused to repeal neutrality laws that made it impossible to help victims of bellicose nations; thus the United States remained a spectator as aggressors went unchecked in Europe and Asia.

British prime minister Neville Chamberlain (1869–1940), joined by the French premier Edouard Daladier (1884–1970) and Mussolini, met with Hitler at Munich in September 1938 to address the crisis. Although the Soviet Union had earlier declared its willingness to come to the aid of Czechoslovakia, Great Britain and France decided to appease Hitler. They agreed to allow Hitler to annex the Sudetenland in return for his guarantee that the rest of Czechoslovakia would remain free. Abandoned by its allies, Czechoslovakia decided not to resist the Nazi takeover of the Sudetenland. As a result, it lost about a third of its population, much of its heavy industry, and important defensive fortifications. Chamberlain declared on his return to London that he had achieved "peace for our time." This peace proved illusory, however, for by March 1939 Hitler and the authoritarian leaders of Hungary and Poland had divided the remaining portion of Czechoslovakia.

Hitler then turned his attention to Lithuania and Poland. He took Memel, a Baltic port with a large German population, from Lithuania and demanded Danzig (which also had a German-speaking population) and other concessions from Poland. British and French leaders, at last convinced that Hitler's word was worthless, announced that they would fight to defend the territorial integrity of Poland, but Hitler, with good reason, doubted their resolve.

Hitler also formed alliances with like-minded aggressive states. Agreements in 1936 and 1937 had created the Berlin-Rome-Tokyo Axis, avowedly an anticommunist alliance, but one that was also intended to coordinate the aggressive activities of the three partner states.

Hitler's most startling diplomatic coup was the Hitler-Stalin Pact of August 1939, in which the two archenemies agreed not to attack each other and to remain neutral should either be attacked by a third party. This agreement protected Hitler from a two-front war in case the British and French should finally take up arms against Germany. It gave Stalin the time he needed to build up Soviet military and industrial strength for what he knew would be an eventual reckoning with Hitler, and it also ensured that he, too, would not have to fight a two-front war with both Germany and Japan. A secret protocol divided Poland between the Soviet Union and Germany and recognized Estonia, Latvia, and Lithuania, three independent states on the Baltic coast, as being within the Soviet sphere of influence. On September 1, 1939, one week after signing the pact, Germany invaded Poland, marking the beginning of World War II in Europe.

World War II and Postwar Settlements

Following recent developments at Lukouchiao, the Japanese have by low and treacherous methods seized our cities . . . and have killed many of our fellow-countrymen. There is no end to the humiliation and insults that they have heaped upon us. . . . Since the Mukden [Manchurian] incident on September 18, 1931, the more indignities we have borne, the more we have yielded, the more violent has Japanese aggression become. . . . Now we have reached the point when we can endure no longer; we will give away no more. The whole nation must rise as one man and fight these Japanese bandits until we have destroyed them and our own life is secure. . . .

*Soldiers! The supreme moment has come. With one heart and purpose advance! Refuse to retreat. Drive out the unspeakably evil invaders and bring about the rebirth of our nation.**

*Chiang Kai-shek, *Resistance and Reconstruction: Messages during China's Six Years of War, 1937–1943* (New York: Harper & Row, 1943), pp. 16, 19.

In 1937 the Japanese army, which had occupied Manchuria six years earlier, struck China again, overrunning its eastern provinces. The head of the Kuomintang (the party that governed China), Chiang Kai-shek, retreated to the interior, where he set up his government. In this excerpt from a speech delivered in 1937, Chiang, appealing to the nationalism of his men, announces that the time has come to take up the challenge to drive the enemy out of China.

Just as Japan meant to dominate East Asia, Hitler's goal was to raise Germany to a preeminent position in

Europe. The Western democracies, distracted and on the defensive, took no positive action for fear of causing a major war. But concessions only whetted Hitler's appetite, and it was soon apparent that he was not content with uniting the Germans under his rule. His occupation of Czechoslovakia demonstrated that his appeal for self-determination was in fact a hollow disguise for a brutal policy of expansion. By overreaching himself, Hitler converted the European democracies from appeasement to resistance.

Japan Launches All-Out War Against China

War began in Asia on July 7, 1937, when Japanese forces attacked a railway junction near Peking. The action came to be known as the Marco Polo Bridge Incident. The Japanese at first hoped to use the incident to extort political and territorial concessions from China, but an aroused Chinese nation insisted that the government refuse further Japanese demands. Thereupon Japan, without declaring formal war, launched an all-out attack, hoping to score a quick victory. In spite of recent modernizing efforts, the Chinese forces were no match for the Japanese army and navy and could only delay enemy advances. Japanese planes bombed civilian targets indiscriminately, just as the Italians had in Ethiopia and the Germans in Spain. The fall of the Chinese capital, Nanking, was followed by frightful atrocities, including the massacre of an estimated 300,000 civilians. By the end of 1938, the entire Chinese coast was under Japanese occupation.

United by the common enemy, the Kuomintang and the Communists stopped their civil war and rallied around Chiang Kai-shek. The government moved up the Yangtze River to mountain-rimmed Chungking, in southwestern China, beyond the reach of Japan's mechanized divisions but not Japanese bombs. Millions of civilians trekked to the interior, taking with them dismantled factories, schools, libraries, and equipment. They destroyed much of what they could not take, leaving a scorched earth for the Japanese occupiers. The retreating Chinese paid a high cost in lives, but such tactics as opening the dikes of the Yellow River slowed down the Japanese advance.

The war continued because the Chinese refused to surrender, and Japan would not abandon its efforts to subdue China completely. The bulk of the Japanese army was pinned down in China and would remain there throughout the war. Even with 2 million troops in China, the Japanese could effectively control only cities and major communication lines. Japanese brutality aroused nationalistic fervor among the hitherto politically apathetic peasants, many of whom became guerrilla fighters. The Japanese were equally unsuccessful in luring important Chinese leaders to collaborate with them. They gave no real power to those who did, merely placing them at the head of puppet governments in occupied areas.

China fought alone until Japan's attack on Pearl Harbor in December 1941. Western powers were sympathetic, but Great Britain and France were preoccupied with the Nazi threat in Europe. The United States fol-

Chinese Resist with Scorched-Earth Policy. One way the Chinese slowed the Japanese advance during World War II was by destroying everything that might help the invaders. Here peasants rip up a road to impede Japanese military transport.

AP/Wide World Photos

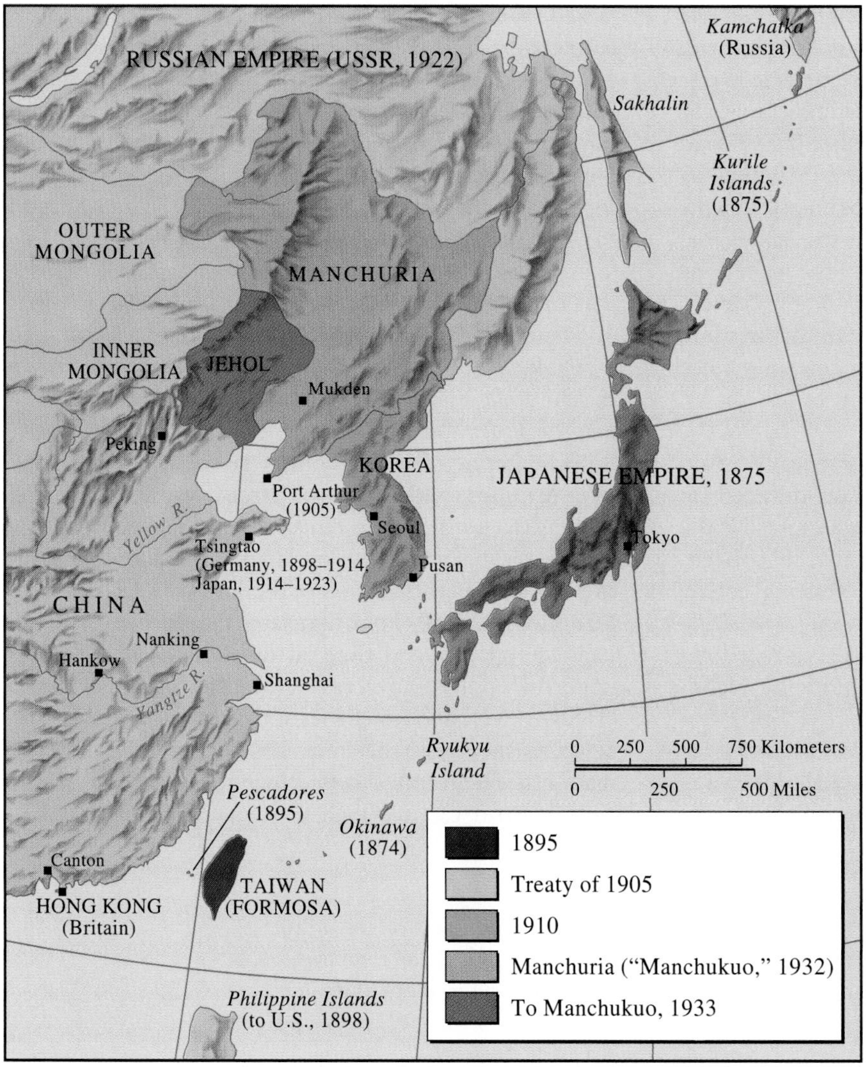

Map 15.2 Japanese Aggression in Asia. Up to 1937 the Japanese were able to conquer large sections of China with little resistance. In that year, however, the Chinese refused to make further concessions, and full-scale war erupted.

lowed an isolationist policy, but in fact, its trade law benefited Japan by allowing it to buy steel and fuel that aided its operations in China. Only the Soviet Union, which feared Japanese designs on its Asian territories, gave substantial aid in the first years in the form of loans, airplanes, and pilots who helped to organize China's air defense.

The outbreak of war in Europe in 1939 initially made China's position even bleaker: the Soviet Union withdrew its assistance to concentrate on the home front, and Great Britain and France, fully occupied in Europe, bent over backward not to offend Japan. The real turning point was Japan's attack on Pearl Harbor and the U.S. controlled Philippines and on British possessions in Southeast Asia. The British and U.S. declaration of war against Japan and similar Chinese actions against Japan and its partners incorporated the war in Asia into the worldwide conflict against Axis aggression. China became part of the China-Burma-India war theater, and Chiang Kai-shek became supreme Allied commander of the China theater.

Axis Advances in Europe

As described previously, Germany, along with the other two aggressor nations, had formed the Berlin-Rome-Tokyo Axis in 1937, ostensibly to contain the expansion of communism. Hitler's next alliance stunned the democratic powers. Untroubled by ideological scruples, in August 1939 Hitler and the Soviet Union signed a nonaggression pact that also included provisions for the division of eastern Europe. Secure that he would not be attacked by the Soviet Union, Hitler ordered his troops to invade Poland on September 1, 1939. To Hitler's surprise, Great Britain and France promptly declared war on Germany.

In stark contrast to the static trench warfare of 1914–1918, the Germans in their first major action introduced new tactics called *blitzkrieg*, meaning "lightning war." The first phase was carried out through the air. The German Luftwaffe knocked out the small Polish air force, while German *stukas*, or dive bombers, demolished rearward communications and spread terror among the civilian population by massive bombardments. The second phase was initiated by heavy tanks, followed by lighter armored divisions. After tearing large gaps in the enemy lines, the fast-moving motorized columns streaked across the Polish plain, often several days ahead of the main body of infantry. The antiquated Polish army fought bravely, but it was torn to shreds. With the Soviet Union invading simultaneously from the east and Great Britain and France unable to help, Polish resistance collapsed in less than a month.

Throughout the autumn there was practically no activity on the western front, and as the war dragged on into the winter of 1939–1940, cynics began to call it the "phony war." During this period the British concentrated on building up their armaments, clearing enemy surface vessels from the ocean, and imposing a blockade on Germany. The French army, expecting another long defensive war, waited complacently behind the elaborately fortified Maginot line.

After the Allies had ignored Hitler's peace offer, he struck without warning in April 1940, seizing Norway and Denmark. Having secured his northern flank, he attacked France through Belgium and the Netherlands so as to outflank the Maginot line. Beginning their blitzkrieg against the West on May 10, German forces quickly breached the defenses of the Netherlands and Luxembourg. The Belgians held out longer, as they were supported by French troops and a small British force. Farther south, German armored columns invaded France through the Ardennes forest, which was thought to be militarily impenetrable, and raced to the channel coast, trapping tens of thousands of French, British, and Belgian troops in Flanders. The retreating Allied forces fell back to Dunkirk, where hundreds of British ships, many of them civilian craft, managed to evacuate some 335,000 men, one-third of whom were French and Belgian.

The heroic rescue operation saved the British army for the future and awakened British pride, but it did nothing to retrieve the situation in France. With the French reeling under the onslaught, Mussolini, anxious to participate in the division of the spoils, declared war on France on June 10. Four days later the Germans entered Paris unopposed, and the new head of the French government, eighty-four-year-old Marshal Philippe Pétain (1856–1951), one-time hero of the battle of Verdun, believed further resistance was hopeless and requested a cease-fire. The terms, dictated by Hitler personally in the same railroad car in which Germany had agreed to an

German Tanks on the Western Front, May 1940. Panzer units like this one went on to cut off the British army in France, eventually forcing its evacuation to Great Britain. These tanks are small and primitive compared to those developed later in the war, but the new technology and tactics they represented were devastating, especially early in the war.

UPI/Corbis-Bettmann

E. T. Archives

"All Behind You, Winston." This cartoon appeared in the London *Evening Standard,* May 10, 1940, the day Winston Churchill took office and formed a national government. Shunned as too rash and controversial a figure in the prewar years, Churchill took an active role in nearly every aspect of the war effort, incessantly demanding more imagination and rapid action from his subordinates. His stirring speeches inspired heroism in the British people standing alone against Hitler's Third Reich.

armistice in 1918, divided France into two zones. The northern half was occupied by German troops, and the rest of the country was placed under a puppet regime with its headquarters at Vichy and headed by Pétain.

Great Britain was left alone to face the might of Hitler's military machine. But under the inspired leadership of Prime Minister Winston Churchill (1874–1965), who took office on May 10, 1940, the British were determined to continue fighting, regardless of the cost. Hitler understood that complete mastery of the air was essential for the safe transport of his invasion force across the channel. After the British rejected a second peace offer, in August 1940 Hitler launched a fierce air attack against Great Britain aimed at destroying the Royal Air Force (RAF).

In the ensuing weeks, the Luftwaffe wreaked massive destruction on the ground but also sustained losses far exceeding those of the RAF. Indeed, the toll on the Luftwaffe was so great that at the start of September the German leaders abandoned their primary objective of bombing air installations and defeating the RAF and began instead to carry out night raids against London and other major southern cities. Some industrial towns like Coventry took a terrible pounding, and parts of London were reduced to rubble, but the exorbitant costs only increased British solidarity and will to resist. By winter, when it was obvious that the air campaign had failed, Hitler postponed indefinitely his plans to invade Great Britain. The battle of Britain was over. The entire nation had played a part in handing Hitler his first military defeat, but none more than the RAF, whose lasting monument was Churchill's eulogy: "Never in the field of human conflict was so much owed by so many to so few."

Frustrated in his air assault on Great Britain, Hitler turned his attention to the Balkans in preparation for his clash with the Soviet Union. By threats and bribes, Hitler had already brought Hungary, Romania, and Bulgaria into the Axis camp in the fall of 1940, but Yugoslavia stubbornly clung to its independence. In the spring of 1941, Hitler's armies quickly subjugated Yugoslavia and unleashed a massive attack against Greece with the object of rescuing Mussolini. In the previous October, Mussolini's armies had invaded Greece, but after initial successes they had been driven back to Albania. In a lightning campaign, the Germans forced the Greeks to surrender on April 23, 1941.

Hitler had found it expedient to sign a nonaggression pact with Stalin, but he had never abandoned his plans for an eventual attack on the Soviet Union as a prerequisite to seizing living space for the German people in the east. Hitler expected to conquer the Soviet Union by the end of the summer. Like Napoleon, he underestimated the vast distances, the bitterly harsh winters, and the capacity of the Soviet soldiers and civilians to endure untold suffering and hardships. The invasion, originally scheduled for May, had to be postponed a month so that German troops could bail out Mussolini from his plight in Greece. The delay may have meant the difference between victory and defeat.

In the early hours of June 22, 1941, Hitler unleashed 3 million men along the entire eastern front from Finland to the Caucasus. It was the start of one of the most savagely fought struggles in the annals of military history. All the early signs indicated that the German blitzkrieg was enjoying the same success in the Soviet

Churchill Addresses Parliament on May 13, 1940

*I would say to the House, as I have said to those who have joined this Government: I "have nothing to offer but blood, toil, tears and sweat." We have before us an ordeal of the most grievous kind. We have before us many, many long months of struggle and of suffering. You ask what is our policy? I can say: It is to wage war, by sea, land and air, with all our might and with all the strength that God can give us; to wage war against a monstrous tyranny, never surpassed in the dark lamentable catalogue of human crime. That is our policy. You ask what is our aim? I can answer in one word: it is victory, victory at all costs, victory in spite of all terror, victory, however long and hard the road may be; for without victory, there is no survival. Let that be realized; no survival for the British Empire, no survival for all that the British Empire has stood for, no survival for the urge and impulses of the ages, that mankind will move forward towards its goal. But I take my task with buoyancy and hope. I feel sure that our cause will not be suffered to fail among men. At this time I feel entitled to claim the aid of all, and I say, "Come then, let us go forward together with our united strength."**

Churchill assumed the reins of government on May 10 in the worst of circumstances. His inaugural speech to Parliament as war leader three days later was intended to instill confidence in a nation shaken by the fall of Europe. Churchill's greatest contribution to winning the war was his oratory, or to be more precise, his speeches, particularly those which dramatized the events of 1940–1941 when Britain had no hope of winning the war alone and only a slender chance of survival unless help arrived from outside.

*Robert Rhodes James, ed., *Winston S. Churchill: His Complete Speeches* (New York: Chelsea House, 1974), vol. 6 (1935–1942), p. 6220.

Union as it had elsewhere. German armored columns slashed deep into Soviet territory, encircling the dazed and disorganized enemy forces and capturing hundreds of thousands of prisoners. As the Germans pressed forward, however, they encountered unexpected resistance, and the drives on Moscow and Leningrad, hampered by an early and severe cold, bogged down. Hitler had expected victory before winter set in, so the Germans were unprepared for the arctic weather. The men froze in their summer uniforms and many suffered from frostbite. Guns would not fire and motorized equipment stalled without antifreeze. The German juggernaut ground to a halt just short of complete victory. It would never regain its initial advantage.

During the first week of December, the Red Army, which had secretly brought fresh troops from Siberia, mounted a huge counteroffensive north and south of Moscow. They drove the Germans back until Hitler gave his troops strict orders not to yield any more ground, even if it meant certain death. The Germans regrouped and stabilized the 1,000-mile front. The Soviet Union had paid an exorbitant price during the early months of the fighting. The Germans occupied the best farmland in the Soviet Union as well as the most important industrial areas. The Red Army had lost hundreds of thousands of men in combat, and nearly 4 million more had been captured. Nevertheless, Hitler had not defeated the Soviet Union by December as he had planned. Thereafter both sides attacked and counterattacked on an unprecedented scale. The Soviet Union would remain the main theater of war until the Allies invaded France in the summer of 1944.

The United States Enters the War

In 1940 Japan faced a serious dilemma. Its army could neither win the war in China nor extricate itself without admitting defeat. In the meantime U.S. public opinion had become so aroused by events in China that Washington had forbidden shipment of scrap iron and oil to Japan and persuaded the Dutch and British to do the same. With these vital supplies cut off, the Japanese military adopted a southern strategy aimed at conquering Southeast Asia so that they could seize the needed oil and other raw materials produced in that region. Japan had already secured de facto control of French Indochina from the puppet Vichy regime. With Great Britain tied down in its desperate struggle against Nazi Germany in Europe, only the United States could challenge Japan's ambitions in Southeast Asia. Negotiations between the two nations became deadlocked when the United States demanded Japanese withdrawal from China.

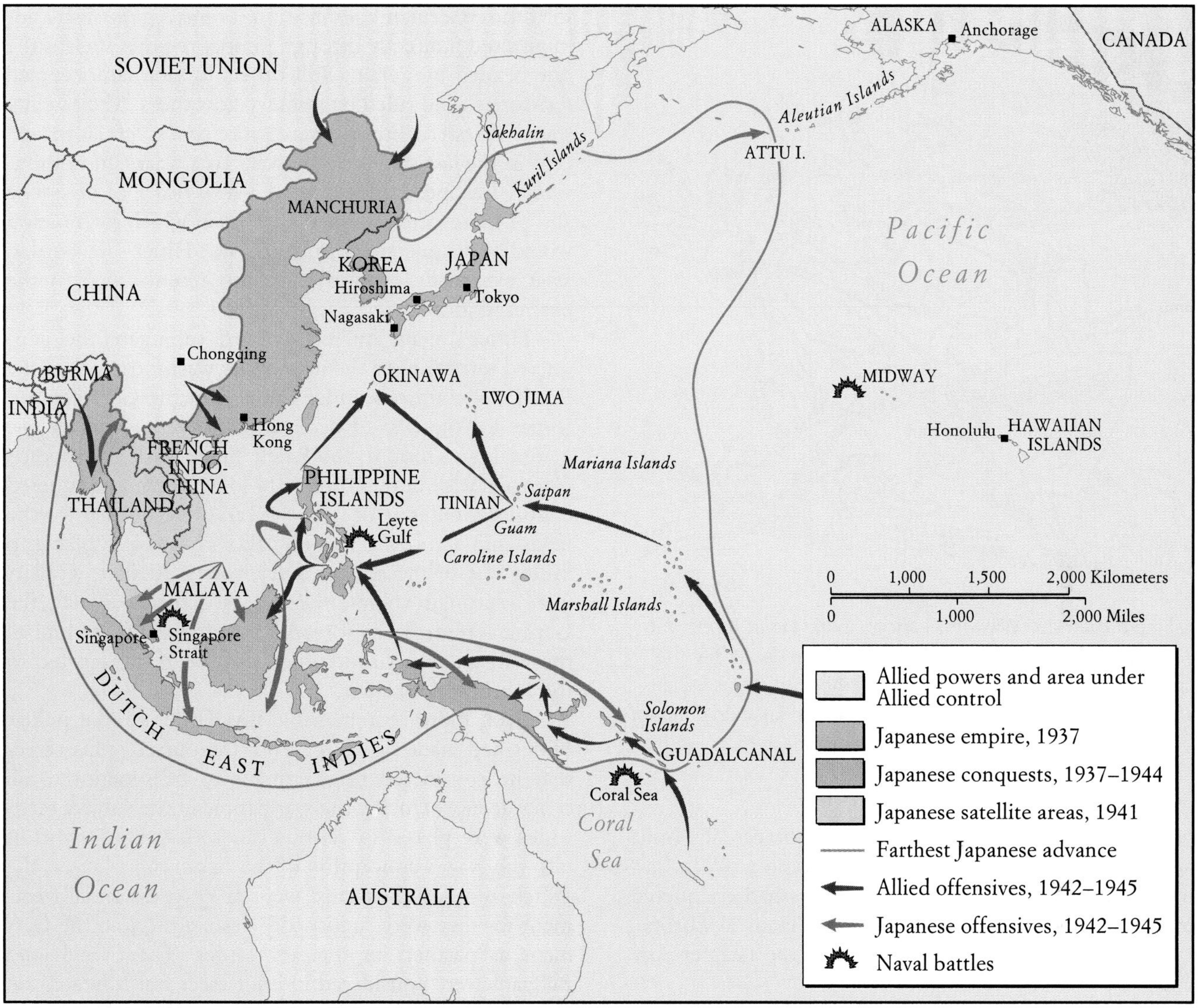

Map 15.3 World War II in Asia and the Pacific. War came to this area in stages, beginning with Japan's invasion of China in 1937. In December 1941 the Japanese attacked British, Dutch, and American possessions. By May 1942, they controlled Southeast Asia and the western Pacific and were even threatening Australia and India. The United States defeated the Japanese by destroying their fleet and bombing their home islands. At the time of surrender, Japanese land forces still held large areas of Asia and the Pacific.

Japan decided to gamble on war with the United States. Its militarists assumed that in a general war the United States would first move against Germany. If Germany won, Japan would be safe; and even if Germany should lose, the Japanese would have bought sufficient time to bring China to its knees and to consolidate their empire in Southeast Asia and the Pacific. Japanese militarists were further convinced that the United States lacked the moral fiber to wage a determined war. Thus, without consulting Japan's Axis allies, Prime Minister and General Hideki Tojo ordered a simultaneous surprise attack on the British, Dutch, and U.S. possessions in Southeast Asia and the Pacific. Japanese forces struck on all fronts on December 7–8, 1941. Carrier-based bombers struck Pearl Harbor in Hawaii, crippling the U.S. navy in a single blow. The United States immediately declared war against Japan; Japan and the other Axis powers responded by declaring war against the United States. With the United States and many nations in the Western Hemisphere involved, World War II was now a truly global conflict.

Japanese war aims initially succeeded brilliantly. In quick succession Japanese forces captured British Malaya and the great British naval base at Singapore, the Dutch East Indies, the U.S.-held Philippines, and British Burma. Independent Thailand bowed to Japanese demands in

Courtesy of the *Japan Times*

Taking It the Hard Way. This cartoon in the *Japan Times and Advertiser* on December 10, 1941, leaves no doubt that the Japanese firmly believed that Pearl Harbor had destroyed the U.S. military capability. Here Japan is shown knocking out not only the United States, but Great Britain and China as well.

order to avoid conquest and became a subject ally. India and Australia were threatened with invasion. Within six months of Pearl Harbor, Japanese forces had conquered more territory in Asia than had the Germans in Europe. Japan euphemistically called its empire the Greater Asia Co-Prosperity Sphere.

Japan's lightning success dealt an irreparable blow to Western imperialism in Asia. However, "Co-Prosperity" and its slogan "Asia for the Asians" soon proved a cruel hoax; those Asians who had hoped that Japan would emancipate them from European rule and grant them freedom found that they had only changed masters. The brutal Japanese military rulers felt superior to their conquered peoples and made exacting demands for raw materials and human resources from the conquered regions. As a result, anti-Japanese resistance rose in all the conquered lands and abetted the growing nationalism of these colonial peoples.

Hitler's "New Order"

By the end of 1941, Hitler was at the pinnacle of his power, having acquired the most extensive empire in European history. The administration of the captive states varied, depending on German aims. A number of areas on Germany's borders like Alsace-Lorraine and Luxembourg were annexed outright to the Reich or set aside for future German colonization. Some regions were administered indirectly through puppet regimes such as the one headed by Pétain. Still others in German-occupied territories were ruled by military governors. The satellite states of eastern Europe were more or less left alone, except in the last stages of the war. To a weary and disillusioned Europe, Hitler offered a new order of discipline and purpose, a refashioned Europe in which each nation would be assigned its fitting role. But Hitler's new order, as it eventually evolved, bore no resemblance to the promised ideal.

Hitler's main interest was to subjugate the conquered territories to the immediate wartime needs of the Reich. All countries under the heel of the Germans had to pay for the cost of occupation as well as deliver raw materials and food to the Reich. Since most able-bodied Germans were at the front or holding down a conquered continent, millions of new workers were needed for the fields and factories. The only labor reservoir available to Hitler was in the occupied territories. At first, workers were recruited voluntarily, but as demand soared, the Germans resorted to forced labor drafts. By the end of the war, millions of foreigners had been transported to the Reich as slave labor.

Even more reprehensible was Hitler's racial policy. Hitler had made no secret from the outset of his career that he considered the Germans to be superior to all other groups. During the war people in the subject territories were placed in various categories. Those who fit into the Nazi's conception of the Aryan race, such as the Dutch and Scandinavians, were given preferential treatment for they were supposedly destined to join the Germans as partners in the new order. The French and Belgians were considered inferior races but tolerated on account of their usefulness in a supportive capacity. In the eyes of the Nazis, the Slavs, classified as subhumans, were fit only for enslavement. Huge numbers of Poles and Russians were herded into camps as forced laborers, condemned to work and live under conditions of filth and misery; many died of exhaustion, starvation, or beatings from guards.

The camps became giant slaughterhouses after Hitler decided to exterminate the Jews, whom he regarded, along with homosexuals and Gypsies, as the lowest species of humanity. Hitler's "Final Solution" was entrusted to the elite SS, which carried out its grisly duties with fanaticism and efficiency. The horrors the Nazis perpetrated were so shocking to the human imagination that even today they can scarcely be believed. In 1941, in Auschwitz, Poland, one of many death camps, the Nazis killed an average of 12,000 people a day. All told, the Nazis murdered 6 million Jews, about 75 percent of the European Jewish population, in the greatest act of genocide in history. It is now referred to as the Holocaust.

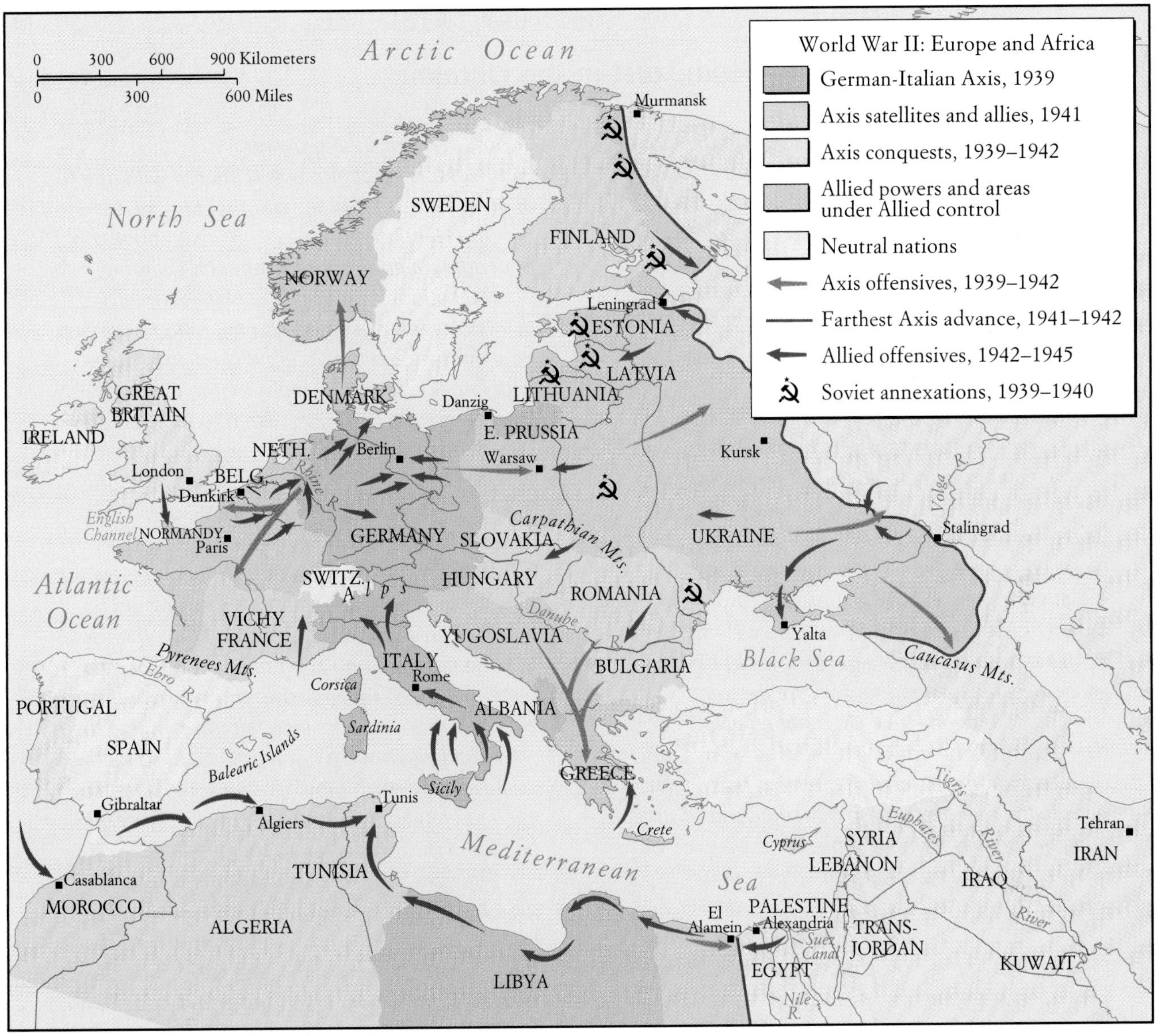

Map 15.4 World War II in Europe and North Africa. In the first phase of the war (1939–1942), Germany and Italy and their allies subjugated most of Europe except for Great Britain and the Soviet Union. In the second stage of the war (1942–1945), powerful U.S. forces arrived in the west and, with the aid of the British, cleared the Mediterranean. They then landed in France and pushed eastward into Germany. Meanwhile, the newly constituted, massive Soviet army drove westward through central Europe and the Balkans, meeting the Western allies in the heart of Germany.

The Home Front

To an even greater extent than World War I, World War II required the cooperation of all sectors of the warring societies. All civilians became involved in the conflict in one way or another. It is estimated that almost as many civilians as military personnel died from enemy action. Aerial bombardments, sieges, wide operational sweeps on the ground, and bloody reprisals by invading armies brought the reality of war directly to tens of millions of people in Europe and Asia. Unlike World War I, the men serving at the front bore no resentment toward those who stayed at home. Everyone was considered to be pulling together and sharing the hardships caused by the war.

The war was more widespread and involved more men in the fighting line and greater weapons of destruction than ever before. Millions of men had to be mobilized and equipped, and guns, tanks, and airplanes had to be turned out as fast as humanly possible. In this total war, central governments assumed great powers as a prerequisite to

Holocaust in the Ukraine

[Public notice in Kiev:] All Yids living in the city of Kiev and its vicinity are to report by 8 o'clock on the morning of Monday, September 29th, 1941, at the corner of Melnikovsky and Dokhturov Streets (near the cemetery). They are to take with them documents, money, valuables, as well as warm clothes, underwear, etc.

Any Yid not carrying out this instruction and who is found elsewhere will be shot. . . .

They started arriving while it was still dark, to be in good time to get seats in the train. With their howling children, their old and sick, some of them weeping, others swearing at each other, the Jews who lived and worked on the vegetable farm emerged on to the street. There were bundles roughly tied woven baskets, boxes of carpenters' tools. . . . Some elderly women were wearing strings of onions hung around their necks like gigantic necklaces—food supplies for the journey. . . .

Then the people in charge started giving orders and shouting, making those who were sitting down stand up and moving them on, pushing the ones in the rear forward, so that some sort of straggling queue was formed. Some of the people's belongings were put down in one place, others in another; there was much pushing and shoving. . . .

At that moment they entered a long corridor formed by two rows of soldiers and dogs. It was very narrow—some four or five feet across. The soldiers were lined up shoulder to shoulder, with their sleeves rolled up, each of them brandishing a rubber club or big stick.

Blows rained down on the people as they passed through.

There was no question of being able to dodge or get away.

Brutal blows, immediately drawing blood, descended on their heads, backs and shoulders from left and right. The soldiers kept shouting: 'Schnell, schnell!' laughing happily, as if they were watching a circus act; they even found ways of delivering harder blows in the more vulnerable places, the ribs, the stomach and the groin. . . .

The poor people, now quite out of their minds, tumbled out into a space cordoned off by troops, a sort of square overgrown with grass. The whole of this grass plot was scattered with articles of underwear, footwear and other clothes.

The Ukrainian police . . . were grabbing hold of people roughly, hitting them and shouting:

'Get your clothes off! Quickly! Schnell!'

Those who hesitated had their clothes ripped off them by force, and were kicked and struck with knuckledusters or clubs by the Germans, who seemed to be drunk with fury in a sort of sadistic rage. . . .

[Back in Kiev] . . . A fourteen-year-old boy, the son of the collective-farm stableman . . . [ran] into the farmyard and was telling the most frightful stories: that they were being made to take all their clothes off; that several of them would be lined up [in a quarry], one behind the other, so as to kill more than one at a time; that the bodies were then piled up and earth thrown over them, and then more bodies were laid on top; that there were many who were not really dead, so that you could see the earth moving, that some had managed to crawl out, only to be knocked over the head and thrown back into the pile. . . .

They packed the hospital patients into the gas-chambers in groups of sixty to seventy, then ran the engines for some fifteen minutes so that the exhaust gases went into the vans. Then the suffocated people were taken out and dropped into a pit. This work went on for several days, quietly and methodically. The Germans were not in a hurry, and took regular hour-long breaks for meals.

The patients in the hospital were not all mad; there were many who were simply being treated for nervous disorders. But they were all buried in the pits of Babi Yar. Most remarkable of all was that after the first horrible days of Babi Yar the destruction of all the patients in an enormous hospital went practically unnoticed and was even taken as a matter of course. . . . *

*A. Anatoli (Kuznetsov), *Babi Yar*, trans. David Floyd (New York: Farrar, Straus and Giroux, 1970), pp. 91, 93, 97, 105, 106, 153.

coordinating the national economy, conducting long-range planning, and ensuring cooperation from every sector of society. The Soviet Union, which had a planned economy, quickly mobilized its human and material resources, pressing into service all civilians between the ages of sixteen and fifty-five, imposing severe rationing, and extending hours for workers. Although the British government responded more slowly, it effectively managed its resources and production distribution, regulated wages and prices, and sponsored much scientific research. During the first two years of the war, the German government refrained from demanding all-out sacrifice from its people, and domestic consumption remained relatively high. Only after it was obvious that the war would drag on did Germany mobilize more systematically.

As in World War I, all belligerent nations tried to maintain patriotic enthusiasm among their civilian populations. All news was censored, and governments waged propaganda campaigns that stressed the righteousness of their cause and exhorted their people to hate the enemy, work harder, and make sacrifices. Examples of intolerance occurred even in the United States, where Americans of Japanese ancestry were interned in camps for the duration of the war simply because of the unjustified fear that they might be disloyal.

Even more than in World War I, large numbers of women came out of their homes and into occupations traditionally dominated by men. In the United States, 200,000 women served in auxiliary branches of the armed forces, and 6 million worked in munitions factories. In some of the occupied countries, women fought in the resistance movement. Russia used women not only in the factories, mines, and railroads but also as combatants. Germany was something of an exception in that Nazi ideology forbade women any role outside the home. Thus few were allowed to replace the men in the fields and the factories.

The War in North Africa and the Invasion of Italy

Soon after Italy entered the war, Mussolini made a bid to wrest control of the eastern Mediterranean from the British. From bases in Ethiopia and Libya, he dispatched an army of 500,000 men against the small, poorly equipped British forces in northeastern Africa. One Italian army overran British Somaliland while another invaded Egypt from Libya with the object of seizing the Suez Canal. In December 1940 the British counterattacked and routed the Italian army, capturing 130,000 prisoners (about four times the number of British soldiers involved

Nazi Victims at Bergen-Belsen. The British, who liberated the concentration camp in April 1945, were horrified by what they found. The camp had been ravaged by a typhus epidemic and thousands of bodies lay unburied, rotting in the sun. Mass graves were dug and bulldozers were brought up to shovel in the dead.

The Home Front. World War II required the greatest outpouring of war matériel in history. As in World War I, women were called on to replace men absent in the service, particularly in the armaments industry. After the war, however, most women returned to traditional domestic roles.

in the attack). Simultaneously, the British drove the Italians out of Somaliland and Ethiopia.

Once again, Hitler came to the rescue of his embattled ally, sending an elite unit, the Afrika Corps, under Field Marshal Erwin Rommel (1891–1944) across the Mediterranean. Rommel, known as the Desert Fox on account of his audacity and mastery of tank warfare, drove back the British, who had been weakened by the dispatch of some 60,000 troops to the Balkans. Rommel might have seized control of Egypt and the entire Middle East if he had been given sufficient forces, but Hitler could not spare them because he was attacking the Balkans and was about to invade Russia.

Forced to retreat late in 1941, Rommel lashed out with a devastating assault the following spring and advanced all the way to El-Alamein, sixty miles from Alexandria where overextended supply lines forced him to call a halt. The lull permitted the British to rebuild their strength, and at the end of October 1942, under a new commander, the egotistical but brilliant General Bernard Montgomery (1887–1976), they were able to take the offensive. It proved successful—the first major British triumph in the war. Montgomery's forces smashed through the German defenses at El-Alamein, driving the invaders headlong into Libya. At this point an Allied army under General Dwight D. Eisenhower (1890–1969) landed in Morocco and Algeria. The Germans were eventually trapped between the Allies advancing from the west and the British from the east. In May 1943 the remnant of Rommel's weary army surrendered.

After clearing the Axis forces from North Africa, the Allies moved quickly to knock dispirited Italy out of the war. In July 1943 the Allies landed in Sicily and, facing only token resistance, conquered the island in less than six weeks. The invasion of Sicily proved fatal to Mussolini, who was forced out of office in a bloodless coup. The new Italian administration negotiated an armistice with General Eisenhower on September 3, one day after Canadian and British troops had established bridgeheads on the mainland.

Hitler reacted by sending as many troops as he could spare to prevent Italy from falling into Allied hands. The Allies found campaigning up the rugged peninsula arduous and costly and did not reach Rome until July 1944. The Germans were not completely expelled from Italy until May the following year, only weeks before Germany's final surrender. In the dying days of the war in Italy, Mussolini and his mistress tried to escape to Switzerland, but they were captured by the partisans and executed. Their corpses were hung upside down in a public square in Milan. It was an inglorious end for a man who had long likened himself to a Roman caesar.

Allied Victory in Europe

The Allies (the United States, Great Britain, the Soviet Union, and China) realized that they had to forge a worldwide alliance and agree on strategic priorities if the Axis powers were to be beaten. From 1942 to 1945, Roosevelt frequently met with Churchill and sometimes also with Stalin and Chiang to coordinate strategy. As Japanese planners had expected, the Allies decided to defeat Germany first, because it represented the greatest threat to Great Britain and the Soviet Union.

With both Great Britain and the Soviet Union already exhausted, the enormous productivity of U.S. industry became the backbone of the Allied war effort. The United States truly became the "Great Arsenal of Democracy" and supplied much of the war matériel used by all the Allies as well as arming 12 million soldiers. Government, military, and private enterprise closely cooperated to sustain the total war effort. By 1945 U.S. military production was more than double that of the combined Axis powers.

First, the U.S. and British navies cleared the seas of marauding German submarines (also called U-boats) that had preyed on Allied shipping, and as a result, large amounts of supplies began to arrive in Great Britain. Next, British and U.S. bombers, protected by fighter planes, flew missions to bomb military installations, industries, transportation networks, and European cities held by the Axis powers. As German air defenses weakened, Germany was forced to relocate factories underground, but as ground transportation was destroyed, these underground factories could not obtain raw materials or ship their products.

LIVES AND TIMES ACROSS CULTURES

What Goes Around Comes Around: Tannenberg and Stalingrad

To check the Russian advance into East Prussia in August 1914, the German High Command sent General Paul von Hindenburg to take charge of the Eighth Army and appointed General Erich Ludendorff as his chief of staff. Ludendorff devised a plan to destroy the Russian army under General Alexander Samsonov invading from the south.

Basing his tactics on Hannibal's spectacular victory at Cannae in 216 B.C.E., Ludendorff moved a corps by rail to the region around Tannenberg to hold Samsonov's army, while sending two corps to envelop it from the flank and rear. Blinded by early Russian successes, Samsonov threw caution to the wind and obligingly walked into the trap. When he attacked, the German center yielded. As he drove ahead, German forces on both sides closed in and virtually encircled his army. The bitter fighting ended three days later with 125,000 Russians dead, wounded, or taken prisoner. Unable to face the tsar, Samsonov shot himself. The battle of Tannenberg offers one of the few examples of the complete destruction of an army. It made popular heroes of Hindenburg and Ludendorff in Germany and, more important, ended Russian plans in East Prussia even more completely than the Marne had stymied German plans in the west.

Thirty years later the Soviet regime avenged Tannenberg. In the spring of 1942 Hitler planned a drive from the Ukraine to Stalingrad on the Volga to prepare the way for his onslaught into the Caucasus, where 75 percent of Soviet oil reserves were located. During the first week in September, the German Sixth Army reached the outskirts of Stalingrad, expecting to take it in short order. The city, renamed after Stalin, was an industrial and transportation center. On orders from Stalin to hold or die, the defenders stood their ground, fighting first over sections of the city, then at close quarters over streets and houses. Casualties on both sides were horrendous. The Germans captured most of the gutted city but could not dislodge about 40,000 Soviet fighters from the industrial section along the Volga.

In mid-November, as the stalled invaders were running short of manpower and munitions, Russian forces under Marshal Georgy Zhukov went over to the offensive. One army attacked to the north of the city while another attacked to the south, the two forming a great pincer. The Germans, led by General Friedrich Paulus, could probably have fought their way out, but Hitler, who had already proclaimed the Soviet Union broken and defeated, would not hear of it. As winter set in, the Germans mounted a rescue operation, but it was halted short of its goal. Isolated, outnumbered, freezing, starving, and half-crazy, the men of the Sixth Army held out for two months. Finally on January 31, 1943 (ironically, the tenth anniversary of Hitler's accession to power), Paulus surrendered what was left of his army—91,000 out of the original 330,000. The Battle of Stalingrad broke the offensive power of the German army. From then on the initiative on the eastern front passed to the Soviet army.

In late 1942 the tide of war began to turn decisively. With British and U.S. air forces inflicting huge damage on the German economy and supply system, Germany could not keep its armed forces adequately supplied. As previously described, British and U.S. units had cleared North Africa of Axis forces by 1943 and followed this victory up by successfully invading Italy. Strengthened by supplies of U.S. and British arms, 6 million Soviet troops began counteroffensives in late 1942. In ferocious fighting that inflicted enormous casualties on both sides, Soviet troops surrounded and then captured German units at the battle of Stalingrad. From that point on, the Soviet forces inexorably pushed the demoralized Germans out of the Soviet Union. They then advanced into Poland and Romania in 1944, with the final goal of invading Germany.

In the summer and autumn of 1944, the Allies began the crucial campaign that ended the war in Europe. On "D Day," June 6, U.S., British, and Canadian forces launched a massive landing on the coast of Normandy in France. German defenders held the Allied forces on the beaches for a month of bitter fighting, but finally were routed. The Normandy landing opened a second front on the European continent. German forces were sent reeling back to Germany from France, Italy, and the eastern front.

By the spring of 1945, Germany was caught in a giant vise. While U.S. and British forces crossed the Rhine River and pressed eastward, Soviet troops captured the Balkans and Hungary and eventually invaded Germany itself. As Soviet forces occupied Berlin, Hitler committed suicide on April 30 in his underground bunker. In accordance with terms laid down by Roosevelt and Churchill at Casablanca in 1942, German forces surrendered unconditionally on May 8, 1945. After nearly six years, the war in Europe had come to an end.

The Defeat of Japan

Victory over Japan was not long delayed. In concentrating on defeating Germany first, the Allies had not abandoned the Pacific entirely to the Japanese. The U.S. war effort was turning out enough war matériel and training enough men to press the war in both theaters. In the spring of 1942, six months after the disaster at Pearl Harbor, the U.S. navy stopped the southward Japanese advance at the Battles of Coral Sea and Midway. These battles ended the threat of a Japanese invasion of Hawaii and Australia and marked a turning point in the Pacific war.

Beginning in June 1943, a two-pronged U.S. counteroffensive struck the Pacific islands where Japan's hold was weakest, leaving the major strongholds to wither away without supplies and reinforcements. With this "island hopping" strategy, the U.S. troops avoided having to engage in numerous scattered offensives, but where fighting occurred, they encountered ferocious resistance for every foot of ground. In the Japanese military code, capture was a disgrace, and usually the only way to dislodge Japanese soldiers from their tunnels and pillboxes was with flamethrowers, hand grenades, and dynamite. By mid-1944 Admiral Chester Nimitz (1885–1966), leading one arm of the U.S. advance, had captured the Marshall Islands and Saipan and Guam in the Marianas, bringing land-based bombers within range of Japanese cities. After a remarkable advance up the coast of New Guinea, General Douglas MacArthur (1880–1964), commanding the other arm, landed on Leyte in October 1944 to reclaim the Philippines for the United States. In February 1945 MacArthur freed Manila.

In the spring of 1945, the move toward the Japanese home islands was being pressed steadily. In March U.S. troops took Iwo Jima and then converged on Okinawa, which was well situated for staging an attack on Japan's main islands. In desperation Japan sent specially trained and indoctrinated pilots on suicide missions to ram their explosive-packed planes directly into U.S. warships. The

D Day. On June 6, 1944, Allied forces launched the greatest sea-to-land invasion in history, crossing the English Channel from Great Britain to assault German fortifications on the coast of Normandy, France. This opened the western front, which, together with the Soviet drive from the east, overwhelmed the Nazi regime in less than a year.

UPI/Corbis-Bettmann

LIVES AND TIMES ACROSS CULTURES

Hollywood and the Two World Wars

Films occasionally shape the public's perception of the past but more often reflect the mood of the society and culture in which they were created. Thus some films have portrayed war in a negative light, while others have seen war as idealistic, courageous, and heroic, providing a powerful medium to mobilize aggressive nationalistic feelings against the enemy.

During the First World War there were no feature movies related to the conflict, only silent news footage shot in war zones. Nearly a decade passed after 1918 before a trend began to take shape—dramatizing and analyzing the war experience in motion pictures. By then the level of disillusionment at the waste and futility of the war in Europe and the United States was significant, and some movies were used to generate revulsion against warfare. No film better conveys the nature of trench warfare and its attendant horrors than *All Quiet on the Western Front* (1930), directed by Lewis Milestone (1895–1980), with Lew Ayres in the starring role. In 1936 Howard Hawks directed *The Road to Glory* (1936), which also graphically portrays the horrific results of the fighting on the western front. A few years later that grim image disappeared from the screen but would return in the post–World War II period. Stanley Kubrick (1928–1999) directed and cowrote *Paths of Glory* (1957), one of the most powerful antiwar movies in the history of Hollywood. With Kirk Douglas in the role of the hero, it is a savage indictment of the French High Command during the First World War.

The only antiwar film made in Hollywood during or after the Second World War, universally depicted as a just and moral conflict, was *Saving Private Ryan* (1998), directed by Stephen Spielberg (1947–). It is so effectively graphic and so emotionally reconstructs the American landing at Omaha beach on D Day that audiences must steel themselves before seeing it. Otherwise, war movies followed a familiar pattern. Movie makers often worked hand in hand with the government to produce movies that not only entertained but were used to build unity through propaganda. Even before the entrance of the United States into the war, there was an effort to overcome the general mood of isolationism by compelling movie audiences to confront the evils of the fascist regime. The films *The Man I Married* (1940), *The Mortal Storm* (1940), *A Yank in the RAF* (1941), and particularly *Underground* (1941) are classic examples. The latter, concentrating on a dedicated group of Germans opposed to Hitler, contains some of the most explicit portrayal of Nazi brutality hitherto seen on the screen.

The early combat films about the Second World War such as *Flying Tigers* (1942), *Pride of the Marines* (1945), and *Bataan* (1943) display a good deal of anti-Japanese feeling. A more evenhanded approach was made in 1970 with the film *Tora!Tora!Tora!* A Darryl Zanuck (1902–1979) production, it is unusual in its recreation of the bombing of Pearl Harbor from the perspective of both the U.S. and Japan. *Midway* (1976) follows a similar line. Most recently, *Pearl Harbor* (2001) uses special effects wizardry to reconstruct the terrible "day of infamy."

Because American troops were absent from the fighting in Europe until the middle of 1944, most of the films involving the Germans came out after the war. The focus is not on vilifying the enemy but on entertaining audiences. Among these are *Twelve O'Clock High* (1950), *Battleground* (1950), *Run Silent, Run Deep* (1958), *The Longest Day* (1962), *The Dirty Dozen* (1967), and *Patton* (1970).

Japanese called these *kamikaze* attacks, recalling the "divine wind" that had turned back the Mongol invaders in 1281. This time, however, the winds failed Japan. The capture of Okinawa and Iwo Jima gave the Americans additional bases from which to launch intense air bombardments of Japan's home islands. Japan's position was now hopeless. Its cities were being leveled by napalm bombs, its navy was no longer a factor, and its overseas garrisons were isolated and defeated. Nevertheless, Japanese military leaders wanted to fight to the finish.

Plans for an invasion of Japan were completed before Germany capitulated. Considering the fanatical resistance shown by the Japanese at Okinawa and elsewhere, casualties for the invading force were expected to run as high as half a million men. But the availability of the atomic bomb, which had been successfully tested in New Mexico, made the costly venture unnecessary. On August 6, 1945, an atomic bomb was dropped on Hiroshima, leveling the city and killing over 50,000 people and maiming 100,000 more. Three days later, while the stunned Japanese still hesitated, a second bomb hit Nagasaki with similar lethal effects. In accordance with its earlier agreement, the Soviet Union declared war against Japan on August 8, just before Japan's surrender and in time to have a voice in the postwar settlement. Soviet troops immediately occupied Manchuria and Korea.

The bombing of Hiroshima and Nagasaki convinced Emperor Hirohito to exert his influence to end the war. On August 14 Hirohito broadcast Japan's acceptance of Allied terms. Germany's government had been dismantled after its unconditional surrender, but the Japanese emperor was allowed to remain to ease the transition and provide for a smooth Allied occupation. Japanese fighting men everywhere obeyed the emperor's command and did not continue to fight as some Allied leaders had feared they might. On September 2 General MacArthur accepted Japan's formal unconditional surrender on the U.S. battleship *Missouri* in Tokyo Bay, ending World War II.

World War II was truly a global war, fought on three continents and on all the oceans. It lasted eight years for China, six for Europe, and nearly four for the United States. It was by far the most destructive war in history. No accurate count can be made of the dead, but perhaps as many as 50 million, both civilians and soldiers, perished. Countless cities in Europe and Asia were flattened or severely damaged. The transportation networks of most belligerent countries were in shambles, and millions of acres of farmland were damaged. The fiscal cost of the war was estimated at $1.5 trillion. The economies of nearly all the belligerents were in ruins, while the survivors were physically and psychologically exhausted.

World War II had an important political consequence as well. It brought to completion a trend that began in 1919—the decline of Europe's power and influence in world affairs. Henceforth global leadership would pass to the United States and the Soviet Union.

Settlements with Germany and Japan

As the victorious Allies began to rebuild their shattered nations, they also had to face the problem of making peace with their former enemies. Since most statesmen were determined not to repeat the error of a quick peace settlement, there was a considerable cooling-off period to allow emotions aroused by the war to subside. Eighteen months passed before even the minor treaties were ready for signing.

Instead of a formal peace conference as after World War I, Allied leaders worked out most issues in a series of conferences during and after the war. These agreements were then formalized in bilateral and multilateral treaties. A consensus on allowing East and West Germany to unify did not occur until 1990. However, territorial disputes between the Soviet Union and Japan remained unsettled.

Regarding Europe, as at Versailles, the victors were primarily concerned with the postwar status of Germany. During the war they had considered permanently dismembering Germany or reducing it to a feeble agricultural region. By 1945, however, the Allies had agreed to retain Germany as a single nation, but they imposed strong safeguards to ensure that it would never again threaten the peace of Europe. Germany was disarmed and divided into four occupation zones: British, U.S., French, and Soviet. The occupying forces were to remain until the German people had been de-Nazified and had set up a government acceptable to all the occupying powers, presumably in three to five years. The victors were initially interested in reparation settlements and agreed that the heavily ravaged Soviet Union would receive the largest share. Soviet authorities dismantled some remaining factories in their zone of occupation and shipped them to the Soviet Union as reparations.

Berlin became a bone of contention among the victors. Although Germany's capital city was situated in the heart of the Soviet zone, the Western powers insisted on sharing in its control. In an awkward arrangement, Berlin was divided into four occupation zones separate from the rest of Germany. The Western powers had the right of access to Berlin by air through the Soviet occupation zone, but they were in a precarious military situation, because the city was far behind the Soviet lines.

A special court convened by the Allies at Nuremberg during 1945–1946 punished Nazi leaders for waging aggressive war and for crimes against humanity. Trials of lesser officials followed. The court set precedents by punishing those responsible for brutal treatment of prisoners and noncombatants and ruled their excuse of "following orders" an insufficient defense. Twelve leading Nazis were condemned to death, the most prominent being Hermann Göring, who cheated the hangman by committing suicide. Seven were imprisoned for terms up to life, and three were acquitted.

The territorial changes mostly affected eastern Europe. The Soviet Union retained the areas first acquired in 1939–1940 and still in its possession at the end of the war: Estonia, Latvia, Lithuania, portions of Romania and Finland, and the eastern half of Poland. It also annexed a province of Czechoslovakia and the northern half of East Prussia. As a result, the Soviet boundary moved dramatically westward. Poland was compensated for its loss in the east by receiving the eastern quarter of Germany. Hitler's allies, Italy, Finland, Hungary, Romania, and Bulgaria were not harshly treated. Their territories were adjusted in minor ways, and they had to pay small reparations. In the west, the German boundary was altered as well. Alsace-Lorraine was returned to France, and Austria was detached from Germany.

Unlike Germany, Japan was not directly governed by the Allied occupation forces. It retained its emperor and government, purged of militarists. U.S. forces occupied Japan under General MacArthur. Although he was Supreme Commander for the Allied Powers (SCAP), MacArthur actually took orders only from the U.S. government. Japan lost all conquests made since the late nineteenth century: the southern Sakhalin and the Kurile Islands went to the Soviet Union; Taiwan and all other Chinese territories were returned to China; Korea was to become independent, while the Ryukyu Islands, with the important Okinawa airbase, were to be administered by the United States. Japan also gave up all its colonial conquests in Southeast Asia and made small reparation payments to its victims there.

MacArthur carried out the SCAP mandate to change Japan from an aggressive, imperialistic nation to a peaceful, democratic one. Japanese militarists who had waged aggressive war and had ordered atrocities against prisoners and conquered civilians were tried at the Tokyo International Court; some, Tojo being the most prominent, were condemned to death, while others were sentenced to prison terms. Another agency oversaw the purge of lesser figures in the government and industrial complex, which had abetted and profited from aggression. Those singled out were forbidden from participating in future policy decisions. Further measures led to the dismantling of Japan's armed forces and to the repatriation of former colonial administrators and settlers.

On January 1, 1946, the emperor made a Declaration of Humanity in which he formally renounced his divine status. General MacArthur and his civilian advisers closely supervised the writing of Japan's new constitution, which was promulgated in 1947 and included a bill of rights. Borrowing passages from the U.S. Constitution, the Bill of Rights, and the Gettysburg address, the constitution placed sovereignty in the hands of the Japanese and provided for a government similar to that of Great Britain. One provision renounced war and the right of belligerency forever and declared that "land, sea, and air forces, as well as other war potential, will never be maintained." Women gained the right to vote and to be elected to office. SCAP also supervised widespread economic, educational, and social reforms that restructured the formerly paternalistic and authoritarian society to a more liberal and individualistic one.

Japan regained full independence in the Treaty of San Francisco in 1951. The treaty was signed by forty-eight of the victor nations. The Soviet bloc nations refused to sign. Neither of China's two governments—the People's Republic (Communist), which controlled mainland China, and the Republic (Nationalists), which ruled Taiwan—was included. Separate treaties were signed between Nationalist China and Japan immediately afterward and between the People's Republic of China and Japan in the 1970s.

Cold War in Europe

On March 31, 1948, the Russians ordered that unless inspectors were permitted to examine passengers and luggage, Western military trains would be not merely delayed but would be turned back. An order also was issued that no freight trains could leave Berlin without a Soviet permit.

The next Soviet move was to stop all passenger trains departing from Berlin. About this time, Americans in Berlin seemed to be the only Westerners who were determined to stay there. French officials repeated the familiar remark that not a single Frenchman would vote to fight for Berlin. The British, believing that Berlin's geographical position makes the city indefensible, opposed an outright showdown. . . .

On June 24 . . . the full extent of the Soviet threat became clear when all rail traffic between Berlin and the West was halted "due to technical difficulties."

During the intermittent traffic stoppages prior to the all-out blockade, we had discovered that airplanes could bring in a surprising amount of essentials. The National Security Council therefore decided that we should enforce only our written agreements for use of specific air corridors. That decision became the inspiration for the fabulous Airlift. . . .

One incongruous aspect of the Airlift epoch was the help which black marketeers brought to Berlin. . . . Black marketeers discovered innumerable ways to move desired goods into the beleaguered city. . . . Luxuries flowed in. . . . As one of my aides remarked to me, "We are a capitalist oasis in a socialist desert!" May 12, 1949 marked the end of the Berlin blockade. . . .

By coincidence, the Berlin blockade was lifted on the same day that two other prolonged negotiations in Germany were also concluded. The French Government completed arrangements to merge the economy of its occupation zone with the economy of the American and British zones. . . .

Today [1964] for better or worse, the German-American alliance has become the key to the American military position in Europe. It seems to me that Americans came out of their German experience as winners on the whole, and the Russians as losers. Even the isolation *of Berlin has worked out more in our favor than the Kremlin's. The Russians inadvertently gave us an outpost one hundred miles inside the Iron Curtain, where the inadequacies of the Communist system show up more conspicuously than anywhere else, in full view of everybody in the world.**

*Robert Murphy, *Diplomat among Warriors* (New York: Doubleday, 1964), pp. 315–323.

The Berlin blockade was the first major crisis in the Cold War. It had the effect of hastening the postwar division of Germany into two separate states—a division that persisted until 1990. In the preceding excerpts from his memoirs, Robert Murphy, a career diplomat with the U.S. State Department, recalled the Berlin crisis in 1948–1949 and its outcome. He was writing from a perspective in which the globe was divided into two warring camps, one dominated by the United States and the other by the Soviet Union. Cold War confrontations and maneuverings between the superpowers dominated global relations after World War II. By 1989 radical changes in the Soviet Union inspired by President Mikhail Gorbachev, crumbling economic systems in the Soviet-dominated eastern European bloc, fears of nuclear annihilation, and *glasnost* (increased openness and communication among the major powers) seemed to mark the end of the Cold War and the beginning of a new, multipolar world.

The Cold War was a complex pattern of competitive, often hostile relationships between the two postwar superpowers—the United States and the Soviet Union—that began in Europe as World War II came to an end and persisted at varying levels of intensity into the 1980s. It involved economic, diplomatic, and military competition between the superpowers and their allies, but never escalated to direct military warfare between the United States and the Soviet Union or to the use of nuclear weapons. During the 1950s and 1960s, the Cold War spread from Europe to Asia, Africa, and Latin America. The United States and the Soviet Union also competed in a global arms race. Eventually, the two powers stockpiled so many nuclear weapons that either could destroy the world in a matter of minutes.

The Beginning of the Cold War: 1945–1949

During World War II, leaders in the United States, Great Britain, and the Soviet Union were already anticipating changes in the postwar world and sought to maximize their respective gains. Great Britain wished to retain its empire and its imperial economic system. The United States wanted not only to maintain its sphere of influence in the Western Hemisphere and Asia, but also to construct a worldwide system of free markets. The Soviet Union had suffered over 20 million wartime dead, and its totalitarian ruler, Joseph Stalin, wanted to dominate eastern Europe and to keep Germany militarily impotent. Moscow also sought to promote Marxism around the world, but without embroiling itself in too many direct involvements or difficulties.

The origins and course of the Cold War continue to be debated heatedly among historians. Whether the United States employed the atomic bomb because it was necessary to win the war or used it primarily to threaten the Soviet Union remains an issue of controversy. Historians and politicians have also differed over whether the United States or the Soviet Union was more aggressive in causing and pursuing the Cold War and whether ideological, military, or economic factors carried the most weight in framing postwar policies.

Relationships among the victorious powers rapidly deteriorated during and after the last two wartime conferences at Yalta and Potsdam in 1945. One major issue was reparations. The United States, whose economy had prospered during the war, was more interested in rebuilding Germany as a potential trading partner than in crushing it economically. In contrast, the Soviet Union, which had been devastated during the war, wished to rebuild its economy mostly with reparations from defeated Germany (along with postwar loans from the United States).

Late in World War II the Soviet army occupied eastern Europe as it drove the Germans out, and Stalin clearly intended to stay there to bolster the Soviet Union's security and strategic position. The Western powers desired the withdrawal of the Soviets and the establishment of democratic governments and free market economies in eastern Europe. To pressure the Soviet Union into opening up eastern Europe, the United States cut off the Lend-Lease program and ended shipments of German industrial supplies to the Soviet Union from Allied occupation zones. The Soviet Union responded by stripping its occupation zone in eastern Germany of industrial plants and materials.

As a result, eastern Europe became the main area of East-West contention in the years immediately after the war. With its occupying troops in the region, the Soviet Union was determined to weld eastern Europe into a buffer zone of friendly nations, or at least friendly governments, to prevent the possibility of future invasions. Despite pressure from the United States to permit free elections and to open up the area to free trade with the Western capitalist nations, the Soviet Union tightened the grip of Communist parties over Poland, Romania, and Bulgaria. A local Communist party also dominated Albania. By 1948 Communist party takeovers had added Hungary and Czechoslovakia to the Soviet sphere. Only Yugoslavia, although Communist, took an independent, nationalistic course under Marshal Josef Tito (1892–1980).

Once in political control, the Soviets began to integrate the economies of the eastern European nations with their own economy. While former British prime minister

Winston Churchill charged that an "iron curtain" had fallen between eastern Europe and the West, Stalin told the Soviet people that they were surrounded by enemies and would have to endure more shortages and cutbacks to maintain their military strength.

The possession of the atomic bomb by the United States also affected postwar relationships. The Soviet Union, which did not then have its own atomic bomb, feared the U.S. weapon, but not enough to back down from defending its interests. Meanwhile, the United States presented the Baruch Plan, under which nations would refrain from making atomic bombs and submit to inspection by an independent international agency. Because the United States and its allies controlled the United Nations, and thus the proposed international agency, the Soviet Union rejected the plan.

As the Soviet Union consolidated its power in eastern Europe, trouble developed in the Mediterranean. Turkey, hoping for Western support, refused a Soviet demand in 1946 and early 1947 for joint Soviet-Turkish supervision of the Bosporus, the waterway connecting the Black Sea to the Aegean Sea. At the same time, Greece was embroiled in a brutal civil war between the corrupt royal government and Communist-dominated guerrillas backed by the Communist regimes in the Balkans. The British, who had been aiding the Greek government in order to keep the Soviet Union out of the Mediterranean, were forced for economic reasons to pull out in 1947. These developments brought in the United States to take up where the British had left off.

AP/Wide World Photos

Joseph Stalin. This portrait shows Stalin as robust, alert, strong-willed, and confident, attributes he worked hard to convey to the West and to his own people. In truth, he was short, insecure, paranoid, and one of the most brutal men in history.

Economic and Political Divisions

The developments in Greece and Turkey, as well as the situation in eastern Europe, caused the Truman administration to reverse the traditional isolationist policy of the United States in international affairs. In the past, U.S. policymakers had taken the position that the nation's interests were best served by staying out of European affairs. Only when U.S. vital interests were threatened, as in the two world wars, had Americans entered into European conflicts. President Harry Truman (1884–1972) moved to reverse 150 years of isolationist sentiment and replace it with a policy whereby the United States adopted a role of global leadership.

By 1947 Truman, a staunch anticommunist, and most of his civilian and military advisers had concluded that the Soviet Union was planning to destroy the "free" (non-Communist) world. Only by active participation could the United States prevent the Soviets from dominating Greece and Turkey. On March 12, 1947, Truman laid out the new principles of U.S. foreign policy in a speech to Congress. In it he advocated U.S. economic aid to Greece and Turkey and to any nation that threatened to come under Communist control. The new policy, called the Truman Doctrine, became crucial in the containment of communism during the following decades.

At the request of the president and after intense lobbying, Congress authorized $150 million in aid to Turkey and $250 million to Greece. With U.S. backing the Turkish government continued to hold out against the Soviet Union. Reorganized and better equipped, the Greek army became more effective against the Communist insurgents, who gave up in 1949 after Yugoslavia cut off vital aid.

Trouble in western Europe quickly produced another major policy innovation, the Marshall Plan. By 1947 despite billions of dollars in U.S. loans, the economy of western Europe had not recovered from wartime devastation. France and Italy in particular were plagued with shortages, inflation, unemployment, and inadequate housing. Out of desperation, many French and Italians voted for Socialist and Communist candidates, who consequently held a number of seats in the cabinets of both governments. In the eyes of the Truman administration, this situation demanded effective U.S. economic intervention.

In June 1947 Secretary of State George Marshall (1880–1959) proposed that the nations of Europe consult with one another and with the United States to determine the amount of economic assistance they needed to rebuild their economies. The Soviet Union, fearful of U.S. economic expansion, prevented eastern European nations from participating. With some reluctance, Congress in 1948 created the European Recovery Program, usually referred to as the Marshall Plan, with an initial outlay of $4 billion. By 1951 Marshall Plan aid had totaled over $13 billion. Most of it went to Great Britain, France, and Italy, whose economies recovered rapidly under its impetus.

The Marshall Plan was a political success as well, assuring the decline of Communist political fortunes in Europe, which had begun to fade even before the implementation of the program. In both Italy and France, voters excluded Communists from cabinet positions after mid-1947, and Communist-led strikes were broken by government action. Hoping for a similar success in the non-Western world, Congress funded the Point Four program in 1950. This program aimed at providing foreign aid to emerging non-Western nations to prevent them from turning to communism as a means to solve their economic problems. The vast infusion of funds that flowed into Europe under the Marshall Plan not only laid the foundations for postwar European prosperity and economic integration but also helped the U.S. economy to grow.

Another development that aided the recovery of western Europe was the formation of the European Economic Community (EEC), popularly called the Common Market. Founded in 1957, and initially including France, Italy, West Germany, the Netherlands, Belgium, and Luxembourg, the Common Market was a customs union that reduced competition among its members and turned western Europe into an open market area. The EEC was so successful that Great Britain and other nations, including Greece, Portugal, and Spain, all sought membership and were later admitted. As European economies grew stronger and relationships among the governments became more cordial, plans were approved for the integration of both European governments and economies by 1992; the new union was known as the European Community, or EC.

The new technology generated by World War II revolutionized both agricultural and industrial production in western Europe. The Common Market allowed goods to circulate freely in western Europe, supplying the demand created by a postwar "baby boom." Rapid economic growth and unprecedented prosperity resulted. Prostrate in 1945, western Europe, especially Germany, was a major competitor of the United States in global markets by 1965.

As the Western nations established more friendly relations with their occupied sections of Germany, the Soviet Union grew increasingly fearful that Germany would again be unified and become a strong, potential military threat. Following some initial maneuvers, the Soviets announced in June 1948 that they had closed "for repairs" those railroads and highways in East Germany set aside to supply Western troops and civilians in West Berlin. The Western governments countered by using the air corridors for the Berlin airlift, or "Operation Vittles," to supply more than 2 million West Berliners and Western troops with food, clothing, coal, and other supplies. The Berlin blockade and airlift dragged on for almost a year before the Soviets conceded defeat and reopened the highways and railroads in May 1949. The immediate crisis was over, but Berlin remained a trouble spot.

In September 1949 the United States and its allies combined the three western zones of occupation in Germany into a German national state as a buffer against the Soviet-controlled eastern sector. Later the western zones became the Federal Republic of Germany (West Germany). U.S., British, and French military forces remained in West Germany, but their role had changed from being anti-German to anti-Soviet.

The Soviet Union countered by organizing its zone into the German Democratic Republic (East Germany). The division of Germany remained in effect for four decades. Thus by the end of the 1940s Europe had effectively been divided into two spheres of influence: one, the Western bloc, was effectively dominated by the United States, and the other, the Eastern bloc, was directly occupied and controlled by the Soviet Union.

By the late 1940s and 1950s, the Cold War had permeated Western and Soviet attitudes. As in other wars, both sides bombarded their publics with propaganda that depicted the other side as bent on destroying their way of life. The mass media, now including television, played a major role. In the totalitarian Soviet bloc, the governments carefully controlled all information received by their citizens, even going to the extreme of jamming outside radio broadcasts. In the Western bloc, the independent press and electronic media generally followed the lead of their governments. Americans were egged on to worry about alleged "subversives," "Commie dupes," "parlor pinks," and "fellow travelers." They became uneasy when the Communists defeated the Nationalist forces in a civil war in China in 1949, and fearful when the new leaders of that nation aided North Korea against the U.S.-supported South Korean government in the Korean War. Congress investigated alleged subversives in the United States and enacted legislation granting government agencies broad powers to combat treasonous organizations. After the mid-1950s, the anticommunist hysteria gradually died down in the United States.

Cold War Military Expansion

The Cold War had a direct military impact on Europe. In 1949 the Truman administration moved to a much more aggressive form of containment when it abandoned its traditional policy of unilateral action and created a system of anti-Soviet alliances and military bases along the Soviet perimeters. Postwar developments that culminated in the

Communists seizing power in Czechoslovakia in 1948 and the Berlin blockade in 1948–1949 convinced U.S. leaders that the Soviet Union represented a permanent aggressive threat in Europe that had to be balanced by a permanent U.S. military presence there.

The Truman administration set up a military alliance called the North Atlantic Treaty Organization (NATO). NATO initially included the United States, Canada, Great Britain, France, West Germany, Iceland, Norway, Denmark, the Netherlands, Belgium, Luxembourg, Portugal, and Italy. Member states agreed to come to one another's aid if attacked. NATO seemed to work so well in countering possible Soviet expansion that it was enlarged to include such questionably North Atlantic nations as Greece and Turkey. The national armed forces of the member nations were incorporated into a unified military operation under the direction of a U.S. commander in chief. The U.S. Strategic Air Command (SAC) established airbases in western Europe and in the non-NATO nations of Spain and Libya. From these bases, U.S. bombers could inflict untold damage on the Soviet Union in case of war.

The U.S.-led encirclement of the Soviet Union in Europe created a series of escalating pressures in Europe. The Soviet Union increased the size of its army in Europe until it greatly outnumbered the NATO forces opposing it. This in effect turned western European nations into hostages in a U.S.-Soviet confrontation, because Europe would be the primary battleground for the superpowers and its people the likely victims of any nuclear explosion. Fear of becoming such a battleground led western European nations to restrain the United States in its stance toward the Soviet Union.

The Cold War entered an even more dangerous phase in 1957, when the Soviets, using a powerful new rocket, launched the first satellite into orbit around the earth. Two months later, they launched an intercontinental ballistic missile (ICBM). The space and missile age had arrived. Americans were predictably alarmed. Having prided

Map 15.5 Post–World War II European Economic Division. In 1949 the Soviet Union and its eighteen eastern European satellites formed the Council for Mutual Economic Assistance (COMECON), while France, West Germany, Italy, Belgium, the Netherlands, and Luxembourg organized the European Economic Community (EEC). The EEC expanded to include most noncommunist European countries, all of which prospered as a result of membership; the Soviet-dominated COMECON did not fare so well.

themselves on leading the world in science and technology, they enthusiastically supported President Dwight D. Eisenhower's decision to pour money into scientific research. A National Aeronautics and Space Administration (NASA) was created to push the United States ahead in the space race. Stung by Democratic charges of a "missile gap," the Eisenhower administration began a major ICBM building program and also constructed submarine-launched missiles (SLM). A U.S. satellite was launched in 1958. By 1963 the United States had 450 missiles and 2,000 bombers capable of striking the Soviet Union versus 50 to 100 Soviet ICBMs and 200 bombers that could reach the United States. The phrases "balance of terror" and, later, "mutually assured destruction" (MAD) came into use.

In 1955 the Soviet Union countered the creation of NATO with its own military alliance system called the Warsaw Pact, which integrated the armed forces of eastern Europe into a unified force under Soviet command. In addition, the Soviets recognized East Germany as an independent state and admitted it into the Warsaw Pact.

People in several satellite nations challenged Soviet hegemony in eastern Europe in the 1950s. Dissatisfaction

Map 15.6 The Cold War in Europe. After World War II, the division of Europe into spheres dominated by the two superpowers was intensified by the NATO and Warsaw Pact alliances and by the arms race. Rival land forces, backed by arrays of nuclear missiles and bombers, faced each other in central Europe, while surface fleets and missile-firing submarines roamed the Atlantic and the Mediterranean. Despite, or because of, Cold War confrontations and military buildups, Europe remained at peace after 1945.

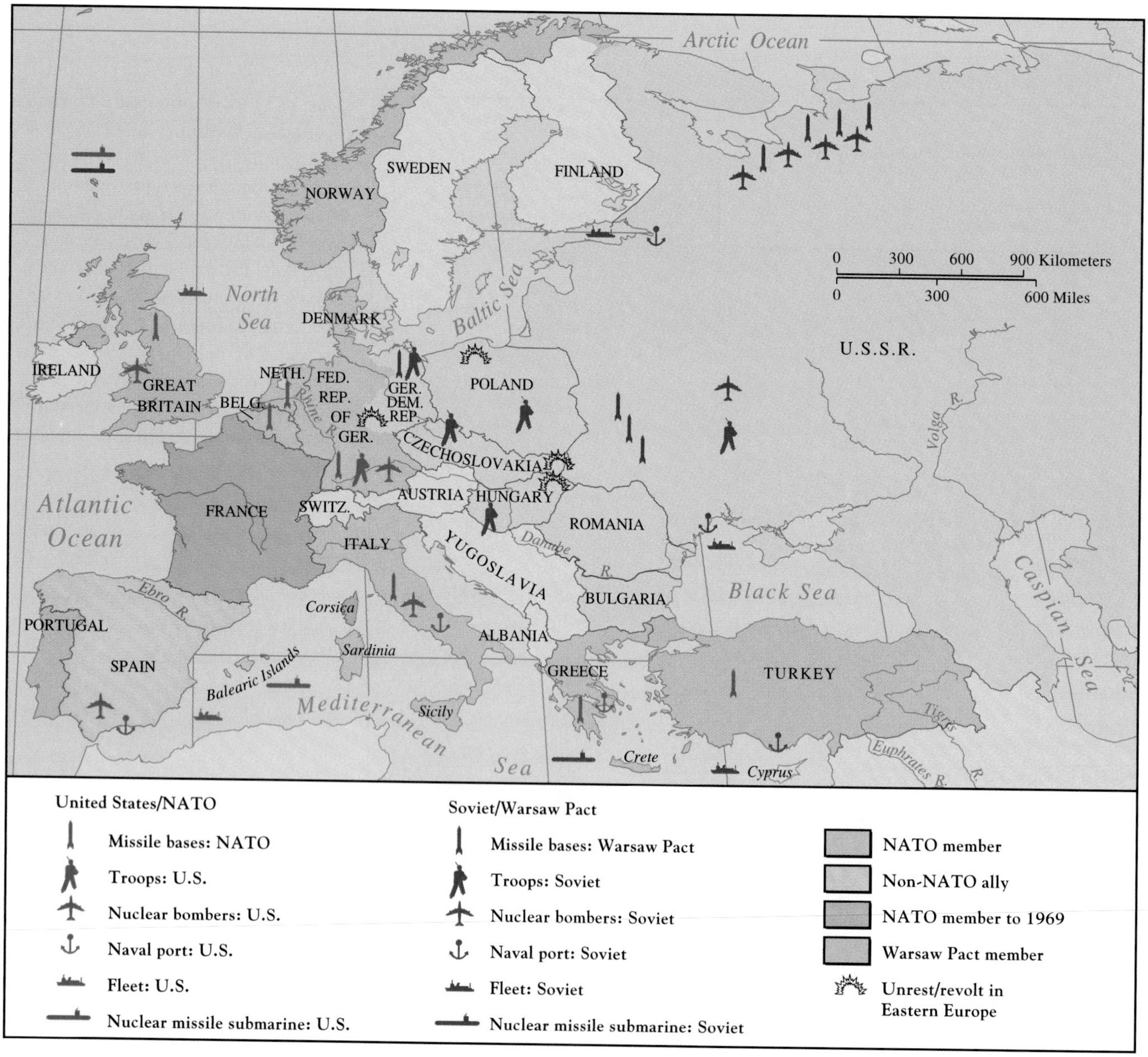

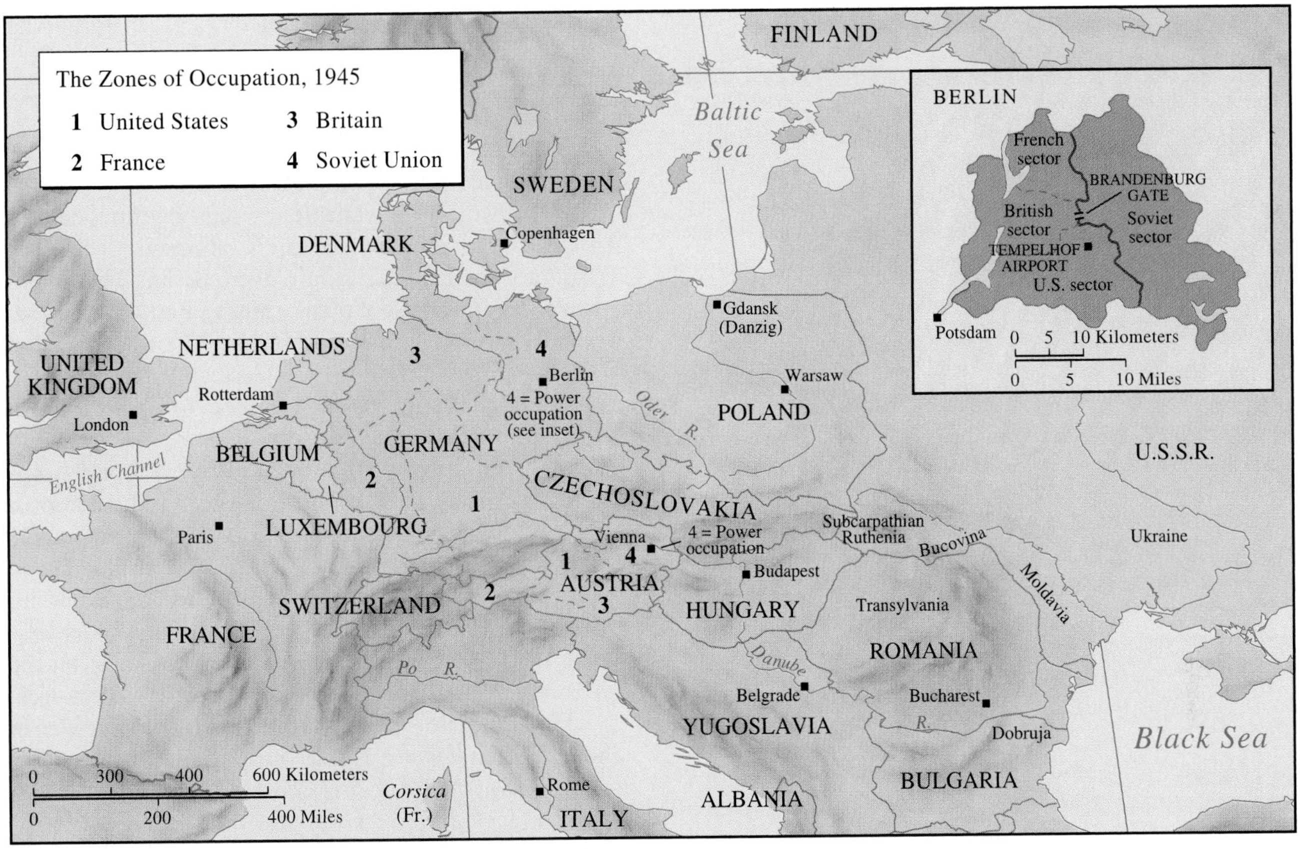

Map 15.7 Zones of Allied Occupation in Germany and Austria, 1945–1955. After World War II, Hitler's Reich was reduced, redivided into Germany and Austria, and occupied by Allied troops. Separate occupation authorities controlled Germany, Austria, and the city of Berlin. The three Western powers had intended the occupation to last only until the German people had a democratic government and no longer threatened their neighbors. But as the Cold War set in, both the Western powers and the Soviet Union began to view this area of Europe as a buffer zone and "their" Germans as future allies in the ongoing competition. The three western zones were consolidated from 1946 to 1949, becoming the Federal Republic of Germany; the Soviet zone became the German Democratic Republic in 1949. In both cases, foreign troops remained as invited allies. By contrast, all occupying forces left Austria when it became independent in 1955. Berlin remained an occupied entity and a dangerous flash point till the end of the Cold War in the early 1990s.

with living conditions, hopes raised by more liberal policies under new Soviet leader Nikita Khrushchev, and encouragement by U.S. propaganda led to riots and other convulsions in East Germany in 1953 and Poland and Hungary in 1956. When the Hungarians announced widespread reforms, including free elections, and said that they would withdraw from the Warsaw Pact, Soviet troops and tanks poured in and surrounded every large city and every important military installation. The United States, distracted by the fighting in the Suez (see Chapter 17) and unwilling to go to war over eastern Europe, was sympathetic to the Hungarian rebels but did not move to intervene on their behalf. The Soviet Union ruthlessly crushed the rebellion, executed independence-minded Hungarian leaders, and maintained its domination over eastern Europe.

In the mid-1950s, the superpowers made several attempts to negotiate their differences. Although mutually suspicious, U.S. president Dwight Eisenhower and Soviet leader Nikita Khrushchev met at a summit conference in Geneva in 1955. The two men agreed to end their occupation of Austria, restore it to independence, and guarantee its neutrality. The Soviet Union also recognized the West German government. The talks had been productive, and they opened the way for future, periodic summit meetings between leaders of the superpowers.

After 1960, however, relations took a turn for the worse, and for a time the two superpowers appeared headed toward nuclear confrontation. In May 1960 the Soviet Union shot down a U.S. high-altitude spy plane (U-2) flying over Soviet territory. The subsequent diplomatic furor, to say nothing of the embarrassment to the U.S. government, led to the cancellation of a planned Eisenhower-Khrushchev summit. It further contributed

1920	
	Fascism in Italy: Benito Mussolini
	Locarno Pact
1930	Japanese militarism and expansionism
	Manchurian incident
	Japan withdraws from League of Nations
	Personalist dictatorships in Latin America
	Nazism: Adolf Hitler becomes chancellor of Germany
	Mussolini invades Ethiopia
	Spanish Civil War: Francisco Franco
	Sino-Japanese War
	Munich Agreement
	Hitler-Stalin Nonaggression Pact
	Hitler invades Poland
1940	
	Japan attacks Pearl Harbor
	The Holocaust: Nazi genocide of Jews
	Atomic bombing of Hiroshima and Nagasaki
	United Nations charter adopted
	End of World War II; beginning of the Cold War
	Truman Doctrine and the Marshall Plan
	Soviet blockade of Berlin
	NATO formed
1950	Warsaw Pact formed
	European Economic Community (EEC) formed in western Europe
1960	
	Construction of the Berlin Wall
1970	

to the election of John F. Kennedy (1917–1963), who promised new programs to restore U.S. prestige.

In 1961 a dangerous crisis flared up in Berlin, a perennial trouble spot. Khrushchev was embarrassed by Berlin, not only because it contained a Western military garrison behind Soviet lines, but also because it was a source of worldwide ridicule, as tens of thousands of East Germans annually fled the Communist regime by crossing from East Berlin into West Berlin. The loss of people was another sore point, causing East Germany severe labor and economic problems. The Soviet Union therefore authorized the East German government to construct the Berlin Wall in August 1961. The wall prevented East Germans from escaping to the West and quickly became the symbol of the Cold War and Communist repression. Tensions mounted and additional U.S. troops were sent into Berlin. President Kennedy traveled to the city to underscore U.S. determination to protect the city, telling an excited crowd, "Ich bin ein Berliner" (I am a Berliner). Although tensions later lessened, Berlin remained a flashpoint, the only spot on the globe where U.S. and Soviet troops were face to face.

Despite these events, Europe saw no major war in the decades following World War II. All nations understood that an attack on a European ally of a superpower meant a general nuclear war. No disastrous miscalculations occurred, because the leaders on both sides had a rather clear idea of each other's interests. As a result, Europeans spent the postwar period worrying that the leaders of the superpowers would lose perspective and destroy them. At the same time, western European economies not only recovered from the devastation of World War II but enjoyed unprecedented levels of prosperity. In comparison, the economies of eastern Europe stagnated, especially in nations with rigid centralized planning. The retreat of Soviet power from eastern Europe resulted in a treaty between the four wartime allies and the two German governments in 1990. The allies agreed to give up their rights in Berlin and Germany and to permit the unification of Germany. Reunited Germany would remain a member of NATO.

Summary and Comparisons

The interwar years saw the rise of totalitarian dictatorships with their doctrinaire ideologies and radical social programs. These regimes varied, yet also shared common traits. Totalitarianism first appeared with the Bolshevik revolution in Russia. Paradoxically, the Soviet regime had much in common with the most anticommunist authoritarian state, Nazi Germany—brutal suppression of dissidents; a single ideology; total domination of the government by the party; a cult of the leader; and an aggressive foreign policy designed to spread the nation's ideology by intimidation or conquest.

The two ideologies, however, were diametrically opposed. Nazism supported an ethnic elite, whereas communism advocated egalitarianism, aiming, at least in theory, for a classless society. The Nazis used their power to induce all classes to cooperate and work in harmony. The Communists, by contrast, sought to eliminate the aristocracy and the bourgeoisie and set up a dictatorship of the proletariat. Finally, the Nazis permitted capitalism and protected the possessions of the landowning class and the industrialists. The Communists suppressed capitalism, nationalizing the land and other means of production.

Among the leading totalitarian states—Japan, Italy, and Germany—the notion grew that armed might could rectify long-standing grievances. Their pact in 1937, the Berlin-Rome-Tokyo Axis, was designed to ensure that each power obtained what it wished, namely, territories to provide space for overcrowding at home as well as badly needed raw materials. As justification for their aggression, they claimed they were out to stop the advances of communism. All respected force and were contemptuous of democratic governments and the League of Nations, which had been set up for the peaceful resolution of international differences.

The first breach in the system of collective security occurred in 1931–1932 when Japan seized Manchuria. The Japanese viewed themselves as superior to other Asians (the same way the Nazis considered Germans the most outstanding people in the world) and believed they were entitled to rule over other peoples. The weakness of the League of Nations was revealed when the democracies took no preventive action and merely scolded Japan.

The failure of the League of Nations to restrain Japan encouraged Italy's Mussolini, who attempted to conquer Ethiopia in 1935 and two years later sent troops to help Franco, an ideological kindred, win the Spanish Civil War. Hitler followed suit, convinced that the time was ripe for a revision of the Treaty of Versailles and for Germany's return to world power status. He first remilitarized the Rhineland, next annexed Austria, and finally dismembered Czechoslovakia at Munich in 1938. In each instance the Western democracies countered totalitarian aggression with a policy of appeasement. Struggling against unemployment and a host of other problems caused by the Great Depression, they were ready to do almost anything to prevent another major war. But appeasement only encouraged further aggression and in the end did not avert war.

World War II differed from World War I in a number of respects. Whereas the underlying and immediate origins of World War I were complex, World War II resulted primarily from the deliberate aggression of the totalitarian states. The first great conflict was static and was fought mainly in the trenches. The second was fully mobile, fought over a greater area of the globe, and more mechanized and scientific in character. In World War I most of the casualties were soldiers, but in World War II as many civilians as troops were killed.

The starting dates for World War II differed in Asia and Europe. Japan struck first by invading China in 1937. China's determined resistance and Japan's inability to bring its campaign in China to a victorious end led to an expansion of the war in Asia. In 1941 Japan's surprise attack on the U.S. fleet at Pearl Harbor in Hawaii and its invasion of British and Dutch colonial holdings in Southeast Asia broadened the war in Asia to include the Western powers.

In the meantime, Hitler concluded a nonaggression pact with the Soviet Union. With his eastern front secure, Hitler attacked Poland in 1939, ignoring British and French warnings that such action would lead to war against them as well. Hitler's military won spectacular successes in eastern and western Europe in 1939 and 1940, until only Great Britain remained. The energetic and inspirational British prime minister, Winston Churchill, doggedly determined to keep on fighting. Hitler's invasion of the Soviet Union in 1941 and Japan's attack against the United States at Pearl Harbor drove these two nations into the conflict on the side of Great Britain. In arduous campaigns the Allies gradually gained the upper hand, first defeating Italy, next Nazi Germany, and then Japan.

The peacemakers after World War II did not follow the same route as their 1919 counterparts. No one in 1945 appeared with a program remotely similar to Wilson's Fourteen Points. The idealism that had heralded the Paris Peace Conference was conspicuously absent in 1945. Moreover, the victors in 1945 paused to gain perspective, unlike the proceedings in Paris, which began in 1919 within two months of the armistice. After World War II, leading Nazi and Japanese leaders were prosecuted and convicted of crimes against humanity. No such trials occurred after World War I.

The United States and the Soviet Union emerged as the two superpowers at the end of World War II. While the United States led the democratic countries of western Europe, the Soviet Union's forces occupied and dominated eastern Europe. The two blocs confronted each other in the Cold War that followed, divided by an iron curtain of Communist governments established by Soviet forces in eastern Europe. Soviet attempts to oust Western occupation forces in Berlin, destabilize Turkey, and aid Communist rebels in Greece led to determined U.S. responses in the Berlin airlift, the Truman Doctrine, and the formation of NATO, which checked Soviet expansion. Economic aid in the form of the Marshall Plan, followed by the formation of the Common Market, revived western Europe's economy and made communism unattractive to most people in that region. The Soviet Union countered with the Warsaw Pact of eastern European nations.

Selected Sources

Baer, George W. *The Test Case: Italy, Ethiopia, and the League of Nations.* 1976. A discussion of the failure of international peacekeeping efforts in the face of totalitarian aggression.

*Bell, P. M. H. *The Origins of the Second World War in Europe.* 1987. A clear survey suitable for undergraduates.

*Benedict, Ruth. *The Chrysanthemum and the Sword: Patterns of Japanese Culture.* 1946. A description of Japanese society prior to World War II by a U.S. anthropologist.

*Bullock, Alan. *Hitler: A Study in Tyranny.* Revised ed. 1962. A good account of the Hitler years as well as of the man.

*Butow, Robert J. C. *Tojo and the Coming of the War.* 1961. An excellent study of Tojo's role in leading Japan to war.

*Carr, Raymond. *The Spanish Tragedy: The Civil War in Perspective.* 1977. A thoughtful analysis of the Spanish Civil War and foreign intervention.

*Chang, Iris. *The Rape of Nanking: The Forgotten Holocaust of World War II.* 1997. Excellent book documenting the horrors Japanese soldiers inflicted on the people of Nanking.

*Clark, Alan. *Barbarossa.* 1965. A lively account of the gigantic struggle between the Soviet Union and Germany.

Costello, John. *The Pacific War.* 1981. An authoritative account of the war between the United States and Japan.

Dulles, Foster Rhea. *American Policy toward Communist China, 1949–1969.* 1972. A good analysis.

Feis, Herbert. *Japan Surrendered: The Atomic Bomb and the End of the War in the Pacific.* 1961. A good account of the end of the war against Japan.

———. *From Trust to Terror: The Onset of the Cold War, 1945–1950.* 1970. An important general treatment.

Gilbert, Martin. *The Holocaust: A History of the Jews of Europe during the Second World War.* 1985. A detailed and well-researched account.

*Hemingway, Ernest. *For Whom the Bell Tolls.* 1940. A novel about the Spanish Civil War by one who took part in it. Also a film.

*Hsiung, James C., and Steven I. Levine, eds. *China's Bitter Victory: The War with Japan, 1937–1945.* 1992. Many experts contributed to this multifaceted book on the most devastating war in Chinese history.

*Iriye, Akira. *The Origins of the Second World War in Asia and the Pacific.* 1987. A clear account.

*Keegan, John. *The Second World War.* 1990. A balanced and well-written study with superb maps and plentiful illustrations.

*Monsarrat, Nicholas. *The Cruel Sea.* 1951. An enthralling novel depicting the destroyer-submarine struggle in the Atlantic. Also a motion picture. Should be seen in conjunction with the German motion picture *Das Boot.*

Rowse, A. L. *Appeasement: A Study in Political Decline, 1933–1939.* 1963. A critical look at the liberal appeasement of aggression in the 1930s.

Sih, Paul K. T., ed. *Nationalist China during the Sino-Japanese War, 1937–1945.* 1970. Many experts contributed to this study of China during the war.

*Smith, Bradley. *Reaching Judgment at Nuremberg.* 1979. An insightful look at the corruption of Nazism. Also a motion picture, *Judgment at Nuremberg.*

*Speer, Albert. *Inside the Third Reich.* 1970. A fascinating biography by Hitler's friend, architect, and minister of armaments. Written during the author's twenty-year imprisonment after his conviction at the Nuremberg trials.

*Taylor, A. J. P. *The Origins of the Second World War.* 1962. The controversial assertion by a noted scholar that Hitler was not the prime instigator of World War II.

*———. *The War Lords.* 1977. A description of the men who directed World War II.

Toland, John. *The Rising Sun: Decline and Fall of the Japanese Empire, 1936–1945.* 1971. A classic on Japanese imperialism leading to defeat.

Triumph of the Will. Riefenstahl, Leni, director. 1935. A striking film of a Nazi rally showing the wide support for Hitler among Germans. Regarded by many as the greatest propaganda film ever produced.

*Wiskemann, Elizabeth. *Fascism in Italy.* 1970. A short, well-written analysis of Mussolini's regime.

*Available in paperback.

Internet Links

Benito Mussolini: What Is Fascism? (1932)
http://www.fordham.edu/halsall/mod/mussolini-fascism.html
An article defining fascism, written by its founding father (and G. Gentile) for the Italian Encyclopedia.

Cybrary of the Holocaust
http://remember.org/
This thorough site provides memoirs of survivors, interviews with experts, historians' analyses, photographic images, bibliography, all manner of documents, and many hyperlinks.

Hiroshima Survivors
http://ftp.std.com/obi/Hiroshima.Survivors
A collection of interviews with sixteen survivors of the bombing of Hiroshima.

The Nanking Massacre, 1937
http://www.fordham.edu/halsall/mod/nanking.html
This eyewitness account by a *New York Times* reporter tells of the Japanese occupation of the capital of the Republic of China and the horrendous atrocities committed by the invading army.

Nuremberg War Crimes Trials
http://www.yale.edu/lawweb/avalon/imt/imt.htm
This vast website, containing key trial documents, is in the process of making available online all twenty-five volumes of the official proceedings.

Winston Churchill: The "Iron Curtain" Speech
http://www.northpark.edu/acad/history/Classes/Sources/Churchill.html
The famous 1946 speech in which Churchill warned the world that "an iron curtain has descended across the Continent."

World War II Timeline Starting Page
http://ac.acusd.edu/History/WW2Timeline/start.html
One of the best online collections of timelines for the war years; covers events nearly day by day with links to images and maps.

Global Conflicts during the Cold War: 1945–1989

16

THE TRIUMPH OF NATIONALIST STRUGGLES FOR INDEPENDENCE
Imperialism in Decline
The British Empire in Asia Collapses
Independent African Nations
The Superpowers and the New Nations

THE COLD WAR IN ASIA AND AFRICA
Communism Wins in China
The Korean War
Escalating War in Vietnam
The Cold War in Africa

CONFLICT IN LATIN AMERICA
Demographic, Economic, and Social Trends
Marxism in a Cold War Context: Castro's Revolution in Cuba
The Cuban Missile Crisis
The United States Combats Marxism throughout Latin America
The Rise of Representative Government in Latin America

SHIFTING WORLD ALLIANCES
The United States since 1960
The Soviet Union from Khrushchev to Gorbachev
European Political Trends
Economic Recovery and Prosperity
Superpower Confrontations and Détentes
The Arms Race and Disarmament

SUMMARY AND COMPARISONS

I say to you today, my friends, so even though we face the difficulties of today and tomorrow, I still have a dream. It is a dream deeply rooted in the American dream. I have a dream that one day this nation will rise up and live out the true meaning of its creed—that we hold these truths to be self-evident, that all men are created equal.

I have a dream that one day on the red hills of Georgia, the sons of former slaves and the sons of former slave-owners will be able to sit down together at the table of brotherhood. . . .

I have a dream that my four little children will one day live in a nation where they will not be judged by the color of their skin but by the content of their character. I have a dream today! . . .

*When we allow freedom to ring, when we let it ring from every village and every hamlet, from every state and every city, we will be able to speed up that day when all of God's children—black men and white men, Jews and Gentiles, Protestants and Catholics—will be able to join hands and sing in the words of the old Negro spiritual, "Free at last, free at last; thank God Almighty, we are free at last."**

*Martin Luther King Jr., "I Have a Dream," August 28, 1963, in David J. Garrow, *Bearing the Cross: Martin Luther King, Jr., and the Southern Christian Leadership Conference* (New York: William Morrow, 1986), pp. 283–284.

In his "I Have a Dream" speech, delivered at the March on Washington in the summer of 1963, Martin Luther King Jr., one of the key leaders of the civil rights movement in the United States, movingly summarized the desire of men and women around the world for equal rights and opportunity. King and others in the movement used many of the nonviolent tactics—boycotts, strikes, sit-ins, marches—advocated by Mohandas Gandhi in his struggle for Indian independence a generation earlier. During the 1950s and 1960s many African Americans struggled to end racial segregation and gain equal access to education, the political system, restaurants, transportation, and a host of other services. The refusal of Rosa Parks, exhausted after a hard day of work, to give up her seat on a public bus to a white man in Birmingham, Alabama, in 1955 spurred a wave of protests and galvanized a generation to demand legislative changes to ensure equal rights. Although racism has remained a persistent problem in the United States and elsewhere, the civil rights movement ended many of the worst abuses of segregation and secured legislative guarantees for equal rights. It inspired human rights advocates among women, other people of color, homosexuals, and many others.

King's demands for freedom were echoed throughout Asia and Africa, where most nations gained their independence from Western imperial powers after World War II, unfortunately often only by violent confrontations and warfare. This chapter traces how the realization of independence in Asian and African nations changed the global balance of power. Many of the newly independent nations faced daunting problems of reconstruction and economic development, and many fell to military dictatorships. Many also struggled to maintain their cultural and religious identities while adapting to Western technology. This chapter also describes the Cold War struggles between the superpowers and their involvement in Asia, Africa, and Latin America, where one of the most dangerous Cold War confrontations—the Cuban Missile Crisis—occurred. Finally, it traces the shifting nature of the economic, political, and military relationships between the Western bloc led by the United States and the Eastern bloc dominated by the Soviet Union through the 1980s.

The Triumph of Nationalist Struggles for Independence

*Long years ago we made a tryst with destiny, and now the time comes when we shall redeem our pledge, not wholly or in full measure, but very substantially. At the stroke of midnight hour, when the world sleeps, India will awake to life and freedom. A moment comes, which comes but rarely in history, when we step out from the old to the new, when an age ends, and when the soul of a nation, long suppressed, finds utterance. . . . The achievement we celebrate today is but a step, an opening of opportunity, to the greater triumphs and achievements that await us.**

*Jawaharlal Nehru on the occasion of Indian independence, 1947, in Michael Brecher, *Nehru: A Political Biography* (London: Oxford University Press, 1961), p. 137.

The eloquence of Jawaharlal Nehru (1889–1964), the first prime minister of independent India, was more than political rhetoric. Nehru's statement celebrated the declaration of Indian independence at the stroke of midnight, August 15, 1947. Few realized that this momentous event heralded the end of colonization and the onset of independence for African and Asian nations. In the twenty years that followed, many leaders across Asia and Africa echoed Nehru's sentiments.

Imperialism in Decline

The scope of the postwar independence movement can scarcely be exaggerated. In the three decades after 1945, Western nations lost their empires in Asia and Africa. In a single generation, former colonies, some of which had been ruled by Europeans for nearly five centuries, gained their independence, and dozens of new nations emerged.

There were precursors to the postwar independence movement, particularly in the evolution of the British Commonwealth of Nations since the second half of the nineteenth century. The Act of Westminster, passed by the British Parliament in 1931, made official the de facto independence of white-dominated dominions of Canada, Australia, New Zealand, and South Africa. The voluntary affiliation of these nations in the Commonwealth under a single monarch did not limit their self-rule. France and the Netherlands, however, did not follow suit in establishing a similar arrangement with their colonies before World War II.

The pattern by which former colonies attained their independence was not uniform, but important similarities existed. Western-educated Asians and Africans led most anticolonial movements. Often these nationalist leaders were highly charismatic figures who embraced and utilized Western ideas, institutions, and weapons to oust the imperial powers.

Some independence movements succeeded in a relatively peaceful fashion. Exhausted by World War II, some European nations found it increasingly hard to justify imperialism and were sometimes glad to rid themselves of colonial entanglements with a minimum of struggle. Others refused to abandon their vested interests abroad.

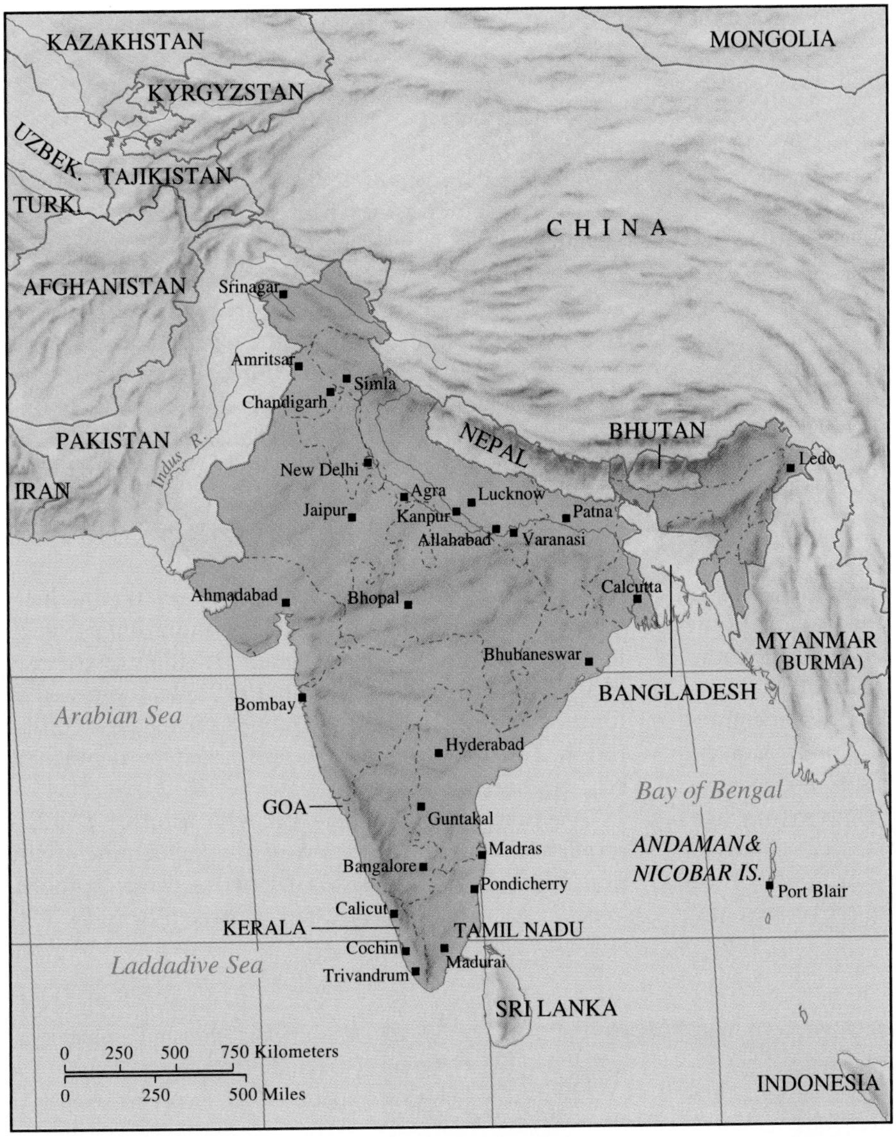

Map 16.1 Present-Day South Asia. In 1947 India and Pakistan obtained independence from Great Britain. Subsequently, Pakistan broke into two separate nations, Pakistan in the west and Bangladesh in the east. The India-Pakistan border remained tense, particularly in the disputed area of Kashmir. China also extended its influence and control along the northern border into Tibet.

The fiercest resistance to independence tended to come in regions where Westerners had settled in substantial numbers. Thus, in regions such as Rhodesia (present-day Zimbabwe), Algeria, and South Africa, African nationalist leaders sometimes had to resort to violence such as bombings and guerrilla warfare to gain freedom. In French-ruled Indochina and Algeria, Portuguese-ruled Mozambique, and the Belgian Congo, indigenous peoples fought protracted wars of liberation to throw off the colonial yoke.

The British Empire in Asia Collapses

The Western-ruled empires that encompassed all of South and Southeast Asia (except Thailand) gave rise to some of the world's first post–World War II independence movements. In the Indian subcontinent and in much of colonial Southeast Asia, militant and sometimes violent mass movements were required to expel the Western imperialists.

The inhabitants of British India, the jewel in Queen Victoria's crown a century earlier, were the first to gain independence. Indian demands, first for autonomy and then for complete independence, had intensified during the twentieth century. After World War I, the Indian National Congress, under Mohandas K. Gandhi's leadership, instituted a series of strikes, economic boycotts, and demonstrations against the British. After World War II, the newly elected British Labour government, long opposed to imperial entanglements, negotiated the final transition to Indian independence.

Both the British and Gandhi originally hoped to achieve independence for a united subcontinent. Unfortunately, religious tensions between Hindus and Muslims, long antedating the arrival of the British, made such a postimperial union impracticable. Muslims feared discrimination in a unified state in which Hindus would heavily outnumber them. A virtual civil war erupted, and mass migrations took place as Hindus rushed toward the safety of Hindu-dominated regions and Muslims moved toward Muslim-dominated areas. Gandhi, the spiritual leader of the nationalist movement, and Jawaharlal Nehru, its tactician, eventually had to settle for the establishment of two separate states: India, which was mostly Hindu, and Pakistan, which was created for the Muslims out of predominantly Muslim regions in the northwestern and northeastern sectors of the subcontinent. Finally, on August 15, 1947, the independence of the two states was proclaimed. Only a few months later, in 1948, a fanatical Hindu, who opposed his efforts to negotiate with the Muslims, assassinated Gandhi.

Nehru became the first prime minister of India. He immediately faced the tasks of quelling the continued border strife with neighboring Pakistan and raising the standard of living for the rapidly growing Indian population. Under the provisions of its 1950 constitution, India became a federal republic and the world's largest democracy. Nehru continued as prime minister until his death in 1964, and his Congress party remained the dominant political force for over forty years.

In 1966, two years after Nehru's death, his daughter Indira Nehru Gandhi (1917–1984; no relation to Mohandas K. Gandhi), was elected prime minister. Following a stunning electoral victory in 1971, Gandhi pushed through a number of authoritarian measures and banned opposition political parties for two years. Gandhi and many within the Congress party firmly supported equality for women and struggled against the oppression of women and children, both of whom were frequently exploited as free labor. Such social policies, particularly a massive state-sponsored program for birth control, alienated many Indians. Deeply entrenched traditions and conservatism, particularly in the countryside where most Indians continued to live, made implementation of government laws and policies difficult. Gandhi lost the election of 1977, but returned to power in the 1980 elections.

In spite of notable strides toward industrialization and increased agricultural productivity, India, with its growing population, continued to face formidable economic problems and troubling sectarian disputes among its many religious and ethnic minorities, especially the Sikhs. After Indira Gandhi's assassination by her Sikh bodyguard in 1984, her son Rajiv was elected Prime minister, thereby continuing the Congress party's and the Nehru-Gandhi family's domination over Indian politics. Voters disgruntled over charges of corruption, inefficiency, and nepotism voted Rajiv Gandhi out of office in 1989, and he was assassinated by Tamil extremists while campaigning for office in 1990. However, except for the two years that Mrs. Gandhi suspended the constitution, India continued to be governed by democratically elected politicians.

Pakistan, too, was plagued with internal political problems. With the partition of the subcontinent, the new Muslim state consisted of two separate sections, West Pakistan and East Pakistan, separated by India. Dif-

AP/Wide World Photos

Jawaharlal Nehru and Mohandas K. Gandhi. Here the leaders of India's independence movement enjoy a relaxed moment on the eve of their country's liberation in 1947. Nehru, a longtime follower of the immensely popular Mahatma, adopted a more formal style of leadership as the first prime minister of the new nation.

ferent ethnic and language groups with little in common except Islam populated East and West Pakistan. East Pakistan, densely populated and extremely poor, was neglected by ruling West Pakistani leaders, and this fueled its political and economic grievances. Mohammed Ali Jinnah (1887–1948), the father of Pakistan, died before a satisfactory constitution could be devised. His weak successors had to contend with land and border disputes with India and Afghanistan. In the face of these problems, the Pakistani military staged a coup in 1958.

The military, heavily dominated by officers from West Pakistan, made no attempt to redress East Pakistani grievances. As a result, serious riots erupted in East Pakistan; and the Awami League, an East Pakistani political party, moved for secession and independence. Indian intervention allowed the party to form the independent state of Bangladesh in 1971. Since its independence, Bangladesh, one of the poorest nations in the world, has suffered recurring floods, famines, political upheavals, and military takeovers.

Under Zulfiqar Ali Bhutto (1929–1979), Pakistan, now confined only to the western sector, enjoyed seven years of civilian rule during the 1970s, but Bhutto was overthrown and executed in a military coup d'état led by General Zia al-Haq. In domestic policy, General Zia instituted stricter adherence to Islamic law, but in foreign relations he maintained a close alliance with the United States. After Zia died in a mysterious helicopter crash, Bhutto's daughter Benazir, heading the Pakistan People's party, was elected prime minister in 1988. The popular Bhutto moved to liberalize the political life of the nation and to make social and economic reforms, but Pakistan continued to face daunting economic problems. In addition, Bhutto and her family were accused of massive corruption and were ousted from office in the 1990s. Benazir Bhutto was the first female head of government in a predominantly Muslim state; indeed women had been elected to the highest political office in few nations at the time. Subsequently, female prime ministers were also elected to office in both Bangladesh and Turkey, two other Muslim states.

Meanwhile, like India and Pakistan, British colonies in Southeast Asia had secured their independence. Following successful fights against guerrilla nationalists, Great Britain granted independence to Burma (present-day Myanmar) and Ceylon (present-day Sri Lanka) in 1948 and to Malaya (present-day Malaysia) in 1957. The most prosperous of these former colonies was the great port and former British naval base of Singapore at the tip of the Malay Peninsula. Singapore, which had a Chinese majority, acquired independence in 1959.

In sharp contrast to the British, the Dutch attempted to retain control of Indonesia. This proved futile, and following a revolt led by Achmad Sukarno (1901–1970), the Dutch granted independence to Indonesians in 1949. After bloody clashes between the strongly entrenched Communist party and the army, Sukarno was ousted from power by General Suharto (1921–) in 1967 in a bloody coup in

Indira Gandhi. Here Indira Gandhi meets with British prime minister Margaret Thatcher outside 10 Downing Street, the residence of British prime ministers. Although Thatcher was politically conservative and Gandhi was pro-Soviet, both were dynamic, forceful leaders.

which hundreds of thousands were killed. Suharto's military dictatorship continued to rule Indonesia until 1998.

The struggle for independence in Indochina was a long and bloody one. The war in Indochina also became part of the Cold War in Asia and will therefore be discussed later in this chapter.

Unlike the situation in Indonesia or Indochina, the Philippines obtained full independence peacefully from the United States in 1946. In the face of a protracted insurgency by Communist rebels, Ferdinand Marcos, who had been elected president in 1965, established martial law. The Marcos regime engaged in widespread nepotism and corruption, allowing the urban middle class and Marcos supporters to prosper while many Filipinos suffered from mounting poverty. As his health failed in the 1980s, Marcos faced a growing opposition movement led by Corazon Aquino (1933–), the widow of a Marcos opponent who had been assassinated. Following allegations of election fraud and massive demonstrations, a military coup ousted Marcos and democracy was restored under the leadership of Aquino. Subsequently, however, democratically elected governments failed to address the ongoing problems of poverty, land reform, and urban slums.

Finally, many Pacific islands also achieved independence in the postwar years. However, some enclaves of Western colonialism have remained, and France, Great Britain, and the United States have all retained a military and administrative presence on scattered Pacific island chains.

Independent African Nations

As they did in Asia, European nations gradually granted independence to their African colonies following World War II. In 1956, the French, suffering from a recent defeat in Indochina and facing a mounting war in neighboring Algeria, granted independence to Morocco and Tunisia. However, they were absolutely determined to retain control of Algeria, which they had held since 1830 and where many French colonists had settled. The French also sought to retain control over the potential wealth of Algeria's petroleum and mineral deposits.

In 1954, the Algerian National Liberation Front (FLN) launched dozens of attacks against French installations throughout the country, and a long and bloody struggle ensued. The French army responded to Algerian guerrilla attacks and urban terrorism by bombing villages, removing people from the countryside into fenced camps, and torturing FLN suspects or sympathizers. The French settlers organized their own terrorist group, the Secret Army Organization (OAS), which killed many Algerians.

The French populace was divided over the issue of Algerian independence, as the people of the United States would later be over Vietnam. After General Charles de Gaulle (1890–1970) became leader of France in 1958, he toured war-torn Algeria and concluded that although France might be able to gain a military victory, in the long run Algeria must be accorded independence. He initiated protracted negotiations with FLN leaders, many of whom were in French prisons.

Meanwhile, the fighting continued to escalate as both sides sought to improve their bargaining positions

"Algérie Française!"

"All-that-France-has-done-in-Algeria" (the hospitals, the roads, the port facilities, the big towns, the beginnings of an industry, and a quarter of the schools that are needed) and "All-that-France-hasn't-done-in-Algeria" (the remaining three quarters of the necessary schools, other industries, and an agricultural plan with the agrarian reform and the technical experts it will call for) form together a sort of explosive compound, to the destructive force of which our accomplishments contribute no less powerfully than our misdeeds.

*And now that the good and the evil that we have done have fused to produce one of the most terrifying time-bombs in the world, quite a number of Frenchmen, it must be admitted, cherish the daydream of leaving Algeria and the Algerians to sort out their own problems as best they can. Well, we undertook to solve those problems, and they are still soluble—at an enormous effort, but not one beyond our means. Without our aid, what ever happens, they will never be solved.**

In the above excerpt, Germaine Tillion, a French anthropologist and member of the French resistance during World War II, expressed her hopes for a resolution to the long and vicious Algerian war. From 1934 to 1940, Tillion worked on scientific missions in Algeria. Although she recognized the shortcomings of French policies in Algeria, she remained convinced that Algeria was part of France and should remain so for the mutual benefit of the French and Algerian people. In this belief she echoed the rallying cry "Algérie Française," or "Algeria is France," which became the slogan for all those seeking a French victory in Algeria. Nevertheless, protracted negotiations between France under the leadership of General Charles de Gaulle and the FLN led to Algerian independence in 1962.

* Germaine Tillion, *Algeria: The Realities* (New York: Knopf, 1958), p. 69.

in the field. The negotiations dragged on until 1962, when Algeria gained its independence. The new government, headed by Ahmed Ben Bella (1919–), faced the formidable task of rebuilding a largely devastated nation. A million Algerians had died in the war, while many others had been forcibly uprooted from their homes, which were then destroyed. Although revenues from a growing petroleum industry helped bolster the economy, successive Algerian governments had to cope with a rapidly growing population, high unemployment, particularly among the young, and declining agricultural output. Ironically, France remained Algeria's major trading partner. Internationally, Algeria took a leadership role among Third World nations. In times of crisis its nonaligned leaders often served as negotiators between Western nations and Arab, Muslim, or African states.

The emergence of independent states in sub-Saharan Africa, most of which was ruled by the British, the French, the Portuguese, and the Belgians, differed markedly from the struggles and independence of states in most of Asia. As the imperial powers gained control in sub-Saharan Africa, they had carved out dozens of small states, many of which had not been independent political entities prior to the imperial age. As a result, the independent nations in Africa—in contrast to those in Asia—often were new political creations that did not have the long national history of their Asian counterparts. In addition, in contrast to Asia, whites had settled in some areas of Africa. These settlers often waged protracted and tenacious struggles to retain their privileged positions and to prevent majority black rule. The following description of African independence struggles will in general follow a geographic pattern from largely French-held western Africa to largely British-dominated eastern Africa and then to central and southern Africa, where the struggles for independence were particularly violent and protracted.

The French controlled a wide band of colonies, collectively known as French West Africa and French Equatorial Africa, that ran south of the Sahara from the Atlantic east to the borders of Egypt and the Sudan. By the mid-twentieth century, Africans in these areas were actively

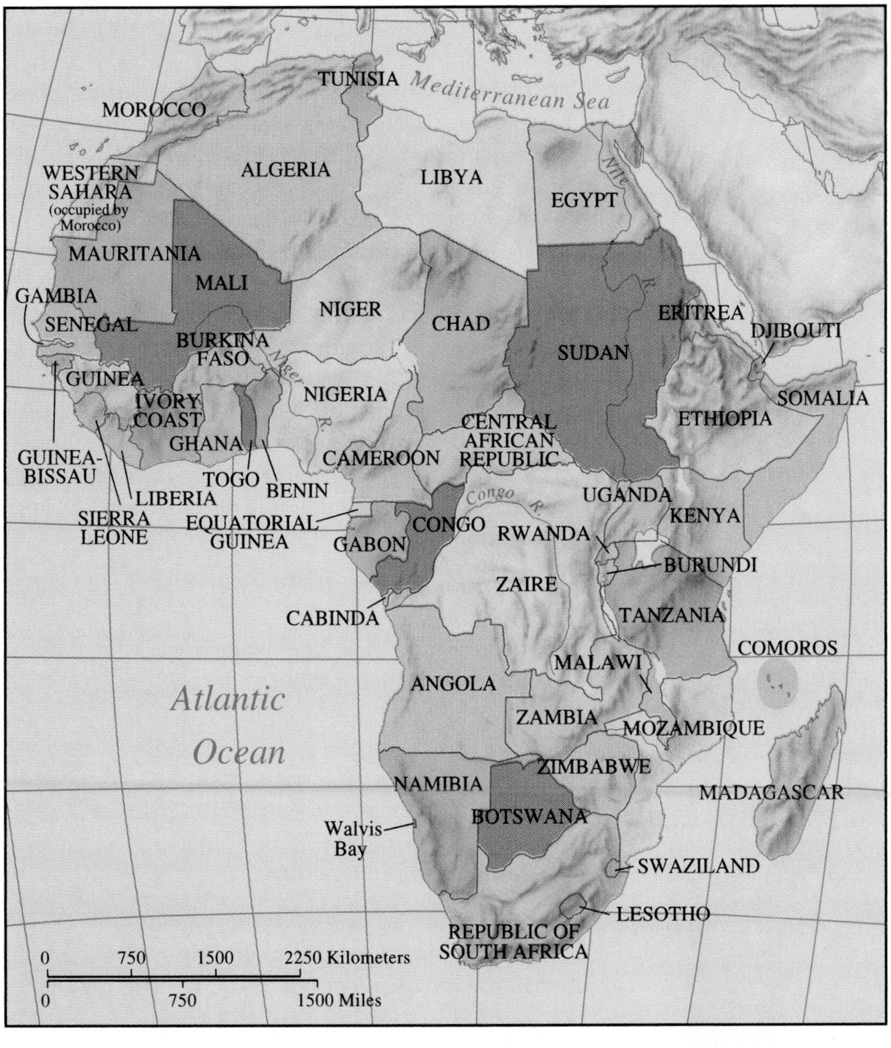

Map 16.2 Africa after World War II. This map depicts the results of the independence movements in northern and central Africa in the 1950s and 1960s and in southern Africa in the 1970s. European powers departed peacefully from their overwhelmingly black colonies, but they had to be pushed out by guerrilla warfare from areas that contained a minority of white settlers. French forces remained by invitation in some former French colonies, and Cuban troops arrived in two instances to support Marxist interests in the Cold War.

pursuing independence. Felix Houphouet-Boigny (1905–1993), a black African planter, doctor, and politician from the small but relatively prosperous Ivory Coast, was one of the most successful and long-lived leaders of the movement for independence in the French colonies. Having served in French governments in Paris, he was an experienced political leader. Together with other African leaders, he organized a West African independence party and worked with liberal and socialist politicians in Paris to end French rule in the area. This objective was achieved with little violence. After a referendum in 1958, the French government under de Gaulle granted limited freedom to most of the colonies, while France retained some political and economic control. The colony of Guinea, under the socialist leader Ahmed Sékou Touré (1922–1984), however, voted for complete independence. In 1960 the rest of French West Africa and French Equatorial Africa secured independence, as did Madagascar, an island off the eastern coast of Africa.

Great Britain's African colonies after World War II consisted of a scattering of territories along the southern edge of French West Africa and a band of colonies down the length of East Africa. With the exception of Kenya, leaders of liberation movements won independence for their countries largely without armed conflict.

Ghana, formerly called the Gold Coast, was the first black colony in Africa to be liberated. Kwame Nkrumah (1909–1972), the leader of Ghana's drive for self-government, had studied in Great Britain and the United States. On his return to the Gold Coast in 1947, he rallied people behind the Convention People's party (CPP), a grassroots, popular African liberation party. Boycotts, strikes, and other measures brought Ghana independence in 1957. Once in power, Nkrumah set the tone for many postindependence African leaders. He created a cult of personality, becoming president for life in 1960, and made the CPP the only legal party. Increasingly, independent African states became one-man dictatorships, one-party states, or military regimes.

In 1960 Nigeria, a large federated state, gained independence from Great Britain. Its petroleum revenues soon made Nigeria comparatively prosperous economically, but internal divisions culminated in 1967 in the attempt of the Igbo peoples in southeastern Nigeria to secede from the union and form the independent nation of Biafra. A violent civil war raged until 1970, when Biafra admitted defeat, and programs for reconstruction began. As in many former British and French colonies, military coups were punctuated by intermittent returns to democracy, as successive governments of Nigeria grappled with persistent economic problems. (The economic and social problems faced by African nations will be described in Chapter 17.)

Two of Great Britain's holdings in East Africa, Tanganyika (present-day Tanzania; this former German colony had been mandated to Britain after World War I) and Uganda, achieved independence during 1961 and 1962 with relatively little violence. In neighboring Kenya, however, the Mau Mau liberation movement was forced to resort to arms in order to dislodge the British settlers who had taken large tracts of the best agricultural land in the Kenyan highlands. Although the Western press greatly exaggerated the extent of the Mau Mau's attacks against the British, mounting violence did hasten Great Britain's moves to withdraw from Kenya. Politically, Kenyan men and women rallied behind Jomo Kenyatta (c. 1897–1978) and the Kenya African Union and sang nationalist songs such as the following:

The white community are foreigners
This land they must quit
And where will you go, their sympathizers
When all the Kikuyu gather?

* * *

We are in every place
The time is flying and never retreats
Our time is flying and never retreats
Our cry is for education
We want our children to learn
Now when there is time.

Faced with armed and political opposition, Great Britain granted Kenya independence in 1963. Kenyatta, a charis-

Jomo Kenyatta. Here Jomo Kenyatta, the Kenyan nationalist leader (in white pants), alights from a truck while in custody during the Mau Mau trials in Kenya. Kenyatta led his nation until his death in 1978.

J. Arya/Camera Press Ltd., London

Independence Must Be Won

Africa will tell the West that today it desires the rehabilitation of Africa, a return to the roots, a revalorization of moral values. The African personality must be expressed: that is the meaning of our policy of positive neutrality. Africa will have no blocs such as you have in Europe. . . .

We have absolutely no intention of letting ourselves be guided by any ideology whatsoever. We have our own ideology, a strong, noble ideology which is the affirmation of the African personality.

We refuse assimilation because assimilation means depersonalizing the African and Africa. So to ally ourselves with this or that bloc, this or that ideology means abandoning our African personality. Never. The imperialists should know that if their policy of assimilating and depersonalizing Africa has succeeded elsewhere, in the other former . . . British, Portuguese, and French colonies, it won't succeed in the Congo. . . . I am convinced that in one month or two you are all going to find honest, capable, competent civil servants throughout the country. There are even some traditional chiefs who are capable; they are illiterate, but tomorrow they will be excellent administrators. . . .

We are going to protect all the citizens. We do not want a bourgeois government that lives at a distance. We are going to go down among the people, speak with the people every time.

*Government policy will be none other than that of the people. It is the people who dictate our actions, and we operate according to the interests and aspirations of the people. Independence is the beginning of a real struggle. . . . Independence must be won for it to be real.**

Addressing the Congolese people, Patrice Lumumba enunciated the national demands for independence from Western imperialists and expressed his inflated hopes for a bright future. Lumumba urged all Third World nations to adopt a neutral course in the Cold War and to avoid foreign entanglements that would limit their own progress. A highly charismatic speaker, Lumumba practiced a fiery brand of nationalism that was opposed by political rivals in the Congo and by foreign powers, including the United States, who feared he would institute socialism in the mineral-rich Congo. Political rivals, with the support of some Western nations, assassinated Lumumba in 1961.

*Patrice Lumumba, *La Pensée Politique de Patrice Lumumba* (Paris, 1963), reprinted in *The African Reader: Independent Africa,* ed. Wildred Cartey and Martin Kilson (New York: Random House, 1970), pp. 87–89.

matic political leader and writer, became the first president; he led Kenya until his death in 1978.

The government encouraged racial harmony among the white settler and Indian minorities and the black majority population with slogans like *harambee* (Let us pull together). During the 1960s and 1970s Kenya was also notable among the newly independent African nations for maintaining its democratic government, but by the 1980s it was dominated by one-party, one-man rule under Daniel arap Moi. Moi's suppression of all political opponents led to numerous popular demonstrations against his regime, but he tenaciously clung to power, claiming that "politics is king."

European colonial holdings in central and southern Africa included the huge Belgian Congo, two large Portuguese territories—Angola and Mozambique—and the British colonies of Northern and Southern Rhodesia. The struggles for independence in most of these colonies were protracted and violent. The Belgian Congo (later renamed Zaire), was important for its valuable copper mines in the Katanga province. At the first sign of agitation for independence, the Belgian government, fearful of becoming mired in colonial wars as France and the Dutch had been, pulled out of the Congo in 1960. Belgium had done little to prepare its colony for independence, however, and left no governmental infrastructure in place. Patrice Lumumba (1925–1961) attempted to rally all Congolese around a program of national unity and neutralism (see the accompanying box), but the Congo's vast mineral wealth attracted other industrialized nations and private corporations. Torn by civil war and troubled by interference from European nations, the Soviet Union, and the United States, Congo became the battleground for Cold War competition in Africa (discussed later in this chapter).

In contrast to Belgium's rapid pullout from the Congo, Portugal refused to consider independence for

Angola or Mozambique. Guerrilla revolts broke out in both colonies in the 1960s. In the long struggle that followed, the autocratic Portuguese government received assistance from its NATO allies, whereas the Marxist leaders of the nationalist guerrilla forces received aid from the Soviet Union's eastern European satellites and Cuba. Angola and Mozambique received their independence in 1975, aided in part by the collapse of the dictatorial government in Portugal.

In Angola, the struggle continued even after independence; the Marxist-led Angolan Liberation Movement (MPLA) was immediately engulfed in a new struggle for supremacy against other nationalist guerrillas from rival ethnic alignments. Both the Republic of South Africa and the United States supported an opposition group led by Jonas Savimbi, while Cuban military forces moved in to prop up the MPLA. After a negotiated compromise, Cuban forces and other foreign supporters, including South Africa, withdrew in the late 1980s. The continued conflicts in southern Africa and struggle for equal rights in the Union of South Africa will be described in detail in Chapter 17.

During the 1960s a similar armed struggle broke out in neighboring Namibia. This former German colony had been mandated to South Africa after World War I. Although the United Nations revoked the South African mandate over Namibia in 1966 and annually condemned its illegal occupation, the South African government refused to withdraw. As a result, a guerrilla revolt led by the South West African People's Organization (SWAPO) started against South Africa. SWAPO received the support of other independent black African nations. In the 1970s and 1980s, members of the Communist bloc supported SWAPO, and newly liberated Angola provided bases and support. South Africa moved to crush the guerrillas and conducted armed "destabilization" raids into Angola itself. In the late 1980s, a fragile cease-fire was achieved, and a negotiated settlement was reached whereby all outside forces were to be withdrawn. In 1989 Namibia had its first free elections and moved toward independence under the elected leadership of SWAPO.

The fates of the two Rhodesias were quite different. Like Kenya and Algeria, both colonies had minority populations of white settlers. As in the other areas, British colonists in the Rhodesias lobbied hard against any form of independence that would allow black majority rule. In 1964, however, the British government imposed a democratic constitution on the settlers of Northern Rhodesia; the new constitution led to the election of a black African president and to the creation of the new nation of Zambia.

White settlers in Southern Rhodesia resisted similar efforts by the British government to impose democracy and black majority rule. In 1965 the white settlers declared their own independence under the white supremacist leader Ian Smith. Only South Africa supported this minority regime. In the face of mounting guerrilla oppo-

AP/Wide World Photos

Namibians Struggle to Vote. In 1989 the first-ever elections in Namibia brought a huge voter turnout; people eagerly cast their votes for the new independent government. Here an elderly woman crawls to the voting place to cast her ballot.

sition against the regime, both Great Britain and the United States sought a negotiated settlement that would grant majority rule. Fifteen years after the whites' unilateral declaration of independence, relatively free elections were finally held, and in 1980 the black African leader Robert Mugabe (1924–) became the first prime minister of the independent nation of Zimbabwe. Thus, by the 1990s independence had been achieved in most of Africa.

The Superpowers and the New Nations

Among other major concerns, the leaders of the world's new nations faced a foreign policy problem of the first magnitude: how to relate to the Cold War confrontation between the United States and the Soviet Union, each of which was supported by a number of allies and satellites. Inevitably, both blocs pressured the recently independent nations to choose sides. The choice presented real difficulties. Both sides claimed to be opposed to imperialism, the United States pointing to its tradition of democratic self-government; the Soviet Union emphasizing the Leninist view that imperialism was a form of capitalist exploitation. Both sides had offered some support to independence movements. The United States pressured its European allies to hasten decolonization, while the Soviet Union provided material support for some guerrilla movements.

Both superpowers wanted the new nations to allow access to their natural resources, to provide sites for military bases, and to render diplomatic support in the United Nations. In return, both superpowers could offer the new nations economic and technological aid, arms, and sometimes military support in their regional struggles. Finally, both could punish nations that rejected their overtures by withdrawing aid or by supporting their enemies.

Most Asian and African countries were fearful of domination by the superpowers and were also disillusioned with both Western capitalism and Soviet communism. Many nations therefore chose to follow nonalignment, the approach taken by India early in the postwar independence era. Nehru, and subsequently the leaders of many of the new states, believed that newly independent and predominantly poor nations were more likely to retain their independence and improve their economies if they avoided firm alliances with either superpower and took stands on international issues on the basis of their own self-interest. Nehru also hoped to pressure the wealthy, industrialized nations into assisting the economic development of the poor nations, thereby achieving a more equitable distribution of goods and services around the world. Thus nonaligned nations, many of which were also part of the Third World bloc, stood apart from the so-called First World of Western nations and the Second World of the Soviet Union and its allies.

The policy of nonalignment and neutrality was formalized with the establishment of the Organization of Nonaligned States at Bandung, Indonesia, in 1955. Thereafter heads of many Asian and African nations and of some Latin American states came together for periodic discussions of common problems. Nehru, Gamal Abdul Nasser of Egypt, and Josef Tito of Yugoslavia became the prominent leaders of the nonaligned movement. In the General Assembly of the United Nations, many Asian and African nations operated as a voting bloc on key issues, where their numbers often outweighed the votes of the industrialized nations.

Some nations, such as India and Egypt, took an officially neutralist stance, but in fact followed a policy that was often pro-Soviet. This infuriated Western leaders like Eisenhower's Secretary of State, John Foster Dulles, who characterized nonalignment as "immoral." During the 1980s Jeane Kirkpatrick, U.S. ambassador to the United Nations, claimed that these nations had a decided tilt against the West and in favor of the Soviet bloc. There was some substance to this charge. India's Indira Gandhi, for example, opposed many U.S. policies and particularly objected to the close relations between the United States and Pakistan. Consequently, she tightened India's alliances with the Soviet Union.

The leaders of former colonies often resented the colonial legacy of the Western nations and indirectly the United States as leader of the Western bloc. Because most of them had no experience with Soviet imperialism, they tended to be less anti-Soviet. Cold War rivalry often moved the United States and the Soviet Union to support opposing sides in the Third World. The Soviet bloc supplied at least some military aid and training, and much rhetorical support, for antiimperialist guerrilla movements during the 1970s and 1980s. The United States, by contrast, in opposing the expansion of communism, often maintained political and economic ties with conservative, pro-Western regimes. This policy often influenced officially nonaligned nations to favor the Soviet Union. Third World leaders also criticized U.S. support for Israel and for the white minority government in South Africa.

The Cold War in Asia and Africa

In 1949 New China was founded and we peasants became masters of the country. Land reform was carried out, with feudalist land ownership abolished and farmland returned to the tillers.

In 1951 the agricultural collectivization movement got underway in my village. We first got organized into mutual-aid production teams and then into elementary agricultural co-operatives and put our farmland into public ownership. The principle of "to each according to his work" was followed.

Long Live the Victory of People's War!

It was on the basis of the lessons derived from the people's wars in China that Comrade Mao Tse-tung, using the simplest and the most vivid language, advanced the famous thesis that "political power grows out of the barrel of a gun." . . .

So long as imperialism and the system of exploitation of man by man exist, the imperialists and reactionaries will invariably rely on armed force to maintain their reactionary rule and impose war on the oppressed nations and peoples. . . .

The history of the people's war in China and other countries provides conclusive evidence that the growth of the people's revolutionary forces from weak and small beginnings into strong and large forces is a universal law of development of the class struggle, a universal law of development of the people's war.

It must be emphasized that Comrade Mao Tse-tung's theory of the establishment of rural revolutionary base areas and the encirclement of cities from the countryside is of outstanding and universal practical importance for the present revolutionary struggles of all the oppressed nations and peoples, and particularly for the revolutionary struggles of the oppressed nations and peoples in Asia, Africa and Latin America against imperialism and its lackeys.

The Chinese revolution provides a successful lesson of making a thorough-going national-democratic revolution under the leadership of the proletariat.

*Ours is the epoch in which world capitalism and imperialism are heading for their doom. . . . The new experience gained in the people's revolutionary struggles in various countries since World War II has provided continuous evidence that Mao Tse-tung's thought is a common asset of the revolutionary people of the whole world. This is the great international significance of the thought of Mao Tse-tung.**

In this article, Marshal Lin Piao, minister of defense in China and, at the time, a close ally of Mao Zedong, extolled Mao's contributions to Marxist revolutionary ideology and his impact on Third World revolutions. In the mid-1960s, when this article was written, Lin and most other revolutionaries were convinced that communism would ultimately triumph over capitalism and that peasant-led revolutions would lead to the establishment of independent socialist nations. In both the Soviet Union and China, however, the Communist party established a dictatorial regime that instituted a form of state capitalism rather than a classless society led by workers. By the 1980s both nations were moving toward privatization and free enterprise, although the Communist party retained its control over the government in China.

*Lin Piao, article distributed by official Chinese press agency, September 1965, reprinted in Henry M. Christman, *Communism in Action: A Documentary History* (New York: Bantam Books, 1969), pp. 341–347.

During those years, since everyone worked hard and the government provided the co-operative with preferential loans and farm tools, production grew rapidly. I remember my family got more than enough wheat that year. We lived quite well during those years.

In 1958 we got organized into the people's commune, which brought about some desirable changes. . . .

In 1966, the chaotic "cultural revolution" began. I could no longer collect firewood or grow melons because these were seen as capitalist undertakings. We peasants, unlike workers who have regular wages, had to work in the fields or we would have had nothing to eat. So our agricultural production continued as usual.

*In retrospect, my life improved steadily after I began working. But I always thought I could have done much better.**

*Wang Xin and Yang Xiabing, "A Peasant Maps His Road to Wealth," *Beijing Review*, 27 (November 12, 1984): 28–30, reprinted in Peter N. Stearns, ed., *Documents in World History*, vol. 2 (New York: Harper & Row, 1988), pp. 143–145.

In this reminiscence, a Chinese peasant who survived the upheavals of war and prospered under the Communist revolution described the sweeping changes in social and economic structures Mao Zedong instituted in the decades following the Communist victory in 1949. This rather positive description offers a striking comparison to the more critical account by a son of Chinese intellectuals presented in a box later in this chapter.

Mao's reliance on peasant support became the model for many Third World liberation movements and revolutions. The United States, as champion of capitalist systems, often saw these movements in Cold War terms as positive gains for communism that would benefit the Soviet Union. The United States, therefore, frequently moved to overthrow or defeat Marxist-dominated regimes in Asia and Africa.

Communism Wins in China

On October 1, 1949, Mao Zedong, the victorious Communist leader in China's civil war, proclaimed the founding of the People's Republic of China. Just as World War I had discredited the Tsarist government in Russia and brought about the triumph of communism under Lenin, World War II exhausted and discredited the Nationalist (Kuomintang) government in China and brought the Chinese Communist party (CCP) to power. Mao had expanded Marx's revolutionary theory by stressing that socialist revolutions could triumph in agricultural as well as industrial nations. Peasants as well as the proletariat could be the revolutionary vanguard. Mao worked effectively with the Chinese peasants, attending to their needs while indoctrinating and organizing them to overthrow the Nationalists. As his following grew, Mao was able, with captured Japanese equipment and some Soviet help, to move from guerrilla warfare to conventional battle tactics that finally destroyed Chiang Kai-shek's forces. Chiang went into exile on the island of Taiwan, where he proclaimed the continuation of his Nationalist government and his determination to return to the mainland in order to liberate China from the Communists.

In different ways, both superpowers misunderstood the successful peasant war in China. The United States, fearing the spread of communism, backed the anticommunist but dictatorial Chiang government. After the embittering experience of the Korean War, the United States ignored the most populous nation on earth and refused to recognize Mao's government. Until 1971 the United States vetoed all attempts to seat the People's Republic in the United Nations, hoping that Chiang could make a comeback from his refuge on the island of Taiwan.

The Soviet Union also misjudged the Chinese situation. Soviet leaders after Stalin refused to recognize Mao as the senior leader of the Communist world or to concede his claim to be the leading Marxist theoretician. The Soviet leaders insisted that Moscow should continue to be the sole interpreter of Marxian theory and viewed Maoist ideology as diversionary. The Chinese Communist government responded that it was the only truly revolutionary force and that the Soviet regime had "gone off the tracks" of true Marxism. In addition, the People's Republic demanded that the Soviet Union return the territories the tsars had taken from the Manchus in the nineteenth century. By the 1960s these issues led to growing tensions between the two great Marxist states. In 1980 China refused to renew the 1950 treaty of alliance with the Soviet Union. The Sino-Soviet border, the longest in the world, also became one of the most heavily guarded. As a result, the Soviet Union found itself facing major enemies in both Europe and Asia.

The Sino-Soviet split marked the beginning of radical changes in China. Already, since 1950 China had

A Young Man Remembers Hard Times

It was in 1960 . . . all China fell on hard times. I was almost seven. Rice, cooking oil, and soybean products were severely rationed, and meat, eggs, flour, and sugar gradually disappeared from the market completely. . . .

Father explained that the rivers and lakes had overflowed and the peasants couldn't grow anything for us to eat. "But you're lucky," he said. "You live in a big capital city, and the Party and Chairman Mao are giving you food from the storage bins. The peasants have to find a way out for themselves."

The situation dragged on and got worse, month after month, until a whole year had passed. . . .

*One day Father came home unusually silent and depressed. . . . Finally he told us that in a commune . . . to the South, nearly an entire Production Team had died of hunger, and there was no one left with enough strength to bury the bodies.**

In this excerpt Liang Heng, whose father was a reporter and whose mother was a ranking cadre in the local police, describes life in an urban area during the massive famine that afflicted vast areas of China between 1959 and 1961, the result of Mao's forcing all farmers into communes. An estimated 30 million people died as a result. Liang's memories differ markedly from the more favorable conclusions given by the peasant in the introductory excerpt.

*Liang Heng and Judith Shapiro, *Son of the Revolution* (New York: Vintage Books, 1984), pp. 17–18.

© Eastfoto

Jiang Qing on Trial. Here Jiang Qing, Mao's widow, is shown at her trial in 1980–1981, when she and her three leading supporters, called the Gang of Four, were tried for crimes committed during the Cultural Revolution. She was placed in a bamboo cage with a sign beside her reading, "The Accused."

nationalized private enterprise, collectivized the land, and gathered peasants into communes; China claimed that all these efforts represented more progress toward a Marxist utopia than Soviet collective farms. The Great Proletarian Cultural Revolution of 1966–1969 was an attempt by Mao to keep China in an extreme revolutionary condition. It was marked by massive purges of so-called revisionists that eliminated many of the best-educated and most effective leaders and brought Mao to supreme power at the expense of his more pragmatic colleagues. Mao's thoughts were embodied in the Little Red Book, which became mandatory reading for all Chinese during this period. The Cultural Revolution resulted in a cult of personality around Mao as extreme as Stalin's had been in the Soviet Union.

After Mao's death in 1976, the Communist government purged the "Gang of Four," headed by Mao's wife, who had risen to power during the Cultural Revolution and had sought to keep China evolving along radical revolutionary lines. As part of their effort to improve China's economy and acquire Western technology, the new leaders improved ties with the West, dismantled the collective farms, and increased private enterprise within China. The Communist party, however, retained strict control over the political apparatus and in the late 1980s smashed movements for increased liberalization and democracy (see Chapter 17).

The Korean War

The Korean War (1950–1953) was a conventional Great Power struggle over spheres of influence. As a result of agreements made during World War II, after the war Japan's former colony, Korea, was split into two occupation zones, divided by the 38th parallel. The Soviet zone in the north expanded its presence in Asia, while the U.S. zone in the south protected Japan. Before the occupation forces left, a Communist dictatorship was established in North Korea and an anticommunist dictatorship emerged in South Korea.

In contrast to its role in Europe, the United States was uncertain over the extent of its commitment in Asia. While the U.S. umbrella definitely covered Japan, Okinawa, and the Philippines, it was not clear whether it also extended to Taiwan, South Korea, and Southeast Asia. Believing that the United States did not intend to protect South Korea, the Soviet Union allowed North Korea to invade the south. North Korean forces quickly overran most of South Korea in June 1950 before a counteroffensive was mounted under the command of the United Nations (UN) but with mostly South Korean and U.S. soldiers. The ensuing struggle expanded the Cold War in Asia. Since South Korea and other U.S. allies in Asia were weaker than the allies of the Soviet Union, the United States had to provide both supplies and its own fighting men to prop up its allies, whereas the Soviet Union needed only to give material aid to keep its allies in the field.

As North Korean forces moved forward, the Truman administration decided that it wished to retain South Korea as a buffer to protect Japan. It exploited the temporary boycott of the United Nations by Soviet representatives and obtained UN agreement to send in U.S. troops and those of other nations to help South Korea. Under the direction of General Douglas MacArthur, UN forces, overwhelmingly U.S. and South Korean, drove the North Koreans back northward close to the border of the People's Republic. Fearing the fall of North Korea and a possible invasion of China, Mao sent Chinese troops into Korea. As a result, the UN forces were driven back into South Korea. By 1951 fighting had bogged down near the original border between the two Koreas. It appeared that U.S. forces could not win a conventional, limited ground war against the Chinese, who could only be defeated by the bombing of Chinese bases or by using nuclear weapons. The use of such tactics would have made war with the Soviet Union a distinct possibility.

The Truman administration concluded that U.S. interests on the Asian mainland were not important enough to risk a third world war. The People's Republic was not bombed, and MacArthur, who had advocated massive bombings and the use of nuclear weapons, was fired when he publicly protested. Agreeing to the stalemate, the combatants signed an armistice in 1953. The cease-fire line, which roughly corresponded to the 38th parallel, remained heavily fortified through the 1990s.

The Korean War was part of the containment policy adopted by the United States after World War II. As part of this policy, the United States signed mutual defense treaties with South Korea, Taiwan, and later South Vietnam. It also established the Southeast Asia Treaty Organization (SEATO), a military alliance of the United States, Great Britain, France, Australia, New Zealand, Thailand, and the Philippines; however, SEATO was never as effective as the North Atlantic Treaty Organization (NATO) in Europe. With its series of regional military alliances—NATO, the Central Treaty Organization (CENTO) in West Asia (the Middle East), and SEATO—the Eisenhower administration believed it had walled in "Communist aggression."

This optimistic view proved illusory. During the 1950s the Soviet Union promoted Marxist-led peasant guerrilla conflicts in much of Southeast Asia. Depending on the circumstances, Marxist guerrillas struck at landlords, colonial authorities, and independent governments. Not understanding the causes of such unrest, the United States focused on the elimination of Marxism and sent Truman Doctrine–style military aid and advisers to bolster unenlightened colonial regimes and authoritarian, anticommunist leaders. In combination with other factors, this aid eliminated insurgency in some areas, but Marxist guerrillas continued to operate in Burma, Thailand, and the Philippines.

By the late 1950s and early 1960s, the Eisenhower and Kennedy administrations were coming to realize that while the United States was trying to maintain its global network of pro-U.S. and anti-Soviet allies, it was also facing mounting demands for social and economic reforms around the world. Leaders in the United States began to see that many of the struggles in Asia, Africa, and Latin America were essentially revolts against economic and social deprivation, rather than support for the Soviet Union in the Cold War. The newly independent, predominantly agricultural, peasant nations of the Third World posed a number of questions for the United States that often seemed to have no satisfactory answers. Should the United States, the bastion of free enterprise and private property, interfere in sovereign states and force land reform? Should the United States support regimes that were often oppressive but were always reliable allies in the Cold War and hope that either by force or domestic reforms they would deal with peasant unrest within their nations? If some of these governments, even with U.S. military and economic aid, still failed to stop peasant movements and Marxist-led guerrillas, should the United States send troops to fight the insurgents in order to save an anti-Soviet regime?

Escalating War in Vietnam

Nowhere were the dilemmas just described more clearly manifested than in Vietnam. After losing to the Viet Minh guerrillas under the Communist leader Ho Chi Minh (1890–1969) at Dien Bien Phu, the French military had reluctantly pulled out of Indochina in 1954; France then granted independence to its former colony. The withdrawal was followed by an international conference at Geneva, where the United States was able to prevent Ho from gaining control of all of Vietnam. Four states emerged in Indochina: Laos, Cambodia, Communist-dominated North Vietnam, and pro-Western South Vietnam. The two Vietnams were divided along the 17th parallel, as Korea was divided near the 38th. By the late 1950s, Communist guerrillas were operating in Laos, and South Vietnam had seen the emergence of Marxist-led groups that resisted the repressive but strongly anticommunist government of Ngo Dinh Diem. The anti-Diem guerrillas were supported by a large section of the peasantry, but at first received little more than moral support from North Vietnam and other Marxist nations. Diem, however, claimed that his opponents were all Viet Cong (Vietnamese Communists) and further claimed that he was being attacked by troops from North Vietnam. He asked the United States for assistance under the Truman Doctrine.

Agreeing with Diem's claims, the Eisenhower and Kennedy administrations sent military equipment and advisers to South Vietnam. As a result, the United States became directly involved in a peasant guerrilla war. Despite U.S. aid, by 1963 the Viet Cong, supplied along the mountainous and jungle-covered Ho Chi Minh Trail with Soviet, North Vietnamese, and Chinese weapons and with other war matériel, had gained control of large sections of South Vietnam.

During 1964–1965, two decisions transformed what had been a predominantly civil war among South Vietnamese into a multinational, full-scale struggle. Most U.S. military and civilian leaders believed that the fall of South Vietnam would be the first "domino" in a process whereby all the Southeast Asian nations would fall one by one. As a consequence, the United States sharply increased its support of the South Vietnamese government by setting up huge supply bases guarded by U.S. troops. After U.S. naval ships off the North Vietnamese coast in the Gulf of Tonkin were allegedly attacked, the Johnson administration sent troops into South Vietnam and began bombing the Ho Chi Minh Trail and the southern section of North Vietnam.

In response, the North Vietnamese began to move many units of their army into South Vietnam to support

Vietnam War. Trying to catch an elusive enemy, U.S. forces in Vietnam transported infantry by helicopter to surprise Viet Cong and North Vietnamese units. The intent was to inflict casualties rather than capture territory, and the attacking forces usually withdrew afterward. Besides helicopter raids, U.S. tactics included patrols, defense of fixed positions, "freefire zones," napalm strikes, and high-altitude carpet bombardment with conventional bombs or Agent Orange used to defoliate the dense jungle.

the Viet Cong. Strictly disciplined, the Communist forces waged a war of attrition against U.S. and South Vietnamese troops. They were willing to suffer heavy casualties and extensive bomb destruction for however long it took to inflict enough casualties on the Americans that the United States lost its will to continue the struggle. Once the Americans withdrew, Vietnam would be united by force into a single Communist state.

As in the Korean War, Cold War considerations dictated U.S. military policy. As the struggle in Vietnam escalated, the world powers tacitly agreed to keep the conflict from triggering a devastating nuclear world war. The Soviet Union and the People's Republic confined themselves to sending supplies and refrained from sending combat units to Vietnam. The United States refrained from employing nuclear weapons and from bombing Soviet supply ships or Chinese supply depots in North Vietnam.

On the Korean Peninsula, it had been possible to draw a battle line from coast to coast, but U.S. forces in Vietnam faced a kaleidoscope of shifting battle lines on the edge of an enormous land mass. Despite building their forces to over half a million men by 1968, the Americans failed to make decisive headway in the war. The South Vietnamese peasants were caught in the middle of the conflict. They had little loyalty to the corrupt and repressive South Vietnamese government and none at all to the foreign Westerners who not only backed the government but also had earlier supported the French. Most peasants were not committed to Marxism either, but at least the Marxists were Vietnamese. Most Americans in the war had little knowledge of or respect for the people of Vietnam. Separated by differences in language, culture, and physical appearance, many Americans regarded Vietnamese and other Asians as alien "gooks." Equally important, the Vietnamese Communists were in the long run more effective in controlling the peasant villages through social contacts, indoctrination, and their daily presence than the Americans were with sporadic raids and "resettlement" programs.

The war reached a turning point in 1968. Just as a large segment of the French public had opposed the war in Algeria, so, too, did influential elements of the U.S. public turn against the war. Antidraft and antiwar disruptions steadily increased. The Nixon administration intensified aspects of the war while systematically withdrawing American troops; protracted negotiations with Hanoi ensued. In 1973 both sides agreed to an armistice and the withdrawal of all foreign troops from South Vietnam. U.S. forces left, and in 1975 North Vietnamese forces and the Vietcong launched a major assault, overrunning South Vietnam in a few weeks. Meanwhile, Communist units also took over in Laos and Cambodia. A major Cold War struggle had come to an end in Asia, but others continued in Africa and Latin America.

"Nam"

The mood was sardonic, fatalistic, and melancholy. I could hear it in our black jokes: "Hey, Bill, you're going on patrol today. If you get your legs blown off can I have your boots?" I could hear it in the songs we sang. Some were versions of maudlin country-and-western tunes like "Detroit City," the refrain of which expressed every rifleman's hope:

I wanna go home, I wanna go home,
O, I wanna go home. . . .

The fighting had not only become more intense, but more vicious. Both we and the Viet Cong began to make a habit of atrocities. One of 1st Battalion's radio operators was captured by an enemy patrol, tied up, beaten with clubs, then executed. . . .

*We paid the enemy back, sometimes with interest. . . . According to those "rules of engagement," it was morally right to shoot an unarmed Vietnamese who was running, but wrong to shoot one who was standing or walking; it was wrong to shoot an enemy prisoner at close range, but right for a sniper at long range to kill an enemy soldier who was no more able than a prisoner to defend himself; it was wrong for infantrymen to destroy a village with white-phosphorus grenades, but right for a fighter pilot to drop napalm on it. Ethics seemed to be a matter of distance and technology. You could never go wrong if you killed people at long range with sophisticated weapons.**

United States soldiers and marines were unprepared for the ground fighting in Vietnam. They had expected to face their enemy in open battle, as in World War II and in Korea. In Vietnam, there were few battlefronts; helicopters flew in troops to spots where the enemy allegedly were concentrated and after combat flew them out again. After ten patrols up the same trail, one second of carelessness on the eleventh patrol meant sudden wounds or death from an antipersonnel mine. The enemy was nowhere and everywhere; the villagers working in the fields claimed to know nothing, but some tossed grenades into U.S. bivouacs at night. After serving for a few months, burnt-out veterans had to be replaced with fresh, but still unprepared, troops.

*Philip Caputo, *A Rumor of War* (New York: Holt, Rinehart & Winston, 1977), pp. 227–230.

The Cold War in Africa

As already noted, both the superpowers, either directly or through intermediary nations such as Israel and Cuba, had become involved in various struggles for independence in central and southern Africa. One major instance was the complex struggle for leadership over the newly independent Congo. The leader of the Congolese nationalists, Patrice Lumumba, was appointed the first prime minister, but as a more radical nationalist, he was feared by conservative Africans and by the West and was eventually assassinated (see the box earlier in the chapter). With Western help, mineral-rich Katanga province seceded and remained independent for two years. Finally, the United Nations was called in to restore order, and a military dictatorship under Sese Seko Mobutu (1930–1997) took over the government. Mobutu carefully balanced demands for Africanization of foreign properties with support for foreign mining interests. Although his regime was notoriously corrupt, Mobotu proved to be one of the most durable African leaders; he styled himself as "President for Life" of the Congo, which he renamed Zaire.

The superpowers also played out their Cold War rivalry in the Horn of Africa in the eastern section of the continent. Its geographic location along the flank of the petroleum-rich Arabian Peninsula and beside the Suez Canal–Red Sea short route between Europe and Asia made the Horn important to both superpowers. Under Emperor Haile Selassie, Ethiopia had remained a largely feudal nation with close ties to the United States, which established a large radar tracking base there. In 1974, after refusing to institute reforms or to acknowledge widespread famine from drought, the emperor was deposed by a group of left-wing army officers. The new Marxist government promptly closed the U.S. base and established close relations with the Soviet Union. However, the impact of the prolonged drought and starvation was only exacerbated by constant civil and border

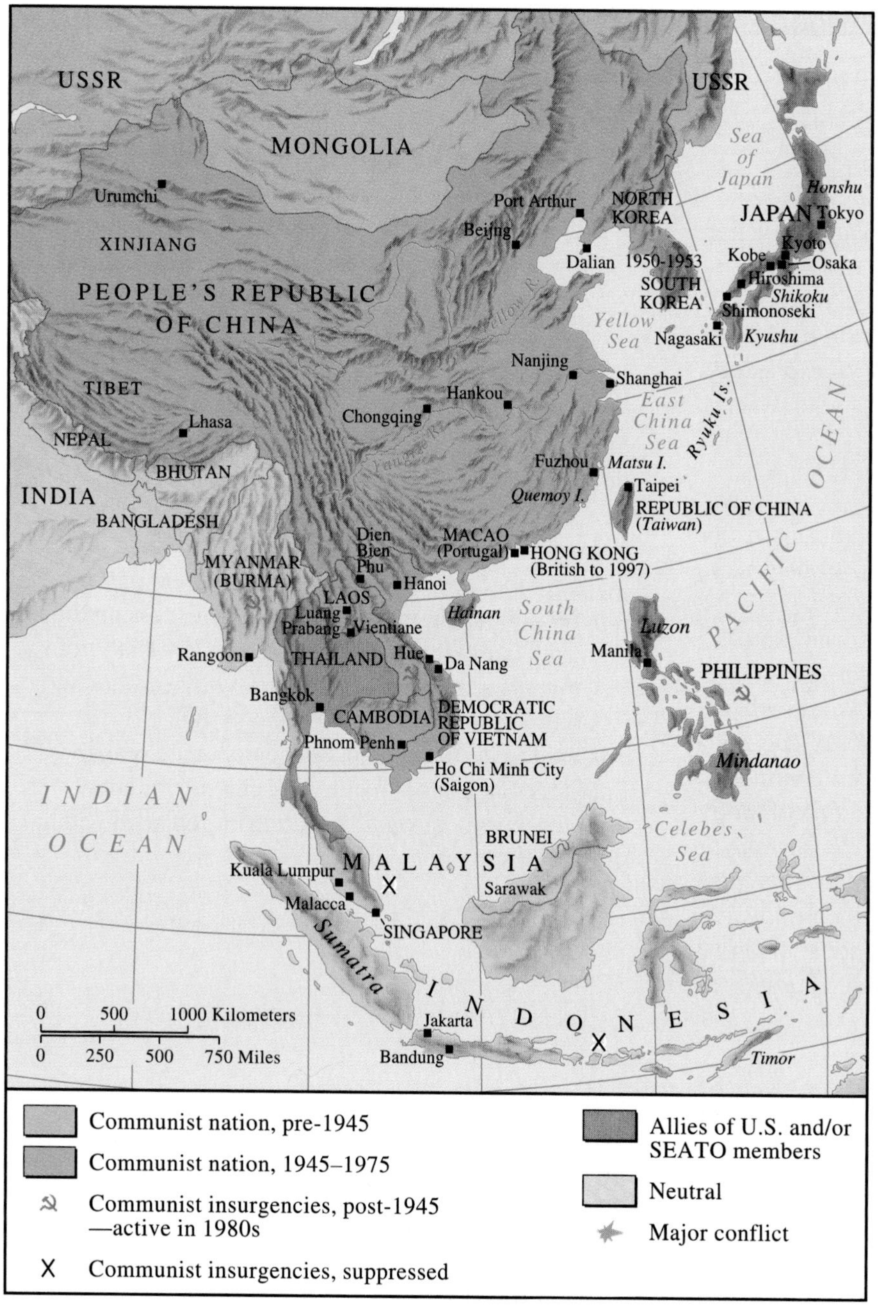

Map 16.3 The Cold War in Asia. After World War II, communism spread into Asia by means of armed struggle, despite resistance by the United States. Communist regimes came to power in China through civil war and in Vietnam, Laos, and Cambodia through armed struggles against the French and the Americans. Only a major military effort by the United States prevented the Communists from taking over all of Korea. Communist guerrillas were also active throughout Southeast Asia; in some nations (for example, Malaysia), the guerrillas were eliminated, but in others, particularly the Philippines, they persisted.

wars. Ethiopia, whether in alliance with the United States or the Soviet Union, remained one of the world's poorest nations.

Neighboring Somalia was also the scene of superpower rivalry. In Somalia a leftist government had established ties with the Soviet Union; however, drought and starvation resulted in a right-wing coup whose leaders then moved closer to the West. In a 180-degree turnabout, the United States, recently ousted from Ethiopia, then moved to support the new Somali military regime. Here, too, the population continued to suffer the ravages of famine and war with Ethiopia. In the late 1980s, when the Soviet Union under Gorbachev moved to disentangle itself from foreign involvements, it reduced economic and political support for the Ethiopian Marxists, and the regime collapsed. As will be described in the following chapter, the Horn of Africa has remained a region of internal wars and extreme poverty.

Conflict in Latin America

I call upon Chairman Khrushchev to halt and eliminate this clandestine, reckless, and provocative threat to world peace and to stabilize relations between our two nations. I call upon him further to abandon this course of world domination and to join in an historic effort to end the perilous arms race and transform the history of man. He has an opportunity now to move the world back from the abyss of destruction—by . . . withdrawing these weapons from Cuba—by refraining from any action which will widen or deepen the present crisis—and then by participating in a search for peaceful and permanent solutions. . . .

*It is difficult to settle or even discuss these problems in an atmosphere of intimidation. That is why this latest Soviet threat—or any other threat which is made either independently or in response to our actions this week—must and will be met with determination. Any hostile move anywhere in the world against the safety and freedom of peoples to whom we are committed . . . will be met by whatever action is needed.**

*John F. Kennedy, in David L. Larson, ed., *The Cuban Crisis of 1962: Selected Documents and Chronology* (Boston: Houghton Mifflin, 1963), pp. 44–45.

On the evening of October 22, 1962, as an anxious American public watched President Kennedy deliver these words on television, the world stood on the brink of atomic holocaust. The two great nuclear-armed superpowers, the United States and the Soviet Union, faced each other in a heart-stopping confrontation issuing out of the installation of Soviet missiles in Cuba aimed at the United States. The Cold War, which had already extended from Europe to Asia, had now shifted its focus to Latin America. In many nations of this region, glaring social inequities had led to domestic unrest. There was also a long-standing resentment of "Yankee Imperialism," a term long applied to U.S. political and economic policies exploiting the resources of Latin America. While some in Latin America supported these policies, many Latin Americans called for social and economic reform at home and for freedom from U.S. economic and political controls. Latin America was therefore fertile ground for the spread of Marxism and for other doctrines that called for social change and for opposition to the United States. From the late 1950s onward, Latin America was often a surrogate battleground for the Cold War superpowers.

Demands for Agrarian Reform

All the peasants want an Agrarian Reform:
so that it is the cows that
are milked . . . not the tenants.
When the sow gives birth
my heart aches;
the son of the landlord
eats my piglets. . . .

The landlord's wife
gave me half a plot (of land);
I did the work
and she took the product.
The boss goes by car
we travel by cart;
these are the delights
of our landlord's rule.
The boss is well-heeled;
we walk about in sandals,
The boss is well dressed;
we are without a stitch . . .

The poor work harder
even than oxen;
the rich do not work
and live like kings.
The priest from my village
told me to wait. . . .
But I cannot endure any more
*I want an "Agrarian Reform."**

Song sung by members of the Peasants' Federation in Ecuador, 1975. This song was also sung in Chile in the 1950s and 60s.

*Hazel Johnson et al., *Third World Lives of Struggle* (London: Heinemann, 1982), pp. 43–44.

Demographic, Economic, and Social Trends

Economically and militarily, Latin America escaped the ravages of World War II, but it continued to suffer from the Great Depression, which caused the prices of its raw exports, mostly foodstuffs and minerals, to drop to all-time lows. The old aristocracy of large landowners and a newly arrived business and professional elite were oriented toward trade with Europe and North America; they exported raw materials and agricultural products in exchange for consumer goods. These leaders gave economic growth, especially industrial output, a high priority after the war. Unfortunately, the interrelated economic, social, and demographic facts of Latin American life made progress very difficult.

Despite a high infant mortality rate, the high birth rate in the region brought a significant population increase to many Latin American nations. In the 1970s the population of Latin America grew at a rate of 2.7 percent

Both photos: © Pablo Corral V/Corbis

Wealth and Poverty in Latin America. The shantytown suburbs, where many live in tar-paper shacks, on the outskirts of Caracas, Venezuela, contrast sharply with the opulent office buildings and luxury apartment complexes at the center of the city. The poverty evident in the shantytown indicates the severe economic and social problems threatening republican government in Venezuela, one of the historically democratic nations of the region. As the populations of the urban centers of Latin America continue to burgeon, such scenes are becoming common.

per year, compared with 0.9 percent for North America and 0.6 percent for Europe. Those children born into *campesino* (country) families faced a serflike existence of labor on the great Latin American estates. Often there was only seasonal employment for these workers, who received low wages and paid high prices at the landowner's store. They lived in dirt-floor shacks with no running water or electricity and had to cope with a polluted public water supply, inadequate medical services, and primitive sanitation. Of course, they had no education and no political rights.

Latin America experienced rapid urbanization as hundreds of thousands of impoverished peasants fled the misery of the countryside in hopes of better opportunities in the cities. In 1930 only one Latin American city had a population of more than a million; by 1997, 29 cities were near or over 1 million. The influx of campesinos put severe strains on the already overburdened city services, particularly housing, transportation, and sanitation. As in the country, many new arrivals could find only part-time work, and many more no work at all. Tar-paper-shack slums increasingly surrounded most Latin American (and, indeed, most Third World) cities, while the rich barricaded themselves and hired armed guards.

Although Latin America as a whole had a higher per capita GNP than most of Africa or West Asia, it lagged behind the rest of the West in industrial development. Political leaders in some nations such as Mexico encouraged domestic industry and even nationalized foreign holdings from the 1930s onward, but the region remained heavily dependent on fluctuating commodity prices for its manufactured and agricultural goods. Declining prices for the region's resource exports, including the petroleum of Mexico and Venezuela during the petroleum glut of the 1980s, hampered plans for road systems, hydroelectric plants, and housing, as well as for improving the standard of living for the impoverished masses. Development loans, coming due when the Latin American nations could least afford to pay them, pushed such large nations as Mexico and Brazil to the verge of bankruptcy.

The burdened Latin American economies might have had some relief if their fast-growing population had constituted a healthy domestic sales market. Instead, postwar population growth in Latin America far exceeded the increase in economic growth; the unemployed and underemployed masses did not have the income to buy the products turned out by the new industrial facilities, and the economic and social gap between the landholding and urban elite and the peasants continued to widen. Throughout Latin America, workers and miners called for higher wages and better working conditions, and some of the normally passive campesinos began to demand improvements in their living conditions, and even land.

Against this backdrop of economic problems, post–World War II Latin American politics embodied a wide spectrum of responses. In many of the smaller, mostly agricultural Latin American nations, the traditional economic elite, supported by the military leaders and by the predominantly conservative Roman Catholic church, ignored the needs of the masses or made only token reforms. The most repressive regimes, as in Paraguay under General Alfredo Stroessner, often banned or repressed unions and workers' organizations. In more industrially developed nations like Mexico, Venezuela, Brazil, Argentina, and Chile, the political authorities, whether authoritarian or republican, accommodated at least some of the demands of the urban workforce. The earlier "personalist" crypto-fascist governments of Vargas and Péron in Brazil and Argentina have already been discussed. By the 1960s, as unrest intensified and took on some aspects of Marxist urban guerrilla terrorism (see below), modern military dictatorships took over in Brazil, Argentina, and Uruguay. Juntas (cliques) of professional officers ruled a number of Latin American nations. They promised stability and order and sometimes brought economic progress, in terms of gross national product and foreign exports. Usually, however, they protected the traditional landholding and business classes and did little to improve the lot of the campesinos or factory workers. Representative government, with honest elections and changes in party control, had been rare in Latin America both before and during World War II.

Costa Rica, Chile, and intermittently Venezuela and Colombia had histories of republicanism, but even in these nations political parties were merely factions of the elite, little concerned with the plight of the masses. After the war, representative government made headway in Brazil, Argentina, and other nations, but often the republican process succumbed to leftist agitation and military takeovers. Consequently, disaffected campesinos and workers who wished to end the inequities in Latin America began to look to revolutionary action instead of republican government.

One possibility was to follow the path of Mexico. The indigenous social revolution in Mexico had made some headway before 1940, but great inequities still existed there, and in the opinion of many, the gap between the rich and the poor in Mexico was about the same as elsewhere in non-Marxist Latin America, and was increasing. Mexico had the forms of representative government but was in fact a one-party dictatorship. In any case, the revolution in Mexico arose out of circumstances peculiar to Mexico and could not necessarily be duplicated in other nations.

As elsewhere around the globe after World War II, many in Latin America considered Marxism, whether revolutionary or evolutionary, to be the best approach to

A Revolutionary Credo

Why does our government have to be . . . isolated, and threatened by destruction and death?

They want, simply, to destroy our revolution in order to continue exploiting the other nations of Latin America. . . . they want to destroy us, because we have had the desire to liberate ourselves economically. They want to destroy us because we have desired to do justice. They want to destroy us because we have concerned ourselves with the humble of our land, because we have cast our lot with the poor of our country. . . .

Revolutions are remedies—bitter remedies, yes. But at times revolution is the only remedy that can be applied to evils even more bitter. . . . The Cuban revolution is already a reality for the history of the world.

What is the outcome of a situation in which misery and hunger lead year by year to more misery and hunger? Can there be any other outcome than that of revolution? . . . This revolution, in the situation of present-day Latin America, can only come by the armed struggle of the peoples. . . .

*We want to convert our work to wealth and welfare for our own people and for other peoples. . . . Our country, our people, and our future are important, but still more important are our 230 million Latin American brothers!**

Fidel Castro here gives the Marxist viewpoint on revolution and social change and on the United States' reaction to it. He stresses economic improvement, not political freedom. Castro also expresses his conviction about the inevitable triumph of Marxism, first in Cuba, then throughout the rest of Latin America.

*Fidel Castro, Labor Day Address, May 1, 1960 (Havana: Cooperativa Obera de Publicidad, 1966), pp. 14, 16–17, 21, in *Fidel Castro Speaks*, ed. M. Kenner and J. Petras (New York: Grove Press, 1969), pp. 151, 159.

CONNECTIONS IN MIGRATION

Families in Cities

Families are the most fundamental units of social life, and they are perhaps the most solid and lasting structures of human society. The ties between parent and child, between spouses, and between siblings are deep. But families have also changed along with other aspects of human society. In the last few centuries, for instance, families have had to adjust to large-scale migration. Young people left their original families and, as voluntary or involuntary migrants, started over, creating new families in new lands.

Since the beginning of the twentieth century, the biggest change affecting family life has been urbanization. Although great cities had existed in earlier times, especially in Eurasia, it was only in the twentieth century that every region of the world came to have its own metropolises.

By 2000, almost half the population of the world lived in cities. The most populous cities, ranging from 10 to 20 million inhabitants, were Bombay, Mexico City, São Paulo, New York, Tokyo, London, Jakarta, Istanbul, Shanghai, and Moscow. Africa, though the least urban of the continents, hosted such massive cities as Cairo, Kinshasa, Lagos, Abidjan, Johannesburg, and Nairobi, ranging in size from 2 to 16 million inhabitants.

Cities grew at a remarkable rate. Hiroshima, which was destroyed by the United States' atomic bomb in 1945, was rebuilt and reached a population of half a million by 1960. Kinshasa, Zaire, with a population of 50,000 in 1960, included over 3 million inhabitants by 1990.

"Home," for most people, was now a neighborhood in the city or suburb, rather than a village or farm. Most people who lived in the city were born in the city, although new migrants continued to stream into each city from near and far.

Urban residence changed the conditions of family life. Work in the city was mostly for wages, and was rarely near home. Whether people go to work on foot or by bicycle, bus, train, or car, the phenomenon of the commute and of rush hour marks life in every city. City life requires literacy for most regular employment, so children have to undergo the socialization of the school in addition to the socialization of their family. The public sector has grown greatly in the city, especially in comparison to villages. If people in villages mainly follow the dictates of family leaders, people in cities must also follow the rules of public institutions, such as accepting conventions for street traffic and for the hours and nature of public services.

The role of family head brings less responsibility and less respect in urban areas than in rural areas. Urban children have many activities outside the home as well as in the family. When urban families focus on gaining property or on building enterprises, family members tend to remain in the urban area. If the family focuses on schooling for the children, the children are more likely to move away after completing their education.

---

1. Consider the changing roles of family life with urbanization as you explore Unit 12 of the Migration CD-ROM. List at least three significant ways in which urbanization changes family structure. Does the impact of urbanization upon the family differ from country to country or from culture to culture?

2. Enter the search term "urbanization" in the InfoTrac Subject Guide. Choose "Periodical references" and read four articles that address the impact of urbanization upon families and/or social structure in general. For each article answer the following: What was the exact phenomenon being discussed or studied? What were the main conclusions of the article? Are the conclusions primarily statements of fact, or do they also include judgments of right and wrong, good and bad?

achieving economic, social, and political justice. However, Leninist communism in the Soviet Union and Maoist communism in the People's Republic of China appeared to many as repellent examples of totalitarianism. Many Latin Americans embraced a broader view of Marxism and worked outside the established Communist parties that were controlled from Moscow or Beijing.

Reform through Marxism was highly problematic in Latin America, however. Not only was it contested by the usual array of economic, social, political, military, and religious elites, it was implacably opposed by the leaders of the United States of America. Most of them did not make fine distinctions among various forms of Marxism; they saw in all Marxists de facto allies of the Soviet Union, and therefore opponents of the United States in the Cold War. Any signs of Marxist power, especially in the Caribbean, essential to the strategic defense of the United States, must be immediately destroyed, or the Soviet Union would enter the Western Hemisphere and outflank the United States to the south.

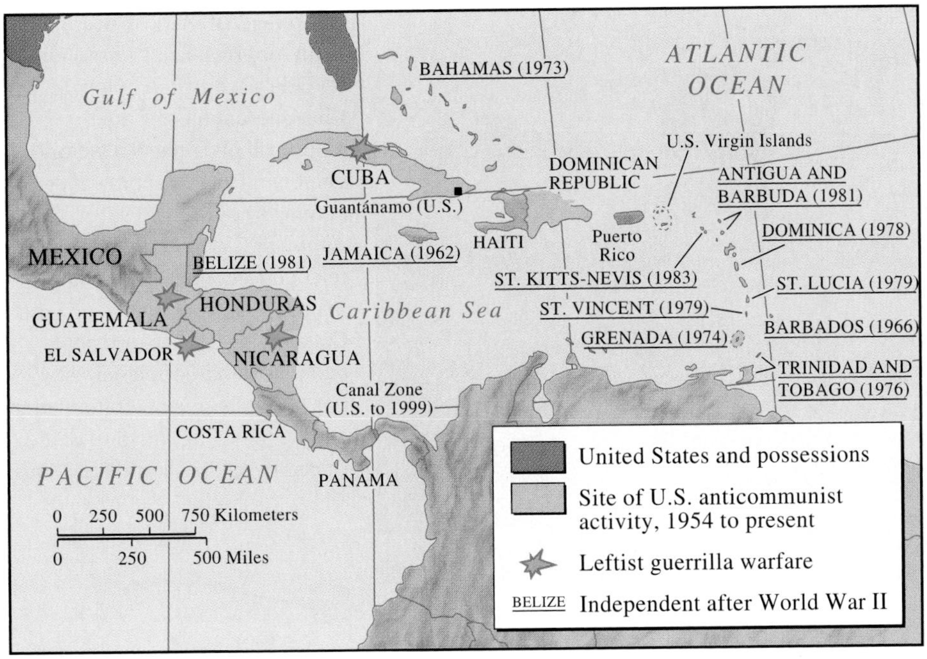

Map 16.4 The Caribbean and Central America after World War II. Two major developments have marked this area. Many colonies of Great Britain became independent, although those held by the French and the Dutch kept their association with the governing nation. At the same time, the United States actively intervened in areas it considered allied with its Cold War rival, the Soviet Union.

The United States used a variety of policies to uproot Marxism in the Caribbean and elsewhere in Latin America. It sometimes engaged in economic warfare against leftist governments through blockade and boycott, hoping an impoverished population would rise against its government. The United States also provided covert assistance, including insurgency training, to conservative opponents seeking to overthrow leftist governments; it also trained and deployed counterinsurgency forces against guerrilla opponents of pro-U.S. regimes. In urgent cases, notably to protect its political and economic interests in the Caribbean, the United States resorted to direct military intervention as it had in its earlier twentieth-century phase of imperialism. The Reagan and Bush administrations pursued a wide range of anti-Marxist policies both overtly and covertly. By and large, the United States was successful in keeping Marxism out of Latin America.

As the decades passed after the war, many U.S. leaders saw with increasing clarity that Marxism drew its strength from the misery of the Latin American masses. Hoping to eliminate the source of Marxist agitation, the United States offered economic aid to entice the governments of Latin America to undertake economic, social, and political reforms. Such programs as the Alliance for Progress and the Inter-American Development Bank failed, however, because most Latin American governments were more fearful of losing power through reform than through Marxist takeover. The United States also moved to shed the image of an old-fashioned imperial power by agreeing in 1978 to give up the Panama Canal Zone and to relinquish control of the canal itself by 2000. Although the latter action was good public relations, U.S. activity in regard to Latin America did little to improve the standard of living for the masses.

Marxism in a Cold War Context: Castro's Revolution in Cuba

The major test for the United States developed during the 1950s when the Cuban government swung abruptly from a moderate right-wing military regime to a left-wing revolutionary dictatorship. Cuba was controlled by Fulgencio Batista, an ally of the U.S. government and of business interests ranging from sugar refining to gambling. Under Batista, Cuban cities enjoyed a relatively high standard of living, but the rural peasantry suffered from seasonal unemployment and inadequate medical and educational facilities. The United States supported Batista because he was strongly anticommunist and pro-United States in domestic and international policies.

In 1959 Fidel Castro, a young Marxist lawyer, gathered enough support to topple Batista's regime. Initially the United States adopted a "wait and see" policy toward Castro's government and hoped that it would institute more liberal reforms and a more efficient government. Castro, however, assumed dictatorial powers and soon announced that his goal was to create a society based on Marxist principles. He nationalized large-scale landholdings, many held by U.S. corporations, closed the casinos (again, many owned by U.S. interests), and made overtures to the Soviet Union for economic aid.

In the climate of the Cold War, the presence of a revolutionary Marxist government close to U.S. borders

A Moment of Marxist Triumph in Latin America. Latin revolutionaries Fidel Castro (center left) and Che Guevara (center right), among others, review a victory parade in Havana shortly after coming to power in 1959. Although Castro clung to power, relentless economic and diplomatic pressures mounted against Cuba by the U.S. government, coupled with poor planning by Castro's government, continued to cripple the living standard of the Cuban people well into the 1990s.

was unacceptable to the Eisenhower administration, which reacted vigorously against the Castro regime by imposing a total embargo on all Cuban products. Castro then set out to make Cuba a model Communist state in the Western Hemisphere. In the following years, Castro's government established a wide range of social services for the poorest Cubans; these included public housing, education, and medical and sanitary care. His efforts, however, were undermined by his failure to diversify Cuba's economy or to increase and expedite the production of sugar, Cuba's main export. Caught in the grip of the U.S. economic embargo, Castro became increasingly dependent on Soviet aid.

Castro also steadfastly refused to open the political system or to allow any dissent. For many, particularly the middle class and intellectuals, the new system was as repressive as the preceding dictatorships; many fled to the United States. As a militant Marxist, Castro tried to export revolution throughout Latin America through peasant and urban guerrilla warfare. Castro's comrade, Ernesto "Che" Guevara, directed several of these efforts and caught the imagination of leftists everywhere. Most of these efforts failed, however, in the face of strong counterrevolutionary measures. Guevara was killed by U.S.-led counterinsurgency forces in Bolivia in 1967.

The Cuban Missile Crisis

Besides imposing the economic embargo and breaking off diplomatic relations, Eisenhower, believing that once the Cubans had a taste of communism they would rebel against it, went another step toward toppling Castro. Following a precedent set in overthrowing the leftist government of Guatemala in 1954, Eisenhower authorized the Central Intelligence Agency (CIA) to recruit and train anti-Castro Cubans to invade Cuba and provide a rallying point for the Cuban population to overthrow Castro.

On entering office in 1961, President John Kennedy reaffirmed the plans for invasion, but stipulated that the United States was not to be involved in the landing itself. In April 1961 anti-Castro forces bombed a Cuban airbase and landed at the Bay of Pigs in Cuba. The Cuban campesinos, whose lives had improved under Castro, did not revolt; instead, they rallied behind the new regime. Kennedy vetoed pleas to provide air support to the invaders, and Cuban militia crushed the invasion. Although the U.S. government for many years publicly denied any complicity in the Bay of Pigs fiasco, the invasion's failure hurt Kennedy's prestige and strengthened his resolve to act more vigorously in any future crisis.

The Bay of Pigs debacle led Khrushchev to view Kennedy as a weak leader. More ominously, it tempted Khrushchev to use Cuba to solve some of his own problems: his colleagues were criticizing him for deficient agricultural production and for letting the United States outstrip the Soviet Union in the missile race. Castro, afraid that the United States would try again to topple him, called for additional support from the Soviet Union. Recently declassified documents and statements made by Soviet and U.S. policy makers during 1989 roundtable discussions reveal that Castro's fears were justified. The United States did have plans to topple the Cuban leader during 1962.

Khrushchev decided to send medium-range bombers and missiles to Cuba to help defend Castro and also to threaten the United States. The missiles would also act as a counterweight to U.S. missiles in Europe and Turkey, which were aimed at key targets in the Soviet Union. In October 1962 U.S. spy planes discovered missile sites

Away from the Brink of Nuclear Holocaust. A U.S. destroyer pulls alongside a Soviet freighter carrying Soviet missiles out of Cuba in November 1962. The U.S. naval blockade of Cuba, although technically an act of war, was one of a series of military threats and diplomatic maneuvers that induced the Soviet Union to withdraw its missiles from Cuba, ending a Cold War crisis that threatened the world with nuclear war.

under construction in Cuba. It is now known that the Soviet Union already had some missiles in Cuba, but they had not been equipped with nuclear warheads.

The Kennedy administration viewed this provocative Soviet move as a direct challenge to its sphere of influence and promptly reacted. Kennedy demanded that the Soviets voluntarily remove the missiles and bombers from Cuba or face their destruction by U.S. air strikes or outright invasion. This was a zero-tolerance matter; the United States was prepared to go to war over the issue. Some Strategic Air Command (SAC) bombers of the U.S. air force were put into the air and others were placed on fifteen-minute alert. President Kennedy also imposed a "quarantine," a peacetime naval blockade of Cuba (by international law an act of war). Latin American nations, at a meeting of the Organization of American States (OAS), supported the blockade. While publicly throwing down the gauntlet, the Kennedy administration was careful not to back the Soviet Union into a corner; it sent word by private channels that in return for Soviet withdrawal, the United States would not attack Cuba, and perhaps would even remove some of its missiles based in Turkey.

For six days people around the world feared war was about to break out between the two superpowers. Fearful of U.S. nuclear superiority, Khrushchev ordered the return of Soviet ships carrying missiles to Cuba. In an exchange of notes, Khrushchev and Kennedy agreed that the Soviet Union would remove the missiles and bombers from Cuba and that the United States would publicly pledge not to invade the island nation. The United States also removed some missiles from Turkey. The armed forces of the two superpowers were ordered to stand down, and nuclear war was avoided. Castro's regime continued into the twenty-first century but became increasingly isolated, impoverished at home, and ineffective abroad.

The United States Combats Marxism throughout Latin America

Marxism in Cuba, with its Cold War associations and risk of thermonuclear destruction, was only the most spectacular instance of U.S.-Marxist confrontation in Latin America. Marxist revolutionary movements broke out regularly throughout Latin America in a twenty-year period from the mid-1950s to the mid-1970s. The big military dictatorships in Brazil, Argentina, and Uruguay, aided in many ways by the United States, crushed Marxism in their own countries.

Besides supporting anti-Marxist governments, the United States also intervened more directly in Latin American nations it perceived as being or becoming Marxist states. The United States intervened covertly in Guatemala in 1954 and militarily in the Dominican Republic in 1965, Grenada in 1983, and Panama (allegedly because of the drug traffic) in 1990.

A striking example of indirect intervention occurred in Chile, which had a long tradition of democracy. A military clique led by General Augusto Pinochet, with U.S. approval and covert support, overthrew the freely elected, left-leaning government of Salvador Allende and killed Allende in 1973. The Pinochet regime brutally purged Allende supporters and imposed strict political and social controls over Chileans. By 1990 representative government had been restored in Chile, and Chileans defeated Pinochet's bid to be elected president.

The main response of the United States to Marxism in Central America, however, centered on the revolutionary government of Nicaragua. In 1978–1979 a broad-based Sandinista guerrilla movement overthrew the dictatorial regime of the Somoza family, which had close ties to the United States. Meanwhile, several Marxist guerrilla groups fought to take over the government of El Salvador, and an intermittent but persistent Marxist uprising continued in Guatemala. President Jimmy Carter recognized and offered aid to the new Sandinista government, which apparently had no ties to the Soviet Union, but his successor, President Ronald Reagan, strongly opposed the Sandinista regime, which by then had implemented a number of socialist reforms. Like Castro in Cuba, the Sandinistas (named after Augusto César Sandino, a Nicaraguan nationalist killed while opposing U.S. occupation of Nicaragua in the 1930s) offered a combination of state socialism and social services to the people.

Map 16.5 Political Trends in South America since World War II. South America was swept by a number of shifting political and social trends in the last half of the twentieth century. A wave of Castroite revolutionary struggles, both rural and urban, broke out in several South American nations, but most were suppressed by forces loyal to traditional elites. More economically advanced nations, such as Argentina, Brazil, and Chile, generally fell under the control of military juntas in the 1960s and 1970s, but returned to representative government by the early 1990s, as did caudillo states such as Paraguay.

Revolution in Central America. Communist guerrillas, many of them mere boys, move out of a town they have captured before a truce is declared in El Salvador. Poverty and misery throughout Latin America brought on many forms of revolution and guerrilla warfare, often led by Marxist elements. The United States actively opposed Marxist movements in Central America and orchestrated military pressure against the Marxist regime in Nicaragua and Communist guerrillas in El Salvador.

As with Cuba, however, U.S. opposition—and Soviet support—stemmed as much from the politics of the intensified Cold War as from the nature of the Nicaraguan revolution.

The Reagan administration believed the Sandinistas were allied with Castro and the Soviet Union and were supporting guerrilla activities in nearby El Salvador. During the 1980s the United States, as it had in Cuba, applied a number of economic sanctions against Nicaragua. In addition, it sponsored the Contras, an anti-Sandinista guerrilla movement, and supported El Salvador's efforts to suppress the leftist guerrillas in that country. During the late 1980s, Costa Rican president Oscar Arias announced a peace plan to resolve the complex conflicts of the region; the various parties involved expressed varying degrees of support for the plan. Largely as a result of the Arias peace plan, free elections were held in Nicaragua in 1990. To the surprise of many political analysts, Daniel Ortega, the Sandinista leader, lost to opposition candidate Violeta Chamorro, who promised a return to capitalism and national reconciliation. When the Sandinistas turned over the reins of power, the Chamorro regime faced the daunting job of unifying the war-torn nation and implementing economic recovery.

The Marxist presence in Central America continued to wane: in Nicaragua, the Sandinistas remained out of power as they lost elections. In the early 1990s a truce brought an end to the fighting in El Salvador. Guerrilla warfare persisted in Guatemala, where another major issue—the political and cultural oppression of the Amerindian population of the Western Hemisphere (see Chapter 17)—became the focus.

The Rise of Representative Government in Latin America

Marxist struggles did not tell the whole story of contemporary Latin American politics. States like Costa Rica and petroleum-rich Venezuela had long-established representative governments. During the 1980s democratic movements increased markedly in the region. Argentina, Brazil, and other Latin American nations moved away from military dictatorships toward working, though fragile, parliamentary regimes. Peru, however, with a checkered history of both authoritarian and republican governments, endured economic problems and mounting revolutionary upheaval. As the revolutionary Shining Path organization stepped up its attacks in both urban and rural areas, Peru drifted from republicanism toward dictatorship.

Thus democratic governments faced many problems in Latin America. Although some of the new democratic regimes continued to thrive, only time would tell whether representative government could solve Latin America's enormous, chronic social and economic problems.

Shifting World Alliances

There has been much agitation, particularly in the American press; over the past several months. I will say to you that the experience I have had personally over the past 25 years with public reactions in the United States has made me less than surprised with the outbursts that pass for opinion. . . .

The United States . . . possesses nuclear weapons without which the fate of the world would be rapidly settled, and France . . . whatever the current inferiority of its means . . . is politically, geographically and morally, [and] militarily essential to the coalition. . . .

In my opinion, the differences of today stem quite simply from the intrinsic changes which have taken place, . . . in the absolute and relative situation of America and France. . . . The situation in France has profoundly changed. Her new institutions have put her in a position to will and to act. Her internal development has brought her prosperity and has caused her to acquire the means of power. . . .

From the political point of view, it is true that the Soviet Bloc retains a totalitarian and threatening ideology, and that even recently . . . the scandal of the Berlin Wall, and the installation of nuclear weapons in Cuba, have shown that, by this fact, peace remains precarious. Meantime, the human evolution in Russia and the satellites, the important economic and social difficulties in the life of these countries, and especially the beginnings of an opposition which is becoming manifest between, on the one hand, a European empire possessing immense Asiatic territories, and which have made it the greatest colonial power of our time, and, on the other, the Empire of China, its neighbor along a distance of 10,000 kilometers, with a population of 700 million, an empire which is indestructible, ambitious, and denuded of everything—all this can, in effect, introduce some new conjunctures in the concerns of the Kremlin and induce it to bring a note of sincerity to the refrain it devotes to peaceful coexistence.

*France, in fact, has believed for a long time that there can come a day when a real détente and even a sincere entente would permit a complete change in the relations between East and West in Europe, and she expects when this day comes . . . to make some constructive proposals with regard to peace, equilibrium, and the destiny of Europe.**

*Charles de Gaulle Press Conference, July 29, 1963, *Discours et messages*, vol. 4, *Pour l'effort, Août 1962–Decembre 1965* (Paris: Plon, 1970), pp. 119–123, reprinted in Charles G. Cogan, *Charles de Gaulle: A Brief Biography with Documents* (New York: St. Martin's, 1996), pp. 205–207.

Thus French President Charles de Gaulle announced France's determination to steer an independent course in the Cold War conflicts between the United States and the Soviet Union. With his profound understanding of political and historical realities, de Gaulle correctly predicted the forthcoming split between the Soviet Union and The People's Republic of China and future changes in Europe. Under de Gaulle, France developed its own nuclear armament program, took independent stances on Asian and African issues, and in 1965 withdrew from NATO, the U.S.-sponsored Western military alliance. His actions illustrated the weakening of the Cold War power blocs in Europe during the 1960s and 1970s. De Gaulle represented a trend in newly prosperous western Europe, which was anxious to be independent from post–World War II tutelage to the United States.

The United States and the Soviet Union, which dominated the globe after World War II, were the most powerful nations in history. They differed strikingly in most respects. Politically, the United States was a nation where citizens enjoyed great freedoms, while the Soviet Union was one of the most authoritarian nations. Militarily, the two seemed to have achieved a rough parity by the 1980s, and both were far stronger than any potential challenger. Despite their might, these two superpowers, like other nations of the Western world, also experienced economic, social, and political problems. Their power was further weakened in the last quarter of the twentieth century by the trend toward independence from superpower domination that spread from western Europe to eastern Europe and the rest of the world. Powerful Asian and European economic blocs also challenged the United States and the Soviet Union.

The United States since 1960

Politically, the people of the United States alternated between support for liberal Democrats and support for conservative Republicans. During the Kennedy-Johnson administrations in the 1960s Americans supported the enactment of liberal legislation, but during Ronald Reagan's two terms in office (1980–1988), many of these trends were reversed.

The 1960s were years of social change in the United States. African Americans spearheaded many of these demands for change. Their leader, Reverend Martin Luther King Jr., advocated tactics of nonviolence, inspired by the teachings of Gandhi, to achieve civil rights. African American advances in civil rights encouraged women, Hispanic Americans, Native Americans, poor Americans, homosexuals, the physically handicapped, and other groups faced with discrimination to make similar demands. The Supreme Court under Chief Justice Earl Warren actively furthered the expansion of civil rights and civil liberties, overturning generations of entrenched discriminatory practice.

The late 1960s and the 1970s was a discouraging and bewildering time for many Americans. There were bitter antiwar protests against U.S. military involvement in Vietnam, and national self-esteem was further undermined by revelations of criminal abuses of power by President Richard Nixon (1913–1994) in the Watergate affair. The repressive tactics that Nixon used against social and anti-

LIVES AND TIMES ACROSS CULTURES

Counterculture in the 1960s and 1970s

During the 1960s and 1970s, many young people in the United States and other Western nations dropped out of so-called mainstream society to experiment with a wide range of countercultural lifestyles. Advocates of alternative lifestyles urged students to "turn on, tune in, and drop out." "Hippy" dress styles of jeans with bell-bottoms, dyed T-shirts, beads, and long hair for both men and women became popular. Many experimented with marijuana and hallucinogenic drugs.

Rock-and-roll bands like the Beatles and the Rolling Stones from England attracted millions of fans around the world. The Grateful Dead gave free concerts in San Francisco, and the city became a mecca for those wanting to live the hippy lifestyle. So-called Deadheads followed the band around on tour in a motley array of cars and vans painted in psychedelic colors. The 1970s were heady times of "sex, drugs, and rock and roll."

At the same time, many students became active in political and social movements. Students in both France and the United States propelled the antiwar movements against the wars in Algeria and Vietnam. University campuses became centers of rebellion against the war in Vietnam as students chanting, "LBJ, LBJ [Lyndon Baines Johnson, the U.S. president], how many kids did you kill today?" joined protests across the country. Young people also joined, and often led, civil rights and feminist movements to demand equal rights for all people, regardless of their race, age, creed, or gender.

war activists and his "dirty tricks" against leaders of the Democratic party led to the conviction of many of his aides for illegal actions and to Nixon's resignation to avoid impeachment in 1974, a first in U.S. history. In addition, soaring prices for petroleum, accelerating inflation, high unemployment, and economic competition from Japanese and other Asian manufacturers also contributed to mounting economic woes in the 1970s.

During the 1960s and 1970s, many young people also experimented with "far-out" dress and hair styles, rock and roll music, sex, and drugs. Others "dropped out" to live the so-called hippie lifestyle in communes. They not only opposed U.S. involvement in the war in Vietnam, but denounced the commercialization of American culture, calling for a return to nature and the return to simpler ways of living.

Although some changes, particularly more relaxed dress styles and new music, entered the mainstream, for the most part the upheavals of the 1970s were temporary. Following the election of President Ronald Reagan (1911–) in 1980, the United States seemed to embark on a new direction and to recover much of its earlier self-confidence. Reagan, a former film actor, was a skilled public speaker who had an instinct for expressing many of the hopes and fears of the U.S. public. Although Reagan supported conservative policies, not all of them succeeded.

The Civil Rights Revolution in the United States. In 1965 Martin Luther King Jr. and Coretta King lead a march protesting racial segregation and other forms of discrimination, both in the South and throughout the nation. Although most African Americans followed King and his peaceful approach based on the principles of the African American churches and on M. K. Gandhi's methods, some turned to violence and to the more radical approaches of Malcolm X and Stokely Carmichael.

© Reuters/Corbis-Bettmann

Gorbachev with Reagan. The leaders of the two superpowers, Mikhail Gorbachev of the Soviet Union and Ronald Reagan of the United States, share a laugh during their first summit in 1985. Gorbachev's reform movement in the Soviet Union and radical changes in eastern Europe in the late 1980s and 1990s ended the Cold War and ushered in a new, challenging era of international relations.

His early promise to balance the budget was abandoned in favor of a huge armaments program that doubled the size of the national debt and left a legacy of indebtedness that worried other industrial nations and contributed to economic strains at home. Reagan also cut or abolished government spending for many social programs. Importantly, he appointed many conservatives to judgeships, including the Supreme Court. The Supreme Court's decisions on police practices and abortion in the late 1980s reflected that conservative trend. In international affairs, Reagan took a strongly anticommunist position. His successor, President George Bush (1924–), although conservative, was less ideologically committed and more pragmatic about economic development and international relations, particularly with the Soviet Union.

The Soviet Union from Khrushchev to Gorbachev

The Soviet Union exhibited more outward domestic stability during the quarter century after 1960 than at any time since the 1917 revolution. However, the stability was deceptive, as it masked many problems that became evident after 1985. From the 1960s to the 1980s, under Communist party control, the economic and political life of the nation remained as strictly controlled and planned as under Stalin. Waste, inefficiency, and mismanagement created enormous problems that lowered productivity. A new affluent, but often corrupt, bureaucracy was another drain on the Soviet economy. Yet, despite the unchanging facade of aging Stalinist rulers, political changes did occur in the Soviet Union. The most apparent change was in leadership style from the crude and heavy-handed Nikita Khrushchev in the 1960s to the more sophisticated, youthful, and urbane Mikhail Gorbachev (1931–) after 1985.

After Khrushchev was forced from office in 1964, Communist party General-Secretary Leonid Brezhnev (1906–1982) dominated the state for almost two decades. Politically, Brezhnev supported career men in the party and in the state bureaucracy. He persecuted dissenters and sent them to labor camps, internal exile, or mental institutions.

Soviet heavy industry continued to grow, but living standards only slowly improved. At enormous economic cost, an expensive armaments program brought the Soviet Union to a position of equality with the United States. Agricultural production remained low, however, and the Soviet Union annually had to import grain, paying for it with hard currency earned through the export of raw materials such as petroleum, gold, and diamonds.

Assuming power in 1985, Mikhail Gorbachev initiated a more subtle and flexible style of Soviet leadership. Gorbachev instituted a program of *glasnost* (openness to the West) and allowed more freedoms for Soviet citizens. His charismatic personality and creative political style brought out cheering crowds during his well-publicized tours to Europe and the United States.

Domestically, Gorbachev advocated a new program of *perestroika* (economic restructuring) to revitalize the sagging Soviet economy by increasing industrial and agricultural production, improving living standards by more efficient methods, lessening corruption, and permitting incentives and some privatization. Hard-liners within the Communist party and many Soviet citizens accustomed to decades of planned economy remained skeptical of these reforms. When the reforms failed to produce the promised improvements in living standards, many people within the Soviet Union became openly critical of the regime, and some minority ethnic groups went so far as to advocate secession from the Soviet Union.

By 1990 mounting restlessness among the many ethnic and religious minorities, which collectively exceeded the population of the politically dominant Great Russians, posed a major threat to Gorbachev's political survival. Gorbachev attempted to balance the opening up of the political system to dissent with reforms aimed at eliminating corruption and inefficiency within the bureaucracy, but he failed, thereby helping to pave the way for the collapse of Communist regimes in eastern Europe and the break-up of the Soviet Union. (The demise of the Soviet Union will be described in the next chapter.)

European Political Trends

The revitalization of democratic political institutions has been one of the most impressive trends in the political life of western Europe since 1945. The claim of the European totalitarian leaders of the interwar years that democracy was doomed proved false. After World War II, free elections and civil liberties flourished in western Europe. Between 1949 and 1969, West Germany's conservative Christian Democratic party, led for many years by the aging anti-Nazi and anticommunist chancellor Konrad Adenauer (1876–1956), guided Germany's return to prosperity and international respectability. Free France's wartime leader, General Charles de Gaulle, in power between 1958 and 1969, brought that nation stability and a return to self-confidence. De Gaulle led France away from its postwar dependency on the United States and toward more independent, individualistic domestic and international policies. (See the introduction to this section for an example of de Gaulle's strongly independent, nationalist rhetoric.)

In the years immediately after World War II, the Labour party dominated British politics. Weakened militarily and economically by the war, Britain, as described in earlier sections of this chapter, reluctantly gave up its imperial holdings and began the long, arduous task of rebuilding its economy. After much debate it also moved toward closer political and economic ties with the rest of Europe by joining the European Economic Community (EEC). During the 1980s the Conservative party under Prime Minister Margaret Thatcher (1925–) dominated the political scene. She was the first female British prime minister and became the longest-serving one since the early nineteenth century.

In the 1980s a new political force, sometimes called the Greens, emerged to challenge the old policies of both the conservative and socialist parties in many European nations. The Greens demanded disarmament, legislation to protect the environment (forests, the ozone layer, and wildlife), and large-scale programs to improve the quality of life. The new party had many active and politically mobilized women in leadership roles and enjoyed growing popularity particularly among the young.

In contrast to the success of the centrist political parties, both Communists on the left and old-fashioned authoritarian regimes of the right were compelled to moderate their ideological programs. Communist parties remained popular in Italy and France, but because of the stigma of their ties to Moscow were unable to win power in national elections. As a result, leaders declared their parties nationalist organizations free of international communism. In Greece, the reign of a military junta, "the colonels," was replaced with a democratic regime. Authoritarian Spain and Portugal were transformed from fascist dictatorships into democracies after the deaths of the aged dictators, Franco and Antonio Salazar, in the 1970s. Spain, under a democratically oriented king, Juan Carlos, who faced down right-wing military rebels gun in hand, and who worked with a Socialist prime minister, provided a striking example of the flexibility, variety, and vitality of political life in Europe.

Until 1989 Soviet military power sustained Communist governments in Soviet satellites in eastern Europe. The Soviets had crushed violent outbreaks in East Germany in 1953 and in Hungary in 1956. In 1968 Brezhnev sent Russian troops into insurgent Czechoslovakia to overthrow a reformist government, but by 1981 Soviet domination over eastern Europe began to fade.

Economic Recovery and Prosperity

A high level of prosperity was the most striking feature of many industrialized nations after World War II. The integration of the economies of the western European nations under the aegis of the European Economic Community (EEC), or Common Market, and, to a lesser degree, of eastern Europe's COMECON was an important element of European economic resurgence.

Although the European Economic Community had originally aimed for full economic integration among its members by 1992, the collapse of the Soviet Union and the resulting economic problems delayed full union; however, the potential economic clout of a unified Europe was tremendous.

During the late 1970s and the early 1980s, Europe suffered from the same global economic decline that already affected the United States. Soaring petroleum prices hurt many European economies, except those of Great Britain and Norway, which derived petroleum from the North Sea. Unemployment rose to unprecedented levels in such wealthy and productive nations as West Germany. Heavy indebtedness to Western banks, meanwhile, pushed several Eastern bloc nations like Poland and Romania to the brink of economic collapse. The failure to provide full, productive employment in peacetime was an ongoing problem for both capitalist and socialist economies until the end of the twentieth century. Neither the conservative remedies of privatization applied by Prime Minister Margaret Thatcher in Great Britain nor the socialist policies of France's President François Mitterand (1916–1996) brought the hoped-for rapid recovery or full employment.

Both Europe and the United States faced formidable competition for world markets from the Pacific rim economic powerhouses of Japan, South Korea, Taiwan, Hong Kong, and Singapore. After World War II, Japan made a phenomenal economic recovery. Under U.S. military occupation, Japan was forced to adopt a democratic constitution patterned on U.S. and British models, and the emperor was forced to renounce his divine status. From the 1950s onward, the conservative Liberal Democratic party dominated Japanese politics and provided extraordinarily stable conditions and state support for economic growth.

Work Regulations in a Japanese Factory

Orientation starts at 8:30. Today, we learn the most important rules:

WORK REGULATIONS:

- *Don't divulge secrets learned during work.*
- *Try hard to increase efficiency and productivity.*
- *Follow instructions concerning your duties.*
- *Go to bed early, get up early, and be cheerful.*
- *Be properly and neatly dressed.*
- *Try to get acquainted with your surroundings quickly.*
- *Pay attention to your safety and security, and follow instructions and regulations.*
- *Ask someone between you to start the work if you don't know it well.*

I arrived yesterday, January 7, 1980, the first working day of Toyota's new year. . . . A big sign in the hall showing "The Number of Toyotas Produced up to the Present" lights up quite impressively. Its electronic panel displays a long row of figures: 29,894,140. . . . This is the total number of vehicles since Toyota shipped out its first real automobile in 1935. . . . Of course, this figure is only as of 11:15 A.M. As I watch, the last digit continually increases. Timing it, I realize that the number is changing every six seconds. . . . The 20 millionth came in July 1976. . . . Watching the figure increase with each passing second, I feel all choked up. I can see it: the conveyor belts moving along mercilessly; the workers moving frantically as they try to keep up. I can hear their sighs. One vehicle every six seconds. The conveyor belts never stop. . . . *

In this excerpt, a Japanese auto worker describes his orientation to work in a huge Toyota plant where workers are considerably more regimented than in Western factories and where rapid production and quality control are emphasized. A neon-lit sign counting auto production, similar to the one described here, was also displayed along a major freeway near Detroit, Michigan.

To protect the U.S. automobile industry from stiff Japanese competition, U.S. automobile manufacturers and the United Auto Workers union pressed the U.S. government to pass legislation requiring Japanese automakers to build automobile plants within the United States and to insist on Japan's self-restriction of exports. Toyota was forced to begin manufacturing in the United States in order to avoid being criticized for flooding the market in the United States and Europe; it was soon followed by a host of other automobile manufacturers from around the world.

*Satoshi Kamata, *In the Passing Lane: An Insider's Account of Life in a Japanese Auto Factory,* ed. and trans. Tatsuru Akimoto (New York: Pantheon, 1982), pp. 10–11, 195–197.

As part of its Cold War strategy, the United States sought to bolster Japanese economic strength in Asia as a counterweight to Communist power in China and Southeast Asia. To this end, the United States assumed most of the economic burden of Japanese defense by placing Japan under its defense umbrella and by retaining military bases on the islands. Free from burdensome military expenditures, Japan was able to devote almost all its technological and financial resources to economic development.

By the 1980s, the Japanese economy, which was geared toward export-oriented growth, had become the second largest in the world. High-quality Japanese goods flooded world markets, and Japanese technology in fields such as robotics and electronics quickly established itself as the most advanced in the world. This economic preeminence provided for unprecedented domestic prosperity for Japanese workers and the industrialized world's lowest rate of unemployment.

Under authoritarian and highly paternalistic governments, Taiwan, Hong Kong, South Korea, and Singapore also launched impressive programs of industrialization. As in Japan, the Confucian work ethic, respect for education, and a tightly knit family structure provided the basis for economic progress. Productivity in these "little dragons" soared. Economic prosperity provided high employment and rising standards of living as wage levels rose rapidly in the 1980s. On the negative side, the lack of government regulations and labor unions also often resulted in poor working conditions, long hours, and lack of protection for workers, particularly women.

The rising economies of western Europe and the Pacific rim nations deprived the United States of the advantage it had enjoyed in manufacturing goods and technology during the two decades following World War II. This loss of preeminence was a shock to Americans and, coupled with soaring military expenditures, resulted in persistent international indebtedness and trade deficits.

In light of the chronic excess of Japanese exports to imports and Japanese trade laws that protected their domestic markets (especially for agricultural goods), many industrialists and workers in the United States pushed for protectionist and stricter limitations on Japanese imports. This slowed, but did not end, Japan's continued economic growth. During the 1980s and early 1990s, domestic political scandals surrounding key politicians caused considerable uneasiness in Japan. During this era Japanese women emerged for the first time as a key political force demanding internal reforms. Nevertheless, until 1997 the Asian Pacific rim nations appeared likely to maintain their key positions in the global economy (see Chapter 17). They also began to explore the possibilities of forming an economic union similar to that in western Europe.

Superpower Confrontations and Détentes

Throughout the Cold War, the superpowers alternated between periods of high tension and periods of détente or rapprochement. Also called "peaceful coexistence" or "competitive coexistence," détente centered on the search by the two superpowers for ways of living together in a dangerous world. Détente flourished in the 1960s but ebbed during the Reagan years in the 1980s.

A dramatic easing of Cold War tensions occurred when the United States accepted the legitimacy of the

Map 16.6 The Global Cold War, 1950s–1980s. This map only hints at the massive, unprecedented outlay of global military power. Both the United States and the Soviet Union spread their forces and weaponry around the globe, challenging each other on the ground in Europe and East Asia, at sea in every ocean, everywhere in the air, including the poles, and even in outer space. China played a secondary "third-party" role. The enormous cost of this global confrontation put heavy strains on the United States and eventually broke down the Soviet economy, bringing the Cold War to an end by the early 1990s.

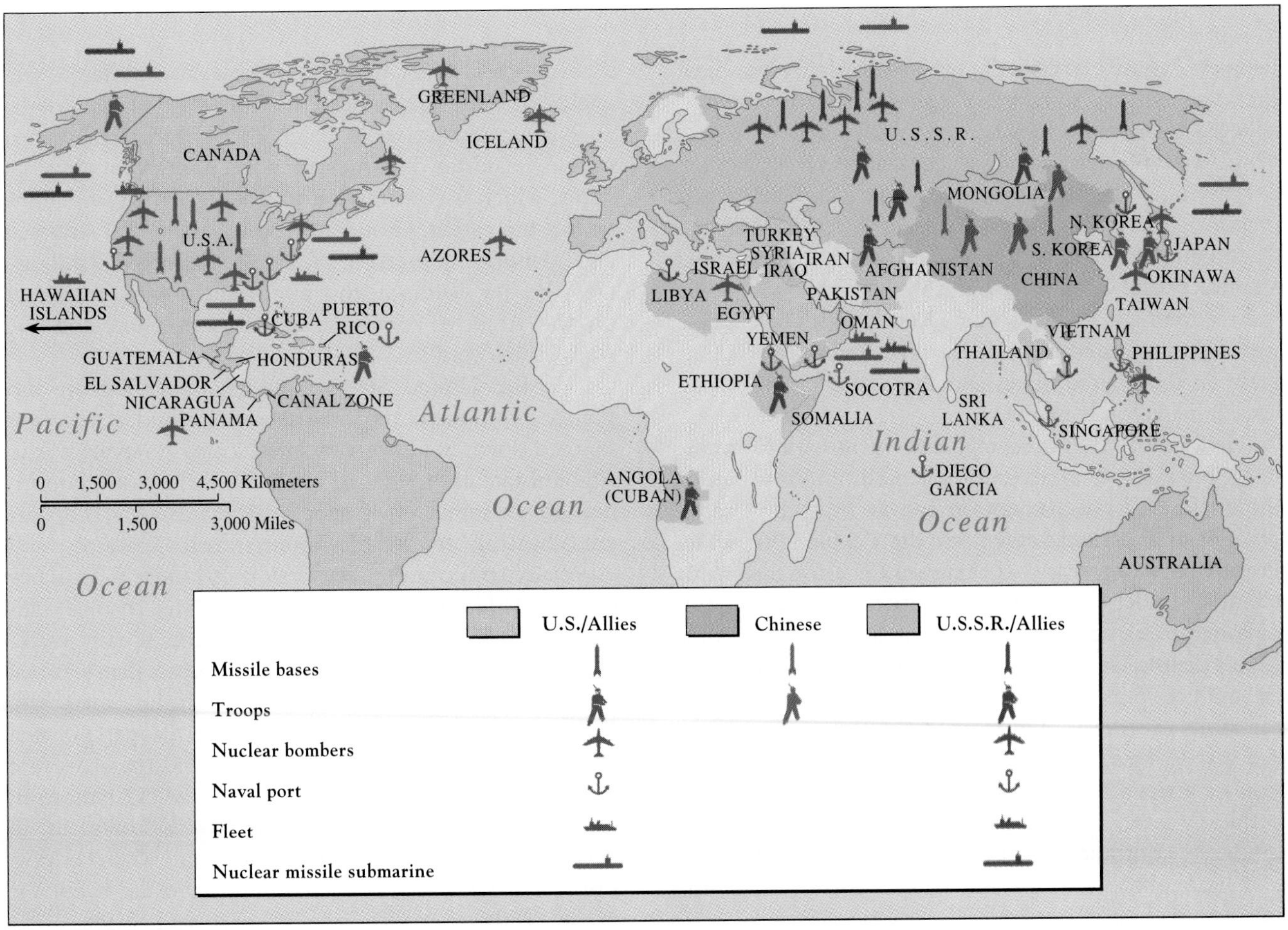

Courtesy of NASA

Man on the Moon. Beginning in 1957, U.S. and Soviet scientists and engineers achieved major breakthroughs in the exploration of space. Manned and unmanned spacecraft were placed into orbit around the earth, and, most exciting to the general populace, the United States put a man on the moon in 1969. Here astronaut Jim Irwin salutes for the camera in 1971.

People's Republic of China in the 1970s. Henry Kissinger, President Nixon's secretary of state and global strategist, believed friendly relations between the United States and China would foster a strong balance of power against the Soviet Union. The U.S. rapprochement with China was a pragmatic one for both U.S. President Richard Nixon and Chairman Mao Zedong. The United States had just ended an unsuccessful war in Vietnam, and the People's Republic was recovering from the Cultural Revolution. The Chinese were also motivated by their fear that improved relations between the United States and the Soviet Union would leave it dangerously isolated.

In 1971, as part of its rapprochement with Communist China, the United States accepted the expulsion of the Nationalist government on Taiwan from the United Nations and its replacement by the People's Republic. President Nixon flew to Peking in 1972 for talks with Chinese leaders. The two countries established full diplomatic relations in 1979. Contacts increased after Mao's death. The Chinese especially sought technological and economic assistance from the United States, and the latter in turn wanted to sell manufactured goods in the vast Chinese market. However, the brutal suppression of liberals in China—demonstrating students were ruthlessly gunned down in Beijing's Tiananmen Square in 1989—continued to strain relations between the two and highlighted the Communist party's determination to retain dictatorial powers.

In other Asian nations, détente also suffered setbacks. In 1979 the Soviet Union, in partial response to an Islamic revolution in neighboring Iran, sent troops into Afghanistan in order to bolster its client government, which was crumbling under the armed onslaught of Muslim rebels. (Both superpowers had vital strategic and economic interests in West Asia. Chapter 17 will discuss the key events in this important region, centering on the Arabian Peninsula, the Persian Gulf, and the Arab-Israeli conflict.)

As the United States discovered in Vietnam and France in Algeria, the Soviets soon found themselves bogged down in a protracted and losing guerrilla war in Afghanistan. By the late 1980s, the futility of a continued Soviet military presence in Afghanistan was apparent. Bowing to hostile international pressures and especially to mounting opposition at home, Gorbachev conceded defeat and withdrew the Soviet troops. This failure in Afghanistan was a blow to the already weakened Soviet Union and contributed to its collapse.

During the early 1980s, Cold War tensions increased. Following his election in 1980, President Reagan pursued a vigorous anti-Soviet policy and escalated the arms race by deploying new nuclear weapons to NATO nations in Europe. Reagan characterized the Soviet Union as an "evil empire" to be opposed whenever and wherever possible. The renewal of U.S. commitment to the Cold War in the 1980s was made easier by Soviet weaknesses.

The Arms Race and Disarmament

All of the superpower confrontations during the Cold War carried with them the possibility of nuclear annihilation due to the stockpiles of atomic weapons accumulated by both the United States and the Soviet Union. Popular demands for improved international relations were prompted by fears of nuclear holocaust held by many people around the world, particularly those in eastern and western European nations. The calls for arms control were reinforced by the cost of maintaining military parity, which became increasingly expensive, even prohibitively so.

After the 1962 Cuban Missile Crisis, a contradictory pattern characterized the arms race. On the one hand, with the long-term motive of reducing the terrible danger of atomic war, the superpowers negotiated a series of international agreements for limiting and controlling weapon systems. Under the Nuclear Test Ban Treaty of 1963, more than 100 nations agreed to stop testing nuclear weapons in the atmosphere, under water, or in space. The Nuclear Nonproliferation Treaty, signed by almost 100 nations, committed its signatories to refrain from developing nuclear weapons of their own. However, the number of nations possessing nuclear weapons continued to proliferate as many refused to be bound by the treaty. France, China, India, and Israel all refused to sign and developed their own nuclear weapons and arsenals. The Strategic Arms Limitation Talks (SALT) of 1972 limited the number of ICBMs (intercontinental ballistic missiles), ABMs (antiballistic missiles), and nuclear missile-firing submarines the two superpowers could deploy. Subsequent agreements between the superpowers banned large underground tests and deployment of missiles on the bottom of the sea or in Antarctica.

On the other hand, while the superpowers agreed to some arms limitations, they both continued to manufacture new generations of arms. The two superpowers enhanced some awesome weapons systems not forbidden by treaty. These included multiple, independently targeted reentry vehicles (MIRVs), which were single rockets bearing a number of nuclear bombs programmed to hit different targets; cruise missiles, which could slip in under enemy radar defenses; and neutron bombs, designed to kill humans with minimum damage to property. By the 1980s the superpowers had the nuclear capabilities to destroy the earth at least twelve times over—the "balance of power" had become the "balance of terror."

Space also became an area of superpower competition. In 1961 Soviet cosmonaut Yuri Gagarin became the first human to orbit the earth, followed into space one year later by U.S. astronaut John Glenn. In 1969 Neil Armstrong was the first person to walk on the moon. By the 1970s the Soviet Union was constructing space platforms, and the United States was sending manned shuttles back

1945	Chinese civil war Indian independence: Jawaharlal Nehru; Pakistan Creation of Israel: Arab-Israeli conflict Chinese Communist victory: Mao Zedong
1950	Korean War Algerian Revolution France withdraws from Indochina Bandung: Third World neutralism Suez crisis Cuban revolution: Fidel Castro
1960	African independence: Jomo Kenyatta, Kwame Nkrumah Cuban Missile Crisis U.S. civil rights movement: Martin Luther King Jr. Cultural Revolution in China War in Vietnam Man on the moon
1970	OPEC becomes a force in global economics and politics Allende's Marxist government overthrown in Chile All Vietnam under communism Women's liberation movement Militant religious movements Sandinistas triumph in Nicaragua
1980	Pacific Rim economic boom Reagan Cold War pressures on Marxists in Nicaragua and El Salvador Mikhail Gorbachev promotes glasnost and perestroika Movement towards democratic governments in Latin America
1991	

and forth between earth and space. Both nations sent space probes deep into the solar system to bring back information about other planets. Space research became part of the arms race, as space platforms and "spy" satellites gathered military information that could be used in future wars.

In spite of support for disarmament, the stockpiles of arms grew in the early 1980s. Although many scientists argued the program was unworkable, President Reagan supported a strategic defense initiative (SDI), the building of an elaborate, space-based system of defenses against nuclear attack, popularly known as "Star Wars." Gorbachev and others objected, partly because SDI would be enormously expensive to build and partly because it was viewed as being fundamentally offensive, not defensive. Gorbachev said of the program, "What we need is Star Peace and not Star Wars."

As the debate continued, Reagan and Gorbachev negotiated the Intermediate Nuclear Forces (INF) treaty (ratified in 1988) that provided for the dismantling of some nuclear systems deployed in Europe. This was the first treaty that actually provided for decreasing existing weaponry.

Summary and Comparisons

The collapse of the European overseas empires was a major trend in the decades following World War II. This great liberation movement freed a third of the world's population from foreign rule and marked a major change in the historical development and relationships between the industrialized West and the largely agricultural, poor nations of Africa, Asia, and Latin America.

Many former colonies in West and East Africa achieved independence with relatively little violence, but the Algerians had to fight a long war of liberation. In southern Africa the struggle for independence was even longer.

In the West there was conflict between the two superpowers, the United States and the Soviet Union, and their respective allies in Europe. During the 1950s to 1980s, relations between the superpowers were largely governed by the rise and fall of détente within the larger framework of the Cold War.

Both the Soviet Union and the United States viewed Asia and Latin America through the lens of the Cold War conflict. In largely agricultural Asia, Africa, and Latin America, the masses generally found Marxists more sympathetic to their problems. Mao Zedong, with peasant support, came to power in China, as did Ho Chi Minh in North Vietnam. In Korea, after a bitter war, the superpowers settled for a stalemate and the division of the country. Later, fearing the spread of communism in Southeast Asia, the United States intervened in South Vietnam. Faced with mounting human and economic costs and strong domestic opposition to the war, the United States ultimately withdrew from Vietnam, just as France reluctantly withdrew from Algeria.

As in China and other parts of Asia, social discontent in Latin America also fueled peasant uprisings and revolutions. Personalist dictatorships and revolutionary regimes were two responses to poverty and the wide gap between rich and poor. The most dangerous Cold War incident occurred in Cuba, where Fidel Castro created a peasant-backed Communist state. A U.S. attempt to overthrow him backfired, and when the Soviet Union intervened to protect him and installed nuclear missiles, the United States took measures that threatened war. Although the Cuban Missile Crisis was defused, the potential for atomic holocaust continued to threaten mass destruction on a scale never thought possible in previous conflicts.

Domestically, social reforms in the 1960s made the United States more truly democratic, while cultural changes swept the nation during the 1960s and 1970s. The Soviet Union appeared to achieve political stability, slow economic growth, and military parity with the United States, but the crumbling of the Soviet Empire by 1989 indicated that many of its gains had been illusionary. Meanwhile, Europe recovered economically, and democracy flourished in western Europe. In eastern Europe, true autonomy came only in the late 1980s, when Gorbachev ended Soviet domination over the region.

Under U.S. tutelage, Japan became a stable democracy and pro-Western force in the Cold War and enjoyed an unprecedented economic recovery following World War II. The United States gradually lost its preeminent economic position as Japan and the "little dragons" of Taiwan, Hong Kong, Korea, and Singapore became economic powerhouses competing successfully against European- and U.S.-manufactured goods and technology. As a result, the global economic balance shifted in the 1980s toward Asia, just as earlier ages of exploration in the fourteenth and fifteenth centuries had shifted the economic bases of power away from the Mediterranean world to Europe, and the growing power of the United States in the nineteenth and early twentieth centuries had shifted power from Europe to the Western Hemisphere. As in Europe, economic gains in the Communist nations were mostly illusory compared with the rapid strides made in capitalist and democratic countries.

During the Cold War, both superpowers developed arsenals capable of destroying the world. Technological developments meant that nations could not only destroy one another, but also threaten the existence of life on the entire planet. However, just as nations had moved toward some arms control after World War I, during the Cold War the superpowers and others took halting steps toward arms control under treaties designed to limit the arms race.

Selected Sources

*Anderson, Thomas P. *Politics in Central America.* 1982. Describes developments in El Salvador, Guatemala, Honduras, and Nicaragua.

Antony, A. *Gandhi-Nehru Dynasty.* 1990. On India's most famous family.

Battle of Algiers. An incredible black-and-white film on the Algerian struggle against the French.

Bhutto, Benazir. *Daughter of Destiny: An Autobiography.* 1989. The first female prime minister of a Muslim country writes about herself.

*Chafe, William H. *The Unfinished Journey: America since World War II.* 3d ed. 1995. Expanded assessment of U.S. history during the Cold War and post–Cold War eras.

*Chinodya, Shimmer. *Harvest of Thorns.* 1991. A dramatic and often humorous story of a young African torn between modern and traditional values.

*Cogan, Charles G. *Charles de Gaulle: A Brief Biography with Documents.* 1996. Readable short biography of a key French leader in the twentieth century.

Collins, Larry, and Dominique La Pierre. *Freedom at Midnight.* 1975. Fascinating account of Indian independence in 1947.

*Davidson, Basil. *Modern Africa: A Social and Political History.* 3d ed. 1994. Balanced narrative of independence struggles in Africa.

"The End of Empires." Multicultural Studies. This 48-minute video, hosted by David Frost, includes interviews with soldiers and civilians who fought for independence in African and Asian nations.

Fejto, F. A. *A History of People's Democracies: Eastern Europe since Stalin.* Trans. D. Weissart. 1973. A survey of communism in eastern Europe prior to the collapse of the Soviet system and the emergence of new states.

Fursenko, Aleksandr, and Timothy Naftali. *One Hell of a Gamble: Khrushchev, Castro, and Kennedy, 1958–1964.* 1997. Detailed account of the most dangerous Cold War confrontation, based on latest materials released since the collapse of the Soviet Union.

*García Márquez, Gabriel. *One Hundred Years of Solitude.* 1971. Complex novel on life in Latin America.

Gorbachev, Mikhail. *Perestroika: New Thinking for Our Country and the World.* 1987. The Soviet leader explains his reform plans.

"Half Lives: History of the Nuclear Age." Films for the Humanities and Sciences. A 56-minute video exploring the nuclear age with balanced discussion of key issues surrounding the arms race and nuclear energy.

*Herring, George. *America's Longest War: The U.S. and Vietnam, 1950–75.* 1979. Well-written, concise, and balanced.

*Horne, Alistair. *A Savage War of Peace: Algeria 1954–1962.* 1977. Moving rendition of Algerian struggle for independence.

"India After Independence." Films for the Humanities and Sciences. A short 21-minute video on India from 1947 to the assassination of Indira Gandhi.

"Jomo Kenyatta." A 12-minute film examining Kenyatta's leadership in Kenya. [Films for the Humanities.]

"Kim Phuo." 1984. A 25-minute film account of a young girl's scarring by napalm during the Vietnam war and her struggle to survive.

"The Legacy of Mao Zedong." Insight Media. 1991. A 30-minute video that traces the impact of Mao and communism in China.

Loth, Wilfried. *The Division of the World 1941–1955.* 1988. Scholarly critique of causes for the Cold War.

"Making Sense of the Sixties." PBS. 1991. A six-part video series on the turbulent sixties with interviews with leading figures from the era.

Martin Luther King, Jr. A 27-minute color video documentary on the Nobel Peace Prize winner and leader of U.S. civil rights movement. [Films for the Humanities.]

*McWilliams, Wayne C., and Harry Piotrowski. *The World Since 1945: Politics, War, and Revolution in the Nuclear Age.* 1987. Comprehensive account of the Cold War and the Third World.

*O'Neill, William. *Coming Apart.* 1971. Spirited account of the United States during the turbulent 1960s.

*Palmer, David Scott, ed. *Shining Path of Peru.* 2d ed. 1994. An updated guide to the organization and program of the revolutionary movement in Peru.

*Patterson, Walter C. *Nuclear Power.* 1976. A lively account of the interconnection of the arms race and the Cold War.

*Powaski, Ronald E. *The Cold War: The United States and the Soviet Union, 1917–1991.* 1998. Cogent narrative of complex interrelationships and conflicts of the two superpowers.

Salisbury, Harrison. *New Emperors: China in the Era of Mao and Deng.* 1992. A masterful analysis of communist China during the last four decades.

**Student Atlas of World Politics.* 1994. Contains accurate current maps and good coverage of independence movements as well as economic and environmental issues.

Szymusiak, Molyda. *The Stones Cry Out: A Cambodian Childhood, 1975–1980.* 1988. Evocative story of terror during Pol Pot regime.

*Available in paperback.

Internet Links

All-African People's Conference: Resolution on Imperialism and Colonialism, Accra, December 5–13, 1958
http://www.fordham.edu/halsall/mod/1958-aapc-res1.html
A formal statement condemning "colonialism and imperialism in whatever shape or form these evils are perpetuated."

Cold War International History Project
http://cwihp.si.edu/cwihplib.nsf
This project of the Woodrow Wilson International Center for Scholars focuses on the Cold War, its crises, major leaders, specific phases, the arms race, and archive materials.

Cuban Missile Crisis (Documents Relating to American Foreign Policy)
http://www.mtholyoke.edu/acad/intrel/cuba.htm
Dozens of important primary documents (memoranda, letters, telegrams) plus expert analyses and interpretive essays by specialists.

Jawaharlal Nehru: Marxism, Capitalism and Nonalignment
http://www.fordham.edu/halsall/mod/1941nehru.html
Reflections of independent India's first prime minister on "Marxism, Capitalism and India's Future (1941)," and "Economic Development and Nonalignment (1956)."

President Lyndon Johnson and Ho Chi Minh: Letter Exchange, 1967
http://www.fordham.edu/halsall/mod/1967-vietnam-letters1.html
Two letters disclosing the ideological chasm that resulted in the prolonged and bloody conflict in Southeast Asia.

The Sixties Project
http://lists.village.virginia.edu/sixties/
Includes personal narratives, primary documents, discussion lists, exhibits, and links to online resources.

COMPARATIVE ESSAY 12

Regionalism and Internationalism

Are we ready to abandon the Monroe Doctrine and leave it to other nations to say how American questions shall be settled and what steps we shall be permitted to take in order to guard our own safety? . . . Are we ready to have other nations tell us by a majority vote what attitude we must assume to immigration or in regard to our tariffs?

Senator Henry Cabot Lodge, speech to Senate in pamphlet, Emory University Library, in Elizabeth Stevenson, *Babbitts and Bohemians: The American 1920s* (New York: MacMillan, 1967), p. 64.

The greatest danger for us of the Western nations . . . is that in our affluence we shall become soft and selfish and self-centered . . . and so complacent that we fail to see the dangers of the wider world in time. . . .

The extent of the dangers is a measure of the need for new effort and for a new sense of urgency, and for new methods. Increasingly we must seek solutions not by old national means but by new international action. The dangers should surely intensify a determination to win freedom from racial discrimination and domination, to settle disputes before violence takes over, to make a new assault on the poverty of more than half the world and . . . to support and strengthen the authority and capacity of the United Nations. Few people will dispute that the dangers exist. The question is whether we understand and care enough to act while there is still time, and time is terribly short.

Hugh Foot, *A Start in Freedom* (London: Hodder and Stoughton, 1964), pp. 231, 246.

These conflicting viewpoints highlight a basic paradox of the post–World War II world. While tribalism, nationalism, and regional loyalties are still strongly felt throughout the world, advanced communications have tied us together in the "Global Village" of interdependence. Senator Lodge's comments are representative of the strong isolationist sentiment held by many in the United States after World War I; Lodge's opposition to U.S. involvement in foreign affairs contributed to the refusal of the U.S. Senate to ratify the Versailles Treaty and of U.S. entry into the League of Nations, the dream project of President Woodrow Wilson. Strong isolationist sentiments are echoed today in the continued opposition among some Americans to the United Nations, except when that organization follows U.S. directives. In contrast, British diplomat Hugh Foot expressed the internationalist viewpoint that stresses the need for cooperation among nations in the latter half of the twentieth century.

Paradoxically, by the year 2000, people in many areas of the world were again espousing narrow ethnic and religious ties. For example, from 1975 to the early 1990s, Maronite Christians and Druze, Sunni, and Shi'i Muslims in Lebanon fought to maintain their separate identities and political power. Similarly, confrontations between ethnic groups in the former Soviet Republic of Azerbaijan threatened to destroy the national unity of that diverse nation. India, too, has been plagued by the sometimes violent separatism of the Sikh minority, while Sri Lanka and Northern Ireland have been torn by ethnic and religious divisions.

On the other hand, stunning advances in transportation and communication technology have tied the world together as never before. Air travel on jet planes has made "globe trotting" commonplace, while satellite transmission, international telephone and telegraph systems, and fax machines enable people around the world to communicate with one another almost instantaneously. These developments have fostered cultural cosmopolitanism and a global economy. Lest the virulent nationalism that led to the world wars resurface, world leaders have turned to strengthening international organizations such as the United Nations and the World Bank to solve national disputes and to encourage international cooperation. Similarly, the Organization of American States (OAS) and the Arab League were created to foster regional cooperation. To promote international trade, most nations joined the General Agreement on Tariffs and Trade (GATT). However, by the 1990s, fear of global economic domination by international corporations and financial institutions had led to a widespread grassroots movement against GATT and similar economic organizations. Similarly, deep-seated national rivalries and emphasis on rights of sovereignty have hampered the efforts of all international organizations.

Since the 1950s, the record of the United Nations has been mixed. On the one hand, it could not prevent wars between Israel and the Arab states or between Iran and Iraq. It also failed to prevent U.S. intervention in Vietnam or the Soviet occupation of Afghanistan. On the other hand, UN peace-keeping forces have helped to prevent full-scale wars in Cyprus and Kashmir. They have also helped in the creation of independent nations; for example,

Libya and Namibia. In addition, the UN has helped negotiate settlements to disputes in Latin America.

International organizations such as the Court of Justice at The Hague and the World Health Organization (WHO) have contributed to the lessening of national rivalries and have channeled creative energies toward the solution of national and human problems. The Court, for example, has settled troublesome disputes about fishing rights in coastal waters, and WHO eradicated smallpox, which had ravaged humanity for centuries. Economic organizations such as the World Bank, the Kuwait Fund for Arab Development, and the Asian Development Bank provide finances for development projects at the international and regional levels. On the negative side, the World Bank has funded grandiose development projects in poor Third World nations to the detriment of smaller, local projects such as clean water and sewage systems.

The European Economic Community (EEC) has been the most effective and successful movement for regional integration in the post World War II era. Beginning with six nations, the membership of the EEC, later just the European Community (EC), now includes all of western Europe; further, the EC has developed affiliate relationships with eastern Mediterranean nations such as Israel, Turkey, and Cyprus. Following the end of the Cold War and the collapse of the Soviet Union, eastern European nations also sought membership in the EC, which has brought unprecedented prosperity to the citizens of its member nations. The EC has also helped to blunt the rivalries that have for so long divided Europe. The success of the EC has inspired other regions to develop similar cooperative ventures, such as the Association of Southeast Asian Nations (ASEAN).

Private multinational corporations have also become major forces in the global economy. Huge multinational corporations such as Exxon, General Motors, Mitsubishi, and Nestlé operate throughout the world. Some, like General Motors, have annual incomes larger than the combined gross national products (GNP) of many poor Southern Hemisphere nations. Their size and wealth place these multinational companies beyond the control of individual governments and international organizations such as the United Nations. For example, nations acting alone have been unable to implement regulations governing the shipment of petroleum by oil tankers. These failures have resulted in major oil spills that caused vast ecological damage from the shores of Alaska to the beaches of France.

Worldwide problems such as pollution, overpopulation, and environmental crises demand global cooperation and financial expenditures far beyond the economic capacity of many poor nations. Whether societies will be able to overcome their national and cultural divisions and cooperate to solve these problems will determine the future of the world.

Life in a Multipolar World: The Post–Cold War Era

17

The world in which we live today is radically different from what it was at the beginning or even in the middle of this century. And it continues to change as do all its components. The advent of nuclear weapons was just another tragic reminder of the fundamental nature of that change. A material symbol and expression of absolute military power, nuclear weapons at the same time revealed the absolute limits of that power.

The problem of mankind's survival and self-preservation came to the fore.

The Soviet Union is prepared to institute a lengthy moratorium of up to 100 years on debt servicing by the least developed countries, and in quite a few cases to write off the debt altogether.

Let us also think about setting up within the framework of the United Nations a center for emergency environmental assistance.

Now let me turn to the main issue—disarmament, without which none of the problems of the coming century can be solved.

The Soviet Union and the United States have built the largest nuclear and missile arsenals. But it is those two countries that, having become specifically aware of their responsibility, were the first to conclude a treaty on the reduction and physical elimination of a portion of their armaments. . . .

*I would like to believe that our hopes will be matched by our joint effort to put an end to an era of wars, confrontation and regional conflicts, to aggressions against nature, to the terror of hunger and poverty as well as to political terrorism. This is our common goal and we can only reach it together.**

*Mikhail Gorbachev, quoted in *The Manchester Guardian Weekly* (December 18, 1988).

In this speech before the United Nations on December 7, 1988, Mikhail Gorbachev, president of the Soviet Union, highlighted the major issues facing the world in the last quarter of the twentieth century; as his remarks make clear, the world today is indeed a global village. While Gorbachev correctly emphasized the need for international cooperation for solving the daunting problems of the twentieth century and for ensuring human progress into the twenty-first, he did not realize that less than two years after delivering this speech he would be forced out of office and the Soviet Union would cease to exist. This chapter will describe the spectacular collapse of the Soviet system and the emergence of numerous—and sometimes conflicting—nations in eastern Europe and the old Soviet republics.

It will also describe the ethnic strife jeopardizing both international peace and economic and social development in Europe and much of Asia and Africa. Other "hot spots" will be discussed with particular reference to the ongoing Israeli-Palestinian-Arab conflict and the ultimately successful struggle for equality and democracy in southern Africa. Both regions saw major upheavals after World War II.

Finally, the chapter will survey urgent problems confronting peoples around the world at the turn of the millennium: struggles for democracy; gender and social inequality; technological, economic, and environmental challenges; and cultural tensions.

The Collapse of the Soviet Union and Changes in Europe

When the idea first came up that I should let my name stand for president of Czechoslovakia, it seemed like an absurd joke. All my life I had opposed the powers that be. I had never held political office. . . .

Slightly less than a month after this shocking proposal was put to me, I was unanimously elected president of my country. It happened quickly and unexpectedly, almost overnight one could say, giving me little time to prepare myself and my thoughts for the job.

It might be said that I was swept into office by the revolution. . . .

The Wall Comes Down. Here enthusiastic crowds of East and West Germans eagerly demolish the Berlin Wall, the hated symbol of the bitter Cold War division of the United States and the Western bloc from the Soviet Union and the Eastern bloc.

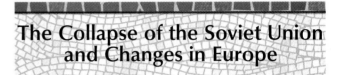

Alexander Avakian/Woodfin Camp & Associates

*The return of freedom to a society that was morally unhinged has produced something we therefore might have expected, but which has turned out to be far more serious than anyone could have predicted: an enormous and dazzling explosion of every imaginable human vice. . . . The authoritarian regime imposed a certain order—if that is the right expression for it—on these vices. . . . This order has now been shattered, but a new order that would limit rather than exploit these vices, an order based on freely accepted responsibility to and for the whole of society, has not yet been built—nor could it have been, for such an order takes years to develop and cultivate.**

*Václav Havel, *Summer Meditations* (New York: Knopf, 1992), pp. xv, 1–2.

Noted playwright, essayist, and political dissident under the Czechoslovakian Communist regime, Václav Havel (1936–) wrote, in his memoirs, about implications of the fall of the Communist regimes in eastern Europe and his unexpected rise to power in post–Communist Czechoslovakia. In 1989, in an almost bloodless, or "velvet" revolution, the people of Czechoslovakia overthrew the repressive Soviet-dominated regime that had held power almost continuously for forty years. Havel was twice elected president of the new Czechoslovakian federated state, but failed to hold the ethnic Czechs and Slovaks together. In the above recollection, he describes the euphoria that swept over the peoples of Europe and elsewhere as authoritarian Communist regimes crumbled under the weight of their own internal corruption and in face of popular opposition. As Havel also explains, however, that euphoria quickly disappeared as the difficult tasks of forging democratic and free market institutions began. Following the collapse of the Communist regimes, old ethnic and religious rivalries, long-dormant racism, economic dislocations, and social disruption emerged to threaten the survival of democratic governments and economic development. At the beginning of the twenty-first century the future still seemed uncertain.

This section will describe the collapse of the Communist regimes in eastern Europe and the end of the Soviet Empire and the resulting political, social, and economic dislocations.

Democracy and Capitalism in Post–Cold War Europe

As it became evident that the Soviet Union would no longer use military force to control its internal affairs, the eastern European nations moved away from Soviet domination and, in generally bloodless revolutions, overthrew the Communist regimes that had governed them for over forty years. The process began in the early 1980s with the formation of the Solidarity opposition party in Poland. In 1989 Solidarity candidates won stunning election victories and entered into a coalition government.

Gallup/Liaison

Václav Havel. A noted playwright and author, Havel was persecuted for voicing his opposition to the old Communist system. After its collapse, he was elected president of Czechoslovakia and remains a leading political force in the Czech Republic.

By the end of 1989, the old, established Communist leaders had been ousted throughout eastern Europe. In 1989 Václav Havel became the president of Czechoslovakia, and in 1990 Lech Walesa (1943–) of the Solidarity party became the president of Poland. By 1991 the Baltic republics, Estonia, Latvia, and Lithuania, had all obtained complete independence from the Soviet Union. In Bulgaria and Romania, coalition or reformist Communist parties emerged. Even Albania, the poorest nation in Europe with the most hard-line Communist regime, instituted a coalition government in 1991.

In an even more stunning development, East and West Germany were reunified. In November 1989, when a new, reformist East German Communist government responded to popular demonstrations by opening the Berlin Wall—the symbol of the Cold War for almost thirty years—millions of East Germans rushed to visit West Berlin and West Germany. The spring 1990 elections in East Germany resulted in a victory for a non-Communist coalition, which promptly agreed to the reunification of Germany under the leadership of Helmut

Maps 17.1 and 17.2 Post–Cold War Europe, 2000. With the collapse of the Soviet Empire, a number of independent nations emerged in eastern Europe and along the Baltic Sea, while the former Soviet republics also declared their independence. By 2000 most of these weak states, with the exception of the Baltic nations, had joined Russia in the Commonwealth of Independent Nations, but many were still threatened by ethnic and religious separatist movements.

Kohl (1930–), leader of the West German Christian Democratic party.

As the new governments across Europe moved to privatize their economies, the era of Soviet domination had clearly ended. In 1991 Soviet forces began to withdraw from eastern Europe, and the Soviet military alliance, the Warsaw Pact, was formally dissolved.

The Soviet Empire Crumbles

Mikhail Gorbachev, general secretary of the Soviet Communist party, sought to reform the corrupt and inefficient Soviet economy and government while preserving the socialist system. Having little experience in the Soviet Republics outside the Russian Republic, Gorbachev underestimated the strength of the ethnic loyalties within the multiethnic Soviet Empire. These troubles, bubbling just below the surface, became evident in 1986 when the Kazakhs, under the banner of "Kazakhstan for the Kazakhs," rioted in Alma-Ata, the Kazakh capital. The Armenians followed in 1988 with the slogan, "One People, One Republic."

As previously noted (Chapter 16), Gorbachev also faced opposition from hard-liners within the Communist party who both opposed the liberalizing reforms he had initiated and feared that the proposed changes would threaten their privileged positions. Others, particularly his rival Boris Yeltsin (1931–), the elected President of the Russian federation, demanded more extensive reforms with the creation of a free market economy. After his election as chairman of the Russian Republic's Supreme Soviet, Yeltsin publicly challenged Gorbachev to expand both political and economic reforms.

Faced by these demands, Gorbachev reluctantly announced his support for a free market economy in the summer of 1991. Gorbachev's apparent intentions to undercut the authority and power of the Communist party caused the hard-liners within the party to move against him. In August 1991, while he was vacationing in the Crimea, Gorbachev was placed under house arrest.

A group of hard-liners, including the KGB (secret police) chief and the defense minister, announced from Moscow that they had taken over the reins of power.

In Moscow, Yeltsin responded by rallying mass demonstrations against the attempted coup. When the military refused to fire on the demonstrators, the coup collapsed and its leaders were imprisoned. A politically weakened Gorbachev returned to power and announced his resignation from the Communist party. In the ensuing backlash against the old Communist party, more and more republics announced their intention to secede from the Soviet Union. The central government, dominated by Russia, was powerless to prevent the breakup. By the end of 1991, Russia, Ukraine, and Belorussia (present-day Belarus) had disbanded the union and formed the Commonwealth of Independent Nations. A number of other republics subsequently joined the loosely organized, decentralized commonwealth union. With no country left to lead, Gorbachev resigned as president in December 1991 and returned to private life. Thus, after more than seventy years, the Soviet Union and its empire had collapsed.

Yeltsin, who had much earlier resigned from the Communist party, continued to head the Russian federation and emerged as the Commonwealth leader until ill health forced him to resign. His hand-chosen successor, Vladimir Putin (1952–), was elected president in 2000. To counter growing opposition and the instability caused by privatization policies, both Yeltsin and Putin increased their executive powers and limited political rights. However, in spite of fierce opposition from more xenophobic Russian nationalists and political dissidents from the old Communist party, Russia continued on the path toward capitalism and increased political participation.

New Economic Alliances and Problems

Throughout the 1990s, privatization in both industrial and agricultural sectors and rising prices caused severe economic dislocation throughout the nations of the old Soviet Empire. Although the Soviet economic system had been inefficient, provided few incentives, and produced goods without consideration of consumer demands and cost effectiveness, it had provided free or low-cost housing, guaranteed employment, transportation, and social services to many citizens. In China, where a similar state-controlled economy operated, the system of guaranteed jobs was called the iron rice bowl. In addition, under Soviet domination, Communist countries had supplied basic needs for one another through extensive trade. For example, within the Soviet Union, Russia had supplied the Ukraine with petroleum at low prices in exchange for grain.

When these programs abruptly stopped, people on fixed incomes, particular the elderly (many of them

AP Photo/Philippe Desmazes, Pool.

Vladimir Putin. The Russian president, Vladimir Putin, arrives in France for an official visit in 2000. Putin faced daunting political and economic problems in Russia and some skepticism in the West over his commitment to democratic reforms.

women) found they no longer had enough money to buy food let alone other basic necessities. Inflation skyrocketed, reaching over 1,000 percent in Poland in the early 1990s (by 1995 it had dropped to a still-high 28 percent). When they could no longer make ends meet, many retired people were forced to sell their guaranteed apartments and to move into cramped quarters with their families or to become homeless. In 1993, Russian women, carrying pictures of Stalin, demonstrated against Yeltsin, demanding a return to family values and government support for the elderly.

As state subsidies and controls disappeared, social problems, crime, declining production, and indebtedness increased. Severe economic hardships led to a broad range of social problems. As health care declined, infectious diseases such as tuberculosis and diphtheria reappeared in Russia and former Soviet republics. By 1999 the death rate in Russia exceeded the birth rate, and population continued to decline. Some Russians, desperate to find scapegoats for their economic and social problems, rallied behind openly racist and anti-Semitic extremists who advocated a return to empire.

Meanwhile, other nations formerly under Soviet domination also experienced economic and social dislocations. West Germany's booming economy was severely strained by its integration with the much poorer and less dynamic East Germany. When East Germans were allowed to exchange their money at a par with the far more stable and valuable West German mark, the nation's huge currency reserves were wiped out. Although citizens of former East Germany generally supported the political and social reforms, many missed such socialist welfare benefits as cheap housing. The integrated economy could not provide jobs for all its new citizens, and unemployment soared. Many in the east also complained that although the stores now carried a wide array of goods, the prices of both consumer goods and basic necessities were much higher. Some, particularly the youth, found outlets for their dissatisfaction by joining neo-Nazi groups or by scapegoating and attacking nonethnic Germans.

Encouraged by the West and international financial institutions such as the International Monetary Fund and the World Bank, the new governments in eastern Europe dismantled their socialist economies, encouraged private enterprise, and established closer ties with the more affluent, capitalist nations of western Europe. At the same time, however, as in Germany, the transition from a Communist to a private enterprise economy was not easy. Poland, Romania and other eastern European nations lacked efficient communication systems, banks, trained personnel, and computer technology. Rising prices, inflation, and unemployment caused severe social dislocations and increased crime and corruption. Some former Communist officials and bureaucrats used their connections and experience to manipulate the systems and to further enrich themselves; some formed so-called mafias that often used illegal methods to gain profit. Other enterprising men and women, however, established flourishing businesses and were confident of future prosperity.

The sweeping changes in eastern Europe also delayed, but did not stop, plans for integration of western European economies and governments that had been established under the Maastricht agreement of 1991. Despite the obstacles, a common currency—the Euro—was put into circulation by the end of the 1990s, and many eastern European and Mediterranean nations sought to become members of the European Union (EU, formerly the European Community). However, before granting membership, the western European nations demanded that further economic reforms and environmental regulations be implemented. By the turn of the twentieth century, the EU, with its 338 million generally well-educated and affluent people, was one of the world's three major economic forces, along with the United States and Japan.

Ethnic Diversity and Conflict

Ethnic rivalries also threatened the political and economic well-being of many nations in Europe and elsewhere. As noted in the introduction to this section, in spite of his enormous efforts, Václav Havel was unable to hold the two ethnic groups in Czechoslovakia together, and in 1993 the nation split along ethnic lines into the Czech Republic and Slovakia.

Yugoslavia was torn apart by ethnic divisions, as rival Macedonians, Slovenians, Croatians, Serbs, and Muslim Bosnians fought one another over national borders and territory. The Bosnian Serbs launched an "ethnic-cleansing" pogrom, laying siege to the city of Sarajevo and many other Muslim-held Bosnian territories, terrorizing civilian inhabitants with random bombings, raids, the raping of women, and mass expulsions. The United States, the European nations, and the United Nations attempted to stop the fighting. Finally, the United States brought the fighting sides together in Dayton, Ohio. The Dayton Accord, 1995, called for a Muslim-Croat Federation and a Serb Republic of Bosnia; NATO forces, including U.S. soldiers, were deployed to keep the fragile peace. When Serbs launched a major offensive in the predominately ethnic Albanian Kosovar region, NATO forces retaliated by bombing Serb territory. NATO troops continued to maintain the fragile peace, but, by 2000, the future of these weak and poor states remained uncertain, while ethnic hatreds continued to escalate.

At the same time, hate crimes against foreign workers, Turks, North Africans, and Asians increased in Germany, France, and elsewhere in Europe. Reactionary political parties in numerous European nations also campaigned for bans or limitations on all immigration by foreign workers or refugees fleeing their own war-torn and impoverished countries. The rise of anti-Semitism was another alarming trend.

In the United States, racism continued to divide citizens, posing an ongoing threat to unity and equal economic development among the multitude of ethnic and racial communities within the nation. Similarly, ethnic strife engulfed Tajikistan, and ethnic and sectarian divisions involving the Tamils in Sri Lanka, minorities in Indonesia and the Philippines, Kurds in Turkey, Iran, and Iraq, and Protestants and Catholics in Northern Ireland undermined the national cohesion of these nations and threatened to Balkanize, or divide them (some of these conflicts will be described in the following sections of this chapter).

The ethnic wars that the United Nations was often called upon to contain or control placed severe strains on its limited budget. Secretary-general Kofi Annan of Ghana urged nations to increase their financial support; he emphasized that the United States, which was heavily in arrears by 2000, needed to fulfill its financial obligation. Annan also warned that the United Nations needed to respond to possible conflicts before thousands and been killed or displaced in full-scale wars. Given that many of the disputes in the Balkans and elsewhere are complex and difficult to resolve, it seems likely that the United Nations, NATO, or other joint national forces will be needed to stop or prevent full-scale wars well into the twenty-first century.

Ongoing Conflict and Changes in West Asia and Africa

The most crucial task which will face the government [the white National Party-led regime] and the ANC will be to reconcile. . . . Such reconciliation will be achieved only if both parties are willing to compromise. The organization will determine precisely how negotiations should be conducted. It may well be that this should be done at least in two stages—the first where the organization and the government will work out together the preconditions for a proper climate for negotiations. Up to now both parties have been broadcasting their conditions for negotiations without putting them directly to each other.

*The second stage would be the actual negotiations themselves when the climate is ripe for doing so. Any other approach would entail the danger of an irremovable stalemate. I . . . hope to see the ANC and the government working closely together to lay the foundations for a new era in our country, in which racial discrimination and prejudice, coercion and confrontation, death and destruction, will be forgotten.**

*Nelson Mandela, *Speeches 1990* (New York: Pathfinder, 1990), p. 18.

In this letter written from prison to South African President P. W. Botha in July 1989, Nelson Mandela outlined a plan for negotiations to resolve the long struggle between the white-dominated South African government and the majority black South African population, which was fighting for an end to apartheid and the establishment of a state based on equal rights and self-determination for all its people. Mandela, the leader of the African National Congress, was addressing the protracted conflict in South Africa, but his analysis is equally applicable to the Arab-Israeli conflict, in which two peoples confronted one another to achieve self-determination. This section will trace the ongoing conflicts in West Asia, with special emphasis on the Arab-Israeli conflict, and the resolution of conflicts in southern Africa, with special emphasis on the Republic of South Africa. Despite strides toward conflict resolution in the 1990s, both regions continued to face major political and economic uncertainties.

The Israeli-Palestinian-Arab Conflict

A legacy of Western imperialism and the Cold War contributed to the tangle of problems in West Asia (the Middle East). After World War II, Great Britain granted full independence to Transjordan (present-day Jordan)

Israeli Declaration of Independence

May 14, 1948: A few minutes later, at exactly 4 P.M., the ceremony began. Ben-Gurion, wearing a dark suit and tie, stood up and rapped a gavel. According to the plan, this was to be the signal for the orchestra . . . to play "Hatikvah." But something went wrong, and there was no music. Spontaneously, we rose to our feet and sang our national anthem. Then Ben-Gurion cleared his throat and said quietly, "I shall now read the Scroll of Independence. . . . Accordingly we, the members of the National Council, representing the Jewish people in the Land of Israel and the Zionist movement, have assembled on the day of the termination of the British mandate for Palestine, and, by virtue of our natural and historic right and of the resolution of the General Assembly of the United Nations, do hereby proclaim the establishment of a Jewish state in the Land of Israel—the State of Israel."

*The State of Israel! My eyes filled with tears, and my hands shook. We had done it . . . Whatever happened now, whatever price any of us would have to pay for it, we had recreated the Jewish national home. The long exile was over.**

In this statement, Golda Meir, a future prime minister of Israel, describes the emotions surrounding the declaration of independence for the new Jewish state in 1948.

*Golda Meir, *My Life* (New York: Dell, 1975), p. 217.

LIVES AND TIMES ACROSS CULTURES

Political Humor

Common people throughout the world have long used humor to express disdain, discontent, and even hatred of politicians and governments. This was, for example, the stock in trade of Aristophanes, whose comedies often satirized the leaders of Athens and their hawkish war policies during the Peloponnesian War. In the ninth century, Arab writers mocked their leaders in satiric essays and poems. The Arabic language lends itself easily to puns and jests; in the Arab world, the Egyptians are particularly famous for making jokes about everything from sex to the bureaucracy, to individual politicians. Arab cartoonists caricature their political leaders much as Garry Trudeau in his Doonesbury comic strip and Art Buchwald in his columns poke fun at Washington politicos.

During the Cold War, jokes about the repressive Soviet regimes, food shortages, and corruption were popular among eastern Europeans. Similarly, Egyptians who opposed Gamal Abdul Nasser's nationalization policies and growing authoritarianism in the 1960s gleefully shared humorous stories that made fun of the regime. The following witticism was particularly popular.

Nasser was walking around the Great Pyramids and the Sphinx at Giza, when the Sphinx called out, "Nasser, Nasser!" Nasser turned around in amazement, crying, "You have been silent for thousands of years. Caesar, Napoleon, the British all came to you, but you refused to speak. Why now do you speak to me?" And the Sphinx replied, "I want an exit visa."

and encouraged Arab nationalism in the neighboring French-held territories of Syria and Lebanon, both of which also received their independence.

Great Britain wanted good relations with the Arab nations because of their strategic locations and their petroleum reserves. The British mandate over Palestine, however, with its majority Palestinian Arab population and growing Jewish minority, who had come mostly from Europe and the United States, posed a problem that defied easy solutions. Jews, pouring into Palestine from the concentration camps of Hitler's Europe, were determined to establish a homeland of their own. To achieve this goal, in the face of frequently hostile British policies, some organized a terrorist underground. The Palestinian Arabs, who accounted for two-thirds of the population and owned 80 percent of the land, were equally determined to defend their rights. Caught in the middle of spiraling violence that their imperial policies had helped to create, the British announced they would leave Palestine in 1948, and turn the entire problem over to the newly formed United Nations. The United Nations recommended the partition of Palestine into a Jewish and an Arab state. Neither side was satisfied with this decision, and fighting between the two conflicting national groups intensified.

When the British left Palestine in 1948, the Jews promptly announced the creation of Israel under the leadership of David Ben-Gurion (1886–1973; see the accompanying box). The Palestinians and the Arab nations refused to recognize the new state, and the first Arab-Israeli war began. The Israelis, better equipped, better trained, more unified, and supported by the United States, defeated their Arab adversaries and expanded their territory by one-third. In the course of the struggle, nearly one million Palestinian Arabs fled their villages and sought refuge in squalid camps in the surrounding Arab states. After the war, fearing that the Palestinians threatened the existence of a Jewish state, Israel refused to allow the Palestinian refugees to return. Meanwhile, the Palestinians remained determined to return to their homes and create a Palestinian state. Without resolution of the core of the conflict, namely, implementation of both Israeli and Palestinian rights, the conflict continued.

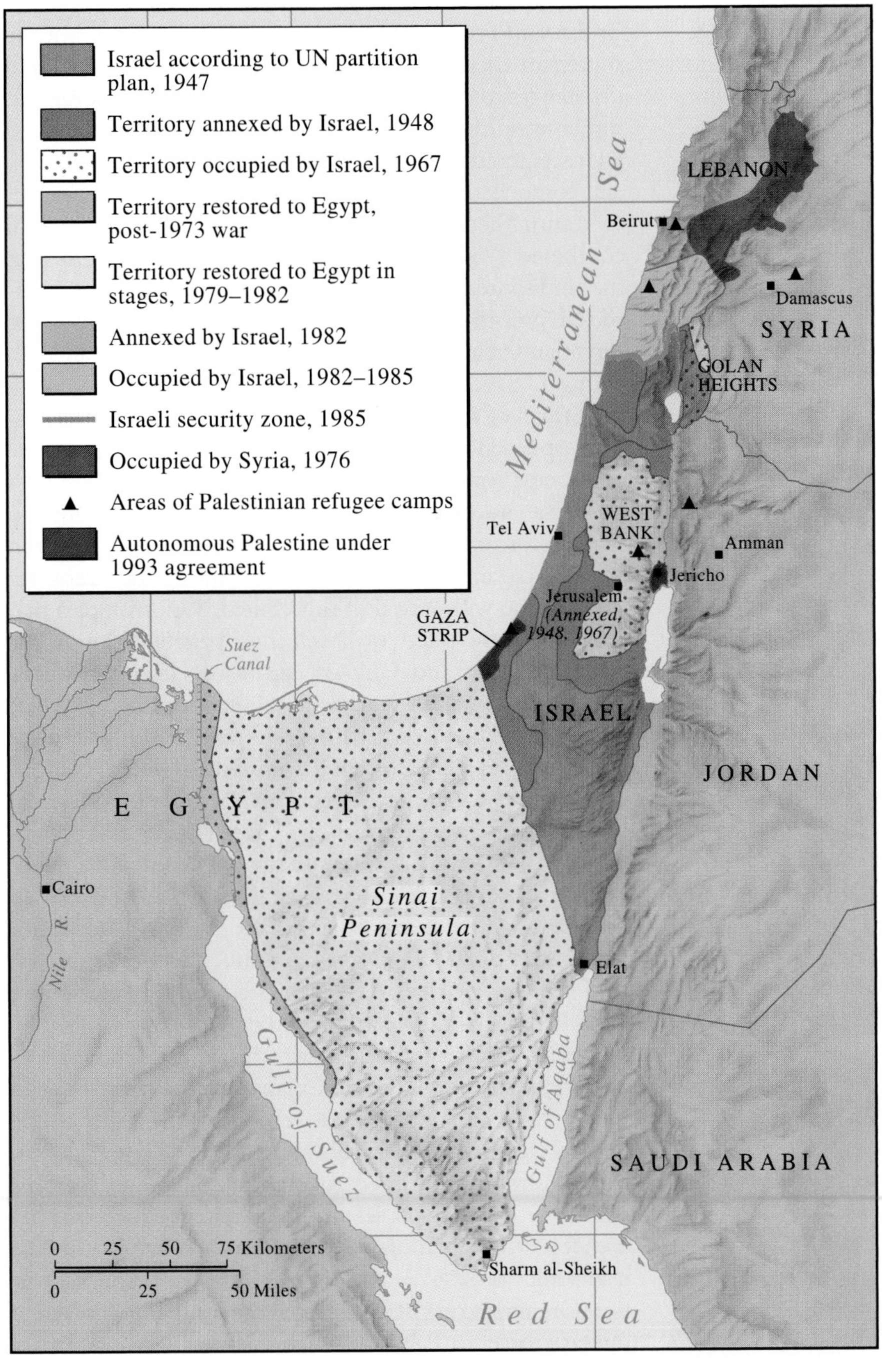

Map 17.3 The Arab-Israeli Conflict. Two basic facts are set out here: Israel's expansions and annexations from 1948 to 1982, and its occupation of, and subsequent withdrawal from, the Sinai Peninsula and most of southern Lebanon. The autonomous areas of the Gaza Strip and Jericho, agreed upon by Israel and the Palestinian Liberation Organization (PLO) in 1993, are also designated. The future of the rest of the West Bank and East Jerusalem, still under Israeli occupation, remains in doubt.

In many ways Israel, established and governed largely by Jews from Europe and North America, was part of the Western world. Nevertheless, it was surrounded by Arab nations and had many Palestinians living within its borders. The hostility of Israel's Arab neighbors brought conflict punctuated by open warfare. The Israeli refusal to permit the creation of a separate Palestinian state was matched by the Arab denial of the right of Israel to exist.

Arab nationalism peaked in the mid-1950s under the charismatic leadership of Gamal Abdul Nasser (Egyptian leader, 1952–1970). In 1952 Nasser led a military revolt that overthrew the corrupt Egyptian King Faruk. Nasser then instituted a number of reforms, including the redistribution of land to the poor and the building of the huge Aswan High Dam to provide water to irrigate more land and electric power for villages and factories to solve Egypt's economic problems. Nasser was a strong supporter of Palestinian rights, and he suspected continued British and French imperialist designs in the region. To counter Western influence, he sought better relations with the Soviet Union and other eastern European nations. In light of the Cold War, the United States viewed Nasser's neutrality with increasing hostility.

The Continuing Arab-Israeli Conflict. During the 1973 war, Israeli troops prepare to counterattack across the Suez Canal. Since 1948 a series of conflicts in West Asia have kept the region in constant turmoil.

When the United States abruptly withdrew its promise to finance the building of the Aswan Dam, Nasser retaliated by nationalizing the Suez Canal, which was controlled by foreign stockholders. Revenues from the canal fees were diverted to build the Aswan Dam, which subsequently was also underwritten by Soviet financial and technical aid. Thus challenged, France, Britain and Israel—all of whom wanted Nasser ousted from power—secretly agreed to take back the canal by force. The subsequent 1956 war resulted in the Israeli occupation of the Sinai Peninsula and the British and French occupation of the Canal Zone, but the successful tripartite invasion was an unmitigated political disaster for the West. Shocked at this apparent return to the nineteenth-century "gunboat diplomacy," the United States entered in rare agreement with the Soviet Union and compelled its NATO allies (Great Britain and France) to return the canal to Egypt. Nasser, whose charges of continued Western imperialism were justified, emerged as the undisputed leader of the Arab world. Following concerted pressure by the United States to withdraw from Egyptian territory, Israel withdrew from the Sinai after securing U.S. recognition of Israeli shipping rights through the Straits of Tiran to the southern port of Elat. Arab nations opposed this concession, and it became a major cause of the next Arab-Israeli war.

With no peace settlement, both sides continued to prepare for the next confrontation. In May 1967, Nasser, hoping to gain increased popularity among the Arabs, requested the withdrawal of the United Nations forces that guaranteed the safety of Israeli ships passing through the Strait of Tiran and Gulf of Aqaba to Israel's southern port. Acting in accordance with regulations providing that troops could be placed in sovereign territory only with the agreement of the affected nation, the United Nations forces withdrew. Israel viewed any move to close the strait to its ships as an act of war. The United States and the Soviet Union attempted to defuse the crisis, but while negotiations were still in process, Israel attacked the key air installations of the major Arab nations. The 1967 Arab-Israeli war, or the Six-Day War, resulted in a stunning Israeli military victory and Israeli occupation of the entire Sinai Peninsula, the Gaza Strip, the West Bank of Jordan, including eastern Jerusalem, which had been under Jordanian jurisdiction, and the Golan Heights, part of Syrian territory. Israel annexed East Jerusalem, proclaiming the unified city its capital. Following this humiliating defeat, some Palestinians turned to guerrilla raids and terrorist strikes to dislodge Israel from the Occupied Territories and force the creation of a Palestinian state. Under the leadership of Yasir Arafat (1929–), the Palestine Liberation Organization (PLO) became the leading political and military force for Palestinian nationalism.

Jimmy Carter Library

Meeting at Camp David. At Camp David in 1978 President Jimmy Carter mediated a formal agreement leading to a full-scale peace treaty between Egypt and Israel in 1979. Here Carter and his wife Rosalyn, President Sadat of Egypt, and Prime Minister Begin of Israel enjoy a light-hearted moment of relaxation from protracted negotiations that stretched over almost two weeks.

Nasser died in 1970, and his successor, Anwar Sadat (1918–1981), promised to secure the return of the Sinai to Egypt. In 1973 the Egyptians launched a surprise attack across the Suez Canal against the occupying Israeli forces. Fighting also ensued along the Golan Heights between Israel and Syria. The 1973 war was not a clear-cut victory for either side. The Israelis beat back Syrian attacks on the Golan Heights, but Egyptian forces were able to cross the Suez Canal and establish a foothold on the eastern bank. With this achievement, Sadat later offered peace and recognition of Israel in return for the Sinai. The settlement, brokered by U.S. President Jimmy Carter in 1978, led to a peace treaty between Egypt and Israel in 1979, but it failed to provide for an independent Palestinian state. The peace settlement did, however, mark a break in the solid front of Arab states against Israel and turned Egypt, formerly a Soviet client, into an ally of the United States.

In 1982, Israel invaded its northern neighbor, Lebanon, which had suffered from a destructive civil war since 1975 and had become a major base for the PLO. Exacerbated by the Palestinian presence, the civil war in Lebanon stemmed largely from social, economic, and sectarian differences among the various Lebanese religious groups. During the summer of 1982, the Israeli army drove into the Lebanese capital, Beirut, forcing the dispersal of the PLO but not its destruction. Even after the 1982 war, the Lebanese failed to settle their differences, and fighting continued until a fragile peace was established in the late 1980s. Meanwhile, Israel continued to hold a so-called security zone in southern Lebanon, the Gaza Strip, and the West Bank and steadily increased the number of Jewish settlers in this predominantly Palestinian territory. The Israeli occupation in southern Lebanon led to a mounting resistance movement by Hezbollah, a Lebanese Muslim movement supported by Iran and sometimes Syria. After protracted violence, Israel withdrew from Lebanese territory in 2000.

Meanwhile, the Palestinians in the Occupied Territories began a campaign of civil disobedience, attacking Israelis with stones and sticks in 1987. The *Intifada,* or uprising, continued unabated in the face of massive repression by the Israelis. In 1988, as the rising spiral of violence continued, the PLO declared Palestinian statehood for the territories of Gaza and the West Bank, the so-called mini-state solution, and recognized Israel's existence (see the accompanying box).

As more and more nations recognized the Palestinian state, the United States reluctantly agreed to mediate between the opposing Israelis and Palestinians and participated in negotiations in 1991. As the negotiations dragged on without results, secret meetings were held between PLO delegates and Israelis that resulted in a stunning Declaration of Principles, whereby the old enemies agreed to recognize one another in September 1993. Further negotiations were to lead to some undefined type of autonomy for the Palestinians in parts of the West Bank and the Gaza Strip, but, once again, the two sides were unable to reach mutually acceptable agreements and the negotiations foundered. Violence between the Palestinians and Israeli settlers in the Occupied Territories escalated and in 1995 a young Israeli violently opposed to any compromise with the Palestinians assassinated Yitzhak Rabin (1922–1995). Although Israel withdrew from some parts of the West Bank and most of the Gaza Strip, major differences over the nature of a Palestinian state, the Israeli settlements, and the status of Jerusalem remained unresolved. Renewed outbreaks of violence in 2000 caused many to conclude that the peace process was dead.

Crises in the Persian Gulf Region

With its vast petroleum reserves and its geopolitical position south of the Soviet Union and astride the intersection between the West and the East, West Asia was of strategic importance to both the superpowers. As a result, during

Palestinian Declaration of Independence

November 15, 1988: Nourished by many strains of civilization and a multitude of cultures and finding inspiration in the texts of its spiritual heritage, the Palestinian Arab people has, throughout history, continued to develop its identity in an integral unity of land and people and in the footsteps of the prophets throughout this Holy Land, the invocation of praise for the Creator high atop every minaret while hymns of mercy and peace have rung out with the bells of every church and temple. . . .

The Palestine National Council hereby declares, in the Name of God and on behalf of the Palestinian Arab people, the establishment of the State of Palestine in the land of Palestine with its capital at Jerusalem. . . .

The State of Palestine, in declaring that it is a peace-loving State committed to the principles of peaceful coexistence, shall strive, together with all other States and peoples, for the achievement of a lasting peace based on justice and respect for rights. . . .

*We give our solemn pledge to continue the struggle for an end to the occupation and the establishment of sovereignty and independence. We call upon our great people to rally to the Palestinian flag, to take pride in it and to defend it so that it shall remain forever a symbol of our freedom and dignity in a homeland that shall be forever free and the abode of a people of free men.**

On November 15, 1988, Chairman Yasir Arafat proclaimed Palestinian independence before the Palestine National Council in Tunis, Tunisia. In many ways his proclamation paralleled Ben-Gurion's declaration of Israeli independence in 1948. Both Israelis and Palestinians seek to exercise their rights to self-determination on the same territory, and therein are the seeds of their ongoing conflict.

*"Palestinian Declaration of Independence," *American-Arab Affairs* (Fall 1988), pp. 182–185.

the Cold War both the Soviet Union and the United States sought to reinforce their alliances with key nations in the region. In addition, most western European nations and Japan depended on petroleum from the region for their energy needs and petrochemical industries. Although the Soviet Union was largely self-sufficient in petroleum, whoever controlled the vital petroleum resources of West Asia clearly held an enormous advantage in the global balance of power.

During the 1960s and 1970s, the Shah in Iran had embarked on an ambitious and costly program of industrialization, and built up a huge military machine. Although urban areas experienced rapid economic development, Iran suffered from mounting inflation, declining agricultural output, political repression, and corruption and nepotism at the highest levels of government. As a result, Iranians from all walks of life, particularly the Shi'i clergy, joined forces to overthrow the Shah. The ousting of the Shah in 1979, through a popular revolution championed by the Islamic leader Ayatollah Ruhollah Khomeini (1900–1989), was a severe blow to U.S. interests. Ayatollah Khomeini and the Shi'i mullahs (clergy) established a strict Islamic state that was hostile to secular Western society, which it viewed as immoral. Since Muslims were often disillusioned by the failures of both Western and Soviet models to improve their societies, many in West Asia and Africa turned to militant Islam. The revolutionary Islamic regime in Iran encouraged and sometimes directly supported militant Islamic movements not only in the Arab world, but elsewhere as well.

Ayatollah Khomeini's attempts to export the Iranian revolution also contributed to the outbreak of a protracted war with neighboring Iraq. The war began in 1980 and dragged on until an uneasy cease-fire was reached in the late 1980s. For both sides the war was a financial and human disaster. Although the war severely strained the Iranian economy, the Islamic state survived both the disasters brought on by the war and the death of Ayatollah Khomeini in 1989.

Iraq emerged from the war with a huge battle-trained army, but with enormous debts. During the war Iraq had been forced to borrow vast amounts of money from oil-rich Arab nations in order to buy arms. The Iraqi regime, under Saddam Hussein (1937–), believed that Iraqis had fought and died in the war in part to protect the Gulf states and Saudi Arabia from possible overthrow by the revolutionary Islamic government of Iran. Consequently, it did not believe it should have to repay the loans. Iraq was also anxious to sell more of its petroleum on world markets to obtain much-needed capital for the rebuilding of its war-damaged infrastructure. When Kuwait began to press for repayment of its loans and massive sales of petroleum by Saudi Arabia and other Gulf states kept the price of petroleum depressed, the Iraqis loudly protested.

After negotiations had failed to resolve these differences, Saddam Hussein took matters into his own hands and launched a massive invasion of Kuwait in August 1990. Most of the international community vigorously condemned the aggression, demanding the immediate withdrawal by Iraq and the return of the Kuwaiti monarchy. With the collapse of the Soviet Union, the United States was the sole superpower, and it was determined to preserve its petroleum and political interests in the region.

Consequently, the United States demanded that economic sanctions be applied against Iraq and that an international coalition under the auspices of the United Nations be organized to force an Iraqi withdrawal by military means. In January 1991, the U.S.-led coalition launched a massive month-long aerial bombardment of Iraq, resulting in numerous Iraqi civilian deaths and widespread destruction. The subsequent ground war into Kuwait by the coalition met with success on all fronts and resulted in the complete withdrawal of Iraqi forces from Kuwait. The war ended with a clear-cut military victory for the coalition and the United States and the return of the pro-West Kuwaiti monarchy.

Although there were uprisings among the Kurds in the north of Iraq and the Shi'i in the south, Saddam Hussein's regime survived. By 2000, after a decade of international sanctions, which caused the death of over 500,000 Iraqi civilians, mostly women and children, the regime was still firmly entrenched in power, and many human rights organizations, Arabs, and Europeans argued that the Iraqi people had suffered enough and that the sanctions should be lifted. The United States and some Arab Gulf states, however, remained committed to maintaining the sanctions indefinitely.

Ayatollah Khomeini. In February 1979, Ayatollah Khomeini returned to Iran following the departure of the Shah and his family. Khomeini was greeted by hundreds of thousands of cheering Iranians, who hailed his leadership in the revolution that overthrew the Shah.

Struggles for Equality in the Republic of South Africa

By 1991, the Republic of South Africa was the only African state still under white minority rule. South Africa's political and economic system continued to be dominated by Afrikaners, descendants of the Dutch settlers or Boers, who outnumbered the generally more tolerant English. After World War II, the Afrikaner government perpetuated its system of strict apartheid, or segregation of the races, and tenaciously refused to grant political rights to the majority black population, which numbered approximately 26 million people by the 1980s.

The goals of apartheid were to segregate the races and to perpetuate white control. A complex set of laws required each race—black Africans, Asians, and people of "mixed races"—to live, go to school, attend church, find recreation, and otherwise spend their lives separate from other races and especially from the whites who ruled them. Interracial marriages were prohibited, and nonwhite South Africans were required to carry special passes. They often had to travel long distances from their segregated living quarters to work at jobs in the white areas.

In the face of mounting international opposition to the denial of political rights to blacks, the Afrikaner South African government created several black African *bantustans* or "homelands." The government then declared many ethnic Africans citizens of these artificial "states" and compelled them to live in these areas. These homelands were enclaves within the territorial confines of South Africa and were invariably established on the poorest land. In the absence of resources, industry, and jobs, a majority of adult black males and women had to leave the homelands to find work in white-dominated areas. Populated mainly by the old, women, and children, the homelands remained desperately poor. President P. W. Botha (1916–), leader of the dominant white

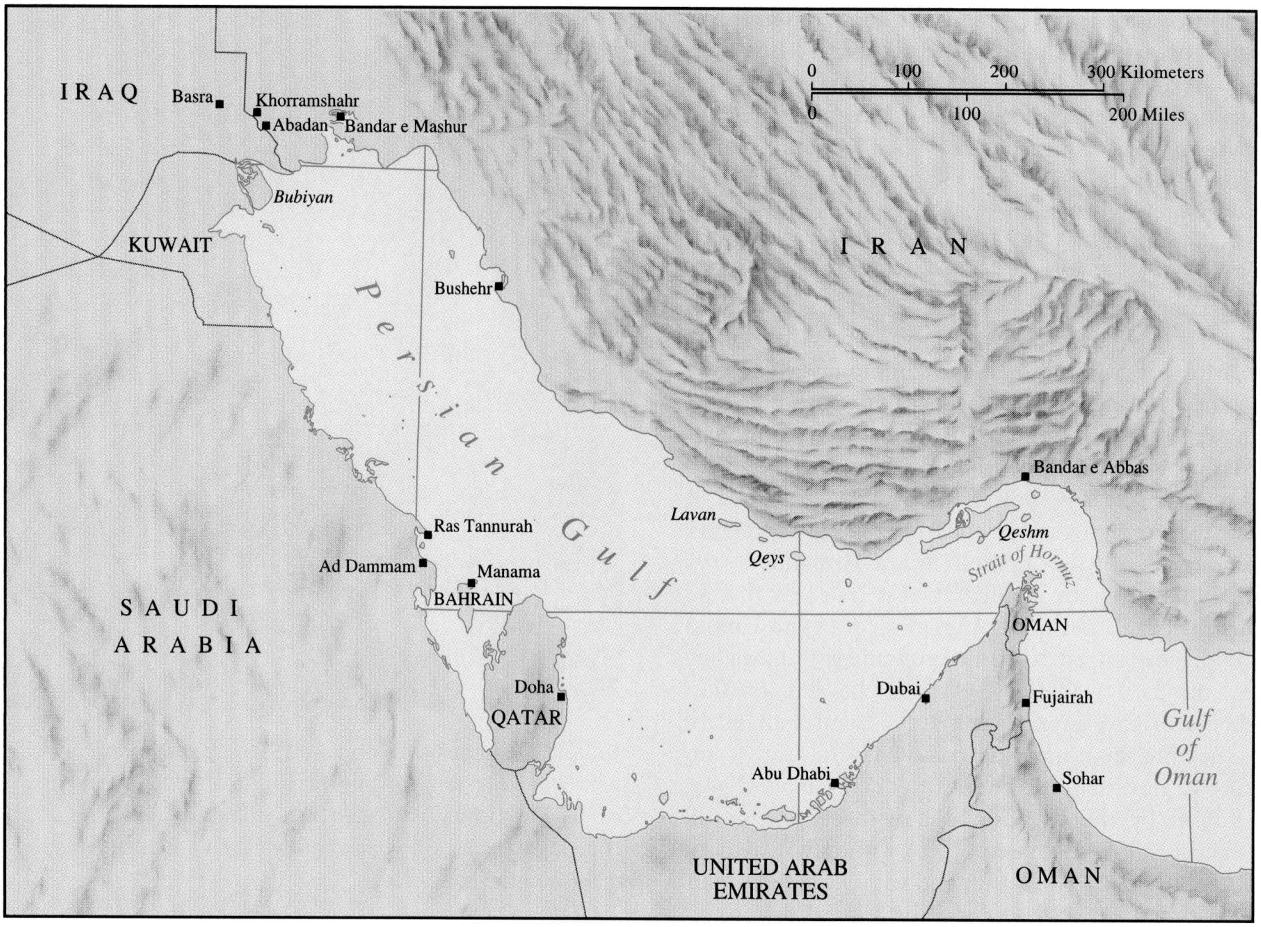

Map 17.4 The Persian Gulf. The gulf, with its vast petroleum reserves and strategic location, became a focus of Cold War rivalry and regional disputes. Iran tried to extend its control of the vital waterway, while Iraq sought to protect and maximize its own interests in the region. As a result, Iran and Iraq fought a long war of attrition in the 1980s. In 1990 Iraq invaded Kuwait but was pushed out by the Allied forces led by the United States in 1991.

political organization, the Nationalist party, inaugurated limited parliamentary reforms in the 1980s to satisfy international criticism. Under these reforms some Asians and people of mixed races were granted limited political participation, but the majority black population remained totally outside the political system.

Beginning in the 1950s, black South Africans responded to apartheid with waves of protests. These demonstrations were ruthlessly crushed by police power, and black political organizations such as the African National Congress (ANC), which was formed in 1912 as one of the first African national movements, were outlawed until 1990. Some opponents of the regime adopted guerrilla warfare as a means of fighting the system. The South African government justified its violent suppression of black African nationalist movements by arguing that they were Communist inspired.

Some black South African activists went underground or into exile in neighboring African states to escape death, persecution, or imprisonment at the hands of the government. ANC leader Nelson Mandela (1918–) spent more than twenty-five years in South African jails for his commitment to the cause of justice and equality for his people. Meanwhile, Nobel Peace Prize winners Albert Luthuli (1898–1967) and Bishop Desmond Tutu (1931–), along with Winnie Mandela, wife of the long-imprisoned ANC leader, continued to work for an end to racial discrimination by generating international support for their cause.

The crisis in South Africa continued to mount in the 1980s as the black townships erupted in violence and Western nations intensified pressure on the government through economic sanctions. The threat of withdrawal of Western investment capital, coupled with strains in the South African economy, compelled the government to promise reforms. After considerable political negotiations, the National party led by Frederik de Klerk (1936–) freed Nelson Mandela, who continued to campaign vigorously

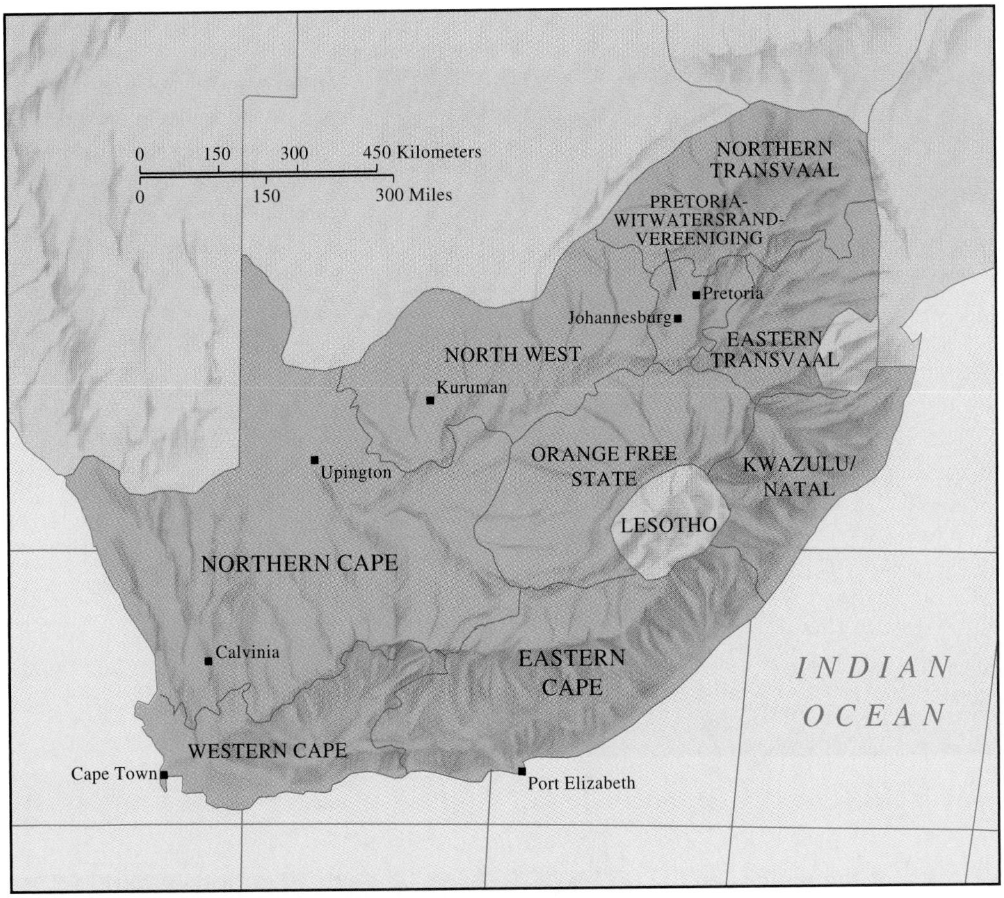

Map 17.5 South Africa. In 1994, in the first elections open to all South Africans, Nelson Mandela won the presidency, ending white minority dominance in the nation. Dire predictions of secession by some tribal groups and whites did not materialize, and the nation remained unified.

for an end to apartheid and full voting rights for the majority black population.

After modifying some apartheid regulations, de Klerk opened negotiations with Mandela and the ANC. The two parties subsequently agreed that voting rights would be granted on the basis of one person, one vote, and those new elections would be held in April 1994. The ANC, which was expected to win a free and open election, campaigned under the simple slogan, "Jobs, Peace, Freedom." Since an estimated 47 percent of the labor force was unemployed, it was not surprising that jobs were the ANC's first priority.

Although some extremists attempted to prevent the elections, a record number of voters turned out for the spring 1994 elections, which resulted in a resounding victory for the ANC. Nelson Mandela became the first South African leader chosen in an election open to all South Africans, and South Africa's first black president. A Truth and Reconciliation Commission was established to investigate those accused of crimes against the opponents of the apartheid system, but South African society largely avoided the racial and ethnic violence that had erupted in so many other nations after the Cold War. South Africa also avoided one-man, dictatorial rule; Mandela willingly turned over the reins of power to others in the ANC when his term in office expired. He did, however, continue to act as a senior diplomat to negotiate peaceful settlements to disputes and the end to civil wars that plagued other Africa nations. On the domestic front, South Africa, like many neighboring African nations, continued to face enormous problems of poverty and unemployment.

Political, Social, and Economic Issues in Africa

The ongoing struggles in the Republic of South Africa also affected neighboring nations; just as the Arab-Israeli conflict had regional implications in West Asia. During the 1980s, in efforts to destabilize regimes hostile to its apartheid system, the white South African government assisted a number of rebel movements in neighboring countries. It also conducted raids into Mozambique and supported a rebel movement so cruel that the entire international community condemned it. In Angola both the United States and South Africa provided arms and money to Jonas Savimbi whose UNITA party waged a protracted civil war against the Soviet- and Cuban-backed Popular Movement for the Liberation of Angola (MPLA) led by Jose Eduardo dos Santos. When dos Santos and the MPLA won free and open elections in

© Reuters/Dave Caulkin/Archive Photos

Nelson Mandela. After his election as president of South Africa, Nelson Mandela traveled around the world to gather international support and economic investment for his nation. Here he jokes with schoolchildren after his speech before both houses of the British Parliament.

1992, Savimbi simply refused to accept the results and resorted to force to achieve political power. In spite of attempted negotiations, fighting continued in much of Angola into 2000. Thus leaders and movements backed by the United States and the West to counter Soviet presence in Africa during the Cold War continued to wage war and threaten democratic, elected governments long after the superpower conflict had ended. Namibia, Angola, Mozambique, and a host of other nations continued to suffer the negative impacts of the Cold War.

As in the Balkans, Northern Ireland, and India, ethnic conflicts also erupted in several central African nations. Genocidal warfare between Hutu and Tutsi populations swept through Rwanda and Burundi and spilled over into neighboring Zaire. The aging Zairian dictator, Mobutu Sese Seko, failed to control the Hutu forces in his nation or to stop outside invasions. Mobutu was forced to resign in 1997, having become a multimillionaire through the theft of Zaire's wealth for over thirty years. The new Zairean government thus inherited a bankrupt nation and faced the seemingly overwhelming job of rebuilding the economy from the ground up. Eritrea and Somalia in the Horn of Africa confronted similar problems of rebuilding war-torn, impoverished nations. Thus the gap between the wealthy, prosperous northern nations of Europe, Japan, and the United and the poor southern states in Africa continued into the twenty-first century.

Major Challenges Confronting the Post–Cold War World

When I got the telegram saying that I was invited by the United Nations [for the International Women's Year Tribunal in Mexico in 1974], I was quite surprised and disconcerted. I called a meeting of the committee and all the compañeras *agreed that it would be good for me to travel. . . .*

During the trip I thought . . . that I'd never imagined I'd be travelling in a plane, and even less to such a far-off country as Mexico. Never, for we were so poor that sometimes we hardly had anything to eat and we couldn't even travel around our own country. . . .

[At the conference] there'd be two groups: one, on the government level, where those upper class ladies would be; and the other, on the non-government level, where people like me would be, people with similar problems, you know, poor people. It was like a dream for me! Goodness, I said to myself, I'll be meeting peasant women and working women from all over the world.

In the Tribunal I learned a lot. . . . In the first place, I learned to value the wisdom of my people even more. There, everyone who went up to the microphone said:

"I'm a professional person, I represent such and such organization. . . ." And bla-bla-bla, they'd begin to give their opinion.

So, I went up and spoke. I made them see that they don't live in our world. I made them see that in Bolivia human rights aren't respected and they apply what we call "the law of the funnel": broad for some, narrow for others. That those ladies who got together to play canasta and applaud the government have full guarantees, full support. But women like us, housewives, who get organized to better our people well, they beat us up and persecute us. They couldn't see the suffering of my people, they couldn't see how compañeras *are vomiting their lungs bit by bit, in pools of blood. They didn't see how underfed our children are. And, of course, they didn't know, as we do, what it's like to get up at four in the morning and go to bed at eleven or twelve at night, just to be able to get all the housework done, because of the lousy conditions we live in.*

*It was . . . a great experience being with so many women and seeing how many, many people are dedicated to the struggle for the liberation of their oppressed peoples.**

*Dimitila Barrios de Chungara, in Hazel Johnson et al., eds., *Third World Lives of Struggle* (London: Heinemann, 1982), pp. 236–242.

In this excerpt, Dimitila Barrios de Chungara, a miner's wife from Bolivia, vividly describes the vast gulf between the rich and the poor and the problems facing peasants and women throughout most of the contemporary world. She was the leader of a Housewives Committee organized to improve the lot of miners in Bolivia. After a military coup in 1980, her organization was banned and she was forced into exile. De Chungara's description provides a human face to the global problems of poverty, development, and struggles for equality described in this section.

Struggles for Democracy

The events of the 1990s indicate that the struggle for democracy is an ongoing one. No one geographic region, people, culture, or religious group seems to have the monopoly either on democracy or dictatorship. The following discussion of the continuing struggle for democratic rights is arranged geographically beginning with Asia and moving to West Asia, Africa, Europe, and the Western Hemisphere.

In Asia the moves toward democracy were mixed. In China, the Communist party stubbornly resisted efforts by the Chinese and international community to democratize. In 1994 the Chinese government detained dissidents for even planning to protest. Even after the death of aged Deng Xiaoping in 1996, the Communist party clung to power, as did the Communist regime in North Korea. By the turn of the century, however, the Chinese regime had released a number of political dissidents, most of whom were forced into exile, and the North Korean regime entered into negotiations to resolve differences with its old opponents, South Korea and Japan.

In Indonesia, the corrupt dictator, General Suharto, was ousted and a fragile, freely elected government was installed in 1998. The new regime quickly moved to end its illegal occupation of East Timor, where since 1975 it had killed over 200,000 people. India, the world's most populous democracy, celebrated 50 years of independence in 1997 and managed to preserve its democratic government despite religious conflict, swelling population, and poverty—a remarkable achievement. The Philippines made some progress in maintaining a democratic government, but the military returned to power in Pakistan.

In West Asia long-term rulers died and were succeeded by their sons in Morocco, Jordan, and Syria. Younger rulers also came to power in several Gulf states. This new generation of rulers inherited authoritarian or dictatorial governments, but promised both political and economic reforms. Whether they will be able to institute meaningful democratic changes remains to be seen. The Islamic Republic dominated by the clergy remained in power in Iran, but the younger generation and many women voters were particularly outspoken in their demands for reforms and more liberal social policies. Although Israel and Turkey continued their democratic institutions, and Lebanon, shattered by years of civil war, reestablished an elected government, many states in the region remained under authoritarian regimes.

In Algeria, when militant Islamic groups seemed certain to win in free elections in the early 1990s, the government cancelled the elections and took firm steps to crush the Islamists, thereby triggering a civil war in which tens of thousands have been killed. The Egyptian government adopted similar martial laws in an increasingly futile effort to stem the tide of Islamic revolution. Meanwhile, the Islamic government in the Sudan failed to resolve the decades-long civil war in that nation and was increasingly isolated by Western nations, which opposed Sudan's militant Islamic program. Much of the mass support for Islamist movements in the Sudan, Algeria, Egypt, and many other Arab nations stemmed from the long-term systematic repression of all other political organizations and the failures of the governments to solve the economic problems, job shortages, rising prices, and increasing gaps between the rich elite and the ever-growing number of poor people. The youth, many of whom were unable to find jobs, were particularly hostile to the failed policies of entrenched governments, and many turned to Islamic movements in hopes that they

Trying to Intimidate the Peasants

The lorry [truck] with the tortured came in. . . . My mother recognized her son, my little brother, among them. All the tortured had no nails and they had cut off part of the soles of their feet. . . . They forced them to walk and put them in a line. They fell down at once. They picked them up again. . . . The officer . . . [said] that he had to be satisfied with our lands, . . . with eating bread and chile, but we mustn't let ourselves be led astray by communist ideas. Saying that all the people had access to everything, that they were content. . . .

The officer ordered the squad to take away those who'd been "punished." . . . They lined up the tortured and poured petrol on them; and then the soldiers set fire to each of them. . . . When the bodies began to burn they began to plead for mercy. . . .

The officer quickly gave the order for the squad to withdraw. . . . They roared with laughter and cried, "Long live the Fatherland! Long live Guatemala! Long live [President] Lucas!" . . .

*[The victims] were Indians, our brothers. . . . Indians are already being killed off by malnutrition, and when our parents . . . make such sacrifices so that we can grow up, then they burn us alive like that.**

*Rigoberta Menchu, *I, Rigoberta Menchu: An Indian Woman in Guatemala*, ed. Elisabeth Bourgos-Debray, trans. Ann Wright (London: Verso, 1984), pp. 176–180.

The ongoing civil war in Guatemala involved relatively few combatants compared to the struggles in Nicaragua, El Salvador, and elsewhere. Nevertheless, this harrowing scene represents several major trends of the twentieth century: the divisive savagery of guerrilla warfare (many Guatemalan soldiers were Amerindians); the struggle between Marxist revolutionaries and the social and political elite (backed by the United States) in Central America; and the centuries-long suppression and exploitation of indigenous peoples throughout the Western Hemisphere by those of white and mestizo ancestry. Inequalities among peoples of different ethnic heritages persisted after the end of the Cold War. In recognition of the struggle by indigenous peoples for equality, the Nobel Peace Prize committee honored Rigoberta Menchu, an illiterate young Quiche woman, who, although her father, mother, and brother had separately met gruesome deaths, had worked for peaceful reforms through publicizing the problems of her people in Guatemala and of Amerindians everywhere. Although Menchu has been criticized for exaggerating and possibly distorting her own history, the struggles for equality among indigenous people, particularly in the Western Hemisphere, persist into the twenty-first century.

would be able to implement much-needed changes. Thus, if free elections were to be held in many of these nations, Islamist parties would probably win.

In sub-Saharan Africa the picture has been similarly mixed. Although over forty of the continent's fifty-two nations have made commitments to democratic reforms, dictators in many nations have simply refused to step down. For example, when their candidate failed to win in open elections, the military in Nigeria simply jailed the winner and put their own man in office. However, by the mid-1990s it was clear that the "Big Man" method of rule was on the way out as Benin, Niger, and Mali in West Africa moved toward democratic governments. By 2000, even Nigeria, which had had a long history of military coups and dictatorships, returned to elected democratic government under President Olusegun Obasanjo. Unfortunately, as noted in the previous section, ethnic conflicts, sometimes resulting in massive bloodshed, impeded and sometimes destroyed the institution of democratic governments.

European nations, as previously noted, either retained or, in the aftermath of the Soviet collapse, instituted democratic governments. However, the democracies in eastern Europe and the former Soviet republics were new and often rather fragile. As in Africa and Asia, economic problems and ethnic disputes also threatened their survival.

In the Western Hemisphere, the industrialized rich nations, particularly the United States and Canada, continued their democratic traditions. But dictatorship remained in Cuba under Castro while martial law in Peru curtailed civil liberties. Likewise, the democracies in Argentina, Colombia, and Brazil were undermined by corruption scandals, inflation, indebtedness, inefficiency, and criminal cartels that often attacked or assassinated elected officials. The events of the 1990s have demonstrated that people around the world can attain and ensure democratic governments only through constant work and vigilance.

Struggles for Gender and Social Equality

Throughout the twentieth century, women around the world have continued to struggle for equality. Just as the struggle for democracy has not made steady progress, so too, women have gained a voice and political and economic power in many nations, but must continue to fight for equality in others. In both rich and poor nations, women are more likely to be poor, and their work remains undervalued and underpaid. The number of women in the work force in industrialized nations continues to grow, and more women head one-parent households. As a result, the structure of family life has changed, and more financial and social demands are being placed on women.

Similarly, children, especially in poor nations, continue to be used as cheap or free labor, receiving little education and few opportunities. As the United Nations has noted, for many children in poor nations, the "march of progress has become a retreat" as increasing numbers are starving or malnourished, uncared for or abandoned.

Although in some traditional societies in West Africa and West Asia, women enjoy more authority and economic power than outside observers have realized, they continue to face many difficulties. Most traditional cultures have bound women to home and family and have made them subordinate to fathers, brothers, or husbands. Women in poor nations are usually "the poorest of the poor," because they lack education, property rights, or opportunity for employment in the modern sectors of the economy. At the same time, as evidence of changing times and customs, women have become presidents and prime ministers in many nations, including India, Israel, Nicaragua, and the Philippines. Benazir Bhutto in Pakistan, Tansu Ciller in Turkey, and Khaleda

Aung San Suu Kyi. Aung San Suu Kyi has been an outspoken opponent of the military dictatorship in Myanmar. In spite of being placed under house arrest for more than six years for her political activities, she has continued her struggle for democracy in Myanmar. She was awarded the Nobel Prize for Peace in 1991. Here she celebrates her freedom from total house arrest in July 1995 with supporters.

Zia of Bangladesh all defied stereotypes of the repressed women of Muslim societies to be elected to the highest offices in their countries. Similarly, in Iran, with a conservative Islamic government, large numbers of women are regularly elected to parliament, and many also hold high government positions. However, in most conservative Muslim nations most women remain subordinate and continue to struggle for equal rights. In contrast, with the exceptions of Great Britain, and a few others such as Norway, Ireland, and Iceland, most Western nations have not elected women to their top political offices. Similarly, although half the voters around the world are women, they hold only 13 percent of the seats in the world's parliaments.

In many nations, women's rights have also been threatened by the growing popularity of militant religious movements that would limit women's social and legal rights. Although in Algeria and elsewhere thousands of women have demanded that their rights be protected and have led public demonstrations against militant Islamic groups, they have gained little and sometimes lost ground. On the other hand, many Christian religious institutions are according women increasing power, for example, by the ordination of the first women priests in the Church of England in 1994; most other Protestant denominations also have women ministers; however, in spite of pressures from many Catholic men and women, the Pope continued to reject the ordination of women as priests in the Catholic church.

Refugees from Ethnic Strife. Famine and starvation continue to be major problems through much of Africa. Here starving Somali children wait in line for food provided by a relief agency in the 1990s.

AP Photo/John Moore

Indigenous peoples around the world, notably in Canada, the United States, and Latin and South America, have also organized to demand equal rights and economic improvements in their communities. For example, beginning in 1993–1994 Mayan Indians in Chiapas state in southern Mexico led a major rebellion demanding land and political reforms, reforms the Mexican government had promised but not delivered for over 40 years. By 2000, under new political leadership, the Mexican government promised reforms and resumed negotiations with Chiapas leaders. Hence, the struggles by indigenous peoples promise to be one of the major global issues well into the twenty-first century.

Technological and Economic Challenges

The twentieth century saw stunning scientific and technological advances (see Chapter 14). As the twenty-first century begins, humans continue to explore and make new discoveries in medicine, space, genetics, technology, armaments, and many other fields. In 2000 scientists announced that they had successfully mapped the human genome; this accomplishment holds the potential for future cures for a myriad of genetic diseases, but also poses complex ethical questions regarding the use of such information about individuals. At the same time, confounding discoveries continue to challenge human knowledge. For example, just as smallpox, a disease that had plagued humans for centuries was eradicated, a new, more deadly disease, AIDS (acquired immune deficiency syndrome), appeared; it has ravaged many societies, and so far no cure has been found.

High costs have also often limited scientific development. For example, the World Health Organization in 1993 estimated that it had the scientific knowledge to eliminate leprosy—a disease that has affected humans since the beginning of recorded history—but it lacked the money to institute the necessary drug treatment and caretaking programs. Similarly, just as tests were under way on promising vaccines to treat malaria, which annually kills 3 million people and infects up to 5 million people in over 100 nations, funding for the program was cut. Because leprosy and malaria generally occur among people in the poor nations of the Southern Hemisphere, the rich nations of the Northern Hemisphere have often minimized money for research and efforts to prevent these deadly diseases. Likewise, many new drugs that offer some relief and prolong life for a wide variety of diseases, for example,

LIVES AND TIMES ACROSS CULTURES

Monumental Structures

Since ancient times, rulers and governments have built monumental structures as evidence of their power, glory, and wealth. The pyramids of Egypt and Mexico and the Great Wall in China are examples of the achievements of past civilizations. During the twentieth century, first Western nations and then countries around the world have continued the tradition of constructing huge dams, bridges, and skyscrapers. Nations vie for the "bragging rights" of having the world's tallest building or largest dam.

Many nations have built massive dams to provide water for irrigation projects and increased hydroelectric power for industrialization and civilian use. When the Aswan Dam in Egypt was built during the 1960s, it was the largest project of its type in the world. But by the 1990s, the Ataturk Dam in Turkey, the Tarbela Dam in Pakistan, and the Three Gorges Dam on the Yangtze River in China all surpassed the older Aswan Dam in size. Although gigantic dams increase nations' economic potential, they also have enormous human and ecological costs. For example, the Three Gorges Dam will displace at least 3 million people.

Bridges and tunnels built to remove barriers to expanding transportation systems are other engineering marvels of the twentieth century. Of the world's seven largest suspension bridges, all built since World War II, two are in Europe, two in the United States, one in Hong Kong, and two in Japan, including the Akashi Kaikyo, which, at 6,529 feet, is the longest of all. Seven of the world's sixteen longest railway tunnels are in Europe, two in the United States, and seven in Japan, including the Seikan, which is 33.5 miles in length.

The United States, the birthplace of the skyscraper, continues to build ever-higher buildings. Of the fourteen structures exceeding 1,000 feet (as a reference point, the Eiffel Tower is 984 feet high), eleven are in the United States. Malaysians boast that their twin towers in Kuala Lumpur are part of the world's highest mosque, several dozen stories high. Meanwhile, Morocco claims to have built one of the world's biggest mosques, while the Ivory Coast brags about having the world's largest cathedral.

In reaction to the negative results of megaprojects, proponents of smaller projects applying "appropriate technology" have argued that "just because a nation can build the world's largest dam or biggest building doesn't mean that it should." Yet those on the "smaller is better" side of the argument have generally failed to dampen the human fascination with ever bigger and more monumental construction projects.

AIDS, are too expensive for the poor, especially in Africa and other developing nations, to afford.

Although the end of the Cold War promised to provide an economic boost to the economies of the industrialized world, particularly in the United States, which had previously spent a large portion of its budget on arms, the anticipated financial gains were slow to materialize. In many rich nations the gaps between the wealthy and the poor continued to widen.

The end of the Cold War did lessen the likelihood of a major nuclear war; however, more nations continued to possess and develop nuclear weapons. Israel, India, and Pakistan developed nuclear capabilities, and the United States continues to fund research on the development of a controversial missile defense system. North Korea was also suspected of having developed nuclear weapons that could threaten the stability of Asia. While some steps have been taken toward disarmament, the proliferation of nuclear weapons around the world remains a major problem. The maintenance and disposal of aging nuclear weapons pose yet another problem; solutions to these problems promise to be complex and costly.

One of the most intractable problems of the contemporary era has been the ever-widening gulf between rich industrialized nations (mostly in the Northern Hemisphere) and poor agricultural nations (mostly in the Southern Hemisphere); economists often referred collectively to these poor nations as the South or Global South and the rich nations as the North. In addition, the gap between the rich and the poor within nations continued to widen. By 1998 the income of more than $1 trillion held by the world's 225 richest people was equal to the income of the poorest 47 percent of the world's population. Three of the richest people—all Americans—had a total worth of the combined gross domestic product (GDP) of the 48 poorest nations.

The newly independent nations of the South face an overwhelming array of difficulties. They are almost all poor by affluent Western standards, and their fast-growing populations cause them to fall behind economically every year. While the nations of the North, including Japan, have attained virtual zero population growth, and even project future population declines, the population of such nations as Kenya doubles every eighteen years. Infertile or overused soil, lack of water, diseases, and low education levels add to the economic problems.

The goal of all poor nations is economic growth, but most of them lack the requirements for industrial development. They are trapped in a cycle of poverty in which lack of capital resulting from low production leads to low savings, which in turn means little or no available capital for future development projects. As producers of raw materials, most poor nations are also limited by the global economy, which is dominated by the nations and multinational corporations of the industrial world that determine the prices of most raw materials.

Prime Minister Jawaharlal Nehru's comment that in economic spheres "India has to run fast so that it might stand still" continues to apply to most poor, developing nations. These nations also lack skilled technicians and are limited by a minimal infrastructure of roads and communication lines. Some have valuable natural resources, but they have often needed foreign financial and technical help to develop them. In some former colonies, the resources are owned by foreign investors who retain the bulk of the profits and send it out of the country. Some nations have attempted to redress this imbalance by expropriations, but foreign investors and industrialized nations have often retaliated by refusing to buy raw materials that have been expropriated.

A key to economic development is, of course, money. Capital for schools and roads, dams and factories, or to hire foreign technicians is indispensable for economic growth. But for these nations the major sources of needed funds are trade, foreign aid, and commercial loans; all are difficult to obtain and often come with strings attached. During the Cold War, the superpowers often insisted on alliances or the granting of facilities for military bases in exchange for economic assistance. With the end of the Cold War the remaining superpower, the United States, faced domestic economic pressures, and was consequently less inclined to provide foreign aid. By 1997 the United States gave about $7 billion in nonmilitary foreign aid, less than one-tenth of 1 percent of the GDP, making it the lowest donor nation among wealthy donor states. During the 1990s, the International Monetary Fund (IMF), the World Bank, and other Western financial institutions demanded that nations privatize and create capitalist economic systems in order to receive assistance. As a result, many nations were forced to cut back on their social and welfare programs that assisted the very poor.

Other nations, such as Peru, Brazil, and Mexico in the Western Hemisphere and Nigeria and others in Africa, remained trapped in a cycle of indebtedness to funding institutions and owed debts far in excess of their ability to pay. Massive debts crippled Latin American development plans and have sometimes brought actual declines in living standards. Decades earlier, M. K. Gandhi had warned that the earth "provides enough for every man's need, but not for every man's greed." Many international, nongovernmental organizations (NGOs) that provide relief assistance to the poor and needy around the world urged that far-reaching debt relief plans be adopted, but some wealthier nations and lending institutions opposed these plans.

Rapid urbanization is another global phenomenon that has caused enormous economic and social problems for many nations. Uncontrolled urban growth has not only undermined village traditions and lowered agricultural output but has produced slums in the cities of poor nations as brutalizing as those found in Europe a century earlier. This growth is caused by the migration of the rural poor to the cities in search of jobs. Many new nations abandoned subsistence farming in favor of growing cash crops such as coffee, sugar, or cocoa for export. Although this shift brought in badly needed foreign capital to finance development, government planners in these nations often did not divide this capital equitably between the urban and rural sectors. Cities, with their educated and politically influential elites, often retained the bulk of the funds needed for overall development. The shift also caused a decline of essential food production and required the import of grain and other agricultural necessities. When the prices paid for the cash crops declined, villages that had once been self-sufficient could not purchase food needed to survive.

In some nations (for example, Colombia, Peru, Myanmar, and Thailand) many impoverished peasants stopped growing traditional food crops in favor of vastly more profitable illicit drugs, which were then sold on the international market for consumption in the industrialized world. More recently, newly independent republics in central Asia have also joined in this lucrative trade. The mounting production and consumption of addicting drugs—opium, heroin, and cocaine—thus became a problem for both wealthy, industrialized nations and poor nations.

A decade before the end of the Cold War, one study presciently concluded that the East-West conflict was not the fundamental division that Washington and Moscow believed it to be. The great divide, according to this view, was the conflict between North and South, between the rich nations of the Northern Hemisphere and the poor nations of the tropics and much of the Southern Hemisphere. A number of leaders, joined by theorists concerned with the future of the globe, were instrumental in effecting a new analysis of the basic economic divisions among nations.

Advocates for the poor nations insist that the poverty of the underdeveloped nations was mainly the result of Western imperial exploitation and, furthermore, that the rich nations should make restitution by offering substantial aid for Third World development. They believe a global redistribution of wealth and technology is necessary, pointing out that while citizens of the richest nations of the world spend $9 billion a year on pet food, they refuse to increase the amounts given to the poorest of the world. Many Western liberals have accepted this analysis, but they balk at its conclusions.

The moral appeal of this argument is powerful, especially when the poverty of the Southern Hemisphere is highlighted by disasters such as the great famines that afflicted parts of Africa in the 1970s. The rich nations, however, have refused to accept the argument that Third World poverty is fundamentally rooted in imperialist exploitation. The United States and other Western nations have pressed the poor nations to follow the Western model of capitalist economic development to secure prosperity. Entrepreneurial efforts and incentives for private economic initiatives have had some effect in Third World nations since 1975.

Despite these many difficulties, some Third World nations of the South have achieved some significant successes since independence. An example is the building of the Aswan High Dam in Egypt, which fulfilled its economic promise in providing electricity and new arable land, even though it has also had unforeseen environmental ramifications. Scientific breakthroughs in agriculture have allowed many nations to feed their rapidly growing populations. The Green Revolution in agriculture resulted in the development of new highly productive strains of rice, corn, and other grains. These have enabled India, formerly the scene of terrible famines, to become largely self-sufficient in grain production. By the 1990s, genetically engineered crops promised to increase productivity even further, but their use also raised environmental and health concerns, and many Europeans rejected any use or sale of modified crops.

Western assistance and well-conceived development policies have enabled some nations to modernize successfully. The development of export industries along the Asian Pacific rim, for example, has allowed South Korea, Taiwan, Hong Kong, and Singapore to escape the poverty that continues to plague many nations in the Southern Hemisphere. As a result, the peoples in these nations enjoy a high standard of living and a lifestyle approaching that of Western nations. Although an economic recession in 1998 battered Asian economies, by the turn of the century most were firmly on the road to recovery.

To secure equitable prices for their raw materials, some nations have formed cartels, or international combines, to regulate output and prices of their raw materials. The Organization of Petroleum Exporting Countries (OPEC) successfully forced a reallocation of revenues from this vital energy source. Oil-rich nations like Saudi Arabia, Venezuela, and Nigeria were able to elevate the world price of petroleum several times over during the 1970s and early 1980s. Although oil prices remained depressed for most of the 1990s when a barrel of oil sold for less than an equal amount of soft drinks, prices rose sharply in 2000. Producing nations then used their petroleum revenues to finance sweeping development projects. For example, Kuwait acquired sufficient wealth to provide a national welfare system for its citizens that included free education through university, low-cost housing and health care, and low- or interest-free loans for new businesses.

Some governments, however, committed too many scarce resources to such "prestige projects" as national airlines, new lavish capital cities, or manufacturing plants—projects that offered few immediate benefits to their predominantly peasant populations. Some nations made important shifts in their priorities after the 1970s. One widely heralded new trend was the shift away from big, expensive industrial projects toward "appropriate technologies" that could be cheaply applied at the village level, using local materials, and requiring little specialized training or expensive repairs. Support for low-impact agriculture or "people-centered" development projects increased. Others continue to ignore the consequences and to indulge in grandiose plans to construct mammoth engineering projects. For example, for China to construct the world's largest dam—the Three Gorges, along the Yangtze River—large areas must be flooded and more than 3 million people must be moved from their homes.Yet another is Libya's Grand Mamade River project to construct 500 miles of pipeline to take water pumped from beneath the Sahara to the Mediterranean coast. In India, work on a huge dam project on the Narmada River was delayed but not canceled despite massive opposition by local peasants and the Japanese government's concern over providing funding for a project that might be damaging to the environment. Critics of these projects argued that they were out of scale with the economic needs of the people they were supposed to benefit and that, furthermore, they posed severe threats to the world's delicate ecological balance. Debates over the relative merits of development projects are legal in democratic India, but they are outlawed in China where opposition to government programs is forbidden.

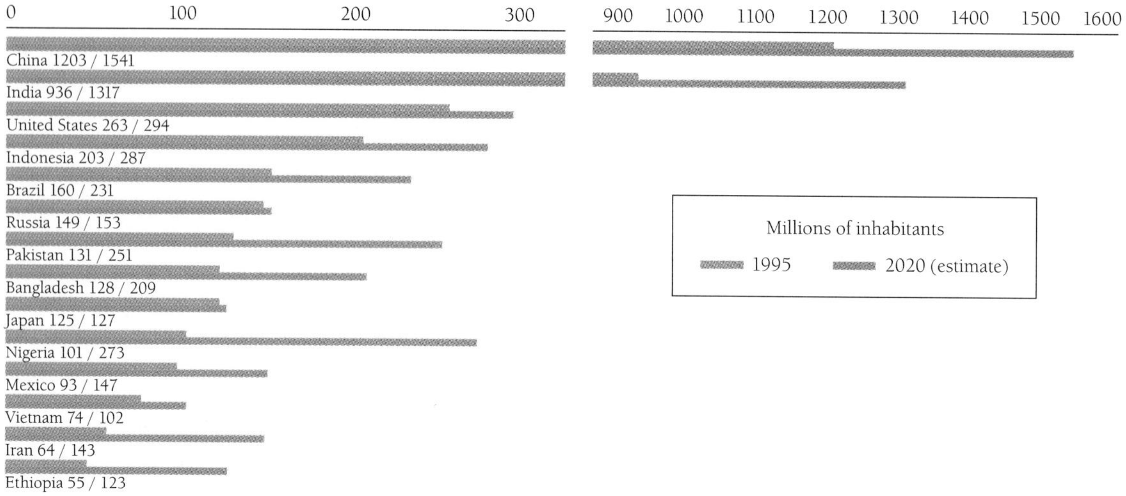

(a) Nations with largest projected populations by 2020

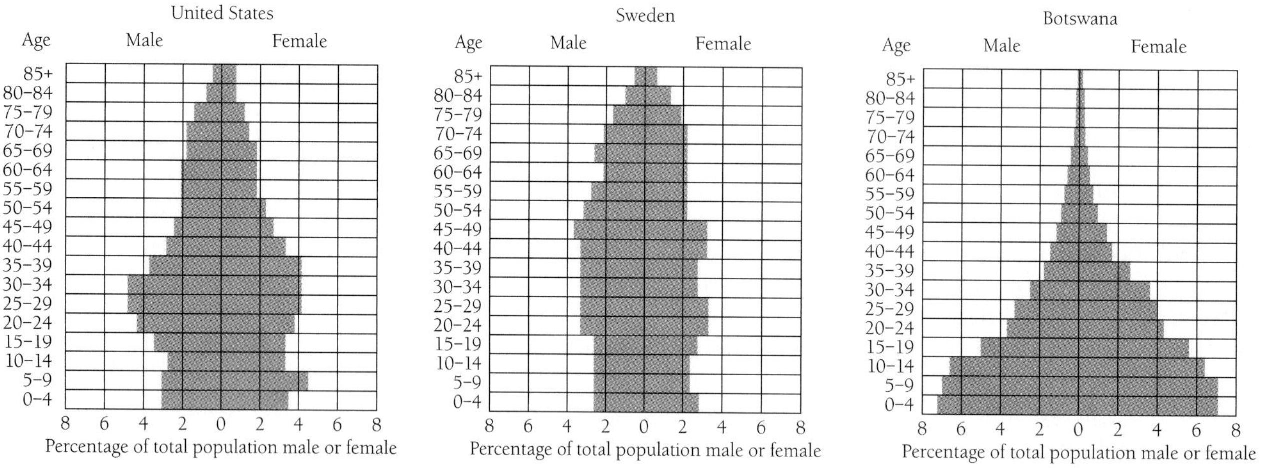

(b) Age distributions

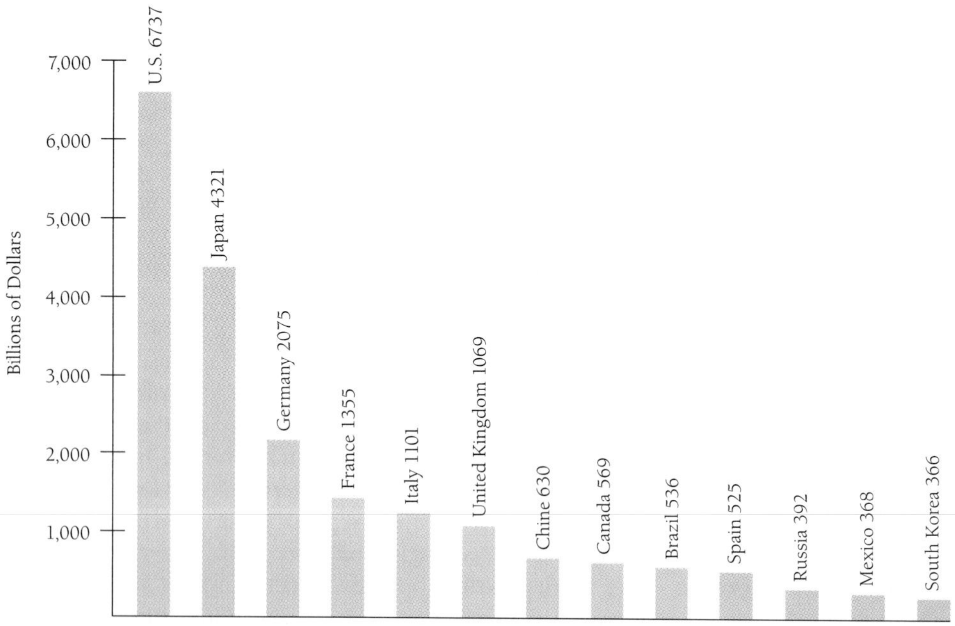

(c) Gross national product (GNP) of several countries

Population and Economic Comparisons around the World. Graph (a) indicates the nations with the largest projected populations by 2020 and (b) the current age distribution of several nations. Graph (c) shows the huge differences in gross national product (GNP) among a number of countries. These are good indications of the relative economic and social welfare of some nations around the world.

LIVES AND TIMES ACROSS CULTURES

Environmental Cleanups

Growing populations and industrialization have made environmental pollution a mounting problem around the world. Cleaning up the trash of a "throw away," consumer society, in addition to its industrial waste and toxic accidents, is expensive and technologically challenging. As early as the 1950s, Rachel Carson, an early environmentalist, warned about the dangers of chemical pesticides and polluted water systems. But environmental degradation is not unique to the twentieth century.

The Roman Empire, for example, deforested large expanses of Africa and western Asia, and later Westerners have decimated or eliminated countless animal and plant species. Until the mid-nineteenth century, the Thames River, which intersects London, was used as the main sewage dump for one of the largest cities in the world. By the 1850s, the stench from the river was so terrible that members of Parliament could smell the pollution from the open windows of the Parliament building. During one hot summer when the odors were particularly bad, they authorized the construction of a sophisticated sanitation system to solve the problem.

In the mid-twentieth century, the river emptying into Lake Erie from Cleveland, Ohio, was so polluted from industrial waste that it actually caught fire! A massive clean-up effort resulted. In recent years, volunteer groups climbed Mount Everest, not in hopes of reaching the summit, but to pick up the debris discarded by hundreds of mountain climbing expeditions. Huge oil spills in Alaska, off the coast of France, and (in 2000) in Brazil, have proven much more difficult to contain. Accidents at atomic energy plants at Three Mile Island in the United States and Chernobyl in the former Soviet Union underscore the dangers and long-term risks to human life and the environment posed by both military and civilian use of nuclear energy.

Driven by poverty and a desperate need for jobs, many poor countries in the Global South have welcomed chemical and other industries that have been heavily regulated or outlawed in the rich northern nations. Although these industries provide much needed jobs, they also destroy both the environment and the health of surrounding populations. For example, the shipyards where huge, outdated ocean-going vessels are dismantled along a six-mile stretch of beach at Alang, India, is one of the most polluted spots on earth. Environmentalists, many from Europe, have called for stricter regulations or the outright banning of such operations. Governments and industrialists in poor nations reply that they provide services that are prohibitively expensive in the West and that poor workers prefer the risks of long-term health problems and pollution to the starvation of their families. Thus the management of human and industrial waste remains a most daunting challenge of the twenty-first century.

From the 1980s, many nations shifted away from government-sponsored economic projects toward entrepreneurial initiatives by private citizens, while central planning gave way to local or grassroots planning. Other new programs earmarked aid for the poorest classes, and guaranteed women equal benefits in education, new jobs, and other opportunities. These trends have offered many people some hope for the future.

Environmental Challenges

By 2000 the world's population exceeded 6 billion and was expected to double within the next fifty years. The world now confronts a myriad of complex ecological crises, many of them related to this population growth. The population explosion, particularly evident in nations in the South, has placed sometimes intolerable strains on many of the earth's resources. Whereas Western nations must cope with problems and expenses associated with aging populations, over half the populations in the nations of the South are under the age of twenty-four. Nations with predominantly young populations of a reproductive age are especially afflicted with rapid population growth, high unemployment, and the need for education. As increasing numbers of people in poor nations flee the countryside in search of better lives in urban areas or emigrate, often illegally, to seek jobs in richer nations, the infrastructures of many cities—for example, Mexico City and Cairo—are strained to the breaking point. In the 1950s Cairo had a population of 1 million; by 2000 it had soared to over 15 million. In addition to massive social dislocations and a frequent drop in agricultural productivity, urbanization also takes away land from agriculture, diverts water supplies, and contributes to further ecological problems.

In spite of technological advances and increased production levels, the world's 6 billion and more people are consuming increasing percentages of finite resources, such as fossil fuels and foodstuffs, while also contributing to more pollution of the earth's atmosphere, soils, oceans, and fresh water supplies. From 1970 to 2000 humans were estimated to have destroyed more than 30 percent of the natural world. The depletion of freshwater resources and global warming are particularly worrisome results. Many of these ecological problems are transnational in nature and can only be resolved through international cooperation on a massive scale. However, nation-states, which emphasize their own self-interest, have often been unwilling or ill-equipped to attack global crises of pollution.

By the 1980s scientists were warning that chemical wastes spewed into the atmosphere might destroy the ozone layer or might also cause a massive warming of the earth—the so-called greenhouse effect—that might, for example, turn the American Midwest into a vast dust bowl and cause rising sea levels to flood the eastern and Gulf coasts. Toxic pollutants have already caused acid rains, which have damaged large tracts of forests in Canada, Germany, Poland, Russia, and other nations.

Meanwhile, burgeoning populations, needing agricultural land, firewood, and money from valuable timber, have deforested large areas of jungles and forests, thereby creating new arid, or desert, regions. The cutting down of the tropical Amazonian rain forest at the rate of a football field every five seconds could threaten climatic conditions and the quality of fresh air throughout the Southern and Northern Hemispheres. Massive destruction of rain forests has caused the extinction of many species of plant and animal life and threatens the survival of many others. Even the disposal of garbage for 6 billion people, particularly the heavy consumers of the industrialized world, has become a major problem.

Industrialization and lack of controls over multinational corporations also have contributed to several major ecological disasters in the late twentieth century. Nuclear accidents at Three Mile Island in the United States and Chernobyl in the Soviet Union demonstrated the very real dangers of nuclear energy and have caused many to question the desirability of further proliferation of nuclear reactors. Similarly, the chemical disaster at Bhopal, India, where toxic gas killed and maimed thousands, demonstrated the dangers of such chemicals. Fourteen years after that accident, survivors continue to suffer, and experts predicted that people would continue to be afflicted with higher rates of cancer for several more decades. Many poor nations are particularly vulnerable to these types of industrial accidents; in their desperate search for outside investment, they have permitted Western corporations to establish plants to produce materials now outlawed in many wealthy nations. Massive oil spills from huge tankers transporting petroleum around the oceans of the world have also resulted in pollution that threatens wildlife and the ecological balance in the Persian Gulf and along the coastlines of Europe, the Gulf of Mexico, and Alaska.

Recognizing these problems, nations have held international conferences and adopted policies to alleviate some of the worst environmental dangers. In 1987, forty-six nations signed a pact to protect the ozone layer by reducing the use of ozone-depleting chlorofluorocarbons. Some critics, however, worried that the measures taken were too little, too late and sought additional international legislation to control and limit the use of such materials. In 1992 representatives from around the world met at an "earth summit" at Rio de Janeiro in Brazil to devise solutions to these environmental challenges. Although sharp disagreements arose between the wealthy, industrialized nations, which opposed programs that might threaten their comfortable lifestyles, and the poor nations, mostly in the Southern Hemisphere, they did agree to consider environmental issues in future development plans. Although an international agreement regarding global warming, believed to be largely caused by increased carbon dioxide levels from burning fossil fuels, was reached in 1998, the United States, one of the largest polluters, was reluctant to address the problem. To protect the environment for future generations, northern nations will have to alter their wasteful consumption, and southern nations will have to stem their rapid population growth.

Many individual nations have enacted laws to control pollution and the dumping of toxic materials. Japan and the Netherlands led the way in recycling waste material. In Israel, highly efficient irrigation systems brought substantial savings in water usage, and Kuwait instituted a technologically complex but efficient system to desalinate seawater, which, however, was largely destroyed during the Gulf War. The use of advanced technology and hydroponics (using water for growing foodstuffs) has increased agricultural output in such nations as the Maldive Islands in the Indian Ocean and Japan. Kenya adopted a national system of soil and water conservation, demonstrating that even a relatively poor nation with limited resources can make impressive strides toward controlling environmental damage. All peoples now face the necessity of protecting the global environment, for as former President Jimmy Carter pointed out, "We're all in the same boat." Protecting the fragile environment against the onslaughts of billions of people and international industrialization is one of the major challenges of the twenty-first century.

Cultural Interactions and Tensions

At the beginning of the twenty-first century, the world is linked together in a vast network of communication systems; the interaction and consequent transformation of societies have resulted not only in profound changes but also in mounting tensions, for example, between those struggling to develop modern secular societies and those adhering to traditional religious values. After World War II, many Western experts predicted that religious values would decline as more societies adopted secular, Western culture. But although people around the world want Western technology and consumer goods, many also are seeking to avoid the Western problems of drug and alcohol abuse, sexual immorality, divorce, and changing family structures. Many also believe that secularization, with the loss of religious commitment, has been the root cause of these social problems.

Predictions regarding the decline of religion around the world have proved false. During the 1990s, religious revivals occurred around the globe. Following the lead of the religiously led Iranian revolution, many militant Muslims in other nations are pushing for a return to government under Islamic law. Similarly, some Orthodox Jews advocate rule by Judaic law in Israel. Some fundamentalist Christian groups in the United States have campaigned for a return to religious values and legal restrictions to control personal lives, schools, films, the media, and the press. Religious and sectarian differences have contributed to ongoing violent struggles in nations as diverse as India, Lebanon, Indonesia, Sri Lanka, and Northern Ireland. In the former Soviet republics, even decades of antireligious policies failed to stamp out Christianity or Islam, and both experienced a revival of adherents following the collapse of the Soviet Union. Unfortunately, religious differences continue to cause wars among people of differing belief systems. Sectarian struggles in the Balkans, Lebanon, and Northern Ireland have led to thousands of deaths and untold property damage.

Religious zealots in many societies have also sought to control culture and the arts. The authors Salman Rushdie and Naguib Mahfouz were condemned by some Muslim clerics for their allegedly anti-Islamic novels, and some Muslim zealots even put a price on Rushdie's head. Similarly, militant Christians condemn many popular music forms, including rap and heavy metal, and call for strict censorship in the electronic media. Conservative religious activists, even in generally open, secular societies such as Great Britain and the United States, support government censorship or limitations of government funding for works of art they deemed blasphemous or pornographic.

The interlocking of global communication systems with broadcasting by satellite, cable television, high-technology telephone and facsimile (fax) systems, e-mail, and computers has made cultural exchanges between people and nations easier than ever. As people of different cultures and artists intermingle and assimilate other types of music, art, designs, and performing arts, new art forms and modes of expression are constantly emerging. Fusions of several cultural traditions are nowhere more apparent than in modern music. Around the world, musicians are adapting African, Latin American, and Western music of all types to create constantly changing and evolving music. Similarly, writers such as Naguib Mahfouz (an Egyptian), Derek Walcott (from St. Lucia in the Caribbean), Gabriel Garcia Márquez (a Colombian), and Wole Soyinka (from Nigeria)—all Nobel Prize winners —are indebted to Western literary forms, but adapt them to their own cultures.

In popular culture, millions around the world enjoy U.S. movie and television productions such as *Star Wars* or MTV. In Russia, Mexican soap operas are enormously popular, while the Chinese demand more popular music and television shows from Hong Kong and Taiwan.

The Persistence of Religion. Although nations around the world have sought to modernize and adapt to new technologies, religion continues to play a major role in the lives of people. In many traditional societies, religious instruction forms the basis of the educational curriculum. Here a young female student in Nigeria reads the Qur'an aloud as her classmates look on.

CONNECTIONS IN CULTURE

Identities in a Global Age

How do we explain and identify ourselves in this global age? Do global connections lead to convergence, making us all the same? Or, do global links cause divergence, leading to new differences and inequalities? Can both happen at once?

In the material world, one side of global connection is the imposition of global trends on localities. Since the early 1970s, radios, stereo equipment, computers of increasing power and decreasing size, and wireless communication devices have spread from centers of manufacture to consumers around the globe. Technology links us all together, yet the differences between the wealthy and the poor have increased substantially over the last 40 years.

Similarly, in the world of ideas, how we define ourselves within our global society is an increasingly complex issue. What shall we assume to be the basic source of identity? Is it one's national birthplace and citizenship? Is it religion, age, gender, economic status, work, or style of cultural expression? Identity operates now on so many levels that it has become a matter of individual choice rather than something assigned by our national and cultural associations.

In an unusual set of events, for example, the local population of Chiapas, Mexico, defined its own identity in a striking mix of local and global terms. This Amerindian population of southern Mexico supported a rebel group (Ejercito Zapatista de Liberación Nacional, or EZLN) that followed up a brief military action in 1994 with a long political struggle against Mexico's central government. Here this small group demanded not independence, but recognition within the larger nation. In making their demands, the Chiapas population relied on the growing consciousness of indigenous peoples throughout the Americas, in the Arctic, the Pacific, and parts of Africa. Their spokesperson, the masked and mysterious Subcomandante Marcos, also relied on Internet communication with allies around the world.

The peasants of Chiapas identified themselves not only as "Indians" or "Maya," but also as citizens of Mexico and as an indigenous people. In so doing, they extended their recognition to other Mexicans and other indigenous peoples, and gained support from all over Mexico and all over the world. Groups and individuals have long asserted their own identities; what is different about the early twenty-first century is that people are more willing to recognize each other's identity.

Who, then, adopts a global identity? If globalization and global consciousness are closely related, then perhaps a growing number of people identify themselves as "humans" or "people," or "citizens of the world." If this is so, does this global identity supplement a national or ethnic identity, or does it diminish or replace it?

The answer leads in two directions. On one side, some people adopt global and cosmopolitan identities, yet without this cutting their local ties. Others acknowledge the growing global connections, but focus on reaffirming their own local identity.

---

1. Explore the Evidence and Narrative sections of Unit 13 in the Migration CD-ROM and look for varying types of identity in this global age. In what cases do people adopt a global identity? In what cases do people adopt a local identity? Do you think these new identities place increased emphasis on tolerance of those who are different, or do they instead increase intolerance?

2. The process of globalization has accelerated in recent years. Enter the search term "globalization" as a Keyword in InfoTrac. Read some representative articles there and develop your own definition of "globalization." Now list the most important economic, political, social, and cultural aspects of globalization. Is globalization necessarily a good thing? What, in your opinion, are the positive and negative aspects of globalism?

Likewise, Japanese-manufactured Nintendo video games fascinate young people from Tokyo to Riyadh, Saudi Arabia, to Kansas City, Kansas. Some nations, however, have sought to limit cultural diffusion and assimilation. For example, France sought to reduce the number of U.S. films shown and tried to stop the entry of English words into the French vocabulary. Nevertheless, such attempts of governments to limit or reduce cultural interactions are constantly impeded by technological advances and the popular demands by their citizens. Clearly, the interactions of cultures and religions will continue, and with expanding technology and global communications, new forms will emerge to amaze, delight, or enrage audiences around the world.

1945	
	First Arab-Israeli War
	Second Arab-Israeli War
1965	Arab-Israeli Six-Day War
	Continuing struggle against apartheid in South Africa
1970	Women's liberation movement
	Fourth Arab-Israeli War
	Iranian Revolution: Ayatollah Khomeini
1980	Fifth Arab-Israeli War The computer age Ecological issues: global warming, acid rain, toxic waste; Green movements Crisis in the Persian Gulf Reunification of Germany Collapse of the Soviet Union Boris Yeltsin; Commonwealth of Independent States Ongoing civil conflict in Northern Ireland Israeli-Palestinian accords Ethnic warfare in Bosnia Nelson Mandela elected president of Union of South Africa
1995	Ongoing ethnic strife: Balkans, India, central Africa Islamist movements Economic prosperity and recessions
1998	

Summary and Comparisons

Between 1989 and 1991, Germany was reunified and the nations of eastern Europe broke away from Soviet domination, privatized their economies, and established closer ties with the richer western European nations.

Mikhail Gorbachev tried to preserve the Soviet system through reforms, but succeeded only in angering and scaring many Communist party hard-liners, who launched an abortive coup against him in 1991. In the ensuing backlash against the Communist party, Gorbachev lost control of the political system and was forced to resign. As the Soviet Union collapsed, many ethnic groups, including Kazakhs, Armenians, and Ukrainians, demanded and attained national independence. Some then formed the loose, decentralized Commonwealth of Independent States. Economic reforms stressing privatization put the new commonwealth on the road to capitalism.

There were, however, social and economic costs. Throughout eastern Europe and the former Soviet republics, prices soared, many people lost both their jobs and the safety net of social welfare programs. Crime and social strife, particularly among differing ethnic and religious groups, became more widespread.

Although western Europe continued to move toward greater economic and political unity, many social problems remained unresolved. Ethnic rivalries ignited full-scale war in the former Yugoslavia. Czechoslovakia split along ethnic lines, while Germany, France, and other nations saw an increase in racism, including anti-Semitism. Canada and India were also threatened with dissolution along ethnic or religious lines. Similar racial and ethnic hatreds also posed problems in the United States.

Political upheaval plagued West Asia and southern Africa. A series of wars led to Israeli victories and expansion of territory, but failed to resolve the continuing struggle for Palestinian self-determination. Negotiations between the Israelis and Palestinians in the 1990s led to mutual recognition, but not an independent Palestinian nation. Consequently, violence in that region continues.

In South Africa, the white minority government and the African National Congress cooperated to dismantle apartheid and to hold open elections based on the principle of "one person, one vote." Nelson Mandela won the presidency and moved to lessen old racial tensions and economic disparities between whites and blacks. But in states neighboring South Africa, armed civil strife disrupted and destabilized elected governments.

The progress of democracy around the world met with mixed success. Dictatorships continued in China, much of West Asia, and parts of South America. On the other hand, the fall of the Soviet Empire brought democracies, though sometimes fragile ones, to eastern

Europe and the former Soviet republics. Democracy began to grow in much of sub-Saharan Africa and South America as well.

The struggle for gender equality and human rights for minorities and indigenous peoples continues around the world. Women are now a significant political force in much of the world and have held the highest offices in many nations, but they still suffer economic and social discrimination in much of the world. Likewise, minorities such as the Kurds in Turkey, Iran, and Iraq; Bosnians; Amerindians; and African Americans still seek full equality and civil rights.

In many poor Asian and African nations, economic growth has come slowly, in part because they lack everything from adequate health care and education to basic industries; they also usually have low production levels in both agriculture and manufacturing. Most are also heavily indebted to Western banks. Technological advances like the Green Revolution and genetically altered seeds have rekindled hopes for the future, but also raise fears about negative environmental impacts.

An ever-growing global population has also strained the planet's finite resources. At the dawn of the twenty-first century, nations everywhere face ecological crises and problems of pollution. Solutions to these complex problems remain elusive.

Finally, the rapidity of social and cultural transformations has heightened tensions between those advocating liberalization and further change and those championing conservative values and religious traditions. Eagerness to acquire modern technology and consumer goods has not altogether supplanted traditional belief systems and cultural values.

Religion remains a compelling force around the world; clashes between secularists and fervent believers have been frequent and sometimes violent. Sophisticated communication systems and advanced technology allow people to learn about other societies and sometimes to adopt their values by fusing many cultural values and styles into new forms. Rapid communication and interactions among peoples around the globe hold the promise of solutions to the economic, developmental, and environmental challenges of the twenty-first century; however, it remains to be seen whether we have sufficient determination to meet those challenges.

Selected Sources

*Aung San Suu Kyi. *Freedom from Fear and Other Writings.* 1991. The Burmese political leader and Nobel laureate pleads for democracy.

Banks, O. *Faces of Feminism.* 1982. A comparison of the U.S. and British feminist movements. Should be read in conjunction with G. W. Lapidus, *Women, Work and Family in the Soviet Union.*

*Caplan, Richard, and John Feffer, eds. *Europe's New Nationalism: States and Minorities in Conflict.* 1996. Useful collection of essays on complex issues.

Carrère d'Encausse, Hélène. *The End of the Soviet Empire.* 1993. A scholarly account of various national movements within the former Soviet Union with an emphasis on the tensions between the Russians and the peoples of their former empire.

Chang, Jung. *Wild Swans: Three Daughters of China.* 1991. On three generations of Chinese women during the twentieth century.

*Critchfield, Richard. *The Golden Bowl Be Broken: Peasant Life in Four Cultures.* Reprinted 1988. Insightful look at daily life in Third World peasant societies.

"A Day With the President." A highly personal 56-minute video of Nelson Mandela as president of South Africa. (Available through First Run/Icarus Films.)

*Filipovic, Zlata. *Zlata's Diary: A Child's Life in Sarajevo.* 1994. A moving account of survival under siege, comparable to Anne Frank's World War II wartime diary. Also on cassette.

*Fisher, Sydney N., and William Ochsenwald. *The Middle East: A History.* 5th ed. Vol. 2. 1997. Readable text with good overview of contemporary West Asia.

*Gaddis, John Lewis. *The United States and the End of the Cold War.* 1994. Incisive essays assessing the impact of the Cold War and its aftermath on U.S. policies.

*Harrison, Paul. *The Greening of Africa; Breaking Through in the Battle for Land and Food.* 1987. Expert analysis of major development problems and possible solutions.

Havel, Václav. *Open Letters: Selected Writings, 1964–1990.* 1991. Personal observations on the changing political scene by the noted Czech writer and politician.

*Head, Bessie. *A Woman Alone: Autobiographical Writings.* 1990. A personal account of struggles by a powerful South African writer.

"In My Country: An International Perspective on Gender." 1993. This 91-minute video focuses on the problems of gender relations and families and features interviews with experts and everyday people from around the world. (Available through Insight Media.)

*Ishinomori. *Shotaro.* 1988. Amusing and informative study of the Japanese economy in comic book format.

Iwao, Sumiko. *The Japanese Woman: Traditional Image and Changing Reality.* 1993. Good discussion of women and gender roles in Japan since 1945.

Liu, Pin-yen. *A Higher Kind of Loyalty: A Memoir of China's Foremost Journalist.* 1990. The memoir of a loyal Communist turned dissident.

Mama Benz: An African Market Woman. This 49-minute video offers a fascinating look at strong, powerful female merchants in West Africa.

Mazrui, Ali A. *Cultural Forces in World Politics.* 1990. Mazrui argues that Western attitudes toward the Third World have been a "dialogue of the deaf." Discusses Islam, Négritude, traditional societies, and gender issues.

*Available in paperback.

"A Republic Gone Mad: Rwanda 1894–1994." A 60-minute video that puts crises in Rwanda and central Africa in a historical perspective. (Available through First Run/Icarus Films.)

"Rigoberta Menchu: Broken Silence." This 25-minute film presents the Nobel Prize winner's reflections on the struggles of indigenous peoples for equality. Menchu is also an outspoken advocate for women's rights.

*Smith, Charles. *Palestine and the Arab-Israeli Conflict.* 4th ed. 1996. Highly readable text on the history of this long-lasting conflict.

**The South Center: An Interdependent World.* 1993. Scholars from around the world discuss North/South relations and the issues of poverty, environmental crises, and political instability.

*Sutcliffe, Bob. *Imperialism after Imperialism.* 1997. Sutcliffe reexamines arguments that imperialism has ended and places the discussion within the context of internationalization of global economies and the issues of feminism, environmental concerns, and social change.

"Understanding Northern Ireland." This 60-minute film traces the ongoing conflict among Protestants, Catholics, and the British in Northern Ireland. [Films for the Humanities.]

Wei, Jingsheng. *The Courage to Stand Alone.* 1997. China's famous dissident speaks out against the government dictatorship.

Weizsäcker, Ernest U. von. *Earth Politics.* 1993. Assesses the 1992 earth summit in Rio de Janeiro with discussion of problems and strategies for the future.

White, Stephen. *After Gorbachev.* 4th ed. 1994. An overview of the dramatic changes that ushered in the collapse of the Soviet Union.

"Women and Islam." A 30-minute video that describes gender issues in the Muslim world with sections on marriage and women's rights. (Available through Films for the Humanities and Sciences.)

"Yugoslavia: Origins of a War." Using archival material and firsthand footage, this 58-minute video traces the causes for the breakup of Yugoslavia and the ensuing ethnic warfare. (Available through First Run/Icarus Films.)

Internet Links

Guide to the Environment
http://environment.about.com/newsissues/environment/
Helpful information about everything from acid rain, climate change, and desertification to organic gardening and parks and camping. Especially strong on the environmental impact of mining industries.

Interview with Rigoberta Menchu Tum
http://www.indians.org/welker/menchu2.htm
A 1992 interview with the Guatemalan refugee and author shortly before she was awarded the Nobel Peace Prize.

Revolution in Eastern Europe: 1989
http://mars.acnet.wnec.edu/~grempel/courses/wc2/lectures/rev89.html
A small anthology of reflections by dissidents and intellectuals on the upheavals in Europe, followed by helpful text on "Eastern Europe in Perspective," "Nationalism," "Terrorism," and "Discontented and Conformist Youth."

U.S. Report on the Middle East
http://www.usrom.com/
Designed by Farid El Khatib, a long-time correspondent and diplomatic editor for several Arab news agencies, this site offers "political, economic and defense news," updated daily from such sources as the U.S. State Department and Middle Eastern ambassadors.

War, Peace and Security Guide: Contemporary Conflicts
http://www.cfcsc.dnd.ca/links/wars/index.html
A handy source of information about regions and countries facing difficult socioeconomic and political problems in the post–Cold War world. A production of the Information Resource Centre of the Canadian Forces College.

Romanizing Chinese Words

Two systems are in current use for romanizing Chinese words. The Wade-Giles system has been in use longer than the Pinying system. Scholars of China use both equally. Newspapers tend to use the Pinying system for the People's Republic and the Wade-Giles system for the Republic of China. This book follows the Wade-Giles system for pre-1949 China and the Pinying system for the post-1949 era. The following table equates some of the Wade-Giles and other conventional spellings with the Pinying spelling used in this text. Since not all words differ in the two systems, only those words that do are included.

Wade-Giles	Pinying	Wade-Giles	Pinying
Canton	Guangzhou	Kwangsi	Guangxi
Ch'an	Chan	Kwangtung	Guangdong
Chao	Zhao	Lao Tzu	Laozi
Chekiang	Zhejiang	Li Po	Li Bo
Chengchow	Zhengzhou	Loyang	Luoyang
Ch'ien-lung	Qianlong	Mao Tse-tung	Mao Zedong
Ch'in	Qin	Nanking	Nanjing
Ching-te Cheng	Jingdezhen	Peking	Beijing
Ch'ing	Qing	Shang-ti	Shangdi
Chou	Zhou	Shantung	Shandong
Chu Hsi	Zhu Xi	Shansi	Shaanxi
Chu Yuan-chang	Zhu Yuanzhang	Shensi	Shanxi
Chungking	Chongqing	Sian	Xi'an
Fukien	Fujian	Sinkiang	Xinjiang
Hangchow	Hangzhou	Sung	Song
Honan	Henan	Szechuan	Sichuan
Hopei	Hebei	T'ang	Tang
Hsiung-nu	Xiongnu	T'ang T'ai-tsung	Tang Taizong
Hung-wu	Hongwu	Taoism	Daoism
K'ang-hsi	Kangxi	Tatung	Dadong
Kansu	Gansu	Tien	Tian
Kiangsi	Jiangxi	Tz'u-hsi	Cixi
Kiangsu	Jiangsu	Wu-ti	Wudi
K'ung Fu-tzu	Kong Fuzi	Yang-tze	Yangzi
Kuomintang	Guomindang	Yung-cheng	Yongzheng

Glossary

Abbasid dynasty The caliphs resident in Baghdad from the 700s C.E. until the tenth century.
Abbot/abbess The male/female head of a monastery/nunnery.
Absolutism A form of government in which the sovereign power or ultimate authority rested in the hands of a monarch who claimed to rule by divine right and was therefore responsible only to God.
Abstractionism A twentieth-century school of painting that rejected traditional representation of external nature and objects.
Academy The school founded by Plato; Aristotle is its most famous student.
Actium, Battle of The decisive 31 B.C.E. battle in the struggle between Octavian and Marc Antony, in which Octavian's victory paved the way for the Principate.
Agincourt The great victory of the English over the French in 1415, during the Hundred Years' War.
Agricultural revolution The substitution of farming for hunting and gathering as the primary source of food by a given people.
Ahimsa Hindu, Buddhist, and Jain doctrine of not harming living creatures.
Ajanta Caves Caves in central India that are the site of marvelous early frescoes inspired by Hinduism and Buddhism.
Allah Arabic title of the one God.
Alliance of 1778 A diplomatic treaty under which France aided the American revolutionaries in their war against Britain.
Anabaptists Radical Protestant reformers who were condemned by both Lutherans and Catholics.
Analects The body of writing containing conversations between Confucius and his disciples that preserves his worldly wisdom and pragmatic philosophies.
Anarchism A political theory that sees all large-scale government as inherently evil and embraces small self-governing communities.
ANC The African National Congress. Founded in 1912, it was the beginning of political activity by South African blacks. Banned by politically dominant European whites in 1960, it was not officially "unbanned" until 1990. It is now the official majority party of the South African government.
Ancien régime The "old government"; the pre-Revolutionary style of government and society in eighteenth-century France.
Angkor Wat A great Buddhist temple complex in central Cambodia, dating to the twelfth-century C.E. Khmer Empire.
Anglo-French entente The diplomatic agreement of 1904 that ended British-French long-standing enmity; known as the Entente Cordiale.
Anglo-Russian Entente The equivalent of the Entente Cordiale between Britain and Russia; signed in 1907.
Animism A religious belief imputing spirits to natural forces and objects.
Anschluss The German term for the 1938 takeover of Austria by Nazi Germany.
Anthropology The study of humankind as a particular species.
Antigonid kingdom One of the Hellenistic successor kingdoms to Alexander the Great's empire.
Anti-Semitism Hostility toward or discrimination against Jews.
Apartheid The Afrikaans term for segregation of the races in South Africa.
Appeasement The policy of trying to avoid war by giving Hitler what he demanded in the 1930s; supported by many in France and Britain.
Archaeology The study of cultures through the examination of artifacts.
Arianism A Christian heresy that taught that Jesus was inferior to God. Though condemned by the Council of Nicaea in 325, Arianism was adopted by many of the Germanic peoples who entered the Roman Empire over the next centuries.
Aristocracy A social governing class based on preeminence of birth.
Arthasastra An early Indian political treatise that sets forth many fundamental aspects of the relationship of rulers and their subjects. It has been compared to Machiavelli's well-known book *The Prince* and has provided principles upon which many aspects of social organization have developed in the region.
Aryans A nomadic pastoral people from Eurasia who invaded the Indus Valley and other regions in about 1500 B.C.E.
Ashikaga clan A noble Japanese family that controlled political power as shoguns from the 1330s to the late 1500s.
Atatürk, Mustafa Kemal The "father of the Turks"; a World War I officer who led Turkey into the modern age and replaced the Ottoman Empire in the 1920s.
Audiencia The colonial council that supervised military and civil government in Latin America.
August 1991 coup The attempt by hard-line Communists to oust Gorbachev and reinstate the Communist party's monopoly on power in the Soviet Union.
***Ausgleich* of 1867** The compromise between the Austro-Germans and Magyars that created the "Dual Monarchy" of Austria-Hungary.
Austro-Prussian War The conflict for mastery of Germany, won by the Bismarck-led Prussian kingdom in 1866.
Authoritarian state A state that has a dictatorial government and some other trappings of a totalitarian state but does not have the same degree of control of the populace and the economy.
Avesta The holy book of the Zoroastrian religion.
Axis Pact The treaty establishing a military alliance between the governments of Germany, Italy, and Japan; signed in 1936.
Axum The center of the ancient Ethiopian kingdom.
Aztec Last of a series of Amerindian masters of central Mexico prior to the arrival of the Spanish; developers of the great city of Tenochtitlán (Mexico City).

Babylon Most important of the later Mesopotamian urban centers.
Babylonian Captivity The transportation of many Jews to exile in Babylon as hostages for the good behavior of the remainder; occurred in the sixth century B.C.E.
Bakufu The military-style government of the Japanese shogun.
Balance of power A distribution of power among several states such that no single nation can dominate the others.
Balfour Declaration The 1917 public statement that Britain was committed to the foundation of a "Jewish homeland" in Palestine after World War I.
Bantu A language spoken by many peoples of central and eastern Africa; by extension, the name of the speakers.
Barbarian Greek for " incomprehensible speaker"; uncivilized.
Battle of the Nations Decisive defeat of the army of Napoleon by combined forces of Prussia, Austria, and Russia in October 1813 at Leipzig in eastern Germany.
Baruch Plan An idea put forth early in the Cold War in which all countries would pledge not to make atomic bombs and to allow international inspections; it was rejected by the Soviet Union.
Bay of Pigs invasion A failed U.S.-backed invasion of Cuba by anti-Castro exiles in 1961.
Bedouin The nomadic inhabitants of interior Arabia; they were the original converts to Islam.
Benedictine Rule The rules of conduct given to his monastic followers by the sixth-century Christian saint Benedict.
Berbers Pre-Arab settlers of northern Africa and the Sahara.
Berlin blockade The 1948–1949 attempt to squeeze the Western allies out of occupied Berlin by the USSR; it failed because of the successful Berlin Airlift of food and supplies.
Berlin Wall The ten-foot-high concrete wall and "death zone" erected by the communist East Germans in 1961 to prevent further illegal emigration to the West.
Bhagavad-Gita The best-known part of the *Mahabharata,* it details the proper relations between the castes and the triumph of the spirit over material creation.
Big bang theory The theory that the cosmos was created by an enormous explosion billions of years ago.
Bill of Rights of 1689 A law enacted by Parliament that established specific rights of English citizens and placed certain limits on royal powers.
Black Death An epidemic of bubonic plague that ravaged most of Europe in the mid-fourteenth century.
Blitzkrieg ("lightning war") A war conducted with great speed and force, as in Germany's advance into Poland at the beginning of World War II.
Bodhisattva In Buddhism, an enlightened being that helps others to reach *nirvana.*
Boer War/Boers The armed conflict, 1899–1902, between the Boers (the Dutch colonists who had been the earliest European settlers of South Africa) and their British overlords; won by the British after a hard fight.
Bohemia Traditional name of the Czech Republic, dating from the tenth century C.E.
Bolsheviks The minority of Russian Marxists led by Lenin who seized dictatorial power in the October Revolution of 1917.
Boule The 500-member council that served as a legislature in ancient Athens.
Bourgeoisie The urban middle class; usually commercial or professional.
Boxer Rebellion A desperate revolt by peasants against the European "foreign devils" who were carving up China in the new imperialism of the 1890s; it was quickly suppressed by Western powers.
Brahman In Hindu theology, the title of the impersonal spirit responsible for all creation.
Brahmin The caste of priests, originally found among the Aryans and later spread to the Indians generally.
Bread and circuses The social policy initiated by Augustus Caesar aimed at gaining the support of the Roman proletariat by supplying them with essential food and entertainment.
Brest-Litovsk Treaty of 1918 The separate peace between the Central Powers and Lenin's government that took Russia out of World War I.
Brezhnev Doctrine The doctrine, enunciated by Leonid Brezhnev, that the Soviet Union had a right to intervene if socialism was threatened in another socialist state; used to justify the use of Soviet troops in Czechoslovakia in 1968.
Bronze Age The period when bronze tools and weapons replaced stone among a given people; generally about 3000–1000 B.C.E.
Burning of the books China's Legalist first emperor attempted to eliminate Confucian ethics by destroying Confucian writings and prohibiting its teaching.
Bushido The samurai code of honor.
Byzantine empire The continuation of the Roman imperium in its eastern provinces until its fall to the Muslim Turks in 1453.

Caliph Arabic for successor (to Muhammad); leader of Islam.
Carthage Rival in the Mediterranean basin to Rome in the last centuries B.C.E.; it was destroyed by Rome.
Caste A socioeconomic group that is entered by birth and can only rarely be exited from.
Caudillo A chieftain (that is, a local or regional strongman) in Latin America.
Central Intelligence Agency A Cold War creation of the United States, this organization, among other activities, sought to overthrow or destabilize countries deemed too receptive to communism.
Chaeronea The battle in 338 B.C.E. in which Philip of Macedon decisively defeated the Greeks and brought them under Macedonian rule.
Ch'an Buddhism Founded by the semilegendary Indian monk Bodhidharma, this Chinese branch of Buddhism (Zen in Japan) focused on meditation and an intuitive understanding of reality.
Chartism A British working-class movement of the 1840s that attempted to obtain labor and political reform.
Chavin Early Peruvian Amerindian culture.
Cheka An abbreviation for the first Soviet secret police.
Chichén Itzá Site in the Yucatan of Mayan urban development in the tenth to thirteenth centuries.
Ch'ing dynasty The Manchu dynasty that ruled China from 1644 to 1911.
City of God, The Written by Augustine in the fifth century C.E., it calls for ultimate allegiance to God, not to earthly rulers.

Civil Code of 1804 Napoleonic law code reforming and centralizing French legal theory and procedures.
Civil constitution of the clergy 1791 law in revolutionary France attempting to force French Catholics to support the new government and bring clergy into conformity with it.
Civil rights The basic rights of citizens, including equality before the law, freedom of speech and press, and freedom from arbitrary arrest.
Civilization A complex, developed culture.
Code Napoleon A system of laws promulgated by Napoleon that upheld many of the ideals of the French Revolution while continuing the subjugation of women and the suppression of unions.
Cold War The ideological conflict between the Soviet Union and the United States after World War II.
Collective farms Large farms created in the Soviet Union by Stalin by combining many small holdings into one large farm worked by the peasants under government supervision.
Command economy The name given to communist economic planning in the Soviet Union after 1929.
Committee of Public Safety The executive body of the Reign of Terror during the French Revolution.
Commonwealth of Independent States (CIS) The loose confederation of eleven of the fifteen former Soviet republics formed after the breakup of the Soviet Union in 1991.
Congress of Vienna A meeting of the major and minor powers of Europe in 1815, called to decide the fate of France and the future of Europe after the defeat of Napoleon. It developed informal structures that kept war in Europe at low levels throughout much of the nineteenth century.
Conquistadores Title given to sixteenth-century Spanish explorers/colonizers in the New World.
Conservatism An ideology based on tradition and social stability that favored the maintenance of established institutions, organized religion, and obedience to authority and resisted change, especially abrupt change.
Consuls Chief executives of the Roman republic; chosen annually.
Contras One side of the 1980s civil war in Nicaragua, it was composed in large part of people loyal to the former dictator Somoza; they fought against the Sandinistas.
Coral Sea, Battle of The naval engagement in the southwest Pacific during World War II that ended the Japanese invasion threat to Australia.
Corpus Juris "Body of the law"; the final Roman law code, produced under the emperor Justinian in the mid-500s C.E.
Cottage industry A system of textile manufacturing in which spinners and weavers worked at home in their cottages using raw materials supplied to them by capitalist entrepreneurs.
Creationism A cosmology based on Christian tradition that holds that the universe was created by an intelligent Supreme Being.
Creole Term used to refer to whites born in Latin America.
Crimean War Conflict fought in the Crimea between Russia on one side and Britain, France, and Turkey on the other, from 1853 to 1856; ended by the Peace of Paris with a severe loss in Russian prestige.
Cultural relativism The belief that no culture is superior to another because culture is a matter of custom, not reason, and derives its meaning from the group holding it.
Culture The human-created environment of a group.
Cuneiform Mesopotamian wedge-shaped writing begun by the Sumerians.
Cynicism A Hellenistic philosophy stressing poverty and simplicity.

Daimyo Japanese nobles who controlled feudal domains under the shogun.
Dasa Sanskrit term for "slave" used by Aryans; refers to the dark skin color of Indus Valley peoples.
D Day June 6, 1944; the invasion of France from the English Channel by combined British and American forces.
Declaration of Independence The 1776 document approved by the Continental Congress in Britain's American colonies; it asserts the colonies' independence from Britain and provides a logical explanation for doing so.
Declaration of the Rights of Man and Citizen The epoch-making manifesto issued by the French Third Estate delegates at Versailles in 1789.
Decolonization The process of becoming free of colonial status and achieving statehood; occurred in most of the world's colonies between 1947 and 1962.
Deductive reasoning Arriving at truth by applying a general law or proposition to a specific case.
Delian League An empire of satellite Greek states under Athens in the fifth century B.C.E.
Democracy A system of government in which the majority of voters decides issues and policy.
Demographic transition The passage of a large group of people from traditional high birthrates to lower ones, induced by better survival rates among children.
Depression A severe, protracted economic downturn with high levels of unemployment.
Descent of Man The 1871 publication by Charles Darwin that applied selective evolution theory to mankind.
Destalinization The policy of denouncing and undoing the most repressive aspects of Stalin's regime; it was begun by Nikita Khrushchev in 1956.
Détente Relaxation of tensions; the term used for the toning down of diplomatic tensions between nations, specifically between the United States and the Soviet Union during the Cold War.
Dharma A code of morals and conduct prescribed for one's caste in Hinduism.
Diaspora The scattering of the Jews from ancient Palestine.
Diffusion theory Description of the spread of ideas and technology through human contacts.
Directory The five-member executive organ that governed France from 1795 to 1799 after the overthrow of the Jacobins and before Napoleon gained control.
Divine right theory The idea that the legitimate holder of the Crown was designated by divine will to govern; personified by King Louis XIV in the seventeenth century.
Domino theory The belief that if the communists succeeded in Vietnam, other countries in Southeast and East Asia would also fall (like dominoes) to communism; a justification for the U.S. intervention in Vietnam.
Dorians Legendary barbaric invaders of Mycenaean Greece in about 1200 B.C.E.

Dream of the Red Chamber The best-known of the eighteenth-century Chinese novels.
Duce, il "The Leader"; title of Mussolini, the Italian dictator.
Duma The Russian legislature created by Tsar Nicolas II.
Dynastic state A state in which the maintenance and expansion of the interests of the ruling family is the primary consideration.

East India Company A commercial company founded with government backing to trade with the East and Southeast Asians. The Dutch, English, and French governments sponsored such companies starting in the early seventeenth century.
Economic nationalism A movement to assert national sovereignty in economic affairs, particularly by establishing freedom from the importation of foreign goods and technology on unfavorable terms.
Edo Name of Tokyo prior to the eighteenth century.
Eightfold Path The Buddha's teachings on attaining perfection.
Emir A provincial official with military duties in Muslim government.
Empirical data Facts derived from observation of the external world.
Empirical method Using empirical data to establish scientific truth.
Enclosure movement An eighteenth-century innovation in British agriculture by which formerly communal lands were enclosed by private landlords.
Encomienda The right to organize unpaid native labor by the earliest Spanish colonists in Latin America; revoked in 1565.
Encyclopédie, The The first encyclopedia; produced in mid-eighteenth-century France by the philosophe Diderot.
Enlightened absolutism An absolute monarchy where the ruler follows the principles of the Enlightenment by introducing reforms for the improvement of society, allowing freedom of speech and the press, permitting religious toleration, expanding education, and ruling in accordance with the laws.
Enlightenment The intellectual reform movement in eighteenth-century Europe that challenged traditional ideas and policies in many areas of theory and practice.
Epicureanism A Hellenistic philosophy advocating the pursuit of pleasure (mental) and avoidance of pain as the supreme good.
Equal field system Agricultural reform favoring the peasants under the T'ang dynasty in China.
Era of Stagnation The period of Brezhnev's government in the Soviet Union (1964–1982), when the Soviet society and economy faced increasing troubles.
Era of Warring States The period of Chinese history between about 500 and 220 B.C.E.; characterized by the breakdown of the central government and near-constant feudal war.
Essenes A Jewish religious group that lived near the Dead Sea at Qumran from around the middle of the second century B.C.E.; some of their ideas were similar to those found in early Christianity.
Estates-General The parliament of France; it was composed of delegates from three social orders: clergy, nobility, and commoners.
Ethnic, Ethnicity The racial, cultural, or linguistic affiliation of an individual or group of human beings.
Ethnic cleansing The policy of killing or forcibly removing people of another ethnic group; used by the Serbs against Bosnian and Kosovar Muslims in the 1990s.
Etruscans The pre-Roman rulers of most of northern and central Italy and cultural models for early Roman civilization.
European Economic Community An organization that blossomed after World War II, it fostered economic cooperation among member states, eventually becoming today's European Union.
Excommunication The act of being barred from the Roman Catholic community by decree of a bishop or the pope.
Existentialism Twentieth-century philosophy that was popular after World War II in Europe; it insists on the necessity to inject life with meaning by individual decisions.
Exodus The Hebrews' flight from the wrath of the Egyptian pharaoh in about 1250 B.C.E.
Extended family Parents and children plus several other kin group members.

Factory Acts Laws passed by Parliament in 1819 and 1833 that began the regulation of hours and working conditions in Britain.
Fallow land Land left uncultivated for a period to recover fertility.
Fascism A political movement in the twentieth century that embraced totalitarian government policies to achieve a unity of people and leader; first experienced in Mussolini's Italy.
Fashoda crisis In 1898 British forces and French forces, both bent on increasing the imperial holdings of their respective countries, came head-to-head in Fashoda in the Sudan. Diplomacy averted a war between the two countries.
Fertile Crescent A belt of civilized settlements reaching from lower Mesopotamia across Syria, Lebanon, and Israel and into Egypt.
Feminism The belief in the social, political, and economic equality of the sexes; also, organized activity to advance women's rights.
Feudal system A mode of government based originally on mutual military obligations between lord and vassal; later often extended to civil affairs of all types; generally supported by landowning privileges.
Final Solution Name given by the Nazis to the wartime massacres of European Jews.
First Consul Title adopted by Napoleon after his coup d'état in 1799.
First Emperor (Shi Huangdi) The founder of the short-lived Qin dynasty (221–205 B.C.E.) and creator of China as an imperial state.
First Industrial Revolution The initial introduction of machine-powered production; began in late-eighteenth-century Britain.
Five Pillars of Islam Popular term for the basic tenets of Muslim faith.
Five-Year Plan First introduced in 1929 at Stalin's command to collectivize agriculture and industrialize the economy of the Soviet Union.
Floating world A term for ordinary human affairs popularized by the novels and stories of eighteenth-century Japan.
Forbidden City The center of Ming and Ching government in Beijing; entry was forbidden to ordinary citizens.

Four Noble Truths The Buddha's doctrine on human fate.
Fourteen Points The outline for a just peace proposed by Woodrow Wilson in 1918.
Franco-Prussian War The 1870–1871 conflict between these two powers, resulting in humiliating defeat for France and German unification.
Frankfurt Assembly A German parliament held in 1848 that was unsuccessful in working out a liberal constitution for a united German state.
Führer, der "The Leader" in Nazi Germany—specifically, Hitler.
Fujiwara clan Daimyo noble clan controlling the shogunate in ninth- to twelfth-century Japan.

Geisha Women in feudal Japan who entertained men with good conversation, dance, singing, and occasional sexual favors; similar to the *hetairai* of ancient Athens.
Gentiles All non-Jews.
Gentry Well-to-do English landowners below the level of the nobility; played an important role in the English Civil War of the seventeenth century.
Geocentric "Earth centered"; theory of the cosmos that erroneously held the Earth to be its center.
Gestapo Hitler's secret police, responsible for intimidating the population and helping to rid Germany of "undesirables" such as Jews and leftists.
Ghana The earliest of the extensive empires in the western Sudan; also a modern African state.
Ghetto Italian name for the quarter restricted to Jews.
Gilgamesh One of the earliest epics in world literature, originating in prehistoric Mesopotamia.
Glasnost The Russian term for "openness"; along with *perestroika,* it was employed to describe the reforms instituted by Gorbachev in the late 1980s in the Soviet Union.
Glorious Revolution of 1688 The English revolt against the unpopular Catholic king James II and the subsequent introduction of certain civil rights restricting monarchic powers.
Golden Horde The Russia-based segment of the Mongol world empire.
Gothic style An artistic style, found mainly in architecture, that came into general European usage during the thirteenth century.
Gracchi brothers Roman noble brothers who as consuls unsuccessfully attempted reform in the late republican era.
Great Depression Originating in 1929 in the United States, this global decline in economic output spread throughout the world, causing high unemployment and political unrest; it was a major reason Hitler came to power in Germany.
Great Elector Frederick William of Prussia (1640–1688); one of the princes who elected the Holy Roman Emperor.
Great Leap Forward Mao Zedong's misguided attempt in 1958–1960 to provide China with an instantaneous industrial base rivaling that of more advanced nations.
Great Proletarian Cultural Revolution The period from 1966 to 1969 when Mao inspired Chinese youth to rebel against all authority except his own; caused great damage to the Chinese economy and culture.
Great Purge The arrest and banishment of millions of Soviet Communist party members and ordinary citizens at Stalin's orders in the mid-1930s for fictitious "crimes against the State and Party."
Great Schism A division in the Roman Catholic church between 1378 and 1417 when two (and for a brief period, three) popes competed for the allegiance of European Christians; a consequence of the Babylonian Captivity of the papacy in Avignon, southern France.
Great Trek The march of the Boers into the interior of South Africa, where they founded the Orange Free State in 1836.
Great Zimbabwe The leading civilization of early southern Africa.
Greens A pro-environment, moderately leftist political movement that began in West Germany in the 1970s and has since spread throughout Europe and to other parts of the world.
Grossdeutsch* versus *Kleindeutsch The controversy over the scope and type of the unified German state in the nineteenth century; *Kleindeutsch* would exclude multinational Austria, and *Grossdeutsch* would include it.
Guild A medieval urban organization that controlled the production and sale prices of many goods and services.

Habsburg dynasty The family that controlled the Holy Roman Empire after the thirteenth century; based in Vienna, they ruled Austria until 1918.
Hacienda A Spanish-owned plantation in Latin America that used native or slave labor to produce export crops.
Hagia Sophia Greek name ("Holy Wisdom") of the cathedral in Constantinople, later made into a mosque by Ottoman Turkish conquerors.
Hajj The pilgrimage to the sacred places of Islam.
Han dynasty The dynasty that ruled China from about 200 B.C.E. to 221 C.E.
Hanoverians The dynasty of British monarchs after 1714 that came from the German duchy of Hanover.
Harappa An early Indus Valley civilization.
Hegira "Flight"; Muhammad's forced flight from Mecca in 622 C.E.; marks the first year of the Muslim calendar.
Heliocentrism Opposite of geocentrism; recognizes the sun as center of the solar system.
Hellenistic A blend of Greek and Asiatic cultures, extant in the Mediterranean basin and Middle East between 300 B.C.E. and about 200 C.E.
Helots Messenian semislaves of Spartan overlords.
Heresy "Wrong" belief in religious doctrines; often severely persecuted by Christian authorities, including the punishment of execution.
Hetairai High-class female entertainer-prostitutes in ancient Greece.
Hieroglyphics Early Egyptian writing consisting of pictographs and symbols for letters and syllables.
Hinayana Buddhism A strict, monastic form of Buddhism claiming a closer link with the Buddha's teaching than Mahayana Buddhism; often called Theravada.
Historiography The writing of history so as to interpret it.
History Human actions in past time, as recorded and remembered.
Hitler-Stalin Pact of 1939 The treaty of nonaggression between Hitler and Stalin in which each agreed to maintain neutrality in any forthcoming war involving the other party.

Hittites An Indo-European people who were prominent in the Middle East around 1200 B.C.E.
Hohenzollerns The dynasty that ruled Prussia-Germany until 1918.
Holocaust The mass executions perpetrated by the Nazi regime of Germany during World War II; its chief victims were 6 million Jews, but hundreds of thousands of gypsies, homosexuals, and others also perished.
Holy Roman Empire First constituted by Charlemagne, the Holy Roman Empire was a concept that served both political and religious purposes; it was eventually controlled by the Habsburgs centered in Austria, but it essentially had lost all its meaning by the early nineteenth century.
Hominid A humanlike creature.
Homo sapiens "Thinking man"; modern human beings.
Hoplites Heavily armed infantry soldiers in ancient Greece in a phalanx formation.
Huguenots French Calvinists, many of whom were forced to emigrate in the seventeenth century.
Humanism The intellectual movement that sees humans as the sole arbiter of their values and purpose.
Hungarian Revolution The Hungarians' attempt to free themselves from Soviet control in October 1956; crushed by the Soviets.
Hyksos A people who invaded the Nile delta in Egypt and ruled it during the Second Intermediate Period around 1600 B.C.E.

Ideographs Written signs conveying entire ideas and not related to the spoken language; used by the Chinese from earliest times.
Iliad The first of the two epics supposedly written by Homer in eighth-century B.C.E. Greece.
Impressionists Members of a Paris-centered school of nineteenth-century painting focusing on light and color.
Individualism Emphasis on and interest in the unique traits of each person.
Indulgence The remission of part or all of the temporal punishment in purgatory due to sin; granted for charitable contributions and other good deeds. Indulgences became a regular practice of the Christian church in the High Middle Ages, and their abuse was instrumental in sparking Luther's reform movement in the sixteenth century.
Inflation A sustained rise in the price level.
Inka Title of the emperor of the Quechuan peoples of Peru prior to arrival of the Spanish.
Indian National Congress Organized in 1885, this secular organization promoted Indian nationalism and lobbied for increased rights of Indians; it became a major force in the struggle for Indian independence.
Inductive reasoning Arriving at truth by reasoning from specific cases to a general law or proposition.
INF (Intermediate Nuclear Forces) Treaty Negotiated by Mikhail Gorbachev and the Reagan administration in the mid-1980s, it removed all medium-range nuclear missiles from Europe.
Inquisition A systematic attempt by the Roman Catholic church to enforce its religious orthodoxy, the Inquisition tortured and executed hundreds of thousands of people suspected of heresy.
Institutes of the Christian Religion John Calvin's major work that established the theology and doctrine of the Calvinist churches; first published in 1536.
Intelligentsia Russian term for a social group that actively influences the beliefs and actions of others, seeking reforms; generally connected with the professions and media.
Iranian Revolution The fundamentalist and anti-Western movement led by the Ayatollah Khomeini that seized power from the shah of Iran through massive demonstrations in 1979.
Iron curtain A metaphor employed by Winston Churchill early in the Cold War, it refers to the divide between western and eastern Europe caused by Soviet domination in the latter region.
Isis A chief Egyptian goddess, represented by the Nile River.
Isolationism A foreign policy in which a nation refrains from making alliances or engaging actively in international affairs.

Jacobins Radical revolutionaries during the French Revolution; organized in clubs headquartered in Paris.
Janissaries An elite troop in the Ottoman army, created originally from Christian boys from the Balkans.
Jesuits Members of the Society of Jesus, a Catholic religious order founded in 1547 to combat Protestantism.
Jewish War A rebellion of Jewish Zealots against Rome in 66–70 C.E.
Jihad Holy war on behalf of the Muslim faith.
Judea One of the two Jewish kingdoms emerging after the death of Solomon when his kingdom was split in two; the other kingdom was Samaria.
Justification by faith Doctrine held by Martin Luther whereby Christian faith alone was the path to heavenly bliss.

Ka'bah The original shrine of pagan Arabic religion in Mecca containing the Black Stone; now one of the holiest places of Islam.
Kali Wife of the Hindu god Shiva, she was both the cosmic mother and the goddess of destruction.
Kamakura shogunate The rule by members of a noble Japanese family from the late twelfth to the mid-fourteenth century in the name of the emperor, who was their puppet.
Kami Shinto spirits in nature.
Kampuchea Native name of Cambodia, a state of Southeast Asia bordered by Thailand and Vietnam.
Karma In Hindu belief, the amounts of good and evil done in a given incarnation.
Karnak The site of a great temple complex along the Nile River in Egypt.
Kashmir A province in northwestern India that Pakistan also claims.
Kellogg-Briand Pact A formal disavowal of war by sixty nations in 1928.
KGB An abbreviation for the Soviet secret police; used after *Cheka* and *NKVD* had been discarded.
Khmers The inhabitants of Cambodia; founders of a large empire in ancient Southeast Asia.
Kiev, Principality of The first Russian state; flourished from about 800 to 1240 C.E., when it fell to Mongols.
Kleindeutsch "Small German"; adjective describing a form of German unification that excluded the multinational Austria; opposite of *Grossdeutsch.*

Knight Type of feudal noble who held title and landed domain only for his lifetime; generally based originally on military service to his overlord.
Korean War 1950–1953 war between the United Nations, led by the United States, and North Korea; precipitated by the invasion of South Korea by North Korea.
Krishna An important Hindu god who gives core religious teachings in the *Bhagavad-Gita*.
Kshatriyas The warrior class of Aryan society.
Kuomintang (KMT) The political movement headed by Chiang Kai-shek during the 1930s and 1940s in China.
Kurds A group of people located in an area comprising eastern Turkey, northern Iraq, northern Syria, and northwest Iran; the Kurds have unsuccessfully sought an independent state and have fought with the governments of Turkey and Iraq.
Kush Kingdom in northeast Africa that had close relations with Egypt for several centuries in the pre-Christian epoch.
Kyoto Ancient capital of the Japanese Empire and seat of the emperor.

Labour party Political party founded in 1906 by British labor unions and others for representation of the working classes.
Laissez-faire "To let alone." An economic doctrine that holds that an economy is best served when the government does not interfere but allows the economy to self-regulate according the forces of supply and demand.
Lascaux Site of Paleolithic cave paintings in France.
Late Manchu Restoration An attempt by Chinese reformers in the 1870s to restore the power of the central government after the suppression of the Taiping rebellion.
Lateran Treaty A 1929 agreement between the pope and Mussolini in which the pope gained substantial sums of money and control over education, while Mussolini gained greater political and economic control of Italy.
League of Nations An international organization founded after World War I to maintain peace and promote amity among nations; the United States did not join.
Lebensraum "Living space." The doctrine, adopted by Hitler, that a nation's power depends on the amount of land it occupies; thus, a nation must expand to be strong.
Legitimacy, principle of The idea that, after the Napoleonic wars, peace could best be reestablished in Europe by restoring legitimate monarchs who would preserve traditional institutions; it guided Metternich at the Congress of Vienna.
Left The reforming or revolutionary wing of the political spectrum; associated originally with the ideals of the radical French Revolution.
Legalism A Chinese philosophy of government emphasizing strong authority.
Legislative Assembly The second law-making body created during the French Revolution; it was dominated by the Jacobins and gave way to the radical Convention.
Legitimacy A term adopted by the victors at the Congress of Vienna in 1815 to explain the reimposition of former monarchs and regimes after the Napoleonic wars.
Lepanto, Battle of Decisive 1571 naval defeat of the Ottomans at the hands of the Habsburgs and Italian city-states; it marked the beginning of the long decline of the Ottomans.
Liberalism An ideology based on the belief that people should be as free from restraint as possible. Economic liberalism is the idea that the government should not interfere in the workings of the economy. Political liberalism is the idea that there should be restraints on the exercise of power so that people can enjoy basic civil rights in a constitutional state with a representative assembly.
Locarno Pact An agreement between France and Germany in 1925.
Long March, the 6,000-mile fighting retreat of the Chinese Communists under Mao Zedong to Shensi province in 1934–1935.
Lyric poetry Poetry that celebrates the poet's emotions.

Maastricht Treaty Signed in 1991 by members of the European Community; committed them to closer political and economic ties.
Macao Portuguese island colony just off China's coast; founded in 1513.
Maghrib or **Maghreb** Muslim northwest Africa.
Magna Carta A "great charter" issued in 1215 by King John of England that gave the aristocracy substantially increased powers, especially over taxation, and created a more uniform justice system.
Mahabharata A Hindu epic poem; a favorite in India.
Mahavira "Great hero." The term refers to Vardhamana, the founder of Jainism in the sixth century B.C.E.
Mahayana Buddhism A more liberal, looser form of Buddhism; originating soon after the Buddha's death, it deemphasized the monastic life and abstruse philosophy in favor of prayer to the Buddha and the bodhisattvas who succeeded him.
Mahdi rebellion A serious rebellion against European rule in the Sudan in the 1890s, led by a charismatic holy man ("mahdi") and ended by his death and British attack.
Mali The African Sudanese empire that was the successor to Ghana in the 1300s and 1400s.
Manchuria Large province of northeastern China, seized in the nineteenth century by Russia and Japan before being retaken by the Maoist government.
Mandarins Chinese scholar-officials who had been trained in Confucian principles and possessed great class solidarity.
Mandate Britain and France governed several Asian and African peoples after World War I, supposedly as agents of the League of Nations.
Mandate of heaven A theory of rule originated by the Chou dynasty in China, emphasizing the connection between an imperial government's rectitude and its right to govern.
Manor An agricultural estate of varying size normally owned by a noble or the clergy and worked by free and unfree peasants/serfs.
Manchu Originally nomadic tribes living in Manchuria who eventually overcame Ming resistance and established the Ching dynasty in seventeenth-century China.
Marathon The battle in 490 B.C.E. in which the Greeks defeated the Persians, ending the first Persian War.
March on Rome A fascist demonstration in 1922 orchestrated by Mussolini as a preliminary step to dictatorship in Italy.
Maritime expeditions (China's) Early fifteenth-century explorations of the Indian and South Pacific Oceans ordered by the Chinese emperor.

Marshall Plan A program proposed by the U.S. secretary of state George Marshall and implemented from 1947 to 1951 to aid western Europe's recovery from World War II.
Marxism The political, economic, and social theories of Karl Marx, which included the idea that history is the story of class struggle and that ultimately the proletariat will overthrow the bourgeoisie and establish a dictatorship en route to a classless society.
Mass education A state-run educational system, usually free and compulsory, that aims to ensure that all children in society have at least a basic education.
Matriarchy A society in which females are dominant socially and politically.
Matrilineal descent Attribution of name and inheritance to children via the maternal line.
Maya The most advanced of the Amerindian peoples who lived in southern Mexico and Guatemala and created a high urban civilization in the pre-Columbian era.
Medes An early Indo-European people who, with the Persians, settled in Iran.
Meiji Restoration The overthrow of the Tokugawa shogunate and restoration of the emperor to nominal power in Japan in 1867.
Mein Kampf *My Struggle;* Hitler's credo, written while serving a prison term in 1924.
Mercantilism A theory of national economics popular in the seventeenth and eighteenth centuries, it aimed at establishing a favorable trade balance through government control of exports and imports as well as domestic industry.
Meritocracy The rule of the meritorious (usually determined by examinations).
Messenian Wars Conflicts between the neighbors Sparta and Messenia that resulted in Sparta's conquest of Messenia around 600 B.C.E.
Messiah A savior-king who would someday lead the Jews to glory.
Mestizo A person of mixed Amerindian and European blood.
Metics Resident foreigners in ancient Athens; not permitted full rights of citizenship, but did receive the protection of the laws.
Mexican Revolution The armed struggle that occurred in Mexico between 1910 and 1920 to install a more socially progressive and populist government.
Middle Kingdom The period in Egyptian history from 2100 to 1600 B.C.E.; followed the First Intermediate Period.
Milan, Edict of A decree issued by the emperor Constantine in 313 C.E. that legalized Christianity and made it the favored religion in the Roman Empire.
Militarism A policy of aggressive military preparedness; in particular, the large armies based on mass conscription and complex, inflexible plans for mobilization that most European nations had before World War I.
Ming dynasty Chinese empire lasting from 1368 to 1644; it overthrew the Mongols and was replaced by the Ch'ing dynasty of the Manchu.
Minoan civilization An ancient civilization that was centered on Crete between about 2000 and about 1400 B.C.E.
Missi dominici Agents of Charlemagne in the provinces of his empire.
Modernism A philosophy of art of the late nineteenth and early twentieth centuries that rejected classical models and values and sought new expressions and aesthetics.
Mohenjo-Daro Site of one of the two chief towns of the ancient Indus Valley civilization.
Moksha In Hinduism, the final liberation from bodily existence and reincarnation.
Monarchy Rule by a single individual, who often claims divine inspiration and protection.
Mongols Name for collection of savage nomadic warriors of Central Asia who conquered most of Eurasia in the thirteenth century.
Mongol yoke A Russian term for the Mongol occupation of Russia, 1240–1480.
Monotheism A religion having only one god.
Monroe Doctrine The announcement in 1823 by U.S. president James Monroe that no European interference in Latin America would be tolerated.
Mughal A corruption of "Mongol"; refers to the period of Muslim rule in India.
Mulatto A person of mixed African and European blood.
Munich Agreement The agreement coming from 1938 meetings between Hitler and the British and French prime ministers that allowed Germany to take much of Czechoslovakia; the agreement confirmed Hitler's belief that the democratic governments would not fight German aggression.
Munich beer-hall putsch The failed attempt by Hitler to seize power by armed force in 1923.
Mutual deterrence The belief that nuclear war could best be prevented if both the United States and the Soviet Union had sufficient nuclear weapons such that even if one nation launched a preemptive first strike, the other could respond and devastate the attacker.
Mycenaens An early and rich Greek culture centered on Mycenae that was destroyed by the "Sea Peoples" and the influx of Dorians from the north.
Mystery religion One of various Hellenistic cults promising immortal salvation of the individual.

Nantes, Edict of A law granting toleration to French Calvinists that was issued in 1598 by King Henry IV to end the religious civil war.
Napoleonic settlement A collective name for the decrees and actions by Napoleon between 1800 and 1808 that legalized and systematized many elements of the French Revolution.
National Assembly The first law-making body during the French Revolution; created a moderate constitutional monarchy.
Nationalism A sense of national consciousness based on awareness of being part of a community—a "nation"—that has common institutions, traditions, language, and customs and that becomes the focus of the individual's primary political loyalty.
Nationalities problem The dilemma faced by the Austro-Hungarian Empire in trying to unite a wide variety of ethnic groups, including, among others, Austrians, Hungarians, Poles, Croats, Czechs, Serbs, Slovaks, and Slovenes in an era when nationalism and calls for self-determination were coming to the fore.

Nationalization The process of converting a business or industry from private ownership to government control and ownership.
Nation-state A form of political organization in which a relatively homogeneous people inhabits a sovereign state, as opposed to a state containing people of several nationalities.
Natural rights Certain inalienable rights to which all people are entitled; include the right to life, liberty, and property, freedom of speech and religion, and equality before the law.
Natural selection The Darwinian doctrine in biology that changes in species derive from genetic changes that confer an enhanced ability to survive and reproduce.
Navigation Acts Laws regulating commerce with the British colonies in North America in favor of Britain.
Nazism The German variant of fascism created by Hitler.
Neanderthal man A species of *Homo sapiens* flourishing between 100,000 and 30,000 years ago and that mysteriously died out; the name comes from the German valley where the first remains were found.
Négritude A literary term referring to the self-conscious awareness of African cultural values; popular in areas of Africa formerly under French control.
Neo-Confucianism An eleventh- and twelfth-century C.E. revival of Confucian thought with special emphasis on love and responsibility toward others.
Neolithic Age The period from about 7000 B.C.E. to the development of metals by a given people.
Nerchinsk, Treaty of A 1714 treaty between China and Russia that settled border issues between the two great powers in eastern Asia.
New China movement An intellectual reform movement in the 1890s that attempted to change and modernize China by modernizing the government.
New Deal The economic policies of U.S. president Franklin Roosevelt; designed to combat the effects of the Great Depression, they included aspects of Keynesian economics and the first significant social welfare programs in the United States.
New Economic Policy (NEP) A policy introduced at the conclusion of the civil war that allowed for partial capitalism and private enterprise in the Soviet Union.
New Kingdom or **Empire** The period from about 1550 to 700 B.C.E. in Egyptian history; followed the Second Intermediate Period. The period from 1550 to about 1200 B.C.E. was the Empire.
Nicheren sect A Japanese sect of Buddhism founded by the monk Nicheren; it stressed its supremacy over other religions and glorified Japan.
Nicaea, Council of A fourth-century conclave that defined essential doctrines of Christianity under the supervision of the emperor Constantine.
Niger River The great river draining most of the African bulge.
Ninety-five Theses The challenge to church authority put forth by Martin Luther in 1517.
Nineveh The main city and later capital of the Assyrian Empire.
Nirvana The Buddhist equivalent of the Hindu *moksha;* the final liberation from suffering and reincarnation.
Nonaligned nations A large group of countries, most of which became independent after World War II, that desired Cold War alliances with neither the United States nor the Soviet Union.
North American Free Trade Agreement (NAFTA) An agreement signed by the United States, Canada, and Mexico in 1993 that liberalized trade among these nations.
North Atlantic Treaty Organization (NATO) An organization founded in 1949 under U.S. aegis as a defense against threatened communist aggression in Europe.
Nuclear family Composed of parents and children only.
Nuclear test ban The voluntary cessation of above-ground testing of nuclear weapons by the United States and the Soviet Union; in existence from 1963 to the present.
Nuremberg Trials Trials conducted in Germany after World War II to determine and punish war guilt among high German officials, resulting in several executions.

October Revolution of 1917 The Bolshevik coup d'etat in St. Petersburg that ousted the Provisional Government and established a communist state in Russia.
Odyssey The second of the two Homeric epic poems, it details the adventures of the homeward-bound Ulysses coming from the siege of Troy; see also *Iliad.*
Oil boycott of 1973 The temporary withholding of oil exports by OPEC members to Western nations with governments friendly to Israel; led to a massive rise in the price of oil and economic dislocation in many countries.
Old Kingdom The period of Egyptian history from 3100 to 2200 B.C.E.
Old regime/old order The political and social system of France in the eighteenth century before the Revolution.
Old Testament The first portion of the Judeo-Christian Bible; the holy books of the Jews.
Oligarchy Rule by a few.
Olmec The earliest Amerindian civilization in Mexico.
Open Door Policy An early-twentieth-century agreement among the major Western powers that all should have access to trade with weakened China.
Opium Wars Conflicts that occurred in 1840–1842 on the Chinese coast between the British and the Chinese over the importation of opium into China. The Chinese defeat began eighty years of subordination to foreigners.
Oracle bones Animal bones used as a primitive writing medium by early Chinese.
Orange Free State One of the two political entities founded after the Boers' Great Trek in South Africa.
Orders/estates The traditional tripartite division of European society based on heredity and quality rather than wealth or economic standing, first established in the Middle Ages and continuing into the eighteenth century; traditionally consisted of those who pray (the clergy), those who fight (the nobility), and those who work (all the rest).
Organization for Pan African Unity (OAU) The present name of the association of African nations founded in 1963 for mutual aid.
Organization of American States (OAS) An organization founded in 1948 under U.S. auspices to provide mutual defense and aid.

Organization of Petroleum Exporting Countries (OPEC) Founded in the 1960s by Arab governments and later expanded to include several Latin American and African members.
Origin of Species, On the Charles Darwin's book that first enunciated the evolutionary theory in biology; published in 1859.
Osiris A chief Egyptian god, ruler of the underworld.
Ostpolitik German term for Chancellor Brandt's 1960s policy of pursuing normalized relations with West Germany's neighbors to the east.
Ostracism In ancient Greece, the expulsion of a citizen for a given period.

Paleolithic Age The period from the earliest appearance of *Homo sapiens* to about 7000 B.C.E., though exact dates vary by area; the Old Stone Age.
Paleontology The study of prehistoric things.
Palestine Liberation Organization (PLO) An organization founded in the 1960s by Palestinians expelled from Israel; until 1994 it aimed at destruction of the state of Israel by any means. Superseded by the autonomous Palestinian Authority created in 1997.
Pan-Arabism A movement after World War I to assert supranational Arab unity, aimed eventually at securing a unified Arab state.
Pan-Africanism The concept of African continental unity and solidarity in which the common interests of African countries transcend regional boundaries.
Panama Canal A canal built across the isthmus of Panama. Completed in 1914 by the United States, it linked the Atlantic and Pacific Oceans, helping international commerce and extending American naval power.
Pantheism A belief that God exists in all things, living and inanimate.
Paris Commune A leftist revolt against the national government after France was defeated by Prussia in 1871; crushed by the conservatives with much bloodshed.
Parthenon The classic Greek temple to Athena on the Acropolis in Athens' center.
Patriarchy A society in which males have social and political dominance.
Patricians *(patres)* The upper class in ancient Rome.
Patronage The practice of awarding titles and making appointments to government and other positions to gain political support.
Pax Mongolica The Mongol peace; between about 1250 and about 1350 in most of Eurasia.
Pax Romana The "Roman peace"; the era of Roman control over the Mediterranean basin and much of Europe between about 31 B.C.E. and 180 C.E. or later.
Peace of Augsburg Pact ending the German religious wars in 1555, dividing the region between Lutheran and Catholic hegemony.
Peaceful coexistence The declared policy of Soviet leader Khrushchev in dealing with the capitalist West after 1956.
Pearl Harbor, bombing of A surprise attack on December 7, 1941 by Japanese planes on the American navy at Pearl Harbor, Hawaii; it brought war between the United States and Japan.
Peasants' Revolt An uprising in southern German states in 1524–1525; it was ruthlessly suppressed after the peasants were denounced by Martin Luther.
Peloponnesian War The great civil war between Athens and Sparta and their respective allies in ancient Greece; fought between 429 and 404 B.C.E. and eventually won by Sparta.
Peon A peasant in semislave status on a hacienda.
Perestroika The Russian term for "restructuring," which, with *glasnost,* was used to describe the reforms instituted by Gorbachev in the late 1980s.
Persepolis With Ecbatana, one of the twin capitals of the Persian Empire in the 500s B.C.E.
Persians An early Indo-European tribe that, along with the Medes, settled in Iran.
Persian Wars The conflict between the Greeks and the Persian Empire in the fifth century B.C.E., fought in two installments and ending with Greek victory.
Petrine succession The doctrine of the Roman Catholic church by which the pope (the bishop of Rome) is the direct successor of St. Peter.
Pharaoh The title of the god-king of ancient Egypt.
Philosophes A French term referring to the writers and activist intellectuals during the Enlightenment.
Phoenicians An ancient seafaring people living along the coast north of Palestine; they dominated trade in the Mediterranean.
Phonetic alphabet A system of writing that matches signs with the sounds of the oral language.
Pictographic script Uses symbols and graphs only, with no alphabet; used in Chinese writing.
Piedmont "Foot of the mountains"; the Italian kingdom that led to the unification of Italy in the mid-nineteenth century.
Platea The land battle that, along with the naval battle of Salamis, ended the Second Persian War with a Greek victory over the Persians.
Plebeians The common people of ancient Rome.
Pogrom Mob violence against local Jews.
Polis The political and social community of citizens in ancient Greece.
Politburo The ruling council of the Soviet Union; it came under the firm control of Joseph Stalin, but reasserted substantial power upon the dictator's death.
Polytheism Belief in many gods.
Popular sovereignty The doctrine that government is created by and subject to the will of the people, who are the source of all political power.
Post-Impressionist A term for late nineteenth-century painting that emphasized color and line in revolutionary fashion.
Praetorian Guard The imperial bodyguard in the Roman Empire and the only armed force in Italy.
Precedent What has previously been accepted in the application of law.
Predestination The belief, associated with Calvinism, that God, as a consequence of his foreknowledge of all events, has predetermined those who will be saved (the elect) and those who will be damned.
Prehistory The long period of human activity prior to the writing of history.

Primogeniture A system of inheritance in which the estate passes to the eldest legitimate son.
Princeps "The First" or "the Leader" in Latin; title taken by Augustus Caesar.
Principate The reign of Augustus Caesar from 27 B.C.E. to 14 C.E.
Proconsuls Provincial governors and military commanders in ancient Rome.
Proletariat Poverty-stricken people without skills; also, a Marxist term for the propertyless working classes.
Provisional Government A self-appointed parliamentary group exercising power in republican Russia from March to October 1917.
Psychoanalysis A psychological technique that employs free associations in the attempt to determine the cause of mental illness.
Ptolemaic Kingdom of Egypt The state created by Ptolemy, one of Alexander the Great's generals, in the Hellenistic era.
Punic Wars The three conflicts between Rome and Carthage that ended with the complete destruction of the Carthaginian Empire and the extension of Roman control throughout the western Mediterranean.
Puranas A collection of mythical stories about Hindu gods and goddesses.
Purdah The segregation of females in Hindu society.
Purgatory In Catholic belief, the place where the soul is purged after death for past sins and thus becomes fit for heaven.
Puritans The English Calvinists who were dissatisfied by the theology of the Church of England and wished to "purify" it.
Pyramid of Khufu (Cheops) The largest pyramid; stands outside Cairo.

Quadruple Alliance The diplomatic pact to maintain the peace established by the Big Four victors of the Napoleonic wars (Austria, Britain, Prussia, and Russia); lasted for a decade.
Quantum theory A theory in physics describing the discontinuous nature of energy. Energy can only come in certain amounts, or quanta.
Quechua The spoken language of the Inka of Peru.
Qur'an The holy scripture of Islam.

Raison d'état The idea that the welfare of the state should be supreme in government policy.
Ramayana A Hindu text that illustrates important aspects of the religion; its heroes, Rama and his wife Sita, are worshiped as the embodiment of the ideal man and woman, especially Sita.
Realpolitik "Politics of reality." Politics based on practical concerns rather than theory or ethics.
Red Guard The youthful militants who carried out the Cultural Revolution in China during the 1960s.
Reform Bill of 1832 Brought about a reform of British parliamentary voting and representation that strengthened the middle class and the urbanites.
Reign of Terror The period (1793–1794) of extreme Jacobin radicalism during the French Revolution.
Relativity theory Einstein's theory that holds, among other things, that (1) space and time are not absolute but are relative to the observer and interwoven into a four-dimensional space-time continuum and (2) matter is a form of energy.
Reparations Money and goods that Germany paid to the victorious Allies after World War I under the Versailles Treaty.
Republican government A form of governing that imitates the Roman *res publica* in its rejection of monarchy.
Reconquista The recapture of Muslim Spain by Christians; it was completed during the reign of Ferdinand and Isabella.
Restoration (English) The period of the 1660s–1680s when Charles II was called by Parliament to take his throne and was thus restored to power.
Revolution A fundamental change in the political and social organization of a state.
Revolutions of 1989 The throwing out of the Communist governments in eastern Europe by popular demand and/or armed uprising.
Rig Veda The oldest of the four Vedas, or epics, brought into India by the Aryans.
Romanov dynasty Ruled Russia from 1613 until 1917.
Rome, Treaty of The pact signed by six western European nations in 1957 that is the founding document of the European Union.
Rubaiyat The verses attributed to the twelfth-century Persian poet Omar Khayyam.
Russo-Japanese War The 1904–1905 conflict that resulted in defeat for Russia, which weakened the position of the Tsar; simultaneously, the international power and prestige of Japan increased substantially.

Safavid The dynasty of Shiite Muslims that ruled Persia from the 1500s to the 1700s.
Sahel The arid belt extending across Africa south of the Sahara; also called the Sudan.
Salamis The naval battle that, with the battle of Platea, ended the Second Persian War with a Greek victory.
SALT (Strategic Arms Limitation Treaty) Two agreements between the United States and the Soviet Union that placed caps on certain types of nuclear weapons.
Samaria One of the two kingdoms into which the Hebrew kingdom was split after Solomon's death; the other was Judea.
Samsara The reincarnation of the soul; a concept shared by Hinduism and Buddhism.
Samurai Japanese warrior-aristocrats of medieval and early modern times.
Sandinistas A left-wing revolutionary group that overthrew the Somoza dictatorship in Nicaragua and found itself the target of the Reagan administration during the 1980s.
Sangha Groupings of Buddhist monks or nuns; one of the "Three Jewels," along with the *dharma* (teachings) and the Buddha.
Sanhedrin The Jewish governing council under the overlordship of Rome.
Sanskrit The sacred language of India; came originally from the Aryans.
Sardinia-Piedmont See Piedmont.
Sati The practice in which a widow committed suicide at the death of her husband in India; also called *suttee*.

Satrapy A province under a governor or *satrap* in the ancient Persian Empire.
Savanna The semiarid grasslands where most African civilizations developed.
Schlieffen Plan The strategic doctrine employed by Germany at the beginning of World War I; it was designed for a two-front war with France and Russia. The bulk of German military forces quickly swept through Belgium into France while fewer forces stayed in the east to hold off the slow-mobilizing Russians.
***Schutzstaffel* (SS)** Hitler's bodyguard; later enlarged to be a subsidiary army and to provide the concentration camp guards.
Scientific method The method of observation and experiment by which the physical sciences proceed.
SDI Strategic Defense Initiative, also known as "star wars." A plan put forth by the Reagan administration to build a space-based missile defense system.
Second Front The reopening of a war front in western Europe against the Axis powers in World War II; eventually accomplished by the invasion of Normandy in June 1944.
Second Industrial Revolution The second phase of industrialization that occurred in the late 1800s after the introduction of electricity and the internal combustion engine.
Second International Association of socialist parties founded in 1889; after the Russian Revolution in 1917, the Second International split into democratic and communist segments.
Secret speech Premier Nikita Khrushchev of the USSR gave an account in February 1956 of the crimes of Josef Stalin against his own people that was supposed to remain secret but was soon known internationally.
Secularism The rejection of supernatural religion as the arbiter of earthly action; emphasis on worldly affairs.
Seleucid kingdom of Persia The successor state to the empire of Alexander the Great in most of the Middle East.
Self-determination The doctrine that the people of a given territory or a particular nationality should have the right to determine their own government and political future.
Self-strengthening The late nineteenth-century attempt by Chinese officials to bring China into the modern world by instituting reforms; it failed to achieve its goal.
Seljuks Turkish converts to Islam who seized the Baghdad government from the Abbasids in the eleventh century.
Semitic Adjective describing a person or language belonging to one of the most widespread of the western Asian groups; among many others, it embraces Hebrew and Arabic.
Seppuku An honorable method of ritual suicide performed by Japanese samurai; it involved disembowelment with a short sword.
Serfdom Restriction of personal and economic freedoms associated with medieval European agricultural society.
Seven Years' War Fought between France and England, with their allies, around the world, 1756–1763; won by England with major accessions of territory to the British Empire.
Shang dynasty The first historical rulers of China; ruled from about 1500 to about 1100 B.C.E.
Shari'a The sacred law of Islam; based on the Qur'an.
Shiite A minority sect of Islam; adherents believe that kinship with Muhammad is necessary to qualify for the caliphate.
Shintoism The earliest religion in Japan, it was polytheistic and stressed the importance of nature; it placed little or no emphasis on theology or ethical conduct.
Shiva An important member of the Hindu pantheon; he, along with his wife Kali (Durga), is both the creator and the destroyer.
Shogunate The government of medieval Japan in which the *shogun*, a military and civil regent, served as the actual leader while the emperor was the symbolic head of the state and religion.
Sikhs Members of a religious group founded in the sixteenth century C.E. by a holy man who sought a middle way between Islam and Hindu belief; centered on the Punjab region in northern India.
Silk Road A route linking China with the Mediterranean region; it opened during the Han dynasty and was an important conduit for ideas and goods.
Sino-Soviet conflict Differences in the nature of socialism were accentuated by conflict over proper policy vis-à-vis the United States in the 1950s and 1960s in the twin capitals of Marxist socialism, Moscow and Beijing.
Six Day War The 1967 conflict between Israel and its neighbors in which Israel gained much territory.
Social Darwinism The misadaptation of Darwinian biology to human societies; it stressed competition and struggle between humans and justified the rule of the powerful over the weak.
Social Democrats Noncommunist socialists who refused to join the Third International and founded independent parties.
Socialism An ideology that calls for collective or government ownership of the means of production and the distribution of goods.
Socratic method A form of teaching that uses a question-and-answer format to enable students to reach conclusions by using their own reasoning.
Solidarity The umbrella organization founded by Lech Walesa and other anticommunist Poles in 1981 to recover Polish freedom; banned for eight years, but continued underground until it was acknowledged as the government in 1989.
Songhai A West African state, centered on the bend of the Niger River, that reached its fullest extent in the sixteenth century before collapsing.
Sophists Wandering scholars and professional teachers in ancient Greece who stressed the importance of rhetoric and tended toward skepticism and relativism.
Soviets Councils of workers' and soldiers' deputies formed throughout Russia in 1917; played an important role in the Bolshevik Revolution.
Spanish Civil War Conflict in Spain lasting from 1936 to 1939 in which authoritarian forces led by Generalissimo Francisco Franco, with the help of Adolf Hitler, triumphed over Republican forces.
Sparta A militaristic Greek city-state that vied with Athens for power in the Peloponnesian War.
Springtime of the Peoples The spring and summer of 1848 when popular revolutions in Europe temporarily succeeded.
Stalingrad, Battle of The 1942 battle that marked the turning point of World War II in Europe.
Stalinist economy Involved the transformation of a retarded agrarian economy to an industrialized one through massive

reallocation of human and material resources directed by a central plan; imposed on the Soviet Union and then, in the first years after World War II, on eastern Europe.
Stamp Act A law enacted by the British Parliament in 1765 that imposed a fee on legal documents of all types and on all books and newspapers sold in the American colonies.
State The term for a territorial, sovereign entity of government.
Stoicism A Hellenistic philosophy that emphasized human brotherhood and natural law as guiding principles.
Stonehenge A Neolithic stone arrangement in southern England with a layout based on astronomical principles.
Successor states Usual term for the several eastern European states that emerged from the Paris Treaty of 1919 as successors to the Russian, German, and Austro-Hungarian Empires.
Sudan The arid belt extending across Africa south of the Sahara; also called the Sahel.
Sudras One of the four classes of Aryan society; included serfs and servants.
Suffrage The right to vote.
Suffragists Those who advocate the extension of the right to vote (suffrage), especially to women.
Sufi Arabic name for a branch of Islamic worship that emphasizes emotional union with God.
Sui dynasty Ruled China from about 580 to about 620 C.E.; ended the disintegration of central government that had existed for the previous 130 years.
Sultanate of Delhi The government and state erected by the conquering Afghani Muslims after 1500 in northern India; immediate predecessor to the Mughal Empire.
Sumerians The creators of Mesopotamian urban civilization.
Sung dynasty The dynasty that ruled China from about 1127 until 1219, when the last ruler was overthrown by the Mongol invaders.
Sunni The majority group in Islam; adherents believe that the caliphate should go to the most qualified individual and should not necessarily pass to the kin of Muhammad.
Supremacy, Act of A law enacted in 1534 by the English Parliament that made the monarch the head of the Church of England.
Swahili A hybrid language based on Bantu and Arabic; used extensively in East Africa.
Sykes-Picot Agreement A secret 1916 pact between the British and French to divide up Ottoman holdings in the Middle East after World War I; at the same time the British were promising Arabs independence after the war.

Taipings Anti-Manchu rebels in China in the 1860s.
Taj Mahal The beautiful tomb built by the seventeenth-century Mughal emperor Jahan for his wife.
Tale of Genji First known novel in Asian, if not world, history; authored by a female courtier about life in the Japanese medieval court.
T'ang dynasty Ruled China from about 620 to about 900 C.E. and began the great age of Chinese artistic and technical advances.
Tao Te Ching "The Way and its Power," a text attributed to Lao Tzu; it discusses the "Tao," the universal source of everything, and also presents ways for attaining the Tao and the best methods of government.
Taoism (Daoism) A nature-oriented philosophy/religion.
Tariffs Duties (taxes) imposed on imported goods; usually imposed both to raise revenue and to discourage imports and protect domestic industries.
Tel el Amarna The site of great temple complexes along the Nile River in Egypt.
Theravada Buddhism A strict monastic form of Buddhism entrenched in Southeast Asia; same as Hinayana Buddhism.
Thermidorean reaction The conservative reaction to the Reign of Terror during the French Revolution.
Third Estate The great majority of Frenchmen: those neither clerical nor noble.
Third International An association of Marxist parties in many nations; inspired by Russian Communists and headquartered in Moscow until its dissolution in 1943.
Third Republic of France The government of France after the exile of Emperor Napoleon III; lasted from 1871 until 1940.
Third Reich The third German empire, self-proclaimed by Hitler. The first was the empire of Charlemagne, the second that of 1871–1918.
Third World A term in use after World War II to denote countries and peoples in underdeveloped, formerly colonial areas of Asia, Africa, and Latin America; the First World was the West under U.S. leadership, and the Second World was the communist states under Soviet leadership.
Thirty Years' War A devastating conflict lasting from 1618–1648, it ravaged central Europe. It involved questions of power and religion, and it ended with an agreement that each ruler would determine the religion in his territory.
Tiananmen Square, massacre on The shooting down of thousands of Chinese who were peacefully demonstrating for relaxation of political censorship by the Communist leaders; occurred in 1989 in Beijing.
Tien The supreme but impersonal deity of Chou dynasty China.
Time of Troubles A fifteen-year period at the beginning of the seventeenth century in Russia when the state was nearly destroyed by revolts and wars.
Titoism The policy of neutrality in foreign policy combined with continued dedication to socialism in domestic policy that was followed by the Yugoslav Marxist leader Tito after his expulsion from the Soviet camp in 1948.
Toltec An Amerindian civilization centered in the Valley of Mexico; succeeded by the Aztecs.
Torah The first five books of the Old Testament; the Jews' fundamental law code.
Tordesillas, Treaty of A 1494 treaty brokered by the pope, it divided the New World between Portugal and Spain, awarding Brazil to Portugal and all the lands west to Spain.
Tories A nickname for nineteenth-century British conservatives; opposite of Whigs.
Totalitarianism The attempt by a dictatorial government to achieve total control over a society's life and ideas.
Trench warfare Warfare in which the opposing forces attack and counterattack from a relatively permanent system of trenches protected by barbed wire; characteristic of World War I.
Trent, Council of The council of Catholic clergy that directed the Counter-Reformation against Protestantism; met from 1545 until 1563.

Triple Alliance A pact concluded in 1882 that united Germany, Austria-Hungary, and Italy against possible attackers; the members were called the Central Powers.
Truman Doctrine The commitment of the U.S. government in 1947 to defend any noncommunist state against attempted communist takeover; proposed by President Harry Truman.
Twelve Tables The first written Roman law code; established about 450 B.C.E.
Tyrant In an ancient Greek *polis* (or an Italian city-state during the Renaissance), a ruler who came to power in an unconstitutional way and ruled without being subject to the law.

Ulema A council of learned men who applied the *shari'a* in Islam; also, a council of religious advisers to the caliph or sultan.
Umayyad dynasty The caliphs resident in Damascus from 661 to 750 C.E.
Uncertainty principle The theory in physics that denies absolute causal relationships of matter and, hence, predictability.
Unequal treaties Chinese name for the diplomatic and territorial arrangements foisted on the weak Ching dynasty by European powers in the nineteenth century; also, the commercial treaties forced on just-opened Japan by the same powers and the United States.
United Nations Created in 1945, it is the world's most extensive international organization.
Upanishads The Hindu holy epics dealing with morals and philosophy.
Utopian socialism The dismissive label given by Marx to previous theories that aimed at establishing a more just and benevolent society.

Vaisyas The landholder and artisan class of Aryan society.
Vassal In medieval Europe, a person, usually a noble, who owed feudal duties to a superior, called a suzerain.
Vedas The four oral epics of the Aryans.
Vernacular The native oral language of a given people.
Versailles, Treaty of Negotiated in 1919, it established the League of Nations, created several new states in Europe, set procedures for imperial control of the Middle East, and imposed harsh punishments upon Germany.
Vichy regime A puppet state in the south of France during World War II, its leaders generally did the bidding of Nazi Germany.
Viet Cong Pro-independence supporters of Ho Chi Minh active in South Vietnam during the Vietnam War.
Viet Minh Ho Chi Minh's North Vietnamese troops.
Vishnu A Hindu god who, through his nine incarnations, saves the world from destruction; in one incarnation he was Krishna, in another Gautama Buddha.
Vizier An official of Muslim government, especially a high Turkish official equivalent to prime minister.

Wandering of peoples A term referring to the migrations of various Germanic and Asiatic tribes in the third and fourth centuries C.E. that brought them into conflict with Rome.
Wars of the Austrian Succession Two 1740s wars between Prussia and Austria that gave important advantages to Prussia and its king, Frederick the Great.
War of the Roses An English civil war between noble factions over the succession to the throne in the fifteenth century.
Warsaw Pact An organization of the Soviet satellite states in Europe; founded under Russian aegis in 1954 to serve as a counterweight to NATO.
Watergate A scandal involving criminal acts by President Nixon; it led to his resignation in 1974.
Waterloo The final defeat of Napoleon in 1815 after his return from Elban exile.
Wealth of Nations, The The short title of the path-breaking work on national economy by Adam Smith; published in 1776.
Weimar Republic The popular name for Germany's democratic government between 1919 and 1933.
Westphalia, Treaty of The treaty that ended the Thirty Years' War in 1648; the first modern peace treaty in that it established strategic and territorial gains as more important than religious or dynastic ones.
Whigs A nickname for British nineteenth-century liberals; opposite of Tories.
"White Man's Burden" A phrase coined by Rudyard Kipling to refer to what he considered the necessity of bringing European civilization to non-Europeans.
World Bank A monetary institution founded after World War II by Western nations to assist in the recovery effort and to aid the Third World's economic development.

Yalta Conference Conference in 1945 where Franklin D. Roosevelt, Josef Stalin, and Winston Churchill (the "Big Three") met to attempt to settle postwar questions, particularly those affecting the future of Europe.
Yamato state The earliest known government of Japan; divided into feudal subdivisions ruled by clans and headed by the Yamato family.
Yin/yang Taoist distinction between the male and female characteristics of the universe.
Yom Kippur War A name for the 1973 conflict between Israel and its Arab neighbors.
Yuan dynasty Official term for the Mongol rule in China, 1279–1368.

Zama, Battle of Decisive battle of the Second Punic War; Roman victory in 202 B.C.E. was followed by absorption of most of the Carthaginian Empire in the Mediterranean.
Zen Buddhism The Japanese form of Ch'an Buddhism.
Zionism A movement founded by Theodor Herzl in 1896 to establish a Jewish national homeland in Palestine.
Zoroastrianism A religion founded by the Persian Zoroaster in the seventh century B.C.E.; characterized by worship of a supreme god, Ahuramazda, who represents the good against the evil spirit, identified as Ahriman.
Zulu wars A series of conflicts between the British and the native Africans in South Africa in the late nineteenth century.

INDEX